COLLINS
GEM
DICTIONARY

RUSSIAN · ENGLISH
ENGLISH · RUSSIAN

Soviet Orthography

Waldemer Schapiro
Fellow of the Institute of Linguistics

HarperCollins*Publishers*

first published in this edition 1963

© William Collins Sons & Co. Ltd. 1958, 1963

latest reprint 1993

ISBN 0 00 458665 4

General Editor
W. T. McLeod

Printed in Great Britain by
HarperCollins Manufacturing, Glasgow

PREFACE

IT is, I think, a fact that an ever-increasing number of English people of all ages are now learning the Russian language. Apart from its usefulness, Russian is a fascinating subject.

In the U.S.S.R. many men, women and school-children are eager to learn English, a language which has been and still is very popular there.

If my efforts in presenting this dictionary prove instrumental in helping the user to delve a little deeper into the Russian language and later to explore the universally recognized Russian classics, my work will not have been in vain.

The grammatical notes given in the introductory pages are provided for quick reference only, as there are available in this country several complete Grammars and Readers by reputable authors.

NOTE TO THE REVISED EDITION

IT has been possible to add several new entries, and a number of corrections have also been made.

As in the Russian-English section, mentioned on page 7, so also in the English-Russian part, omissions have had to be affected.

In order, however, to accommodate a maximum number of entries in the small format of a pocket dictionary, it became imperative for me to resort to an identical procedure.

Many words with such negative prefixes as 'anti', 'in', 'im', 'un', or suffixes such as 'less', or repetitive particles 're' and 're-', also the reflexive pronoun 'self', had to be omitted.

It is hoped that users of this dictionary, realizing our difficulties, will spend a few extra seconds in looking up the affirmative or other forms of the required word and add the appropriate particles themselves.

For their benefit, here are the Russian equivalents: anti = анти or противо; in, im = не; less = без or бес (бес with an 'c' is used when the word begins with any of the following consonants: к, п, с, т, х, ц, ч, ш, and без with a 'з' for all vowels and remaining consonants); re- and пере-, при (these should be employed cautiously); self = само; un = без, не, раз, рас.

I wish to express my thanks to Mr. A. N. Wilkinson for his help and advice when the work was first envisaged.

I would like to extend to the publishers in Moscow my appreciation of their dictionaries which I used as a reference guide.

Thorpe Bay, 1963.   W. SCHAPIRO

ARRANGEMENT

EACH key-word is printed in a clear bold type and is followed by its phonetic transcription (see p. 10 for Russian and p. 384 for English) enclosed in square brackets. It is hoped that this will prove of real value to the user in assisting him to pronounce each language with ease and comparative accuracy. The 'Guide to Pronunciation' has been devised after considerable thought, research and consultation with experts in this field of study.

Next come the parts of speech, abbreviated and in italic type (see pp. 11 and 12 for List of Abbreviations).

Then follow the definitions, a comma divides synonyms or near-synonyms placed in alphabetical order; a semi-colon is used to signify a different meaning, which often has no connection whatsoever with the first translation.

Explanatory words, printed in italics and enclosed in round brackets, are added where it is necessary to clarify a meaning which might otherwise appear ambiguous.

Subsidiary words are also printed in bold type and a phonetic transcription is given likewise. A short dash standing alone represents the repetition of the key-word without alteration, but where a prefix or suffix is added the additional letters are printed close up to a bold hyphen.

Where the key-word is a Russian verb, this is nearly always of the Imperfective Aspect, in which case its Perfective Aspect is given in light type enclosed in round brackets.

Where the Perfective Aspect is denoted by a prefix added to the Imperfective Aspect without alteration, only the prefix is given followed by a hyphen to represent the remainder of the word; in all other cases the verb is given in full.

A note explaining the Russian Aspects will be found on p. 6.

There are some words in Russian which may be given an entirely different meaning merely by shifting the stress from one syllable to another, for example, мука [mōō-ka], torment, and мука [mōō-ká] flour. The tonic accent is therefore of great importance, and it has been indicated in the phonetic transcription by an acute accent placed on the vowel in the syllable to be stressed.

Where, however, a vowel already carries a horizontal stroke denoting a long vowel, this automatically becomes a stressed syllable, for all long vowels are stressed in Russian, and it therefore needs no further indication. (See above example.)

4

CONTENTS
СОДЕРЖАНИЕ

GRAMMATICAL NOTES

The Verbal Aspects

There are only three tenses in Russian—Present, Past, Future—and to compensate for this deficiency the verb has two forms or Aspects: the Imperfective and the Perfective. The former is used to express continuity of action and the latter, an action which has been completed.

This is, of course, a subject needing careful study, and a Grammar should be consulted for further information.

The Genders

There are three genders in Russian: masculine, feminine and neuter. Apart from the exceptions, which are few, genders are easily recognized.

1. All nouns ending with a consonant or the semi-vowel **-й** are masculine. There are no exceptions. A few words ending in **-ь** (the 'soft sign', which palatalizes the preceding consonant and is normally a feminine ending) are masculine. These include:

(a) Nine names of months—the other three have normal masculine endings.

(b) Nouns formed from infinitives of verbs by replacing the ending **ть** with the suffix **-тель**; e.g. **учить** (to teach) becomes **учитель** (teacher).

(c) An alphabetical list of other exceptions: **алтарь**, altar; **бемоль**, flat (b); **бинокль**, opera-glasses; **бредень**, drag-net; **будень**, working day; **букварь**, spelling book; **вексель**, bill of exchange; **витязь**, knight; **вождь**, chieftain; **гребень**, comb; **день**, day; **зверь**, wild animal; **кашель**, cough; **кисель**, fruit jelly; **козырь**, trump; **корабль**, ship; **корень**, root; **кремль**, citadel; **ливень**, downpour; **локоть**, elbow; **ломоть**, slice; **миндаль**, almond; **ноль**, nil; **огонь**, fire, бенгаль; **пекарь**, baker; **погибель**, ruin; **поршень**, piston; **псалтырь**, Psalter; **рубль**, rouble; **соболь**, sable; **студень**, jelly; **уголь**, coal; **фитиль**, wick; **хрусталь**, crystal; **циркуль**, compass; **щавель**, sorrel; **якорь**, anchor; **янтарь**, amber; **ясень**, ash.

(d) A few words ending in **-я** and describing a male, such as **дядя**, uncle.

2. Words ending in **-а, -ь, -я** are feminine. There are a few exceptions with the **-а** termination. The exceptions with **-ь** and **-я** are those given as masculine or neuter in 1 and 3.

3. The neuter terminations are **-е, -ё, -о** and very few in **-я**, usually preceded, by **м**, such as **время**, time.

Articles

Strange as it may seem, there are no articles in the Russian language, and no change takes place in Russian nouns to indicate whether they are used in a definite or indefinite sense; the particular meaning implied may usually be understood from the context. Consequently, when translating into Russian, articles are simply ignored.

Prefixes and Suffixes

Russian may be truly described as a language of prefixes, inflexions and suffixes, and aided by these a Russian can express his thoughts with great accuracy and indicate precise shades of meaning.

Prefixes. These are used principally to form the perfective aspect of imperfective verbs. Space does not permit a full description of these prefixes, but the following examples will clearly show how very useful they are:

Prefix	Implication
в-	inward movement
вс-	upward movement
вы-	outward movement
за-	beginning, starting
на-	sense of quantity, sufficiency
о-, об- or обо-	sense of movement around or about
от-, ото-	sense of moving away from
пере-	expresses repetition
по-	denotes an action completed
под-	motion under or towards
при-	sense of arriving
про-	through
раз-, рас-	finality
у-	denotes losing sight of, disappearing

Mention should be made here that all the verbs beginning with prefixes could not be accommodated in this dictionary; for example there are at least a further 500 words beginning with без-, бес- or не- (*in-, im- without, less*). In such cases look for the word minus the prefix and then add to its meaning the equivalent appropriate negative particle.

Suffixes. Apart from those used as endings in declensions, suffixes are usually employed to denote augmentation or diminution. By adding, for instance, the particles -ище or -ина to some nouns, enormity or unreasonable dimensions are imputed; whereas by adding the particles -ец, -ик, -ок,

7

-чик the object is reduced to a minute size in one's imagination, and words so formed often serve as an expression of endearment.

Declensions

Nouns, adjectives and pronouns are declined in Russian. There are six cases:

Nominative, used for the subject of a sentence.
Genitive, showing possession.
Dative, used for the indirect object of a sentence.
Accusative, used for the object of a sentence.
Instrumental, denoting means, instrument or agency.
Prepositional. This case is always preceded by a preposition. It should be noted that such prepositions as **в** (in) and **на** (on), when governing this case, answer the question 'where', but when governing the accusative case, they answer the question 'whither'.

Adjectives

There are two forms of adjectives: the *attributive*, which precedes the noun, and the *predicative*, which follows it. It is the *attributive* form which declines, and it agrees in number, gender and case with the noun it qualifies.

The masculine nominative endings are **-ый** and **-ий**; the feminine, **-ая** and **-яя**; and the neuter, **-ое** and **-ее**.

Adverbs

As adverbs may be formed from adjectives by changing the adjectival endings **-ый** and **-ий** into **-о**, it would be purposeless to list them all. Only those so formed which have a limited or unusual meaning are given. Adverbs not formed from adjectives are, of course, included in this dictionary.

Verbs

The following generalities apply to the majority of Russian verbs, but the reader should consult a Grammar to acquaint himself with the comparatively few exceptions.

Most verbs have one of the three following infinitive endings: **-ать**, **-ить** and **-ять**; a few end in **-ть** and **-чь**; it will be noted, that with the exception of **-ти**, they all have **ь** as their final ending. The present tense (used only in the imperfective aspect) is formed by removing the infinitive particle **-ть** and adding the following endings:

		-ать ог **-ять**	**-ить**
1st person sing.		**-ю**	**-ю** (ог **-у**)
2nd ,, ,,		**-ешь**	**-ишь**
3rd ,, ,,		**-ет**	**-ит**
1st ,, *plur.*		**-ем**	**-им**
2nd ,, ,,		**-ете**	**-ите**
3rd ,, ,,		**-ют (-ут)**	**-ят (-ат)**

For the past tense, in both the aspects, all one has to do is to change the infinitive ending to **-л** in the singular and **-ли** in the plural; the third person singular has a feminine ending **-ла** and a neuter one **-ло**. Some irregular and other verbs undergo various changes.

The future tense in the imperfective aspect is formed by conjugating the future of the verb 'to be' with the infinitive, e.g.:

я буду	**читать**	I shall read
ты будешь	,,	thou wilt read
он будет	,,	he will read
мы будем	,,	we shall read
вы будете	,,	you will read
они будут	,,	they will read

The future of the perfective aspect is conjugated like the present tense of imperfective verbs.

The Auxiliary Verb **быть** (to be). In the present tense only the third person singular and rarely the third person plural are used, and then only for emphasis or when it is translated into English by *has* and not *is*:

в этом городе есть вокзал—there *is* a station in this town.

У меня есть словарь—I have a dictionary (*lit*. 'at me is').

To compensate for this deficiency, the personal pronouns **я** (I), etc. may also mean 'I am', etc.
In addition to the aspects already dealt with, there are both reflexive and reciprocating verbs. These are formed by adding to the infinitive the suffix **-ся**, which is an abbreviation of **себя**, oneself, e.g. **мыться**, to wash oneself, whereas **мыть** means 'to wash'. The reciprocating form, as the word implies must apply to two or more people, as for instance, **драться**, to fight.

In conclusion it is stressed that a Grammar should be consulted for amplification of the points already discussed, and in particular for information regarding moods, participles, gerunds, etc., which it has not been possible to mention in so short a grammatical summary.

GUIDE TO PRONUNCIATION OF
RUSSIAN WORDS

Russian Alphabet		Symbol	Examples
А	**а**	ā long and stressed	father
		a short and unstressed	baron
Б	**б**	b	bat
В	**в**	v	vat
Г	**г**	g	get
Д	**д**	d	dog
Е	**е**	ye	yet
		e	enter
Ё	**ё**	yo	yonder
		o	orange
Ж	**ж**	zh	vision
З	**з**	z	zebra, rose
И	**и**	ē long and stressed	beer, meet
		i short unstressed;	
		sometimes stressed	sit
		after ж, ч, ш, щ	
Й	**й**	y	yellow
К	**к**	k	king
Л	**л**	l	stool
М	**м**	m	man
Н	**н**	n	nut
О	**о**	o stressed	pot
		a unstressed	baron
		ŏ final or in final	
		syllables, unstressed	motor
П	**п**	p	pat
Р	**р**	r	error
С	**с**	s	sum
Т	**т**	t	top
У	**у**	ōō long and stressed	moon
		ōō short, unstressed	book
Ф	**ф**	f	fit
Х	**х**	ch	as in Scottish 'Loch'
Ц	**ц**	ts	mats
Ч	**ч**	ch	chair
Ш	**ш**	sh	shut
Щ	**щ**	shch	ashchurch
Ъ	**ъ**	—	(silent)
Ы	**ы**	ă (indeterminate vowel)	about

10

Russian		Symbol	Examples
ЫЙ ый		ăy This diphthong has no equivalent in English.	equals a combination of the *a* in 'about' with the *y* in 'body'.
Ь ь		′ denotes a palatalized sound*	as the *t* in 'tulip' or the *n* in 'onion'.
Э э		ҫ a more open *e* than is generally used in English	as the *a* in 'any'.
Ю ю		yōō long and stressed yŏŏ short, unstressed	mute, few unite
Я я		yă long and stressed	yard

* In *spoken* Russian, a *slight* softening of many consonants when followed by the vowel '**и**' is discernible.

ABBREVIATIONS

СОКРАЩЕНИЯ

adjective	*adj.*	прилагательное
adverb	*adv.*	наречие
anatomy	*anat.*	анатомия
architecture	*arch.*	архитектура
astronomy	*astr.*	астрономия
biblical	*bibl.*	библейский
biology	*biol.*	биология
botany	*bot.*	ботаника
chemistry	*chem.*	химия
colloquial	*coll.*	разговорное выражение
commercial	*com.*	коммерческий термин
conjunction	*conj.*	союз
ecclesiastical	*eccl.*	церковное выражение
electrical	*electr.*	электрический
exclamation	*excl.*	восклицание
feminine	*f.*	женского рода
figurative	*fig.*	фигуральный
geography	*geog.*	география
geology	*geol.*	геология
grammatical	*gram.*	граматический

11

interjection	*interj.*	междометие
legal	*leg.*	юридическое выражение
masculine	*m.*	мужского рода
mathematics	*math.*	математика
mechanics	*mech.*	механика
medical	*med.*	медицинский
military	*mil.*	военное дело
mineral	*min.*	минерал
music	*mus.*	музыка
mythology	*myth.*	мифология
nautical	*naut.*	морской термин
naval	*nav.*	флотский термин
neuter	*n.*	среднего рода
numeral	*num.*	цифра
philosophy	*phil.*	философия
phonetic	*phon.*	фонетический
physiology	*physiol.*	физиология
plural	*pl.*	множественное число
poetical	*poet.*	поэтический
political	*polit.*	политический
preposition	*prep.*	предлог
pronoun	*pron.*	местоимение
railway	*rail.*	железнодорожный термин
religion	*relig.*	религия
singular	*sing.*	единственное число
substantive	*s.*	существительное
technical	*tech.*	технический
theatrical	*theat.*	театральный
typographical	*typ.*	типографический термин
verb	*v.*	глагол
verb intransitive	*vi.*	непереходный глагол
verb reflexive	*vr.*	возвратный глагол
verb transitive	*vt.*	переходный глагол
verb transitive and intransitive	*vt.i.*	переходный и непереходный глагол
vocative	*voc.*	звательный
zoology	*zool.*	зоология

RUSSIAN-ENGLISH
DICTIONARY

a [ă] *conj.* but; and; or; *interj.* ah!

абажур [a-ba-zhōōr] *sm.* lamp-shade

абака [a-bă-ka] *sf.* abacus

аббат [ab-bằt] *sm.* abbot

аббата [a-ba-tă] *sf.* abbacy; сан — [săn —] abbotship

аббатиса [a-ba-t'ĕ-sa] *sf.* abbess [abbey]

аббатство [a-băt-stvŏ] *sn.*

абдикация [ab-di-kă-tsya] *sf.* abdication

аберрация [a-ber-ră-tsya] *sf.* aberration

абзац [ăb-zats] *sm.* paragraph; делать — [dyĕ-lat' —] *typ.* to indent

абитуриент [a-bi-tōō-ryént] *sm.* matriculating student

абиссинец [a-bi-s'ĕ-nyets] *sm.*, абиссинка [a-bi-s'ĕn-ka] *sf.* Abyssinian

абиссинский [a-bi-s'ĕn-ski] *adj.* Abyssinian

абонемент [a-ba-nye-myént] *sm.* subscription; season ticket

абонент [a-ba-nyént] *sm.* subscriber

абонировать [a-ba-n'ĕ-ra-vat'] *vi.* to subscribe (*to a journal, etc.*)

абордаж [a-bar-dăzh] *sm. naut.* boarding; взять на —

[vzyăt' na —] to grapple; -ный крюк [-năy kryŏŏk] grapnel

аборигены [a-ba-ri-gé-nă] *sm. pl.* aborigines; *sing.* native

аборт [a-bórt] *sm.* abortion; miscarriage

абортивный [a-bar-t'ĕv-năy] *adj.* abortive

абрикос [a-bri-kós] *sm.* apricot; -ный [-năy] *adj.* apricot

абрис [ăb-ris] *sm.* outline

абсент [ab-syént] *sm.* wormwood; absinthe

абсолютный [ab-sa-lyōōt-năy] *adj.* absolute, sheer, utter; - слух [- slōōch] *mus.* absolute pitch

абсорбировать [ab-sar-b'ĕ-ra-vat'] *vt.* to absorb

абсорбция [ab-sórb-tsya] *sf.* absorption

абстрактный [ab-străkt-năy] *adj.* abstract; discrete

абсурд [ab-sŏŏrd] *sm.* absurdity

абсурдный [ab-sŏŏrd-năy] *adj.* absurd, inept

аванпост [a-van-póst] *sm.* outpost

аванс [a-văns] *sm.* (*money*) deposit; делать авансы [dyĕ-lat' a-văn-că] to make advances (*courtship*)

авансцена [a-van-stsyé-na] *sf.* proscenium

авантажный [a-van-tázh-năy] *adj.* showing to advantage

авантюрный [a-van-tyŏŏr-năy] *adj.* venturesome

авария [a-vá-rya] *sf.* damage, wreck; injury; *com.* average

авгур [av-gŏŏr] *sm.* augur, soothsayer

август [áv-gŏŏst] *sm.* August

августейший [av-gŏŏ-styéy-shi] *adj.* august, majestic

авиаматка [a-via-mát-ka] *sf.* aircraft carrier

авианосец [a-via-nó-syets] *sm.* aircraft carrier

авиатор [a-viǎ-tŏr] *sm.* airman, aviator, flier

авиационный [a-via-tsión-năy] *adj.* air-, aviatic

авиация [a-viǎ-tsya] *sf.* aviation

авиз [a-v'ēz] *sm.* advice note

авось [a-vós'] *adv.* maybe, perhaps; **на —** [nǎ —] in a leisurely manner; **пойти на —** [pay-t'ē na —] to risk haphazardly

аврора [a-vró-ra] *sf.* aurora

австралиец [av-stra-l'ē-yets] *sm.*, **австралийка** [av-stra-l'ē-ka] *sf.* Australian

австралийский [av-stra-l'ēs-ki] *adj.* Australian

австриец [av-str'ē-yets] *sm.*, **австрийка** [av-strē-ka] *sf.* Austrian

австрийский [av-strē-ski] *adj.* Austrian

автобиограф [af-ta-bió-graf] *sm.* autobiographer

автобиографический [af-ta-bia-gra-f'ē-ches-ki] *adj.* autobiographical

автобиография [af-ta-bia-grá-fya] *sf.* autobiography

автократия [af-ta-krá-tya] *sf.* autocracy

автоматический [af-ta-ma-t'ē-ches-ki] *adj.* automatic

автомобиль [af-ta-ma-b'ēl'] *sm.* limousine, motor-car

автономия [af-ta-nó-mya] *sf.* autonomy

автономный [af-ta-nóm-năy] *adj.* autonomous

автор [áf-tŏr] *sm.* author

авторизованный [af-ta-ri-zó-van-năy] *adj.* authorized

авторство [áf-tar-stvŏ] *sn.* authorship

авторитет [af-ta-r'i-tyét] *sm.* authority

агент [a-gyént] *sm.* agent; factor

агентство [a-gyént-stvŏ] *sn.* agency (*business*)

агентура [a-gyen-tŏŏ-ra] *sf.* agency (*occupation*)

агитатор [a-gi-tá-tŏr] *sm.* agitator, propagandist

агитировать [a-gi-t'ē-ra-vat'] *vi.* (*polit.*) to agitate

агнец [ag-nyéts] *sm.* lamb; offering

агония [a-gó-nya] *sf.* agony; struggle

агонировать [a-ga-n'ē-ra-vat'] *vt.* to agonize; *fig.* to torture

аграрий [a-grá-ri] *sm.* agrarian; landowner; *pl. only*, the landed class

аграрный [a-grár-năy] *adj.* (*polit.*) agrarian

агрессия [a-gres-s'ēv-nŏst'] *sf.* aggression; aggressiveness

агрессивный [a-gres-s'ēv-năy] *adj.* aggressive

агрикультура [a-gri-kŏŏl'-tŏŏ-ra] *sf.* agriculture, farming

ад [ăd] *sm.* hell, inferno; **адский** [ăd-ski] *adj.* hellish, infernal

адвокат [ad-va-kăt] *sm.* barrister; solicitor, lawyer; **стать -ом** [stăt' -ŏm] to be called to the bar

административный [ad-m'i-n'i-stra-t'ĕv-năy] *adj.* administrative

администрация [ad-m'i-n'i-strā-tsya] *sf.* administration

адмирал [ad-m'i-răl] *sm.* admiral; **вице –** [v'ĕ-tse –] vice-admiral; **контр –** [kóntr –] rear-admiral; **полный –** [pól-năy –] Admiral of the Fleet

адмиралтейство [ad-m'i-ral-tyéy-stvŏ] *sn.* Admiralty

адрес [ă-dres] *sm.* address

адресат [a-dre-săt] *sm.* addressee

адресный [a-dryés-năy] *adj.* address

адресовать [a-dre-sa-văt'] *vt.* to address, direct

адъютант [a-dyŏŏ-tănt] *sm.* aide-de-camp; **старший –** [stărshi –] adjutant

ажур [a-zhŏŏr] *sm.* open-work; **-ная строчка** [-na-ya stróch-ka] hemstitch

азарт [a-zărt] *sm.* danger; risk; **-но** [-nŏ] *adv.* rashly; **-ный** [-năy] *adj.* risky; venturesome

азбука [ăz-bŏŏ-ka] *sf.* alphabet; **азбучная истина** [ăz-bŏŏch-na-ya ĕ-st'i-na] truism

азиат [a-ziăt] *sm.,* **-ка,** *sf.* Asian

азиатский [a-ziăt-ski] *adj.* Asiatic, oriental

азот [a-zót] *sm.* nitrogen; **закись азота** [ză-k'is' a-zóta] nitrous oxide; **азотистая кислота** [a-za-t'ĕ-sta-ya k'is-la-tă] nitrous acid

аист [ă-ist] *sm.* stork

ай! [ăy] *excl.* oh!

айва [ay-vă] *sf.* quince; japonica

академик [a-ka-dyé-mik] *sm.* academician

академический [a-ka-dye-m'ĕ-ches-ki] *adj.* academic (al)

академия [a-ka-dyé-mya] *sf,* academy; **– Наук** [– na-ŏŏk] (in the U.S.S.R.) The Academy of Sciences; **– Художеств** [– chŏŏ-dó-zhestv] Academy of Arts

акация [a-kă-tsya] *sf.* acacia

акварелист [a-kva-rye-l'ĕst] *sm.* painter in water-colours

акварель [a-kva-ryél'] *sf.* water-colour

акведук [a-kvye-dŏŏk] *sm.* aqueduct, conduit

акклиматизация [a-kl'i-ma-t'i-ză-tsya] *sf.* acclimatization

акклиматизировать [a-kl'i-ma-t'i-z'ĕ-ra-vat'] *vt.* to acclimatize; **-ся** [-sya] *vi.* to become acclimatized

аккомпанемент [ak-kam-pa-nye-myént] *sm. mus.* accompaniment

аккомпаниатор [ak-kam-pa-niă-tŏr] *sm. mus.* accompanist

аккомпанировать [ak-kam-pa-n'ĕ-ra-vat'] *vt.* to accompany

аккорд [a-kórd] *sm.* accord;

chord; **-ная плата** [-na-ya plá-ta] *com.* payment in full

аккредитив [ak-krye-d'i-t'ēv] *sm.* letter of credit

аккредитовать [ak-krye-d'i-t'ē-ra-vat'] *vt.* to accredit

аккумулировать [ak-kōō-mōō-l'ē-ra-vat'] *vt.i.* to accumulate

аккумуляция [ak-kōō-mōō-lyá-tsya] *sf.* accumulation

аккуратность [ak-kōō-rát-nŏst'] *sf.* accuracy, exactness; punctuality, regularity; neatness, tidiness

аккуратный [ak-kōō-rát-nǎy] *adj.* accurate, exact; neat

акр [ākr] *sm.* acre

акрида [a-krē-da] *sf.* locust

акробат [a-kra-bắt] *sm.* acrobat, contortionist; tumbler

акростих [a-kra-st'ēçh] *sm.* acrostic

аксельбант [āk-syel'-bant] *sm.* shoulder-knot

акт [ākt] *sm.* *theat.* act; deed; bill; **– в учебном заведении** [– vōō-chéb-nŏm za-vye-dyé-ni'i] Speech Day; **-овый зал** [āk-to-vǎy zāl] Assembly Hall

актёр [ak-tyór] *sm.* actor, player, performer; **главный** [– gláv-nǎy –] leading man

актёрство [ak-tyór-stvŏ] *sn.* profession of an actor

актив [ak-t'ēv] *sm.* assets; **– и пассив** [– i pas-s'ēv] assets and liabilities

активист [ak-t'i-v'ēst] *sm.* (in U.S.S.R.) active member

активность [ak-t'ēv-nŏst'] *sf.* activity

активный [ak-t'ēv-nǎy] *adj.* active, industrious

актриса [ak-tr'ē-sa] *sf.* actress, comedienne; **главная** [ak-tr'ē-sa –] leading lady

актуальность [ak-tōō-ál'-nŏst'] *sf.* actuality, realism

актуальный [ak-tōō-ál'-nǎy] *adj.* essential; instant; **актуальные условия** [ak-tōō-ál'-nǎ-ye ōō-slṓ-vi-ya] present conditions

акула [a-kōō-la] *sf.* dog-fish; shark

акушёр [a-kōō-shór] *sm.* obstetrician; **-ка** [-kā] *sf.* midwife

акушёрство [a-kōō-shór-stvŏ] *sn.* midwifery

акцент [ak-tsyént] *sm.* accent; **изысканный** [i-zắs-kan-nǎy –] refined pronunciation

акцентирование [ak-tsyent'ē-ra-va-nye] *sn.* accentuation

акцентировать [ak-tsyent'ē-ra-vat'] *vt.* to accentuate

акцепт [ak-tsyépt] *sm. com.* acceptance

акцидентный [ak-ts'i-dyént-nǎy] *adj.* accidental

акциз [ak-tsēz] *sm.* excise; **сборщик -а** [zbór-shchik -a] exciseman

акционер [ak-tsio-nyér] *sm.* shareholder, stockholder; **-ное общество** [-na-ye ób-shchest-vŏ] limited company; **Акц. Об-во,** Co., Ltd.

акция [āk-tsya] *sf. com.* share

аладья [a-lá-dya] *sf.* fritter

албанец [al-bá-nyets] *sm.*, **албанка** [al-bán-ka] *sf.* Albanian

албанский [al-bán-ski] *adj.* Albanian

алгебра [ál-geb-ra] *sf.* algebra

аленький [á-lyen'-ki] *adj.* reddish

алеть [a-lyét'] *vi.* to reden; to glow

алжирец [al-zhé-ryets] *sm.*, **алжирка** [al-zhér-ka] *sf.* Algerian

алжирский [al-zhér-ski] *adj.* Algerian

алименты [a-l'i-myén-tă] *sm. pl.* alimony

алкание [al-kā-nye] *sn.* hunger; *fig.* craving

алкать [al-kāt'] (вз–) *vi.* to hunger; crave (for)

аллея [al-lyé-ya] *sf.* alley, avenue

аллилуя [al-l'i-lōō-ya] *sf.* hallelujah

аллитерация [al-l'i-tye-rā-tsya] *sf.* alliteration

аллюр [al-lyōōr] *sm.* gait, pace; step; **бешеный –** [byé-she-năy –] breakneck speed

алмаз [al-māz] *sm.* diamond; **-ный** [-năy] *adj.* adamant

алтарь [al-tār'] *sm.* altar; chancel; apse (*in Orthodox churches*)

алфавит [al-fā-vit] *sm.* alphabet; **-ный** [-năy] *adj.* alphabetical; **-ный указатель** [-năy ōō-ka-zā-tyel'] *sf.* alphabetical index

алхимик [al-chĕ-mik] *sm.* alchemist

алчность [álch-nŏst'] *sf.* avarice, cupidity; greed

алчный [álch-năy] *adj.* avid, greedy

алый [ā-lăy] crimson; **алая роза** [ā-la-ya ró-za] damask rose

альбом [al'-bóm] *sm.* album; scrapbook

альманах [al'ma-nāch] *sm.* almanac, calendar

альпари [al'-pa-rē] *adv.* at par

альпийский [al'-p'ē-ski] *adj.* alpine

альпинист [al'-p'i-n'ĕst] *sm.* alpinist

альт [āl't] *sm.* alto, contralto (*voice*); viola (*instrument*)

альтруизм [al'-trōō-ēzm] *sm.* generosity, unselfishness

аляповатость [a-lya-pa-vāt-nŏst'] *sf.* awkwardness

аляповатый [a-lya-pa-vā-tăy] *adj.* clumsy; coarse

амазонка [a-ma-zón-ka] *sf.* horsewoman; riding-habit

амбар [am-bār] *sm.* barn, granary; warehouse

амбиция [am-b'ē-tsya] *sf.* ambition; **вломиться в амбицию** [vla-'mĕt'-sya vam-b'ē-tsyōō] to ride the high horse

амбра [ám-bra] *sf.* amber; **серая –** [syé-ra-ya –] ambergris

амбулатория [am-bōō-la-tó-rya] *sf.* dispensary, ambulance

американец [a-mye-ri-kā-nyets] *sm.*, **американка** [a-mye-ri-kăn-ka] *sf.* American

американский [a-mye-ri-kăn-ski] *adj.* American

аминь [a-m'ĕn'] *interj.* amen

амнистия [am-n'ē-stya] *sf.* amnesty

аморфный [a-mórf-năy] *adj.* amorphous, shapeless

ампула [am-plōō-a] *sf. theat.* line, type (*of business*)

ампутировать [am-pōō-t'ē-ra-vat'] *vt.* to amputate

амуниция [a-mŏŏ-nē-tsya] *sf.* ammunition; munitions

амурничать [a-mŏŏr-n'i-chat'] *vt.* to court

анализ [a-na-l'ēz] *sm.* analysis; parsing

анализировать [a-na-l'i-z'ē-ra-vat'] *vt.* to analyse; to parse

аналогичный [a-na-la-g'ēch-nǎy] *adj.* analogous

ананас [a-na-nâs] *sm.* pineapple

ангар [an-gâr] *sm.* hangar

ангел [ân-gel] *sm.* angel; -хранитель [- -chra-n'ē-tyel'] guardian angel; -очек [-óchek] *sm.* cherub

ангельский [ân-gel'-ski] *adj.* angel-, angelic

ангина [an-g'ē-na] *sf.* quinsy, tonsillitis

английский [an-gl'ē-ski] *adj.* English; **английская болезнь** [an-gl'ē-ska-ya ba-lyézn'] *sf.* rickets; - **соль** [- sól'] *sf.* Epsom salts

англичанин [an-gl'i-chân'in] *sm.* Englishman; **англичанка** [an-gl'i-chân-ka] *sf.* Englishwoman; **англичане** [an-gl'i-châ-nye] *sm. pl.* Englishmen; the English (*people*)

анкета [an-kyé-ta] *sf.* form, questionnaire

анналы [an-nâ-lǎ] *sm. pl.* annals, records

аннулирование [an-nŏŏ-l'ē-ra-va-nye] *sn.* abrogation, cancellation; dissolution; nullification

аннулировать [an-nŏŏ-l'ē-ra-vat'] *vt.* abrogate, annul

аномалия [a-na-mâ-lya] *sf.* anomaly; **умственная** -

[ŏŏm-stvyen-na-ya -] aberration

анонимный [a-na-n'ēm-nǎy] *adj.* anonymous

анонс [a-nóns] *sm.* notice

анормальность [a-nar-mâl'-nòst] *sf.* abnormality

антенна [an-tyén-na] *sf.* aerial; antenna

антипатичный [an-t'i-pa-t'ēch-nǎy] *adj.* antipathetic

антипатия [an-ti-pâ-tya] *sf.* antipathy, aversion

античный [an-t'ēch-nǎy] *adj.* antique

антология [an-ta-ló-gya] *sf.* anthology

антракт [an-trâkt] *sm.* interlude

анташа [an-trâ-sha] *sf.* caper, gambol

антрекот [an-tre-kót] *sm.* chop (*mutton, etc.*)

антрепренёр [an-tre-pre-nyór] *sm. theat.* impresario; backer of plays, shows, etc.; manager of theatrical company

антресоль [an-tre-sól'] *sf.* attic

анчоус [an-chó-ŏŏs] *sm.* anchovy

анютины глазки [a-nyŏŏ-t'ē-nǎ glâz-ki] *s. pl.* pansy

апатичный [a-pa-t'ēch-nǎy] *adj.* apathetic, languid

апельсин [a-pyel'-s'ēn] *sm.* orange; **-овый цвет** [-vǎy tsvyet] *sm.* orange blossom; **-овое варенье** [-a-va-ye va-ryé-nye] *sn.* marmalade

апендицит [a-pyen-di-tsēt] *sm.* appendicitis

апликке [a-pli-ké] *sn.* coated, plated

аплодировать [a-pla-d'ē-ra-vat'] *vi.* to applaud, clap

аплодисмент [a-pla-d'is-myént] *sm.* acclamation, applause

апломб [a-plómb] *sm.* self-possession

апогей [a-pa-géy] *sm.* apogee; climax, highest point

апология [a-pa-ló-gya] *sf.* apologetics

апостол [a-pós-tŏl] *sm.* apostle

апостольский [a-pas-tól'-ski] *adj.* apostolic

аппарат [ap-pa-rāt] *sm.* apparatus

аппетит [ap-pye-t'ēt] *sm.* appetite

апрель [a-pryél] *sm.* April

апсида [ap-s'ē-da] *sf.* apse, tribune

аптека [ap-tyé-ka] *sf.* chemist's shop, pharmacy; dispensary

аптекарь [ap-tyé-kar'] *sm.* chemist, pharmacist

аптечка [ap-tyéch-ka] *sf.* first-aid box

араб [a-ráb] *sm.*, **-ка** [-ka] *sf.* Arabian; **-ский** [-ski] *adj.* Arabian

аранжировка [a-ran-zhi-róv-ka] *sf. mus.* arrangement

арап [a-ráp] *sm.* negro

арапник [a-ráp-n'ik] *sm.* long whip

арбитраж [ar-bi-trázh] *sm.* arbitration; **-ный суд** [-náy sōōd] Court of Referees

арбуз [ar-bōōz] *sm.* watermelon

аргентинец [ar-gyen-t'ē-nyets] *sm.*, **аргентинка** [argyen-t'ēnka] *sf.* Argentinian

аргентинский [ar-gyen-t'ēn-ski] *adj.* Argentine

арго [ar-gó] *sn.* slang

арена [a-ryé-na] *sf.* arena, ring

аренда [a-ryén-da] *sf.* tenantry

арендатор [a-ryen-dā-tŏr] *sm.* tenant

арендатура [a-ryen-da-tōō-ra] *sf.* tenancy

арест [a-ryést] *sm.* arrest; seizure; sequestration

арестант [a-ryes-tānt] *sm.* convict, prisoner

арестантская [a-ryes-tānt-ska-ya] *adj. as sf.* lock-up *(detention room)*

арестовывать [a-ryes-tō-vă-vat'] (**арестовать**) *vt.* to arrest

аристократия [a-ris-ta-krā-tya] *sf.* aristocracy

арифметика [a-rif-myé-t'i-ka] *sf.* arithmetic

ария [ā-rya] *sf. mus.* air, aria, tune

арка [ār-ka] *sf.* arch

аркан [ar-kān] *sm.* lasso; **ловить -ом** [la-v'ét' -ŏm] to lasso

армеец [ar-myé-yets] *sm.* regular soldier

армия [ār-mya] *sf.* army; **– спасения** [– spa-syé-na –] Salvation Army; **Красная –** [krās-na-ya –] the Red Army

армяк [ar-myāk] *sm.* peasant's overcoat

армянин [ar-myā-n'in] *sm.*, **армянка** [ar-myān-ka] *sf.*

армянский [armyān-ski] *adj.* Armenian

аромат [a-ra-māt] *sm.* aroma, odour, perfume, scent

ароматический [a-ra-ma-t'ē-ches-ki] *adj.* aromatic; **– воздух** [– vóz-dŏŏch] balmy air

арсенал [ar-sye-nál] *sm.* arsenal; **морской** [mar-skóy –] dockyard

артачиться [ar-tǎ-chit'-sya] *vi.* to be unwilling; to jib

артачливый [ar-tǎ-chl'í-vǎy] *adj.* stubborn

артель [ar-tyél'] *sf.* workmen's association

артельщик [ar-tyél'-shchik] *sm.* member of a workmen's association; porter

артикул [ar-t'i-kŏŏl] *sm.* articles of war

артист [ar-t'ēst] *sm.* artist; **оперный** [–ó-pyer-nǎy –] opera singer; **балетный** [ba-lyét-nǎy –] ballet-dancer

артистический [ar-t'is-t'ē-ches-ki] *adj.* artistic

артишок [ar-t'i-shók] *sm.* artichoke

артрит [ar-trēt] *sm.* arthritis

арфа [ár-fa] *sf.* harp

арфист [ar-fēst] *sm.*, **-ка,** [–ches-ki] *adj.* harpist

архангел [ar-chán-gyel] *sm.* archangel

археолог [ar-chye-a-lóg] *sm.* archaeologist

археология [ar-chye-a-ló-gya] *sf.* archaeology

архив [ar-chēv] *sm.* archive; chancery; **государственный –** [ga-sŏŏ-dár-stvyen-nǎy –] Record Office

архиварнус [ar-chi-vá-riŏŏs] *sm.* keeper of records

архидиакон [ar-chi-dyá-kŏn] *sm.* archdeacon

архиепископ [ar-chi-ye-p'ēs-kŏp] *sm.* archbishop

архиерей [ar-chi-ye-ryéy] *sm.* bishop

архимандрит [ar-chi-man-drēt] *sm.* superior of an Orthodox monastery

архипелаг [ar-chi-pye-lág] *sm.* archipelago

архитектор [ar-chi-tyék-tŏr] *sm.* architect

архитектура [ar-chi-tyek-tŏŏ-ra] *sf.* architecture

аршин [ar-shín] *sm.* = 28 inches

ассоциация [as-sa-tsyǎ-tsya] *sf.* association

астматический [a-stma-t'ē-ches-ki] *adj.* asthmatic

астра [ás-tra] *sf.* aster

астральный [as-trál'-nǎy] *adj.* astral, starry

атаковать [a-ta-ka-vát'] *vt.* to assault, attack, charge

ателье [a-te-lyé] *sn.* studio (*artist's*)

атлас [ắt-las] *sm.* atlas

атлас [at-lắs] *sm.* satin

атлет [at-lyét] *sm.* athlete

атлетический [at-lye-t'ē-ches-ki] *adj.* athletic

атмосфера [at-mas-fyé-ra] *sf.* atmosphere

атмосферический [at-mas-fye-r'ē-ches-ki] *adj.* atmospheric

аттестат [at-tyes-tát] *sm.* testimonial

аттестация [at-tyes-tǎ-tsya] *sf.* attestation; character

аттестовать [at-tyes-ta-vát'] *vt.i.* to testify

аудиенция [a-ŏŏ-dyén-tsya] *sf.* audience

аудитория [a-ŏŏ-d'i-tó-rya] *sf.* auditorium

аукцион [a-ŏŏk-tsión] *sm.* auction; **-ный зал** [-nǎy

zäl] *sm.* sale-room; **-щик** [-shchik] *sm.* auctioneer;

молоток -щика [malatók -shchi-ka] *sf.* auctioneer's hammer

афера [a-fyé-ra] *sf.* speculation

аферист [a-fye-r'ëst] *sm.* speculator; **-ка** [-ka] *sf.* adventuress

афиша [a-fē-sha] *sf.* bill, poster

афишировать [a-fi-shē-ravat'] *vt.* to display (*posters*)

африканец [a-fri-kä-nyets] *sm.*, **африканка** [a-fri-känka] *sf.* African

африканский [a-fri-känski] *adj.* African

аффектация [af-fek-tätsya] *sf.* affectation, pretence

ах! [äch] *interj.* ah!

аханье [ä-cha-nye] *sn.* moan, moaning

ахать [ä-chat'] *vi.* to groan, moan

ахинея [a-ch'i-nyé-ya] *sf.* nonsense; cock-and-bull story

ахти! [ach-t'ē] *interj.* alas!

аэродром [a-ɇ-ra-dröm] *sm.* aerodrome

аэронавтика [a-ɇra-näf-t'ika] *sf.* aeronautics

аэроплан [a-ɇra-plän] *sm.* aeroplane

аэростат [a-ɇra-stät] *sm.* balloon

аэростатика [a-ɇra-stä-t'ika] *sf.* aerostatics

Б

б, бы [b, bä] *gram.* (*used with the conditional and subjunctive moods*); should, would; may, might

ба! [bä] *interj.* bah!

баба [bä-ba] *sf.* woman (*country usage*); (when applied to men, it is derogatory and means 'effeminate'); **- яга** [- ya-gä] *sf.* Russian mythical witch; hag; **снежная -** [snyézh-na-ya -] *sf.* snowman; **бабий** [bäbi] *adj.* womanish (*derisive*); **бабье лето** [bä-bye lyé-to] *sn.* Indian Summer

бабка [bäb-ka] *sf.* grandmother; pastern (*of a horse*); knucklebone(s); chuck; piledriving weight; rod for metal forging; **повивальная -** [pa-v'i-väl'-na-ya -] *sf.* midwife; **ночная -** [nach-nä-ya -] *sf.* moth

бабочка [bä-bach-ka] *sf.* butterfly

бабушка [bä-bŏŏsh-ka] *sf.* grandma, granny; **вот тебе - !** [vot tye-bé -] well, I never! **бабушкины сказки** [bä-bŏŏsh-k'i-nä skäz-ki] old wives' tales

багаж [ba-gäzh] *sm.* luggage

багроветь [ba-gra-vyét'] *vi.* to redden

багровый [ba-gró-väy] *adj.* blood-red

база [bä-za] *sf.* base; **- колонны** [- ka-lón-nä] *sf.* arch, pedestal

базар [ba-zär] *sm.* market; **-ный** [-näy] *adj. fig.* cheap

базис [bä-z'is] *sm.* base, basis

баиньки [bä-in'-ki] *pl.* hush-a-by; **баюшки-баю** [bä-yŏŏsh-ki-ba-yŏŏ] Russian lullaby

байдарка [bay-där-ka] *sf.* canoe

байка [bāy-ka] *sf.* baize

байковое одеяло [bāy-ka-vo-ye a-dye-yā-lŏ] *sn.* blanket.

бак [bāk] *sm.* cistern, tank; *naut.* forecastle

бакалейщик [ba-ka-lyéy-shchik] *sm.* grocer

бакалея [ba-ka-lyé-ya] *sf.* grocer's shop; **бакалейные товары** [ba-ka-lyéy-nă-ye ta-vā-rā] *sm. pl.* groceries

бакан [ba-kān] *sm.* beacon, buoy

бакалавр [ba-ka-lāvr] *sm.* bachelor (*degree*)

баклага [ba-klā-ga] *sf.* wooden vessel; flask

баклажан [ba-kla-zhān] *sm.* aubergine, eggplant

баклушничать [ba-klōōsh-n'i-chat] *vi.* to hang about, linger

бактериолог [bak-tye-rió-lŏg] *sm.* bacteriologist

бактериология [bak-tye-ria-ló-gya] *sf.* bacteriology

бактерия [bak-tyé-rya] *sf.* bacterium

бакшиш [bak-shísh] *sm.* tip (*for service rendered*)

бал [bāl] *sm.* ball (*dancing*); **костюмированный** – [ka-styōō-m'i-ró-van-năy –] masked ball

балаболка [ba-la-ból-ka] *sf.* small ornament; *fig.* chatterbox

балаган [ba-la-gān] *sm.* booth

балаганить [ba-la-gā-n'it] *vi.* to play the fool

балаганщик [ba-la-gān-shchik] *sm.* showman

балагур [ba-la-gōōr] *sm.* joker

балагурить [ba-la-gōō-r'it] *vi.* to joke

баламутить [ba-la-mōō-t'it] *vt.* to stir up (*water*); to muddle; *fig.* to disturb

баланс [ba-lāns] *sm. com.* balance; **– счетов** [– sche-tóv] balance-sheet; **подвести** – [pad-vyes-t'ē –] to strike a balance

балансир [ba-lan-s'ĕr] *sm. tech.* beam; bob

балансировать [ba-lan-s'ē-ra-vat'] *vt.* to balance

балахон [ba-la-chón] *sm.* smock

балбес [bal-byés] *sm.* dunce; idler

балбесничать [bal-byés-n'i-chat] *vi.* to waste time, idle

балда [baldā] *sf.* knob; heavy hammer; *fig.* blockhead

балдахин [bal-dā-chin] *sm.* canopy

балетчик [ba-lyét-chik] *sm.* ballet-dancer; **балетчица** [ba-lyét-chi-tsa] *sf.* ballerina

балка [bāl-ka] *sf.* narrow gorge; girder; joist

балкон [bal-kón] *sm.* balcony

балл [bāl] *sm.* mark (*unit of merit*)

баллада [bal-lā-da] *sf.* ballad

баллистика [bal-l'ēs-t'i-ka] *sf.* ballistics

баллотирование [bal-la-t'ē-ra-va-nye] *sn.* ballot

баллотировать [bal-la-t'ē-ra-vat'] *vt.i.* to poll, vote

баловать [ba-la-vāt] *vi. fig.* to spoil (*a child*)

баловаться [bā-la-vat'-sya] *vi.* to have fun, play about

баловень [bă-lo-vyen'] *sm.* pet (*child*)

баловник [ba-lov-n'ík] *sm.* naughty child, rascal

баловство [ba-lav-stvó] *sn.* overindulgence; naughtiness

балык [ba-lǎk] *sm.* cured sturgeon

бальзам [bal'-zăm] *sm.* balm, balsam; flowering plant

бальзамировка [bal'-zam'i-róv-ka] *sf.* embalmment

бальный [bǎl'-năy] *adj.* ball-, dance-

балюстрада [ba-lyŏŏ-strá-da] *sf.* balustrade; banister

бамбук [bam-bŏŏk] *sm.*bamboo; **-овая трость** [-a-va-ya trost'] *sf.* bamboo cane

банальность [ba-năl'-nŏst'] *sf.* commonplace; platitude

банальный [ba-năl'-năy] *adj.* hackneyed, trite

банда [băn-da] *sf.* gang

бандаж [ban-dăzh] *sm.* bandage; truss; tyre (*of wheel*)

бандероль [ban-dye-ról'] *sf.* wrapper; **посылать -ю** [pa-sǎ-lăt' -yŏŏ] to send by book-post

банк [bănk] *sm.* bank (*financial*); card game

банка [băn-ka] *sf.* jar (*container*); *med.* cupping-glass; *geog.* bank, shoal; *naut.* bank, thwart

банкет [ban-kyét] *sm.* banquet; **-ная икра** [-na-ya i-krǎ] first quality caviar

банкир [ban-k'ér] *sm.* banker

банкнота [bank-nó-ta] *sf.* banknote

банкрот [ban-krót] *sm.* bankrupt

банкротство [ban-krót-stvó] *sn.* bankruptcy; failure

бант [bănt] *sm.* bow, knot; **-овая складка** [-ó-va-ya sklǎd-ka] *sf.* pleat

банщик [băn-shchik] *sm.* public-baths attendant; **бан-щица** [băn-shchi-tsa] *sf.* female attendant

баня [bă-nya] *sf.* bath, baths; **паровая -** [pa-ra-vă-ya -] Turkish bath

барабан [ba-ra-băn] *sm.* drum; reel; **кожа -а** [kó-zha -a] drumhead

барабанить [ba-ra-bă-n'it'] *vt.* to drum

барабанщик [ba-ra-băn-shchik] *sm.* drummer

баран [ba-răn] *sm.* ram, sheep; battering ram

баранина [ba-ră-n'i-na] *sf.* mutton

баранка [ba-răn-ka] *sf.* dry biscuit

баранок [ba-ră-nŏk] *sm.* plane (*tool*)

баранчик [ba-răn-chik] *sm.* cowslip

барахлиться [ba-rach-l'ét'-sya] *vi.* to be fooling

барахло [ba-rach-ló] *sn.* trash

барахолка [ba-ra-chól-ka] *sf.* jumble sale

барахтанье [ba-rach-tă-nye] *sn.* floundering

барахтаться [ba-răch-tat'-sya] *vi.* to struggle (*in water*); to be helpless [lamb

барашек [ba-ră-shek] *sm.*

барашки [ba-răsh-ki] *sm. pl.* fleecy clouds; white horses (*waves*)

барашковый [ba-răsh-ko-văy] *adj.* lambskin-, made from lambskin

барда [bar-dă] *sf.* grain(s) (*after fermentation*)

баржа [bār-zha] *sf.* barge; *nav.* pinnace

барин [bā-r'in] *sm.* gentleman; **жить -ом** [zhit' -ōm] to live like a lord

барич [bā-r'ich] *sm.* nobleman's son; master

барка [bā-rka] *sf.* bark, barque

баркас [bar-kās] *sm.* barge, launch

барочник [bā-rach-n'ik] *sm.* bargee

барс [bārs] *sm.* panther

барский [bār-ski] *adj.* lordly

барсук [bar-sōōk] *sm.* badger

бархат [bār-chat] *sm.* velvet; **-истый** [-'ēs-tăy] *adj.* velvety; **-ный** [-năy] *adj.* velvet, made from velvet

барщина [bār-shchi-na] *sf.* corvée, unpaid labour

барыня [bā-rä-nya] *sf.* lady, nobleman's wife

барыш [ba-rāsh] *sm.* gain, profit; **получить** – [pa-lōō-chēt' –] to make a business deal

барышник [bā-räsh-n'ik] *sm.* horse-dealer; profiteer

барышничество [bā-räsh-n'i-chest-vŏ] *sn.* corrupt dealings; profiteering

барышня [bā-räsh-nya] *sf.* miss, young lady

баснописец [ba-sna-p'ē-syets] *sm.* fabler, fabulist, writer of fables

баснословный [ba-sna-slóv-năy] *adj.* fabulous, incredible; legendary

басня [bās-nya] *sf.* fable

басовый [ba-só-văy] *adj. mus.* bass; **– ключ** [– klyōóch] bass clef

басон [ba-són] *sm.* braid, fringe, galloon, tape

бассейн [ba-syéyn] *sm.* reservoir; basin (*of river*); *coll.* watershed; **– для плавания** [– dlya plä-va-nya] swimming pool; **каменноугольный –** [ka-myen-na-ōō-gól'-năy –] coal-field(s)

баста [bāsta] *excl.* enough!

бастовать [bas-ta-vāt'] *vi.* to stop work, strike

бастующий [bas-tōō-yōō-shchi] *adj. as sm.* striker

басурман [ba-sōōr-mān] *sm.* pagan

басурманство [ba-sōōr-män-stvŏ] *sn.* paganism

батарея [ba-ta-ré-ya] *sf.* battery

батенька [bā-tyen-ka] *sm.* old chap (*endearing*)

батист [ba-t'ēst] *sm.* cambric

батог [ba-tóg] *sm.* thick stick

батожок [ba-ta-zhók] *sm.* maul-stick, rest-stick

батрак [ba-trāk] *sm.* drudge, hack; farmhand; *fig.* hireling

батрачить [ba-trā-chit'] *vi.* to drudge, labour

батюшка [bā-tyōōsh-ka] *sm.* dad; Father (*to priest*)

батюшки! [bā-tyōōsh-ki] *excl.* goodness me!

баул [ba-ōōl] *sm.* workbox

бахвал [ba-chvāl] *sm.* swaggerer

бахвалиться [ba-chva-l'ēt'-sya] *vi.* to brag

бахрома [ba-chró-ma] *sf.* fringe; scalloping

бахча [bach-chā] *sf.* melon field, melon plot

бацать [ba-tsāt'] (бацнуть) *vt.* to hit, slap; bang indiscriminately

башенка [bā-shen-ka] *sf.*

small tower; turret; *coll.* pepperbox

башлык [ba-shlák] *sm.* hooded cloak

башмак [bash-mák] *sm.* shoe; *tech.* brake-shoe; **под её башмаком** [pad yeyó bash-ma-kóm] tied to her apron; **грубый –** [grōō-báy –] brogue

башмачник [bash-mách-n'ik] *sm.* cobbler, shoemaker

башня [básh-na] *sf.* tower; **водопроводная –** [va-da-pra-vód-na-ya –] water-tower

бдение [bdýe-nye] *sn.* vigil, watch

бдеть [bdyét'] *vi.* to keep vigil, watch

бдительность [bd'é-tyel'-nóst'] *sf.* vigilance

бдительный [bd'é-tyel'-náy] *adj.* alert; vigilant, watchful; *fig.* open-eyed

бег [byég] *sm.* run; race; **быстрый –** [bás-trăy –] career, rapid running; **короткий –** [ka-rót-ki –] sprint

бега [bye-gá] *sm. pl.* races; **быть на -х** [bát' na -<u>ch</u>] to be in hiding

бегать [bye-gat'] (за-) *vi.* to run

бегающий [bye-ga-yōō-shchi] *adj.* cursorial

бегемот [bye-ge-mót] *sm.* hippopotamus

беглец [bye-glyéts] *sm.* fugitive, runaway

беглость [bye-glóst'] *sf.* fluency

беглый [bye-glăy] *adj.* fluent

беговой [bye-ga-vóy] *adj.* race-, racing-; **– ипподром**

[– ip-pa-dróm] *sm.* racecourse; **беговая лошадь** [bye-ga-vá-ya ló-shad'] *sf.* race-horse

беготня [bye-gat-nyá] *sf.* bustle, scurry

бегство [byég-stvŏ] *sn.* flight, hasty retreat; **обратить в –** [a-bra-t'ĕt' v –] to rout

бегун [bye-gōōn] *sm.* runner

беда [bye-dá] *sf.* misfortune, mishap

бедерный [bye-dýer-náy] *adj.* femoral

беднеть [byed-nyét'] (o-) *vi.* to become poor

бедность [byed-nost'] *sf.* poverty; bareness

беднота [byed-na-tá] *sf.* destitution; the poor

бедняга [byed-nyá-ga] *sm.* poor creature

бедняк [byed-nyák] *sm.* pauper; poor person

бедовый [bye-dó-văy] *adj.* mischievous; naughty

бедокурить [bye-da-kōō-r'it'] *vi.* to frolic; to play pranks

бедренный [byed-drye-náy] *adj.* femoral; **бедренная кость** [byed-drye-na-ya kost'] *sf.* thigh-bone

бедро [bye-dró] *sn.* hip, thigh; femur; haunch

бедствие [byéd-stvye] *sn.* distress; calamity; disaster; tribulation

бедствовать [byéd-stva-vat'] *vi.* to be in dire need

бежать [bye-zhát'] (по-) *vi.* to run; **время бежит** [vrýe-mya bye-zhít] time flies

беженец [byé-zhe-nyets] *sm.* **беженка** [bye-zhen-ka] *sf.* refugee

без [byéz] *prep.* without; **ясно без слов** [yás-nŏ byéz slov] it goes without saying; less, minus

безалаберность [byez-a-lá-byer-nŏst'] *sf.* disorder; inconsistency

безалаберный [byez-a-lá-byer-năy] *adj.* inconsistent, orderless; careless, negligent

безапелляционный [byez-appel-lya-tsiŏn-năy] *adj.* peremptory

безбедность [byez-byéd-nŏst'] *sf.* competence

безбедный [byez-byéd-năy] *adj.* comfortably off

безбожие [byez-bó-zhye] *sn.* atheism, ungodliness

безбожник [byez-bózh-n'ik] *sm.* atheist

безбожный [byez-bózh-năy] *adj.* irreligious, ungodly

безбоязненность [byez-ba-yáz-nyen-nŏst'] *sf.* bravery; fearlessness

безбрачие [byez-brá-chye] *sn.* celibacy; *biol.* agamy

безбрежность [byez-bryézh-nŏst'] *sf.* infinity; vastness

безбрежный [byez-bryézh-năy] *adj.* boundless, unlimited

безвинный [byez-v'ĕn-năy] *adj.* innocent

безвкусный [byez-vkōōs-năy] *adj.* insipid; tasteless

безвлажный [byez-vlázh-năy] *adj.* dry, parched

безвозмездный [byez-vaz-myézd-năy] *adj.* gratuitous

безволосый [byez-va-ló-săy] *adj.* bald, hairless

безволие [byez-vó-lye] *sn.* lacking in will-power; weak-

ness of character

безвредность [byez-vryéd-nŏst'] *sf.* harmlessness; innocence

безвредный [byez-vryéd-năy] *adj.* harmless, innocent, innocuous

безвременность [byez-vryé-myen-nŏst'] *sf.* prematurity

безвременный [byez-vryé-myen-năy] *adj.* untimely; premature

безглавый [byez-glá-văy] *adj.* headless

безгласный [byez-glás-năy] *adj.* mute, voiceless

безголовый [byez-ga-ló-văy] *adj.* brainless

безграмотность [byez-grá-mat-nŏst'] *sf.* illiteracy

безграмотный [byez-grá-mat-năy] *adj.* ignorant, illiterate

безгрешный [byez-gryésh-năy] *adj.* innocent, sinless

бездействие [byez-dyéy-stvye] *sn.* inactivity, slackness

безделица [byez-dyé-l'i-tsa] *sf.* trifle, triviality

безделушка [byez-dye-lōōsh-ka] *sf.* knick-knack

безделье [byez-dyé-lye] *sn.* idleness, laziness

бездельник [byez-dyél'-n'ik] *sm.* idler, loafer

бездельничать [byez-dyél'-n'i-chat'] *vi.* to be idle

безденежность [byez-dyé-nyezh-nŏst'] *sf.* impecuniosity

безденежный [byez-dyé-nyezh-năy] *adj.* penniless

бездеятельность [byez-dyé-ya-tyel'-nŏst'] *sf.* inactivity; inaction; inertness

бездна [byézd-na] *sf.* chasm; gulf; – **волнений** [– val-nyé-n'i] a sea of troubles; *coll.* a heap, an enormous number

бездольный [byez-dól-nǎy] *adj.* unfortunate, unlucky

бездомник [byez-dóm-n'ik] *sm.* homeless person; abandoned child; waif

бездомный [byez-dóm-nǎy] *adj.* homeless; **бездомные дети** [byez-dóm-nǎ-ye dyé-t'i] waifs and strays

бездорожье [byez-da-ró-zhye] *sn.* road not admitting traffic; 'no thoroughfare'

бездушный [byez-dōōsh-nǎy] *adj.* heartless, soulless; callous

безжалостный [byez-zhá-last-nǎy] *adj.* merciless; ruthless

безжизненный [byez-zhíz-nye-nǎy] *adj.* inanimate; lifeless

беззаботный [byez-za-bót-nǎy] *adj.* lighthearted, unconcerned; careless, reckless

беззаконник [byez-za-kón-n'ik] *sm.* lawbreaker, transgressor

беззаконность [byez-za-kón-nöst'] *sf.* lawlessness; illegality

беззастенчивый [byez-za-styén-chi-vǎy] *adj.* impudent, shameless

беззащитный [byez-za-shchít-nǎy] *adj.* defenceless

беззвучный [byez-zvōōch-nǎy] *adj.* soundless

безземельный [byez-zye-myél'-nǎy] *adj.* landless

безмала [byez-mā-la] *adv.* almost, nearly

безместный [byez-myést-nǎy] *adj.* without a place

безмятежность [byez-mya-tyézh-nöst'] *sf.* serenity

безмятежный [byez-mya-tyézh-nǎy] *adj.* serene, undisturbed

безнадёжный [byez-na-dyózh-nǎy] *adj.* despairing, hopeless

безначалие [byez-na-chā-lye] *sn.* chaos, disorder

безнравственность [byez-nráv-stvyen-nöst'] *sf.* immorality

безнравственный [byez-nráv-stvyen-nǎy] *adj.* immoral, wicked

безобразие [byez-a-brā-zye] *sn.* indecency; ugliness; **что за** – [shtó za –] what a shame!

безобразный [byez-a-brāz-nǎy] *adj.* hideous, monstrous, unseemly

безоговорочный [byez-a-ga-vó-roch-nǎy] *adj.* unconditional

безопасность [byez-a-pás-nost'] *sf.* safety; security

безопасный [byez-a-pás-nǎy] *adj.* safe, secure

безоружный [byez-a-rōōzh-nǎy] *adj.* defenceless; unarmed

безостановочный [byez-a-sta-nó-vach-nǎy] *adj.* ceaseless, endless; – **перелёт** [– pye-rye-lyót] *sm.* non-stop flight

безответный [byez-at-vyét-nǎy] *adj.* timid

безответственный [byez-at-vyét-stvyen-nǎy] *adj.* irresponsible

безотлучный [byez-atlōōch-nǎy] *adj.* ever present

безошибочный [byez-a-shí-bach-nǎy] *adj.* faultless, infallible

безработица [byez-ra-bót'i-tsa] *sf.* unemployment

безработный [byez-ra-bót-nǎ(-ye] *sm. pl.* the unemployed

безраздельный [byez-raz-dyél'-nǎy] *adj.* inseparable

безразличие [byez-raz-l'e-chye] *sn.* apathy, indifference

безразличный [byez-raz-l'éch-nǎy] *adj.* impartial, indifferent; **мне безразлично** [mnye byez-raz-l'éch-nō] it is all the same to me

безропотность [byez-ró-pat-nōst'] *sf.* resignation, submissiveness

безрукавка [byez-rōō-kǎv-ka] *sf.* sleeveless vest

безударный [byez-ōō-dǎr-nǎy] *adj.* unaccented, unstressed; *gram.* atonic

безукоризненный [byez-ōō-ka-r'ěz-nyen-nǎy] *adj.* irreproachable; blameless

безуметь [byez-ōō-myét'] *vi.* to go mad

безумец [byez-ōō-myets] *sm.* madman

безумие [byez-ōō-mye] *sn.* insanity; lunacy; folly

безумный [byez-ōōm-nǎy] *adj.* crazy, frantic, mad; **безумные цены** [byez-ōōm-ná-ye tsyé-nǎ] extravagant prices

безумство [byez-ōōm-stvŏ] *sn.* insanity

безукоснность [byez-ōō-slóv-nōst'] *sf.* certainty

безусловный [byez-ōō-slóv-nǎy] *adj.* positive; unconditional

безуспешный [byez-ōō-spyésh-nǎy] *adj.* unsuccessful

безусый [byez-ōō-sǎy] *adj.* moustacheless; *fig.* very young, 'green'

безъязычный [byez-ya-zǎch-nǎy] *adj.* tongueless; *fig.* dumb, speechless

безымённый [byez-ǎ-myón-nǎy] *adj.* anonymous; nameless

бекар [bye-kǎr] *sm. mus.* natural (*cancelling* ♯ *or* ♭)

белёный [bye-lyó-nǎy] *adj.* bleached

белеть [bye-lyét'] *vi.* to whiten; to fade

белиберда [bye-l'i-byer-dǎ] *sf.* absurdity, nonsense; rot; **какая – !** [ka-kǎ-ya –] what rot!

белизна [bye-l'iz-nǎ] *sf.* whiteness

белильня [bye-l'ěl'-nya] *sf.* bleaching factory

белить [bye-l'ét'] *vi.* to bleach, whitewash; to white

белка [byél-ka] *sf.* squirrel

беллетрист [bye-lye-trēst] *sm.* novelist

беллетристика [bye-lye-tr'ēs-t'i-ka] *sf.* belles-lettres, literary works

белок [bye-lók] *sm.* albumen

белокалильный [bye-lo-ka-l'él-nǎy] *adj.* incandescent, white hot

белокурый [bye-la-kōō-rǎy] *adj.* blond, fair

белолицый [bye-la-l'é-tsǎy] *adj.* of a fair complexion

белоснежный [bye-la-snyézh-nǎy] *adj.* snow-white

белотелый [bye-la-tyé-lǎy] *adj.* fair-skinned

белошвейка [bye-la-shvyéy-ka] *sf.* seamstress; needle-woman

белошвейная [bye-la-shvyéy-na-ya] *sf.* sewing work-room

белый [byé-lăy] *adj.* white; **белые стихи** [byé-lă-ye st'i-chē] blank verse

бельгиец [byel'-gē-yets] *sm.* Belgian

бельгийка [byel'-gē-ka] *sf.* Belgian

бельгийский [byel'-gēs-ki] *adj.* Belgian

бельё [byel'-yó] *sn.* linen; underwear; **постельное –** [pas-tyél'-na-ye –] bedding; **столовое –** [sta-la-vó-ye –] table-linen

бельэтаж [byel'-e-tázh] *sm. theat.* first floor; dress-circle

белянка [bye-lyán-ka] *sf.* mushroom; fair-faced woman

бемоль [bye-mól'] *sm. mus.* flat (♭)

бенефициант [bye-ne-fi-tsyánt] *sm.* beneficiary

бердыш [byer-dăsh] *sm.* pole-axe

берег [byé-ryeg] *sm.* shore; **на берегу** [na bye-rye-gōō] ashore

бередить [bye-rye-d'ét'] *vt.* to irritate; to re-open (as a wound); to rip up

бережённый [bye-rye-zhón-năy] *adj.* well protected

бережливость [bye-ryezh-l'é-vost'] *sf.* parsimony, thrift

бережливый [bye-ryezhl'é-văy] *adj.* frugal, thrifty

бережность [byé-ryezh-nóst'] *sf.* heed, prudence

бережный [byé-ryezh-năy] *adj.* cautious

берёза [bye-ryó-za] *sf.* birch; **плакучая –** [pla-kōō-cha-ya –] weeping birch

беременеть [bye-ryé-mye-nyet'] *vt.i.* to conceive, become pregnant

беременная [bye-ryé-myen-na-ya] *adj.* enceinte, pregnant; *sf.* expectant mother

беременность [bye-ryé-myen-nóst'] *sf.* pregnancy

беречь [bye-ryéch'] (по-) *vt.* to look after, take care of; to respect; **-ся** [-sya] *vi.* to beware, mind; **берегитесь собаки!** [bye-rye-g'ě-tyes' sa-bá-ki] beware of the dog!

берлога [byer-ló-ga] *sf.* den, lair

бес [byes] *sm.* demon; **бесёнок** [bye-syó-nŏk] imp

беседа [bye-syé-da] *sf.* conversation, talk

беседка [bye-syéd-ka] *sf.* arbour, bower, summer-house

беседовать [bye-syé-da-vat'] (по-) *vi.* to chat, converse (in company)

бесить [bye-s'ĕt'] (вз-) *vt.* to infuriate

бескозырка [byez-kó-zăr-ka] *sf.* without trump (cards); **бескозырная игра** [byes-kó-zăr-na-ya i-grá] no trumps

бесконечность [byes-ka-nyéch-nost'] *sf.* eternity, infinity; the infinite; endlessness

бесконечный [byes-ka-nyéch-năy] *adj.* endless, everlasting, infinite, interminable; **бесконечномалая величина** [byes-ka-nyech-nŏ-má-la-ya vye-l'i-chi-nā] *math.* infinitesimal value

бескорыстный [byes-ka-rást-năy] *adj.* disinterested, unbiased

бескровие [byes-kró-vye] *sn.* anaemia

бескровный [byes-króv-năy] *adj.* anaemic, bloodless, pale, sickly-looking

бескручинный [byes-króo-chēn-năy] *adj.* carefree

беснование [byes-na-vā-nye] *sn.* anger, rage, vehemence

бесноватый [byes-na-vā-tăy] *adj.* demoniac, possessed with an evil spirit

бесноваться [byes-na-vat'-sya] *vi.* to rage; to be violent, to lose one's temper

бесовщина [bye-sav-shché-na] *sf.* devilry, iniquity

беспамятность [byes-pā-myat-nŏst'] *sf.* forgetfulness

беспамятный [byes-pā-myat-năy] *adj.* forgetful; unconscious

беспамятство [byes-pā-myat-stvŏ] *sn.* unconsciousness; **впасть в —** [vpast' v —] to lose consciousness

беспардонный [byes-par-dón-năy] *adj.* desperate, merciless; *coll.* impudent

беспартийный [byes-par-t'ē-năy] *adj.* non-party; independent

беспатентный [byes-pa-tyént-năy] *adj.* unlicensed

беспересадочный [byes-pye-rye-sā-dach-năy] *adj.* through (*train*); direct; **— билет** [— b'i-lyét] *sm.* through ticket

беспечность [byes-pyéch-nŏst'] *sf.* carelessness, unconcern

беспечный [byes-pyéch-năy] *adj.* heedless, unconcerned; careless; **беспечное существование** [byes-pyéch-na-ye sŏŏ-shche-stva-nye] a secure existence

бесплатность [byes-plát-nŏst'] *sf.* gratis, without payment

бесплатный [byes-plát-năy] *adj.* free (*of charge*), gratuitous

бесплодие [byes-pló-dye] *sn.* barrenness; infertility

бесплодность [byes-plód-nŏst'] *sf.* fruitlessness

бесплодный [byes-plód-năy] *adj.* barren, fruitless, sterile

бесповоротность [byes-pa-va-rót-nŏst'] *sf.* irrevocability

бесповоротный [byes-pa-va-rót-năy] *adj.* irrevocable, unalterable

бесподобный [byes-pa-dób-năy] *adj.* unrivalled; 'second to none'

беспокойный [byes-pa-kóy-năy] *adj.* fidgety, restless; **— ребёнок** [— rye-byó-nŏk] a troublesome child; **— взгляд** [— vzglyad] an anxious look

беспокойство [byes-pa-kóy-stvŏ] *sn.* trouble, unrest; disturbance, turmoil

беспокоить [byes-pa-kó-it'] (o-) *vt.* to bother, disturb, harass; **-ся** [-sya] *vi.* to fret, worry; to feel uneasy

бесполезность [byes-pa-lyéz-nŏst'] *sf.* uselessness

бесполезный [byes-pa-lyéz-nǎy] *adj.* unavailing, useless; **бесполезное начинание** [byes-pa-lyéz-na-ye na-chi-nǎ-nye] *sn. coll.* fool's errand

бесполый [byes-pó-lǎy] *adj.* asexual; *bot.* neuter; *biol.* agamous

беспомощность [byes-pó-mashch-nòst'] *sf.* helplessness, inability

беспомощный [byes-pó-mashch-nǎy] *adj.* helpless

беспорочный [byes-pa-róch-nǎy] *adj.* blameless, immaculate, perfect; **беспорочное зачатие** [byes-pa-róch-na-ye za-chǎ-tye] Immaculate Conception

беспорядок [byes-pa-ryǎ-dòk] *sm.* confusion, disorder; **в беспорядке** [vbyes-pa-ryǎd-ke] all over the place, a mix-up; **беспорядки** [byes-pa-ryǎd-kij] *sm. pl.* disorders, riot, upheaval

беспорядочность [byes-pa-ryǎ-dach-nòst'] *sf.* promiscuity

беспорядочный [byes-pa-ryǎ-dach-nǎy] *adj.* disorderly, irregular, promiscuous

беспочвенный [byes-póch-vyen-nǎy] *adj.* groundless, unfounded; fictitious

беспошлинный [byes-pósh-l'in-nǎy] *adj.* duty free

беспощадный [byes-pa-shchǎd-nǎy] *adj.* pitiless, relentless, unmerciful

бесправие [byes-prǎ-vye] *sn.* lawlessness; despotism; capriciousness; want of justice

бесправный [byes-prǎv-

nǎy] *adj.* arbitrary, lawless; discretionary

беспредметный [byes-pryed-myét-nǎy] *adj.* aimless

беспрепятственный [byes-prye-pǎt-stvyen-nǎy] *adj.* unimpeded, unobstructed

беспрерывность [byes-prye-rǎv-nòst'] *sf.* continuity, perpetuity

беспрерывный [byes-prye-rǎv-nǎy] *adj.* continued, incessant

беспризорный [byes-pr'i-zór-nǎy] *adj.* derelict; – **ребёнок** [– rye-byó-nòk] *sm.* street arab

беспримерный [byes-pr'i-myér-nǎy] *adj.* unprecedented; without equal

беспринципный [byes-pr'in-ts'ěp-nǎy] *adj.* unprincipled, unscrupulous

беспристрастный [byes-pr'i-strǎst-nǎy] *adj.* impartial, unbiased

бесприютный [byes-pr'i-yóot-nǎy] *adj.* homeless

беспробудный [byes-pra-bóod-nǎy] *adj.* sound (*as sleep*); – **сон** [– son] *fig.* eternal sleep, death

беспроволочный [byes-pró-va-lach-nǎy] *adj.* wireless

беспросветный [byes-pra-svyét-nǎy] *adj.* gloomy; without a ray of hope; **беспросветная тьма** [byes-pra-svyé't-na-ya t'mǎ] *sf.* utter darkness

беспутник [byes-póot-n'ik] *sm.* debauchee

беспутный [byes-póot-nǎy] *adj.* disreputable, licentious

бессвязанный [byes-svyǎzan-náy] *adj.* disconnected, incoherent

бессемейный [byes-sye-myéy-nay] *adj.* single, unmarried; childless

бессемянный [byes-sye-myán-nay] *adj.* seedless; acotyledonous

бессердечный [byes-syer-dyéch-nay] *adj.* heartless, pitiless

бессилие [byes-s'ē-lye] *sn.* feebleness, weakness; inability; **половое** – [pa-la-vó-ye –] impotence

бессильный [byes-s'ēl'-nay] *adj.* powerless, weak; impotent

бесславный [byes-sláv-nay] *adj.* inglorious; shameful

бесследный [byes-slyéd-nay] *adj.* untraceable; **он исчез бесследно** [on is-chéz byes-slyéd-no] he vanished into thin air

бессловный [byes-slóv-nay] *adj.* dumb; speechless

бессменный [byes-smyén-nay] *adj.* permanent

бессмертие [byes-smyér-tye] *sn.* immortality

бессмертник [byes-smyért-n'ik] *sm. bot.* immortelle

бессмертный [byes-smyért-nay] *adj.* immortal, undying

бессмысленность [byes-smás-lyen-nŏst'] *sf.* absurdity, foolishness, nonsense

бессмысленный [byes-smás-lyen-nay] *adj.* absurd, nonsensical, senseless

бессовестность [byes-só-vyest-nŏst'] *sf.* dishonesty, shamefulness

бессовестный [byes-só-vyest-nay] *adj.* shameful, unscrupulous

бессодержательный [byes-sa-dyer-zhá-tyel'-nay] *adj.* empty, devoid of substance

бессонница [byes-són-n'i-tsa] *sf.* insomnia; sleeplessness

бесспорный [byes-spór-nay] *adj.* indisputable, undebatable

бессрочный [byes-sróch-nay] *adj.* timeless, without limit

бесстрастие [byes-strás-tye] *sn.* indifference; apathy

бесстрастный [byes-strást-nay] *adj.* indifferent; phlegmatic

бесстрашный [byes-strásh-nay] *adj.* daring, fearless

бесстыдник [byes-stád-n'ik] *sm.* shameless person

бесстыдный [byes-stád-nay] *adj.* cheeky, immodest; lewd; obscene

бестолковый [byes-tal-kó-vay] *adj.* fatuous; silly, stupid

бесцветность [byes-tsvyét-nŏst'] *sf.* devoid of colour

бесцветный [byes-tsvyét-nay] *adj.* colourless; expressionless; achromatic

бесцельный [byes-tsyél'-nay] *adj.* aimless, purposeless

бесценный [byes-tsyén-nay] *adj.* invaluable, priceless

бесценок [byes-tsyé-nŏk] *sm.* 'dirt-cheap' article; **купить (продать) за** – [kŏŏ-p'ét' (pra-dát') za –] to buy (sell) for a trifle

бесцеремонный [byes-tsye-rye-món-nǎy] *adj.* off-handed, unceremonious

бесчеловечность [byes-che-la-vyéch-nǒst'] *sf.* barbarity, inhumanity

бесчестие [byes-chés-tye] *sn.* dishonour, infamy

бесчестить [byes-chés-t'it'] *vt.* to disgrace, dishonour

бесчестность [byes-chést-nǒst'] *sf.* dishonesty, wickedness

бесчисленный [byes-chés-lyen-nǎy] *adj.* countless, numberless; innumerable

бесчувственность [byes-chóov-stvyen-nǒst'] *sf.* insensibility, numbness; devoid of feeling

бетон [bye-tón] *sm.* concrete

бешенство [byé-shen-stvǒ] *sn.* madness, rage; hydrophobia; rabies

библейский [b'i-bléy-ski] *adj.* biblical, scriptural

библиография [b'i-bl'ia-grá-fya] *sf.* bibliography

библиотека [b'i-bl'ia-tyé-ka] *sf.* library

библиотекарь [b'i-bl'ia-tyé-kar'] *sm.* librarian

библия [b'é-blya] *sf.* Bible, Scriptures

бидон [b'i-dón] *sm.* can, container

биение [b'i-yé-nye] *sn.* beat, pulse, throb; beating

билет [b'i-lyét] *sm.* ticket; **билетная касса** booking-office

бинокль [b'i-nókl'] *sm.* opera-glasses; **полевой** – [pa-lye-vóy –] field-glasses

бинт [b'ent] *sm.* bandage

бинтовать [b'in-ta-vát'] (за-) *vt.* to bandage, swathe

биография [b'i-a-grá-fya] *sf.* biography

биология [b'i-a-ló-gya] *sf.* biology

биржа [b'ér-zha] *sf.* stock-exchange; **биржевой маклер** [b'ir-zhe-vóy mák-lyer] *sm.* stock-broker

бирка [b'ér-ka] *sf.* score, tally

бирюза [b'i-ryōó-zá] *sf.* turquoise

бирюзовый [b'i-ryōó-zó-vǎy] *adj.* turquoise

бирючина [b'i-ryōó-chi-na] *sf.* privet

бисер [b'é-syer] *sm.* (collective) beads, cheap pearls; **бисерина** [b'é-sye-r'i-na] *sf.* glass bead

бисировать [b'i-s'é-ra-vat'] *vt.* to encore

бисквит [b'is-kv'ét] *sm.* biscuit; **бисквитный рог** [b'is-kv'ét-nǎy p'i-róg] sponge-cake

битва [b'ét-va] *sf.* battle, fight

биток [b'i-tók] *sm.* beetle, ramming tool; beef cutlet

битый [b'i-tǎy] *adj.* beaten; cracked (of crockery, etc.); **битые сливки** [b'é-tǎ-ye sl'év-k'i] whipped cream

бить [b'ét'] (по-) *vt.* to beat, thrash; to strike (as clock); – **отбой** [– at-bóy] to sound a retreat

битье [b'i-tyó] *sn.* beating, flogging

биться [b'ét-sya] *vi.* to beat, throb, thump; to strive

битюк [b'i-tyōók] *sm.* Russian cart-horse

бич [b'éch] *sm.* lash, whip fig. pest, plague

бичевать [b'i-che-vät'] *vt.* to flog, lash; to tow

бичёвка [b'i-chóv-ka] *sf.* twine, whipcord

благо [blä-gŏ] *sn.* blessing; **общее** – [ób-shche-ye –] common weal

благоверный [bla-ga-vyér-nӑy] *adj. as sm.* husband (*jokingly*); **благоверная** [bla-ga-vyér-naya] *sf.* wife; (*literal translation*—blessedly true)

Благовещение [bla-ga-vyé-shche-nye] *sm.* Annunciation

благовидный [bla-ga-v'éd-nӑy] *adj.* comely, of good appearance; – **предлог** [– pryed-lóg] plausible excuse

благоволение [bla-ga-va-lyé-nye] *sn.* benevolence; favour

благовоние [bla-ga-vó-nye] *sn.* aroma, fragrance

благовонность [bla-ga-vón-nŏst'] *sf.* fragrancy

благовонный [bla-ga-vón-nӑy] *adj.* aromatic

благовоспитанность [bla-ga-vas-p'ē-tan-nŏst'] *sf.* good breeding, politness

благовоспитанный [bla-ga-vas-p'ē-tan-nӑy] *adj.* good-mannered, polite, well-bred

благоговейный [bla-ga-gav'éy-nӑy] *adj.* reverent

благоговение [bla-ga-gav'é-nye] *sn.* reverence, veneration

благодарить [bla-ga-da-r'ēt'] (по–) *vt.* to thank

благодарность [bla-ga-där-nŏst'] *sf.* gratitude, thanks; **в** –, in acknowledgment;

не стоит благодарности [nye stó-it bla-ga-där-nŏst'i] don't mention it

благодарный [bla-ga-där-nӑy] *adj.* grateful, thankful

благоденствие [bla-ga-dyén-stvye] *sn.* bliss; prosperity

благоденственный [bla-ga-dyén-stvyen-nӑy] *adj.* blissful; prosperous, thriving

благодетель [bla-ga-dyé-tyel'] *sm.* benefactor

благодеяние [bla-ga-dye-yä-nye] *sn.* benefaction, blessing; benefit

благодушие [bla-ga-dōō-shye] *sn.* complacency, magnanimity, placidity

благодушный [bla-ga-dōōsh-nӑy] *adj.* complacent, placid; calm, undisturbed

благожелательный [bla-ga-zhe-lâ-tyel'-nӑy] *adj.* benevolent, charitable, well-disposed

благозвучие [bla-ga-zvōō-chye] *sn.* euphony

благозвучный [bla-ga-zvōōch-nӑy] *adj.* harmonious, melodious

благой [bla-góy] *adj.* favourable, good, honourable

благолепие [bla-ga-lyé-pye] *sn.* grandeur, magnificence, splendour

благолепный [bla-ga-lyép-nӑy] *adj.* magnificent, splendid; pompous

благонадёжность [bla-ga-na-dyózh-nŏst'] *sf.* confidence; reliability

благонадёжный [bla-ga-na-dyózh-nӑy] *adj.* dependable, reliable

благонамеренный [bla-ga-na-myé-ryen-nǎy] *adj.* well-meant

благонравный [bla-ga-nráv-nǎy] *adj.* decent, moral, well-behaved

благообразный [bla-ga-ab-ráz-nǎy] *adj.* comely, pleasant, sightly

благополучный [bla-ga-pa-lóóch-nǎy] *adj.* felicitous, fortunate; safe, secure

благоприличие [bla-ga-pr'i-l'ē-chye] *sn.* decency, propriety

благоприятный [bla-ga-pr'i-yát-nǎy] *adj.* favourable, hopeful, propitious

благоразумие [bla-ga-ra-zōō-mye] *sn.* discreetness, common sense

благоразумный [bla-ga-ra-zōōm-nǎy] *adj.* prudent, reasonable, wise

благородный [bla-ga-ród-nǎy] *adj.* honourable; noble

благословение [bla-ga-sla-vyé-nye] *sn.* benediction, blessing

благословлять [bla-ga-slav-lyát'] (благослови́ть) *vt.* to bless

благостный [blá-gast-nǎy] *adj.* good, kind-hearted

благотворение [bla-ga-tva-ryé-nye] *sn.* charitable deed

благотворитель [bla-ga-tva-r'é-tyel'] *sm.* philanthropist

благотворность [bla-ga-tvór-nǒst'] *sf.* charity

благоустройство [bla-ga-ōō-stróy-stvǒ] *sn.* public welfare

благочестие [bla-ga-chés-tye] *sn.* devotion

благочестный [bla-ga-

chést-nǎy] *adj.* devout, pious, religious

блаженство [bla-zhén-stvǒ] *sn.* beatitude, felicity

блажлвый [blazh-l'ē-vǎy] *adj.* capricious; crazy

бланшировать [blan-shē-ra-vat'] *vt.* to blanch

блевать [blye-vát'] (с-) *vi.* to vomit

блевота [blye-vó-ta] *sf.* fit of sickness

блевотина [blye-vó-t'i-na] *sf.* puke

бледнеть [blyed-nyét'] (по-) *vi.* to become pale, lose colour

бледнить [blyed-n'ēt'] *vi.* to render colourless

бледноватый [blyed-na-vá-tǎy] *adj.* palish, whitish (*complexion*); faint (*colour*); dim (*light*)

бледность [blyed-nǒst'] *sf.* paleness, pallor

бледный [blyéd-nǎy] *adj.* pale, wan, white

блёклый [blyók-lǎy] *adj.* faded, withered

блеск [blyésk] *sm.* glitter, lustre; brilliance; **дешёвый** ‒ [dye-shó-vǎy ‒] cheap glitter; tinsel, tawdry brilliance

блестеть [blyes-tyét'] (за-) *vi.* to glitter, shine, sparkle

блёстка [blyóst-ka] *sf.* spangle

блестящий [blyes-tyá-shchi] *adj.* brilliant, lustrous, resplendent

блеяние [blye-yá-nye] *sn.* bleating

блеять [blye-yát'] (за-) *vi.* to bleat

ближайший [bl'i-zháy-shi]

adj. very near; the next one, proximate; – **родственник** [– ród-stvyen-n'ik] *sm.* next of kin

ближний [bl'ézh-n'i] *adj.* near, nigh; sm. neighbour

близ [bl'éz] *adv.* in the neighbourhood; close to

близиться [bl'i-z'ét'-sya] *vi.* to approach, come near, come up to

близкий [bl'éz-ki] *adj.* close by, near to; familiar, intimate

близлежащий [bl'iz-lye-zhá-shchi] *adj.* adjacent, adjoining to

близна [bl'iz-ná] *sf.* flaw

близнец [bl'iz-nyéts] *sm.* twin; **Близнецы** [bl'iz-nye-tsá] sign of the zodiac; **созвездие Близнецов** [sa-zvyéz-dye   bl'iz-nye-tsóv] Gemini

близорукий [bl'i-za-róó-ki] *adj.* short-sighted; myopic

близость [bl'é-zóst'] *sf.* nearness, vicinity; intimacy; propinquity; **по близости** [pa bl'é-zas-t'i] near at hand; within reach   (*painting*)

блик [bl'ék] *sm.* high light (*in painting*)

блин [bl'én] *sm.* pancake

блиндаж [bl'in-dázh] *sm. mil.* blindage; shelter

блистательный [bl'i-stá-tyel'-näy] *adj.* radiant

блистать [bl'i-stát'] *vt.i.* to shine; be conspicuous; – **красотой** [– krasa-tóy] be radiant with beauty

блок [blok] *sm.* pulley, sheave; *polit.* bloc

блокировать [bla-k'é-ra-vat'] *vt.* to blockade, obstruct

блокнот [blak-nót] *sm.* writing pad

блондин [blan-d'én] *sm.* blond; **блондинка** [bland'én-ka] *sf.* blonde

блоха [bla-chá] *sf.* flea

блуд [blóód] *sm.* lechery

блудить [blóó-d'ét'] *vi.* to rove, wander

блудливый [blóód-l'é-väy] *adj.* roguish

блудный [blóód-näy] *adj.* profligate, reckless; – **сын** [– sän] *sm.* prodigal son

блуждание [blóózh-dá-nye] *sn.* errancy; roaming, wandering

блуза [blóó-za] *sf.* blouse

блузник [blóóz-n'ik] *sm. fig.* labourer

блюдечко [blyoo-dyech-kó] *sn.* saucer   [(*food*)

блюдо [blyoo-dó] *sn.* course

блюсти [blyoo-st'é] (со-) *vt.* to guard, keep; observe; preserve

блюститель [blyoo-st'é-tyel'] *sm.* guardian, keeper

бляха [blya-chá] *sf.* number-plate

боа [bóá] *sm.* fur wrap, necklet; *zool.* boa

боб [bob] *sm.* bean; **турецкий** – [tóó-ryéts-ki –] kidney-bean, French bean; **остаться на бобах** [as-tát'-sya na ba-bách] to be left in the lurch

бобовник [ba-ba-v'ék] *sm.* bean-stalk

бобовые растения [ba-bó-vä-ye ras-tyé-nya] *sn.pl.* leguminous plants

бобёр [bo-byór] *sm.* beaver

Бог [bog] God, Lord, Almighty; **дай** –! [däy –] God grant! **сохрани** –! [sa-chran'é –] God forbid! **ради**

Бога! [rā-d'i bó-ga] for Heaven's sake! **слава Богу!** [slá-va bó-gŏŏ] thanks be to God!

богадельня [ba-ga-dyél'-nya] *sf.* alms-house, poorhouse

богатей [ba-ga-tyéy] *sm. coll.* wealthy man

богатеть [ba-ga-tyét'] (о-) *vi.* to become rich; to thrive

богатство [ba-gát-stvŏ] *sn.* fortune; riches; wealth

богатый [ba-gā-täy] *adj.* rich, wealthy

богатырский [ba-ga-tǎr-ski] *adj.* heroic, valiant; **– сон** [– son] *sm.* sound sleep

богатырство [ba-ga-tǎr-stvŏ] *sn.* chivalry

богатырь [ba-ga-tǎr'] *sm.* hero (*Russian folklore*); valiant knight

богач [ba-gāch] *sm.* one possessing riches

богачи [ba-ga-chē] *sm. sf. pl.* the rich

богиня [ba-gē-nya] *sf.* goddess

богобоязненность [ba-ga-ba-yāz-nyen-nŏst'] *sf.* fear of God

богомаз [ba-ga-māz] *sm. coll.* painter of ikons

богомерзкий [ba-ga-myérz-ki] *adj.* ungodly

богомолец [ba-ga-mó-lyets] *sm.* pilgrim

богопочитание [ba-ga-pa-chi-tā-nye] *sn.* the worship of God

Богородица [ba-ga-ró-d'i-tsa] *sf.* Our Lady, Virgin Mary

богослов [ba-ga-slóv] *sm.* theologian

богословие [ba-ga-sló-vye] *sn.* divinity; theology

богослужение [ba-ga-slŏŏ-zhé-nye] *sn.* divine service

боготворение [ba-ga-tva-ryé-nye] *sn.* deification; worship (*of idols*)

богохульник [ba-ga-chŏŏl'-n'ik] *sm.* blasphemer

богохульный [ba-ga-chŏŏl'-näy] *adj.* blasphemous, profane

богоявление [ba-ga-ya-vlyé-nye] *sn.* Epiphany

бодать [ba-dāt] *vt.* to butt; to gore

бодало [ba-d'ē-lŏ] *sn.* goad

бодрый [bó-dräy] *adj.* cheerful, jolly; **– духом** [– dŏŏ-chŏm] in good spirits

боевой [ba-ye-vóy] *adj.* battle-, war-; **боевые запасы** [ba-ye-vǎ-ye za-pā-sǎ] *sm. pl.* ammunition

боёк [ba-yók] *sm.* firing pin

боец [ba-yéts] *sm.* fighter, soldier, warrior

божба [bazh-bā] *sf.* oath

боже [bó-zhe] *voc.* O God! **– мой!** [– moy] oh, dear me!

божественность [ba-zhést-vyen-nŏst'] *sf.* heavenliness

божественный [ba-zhést-vyen-näy] *adj.* divine, heavenly

божество [bó-zhest-vŏ] *sn.* deity, divinity

божий [bó-zhi] *adj.* God's; **с Божьей помощью** [sbó-zhyey po-ma-shchyŏŏ] God willing; **божья коровка** [bó-zhya ka-róv-ka] *sf.* ladybird

бой [bóy] *sm.* fight; *mil.* conflict, engagement; striking (*of clock*)

бой-баба [bóy-ba-ba] *sf.* abusive woman

бойкий [bóy-ki] *adj.* dashing, pert; smart; glib

бойкость [bóy-kŏst'] *sf.* smartness; impudence, sauciness; glibness

бойница [bóy-n'i-tsa] *sf.* embrasure, opening; loophole

бойня [bóy-nya] *sf.* slaughter-house, shambles; *fig.* massacre, slaughter

бок [bok] *sm.* side; *anat.* flank; *(also arch. and mil.)* **--о--** [--а--] side-by-side; **колоть в боку** [ka-ló-tye vba-kōō] stitch in the side; **с боку на --** [sbó-kōō na --] from side to side; **боком** [bó-kŏm] sideways

бокал [ba-kāl] *sm.* drinking cup; goblet; champagne-glass

боковой [ba-ka-vóy] *adj.* lateral; oblique; **боковая улица** [ba-ka-vā-ya ōō-l'i-tsa] *sf.* by-road

боковушки [ba-ka-vōōsh-ki] *sf. pl. typ.* margins

боксировать [bak-s'ē-ra-vat'] *vi.* to box

болван [bal-ván] *sm.* blockhead, stupid person; dummy *(cards)*

болванка [bal-ván-ka] *sf.* block, mould, ingot of pig-iron

болгарин [bal-gá-rin] *sm.* **болгарка** [bal-gár-ka] *sf.* Bulgarian

болгарский [bal-gár-ski] *adj.* Bulgarian

более [bó-lye-ye] *adv.* more; **-- всего** [-- vsye-vó] most of all

болезненный [ba-lyéz-nyen-nǎy] *adj.* ailing, sickly; morbid

болезнь [ba-lyézn'] *sf.* illness; malady; **морская --** [mar-skā-ya --] sea-sickness; **очаг болезни** [a-chāg ba-lyéz-n'i] seat of disease; **одр болезни** [ódr ba-lyéz-n'i] sick-bed

болеть [ba-lyét'] *vi.* to ache; to ail, to be ill

болотина [ba-la-t'é-na] *sf.* fen, marshland

болотный [ba-lót-nǎy] *adj.* marshy, swampy

болото [ba-ló-tŏ] *sn.* bog, marsh

болтать [bal-tāt'] (вз--) *vt.* to shake, stir *(liquids)*; to chat, gossip

болтливый [balt-l'é-vǎy] *adj.* chatty, talkative

болтовня [bal-tav-nyá] *sf.* chat, gossip, talk; rigmarole

болтун [bal-tōōn] *sm.* chatter-box

болтушка [bal-tōōsh-ka] *sf.* scrambled egg; talkative woman

боль [bol'] *sf.* pain

больница [bal'-n'é-tsa] *sf.* hospital, infirmary

больно [ból'-nŏ] *adv.* painfully; **он -- горяч** [on -- ga-ryách] he is very hot-tempered

больной [bal'-nóy] *adj.* ill, sick; *as sm.* sick person

больные [bal'-nǎ-ye] *sm. pl.* the sick

больше [ból'-she] *adv.* more

большинство [bal'-shin-stvó] *sn.* majority

большой [bal'-shóy] *adj.* bulky; great; large; **боль--**

шая буква [bal'-sha-ya bŏŏk-va] capital letter

болячка [ba-lyäch-ka] sf. skin eruption

бомба [bóm-ba] sf. bomb

бомбардировать [bam-bar-d'i-ra-vät'] vt. to bombard

бомбардировка [bam-bar-d'i-róv-ka] sf. bombardment

бомбардировщик [bam-bar-d'i-róv-shchik] sm. bomber

бомбовоз [bam-ba-vóz] sm. bomber (aeroplane)

бона [bó-na] sf. bonus

бондарить [ban-dä-r'it'] vt. to cooper

бондарня [ban-där-nya] sf. cooperage

бондарь [bón-dar'] sm. cooper

борец [ba-ryéts] sm. wrestler; bot. aconite

борзая [bar-zä-ya] sf. greyhound

борзописец [bar-za-p'é-syets] sm. hack-writer

борзый [bór-zǎy] adj. fleet, swift

бормотание [bar-ma-tä-nye] sm. mumbling

бормотать [bar-ma-tät'] vi. to mumble, mutter

боров [bó-rŏv] sm. boar, hog; horizontal flue

борода [ba-ra-dä] sf. beard

бородавка [ba-ra-däv-ka] sf. wart

бородчатый [ba-rad-chä-tǎy] adj. wartlike; бородчатая трава [ba-rad-chä-ta-ya tra-vä] sf. nipple-wart

бородатый [ba-ra-dä-tǎy] adj. bearded

бородка [ba-ród-ka] sf. cuneiform peak; goatee

бородок [ba-ra-dók] sm.

puncher (tool)

борозда [ba-raz-dä] sf. furrow

бороздить [ba-raz-d'ét'] vt. to furrow, plough

борона [ba-ra-nä] sf. harrow

бороновать [ba-ra-na-vät'] vt. to harrow

бороться [ba-rót'-sya] vi. to struggle; wrestle; – за что-либо [– za shtó-l'i-bŏ] to contest

борт [bort] sm. border, hem, rim (of material, dress); brim (of hat); cushion (of billiard table)

борщ [borshch] sm. Russian soup (beetroot and cabbage)

борьба [bar'-bä] sf. contest, fight; strife

босой [ba-sóy] adj. barefooted

босоножка [ba-sa-nózh-ka] sf. barefooted dancer

босяк [ba-syäk] sm. tramp

ботаник [ba-tä-n'ik] sm. botanist

ботаника [ba-tä-n'i-ka] sf. botany

ботанический [ba-ta-n'é-ches-ki] adj. botanical

ботва [bat-vä] sf. leaf of beet; pot-herb

ботик [bó-t'ik] sm. over-shoe; yawl

ботинок [ba-t'é-nok] sm. boot; пара ботинок [pä-ra ba-t'é-nŏk] pair of boots

ботфорты [bat-fór-tǎ] sm. pl. jack-boots, Wellingtons

бочаг [ba-chäg] sm. pool

бочёнок [ba-chó-nŏk] sm. small barrel, keg, cask

бочка [bóch-ka] sf. barrel, tub; tun; вино из бочки [v'i-nó iz bóch-ki] wine from the wood

боязливость [ba-ya-zl'ē-vŏst'] *sf.* apprehensiveness, timidity

боязливый [ba-ya-zl'ē-vǎy] *adj.* fearful, timorous

боязнь [ba-yäzn'] *sf.* fear, fright

боярышник [ba-yǎ-rǎsh-n'ik] *sm.* hawthorn

бояться [ba-yät'-sya] *vi.* to be afraid

брага [brä-ga] *sf.* home-made beer

бражничать [brǎzh-n'i-chat'] *vi.* to drink to excess; to revel

брак [bräk] *sm.* marriage; matrimony

бракованный [bra-kó-van-nǎy] *adj.* defective, spoiled (*during manufacture*)

браконьер [bra-ka-nyér] *sm.* poacher

бракосочетание [bra-ka-so-che-tä-nye] *sn.* nuptials, wedding

бранить [bra-n'èt'] (по-) *vt.* to rebuke, scold

бранчливый [bran-chl'ē-vǎy] *adj.* quarrelsome

брат [brät] *sm.* brother; **двоюродный –** [dva-yōō-rad-nǎy –] cousin

братание [bra-tä-nye] *sn.* fraternization

брататься [bra-tät'-sya] *vi.* to fraternize

братия [brä-tya] *sf.* brotherhood, fraternity; brethren

братский [brät-ski] *adj.* brotherly, fraternal

братство [brät-stvŏ] *sn.* confraternity, fellowship

брать [brät'] (взять) *vt.* to take

брачный [bräch-nǎy] *adj.* conjugal, nuptial

бревно [bryev-nó] *sn.* beam, joist; log

бред [bryed] *sm.* delirium; frenzy; **быть в бреду** [bắt' vbrye-dóō] to be delirious

бредень [bryé-dyen] *sm.* drag-net

бредни [bryéd-n'i] *sf. pl.* nonsense

брезгать [bryéz-gat'] *vi.* to be fastidious, squeamish

бремя [bryé-mya] *sn.* burden, load; **снять –** [snyät' –] to exonerate

брехать [brye-chat'] (брехнуть) *vi.* to bark, yelp; to boast

брехун [brye-chōōn] *sm.* boaster, bragger

брешь [bryésh] *sf.* breach, gap; flaw

бригада [bri-gä-da] *sf.* brigade

британец [bri-tä-nyets] *sm.* Britisher

британский [bri-tän-ski] *adj.* British; Britannic

бритва [brit-va] *sf.* razor; **безопасная –** [bez-a-pás-na-ya –] safety razor

бритый [brí-tǎy] *adj.* clean-shaven

брить [brít'] (по-) *vt.* to shave; **-ся** [-sya] *vr.* to shave oneself

бритьё [bri-tyó] *sn.* shaving

бровь [brov'] *sf.* eyebrow

брод [brod] *sm.* ford

бродило [bra-d'ē-lŏ] *sn.* leaven

бродильный [bra-d'ĕl'-nǎy] *adj.* fermentative

бродить [bra-d'ēt'] *vt.i.* to ferment, work; to rove, wander; to stroll

бродяга [bra-dyá-ga] *sm.* vagabond; tramp; **бродячая собака** [bra-dyá-cha-ya sa-bā-ka] stray dog

брожение [bra-zhé-nye] *sn.* fermentation; discontent

броневик [bra-nye-v'ēk] *sm.* armoured car

броненосец [bra-nye-nó-syets] *sm.* battleship; *zool.* armadillo

броненосный [bra-ny -nós-nǎy] *adj.* armoured, iron-clad

бронза [brón-za] *sf.* bronze

броня [bró-nya] *sf.* armour, coat of mail; quota of apprentices

бросание [bra-sā-nye] *sn.* hurling, throwing

бросать [bra-sāt'] (бросить) [bró-sit'] *vt.* to fling, throw; to leave off, give up; – в жар [– vzhār] to go hot and cold; –ся [-syá] *vi.* to make a dash for; to throw oneself

брошенный [bró-shen-nǎy] *adj.* abandoned, deserted

брошировка [bra-shi-róv-ka] *sf. typ.* stitching

брошировать [bra-shi-ro-vāt'] *vt. typ.* to stitch

брошь [brosh'] *sf.* brooch

брошюра [bra-shōō-ra] *sf.* pamphlet

брульон [brōō-lyón] *sm.* rough copy

брус [brus] *sm.* longitudinal joist; **брусковое железо** [brōōs-kó-vǒ-ye zhe-lyé-zǒ] bar-iron

брусок [brōō-sók] *sm.* ingot; **точильный** – [ta-chēl'-nǎy –] whetstone

брусья [broo-syā] *sf.* crossbar

брутто [brōō-tǒ] *sn.* gross weight

брызгалка [brăz-gāl-ka] *sf.* syringe; sprayer (*for scent, etc.*)

брызганье [brăz-ga-nye] *sn.* splashing; sprinkling; patter (of rain)

брызгать [brăz-gat'] (брызнуть) [brăz-nut'] *vi.* to splash; to spatter; to squirt; to sputter

брыкать [brǎ-kāt'] (брыкнуть) [brǎk-nút'] *vt.* to kick; **брыкливая лошадь** [brǎ-kl'ě-va-ya ló-shad'] *sf.* bucking horse

брысь! [brǎs'] *interj.* begone!

брюзга [bryōōz-gā] *sf.* grumbler

брюзгливый [bryōōz-gl'ě-vǎy] *adj.* morose; *coll.* grumpy

брюква [bryōōk-va] *sf.* turnip; **шведская** – [shvyéd-ska-ya –] swede

брюки [bryōō-ki] *sf. pl.* trousers; breeches; pants

брюнет [bryōō-nyét] *sm.* man of dark complexion; **-ка,** *sf.* brunette

брюхо [bryōō-chó] *sn.* abdomen; paunch

брюшной [bryōōsh-nóy] *adj.* abdominal

бубны [bōōb-nǎ] *sf. pl.* diamonds (cards)

бугор [bōō-gór] *sm.* hill, mound

бугристый [bōō-grě-stǎy] *adj.* hilly

будень [bōō-dyen'] *sm.* weekday; working-day

будет! [bōō-dyet] *interj.* enough! stop it! that will do!

будильник [bōō-d'ēl'-n'ik] *sn.* alarm-clock

будить [bōō-d'ět'] (про-,

раз-) *vt.* to wake; to call; to rouse

будка [bŏŏd-ka] *sf.* booth, stall; **караульная** – [ka-ra-ŏŏl´-na-ya –] sentry-box; **собачья** – [sa-bā-chya –] dog-kennel

будный [bŏŏd-năy] *adj.* trivial

будоражить [bŏŏ-da-ră-zhit´] (вз–) *vt.* to disturb

будто [bŏŏd-tŏ] *conj.* as if, as though

будущее [bŏŏ-dŏŏ-shche-ye] *sn.* the future; – **время** [– vrýe-mya] *gram.* future tense

будущий [bŏŏ-dŏŏ-shchiy] *adj.* future, next

буерак [bŏŏ-ye-răk] *sm.* ravine

бузина [bŏŏ-z´i-nā] *sf. bot.* elder

буйвол [bŏŏy-vŏl] *sm.* buffalo

буйность [bŏŏy-nŏst´] *sf.* fury, violence

буйство [bŏŏy-stvŏ] *sn.* tumult, uproar

бук [bŏŏk] *sm.* beech

буква [bŏŏk-va] *sf.* character, letter; *typ.* type; **гласная** – [glās-na-ya –] vowel; **согласная** – [sa-glās-na-ya –] consonant; **начальная** – [na-chāl´-na-ya –] initial letter; **прописная** – [pra-p´is-nā-ya –] capital letter, upper case; **строчная** – [strach-nā-ya –] small letter, lower case

буквальный [bŏŏk-vāl´-năy] *adj.* literal, word for word

букварный [bŏŏk-văr-năy] *adj.* alphabetical

букварь [bŏŏk-văr´] *sm.* spelling book

буквица [bŏŏk-v´ē-tsa] *sf.* cowslip

букет [bŏŏ-kyét] *sm.* bouquet, nosegay, posy; aroma, bouquet (*of wine, etc.*)

букинист [bŏŏ-k´i-n´ēst] *sm.* second-hand book dealer

букля [bŏŏk-lya] *sf.* lock of hair, ringlet

буксирование [bŏŏk-s´ē-ra-va-nye] *sn.* towing

булавка [bŏŏ-lăv-ka] *sf.* pin; **английская** – [an-gl´ē-ska-ya –] safety pin

булочка [bŏŏ-lach-ka] *sf.* small French roll, bun

булочная [bŏŏ-lach-na-ya] *sf.* bakery

булочник [bŏŏ-lach-n´ik] *sm.* baker

булыжник [bŏŏ-lăzh-n´ik] *sm.* cobble-stone

бульвар [bŏŏl´-văr] *sm.* avenue, boulevard

булькать [bŏŏl´-kăt] *vi.* to gurgle

бульон [bŏŏ-l´ón] *sm.* broth

бумага [bŏŏ-mă-ga] *sf.* paper; **копировальная** – [ka-p´i-ra-văl´-na-ya –] carbon paper; **газетная** – [ga-zýet-na-ya –] news-print; **нотная** – [nót-na-ya –] *mus.* manuscript; **почтовая** – [pach-tó-va-ya –] note-paper; **промокательная** – [pra-ma-kă-tyel´-na-ya –] blotting paper; **стеклянная** – [styek-lyăn-na-ya –] sand paper; **хлопчатая** – [chlap-chă-ta-ya –] cotton

бумагопрядильня [bŏŏ-ma-ga-prya-d´ěl´-nya] *sf.* cotton-mill

бумажка [bŏŏ-măzh-ka] *sf.* slip of paper

бумажник [bōō-mázh-n'ik] *sm.* pocket-book

бумажный [bōō-mázh-nǎy] *adj.* paper

бумазея [bōō-ma-zyé-ya] *sf.* fustian; eider-down

бунт [bōōnt] *sm.* rebellion, uprising; *mil.* mutiny; riot; bale, bundle

бунтарь [bōōn-tár'] *sm.* rioter

бунтовщик [bōōn-tov-shchík] *sm.* rebel; mutineer

бур [bōōr] *sm.* auger (*tool*); Boer

бурав [bōō-ráv] *sm.* gimlet

буравить [bōō-rá-v'it'] (про-) *vt.* to bore, pierce

буран [bōō-rán] *sm.* snow-storm

буревестник [bōō-rye-vyést-n'ik] *sm.* petrel

бурение [bōō-ré-nye] *sn.* boring, drilling

буркать [bōōr-kat] (буркнуть) *vt.* to speak indistinctly

бурливый [bōōr-l'é-vǎy] *adj.* stormy, tempestuous

бурный [bōōr-nǎy] *adj.* boisterous, violent

бурчание [bōōr-chá-nye] *sn.* rumbling; muttering

бурый [bōō-rǎy] *adj.* brown, fallow

буря [bōō-rya] *sf.* storm, tempest

бусинка [bōō-s'in-ka] *sf.* bead; **бусы** [bōō-sä] *sf. pl.* beads

бутафор [bōō-ta-fór] *sm. theat.* property-master

бутафория [bōō-ta-fó-rya] *sf. theat.* properties

бутерброд [bōō-ter-brod] *sm.* sandwich

бутоньерка [bōō-ta-nyér-ka] *sf.* button-hole

бутылка [bōō-tál-ka] *sf.* bottle

бутыль [bōō-tál'] *sf.* flagon; carboy

буфет [bōō-fyét] *sm.* sideboard; buffet, refreshment room

буфетчик [bōō-fyét-chik] *sm.* barman; butler

буфетчица [bōō-fyét-chi-tsa] *sf.* barmaid

бухгалтер [bōōch-gál-tyer] *sm.* book-keeper

бухгалтерия [bōōch-gal-tyé-rya] *sf.* book-keeping; counting-house

бухта [bōōch-ta] *sf.* bay, cove, creek; coil (*of rope*)

бухточка [bōōch-tach-ka] *sf.* basin, inlet

буян [bōō-yán] *sm.* bully, ruffian; landing place

бывалый [bǎ-vá-lǎy] *adj.* former

бывать [bǎ-vát] *vi.* to happen, occur; to frequent

бывший [bǎv-shi] *adj.* late, quondam

бык [bǎk] *sm.* bull, ox; pier

былинка [bǎ-l'én-ka] *sf.* blade of grass

былой [bǎ-lóy] *adj.* by-gone; **в былые времена** [vbǎ-lá-ye vrye-mye-ná] in former days

быль [bǎl'] *sf.* fact, reality, true story

быстроногий [bǎ-stra-nó-gi] *adj.* light-footed, nimble

быстрота [bǎ-stra-tá] *sf.* quickness, rapidity

быстроходный [bǎ-stra-chód-nǎy] *adj.* high-speed

быстрый [bǎ-strǎy] *adj.* fast, rapid, speedy

быт [bǎt] *sm.* mode of life

бытие [bǎ-tyé] *sn.* existence;
Книга Бытия [kn'ē-ga bǎ-tyǎ] Genesis

бытописатель [bǎ-ta-p'i-sǎ-tyel'] *sm.* historian

быть [bǎt'] *aux. v.* to be;
как –? [kak –] what is one to do? **может –** [mó-zhet –] perhaps

бычачий [bǎ-chā-chi] *adj.* bovine

бычок [bǎ-chók] *sm.* young bull, steer; bullhead (*fish*)

бювар [byoo-vār] *sm.* blotting-pad

бюджет [byood-zhét] *sm.* budget

бюджетный [byood-zhét-nǎy] *adj.* budgetary

бюллетень [byoo-lye-tyén'] *sm.* bulletin

бюро [byoo-ró] *sn.* bureau, office; **справочное –** [sprā-vach-na-ye –] information office

бюрократия [byoo-ra-krā-tya] *sf.* bureaucracy

бюст [byoost] *sm.* bust; **-гальтер** [-gāl'-tyer] brassière

В

в [v] **во** [vŏ] *prep.* in: **в Англии** [vān-glii] in England;
в этом году [vé-tam ga-dŏō] this year; into, to:
идти в город [it-t'ē vgó-rŏd] to go into town; **поехать в Париж** [ra-yé-chat' vpa-rēzh] to go to Paris; for: **уехать в Лондон** [ōō-yé-chat' vlón-dŏn] to leave for London; at: **в театре** [vtye-ā-trye] at the

theatre; on: **во вторник** [va ftór-n'ik] on Tuesday

вабильщик [vab-bēl'-shchik] *sm.* falconer

вабить [vā-b'ít] *vt.* to lure

вагон [va-gón] *sm.* railway carriage; van

вагонетка [va-ga-nyét-ka] *sf.* trolley

вагранка [va-grān-ka] *sf.* cupola

важничать [vāzh-n'i-chat'] (за-) *vi.* to put on airs; appear important

важность [vāzh-nŏst'] *sf.* importance, significance, weight; **эка –!** [éka –] does not mean a thing!

важный [vāzh-nǎy] *adj.* important; grave

ваза [vā-za] *sf.* bowl, vase

вакансия [va-kān-sya] *sf.* vacancy

вакантный [va-kānt-nǎy] *adj.* vacant

вакация [va-kā-tsya] *sf.* holidays, vacation

вакса [vāk-sa] *sf.* blacking

вакцинация [vak-tsi-nā-tsya] *sf.* vaccination

вал [val] *sm.* roller; bulwark, rampart; shaft; spindle; billow, wave

валёк [va-lyók] *sm.* battledore

валет [va-lyét] *sm.* knave (*cards*)

валик [vā-ik] *sm.* bolster; small cylinder

валить [va-l'ét] (по-) *vt.* to overturn, throw down; to fell

валка [vāl-ka] *sf.* cutting down, felling

валкий [vāl-ki] *adj.* faltering, shaky

валлиец [val-l'ē-yets] *sm.* Welsh, Welshman

валлийский [val-l'ês-ki] *adj.* Welsh

валовой [va-la-vóy] *adj.* gross; wholesale; **валовая прибыль** [va-la-vá-ya pr'ê-bál'] *sf.* gross profit; **валовая сумма** [va-la-vá-ya sōō-ma] total sum

валторна [val-tór-na] *sf. mus.* French horn

валун [va-lōōn] *sm.* boulder

вальдшнеп [val'd-shnyép] *sm.* woodcock

вальс [val's] *sm.* waltz

вальсировать [val'-s'ê-ra-vat'] (про-) *vi.* to waltz

вальцовка [val'-tsóv-ka] *sf.* rolling

валюта [va-lyōō-ta] *sf.* rate; currency

валять [va-lyát'] (на-) *vt.* to roll; to knead

валяться [va-lyát'-sya] *vi.* to loll about, roll, tumble

вам [vām] *pr.* to you, for you

ванна [ván-na] *sf.* bath, bathtub

ванная [ván-na-ya] *sf.* bathroom

ванты [ván-tä] *sf. pl. naut.* shrouds

вар [vär] *sm.* tar; wax

варвар [vär-var] *sm.* barbarian

варварский [vär-var-ski] *adj.* barbarous, cruel

варварство [vär-var-stvó] *sn.* barbarism, cruelty

варево [vä-rye-vó] *sn.* broth, soup; concoction

варенец [va-ryé-nyets] *sm.* fermented milk

вареники [va-ryé-ni-ki] *sm. pl.* Russian curd dumplings

варенье [va-ryé-nye] *sn.* jam, preserves

варить [va-r'ět'] (с-) *vt.* to boil, cook, poach; to brew

варка [vär-ka] *sf.* boiling, cooking

варница [vär-n'i-tsa] *sf.* boiler-house; brewery; salt-works

вас [väs] *pron.* you (accusative)

василёк [va-s'i-lyók] *sm.* cornflower [wadding

вата [vä-ta] *sf.* cotton-wool,

ватный [vät-näy] *adj.* quilted, wadded

ватрушка [va-trōōsh-ka] *sf.* curd tart

вафля [väf-lya] *sf.* wafer

вахня [väkh-nya] *sf.* haddock

вахта [väkh-ta] *sf. naut.* lookout, watch

ваш [väsh] *pron.* your, yours

вайло [va-yä-lö] *sn.* chisel

ваяние [va-yä-nye] *sn.* carving, chiselling

ваятель [va-yä-tyel'] *sm.* carver, modeller, sculptor

ваять [va-yät'] (из-) *vt.* to chisel, model

вбегать [vbye-gät'] (вбежать) *vi.* to run in(to)

вбивать [vb'i-vät'] (вбить) *vt.* to hammer, wedge

вбирать [vb'i-rät'] (вобрать) *vt.* to absorb, soak up; imbibe, inhale

вбирание [vb'i-rä-nye] *sn.* absorbing, soaking up; inhalation

вблизи [vbl'i-z'ě] *adv.* not far from, near at hand, in the vicinity

вваливаться [vä-l'i-vat'-sya] (ввалиться) *vi.* to flock; to tumble into

введение [vye-dyé-nye] *sn.* introduction, preface; preamble

ввергать [vyer-gát'] (ввергнуть) vt. to precipitate

ввёртывать [vyór-tă-vat'] (ввертеть) vt. to turn, twist in; – словцо [– slav-tsó] to put in a (small) word

вверх [vyérch] adv. up, upward; – дном [– dnom] upside down

вверху [vyer-choó] adv. above; overhead

вверять [vye-ryát'] (вверить) vt. to entrust; to confide

ввиду [v'i-doó] adv. as; in view of

ввинчивать [v'ĕn-chi-vat'] (ввинтить) vt. to screw in

вводить [va-d'ĕt'] (ввести) to introduce, lead in; to insert, interpolate

вводный [vód-năy] adj. introductory, prefatory; parenthetic

ввоз [voz] sm. importation

ввозить [va-z'ĕt'] (ввезти) vt. to import; to bring in

вволакивать [va-lā-k'i-vat'] (вволочить) vt. to drag in

вволю [vó-lyóo] adv. to one's heart's content

ввязывать [vyā-ză-vat'] (ввязать) vt. to tie in; to knit in; fig. to entangle, involve; –ся [-sya] vi. to meddle; become implicated

вгиб [vg'ib] sm. an inward bend

вглубь [vglŏób'] adv. deep into

вглядываться [vglyā-dă-vat'-sya] vi. to peer, stare into; to observe, take stock of

вгонять [vga-nyát'] (вогнать) vt. to drive in

вдаваться [vda-vát'-sya] vi.

to jut out, cut into

вдавливать [vdāv-l'i-vat'] (вдавить) vt. to crush, press

вдали [vda-l'ĕ] adv. beyond, far off; держаться – [dyer-zhát'-sya] to keep aloof

вдаль [vdāl'] adv. into the distance, into space

вдвое [vdvó-ye] adv. doubly, twice, two-fold; – больше [– ból'-she] twice as much

вдвоём [vdva-yóm] pron. both, the two of us, two together

вдевать [vdye-vát'] (вдеть) vt. to thread through

вдёргивать [vdyór-gi-vat'] vt. to draw in, pull in

вдобавок [vda-bā-vŏk] adv. in addition, besides, furthermore

вдова [vda-vā] sf. widow; соломенная – [sa-ló-myen-na-ya –] grass widow

вдовец [vda-vyéts] sm. widower

вдоволь [vdó-val'] adv. enough, plenty

вдоль [vdol'] adv. along, by; longways; thoroughly

вдохновение [vdach-na-vyé-nye] sn. inspiration

вдохновлять [vdach-na-vlyát'] (вдохновить) vt. to infuse; to inspire

вдохновляться [vdach-na-vlyát'-sya] vi. to be inspired

вдребезги [vdrye-byez-gi] adv. smashed into fragments

вдруг [vdrŏóg] adv. suddenly; without warning

вдувать [vdŏó-vát'] (вдунуть) vt. to blow in

вдумчивость [vdŏóm-chi-vóst'] sf. pensiveness, thoughtfulness

вдумчивый [vdōm-chi-vày] *adj.* meditative

вдумываться [vdōō-mă-vat'-sya] *vi.* to ponder over

вдыхать [vdă-chàt'] (вдохнуть) *vt.* to inhale

вдыхание [vdă-chā-nye] *sn.* inhalation

вегетарианец [ve-ge-ta-ryā-nyets] *sm.* vegetarian

ведать [vyé-dàt'] *vt.* to know; to control, manage

ведение [vyé-dye-nye] *sn.* knowledge; authority

ведение [ve-dyé-nye] *sn.* managing; – дела [– dyé-la] transaction; – счетов [– sche-tóv] book-keeping; – хозяйства [– cha-zyāy-stva] house-keeping

ведомость [vyé-da-mŏst'] *sf.* journal, list, report; ведомости [vyé-da-mas-t'i] news; newspaper

ведомство [vyé-dam-stvŏ] *sn.* department, office; военное [– va-yén-na-ye –] War Office; судебное [– sōō-dyéb-na-ye –] law court; legal department (*in Russia*)

ведро [vye-dró] *sn.* bucket, pail

вёдро [vyó-drŏ] *sn. coll.* fine weather

ведун [vye-dōōn] *sm.* wizard

ведь [vyed'] *conj.* but, of course, why; well (*used only in conjunction with other words; no particular meaning alone*)

ведьма [vyéd'-ma] *sf.* hag, witch

веер [vyé-yer] *sm.* fan

веерообразный [vye-yep-za-abrāz-nãy] *adj.* fan-shaped

вежливость [vyé-zhl'i-vŏst']

sf. courtesy, politeness

вежливый [vyé-zhl'i-vãy] *adj.* civil, gallant, polite

везде [vyez-dyé] *adv.* everywhere; anywhere; – и всюду [– i vsyōō-dōō] here, there and everywhere

вездесущность [vyez-dye-sōōshch-nŏst'] *sf.* omnipresence

везти [vyez-t'é] (по-) *vt.* to carry, transport; ему не везёт [ye-mōō nye vye-zyót] he has no luck

век [vyék] *sm.* age, century; eternity; в кои-то веки [vka-ēta vyé-k'i] once in a blue moon; на веки вечные [na vyé-k'i vyéch-nã-ye] for ever and ever

веко [vyé-kã] *sn.* eyelid

вековечный [vye-ka-vyéch-nãy] *adj.* everlasting

вексель [vék-syel'] *sm.* bill of exchange, draft

векша [vyék-sha] *sf.* squirrel

велеть [vye-lyét'] (по-) *vt.* to command, order, tell

великан [vye-l'i-kān] *sm.* giant

великий [vye-l'é-ki] *adj.* great; – пост [– post] Lent; великая пятница [vye-l'é-ka-ya pyāt-n'i-tsa] Good Friday

великобританский [vye-l'i-ka-bri-tān-ski] *adj.* British

великовозрастный [vye-l'i-ka-vóz-rast-nãy] *adj.* overgrown

великодушие [vye-l'i-ka-dōō-shye] *sn.* generosity, magnanimity

великодушный [vye-l'i-ka-dōōsh-nãy] *adj.* generous, liberal

великолепие [vye-l'i-ka-lyé-pye] sn. dignity, grandeur, splendour

великолепный [vye-l'i-ka-lyép-nåy] adj. glorious; magnificent, superb

великопостный [vye-l'i-ka-póst-nåy] adj. Lenten

величавость [vye-l'i-chå-vöst'] sf. dignity

величавый [vye-l'i-chå-våy] adj. dignified, majestic

величайший [vye-l'i-chåy-shi] adj. greatest, paramount, supreme

величать [vye-l'i-chåt'] vt. to extol, glorify, praise

величественность [vye-l'é-chest-vyen-nöst'] sf. exaltation, stateliness

величественный [vye-l'é-chest-vyen-nåy] adj. grand, stately

величество [vye-l'é-chest-vö] sn. majesty

величие [vye-l'é-chye] sn. greatness, magnificence

величина [vye-l'i-chi-nå] sf. largeness; size; math. quantity, value [cycle-track

велодром [vye-la-dróm] sm.

велосипед [vye-la-s'i-pyéd] sm. bicycle

велосипедист [vye-la-s'i-pye-d'ést] sm. cyclist

велюр [vye-lyör] sm. velours

вена [vyé-na] sf. vein; **воспаление вен** [vas-pa-lyé-nye vyen] phlebitis

венгерец [vyen-gyé-ryets] sm., **венгерка** [vyen-gyér-ka] sf. Hungarian

венгерский [vyen-gyér-ski] adj. Hungarian

венерический [vye-nye-r'é-ches-ki] adj. venereal

венец [vyé-nyets] sm. crown, wreath

венечный [vye-nyech-nåy] adj. anat. coronal

вензель [vyén-zyel'] sm. initials (monogram)

веник [vye-n'ik] sm. broom

веничек [vye-n'i-chek] sm. bot. panicle

венок [vye-nók] sm. garland, wreath; chaplet (on head)

вентилировать [vyen-t'i-l'é-ra-vat'] vt. to ventilate

вентилятор [vyen-t'i-lyå-tör] sm. fan, ventilator

вентиляция [vyen-t'i-lyå-tsya] sf. ventilation

венчание [vyen-chå-nye] sn. wedding

венчать [vyen-chåt'] (y-) to marry; **-ся** [-sya] vi. to be married

венчик [vyén-chik] sm. halo, nimbus; bot. corolla

вепрь [vyépr'] sm. wild boar

вера [vyé-ra] sf. belief, faith, religion, trust

верба [vyér-ba] sf. cobbler's thread [camel

верблюд [vyer-blyóod] s.

верёвка [vye-róv-ka] sf. cord, rope, string

веред [vye-ryed] sm. boil, sore

ережжание [vye-ryez-zhå-nye] sn. whimpering

вереница [vye-rye-n'é-tsa] sf. file, line, row

вереск [vyé-ryesk] sm. heather

веретено [vye-rye-tye-nó] sn. spindle; shank

верея [vye-rye-yå] sf. gatepost

вериги [vye-r'é-gi] sf. pl. chains, fetters, irons

верить [vyé-r'it'] (по-) vi. to believe, to trust

верно [vyér-nŏ] *adv.* faithfully, truly; correctly, rigidly; **верно!** that's it! quite right!

верноподданный [vyer-na-pód-dan-năy] *adj.* loyal; *sm.* loyal subject

верность [vyer-nŏst'] *sf.* fidelity, loyalty; truth

вернуть [vyer-nōōt'] *vt.* to recall; **-ся** [-sya] *vi.* to come back, return

верный [vyér-năy] *adj.* faithful, true

веровать [vyé-ra-vat'] *vi.* to have faith in

вероисповедание [vye-ra-is-pa-vye-dá-nye] *sn.* creed, religion

вероломный [vye-ra-lóm-năy] *adj.* disloyal, false, treacherous

вероломство [vye-ra-lóm-stvŏ] *sn.* perfidy, treachery

веротерпимый [vye-ra-tyer-p'é-măy] *adj.* tolerant

вероучение [vye-ra-ōō-ché-nye] *sn.* religious doctrine

вероятность [vye-ra-yát-nŏst'] *sf.* probability

вероятный [vye-ra-yát-năy] *adj.* likely

верстак [vyer-sták] *sm.* joiner's bench

верстатка [vyer-stát-ka] *sf. typ.* composing stick

верстать [vyer-stát'] (по-) *vt. typ.* to impose

вертел [vyer-tyél] *sm.* spit (*for roasting*)

вертеть [vyer-tyét'] (по-) *vt.* to turn, twist

вертлявый [vyer-tlyă-văy] *adj.* fidgety, restless

вертолёт [vyer-ta-lyót] *sm.* helicopter

верфь [vyerf'] *sf.* dockyard, wharf

верх [vyerch] *sm.* top, upper part; *fig.* upperhand

верховный [vyer-chóv-năy] *adj.* supreme

верхом [vyer-chóm] *adv.* on horseback; [vyér-chŏm] *adv.* heaped, quite full

верхушка [vyer-chōōsh-ka] *sf.* peak, top

верчение [vyer-ché-nye] *sn.* boring, turning

верша [vyér-sha] *sf.* fishing basket

вершина [vyer-shē-na] *sf.* summit

вес [vyés] *sm.* tare; weight

веселить [vye-sye-l'ět'] (раз-) *vt.i.* to cheer, gladden, rejoice; **-ся** [-sya] *vi.* to enjoy oneself, to be merry

весёлость [vye-syó-lŏst'] *sf.* hilarity, merriment

весёлый [vye-syó-lăy] *adj.* gay, jolly

веселье [vye-syé-lye] *sn.* gaiety, merriment

весить [vyé-s'it'] *vt.* to weigh

веский [vyés-ki] *adj.* weighty

вескость [vyés-kŏst'] *sf.* weight

весло [vyes-ló] *sn.* oar; scull; [paddle

весна [vyes-ná] *sf.* spring;

весною [vyes-nó-yōō] in spring

веснушка [vyes-nōōsh-ka] *sf.* freckle

вести [vyes-t'ě] (по-) *vt.* to conduct, lead; keep; carry on

вестник [vyést-n'ik] *sm.* herald, messenger

весть [vyést'] *sf.* item of news, tidings

весы [vye-sá] *sm. pl.* scales; weighing machine

весь [vyés'] *s.*, *adj.* all, total, whole

весьма [vyes'-má] *adv.* exceedingly, very, very much

ветвь [vyetv'] *sf.* branch (*of tree*); shoot, sprig, twig

ветер [vyé-tyer] *sm.* wind; **сквозной** – [skvaz-nóy –] draught

ветеринарный [vye-tye-r'i-nár-nǎy] *adj.* veterinary

ветерок [vye-tye-rók] *sm.* breeze

ветка [vyét-ka] *sf.* rail. branch-line; twig

ветла [vyet-lá] *sf.* willow

ветошник [vyé-tǎsh-n'ik] *sm.* rag-merchant

ветошь [vyé-tǒsh] *sf.* old clothes, rags

ветреник [vyé-trye-n'ik] *sm.* nincompoop; **ветреница** [vyé-trye-n'i-tsa] *sf.* light-hearted woman; *bot.* anemone

ветреность [vyé-trye-nǒst'] *sf.* fickleness, frivolity, thoughtlessness

ветреный [vyé-trye-nǎy] *adj.* wind-, windy; flighty, thoughtless

ветрянка [vye-tryǎn-ka] *sf.* windmill

ветхий [vyét-chi] *adj.* ancient, aged; dilapidated; enfeebled

ветхость [vyé-chǒst'] *sf.* decay; oldness; decrepitude, infirmity

ветчина [vyet-chi-ná] *sf.* ham

веха [vyé-cha] *sf.* landmark

вечер [vyé-cher] *sm.* evening; **вечеринка** [vye-che-r'én-ka] evening party; **вечером** [vyé-che-rǒm] *adv.* in the evening

вечерня [vye-chér-nya] *sf.* vespers

вечность [vyéch-nǒst'] *sf.* eternity

вечный [vyéch-nǎy] *adj.* eternal; endless

вешалка [vyé-shal-ka] *sf.* clothes-stand, coat-hanger, peg; tab

вешать [vye-shat'] (повесить) *vt.* to hang, hang up, suspend; to weigh

вешний [vyésh-n'i] *adj.* vernal

вещание [vye-shchǎ-nye] *sn.* prediction, utterance

вещатель [vye-shchǎ-tyel'] *sm.* diviner

вещать [vye-shchǎt'] *vi.* to prophesy

вещественность [vye-shchést-vyen-nǒst'] *sf.* substantiality

вещественный [vye-shchést-vyen-nǎy] *adj.* material, real

вещество [vye-shche-stvó] *sn.* essence, reality, substance

вещь [vyeshch'] *sf.* object, thing; **вещи** [vyé-shchi] belongings, luggage, things

веять [vyé-yat'] (по-) *vi.* to blow; to winnow

вжимать [vzhi-mát'] (вжать) *vt.* to force in, push in, squeeze in

взад [vzad] *adv.* back, backwards; – **и вперёд** [– ĭ fpe-ryód] up and down, to and fro

взаём [vza-yóm] *adv.* on credit

взаимный [vza-ím-nǎy] *adj.* mutual, reciprocal

взаимодействие [vza-íma-dyést-vye] *sn.* interaction, interplay; reciprocity

взаимопомощь [vza-ima-pó-móshch'] *sf.* mutual aid

взамен [vza-myén] *adv.* in exchange for, instead of, in return for

взаперти [vza-pyer-t'é] *adv.* under lock and key

взбалтывать [vzbál-tǎ-vat'] (взболтáть) *vt.* to shake up, stir

взбегать [vzbye-gát'] (взбежáть) *vi.* to run up

взбелениться [vzbye-lyé-n'ét'-sya] *vi.* to get angry, frantic

взбеситься [vzbye-s'ét'-sya] *vi.* to go mad (*especially of dog*); to become furious

взбешённый [vzbye-shón-nǎy] *adj.* furious, violent

взбивать [vzb'i-vát'] (взбить) *vt.* to beat up, churn, whip; — **постель** [— pa-stýél'] to shake up bedding

взбираться [vzb'i-rát'-sya] (взобрáться) *vi.* to ascend, climb up

взбрасывать [vzbrá-sǎ-vat'] (взбрóсить) *vt.* to throw up

взбунтоваться [vzbōōn-ta-vát'sya] *vi.* to mutiny, revolt

взбучка [vzbōōch-ka] *sf.* reprimand; **дать взбучку** [dat' vzbōōch-kōō] to tell one off; **получить взбучку** [pa-lōō-chit' vzbōōch-kōō] to become involved in a row, dispute, etc.

взвешивание [vzvyé-shi-va-nye] *sn.* weighing; weighing-in

взвешивать [vzvyé-shi-vat'] (взвéсить) *vt.* to weigh; to consider

взвивать [vzvi-vát'] (взвить) *vt.* to raise (*as bird in the air*); to raise (*as curtain*)

взвизгивать [vzvízg-gi-vat'] (взвúзгнуть) *vi.* to scream, squeak; to howl (*as dog*)

взвинчивать [vzv'ēn-chi-vat'] (взвинчúть) *vt.* to excite, rouse; inflate (*prices*)

взвод [vzvod] *sm.* platoon; section (*in army*)

взволновать [vzval-na-vát'] *vt.* to agitate, upset; to disturb; to stir

взгляд [vzglyád] *sm.* glance, look; outlook

взглядывать [vzglyá-dǎ-vat'] (взглянýть) *vi.* to glance at, look at

взгорье [vzgó-rye] *sn.* hill

вздёргивать [vzdyór-gi-vat'] (вздёрнуть) *vt.* to hitch up, jerk up, pull up

вздор [vzdor] *sm.* nonsense, trash

вздорность [vzdór-nòst'] *sf.* absurdity

вздорный [vzdór-nǎy] *adj.* absurd, nonsensical

вздорожание [vzda-ra-zhá-nye] *sn.* price increase

вздох [vzdoch] *sm.* gasp; sigh

вздрагивать [vzdrá-gi-vat'] (вздрóгнуть) *vi.* to start (*involuntary movement*); to flinch, wince

вздремнуть [vzdryem-nōōt'] *vi.* to doze, have a nap

вздувать [vzdōō-vát'] (вздуть) *vt.* to blow, fan (*a fire*)

вздумать [vzdōō-mat'] *vt.* to take into one's head; to occur to one

вздыматься [vzdǎ-mát'-sya] *vi.* to rise (*as clouds*); to heave (*chest*)

вздыхатель [vzdă-<u>chă</u>-tyel'] *sm. fig.* suitor, sweetheart

вздыхать [vzdă-<u>chăt</u>](вздохнуть) *vi.* to sigh; to long for

взимать [vz'i-măt'] *vt.* to collect, gather, raise

взламывать [vzlă-mă-vat'] *vt.* to force open, wrench

взлелеять [vzlye-lyé-yat'] *vt.* to bring up, nurture

взлёт [vzlyót] *sm.* upward flight

взлом [vzlom] *sm.* housebreaking; forcing open

взломщик [vzlóm-shchik] *sm.* burglar

взмах [vzmach] *sm.* flapping; upward swing; stroke

взмахивать [vzmă-chi-vat'](взмахнуть) *vt.* to beat, flap (*wings*); to swing

взмёт [vzmyot] *sm.* first ploughing

взметнуть [vzmyet-nóōt] *vt.i.* to flap (*as with wings*); to fling (*as one's arms*)

взмолиться [vzma-l'ět'-sya] *vi.* to beseech, cry out, implore

взморье [vzmó-rye] *sn.* beach, sea-shore; estuary

взмыленный [vzmă-lyén-năy] *adj.* foamy, soapy

взнос [vznos] *sm.* fee, payment; instalment; deposit; contribution

взнуздывать [vznōōz-dă-vat'] (взнуздать) *vt.* to bridle; to control, curb

взор [vzor] *sm.* gaze, glance, look

взрастать [vzras-tăt'] (взрасти) *vi.* to grow up

взрезывать [vzryé-ză-vat'] (взрезать) *vt.* to cut open, slit; dissect

взрослый [vzrós-lăy] *adj.* adult, grown-up

взрыв [vzrăv] *sm.* explosion; burst (*of applause*); outbreak (*of excitement*); peal (*of laughter*)

взрывать [vzră-văt'] *vt.* to dig up, turn up (*soil*); to explode

взывать [vză-văt'] (воззвать) *vt.* to appeal, invoke

взыскивать [vzăs-k'i-vat'] (взыскать) *vt.* to exact, extort

взятие [vzyă-tye] *sn.* capture, taking

взятка [vzyăt-ka] *sf.* bribe; trick (*cards*)

взяточничество [vzyă-tach-n'i-chest-vŏ] *sn.* bribery

взяться [vzyat'-sya] *vi.* to undertake (*take upon oneself a task, etc.*); — за работу [— za ra-bó-tōō] to start work; — за оружие [— za a-rōō-zhye] to take up arms

вид [v'id] *sm.* aspect, view; appearance; kind, sort, species

видение [v'i-dyé-nye] *sn.* sight, vision; apparition; phantom

видеть [v'ĕ-dyet] (у-) *vt.* to perceive, see; to behold, view

видимый [v'ĕ-d'i-măy] *adj.* apparent, visible; clear; evident

видно [v'ĕd-nŏ] *adv.* apparently, evidently

видный [v'ĕd-năy] *adj.* conspicuous, prominent

видоизменять [v'i-do-iz-mye-nyăt'] *vt.* to alter, change; to vary

визг [v'ĕzg] *sm.* scream, shriek, squeal; yelp; screaming, *etc.*

визжать [v'iz-zhát'] (за-) *vi.* to scream, shriek

визитка [v'i-z'étka] *sf.* morning coat

вилка [v'ĕl-ka] *sf.* fork

вилочка [v'ĕ-lach-ka] *sf.* wishbone; small fork

вилы [v'ĕ-lȳ] *sf. pl.* pitchfork

вилять [v'i-lyát'] *vi.* to wag, wriggle; to prevaricate

вина [v' inā] *sf.* fault, guilt; **поставить в вину** [pa-stā-v'it' vv'i-nōō] to incriminate

винительный [v'i-n'ĕ-tyel'-nāy] *adj. gram.* accusative

винить [v'i-n'ĕt'] (об-) *vt.* to accuse, impute

вино [v'i-nó] *sn.* wine

виноватый [v'i-na-vā-tāy] *adj.* culpable, guilty; **виноват!** [v'i-na-vāt] excuse me, please! so sorry! I beg your pardon!

виновник [v'i-nóv-n'ik] *sm.* culprit

виноград [v'i-na-grād] *sm.* grapes, vine

виноградарство [v'i-na-grā-dar-stvŏ] *sn.* viticulture

виноградник [v'i-na-grād-n'ik] *sm.* vineyard

виноделие [v'i-na-dyé-lye] *sn.* vine-growing

винокур [v'i-na-kōōr] *sm.* distiller; **винокуренный завод** [v'i-na-kōō-ryen-nāy zavód] distillery

винт [v'int] *sm.* screw; **винтик** [v'in-t'ik] *sm.* tiny screw

винтить [v'i-nt'ét'] (за-) *vt.* to screw

винтовка [v'in-tóv-ka] *sf.* rifle

винтовой [v'in-ta-vóy] *adj.* spiral

виолончель [vio-lon-chél'] *sf. mus.* violoncello, 'cello

вирша [v'ĕr-sha] *sf.* doggerel

виселица [v'ĕ-sye-l'i-tsa] *sf.* gallows, scaffold

висеть [v'i-syét'] (повис-нуть) *vi.* to be hanging, suspended

вислоухий [v'i-sla-ōō-chi] *adj.* lop-eared

висок [v'i-sók] *sm. anat.* temple

високосный год [v'i-sa-kós-nāy god] *sm.* leap year

височный [v'i-sóch-nāy] *adj.* temporal (*of the head*)

висюлка [v'i-syōōl-ka] *sf.* pendant

витать [v'i-tāt'] *vi.* to be absent-minded; to dwell

витиеватый [v'i-tye-vā-tāy] *adj.* ornate; eloquent; florid

витрина [v'i-tr'ēna] *sf.* shop-window; show-case

Виттова пляска [v'ĕt-ta-va plyás-ka] *sf.* St. Vitus's dance

вить [v'ĕt'] (с-) *vt.* to twist, wind; to weave

витязь [v'ĕ-tyaz'] *sm.* knight

вихор [v'i-chór] *sm.* forelock

вихрь [v'ĕchr'] *sm.* whirlwind; *fig.* vortex

вишнёвый [v'ish-nyó-vāy] *adj.* cherry; **сад** [– sad] *sm.* cherry orchard; **вишнёвая наливка** [v'ish-nyó-va-ya na-l'ĕv-ka] *sf.* cherry-brandy

вишня [v'ĕsh-nya] *sf.* cherry; cherry-tree

вишь! [v'ĕsh'] *interj.* look! there! – **какая!** [– ka-kā-ya] what a strange girl!

вкапывать [vkā-pā-vat']

(вкопа́ть) *vt.* to dig in, drive in

вка́тывать [vka-tǎ-vat'] (вкати́ть) *vt.* to roll in, wheel in

вклад [vklád] *sm.* deposit, investment; contribution, donation

вкла́дчик [vklád-chik] *sm.* depositor, investor

вкла́дывать [vklā-dǎ-vat'] (вкласть) *vt.* to enclose; to invest; to put into

вкле́ивать [vklyé-i-vat'] (вкле́ить) *vt.* to glue in, paste in, stick in

вкле́йка [vkléy-ka] *sf.* inset

включа́ть [vklyōō-chát'] (включи́ть) *vt.* to include; insert

включи́тельно [vklyōō-ché-tyel'-nŏ] *adv.* inclusively

вкола́чивание [vka-lā-chi-va-nye] *sn.* driving in, hammering in

вконе́ц [vka-nyéts] *adv.* completely, entirely, wholly; altogether, quite

вкореня́ть [vka-rye-nyát'] (вкорени́ть) *vt.* to enroot, implant firmly; to impress

вкось [vkos'] *adv.* askew, crookedly, obliquely

вкра́дчивый [vkrád-chi-vǎy] *adj.* ingratiating, insinuating; cheating

вкра́тце [vkrá-tsye] *adv.* briefly, in short, terse

вкруг [vkrōōg] *adv.* around

вкруту́ю [vkrōō-tōō-yōō] *adv.* hard-boiled (*egg*)

вкус [vkōōs] *sm.* relish, taste; style

вку́сный [vkōōs-nǎy] *adj.* savoury, tasty; palatable; delicious

вкуша́ть [vkōō-shat'] (вкуси́ть) *vt.* to partake, taste; to enjoy

вла́га [vlá-ga] *sf.* dampness, moisture

влага́лище [vla-gā-l'i-shche] *sn. anat., bot.* vagina

владе́лец [vla-dyé-lyets] *sm.* owner, proprietor

владе́тель [vla-dyé-tyel'] *sm.* governor, ruler; possessor; sovereign

владе́ть [vla-dyét'] (за-) *vt.* to own, possess; to govern

влады́чество [vla-dǎ-chest-vŏ] *sn.* lordship (*title*); dominion

вла́жность [vlázh-nŏst'] *sf.* dampness, humidity; moisture

вла́мываться [vlā-mǎ-vat'-sya] (влами́ться) *vi.* to break into; to enter with violence

власть [vlast'] *sf.* power, rule; authority

влачи́ть [vla-chét'] (про-) *vt.* to drag, draw

вле́во [vlyé-vŏ] *adv.* to the left

влеза́ть [vlye-zát'] (влезть) *vi.* to climb in, creep in

влепля́ть [vlyep-lyát'] (влепи́ть) *vt.* to stick, glue in

влета́ть [vlye-tát'] (влете́ть) *vi.* to fly in

влече́ние [vlye-ché-nye] *sn.* craving, desire; inclination; impulse

влечь [vlyéch'] (по-, у-) *vt.* to involve; to bring; to attract

влива́ть [vl'i-vát'] (влить) *vt.* to pour into; to infuse; to fall into (*river into sea*)

влия́ние [vl'i-yā-nye] *sn.* influence; authority

влиятельный [vl'i-yá-tyel'-năy] *adj.* influential

влиять [vl'i-yát'] (по-) *vt.* to influence

вложение [vla-zhé-nye] *sn.* enclosure

влопаться [vló-pat'-sya] *vi. coll.* to get oneself into trouble; put one's foot in it

влюблённый [vlyŏŏb-lyónnăy] *adj.* in love; amorous *sm.* lover, sweetheart; **быть влюблённым** [bắt' vlyŏŏb-lyón-nám] to be in love

влюбляться [vlyŏŏb-lyát'-sya] *vi.* to fall in love

вмазывать [vmá-ză-vat'] (вмазать) *vt.* to cement, fasten with putty

вменение [vmye-nyé-nye] *sn.* imputation

вменять [vmye-nyát'] (вменить) *vt.* to ascribe, impute

вместе [vmyés-tye] *adv.* together

вместительность [vmyest'é-tyel'-nŏst'] *sf.* spaciousness

вместительный [vmyest'é-tyel'-năy] *adj.* roomy

вместо [vmye-stŏ] *adv.* instead, in place of

вмешательство [vmyeshá-tyel'-stvŏ] *sn.* interference; intervention

вмешивать [vmyé-shi-vat'] (вмешать) *vt.* to implicate, involve; **-ся** [-sya] *vi.* to interfere, intervene; to meddle in other people's affairs

вмещать [vmye-shchát'] *vt.* to contain, hold

вмиг [vm'ég] *adv.* instantly

внаём [vna-yóm] *adv.* to be let, for hire; **взять -** [vzyat' -] to hire, rent

вначале [vna-chá-lye] *adv.* at first

вне [vnyé] *adv.* outside; **быть - себя** [sye-byá] to be in a temper; **- дома** [- dó-ma] out of doors

внедрять [vnye-dryát'] (внедрить) *vt.* to embed; to instil

внезапный [vnye-záp-năy] *adj.* sudden, unexpected; **внезапное начало** [vnye-záp-na-ye na-chá-lŏ] outbreak

внесение [vnye-sé-nye] *sn.* entry (*in book*); insertion

внешний [vnyésh-n'i] *adj.* external, outward

внешность [vnyésh-nŏst'] *sf.* exterior

вниз [vn'éz] *adv.* down, downwards; **внизу** [vn'i-zŏŏ] *adv.* below, downstairs; at the bottom

вникать [vn'i-kát'] (вникнуть) *vi.* to look into; to investigate

внимание [vn'i-má-nye] *sn.* attention, care, regard

внимательный [vn'i-má-tyel'-năy] *adj.* attentive; thoughtful

вновь [vnó-vye] *adv.* recently; new

вновь [vnov'] *adv.* afresh, anew, over again

вносить [vna-s'ét'] (внести) *vt.* to carry in, get in; to book, enter

внук [vnŏŏk] *sm.* grandson

внутренний [vnŏŏ-tryen-n'i] *adj.* inner, internal

внутренность [vnŏŏ-tryen-nŏst'] *sf.* interior

внутри [vnŏŏ-tr'é] *adv.* inside, within

внучка [vnŏŏch-ka] *sf.* granddaughter

внушать [vnōō-shāt'] (внушить) *vt.* to infuse, inspire; to suggest

внушение [vnōō-shé-nye] *sn.* inspiration; suggestion

внятный [vnyāt-náy] *adj.* audible, distinct

во [va] *prep.* in (*used before words beginning with certain combinations of consonants*)

вобла [vób-la] *sf.* roach

вовлекать [va-vlye-kāt'] (вовлечь) *vt.* to implicate; to involve; to confuse, mislead

во-время [vó-vrye-mya] *adv.* in time

вовсе [vóv-sye] *adv.* altogether, completely; at all; – нет [– nyet] not at all

вогнутый [va-gnōō-táy] *adj.* concave; bent in

вод [vod] *sm.* breeding, rearing

вода [va-dā] *sf.* water; ехать водою [yé-chat' va-dó-yōō] to go by water; воды [vó-dā] *pl.* watering place

водворение [vad-va-ryé-nye] *sn.* establishment; settlement; installation

водворять [vad-va-ryāt'] (водворить) *vt.* to establish, to install; -ся [-sya] *vi.* to settle down

водить [va-d'ēt'] (по-) *vt.* to conduct, guide; to run (*a concern*)

водка [vód-ka] *sf.* vodka (*made from rye*)

водный [vód-náy] *adj.* water; водная окись [vód-na-ya ó-k'is'] hydrate

водобоязнь [va-da-ba-yāzn'] *sf.* hydrophobia

водовместилище [va-da-

водовоз [va-da-vóz] *sm.* water-carrier

водоворот [va-da-va-rót] *sm.* whirlpool

водоём [va-da-yóm] *sm.* cistern, tank; reservoir

водоизмещение [va-da-iz-mye-shché-nye] *sn.* displacement, tonnage

водокачка [va-da-kāch-ka] *sf.* pumping-station; watertower; pump

водолаз [va-da-lāz] *sm.* diver

Водолей [va-da-lyéy] *sm.* Aquarius

водолечебный [va-da-lye-chéb-náy] *adj.* hydropathic

водомер [va-da-myér] *sm.* hydrometer

водонепроницаемый [va-da-nye-pro-n'i-tsā-ye-máy] *adj.* watertight

водоосвящение [va-da-asvya-shché-nye] *sn.* consecration

водопад [va-da-pād] *sm.* waterfall

водопой [va-da-póy] *sm.* trough

водопровод [va-da-pra-vód] *sm.* aqueduct; conduit

водопроводчик [va-da-pra-vód-chik] *sm.* plumber

водород [va-da-ród] *sm.* hydrogen

водоросль [va-da-rósl'] *sf.* seaweed

водоснабжение [va-da-snab-zhé-nye] *sn.* water-supply

водоспуск [va-da-spōōsk] *sm.* sluice

водосток [va-da-stók] *sm.* drain; gutter

водружать [va-drōō-zhāt'] *vt.* to erect, set-up; to hoist

водянка [va-dyán-ka] *sn. med.* dropsy

водяной [va-dya-nóy] *adj.* aquatic

воевать [va-ye-vát'] *vi.* to wage war

воедино [va-ye-d'ē-nŏ] *adv.* together; united

военачальник [va-ye-na-chál'-n'ik] *sm.* commander-in-chief

военнопленный [va-yen-na-plyén-nay] *sm.* prisoner of war

военные [va-yén-nă-ye] *adj. pl.* military; – **действия** [– dyéy-stv'i-ya] *sn. pl.* hostilities; – **запасы** [– za-pá-să] *sm. pl.* munitions; *as s.pl.* the military

военный [va-yén-nay] *adj.* military; – **флот** [– flot] navy

вожак [va-zhák] *sm.* leader; conductor

вожделение [vazh-dye-lyé-nye] *sn.* desire, longing

вождь [vozhd'] *sm.* chieftain; leader

вожжа [vazh-zhá] *sf.* rein, reins

воз [voz] *sm.* cart-load; load

возбранять [vaz-bra-nyát'] *vt.* to forbid, prohibit

возбудитель [vaz-bŏŏ-d'ē-tyel'] *sm.* instigator

возбудительный [vaz-bŏŏ-d'ē-tyel'-nay] *adj.* exciting, stimulating

возбуждать [vaz-bŏŏzh-dát'] (возбудить) *vt.* to arouse, excite, stimulate

возбуждение [vaz-bŏŏzh-nye] *sn.* incitement, stimulation; excitement

возведение [vaz-vye-dyé-nye] *sn.* raising; advancement, promotion

возвеличение [vaz-vye-l'i-ché-nye] *sn.* exaltation, glorification

возвещать [vaz-vye-schát'] (возвестить) *vt.* to announce, proclaim

возвещение [vaz-vye-shché-nye] *sn.* announcement

возвратный [vaz-vrát-nay] *adj.* returning, recurring; – **глагол** [– gla-gól] *gram.* reflexive verb

возвращать [vaz-vra-shchát'] (возвратить) *vt.* to return; to restore; to recall; – **ся** [–sya] *vi.* to come back

возвышать [vaz-vă-shát'] (возвысить) *vt.* to lift up, raise; to elevate; to increase (*price*); to advance (*in position, rank*)

возвышение [vaz-vă-shé-nye] *sn.* elevation, raising

возвышенный [vaz-vǎ-shen-nay] *adj.* elevated, lofty; dignified

возглас [vóz-glas] *sm.* exclamation

возглашать [vaz-gla-shát'] (возгласить) *vt.* to exclaim; to proclaim

возгонка [vaz-gón-ka] *sf.* sublimation

возгораемый [vaz-ga-rá-ye-may] *adj.* inflammable

воздавать [vaz-da-vát'] (воздáть) *vt.* to render, to restore; to reward

воздаяние [vaz-da-yá-nye] *sn.* requital, reward; retribution

воздействие [vaz-dyéy-stvye] *sn.* influence; reaction

возделывание [vaz-dyé-la-va-nye] *sn.* cultivation, tillage

воздерживаться [vaz-dyér-zhi-vat'-sya] (воздержа́ться) *vt.* to abstain, restrain; forbear, refrain

воздержность [vaz-dyér-zhnŏst'] *sf.* abstinence, moderation, temperance; полная – [pól-na-ya –] teetotalism

воздух [vóz-dōŏch] *sm.* air, atmosphere; на во́льном -е [na-vól'-nŏm -ye] in the open air, out of doors

воздухоплавание [vaz-dōŏ-cha-plǎ-va-nye] *sn.* aeronautics

воздушный [vaz-dōŏsh-nǎy] *adj.* aerial, air, airy

возжигать [vaz-zhi-gát'] (возже́чь) *vt.* to kindle, light; to excite

воззвание [vaz-zvá-nye] *sn.* appeal; proclamation

воззрение [vaz-zryé-nye] *sn.* opinion, view; consideration

возить [va-z'ět'] (по-) *vt.* to carry, convey, transport; to cart, draw

возлагать [vaz-la-gát'] (возложи́ть) *vt.* to lay upon, rest on; to confer; to entrust

возле [vóz-lye] *prep.* beside, near; close to

возлежать [vaz-lye-zhát'] (возле́чь) *vi.* to recline

возликовать [vaz-l'i-ka-vát'] *vi.* to rejoice, triumph

возложение [vaz-la-zhé-nye] *sn.* imposition

возлюбленный [vaz-lyōŏb-lyen-nǎy] *adj.* beloved, dear; *sm.* lover, sweetheart

возмездие [vaz-myéz-dye] *sn.* retribution; requital

возмечтать [vaz-myech-tát'] *vi.* to be conceited

возмещать [vaz-mye-shchát'] (возмести́ть) *vt.* to compensate, repay; make amends; to indemnify

возмещение [vaz-mye-shché-nye] *sn.* compensation, reparation

возможный [vaz-mózh-nǎy] *adj.* feasible, possible; practicable

возмужалый [vaz-mōŏ-zhǎ-lǎy] *adj.* adult, grown-up, mature

возмутительный [vaz-mōŏ-t'ě-tyel'-nǎy] *adj.* outrageous, scandalous

возмущать [vaz-mōŏ-shchát'] (возмути́ть) *vt.* to anger, stir up; to cause revolt

возмущение [vaz-mōŏ-shché-nye] *sn.* insurrection, mutiny, revolt

вознаграждать [vaz-na-grazh-dát'] (вознагради́ть) *vt.* to recompense, reward; to compensate; – за поте́рю [– za pa-tyé-ryōŏ] to make good a loss

вознаграждение [vaz-na-grazh-dyé-nye] *sn.* recompense, reward; fee, pay, remuneration

Вознесение [vaz-nye-syé-nye] *sn.* Ascension

возникать [vaz-n'i-kát'] (возни́кнуть) *vi.* to appear, arise, occur, spring up

возникновение [vaz-n'i-kna-vé-nye] *sn.* outbreak; appearing, arising

возносить [vaz-na-s'ét'] (вознести́) *vt.* to lift up, raise; to extol, praise; – моли́тву [– ma-l'ět-vōŏ] to offer a prayer

возношение [vaz-na-shé-nye] sn. elevation, exaltation; praise; pride

возня [vaz-nyá] sf. trouble; annoyance, nuisance

возобновление [va-zab-na-vlyé-nye] sn. renewal, resumption

возобновлять [va-zab-na-vlyát'] (возобновить) vt. to renew, resume; to renovate

возок [va-zók] sm. closed sleigh

возрадоваться [vaz-rá-da-vat'-sya] vi. to rejoice

возражать [vaz-ra-zhát'] (возразить) vi. to object; to oppose; to retort

возражение [vaz-ra-zhé-nye] sn. objection; refutation

возраст [vóz-rast] sm. age; growth; **одного -а** [ad-na-vó -a] of the same age; **войти в полный -** [vay-t'é vpól-nɐy -] to become of age

возрастать [vaz-ras-tát'] (возрасти) vi. to grow up; increase

возрождать [vaz-razh-dát'] (возродить) vt. to regenerate

возрождение [vaz-razh-dýé-nye] sn. rebirth; revival; **эпоха Возрождения** [e-pó-cha vaz-razh-dýé-nya] Renaissance

возчик [vóz-chik] sm. carrier, carter; driver

возыметь [va-ză-myét'] vt. to consider; **- желание** [- zhe-lá-nye] to set one's heart upon

воин [vó-in] sm. soldier, warrior

воинский [vó-in-ski] adj. martial, military; troop (train, etc.)

воинственный [va-ěn-stvyen-nɐy] adj. valiant, warlike; truculent

воистину [va-ês-t'i-nŏŏ] adv. indeed, truly, verily

вой [voy] sm. howl, whining

войлок [vóy-lŏk] sm. felt

война [voy-ná] sf. war, warfare; **вести войну** [vyes-t'é vay-nŏŏ] to wage war

войско [vóy-skŏ] sn. army, military, troops

вокальный [va-kál'-nɐy] adj. vocal

вокзал [vag-zál] sm. railway station

вокруг [va-krŏŏg] adv. about, around, round

вол [vol] sm. bull, ox

волан [va-lán] sm. shuttlecock; flounce

волглый [vól-glɐy] adj. humid, moist

волдырь [val-dár'] sm. blister; boil, lump, swelling

волк [volk] sm. wolf; **волкодав** [val-ka-dáv] wolf-dog

волна [val-ná] sf. billow, wave

волнение [val-nýé-nye] sn. emotion; agitation; tumult; commotion, disturbance; **- моря** [- mó-rya] heavy seas

волнистый [val-n'é-stɐy] adj. ripply, wavy; undulating; curly (hair)

волнолом [val-na-lóm] sm. breakwater

волокнистый [va-lak-n'és-tɐy] adj. fibrous

волокно [va-lak-nó] sn. fibre; filament

волос [vó-lŏs] sm. hair; pl. **волосы** [vó-lŏ-sǎ]

волосатый [va-la-sā-tăy] adj. hairy, shaggy

волосок [va-la-sók] sm. hair-spring; filament

волочение [va-la-ché-nye] sn. dragging, trailing

волочить [va-la-chét'] (по-) vt. to drag, draw, trail

волхвование [val-chva-vā-nye] sn. magic, sorcery

волчёнок [val-chó-nŏk] sm. wolf-cub

волчок [val-chók] sm. humming-top

волшебник [val-shéb'n'ik] sm. magician

волшебный [val-shéb-năy] adj. fairy, magical

вольно [vól'-nŏ] adv. freely; mil. stand at ease!

вольнодумец [val'-na-dōō-myets] sm. freethinker

вольнонаёмный [val'-na-na-yóm-năy] adj. hired, mercenary

вольнослушатель [val'-na-slōō-sha-tyel'] sm. external student

вольность [vól'-nŏst'] sf. freedom, liberty; licence (poetic)

вольный [vól'-năy] adj. free; – **каменщик** [= kā-myen-shchik] freemason

воля [vó-lya] sf. will, will-power; freedom; **волей-неволей** [vó-lyey-nye-vó-lyey] willy-nilly

вон [von] adv. out; there; away; yonder; **пошёл –!** [pa-shól –] get out! be off!

вонзать [van-zát'] (вонзить) vt. to drive in, thrust

вонь [von'] sf. stench

вонючка [va-nyôō-chka] sf. zool. skunk

вонять [va-nyăt'] vi. to stink

воображать [va-a-bra-zhăt'] (вообразить) vt. to conceive, fancy, imagine

воображение [va-a-bra-zhé-nye] sn. fancy, imagination

вообще [va-ab-shché] adv. generally

воодушевление [va-a-dōō-she-vlyé-nye] sn. enthusiasm; ardour; animation

воодушевлять [va-a-dōō-she-vlyăt'] vt. to inspire; to animate

вооружать [va-a-rōō-zhăt'] (вооружить) vt. to arm, to equip; –**ся** [-sya] vi. to take up arms; to revolt

вооружение [va-a-rōō-zhé-nye] sn. arming; armament; equipment

воочию [va-óchi-yōō] adv. seemingly

во-первых [va-pyér-vǎch] adv. firstly, primarily

вопить [va-p'ět'] (вз-) vi. to lament, mourn; to sob; to cry out

воплощать [va-pla-shchăt'] (воплотить) vt. to embody, incarnate

вопреки [va-prye-k'ě] adv. contrary to, despite

вопрос [va-prós] sm. query, question; interrogation

вопросительный [va-pra-s'ě-tyel'-năy] adj. interrogative; – **знак** [-znăk] note of interrogation, question mark

вопросник [va-prós-n'ik] sm. questionnaire

вопросный [va-prós-năy] adj. questionable

вор [vor] sm. burglar; thief

воркова́ть [var-ka-vát'] (за-) *vi.* to coo

воркотня́ [var-kat-nyá] *sf.* grumbling

воробе́й [va-ra-byéy] *sm.* sparrow; - саме́ц [- sá-myets] cock-sparrow; - са́мка [- sám-ka] hen-sparrow

ворова́ть [va-ra-vát'] (с-) *vt.* to steal

воровство́ [va-rav-stvó] *sn.* theft; larceny

ворожба́ [va-razh-bá] *sf.* fortune-telling

ворожи́ть [va-ra-zhét'] (по-) *vt.* to tell fortunes, to divine

во́рон [vó-rŏn] *sm.* raven

воро́на [va-ró-na] *sf.* crow

вороно́ить [va-ra-n'ét'] *vt.* to burnish

воро́нка [va-rón-ka] *sf.* funnel; crater; eddy

во́рот [vó-rŏt] *sm.* collar; capstan, windlass

воро́та [va-ró-ta] *sf.* gate, gateway

вороти́ть [va-ra-t'ét'] (по-) *vt.* to call back; -ся [-sya] *vi.* to return

воротни́к [va-rat-n'ék] *sm.* collar, neckband

во́рох [vó-rŏch] *sm.* heap, pile

вороча́ть [va-ra-chát'] (воро́тить) *vt.* to roll, turn

ворс [vors] *sm.* nap, pile (*of velvet, etc.*)

ворси́льна [var-s'él'-na] *sf.* carding-comb

ворси́ть [var-s'ét'] (на-) *vt.* to raise nap

ворся́нка [var-syán-ka] *sf.* teasel

ворча́ть [var-chát'] (за-) *vi.* to grumble; to growl

во́семдесят [vó-syem-dye-syat] *num.* eighty

восемна́дцать [va-syem-nád-tsat'] *num.* eighteen

во́семь [vó-syem'] *num.* eight

восемьсо́т [va-syem'-sót] *num.* eight hundred

воск [vosk] *sm.* wax

восклица́ние [vas-kl'i-tsá-nye] *sn.* exclamation

восклица́тельный [vas-kl'i-tsá-tyel'-nǎy] *adj.* exclamatory; - знак [- znäk] *sm.* exclamation mark

воскресе́ние [vas-krye-syé-nye] *sn.* resurrection; ве́рбное [- vyérb-na-ye -] Palm Sunday; све́тлое [svyét-la-ye] Easter Sunday

воскресе́нье [vas-krye-syé-nye] *sn.* Sunday

воскуря́ть [vas-kŏŏ-ryát'] (воскури́ть) *vt.* to fumigate

воспале́ние [vas-pa-lyé-nye] *sn.* inflammation; - лёгких [- lyóch-k'ich] pneumonia

воспаря́ть [vas-pa-ryát'] (воспари́ть) *vi.* to soar

воспева́ть [vas-pye-vát'] (воспе́ть) *vt.* to chant; to praise; to sing

воспита́ние [vas-p'i-tá-nye] *sn.* education, upbringing

воспита́тель [vas-p'i-tá-tyel'] *sm.* teacher, tutor; instructor

воспи́тывать [vas-p'é-tä-vat'] (воспита́ть) *vt.* to bring up, educate

воспламене́ние [vas-pla-mye-nyé-nye] *sn.* ignition

воспламеня́ть [vas-pla-mye-nyát'] *vt.* to inflame

воспо́льзоваться [vas-pól'-

za-vat'-sya] vi. to profit by, take advantage of, avail oneself of

воспоминание [vas-pa-m'i-ná-nye] sn. remembering, recollection, reminiscence

воспретительный [vas-prye-t'é-tyel'-nǎy] adj. forbidding, prohibitive

воспрещать [vas-prye-shchát'] (воспретить) vt. to forbid, prohibit

восприемник [vas-pr'i-yém-n'ik] sm. godfather

восприемница [vas-pr'i-yém-n'i-tsa] sf. godmother

восприимчивый [vas-pr'i-ém-chi-vǎy] adj. receptive, susceptible

восприятие [vas-pr'i-yǎ-tye] sn. perception; assumption

воспротивиться [vas-pra-t'i-vět'-sya] vt.i. to oppose, resist

восстание [vas-stá-nye] sn. rebellion, revolt

восстановление [vas-ta-na-vlyé-nye] sn. recovery, restoration

восток [va-stók] sm. east; orient; **Средний** – [sryéd-n'i–] Middle East; **Дальний** – [dǎl'-n'i –] Far East

восторг [va-tórg] sm. delight, ecstasy, rapture

восточный [vas-tóch-nǎy] adj. eastern, oriental

восхваление [vas-chva-lyé-nye] sn. praising; eulogy

восхвалять [vas-chva-lyát'] (восхвалить) vt. to commend; praise

восхитительный [vas-chi-t'é-tyel'-nǎy] adj. charming, delightful; delicious

восхищение [vas-chi-shché-

nye] sn. admiration, ravishment

восход [vas-chód] sm. ascent; rising; – **солнца** [– són-tsa] sunrise

восшествие [vas-shést-vye] sn. accession; ascent

восьмой [vas'-móy] num. eighth

вот [vot] adv. here; there; **вот!** here (there) you are! – **тебе раз!** [– tye-bye ráz] Well, I never!

вошь [vosh'] sf. louse

вояжёр [va-ya-zhór] sm. commercial traveller

впадать [fpa-dát'] (впасть) vi. to fall in, flow into; – **в грех** [– vgryéch] to lapse into sin

впадение [fpa-dyé-nye] sn. issue, mouth (of river)

впадина [fpá-d'i-na] sf. cavity, hollow; pit

впаивать [fpá-i-vat'] (впаять) vt. to solder in

впалый [fpá-lǎy] adj. hollow, sunken

вперёд [fpe-ryód] adv. ahead, forward, onward

впереди [fpe-rye-d'é] adv. in front of, ahead of; before

вперемежку [fpe-rye-myésh-kŏŏ] adv. confusedly; pell-mell

впечатление [fpe-cha-tlyé-nye] sn. impression, sensation; inculcation

впивать [fp'i-vát'] (впить) vt. to imbibe; to absorb

вписывать [fp'é-sǎ-vat'] (вписать) vt. to enter (in book); to inscribe; to register

впитывать [fp'é-tǎ-vat'] (впитать) vt. to absorb, soak up

вплотную [fplat-nōō-yōō] *adv.* closely, firmly

вплоть [fplot'] *adv.* almost to the end, till, up to; close to

вплывать [fplă-vāt'] (вплыть) *vi.* to sail in (of ships); to swim in

вполголоса [fpal-gó-la-sa] *adv.* in a whisper

вползать [fpal-zāt'] (вползти) *vi.* to creep in; to worm into

вполне [fpal-nyé] *adv.* entirely, fully, quite, totally

вполовину [fpal-a-ví-nōō] *adv.* half, in half, half-way

впопад [fpa-păd] *adv.* opportunely, well-timed

впору [fpó-rōō] *adv.* at the right time; fittingly

впоследствии [fpa-slyéd-stv'ii] *adv.* afterwards, later

впотьмах [fpat'-măch] *adv.* in the dark

вправду [fpráv-dōō] *adv.* indeed, really, truly; seriously

вправлять [fprav-lyāt'] (вправить) *vt.* to set (a bone, a dislocation)

вправо [fpră-vò] *adv.* to the right; turn right!

впрах [fprăch] *adv.* totally, utterly

впредь [fpryéd'] *adv.* henceforth, in future

впроголодь [fpró-ga-lŏd'] *adv.* half starving; **жить** – [zhit' –] exist from hand to mouth

впросак [fpra-săk] *adv.* be in difficulty, in a dilemma

впросонках [fpra-són-kach] *adv.* half asleep

впрочем [fpró-chem] *adv.* besides, however, otherwise

впрыгивать [fpră-gi-vat']

(впрыгнуть) *vi.* to jump in

впрыскивание [fprăs-ki-va-nye] *sn.* injecting, syringing

впуск [fpōōsk] *sm.* admittance

впускать [fpōōs-kāt'] (впустить) *vt.* to admit, let in

впустую [fpōōs-tōō-yōō] *adv.* to no purpose, in vain

впутывать [fpōō-ti-vat'] (впутать) *vt.* to entangle, implicate; **-ся** [-sya] *vi.* to interfere, meddle

враг [vrăg] *sm.* enemy, foe

вражда [vrazh-dā] *sf.* animosity, enmity; hostility

враждебный [vrazh-dyéb-năy] *adj.* hostile

враз [vrăz] *adv.* suddenly

вразрез [vraz-ryéz] *adv.* contrary

вразумительный [vra-zoo-m'ĕ-tyel'-năy] *adj.* perspicuous; intelligible

вразумлять [vra-zōōm-lyāt'] (вразумить) *vt.* to comprehend; to explain, teach; to make listen to reason

враки [vrā-ki] *pl.* idle talk, lies

враль [vral'] *sm.* fibber, liar; humbug

вратарь [vra-tār'] *sm.* goalkeeper

врасплох [vras-plóch] *adv.* by surprise, unawares, unexpectedly

врать [vrăt'] (со-) *vi.* to tell lies

врач [vrăch] *sm.* physician

врачебный [vra-chéb-năy] *adj.* medical

вращательный [vra-shchā-tyel'năy] *adj.* rotatory

вращать [vra-shchāt'] *vt.* to revolve, turn; to roll (eyes)

вред [vryéd] *sm.* harm, hurt; damage, injury

вредить [vrye-d'ět] (по-вредить) *vt.* to harm, injure

вредность [vryéd-nŏst'] *sf.* perniciousness

вредный [vryéd-năy] *adj.* harmful, hurtful, injurious

временно [vryé-myen-nŏ] *adv.* provisionally, temporarily

временный [vryé-myen-năy] *adj.* temporary; acting

время [vryé-mya] *sn.* time; *gram.* tense; **времена** [vrye-mye-ná] *pl.* times; contemporary conditions

времяисчисление [vrye-mya-is-chi-slyé-nye] *sn.* chronology

времяпрепровождение [vrye-mya-prye-pra-vazh-dyé-nye] *sn.* pastime

врождённый [vrazh-dyón-năy] *adj.* inherent, innate, native; natural

врозницу [vróz-n'i-tsŏo] *adv.* by retail; separately

врубать [vrŏo-bát] (вру-бить) *vt.* to cut in, hew in

врун [vrŏon] *sm.*, **врунья** [vrŏo-nya] *sf.* liar

вручать [vrŏo-chát] (вру-чить) *vt.* to deliver, hand in; to entrust

вручение [vrŏo-ché-nye] *sn.* delivery, handing in

вряд ли [vryăd l'i] *adv.* hardly, scarcely

всадник [fsăd-n'ik] *sm.* equestrian, horseman, rider

всаживать [fsá-zhi-vat'] (всадить) *vt.* to plant in, stick in; to seat

всасывать [fsá-să-vat'] (всо-сáть) *vt.* to absorb, suck up

все [fsyé] *s.*, *pron.* all, everybody

всё [fsyó] *s.*, *pron.*, *adj.*, *adv.* all, everything, the whole; all the time, always, any, entirely, quite; **всего на -** [fsye-vó na -] everything considered

всеведущий [fsye-vyé-dŏo-shchi] *adj.* omniscient

всевозможный [fsye-vaz-mózh-năy] *adj.* all kinds; different, various

всегда [fsyeg-dá] *adv.* always, constantly, ever; **раз на -** [raz na -] once for all

всегдашний [fsyeg-dá-shni] *adj.* constant; usual; customary

всеизвестный [fsye-iz-vyést-năy] *adj.* well-known

вселенная [fsye-lyén-na-ya] *sf.* universe, world

вселенский [fsye-lyén-ski] *adj.* universal; *eccl.* oecumenical

вселять [fsye-lyát'] (вселить) *vt.* to settle; to inspire

всемирный [fsye-m'ér-năy] *adj.* universal

всенародный [fsye-na-ród-năy] *adj.* general, public

всенощная [fsyé-nashch-na-ya] *sf.* evening service; midnight mass; vespers

всеобщий [fsye-ób-shchi] *adj.* common, general

всепрощение [fsye-pra-shché-nye] *sn.* amnesty; general pardon

всердцах [fsyerd-tsăch] *adv.* angrily

всероссийский [fsye-rass-sí-ski] *adj.* All-Russian

всё-таки [fsyó-ta-ki] *adv.* however, nevertheless, still

всецело [fsye-tsyé-lä] *adv.* completely, wholly

всечасный [fsye-chäs-näy] *adj.* hourly

всеядный [vsye-yád-näy] *adj.* omnivorous

вскакивать [fskä-k'i-vat'] (вскочить) *vi.* to leap up, spring up

вскапывать [fskä-pä-vat'] (вскопать) *vt.* to dig up

вскарабкиваться [fska-ráb-k'i-vat'-sya] (вскарабкаться) *vi.* to clamber up, climb up

вскармливать [fskär-ml'i-vat'] (вскормить) *vt.* to bring up, feed, rear; to nurse

вскачь [fskäch'] *adv.* at a gallop

вскипать [fsk'i-pät'] (вскипеть) *vi.* to boil up; to fly into a rage

вскользь [fskol'z] *adv.* slightly; superficially

вскоре [fskó-rye] *adv.* presently, shortly

вскормленник [fskór-mlyen-n'ik] *sm.* foster-son

вскрикивать [fskr'ĕ-ki-vat'] (вскричать) *vi.* to cry out; to shriek

вскрытие [fskrä-tye] *sn.* opening; uncovering; turning up [hind

вслед [fslyed] *adv.* after, by

вследствие [fslyéd-stvye] *adv.* consequently

вслух [fslóōch] *adv.* aloud, audibly

вслушиваться [fslōō-shi-vat'-sya] (вслушаться) *vi.* to listen to, pay attention

вспахивать [fspä-chi-vat'] (вспахать) *vt.* to plough-up

вспашка [fspäsh-ka] *sf.* ploughing, tillage

всплакнуть [fspläk-nōōt'] *vi.* to shed a tear

всплошную [fsplash-nōō-yōō] *adv.* close together; without interruption

всполаскивать [fspa-läs-k'i-vat'] (всполоскать) *vt.* to rinse, wash out

всполашивать [fspa-lä-shi-vat'] (всполошить) *vt.* to warn; to raise an alarm

вспоминать [fspa-m'i-nät'] (вспомнить) *vt.* to recollect, remember

вспомогательный [fspa-ma-gä-tyel'-näy] *adj.* auxiliary; subsidiary

вспомоществование [fspa-ma-shche-stva-vä-nye] *sn.* assistance, help, relief

вспугивать [fspōō-gi-vat'] (вспугать) *vt.* to frighten, startle

вспучивать [fspōō-chi-vat'] *vt.* to distend

вспыльчивый [fspäl'-chi-väy] *adj.* hasty, passionate, quick-tempered

вспыхивать [fspä-chi-vat'] (вспыхнуть) *vi.* to flare up; to burst into flames; to break out

вспышка [fspäsh-ka] *sf.* outburst

вставать [fsta-vät'] (встать) *vi.* to get up, stand up, rise; **— на ноги** [– nä nä-gi] to get a footing

вставка [fstäv-ka] *sf.* insertion, inset

вставлять [fstav-lyät'] (вставить) *vt.* to fit in, insert, set in; **вставной зуб** [vstav-nóy zōōb] false tooth

встарину [fsta-ri-nōō] *adv.* in days gone by

встрёпанный [fstryó-pan-näy] *adj.* dishevelled, ruffled

встреча [fstryé-cha] *sf.* meeting; welcome

встречать [fstrye-chát'] (встрéтить) *vt.* to meet; to greet; to welcome

вступать [fstoō-pát'] (вступúть) *vi.* to enter, step in

вступúтельный [fstoō-p'é-tyel'-näy] *adj.* introductory, inaugural

вступлéние [fstoō-plé-nye] *sn.* prelude; entry, opening; introduction

всходить [fscha-d'ét'] *vi.* to ascend, mount [shoots

всходы [fschó-dä] *pl.* corn

всыпáть [fsä-pát'] (всыпáть) *vt.* to fill; to add

всюду [fsyoō-doō] *adv.* everywhere

всякий [fsyä-ki] *pron.* anybody, each

всячески [fsyä-ches-ki] *adv.* in every way

всяческий [fsyä-ches-ki] *adj.* of all kinds

втайне [ftäy-nye] *adv.* secretly

втеснять [ftye-snyát'] (втеснúть) *vt.* to squeeze

втирание [ft'i-rä-nye] *sn.* friction, rubbing

втихомолку [ft'i-cha-mólkoō] *adv.* stealthily

вторжéние [ftar-zhé-nye] *sn.* intrusion, invasion

вторник [ftór-n'ik] *sm.* Tuesday

второй [fta-róy] *num.* second

второстепéнный [fta-ra-stye-pyén-näy] *adj.* secondary; second rate

втулка [ftoōl-ka] *sf.* bush; hub; plug

втягивать [ftyá-gi-vat'] (втянúть) *vt.* to draw in, pull in; to implicate

вуаль [voō-ál'] *sf.* veil

вулкан [voōl-kán] *sm.* volcano

вход [fchod] *sm.* entrance, entry; access

входить [fcha-d'ét'] (войтú) *vi.* to enter; walk in [day

вчера [íche-rä] *adv.* yesterday

вчерне [fcher-nvé] *adv.* in the rough, unprepared

въéдчивый [vyéd-chi-väy] *adj.* corrosive

въезд [vyézd] *sm.* avenue, drive, entrance

въезжáть [vyez-zhát'] (въéхать) *vt.* to drive in, ride in

въявь [vyäv'] *adv.* in reality

вы [vä] *pron.* you

выбáлтывать [vä-bál-tä-vat'] (выболтать) *vt.* to disclose, divulge; to tell tales

выбегáть [vä-bye-gát'] (выбежать) *vi.* to run out

выбелúвать [vä-byé-l'i-vat'] (выбелить) *vt.* to bleach, whiten; to whitewash

выбирáть [vä-b'i-rát'] (выбрать) *vt.* to select; to elect

выборка [vä-bar-ka] *sf.* choice, selection

выборы [vä-ba-ri] *sm.pl.* elections

выбранить [vä-bra-n'it'] *vt.* to reprimand, scold

выварка [vä-var-ka] *sf.* extraction (*by boiling*)

вывод [vä-vód] *sm.* conclusion, deduction, inference

выводить [vä-va-d'ét'] (вывести) *vt.* to bring out, lead out [tion

вывоз [vä-vóz] *sm.* exportation

выворот [vä-va-rót] *sm.* reverse (*wrong side*); на - [na -] *adv.* inside out

выгибать [vă-gi-bát'] (вы́гнуть) vt. to bend, curve

выглаживать [vă-glá-zhi-vat'] (вы́гладить) vt. to iron, smooth; to polish

выговор [vă-gă-vôr] sm. pronunciation; censure, rebuke

выгода [vă-ga-da] sf. advantage, benefit, profit

выгодный [vă-gad-năy] adj. gainful, remunerative; beneficial

выгрузка [vă-grōōz-ka] sf. unloading; disembarkation

выдавать [vă-da-vát'] (вы́дать) vt. to distribute; to betray

выдача [vă-da-cha] sf. delivery, handing out; payment; extradition

выдающийся [vă-da-yōō-shchi-sya] adj. prominent

выделка [vă-dyel-ka] sf. finish, preparation; manufacture

выделять [vă-dye-lyát'] (вы́делить) vt. to allot, to share out

выдержка [vă-dyer-zhka] sf. extract, passage; firmness, endurance

выдумка [vă-dōōm-ka] sf. invention; fabrication, fiction

выдумщик [vă-dōōm-shchik] sm. inventor; boaster, liar

выдыхание [vă-dă-chá-nye] sn. exhalation

выезд [vă-yezd] sn. departure

выездчик [vă-yezd-chik] sm. horse-trainer

выезжать [vă-yez-zhát'] (вы́ехать) vi. to drive out, to ride out; to depart

выжигать [vă-zhi-gát'] (вы́жечь) vt. to burn out; to cauterize

выжидательный [vă-zhi-dá-tyel'-năy] adj. expectant

выздоровление [vă-zda-ra-vlyé-nye] sn. convalescence, recovery

вызов [vă-zŏv] sm. call; subpoena; summons

выигрывать [vă-ĕ-gră-vat'] (вы́играть) vt. to gain, win

выкидыш [vă-k'i-dăsh] sm. miscarriage; abortion

выкройка [vă-kray-ka] sf. cutting out; pattern

выкуп [vă-kŏŏp] sm. redemption; ransom

вылазка [vă-laz-ka] sf. excursion, outing, ramble; mil. sally, sortie

вылезать [vă-lye-zát'] (вы́лезть) vi. to crawl out, creep out; to fall out (as hair)

вылет [vă-lyet] sm. flight; departure

вылечивать [vă-lyé-chi-vat'] (вы́лечить) vt. to cure, heal

выливать [vă-l'i-vát'] (вы́лить) vt. to pour out

вымазывать [vă-mă-ză-vat'] (вы́мазать) vt. to grease, oil, smear; to soil

вымогательство [vă-ma-gá-tyel'-stvŏ] sn. extortion

вымучивать [vă-mōō-chi-vat'] (вы́мучить) vt. to extort; to torment; to worry

вымысел [vă-mă-syel] sm. fiction; invention

вымя [vă-mya] sn. udder

выносить [vă-na-s'ĕt'] (вы́нести) vt. to bear, support; undergo

выправка [vå-prav-ka] sf. correction

выпуклость [vă-pŏŏ-klŏst'] sf. convexity; protuberance

выпуск [vǎ-pŏŏsk] *sm.* issue; outlet; omission; number (*of journal, periodical, etc.*)

вырабатывать [vǎ-ra-bā-tā-vat'] (выработать) *vt.* to work out; to perfect

выражать [vǎ-ra-zhāt'] (выразить) *vt.* to convey, express (*an idea*)

выражение [vǎ-ra-zhé-nye] *sn.* expression; countenance; term (*musical, technical, etc.*)

выразительный [vǎ-ra-z'ĕ-tyel'-nǎy] *adj.* expressive, significant; emphatic

вырезка [vǎ-ryez-ka] *sf.* cut, pattern; rumpsteak

вырождение [vǎ-razh-dyé-nye] *sn.* degeneration; deterioration

вырослый [vǎ-ras-lǎy] *adj.* grown-up

выручка [vǎ-rŏŏch-ka] *sf.* release; proceeds (*of sale*); till (*money drawer*)

вырываться [vǎ-rǎ-vāt'-sya] *vi.* to free oneself, escape; to break out

высадка [vǎ-sad-ka] *sf.* transplanting; disembarkation, landing

высекать [vǎ-sye-kāt'] (высечь) *vt.* to cut, hew; to carve; to fell

выселение [vǎ-sye-lyé-nye] *sn.* eviction; emigration; removal

высказываться [vǎs-kā-zǎ-vat'-sya] *vi.* to express one's views

выслушивать [vǎ-slŏŏ-shi-vat'] (выслушать) *vt.* to hear out, to listen to; *med.* to examine

высокий [vǎ-só-ki] *adj.* high, lofty, tall; superior

высоковатый [vǎ-sa-ka-vā-tǎy] *adj.* rather high, somewhat tall

высокомерие [vǎ-sa-ka-myé-rye] *sm.* haughtiness, presumption, pride

высокопреподобный [vǎ-sa-ka-prye-pa-dób-nǎy] *adj.* right reverend

высокородный [vǎ-sa-ka-ród-nǎy] *adj.* right honourable

высота [vǎ-sa-tā] *sf.* altitude, height; pitch

высочайший [vǎ-sa-chāy-shi] *adj.* Highness

выставка [vǎ-stav-ka] *sf.* exhibition, show; display

выступ [vǎ-stŏŏp] *sm.* projection, protuberance

выстрел [vǎ-stryel] *sm.* report (*sound*), shot; gunfire

высылка [vǎ-sǎl-ka] *sf.* banishment, exile; sending off

высыпать [vǎ-sǎ-pāt'] (высыпать) *vt.* to empty, scatter; to break out (*disease, epidemic*); to throng

высыхать [vǎ-sǎ-chāt'] (высохнуть) *vi.* to dry up; to parch, wither

высь [vǎs'] *sf.* height, summit

вытачивать [vǎ-tā-chi-vat'] (выточить) *vt.* to grind, sharpen [leakage

вытечка [vǎ-tyech-ka] *sf.*

вытьё [vǎ-tyó] *sn.* cry, howl, howling

выучивать [vǎ-ŏŏ-chi-vat'] (выучить) *vt.* to learn up; to teach

выход [vǎ-chod] *sm.* exit, way out; outlet; issue

выходить [vǎ-cha-d'ĕt'] (выйти) *vi.* to go out, walk out; to appear, come out

выходка [vǎ-chad-ka] *sf.* escapade, prank; ramble

выхухоль [vǎ-choō-chól'] *sm.* musk-rat; **выхухолевый мех** [vǎ-choō-chó-lye-văy myéch] musquash

выцарапывать [vǎ-tsa-rǎ-pǎ-vat'] (**выцарапать**) *vt.* to scratch, scratch out (*not erase*)

вычёркивать [vǎ-chór-k'i-vat'] (**вычеркнуть**) *vt.* to cross out, strike out; to cancel; to obliterate

вычернивать [vǎ-chér-n'i-vat'] (**вычернить**) *vt.* to blacken; to stain

вычески [vǎ-ches-ki] *sf. pl.* combings

вычет [vǎ-chet] *sm.* deduction, discount

вычисление [vǎ-chis-lye-nye] *sn.* calculation, reckoning

вычитание [vǎ-chi-tǎ-nye] *sn.* subtraction

вычищать [vǎ-chi-shchat'] (**вычистить**) *vt.* to cleanse

вычурный [vǎ-choōr-nǎy] *adj.* affected, pretentious; florid (*style*)

вышеуказанный [vǎ-she-oō-kǎ-zan-nǎy] *adj.* aforesaid, foregoing

вышеупомянутый [vǎ-she-oō-pa-myǎ-noō-tǎy] *adj.* above-mentioned

вышибать [vǎ-shi-bǎt'] (**вышибить**) *vt.* to chuck out; to smash in

вышивание [vǎ-shi-vǎ-nye] *sn.* embroidery, fancy work, needle-work

вышина [vǎ-shi-nǎ] *sf.* height; elevation

вышка [vǎsh-ka] *sf.* garret, loft; tower

выщупывать [vǎ-shchoō-pǎ-vat'] (**выщупать**) *vt.* to feel, probe, touch

выявлять [vǎ-ya-vlyǎt'] (**выявить**) *vt.* to expose; to show; to proclaim

выяснять [vǎ-ya-snyǎt'] (**выяснить**) *vt.* to explain, make clear; to ascertain

вьюга [vyoō-ga] *sf.* snow-storm

вьюжный [vyoōzh-nǎy] *adj.* stormy

вьюк [vyoōk] *sm.* bale, load, pack; burden

вьюшка [vyoōsh-ka] *sf.* damper

вяжущий [vyǎ-zhoō-shchi] *adj.* astringent, binding

вяз [vyäz] *sm.* elm

вязание [vyǎ-za-nye] *sn.* binding; knitting

вязать [vyǎ-zat'] (с-) to bind, knit, tie

вязкость [vyäz-kǒst'] *sf.* viscosity

вязнуть [vyaz-noōt'] (у-, за-) *vi.* to stick in

вязь [vyäz'] *sf. typ.* ligature

вяление [vya-lyé-nye] *sn.* air-drying, sun-drying; curing; jerking (*of beef*)

вялый [vyä-lǎy] *adj.* flabby, limp, sluggish; lifeless

вянуть [vyä-noōt'] (за-) *vi.* to droop, fade, wither

Г

гавань [ga-vǎn'] *sf.* harbour, port; *poet.* haven

гага [gä-ga] *sf.* eider; **гагачий пух** [ga-gǎ-chi poōch] eider-down гад [gād] *sm.* reptile; *fig.* mean person

гадалка [ga-dāl-ka] *sf.* fortune-teller

гаданне [ga-dā-nye] *sn.* divination, fortune-telling

гадать [ga-dāt'] (по-, y-) *vi.* to tell fortunes; to guess; to surmise

гадательный [ga-dā-tyel'-năy] *adj.* conjectural

гадина [gā-d'i-na] *sf.* reptile; trash; *fig.* repulsive person

гадить [gā-d'it'] (на-) *vt.* to soil, spoil; to damage

гадкий [gād-ki] *adj.* bad, wicked

гадость [gā-dŏst'] *sf.* badness, foulness, poor stuff; filth

гадюка [ga-dyŏŏ-ka] *sf.* adder, viper

гаер [gā-yer] *sm.* buffoon, mountebank

гаерничать [gā-yer-n'i-chat'] *vi.* to act the fool

гаерство [gā-yer-stvŏ] *sn.* tomfoolery

газ [gāz] *sm.* gauze; gas;
веселящий – [vye-sye-lyā-shchi –] laughing gas;
слезоточивый – [slye-za-ta-chē-văy –] tear gas

газета [ga-zyé-ta] *sf.* journal; newspaper

газетчик [ga-zyét-chik] *sm.* news-boy

газовый [gā-za-văy] *adj.* gaseous [gas-meter

газомер [ga-za-myér] *sm.*

газообразный [ga-za-ab-rāz-năy] *adj.* gaseous

гайка [gāy-ka] *sf. tech.* nut

галантерея [ga-lan-tye-ryé-ya] *sf.* haberdashery

галантность [ga-lānt-nŏst'] *sf.* gallantry

галдёж [gal-dyŏzh] *sm.* din, noise, row

галера [ga-lyé-ra] *sf. hist.* galley; Russian barge

галёрка [ga-lyór-ka] *sf. theat.* gallery

галка [gāl-ka] *sf.* jackdaw

галлерея [gal-lye-ryé-ya] *sf.* gallery (*as picture gallery, etc.*)

галопировать [ga-la-p'ē-ra-vat'] *vi.* to gallop, scamper

галоша [ga-lŏ-sha] *sf.* galosh, overshoe

галс [gals] *sm. naut.* tack

галстук [gāl-stŏŏk] *sm.* neck-tie

галька [gāl'-ka] *sf.* pebble, shingle

гамаша [ga-mā-sha] *sf.* gaiter, legging

гамма [gām-ma] *sf. mus.* scale

гарантировать [ga-ran-t'ē-ra-vat'] *vt.* to guarantee, secure, warrant

гардемарин [gar-dye-ma-r'ēn] *sm.* midshipman

гардероб [gar-dye-rób] *sm.* wardrobe; cloak-room

гардеробщик [gar-dye-rób-shchik] *sm.* cloak-room attendant

гармонизировать [gar-ma-n'i-z'ē-ra-vat'] *vt.* to harmonize

гармония [gar-mó-nya] *sf.* harmony

гарнизон [gar-n'i-zón] *sm.* garrison

гарнитур [gar-n'i-tŏŏr] *sm.* fittings, trimmings

гарт [gārt] *sm. typ.* metal; *typ.* pie

гарус [gā-rŏŏs] *sm.* worsted yarn

гарь [gar'] *sf.* smell of burning

гас [gäs] *sm.* braid

гасильник [ga-s'ěl'-nik] *sm.* extinguisher

гасить [ga-s'ět'] (по-) *vt.* to extinguish

гастрический [ga-str'ě-ches-ki] *adj.* gastric

гастроль [ga-stról'] *sf.* theat. starring; touring

гауптвахта [gaőpt-väch-ta] *sf. mil.* guard-room

гвалт [gvalt] *sm.* disturbance, riot

гвардеец [gvar-dýé-yets] *sm.* guardsman

гвардия [gvär-dya] *sf.* household troops; **Красная –** [kräs-na-ya –] Red Guards; **лейб––** [lýéyb––] Life-Guards

гвоздика [gvaz-d'ě-ka] *sf.* clove (spice); red carnation

гвоздь [gvčzd'] *sm.* nail; spike

где [gdyé] *adv.* where; **––либо** [––l'ě-bŏ], **––нибудь** [––n'i-bŏŏd'], **––то** [––ta] somewhere

геена [ge-yé-na] *sf.* Gehenna, hell

гемма [gýém-ma] *sf.* gem

геморрой [gye-ma-róy] *sm.* haemorrhoids, piles

генерал [ge-ne-räl] *sm.* general

генеральный [ge-ne-räl'-näy] *adj.* general

гениальность [ge-nyäl'-nőst'] *sf.* genius, talents

геральдика [ge-räl'-d'i-ka] *sf.* heraldry

герань [ge-rän'] *sf.* geranium

герб [gýérb] *sm.* coat of arms; stamp

гербовник [ger-bóv-n'ik] *sm.* book of heraldry

гербовый [gér-bo-väy] *adj.* armorial

германец [ger-mä-nyets] *sm.* German, Teuton

германский [ger-män-ski] *adj.* Germanic, Teutonic

героиня [ge-ra-ě-nya] *sf.* heroine

героический [ge-ra-ě-ches-ki] *adj.* heroic

герой [ge-róy] *sm.* hero

геройство [ge-róy-stvŏ] *sn.* heroism

герундий [ge-rŏŏn-d'i] *sm. gram.* gerund

герцог [gér-tsog] *sm.* duke

герцогиня [ger-tsa-g'ě-nya] *sf.* duchess

герцогство [gér-tsŏg-stvŏ] *sn.* duchy

гибель [g'ě-byel'] *sf.* catastrophe, ruin; wreck

гибельный [g'ě-byel'-näy] *adj.* disastrous, ruinous

гибкий [g'ěb-ki] *adj.* flexible, supple

гибкость [g'ěb-kŏst'] *sf.* flexibility, pliability

гибнуть [g'ib-nŏŏt'] (по-) *vt.* to perish, rot

гигантский [g'i-gänt-ski] *adj.* gigantic

гигиена [g'i-g'i-yé-na] *sf.* hygiene

гидравлика [g'i-dräv-l'i-ka] *sf.* hydraulics

гиена [g'i-yé-na] *sf.* hyena

гиль [g'ěl'] *sf.* nonsense, rubbish

гильдия [g'ěl'-dya] *sf.* guild

гильза [g'ěl'-za] *sf.* cartridge case

гимн [g'ěmn] *sm.* anthem, hymn

гимназия [g'im-nā-zya] *sf.* college, grammar school, high school

гимнастика [g'im-nāst'i-ka] *sf.* gymnastics

гипнотизировать [g'ip-nat'i-z'ē-ra-vat'] *vt.* to hypnotize

гиппопотам [g'i-pa-pa-tām] *sm.* hippopotamus

гипс [g'ēps] *sm.* gypsum

гираф [g'i-rāf] *sm.* giraffe

гирло [g'ēr-lŏ] *sn.* estuary

гирлянда [g'ir-lyān-da] *sf.* garland, wreath

гиря [g'ē-rya] *sf.* weight

гитара [g'i-tā-ra] *sf.* guitar

гичка [g'ēch-ka] *sf.* gig

глава [gla-vā] *sf.* chief, head, headmaster, principal; cupola; chapter

главный [glāv-nǎy] *adj.* main, supreme

глагол [gla-gól] *sm.* verb; **вспомогательный** – [vspa-ma-gā-tyel'-nǎy –] auxiliary verb; **переходный** – [pye-rye-chód-nǎy –] transitive verb; **непереходный** – [nye-pye-rye-chód-nǎy –] intransitive verb

гладить [glā-d'it'] (с-) *vt.* to iron, smooth out; to polish

гладкий [glād-ki] *adj.* even, plane, smooth

глаз [glāz] *sm.* eye

глазеть [gla-zyét'] (по-) *vi.* to gaze, stare

глазной [glaz-nóy] *adj.* ocular; – **врач** [– vrach] oculist; **глазное яблоко** [glāz-na-ye yā-bla-ko] eyeball

глазунья [gla-zōo-nya] *sf.* poached eggs, fried eggs

гласить [gla-s'ēt'] (воз-) *vi.* to declare, say

гласный [glās-nǎy] *adj.* public; known, notorious; *as sm.* town-councillor; **гласная буква** [glās-na-ya bŏŏk-va] *sf.* vowel

глашатай [gla-shā-tay] *sm.* town-crier; *fig.* mouthpiece

глетчер [glyét-cher] *sm.* glacier

глина [gl'ē-na] *sf.* clay

глист [gl'ēst] *sm.* tapeworm

глобус [gló-bŏŏs] *sm.* globe

глодать [gla-dāt'] *vt.* to gnaw, nibble

глоссарий [glas-sā-ri] *sm.* glossary

глотать [gla-tāt'] (проглоти́ть) *vt.* to swallow

глотка [glót-ka] *sf.* throat; *med.* pharynx; **во всю глотку** [va vsyŏŏ glót-kŏŏ] at the top of one's voice

глоток [gla-tók] *sm.* draught, mouthful

глохнуть [glóch-nŏŏt'] (о-) *vi.* to become deaf; to wither

глубина [glŏŏ-b'i-nā] *sf.* depth, profundity

глубокий [glŏŏ-bó-ki] *adj.* deep; extreme; profound

глубокомысленный [glŏŏ-ba-ka-mǎs-lyen-nǎy] *adj.* thoughtful

глумление [glum-lyé-nye] *sn.* derision, mockery

глупец [glŏŏ-pyéts] *sm.* fool, simpleton

глуповатый [glŏŏ-pa-vā-tǎy] *adj.* somewhat stupid

глупость [glŏŏ-pŏst'] *sf.* foolishness, stupidity; nonsense

глухарь [glŏŏ-chār'] *sm.* wood-grouse

глуховатый [glŏŏ-cha-vā-]

тый *adj.* hard of hearing; rather deaf

глухой [gloo-chóy] *adj.* deaf; voiceless (*sound*)

глухонемой [gloo-cha-nye-móy] *adj.* deaf and dumb

глухота [gloo-cha-tá] *sf.* deafness

глушитель [gloo-shé-tyel] *sm. tech.* silencer

глушить [gloo-shét'] (о-) to deafen; to stun

глушь [gloosh] *sf.* thicket; solitary place

глыба [glá-ba] *sf.* lump; clod; heap

глядеть [glya-dyét'] (по-) *vi.* to look, peer, see

глянуть [glya-nóot'] *vi.* to throw a glance

глянцевитый [glyan-tse-vʹé-tåy] *adj.* glossy, lustrous

гнать [gnat'] (по-) to chase, drive; to hunt, pursue

гнев [gnyév] *sm.* anger, rage

гневаться [gnyé-vat'-sya] *vi.* to be angry, to be enraged

гнездо [gnyez-dó] *sn.* nest

гнести [gnyes-tʹé] *vt.* to press, squeeze; to harass, oppress

гнида [gnʹé-da] *sf.* nit

гниение [gnʹi-yé-nye] *sn.* decaying, rotting

гнилой [gnʹi-lóy] *adj.* putrid, rotten

гнилость [gnʹé-lŏst] *sf.* rot

гной [gnóy] *sm.* matter, pus

гнойный [gnóy-nåy] *adj.* purulent; blear (*nasal*)

гнусавый [gnŏŏ-sá-våy] *adj.*

гнусный [gnŏŏs-nåy] *adj.* abominable, base, hideous

гнуть [gnŏŏt'] (за-, со-) *vt.* to bend, curve, inflect

гобой [ga-bóy] *sm.* oboe

говор [gó-vŏr] *sm.* rumour;

talk; **местный** – [myést-náy –] dialect; jargon

говорить [ga-va-rʹét'] (сказать) *vt.* to say, speak, tell

говорливый [ga-var-lʹé-våy] *adj.* chatty, talkative

говорун [ga-va-rŏŏn] *sm.*, **говорунья** [ga-va-rŏŏ-nya] *sf.* chatterbox

говядина [ga-vyá-dʹi-na] *sf.* beef

гоготать [ga-ga-tát'] (за-) *vi.* to roar with laughter

год [god] *sm.* year

годиться [ga-dʹét'-sya] (при-) *vi.* to become, fit, suit

годичный [ga-dʹéch-náy] *adj.* annual, yearly

годный [gŏŏd-náy] *adj.* suitable; **никуда не** – [nʹi-kŏŏ-dá nye –] good for nothing, useless

годовик [ga-da-vʹék] *sm.* yearling

годовщина [ga-dav-shchí-na] *sf.* anniversary

голенастый [ga-lye-nás-tåy] *adj.* long-legged

голень [gó-lyen] *sf.* shin

голизна [ga-lʹéz-na] *sf.* nudity

голландец [gal-lán-dyets] *sm.* Dutchman; **голландка** [gal-lánd-ka] *sf.* Dutchwoman

голландский [gal-lánd-ski] *adj.* Dutch

голова [ga-la-vá] *sf.* head

головка [ga-lóv-ka] *sf.* small head; nail-head, pin-head

головной [ga-lav-nóy] *adj. med.* cephalic; – **убор** [– ŏŏ-bór] *sm.* head-dress; **головная боль** [ga-lav-ná-ya bol'] *sf.* headache

головокружение [ga-la-va-krŏŏ-zhé-nye] *sn.* giddiness

головоломка [ga-la-va-lóm-ka] *sf.* puzzle; brain-racking work

головорез [ga-la-va-ryéz] *sm.* ruffian, villain

голод [gó-lŏd] *sm.* famine; hunger

голодать [ga-la-dát'] (про-) *vi.* to hunger, starve

голодание [ga-la-dá-nye] *sn.* starvation

голодный [ga-lód-năy] *adj.* hungry

голодовка [ga-la-dóv-ka] *sf.* hunger-strike

голос [ga-lŏs] *sm.* voice; tone; vote; *mus.* part

голосить [ga-la-s'ĕt'] *vi.* to vociferate

голословный [ga-la-slóv-năy] *adj.* unfounded

голосовать [ga-la-sa-vát'] *vt.* to vote

голубец [ga-lŏŏ-byéts] *sm.* mountain-blue colour; sparrow-hawk

голубизна [ga-lŏŏ-b'ĕz-na] *sf.* azure colour

голубиный [ga-lŏŏ-b'ĕ-năy] *adj.* dovelike

голубка [ga-lŏŏb-ka] *sf.* hen-pigeon; *fig.* darling, pet

голубой [ga-lŏŏ-bóy] *adj.* sky-blue

голубушка [ga-lŏŏ-bŏŏsh-ka] *sf.* darling, dearest

голубчик [ga-lŏŏb-chik] *sm.* darling, dearest

голубь [gó-lŏŏb'] *sm.* pigeon; **гонный** – [gón-năy –] homing pigeon; **почтовый** – [pach-tó-văy –] carrier pigeon

голубятник [ga-lŏŏ-byát-n'ik] *sm.* pigeon-fancier

голубятня [ga-lŏŏ-byát-nya] *sf.* pigeonry

голый [gó-lăy] *adj.* bare, naked; neat (*as alcohol*); empty (*words*)

голыш [ga-lásh] *sm.* pebble, shingle; *coll.* wretched fellow

голь [gól'] *sf.* bareness; nakedness, nudity; poverty

гонение [ga-nyé-nye] *sn.* persecution

гонец [ga-nyéts] *sm.* courier, messenger

гонка [gón-ka] *sf.* race, regatta; chase; reprimand

гончар [gan-chár] *sm.* potter; **гончарное искусство** [gan-chár-nŏ-ye is-kŏŏs-stvŏ] ceramics

гончарня [gan-chár-nya] *sf.* pottery (*workshop*)

гончая [gón-chaya] *adj. and sf.* hunting dog; gun-dog; harrier

гонщик [gón-shchik] *sm.* racer, runner

гонять [ga-nyát'] (по-) *vt.* to chase, hunt

гора [ga-rá] *sf.* mountain; **на гору** [ná-ga-rŏŏ] uphill; **под гору** [pód-ga-rŏŏ] downhill

гораздо [ga-ráz-dŏ] *adv.* by far, much

горб [gorb] *sm.* hump; back

горбатый [gar-bá-tăy] *adj.* hunchbacked

горбатость [gar-bá-tŏst'] *sf.* gibbosity

горбун [gar-bŏŏn] *sm.*, **горбунья** [gar-bŏŏ-nya] *sf.*, hunchback

горделивый [gar-dye-l'ĕ-văy] *adj.* haughty, proud

гордиться [ga-d'ĕt'-sya] *vi.* to be proud, take pride in

гордость [gór-dŏst'] *sf.* pride

горе [gó-rye] *sn.* grief, sorrow; misfortune; woe!

горевать [ga-rye-vát'] *vi.* to grieve; to lament

горелка [ga-ryél-ka] *sf.* burner

горение [ga-ryé-nye] *sn.* combustion

горестный [gó-ryest-năy] *adj.* sad, sorrowful

гореть [ga-ryét'] (с-) *vi.* to burn, glow [taineer-

горец [gó-ryets] *sm.* moun-

горечь [gó-ryech'] *sf.* bitterness (*taste*)

горжетка [ga-zhét-ka] *sf.* necklet

горизонт [ga-ri-zónt] *sm.* horizon

горизонтальный [ga-ri-zón-tál'-năy] *adj.* horizontal

гористый [ga-rěs-tăy] *adj.* mountainous

горлица [ga-lě-tsa] *sf.* turtle-dove

горло [gór-lŏ] *sn.* throat

горн [gorn] *sm.* forge, furnace; *mus.* horn

горний [gór-n'i] *adj.* heavenly

горничная [gar-n'ĕch-naya] *sf.* chambermaid, maid

горнозаводский [gor-na-za-vód-ski] *adj.* mining

горнорабочий [gor-na-ra-bó-chi] *sm.* miner

горностай [gor-na-stáy] *sm.* ermine, stoat

горный [gór-năy] *adj.* mountainous

город [gó-rŏd] *sm.* town, city; **за городом** [zā-go-ró-dŏm] in the suburbs

городить [ga-ra-d'ét'] (за-) *vt.* to fence, hedge in

городской [ga-rad-skóy] *adj.*

urban; **– голова** [– ga-la-vá] mayor

горожанин [ga-ra-zhá-n'in] *sm.* citizen; townsman

горох [ga-róch] *sm.* pea

гороховый [ga-ró-chŏ-văy] *adj.* pea-green

горсть [gorst'] *sf.* handful; hollow of hand

гортань [gar-tán'] *sf.* larynx

гортанный [gar-tán-năy] *adj.* throaty; *phon.* guttural; *med.* laryngeal

горчица [gar-chē-tsa] *sf.* mustard

горчичник [gar-chēch-nik] *sm.* mustard-plaster

горчичный [gar-chēch-năy] *adj.* mustard-

горшечник [gar-shéch-nik] *sm.* potter

горшок [gar-shók] *sm.* pot

горький [gór'-k'i] *adj.* bitter

горьклый [gór'-klăy] *adj.* rancid

горьковатый [gar'-ka-vá-tăy] *adj.* rather bitter

горючее [ga-ryōō-che-ye] *sn.* fuel

горючесть [ga-ryōō-chest'] *sf.* combustibility, inflammability; **горючие слёзы** [ga-ryōō-chi-ye slyó-ză] scalding tears

горячечный [ga-ryā-che-năy] *adj.* feverish; **– бред** [– bryed] delirium

горячиться [ga-rya-chét'sya] *vi.* to become heated; to be angry

горячка [ga-ryāch-ka] *sf.* burning fever

госпиталь [gos-pi-tál'] *sm.* military hospital

господин [gas-pa-d'ĕn] *sm.* Mister; gentleman; **г-н,** Mr *pl.* **господа** [gas-pa-dá] Messrs. (Messieurs), gentlemen; **господа!** Ladies and Gentlemen!

господский [gas-pód-ski] *adj.* lord's, manorial; **– дом** [– dom] manor-house

господствовать [gas-pódstvŏ-vat'] *vi.* to dominate, rule

Господь [gas-pód'] *sm.* God, Lord; *voc.* **Господи!** [góspa-d'i] O Lord; dear me! good gracious! **молитва Господня** [ma-lĭt-va gaspód-nya] the Lord's prayer

госпожа [gas-pa-zhá] *sf.* mistress; **г-жа**, Mrs.

гостеприимный [gas-tyepri-ĕm-nǎy] *adj.* hospitable

гостеприимность [gas-tyepri-ĕm-nŏst'] *sf.* hospitality

гостиная [gas-t'ĕ-na-ya] *sf.* drawing-room, parlour

гостиница [gas-t'ĕ-ni-tsa] *sf.* hotel, inn; restaurant; **содержатель гостиницы** [sa-dyer-zhá-tyel' gas-t'ĕnĭtsa] hotelkeeper, innkeeper, landlord; restaurateur; **гостиный двор** [gas-t'ĕ-nǎy dvor] arcade, bazaar, stores

гостить [gas-t'ĕt'] *vi.* to visit (*as guest*), stay with friends

гость [gost'] *sm.* guest, visitor

государство [ga-sŏŏ-dárstvŏ] *sm.* kingdom, state; government

государь [ga-sŏŏ-dár'] *sm.* sovereign; **милостивый** [mi-lŏs-t'ĕ-vǎy –] 'Dear Sir'

готовить [ga-tó-vit'] (**при-**) *vt.* to prepare, provide; to cook, dress

готовность [ga-tóv-nŏst'] *sf.*

readiness, willingness; disposition; preparedness; **выражать** – [vǎ-ra-zhát' –] to offer

готовый [ga-tó-vǎy] *adj.* prepared, ready; willing; finished

грабёж [gra-byózh] *sm.* robbery; plundering, pillage

грабитель [gra-bĕ-tyel'] *sm.* robber

грабить [grá-bit'] *vt.* to plunder, ransack, rob

грабли [gráb-l'i] *sf. pl.* rake (*for hay*)

гравёр [gra-vyór] *sm.* engraver

гравий [grá-vi] *sm.* gravel

гравировать [gra-vĕ-róvat'] *vt.* to engrave, etch

гравюра [gra-vyŏŏ-ra] *sf.* engraving

град [grad] *sm.* hail, sleet

градина [gra-d'ĕ-na] *sf.* hailstone

градирование [gra-d'ĕ-ra-va-nye] *sn.* graduation

градус [grá-dŏŏs] *sm.* degree (°)

градусник [grá-dŏŏs-n'ik] *sm.* thermometer

гражданин [grazh-da-n'ĕn] *sm.* **гражданка** [grazh-dán-ka] *sf.* citizen, subject

гражданский [grazh-dánski] *adj.* civic, civil; social; **гражданская печать** [grazh-dán-skaya pe-chát'] *typ.* roman type

гражданство [grazh-dánstvŏ] *sn.* citizenship

грамматика [gram-mát'ika] *sf.* grammar

грамматический [gramma-t'ĕ-chesk-ki] *adj.* grammatical

грамота [grá-ma-ta] *sf.* reading and writing, the three R's; deed, document, record

грамотник [grá-mat-n'ik] *sm.* an educated person

грамотность [grá-mat-nŏst'] *sf.* literacy

грамотный [grá-mat-năy] *adj.* literate

гранат [gra-nát] *sm.* pomegranate; garnet

граната [gra-ná-ta] *sf.* hand grenade, shell

гранёный [gra-nyó-năy] *adj.* faceted

гранильный [gra-n'ĕl'-năy] *adj.* polishing

гранильщик [gra-n'ĕl'-shchik] *sm.* cutter of gems, lapidary

гранит [gra-nĕt] *sm.* granite

гранить [gra-n'ĕt'] (вы-) *vt.* to cut facets; to grind

граница [gra-n'ĕ-tsa] *sf. polit.* frontier; boundary; border; limit; **за границу** [za-gra-n'ĕ-tsŏo] abroad

граничить [gra-n'ĕ-chit'] *vi.* to border on; *fig.* to verge on

грапка [grap-ka] *sf. typ.* galley; galley-proof, slip

грань [grán'] *sf.* facet, surface (*of stone*); border, verge

граф [gráf] *sm.* count, earl

графа [gra-fá] *sf.* column (*newspaper, etc.*)

графика [grá-fi-ka] *sf.* graphic arts

графин [gra-fĕn] *sm.* carafe

графиня [gra-fĕ-nya] *sf.* countess

графит [gra-fĕt] *sm.* graphite

графический [gra-fĕ-cheski] *adj.* graphic

графство [gráf-stvŏ] *sn.* earldom; county

грациозный [gra-tsióznăy] *adj.* graceful

грация [grá-tsya] *sf.* grace, gracefulness

грач [grách] *sm.* rook

гребень [gré-ben'] *sm.* comb ridge; crest; **частый** - [chás-tăy -] tooth-comb

гребец [gre-byéts] *sm.* rower, oarsman

гребешок [gre-bye-shók] *sm.* small comb

грёза [gryó-za] *sf.* dream; day-dream, fancy; **мир** - [mir gryóz] dreamland

грезить [gryé-zit'] *vi.* to dream; to meditate, ponder

грек [gryék] *sm.*, **гречанка** [grye-chán-ka] *sf.* Greek

греческий [gryé-ches-ki] *adj.* Greek, Grecian

грелка [gryél-ka] *sf.* hot-water bottle, warming-pan

греметь [grye-myét'] (за-) *vi.* to thunder; to roar, rumble; to resound; **гром гремит** [grom grye-mĕt] it thunders

гремучий [grye-mŏŏ-chi] *adj.* thundering; rattling; detonating; – **газ** [– gáz] fire-damp; **гремучая змея** [grye-mŏŏ-cha-ya zmyé-ya] rattlesnake

гремушка [grye-mŏŏsh-ka] *sf.* child's rattle

гренок [grye-nók] *sm.* rusk, toast

грести [grye-stĕ] *vt.* to row; to paddle; to rake

греть [gryét'] (на-) *vt.* to heat, warm

грех [gryech] *sm.* sin; guilt; **первородный** – [pyer-varód-năy —] original sin; **отпущение грехов** [at-pŏŏ-shché-nye gryé-chŏv] remission of sins; absolution

греховный [grye-chóv-năy] adj. sinful

грецкий орех [gryéts-ki aryéch] sm. walnut

грешить [grye-shět'] (co-) vi. to sin, to do wrong

грешник [gryésh-nik] sm., **грешница** [gryésh-ni-tsa] sf. sinner; offender

грешный [gryésh-năy] adj. sinful; guilty

гриб [grib] sm. bot. fungus; mushroom; toadstool

грива [grě-va] sf. mane; crest; fig. head of hair

гривенник [grě-vyen-n'ik] sm. ten copecks (silver)

грим [grim] sm. theat. make-up

гримёр [gri-myór] sm. theat. make-up artist

гримировать [gri-m'ě-ra-vat'] vt. to make up (some-one)

гримаса [gri-mā-sa] sf. grimace

гримасничать [gri-más-n'i-chat'] vi. to grimace, pull faces

грипп [grip] sm. influenza

гриф [grif] sm. mus. finger board; neck (violin, etc.); zool. griffin, vulture

грифель [grě-fel'] sm. slate-pencil; **-ная доска** [-naya daská] slate

гроб [grob] sm. grave; coffin; **-ница** [-n'ě-tsa] sf. tomb; shrine; **-овщик** [-av-shchěk] sm. coffin-maker; undertaker; **-окопатель** [-aka-pā-tyel'] sm. grave-digger

гроза [gra-zā] sf. storm; calamity; terror

гроздь [grozd'] sm. bunch (as grapes); cluster

грозить [gra-zět'] vi. to menace, threaten

грозный [gróz-năy] adj. threatening; rigorous; formidable

грозящий [gra-zyā-shchi] adj. imminent (danger)

гром [grom] sm. thunder; **удар грома** [ŏŏ-dăr gró-ma] thunder-clap

громада [gra-mā-da] sf. bulk, mass

громадность [gra-mād-nŏst'] sf. enormity, vastness

громадный [gra-mād-năy] adj. massive, vast

громила [gra-mě-la] sm. burglar

громить [gra-mět'] (раз-) vt. to destroy, ruin

громкий [gróm-ki] adj. loud; boisterous; fig. renowned

громко [gróm-kŏ] adv. aloud; **-говоритель** [-ga-va-ě-tyel'] sm. loud-speaker

громоздить [gra-maz-d'ět'] (на-) vt. to pile up; to lumber up

громоздкий [gra-mózd-ki] adj. bulky, cumbersome

громоотвод [gra-ma-at-vód] sm. fig. lightning conductor

гроссбух [grós-bŏŏch] sm. ledger

грохнуть [gróch-nŏŏt'] vt. to let fall heavily; to crash

грохот [gró-chŏt] sm. roll (drum); crash, roar

грубеть [grŏŏ-byét'] (за-) vi. to harden; become coarse, become rude

грубить [grŏŏ-bēt'] (на-) *vi.* to offend, be rude

грубиян [grŏŏ-byān] *sm.* vulgar person, ruffian

грубый [grŏŏ-băy] *adj.* rough, rude; coarse, crude

грудастый [grŏŏ-dās-tăy] *adj.* broad-chested

грудинка [grŏŏ-d'én-ka] *sf.* brisket

грудь [grŏŏd'] *sf.* breast, chest; bosom

груз [grŏŏz] *sm.* load, burden; weight; cargo, freight; shipment

грузило [grŏŏ-zē-lŏ] *sn.* plumb, plumb-line; plummet

грузин [grŏŏ-zēn] *sm.* Georgian; **-ский** [-ski] *adj.* Georgian

грузить [grŏŏ-zēt'] (по-) *vt.* to load, ship; to embark

грузный [grŏŏz-năy] *adj.* laden; massive

грузовик [grŏŏ-za-v'ĕk] *sm.* motor lorry, truck

грузовщик [grŏŏ-zav-shchĕk] *sm.* charterer, shipper

грунт [grŏŏnt] *sm.* ground, soil

группа [grŏŏ-pa] *sf.* group

группировка [grŏŏ-pi-róv-ka] *sf.* classification; grouping

грустный [grŏŏst-năy] *adj.* melancholy, mournful

грусть [grŏŏst'] *sf.* grief, sorrow

груша [grŏŏ-sha] *sf.* pear; pear-tree

грушевидный [grŏŏ-she-v'ĕd-năy] *adj.* pear-shaped

грыжа [grŏ-zha] *sf.* hernia, rupture

грызение [grŏ-zyé-nye] *sn* nibbling

грызня [grăz-nyā] *sf.* brawl

грызть [grăzt'] (раз-) *vt.* to gnaw

грызун [gră-zŏŏn] *sm.* rodent; *fig.* quarrelsome person

гряда [gryă-da] *sf.* border (*flowers*); row (*of vegetables*); ridge (*of mountain*); bank (*of clouds*)

грядиль [gră-dil'] *sm.* plough-beam

грязнить [gryaz-n'ēt'] (за-) *vt.* to dirty, soil

грязный [gryāz-năy] *adj.* dirty, filthy, muddy

грязь [gryăz'] *sf.* dirt, filth, mud

губа [gŏŏ-bā] *sf.* lip; **заячья** – [zăya-chya –] hare-lip; bay, gulf; **-стый** [-stăy] thick-lipped

губернатор [gŏŏ-ber-nā-tŏr] *sm.* governor

губерния [gŏŏ-bér-nya] *sf* district *or* local government, county (*term no longer used in the USSR*)

губитель [gŏŏ-b'ĕ-tyel'] *sm.,* **-ница** [-n'itsa] *sf.* one who destroys, injures, ruins; **-ный** [-năy] *adj.* destructive, pernicious

губить [gŏŏ-bēt'] (по-) *vt.* to destroy, ruin, undo; to spoil (*crops, etc.*)

губка [gŏŏb-ka] *sf.* sponge; tiny lip

губной [gŏŏb-nóy] *adj. phon.* labial

губчатый [gŏŏb-chā-tăy] *adj.* spongy; fungoid

гувернантка [gŏŏ-ver-nānt-ka] *sf.* governess [tutor

гувернёр [gŏŏ-ver-nyór] *sm.*

Д

гудение [goo-dyé-nye] *sn.* drone, hum

гудеть [goo-dyét'] (за-) *vi.* to buzz, hum; to hoot

гудок [goo-dók] *sm.* hooter

гул [gool] *sm.* boom, rumble; **-кий** [-ki] *adj.* hollow; resounding

гульба [gool'-ba] *sf.* revelry

гуляка [goo-lyá-ka] *sm. and f.* idler, stroller

гулянье [goo-lyá-nye] *sn.* walking; promenading

гулять [goo-lyát'] (по-) *vi.* to walk

гуманность [goo-mán-nóst'] *sf.* humanity

гумми [goom-mi] *sn.* gum

гумно [goom-nó] *sn.* threshing-floor

гурт [goort] *sm.* drove; herd; flock

гуртовщик [goor-tav-shchík] *sm.* drover; wholesale merchant

гусак [goo-sák] *sm.* gander

гусеница [goo-sye-n'i-tsa] *sf.* caterpillar

гусёнок [goo-syónŏk] *sm.* gosling

гусли [goos-l'i] *sf. pl.* dulcimer, psaltery

гусляр [goos-lyár] *sm.* dulcimer player

густеть [goos-tyét'] (за-) *vi.* to condense; to thicken

густой [goos-tóy] *adj.* dense, thick; deep (*colour*)

густота [goos-ta-tá] *sf.* density, thickness; depth

гусь [goos'] *sf.* goose

гусятина [goo-syá-t'i-na] *sf.* goose-meat

гуща [goo-shcha] *sf.* dregs, sediment; residue

да [dá] *adv.* yes; *conj.* and; but

дабы [dá-bǔ] *conj.* as, because, in order to, in order that

давать [da-vát'] (дать) *vt.* to give; to bestow; to allow; to permit; **- знать** [- znát'] to inform

давить [da-vět'] (раз-) *vt.* to press, squash, squeeze; **-ся** [-sya] to choke

давка [dáv-ka] *sf.* crowding, pressing; traffic jam

давление [dav-lyé-nye] *sn.* enforcement, pressure, stress; *tech.* thrust

давний [dáv-ni] *adj.* of old, of long standing, old-established

давнишний [dav-n'ésh-ni] *adj.* ancient

давно [dav-nó] *adv.* long ago

давность [dáv-nóst'] *sf.* antiquity, remoteness

даже [dá-zhe] *adv.* even

дакать [dá-kat'] *vi.* to answer always in the affirmative, to say yes habitually, submit

далее [dá-lye-ye] *adv.* farther, further; **и т.д.,** etc.

далёкий [da-lyó-ki] *adj.* distant, far, remote

далеко [da-lye-kó] *adv.* far, far off, a long way away; **- не** [-nye] not at all, far from it

даль [dál'] *sf.* great distance

дальний [dál'-ni] *adj.* distant; **самый -** [sá-mǎy -] far

дальнобойный [dal'-na-bóy-nǎy] *adj.* long range

дальновидный [dal'-na-v'ĕd-năy] *adj.* clear-sighted; far-seeing

дальновидность [dal'na-v'ĕd-nŏst'] *sf.* foresight; insight

дальнозоркий [dal'na-zór-ki] *adj.* long-sighted

дальнозоркость [dal'-na-zór-kŏst'] *sf.* presbyopia

дальность [dal'nŏst'] *sf.* distance; range

дальше [dál'-she] *adv.* farther, further; beyond; – ! continue! proceed!

дама [dā-ma] *sf.* lady; queen (*cards*)

дамба [dām-ba] *sf.* dam, dike, embankment, sea-wall

дамка [dām-ka] *sf.* king (*draughts*)

дамский [dām-ski] *adj.* lady's

данник [dān-n'ik] *sf.* tributary

данные [dān-nă-ye] *sn. pl.* data, facts

данный [dān-năy] *adj.* given; present; в – момент [v – ma-myént] at present

дантист [dan-t'ēst] *sm., -ка, sf.* dentist

дань [dān'] *sf.* tax; tribute; contribution

дар [dār] *sm.* gift, present; grant; святые дары [svya-tắye da-rắ] Holy Sacraments

даритель [da-rē-tyel'] *sm., -ница* [-n'i-tsa] *sf.* donor

дарить [da-rēt'] *vt.* to give, present; to make a present; to grant

дармоед [dar-ma-yéd] *sm.* drone, parasite, sponger

даровитый [da-ra-vē-tăy] *adj.* clever, gifted, talented

даровой [da-ra-vóy] *adj.* gratuitous; free; – стол [– stol] free board; [in vain

даром [dā-rŏm] *adv.* gratis; in vain

дароносица [da-ra-nó-si-tsa] *sf.* monstrance; pyx

дательный [dā-tyel'-năy] *adj. gram.* dative; – падеж [– pa-dyézh] dative case

датский [dāt-ski] *adj.* Danish

датчанин [dat-chá-n'in] *sm.,* **датчанка** [dat-chán-ka] *sf.* Dane

дача [dā-cha] *sf.* giving, payment; villa; summer residence; дачная жизнь [dách-naya zhizn'] country life

два [dvā] *num.* two

двадцатилетие [dvad-tsa-t'i-lyé-tye] *sn.* twentieth anniversary

двадцатый [dvad-tsá-tăy] *num.* twentieth

двадцать [dvād-tsat'] *num.* twenty

двенадцать [dvye-nád-tsat'] *num.* twelve

дверца [dvyér-tsa] *sf.* door of a carriage, car, oven, *etc.*

дверь [dvyer'] *sf.* door; входная – [vchad-nā-ya –] front-door; запасная – [za-pas-nā-ya –] emergency exit

двести [dvyé-st'i] *num.* two hundred

движение [dv'ĕ-ga-nye] *sn.* moving; stirring

двигатель [dv'ĕ-ga-tyel'] *sm.* engine, motor; propeller

двигать [dv'ĕ-gat'] (**двинуть**) *vt.* to move, stir; to set in motion; **-ся** [-sya] to taxi (*on land or water*)

движение [dv'i-<u>zhé</u>-nye] *sn.* motion, movement; **сила движения** [sē-la dv'i-<u>zhé</u>-nya] impetus

двоеобрачие [dvaye-brá-chye] *sn.* bigamy

двоеобрачный [dvaye-brách-nǎy] *adj.* bigamous

двоедушие [dvaye-dōō-shye] *sn.* duplicity, false-hood; double-dealing

двоедушный [dvaye-dōōsh-nǎy] *adj.* deceitful, false, two-faced

двоеженец [dvaye-zhé-nyets] *sm.* bigamist

двоеточие [dvaye-tó-chye] *sn. gram.* colon; diaresis

двоить [dva-ét'] (с-) *vt.* to double

двойка [dvóy-ka] *sf.* pair; deuce (*cards*)

двойной [dvay-nóy] *adj.* double, twofold, two-ply

двойня [dvóy-nya] *sf.* pl. twins

двойственность [dvóy-stven-nŏst'] *sf.* duplicity

двор [dvor] *sm.* court, yard

дворец [dva-ryéts] *sm.* palace

дворник [dvór-n'ik] *sm.* door-keeper, house-porter

дворня [dvór-nya] *sf.* domestic staff

дворняжка [dvar-nyá<u>zh</u>-ka] *sf.* mongrel, yard-dog

дворцовой [dvar-tsa-vóy] *adj.* palatial

дворянин [dva-rya-n'én] *sm.* nobleman

дворянство [dva-ryán-stvŏ] *sn.* nobility

двоюродный [dva-yōō-rad-nǎy] *adj.* – **брат** [– brát] *sm.,* **двоюродная сестра** [dva-yōō-rad-na-ya ses-trá] *sf.* first cousin

двояко [dva-yā-kŏ] *adv.* in two ways

двугласный [dvŏō-glás-nǎy] *adj.* – **звук** [– zvŏŏk] diphthong

двукратный [dvŏŏ-krát-nǎy] *adj.* reiterated; twofold

двулетний [dvŏŏ-lyét-ni] *adj.* biennial

двуличный [dvŏŏ-l'éch-nǎy] *adj.* hypocritical

двуногий [dvŏŏ-nó-gi] *adj.* biped

двусложный [dvŏŏ-sló<u>zh</u>-nǎy] *adj.* disyllabic

двусмысленный [dvŏŏ-smás-lyen-nǎy] *adj.* ambiguous

двусторонний [dvŏŏ-sta-rón-n'i] *adj.* bilateral

двухместный [dvŏŏ<u>ch</u>-myést-nǎy] *adj.* two-seated

двухмесячный [dvŏŏ<u>ch</u>-myé-syach-nǎy] *adj.* bi-monthly

двухнедельный [dvŏŏ<u>ch</u>-nye-dyél'-nǎy] *adj.* fort-nightly

двухэтажный [dvŏŏ<u>ch</u>-eta<u>zh</u>-nǎy] *adj.* two-storeyed

дебаркадер [de-bar-ka-dyér] *sm.* platform (*railway*); landing-stage

дебатировать [de-ba-t'é-ra-vat'] *vi.* to debate

дебелость [dye-byé-lŏst'] *sf.* corpulence, stoutness

дебелый [dye-byé-lǎy] *adj.* plump, solid

дебри [dyé-bri] *pl.* thicket; glen; jungle

дебушировать [de-bŏō-shé-ra-vat'] *vi. mil.* to debouch

дебютировать [de-byōōt'ĕ-ra-vat'] vi. to make a first appearance

дева [dyé-va] sf. maid; virgin; **старая –** [stá-ra-ya –] spinster; **Пресвятая –** [prye-svya-tā-ya –] The Holy Virgin

девать [dye-vāt'] (деть) vi. to place, put; **-ся** [-sya] vi. to take refuge

деверь [dye-ver'] sm. brother-in-law

девиз [dye-vēz] sm. device, motto; slogan

девица [dye-v'ĕ-tsa] sf. girl, maiden

девический [dye-v'ĕ-ches-ki] adj. girlish

девичество [dye-v'ĕ-ches-tvŏ] sn. maidenhood

девичник [dye-v'ĕch-nik] sm. wedding-eve

девочка [dyé-vach-ka] sf. little girl

девственный [dyév-stven-nǎy] adj. innocent; virgin

девушка [dyé-vŏŏsh-ka] sf. young lady

девяносто [dye-vya-nós-tŏ] num. ninety

девятый [dye-vyā-tǎy] num. ninth

девять [dyé-vyat] num. nine

девятьсот [dye-vyat'-sót] num. nine hundred

дёготь [dyó-gŏt'] sm. tar

дед [dyed] sm. grandfather; **рождественский –** [razh-dyést-vyen-ski –] Father Christmas; **-ушка** [-ŏŏsh-ka] grandad

деепричастие [dye-ye-pri-chās-tye] sn. gram. gerund

дежурить [dye-zhŏŏ-rit'] vi. to be on duty

дежурный [dye-zhŏŏr-nǎy] adj. on duty; **офицер** [– afi-tsyér] orderly officer

дезертировать [dye-zer-

t'ĕ-ra-vat'] vt.i. to desert

действенный [dyéyst-ven-nǎy] adj. efficient

действие [dyéy-stvye] sn. action, operation, efficacy, influence; theat. act

действительный [dyey-stvē-tyel'-nǎy] adj. actual, real; efficacious; leg. valid

действовать [dyéy-stva-vat'] (по–) vi. to act, function

действующий [dyéy-stvŏŏ-yŏŏ-shchi] adj. active; **действующие лица** [dyéy-stvŏŏ-yŏŏ-shchiye l'ĕ-tsa] dramatis personae

дека [dyé-ka] sf. mus. sounding board

декабрь [dye-kābr'] sm. December

декан [dye-kān] sm. dean; **-ат** [-āt] deanery

декламатор [dye-kla-mā-tŏr] sm. reciter

декламация [dye-kla-mā-tsya] sf. declamation, recitation, verse-speaking

декламировать [dye-kla-mē-ra-vat'] vt. to recite

декларация [dye-kla-rā-tsya] sf. declaration

декольте [de-kol'-té] sn. low-necked dress

декрет [de-krýet] sm. decree

делать [dye-lat'] (с-) vt. to do; to make

делегация [dye-le-gā-tsya] sf. delegation

дележ [dye-lyózh] sm. division; sharing

деление [dye-lyé-nye] sn. arith. division; sharing

делец [dye-lyéts] sm. business-man

деликатность [dye-li-kāt-nŏst'] sf. delicacy

деликатный [dye-li-kát-nǎy] adj. delicate, dainty; fragile

делимое [dye-lʼē-ma-ye] sn. math. dividend

делимость [dye-lʼē-mõst'] sf. divisibility

делимый [dye-lʼē-mǎy] adj. divisible

делитель [dye-lʼē-tyel'] sm. math. divisor

делить [dye-lʼēt'] (раз-) vt. to divide, share

делишки [dye-lʼēsh-ki] s. pl. affairs; как –? how are things?

дело [dyé-lô] sn. affair, business, concern; в чём –? [vchóm –] What's the trouble?

деловой [dye-la-vóy] adj. business-like

делопроизводство [dye-la-pra-iz-vód-stvŏ] sn. production and administrative management

дельность [dyél'-nõst'] sf. capability, shrewdness

дельта [dyél'-ta] sf. delta

дельфин [dyel'-fēn] sm. dolphin

делянка [dye-lyán-ka] sf. allotment, plot of land

демобилизация [dye-ma-bi-li-zā-tsya] sf. demobilization

демократический [de-ma-kra-tē-ches-ki] adj. democratic

демократия [de-ma-krā-tya] sf. democracy

демонстрировать [de-man-strē-ra-vat'] vi. to demonstrate

денежный [dyé-nyezh-nǎy] adj. monetary; pecuniary; fam. well-off

денница [dyen-nē-tsa] sf. poet. dawn; morning star

денщик [dyén-shchik] sm. batman

день [dyen'] sm. day; будний – [bōōd-ni'] – week-day; добрый – ! [dó-brǎy –] Good day! Good afternoon! – рождения [– razh-dyé-nya] birthday

деньги [dyén'-gi] sf. pl. money; currency; карманные [– kar-mán-nǎye –] pocket money

департамент [de-par-tā-myent] sm. department

депеша [de-pyé-sha] sf. despatch; telegraphic message

депо [de-pó] sn. depot

депутат [de-pōō-tāt] sm. delegate, deputy, representative

депутация [de-pōō-tā-tsya] sf. delegation, deputation

дёргать [dyór-gat'] (дёрнуть) vt. to drag, pull, pull out; -ся [-sya] to twitch

деревенский [dye-re-vyén-ski] adj. rural, rustic; – житель [– zhē-tyel'] countryman, villager

деревня [dye-ryév-nya] sf. village; country

дерево [dyé-re-vŏ] sn. tree; wood; красное – [krās-na-ye –] mahogany; чёрное – [chór-na-ye –] ebony

деревушка [dye-re-vōōsh-ka] sf. hamlet

деревянный [dye-re-vyán-nǎy] adj. wooden

держава [dyer-zhā-va] sf. power, state; dominion

державный [dyer-zhāv-nǎy] adj. powerful, potent, reigning, sovereign

держаный [dyér-zha-nǎy] adj. second-hand, used

держать [dyer-zhát'] (по-) *vt.* to detain; to hold, keep;
– пари [– pa-rḗ] to bet, stake; **– вправо!** [– vprá-vŏ] Keep to the right! **–влево!** [– vlyé-vŏ] Keep to the left! **-ся** [-sya] *vi.* to adhere to

дерзать [dyer-zát'] (дерзнýть) *vi.* to dare, presume; to venture

дерзкий [dyérs-ki] *adj.* audacious, impudent; bold, daring

дерзость [dyér-zŏst'] *sf.* insolence, sauciness

дёрн [dyórn] *sm.* turf

дернистый [dyer-n'é-stăy] *adj.* grassy, turfy

дерюга [dye-ryōō-ga] *sm.* canvas, sackcloth

десерт [de-sért] *sm.* dessert

десна [dyes-ná] *sf.* gum

деспотический [des-pa-t'é-ches-ki] *adj.* despotic

десть [dyest'] *sf.* quire (*paper*)

десятилетие [dye-sya-t'i-lyé-tye] *sn.* decade

десятичный [dye-sya-t'éch-năy] *adj.* decimal

десять [dyé-syat'] *num.* ten

десятый [dye-syá-tăy] *num.* tenth

деталь [dye-tál'] *sf.* detail; particulars

детвора [dye-tva-rá] *s. pl. coll.* a group of children

детёныши [dye-tyó-năsh] *sm.* the young of animals

дети [dyé-t'i] *sn. pl.* children

детородный [dye-ta-ród-năy] *adj.* genital

деторождение [dye-ta-razhdyé-nye] *sn.* child-birth

детоубийство [dye-ta-ōō-bḗ-stvŏ] *sn* infanticide

детсад [dyet-sád] *sm.* kinder-garten

детский [dyét-ski] *adj.* child's, children's; childish

детская [dyét-skaya] *sf.* child's nursery

детство [dyét-stvŏ] *sn.* child-hood, infancy

дефективный [dye-fek-t'ēv-năy] *adj.* defective

дефилировать [dye-fi-l'ḗ-ra-vat'] (про-) *vi.* to defile

дефис [de-fḗs] *sm. typ.* hyphen

дешеветь [dye-she-vyét'] (по-) *vi.* to become cheaper, to fall in price; to depreciate

дешевизна [dye-she-v'ēz-na] *sf.* cheapness; bargain prices

дешевить [dye-she-v'ét'] (про-) *vt.* to undercharge; to undervalue

дешёвка [dye-shóv-ka] *sf.* bargain, cheap article(s)

дёшево [dyó-she-vŏ] *adv.* cheaply

дешёвый [dye-shó-văy] *adj.* cheap; inexpensive

дешифрировать [dye-shifrḗ-ra-vat'] *vt.* to decipher

деяние [dye-yá-nye] *sn.* action, deed

деятель [dyé-ya-tyel'] *sm.* promoter; doer, worker; **государственный** – [ga-sōō-dár-stven-năy –] statesman

деятельный [dyé-ya-tyel'-năy] *adj.* active, agile, energetic

деятельность [dyé-ya-tyel'-nŏst'] *sf.* activity, work; **общественная** – [ab-shchést-vyen-naya –] public work, social work

джут [dzhōōt] *sm.* jute

диабет [dia-bét] *sm.* diabetes

диагноз [diag-nóz] *sm.* diagnosis

диагональный [dia-ga-nál'-nǎy] *adj.* diagonal

диаграмма [dia-grám-ma] *sf.* diagram, figure

диалект [dia-lyékt] *sm.* dialect; **-ический** [-éches-ky] dialectical

диалог [dia-lóg] *sm.* dialogue

диаметр [dia-myétr] *sm.* diameter

дива [d'é-va] *sf. theat.* star; great opera singer

диван [d'i-ván] *sm.* divan, ottoman, sofa

диверсия [di-vér-sya] *sf. mil.* diversion

дивертисмент [di-ver-tis-myént] *sm.* entertainment, variety show

дивизия [di-vé-zya] *sf. mil.* division

дивить [d'i-v'ét] (y-) *vt.* to astonish, surprise; **-ся** [-sya] *vi.* to wonder; to be surprised

дивный [d'év-nǎy] *adj.* marvellous; delicious

диво d'é-vò] *sm.* prodigy; **что за** – ! [shto za –] how strange!

диез [dyéz] *sm. mus.* sharp (♯)

диета [diyé-ta] *sf.* diet

дикарь [d'i-kár] *sm.* дикарка [d'i-kár-ka] *sf.* savage. wild person, unsociable person

дикий [d'é-ki] *adj.* savage, wild; untamed; unsociable

дикобраз [d'i-ka-bráz] *sm.* porcupine

диковинный [d'i-ka-v'én-nǎy] *adj.* odd, unusual

дикость [d'é-kǒst] *sf.* savagery, wildness; absurdity

диктатура [d'ik-ta-tōō-ra] *sf.* dictatorship

диктовать [d'ik-ta-vát] (про-) *vt.i.* to dictate

диктовка [d'ik-tóv-ka] *sf.* dictation

дикция [d'ĕk-tsya] *sf.* diction, elocution

дилетантский [d'i-lye-tánt-ski] *adj.* amateurish

дилижанс [di-li-zháns] *sm.* stage-coach; **почтовый** [pach-tó-vǎy –] mail-coach

диоцез [dia-tsyéz] *sm.* diocese

диплом [di-plóm] *sm.* diploma

дипломатический [di-pla-ma-t'é-cheski] *adj.* diplomatic

дипломатия [di-pla-mátya] *sf.* diplomacy

директива [d'i-rek-t'é-va] *sf.* directions, instructions

директор [d'i-rék-tǒr] *sm.* director, manager; chief, headmaster; **почт-** [pocht-] Postmaster General

директорство [d'i-rék-tar-stvǒ] *sn.* directorship

директриса [d'i-rek-trē-sa] *sf.* headmistress

дирекция [d'i-rék-tsya] *sf.* directorate, management; board of directors

дирижёр [di-ri-zhyór] *sm.* bandmaster, conductor

дирижировать [di-ri-zhé-ra-vat'] *vt.i.* to conduct

дискант [dis-kánt] *sm.* soprano voice, treble

дисконт [dis-kónt] *sm.* discount

дискуссия [dis-kōōs-sya] *sf.* debate, discussion; argument

дистиллировать [di-stil-l'é-ra-vat'] *vt.* to distil

дисциплинарный [dis-tsi-pli-nâr-nǎy] *adj.* disciplinary

дитя [d'i-tyã] *sn.* child

дичать [d'i-chãt'] *vi.* to run wild; to be unsociable

дичь [d'ěch'] *sf.* game, hunted animals; thicket; lonely spot; nonsense; **какая** —! [ka-kã-yá —] rubbish!

длань [dlǎn'] *sf.* palm (*of hand*)

длина [dl'i-nã] *sf.* length

длинный [dl'ěn-nǎy] *adj.* long

длинноватый [dl'in-nǎ-vã-tǎy] *adj.* rather long, longish

длительный [dl'ě-tyel'-nǎy] *adj.* lingering, protracted

длить [dl'ět'] (про-) *vt.* to lengthen; to prolong; to delay; **-ся** [-sya] *vi.* to endure, last

для [dlyã] *prep.* for, to; **— того** [— ta-vó] therefore; **— чего?** [— chye-vó] Why? What for? **— того чтобы** [— ta-vó shtó-bǎ] in order to, so that

дневать [dnye-vãt'] (про-) *vi.* to spend the day

дневник [dnyev-n'ěk] *sm.* diary, journal; **вести —** [vyes-t'ě —] to keep a diary

дневной [dnyev-nóy] *adj.* diurnal; **— спектакль** [— spek-tãkl'] matinée

днём [dnyóm] *adv.* in the daytime

дно [dno] *sn.* bottom (*as of the sea, etc.*); ground; **итти ко дну** [it'ě ka-dnóо] to sink

до [do] *prep.* before; to; as far as; until; *sn. mus.* C

добавление [da-ba-vlyé-nye] *sn.* addition, appendix; rider

добавлять [da-ba-vlyãt'] (добавить) *vt.* to add to, append

добавок [da-bã-vók] *sm.* addition; make-weight

добавочный [da-bã-vach-nǎy] *adj.* additional, supplementary

добегать [da-bye-gãt'] *vt.* to reach, run up to

добивать [da-b'i-vãt'] (добить) *vt.* to kill; to finish; to drive home (*as nail*); **-ся** [-sya] *vi.* to endeavour; *vt.* to attain; to seek

добирать [da-b'i-rãt'] (добрать) *vt.* to collect, gather

доблестный [dó-blyest-nǎy] *adj.* brave, heroic, valiant

доблесть [dó-blyest'] *sf.* heroism, valour

добро [da-bró] *sn.* well-being; goods, property; **—!** fine! splendid!

доброволец [da-bra-vó-lyets] *sm.* volunteer

добровольный [da-bra-vól'-nǎy] *adj.* voluntary, willing

добродетель [da-bra-dyé-tyel'] *f.* virtue

добродушие [da-bra-dōō-shye] *sn.* kindness; good nature

доброжелатель [da-bra-zhe-lã-tyel'] *sm.* patron, well-wisher

доброкачественный [da-bra-kã-chest-vyen-nǎy] *adj.* of good quality, sound; genuine (*of goods*)

добронравие [da-bra-nrã-vye] *sn.* exemplary behaviour

добропорядочный [da-bra-pa-ryã-dach-nǎy] *adj.* respectable

добросердечный [da-bra-syer-dyéch-nǎy] *adj.* kind-hearted

добросовестный [da-bra-só-vyest-nǎy] *adj.* conscientious, dutiful, scrupulous

доброта [da-bra-tá] *sf.* goodness, kindness; good quality

добрый [dó-bray] *adj.* good, kind

добряк [da-bryák] *sm.* good-natured man; *coll.* good sort

добрячка [da-bryách-ka] *sf.* kindly woman

добывать [da-be-vát'] (добыть) *vt.* to extract, mine; to acquire, gain, secure

добыча [da-bá-cha] *sf.* extraction; booty; prey; gain, profit; *naut.* prize

доверенность [da-vyé-ren-nǒst'] *sf.* trust; warrant of attorney; complete authority

доверие [da-vyé-rye] *sn.* confidence, reliance

доверху [dó-ver-chǒŏ] *adv.* up to the top

доверчивый [da-vyér-chi-vǎy] *adj.* confiding, credulous

довершать [da-vyer-shát'] *vt.* to attain perfection; to accomplish

доверять [da-vye-ryát'] (доверить) *vt.* to confide, trust; to entrust; to depend

довод [dó-vǒd] *sm.* argument, point of view; proof; reason

доводить [da-va-d'ét'] (довести) *vt.* to bring *or* lead up to; to see it through

довоенный [da-va-yén-nǎy] *adj.* pre-war

довольно [da-vól'-nǒ] *adv.* enough, sufficiently; rather

довольный [da-vól'-nǎy] *adj.* content, pleased, satisfied

довольствие [da-vól'-stvye] *sn.* sufficiency; *mil.* provision, ration

довольство [da-vól'-stvǒ] *sn.* contentment; prosperity

догадка [da-gád-ka] *sf.* conjecture, surmise

догадливость [da-gád-l'i-vǒst'] *sf.* ingenuity, shrewdness

догадливый [da-gá-dl'i-vǎy] *adj.* ingenious, shrewd

догадываться [da-gá-dǎ-vat'-sya] (догадаться) *vi.* to guess; to suspect

доглядеть [da-glya-dyét'] *vt.* to notice, watch

договаривать [da-ga-vá-ri-vat'] (договорить) *vt.* to speak out; to conclude speaking; **-ся** [-sya] *vi.* to negotiate; to contract, come to terms

договор [da-ga-vór] *sm.* agreement, contract; treaty

догонять [da-ga-nyát'] (догнать) *vt.* to overtake; run down

догорать [da-ga-rát'] (догореть) *vi.* to burn low, burn out

додача [da-dá-cha] *sf.* addition, supplement

доделывать [da-dyé-lǎ-vat'] (доделать) *vt.* to touch up

доезжать [da-yez-zhát'] (доехать) *vi.* to arrive (*at*), reach (*a destination*); drive up to

доение [da-yé-nye] *sn.* milking

дожаренный [da-zhá-ren-nǎy] *adj.* thoroughly cooked, roasted *or* fried

дождевик [dazh-dye-v'ěk] sm. raincoat; kind of fungus

дождевой [dazh-dye-vóy] adj. rainy

дождить [dazh-d'ět'] vi. to rain; **дождит** [dazh-d'ět] it is raining

дождь [dozhd'] sm. rain

доживать [da-zhi-vát'] (дожить) vi. to attain, to reach (a desired goal), live to witness (a great event, etc.)

доза [dó-za] sf. dose, draught, potion

дозволение [daz-va-lyé-nye] sn. concession, leave, permission

дозволять [daz-va-lyát'] (дозволить) vt. to allow, grant, permit

дознавать [daz-na-vát'] (дознать) vt. to ascertain

дознание [da-znā-nye] sn. inquiry, investigation

дозор [da-zór] sm. patrol

дозревание [da-zre-vā-nye] sn. ripening

доить [da-ět'] vt. to milk

дойник [dóy-n'ik] sm. milk-pail

доказательный [da-ka-zā-tyel'-năy] adj. conclusive

доказательство [da-ka-zā-tyel'-stvŏ] sn. proof, testimony

доказывать [da-kǎ-ză-vat'] (доказать) vt. to attest, demonstrate, prove

доклад [da-klād] sm. announcement, report

доктор [dŏk-tŏr] sm. doctor, physician; – прав [– práv] doctor of laws; -ша [-sha] sf. lady-doctor

докуда [da-kōō-da] adv. how far? until when?

докука [da-kōō-ka] sm. annoyance, vexation

докучливый [da-kōō-chl'i-văy] adj. irksome, tiresome

долбить [dal-bět'] (выдолбить) vt. to chisel, gouge; to peck (as birds); to swot

долг [dolg] sm. duty; debt; obligation; **долги** [dal-gě] pl. arrears, liabilities; **в долгах** [vdal-gāch] in debt

долгий [dól-gi] adj. long, prolonged

долговатый [dal-ga-vā-tăy] adj. rather long

долговременный [dal-ga-vryé-men-năy] adj. protracted

долголетие [dal-ga-lyé-tye] sn. longevity

долгосрочный [dal-ga-sróch-năy] adj. long-dated

долетать [da-lye-tāt'] (долететь) vi. to arrive (by air)

должник [dal-zhn'ěk] sm. debtor

должность [dól-zhnŏst'] sf. appointment, job, situation

должный [dól-zhnăy] adj. due, owing; proper

долина [da-l'ē-na] sf. valley; dale

долой [da-lóy] adv. down

долото [da-la-tó] sn. chisel, gouge

долька [dól'-ka] sf. lobule; tiny portion

доля [dó-lya] sf. part, share, quota; lobe

дом [dom] sm. house; home

дома [dó-ma] adv. at home

домашние [da-māsh-nye] sm. pl. the household

домашний [da-māsh-ni] adj. domestic; home-made; homely

домик [dó-mik] *sm.* cottage

домкрат [dam-krát] *sm. tech.* jack

домна [dóm-na] *sf.* blast-furnace

домовитый [da-ma-v'ě-tăy] *adj.* economic, thrifty

домовладелец [da-ma-vla-dýé-lyets] *sm.* landlord, proprietor

домоводство [da-ma-vód-stvŏ] *sn.* house-keeping

домогаться [da-ma-gát'-sya] *vi.* to solicit, woo

домой [da-móy] *adv.* home, homewards

домоправитель [da-ma-pra-vě-tyel'] *sm.* steward

домосед [da-ma-syéd] *sm.* stay-at-home

домочадцы [da-ma-chád-tsă] *sm. pl.* members of a household

донашивать [da-ná-shi-vat'] *vt.* to wear out (*clothing, etc.*)

донесение [da-nye-syé-nye] *sn.* dispatch, report

донос [da-nós] *sm.* denunciation; information

доносить [da-na-sět'] (доне-сти́) *vt.* to denounce, inform against

доносчик [da-nós-chik] *sm.* informer; sneak

доныне [da-ná-nye] *adv.* hitherto

допивать [da-pi-vát'] (допи́ть) *vt.* to drink up

доплата [da-plá-ta] *sf.* supplementary payment; excess fare

дополнительный [da-pal-n'ě-tyel'-năy] *adj.* complementary; supplementary

дополуденный [da-pa-lōō-

dyen-năy] *adj.* antemeridian

допрос [da-prós] *sm.* interrogation; inquest; **крестный** – [kryést-năy –] cross-examination

допуск [dó-pŏŏsk] *sm.* admittance

допускать [da-pŏŏs-kát'] (допусти́ть) *vt.* to admit; to allow, permit; to tolerate

допустимый [da-pŏŏs-t'ě-măy] *adj.* admissible

дорога [da-ró-ga] *sf.* road, path, way; **большая** – [bal'-shā-ya –] highway; **железная** – [zhe-lyéz-na-ya –] railway

дороговатый [da-ra-ga-vá-tăy] *adj.* rather dear (*price*)

дороговизна [da-ra-ga-v'ěz-na] *sf.* costliness, high prices

дорогой [da-ra-góy] *adj.* dear, expensive; darling, dear

дородный [da-ród-năy] *adj.* corpulent, stout; burly

дорожать [da-ra-zhát'] *vt.* to rise in price

дорожить [da-ra-zhět'] *vt.* to esteem, prize, value

дортуар [dar-tōōár] *sm.* dormitory

досада [da-sá-da] *sf.* annoyance; disappointment; vexation; pity; **какая** – ! [ka-kā-ya –] what a pity!

досаждать [da-sazh-dát'] (досади́ть) *vi.* to annoy, bother; to provoke

доска [das-ká] *sf.* board, plank; **классная** – [klás-sna-ya –] blackboard

доскональный [das-ka-nál'-năy] *adj.* exact; punctual; thorough

дословный [da-slóv-năy] *adj.* literal, verbatim

досматривать [da-smá-tri-vat'] (досмотре́ть) vt. to inspect (luggage, etc.); to look into thoroughly

досмотр [da-smótr] sm. inspection (of goods)

досрочный [da-sróch-näy] adj. before end of term; premature

доставать [da-sta-vát'] (доста́ть) vt. to get, obtain, procure

доставка [da-stáv-ka] sf. delivery, supply (goods)

доставлять [da-stav-lyát'] (доста́вить) vt. to deliver, transmit; to furnish, supply

достаток [da-stá-tök] sm. abundance, sufficiency, welfare

достаточный [da-stá-tach-näy] adj. adequate; sufficient

достигать [da-st'i-gát'] (дости́гнуть) vt. to attain

достижение [da-st'i-zhé-nye] sn. achievement; progress

достоверный [da-sta-vyér-näy] adj. authentic; trustworthy

достоинство [da-stóin-stvö] sn. merit, virtue; dignity; высокое – [vä-só-kaye –] excellence

достойный [da-stóy-näy] adj. meritorious

достопамятный [da-sta-pá-myat-näy] adj. memorable

достопримечательный [da-sta-pri-mye-chá-tyel'-näy] adj. noteworthy, remarkable

достояние [da-sta-yá-nye] sn. property; fortune

доступ [dós-tööp] sm. access, approach

доступный [da-stóöp-näy] adj. accessible

досуг [da-sóog] sm. leisure; на -е [na -ye] at leisure

досыта [dó-sä-ta] adv. until satiated, to repletion

досюда [da-syóö-da] adv. up to here

досягаемость [da-sya-gá-ye-möst'] sf. reach; mil. range

дотация [da-tá-tsya] sf. grant, subsidy

дотрагиватья [da-trá-gi-vat'-sya] (дотро́нуться) vi. to touch

дотуда [da-tóö-da] adv. up to there

дохлый [dóch-läy] adj. dead

дохлятина [dach-lyá-t'i-na] sf. garbage; carrion

дохнуть [dóch-nöot'] vi. to die; to perish (animals)

дохнуть [dach-nóöt'] vi. to breathe; to exhale

доход [da-chód] sm. income, profit; revenue; валовой – [va-la-vóy –] gross receipts; чистый – [chës-täy –] net profit

доходный [da-chód-näy] adj. lucrative

доцент [da-tséynt] sm. lecturer, reader

дочка [dóch-ka] sf. small daughter

дочь [doch'] sf. daughter

дошкольный [da-shkól'-näy] adj. pre-school

дошлый [dósh-läy] adj. experienced; skilful; cunning

драгоценный [dra-ga-tsyén-näy] adj. precious (as gem, jewel, stone, etc.); invaluable

драже [dra-zhé] sm. sugar [plum

дразнить [draz-n'ět'] (раз-) *vt.* to tease; to mock, provoke

драка [drā-ka] *sf.* fight, scuffle

драма [drā-ma] *sf.* drama

драматический [dra-ma-t'ě-ches-ki] *adj.* dramatic(al)

драматург [dra-ma-tōōrg] *sm.* playwright

драный [drā-năy] *adj.* ragged, tattered

драп [drāp] *sm.* thick woollen cloth

драпировка [dra-pi-róv-ka] *sf.* drapery, hangings

драпировщик [dra-pi-róv-shchik] *sm.* upholsterer

драть [drāt'] (разо-) *vt.* to tear; to flog, thrash; – **горло** [– gór-lŏ] to roar

драться [drāt'sya] *vi.* to be involved in a scrimmage; to scuffle

драчливый [dra-chl'ě-văy] *adj.* pugnacious

драчун [dra-chōōn] *sm.*, **драчунья** [dra-chōō-nya] *sf.* bully

дребедень [dre-bye-dyén'] *sf.* nonsense, trash

древесина [dre-vye-s'ě-na] *sf.* wood

древесный [dre-vyés-năy] *adj.* arboreal, woody; – **уголь** [– ōō-gŏl'] charcoal

древко [dryév-kŏ] *sn.* shaft, staff; tent-pole

древнееврейский [drev-nye-ye-vryéy-ski] *adj.* Hebrew

древний [dryév-n'i] *adj.* ancient, antique

древность [dryév-nŏst'] *sf.* antiquity

дрезина [dre-z'ě-na] *sf.* trolley

дрек [drek] *sm. naut.* grapnel

дремать [dre-māt'] (вз-) *vi.* to doze

дремота [dre-ma-tā] *sf.* drowsiness

дремучий [dre-mōō-chi] *adj.* dense, thick (as forest)

дресва [dres-vā] *sf.* gravel

дрессировать [dres-sě-ra-vāt'] *vt.* to coach, train, break in

дрессировщик [dres-si-róv-shchik] *sm.* trainer

дробинка [dra-běn-ka] *sf.* pellet

дробить [dra-bět'] (раз-) *vt.* to crush, granulate, pulverize

дробный [dró́b-năy] *adj.* fractional; broken up

дробь [drob'] *sf.* small shot; *math.* fraction

дрова [dra-vā] *sn. pl.* firewood, wood

дровни [dróv-n'i] *sf. pl.* peasant's sledge

дровосек [dra-va-syék] *sm.* lumberman, woodman

дровяник [dra-vya-n'ěk] *sm.* firewood dealer; timber-merchant

дроги [dró-gi] *sf. pl.* hearse

дрожание [dra-zhā-nye] *sn.* trembling; vibration

дрожжи [dró-zhi] *sf. pl.* yeast

дрожки [dró́zh-ki] *sf. pl.* "droshky", horse-drawn carriage; racing sulky

дрожь [drozh'] *sf.* shivering, shuddering

дрозд [drozd] *sm.* thrush

дроссель [drós-syel'] *sf. tech.* throttle

дротик [dró-t'ik] *sm.* javelin

друг [drŏŏg] *sm.* friend; –а each other

другой [drŏŏ-góy] *adj.* another, other; **другие** [drŏŏ-gĕ-ye] others

дружба [drŏŏzh-ba] *sf.* friendship

дружелюбие [drŏŏ-zhe-lyŏŏb-ye] *sn.* friendliness, kindness

дружелюбный [drŏŏ-zhe-lyŏŏb-năy] *adj.* amicable; benevolent

дружно [drŏŏzh-nŏ] *adv.* in a friendly manner

дружный [drŏŏzh-năy] *adj.* amicable, friendly

дрыгать [dră-gát'] (дрыгнуть) *vi.* to jerk, twitch

дряблый [dryá-blăy] *adj.* flabby, limp, shrivelled

дрянной [dryan-nóy] *adj.* worthless; wretched

дрянь [dryán'] *sf.* trash; *coll.* rotter

дряхлость [dryáchs-lost'] *sf.* decrepitude

дуб [dŏŏb] *sm.* oak, oak-tree

дубильня [dŏŏ-bél'-nya] *sf.* tannery

дубина [dŏŏ-bē-na] *sf.* bludgeon, club; *fig.* blockhead, dolt

дублёр [dŏŏb-lyór] *sm. theat.* understudy

дубняк [dŏŏb-nyák] *sm.* oak-grove

дубовый [dŏŏ-bó-văy] *adj.* oaken

дубровка [dŏŏbróv-ka] *sf.* germander

дуга [dŏŏ-gá] *sf.* arc; arch

дудка [dŏŏd-ka] *sf.* fife, reed-pipe; **дудки!** *interj.* fiddle-sticks!

дуло [dŏŏ-lŏ] *sn.* bore, muzzle

дульце [dŏŏl'-tse] *sn.* mouth-piece (*for wind instruments*)

дума [dŏŏ-ma] *sf.* thought, idea; council (*pre-Com. regime*); elegy

думать [dŏŏ-mat'] (по-) *vt.i.* to think

думка [dŏŏm-ka] *sf. coll.* small pillow

дуплистый [dŏŏ-pl'és-tăy] *adj.* hollow

дура [dŏŏ-ra] *sf.* stupid woman

дурак [dŏŏ-rák] *sm.* fool, idiot

дурачить [dŏŏ-rá-chit'] *vi.* to play the fool

дурманить [dŏŏr-má-n'it'] *vt.* to stupefy

дурной [dŏŏr-nóy] *adj.* bad, wicked; ugly

дурь [dŏŏr'] *sf.* folly

дуть [dŏŏt'] (по-) *vi.* to blow; **здесь дует** [zdyes' dŏŏ-yet] here it is draughty

дуться [dŏŏt'-sya] *vi.* to pout, sulk

дух [dŏŏch] *sm.* mind, spirit; aroma, odour; **святой –** [svya-tóy –] Holy Ghost

духи [dŏŏ-chi] *sm. pl.* spirits, goblins

духи [dŏŏ-chē] *sm. pl.* perfume, scent

духов день [dŏŏ-chŏv dyen'] *sm.* Whit Monday

духовенство [dŏŏ-cha-vyénstvŏ] *sn.* clergy, priesthood

духовник [dŏŏ-chav-n'ék] *sm.* confessor

духовный [dŏŏ-chóv-năy] *adj.* spiritual

духовой [dŏŏ-cha-vóy] *adj.* wind (*of instrument*)

духота [dŏŏ-cha-tá] *sf.* closeness, oppressiveness

душ [dŏŏsh] *sm.* shower-bath

душа [dŏŏ-shā] *sf.* mind; soul, spirit

душевный [dŏŏ-shév-nǎy] *adj.* cordial; sincere; mental

душегрейка [dŏŏ-she-gréy-ka] *sf.* warm jacket (*woman's*)

душегубец [dŏŏ-she-gŏŏ-byets] *sm.* homicide

душенька [dŏŏ-shen'-ka] *sf.* darling

душистый [dŏŏ-shēs-tǎy] *adj.* fragrant

душить [dŏŏ-shēt'] (y-) *vt.* to choke, smother, suffocate; to perfume

душник [dŏŏ-shn'ik] *sm.* air-hole, ventilator

душный [dŏŏsh-nǎy] *adj.* close, oppressive, stuffy

дуэль [dŏŏ-él'] *sf.* duel

дуэт [dŏŏ-ét] *sm.* duet

дыба [dá-ba] *sf.* gibbet; rack

дыбом [dǎ-bŏm] *adv.* rearward; stand on end (*as of hair*)

дым [dǎm] *sm.* smoke

дымить [dǎ-mēt'] (за-) *vt.i.* to smoke (*as chimney, etc.*)

дымка [dǎm-ka] *sf.* mist

дымный [dǎm-nǎy] *adj.* smoky

дымоход [dǎma-chód] *sm.* chimney

дыня [dǎ-nya] *sf.* melon

дыра [dǎ-rá] *sf.* hole, tear

дырявый [dǎ-ryá-vǎy] *adj.* full of holes

дыхание [dǎ-chá-nye] *sn.* breathing, respiration; gasp

дыхательный [dǎ-chá-tyel'-nǎy] *adj.* respiratory

дышать [dǎ-shát'] *vi.* to breathe

дышло [dǎ-shló] *sn.* beam, pole, shaft; connecting rod

дьявол [dyá-vŏl] *sm.* devil; fiend; *coll.* the deuce!

дьявольский [dyǎ-val'-ski] *adj.* diabolical

дьякон [dyǎ-kŏn] *sm.* deacon

-исса [-ēsa] *sf.* deaconess

дьячок [dya-chók] *sm.* sacristan, sexton

дюжина [dyŏŏ-zhi-na] *sf.* dozen

дюжинный [dyŏŏ-zhin-nǎy] *adj.* common, ordinary

дюйм [dyŏŏim] *sm.* inch

дягиль [dyǎ-gil'] *sf.* angelica

дядя [dyǎ-dya] *sm.* uncle

дятел [dyǎ-tyel] *sm.* woodpecker

дятлина [dyǎt-lina] *sf.* clover

Е

евангелие [evan-gé-lye] *sn.* Gospel

евангелист [evan-ge-l'ēst] *sm.* evangelist

еврей [ye-vréy] *sm.* Israelite, Jew; **-ка** *sf.* Jewess; **-ский** [– ski] *adj.* Jewish

еврейство [ye-vréy-stvŏ] *sn.* Jewry

европеец [ye-vra-pyé-yets] *sm.* European

европейский [ye-vra-pyéy-ski] *adj.* European

егда [yeg-dá] *adv.* though, when

егерь [yé-ger'] *sm.* hunter, sportsman; infantry soldier

египетский [ye-gē-pet-ski] *adj.* Egyptian

египтянин [ye-gip-tyá-n'in] *sm.* Egyptian

его [ye-vó] *pron.* him; *poss. adj. and pron.* his, its

егоза [ye-gó-za] *sm.*, *f.* fidget, unruly child

еда [ye-dá] *sf.* edibles, food, meal

едва [yed-vá] *adv.* hardly, scarcely; **– не** [– nyé] almost, nearly

единение [ye-d'i-nyé-nye] *sn.* accord; union; unity

единица [ye-d'i-n'é-tsa] *sf.* unit

единичный [ye-d'i-n'éch-nǎy] *adj.* one, single; isolated

единоборство [ye-d'i-na-bór-stvŏ] *sn.* single combat

единобрачие [ye-d'i-na-brá-chye] *sn.* monogamy

единовластие [ye-d'i-na-vlá-stye] *sn.* monarchy

единогласие [ye-d'i-na-glá-sye] *sn.* accord, unanimity

единогласный [ye-d'i-na-glás-nǎy] *adj.* unanimous; unison

единодержавие [ye-d'i-na-dyer-zhá-vye] *sn.* autocracy

единодушие [ye-d'i-na-dŏō-shye] *sn.* accord, harmony

единомыслие [ye-d'i-na-mǎs-lye] *sn.* concord

единомышленник [ye-d'i-na-mǎsh-lyen-n'ik] *sm.* adherent, partisan

единообразие [ye-d'i-na-abrá-zye] *sn.* uniformity

единорог [ye-d'i-na-róg] *sm.* unicorn

единственный [ye-d'én-stven-nǎy] *adj.* only, sole, unique

единство [ye-d'én-stvŏ] *sn.* unity, oneness

едкий [yéd-ki] *adj.* caustic,

corrosive; *coll.* sarcastic

её [ye-yó] *pron.* her, hers

ёж [yozh] *sm.* hedgehog; urchin

ежевика [ye-zhe-v'é-ka] *sf.* blackberry, bramble

ежегодник [ye-zhe-gód-n'ik] *sm.* almanac, annual

ежегодный [ye-zhe-gód-nǎy] *adj.* annual, yearly

ежедневный [ye-zhe-dnyév-nǎy] *adj.* daily

ежели [ye-zhe-l'i] *conj.* if, in case

ежемесячный [ye-zhe-myé-svach-nǎy] *adj.* monthly

ежеминутный [ye-zhe-minŏōt-nǎy] *adj.* constantly every minute, repeatedly

еженедельный [ye-zhe-nye-dyél'-nǎy] *adj.* weekly

ежеиощный [ye-zhe-nóshch-nǎy] *adj.* nightly

ежечасный [ye-zhe-chás-nǎy] *adj.* hourly

ёжиться [yó-zhit'-sya] *vi.* to shrink, shrivel

езда [yez-dá] *sf.* drive; ride; journey; driving, riding

ездить [yéz-d'it'] *vi.* to travel

ездок [yez-dók] *sm.* rider

ей [yey] *pron.* to her

еле [ye-lyé] *adv.* hardly, scarcely; **еле-еле**, *adv.* narrowly, scarcely enough time

елей [ye-lyéy] *sm.* anointing, unction

ёлка [yól-ka] *sf.* small fir-tree

ель [yél'] *sf.* fir

ёмкий [yóm-ki] *adj.* capacious, roomy

ёмкость [yóm-kŏst'] *sf.* capacity

ему [ye-mŏō] *pron.* to him

епархия [ye-pár-chya] *sf.* diocese; see

епархияльный [ye-par-chyā'l-năy] *adj.* diocesan

епископ [ye-pēs-kŏp] *sm.* bishop

епископство [ye-pēs-kap-stvŏ] *sn.* bishopric, episcopacy

епитимия [ye-pi-ti-mē-ya] *sf.* penance

еретичество [ye-re-tē'-chest-vŏ] *sn.* heresy

ёрзать [yór-zat'] *vi.* to be restless

ермолка [yer-mól-ka] *sf.* skull-cap

ерунда [ye-rŏŏn-dā] *sf.* nonsense

если [yé-sl'i] *conj.* if

естественный [yes-tyéstven-năy] *adj.* natural

естество [yes-tyes-tvó] *sn.* substance

естествознание [yes-tyestva-znā-nye] *sn.* natural history, natural science

есть [yest'] (съесть) *vt.* to eat

есть [yest'] *auxiliary v.* is, there is, there are

ефрейтор [efréy-tŏr] *sm.* corporal

ехать [yé-chat] *vi.* to drive, ride

ехидна [ye-chēd-na] *sf.* viper

ехидный [ye-chēd-năy] *adj.* malicious

ещё [ye-shchó] *adv.* mo:e; again; still; yet; **-бы!** [-bă] what next!

ею [yé-yŏŏ] *pron.* by her, with her

Ж

жаба [zhā-ba] *sf.* toad; angina pectoris; tonsilitis

жабо [zha-bó] *sn.* frill, jabot

жабры [zhā-brā] *sf. pl.* gills

жаворонок [zhā-va-rŏ-nŏk] *sm.* skylark

жадничать [zhā-dn'i-chat'] *vi.* to be greedy

жадность [zhād-nŏst'] *sf.* avarice, greed, thirst

жадный [zhād-năy] *adj.* greedy; craving

жажда [zhāzh-da] *sf.* thirst; craving; lust

жаждать [zhāzh-dat'] *vi.* to be thirsty; to crave (*for*); to desire intensely

жакет [zha-kyét] *sm.* coat, jacket; **-ка,** *sf.* coatee

жалеть [zha-lyét'] (по-) *vi.* to feel sorry (*for someone*); to regret, sympathize; *vt.* to spare

жалить [zhā-l'it'] (у-) *vi.* to prick, sting; *fig.* to taunt

жалкий [zhāl-ki] *adj.* miserable, pitiful, sad

жалко [zhāl-kŏ] *adv.* most pitiful

жало [zhā-lŏ] *sn.* sting

жалоба [zhā-la-ba] *sf.* complaint, grievance

жалобный [zhā-lab-năy] *adj.* mournful, sorrowful; plaintive

жалобщик [zhā-lab-shchik] *sm.* plaintiff; prosecutor

жалование [zhā-la-va-nye] *sn.* grant; gratuity

жалованье [zhā-la-va-nye] *sn.* pay, salary, wages

жаловать [zhā-la-vat'] *vt.* to bestow, confer, grant; to favour; **-ся** [-sya] *vi.* to complain, grumble; to deplore, lament

жалостливый [zhā-lŏstl'i-văy] *adj.* compassionate; pitiful

жалость [zhā-löst] *sf.* compassion; mercy, pity

жаль [zhāl'] *sf.* compassion; как -! what a pity! мне его - [mnyé ye-vó -] I am sorry for him

жанр [zhānr] *sm.* style

жар [zhār] *sm.* ardour; heat; fever; embers [heat

жара [zha-rā] *sf.* summer

жаргон [zhar-gón] *sm.* jargon, slang

жардинерка [zhar-d'i-nyér-ka] *sf.* flower-stand

жаренье [zhā-re-nye] *sn.* frying; roasting; toasting

жарить [zhā-r'it'] (с-) *vt.* to fry, grill, roast, toast; to burn, scorch

жаркий [zhār-ki] *adj.* hot; ardent

жаркое [zhar-kóye] *sn.* roast meat; braised pieces of meat with gravy, *etc.*

жаровня [zha-róv-nya] *sf.* brazier

жатва [zhāt-va] *sf.* crop, harvest; harvesting

жать [zhāt'] (с-) *vt.* to gather in; to harvest, reap; to nip, squeeze, wring; to pinch (*as shoes*); - руку [- rōō-kōō] to shake hands; *fig.* to oppress

жвачка [zhvāch-ka] *sf.* cud; rumination

жгут [zhgōōt] *sm.* braid, plait

жгучий [zhgōō-chi] *adj.* burning, stinging

ждать [zhdāt'] (подо-) *vt.* to wait; to expect

же *or* **ж** [zhe] *conj.* but, however

жевание [zhe-vā-nye] *sn.* mastication; rumination

жевать [zhe-vāt'] *vt.* to chew, masticate, munch, ruminate

жезл [zhezl] *sm.* mace, wand; staff; sceptre; baton

желание [zhe-lā-nye] *sn.* wish; desire, longing

желательный [zhe-lā-tyel'-năy] *adj.* desirable

желать [zhe-lāt'] (по-) *vt.* to want, wish; to long for

желвак [zhel-vāk] *sm.* tumour, swelling

железа [zhe-lye-zā] *sf.* gland

железистый [zhe-lye-zēs-tăy] *adj.* glandular; ferriferous

желёзка [zhe-lyŏz-ka] *sf.* glandule

железная дорога [zhe-lyéz-na-ya da-ró-ga] *sf.* railway; подземная - - [pad-zyém-na-ya - -] the Underground

железнодорожный [zhe-lyez-na-da-rózh-năy] *adj.* railway

железный [zhe-lyéz-năy] *adj.* iron, ferrous

железняк [zhe-lyez-nyāk] *sm.* iron-clay, iron-ore; clinker

железо [zhe-lyé-zŏ] *sn.* iron; -делательный завод [-dye-lā-tyel'-năy za-vód] iron-foundry

жёлобок [zhó-lo-bok] *sm.* *tech.* groove; gutter; trough

желобить [zhe-la-bét'] *vt.* to groove, hollow out

жёртенький [zhól-tyen'-ki] *adj.* yellowish

желтеть [zhel-tyét'] (по-) *vi.* to become yellow

желтить [zhel-tét'] (вы-) *vt.* to paint yellow

желтоватый [zhel-ta-vā-

желток [zhel-tók] *sm.* yolk

желтофиоль [zhel-ta-fiól'] *sf.* wallflower

желтуха [zhel-tōō-cha] *sf.* jaundice; ragwort

жёлтый [zhól-tăy] *adj.* yellow

желудок [zhe-lōō-dŏk] *sm.* stomach; **несварение желудка** [nye-sva-ré-nye zhe-lōōd-ka] indigestion

жёлчность [zhól-chnŏst] *sf.* biliousness

жёлчь [zholch] *sf.* bile, gall

жеманный [zhe-mán-năy] *adj.* affected, finical, prudish

жемчуг [zhém-chōōg] *sm.* pearl

жена [zhe-nā] *sf.* wife

женатый [zhe-nā-tăy] *adj.* married (*of man only*)

женить [zhe-n'ét'] *vt.* to marry; **-ся** [sya] to get married

женитьба [zhe-n'ét-ba] *sf.* marriage, wedding

жених [zhe-n'éch] *sm.* bridegroom, fiancé

женоненавистник [zhena-nye-na-v'ést-n'ik] *sm.* woman-hater

женоподобный [zhe-na-pa-dób-năy] *adj.* effeminate, womanish

женский [zhén-ski] *adj.* female, feminine; womanly

женственность [zhén-stvyen-nŏst'] *sf.* femininity, womanhood

женщина [zhén-shchi-na] *sf.* woman

жердь [zherd'] *sf.* perch, pole

жеребёнок [zhe-re-byó-nŏk] *sm.* foal

жеребец [zhe-re-byéts] *sm.* stallion

жеребчик [zhe-réb-chik] *sm.* colt

жеребьёвка [zhe-re-byóv-ka] *sf.* distribution by lots

жерло [zher-ló] *sn.* crater; muzzle; aperture

жернов [zhér-nŏv] *sm.* millstone

жертва [zhér-tva] *sf.* oblation, sacrifice; victim

жертвенник [zhér-tvyen-n'ik] *sm.* altar

жертвовать [zhér-tva-vat'] *vt.* to offer, sacrifice

жеруха [zhe-rōō-cha] *sf.* watercress

жёсткий [zhóst-ki] *adj.* harsh, tough; rigid

жестокий [zhes-tó-ki] *adj.* brutal, heartless, merciless

жестокость [zhes-tó-kŏst] *sf.* cruelty, ferocity

жесть [zhest'] *sf.* tin, tin-plate

жестяник [zhes-tyă-n'ik] *sm.* tinsmith

жестянка [zhes-tyăn-ka] *sf.* can, tin

жечь [zhech'] (с-) *vt.* to burn, consume; to scorch

жжение [zhé-nye] *sn.* burning, consuming

жжёнка [zhón-ka] *sf.* hot punch

жив [zhiv] *adj.* in being, active, lively

живительный [zhi-vé-tyel'-năy] *adj.* restorative, vivifying

живность [zhév-nŏst'] *sf.* fowl, poultry; livestock

живодёр [zhi-va-dyór] *sm.* slaughterer; **-ня** [-nya] slaughterhouse

живой [zhi-vóy] *adj.* animate; lively; vivid

живописец [zhi-va-p'ḗsyets] *sm.* artist, painter

живописный [zhi-va-p'ḗsnăy] *adj.* pictorial, picturesque

живопись [zhi-va-p'ês'] *sf.* pictorial art

живость [zhē-vŏst'] *sf.* animation, vivacity

живот [zhi-vót] *sm.* abdomen, belly

животик [zhi-vó-t'ik] *sm.* tummy

животноводство [zhi-vat-na-vód-stvŏ] *sn.* cattle-breeding

животное [zhi-vót-nŏ-ye] *sn.* animal, beast; brute

животный [zhi-vót-năy] *adj.* animal, bestial; brutal

живучий [zhi-vōō-chi] *adj.* tenacious

живущий [zhi-vōō-shchi] *adj.* living

жидкий [zhíd-ki] *adj.* liquid, watery; scanty

жидкость [zhíd-kŏst'] *sf.* fluidity; liquid

жизнедеятельность [zhiz-nye-dyé-ya-tyel'-nŏst'] *sf.* activity

жизненность [zhíz-nyen-nŏst'] *sf.* life, vitality

жизненный [zhíz-nyen-năy] *adj.* vital

жизнеописание [zhiz-nye-api-sā-nye] *sn.* biography

жизнерадостный [zhiz-nye-rá-dast-năy] *adj.* buoyant, joyous

жизнеспособный [zhiz-nye-spa-sób-năy] *adj.* capable of living, viable

жизнь [zhizn'] *sf.* life, life-time; existence, living

жила [zhí-la] *sf.* tendon, vein; nerve; lode; *fig.* extortioner

жилет [zhi-lyét] *sm.* waistcoat

жилец [zhi-lyéts] *sm.* **жилица** [zhi-l'í-tsa] *sf.* lodger

жилистый [zhi-l'ês-tăy] *adj.* sinewy

жилище [zhi-l'ě-shche] *sn.* dwelling, residence; lodgings; apartment; *mil.* quarters

жилой [zhi-lóy] *adj.* habitable

жильё [zhi-lyó] *sn.* habitation

жимолость [zhí-ma-lŏst'] *sf.* honeysuckle

жир [zhir] *sm.* fat, grease; suet, tallow

жираф [zhi-ráf] *sm.* giraffe

жиреть [zhi-l'i-tsa] (за-) *vi.* to fatten; to grow stout

жирный [zhír-năy] *adj.* greasy, oily; rich (*of food*); obese; *typ.* bold

жирноватый [zhir-na-vá-tăy] *adj.* somewhat fat

жировик [zhi-ra-v'ěk] *sm.* tumour; French chalk

житейский [zhi-tyéy-ski] *adj.* worldly

житель [zhi-tyel'] *sm.*, **-ница** [-n'í-tsa] *sf.* inhabitant, resident

жительство [zhí-tyel'-stvŏ] *sn.* domicile, habitation

житница [zhí-tn'i-tsa] *sf.* granary

жито [zhí-tŏ] *sn.* corn, grain

жить [zhit'] (по-) *vi.* to live; to dwell; to subsist; **жил-был** [zhil-bál] once upon a time there lived . . .

житьё [zhi-tyó] *sm.* existence; —бытьё [—bǎ-tyó] way of living

жмурить [zhmŏŏ-rit'] *vt.* to screw up one's eyes

жмурки [zhmŏŏr-ki] *sf. pl.* blind-man's-buff

жнейка [zhnyéy-ka] *sf.* harvester (*machine*)

жнец [zhnyéts] *sm.* harvester, reaper [ble

жнивьё [zhn'i-vyó] *sn.* stub-

жокей [zhó-key] *sm.* jockey

жолоб [zhó-lŏb] *sm.* shoot; *tech.* groove; furrow; gutter

жолудь [zhó-lŏŏd] *sm.* acorn

жранье [zhra-nyó] *sf.* gluttony

жрать [zhrát] (со—) *vt.* to eat greedily, devour, gorge

жребий [zhryé-bi] *sm.* lot; *fig.* destiny, fate

жрец [zhryéts] *sm.* priest

жреческий [zhryé-ches-ki] *adj.* priestly; Druidical

жречество [zhryé-ches-tvŏ] *sn.* priesthood; Druidism

жужелица [zhŏŏ-zhe-l'i-tsa] *sf.* cockchafer; slag

жужжать [zhŏŏzh-zhát'] (за—) *vi.* to drone, buzz, hum

жук [zhŏŏk] *sm.* beetle

жулик [zhŏŏ-l'ik] *sm.* crook, rogue, swindler

жупел [zhŏŏ-pyel] *sm.* bogy

журавль [zhŏŏ-rávl'] *sm.* crane (*bird*)

журить [zhŏŏ-rét'] (по—) *vt.* to censure, reprimand

журнал [zhŏŏr-nál] *sm.* journal, magazine, review; log-book

журналист [zhŏŏr-na-l'ést] *sm.* journalist, reporter

журналистика [zhŏŏr-na-l'és-ti-ka] *sf.* journalism

журфикс [zhŏŏr-fíks] *sm.* an at-home

журчать [zhŏŏr-chát'] (за—) *vi.* to murmur

жуткий [zhŏŏt-ki] *adj.* frightful

жуть [zhŏŏt'] *sf.* fright, horror, terror

З

за [zā] *prep.* behind, beyond; for; at, by

забава [za-bā-va] *sf.* amusement, diversion, pastime

забавлять [za-ba-vlyát'] *vt.* to amuse, entertain

забавник [za-bāv-n'ik] *sm.* amusing fellow, good company

забавный [za-bāv-nǎy] *adj.* amusing, entertaining

забастовать [za-ba-sta-vát'] *vi.* to go on strike

забастовка [za-ba-stóv-ka] *sf.* strike; cessation of work

забастовщик [za-ba-stóv-shchik] *sm.* striker

забвение [zab-vé-nye] *sn.* oblivion

забегать [za-bye-gát'] (за-бежáть) *vi.* to drop in; to call on; *fig.* to forestall

забеливать [za-byé-li-vat'] (забели́ть) *vt.* to whiten; to whitewash

забивать [za-bi-vát'] (за-би́ть) *vt.* to hammer in

забирать [za-bi-rát'] (за-брáть) *vt.* to take up; carry away

забитый [za-bé-tǎy] *adj.* beaten, oppressed

забияка [za-byā-ka] *sm., sf.* quarrelsome person

заблуждаться [za-blŏozh-dăt'-sya] (заблудиться) vi. to go astray; fig. to err; labour under a delusion

заблуждение [za-blŏozh-dyé-nye] sn. delusion, fallacy

забодать [za-ba-dăt'] vt. to gore

забой [za-bóy] sm. weir

забойник [za-bóy-n'ĭk] sm. tech. beetle

заболачивать [za-ba-lă-chi-vat'] vt. to bog up, swamp

заболеваемость [za-ba-lye-vă-ye-mŏst'] sf. morbidity

заболевание [za-ba-lye-vă-nye] sn. illness

заболевать [za-ba-lye-vắt'] (заболеть) vi. to be taken ill

забор [za-bór] sm. fence; enclosure; money paid in advance; goods on credit; **-ная книжка** [-na-ya kn'ĕzh-ka] ration-book

забота [za-bó-ta] sf. anxiety, care; worry

заботиться [za-bó-t'it'-sya] vi. to take care of someone

заботливый [za-bót-l'i-văy] adj. careful, thoughtful

забраковать [za-bra-ka-vắt'] vi. to refuse, reject

забрало [za-bră-lŏ] sn. visor, beaver (of helmet)

забрасывать [za-bră-să-vat'] (забросить) vt. to abandon; to neglect; to cast away

забронировать [za-bra-n'ē-ra-vat'] vt. to reserve

заброшенность [za-bró-shen-nŏst'] sf. abandonment, desertion

забывать [za-bă-vắt'] (забыть) vt. to forget

забывчивый [za-bắv-chi-văy] adj. forgetful

забытьё [za-bă-tyó] sn. drowsiness; unconsciousness

завал [za-văl] sm. obstruction; stoppage; constipation

заваливать [za-vă-l'i-vat'] (завалить) vt. to heap up; encumber; to clog up

заваль [za-văl'] sf. shop-soiled goods

заваривать [za-vă-ri-vat'] (заварить) vt. to brew, boil; tech. to weld

заведение [za-vye-dyé-nye] sn. establishment; institution; custom, usage

заведование [za-vyé-da-va-nye] sn. administration, management, superintendence

заведовать [za-vyé-da-vat'] vi. to manage

заведомо [za-vyé-dŏ-mŏ] adv. knowingly

заведующий [za-vyé-dŏo-yŏo-shchi] sm. chief, manager

заверение [za-vye-ryé-nye] sn. assertion; assurance

заверитель [za-vye-r'ē-tyel'] sm. witness

завёртывать [za-vyór-tă-vat'] (завернуть) vt. to envelop, wrap up; screw up

завершать [za-vyer-shăt'] vt. to conclude; to complete

завершение [za-vyer-shé-nye] sn. completion; end

заверять [za-vye-ryắt'] (заверить) vt. to assure; to ensure; to witness

завеса [za-vyé-sa] sf. curtain; screen; veil

завет [za-vyét] sm. legacy; precept; testament

заветный [za-vyét-năy] adj. testamentary; sacred; ardent

завещание [za-vye-shchă-nye] sn. testament, will

завещатель [za-vye-shchá-tyel'] *sm.* testator

завещать [za-vye-shchát'] *vt.* to bequeath

завзятый [za-vzyá-tăy] *adj.* incorrigible, obstinate; inveterate; outspoken

завивать [za-vi-vát'] (за-вить) *vt.* to coil, wave (*hair*); to wind up

завивка [za-v'év-ka] *sf.* curling; hair-waving

завидный [za-v'éd-năy] *adj.* enviable

завидовать [za-v'é-da-vat'] (по-) *vi.* to envy, to be envious

завинчивать [za-v'én-chi-vat'] (завинтить) *vt.* to screw down

завиральный [za-v'i-rál'-năy] *adj.* absurd, foolish

завираться [za-v'i-rát'-sya] (завраться) *vi.* to talk haphazardly

зависеть [za-v'é-syet'] *vi.* to depend on, be dependent on

зависимость [za-v'é-s'i-mŏst'] *sf.* dependence, subordination

зависимый [za-v'é-s'i-măy] *adj.* dependent, subordinate

завистливый [za-v'ést-l'i-văy] *adj.* jealous

завистъ [zá-v'ist'] *sf.* envy, jealousy

завиток [za-v'é-tŏk] *sm.* coil, curl; flourish; *arch.* volute

завладевать [za-vla-dye-vát'] (завладеть) *vt.i.* to take possession of; confiscate

завлекать [za-vlye-kát'] (завлечь) *vt.* to allure, tempt

завод [za-vód] *sm.* factory, works

заводить [za-va-d'ét'] (завести) *vt.* to wind up (*watch, etc.*); to introduce, set-up; to establish, found

заводский [za-vód-ski] *adj.* pertaining to factory

заводчик [za-vód-chik] *sm.* manufacturer, proprietor of factory

завоевание [za-va-ye-vá-nye] *sn.* conquest

завоеватель [za-va-ye-vá-tyel'] *sm.* conqueror

завоёвывать [za-va-yó-vă-vat'] (завоевать) *vt.* to conquer

завоз [za-vóz] *sm.* naut. hawser, tow-line

завозить [za-va-z'ét'] (завезти) *vt.* to convey, transport

заволакивать [za-va-lá-ki-vat'] *vt.* to cloud over; to bedim

завораживать [za-va-rá-zhi-vat'] (заворожить) *vt.* to bewitch, charm

заворачивать [za-va-rá-chi-vat'] (заворотить) *vt.* to turn, turn in, turn up; to roll up (*sleeve*)

заворот [za-va-rót] *sm.* facing (*on wearing apparel*)

завсегда [za-vsyeg-dá] *adv.* always, ever

завсегдатай [za-vsyeg-dá-tay] *sm.* frequenter, habitual caller, visitor

завтра [záv-tra] *adv.* to-morrow

завтрак [záv-trak] *sm.* breakfast; mid-morning lunch

завтракать [záv-tra-kat'] (по-) *vi.* to breakfast

завтрашний [záv-trash-n'i] *adj.* tomorrow's

завывать [za-vȧ-vȧt'] (за-
выть) *vi.* to start howling,
moaning

завязка [za-vyáz-ka] *sf.* bandage, string; plot (*in play*)

завязывать [za-vyá-zȧ-vȧt']
(завязать) *vt.* to bind, knot,
tie; to start (*an argument, etc.*)

завязь [zá-vyaz'] *sf. bot.* ovary

завялый [za-vyá-lăy] *adj.*
faded, withered

загадка [za-gád-ka] *sf.* puzzle, riddle

загадочный [za-gá-dach-
năy] *adj.* enigmatic(al),
mysterious

загадывать [za-gá-dȧ-vȧt']
(загадать) *vt.* to conjecture,
guess; to set a riddle

загаживать [za-gá-zhi-vȧt']
(загадить) *vt.* to soil; to foul

загар [za-gár] *sm.* sunburn,
tan

загасать [za-ga-sát'] (за-
гаснуть) *vi.* to extinguish; to
switch off, turn off

загашать [za-ga-shát'] (за-
гасить) *vt.* to quench; to
smother

загибать [za-gi-bát'] (за-
гнуть) *vt.* to bend, fold

заглавие [za-glá-vye] *sm.*
heading, title; **заглавный
лист** [za-gláv-năy list] title-
page

заглаживать [za-glá-zhi-
vȧt'] (загладить) *vt.* to make
even, level, smooth; *fig.* to
expiate

заглаза [za-gla-zá] *adv.* behind one's back; amply

заглохнуть [za-glóch-nŏŏt']
vi. to be smothered; to become overgrown (*garden*)

заглушать [za-glŏŏ-shát']
(заглушить) *vt.* to deafen,

stun; to deaden, overpower,
suppress

заглядывать [za-glyá-dȧ-
vȧt'] (заглянуть) *vi.* to peep
in; to drop in (*as friend, for a
moment*); **-ся** [-sya] to gape,
stare at; to contemplate

загнивание [za-gni'i-vȧ-
nye] *sn.* suppuration; *fig.*
decay

заговор [zá-ga-vŏr] *sm.* conspiracy, plot

заговорщик [za-ga-vór-
shchik] *sm.* conspirator, plotter

заголовок [za-ga-ló-vŏk] *sm.*
rubric; superscription

загон [za-gón] *sm.* driving of
cattle; enclosure; sheep fold;
fig. oppression; **-щик**
[-shchik] *sm.* drover

загонять [za-ga-nyát'] (за-
гнать) *vt.* to drive in; to pen;
fig. to harass, to heckle

загораживать [za-ga-rá-
zhi-vȧt'] (загородить) *vt.*
to enclose, fence in; to jam,
obstruct; to barricade

загорать [za-ga-rát'] (за-
гореть) *vi.* to become sunburnt; **-ся** [-sya] to catch
fire

загорелый [za-ga-ryé-lăy]
adj. sunburnt, tanned

загородка [za-ga-ród-ka] *sf.*
partition, screen

загородный [zá-ga-rad-
năy] *adj.* suburban

заготавливать [za-ga-tá-
vl'i-vȧt'] *vt.* to make ready,
prepare; to purvey

заготовка [za-ga-tóv-ka] *sf.*
storing, providing, supply-
ing (*provisions, etc.*)

заготовлять [za-ga-ta-
vlyát'] (заготовить) *vt.* to

procure (supplies); to buy in (provisions)

заграждать [za-grazh-dát'] (заградить) vt. to block, obstruct

заграницей [za-gra-n'é-tsey] adv. abroad

заграничный [za-gra-n'éch-năy] adj. foreign; beyond one's frontier

загребать [za-gre-bát'] (загрести) vt. to rake, scrape together; to bury; vi. to start rowing (boat)

загривок [za-grĕ-vŏk] sm. nape of neck; withers

загромождение [za-gra-mazh-dyé-nye] sn. obstruction

загрубелый [za-grŏŏ-byé-lăy] adj. callous, hardened; inveterate

загружать [za-grŏŏ-zhát'] (загрузить) vt. to burden, load; to encumber

загрузка [za-grŏŏz-ka] sf. charge, load

загрязнение [za-gryaz-nyé-nye] sn. pollution; soiling

загубить [za-gŏŏ-bĕt'] vt. to destroy, ruin; to waste

зад [zad] sm. back, hind part; croup (of horse); **-ом** [zá-dŏm] adv. backwards

задабривать [za-dá-bri-vat'] (задобрить) vt. to cajole, coax

задавать [za-da-vát'] (задать) vt. to propose, put; to set (task, etc.)

задавливать [za-dá-vl'i-vat'] (задавить) vt. to knock down (a person by a vehicle), to run over; to crush

задание [za-dá-nye] sn. task

задаром [za-dá-rŏm] adv.

dirt-cheap; purposeless, in vain

задаток [za-dá-tŏk] sm. deposit (on goods, etc.)

задача [za-dá-cha] sf. math. problem, proposition; undertaking

задвигать [za-dv'i-gát'] (задвинуть) vt. to bar, bolt; to shut (a drawer, etc.)

задвижка [za-dv'ĕzh-ka] sf. bar, bolt

задворки [za-dvór-ki] pl. backyard; **на задворках**, in the background

задевать [za-dye-vát'] (задеть) vt. to catch hold of; to be caught in; to knock against; to graze; fig. to provoke, vex

задёргивать [za-dyór-gi-vat'] (задёрнуть) vt. to draw (curtains, etc.), to pull (reins, etc.)

задержание [za-dyer-zhá-nye] sn. delay; detention; retention; mus. suspension

задерживать [za-dyér-zhi-vat'] (задержáть) vt. to detain; to retard; to embargo

задержка [za-dyér-zhka] sf. check, delay; impediment

задирать [za-d'i-rát'] (задрáть) vt. to start scratching, tearing; **– нос** [– nos] to be haughty, put on airs

задний [zád-ni] adj. back, rear

задник [zád-n'ik] sm. counter (of shoe); dicky (of a carriage)

задолго [za-dól-gŏ] adv. long before; in good time

задолжать [za-dal-zhát'] vt. to run into debt

задор [za-dór] *sm.* fervour; passion; **-ный** [-nǎy] *adj.* provocative; full of life

задумчивый [za-dōōm-chi-vǎy] *adj.* pensive, thoughtful

задумчивость[za-dōōm-chi-vǒst'] *sf.* pensiveness, reverie

задумывать [za-dōō-mǎ-vat'] (задумать) *vt.* to intend; to plan, scheme; **-ся** [-sya] *vi.* to meditate, ponder

задушевный [za-dōō-shév-nǎy] *adj.* cordial; intimate; sincere [to suffocate

задушить [za-dōō-shēt'] *vt.*

заедание [za-ye-dā-nye] *sn. tech.* jamming

заезжий [za-yéz-zhi] *adj.* occasional (*as guest, visitor*); *sm.* casual caller; stranger

заём [za-yóm] *sm.* loan

заёмщик [za-yóm-shchik] *sm.* borrower

заживать [za-zhi-vát'] (зажить) *vi.* to heal up; to work off (*a debt*); to earn

заживление [za-zhi-vlyé-nye] *sn.* healing

заживо [zā-zhi-vǒ] *adv.* during one's lifetime

зажигалка [za-zhi-gál-ka] *sf.* cigarette-lighter

зажигательный [za-zhi-gā-tyel'-nǎy] *adj.* incendiary

зажигать [za-zhi-gát'] (зажечь) *vt.* to ignite, light, set fire to; to strike (*a match*)

зажим [za-zhēm] *sm.* clamp, clutch; suppression

зажимать [za-zhi-mát'] (зажать) *vt.* to grip, squeeze

зажин [za-zhīn] *sm.* beginning of harvest-time

зажиток [za-zhi-tǒk] *sm.* earnings, wages

зажиточный [za-zhi-tach-

nǎy] *adj.* well-off; prosperous

зазноба [za-znó-ba] *sf.* chil-blain; *coll.* sweetheart

зазор [za-zór] *sm.* disgrace, shame; chink

зазубривать [za-zōō-bri-vat'] (зазубрить) *vt.* to swat; to jag, notch

зазывать [za-zǎ-vát'] (за-звать) *vt.* to call in, invite

заика [za-éka] *sm.* stammerer, stutterer

заикание [za-i-kā-nye] *sn.* stammering, stuttering; speech impediment

заимодавец [za-i-ma-dā-vyets] *sm.* creditor; lender

заимствовать [za-ēm-stva-vat'] (по-) *vt.* to borrow

заискивать [za-ēs-ki-vat'] (заискать) *vi.* to favour, ingratiate

закадычный [za-kā-dăch-nǎy] *adj.* intimate

заказ [za-káz] *sm.* command, order; **делать на –** [dyé-lat' na –] to make to measure

заказной [za-ka-znóy] *adj.* bespoke; registered

заказчик [za-káz-chik] *sm.* client, customer

заказывать [za-kā-zǎ-vat'] (заказать) *vt.* to order; to bespeak

закаиваться [za-kā-i-vat'-sya] (закаяться) *vi.* to give up, renounce, repudiate

закал [za-kál] *sm.* hardening, tempering

закалённый [za-ka-lyón-nǎy] *adj.* hardened, tem-pered; weather-beaten; *coll.* 'hard as nails'

закаливать [za-kā-l'i-vat'] (закалить) *vt.* to harden, to temper

закалывать [za-kä-lä-vat'] (заколо́ть) vt. to slay, stab; to kill, slaughter

закаменелый [za-ka-mye-nyé-läy] adj. petrified

заканчивать [za-kän-chi-vat'] (зако́нчить) vt. to conclude, complete, finish

закапывать [za-kä-pä-vat'] (закопа́ть) vt. to dig in, inter; to fill up (with earth)

закармливание [za-kärm'li-i-va-nye] sn. fattening; overfeeding

закат [za-kät] sm. setting (of sun, etc.); fig. decline, sinking

закатывать [za-kä-ti-vat'] (закати́ть) vt. to roll (a barrel, etc.), (one's eyes); to send or condemn (to prison)

закваска [za-kväs-ka] sf. ferment, leaven; fig. disposition

закидывать [za-kē-dä-vat'] (заки́нуть) vt. to cast, throw; toss (one's head) [acidity

закись [zä-k'is'] sf. acid,

заклад [za-kläd] sm. mortgage, pawn; bet, stake; **-чик** [-chik] sm. mortgager

закладка [za-kläd-ka] sf. bookmark; harnessing (of horses); laying (foundation-stone, etc.)

закладывать [za-klä-dä-vat'] vt. to pawn; to mortgage; to pledge; to lay; to harness

заклеивать [za-klyé-i-vat'] vt. to glue up, to paste up

заклёпка [za-klyóp-ka] sf. rivet

заклёпывать [za-klyó-pä-vat'] (заклепа́ть) vt. to clench; to rivet

заклинать [za-kl'i-nät'] vt. to conjure, invoke

заклинание [za-kl'i-ná-nye] sn. invocation

заклинить [za-kl'i-n'ēt'] vt. to wedge

заключать [za-klyōō-chät'] (заключи́ть) vt. to confine, shut in; to deduce, infer

заключение [za-klyōō-ché-nye] sn. conclusion, deduction, inference; resolution (at a meeting, etc.); imprisonment

заключённый [za-klyōō-chón-näy] adj. confined; sm. prisoner

заключительный [za-klyōō-chē-tyel'-näy] adj. conclusive, final

заклятый [za-klyä-täy] adj. sworn; - **враг** [- vräg] mortal enemy

заковывать [za-kó-vä-vat'] (закова́ть) vt. to shackle

закон [za-kón] sm. law; statute

законность [za-kón-nöst'] sf. legality, validity

законоведение [za-ka-na-vyé-dye-nye] sn. jurisprudence

законовед [za-ka-na-vyéd] sm. lawyer; jurist

законодатель [za-ka-na-dä-tyel'] sm. legislator

законопреступление [za-ka-na-pre-stōō-plyé-nye] sn. law-breaking, transgression of the law

законорождённый [za-ka-na-razh-dyón-näy] adj. legitimate (of birth)

закоптелый [za-kap-tyé-läy] adj. smoky, smutty, sooty

закоренелый [za-ka-re-nyé-läy] adj. deep-rooted, inveterate [ka zl'

закорючка [za-ka-ryōōch-

hook, crook; *fig.* hitch, obstacle; *coll.* flourish

закоснелый [za-ka-snyé-lăy] *adj.* obdurate, stubborn

закоулок [za-ka-ŏŏ-lŏk] *sm.* nook, retreat, secluded corner

закоченелый [za-ka-che-nyé-lăy] *adj.* chilled; stiff

закрадываться [za-krá-dă-vat'-sya] *vi.* to sneak in

закраивать [za-krá-i-vat']*vt.* to cut out; to make patterns

закранна [za-krái-na] *sf.* border, edge, margin; flange

закрашивать [za-krá-shi-vat'] (закрасить) *vt.* to paint over; to cover up defects

закреплять [za-kre-plyát'] (закрепить) *vt.* to fasten; to strengthen; toratify; tosecure

закривлять [za-kriv-lyát'] (закривить) *vt.* to bend, distort

закройщик [za-króy-shchik] *sm.* tailor's cutter

закром [ză-króm] *sm.* bin, corn-bin; hutch

закручивать [za-krŏŏ-chi-vat'] (закрутить) *vt.* to twist; **-ся** [-sya] *vi.* to writhe

закрывать [za-krä-vát'] (закрыть) *vt.* to close, shut; to conceal, cover

закрытие [za-krä-tye] *sn.* closing, shutting; close (*of season, etc.*)

закулисный [za-kŏŏ-l'és-năy] *adj.* behind the scenes; *fig.* underhand

закупать [za-kŏŏ-pát'] (закупить) *vt.* to buy in; purchase

закупка [za-kŏŏp-ka] *sf.* purchase goods bought

закупоривать [za-kŏŏ-pó-ri-vat'] *vt.* to cork, stop up

закупщик [za-kŏŏp-shchik] *sm.* buyer

закуривать [za-kŏŏ-ri-vat'] (закурить) *vt.* to start smoking (*a cigarette, etc.*); to fill with smoke

закуска [za-kŏŏs-ka] *sf.* snack; hors d'œuvre

закусывать [za-kŏŏ-să-vat'] (закусить) *vt.* to bite (*one's lip, tongue*) a meal; *mil.* hors to camouflage

закутывать [za-kŏŏ-tă-vat'] (закутать) *vt.* to wrap up; *mil.* to camouflage

зал [zăl] *sm.*, **зала** [ză-la] *sf.* hall (*for meetings, dances, etc.*)

залавок [za-lă-vŏk] *sm.* locker

залежалый [za-lye-zhá-lăy] *adj.* spoiled through neglect

залежь [ză-lyezh'] *sf.* soiled goods; *geol.* bed, deposit, seam

залив [za-l'év] *sm.* bay, gulf

заливать [za-l'i-vát'] (залить) *vt.* to pour over

залог [za-lóg] *sm.* deposit; *gram.* voice (*verbal forms*)

заложник [za-lózh-n'ik] *sm.* hostage

залп [zălp] *sm.* discharge, volley

залучать [za-lŏŏ-chát'] (лучить) *vt.* to decoy, entice

замазка [za-măz-ka] *sf.* cement, putty

замаливать [za-mă-l'i-vat'] *vi.* to atone

замалчивать [za-măl-chi-vat'] (замолчать) *vt.* to conceal, hush-up

заманивать [za-mă-n'i-vat'] (заманить) *vt.* to allure, seduce

заманчивость [za-măn-chi-vŏst'] *sf.* temptation

замаскировать [za-mas-kě-ra-vat'] *vt.* to disguise; to mask

замаслить [za-mā-sl'i-vat'] *vt.* to grease, oil

заматывать [za-mā-tā-vat'] (замотáть) *vt.* to wind

замачивать [za-mā-chi-vat'] (замочить) *vt.* to steep; to wet

замашка [za-másh-ka] *sf.* habit, manner, way

замащивать [za-mā-shchi-vat'] (замостить) *vt.* to pave

замедление [za-mye-dlýé-nye] *sn.* delay, slowing down

замена [za-myé-na] *sf.* replacement, substitution

заменять [za-mye-nyát'] (заменить) *vt.* to replace, substitute

замерзание [za-myer-zā-nye] *sn.* congelation, freezing

замёрзлый [za-myórz-lăy] *adj.* congealed; frozen

замертво [za-myer-tvó] *adv.* in a dead faint; senselessly

заместитель [za-mye-st'é-tyel'] *sm.* deputy, proxy, substitute

заметаться [za-mye-tāt'-sya] *vi.* to turn and turn about (*as one ill in bed*)

заметка [za-myét-ka] *sf.* paragraph [notes

заметки [za-myét-ki] *sf. pl.*

заметный [za-myét-năy] *adj.* noticeable, visible

замечательный [za-mye-chā-tyel'-năy] *adj.* remarkable, striking

замечать [za-mye-chāt'] (заметить) *vt.* to notice, observe, remark

замешательство [za-mye-shā-tyel'-stvó] *sn.* confusion, embarrassment

замешивать [za-myé-shi-vat'] (замешáть) *vt.* to mix; to confuse, involve

замещáть [za-mye-shchāt'] (заместить) *vt.* to supersede

заминáть [za-m'i-nāt'] (замять) *vt.* to suppress; to stamp out; to hush up; to change (*subject*)

замирáть [za-m'i-rāt'] (замерéть) *vi.* to become feeble; to sink

замирéние [za-m'i-ré-nye] *sn.* cessation of hostilities; pacification; peace treaty

замкнутый [zam-knóo-tăy] *adj.* retired, secluded

замкнутость [zam-knóo-tóst'] *sf.* reticence

замок [za-mók] *sm.* lock; висячий – [vi-syā-chi –] padlock

замок [zāmŏk] *sm.* castle

замокáть [za-ma-kāt'] (замóкнуть) *vi.* to be drenched

замолвить [za-mal-v'ēt'] to intercede

замолкáть [za-mal-kāt'] (замóлкнуть) *vi.* to become silent

замораживать [za-ma-rā-zhi-vat'] *vt.* to freeze

заморить [za-ma-r'ēt'] *vi.* to starve

замороженный [za-ma-ró-zhen-năy] *adj.* iced

заморозки [za-ma-raz-ki] *sm. pl.* early autumn frost

заморский [za-mor-ski] *adj.* ultramarine; *fig.* foreign; queer-looking

замуж [zā-mōozh] *adv.* выходить – [vă-cha-d'ět' –] to get married (*applied to woman*)

замужем [zā-mōo-zhem] *adv.* married (*of woman*)

замужняя [za-mōōzh-nya-ya] *sf.* married woman

замучивать [za-mōō-chi-vat'] (замучить) *vt.* to tire out; to torment; *coll.* to sweat

замша [zām-sha] *sf.* chamois-leather

замывать [za-mă-văt'] *vt.* to wash off

замыкать [za-mă-kăt'] (замкнуть) *vt.* to lock, to lock up; to close up

замысел [zā-mǐ-sel] *sm.* intention, project; conception

замысловатый [za-mǐ-sla-vā-tăy] *adj.* complex; ingenious

замышлять [za-mǐsh-lyăt'] (замыслить) *vt.* to design, plot; to contemplate

замять [za-myăt'] *vt.* to hush up, suppress

занавес [zā-na-vyes] *sm.* curtain

занашивать [za-nā-shi-vat'] (заносить) *vt.* to wear out (*clothes*)

занимательный [za-n'i-mă-tyel'-năy] *adj.* diverting, interesting

занимать [za-n'i-măt'] (занять) *vt.* to borrow; to occupy (*a house, etc.*); **-ся** [-sya] *vt.* to engage in, occupy one's time with; to study; to work at

заново [zā-na-vŏ] *adv.* anew

заноза [za-nŏ-za] *sf.* splinter; *fig.* heart-ache

занос [za-nós] *sm.* snow-drift

заносить [za-na-sět'] (занести) *vt.* to enter (*in ledger, etc.*), to write down; to carry away; to drift (*snow*)

заносный [za-nós-năy] *adj.* imported

заносчивый [za-nós-chi-văy] *adj.* presumptuous; supercilious

занятие [za-nyā-tye] *sn.* job, occupation, pursuit

заодно [za-ad-nŏ] *adv.* mutually; unanimously

заострённый [za-as-tryón-năy] *adj.* peaked, pointed, sharp

заочный [za-óch-năy] *adj.* out of sight; behind one's back

запад [zā-pad] *sm.* west; **-ный** [-năy] *adj.* westerly, western; **к западу** [kză-pa-dōō] westwards

западня [za-pad-nyā] *sf.* snare, trap

запаздывать [za-pāz-dă-vat'] (запоздать) *vi.* to be late, to retard

запаивать [za-păi-vat'] *vt.* to seal up, solder, weld

запал [za-pāl] *sm.* fuse, vent, touch-hole (*in firearms*); ignition; heaves (*of horse*)

запаливать [za-pă-l'i-vat'] (запалить) *vt.* to set fire to, kindle, light

запальчивый [za-păl'-chi-văy] *adj.* passionate, vehement

запас [za-pās] *sm.* stock, store, provision, supply; *mil.* reserve; margin; **- товаров** [- ta-vă-rŏv] stock-in-trade; **-ный выход** [-năy vă-chŏd] emergency exit

запах [zā-pach] *sm.* odour, smell; scent

запашка [za-pāsh-ka] *sf.* tillage

запев [za-pyév] *sm.* opening bars of song

запевала [za-pye-vá-la] *sm.* choir master

запевать [za-pye-vát'] (запеть) *vt.* to strike up a tune

запечатлевать [za-pye-chat-lye-vát'] *vt.* to engrave, imprint, to impress

запечатывание [za-pye-chá-ta-va-nye] *sn.* sealing up; imprinting

запинка [za-p'ēn-ka] *sf.* hesitation (*in speech*)

запирательство [za-pi-rá-tyel'-stvŏ] *sm.* denial, disavowal

запирать [za-pi-rát'] (запереть) *vt.* to close, fasten, lock; -ся [-sya] *vi.* to shut oneself up

записка [za-p'ès-ka] *sf.* note; short letter; memorandum

запись [zá-pis'] *sf.* document, record; inscription

заплата [za-plá-ta] *sf.* payment; patch

заплечье [za-plyé-chye] *sn.* shoulder-blade

заповедный [za-pa-vyéd-näy] *adj.* forbidden

заповедывать [za-pa-vyé-dä-vat'] (заповедать) *vt.* to forbid prohibit; to command

заповедь [zá-pa-vyed'] *sf.* commandment

заподозревать [za-pa-da-zre-vát'] (заподозрить) *vt.* to suspect

запоздалый [za-paz-dá-läy] *adj.* belated

запоминать [za-pa-mi-nát'] (запомнить) *vt.* to remember

запонка [zá-pan-ka] *sf.* button, link, stud

запор [za-pór] *sm.* constipation; bolt, lock

запотелый [za-pa-tyé-läy]

заправский [za-práv-ski] *adj.* genuine

запрашивать [za-prä-shi-vat'] (запросить) *vt.* to inquire; to overcharge

запретительный [za-pre-t'ē-tyel'-näy] *adj.* prohibitive

запрещать [za-pre-shchát'] (запретить) *vt.* to forbid, prohibit

запрещение [za-pre-shche-nye] *sn.* interdiction; *leg.* distraint

запрос [za-prós] *sm.* inquiry; overcharging

запросто [zā-pras-tŏ] *adv.* unceremoniously

запруда [za-prōō-da] *sf.* dam, dike; weir; mill-pond

запруживать [za-prōō-zhi-vat'] *vt.* to embank

запрягать [za-prya-gát'] (запрячь) *vt.* to harness

запугивать [za-pōō-gi-vat'] (запугать) *vt.* to frighten, scare

запускать [za-pōōs-kát'] (запустить) *vt.* to neglect

запустелый [za-pōō-styé-läy] *adj.* desolate

запутанный [za-pōō-tan-näy] *adj.* intricate

запутывать [za-pōō-tä-vat'] (запутать) *vt.* to entangle; to perplex

запущенный [za-pōō-shchen-näy] *adj.* neglected

запястье [za-pyá-stye] *sn.* wrist; bracelet, wristband

запятая [za-pya-tä-ya] *sf.* comma

зарабатывать [za-ra-bá-tä-vat'] (заработать) *vt.* to earn

заработок [za-ra-bó-tŏk] *sm.* earnings, emoluments

заражать [za-ra-zhát'] (заразить) vt. to contaminate, infect

зараз [za-ráz] adv. simultaneously

зараза [za-rá-za] sf. infection

заразительный [za-ra-z'ē-tyel'-năy] adj. contagious, infectious

заранее [za-rä-nye-ye] adv. beforehand, in good time

зарево [zá-rye-vŏ] sn. glow

зарекаться [za-re-kát'-sya] (заречься) vi. to renounce

зариться [zá-rit'-sya] vi. to envy; to long for

зарница [zar-n'ē-tsa] sf. summer-lightning

заровнять [za-rav-nyát'] vt. to level up; to flatten

зародыш [za-ró-dăsh] sm. germ, seed; foetus

зарождать [za-razh-dát'] (зародить) vt. to bear, conceive

зарождение [za-razh-dyé-nye] sn. conception; fig. origin

зарок [za-rók] sm. oath, vowing

заросль [zá-rŏsl'] sf. overgrowth (in garden); weeds; thicket

зарубать [za-rŏŏ-bát'] (зарубить) vt. to hack, hew; to notch

зарубка [za-rŏŏb-ka] sf. incision, notch

зарубежный [za-rŏŏ-byézh-năy] adj. beyond the frontier

заручаться [za-rŏŏ-chát'-sya] vi. to vouch

заря [za-ryá] sf. glow;
  вечерняя – [vye-chér-nya-ya –] sunset; twilight;
  утренняя – [ŏŏtren-nya-

ya –] sunrise; dawn; mil. retreat, reveille; tattoo

заряд [za-ryäd] sm. charge, loading (of arms), sf. charging, loading

засада [za-sä-da] sf. ambush

засадка [za-säd-ka] sf. planting

засаживать [za-sä-zhi-vat'] (засадить) vt. to plant; – **за работу** [– za ra-bó-tŏŏ] to set to work; to imprison

засаливать [za-sä-l'i-vat'] (засалить) vt. to put into salt, to pickle; to make greasy; to soil

засаривать [za-sä-ri-vat'] (засорить) vt. to block up (as drains, etc.); to litter

засветло [zá-svyet-lŏ] adv. by daylight

засвидетельствовать [za-svi-dyé-tyel'-stva-vat'] vt. to attest; to witness; to testify

засев [za-syév] sm. sowing; seed; sown area

заседание [za-sye-dä-nye] sn. conference, meeting, session

заседать [za-sye-dät'] vi. to take part in a conference, etc.

засека [za-syé-ka] sf. abatis; warren

заселение [za-sye-lyé-nye] sn. colonization, population

заселять [za-sye-lyät'] (заселить) vt. to colonize, populate

засилие [za-sē-lye] sn. preponderance

заслонка [za-slón-ka] sf. oven-door

заслонять [za-sla-nyát'] vt. to shield, screen

заслуга [za-slŏŏ-ga] sf. merit, reward; service rendered

заслуживать [za-slŏŏ-zhi-

vat'] (заслужи́ть) vt. to deserve, merit

засма́тривать [za-smā-tri-
vat'] (засмотре́ть) vt. to look
into; **-ся** [-sya] vi. to look at
something with admiration

засо́в [za-sóv] sm. bar, bolt

засо́вывать [za-só-vă-vat']
(засу́нуть) vt. to push into,
thrust   [salting

засо́л [za-sól] sm. pickling,

засоря́ть [za-sa-ryāt'] vi. to
litter; to obstruct

засо́с [za-sós] sm. quagmire

заста́ва [za-stā-va] sf. gate,
gates; turnpike; mil. outpost

заста́вка [za-stáv-ka] sf. typ.
illumination

заставля́ть [za-stav-lyāt']
(заста́вить) vt. to compel,
force; to coerce; to block up

застаре́лый [za-sta-ryé-
lăy] adj. neglected; in-
veterate; med. chronic

застёгивать [za-styó-gi-
vat'] (застегну́ть) vt. to
button up, to do up, to fasten

застёжка [za-styózh-ka] sf.
clasp, snap

застекли́ть [za-styek-l'ét']
vt. to glaze

засте́нчивость [za-styén-
chi-vŏst'] sf. bashfulness,
shyness, timidity

засто́й [za-stóy] sm. stagnation; crisis, depression

застрахова́ние [za-stra-
cha-vā-nye] sn. insurance

застра́щивать [za-strā-
shchi-vat'] (застраща́ть) vt.
to intimidate

застужа́ть [za-stoo-zhi-
vat'] (застуди́ть) vt. to chill,
make cold; **-ся** [-sya] to
catch cold   [axe, spade

за́ступ [zá-stŏŏp] sm. pick-

заступа́ться [za-stŏŏ-pắt'-
sya] vi. to intercede, plead;
to defend

засту́пник [za-stŏŏp-n'ik]
sm. defender; patron

застыва́ть [za-sti-vāt'] (за-
сты́нуть) vt.i. to congeal,
set; to shrink (from fright)

застыди́ться [za-stă-d'ét'-
sya] vi. to be ashamed

засуди́ть [za-sŏŏ-d'ét'] vt. to
condemn

засу́ха [zắ-sŏŏ-cha] sf.
drought, dryness

засуши́вать [za-sŏŏ-shi-
vat'] (засуши́ть) vt. to dry up

засыпа́ть [za-să-pat'] vt. to
strew; to shower (with gifts)

засыпа́ть [za-să-pāt'] vi. to
fall asleep

засыха́ть [za-să-chát'] (за-
со́хнуть) vi. to dry; to dry up
(from heat), shrivel up

заска́кивать [za-tās-ki-vat']
(затащи́ть) vt. to drag away

затво́р [za-tvór] sm. seclusion;
-ник [-n'ik] sm. hermit,
recluse

затво́рничество [za-tvór-
n'i-che-stvŏ] sn. seclusion;
solitary life

затворя́ть [za-tva-ryát']
(затвори́ть) vt. to close, shut

затева́ть [za-tye-vát'] vt. to
devise, suggest

зате́м [za-tyém] adv. then,
thereupon; subsequently

затемня́ть [za-tyem-nyát']
(затемни́ть) vt. to darken; to
obscure; to eclipse

зате́я [za-tyé-ya] sf. enterprise, undertaking

зати́шье [za-t'ē-shye] sn.
calmness, lull

затме́ние [za-tmyé-nye] sn.
eclipse

зато́ [za-tó] adv. whereas

затоваривание [za-ta-vā-ri-va-nye] *sn.* over-production

затонуть [za-ta-nōōt'] *vi.* to be submerged; to sink

затор [za-tór] *sm.* congestion, jam, obstruction; mash

затрата [za-trā-ta] *sf.* disbursement, expenditure, outlay

затребовать [za-tryé-bavat'] *vt.* to order; to require

затруднение [za-trōōd-nyé-nye] *sn.* difficulty; inconvenience

затруднять [za-trōōd-nyāt'] (затруднить) *vt.* to embarrass, hamper, hinder

затхлый [zăt-chláy] *adj.* close, musty, stuffy

затылок [za-tǎ-lŏk] *sm.* nape

затычка [za-tǎch-ka] *sf.* plug, stopper; *fig.* stop-gap

затягивать [za-tyā-gi-vat'] (затянуть) *vt.* to tighten; to implicate

затяжка [za-tyǎzh-ka] *sf.* tightening; delay, protraction

заулок [za-ōō-lók] *sm.* side-street, lane

заумный [za-ōōm-nǎy] *adj.* meaningless

заурядный [za-ōō-ryād-nǎy] *adj.* commonplace

заутреня [za-ōō-tre-nya] *sf.* morning service, matins

заушница [za-ōōsh-n'i-tsa] *sf.* mumps

зафрахтовать [za-frach-ta-vat'] *vt.* to freight

захват [za-chvát] *sm.* plunder, seizure

захватывать [za-chvá-tǎvat'] (захватить) *vt.* to encroach, to usurp

заход [za-chód] *sm.* setting (of *sun*); stopping, touching (as *ship, etc.*)

заходить [za-cha-d'ēt'] (зайти) *vi.* to go in

захудалый [za-chōō-dā-lǎy] *adj.* impoverished, shabby

зацеплять [za-tsye-plyāt'] (зацепить) *vt.* to hook; *tech.* to engage, gear

зачастую [za-chās-tōō-yōō] *adv.* frequently

зачаточный [za-chā-tach-nǎy] *adj.* rudimental

зачем [za-chyém] *adv.* why, what for

зачёркивать [za-chór-ki-vat'] (зачеркнуть) *vt.* to cross out, strike out

зачёсывать [za-chó-sǎ-vat'] (зачесать) *vt.* to comb, brush back one's hair

зачёт [za-chót] *sm.* examination, 'exams'; сдавать – [zda-vāt' –] to sit for an exam; сдать [zdāt' –] to pass an exam; в – [vza-chót] in part payment

зачинить [za-chi-n'ēt'] *vt.* to mend, repair, patch

зачисление [za-chi-slyé-nye] *sn.* enlistment, enrolment

зачислять [za-chi-slyāt'] (зачислить) *vt.* to enlist; to enrol; to include, count in

зачумление [za-chōōm-lyé-nye] *sn.* infection; tainting

зашеек [za-shé-yek] *sm.* nape

зашибать [za-shi-bāt'] (зашибить) *vt.* to bruise, hurt

зашифровать [za-shi-fra-vāt'] *vi.* to cipher, write in code

зашпилить [za-shpē-l'it'] *vt.* to pin up

заштатный [za-shtāt-nǎy] *adj.* supernumerary; unattached

заштопывать [za-shtó-pä-vat'] (заштопать) *vt.* to darn

защёлка [za-shchól-ka] *sf.* latch, trigger, pawl

защемить [za-shche-mét'] *vt.* to jam

защита [za-shchí-ta] *sf.* defence; protection, safeguard

защитник [za-shchét-n'ik] *sm.* defender; champion

защищать [za-shchi-shchát'] (защитить) *vt.* to defend, guard, shield; to advocate

заявка [za-yáv-ka] *sf.* claim, demand

заявление [za-ya-vlýé-nye] *sn.* declaration, statement

заявлять [za-ya-vlýát'] (заявить) *vt.* to declare, testify

заяц [zá-yats] *sm.* hare

звание [zvá-nye] *sn.* calling, condition, vocation

званый [zvá-näy] *adj.* invited, summoned; – вечер [– vyé-cher] (evening) party, banquet

звать [zvát'] (по-) *vt.* to call, summon

звезда [zvyez-dá] *sf.* star

звёздный [zvyózd-näy] *adj.* starry

звездочёт [zvyez-da-chót] *sm.* astrologer; stargazer

звёздочка [zvyóz-dach-ka] *sf.* asterisk

звенеть [zvye-nyét'] (за-) *vi.* to ring, sound, tinkle

звено [zvye-nó] *sn.* link

зверинец [zvye-rĕ-nyets] *sm.* menagerie

зверолов [zvye-ra-lóv] *sm.* trapper

зверский [zvyér-ski] *adj.* brutal, ferocious

зверь [zvyér'] *sm.* wild beast

звон [zvon] *sm.* chime, peal, ringing [ringer

звонарь [zva-nár'] *sm.* bell-

звонить [zva-n'ét'] (по-) *vt.* to ring; to toll

звонкий [zvón-ki] *adj.* clear, resounding, sonorous; *phon.* voiced; **звонкая монета** [zvón-ka-ya mo-nýé-ta] hard cash

звонок [zva-nók] *sm.* bell, hand-bell

звук [zvook] *sm.* sound, tone

звучать [zvoo-chát'] (про-) *vi.* to sound; to ring (*false, true*) [sonorous

звучный [zvóoch-näy] *adj.*

здание [zdá-nye] *sn.* building, house

здесь [zdyes'] *adv.* here; 'local' (*on letters*)

здешний [zdyésh-ni] *adj.* native, resident

здороваться [zda-ró-vat'-sya] (по-) *vt.* to greet

здоровенный [zda-ra-vyén-näy] *adj.* hardy, robust

здорово [zdó-ra-vŏ] *adv.* splendid! well done!

здоровый [zda-ró-väy] *adj.* healthy, sound

здоровье [zda-ró-vye] *sn.* health; **на здоровье!** [na-zda-ró-vye] good health!

здравница [zdráv-n'itsa] *sf.* health resort; sanatorium

здравомыслие [zdra-va-mä-slye] *sn.* common sense

здравоохранение [zdra-va-ochra-nyé-nye] *sn.* National Health Insurance

здравотдел [zdra-va-at-dyél] *sm.* Health Department

здравствуйте [zdráv-stvŏ-tye] good morning, good-afternoon; how do you do

здравый [zdrǎ-văy] *adj.* sane, sensible, sound

зев [zyev] *sm.* jaw, mouth; pharynx

зевать [zye-vát'] (зевнýть) *vi.* to yawn

зеленщик [zye-lyen-shchík] *sm.* greengrocer

зелёный [zye-lyó-năy] *adj.* green

зелень [zyé-lyen'] *sf.* greens, vegetables; verdure

землевладелец [zye-mlye-vla-dyé-lyets] *sm.* landowner

земледелец [zye-mlye-dyé-lyets] *sm.* landworker

земледелие [zye-mlye-dyé-lye] *sn.* agriculture

землекоп [zye-mlye-kóp] *sm.* navvy (land)

землетрясение [zye-mlye-trya-syé-nye] *sn.* earthquake

землечерпалка [zye-mlye-cher-pǎl-ka] *sf.* dredge

земля [zye-mlyá] *sf.* earth, land, soil

земляника [zye-mlyá-ni-ka] *sf.* wild strawberry

зеница [zyé-n'i-tsa] *sf.* pupil (of eye)

зеркало [zyér-ka-lŏ] *sn.* mirror

зерно [zyer-nó] *sn.* grain, kernel, seed

зернистый [zyer-n'ĕ-stǎy] *adj.* granular

зима [z'i-mǎ] *sf.* winter

зимний [z'ĕm-n'i] *adj.* hibernal, winter-; wintry

зимовать [z'i-ma-vǎt'] (про-) *vi.* to winter; to hibernate

зияние [zi-yǎ-nye] *sn.* gaping

злак [zlǎk] *sm.* cereal, grass, herb

златоустый [zla-ta-ōō-stǎy] *adj.* eloquent

злачный [zlǎch-nǎy] *adj.* grassy, herbaceous

злить [z'l'ĕt] *vt.* to irritate, tease

зло [zlo] *sn.* evil, harm, wrong; mischief; malice; *adv.* spitefully, wickedly

злоба [zló-ba] *sf.* malice, wickedness

зловещий [zla-vyé-shchi] *adj.* ominous

зловредный [zla-vryéd-năy] *adj.* mischievous, pernicious

злодей [zla-d'éy] *sm.* rogue, villain

злой [zlóy] *sm.* angry, wicked

злокачественный [zla-kà-chest-vyen-nǎy] *adj.* malignant

злонравие [zla-nrǎ-vye] *sn.* ill-temper

злость [zlost'] *sf.* wickedness

злоупотреблять [zla-ōōpa-trye-blyǎt'] *vt.* to abuse; to betray; to misuse

злоязычие [zlo-ya-zǎ-chye] *sn.* slander

змей [zmyey] *sm.* dragon, serpent

змея [zmye-yǎ] *sf.* snake, viper

знак [znak] *sm.* mark, sign, symbol

знакомство [zna-kóm-stvŏ] *sn.* acquaintance

знакомый [zna-kŏ-mǎy] *adj.* familiar, known; *sm.* acquaintance (person)

знаменатель [zna-mye-nǎ-tyel'] *sm.* denominator

знаменательный [zna-mye-nǎ-tyel'-nǎy] *adj.* noteworthy, significant

знаменитость [zna-mye-n'ĕ-tŏst'] *sf.* eminence, fame

знамени́тый [zna-mye-n'é-tăy] *adj.* celebrated, famous

знамено́сец [zna-mye-nó-syets] *sm.* standard-bearer

зна́мя [zná-mya] *sn.* banner; ensign; standard

зна́ние [zná-nye] *sn.* knowledge; skill

зна́тность [znát-nŏst'] *sf.* eminence, notability

зна́тный [znát-năy] *adj.* distinguished, illustrious

знато́к [zna-tók] *sm.* connoisseur, expert

знать [znat'] (y-) *v.* to know; to be aware of

значе́ние [zna-ché-nye] *sn.* meaning, sense; significance

значи́тельный [zna-ché-tyel'-năy] *adj.* important, significant

зна́чить [zná-chit'] *vt.* to mean, signify

значо́к [zna-chók] *sm.* badge, emblem

знаю́щий [zná-yŏŏ-shchiy] *adj.* knowing, skilful; learned

знобить [zna-bét'] (за-) *vt.* to chill, freeze; to shiver

зной [znóy] *sm.* sultriness

зоб [zob] *sm. med.* goiter; crop, craw (*of birds*)

зов [zov] *sm.* call, summons

зола́ [za-lá] *sf.* ash(es), ember(s)

золо́вка [za-lóv-ka] *sf.* sister-in-law (*husband's sister*)

золоти́льщик [za-la-t'él'-shchik] *sm.* gilder

золоти́ть [za-la-t'ét'] (по-) *vt.* to gild

зо́лото [zó-la-tŏ] *sn.* gold; **-носный** [-nós-năy] *adj.* auriferous

золото́й [za-la-tóy] *adj.* golden

золоту́ха [za-la-ta-ŏŏ-cha] *sf.* scrofula

золоче́ние [za-la-ché-nye] *sn.* gilding

Золу́шка [zó-lŏŏsh-ka] *sf.* Cinderella

зо́на [zó-na] *sf.* area, zone

зо́нтик [zón-t'ik] *sm.* umbrella; parasol, sunshade

зоо́лог [za-ó-lŏg] *sm.* zoologist; **-и́ческий** [-ĕ-ches-kiy] *adj.* zoological

зооло́гия [za-a-ló-gya *sf.* zoology

зо́ркий [zór-kiy] *adj.* far-sighted, vigilant

зре́лище [zryé-l'i-shche] *sn.* show, spectacle

зре́лость [zryé-lŏst'] *sf.* maturity, ripeness

зре́лый [zryé-lăy] *adj.* ripe

зре́ние [zryé-nye] *sn.* eyesight, vision; **в поле зрения** [vpó-lye zryé-nya] within eyeshot; **вне -** [vnyé -] out of sight; **обман -** [ab-mán -] optical illusion; **точка -** [tóch-ka -] point of view

зри́тель [zr'é-tyel'] *sm.* onlooker, spectator; playgoer; **-ный** [-năy] *adj.* visual

зря [zryă] *adv.* at random

зуб [zŏŏb] *sm.* tooth; **-но́й** [-nóy] *adj.* dental; **зубно́й врач** [zŏŏb-nóy vrách] dentist

зуба́стый [zŏŏ-bá-stăy] *adj.* large-toothed

зубе́ц [zŏŏ-byéts] *sm.* cog; jag; tooth-like projection

зубовраче́ние [zŏŏ-ba-vra-ché-nye] *sn.* dentistry

зубочи́стка [zŏŏ-ba-chést-ka] *sf.* toothpick; toothbrush

зубр [zŏŏbr] *sm.* bison

зубри́ть [zŏŏ-brét'] (вы-) *vt.* to cram, swot

зубчатый [zŏŏb-chá-tăy] *adj.* jagged, notched, toothed

зуд [zŏŏd] *sm.* itch(ing)

зудеть [zŏŏ-dyét'] *vi.* to itch

зудить [zŏŏ-d'ět'] *vi.* to nag

зыбкий [záb-ki] *adj.* marshy; shaky, unsteady

зыбь [záb'] *sf.* marsh; surge

зычность [zách-nŏst'] *sf.* shrieking, shouting

зябкий [zyáb-ki] *adj.* chilly, feeling the cold

зяблик [zyá-bl'ik] *sm.* chaffinch

зять [zyát'] *sm.* brother-in-law; son-in-law

И

и [ē] *conj.* and; but; although

ибо [ébŏ] *conj.* as, because

ива [ē-va] *sf.* willow

ивняк [iv-nyák] *sm.* osier-bed

иволга [ē-val-ga] *sf.* oriole

игла *or* **иголка** [i-glá, i-gól-ka] *sf.* needle; quill; thorn

иглистый [i-gl'ís-tăy] *adj.* needle-like; prickly, thorny

игольник [i-gól'-n'ik] *sm.* needle-book, needle-case

иго [ĭgŏ] *sn.* yoke

игорный [i-gór-năy] *adj.* gambling, playing

игра [i-grá] *sf.* game; sport

играть [i-grát'] *vi.* to play; to act, perform

игривый [i-grĭ-văy] *adj.* frolicsome, playful

игристый [i-grĭs-tăy] *adj.* sparkling

игрок [i-grók] *sm.* player (*of games, etc.*)

игрушка [i-grŏŏsh-ka] *sf.* toy

игумен [i-gŏŏ-myen] *sm.* abbot; **-ья** [-ya] *sf.* abbess, Mother superior

идеализировать [i-dye-a-lí'z'ē-ra-vat'] *vt.* to idealize

идеальный [i-dye-ál'-năy] *adj.* ideal

идентичный [i-dyen-t'éch-năy] *adj.* identical

идея [i-dyé-ya] *sf.* conception, idea, notion

идиот [i-dyót] *sm.* idiot

идол [ē-dŏl] *sm.* idol, image

идти [i-t'ē] *vi.* to go

иждивение [izh-d'i-vyé-nye] *sn.* cost(s), expense(s)

иждивенец [izh-d'i-vyé-nyets] *sm.* dependant

из [iz] *prep.* from, out of, through

изба [iz-bá] *sf.* cottage, hut, [log cabin

избавитель [iz-ba-vĕ-tyel'] *sm.* liberator, rescuer

избавление [iz-ba-vlyé-nye] *sn.* liberation, rescue

избавлять [iz-ba-vlyát'] (избавить) *vt.* to free, release; to save, rescue

избаловывать [iz-ba-ló-vă-vat'] (избаловать) *vt.* to fondle, pet, spoil (*children*)

избегать [iz-bye-gát'] (избежать) *vi.* to avoid, elude; to refrain

избиение [iz-bi-yé-nye] *sn.* massacre; extermination

избиратель [iz-bi-rá-tyel'] *sm.* elector, voter

избирательный [iz-bi-rá-tyel'-năy] *adj.* electoral

избирать [iz-bi-rát'] (избрать) *vt.* to elect; to choose

избитый [iz-b'é-tăy] *adj.* hackneyed

избрание [iz-brá-nye] *sn.* election; choice

избыток [iz-bá-tŏk] *sm.* abundance; surplus

избыточный [iz-bá-tach-năy] *adj.* superfluous, surplus

изведывать [iz-vyé-dă-vat'] *vt.* to find out; to investigate

изверг [ēz-vyerg] *sm.* monster, tyrant

извергать [iz-vyer-gát'] (извергнуть) *vt.* to erupt; to exclude, expel; to vomit

извержение [iz-vyer-zhe-nye] *sn.* eruption; *med.* discharge, excretion

известие [iz-vyé-stye] *sn.* information, news; tidings

известность [iz-vyést-nŏst] *sf.* fame, repute

известный [iz-vyést-năy] *adj.* famous, well-known

известняк [iz-vyest-nyák] *sm.* limestone

известь [ēz-vyest'] *sf.* lime

извещать [iz-vye-shchát'] *vi.* to advise, announce; to inform

извещение [iz-vye-shche-nye] *sn.* notification

извив [iz-v'ēv] *sm.* bend

извинение [iz-vi-nyé-nye] *sn.* apology, excuse, pardon

извинять (iz-vi-nyát') (извинить) *vt.* to excuse, pardon

извлекать [iz-vlye-kát'] (извлечь) *vt.* to extract; to elicit; to derive

извлечение [iz-vlye-ché-nye] *sn.* extraction; abstract; summary

извне [iz-vnyé] *adv.* externally, from without

извод [iz-vód] *sm.* waste (money, time)

изводить [iz-va-d'ēt'] (извести) *vt.* to exhaust, use up, overwork

извозчик [iz-vóz-chik] *sm.* cabman

изворотливый [iz-va-rót-l'i-văy] *adj.* resourceful

извращать [iz-vra-shchát'] (извратить) *vt.* to misinterpret; to corrupt

извращение [iz-vra-shché-nye] *sn.* distortion

изгиб [iz-g'ēb] *sn.* bend, curve

изгнание [iz-gná-nye] *sn.* banishment, expulsion

изгнанник [iz-gnán-nik] *sm.* exile

изголовье [iz-ga-ló-vye] *sn.* head (of bedstead)

изгонять [iz-ga-nyát'] (изгнать) *vt.* to banish, exile

изготавливать [iz-ga-tá-vli-vat'] (изготовить) *vt.* to prepare; to execute (an order)

издавать [iz-da-vát'] (издать) *vt.* to exhale; to emit; to produce; to issue, publish; to promulgate

издавна [ēz-dav-na] *adv.* long since

издалека [iz-da-lye-ká] и **издали** [ēz-da-l'i] *adv.* from afar

издание [iz-dá-nye] *sn.* edition, issue, publication

издатель [iz-dá-tyel'] *sm.* publisher

изделие [iz-dyé-lye] *sn.* manufactured article, ware

издержки [iz-dyérzh-ki] *pl.* costs; expenses

издыхать [iz-da-chát'] (издохнуть) *vi.* to die (of animals only)

изживать [iz-zhi-vát'] (изжить) *vt.* to exterminate

изжога [iz-zhó-ga] *sf.* heartburn

излагать [iz-la-gát'] (изложи́ть) *vt.* to elucidate, expound

изла́мывать [iz-lā-mȧ-vat'] (изломи́ть) *vt.* to break, smash

излече́ние [iz-lye-ché-nye] *sn.* recovery (*from illness*)

изле́чивать [iz-lyé-chi-vat'] (излечи́ть) *vt.* to cure, heal

излечи́мый [iz-lye-chē-māy] *adj.* curable

изли́шек [iz-l'é-shek] *sm.* surplus; excess

изли́шний [iz-l'ésh-ni] *adj.* superfluous, unnecessary

излия́ние [iz-l'i-yā-nye] *sn.* effusion

изло́м [i-zlóm] *sm.* fracture; **-анный**[-an-nāy] *adj.* broken

излуче́ние [iz-lōō-ché-nye] *sn.* emanation, origin

излю́бленный [iz-lyōō-blyen-nāy] *adj.* favourite

изма́зывать [iz-mā-zȧ-vat'] (изма́зать) *vt.* to grease, oil, smear

изма́лывать [iz-mā-lȧ-vat'] *vt.* to grind

изма́ять [iz-mā-yat'] *vi.* to overwork; **-ся** [-sya] *vt.* to be exhausted

изме́на [iz-myé-na] *sf.* treachery, treason

измене́ние [iz-mye-nyé-nye] *sn.* change, variation

изме́нник [iz-myén'nik] *sm.* betrayer, traitor

изме́нчивость [iz-myén-chi-vŏst'] *sf.* variability; inconstancy; fickleness

изменя́ть [iz-mye-nyāt'] (измени́ть) *vt.* to alter, change, modify; to betray

измере́ние [iz-mye-ryé-nye] *sn.* measurement; dimension

измеря́ть [iz-mye-ryāt'] (изме́рить) *vt.* to measure; to survey; to gauge

измождённый [iz-mazh-dyón-nāy] *adj.* emaciated, macerated

изма́лачивать [iz-ma-lā-chi-vat'] (измолоти́ть) *vt.* to thresh

изморозь [ĕz-ma-rŏz'] *sf.* hoarfrost; rime

изморось [ĕz-ma-ros'] *sf.* drizzle; sleet

изму́чивать [iz-mōō-chi-vat'] (изму́чить) *vt.* to torment, weary; to harass

изна́нка [iz-nān-ka] *sf.* reverse, wrong side

изнаси́лование [iz-na-s'ē-la-va-nye] *sn.* violation

изне́женный [iz-nyé-zhen-nāy] *adj.* effeminate; delicate, sensitive

изнемога́ть [iz-nye-ma-gāt'] (изнемо́чь) *vi.* to succumb

изно́с [iz-nós] *sm.* wear-and-tear

изно́шенный [iz-nó-shen-nāy] *adj.* threadbare

изнутри́ [iz-nōō-trí] *adv.* internally, from within

изоби́лие [i-za-bē-lye] *sn.* abundance; profusion

изоби́льный [i-za-bél'-nāy] *adj.* plentiful

изобличе́ние [i-za-bl'i-ché-nye] *sn.* accusation, conviction

изобража́ть [i-za-bra-zhát'] (изобрази́ть) *vt.* to render, represent; to portray

изобрета́тель [i-za-bre-tā-tyel'] *sm.* inventor

изобрета́тельный [i-za-bre-tā-tyel'-nāy] *adj.* ingenious, resourceful

изобретение [i-za-bre-tyé-nye] *sn.* invention

изоляция [i-za-lyá-tsya] *sf.* isolation

изорванный [i-zór-van-năy] *adj.* tattered

изорвать [i-zar-vát'] *vt.* to tear

изразец [ē-zra-zyéts] *sm.* tile

израсходовать [iz-ras-chó-da-vat'] *vt.* to spend

изредка [ēz-ryed-ka] *adv.* rarely

изречение [iz-rye-ché-nye] *sn.* dictum; sentence

изрядный [iz-ryád-năy] *adj.* tolerable [tic

изувер [i-zŏŏ-vyér] *sm.* fanatic

изувечение [i-zŏŏ-vye-ché-nye] *sn.* mutilation

изумительный [i-zŏŏ-mē'-tyel'-năy] *adj.* amazing, wonderful

изумление [i-zŏŏ-mlyé-nye] *sn.* amazement, surprise, wonder

изумруд [i-zŏŏm-rŏŏd] *sm.* emerald

изустно [i-zŏŏst-nŏ] *adv.* orally, verbally

изучать [i-zŏŏ-chát'] (изучи́ть) *vt.* to learn, study

изъездить [iz-yéz-dit'] *vt.* to travel all over

изъязвление [iz-yaz-vlyé-nye] *sn.* ulceration

изъян [iz-yān] *sm.* defect, flaw

изъятие [iz-yā-tye] *sn.* exception, exemption

изыскание [i-zăs-kā-nye] *sn.* investigation; research

изысканность [i-zăs-kan-nŏst'] *sf.* daintiness; refinement

изюбр [i-zyŏŏbr] *sm.* roebuck

изюм [i-zyŏŏm] *sm.* raisin(s), sultana(s)

изящество [i-zyā-shchest-vŏ] *sn.* elegance, gracefulness, smartness

изящный [i-zyáshch-năy] *adj.* elegant, refined; **изящные искусства** [i-zyáshch-năye is-kŏŏs-stva] the fine arts

Иисус [i-sŏŏs] Jesus

икать [i-kāt'] (икнуть) *vi.* to hiccup

икона [i-kó-na] *sf.* icon, image

икота [i-kó-ta] *sf.* hiccup

иконоборец [i-ka-na-bó-ryets] *sm.* iconoclast

иконостас [i-ka-na-stás] *sm.* altar-screen

икра [i-krá] *sf.* hard roe; caviare; calf (*of leg*)

ил [ēl] *sm.* silt, slime

или [ē-l'i] *conj.* or; either

иллюзорный [il-lyŏŏ-zór-năy] *adj.* illusive

иллюстрация [il-lyŏŏ-strá-tsya] *sf.* illustration

иллюстрированный [il-lyŏŏ-stri-ró-van-năy] *adj.* illustrated, pictorial

ильм [ēl'm] *sm.* elm (-tree)

имбирь [im-bēr'] *sm.* ginger

имение [i-myé-nye] *sn.* estate, possessions, property

именинник [i-mye-n'én-n'ik] *sm.* one whose nameday it is

именины [i-mye-n'é-nă] *sf. pl.* name's day; saint's day

именно [ē-myen-nŏ] *adv.* namely; viz.; particularly

именной [i-myen-nóy] *adj.* nominal

именовать [i-mye-na-vát'] (на-) *vt.* to name, nominate

иметь [i-myét'] *vt.* to have; to possess

имеющийся [i-myé-yŏŏ-shchi-sya] *adj.* available

ими [ē-m'i] *pron.* by them

империя [im-pé-rya] *sf.* empire

имущество [i-mŏŏ-shchest-vŏ] *sn.* belongings, property

имя [ē-mya] *sn.* name; noun

иначе [i-nä-che] *adv.* otherwise; else

индеец [in-dyé-yets] *sm.* Indian; **индианка** [in-d'iän-ka] *sf.* Indian woman (*American, Red*) [turkey-hen

индейка [in-d'yéy-ka] *sf.*

индейский [in-dyéy-ski] *adj.* Indian (*American, Red*)

индивидуальный [in-d'i-vi-dŏŏ-äl'-năy] *adj.* individual, personal [dian

индиец [in-d'ē-yets] *sm.* In-

индийский [in-d'ēs-ki] *adj.* Indian

индуктивный [in-dŏŏk-t'ēv-năy] *adj.* inductive

индус [in-dŏŏs] *sm.* Hindu

индустрия [in-dŏŏs-trya] *sf.* industry [cock

индюк [in-dyŏŏk] *sm.* turkey-

иней [ē-nyey] *sm.* hoar-frost

инженер [in-zhe-nér] *sm.* engineer; **-ный** [-năy] *adj.* engineer's, engineering

инжир [in-zhér] *sm.* dried fig

инициал [i-n'i-tsyäl] *sm.* initial

иноверец [i-na-vyé-rets] *sm.* dissenter, heterodox

иноверие [i-na-vyé-rye] *sn.* dissent, heterodoxy

иногда [i-nag-dä] *adv.* now and then, occasionally

иноземец [i-na-zyé-mets] *sm.* alien, stranger

иной [i-nóy] *adj.* other; some

инок [ē-nŏk] *sm.* monk; **-иня** [ē-nya] *sf.* nun

иносказательный [i-na-ska-zä-tyel'-năy] *adj.* allegorical

иностранец [i-na-strä-nyets] *sm.* foreigner

инспекция [in-spék-tsya] *sf.* inspection

инструкция [in-strŏŏk-tsya] *sf.* instruction

интерес [in-tye-rés] *sm.* interest

интересный [in-tye-rés-năy] *adj.* interesting

интересоваться [in-tye-re-sa-vät'-sya] *vi.* to take an interest in

интермедия [in-ter-mé-dya] *sf.* interlude

интернат [in-ter-nät] *sm.* boarding school

интернациональный [in-ter-na-tsya-näl'-năy] *adj.* international

интимный [in-t'ēm-năy] *adj.* intimate

информация [in-far-mä-tsya] *sf.* information

инъекция [i-nék-tsya] *sf.* injection

иод [iód] *sm.* iodine

иота [ió-ta] *sf.* iota, jot

иприт [ip-rét] *sm.* mustard gas

ирбис [ir-bēs] *sm.* lynx

ирис [ē-ris] *sm.* iris, fleur-de-lis

ирландец [ir-län-dyets] *sm.* Irishman; **ирландка** [ir-länd-ka] *sf.* Irishwoman

ирландский [ir-länd-ski] *adj.* Irish

иронический [i-ra-n'ē-ches-ki] *adj.* ironical

ирония [i-ró-nya] *sf.* irony

иск [ĕsk] *sm.* action, claim, suit

искажать [is-ka-zhát'] (исказить) *vt.* to alter, disfigure, distort; to jam (radio); to misrepresent

искатель [is-ká-tyel'] *sm.* searcher, seeker

искательный [is-ká-tyel'-năy] *adj.* cringing; lowly

искать [is-kát'] (по-) *vt.* to look for, seek

исключать [is-klyŏŏ-chát'] *vt.* to except, exclude; to expel, turn out

исключение [is-klyŏŏ-ché-nye] *sn.* exception; exclusion; expulsion

исключительный [is-klyŏŏ-ché-tyel'-năy] *adj.* exceptional; exclusive

исковеркать [is-ka-vyer-kát'] *vt.* to mutilate; to corrupt

искомкать [is-kam-kát'] *vt.* to crumble

искомый [is-kó-măy] *adj.* looked for, sought for; **искомое число** [is-kó-ma-ye chi-sló] unknown quantity

исконный [is-kón-năy] *adj.* primordial

искоренение [is-ka-re-nyé-nye] *sn.* eradication, extermination

искоса [ĕs-ka-sa] *adv.* askance, askew

искра [ĕs-kra] *sf.* spark; *fig.* glimmer

искренний [ĕs-kryen-n'i] *adj.* frank, sincere, true

искривление [ĕs-kriv-lyé-nye] *sn.* curvature, wryness

искромсать [is-kram-sát'] *vt.* to chop up, mince

искупать [is-kŏŏ-pát'] (ис-

купить) *vt.* to atone, redeem

искупление [is-kŏŏ-plyé-nye] *sn.* expiation, redemption

искус [is-kŏŏs] *sm.* ordeal, trial; temptation; novitiate, probation [expert

искусник [is-kŏŏs-n'ik] *sm.*

искусный [is-kŏŏs-năy] *adj.* dexterous, skilful

искусственный [is-kŏŏst-vyen-năy] *adj.* artificial, imitated; synthetic

искусство [is-kŏŏs-stvŏ] *sn.* art; craft

исландец [is-slán-dyets] *sm.*, **исландка** [is-lánd-ka] *sf.* Icelander

исландский [i-slánd-ski] *adj* Icelandic

испанец [is-pá-nyets] *sm.* Spaniard; **испанка** [is-pán-ka] *sf.* Spanish woman

испанский [is-pán-ski] *adj.* Spanish

испарение [is-pa-ryé-nye] *sn.* evaporation

испарина [is-pá-ri-na] *sf.* perspiration, sweat

испаритель [is-pa-r'é-tyel'] *sm.* evaporator

испепелять [is-pye-pye-lyát'] *vt.* to incinerate

испитой [is-p'i-tóy] *adj.* lean, meagre; hollow-cheeked

исповедник [is-pa-vyéd-n'ik] *sm.* confessor

исповедовать [is-pa-vyé-da-vat'] (исповедать) *vt.* to confess; to profess

исповедь [is-pa-vyed'] *sf.* confession

исподволь [ĕs-pad-vŏl'] *adv.* gradually, leisurely

исподлобья [is-pad-ló-bya] *adv.* frowningly

исподтишка [is-pad-t'ish-kå] *adv.* stealthily, underhandedly

исполнение [is-pal-nýe-nye] *sn.* accomplishment, fulfilment; *mus.* execution

исполнительный [is-pal-n'ē-tyel'-nåy] *adj.* attentive, punctual; executive

исполнять [is-pal-nyāt'] (исполнить) *vt.* to carry out (a task), to execute, fulfil

использовать [is-pól'-za-vat'] *vt.* to make use of, profit by; to consume (one's energy, etc.)

испорченный [is-pór-chen-nåy] *adj.* bad, rotten, spoiled; depraved, corrupt

исправление [is-prav-lýe-nye] *sn.* amendment, correction, improvement

исправлять [is-prav-lyāt'] (исправить) *vt.* to amend, correct, rectify, revise

исправный [is-prāv-nåy] *adj.* exact, prompt

испражняться [is-prazh-nyāt'-sya] *vi.* to evacuate, defecate; to excrete

испрашивать [is-prā-shi-vat'] (испросить) *vt.* to beg, solicit

испробовать [is-pró-ba-vat'] *vt.* to test, try; to taste

испуг [is-pŏŏg] *sm.* fright, scare; **-аться** [-āt'-sya] to become frightened, scared

испытание [is-på-tā-nye] *sn.* essay, test, trial; experiment

испытанный [is-på-tan-nåy] *adj.* tested, well-tried

исследование [is-slýe-da-va-nye] *sn.* investigation, research

исстари [ēs-sta-ri] *adv.* from time immemorial

иступление [is-stŏŏp-lýe-nye] *sn.* delirium; frenzy; rage; ecstasy

иссушать [is-sŏŏ-shāt'] (иссушить) *vt.* to shrink, wither

иссыхать [is-så-chāt'] (иссохнуть) *vi.* to dry up, wither away

истаять [is-tā-yat'] *vi.* to melt, thaw; *fig.* to pine, waste away

истекать [is-tye-kāt'] (истечь) *vi.* to elapse, expire

истерзать [is-tyer-zāt'] *vt.* to tear up into shreds

истерика [is-tyé-ri-ka] *sf.* hysterics

истец [is-tyéts] *sm.* petitioner, plaintiff

истечение [is-tye-ché-nye] *sn.* outflow; expiration (time); *med.* flux

истина [ēs-t'i-na] *sf.* truth

истинный [ēs-t'in-nåy] *adj.* veritable

истовый [ēs-ta-våy] *adj.* earnest, fervent

исток [is-tók] *sm.* source

истолкование [is-tal-ka-vā-nye] *sn.* explanation, interpretation

истолкователь [is-tal-ka-vā-tyel'] *sm.* commentator

истома [is-tó-ma] *sf.* exhaustion, lassitude

исторгать [is-tar-gāt'] (исторгнуть) *vt.* to extort, wrench

историк [is-tó-rik] *sm.* historian

исторический [is-ta-rē-ches-ki] *adj.* historic(al)

история [is-tó-rya] *sf.* history; story, yarn

источник [is-tóch-n'ik] *sm.* origin, source; spring

истошный [is-tósh-nǎy] *adj.* distressing, heart-rending

истощение [is-ta-shché-nye] *sn.* exhaustion

истреблять [is-tryeb-lyát'] *vt.* to destroy, exterminate

истукан [is-tōō-kán] *sm.* idol

истязать [is-tya-zát'] *vt.* to torment, torture

исход [is-chód] *sm.* issue, outlet; **Книга Исхода** [kn'ē-ga -a] Exodus

исходный [is-chód-nǎy] *adj.* initial

исцелять [is-tsye-lyát'] (**исцелить**) *vt.* to cure, heal; restore (*health*)

исчезать [is-che-zát'] (**исчéзнуть**) *vi.* to disappear

исчисление [is-chi-slyé-nye] *sn.* calculation

исщепать [is-shche-pát'] *vt.* to chip, splinter

итак [i-ták] *conj.* so, thus; and now . . .

итальянец [i-ta-lyā-nyets] *sm.*, **итальянка** [i-ta-lyān-ka] *sf.* Italian

итальянский [i-ta-lyān-ski] *adj.* Italian

итог [i-tóg] *sm.* (sum) total; **в итоге** [vi-tó-gye] to sum up

итти [it-t'é] (**пойти**) *vi.* to go; to suit; **это ему идёт** [eta yemōō i-dyót] it suits him

иудей [yōō-dyéy] *sm.* Israelite; **-ский** [-ski] *adj.* Judaic; **-ство** [-stvō] *sn.* Judaism

их [ēch] *pron.* their, theirs

ишиас [ē-shi-as] *sm.* sciatica

ищейка [i-shchéy-ka] *sf.* police-dog, blood-hound

июль [yōōl'] *sm.* July

июнь [yōōn'] *sm.* June

К

к *or* **ко** [k, ka] *prep.* to, towards; by; for

кабак [ka-bák] *sm.* inn, public-house

кабала [ka-bā-lá] *sf.* bondage

кабатчик [ka-bát-chik] *sm.* publican

кабачок [ka-ba-chók] *sm.* egg-plant; vegetable marrow

кабель [ká-byel'] *sm.* cable

кабестан [ka-bye-stán] *sm.* capstan

кабина [ka-b'ē-na] *sf.* cabin

кабинет [ka-bi-nyét] *sm.* cabinet; study

каблук [ka-blōōk] *sm.* heel (of shoe)

кавалерство [ka-va-lyér-stvō] *sn.* knighthood

каверзник [ka-vyér-znik] *sm.* intriguer, trickster

кавычка [ka-vách-ka] *sf.* quotation mark, inverted comma

кадить [ka-d'ēt'] (**по-**) *vt.* to incense; *fig.* to flatter

кадка [kád-ka] *sf.* tub, vat

кадык [ka-dák] *sm.* Adam's apple

каждый [kázh-dǎy] *pron.* each, everyone

казак [ka-zák] *sm.* Cossack

казачка [ka-zách-ka] *sf.* Cossack woman

казарма [ka-zár-ma] *sf.* barracks

казаться [ka-zát'-sya] *vi.* to appear, seem; **кажется** [ká-zhet-sya] it seems

казачок [ka-za-chók] *sm.* Russian dance

казённый [ka-zyón-nǎy] *adj.* fiscal

казна [kaz-nā] sf. exchequer, treasury; mil. breech

казначей [kaz-na-chéy] sm. cashier, treasurer

казнить [kaz-n'ět'] vt. to execute, put to death

казнокрадство [kaz-na-krād-stvó] sn. embezzlement of public funds

казнь [kāzn'] sf. execution, death penalty

кайма [kay-mā] sf. border, edging, selvage

как [kāk] adv. how; as, like; – будто [– bōōd-tō] as though; – бы не [– bǎ nye] lest; – нибудь [– n'i-bōōd'] somehow; – раз [– rāz] exactly

какао [ka-kā-ō] sm. cocoa

какой [ka-kóy] pron. what? which?

каламбур [ka-lam-bōōr] sm. pun

каландр [ka-lāndr] sm. calender

каланча [ka-lan-chā] sf. watch-tower

калека [ka-lyé-ka] sm. and f. cripple

календарь [ka-lyen-dār'] sm. calendar; almanac

каление [ka-lyé-nye] sn. incandescence

калёный [ka-lyó-nǎy] adj. red-hot; tempered

калечить [ka-lyé-chit'] (ис-) vt. to cripple, maim

калитка [ka-l'ět-ka] sf. wicket-gate

калька [kal'-ka] sf. tracing-paper

калькировать [kal'-kě-ra-vat'] vt. to trace

калькуляция [kal-kōō-lyā-tsya] sf. calculation

кальсоны [kal'-só-nā] sm. pl. drawers, pants, trunks

камвольный [kam-vól'-nǎy] adj. worsted

камедистый [ka-mye-d'ēs-tǎy] adj. gummy, resinous

камедь [ka-myéd'] sf. gum, resin

камелёк [ka-mye-lyók] sm. fire-place

каменеть [ka-mye-nyét'] (o-) vi. to become petrified, turn into stone

каменистый [ka-mye-n'ēs-tǎy] adj. hardened, firm

каменный [kā-myen-naǎy] adj. stone, stony; – век [– vyek] stone-age; **каменная кладка** [kā-myen-na-ya klād-ka] masonry

каменоломня [ka-mye-na-lóm-nya] sf. quarry

каменщик [kā-myen-shchik] sm. stone-mason; brick-layer

камень [kā-myen'] sm. stone; rock

камера [kā-mye-ra] sf. room; ward; cell; chamber

камергер [ka-myer-gér] sm. chamberlain

камердинер [ka-myer-dě-nyer] sm. valet

камеристка [ka-mye-rēst-ka] sf. lady's maid

камертон [ka-myer-tón] sm. tuning-fork

камзол [kam-zól] sm. camisole

камилавка [ka-m'i-lāv-ka] sf. calotte, skull-cap

камин [ka-m'ēn] sm. fire-place; mantelpiece

камнеломка [ka-mnye-lóm-ka] sf. rock plant

каморка [ka-mór-ka] sf. cabin, closet, tiny room

кампания [kam-pá-nya] *sf.* campaign

камфора [kạm-fa-rã] *sf.* camphor

камфорка [kam-fór-ka] *sf.* oil-lamp, spirit-lamp

камчатка [kam-chát-ka] *sf.* damask

камыш [ka-mắsh] *sm.* cane; reed, rush

канава [ka-ná-va] *sf.* ditch, gutter; drain

канализация [ka-na-l'i-zã-tsya] *sf.* drainage, sewerage

канальство [ka-nál'-stvŏ] *sn.* knavery, villainy

каналья [ka-ná-lya] *sm., f.* rascal, rogue

канарейка [ka-na-réy-ka] *sf.* canary

канат [ka-nát] *sm.* cable, rope; **-чик** [-chik] *sm.* rope-maker

канаус [ka-nã-ōŏs] *sm.* taffeta

канва [kan-vã] *sf.* canvas; *fig.* design, groundwork

кандалы [kan-da-lã] *sf. pl.* shackles; manacles

канделябр [kan-dye-lyãbr] *sm.* candelabrum

кандидат [kan-d'i-dãt] *sm.,* **-ка,** *sf.,* **-ура** [-ōōra] *sf.* candidature

каникулы [ka-n'ẽ-kōō-lă] *sf. pl.* school holidays, vacation

канитель [ka-n'i-tyél'] *sf.* gold *or* silver thread; bullion; *fig.* protracted proceedings

канифоль [ka-n'i-fól'] *sf.* rosin

канонерка [ka-na-nyér-ka] *sf.* gun-boat

канонизировать [ka-na-n'ẽ-ra-vat'] *vt.* to canonize

кантор [kãn-tŏr] *sm.* precentor

канун [ka-nōōn] *sm.* eve, vigil; **на - е . . .** [na -ye] on the eve of . . .

каифорка [kan-fór-ka] *sf.* top of a samovar

канцелярист [kan-tse-lya-rĕst] *sm.* clerk

канцелярия [kan-tse-lyã-rya] *sf.* chancery; office

канцелярский [kan-tse-lyãr-ski] *adj.* clerical

канцлер [kãn-tslyer] *sm.* chancellor; **- казначейства** [- kaz-na-chéy-stva] Chancellor of the Exchequer

капать [kã-pat'] *vi.* to drip, trickle

капелла [kap-pél-la] *sf.* chapel; **-н** [-n] *sm.* chaplain

капель [kã-pyel'] *sf.* dripping, dropping, trickling; **-ка,** *sf.* tiny drop

капельдинер [ka-pyel'-dĕnyer] *sm.* usher (*in theatre*)

каперство [kã-pyer-stvŏ] *sn.* privateering

каперсы [kã-pyer-sä] *sm. pl.* capers

капиллярный [ka-pil-lyãr-nãy] *adj.* capillary

капитальный [ka-pi-tãl'-nãy] *adj.* substantial; thorough; fundamental

капитан [ka-pi-tãn] *sm.* captain; **-ша** [-sha] *sf.* captain's wife

капитель [ka-pi-tyél'] *sf. arch.* capital; *typ.* capital letter

капитул [ka-pĕ-tōŏl] *sm.* chapter (*of an order*)

капкан [kap-kãn] *sm.* trap

капля [kã-plya] *sf.* blob, drop

капор [kă-pŏr] *sm.* hood, cape

капот [ka-pót] *sm.* lady's dressing-gown

капрал [ka-prál] *sm.* corporal

каприз [ka-préz] *sm.* caprice, fancy, whim

капризничать [ka-préz-ni-chát'] (за-) *vi.* to be capricious, naughty

капризный [ka-préz-năy] *adj.* capricious, whimsical; naughty (*of children*)

капуста [ka-pŏŏs-ta] *sf.* cabbage; **брюссельская** - [bryŏŏs-syél'-ska-ya -] Brussels sprouts; **кудрявая** - [kŏŏ-dryá-va-ya -] savoy; **цветная** - [tsvyet-ná-ya -] cauliflower

капут [ka-pŏŏt] *sm. coll.* it's all up!, no good!

капюшон [ka-pyŏŏ-shón] *sm.* cowl

карабкаться [ka-ráb-kat'-sya] (вс-) *vi.* to climb, scramble

каракули [ka-rá-kŏŏ-l'i] *sf. pl.* scrawl, scribble

каракуль [ka-ra-kŏŏl'] *sf.* astrakhan

карамболь [ka-ram-ból'] *sm.* cannon (*billiards*)

карандаш [ka-ran-dásh] *sm.* pencil

карантин [ka-ran-t'ēn] *sm.* quarantine

карапуз [ka-ra-pŏŏz] *sm.* small person, dwarf; tot

карась [ka-rás'] *sm.* carp

карать [ka-rát'] (по-) *vt.* to chastise

караул [ka-ra-ŏŏl] *sm.* guard, sentry; 1! help!; -**ка,** *sf.* sentry-box; -**ьня** [-'nya] *sf.* guard-room

кардинальный [kar-d'i-nál'-năy] *adj.* cardinal, principal

карета [ka-ryé-ta] *sf.* carriage, coach

карий [kă-ri] *adj.* brown, hazel

карикатура [ka-r'i-ka-tŏŏ-ra] *sf.* caricature, cartoon

каркать [kăr-kat'] (кар-кнуть) *vi.* to croak

карлик [kar-l'ik] *sm.* dwarf; -**овый** [ó-văy] *adj.* diminutive

карлук [kar-lŏŏk] *sm.* isinglass

кармазин [kar-má-z'ēn] *adj., sm.* crimson

карман [kar-mán] *sm.* pocket

карманник [kar-mán-n'ik] *sm.* pickpocket

карманный [kar-mán-năy] *adj* pocket-, pockety

карниз [kar-n'ēz] *sm.* cornice

карпетка [kar-pyét-ka] *sf.* shoe-sock

карта [kăr-ta] *sf.* card; map; menu

картавить [kar-tá-vit'] *vi.* to lisp

картёжник [kar-tyózh-n'ik] *sm.* card-player; gambler

картина [kar-t'é-na] *sf.* picture; painting; illustration

картинный [kar-t'én-năy] *adj.* pictorial

картон [kar-tón] *sm.* cardboard, pasteboard; -**ка,** *sf.* band-box, hat-box

картофель [kar-tó-fyel'] *sm. pl.* potatoes; **жареный** - [zhā-re-na -] chips

карточка [kăr-tach-ka] *sf.* small card; visiting-card

картошка [kar-tósh-ka] *sf. sing.* potato

картуз [kar-tōōz] *sm.* cap; cartridge; paper-bag

карусель [ka-rōō-syél'] *sm.* roundabout; fair ground

карцер [kár-tsyer] *sm.* detention-room (*usually in schools*)

карьер [ka-ryér] *sm.* gallop; **-ом,** at full-speed

карьера [ka-ryé-ra] *sf.* career

касание [ka-sá-nye] *sn.* math. contact

касательно [ka-sá-tyel'-nŏ] *adv.* concerning; **-ная линия** [-na-ya l'ē-nya] tangent

касаться [ka-sát'-sya] *vi.* to touch upon (*a subject*); to concern, to relate; to refer

каскад [kas-kád] *sm.* waterfall

касса [kás-sa] *sf.* cash-box; booking office; till; *typ.* case; **сберегательная —** [zbye-re-gä-tyel'-na-ya —] savings-bank

кассир [kas-sēr] *sm.* cashier; booking clerk

кассировать [kas-sē-ra-vat'] *vt.* to annul, reverse

касторка [kas-tór-ka] *sf.* castor-oil

кастрюля [kas-tryōō-lya] *sf.* saucepan

катальщик [ka-tál'-shchik] *sm.* skater

катанье [ka-tá-nye] *sn.* driving (*in car, etc.*); rolling, wheeling; skating

катар [ka-tár] *sm.* catarrh

катать [ka-tát'] (по-) *vt.i.* to mangle; to roll; to skate; to take for a drive; **-ся** [-sya] *vi.* to go for a drive; to go skating

категория [ka-tye-gó-rya] *sf.* category

катехизис [ka-tye-chē-zis] *sm.* catechism

каток [ka-tók] *sm.* skating-rink; mangle, rolling press

католик [ka-tó-l'ik] *sm.* Roman-Catholic

католический [ka-ta-l'ē-ches-ki] *adj.* catholic

католичество [ka-ta-l'ē-tvŏ] *sn.* catholicism

каторга [ká-tar-ga] *sf.* penal servitude

каторжник [ká-tar-zhn'ik] *sm.* convict; **каторжные работы** [ka-tar-zhnă-ye ra-bó-tă] hard labour

катушка [ka-tōōsh-ka] *sf.* bobbin, reel, spool; roll (*of paper*)

каустический [ka-ōōs-t'ē-ches-ki] *adj.* caustic

каучук [ka-ōō-chōōk] *sm.* india-rubber

кафедра [ka-fyéd-ra] *sf.* pulpit; chair (*professorship*)

кафтан [kaf-tán] *sm.* peasant's long coat

качалка [ka-chál-ka] *sf.* rocking-chair

качать [ka-chát'] (по-) *vt.* to rock, swing; to shake (*one's head*)

качель [ka-chél'] *sf.* see-saw, swing

качество [ká-chest-vŏ] *sn.* quality; capacity

каша [ká-sha] *sf.* gruel, porridge; *fig.* jumble, muddle

кашевар [ka-she-vär] *sm.* army cook

кашель [ká-shel'] *sm.* cough

кашица [ká-shi-tsa] *sf.* pulp

кашка [käsh-ka] *sf.* infant's food; clover

кашлять [käsh-lyat'] *vi.* to cough

кашне [kash-nyé] *sn.* muffler scarf; comforter

каштан [kash-tán] *sm.* chest-nut; **-овый** [-a-vǎy] *adj.* auburn, nut-brown

каюта [ka-yōō-ta] *sf.* cabin

каютюнга [ka-yōōt-yōōn-ga] *sm.* cabin-boy

каяться [ká-yat'-sya] (по-) *vi.* to regret, repent

кающийся [ká-yōō-shchi-sya] *adj.* contrite, penitent, repentant

квадрат [kva-drát] *sm.* square

квадратура [kva-dra-tōō-ra] *sf.* quadrature

квакать [kvá-kat'] (за-) *vi.* to croak, quack

квалифицировать [kva-l'i-fi-tsē-ra-vat'] *vt.* to qualify

кварта [kvár-ta] *sf.* quart; *mus.* fourth

квартал [kvar-tál] *sm.* district, quarter, ward

квартет [kvar-tyét] *sm. mus.* quartet

квартира [kvar-t'ē-ra] *sf.* apartment, lodgings, residence; **-нт** [-ánt] *sm.*, **-нтка** [-ántka] *sf.* lodger

квартировать [kvar-t'ē-ra-vat'] *vi.* to lodge, reside

квас [kvás] *sm.* Russian cider (made from rye flour and malt)

квасить [kvá-sit'] *vt.* to ferment, make sour

квасцы [kvas-tsá] *sm. pl.* alum

кваша [kvá-sha] *sf.* leaven

квашня [kvash-nyá] *sf.* kneading-trough

кверху [kvyer-chōō] *adv.* up, upwards

квинта [kv'ēn-ta] *sf. mus.* fifth

квинтет [kv'in-tyét] *sm. mus.* quintet

квит(ы) [kv'ē-t(ä)] *adj. pl.* quits

квитанция [kv'i-tán-tsya] *sf.* receipt

кегельбан [ké-gyel'-ban] *sm.* skittle-alley

кегль [kégl'] *sf. typ.* point, size (of type)

кегля [ké-glya] *sf.* skittle

кедр [kedr] *sm.* cedar, cedar-tree

келейный [ke-lyéy-nǎy] *adj.* cellular; private, secret

кельнер [kél'-nyer] *sm.* waiter; **-ша** [-sha] *sf.* waitress

келья [ké-lya] *sf.* cell

кем [kyem] *pron.* by whom

керамика [ke-rá-mi-ka] *sf.* ceramics

керосин [kye-ra-s'ēn] *sm.* petroleum

кивать [ki-vát'] (кивнуть) *vi.* to beckon, nod

кидать [ki-dát'] (кинуть) *vt.* to fling, throw; to abandon, leave

кий [kē] *sm.* billiard-cue

кикимора [ki-kē-ma-ra] *sf.* ghost, phantom; brownie

киль [kēl'] *sm.* keel

килька [kēl'-ka] *sf.* sprat

кинжал [kin-zhál] *sm.* dagger

кино [ki-nó] *sn.* cinema

кипа [ké-pa] *sf.* bale; stack

кипение [ki-pyé-nye] *sn.* boiling; effervescence

кипеть [ki-pyét'] (за-) *vi.* to boil, effervesce; to seethe

кипучий [ki-pōō-chi] *adj.* fervent, intense; boiling, foaming

кипятильник [ki-pya-t'ēl'-nik] *sm.* boiler

кириллица [ki-rēl-li-tsa] *sf.* Cyrillic (Russian) alphabet

кирка [kir-kā] *sf.* pickaxe

кирпич [kir-pēch] *sm.* brick

кисель [ki-syél'] *sm.* sour fruit jelly; **морской –** [mar-skóy –] jellyfish

кисет [ki-syét] *sm.* tobacco-pouch

кисея [ki-sye-yā] *sf.* muslin

киска [kēs-ka] *sf.* pussy-cat

кисловатый [ki-sla-vā-tăy] *adj.* sourish, tartish

кислород [ki-sla-ród] *sm.* oxygen

кислость [kē-slóst'] *sf.* acidity

кислый [kē-slăy] *adj.* sour, tart

киста [kē-sta] *sf.* cyst

кистень [ki-styén'] *sm.* bludgeon

кисточка [kē-stŏch-ka] *sf.* small brush; tassel

кисть [kēst'] *sf.* wrist; paintbrush; bunch, cluster (*of grapes*); tassel

кит [kēt] *sm.* whale

китаец [ki-tā-yets] *sm.* Chinaman; **китаянка** [ki-ta-yān-ka] *sf.* Chinese woman

китайский [ki-tāy-ski] *adj.* Chinese

кичиться [ki-chēt'-sya] *vi.* to swagger, swank

кичливый [kich-l'ē-văy] *adj.* conceited, vain

кишеть [ki-shét'] (за–) *vi.* to swarm

кишечник [ki-shéch-n'ik] *sm.* bowels, intestines

кишка [kish-kā] *sf.* gut, intestine; garden hose

кишмиш [kish-mēsh] *sm.* currant(s)

клавиатура [kla-vi-a-tōō-ra] *sf. mus.* finger-board, keyboard

клавиш [klā-vish] *sm.* key, ivory (*of piano*)

клад [klād] *sm.* hidden treasure

кладбище [klād-bi-shche] *sn.* cemetery, churchyard

кладка [klād-ka] *sf.* laying, piling

кладовая [kla-da-vā-ya] *sf.* larder, pantry

кланяться [klā-nyat'-sya] (поклониться) *vi.* to bow, greet, salute; to humble oneself

клапан [klā-pan] *sm.* valve; vent

кларнет [klar-nyét] *sm.* clarinet

класс [klās] *sm.* class, form; **-ик** [-ik] *sm.* classic (*a classic writer*)

классификация [klas-si-fi-kā-tsya] *sf.* classification

класть [klāst'] (положить) *vt.* to deposit, lay, place, put

клёв [klyov] *sm.* bait, bite, biting (*in angling*)

клевать [klye-vāt'] *vt.* to peck, pick; to bite, nibble

клевер [klyé-ver] *sm.* clover

клевета [klye-ve-tā] *sf.* defamation, slander

клеветать [klye-ve-tāt'] (на–) *vi.* to libel, slander

клеветник [klye-vet-n'ēk] *sm.* slanderer

клеёнка [klye-yón-ka] *sf.* oilcloth

клей [klyéy] *sm.* glue, gum

клеить [klyé-it'] (с–) *vt.* to glue, paste, stick

клейкость [klyéy-kŏst'] *sf.* viscosity

клеймо [klyey-mō] *sn.* brand, trade-mark

клейстер [klyéy-ster] *sm.* paste

клён [klyón] *sm.* maple

клепать [klye-pát'] (за-) *vt.* to rivet; to slander

клёпка [klyóp-ka] *sf.* riveting; cooper's lag, stave

клетка [klyét-ka] *sf.* cage, coop; check (*on material*); *biol.* cell

клетчатый [klyet-chá-tǎy] *adj.* checked (*material*)

клёцка [klyóts-ka] *sf.* dumpling

клещи [klye-shchē] *sm. pl.* nippers, pincers; tongs

кливер [klē-vyer] *sm. naut.* jib

клиент [kl'i-yént] *sm.* client; **-ура** [-ōōra] *sf.* clientele

клика [kl'é-ka] *sf.* clique, faction

кликать [kl'é-kat'] *vt.* to call

климат [kl'é-mat] *sm.* climate

клин [kl'en] *sm.* wedge

клиника [kl'é-n'i-ka] *sf.* clinic

клинический [kl'i-n'é-ches-ki] *adj.* clinical

клинок [kl'i-nók] *sm.* steel blade

клинообразный [kl'i-na-ab-ráz-nǎy] *adj.* cuneiform

клинопись [kl'i-na-p'ēs'] *sf.* cuneiform characters

клир [kl'ēr] *sm.* clergy; **-ик** [-ik] *sm.* cleric; **-ос** [-ós] *sm.* chancel; **-ошанин** [-a-shán'in] *sm.* chorister

клистир [kl'i-st'ēr] *sm.* enema

клич [kl'ēch] *sm.* call, cry, shout; **-ка** *sf.* nick-name

клише [kli-shé] *sn. typ.* block, stereo

клобук [kla-bōōk] *sm.* cowl, hood

клок [klok] *sm.* flock, rag, tuft

клокот [kló-kŏt] *sm.* bubbling, gurgling

клонить [kla-n'ēt'] (на-) *vt.* to lean, incline

клоп [klop] *sm.* bug

клохтать [klach-tát'] *vi.* to chuckle, cluck

клочковатый [klach-ka-vá-tǎy] *adj.* flaky, flocky, patchy, shred-like

клуб [klōōb] *sm.* club (*meeting-place*); puff; cloud of smoke

клубника [klōōb-n'é-ka] *sf.* garden strawberry

клубок [klōō-bók] *sm.* ball (*of thread, etc.*); knot, tangle

клумба [klōōm-ba] *sf.* flower-bed

клык [klǎk] *sm.* tusk; canine tooth, fang

клюв [klyōōv] *sm.* beak, bill

клюз [klyōōz] *sm.* hawse

клюка [klyōō-ká] *sf.* crutch

клюква [klyōōk-va] *sf.* cranberry

ключ [klyōōch] *sm.* key; *mus.* clef; **гаечный –** [gá-yech-nǎy –] spanner; **английский –** [an-glʹés-ki –] monkey-wrench; **-арь** [-ár'] *sm.* sacristan; steward; **-ник** [-n'ik] *sm.* caretaker

ключица [klyōō-ché-tsa] *sf.* collar-bone

клюшка [klyōōsh-ka] *sf.* club (golf)

клякса [klyák-sa] *sf.* blot

клянчить [klyän-chit'] *vt.* to beg; to importune

клясть [klyäst'] *vt.* to curse; **-ся** [-sya] *vi.* to swear, vow; to take an oath

клятва [klyät-va] *sf.* oath, vow

клятвопреступление [klyat-va-pre-stoop-lyé-nye] *sn.* perjury

кляуза [klyáóö-za] *sf.* quibble; gossip, intrigue

книга [kn'é-ga] *sf.* book

книгоиздательство [kn'i-ga-iz-dá-tyel'-stvŏ] *sn.* publishing house

книгопечатание [kn'i-ga-pye-chá-ta-nye] *sn.* book-printing, typography

книгопродавец [kn'i-ga-pra-dá-vyets] *sm.* bookseller

книжный [kn'í-gŏ-chi] *sm. coll.* book-worm

книжечка [kn'é-zhech-ka] *sf.* booklet

книжка [kn'ésh-ka] *sf.* small book, pocket-book

книжник [kn'ézh-n'ik] *sm.* second-hand book-dealer; scribe

книжный [kn'ézh-năy] *adj.* bookish

книзу [kn'é-zŏŏ] *adv.* downwards

кнопка [knóp-ka] *sf.* button, knob, press-stud

кнут [knŏŏt] *sm.* whip; **-овище** [-a-vé-shche] *sn.* whiphandle

княгиня [knya-gé-nya] *sf.* princess

княжение [knya-zhé-nye] *sn.* reign

княжеский [knyá-zhes-ki] *adj.* princely

князь [knyáz'] *sm.* prince

ко [kŏ] *prep.* to, towards; by; for

коалиция [ka-a-l'é-tsya] *sf.* coalition

кобель [ka-byél'] *sm.* dog

кобура [ka-bŏŏ-ra] *sf.* holster

кобыла [ka-bÁ-la] *sf.* mare

кобылка [ka-bÁl-ka] *sf.* filly; *mus.* bridge

кованый [kó-va-năy] *adj.* forged; shod

коварный [ka-vár-năy] *adj.* artful, crafty

ковать [ka-vát'] (c-) *vt.* to forge, hammer; to shoe (*hoofs*)

ковёр [ka-vyór] *sm.* carpet; rug

коверкать [ka-vyér-kat'] (ис-) *vt.* to distort, mangle

ковка [kóv-ka] *sf.* forging, shoeing

коврига [kav-ré-ga] *sf.* round loaf

коврижка [kav-rézh-ka] *sf.* gingerbread

коврик [kóv-rik] *sm.* hearthrug

ковчег [kav-chég] *sm.* ark; shrine

ковш [kovsh] *sm.* ladle, scoop; bucket

ковылять [ka-vă-lyát'] *vi.* to hobble, limp; to toddle; to stump

ковырять [ka-vă-ryát'] *vt.* to pick (*teeth*), scour out; to tinker

когда [kag-dá] *adv.* when; **--либо** [—l'i-bŏ] sometime or other; **--то** [—ta] formerly, once

кого [ka-vó] *pron.* whom; **— бы ни** [— bă n'i] whomsoever

коготь [kó-gŏt'] *sm.* claw, nail, talon

когти [kóch-t'i] *sm. pl. fig.* clutches

кое-где [kó-ye-gdye] *adv.* somewhere; **--как** [—kák] somehow; haphazardly;

-кто [—chto] someone; **-куда** [—kōō-dā] somewhere; **—что** [—shto] something

кожа [kó-zha] *sf.* skin; leather; hide; **-ный** [-năy] *adj.* leather-, leathern

кожевник [ka-zhév-n'ik] *sm.* currier. tanner

кожевня [ka-zhév-nya] *sf.* tannery

кожица [kó-zhi-tsa] *sf.* pellicle, film; peel, rind

кожный [kózh-năy] *adj.* cutaneous

кожура [ka-zhōō-rā] *sf.* peel, rind

кожух [ka-zhōōch] *sm.* peasant's fur-coat

коза [ka-zā] *sf.* nanny-goat

козёл [ka-zyól] *sm.* billy-goat

козерог [ka-zye-róg] *sm.* Capricorn

козетка [ka-zyét-ka] *sf.* settee

козлёнок [ka-zlyó-nŏk] *sm.* kid (*young goat*)

козлы [kóz-lä] *sm. pl.* trestle, vaulting-horse

козни [kóz-n'i] *sf. pl.* ambush, traps; intrigues

козырёк [ka-ză-ryók] *sm.* peak of cap

козырь [kó-zăr'] *sm.* trump

койка [kóy-ka] *sf.* berth, cot; hammock

кокетка [ka-kyét-ka] *sf.* flirt

кокетничать [ka-kyét-n'i-chat'] *vi.* to flirt

коклюш [ka-klyōōsh] *sm.* whooping cough

коклюшка [ka-klyōōsh-ka] *sf.* bobbin

кокос [ka-kós] *sm.* coco-nut

кокс [koks] *sm.* coke

кол [kol] *sm.* picket, post, stake

колбаса [kal-ba-sā] *sf.* salame, sausage

колбасник [kal-bās-n'ik] *sm.* sausage-purveyor

колдовать [kal-da-vāt'] *vi.* to practise sorcery

колдовство [kal-dav-stvó] *sn.* magic, witchcraft

колдун [kal-dōōn] *sm.* magician, sorcerer; **-ья** [-ya] *sf.* witch

колебание [ka-lye-bā-nye] *sn.* oscillation; fluctuation; hesitation

колебательный [ka-lye-bā-tyel'-năy *adj.* oscillating, vibrating

коленкор [ka-lyen-kór] *sm.* calico

колено [ka-lyé-nŏ] *sn.* knee

коленопреклонение [ka-lye-na-pre-kla-né-nye] *sn.* genuflexion

колёсник [ka-lyós-n'ik] *sm.* wheelwright

колесо [ka-lye-só] *sn.* wheel

колечко [ka-lyéch-kŏ] *sn.* ringlet

колея [ka-lyé-ya] *sf.* rut, track

количество [ka-l'ē-chest-vŏ] *sn.* amount, number

колка [kól-ka] *sf.* cleaving

колкий [kól-ki] *adj.* prickly; cleavable; *fig.* poignant

коллективный [kal-lyek-t'ēv-năy] *adj.* collective

коллекция [kal-lyék-tsya] *sf.* collection

коловорот [ka-la-va-rót] *sm.* *tech.* brace

колода [ka-ló-da] *sf.* block, log; pack (*cards*)

колодец [ka-ló-dyets] *sm.* well

колодка [ka-lód-ka] *sf.* shoetree; last

колокол [kó-la-kŏl] *sm.* bell

колокольня [ka-la-kól'-nya] *sf.* steeple; bell-tower

колокольчик [ka-la-kól'-chik] *sm.* hand-bell; bluebell

коломазь [ka-la-máz'] *sf.* lubricating oil

колонна [ka-lón-na] *sf.* pillar; *mil.* column

колос [kó-lŏs] *sm.* ear of corn, spike

колотить [ka-la-t'ĕt'] (по-) *vt.* to thrash

колоть [ka-lót'] (рас-) *vt.* to break up, pierce, stab, thrust

колпак [kal-pák] *sm.* nightcap; cap, cowl; *fig.* simpleton

колун [ka-lōōn] *sm.* axe

колыбель [ka-lă-byél'] *sf.* cradle

колышек [kó-lă-shek] *sm.* peg

кольцо [kal'-tsó] *sn.* ring; *tech.* collar, split-ring

кольчатый [kal'-chă-tăy] *adj.* annular

кольчуга [kal'-chōō-ga] *sf.* coat of mail

колючий [ka-lyōō-chi] *adj.* prickly, thorny

коляда [ka-lyă-da] *sf.* Christmas carol

колядовать [ka-lyă-da-vat'] *vi.* to sing carols in the streets

коляска [ka-lyăs-ka] *sf.* carriage

ком [kom] *sm.* clot, lump; ball (*snow*)

команда [ka-mán-da] *sf.* mil. command

комар [ka-már] *sm.* gnat, mosquito

комбинировать [kam-bi-n'ĕ-ra-vat'] *vt.* to combine

комедия [ka-mé-dya] *sf.* comedy

комель [kó-myel'] *sm.* butt-end

комиссар [ka-mis-sár] *sm.* commissary

комиссия [ka-mĕs-sya] *sf.* commission

комитет [ka-mi-tyét] *sm.* committee

комический [ka-mĕ-ches-ki] *adj.* comic

комичный [ka-mĕch-năy] *adj.* ridiculous

комкать [kóm-kat'] (с-) *vt.* to crumple

коммерсант [kam-myer-sänt] *sm.* wholesale merchant

коммерция [kam-myér-tsya] *sf.* commerce, trade

коммерческий [kam-myér-ches-ki] *adj.* commercial

коммивояжёр [kam-mi-va-ya-zhyór] *sm.* commercial traveller

комната [kóm-na-ta] *sf.* room

комод [ka-mód] *sm.* chest of drawers, tall-boy

компания [kam-pá-nya] *sf.* business company

компаньон [kam-pa-nyón] *sm.*, -ка, *sf.* companion

компетенция [kam-pe-tén-tsya] *sf.* competence

компилировать [kam-pi-l'ĕ-ra-vat'] *vt.* to compile

компилятор [kam-pi-lyă-tör] *sm.* compiler

комплект [kam-plyékt] *sm.* complement, set

комплектование [kam-plyek-ta-vă-nye] *sn.* recruitment

комплекция [kam-plyék-tsya] *sf.* constitution

композитор [kam-pa-zĕ-tör] *sm.* composer

композиция [kam-pa-zé-tsya] *sf.* mus. composition

компонировать [kam-pa-n'ě-ra-vat'] *vt.* mus. to compose

компот [kam-pót] *sm.* mixed stewed fruit

кому [ka-móō] *pron.* to whom

кон [kon] *sm.* stake (*in games*), lead, turn

конверт [kan-vyért] *sm.* envelope

конвой [kan-vóy] *sm.* convoy, escort, guard

кондитер [kan-d'é-tyer] *sm.* confectioner, pastrycook; **-ская** [-ska-ya] *sf.* confectioner's shop

коневодство [ka-nye-vódstvŏ] *sn.* horse-breeding

конёк [ka-nyók] *sm.* pony; hobby; ridge (*of roof*)

конец [ka-nyéts] *sm.* conclusion, end; termination

конечно [ka-nyéch-nŏ] *adv.* certainly, of course

конечность [ka-nyéch-nŏst'] *sf.* limit; extremity, tip

конечный [ka-nyéch-náy] *adj.* final, ultimate; terminal

конина [ka-ně-na] *sf.* horse-meat

конкурент [kan-kŏō-ryént] *sm.* competitor, rival

конкурс kán-kŏōrs] *sm.* meeting of creditors

конница [kón-n'i-tsa] *sf.* cavalry

конозаводство [kan-na-za-vód-stvŏ] *sn.* stud-farm

коновал [ka-na-vál] *sm.* veterinary surgeon

конопля [ka-na-plyä] *sf.* hemp

коносамент [ka-na-sa-myént] *sm.* bill of lading

консерватория [kan-ser-va-tō-rya] *sf.* conservatoire

консервы [kan-syér-vǎ] *sm. pl.* preserved foods

консервировать [kan-syer-v'ě-ra-vat'] *vt.* to conserve, preserve

конский [kón-ski] *adj.* equine

конспект [kan-spyékt] *sm.* abstract; epitome; précis; synopsis

конструировать [kan-strŏō-ě-ra-vat'] *vt.* to construct, design

консульство [kón-sŏōl'-stvŏ] *sn.* consulate

контора [kan-tó-ra] *sf.* bureau, counting-house, office

конторка [kan-tór-ka] *sf.* desk

конторщик [kan-tór-shchik] *sm.* office clerk

контрабас [kon-tra-bás] *sm.* double-bass

контр-адмирал [kóntr-ad-mi-rál] *sm.* rear-admiral

контракт [kan-trákt] *sm.* business agreement

контрминоносец [kontr-mi-na-nó-syets] *sm.* destroyer, torpedo-boat

контролёр [kon-tro-lyór] *sm.* inspector

контролировать [kon-tro-l'ě-ra-vat'] *vt.* to check, superintend

контроль [kon-tról'] *sm.* control, check, supervision

контузия [kan-tōō-zya] *sf.* shell-shock

конура [ka-nōō-ra] *sf.* kennel; *fig.* hovel

конус [kó-nōōs] *sm.* cone

конфета [kan-fyé-ta] *sf.* sweetmeat

конфузить [kan-fōō-zit'] (с-) *vt.* to confuse, perplex

концерт [kan-tsyért] *sm.* concert; concerto

концовка [kan-tsóv-ka] *sf.* tail-piece; colophon

кончать [kan-chát'] (кóнчить) *vt.* to end, finish, terminate

кончик [kón-chík] *sm.* point, tip

кончина [kan-chê-na] *sf.* decease

конь [kon'] *sm.* horse, steed; knight (*chess*)

конюх [kó-nyōōch] *sm.* groom; ostler

конюшня [ka-nyōōsh-nya] *sf.* stable, mews

копа [ka-pá] *sf.* heap; =60 sheaves

копать [ka-pát'] (вы-) *vt.* to dig, excavate

копейка [ka-péy-ka] *sf.* copeck (*about a farthing*)

копёр [ka-pyór] *sm.* pile-driver

копилка [ka-p'ĕl-ka] *sf.* money-box

копировать [ka-p'ê-ra-vat'] (с-) *vt.* to copy, duplicate

копить [ka-p'ét'] (на-) *vt.* to hoard, save up, store up

копия [kô-pya] *sf.* copy, transcript

копна [kap-ná] *sf.* rick (*of hay*); – волос [–va-lós] shock of hair

копотливый [ka-pat-l'ê-văy] *adj.* sluggish

копоть [kó-pŏt'] *sf.* soot; lampblack

копошиться [ka-pa-shét'-sya] (за-) *vi.* to swarm; to crawl; *coll.* to potter about

коптеть [kap-tyét'] (за-) *vi.* to smoke (*as lamp, etc.*)

коптить [kap-t'ét'] (вы-) *vt.* to smoke (*fish, etc.*)

копченье [kap-ché-nye] *sn.* curing, smoking

копыто [ka-pá-tŏ] *sn.* hoof

копь [kop'] *sf.* mine, pit

копьё [ka-pyó] *sn.* lance, spear

копьеносец [ka-pye-nó-syets] *sm.* lancer, spearman

кора [ka-rá] *sf.* bark, rind; cortex; crust

корабельный [ka-rä-byel'-năy] *adj.* naval; ship's; – плотник [–plót-n'ik] shipwright

кораблекрушение [ka-rab-lye-krōō-shé-nye] *sn.* shipwreck

кораблестроение [ka-rab-lye-stra-yé-nye] *sn.* shipbuilding

кораблик [ka-ráb-l'ik] *sm.* small ship

корабль [ka-rábl'] *sm.* ship, vessel; военный – [va-yén-năy –] warship

коралл [ka-rál] *sm.* coral

коренастый [ka-rye-nás-tăy] *adj.* stocky, thick-set

коренной [ka-ryen-nóy] *adj.* fundamental, radical, root-

корень [kó-ryen'] *sm.* root

корешок [ka-rye-shók] *sm.* counterfoil

корзина [kar-z'ê-na] *sf.* basket, hamper

корить [ka-r'êt] (у-) *vt.* to reproach

корица [ka-r'ê-tsa] *sf.* cinnamon

коричневый [ka-r'êch-nye-văy] *adj.* brown

корка [kór-ka] *sf.* crust (*of bread*); peel; rind; scab

корм [korm] *sm.* food; fodder

корма [kar-mā] *sf. naut.* stern; **за кормой** [za kar-móy] *adv.* astern

кормёжка [kar-myózh-ka] *sf.* feed

кормилец [kar-m'ē-lyets] *sm.* bread-winner

кормилица [kar-m'ē-l'i-tsa] *sf.* nurse, wet nurse

кормило [kar-m'ē-lŏ] *sn.* helm, rudder

кормить [kar-m'ēt'] (на-) *vt.* to feed, nourish; **-ся** [-sya] *vi.* to live, subsist

кормление [kar-mlyé-nye] *sn.* feeding, nourishing; lactation

кормушка [kar-mōōsh-ka] *sf.* rack

кормчий [kórm-chi] *sm.* helmsman

корнать [kar-nāt'] (o-) *vt.* to crop, prune

корнишон [kar-n'i-shón] *sm.* gherkin

коробейник [ka-ra-byéy-n'ik] *sm.* pedlar

коробить [ka-ró-b'it'] *vt.* to warp; *fig.* to jar upon; **-ся** [-sya] *vi.* to bend, contract, shrivel

коробка [ka-rób-ka] *sf.* box, case

коробление [ka-rab-lyé-nye] *sn.* warping

корова [ka-ró-va] *sf.* cow; **дойная –** [dóy-na-ya –] milch cow

коровай [ka-ra-váy] *sm.* loaf

коровий [ka-ró-vi] *adj.* cow-, cow's; cowish

коровник [ka-róv-n'ik] *sm.* cowshed

коровница [ka-róv-n'i-tsa] *sf.* dairy-maid

королева [ka-ra-lyé-va] *sf.* queen

королевский [ka-ra-lyév-ski] *adj.* regal, royal

королевство [ka-ra-lyév-stvŏ] *sn.* kingdom

королёк [ka-ra-lyók] *sm.* wren; blood-orange

король [ka-ról] *sm.* king

коромысло [ka-ra-mâs-lŏ] *sn.* yoke (*for carrying*); beam (*balance*); rocking-shaft

корона [ka-ró-na] *sf.* crown; coronet

коронация [ka-ra-nā-tsya] *sf.* coronation

короста [ka-rós-ta] *sf.* scab

короткий [ka-rót-ki] *adj.* brief, short

коротко [kó-rat-kŏ] *adv.* briefly

короткость [ka-rót-kŏst] *sf.* shortness

корпеть [kar-pyét'] (про-) *vi.* to plod, work hard (*at*); to pore (*over a book, etc.*)

корпия [kór-pya] *sf.* lint

корпус [kór-pŏōs] *sm.* body; building; army corps; *typ.* long primer

корректировать [kar-ryek-t'ē-ra-vat'] *vt.* to read, correct printer's proofs

корректный [kar-ryékt-nây] *adj.* correct, proper

корректор [kar-ryék-tŏr] *sm.* proof-reader

корректура [kar-ryék-tōō-ra] *sf.* printer's proof

корреспонденция [kar-ryes-pon-dyén-tsya] *sf.* correspondence

кортеж [kar-tyézh] *sm.* procession, retinue

кортик [kór-t'ik] *sm.* cutlass, dirk

корточки [kór-tach-ki] *sf. pl.* knees drawn up; **на корточках** [na kór-tach-kach] squatting

корча [kór-cha] *sf.* convulsions; cramp; spasm

корчага [kar-chă-ga] *sf.* large earthen pot

корчёвка [kar-chóv-ka] *sf.* clearing, uprooting

корчить [kór-chit'] (с-) *vt.* to contort; to grimace; **-ся** [-sya] *vi.* to squirm, wriggle

корчма [kar-chmă] *sf.* inn, public-house

корчмарь [karch-măr'] *sm.* innkeeper, publican

корыстный [ka-răst-nay] *adj.* mercenary

корыстолюбивый [ka-răs-ta-lyŏŏ-bĕ-vǎy] *adj.* covetous

корыто [ka-ryă-tŏ] *sn.* trough

корь [kor'] *sf.* measles

корявый [ka-ryă-vǎy] *adj.* rugged, uneven; awkward

коряга [ka-ryă-ga] *sf.* snag

коса [ka-să] *sf.* scythe; plait, tress; spit (of land)

косарь [ka-săr'] *sm.* mower; chopper; reaper

косвенный [kós-vyen-nǎy] *adj.* indirect, oblique

косец [ka-syéts] *sm.* mower, hay-maker, reaper

косить [ka-s'ĕt'] *vt.* to mow; to squint

косичка [ka-s'ĕch-ka] *sf.* pigtail

косматый [kas-mă-tǎy] *adj.* shaggy

космы [kós-mǎ] *sf. pl.* locks (*hair*)

коснеть [kas-nyét'] *vi.* to remain, to stagnate

косноязычный [kas-na-ya-zăch-nǎy] *adj.* tongue-tied

косный [kós-nǎy] *adj.* inert; stagnant

косо [kó-sŏ] *adv.* askance, obliquely

костенеть [kas-tye-nyét'] (о-) *vi.* to become numb; to stiffen

костёр [kas-tyór] *sm.* bonfire, camp-fire

костлявый [kast-lyă-vǎy] *adj.* bony

костоправ [kas-ta-prăv] *sm.* bonesetter

костыль [kas-tăl'] *sm.* crutch

кость [kost'] *sf.* bone; **игральная** – [i-grăl'-na-ya –] *die* (*sing. of* dice); **слоновая** – [sla-nó-va-ya –] ivory

костюм [kas-tyŏŏm] *sm.* costume, suit

костюмёр [kas-tyŏŏ-myór] *sm.* costumier

костяк [kas-tyăk] *sm.* skeleton

косуля [ka-sŏŏ-lya] *sf.* roe (*deer*)

кот [kot] *sm.* tom-cat

котёл [ka-tyól] *sm.* boiler, cauldron, kettle

котельщик [ka-téyl'-shchik] *sm.* boiler-maker

котёнок [ka-tyó-nŏk] *sm.* kitten

котировка [ka-t'i-róv-ka] *sf.* quotation

котлета [kat-lyé-ta] *sf.* meat cutlet, chop

котловина [kat-la-v'ĕ-na] *sf.* crater, hollow, valley

котомка [ka-tóm-ka] *sf.* wallet; knapsack

который [ka-tó-rǎy] *pron.* what, which, who (*rel.*, *interr.*); that; – **час?** [– chăs] what is the time?

кофе [kó-fye] *sn.* coffee

кофейник [ka-fyéy-n'ik] *sm.* coffee-pot

кофейня [ka-fyéy-nya] *sf.* café, coffee-house

кофта [kóf-ta] *sf.* woman's jacket

кочан [ka-chán] *sm.* heart of cabbage, lettuce, etc.

кочевать [ka-che-vát'] *vi.* to wander, to roam from place to place

кочевник [ka-chév-n'ik] *sm.* wanderer

кочевой [ka-che-vnóy] *adj.* nomadic

кочегар [ka-che-gár] *sm.* fireman, stoker

коченеть [ka-che-nyét'] (о-) *vi.* to be benumbed; to become chilled

кочерга [ka-cher-gá] *sf.* poker

кочерыжка [ka-che-rázh-ka] *sf.* cabbage-stalk

кочка [kóch-ka] *sf.* hillock

кочковатый [kach-ka-vá-tăy] *adj.* hilly, abounding in hillocks

кошачий [ka-shá-chi] *adj.* catlike, cat's, feline

кошелёк [ka-she-lyók] *sf.* purse

кошка [kósh-ka] *sf.* cat

кошмар [kash-már] *sm.* nightmare

краги [krá-gi] *sm. pl.* gaiters, leggings

кража [krá-zha] *sf.* larceny; theft

край [kráy] *sm.* border, rim; brink, edge; country, region; **-не** [-nye] *adv.* extremely, urgently; **-ний** [-n'i] *adj.* extreme; utmost; **-ность** [-nŏst'] *sf.* exigence; extremity; need

кран [krăn] *sm.* tap; cock; crane

крап [krăp] *sm.* speck(s); markings on book covers; *bot.* madder

крапать [kră-pat'] *vt.* to marble; to sprinkle; *vi.* to trickle

крапива [kra-p'é-va] *sf.* nettle

крапивник [kra-p'ēv-n'ik] *sm.* wren

крапивница [kra-p'ēv-n'i-tsa] *sf.* nettle-rash

крапчатый [krap-chá-tăy] *adj.* freckled, spotted

краса [kra-sá] *sf.* beauty; embellishment, ornament; **-вец** [-vyets] *sm.* handsome man; **-вица** [-v'i-tsa] *sf.* beautiful woman

красивый [kra-s'ē-văy] *adj.* handsome, pretty

красильный [kra-s'ēl'-năy] *adj.* tinctorial

красильня [kra-s'ēl'-nya] *sf.* dyers (factory)

красильщик [kra-s'ēl'-shchik] *sm.* dyer; house-painter

красить [kră-sit'] (вы-) *vt.* to colour; to dye; to paint; to stain; *fig.* to adorn, embellish

краска [krás-ka] *sf.* colour, dye; hue

краснеть [kras-nyét'] (по-) *vi.* to blush, colour, redden

красноармеец [kras-nŏ-ar-myé-yets] *sm.* soldier of the Red Army

красноватый [kras-na-vá-tăy] *adj.* reddish

красноречивый [kras-na-rye-chē-văy] *adj.* eloquent, fluent

краснуха [kras-nŏŏ-cha] *sf.* German measles

красный [krás-năy] *adj.* red; *fig.* bright, fine; revolutionary; **красная горка** [krás-na-ya gór-ka] first Sunday after Easter; **-строка** [- stra-ká] new paragraph

красоваться [kra-sa-vát'-sya] *vi.* to show off

красота [kra-sa-tá] *sf.* beauty

красочный [krá-sach-năy] *adj.* graphic, picturesque, vivid

красть [krást'] (у-) *vt.* to steal; **-ся** [-sya] *vi.* to creep, sneak [concise

краткий [krát-ki] *adj.* brief, brevity, shortness

краткость [krát-kŏst'] *sf.* brevity, shortness

кратный [krát-năy] *adj. comm.* short-dated

крах [krách] *sm.* bankruptcy, crash, failure [starch

крахмал [krach-mál] *sm.* starch

крахмалить [krach-má-l'it'] (на-) *vt.* to starch

крашение [kra-shé-nye] *sf.* dyeing

краюха [kra-yŏŏ-cha] *sf.* end crust of a loaf

креветка [krye-vyét-ka] *sf.* shrimp

кредит [krye-d'ét] *sm.* credit; **-ив** [-év] *sm.* letter of credit; **-оспособность** [-a-spasób-nŏst'] *sf.* solvency

крейсер [kréy-ser] *sm.* cruiser; **линейный** [li-nyéynăy -] battle cruiser

крем [kryém] *sm.* cream; **-овый** [-a-văy] *adj.* cream-coloured, creamy

крематорий [krye-ma-tó-ri] *sm.* crematorium

кремация [kre-má-tsya] *sf.* cremation [flint

кремень [kryé-myen'] *sm.*

кремль [kryéml'] *sm.* citadel

крен [kryen] *sm. naut.* heel, list, lurch

кренить [krye-n'ét'] *vt.* to heel over; **-ся** [-sya] *vi.* to careen, heel, list

креп [kryép] *sm.* crape; crêpe

крепительный [krye-p'étel'-năy] *adj.* invigorating

крепить [krye-p'ét'] *vt.* to fortify, strengthen

крепкий [kryép-ki] *adj.* solid, strong, tough

крепость [krye-pŏst'] *sf.* fortress, stronghold; firmness, strength

крепыш [krye-pásh] *sm. coll.* robust person

кресло [kryés-lŏ] *sn.* easy-chair, armchair; stall (*in theatre*)

крест [kryést] *sm.* cross

крестильный [kryes-t'él'-năy] *adj.* baptismal

крестины [kryes-t'é-nă] *sf. pl.* baptism, christening

крестить [kryes-t'ét'] *vt.* to baptize, christen; **-ся** [-sya] *vi.* to be christened; make the sign of the cross

крестник [kryést-n'ik] *sm.* god-child (*son*); **крестница** [kryést-n'i-tsa] *sf.* god-child (*daughter*)

крёстный [kryóst-năy] *adj.* of the Cross; **- отец** [- a-tyéts] *sm.* godfather; **крёстная мать** [kryóst-na-ya mát'] *sf.* godmother

крестоносец [kryes-ta-nósyets] *sm.* crusader

крестьянин [kryes-tyán'in] *sm.* peasant

крестьянский [kryes-tyắn-ski] *adj.* peasant's, rustic

крестьянство [kryes-tyắn-stvŏ] *sn.* peasantry

крещение [krye-shché-nye] *sn.* christening ceremony

кривда [kr'ēv-da] *sf. coll.* falsehood, injustice

кривить [kri-vĕt'] (с-) *vt.* to bend; to distort

кривляться [kriv-lyắt-sya] *vi.* to grimace, come

кривой [kri-vóy] *adj.* crooked, curved

криводушный [kri-va-dŏŏsh-nǎy] *adj.* insincere, hypocritical

кривошип [kri-va-shíp] *sm. tech.* crank

кризис [krí-zis] *sm.* crisis

крик [krēk] *sm.* cry, shout

крикливый [krik-l'ē-vǎy] *adj.* clamorous, noisy

крикун [kri-kŏŏn] *sm. -ья* [-ya] *sf.* noisy person

критика [krē-t'i-ka] *sf.* criticism

критиковать [kri-t'i-ka-vát'] *vt.* to criticize

кричать [kri-chát'] (крикнуть) *vi.* to call out; shout

кров [krov'] *sm.* roof, shelter

кровавый [kra-vá-vǎy] *adj.* bloody, sanguinary

кровать [kra-vát'] *sf.* bed, bedstead

кровля [króv-lya] *sf.* roofing

кровожадный [kra-va-zhắd-nǎy] *adj.* blood-thirsty

кровоизлияние [kra-va-iz-l'i-yắ-nye] *sn.* haemorrhage

кровопереливание [kra-va-pye-re-l'i-vắ-nye] *sn.* blood transfusion

кровопролитие [kra-va-pra-l'ē-tye] *sn.* bloodshed

кровопускание [kra-va-pŏŏs-kắ-nye] *sn.* bleeding

кровь [krov'] *sf.* blood; **кровяная колбаса** [kra-vya-nắ-ya kal-ba-sắ] black pudding

кроить [kra-ēt'] *vt.* to cut out (*tailoring*)

кройка [króy-ka] *sf.* cutting out (*tailoring*)

кролик [kró-l'ik] *sm.* rabbit

крольчатник [kral'-chắt-n'ik] *sm.* rabbit-hutch

кроме [kró-mye] *prep.* except

кромка [króm-ka] *sf.* edge; selvage

кромсать [kram-sắt'] (pac-) *vi.* to shred, to tear into pieces

кронштейн [kran-shtéyn] *sm.* corbel; bracket; holder

кропать [kra-pát'] (с-) *vt.* to scribble

кропильница [kra-p'ēl'-n'i-tsa] *sf.* font

кропить [kra-p'ēt'] *vt.* to besprinkle

кропотливый [kra-pat-l'ē-vǎy] *adj.* painstaking

крот [krot] *sm.* mole

кроткий [krót-ki] *adj.* gentle, meek, mild

кротовина [kra-ta-v'ē-na] *sf.* mole-hill

кротость [kró-tǒst'] *sf.* meekness; kindness

крохотить [kra-cha-t'ĕt'] *vt.* to crumb, crumble; to mince

крошить [kra-shĕt'] (на-) *vt.* to hash

крошка [krósh-ka] *sf.* crumb

круг [krŏŏg] *sm.* group, set; circle, ring

кругловатый [krŏŏg-la-vắ-tǎy] *adj.* roundish

круглый [krŏŏg-lǎy] *adj.* globular, round

круговой [kroo-ga-vóy] adj. circular

кругозор [kroo-ga-zór] sm. horizon; scope; outlook

кругом [kroo-góm] adv. around; fig. entirely

кругом [kroo-góm] adv. in a ring, in a whirl

кружево [kroo-zhe-vŏ] sn. lace

кружить [kroo-zhét'] (за-) vt. to spin round, turn

кружка [kroozh-ka] sf. jug, mug, tankard

круп [kroop] sm. med., croup; crupper (horse's)

крупа [kroo-pá] sf. pl. groats

крупный [kroop-năy] adj. big, large; coarse

крутизна [kroo-t'ĕzna] sf. steepness; precipice

крутить [kroo-t'ĕt'] (за-) vt. to twist, wring; to roll; to twirl

крутой [kroo-tóy] adj. steep

кручина [kroo-chĕ-na] sf. affliction, sorrow

крушение [kroo-shé-nye] sn. ruin, wreck

крушить [kroo-shĕt'] vt. to destroy, shatter

крыжовник [kra-zhóv-n'ik] sm. gooseberry

крылатый [kra-lă-tăy] adj. winged

крыло [kra-ló] sn. wing

крыльцо [krăl'-tsó] sn. flight of steps; porch

крымский [krăm-ski] adj. Crimean

крымчак [krăm-chăk] sm. Crimean

крынка [krăn-ka] sf. milk-jug

крыса [kră-sa] sf. rat

крысолов [kră-sa-lóv] sm. rat-catcher

крысоловка [kră-sa-lóv-ka] sf. rat-trap

крыть [krăt'] (по-) vt. to cover; to trump; **-ся** [-sya] vi. to be covered; to hide oneself

крыша [krá-sha] sf. roof

крышка [krăsh-ka] sf. cover, lid, top [tour

крюк [kryook] sm. hook; de-

крючник [kryóoch-n'ik] sm. stevedore [hook

крючок [kryoo-chók] sm.

кряж [kryăzh] sm. mountain range, ridge; stump

кряхтеть [kryach-tyét'] (за-) vi. to groan

кстати [kstăt'i] adv. apropos, opportunely, relevantly

ктитор [kt'ĕ-tŏr] sm. church-warden

кто [chto] pron. who

куб [koob] sm. cube

кубарь [koo-bár'] sm. humming top, peg-top

кубок [koo-bŏk] sm. bowl, beaker

кувшин [koov-shín] sm. water-jug

кувыркать [koo-văr-kát'] (кувыркнуть) vt. to overturn, upset

куда [koo-dá] adv. where, whither

кудреватый [koo-drye-vă-tăy] adj. florid, ornate

кудри [koo-dri] sf. pl. curls, curly hair

кудрявый [koo-drya-văy] adj. curly, frizzy

кузнец [kooz-nyéts] sm. smith, blacksmith, farrier

кузнечик [koóz-nyé-chik] sm. grasshopper

кузница [kōōz-n'é-tsa] *sf.* forge, smithy

кузов [kōō-zöv] *sm.* pannier; body, frame (*of vehicle*)

кукла [kōōk-la] *sf.* doll

кукуруза [kōō-kōō-rōō-za] *sf.* maize, Indian corn

кукушка [kōō-kōōsh-ka] *sf.* cuckoo

кулак [kōō-lák] *sm.* fist; cam, cog; rich peasant

кулачный [kōō-lách-năy] *adj.* fistic(al)

кулёк [kōō-lyók] *sm.* mat-bag

кулинарный [kōō-l'i-nár-năy] *adj.* culinary

кулиса [kōō-l'í-sa] *sf.* theat. wings; side-scene; tech. coulisse

кулич [kōō-l'éch] *sm.* Easter cake

кулуары [kōō-lōō-á-ră] *sm. pl.* lobby

культ [kōōl't] *sm.* cult, worship

культивировать [kōōl'-t'i-vē-ra-vat'] *vt.* to cultivate

культура [kōōl'-tōō-ra] *sf.* culture

культурный [kōōl'-tōōr-năy] *adj.* cultural

кум [kōōm] *sm.* godfather; -а [-á] *sf.* godmother

кумач [kōō-mách] *sm.* red bunting

кумжа [kōōm-zha] *sf.* salmon-trout

кумир [kōō-m'ér] *sm.* idol

кумушка [kōō-mōōsh-ka] *sf.* gossip

кунжут [kōōn-zhōōt] *sm.* sesame

куница [kōō-n'é-tsa] *sf.* marten

купальный [kōō-pál'-năy] *adj.* bathing-, fit for bathing

купальня [kōō-pál'-nya] *sf.* bath, bathing-place

купальщик [kōō-pál'-shchik] *sm.* bath-attendant

купанье [kōō-pá-nye] *sm.* bathing

купать [kōō-pát'] (вы-) *vt.* to bathe; -ся [-sya] *vi.* to bathe

купе [kōō-pyé] *sn.* railway compartment

купель [kōō-pyél'] *sm.* baptismal font

купец [kōō-pyéts] *sm.* merchant

купеческий [kōō-pyé-ches-ki] *adj.* mercantile

купить [kōō-p'ét'] *vt.* to buy

куплет [kōō-plyét] *sm.* couplet

купля [kōōp-lya] *sf.* purchase

купюра [kōō-pyōō-ra] *sf.* excision

кураж [kōō-rázh] *sm.* courage; -иться [-it'-sya] *vi.* to bully; to swagger

куранты [kōō-rán-tă] *sm. pl.* chimes

курган [kōōr-gán] *sm.* barrow; burial mound; tumulus

курение [kōō-ryé-nye] *sn.* smoking; fumigation

курёнок [kōō-ryó-nŏk] *sm.* chicken

курилка [kōō-r'él-ka] *sf.* smoke-room

курильница [kōō-r'él'-ni-tsa] *sf.* censer

курильщик [kōō-r'él'-shchik] *sm.* smoker

куриный [kōō-r'é-năy] *adj.* hen's, gallinaceous

курить (по-) [kōō-r'ét'] *vt.* to smoke (*cigarettes, etc.*)

курица [kōō-ri-tsa] *sf.* hen

куроводство [kōō-ra-vód-stvŏ] *sn.* poultry-farm

курок [kŏŏ-rók] *sm.* cock (of gun)

куролесить [kŏŏ-ra-lyé-sit'] *vi.* to play pranks

куропатка [kŏŏ-ra-pát-ka] *sf.* partridge

курорт [kŏŏ-rórt] *sm.* health-resort

курослеп [kŏŏ-ra-slyép] *sm.* buttercup

курочка [kŏŏ-rach-ka] *sf.* pullet

курс [kŏŏrs] *sm.* course; policy; rate of exchange

курсив [kŏŏr-s'ēv] *sm.* typ. italic

курсировать [kŏŏr-s'ē-ra-vat'] *vt.* to ply

курточка [kŏŏr-tach-ka] *sf.* lady's jacket

курчавый [kŏŏr-chā-văy] *adj.* curly, brittle

курьёзный [kŏŏr-ryóz-năy] *adj.* curious, strange

курятина [kŏŏ-ryā-t'i-na] *sf.* fowl

курятник [kŏŏ-ryāt-n'ik] *sm.* poultry-house

курящий [kŏŏ-ryā-shchi] *sm.* smoker

кус [kŏŏs] *sm.* morsel

кусать [kŏŏ-sāt'] (укусить) *vt.* to bite, to nibble

кусок [kŏŏ-sók] *sm.* bit, piece

кусочек [kŏŏ-só-chek] *sm.* small piece

куст [kŏŏst] *sm.* bush, shrub; **-арник** [-ār-n'ik] *sm.* brush-wood, shrubbery

кустарь [kŏŏs-tār'] *sm.* amateur craftsman

кустарный [kŏŏs-tār-năy] *adj.* home-made

кутать [kŏŏ-tat'] (за-) *vt.* to wrap up; **-ся** [-sya] *vr.* to wrap oneself up

кутёж [kŏŏ-tyó*zh*] *sm.* carouse

кутерма [kŏŏ-tyer-mā] *sf.* inclement weather; *fig.* commotion, stir

кутить [kŏŏ-t'ēt'] (за-) *vi.* to revel

кухарка [kŏŏ-chār-ka] *sf.* cook (female)

кухня [kŏŏch-nya] *sf.* kitchen

кухонный [kŏŏ-chōn-năy] *adj.* culinary, kitchen-

куча [kŏŏ-cha] *sf.* heap, pile; throng

кучер [kŏŏ-cher] *sm.* coachman, driver

куш [kŏŏsh] *sm.* sum (of money); stake; *interj.* down! (as to a dog)

кушак [kŏŏ-shāk] *sm.* belt, girdle, sash

кушанье [kŏŏ-sha-nye] *sn.* dish, fare, food

кушать [kŏŏ-shat'] (по-) *vt.* to eat; **пожалуйста –!** [pa-*zh*āl-sta –] (please) dinner is served!

кушетка [kŏŏ-shét-ka] *sf.* couch

Л

лабаз [la-bāz] *sm.* corn-shop

лабазник [la-bāz-n'ik] *sm.* corn-merchant

лаванда [la-vān-da] *sf.* lavender

лавина [la-v'ē-na] *sf.* avalanche

лавировать [la-v'ē-ra-vat'] *vi. naut.* to tack, veer; *fig.* to manœuvre

лавка [lāv-ka] *sf.* bench; shop

лавочник [lā-vach-n'ik] *sm.* shopkeeper

лавр [lávr] *sm.* laurel

лаг [lág] *sm. naut.* log

лага [lá-ga] *sf. tech.* bolster

лагерь [lá-gyer'] *sm.* camp, encampment

лад [lád] *sm.* accord, harmony; fretwork; **петь в –** [pyét' v –] to sing in tune

ладан [lá-dan] *sm.* incense

ладить [lá-d'it'] *vi.* to agree, be on good terms

ладно [lád-nŏ] *adv.* in concord, in tune; **–!** all right! very well! O.K.!

ладный [lád-năy] *adj.* harmonious; suitable

ладонь [la-dón'] *sf. anat.* palm

ладья [la-dyá] *sf.* castle (*chess*)

лаз [láz] *sm.* manhole

лазарет [la-za-ryét] *sm.* field ambulance; infirmary

лазить [lá-z'it'] (c–) *vi.* to clamber, creep

лазурь [la-zŏŏr'] *sf.* azure

лазутчик [la-zŏŏt-chik] *sm. mil.* scout

лай [láy] *sm.* bark, barking, yelp

лайка [láy-ka] *sf.* doe-skin; Eskimo dog, husky

лак [lák] *sm.* lacquer, varnish

лакать [la-kát] *vt.* to lap; to swill

лакание [lá-ka-nye] *sn.* lapping

лакей [la-kéy] *sm.* footman

лакировать [la-k'ĕ-ra-vat] *vt.* to varnish

лакировка [la-k'i-róv-ka] *sf.* varnishing

лакомка [lá-kam-ka] *sm.f.* gourmand

лакомство [lá-kam-stvŏ] *sn.* dainties, delicacies

лакомный [lá-kam-năy] *adj.* tasty; sweet-toothed

лакрица [la-krē-tsa] *sf.* liquorice

лампа [lám-pa] *sf.* lamp; **–да** [–da] *sf.* ikon-lamp

лангуст [lan-gŏŏst] *sm.* lobster

ландыш [lán-dăsh] *sm.* lily of the valley

лань [lán] *sf.* deer, doe; hind

лапа [lá-pa] *sf.* paw; pad

лапушка [lá-push-ka] *sf.* darling

лапчатый [lap-chá-tăy] *adj.* web-footed

лапша [lap-shá] *sf.* vermicelli soup

ларёк [la-ryók] *sm.* booth, stall

ларец [la-ryéts] *sm.* coffer, small chest

ларь [lár'] *sm.* bin, trunk

ласка [lás-ka] *sf.* caress, endearment; weasel

ласкатель [las-ká-tyel'] *sm.* flatterer

ласкательный [las-kă-tyel'-năy] *adj.* caressing

ласкать [las-kát] (по–) *vt.* to caress, fondle, pet

ласковость [lás-ka-vŏst'] *sf.* affability, tenderness

ласковый [lás-ka-văy] *adj.* affectionate; kind

ластиться [las-t'ét'-sya] *vi.* to fawn

ласточка [lás-tach-ka] *sf.* swallow

лата [lá-ta] *sf.* patch (*mending*)

латать [la-tat'] *vt.* to patch

латинский [la-t'ēn-ski] *adj.* Latin

латка [lát-ka] *sf.* patch, piece; stew-pan

латук [la-tŏŏk] *sm.* lettuce

латунь [la-tŏŏn'] *sf.* brass

латы [lá-tă] *sf. pl.* cuirass

латынь [la-tăn'] *sf.* Latin

лафет [la-fyét] *sm.* gun-carriage

лачуга [la-chŏŏ-ga] *sf.* hovel, shanty

лаять [lā-yat'] *vi.* to bark

лганьё [lga-nyó] *sn.* lies, lying

лгать [lgat'] (co-) *vi.* to lie, tell lies

лгун [lgōōn] *sm.* **-ья** [-ya] *sf.* liar

лебёдка [lye-byód-ka] *sf.* female swan; capstan, winch

лебедь [lyé-bed'] *sm.* swan

лебяжий [lye-byá-zhi] *adj.* swanlike, swan's

лев [lyev] *sm.* lion

левкой [lyev-kóy] *sm.* stock, wallflower

левша [lyev-shá] *sm.* left-handed person

левый [lyé-vǎy] *adj.* left

легальность [lye-gál'-nŏst'] *sf.* legality

легальный [lye-gál'-nǎy] *adj.* legal

лёгкие [lyóch-ki-ye] *sn. pl.* lights (*of animals*)

лёгкий [lyóch-ki] *adj.* easy, light; slight; simple

легко [lyech-kó] *adv.* lightly, softly; easily; **-ватый** [-vá-tǎy] *adj.* rather easy; **-верие** [-vyé-rye] *sn.* credulity

лёгкое [lyóch-ka-ye] *sn.* lung

легкомысленный [lyoch-ka-mǎs-lyen-nǎy] *adj.* flippant, thoughtless

лёгкость [lyóch-kŏst'] *sf.* lightness; ease; frivolity

лёгочный [lyó-gach-nǎy] *adj.* pulmonary

легчать [lyech-chát'] (по-) *vi.* to lighten (*in weight*); to mitigate

лёд [lyod] *sm.* ice

леденец [lye-dye-nyéts] *sm.* sugar candy

леденить [lye-dye-n'ět'] *vt.* to freeze

ледник [lyéd-n'ik] *sm.* ice-box, ice-house; refrigerator

ледник [lyed-n'ěk] *sm.* glacier

ледокол [lye-da-kól] *sm.* ice-breaker

ледяной [lye-dya-nóy] *adj.* glacial, icy

лежалый [lye-zhá-lǎy] *adj.* musty, old, stale (*of eatables*)

лежать [lye-zhát'] (по-) *vi.* to lie, recline, repose; to be laid up

лежачий [lye-zhá-chi] *adj.* lying prone; prostrate; recumbent

лежень [lyé-zhen'] *sm. tech.* ledger, sleeper; foundation beam

лезвие [lyéz-vye] *sn.* blade, edge

лезть [lyézt'] (по-) *vi.* to ascend, scale

лейка [lyé-ka] *sf.* watering-can

лекало [lye-kä-lŏ] *sn.* form, mould

лекарственный [lye-kár-stvyen-nǎy] *adj.* medicinal

лекарство [lye-kár-stvŏ] *sn.* medicine

лектор [lyék-tŏr] *sm.* lecturer, reader; **-ство** [-stvŏ] *sn.* lectureship

лекция [lyék-tsya] *sf.* lecture

лелеять [lye-lyé-yat'] *vt.* to cherish, foster, nurse; to pamper

лемех [lyé-myech] *sm.* ploughshare

лён [lyón] *sm.* flax

ленивец [lye-n'ě-vets] *sm.* idler, lazy person; sloth

ленивый [lye-n'ě-vǎy] *adj.* idle, lazy, sluggish

лениться [lye-n'ĕt'-sya] (по-) *vi.* to be idle, lazy

леность [lyé-nŏst'] *sf.* indolence

лента [lyén-ta] *sf.* band, ribbon; tape

лентяй [lyen-tyáy] *sm.*, **-ка** *sf.* lazy person

лень [lyén'] *sf.* idleness, laziness

лепесток [lye-pes-tók] *sm.* [petal]

лепетание [lye-pe-tá-nye] *sn.* chattering; murmur

лепёшка [lye-pyósh-ka] *sf.* pancake; lozenge

лепить [lye-p'ĕt'] (с-) *vt.* to model; to sculpture; **-ся** [-sya] *vi.* to cling to

лепка [lyép-ka] *sf.* modelling

лепной [lyep-nóy] *adj.* plastic

лепта [lyép-ta] *sf.* mite

лес [lyés] *sm.* forest, wood

леса [lye-sá] *sm. pl.* woodlands; scaffolding; fishing-line

лесистый [lye-sĕs-tăy] *adj.* timbered, woody

лесник [lye-s-n'ĕk] *sm.* forester

лесничество [lyes-n'ĕ-chest-vŏ] *sn.* forestry

лесной [lyes-nóy] *adj.* silvan

лесопильня [lyes-na-p'ĕl'-nya] *sf.* saw-mill

лесопромышленность [lyes-na-pra-măsh-lyen-nŏst'] *sf.* timber industry

лесоводство [lye-sa-vód-stvŏ] *sn.* forestry; sylviculture

лестница [lyést-n'i-tsa] *sf.* staircase, stairs; ladder

лестный [lyést-năy] *adj.* complimentary

лесть [lyést'] *sf.* adulation, flattery

лёт [lyót] *sm.* flight; **на лету** [na lye-tōō] in flight

лета [lye-tá] *pl.* age, years

летание [lye-tá-nye] *sn.* flying

летать [lye-tát'] (по-) *vi.* to fly; to navigate (*plane*)

лететь [lye-tĕt'] (по-) *vi.* to fly (*bird*); to tear along

летний [lyét-ni] *adj.* summer-, summery

лето [lye-tó] *sn.* summer; year; **-м** [-m] in summer

летопись [lyé-ta-p'is'] *sf.* annals, chronicle

летосчисление [lye-ta-schis-lyé-nye] *sn.* chronology

летун [lye-tōōn] *sm.* flyer

летучий [lye-tōō-chi] *adj.* flying; volatile

лётчик [lyót-chik] *sm.* airman

лечебница [lye-chéb-n'i-tsa] *sf.* hospital

лечебный [lye-chéb-năy] *adj.* medical; medicinal

лечение [lye-ché-nye] *sn.* cure, healing; treatment

лечить [lye-chĕt'] *vt.* to cure

лец [lyeshch] *sm.* bream

лещадь [lye-shchăd'] *sf.* slab

лещина [lye-shché-na] *sf.* hazel

лже- [lzhye] *prefix.* false-, mock-, pseudo-; **-свидетельство** [-sv'i-dyé-tyel'-stvŏ] *sn.* perjury

лжец [lzhets] *sm.* liar

лживость [lzhĕ-vŏst'] *sf.* falsehood, mendacity

лживый [lzhĕ-văy] *adj.* deceitful

ли [l'ĕ] *interrog. particle,* if, whether; *conj.,* **ли . . . ли,** either . . . or . . . (ли *cannot commence a sentence, use* **если**)

либеральность [l'i-bye-rál'-nŏst'] sf. liberal views

либо [l'ē-bŏ] adv. or; - . . . - . . . either - . . . or . . .

ливень [l'ē-vyen] sm. downpour, heavy shower

ливрея [l'iv-ré-ya] sf. livery

лига [l'ē-ga] sf. league (distance); confederacy, guild

лигатура [l'i-ga-tōō-ra] sf. alloy; med., typ. ligature

лизать [l'i-zát'] (лизнуть) vt. to lick

лизоблюд [l'i-za-blyŏ̄d] sm. sponger

лик [l'ēk] sm. countenance; image; naut. leech

ликовать [l'i-ka-vát'] (воз-) vt.i. to acclaim; to rejoice; to triumph

ликующий [l'i-kōō-yōō-shchi] adj. jubilant, triumphant

лилейный [l'i-lyéy-năy] adj. lily-white

лилия [l'ē-lya] sf. lily

лиловый [l'i-ló-văy] adj. lilac, violet (colour)

лиман [l'i-mán] sm. bay; estuary

лимон [l'i-món] sm. lemon

лингвистика [l'in-gvēs-t'i-ka] sf. linguistics

линевать [l'i-nye-vát'] (на-) vt. to draw parallel lines

линейка [l'i-nyéy-ka] sf. ruler; typ. setting-rule

линейный [l'i-nyéy-năy] adj. linear

линза [l'ēn-za] sf. lens

линия [l'ē-nya] sf. line

линялый [l'i-nyá-lăy] adj. discoloured, faded; moulted

линять [l'i-nyát'] (по-) vi. to fade; to moult

липа [l'ē-pa] sf. lime-tree

липкий [l'ēp-ki] adj. clammy, sticky (cosity)

липкость [l'ēp-kŏst'] sf. viscosity

липнуть [l'ēp-nōōt'] (при-) vi. to stick to; adhere to

липняк [l'ip-nyák] sm. lime-grove

лира [l'ē-ra] sf. lyre

лирик [l'ē-rik] sm. lyric poet; -a, lyric poetry

лирический [l'i-rē-ches-ki] adj. lyrical

лиса [l'i-sá] sf. fox

лисёнок [l'i-syó-nŏk] sm. young fox

лисий [l'ē-si] adj. fox-, fox-like, vulpine

лисица [l'i-sē-tsa] sf. fox, vixen

лист [l'ēst] sm. leaf; blade; sheet; -ва [-vá] sf. foliage, leaves

лиственница [l'ēst-vyen-n'i-tsa] sf. larch

листик [l'ēs-t'ik] sm. small leaf, single sheet

листок [l'is-tók] sm. leaflet, news-sheet

литавра [l'i-tá-vra] sf. kettle-drum

лития [l'i-tá-nya] sf. litany

литейня [l'i-tyéy-nya] sf. foundry

литейщик [l'i-tyéy-shchik] sm. founder, smelter

литера [l'ē-tye-ra] sf. typ. letter, type

литератор [l'i-tye-rá-tŏr] sm. man of letters

литература [l'i-tye-ra-tōō-ra] sf. literature

литературный [l'i-tye-ra-tōōr-năy] adj. literary

литовец [l'i-tó-vyets] sm., **литовка** [l'i-tóv-ka] sf. Lithuanian

литовский [l'i-tóv-ski] *adj.* Lithuanian

литургия [l'i-tōōr-gya] *sf.* liturgy, mass

лить [l'ět'] (по-) *vt.* to pour; to shed; to spill; to cast, mould

литьё [l'i-tyó] *sn.* casting, founding, moulding

лиф [l'ĕf] *sm.* bodice; **-чик** [-chik] *sm.* slip, under-bodice

лихва [l'ich-vá] *sf.* interest, profit; usury

лихо [l'ē-chó] *sn.* evil, grudge, malice; **-дей** [-dyéy] malicious person; **-имец** [-ē-myets] *sm.* extortioner

лихой [l'i-chóy] *adj.* bold, spirited; evil

лихорадка [l'i-cha-rád-ka] *sf.* fever

лихорадочный [l'i-cha-rá-dach-năy] *adj.* feverish

лицевой [l'i-tse-vóy] *adj.* facial

лицезрение [l'i-tse-zré-nye] *sn.* aspect; contemplation; perception

лицей [l'i-tséy] *sm.* college; Lyceum

лицемер [l'i-tse-myér] *sm.* hypocrite; **-ие** [-ye] *sn.* hypocrisy

лицеприятный [l'i-tse-pri-yát'năy] *adj.* partial

лицо [l'i-tsó] *sn.* face; person; **лицом к лицу** [l'i-tsóm-kl'i-tsōō] face-to-face

личина [l'i-chē-na] *sf.* guise

личинка [l'i-chēn-ka] *sf.* larva; grub; maggot

личность [l'ĕch-nŏst'] *sf.* personality

личный [l'ĕch-năy] *adj.* individual, personal

лишай [l'i-sháy] *sm. bot.* lichen; *med.* tetter

лишать [l'i-shát'] (лишить) *vt.* to defraud, deprive

лишек [l'ē-shek] *sm.* excess, surplus

лишенец [l'i-shē-nyets] *sm.* disfranchised person

лишение [l'i-shē-nye] *sn.* deprivation; forfeiture, loss

лишний [l'ĕsh-n'i] *adj.* superfluous; spare; unnecessary

лишь [l'ĕsh] *adv.* only; *conj.* as soon as

лоб [lob] *sm.* brow, forehead; **-астый** [-ās-tăy] *adj.* having a high forehead

лобзик [lób-zik] *sm.* fretsaw

лобный [lób-năy] *adj.* frontal

ловец [la-vyéts] *sm.* hunter

ловить [la-v'ēt'] (поймать) *vt.* to catch, hunt

ловкач [lav-kách] *sm.* dodger

ловкий [lóv-ki] *adj.* adroit, dexterous; shrewd

ловкость [lóv-kŏst'] *sf.* dexterity; skill

ловля [lóv-lya] *sf.* catching, hunting

ловушка [la-vōōsh-ka] *sf.* trap

логика [ló-gi-ka] *sf.* logic

логичный [la-gēch-năy] *adj.* logical

логовище [ló-ga-v'i-shche] *sn.* den, lair

лодка [lód-ka] *sf.* boat

лодочник [ló-dach-n'ik] *sm.* boatman; ferryman

лодыжка [la-dắzh-ka] *sf.* ankle

ложа [ló-zha] *sf. theat.* box; lodge (*as masonic, etc.*)

ложиться [la-zhít'-sya] (лечь) *vi.* to lie down; **- спать** [- spăt'] to go to bed

ложка [lózh-ka] *sf.* spoon

ложный [lózh-nay] *adj.* fallacious, false

ложь [lozh'] *sf.* falsehood, lie

лоза [la-zá] *sf.* rod, twig; **виноградная —** [vi-na-grád-na-ya —] vine

лозунг [ló-zōong] *sm.* password; slogan

локальный [la-kál'-nay] *adj.* local

локомобиль [la-ka-ma-b'él'] *sm.* steam-engine, tractor

локон [ló-kŏn] *sm.* curl, lock, ringlet

локоть [ló-kŏt'] *sm.* elbow

лом [lom] *sm.* fragments, scrap; crow-bar

ломать [la-mát'] (c-) *vt.* to break, fracture, smash; to break down, demolish

ломбард [lam-bárd] *sm.* pawnshop

ломкий [lóm-ki] *adj.* brittle, fragile

ломовик [la-ma-v'ék] *sm.* cart-horse; drayman

ломота [la-mó-ta] *sf.* rheumatic pain

ломоть [la-mót'] *sm.* slice

лоно [ló-nŏ] *sn.* bosom, lap

лопасть [ló-past'] *sf.* paddle; fan; lobe

лопата [la-pá-ta] *sf.* shovel, spade

лопатка [la-pát-ka] *sf.* small shovel; scoop; trowel; shoulder-blade

лопать [ló-pat'] (лóпнуть) *vt.* to burst, to explode; **-ся** [-sya] *vi.* to burst, crack, split

лосина [la-s'é-na] *sf.* chamois-leather

лоск [losk] *sm.* gloss, lustre

лосось [ló-sŏs'] *sm.* salmon

лось [los'] *sm.* elk

лотерея [la-tye-ré-ya] *sf.* lottery, raffle

лоток [la-tók] *sm.* hawker's tray; gutter

лохань [la-chán'] *sf.* wash-tub

лохматый [lach-má-tay] *adj.* dishevelled, shaggy

лохмотья [lach-mó-tya] *sn. pl.* rags, tatters

лоция [ló-tsya] *sf.* sailing directions

лоцман [lóts-man] *sm.* pilot

лошадь [ló-shad'] *sf.* horse

лошак [la-shák] *sm.* mule

лощина [la-shché-na] *sf.* dell, hollow

лощить [la-shchét'] (вы́-) *vt.* to gloss, polish

луб [lōob] *sm.* bast

лубок [lōo-bók] *sm.* splint

луг [lōog] *sm.* meadow

лудильщик [lōo-d'él'-shchik] *sm.* tinsmith

лужа [lōo-zha] *sf.* pool, puddle

лужайка [lōo-zháy-ka] *sf.* grass-plot; lawn

луза [lōo-za] *sf.* pocket of billiard table

лук [lōok] *sm.* bow (*weapon*); onion

лукавство [lōo-káv-stvŏ] *sn.* slyness

луковица [lōo-ka-vi-tsa] *sf.* bulb; onion

луна [lōo-ná] *sf.* moon

лунный [lōon-nay] *adj.* lunar

лупа [lōo-pa] *sf.* magnifying glass

лупить [lōo-p'ét'] (об-) *vt.* to peel; to beat, thrash; **-ся** [-sya] *vi.* to come off, peel off

луч [lōoch] *sm.* beam, ray

лучезарный [lōo-che-zár-nay] *adj.* radiant

лучина [lōo-ché-na] *sf.* splinter

лучистый [lōō-chēs-tăy] *adj.* radial, radiant

лучиться [lōō-chít'-sya] *vi.* to beam, shine brightly

лучший [lōōch-shĭ] *adj.* best

лущение [lōō-shché-nye] *sn.* husking, shelling

лущить [lōō-shchět'] (вы-) *vt.* to husk, scale, shell; to crack

лыжа [lǎ-zha] *sf.* ski, snow-shoe

лыжник [lázh-n'ik] *sm.* skier

лысеть [lǎ-syét'] *vi.* to grow bald

лысина [lǎ-s'i-na] *sf.* bald patch; star (*on animal*)

лысый [lá-săy] *adj.* bald

львиный [l'vĕ-năy] *adj.* leonine, lion's

львица [l'vĕ-tsa] *sf.* lioness

льгота [l'gó-ta] *sf.* exemption, immunity; privilege

льдина [l'd'ē-na] *sf.* block of ice

льдистый [l'dĕs-tăy] *adj.* icy

льняной [l'nya-nóy] *adj.* flaxen; linseed

льстец [l'styets] *sm.* flatterer

льстивый [l'st'ĕ-văy] *adj.* flattering

льстить [l'stĕt'] *vi.* to flatter

любезник [lyŏŏ-byéz-n'ik] *sm.* gallant, wooer

любезничать [lyŏŏ-byéz-n'i-chat] *vi.* to court, pay compliments, seek favours

любезный [lyŏŏ-byéz-năy] *adj.* civil, obliging; polite; dear, kind

любезность [lyŏŏ-byéz-nŏst'] *sf.* courtesy, kindness

любимец [lyŏŏ-b'ĕ-myets] *sm.*, **любимица** [lyŏŏ-b'ĕ-mi-tsa] *sf.* darling, favourite, pet

любимый [lyŏŏ-b'ĕ-măy] *adj.* beloved

любитель [lyŏŏ-b'ĕ-tyel'] *sm.*, **-ница** [-n'i-tsa] *sf.* amateur

любить [lyŏŏ-b'ĕt'] (по-) *vt.* to love; to like

любоваться [lyŏŏ-ba-vát'-sya] (по-) *vi.* to admire

любовник [lyŏŏ-bóv-n'ik] *sm.*, **любовница** [lyŏŏ-bóv-n'i-tsa] *sf.* lover, sweetheart

любовный [lyŏŏ-bóv-năy] *adj.* amorous

любовь [lyŏŏ-bóv'] *sf.* love

любознательный [lyŏŏ-ba-znǎ-tyel'-năy] *adj.* curious, eager

любой [lyŏŏ-bóy] *adj.* any, whichever

любопытный [lyŏŏ-ba-pát-năy] *adj.* inquisitive

любопытство [lyŏŏ-ba-strás-tye] *sn.* lust

любостраcтный [lyŏŏ-ba-strást-năy] *adj.* lecherous

любостяжательный [lyŏŏ-ba-stya-zhá-tyel'-năy] *adj.* avaricious, greedy

любящий [lyŏŏ-byă-shchi] *adj.* affectionate, loving

люди [lyŏŏ-d'i] *sm. pl.* people

людный [lyŏŏd-năy] *adj.* crowded, populous

людская [lyŏŏd-skă-ya] *sf.* servants' hall

людской [lyŏŏd-skóy] *adj.* human; people's

люк [lyŏŏk] *sm.* hatch, trap-door

люлька [lyŏŏl'-ka] *sf.* cradle, cot; pipe (*smoker's*)

лютик [lyŏŏ-t'ik] *sm.* buttercup

лютый [lyŏŏ-tăy] *adj.* ferocious, fierce, severe

ля [lyă] *sn. mus.* A

лягавая [lya-gă-va-ya] *adj. as sf.* hound; setter

лягавый [lya-gă-văy] *adj.* hound-like

лягать [lya-găt'] (**лягнуть**) *vi.* to kick

лягушка [lya-gōōsh-ka] *sf.* frog

ляжка [lyázh-ka] *sf.* haunch, thigh

лязг [lyäzg] *sm.* clank, noise, rattle

лямка [lyäm-ka] *sf.* strap; **тянуть на -ах** [tya-nōōt' na -ach] in tow; **тянуть лямку** [tya-nōōt' lyäm-kōō] *coll.* to drudge, toil

М

магазин [ma-ga-z'ēn] *sm.* shop, store, warehouse

магистр [ma-gēstr] *sm.* Master (*university degree*); **- искусств** [- is-kōōstv] M.A.; head of religious orders

магистральный [ma-gi-străl'-năy] *adj.* leading, main, principal

магистрант [ma-gi-stränt] *sm.* undergraduate

магнетический [ma-gnye-t'ē-ches-ki] *adj.* magnetic

магнит [mag-n'ēt] *sm.* magnet

мажор [ma-zhór] *sm. mus.* major

мазать [ma-zat'] (на-, по-) *vt.* to anoint; to smear

мазилка [ma-z'ēl-ka] *sf.* brush; dauber

мазь [măz'] *sf.* grease, ointment

май [măy] *sm.* May

майор [ma-yór] *sm. mil.* major; **-ство** [-stvó] *sn.* rank of major; **-ша** [-sha] *sf.* major's wife

майский [măy-ski] *adj.* of May, May-

мак [măk] *sm.* poppy

макать [ma-kăt'] (**макнуть**) *vt.* to dip, soak

маклер [ma-klyer] *sm.* stock broker

маковка [mă-kav-ka] *sf.* crown (*of head*); cupola; summit

макрель [ma-kryél'] *sf.* mackerel

максимально [ma-ksi-măl'-nŏ] *adv.* at most; as much as possible

макулатура [ma-kōō-la-tōō-ra] *sf.* waste paper; trashy books; *typ.* mackled sheet

малевать [ma-lye-văt'] (на-) *vt.* to daub, whitewash

малейший [ma-lyéy-shi] *adj.* least, slightest

маленький [mă-lyen'-ki] *adj.* little, small; diminutive

малец [mă-lyets] *sm.* lad

малина [ma-l'ē-na] *sf.* raspberry

малинник [ma-l'ēn-n'ik] *sm.* raspberry-bush

малиновка [ma-l'ē-nav-ka] *sf.* robin

малиновый [ma-l'ē-na-văy] *adj.* raspberry-; crimson

малка [măl-ka] *sf. tech.* bevel

мало [mă-la] *adv.* few, little; **-по-малу** [-pa-mă-lōō] by degrees

маловажный [ma-la-văzh-năy] *adj.* unimportant

маловато [ma-la-vă-tŏ] *adv.* insufficiently

малограмотный [ma-la-gră-mat-năy] *adj.* semi-educated

малодушный [ma-la-dōōsh-năy] *adj.* faint-hearted

малоимущий [ma-la-i-mōō-shchi] *adj.* needy, poor

малокровие [ma-la-kró-vye] *sn.* anaemia

малокровный [ma-la-króv-nǎy] *adj.* anaemic

малолетний [ma-la-lyét-n'i] *adj.* under age; juvenile

малолетство [ma-la-lyét-stvǒ] *sn.* infancy, minority

малорослый [ma-la-rós-lǎy] *adj.* under-sized

малость [mǎ-lŏst'] *sf.* small-ness, trifle

малоценный [ma-la-tsyén-nǎy] *adj.* cheap, of little value

малый [mǎ-lǎy] *adj.* little, small; **бесконечно –** [byes-ka-nyéch-nǒ –] infinitesimal; *fig.* little fellow, good lad

малыш [ma-lǎsh] *sm.* mite, tot; kiddy

мальва [mǎl'-va] *sf.* holly-hock

мальчик [mǎl'-chik] *sm.* boy, youngster

мальчишка [mal'-chésh-ka] *sm.* nipper, urchin

малютка [ma-lyŏŏt-ka] *sm., f.* baby, tiny tot

маляр [ma-lyǎr] *sm.* painter and decorator

мандрил [man-drél] *sm.* ba-boon

маневрировать [ma-nye-vrē-ra-vat'] *vt.* to manœuvre; to shunt

манеж [ma-nyézh] *sm.* riding-school

манера [ma-nyé-ra] *sf.* man-ner, style, way; **манеры** [ma-nyé-rǎ] *sf. pl.* manners; behaviour

манерка [ma-nyér-ka] *sf.* soldier's canteen, mess-tin

манерность [ma-nyér-nŏst] *sf.* affectation, mannerism

манжета [man-zhé-ta] *sf.* cuff

манить [ma-n'ēt'] (при-) *vt.* to attract; to beckon; to en-tice

манишка [ma-n'ésh-ka] *sf.* dicky, false shirt-front

мантия [mǎn-tya] *sf.* gown, mantle, robe

марал [ma-rǎl] *sm.* stag

марать [ma-rǎt'] (за-) *vt.* to smear, soil; to daub; to scribble

марганец [mǎr-ga-nyets] *sm.* manganese

маргаритка [mar-ga-rét-ka] *sf.* daisy

марево [mǎ-rye-vǒ] *sn.* mirage

марена [ma-ryé-na] *sf.* mad-der

маринад [ma-ri-nǎd] *sm.* pickles

мариновать [ma-ri-na-vǎt'] *vt.* to pickle, preserve (*in vinegar*)

маринованный [ma-ri-nó-van-nǎy] *adj.* pickled

марка [mǎr-ka] *sf.* stamp; mark; **почтовая –** [pach-tó-va-ya –] postage-stamp; **торговая –** [tar-gó-va-ya –] trade-mark

марля [mǎr-lya] *sf.* gauze

март [mǎrt] *sm.* March

марш [mǎrsh] *sm.* march

маршировать [mar-shē-ra-vat'] *vi.* to march

маршрут [marsh-rōōt] *sm.* route-march; itinerary

маска [mǎs-ka] *sf.* guise, mask

маскарад [mas-ka-rǎd] *sm.* fancy-dress ball

масленица [mãs-lye-n'i-tsa] *sf.* Shrove-tide; carnival

маслёнка [mas-lyón-ka] *sf.* butterdish; oil-can

маслина [mas-l'ē-na] *sf.* olive

маслить [mãs-l'it'] (за-) *vt.* to butter, oil

масло [mãs-lŏ] *sn.* butter; oil

маслобойка [mas-la-bóy-ka] *sf.* churn

маслобойня [mas-la-bóy-nya] *sf.* creamery; oil-mill

масон [ma-són] *sm.* free-mason

масонский [ma-són-ski] *adj.* masonic

масонство [ma-són-stvŏ] *sn.* freemasonry

масса [mãs-sa] *sf.* heap, lot, mass

массажист [mas-sa-zhēst] *sm.* masseur; -ка, *sf.* masseuse

массивный [mas-s'ēv-nǎy] *adj.* massive, solid

массировать [mas-s'ē-ra-vat'] *vt.* to massage; to knead

мастер [mãs-tyer] *sm.* artisan, craftsman; master; skilled worker; foreman

мастерская [mas-tyer-skã-ya] *sf.* workshop

мастерской [mas-tyer-skóy] *adj.* skilful, workmanlike

мастерство [mas-tyer-stvó] *sn.* craftsmanship, skill

мастика [mas-t'ēka] *sf.* mastic; chewing gum

маститый [mas-t'ē-tǎy] *adj.* venerable

масть [mãst'] *sf.* suit of cards

масштаб [mas-shtãb] *sm.* scale, standard

мат [mãt] *sm.* checkmate, mate

математик [ma-tye-mã-t'ik] *sm.* mathematician; -ка, *sf.* mathematics

материал [ma-tye-ryãl] *sm.* material; stuff

материк [ma-tye-r'ēk] *sm.* continent, mainland; -овый [-óvǎy] *adj.* continental

материнский [ma-tye-rěn-ski] *adj.* maternal

материнство [ma-tye-rěn-stvŏ] *sn.* motherhood

материя [ma-tyé-rya] *sf.* matter, substance; cloth, fabric, material

материчатый [ma-tyer-chã-tǎy] *adj.* textile, of textile

матка [mãt-ka] *sf.* womb; dam (*of animals*); queen (*of bees*)

матовый [mã-ta-vǎy] *adj.* dull, mat

маточник [mã-tach-n'ik] *sm.* ovary; cell (*of queen-bee*)

матрац [mat-rãts] *sm.* mattress

матрица [mat-r'ē-tsa] *sf.* *typ.* matrix

матрос [ma-trós] *sm.* sailor

мать [mãt'] *sf.* mother

мах [mãch] *sm.* stroke, swing

махать [ma-chãt'] (махнуть) *vt.* to wave; to wag; to flap

махинация [ma-chi-nã-tsya] *sf.* machination, plot

маховик [ma-cha-v'ēk] *sm.* fly-wheel

мачеха [mã-che-cha] *sf.* step-mother

мачта [mãch-ta] *sf.* mast

машина [ma-shē-na] *sf.* engine, machine

машинальный [ma-shi-nãl'-nǎy] *adj.* mechanical

машинист [ma-shi-n'ēst] *sm.*, **-ка** [-ka] *sf.* machinist; typist; machine-minder

машинка [ma-shēn-ka] *sf.* typewriter

маяк [ma-yāk] *sm.* beacon, lighthouse

маятник [mā-yat-n'ik] *sm.* pendulum

маяться [mā-yat'-sya] *vi.* to pine, suffer

мгла [mglā] *sf.* haze, mist

мглистый [mgl'ēs-tăy] *adj.* clouded, misty

мгновение [mgna-vyé-nye] *sn.* instant, moment

мгновенный [mgna-vyén-năy] *adj.* instantaneous, momentary

мебель [mé-byel] *sf.* piece of furniture; *coll.* furniture

мебельщик [mé-byel'-shchik] *sm.* furniture-dealer; cabinet-maker

меблировать [me-bl'ē-ra-vat'] (об-) *vt.* to furnish; to upholster

меблировка [me-bl'i-róv-ka] *sf.* furnishing; upholstering; furniture

меблировщик [me-bl'i-róv-shchik] *sm.* upholsterer

мёд [myód] *sm.* honey; mead

медаль [mye-dāl'] *sf.* medal; **-ер** [-yér] *sm.* medalist

медведка [myed-vyéd-ka] *sf.* truck

медведь [myed-vyéd'] *sm.* bear; **белый** [-byé-lăy -] polar bear; **серый** [-syé-răy -] grizzly bear

медвежонок [myed-vye-zhó-nŏk] *sm.* bear-cub

медвежий [myed-vye-zhī] *adj.* bear-like, ursine; *fig.* awkward, rough, surly

медслянка [mye-dye-lyān-ka] *sf.* mastiff (*dog*)

медик [myé-d'ik] *sm.* medical student

медицина [mye-d'i-tsē-na] *sf.* medicine

медицинский [mye-d'i-tsēn-ski] *adj.* medical

медленный [myé-dlyen-năy] *adj.* backward, dilatory, slow

медлить [mye-dl'ēt'] (по-) *vi.* to delay, linger, tarry

медник [myéd-n'ik] *sm.* brazier; coppersmith

медный [myéd-năy] *adj.* coppery, cupreous

медовый [mye-dó-văy] *adj.* of honey, honeyed; **- месяц** [-myé-syats] honeymoon

медоносный [mye-da-nós-năy] *adj.* honey-sweet, mellifluous

медь [myed'] *sf.* copper; **жёлтая** [-zhól-ta-ya -] brass

медянка [mye-dyān-ka] *sf.* grass-snake; verdigris

межа [mye-zhā] *sf.* boundary

междометие [myezh-da-myé-tye] *sn.* interjection

между [myezh-dōō] *prep.* among, between; **- тем** [- tyém] whereas; **- прочим** [- pró-chim] by the way, in passing

международный [myezh-dōō-na-ród-năy] *adj.* international

межевание [mye-zhe-vā-nye] *sn.* survey; measuring, surveying

межевать [mye-zhe-vāt'] (на-, от-) *vt.* to survey

мел [myel] *sm.* chalk

мелкий [myél-kăy] *adj.* shallow; fine, minute; *fig.* petty

меловой [mye-la-vóy] *adj.* chalky

мелодичный [mye-la-d'échnăy] *adj.* melodious, tuneful

мелодия [mye-ló-dya] *sf.* melody, tune

меломан [mye-la-mán] *sm.* music-lover

мелочность [myé-lăchnŏst'] *sf.* meanness, pettiness

мелочный [myé-lach-năy] *adj.* mean, petty; narrow-minded

мелочь [myé-lŏch] *sf.* detail, trifle; small change

мель [myél] *sf.* sand-bank; **на мель** [nă myel'] aground

мелькать [myel'-kát] (**мелькнуть**) *vi.* to flash, gleam, glisten

мельком [myel'kóm] *adv.* hastily, rapidly

мельник [myel'-n'ik] *sm.* miller

мельница [myél'-n'i-tsa] *sf.* mill

мельничный [myél'-n'ichnăy] *adj.* mill-

мельчать [myel'-chát] (**из-**) *vi.* to diminish; to become petty

мельчить [myel'-chét'] (**из-**) *vt.* to grind, pound

мелюзга [mye-lyŏōz-gá] *sf.* fry, small fry

мемуары [mye-mŏōä-ră] *pl.* memoirs

мена [myé-na] *sf.* barter, exchange

менее [myé-nye-ye] *adv.* less, under; **тем не** – [tyem nye –] none the less; **– пяти лет** [– pya-t'ĕ lyet] under five (*years of age*)

менестрель [mye-nyestryél'] *sm.* minstrel

меньше [myén'-she] *adj., adv.* less, smaller

меньшинство [myen'-shinstvó] *sn.* minority

меню [mye-nyŏō] *sn.* bill of fare

меня [mye-nyä] *pron.* me, of me, myself; **у** – [ŏō –] I have

менять [mye-nyát] *vt.* to change, vary; to exchange; **ся** [-sya] *vi.* to alter, change; to fluctuate

мера [myé-ra] *sf.* gauge, measure; **сверх меры** [svyérch myé-rä] excessively

мережа [mye-ré-zha] *sf.* fishing-net

мережка [mye-rézh-ka] *sf.* open-work

мерещиться [mye-re-shchét'-syä] (**по-**) *vi.* to glimmer; to appear dimly, to seem

мерзавец [myer-zä-vyets] *sm.* rogue, villain

мерзавка [myer-zäv-ka] *sf.* vile creature

мёрзнуть [myer-znŏōt'] *vi.* to freeze; to shiver

мерзостный [myér-zast-năy] *adj.* detestable

мерзость [myér-zŏst'] *sf.* abomination, meanness

мерило [mye-rĕ-lŏ] *sn.* scale, standard

мерить [myé-rit'] *vt.* to measure; to survey

мерка [myér-ka] *sf.* measure, measuring; **по мерке** [pa myér-ke] bespoke, made to measure

меркнуть [myér-knŏōt'] (**по-**) *vi.* to fade

мерлан [myer-lán] *sm.* whiting (*sea-fish*)

мерлушка [myer-lōōsh-ka] *sf.* lambskin

мерный [myér-năy] *adj.* measured; rhythmic

мероприятие [mye-ra-pr'i-yá-tye] *sn.* legislative measure

мертвенность [myér-tvyen-nŏst'] *sf.* deathly paleness; ghastliness

мертвенный [myér-tvyen-năy] *adj.* deathly, ghastly, wan

мертветь [myer-tvyét'] *vi.* to become numb

мертвец [myer-tvyéts] *sm.* corpse; ghost; **-кая** [-káya] *sf.* mortuary

мертвечина [myer-tvye-ché-na] *sf.* garbage

мертвить [myer-tvét'] *vt.* to deaden

мертворождённый [myer-tva-razh-dyón-năy] *adj.* still-born

мёртвый [myór-tvăy] *adj.* dead

мертель [myér-tyel'] *sf.* mortar

мерцание [myer-tsá-nye] *sn.* blinking, twinkling

месиво [myé-si-vŏ] *sn.* mash; *fig.* jumble, medley

месить [mye-s'ét'] (раз-, с-) *vt.* to knead

месса [myés-sa] *sf.* Mass

местечко [myes-tyéch-ko] *sn.* hamlet; small town

мести [myes-t'é] (вы-) *vt.* to sweep

местность [myést-nŏst'] *sf.* district, locality; country

местный [myést-năy] *adj.* local

место [myés-tŏ] *sn.* place, space; locality, site; job, situation; **-жительство** [-zhé-tyel'-stvŏ] *sn.* domicile;

residence; **-имение** [-i-myé-nye] *sn.* pronoun; **-рождение** [-razh-dyé-nye] *sn.* birthplace; seam, layer

месть [myést'] *sf.* vengeance

месяц [mye-syats] *sm.* month; moon; **медовый —** [mye-dó-văy —] honeymoon

месячный [mye-syach-năy] *adj.* lunar, monthly

металл [mye-tál] *sm.* metal; **-ический** [-é-ches-ki] metallic; **-ург** [-ōōrg] *sm.* metallurgist

метание [mye-tá-nye] *sn.* throwing, tossing

метательный снаряд [mye-tă-tyel'-năy sna-ryăd] *sm.* missile, projectile

метать [mye-tát'] *vt.* to fling, throw

метёлка [mye-tyól-ka] *sf.* whisk; panicle

метель [mye-tyél'] *sf.* snow-storm

метельчатый [mye-tyel'-chă-tăy] *adj.* panicular

метельщик [mye-tyél'-shchik] *sm.* road-sweeper

метение [mye-tyé-nye] *sn.* sweeping

метис [mye-t'ēs] *sm.* mongrel; half-breed

метисация [mye-t'i-sá-tsya] *sf.* cross-breeding

метить [mye-t'it'] (на-) *vt.* to mark; to aim at

метка [myét-ka] *sf.* mark, sign

метла [myet-lá] *sf.* broom

метловище [mye-tla-v'ē-shche] *sn.* broom-handle, broom-stick

метод [mye-tód] *sm.* method; **-ичный** [-'éch-năy] *adj.* methodical, orderly метр [myetr] *sm.* meter

метранпаж [metr-an-pázh] *sm. typ.* clicker, make-up man

метрика [myé-tri-ka] *sf.* birth-certificate; metrics

метрический [mye-tré-ches-ki] *adj.* metrical

мётчик [myót-chik] *sm.* screw-tap; marker (*billiards*)

мех [myech] *sm.* fur; *pl.* bellows; skin (*for wine, etc.*)

механик [mye-chá-n'ik] *sm.* engineer, mechanic

меховой [mye-cha-vóy] *adj.* fur-, furry

меховщик [mye-chav-shchĕk] *sm.* furrier

меч [myéch] *sm.* sword

мечеть [mye-chét'] *sf.* mosque

мечта [mye-tá] *sf.* day-dream, illusion; *pl.* reverie

мечтатель [myech-tá-tyel'] *sm.* dreamer; -ный [-náy] *adj.* dreamy, moony, pensive

мечтать [myech-tát'] (по-) *vi.* to day-dream

мешалка [mye-shál-ka] *sf.* mixer, stirrer

мешать [mye-shát'] (пере-) *vt.* to mix, stir; (по-) *vi.* to disturb, hinder

мешкать [myésh-kat'] (за-) *vi.* to loiter, tarry

мешковатый [myesh-ka-vá-tăy] *adj.* baggy; clumsy

мешок [mye-shók] *sm.* bag, sack

мещанин [mye-shcha-n'én] *sm.* citizen, commoner; (*now referred to as a bourgeois*)

мзда [mzdá] *sf.* remuneration, reward; bribe

мздоимец [mzda-é-myets] *sm.* extortioner

мздоимство [mzda-ém-stvŏ] *sn.* bribery, venality

ми [mĕ] *sn. mus.* E

миг [m'ĕg] *sm.* instant, moment

мигать [m'i-gát'] (мигнуть) *vi.* to blink, wink

мигом [m'ĕ-gŏm] *adv.* in the twinkling of an eye

мизинец [m'i-z'é-nyets] *sm.* little finger, little toe

миленький [m'ĕ-lyen'-ki] *adj.* gentle; darling; pretty

миловать [m'ĕ-la-vat'] (по-) *vt.* to show mercy; to forgive; [m'i-la-vát'] *vt.* to caress, fondle

милосердие [m'i-la-syér-dye] *sn.* charity, clemency, compassion

милосердный [m'i-la-syérd-năy] *adj.* merciful

милостивец [m'i-las-t'é-vyets] *sm.* benefactor

милостивый [m'i-las-t'é-văy] *adj.* gracious

милостыня [m'i-las-tă-nya] *sf.* alms, charity

милость [m'ĕ-lóst'] *sf.* favour, grace; ваша – [vá-sha –] your Honour, your Worship; милостью Божиею [m'ĕ-las-tyŏŏ bó-zhi-ye-yŏŏ] by the Grace of God

милый [m'ĕ-lăy] *adj.* amiable; beloved, dear; kind, pleasant; *as sm.*, sweetheart

миля [m'ĕ-lya] *sf.* mile; расстояние в милях [ras-sta-yá-nye vm'ĕ-lyach] milage

мимика [m'ĕ-mi-ka] *sf.* mimicry; gesticulation

мим [m'ĕm] *sm.* mime

мимо [m'ĕ-mŏ] *adv.* by, passing by, past; -ходом [-chó-dŏm] *adv.* by the way, in passing

мина [m'ĕ-na] *sf.* countenance, look; mine; torpedo

миндаль [m'in-dál'] *sm.* almond(s); almond-tree

минералогия [m'i-nye-ra-ló-gya] *sf.* mineralogy

минеральный [m'i-nye-rál'-nåy] *adj.* mineral

министр [m'i-n'éstr] *sm.* minister (*not ecclesiastical*)

министерство [m'i-n'i-styér-stvö] *sn.* ministry

минование [m'i-na-vā-nye] *sn.* avoidance

миновать [m'i-na-vāt'] (**минýть**) *vt.* to avoid, escape; to pass

минога [m'i-nó-ga] *sf.* lamprey

миномёт [m'i-na-myót] *sm.* mine-thrower

миноносец [m'i-na-nó-syets] *sm.* torpedo-boat

минор [m'i-nór] *sm. mus.* minor key; **-ный** [-nåy] *adj.* minor

минувшее [m'i-nōōv-she-ye] *sn.* the past

минувший [m'i-nōōv-shi] *adj.* last, past; bygone

минус [m'ē-nōōs] *sm.* minus

минута [m'i-nōō-ta] *sf.* minute; instant, moment

минутный [m'i-nōōt-nåy] *adj.* momentary; transient

мир [m'ēr] *sm.* peace; universe, world

мирволить [m'ir-vó-l'it'] *vi.* to connive

мирить [m'i-r'ēt'] (по-) *vt.* to mediate, reconcile; **-ся** [-sya] *vi.* to become reconciled, to make one's peace; to tolerate

мирный [m'ēr-nåy] *adj.* peaceful, peace-; **-договор** [- da-ga-vór] peace treaty

мировоззрение [m'i-ra-vaz-

zryé-nye] *sn.* world-conception, world-outlook; creed

мироед [m'i-ra-yéd] *sm.* parasite

мироздание [m'i-ra-zdā-nye] *sn.* creation

миролюбивый [m'i-ra-lyōō-b'ē-vày] *adj.* peaceable

миротворец [m'i-ra-tvó-ryets] *sm.* peacemaker

мирской [m'ir-skóy] *adj.* secular, worldly

миряне [m'i-ryā-nye] *sm. pl.* the laity

мирянин [m'i-ryā-n'in] *sm.* layman

миска [m'ēs-ka] *sf.* basin, tureen

миссионер [m'is-sia-nyér] *sm.* missionary; **-ский** [-ski] *adj.* missionary

миссия [m'ēs-sya] *sf.* mission; legation

миф [m'ēf] *sm.* myth; **-ология** [-a-ló-gya] *sf.* mythology

мишень [m'i-shén'] *sf.* target; **глазок мишени** [glazók m'i-shé-n'i] bull's eye

мишка [m'ēsh-ka] *sm.* Bruin; Teddy bear

мишура [m'i-shōō-rā] *sf.* tinsel

мишурный [m'i-shōōr-nåy] *adj.* flashy, gaudy

младенец [mla-dyé-nyets] *sm.* baby, infant

младенческий [mla-dyén-ches-ki] *adj.* infantile

младенчество [mla-dyén-chest-vö] *sn.* babyhood, infancy

младший [mlād-shi] *adj.* junior, younger

млекопитающий [mlye-ka-p'i-tā-yōō-shchi] *adj.* mammiferous

млеть [mlyét'] *vi.* to court; to become numb

млечный [mlyéch-nǎy] *adj.* lactic

мне [mnyé] *pron.* me, to me

мнение [mnyé-nye] *sn.* opinion

мнимо [mn'ě-mǒ] *adv.* apparently

мнимый [mn'ě-mǎy] *adj.* imaginary, pretended

мнить [mn'ět'] *vi.* to imagine, seem, suppose

многие [mnó-gi-ye] *adj.* many, several

много [mnó-gǒ] *adv.* great deal, lot(s), many, much; **-брачие** [-brǎ-chye] *sn.* polygamy; **-вато** [-vǎ-tǒ] *adv.* rather too much; **-женец** [-zhé-nyets] *sm.* polygamist; **-значительный** [-zna-chě-tyel'-nǎy] *adj.* significant; **-кратный** [-krǎt-nǎy] *adj.* frequent, reiterated; **-язычный** [-ya-zǎch-nǎy] *adj.* polyglot

множественный [mnó-zhest-vyen-nǎy] *adj.* plural

множество [mnó-zhest-vǒ] *sn.* multitude

множить [mnó-zhit'] (у-) *vt.* to multiply

множитель [mna-zhě-tyel'] *sf.* factor, multiplier

мной, мною [mnóy, mnó-yōó] *pron.* by me

могила [ma-g'é-la] *sf.* grave, tomb

могильщик [ma-g'ěl'-shchik] *sm.* grave-digger, sexton

могучий [ma-gōō-chi] *adj.* mighty, powerful

могущество [ma-gōō-shchest-vǒ] *sn.* might, potency, power

мода [mō-da] *sf.* fashion, vogue

модель [ma-dyél'] *sf.* model, pattern; **-ный** [-nǎy] *adj.* fashionable

модистка [ma-d'ěst-ka] *sf.* milliner

модный [mód-nǎy] *adj.* fashionable, stylish

может быть [mō-zhet bǎt'] perhaps, it is possible, one can, one may

мозг [mozg] *sm.* brain; **-овитый** [-a-v'é-tǎy] brainy; **-овой** [-a-vóy] *adj.* cerebral

мозоль [ma-zól'] *sf.* bunion, corn

мой [móy] *pron.* mine, my

мойка [móy-ka] *sf. tech.* washing

мокнуть [mak-nōōt'] (про-) *vt.i.* to drench, soak

мокроватый [ma-kra-vǎ-tǎy] *adj.* moist, wettish

мокрота [ma-kra-tǎ] *sf.* humidity, moisture, wet; [ma-kró-ta] *sf.* phlegm

мокрый [mók-rǎy] *adj.* wet

мол [mol] *sm.* breakwater, jetty, pier; *coll.* 'they say'

молва [mal-vǎ] *sf.* report, rumour; gossip

молвить [mól-v'it] (про-) *vt.* to utter

молебен [ma-lyé-ben] *sm.* Te Deum, thanksgiving service

моления [ma-lyél'-nya] *sf.* [chapel

молитва [ma-l'ět-va] *sf.* prayer

молитвенник [ma-l'ét-vyen-n'ik] *sm.* prayer-book

молить [ma-l'ět'] *vt.* to beseech, implore, pray; **-ся** [-sya] *vi.* to offer prayers

молкнуть [mal-knōōt'] *vi.* to become silent

молниеотвод [mal-nye-at-vód] *sm.* lightning-conductor

молния [mól-nya] *sf.* lightning; flash

молодёжь [ma-la-dyózh'] *sf.* youth, young people

молодец [ma-la-dyéts] *sm.* brave fellow, lad

молодить [ma-la-d'ét'] *vt.* to rejuvenate

молодожёны [ma-la-da-zhó-nä] *pl.* newly-married couple

молодой [ma-la-dóy] *adj.* young

молодость [mó-la-dŏst'] *sf.* youthfulness

моложавый [ma-la-zhä-väy] *adj.* young-looking

молоки [ma-ló-ki] *sn. pl.* soft roe

молоко [ma-la-kó] *sn.* milk

молот [mó-lŏt] *sm.* mallet

молотилка [ma-la-t'él-ka] *sf.* threshing-machine

молотить [ma-la-t'ét'] *vt.* to thresh

молоток [ma-la-tók] *sm.* hammer

молоть [ma-lót'] *vt.* to grind, mill

молотьба [ma-lat'-bä] *sf.* threshing

молочная [ma-lóch-na-ya] *sf.* dairy

молочник [ma-lóch-n'ik] *sm.* milk-jug; milkman

молочница [ma-lóch-n'i-tsa] *sf.* dairymaid; *med.* thrush

молочный [ma-lóch-näy] *adj.* dairy-, lactic, milk-, milky; –**брат** [– brät] foster-brother

молча [mól-cha] *adv.* in silence, silently

молчаливый [mal-cha-l'é-väy] *adj.* reticent, taciturn

молчание [mal-chä-nye] *sn.* silence

молчать [mal-chät'] (за–) *vi.* to keep quiet, to be silent

моль [mol'] *sf.* moth

мольба [mal'-bä] *sf.* entreaty, request

мольберт [mól'-bert] *sm.* easel

моментальный [ma-myen-täl'-näy] *adj.* instant

монархия [ma-när-chya] *sf.* monarchy

монастырь [ma-na-står'] *sm.* cloister; convent, friary, monastery, nunnery

монастырский [ma-na-står-ski] *adj.* monastic

монах [ma-näch] *sm.* friar, monk; –**иня** [–ē-nya *sf.* nun

монета [ma-nyé-ta] *sf.* coin

монетный [ma-nyét-näy] *adj.* monetary

монотонный [ma-na-tón-näy] *adj.* monotonous

монтаж [mon-täzh] *sm.* assembly, erecting

монтёр [mon-työr] *sm.* fitter

монтировать [man-t'ē-ra-vat'] *vt.* to assemble, erect, fit

мор [mor] *sm.* pestilence, plague

мораль [ma-räl'] *sf.* ethics, morality, morals; –**ный** [–näy] *adj.* moral

мораторий [ma-ra-tó-ri] *sm.* moratorium

моргать [mar-gät'] (морг-нуть) *vi.* to blink, wink

морда [mór-da] *sf.* muzzle, snout; ugly face

море [mó-rye] *sn.* sea

мореплавание [ma-rye-plä-va-nye] *sn.* navigation

мореплавательный [ma-rye-pla-vă-tyel'-năy] *adj.* nautical

морж [morzh] *sm.* walrus

морить [ma-r'ĕt'] (за-) *vt.* to famish, starve; to destroy, exterminate; to torment

морковь [mar-kóv'] *sf.* carrot

мороженик [ma-ró-zhe-n'ik] *sm.* ice-cream vendor

мороженое [ma-ró-zhe-na-ye] *sn.* ice-cream

мороз [ma-róz] *sm.* frost

морозить [ma-ró-z'it'] (за-) *vt.* to congeal, freeze

морозный [ma-róz-năy] *adj.* frost-, frosty

моросить [ma-ra-s'ĕt'] *vi.* to drizzle

морочить [ma-ró-chit] *vt.* to deceive; to annoy, worry; *coll.* to pull someone's leg

морской [mar-skóy] *adj.* marine, maritime, naval, sea-

мортира [mart'ě-ra] *sf.* mortar; **окопная** = [akóp-na-ya =] trench mortar

морщина [mar-shchě-na] *sf.* crease, fold; furrow; wrinkle

морщинистый [mar-shchě-n'is-tăy] *adj.* creasy, wrinkled; full of wrinkles

морщить [mar-shchět'] (с-) *vt.* to purse, wrinkle

моряк [ma-ryák] *sm.* seaman

москательщик [mas-ka-tyél'-shchik] *sm.* chandler

мост [most] *sm.* bridge

мостить [mas-t'ĕt'] (вы-) *vt.* to pave

мостки [mast-kē] *sm. pl.* foot-bridge, foot-path

мостовая [mas-ta-vă-ya] *sf.* pavement; roadway

мот [mot] *sm.* prodigal

мотать [ma-tăt'] (про-) *vt.*

to reel, wind; to squander, waste

мотив [ma-t'ěv] *sm.* cause, reason; *mus.* tune

мотовило [ma-ta-v'ě-lŏ] *sn.* reel, winder [skein

моток [ma-tók] *sm.* hank, [skein

моторный [ma-tór-năy] *adj.* motor-, motorized

мотоциклет [ma-ta-tsik-lyét] *sm.* motor-cycle

мотыга [ma-tă-ga] *sm.* hoe, mattock

мотылёк [ma-tă-lyók] *sm.* butterfly [crank

мотыль [ma-tăl'] *sm. tech.* crank

мох [moch] *sm.* moss

мохнатый [mach-nă-tăy] *adj.* hairy, shaggy; napped

моча [ma-chă] *sf.* urine

мочение [ma-ché-nye] *sm.* soaking, wetting

мочить [ma-chét'] (на-) *vt.* to moisten, soak, wet

мочка [móch-ka] *sf.* macerating, wetting; lobe (*of ear*)

мочь [moch'] *vi.* to be able; *sf.* might, power

мошенник [ma-shén-n'ik] *sm.* rogue, scoundrel

мошенничать [ma-shén-n'i-chat'] *vi.* to cheat, swindle, trick

мошка [mósh-ka] *sf.* midge; -**ра** [-ră] swarm of midges

мощный [móshch-năy] *adj.* powerful, robust

мощь [moshch'] *sf.* strength, vigour

мразь [mrăz'] *sf.* dirt, filth; wretched person

мрак [mrăk] *sm.* gloom, obscurity

мрамор [mră-mór] *sm.* marble

мрачность [mrăch-nòst'] *sf.* darkness, gloom

мрачный [mrâch-năy] *adj.* dreary, sombre

мстить [mst'êt'] (отомсти́ть) *vt.* to avenge

мудрёный [mŏŏ-dryó-năy] *adj.* abstruse, ingenious, subtle

мудрец [mŏŏd-ryéts] *sm.* sage, wise man

мудрый [mŏŏd-răy] *adj.* wise

мудрость [mŏŏd-rŏst'] *sf.* wisdom [man]

муж [mŏŏzh] *sm.* husband;

мужаться [mŏŏ-zhât'-sya] *vi.* to take courage

мужественный [mŏŏ-zhest-vyen-năy] *adj.* manly, masculine

мужество [mŏŏ-zhest-vŏ] *sn.* manliness; courage, fortitude

мужик [mŏŏ-zhík] *sm.* peasant

мужской [mŏŏzh-skóy] *adj.* male, man's; *gram.* masculine (*gender*)

мужчина [mŏŏzh-chē-na] *sm.* man

музей [mŏŏ-zyéy] *sm.* museum

музыка [mŏŏ-ză-ka] *sf.* music; **-льный** [-ǎl'-năy] *adj.* musical; **-нт** [-ânt] *sm.* musician

мука [mŏŏ-ka] *sf.* anguish, torment

мука [mŏŏ-kâ] *sf.* flour; meal

мул [mŏŏl] *sm.* mule

мумия [mŏŏ-mya] *sf.* mummy

мундир [mŏŏn-d'êr] *sm.* military uniform

мундштук [mŏŏnd-shtŏŏk] *sm.* cigarette-holder, mouthpiece; bit

муравей [mŏŏ-ra-vyéy] *sm.* ant; **-ник** [-n'ik] *sm.* ant-hill

муравить [mŏŏ-râ-v'it] *vt.* to glaze

мурашки [mŏŏ-râsh-ki] *sf. pl. coll.* the creeps

мурлыкать [mŏŏr-lá-kat'] (мурлы́кнуть) *vi.* to purr

мускат [mŏŏs-kât] *sm.* nutmeg; muscatel

мускул [mŏŏs-kŏŏl] *sm.* muscle; **-истый** [-ēs-tăy] *adj.* muscular

мускус [mŏŏs-kŏŏs] *sm.* musk

мусор [mŏŏ-sór] *sm.* dust, rubbish, scrap

мусорить [mŏŏ-só-rit'] *vt.* to litter

мутить [mŏŏ-t'êt'] (c-) *vt.* to disturb

мутный [mŏŏt-năy] *adj.* dull; muddy; turbid

муфта [mŏŏf-ta] *sf.* muff; clutch; coupling

муха [mŏŏ-cha] *sf.* fly; **-ловка** [-lóv-ka] *sf.* fly-catcher

мухортый [mŏŏ-chór-tăy] *adj.* bay (*of horse*)

мучение [mŏŏ-ché-nye] *sn.* agony, pain

мученик [mŏŏ-che-n'ik] *sm.* martyr

мучитель [mŏŏ-ché-tyel'] *sm.* tormentor; **-ный** [-năy] *adj.* acutely painful, excruciating, poignant

мучить [mŏŏ-chét'] (по-) *vt.* to distress, harass, torment

мушка [mŏŏsh-ka] *sf.* beauty spot (*on face*); blister; sight (*on rifle*)

мушкет [mŏŏsh-két] *sm.* musket; **-ёр** [-yór] *sm.* musketeer

мчать [mchât'] (по-) *vt.* to bolt (*of horse*); to hurry away, tear along

мщение [mshché-nye] *sn.* vengeance

мы [mä] *pron.* we

мыза [mä-za] *sf.* country-house, farmstead

мыкать [mä-kat'] *vt.* to hackle; — **горе** [– gó-rye] to live in misery

мылить [mä-l'it'] (на-) *vt.* to lather, soap

мыло [mä-lŏ] *sn.* soap; foam (*on horses*)

мыльница [mäl'-n'i-tsa] *sf.* soap-dish

мыльный [mäl'-năy] *adj.* soapy; foamy

мыс [mäs] *sm.* promontory

мысленный [mäs-lyen-năy] *adj.* fancied; mental, of thought

мыслитель [mäs-l'ē-tyel'] *sm.* thinker

мыслить [mäs-l'it'] (по-) *vi.* to reflect, think

мысль [mäsl'] *sf.* conception, reflection, thought

мыслящий [mäs-lya-shchi] *adj.* thinking; intellectual (*also as noun*)

мытарство [mä-tär-stvŏ] *sn.* tribulation; trying experience

мыть [mät'] (по-) *vt.* to wash; -**ся** [-sya] *vr.* to wash oneself

мычать [mä-chät'] *vi.* to bellow, low, moo

мышеловка [mä-she-lóv-ka] *sf.* mouse-trap

мышление [mä-shlé-nye] *sn.* pondering, thinking; mentality

мышца [mäsh-tsa] *sf.* muscle

мышь [mäsh'] *sf.* mouse; летучая — [lye-tōō-cha-ya –] bat

мышьяк [mä-shyäk] *sm.* arsenic

мэр [mer] *sm.* mayor; -**ия** [-ya] *sf.* town-hall

мягкий [myäch-ki] *adj.* soft; mild

мягкость [myäch-kŏst'] *sf.* mildness, softness, tenderness

мягчение [myagh-ché-nye] *sn.* softening

мягчительный [myach-ché-tyel'-năy] *adj.* emollient

мягчить [myach-chét'] (с-) *vt.* to soften

мякина [mya-k'é-na] *sf.* chaff, husks

мякиш [myä-kish] *sm.* crumb (*soft inner part of bread*)

мясистый [mya-s'ĕs-tăy] *adj.* fleshy; pulpy

мясник [myas-n'ék] *sm.* butcher

мясо [myä-sŏ] *sn.* flesh; meat; -**рубка** [-rŏŏb-ka] *sf.* mincer

мята [myä-ta] *sf.* mint; перечная — [pyé-rech-na-ya –] peppermint

мятеж [mya-tyézh] *sm.* mutiny, rebellion; -**ник** [-n'ik] *sm.* rebel

мятежный [mya-tyézh-năy] *adj.* restless; rebellious

мять [myät'] *vt.* to disarrange, rumple; to trample

мяукать [mya-ōō-kat'] (мяукнуть) [mya-úknut'] *vi.* to mew, squall

мяч [myäch] *sm.* ball

Н

на [nä] *prep.* at; by; on, upon; to, towards

набавлять [na-bav-lyät'] (набавить) [na-bav-it'] *vt.* to add, increase

набалдашник [na-bal-dáshn'ik] *sm.* knob

набат [na-bát] *sm.* alarm, alarm signal

набег [na-byég] *sm.* invasion, raid

набегать [na-bye-gát'] (набежáть) *vi.* to come up against, to stumble over; flow in

набело [nā-bye-lŏ] *adv.* cleanly, fairly

набережная [nā-bye-rezh-na-ya] *sf.* quay, wharf

набивать [na-b'i-vát'] (на-бить) *vt.* to cram, fill, pack; to print (*textiles*)

набивка [na-bêv-ka] *sf.* filling, padding, stuffing

набирать [na-b'i-rát'] (на-брáть) *vt.* to collect, gather; to inlay, veneer; *typ.* to compose

наблюдатель [na-blyŏŏ-dá-tyel'] *sm.* observer, spectator; overseer; **-ный** [-năy] *adj.* observant

наблюдать [na-blyŏŏ-dát'] *vt.* to observe, watch; to eye; to look after

наблюдение [na-blyŏŏ-dyé-nye] *sn.* observation; watchfulness

набожный [nā-bazh-năy] *adj.* devout, pious

набойщик [na-bóy-shchik] *sm.* linen-printer

набор [na-bór] *sm.* assemblage, collection, set; recruitment; *typ.* composition; **-ная** [-na-ya] *sf.* composing room; **-щик** [-shchik] *sm.* compositor

набрасывать [na-brá-să-vat'] (набросáть) *vt.* to outline roughly, sketch; **-ся**

[-sya] *vi.* to attack, to throw oneself upon

набросок [na-bró-sŏk] *sm.* rough sketch; unedited MS.

наваливать [na-vā-l'i-vat'] (навалить) *vt.* to heap up, pile up; to overload; **-ся** [-sya] *vi.* to lean on someone

навар [na-vár] *sm.* fat; beef-tea

наваривать [na-vā-ri-vat'] (наварить) *vt.* to brew; to cook

наведение [na-vye-dyé-nye] *sn.* inference; directing

наведываться [na-vyé-dă-vat'sya] (наведáться) *vi.* to make inquiries; to visit

навеки [na-vyé-ki] *adv.* for good, for ever; eternally

наверно [na-vyér-nŏ] *adv.* surely; certainly

наверху [na-vyer-chŏŏ] *adv.* above, upstairs

навес [na-vyés] *sm.* awning; canopy; penthouse

навет [na-vyét] *sm.* slander; **-ный** [-năy] *adj.* slanderous

наветренный [na-vyét-ren-năy] *adj.* windward

навещать [na-vye-shchát'] *vt.* to call on, visit

навивать [na-v'i-vát'] (на-вить) *vt.* to roll, wind; to stack

навлекать [na-vlye-kát'] (на-влéчь) *vt.* to cause; to incur

наводить [na-va-d'ét'] (навести) *vt.* to aim at, point at; to erect; to guide; to look up (*in book*, *etc.*)

наводнение [na-vad-nyé-nye] *sn.* flood, inundation

наводнять [na-vad-nyát'] (наводнить) *vt.* to flood, inundate

навождение [na-vazh-dyé-nye] *sn.* obsession, temptation; delusion

навоз [na-vōz] *sm.* manure

навозить [na-vó-z'it'] *vt.* to manure

навозить [na-va-z'ět'] *vt.* to cart, convey; to import

наволочка [nä-va-lach-ka] *sf.* pillow-case

навострить [na-va-strět'] *vt.* to sharpen

навряд [na-vryäd] *adv.* hardly, scarcely; unlikely

навсегда [na-vsyeg-dä] *adv.* always

навстречу [na-vstré-chōō] *adv.* towards; **итти** – [it-t'ě –] to go to meet someone

навыворот [na-vǎ-va-rŏt] *adv.* inside out

навык [nä-vǎk] *sm.* custom, habit

навыкать [na-vǎ-kät'] (**навыкнуть**) *vi.* to get accustomed

навылет [na-vǎ-lyet] *adv.* through

навязчивый [na-vyäz-chi-väy] *adj.* obtrusive

навязчивость [na-vyäz-chi-vŏst'] *sf.* obtrusiveness

навязывать [na-vyä-zǎ-vat'] (**навязать**) *vt.* to attach, fasten, tie; **-ся** [-sya] *vi.* to intrude, force oneself upon someone

нагайка [na-gǎy-ka] *sf.* whip

нагар [na-gär] *sm.* snuff (of candle); residue; scale

нагибать [na-gi-bät'] (**нагнуть**) *vt.* to bend

нагишом [na-gi-shóm] *adv.* stark naked

наглазники [na-gläz-n'i-ki] *sm. pl.* blinkers

наглец [nag-lyéts] *sm.* impudent person

наглость [näg-lŏst] *sf.* impudence, insolence

наглухо [nä-glōō-chŏ] *adv.* hermetically, tightly

наглый [näg-lǎy] *adj.* insolent, pert

наглядный [nag-lyäd-nǎy] *adj.* descriptive, graphic

нагнетать [nag-nye-tät'] *vt.* to force, press

нагноение [nag-na-yé-nye] *sn.* suppuration

наговор [na-ga-vór] *sm.* denunciation

нагой [na-góy] *adj.* bare, nude

нагоняй [na-ga-nyäy] *sm.* reprimand

нагонять [na-ga-nyät'] (**нагнать**) *vt.* to overtake

нагорный [na-gór-nǎy] *adj.* mountainous

нагорье [na-gó-rye] *sn.* highlands, uplands

наготавливать [na-ga-täv-l'i-vat'] *vt.* to prepare on a large scale; to obtain a quantity of stores

награда [na-grä-da] *sf.* remuneration, reward; prize

награждать [na-grazh-dät'] (**наградить**) *vt.* to reward; *fig.* to endow

нагревать [na-gre-vät'] (**нагреть**) *vt.* to heat, warm

нагрудник [na-grōōd-n'ik] *sm.* bib; breastplate

нагружать [na-grōō-zhät'] (**нагрузить**) *vt.* to load

нагрузка [na-grōōz-ka] *sf.* lading; cargo; shipment; stowage

нагрянуть [nag-ryá-nōōt'] vi. to attack unexpectedly; to surprise; to happen

над [nad] prep. above, over

надавливать [na-dáv-l'i-vat'] (надавить) vt. to press, squeeze

надбавка [nad-báv-ka] sf. increase, rise (in price or wages); outbidding

надбавлять [nad-bav-lyát'] (надбáвить) vt. to add, increase; to outbid

надбавочный [nad-bá-vach-nây] adj. additional, supplementary

надвигающийся [nad-v'i-gá-yōō-shchi-sya] adj. approaching; imminent

надгробие [nad-gró-bye] sm. epitaph

надевать [na-dye-vát'] (надéть) vt. to put on; to harness; – траур [– trá-ōōr] to go into mourning

надежда [na-dézh-da] sf. hope, trust; reliance

надёжность [na-dyózh-nóst'] sf. reliability; safety

надёжный [na-dyózh-nây] adj. reliable, trustworthy

надел [na-dyél] sm. allowance, share

наделять [na-dye-lyát'] (надели́ть) vt. to allot, dispense; to impart

надёргивать [na-dyór-gi-vat'] (надёргать) vt. to pluck out

надеяться [na-dyé-yat'-sya] vi. to hope, trust

надземный [nad-zyém-nây] adj. above-ground, overhead

надзиратель [nad-z'i-rá-tyel'] sm. inspector, overseer, supervisor

надзирать [nad-z'i-rát'] vi. to supervise

надзор [nad-zór] sm. control, inspection, supervision

надлежащий [nad-lye-zhá-shchi] adj. due; requisite

надлом [nad-lóm] sm. fracture; wretchedness

надменность [nad-myén-nóst'] sf. arrogance, pride

надменный [nad-myén-nây] adj. haughty, supercilious

на-днях [na-dnyách] adv. before long, in the near future; in a day or so; lately, recently

надо [ná-dō] adv. necessarily, one ought; **так ему и –!** [ták ye-mōō i –] it serves him right!

надобность [ná-dab-nóst'] sf. necessity, requirement

надобный [ná-dab-nây] adj. needful, requisite

надоедать [na-da-ye-dát'] (надоéсть) vi. to annoy, bother, tire

надоедливый [na-da-yéd-l'i-vây] adj. irksome, tiresome

надолго [na-dól-gō] adv. for a long spell

надпись [nad-p'is'] sf. inscription, superscription; endorsement

надрез [nad-ryéz] sm. cut, incision; notch

надрыв [nad-rắv] sm. rent, small tear; anguish; strain

надрываться [nad-rắ-vát'-sya] vi. to hurt oneself (by lifting); to overstrain

надсматривать [nad-smá-tri-vat'] (надсмотрéть) vi. to inspect, survey

надсмотр [nad-smótr] *sm.* control, supervision

надсмотрщик [nad-smótr-shchik] *sm.* overseer

надстрочный [nad-stróch-nǎy] *adj.* interlinear; diacritical

надувание [na-dŏŏ-vá-nye] *sn.* inflation

надувательство [nadŏŏ-vá-tyel'-stvǒ] *sn.* cheating, trickery

надувать [na-dŏŏ-vát'] (надуть) *vt.* to blow up, inflate; to cheat

надушить [na-dŏŏ-shét'] *vt.* to sprinkle scent about

надышать [na-dǎ-shát'] *vt.* to breathe into; **-ся** [-sya] *vi.* to inhale

наедаться [na-ye-dát'-sya] (наесться) *vi.* to eat one's fill

наедине [na-ye-d'i-nyé] *adv.* alone, privately

наезд [na-yézd] *sm.* incursion, inroad; flying visit

наездник [na-yézd-n'ik] *sm.* jockey, rider

наезжать [na-yez-zhát'] (наехать) *vi.* to collide; to come across

наём [na-yóm] *sm.* hire, rent; **сдавать в –** [zda-vát' v –] to let

наёмный [na-yóm-nǎy] *adj.* hired

наждак [nazh-dák] *sm.* emery

нажива [na-zhé-va] *sf.* gain, profit

наживать [na-zhi-vát'] (нажить) *vt.* to acquire (*money*); to contract (*an illness*)

наживка [na-zhév-ka] *sf.* bait

нажим [na-zhém] *sm.* pressure

нажимать [na-zhi-mát']

(нажать) *vt.* to nip, press, squeeze

нажраться [na-zhrát'-sya] *vi.* to overeat

назад [na-zád] *adv.* back, backwards; ago; **–!** stand back!

назальный [na-zál'-nǎy] *adj.* nasal (*sound*)

назади [na-za-d'é] *adv.* behind

название [na-zvá-nye] *sn.* denomination, name; title (*of books, etc.*)

назидательный [na-zi-dá-tyel'-nǎy] *adj.* edifying

назло [na-zló] *adv.* in spite of, maliciously

назначать [na-zna-chát'] (назначить) *vt.* to appoint, designate; to fix (*date, time*)

назначение [naz-na-ché-nye] *sn.* appointment; nomination

назойливый [na-zóy-l'i-vǎy] *adj.* intrusive, persistent

назубок [na-zŏŏ-bók] *sm.* coarse file

называть [na-zǎ-vát'] (назвать) *vt.* to call, name, term

наивный [na-év-nǎy] *adj.* naïve, unaffected

наизнанку [na-iz-nán-kŏŏ] *adv.* inside out

наизусть [na-i-zŏŏst'] *adv.* from memory

наилучший [na-i-lŏŏch-shi] *adj.* the best

наименее [na-i-myé-nye-ye] *adv.* least

наименование [na-i-mye-na-vá-nye] *sn.* denomination, nomenclature

найдёныш [nay-dyó-nǎsh] *sn.* foundling

наказ [na-káz] *sm.* decree, order; mandate

наказание [na-ka-zā-nye] *sn.* punishment

наказывать [na-kā-ză-vat'] (наказа́ть) *vt.* to chastise, punish

накал [na-kāl] *sm.* incandescence, white heat

накаливать [na-kā-l'i-vat'] (накали́ть) *vt.* to render incandescent

накалывать [na-kā-lă-vat'] *vt.* to cleave, split; to prick

накануне [na-ka-nōō-nye] *adv.* on the eve

накидка [na-k'ēd-ka] *sf.* cape; cloak; mantle

накидывать [na-k'ē-dă-vat'] (наки́нуть) *vt.* to slip on, throw over (*clothes*)

накипь [nā-k'ip'] *sm.* foam, scum

накладка [na-klād-ka] *sf.* dress-trimming; false hair

накладная [na-klad-nā-ya] *sf.* invoice

накладывание [na-klā-dă-va-nye] *sn.* laying on; superposition

наклейка [na-klyéy-ka] *sf.* a thing glued or pasted on

наклон [nak-lón] *sm.* incline, slope; incidence

наклонение [na-kla-nyé-nye] *sn.* inclination; *gram.* mood

наковальня [na-ka-vāl'-nya] *sf.* anvil

накожный [na-kózh-năy] *adj.* cutaneous

наконец [na-ka-nyéts] *adv.* at last, finally

наконечник [na-ka-nyéch-n'ik] *sm.* point, tag, tip; ferrule

накопление [na-kap-lyé-nye] *sn.* accumulation, mass, hoard

накрепко [nă-kryep-kŏ] *adv.* firmly, strongly

накрест [nă-kryest] *adv.* across, crosswise

накрывать [na-kră-vat'] (накры́ть) *vt.* to cover; to lay, spread

налагать [na-la-gāt'] (наложи́ть) *vt.* to impose, inflict

налево [na-lyé-vŏ] *adv.* left, on the left, to the left

налегке [na-lyech-kyé] *adv.* lightly, scantily; without luggage

налёт [na-lyót] *sm.* raid, swoop; efflorescence

налетать [na-lye-tāt'] (налете́ть) *vi.* to rush at, swoop down

налив [na-l'ēv] *sm.* sap, juice

наливать [na-l'i-vat'] (нали́ть) *vt.* to fill up, pour in

наливной [na-l'iv-nóy] *adj.* clear; juicy

наличие [na-l'ē-chye] *sn.* availability; presence

наличность [na-l'ēch-nŏst'] *sf.* ready cash

налог [na-lóg] *sm.* duty, imposition, rates, tax

налой [na-lóy] *sm.* lectern

нам [năm] *pron.* us, to us

намёк [na-myók] *sm.* hint, intimation

намекать [na-mye-kāt'] (намекну́ть) *vt.* to allude, insinuate

намереваться [na-mye-re-vat'sya] *vt.* to intend

намерение [na-mye-ré-nye] *sn.* design, intention, purpose

наместник [na-myést-n'ik] *sm.* deputy

намечать [na-mye-chāt'] *vt.* [to mark

нами [nā-m'i] *pron.* by us, through us

намордник [na-mórd-n'ik] *sm.* muzzle

наморщивать [na-mór-shchi-vat'] *vt.* to frown; to wrinkle

наниматель [na-n'i-má-tyel'] *sm.* employer, hirer; tenant

нанимать [na-n'i-mát'] (нанять) *vt.* to engage; to hire; to rent

наоборот [na-a-ba-rót] *adv.* contrary, inversely

наобум [na-a-bōom] *adv.* at random

нападать [na-pa-dát'] (напасть) *vt.* to assault, attack

нападение [na-pa-dyé-nye] *sn.* offensive

нападки [na-pád-ki] *sf. pl.* aggression; attacks (*in the press*); persecution

напасть [na-pást'] *sf.* calamity, disaster, misfortune

напев [na-pyév] *sm.* air, melody, tune

напевать [na-pye-vát'] (напеть) *vt.* to hum, croon, sing

напекать [na-pye-kát'] (напечь) *vt.* to bake (*in quantity*); to scorch

наперсник [na-pyérs-n'ik] *sm.* confidant, favourite

напёрсток [na-pyórs-tŏk] *sm.* thimble

напилок [na-p'ē-lŏk] *sm.* file, rasp

напильник [na-p'ēl'-n'ik] *sm.* small file

напиток [na-p'ē-tŏk] *sm.* beverage

напитывать [na-p'ē-tă-vat'] (напитать) *vt.* to satiate; to saturate

наплечие [na-plyé-chye] *sn.* shoulder-strap

наплыв [na-plắv] *sm.* abundance; influx; excrescence

наповал [na-pa-vál] *adv.* outright

напоказ [na-pa-káz] *adv.* showing off

наполнять [na-pal-nyát'] (наполнить) *vt.* to fill; to crowd

наполовину [na-pa-la-v'ē-nōo] *adv.* by halves, in half

напоминание [na-pa-m'i-ná-nye] *sn.* reminding

напоминать [na-pa-m'i-nát'] (напомнить) *vt.* to recall, remind

напор [na-pór] *sm.* pressure, stress

напоследок [na-pas-lyé-dŏk] *adv.* at last, in conclusion, in the long run

направка [na-práv-ka] *sf.* setting (*blades, etc.*)

направление [na-prav-lyé-nye] *sn.* direction; trend

направлять [na-prav-lyát'] (направить) *vt.* to direct; to relegate; to set

направо [na-prá-vŏ] *adv.* right, to the right

напрасно [na-prás-nŏ] *adv.* to no purpose, uselessly, vainly

например [na-pr'i-myér] *adv.* for instance

напрокат [na-pra-kát] *adv.* on hire

напролёт [na-pra-lyót] *adv.* right through, throughout

напролом [na-pra-lóm] *adv.* straight on

напропалую [na-pra-pa-lōō-yōō] *adv.* at random; recklessly

напротив [na-pró-t'iv] *prep.* facing, opposite; *adv.* on the contrary

напряжение [na-prya-zhé-nye] *sn.* effort, strain, tension

напряжённый [na-prya-zhón-nǎy] *adj.* strenuous; tense

напульсник [na-pōōl's-n'ik] *sm.* wristlet

напыщенность [na-pǎ-shchen-nóst'] *sf.* pomposity

наравне [na-rav-nyé] *adv.* on a par, on equal terms, equally

нарезка [na-ryéz-ka] *sf.* indentation, incision; thread, worm

нарекание [na-rye-ká-nye] *sn.* blame, reproach

наречие [na-ryé-chye] *sn.* dialect; *gram.* adverb

нарицательный [na-r'i-tsátyel'-nǎy] *adj.* nominal; *gram.* appellative

народ [na-ród] *sm.* folk, nation, people; **-ность** [-nóst'] *sf.* nationality; **-ный** [-nǎy] *adj.* national, people's, popular

народоведение [na-ra-davye-dyé-nye] *sn.* ethnology

народовластие [na-ra-da-vlá-stye] *sn.* democracy

народосчисление [na-ra-da-schis-slyé-nye] *sn.* census

нарост [na-róst] *sm.* excrescence

нарочитый [na-ra-ché-tǎy] *adj.* deliberate, intentional; considerable; *coll.* eminent

нарочно [na-róch-nŏ] *adv.* purposely

нарочный [na-róch-nǎy] *adj.* intentional; *sm.* messenger

нарта [nǎr-ta] *sf.* sledge

наружа [na-rōōzh-nóst'] *sf.* exterior; appearance; outward aspect

наружный [na-rōōzh-nǎy] *adj.* exterior, external, outside

наружу [na-rōō-zhōō] *adv.* outwardly

нарукавник [na-rōō-káv-n'ik] *sm.* oversleeve; armlet

наручник [na-rōōch-n'ik] *sm.* handcuff

нарушать [na-rōō-shát'] (нарушить) *vi.* to infringe, transgress, violate

нарушение [na-rōō-shé-nye] *sn.* breach, transgression

нарцисс [nar-tsés] *sm.* narcissus; жёлтый – [zhól-tǎy –] daffodil

нарыв [na-rǎv] *sm.* abscess, ulcer, sore

нарывать [na-rǎ-vát'] (нарвать) *vt.* to fester, gather; to pick, pluck

наряд [na-ryǎd] *sm.* attire, dress, finery; **-ный** [-nǎy] *adj.* elegant, smart

наряжать [na-rya-zhát'] (нарядить) *vt.* to array, dress up

насаждать [na-sazh-dát'] *vt.* to plant; to propagate; to spread

наседка [na-syéd-ka] *sf.* sitting hen

насекать [na-sye-kát'] (насечь) *vt.* to incise, notch

насекомое [na-sye-kó-ma-ye] *sn.* insect

население [na-sye-lyé-nye] *sn.* population

насестка [na-syést-ka] *sf.* perch, roost

насиживать [na-s'ě-zhi-vat'] *vi.* (насидеть) to hatch, sit

насилие [na-s'ě-lye] *sn.* force, violence

насильно [na-s'ěl'-nŏ] *adv.* forcibly

насквозь [na-skvóz'] *adv.* through, throughout

наскок [na-skók] *sm.* sudden attack, swoop

насколько [na-skól'-kŏ] *adv.* how much? to what extent?; as far as

наскоро [nă-ska-rŏ] *adv.* hastily, hurriedly

наслаждаться [na-slazh-dát'-sya] (насладиться) *vt.* to enjoy; *vi.* to enjoy oneself; to delight in; to revel

наслаждение [na-slazh-dyé-nye] *sn.* delight, enjoyment, pleasure

наследие [na-slyé-dye] *sn.* heritage; legacy

наследник [na-slyéd-n'ik] *sm.* heir

наследственный [na-slyéd-stven-năy] *adj.* hereditary

наследство [na-slyéd-stvŏ] *sn.* inheritance

наслоение [na-sla-yé-nye] *sn.* stratum; stratification

наслышка [na-slásh-ka] *sf.* hearsay

насмешка [na-smyésh-ka] *sf.* mockery, sneer

насмешливость [na-smyésh-l'i-vŏst'] *sf.* derision

насморк [năs-mórk] *sm.* catarrh, head-cold

насос [na-sós] *sm.* pump

наставление [na-stav-lyé-nye] *sn.* precept

настаивать [na-stá-i-vat'] (настоять) *vt.* to insist, urge

настежь [ná-styezh'] *adv.* wide open

настой [na-stóy] *sm.* infusion

настойчивый [na-stóy-chi-văy] *adj.* persistent

настолько [na-stól'-kŏ] *adv.* so much, thus far

настороже [na-sta-ra-zhé] *adv.* cautiously; on guard

настоятель [na-sta-yă-tyel'] *sm.* prior, superior

настоятельный [na-sta-yă-tyel'-năy] *adj.* imperative, urgent

настоящий [na-sta-yă-shchi] *adj.* actual, present; genuine, real

настрого [nă-stra-gŏ] *adv.* severely

настроение [na-stra-yé-nye] *sn.* mood

настройка [na-stróy-ka] *sf.* tuning

настройщик [na-stróy-shchik] *sm.* piano-tuner

наступательный [na-stŏŏ-pă-tyel'-năy] *adj.* aggressive; *mil.* offensive

наступление [na-stŏŏp-lyé-nye] *sn.* approach, coming; *mil.* attack, offensive

насущный [na-sŏŏshch-năy] *adj.* daily

насчёт [na-schót] *prep.* concerning

насчитывать [na-schё-tă-vat'] (насчитать) *vt.* to count, number, reckon

насыпать [na-să-pát'] (насыпать) *vt.* to fill, put in

насыпь [nă-săp'] *sf.* dam, dike; embankment, mound

насыщать [na-să-shchát'] (насытить) *vt.* to satiate, satisfy; to saturate

наталкивать [na-tăp-l'i-vat'] (натопить) *vt.* to heat intensely; to melt

натаскивать [na-tăs-ki-vat'] (натаскать) *vt.* to coach; to train (dogs)

натиск [nă-t'isk] *sm.* attack, charge, onslaught

натощак [na-ta-shchák] *adv.* on an empty stomach

натуга [na-tōō-ga] *sf.* effort, strain

натуго [na-tōō-gŏ] *adv.* tightly

натура [na-tōō-ra] *sf.* nature; disposition

натуральный [na-tōō-rál'-năy] *adj.* natural

натурщик [na-tōōr-shchik] *sm.* living model, sitter

натюрморт [na-tyōōr-mórt] *sm.* still life

натягивать [na-tyá-gi-vat'] *vt.* (натянуть) to draw on, pull on; to tighten

натяжка [na-tyázh-ka] *sf.* quibble; stretching

натянутый [na-tyá-nōō-tăy] *adj.* tense, tight

наугад [na-ōō-gád] *adv.* haphazardly

наугольник [na-ōō-gól'-n'ik] *sm.* corner wardrobe; bevel, square (*instruments*)

наудачу [na-ōō-dá-chōō] *adv.* by chance

наука [na-ōō-ka] *sf.* science

научать [na-ōō-chát'] (научить) *vt.* to instruct, teach; -ся [-sya] *vi.* to learn

научный [na-ōōch-năy] *adj.* scientific

наушник [na-ōōsh-n'ik] *sm.* ear-protector; informer

нахал [na-chál] *sm.* shameless person

нахальный [na-chál'-năy] *adj.* cheeky, impudent

нахальство [na-chál'-stvŏ] *sn.* impudence

нахлебник [na-chlyéb-n'ik] *sm.* boarder

находить [na-cha-d'ét'] (найти) *vt.* to discover; to find

находка [na-chód-ka] *sf.* finding, something found; windfall

находчивый [na-chód-chi-văy] *adj.* quickwitted; resourceful

национальный [na-tsyo-nál'-năy] *adj.* national

нация [ná-tsya] *sf.* nation

начало [na-chá-lŏ] *sn.* beginning; basis; origin

начальник [na-chál'-n'ik] *sm.* chief, head, superior; commander; headmaster

начальный [na-chál'-năy] *adj.* elementary; first, initial

начальство [na-chál'-stvŏ] *sn.* administration; authority

начатки [na-chát-ki] *sm. pl.* elements, rudiments

начерно [na-cher-nó] *adv.* in the rough (*unfinished sketch, unprepared copy, etc.*)

начертание [na-cher-tá-nye] *sn.* outline, sketch, tracing

начёт [na-chót] *sm.* deficit; miscalculation

начётчик [na-chót-chik] *sm.* biblical scholar

начинание [na-chi-ná-nye] *sn.* beginning; enterprise, undertaking

начинать [na-chi-nát'] (начать) *vt.* to begin; to initiate

начинающий [na-chi-ná-yōō-shchi] *adj.* beginning, beginner's; *sm.* beginner

начинка [na-chin-ka] *sf.* filling, stuffing (*culinary*)

начисто [ná-chis-tŏ] *adv.* cleanly, fairly

начитанность [na-chē-tan-nŏst'] *sf.* erudition, scholarship

начитанный [na-chē-tan-năy] *adj.* learned, well-read

наш [nâsh] *pron.* our, ours;
по нашему [pa nâ-she-mŏŏ]
in our opinion, in our way

нашейник [na-shéy-n'ik
sm. frill; neck-band

нашествие [na-shést-vye]
sn. invasion

нашивка [na-shêv-ka] *sf.*
something sewn on; *mil.*
chevron, stripe

наяву [na-ya-vŏŏ] *adv.* in
reality

не [nye] *adv.* not; no; *neg.*
particle dis-, in-, mis-, un-;
pron. none

небесный [nye-byés-nåy]
adj. celestial

неблагодарный [nye-bla-
ga-dâr-nåy] *adj.* thankless,
ungrateful

неблагонадёжный [nye-
bla-ga-na-dyŏzh-nåy] *adj.*
unreliable

неблагородный [nye-bla-
ga-ród-nåy] *adj.* ignoble

неблагосклонный [nye-
bla-ga-sklón-nåy] *adj.* ill-
disposed

небо [nyé-bŏ] *sn.* heaven; sky

нёбо [nyó-bŏ] *sn.* palate

нёбный [nyób-nåy] *adj.*
palatal

небосвод [nye-ba-svód] *sm.*
firmament

небоскрёб [nye-ba-skryób]
sm. skyscraper

небрежный [nye-bryézh-
nåy] *adj.* careless, negligent

небывалый [nye-bă-vá-
låy] *adj.* unprecedented

небылица [nye-bå-l'i-tsa] *sf.*
fable, fiction

невдалеке [nye-vda-lye-
kyé] *adv.* not far off

неведение [nye-vye-dyé-
nye] *sn.* ignorance

неведомый [nye-vyé-da-
måy] *adj.* unknown

невежа [nye-vyé-zha] *sm.*, *f.*
ill-mannered person

невежда [nye-vyézh-da]
sm., *f.* ignoramus

невежественный [nye-
vyé-zhest-vyen-nåy] *adj.* ignorant, illiterate

невежливый [nye-vyézh-
l'i-våy] *adj.* rude, uncivil

неверность [nye-vyér-nŏst']
sf. falseness; infidelity

неверный [nye-vyér-nåy]
adj. unfaithful

невероятный [nye-vye-ra-
yát-nåy] *adj.* incredible

неверующий [nye-vyé-rŏŏ-
yŏŏ-shchi] *adj.* irreligious;
sm. infidel

невеста [nye-vyés-ta] *sf.*
bride

невестка [nye-vyést-ka] *sf.*
fiancée; daughter-in-law; sister-in-law

невзгода [nye-vzgó-da] *sf.*
adversity, ill-luck

невзрачный [nye-vzrâch-
nåy] *adj.* insignificant, plain

невидаль [nye-v'i-dal'] *sf.*
prodigy, wonder

невидимый [nye-v'ĕ-d'i-
måy] *adj.* invisible

невинный [nye-v'ĕn-nåy]
adj. innocent

невнятный [nye-vnyát-nåy]
adj. inarticulate, inaudible

невозвратный [nye-vaz-
vrát-nåy] *adj.* irrevocable

невоздержный [nye-vaz-
dyérzh-nåy] *adj.* intemperate

невозможный [nye-vaz-
mózh-nåy] *adj.* impossible

невозмутимый [nye-vaz-
mŏŏ-t'ĕ-måy] *adj.* calm, cool,
imperturbable

неволя [nye-vó-lya] *sf.* bondage, captivity

невооружённый [nye-va-roō-zhón-nǎy] *adj.* unarmed

невралгия [nyev-rāl-gya] *sf.* neuralgia

неврит [nye-vrít] *sm.* neuritis

невтерпёж [nye-tyer-pyózh] *adv.* unbearably

невыгода [nye-vǎ-ga-da] *sf.* disadvantage

негде [nyég-dye] *adv.* nowhere; no room

негласно [nye-glás-nǒ] *adv.* secretly

негодник [nye-gód-n'ik] *sm.* reprobate

негодный [nye-gód-nǎy] *adj.* worthless

негодяй [nye-ga-dyáy] *sm.*, scoundrel, wretch

негр [nyégr] *sm.* negro.

негритянка [nye-gri-tyán-ka] *sf.* negress

неграмотность [nye-grá-mat-nǒst'] *sf.* illiteracy

недавний [nye-dǎv-n'i] *adj.* late, recent

недаром [nye-dǎ-rǒm] *adv.* not in vain

недвижимый [nye-dv'ě-zhi-mǎy] *adj.* immovable; motionless

неделимый [nye-dye-l'ě-mǎy] *adj.* indivisible

неделовой [nye-dye-la-vóy] *adj.* unbusinesslike

недельный [nye-dyél'-nǎy] *adj.* weekly

неделя [nye-dyé-lya] *sf.* week; **страстная** — [strást-na-ya —] Passion-week, Holy-week

недобросовестный [nye-da-bra-só-vyest-nǎy] *adj.* dishonest, unscrupulous

недобрый [nye-dób-rǎy] *adj.* unkind

недоверие [nye-da-vyé-rye] *sn.* mistrust

недовес [nye-da-vyés] *sm.* short weight

недовольный [nye-da-vól'-nǎy] *adj.* discontented

недозволенный [nye-daz-vó-lyen-nǎy] *adj.* unlawful, unauthorized

недоимка [nye-da-ěm-ka] *sf.* arrears

недопустимый [nye-da-roōs-t'é-mǎy] *adj.* inadmissible

недоразумение [nye-da-ra-zoō-myé-nye] *sn.* misunderstanding

недород [nye-da-ród] *sm.* bad harvest

недосмотр [nye-da-smótr] *sm.* oversight

недоставать [nye-da-sta-vát'] (недостать) *vi.* to lack, to be short

недостаток [nye-da-stá-tŏk] *sm.* deficiency, scarcity, want

недостаточный [nye-da-stá-tach-nǎy] *adj.* inadequate

недоступный [nye-da-stoōp-nǎy] *adj.* unapproachable

недотрога [nye-da-tró-ga] *sm., f.*, *coll.* sensitive person

недоумевать [nye-do-oō-mye-vát'] *vi.* to be perplexed

недочёт [nye-da-chót] *sm.* deficiency, deficit

недра [nyé-dra] *sf.* bosom; **— земли** [— zyem'-lê] bowels of the earth

недруг [nyé-droōg] *sm.* enemy

недуг [nyé-doōg] *sm.* ailment

нежданный [nye-zhdán-nåy] *adj.* unexpected

нежели [nyé-zhe-l'i] *conj.* than

неженатый [nye-zhená-tåy] *adj.* unmarried (*man*); *sm.* bachelor

неженка [nyé-zhen-ka] *sf.* effeminate person

нежный [nyézh-nåy] *adj.* affectionate; delicate, tender

незабудка [nye-za-bóod-ka] *sf.* forget-me-not

независимый [nye-za-v'é-s'i-måy] *adj.* independent

незаконный [nye-za-kón-nåy] *adj.* illegal, unlawful; illegitimate

незамужняя [nye-za-móozh-nya-ya] *adj.* unmarried (*woman*); *sf.* spinster

незаметный [nye-za-myét-nåy] *adj.* imperceptible

незанятый [nye-zá-nya-tåy] *adj.* unoccupied

незапамятный [nye-za-pá-myat-nåy] *adj.* immemorial

нездоровый [nye-zda-ró-våy] *adj.* ill, indisposed

незнакомец [nye-zna-kó-myets] *sm.* stranger

незначительный [nye-zna-ché-tyel'-nåy] *adj.* insignificant

незрелый [nye-zryé-låy] *adj.* immature, unripe

незримый [nye-zr'é-måy] *adj.* invisible

неизбежный [nye-iz-byézh-nåy] *adj.* inevitable, unavoidable

неизведанный [nye-iz-vyé-dan-nåy] *adj.* inexperienced

неизвестный [nye-iz-vyést-nåy] *adj.* obscure; unknown

неимущий [nye-i-móo-shchi] *adj.* indigent, poor

неимоверный [nye-i-ma-vyér-nåy] *adj.* incredible

неисправимый [nye-is-pra-v'é-måy] *adj.* incorrigible

неистовый [nye-és-ta-våy] *adj.* frantic, furious

нейтральный [nyey-trál'-nåy] *adj.* neutral

некий [nyé-ki] *adj.* one, some

некогда [nyé-kag-da] *adv.* formerly; lacking time

некоторый [nyé-ka-to-råy] *adj.* certain, some

некролог [nye-kra-lóg] *sm.* obituary (*notice*)

некстати [nye-kstá-t'i] *adv.* irrelevantly, untimely

некто [nyék-tö] *pron.* someone

некуда [nye-kóo-da] *adv.* nowhere (*to go, put, etc.*)

некурящий [nye-kóo-rya-shchi] *adj.* non-smoking; *sm.* non-smoker

нелепый [nye-lyé-påy] *adj.* absurd, foolish

неловкий [nye-lóv-ki] *adj.* awkward, clumsy

нельзя [nyel'-zyá] (*impersonal expression*) not allowed; – ! you must not!; – входить [– fcha-d'ét'] entry prohibited!

нелюдимый [nye-lyöö-dé-måy] *adj.* unsociable

немедленно [nye-myéd-lyen-nö] *adv.* immediately

немец [nyé-myets] *sm.*, **немка** [nyém-ka] *sf.* German

немецкий [nye-myéts-ki] *adj.* German

немилость [nye-m'é-löst'] *sf.* disfavour, disgrace

неминуемый [nye-m'i-nŏŏ-ye-măy] *adj.* inevitable

немногие [nye-mnŏ-gi-ye] *adj. pl.* few, not many

немой [nye-móy] *adj.* dumb, mute; speechless

ненависть [nye-nă-v'ist'] *sf.* abhorrence, hatred

ненаглядный [nye-na-glyăd-năy] *adj.* beloved, charming

ненароком [nye-na-ró-kŏm] *adv.* unintentionally

ненастный [nye-năst-năy] *adj.* bad, foul (*of weather*); rainy

необдуманный [nye-ab-dŏŏ-ma-năy] *adj.* inconsiderate, rash, thoughtless

необозримый [nye-a-ba-zr'ĕ-măy] *adj.* boundless, immense

необработанный [nye-ab-ra-bó-tan-năy] *adj.* uncultivated; crude

необразованный [nye-ab-ra-zó-van-năy] *adj.* uneducated

необходимый [nye-ab-cha-d'ĕ-măy] *adj.* indispensable, necessary

неожиданный [nye-a-zhĕ-dan-năy] *adj.* unexpected

неоплатный [nye-a-plăt-năy] *adj.* insolvent

неосновательный [nye-a-sna-vă-tyel'-năy] *adj.* groundless, unfounded

неотделимый [nye-at-dye-l'ĕ-măy] *adj.* inseparable

неоткуда [nyé-at-kŏŏ-da] *adv.* from nowhere

неотложный [nye-at-lózh-năy] *adj.* pressing, urgent

неохота [nye-a-chó-ta] *sf.* reluctance

неоценимый [nye-a-tsye-n'ĕ-măy] *adj.* inestimable

непарный [nye-păr-năy] *adj.* odd

неплатёж [nye-pla-tyózh] *sm.* non-payment

неплодородный [nye-pla-da-ród-năy] *adj.* barren

неповоротливый [nye-pa-va-rót-l'i-văy] *adj.* clumsy

непогода [nye-pa-gó-da] *sf.* inclement weather

неподдельный [nye-padd-dyél'-năy] *adj.* genuine, real

неподчинение [nye-pad-chi-nyé-nye] *sn.* insubordination

неполный [nye-pól-năy] *adj.* incomplete

непорядок [nye-pa-ryă-dŏk] *sm.* disorder

непорядочный [nye-pa-ryă-dach-năy] *adj.* dishonourable

непоседа [nye-pa-syé-da] *sm., f.* fidget

непосредственный [nye-pa-sryéd-stven-năy] *adj.* direct; immediate; spontaneous

неправда [nye-prăv-da] *sf.* falsehood

неправильный [nye-pră-v'il'-năy] *adj.* defective, irregular, wrong

неправый [nye-pră-văy] *adj.* unjust

непременно [nye-prye-myén-nŏ] *adv.* without fail

непременный [nye-prye-myén-năy] *adj.* indispensable; permanent

непрерывный [nye-prye-răv-năy] *adj.* continuous, unbroken, uninterrupted

неприязнь [nye-pr'i-yăzn'] *sf.* enmity

неприятель [nye-pr'i-yǎ-tyel'] *sm.* enemy

непроницаемый [nye-pra-n'i-tsǎ-ye-mǎy] *adj.* impenetrable

неравномерный [nye-rav-na-myér-nǎy] *adj.* disproportionate; irregular

нерадение [nye-ra-dyé-nye] *sn.* carelessness, negligence

неразрушимый [nye-raz-rōō-shé-mǎy] *adj.* indestructible

неразумный [nye-ra-zōōm-nǎy] *adj.* unreasonable

нерасположение [nye-ras-pa-la-zhé-nye] *sn.* indisposition

нерастворимый [nye-ras-tva-r'é-mǎy] *adj.* insoluble

нерв [nyérv] *sm.* nerve; **-ный** [-nǎy] *adj.* nervous

нервность [nyérv-nǒst'] *sf.* nervousness

нередко [nye-ryéd-kǒ] *adv.* frequently

нерешительность [nye-rye-shé-tyel'-nǒst'] *sf.* indecision

нерпа [nyér-pa] *sf. zool.* seal

несварение [nye-sva-ryé-nye] *sn.* indigestion

несвежий [nye-svyé-zhi] *adj.* stale

несвязный [nye-svyǎz-nǎy] *adj.* incoherent

несгораемый [nye-zga-ryǎ-ye-mǎy] *adj.* fire-proof

несение [nye-syé-nye] *sn.* bearing, deportment

несессер [ne-se-sér] *sm.* dressing-case

несколько [nyé-skal'-kǒ] *adv.* somewhat; few, some

нескромный [nye-skróm-nǎy] *adj.* immodest

несложный [nye-slózh-nǎy] *adj.* simple

несмотря [nye-sma-tryǎ] *adv.* notwithstanding

несмываемый [nye-smǎ-vǎ-ye-mǎy] *adj.* indelible

несогласие [nye-sa-glǎ-sye] *sn.* discord, variance

несомненно [nye-sam-nyén-no] *adv.* undoubtedly

неспособный [nye-spa-sób-nǎy] *adj.* incapable; dull

несправедливость [nye-spra-vyed-l'é-vǒst'] *sf.* injustice

нести [nye-st'é] (по-) *vt.* to carry; to lay; to reek

нестись [nye-st'és'] *vi.* to rush along

несчастный [nye-schǎst-nǎy] *adj.* unlucky

несчастье [nye-schǎ-stye] *sn.* adversity, misfortune; calamity

несчётный [nye-schót-nǎy] *adj.* innumerable

несъедобный [nye-sye-dób-nǎy] *adj.* inedible

нет [nyét] *adv.* no, not; there is (are) not; **у меня – [**ōō-mye-nyǎ –] I have not

нетерпеливость [nye-tyer-pye-l'é-vǒst'] *sf.* impatience

нетрезвый [nye-tryéz-vǎy] *adj.* intoxicated

неудача [nye-ōō-dǎ-cha] *sf.* failure

неудобный [nye-ōō-dób-nǎy] *adj.* inconvenient

неужели [nye-ōō-zhé-l'i] *adv.* indeed? really?

неумелый [nye-ōō-myé-lǎy] *adj.* unskilful

неутомимый [nye-ōō-ta-m'é-mǎy] *adj.* untiring

неф [nyef] *sm.* nave

нефть [nyéft'] *sf.* mineral-oil, petroleum

нехорошо [nye-cha-ra-shó] *adv.* badly

нечаянно [nye-chā-yan-nŏ] *adv.* incidentally

нечёткий [nye-chót-ki] *adj.* illegible

нечистый [nye-chés-tăy] *adj.* impure, unclean

нечто [nyéch-tŏ] *pron.* something

нешуточный [nye-shōō-tach-năy] *adj.* grave, serious

нещадный [nye-shchād-năy] *adj.* merciless

неявка [nye-yāv-ka] *sf.* absence, default

ни [n'i] *conj.* not; neither, nor; whatever

нива [n'ē-va] *sf.* cornfield

нигде [n'ig-dyé] *adv.* nowhere

нижайший [n'i-zhái-shi] *adj.* most humble; lowest; mean

ниже [n'ē-zhe] *adj.* below, less, under

нижний [n'ēzh-ni] *adj.* inferior; lower; **—этаж** [—-ę-tázh] ground floor; **Нижняя Палата** [n'ēzh-nya-ya pa-lā-ta] Lower House, House of Commons

низ [n'ēz] *sm.* bottom, ground floor; *med.* stool; **—ы** [n'i-ză] *sm. pl.* lowest classes

низать [n'i-zát'] *vt.* to string, thread

низведение [n'iz-vye-dyé-nye] *sn.* degradation

извергать [n'iz-vyer-gát'] (низвергнуть) *vt.* to precipitate; to subvert

низкий [n'ēz-ki] *adj.* base, mean; low

низлагать [n'iz-la-gát'] (низложить) *vt.* to depose

низость [n'ē-zŏst'] *sf.* baseness, meanness

никак [n'i-kāk] *adv.* by no means

никакой [n'i-ka-kóy] *pron.* none, any

никогда [n'i-kag-dā] *adv.* never

никто [n'ik-tó] *pron.* nobody

никуда [n'i-kŏŏ-dā] *adv.* nowhere

нисколько [n'i-skól'-kŏ] *adv.* not at all, not in the least

ниспровержение [n'is-pra-vyer-zhé-nye] *sn.* overthrowing, subversion

нитка [n'ēt-ka] *sf.* thread

ничего [n'i-che-vó] *sn.* nothing; *coll.* it does not matter, never mind

ничто [n'i-chtó] *sn.* nothingness

ничтожный [n'ich-tózh-năy] *adj.* insignificant

ничья [n'i-chyā] *sf.* draw, tie (*in sport, etc.*)

нищий [n'ē-shchi] *sm.* beggar, pauper; *adj.* beggarly; indigent

но [no] *conj.* but

новейший [na-vyéy-shi] *adj.* latest, modern

новизна [na-v'iz-nā] *sf.* novelty; newness

новобранец [na-va-brā-nyets] *sm.* recruit

новобрачные [na-va-brāch-nă-ye] *adj.* newly-married, *s.pl.* newly-married couple

нововведение [na-va-vve-dyé-nye] *sn.* innovation

новоселье [na-va-syé-lye] *sn.* house-warming

новость [nó-vŏst'] *sf.* news, tidings

новый [nó-vǎy] *adj.* new

новь [nov'] *sf.* virgin soil

нога [na-gä] *sf.* foot; leg; **идти в ногу** [it-t'ẽ vnó-gōō] to keep in step

ноготки [na-gat-k'ẽ] *s. pl.* marigold

ноготь [nó-gŏt'] *sm.* finger-nail, toe-nail

нож [nozh] *sm.* knife

ножка [nózh-ka] *sf.* leg (*of chair, etc.*); stalk; stem (*of glass*) [*pl.* scissors

ножницы [nózh-n'i-tsä] *sf. pl.* scabbard, sheath

ножны [nózh-nǎ] *sf. pl.* scabbard, sheath

ноздря [naz-dryä] *sf.* nostril

ноль [nol'] *sm.* nil, zero

номер [nó-myer] *sm.* number

нора [na-rä] *sf.* burrow, lair

норвежец [nar-vyé-zhets] *sm.*, **норвежка** [nar-vyézh-ka] *sf.* Norwegian

норвежский [nar-vyézh-ski] *adj.* Norwegian

норка [nór-ka] *sf.* mink

нормальный [nor-mäl'-näy] *adj.* normal

норов [nó-rŏv] *sm.* custom, habit; caprice; obstinacy

норовистый [na-ra-v'ẽs-täy] *adj.* capricious, stubborn, touchy

нос [nos] *sm.* nose; **-астый** [-äs-täy] *adj.* large-nosed, long-nosed; *coll.* nosy

носилка [na-s'ẽl-ka] *sf.* barrow; stretcher

носильщик [na-s'ẽl'-shchik] *sm.* carrier, porter

носитель [na-s'ẽ-tyel'] *sm.* bearer

носить [na-s'ẽt'] *vt.* to bear; to carry; to wear

ноский [nós-ki] *adj.* durable, lasting

носкость [nós-kŏst'] *sf.* durability, strength

носовой [na-sa-vóy] *adj.* nasal

носок [na-sók] *sm.* toe of shoe; shoe-sock; nozzle; sock

носорог [na-sa-róg] *sm.* rhinoceros

нота [nó-ta] *sf. mus.* note

ноты [nó-tǎ] *sf. pl.* sheet-music

ночевать [na-che-vät'] (пере-) *vi.* to stay (*sleep*) the night

ночлег [nach-lyég] *sm.* lodging (*for the night*)

ночник [nach-n'ẽk] *sm.* night-light

ночной [nach-nóy] *adj.* nocturnal

ночь [noch'] *sf.* night; **-ю** [-yōō] at night

ноша [nó-sha] *sf.* burden; load

ноябрь [na-yäbr'] *sm.* November

нрав [nräv] *sm.* character, disposition; **-ы** [-ǎ] *pl.* manners, morals

нравиться [nrä-v'it'-sya] (по-) *vi.* to please; to like

нравоучение [nra-va-ōō-ché-nye] *sn.* ethics

нравственный [nräv-stvyen-nǎy] *adj.* moral

ну [nōō] *interj.* now then! well! [some

нудный [nōōd-näy] *adj.* tiresome

нужда [nōōzh-dä] *sf.* necessity, want

нуждаться [nōōzh-dät'-sya] *vi.* to be in need; to require; to be short of

нуждающийся [nōōzh-dä-yōō-shchi-sya] *adj.* destitute, poor

нужный [nōo̱zh-năy] *adj.* necessary, requisite

нуль [nōol'] *sm.* nil, nought, zero

нумеровать [nōo-mye-ra-vāt'] *vt.* to number

ныне [nā-nye] *adv.* at present

нынешний [nā-nyesh-ni] *adj.* current

нырять [nă-ryāt'] (ныр-нýть) *vi.* to dive, duck, plunge

ныть [năt'] (за-) *vi.* to sob, whine; to ache

нюх [nyōo̱ch] *sm.* flair; scent

нюхание [nyōo̱-cha-nye] *sn.* smelling, sniffing

нюхательный табак [nyōo̱-chā-tyel'-năy tabāk] snuff

нюхательная соль [nyōo̱-chā-tyel'-na-ya sol'] *sf.* smelling salts

нюхать [nyōo̱-chat] (по-) *vt.i.* to smell, sniff

нянчение [nyan-ché-nye] *sn.* nursing

нянчить [nyăn-chit'] *vt.* to pet, nurse

няня [nyā-nya] *sf.* nurse

О

о, об, обо [a, ab, óbŏ] *prep.* about, concerning, of

оба [ó-ba] *adj.*, *adv.* both

обагрять [a-ba-gryāt'] (обагрѝть) *vt.* to redden; to stain

обаяние [a-ba-yā-nye] *sn.* charm, fascination

обаятельный [a-ba-yā-tyel'-năy] *adj.* charming, enchanting

обвал [ab-vāl] *sm.* collapse; landslide; **снежный —** [snyé̱zh-năy —] avalanche

обваливать [ab-vā-l'i-vat'] (обвáлить) *vt.* to crumble; **-ся** [-sya] *vi.* to collapse

обваривать [ab-vā-ri-vat'] (обварѝть) *vt.* to scald

обвес [ab-vyés] *sm.* short weight

обветренный [ab-vyét-ryen-năy] *adj.* weather-beaten

обветшалый [ab-vyet-shā-lăy] *adj.* decayed, worn out

обвивать [ab-v'i-vāt'] *vt.* to entwine, wind

обвинение [ab-v'i-nyé-nye] *sn.* accusation, charge

обвинитель [ab-v'i-n'ē-tyel'] *sm.* accuser, prosecutor; **-ница** [-n'i-tsa] *sf.* accuser, prosecutrix

обвинять [ab-v'i-nyāt'] (обви-нѝть) *vt.* to accuse, charge

обвислый [ab-v'ēs-lăy] *adj.* drooping, flabby

обводить [ab-va-d'ēt'] (обвестѝ) *vt.* to encircle, outline

обводнить [ab-vad-n'ēt'] *vt.* to irrigate

обволакивать [ab-va-l'ā-k'i-vat'] *vt.* to envelop, wrap

обгорелый [ab-ga-ryé-lăy] *adj.* charred, scorched

обдавать [ab-da-vāt'] (обдáть) *vt.* pour over

обделка [ab-dyél-ka] *sf.* fashioning, mounting, setting

обделывать [ab-dyé-lă-vat'] (обдéлать) *vt.* to arrange, fashion, finish

обделять [ab-dye-lyāt'] *vt.* to be unfair, to cheat

обдёрганный [ab-dyór-gan-năy] *adj.* shabby

обдирать [ab-d'i-rāt'] *vt.* to peel, skin

обдуманный [ab-dōō-man-năy] *adj.* well thought out

обдумывать [ab-dōō-mă-vat'] (обдумать) *vt.* to consider, to think; to ruminate

обед a-byéd]*sm.* dinner, lunch

обедать [a-byé-dat'] (по-) *vi.* to dine

обедневший [a-byed-nyév-shi] *adj.* impoverished

обеднять [a-byed-nyát'] *vt.* to impoverish; make scanty

обедня [a-byéd-nya] *sf.* Mass

обеззараживание [a-byezz-a-rá-zhi-va-nye] *sn.* disinfection

обеззараженный [a-byez-zye-myé-lyen-năy] *adj.* landless

обезображивание [a-byez-a-bra-zhi-vă-nye] *sn.* mutilation

обезоружение [a-byez-a-rōō-zhé-nye] *sn.* disarmament

обезьяна [a-bye-zyá-na] *sf.* monkey

обезьянничать [a-bye-zyá-n'i-chat'] *vt.* to ape

оберегать [a-bye-rye-gát'] (оберечь) *vt.* to guard, defend, protect

обер-прокурор [o-ber-pro-kōō-rór] *sm.* Attorney-General

обёртка [a-byórt-ka] *sf.* casing, wrapper

обёртывать [a-byór-tă-vat'] *vt.* to envelop, wrap up; -ся [-sya] *vi.* to turn round; *fig.* to wriggle out

обескровленный [a-byes-króv-lyen-năy] *adj.* bloodless

обеспечение [a-byes-pye-ché-nye] *sn.* guarantee, security

обеспеченный [a-byes-pyé-chen-năy] *adj.* secure, well provided for

обессмертить [a-byes-smyér-t'it'] *vt.* to immortalize

обесценивать [a-byes-tsyé-n'i-vat'] (обесценить) *vt.* to cheapen, depreciate; underrate

обет [a-byét] *sm.* promise, vow

обещать [a-bye-shchát'] *vt.* to promise

обжаловать [ab-zhá-la-vat'] *vt.* to appeal; to complain; to lodge a complaint

обжиг [ób-zhig] *sm.* kilning

обжигать [ab-zhi-gát'] (обжечь) *vt.* to burn, scorch; to bake (*bricks, etc.*); -ся [-sya] *vi.* to burn oneself

обжора [ab-zhó-ra] *sm., f.* glutton

обжорство [ab-zhór-stvó] *sn.* greediness

обзор [ab-zór] *sm.* review, survey

обивка [a-b'ĕv-ka] *sf.* upholstery

обида [a-b'ē-da] *sf.* insult, offence

обижать [a-b'i-zhát'] (обидеть) *vt.* to offend

обилие [a-b'ē-lye] *sn.* abundance

обильный [a-b'ĕl'-năy] *adj.* abundant, copious, profuse

обиняк [a-b'i-nyák] *sm.* circumlocution; говорить -ами [ga-va-rét' -a-mi) to beat about the bush

обирать [a-b'i-rát'] *vt.* to gather, pick; to plunder

обитание [a-b'i-tă-nye] *sm.* dwelling, residing

обитатель [a-b'i-tä-tyel'] *sm.* inhabitant, resident; inmate

обитель [a-b'i-tät'] *vi.* to inhabit; reside, dwell

обитель [a-b'ě-tyel'] *sf.* cloister, convent, monastery

обитый [a-b'i-täy] *adj.* padded; studded; upholstered

обиход [a-b'i-chód] *sm.* custom, habit; **домашний** – [da-mâsh-ni –] housekeeping; **-ный** [-näy] *adj.* daily; household-; colloquial

облагать [a-bla-gät'] (обложить) *vt.* to besiege, blockade; to tax

обладать [a-bla-dät'] *vt.* to possess

облако [ó-bla-kö] *sn.* cloud

обламывать [a-blä-mä-vat'] (обломать) *vt.* to break down, break off

областной [ab-last-nóy] *adj.* district-; provincial; regional; territorial

область [ób-last'] *sf.* district, province, region; domain; *fig.* tract

облачать [a-bla-chät'] (облачить) *vt.* to array; to invest with

облачение [a-bla-ché-nye] *sn.* vestments

облачный [ó-blach-näy] *adj.* cloudy

облегчать [ab-lyech-chät'] (облегчить) *vt.* to facilitate, lighten, relieve

облегчение [ab-lyech-ché-nye] *sn.* alleviation, relief

облив [ab-l'ěv] *sm.* glazing

обливать [ab-l'i-vät'] (облить) *vt.* to pour over

облик [ób-l'ik] *sm.* countenance, face, figure

обличать [ab-l'i-chät'] (обличить) *vt.* to detect, disclose; to discover

обличение [ab-l'i-ché-nye] *sn.* accusation; unmasking

обложение [ab-la-zhé-nye] *sn.* assessment; taxation

обложка [ab-lózh-ka] *sf.* book-jacket

обломок [ab-ló-mök] *sm.* fragment, splinter, stump

обмазка [ab-máz-ka] *sf.* coating (of paint, etc.); greasing; putty

обман [ab-män] *sm.* deceit, fraud; illusion

обманный [ab-män-näy] *adj.* fraudulent

обманщик [ab-män-shchik] *sm.* charlatan, cheat; impostor

обманывать [ab-mä-nä-vat'] (обмануть) *vt.i.* to cheat, deceive, swindle

обмен [ab-myén] *sm.* barter, exchange, interchange

обмер [ab-myér] *sm.* measure, measurement

обморок [ób-ma-rök] *sm.* fainting; **падать в** – [pâ-dat' v–] to faint, swoon

обмундировка [ab-möon-d'i-róv-ka] *sf.* equipment, outfit

обнажённый [ab-na-zhón-näy] *adj.* bare, uncovered

обнародовать [ab-na-ró-da-vat'] *vt.* to proclaim, promulgate, publish

обнашивать [ab-nä-shi-vat'] (обносить) *vt.* to carry, serve; to enclose

обнимать [ab-n'i-mät'] (обнять) *vt.* to embrace; to hug

обнищалый [ab-n'i-shchä-läy] *adj.* impoverished

обновление [ab-nav-lyé-nye] *sn.* renovation, restoration

обноски [ab-nós-ki] *sm. pl.* cast-off clothing

обобщать [a-bab-schchát'] (обобщи́ть) *vt.i.* to generalize

обогащать [a-ba-ga-schchát'] (обогати́ть) *vt.* to enrich

обоготворять [a-ba-ga-tva-ryát'] *vt.* to idolize, worship

обогревание [a-ba-grye-vá-nye] *sn.* warming

обод [a-bód] *sm.* hoop, rim; -ок, *sm.* circle, ring

ободрение [aba-dryé-nye] *sn.* encouragement

обожатель [a-ba-zhá-tyel'] *sm.* admirer; worshipper

обожать [a-ba-zhát'] *vt.* to adore, worship

обоз [a-bóz] *sm. mil.* baggage transport; a fleet of vans; transport

обозначение [a-baz-na-ché-nye] *sn.* designation; symbol

обозрение [a-ba-zryé-nye] *sn.* review, survey; *theat.* revue

обои [a-bó-i] *sm. pl.* hangings, wallpaper

обойщик [a-bóy-shchik] *sm.* paper-hanger and decorator; upholsterer

оболочка [a-ba-lóch-ka] *sf.* cover, envelope, wrapper; film, membrane

обольщение [a-bal'-shché-nye] *sn.* enticement

оборванец [a-bar-vá-nyets] *sm.* tramp

оборка [a-bór-ka] *sf.* flounce

оборона [a-ba-ró-na] *sf.* defence

оборот [a-ba-rót] *sm.* turn; rotation; turn-over (*trade*)

оборотливый [a-ba-rót-'li-vǎy] *adj.* dexterous, resourceful

оборудование [a-ba-róō-da-va-nye] *sn.* equipping; equipment, outfit

обоюдный [a-ba-yōōd-nǎy] *adj.* reciprocal

обрабатывать [a-bra-bá-tǎ-vat'] (обработать) *vt.* to cultivate, farm

образ [ób-raz] *sm.* form; image; icon; manner

образец [ab-ra-zyéts] *sm.* pattern, sample, specimen

образование [ab-ra-za-vá-nye] *sn.* culture, education, instruction; organization

образованный [ab-ra-zó-van-nǎy] *adj.* cultured, educated, well-read

образовательный [ab-ra-za-vá-tyel'-nǎy] *adj.* educational

образок [ab-ra-zók] *sm.* small picture of a saint

образцовый [ab-raz-tsó-vǎy] *adj.* exemplary; standard

образчик [a-bráz-chik] *sm.* pattern; sample, specimen

обратный [ab-rát-nǎy] *adj.* converse, inverted; return

обращать [a-bra-schát'] (обрати́ть) *vt.* to change, convert, transform; – внимание [– vni'-mǎ-nye] to pay attention; -ся [-syá] *vi.* to address (*someone*), appeal, apply

обращение [a-bra-schché-nye] *sn.* circulation; rotation; dealing – [dōōr-nó-ye –] ill-treatment

обрез [ab-ryéz] *sm.* edge, (*of book*) *typ.* size; -ки [-k'i] *sm. pl.* clippings, scraps

обрекать [ab-rye-kát'] (об-
ре́чь) vt. to devote, doom;
to consecrate; **-ся** [-sya] vi.
to devote oneself

обременять [ab-rye-mye-
nyát'] (обремени́ть) vt. to
overburden, overtax; to en-
cumber

обрече́ние [ab-rye-ché-
nye] sn. consecration

обро́сший [ab-rós-shi] adj.
overgrown

обруба́ть [ab-rōō-bát'] (об-
руби́ть) vt. to cut round,
trim; to hem

обру́бок [ab-rōō-bŏk] sm.
log, stump, trunk

о́бруч [ób-rōŏch] sm. hoop,
ring; **-ник** [-n'ik] sm. cooper

обруче́ние [ab-rōō-ché-nye]
sn. betrothal

обру́шивать [ab-rōō-shi-
vat'] (обру́шить) vt. to de-
molish, destroy

обры́в [ab-rýv] sm. precipice

обрыва́ть [ab-rä-vát'] (обор-
ва́ть) vt. to pluck, tear

обря́д [ab-ryád] sm. cere-
mony, rite; **-ный** [-náy] adj.
ceremonial, ritual

обса́харивать [ab-sä-cha-
r'i-vat'] (обса́харить) vt. to
sprinkle over with sugar, to
ice

обсле́довать [ab-slyé-da-
vat'] vt. to inspect, investi-
gate

обстано́вка [ab-sta-nóv-ka]
sf. furnishings, furniture;
fig. atmosphere, conditions

обстоя́тельный [ab-sta-ya-
tyel'-näy] adj. reliable,
thorough; circumstantial

обстоя́тельство [ab-sta-ya-
tyel'-stvŏ] sn. circumstance,
reason, situation

обстре́л [ab-stryél] sm. bom-
bardment

обстре́ливать [ab-stryé-l'i-
vat'] vi. to open fire

обступа́ть [ab-stōō-pát']
(обступи́ть) vt. to surround

обсужда́ть [ab-sōōzh-dát']
(обсуди́ть) vt. to consider,
discuss; coll. to settle (an
argument)

обсужде́ние [ab-sōōzh-dyé-
nye] sn. consideration; debate

обсыха́ть [ab-sä-chát'] (об-
со́хнуть) vi. to get dry

обта́чка [ab-tách-ka] sf. ro-
tating, turning

обтя́жка [ab-tyázh-ka] sf.
covering, stretching

о́бувь [ó-bŏŏv'] sf. footwear

обу́гливание [a-bōō-gl'i-
vä-nye] sn. carbonization

обу́здывать [a-bōōz-dä-
vat'] (обузда́ть) vt. to bridle,
curb; to break in (animals);
fig. to restrain

о́бух [a-bóōch] sm. butt; haft

обхва́т [ab-chvát] sm. cir-
cumference, girth

обхо́д [ab-chód] sm. beat (of
policeman, etc.); round (of
milkman, etc.); circuit, tour
обходно́й [ab-chód-näy]
adj. roundabout

обхожде́ние [ab-chazh-dyé-
nye] sn. treatment, way's

обша́ривать [ab-shá-r'i-
vat'] (обша́рить) vt. to ran-
sack, search

обшива́ть [ab-shi-vát'] (об-
ши́ть) vt. to hem, sew round,
trim

обши́вка [ab-shév-ka] sf.
hem, trimming, welt; board-
ing, veneering

обши́рность [ab-shér-nŏst']
sf. vastness

обширный [ab-shér-năy] *adj.* enormous, spacious

общаться [ab-shchát'-sya] *vi.* to associate, communicate (with)

общедоступный [ab-shche-da-stóop-năy] *adj.* accessible to all

общежитие [ab-shche-zhí-tye] *sn.* communal living; hostel

общеизвестный [ab-shche-iz-vyést-năy] *adj.* generally known, popular

общение [ab-shchē-nye] *sn.* communion

общепринятый [ab-shche-pr'è-nya-tăy] *adj.* universally adopted

общественный [ab-shché-stven-năy] *adj.* public, social

общество [ób-shchest-vŏ] *sn.* community, society; association, company

общий [ób-shchi] *adj.* common, general, public

община [ab-shchē-na] *sf.* parish; fraternity

объединение [ab-ye-d'i-nyé-nye] *sn.* joining, union

объедки [ab-yéd-ki] *pl.* leavings

объект [ab-yékt] *sm.* object; **-ивный** [-'ěv-năy] *adj.* objective; phenomenal

объём [ab-byóm] *sm.* bulk, volume; capacity

объявитель [ab-ya-v'ě-tyel'] *sm.* announcer

объявление [ab-yav-lyé-nye] *sn.* announcement, advertisement, declaration

объявлять [ab-yav-lyát'] (объявить) *vt.* to advertise, announce; to declare; to notify

объяснять [ab-yas-nyát'] (объяснить) *vt.* to explain, expound

объяснительный [ab-yas-n'ě-tyel'-năy] *adj.* explanatory

объятие [ab-yă-tye] *sn.* embrace

обыватель [a-bă-vă-tyel'] *sm.* inhabitant, resident

обыкновенный [a-băk-na-vyén-năy] *adj.* customary, usual; ordinary, plain

обыск [ó-băsk] *sm.* search

обычай [a-bă-chay] *sm.* custom, mode

обязанность [a-byă-zan-nŏst'] *sf.* duty, obligation

обязанный [a-byă-zan-năy] *adj.* obligatory

овация [a-vă-tsya] *sf.* ovation

овёс [a-vyós] *sm.* oat(s)

овин [a-v'ěn] *sm.* barn

овощи [ó-va-shchi] *sm. pl.* vegetables [meal

овсянка [av-syăn-ka] *sf.* oatmeal

овца [av-tsá] *sf.* ewe, sheep

овцеводство [av-tse-vód-stvŏ] *sn.* sheep-breeding

овчарка [av-chăr-ka] *sf.* sheep-dog

овчина [av-chē-na] *sf.* sheepskin

оглавление [a-glav-lyé-nye] *sn.* table of contents

оглавлять [a-glav-lyát'] *vt.* to index

оглушать [a-glóoshăt'] (оглушить) *vt.* to deafen

оглядывать [a-glyă-dă-vat'] *vt.* to examine, look over

огневой [a-gne-vóy] *adj.* igneous; *fig.* ardent, fiery

огнетушитель [a-gne-tŏŏ-shē-tyel'] *sm.* fire-extinguisher

огнеупорный [a-gnye-ōō-pór-nǎy] adj. fire-proof

оговор [a-ga-vór] sm. denunciation; slander

оговорка [a-ga-vór-ka] sf. clause, proviso; stipulation

огонь [a-gón] sm. fire; **пушечный** — [pōō-shech-nǎy —] gunfire

огород [a-ga-ród] sm. kitchen-garden, market-garden; **-ник** [-n'ik] sm. market-gardener

огорошить [a-ga-ró-shit] vt. to embarrass; to surprise

огорчать [a-gar-chát] (огорчить) vt. to distress, grieve; **-ся** [-sya] vi. to be distressed

огорчение [a-gar-ché-nye] sn. affliction, concern, distress

ограда [a-grá-da] sf. enclosure, fence

ограждать [a-grazh-dát] (оградить) vt. to fence, wall-in; to defend, guard

ограничение [a-gra-n'i-ché-nye] sn. limitation, restriction

ограничивать [a-gra-n'é-chi-vat] (ограничить) vt. to confine, limit

огромный [a-gróm-nǎy] adj. huge, immense

огурец [a-gōō-ryéts] sm. cucumber

ода [ó-da] sf. ode

одаривать [a-dā-r'i-vat] (одарить) vt. to endow; to shower with gifts

одевать [a-dyé-vát] (одеть) vt. to clothe, dress

одежда [a-dyézh-da] sf. clothing, dress, garments

одёр [a-dyór] sm. jade (horse)

одеяло [a-dye-yā-lō] sn. bed-cover, blanket, eider-down

одеяние [a-dye-yā-nye] sn. attire, garment

один [a-d'ēn] num., pron. a, one

одинаковый [a-d'i-nā-ka-vǎy] adj. identical, same

одиннадцать [a-d'ēn-nad-tsat] num. eleven

одинокий [a-d'i-nó-ki] adj. lonely, solitary; single

одиночество [a-d'i-nó-chest-vō] sn. loneliness, solitude

однажды [ad-názh-dǎ] adv. once

однако [ad-nā-kō] adv. but, however, yet

одноактный [ad-na-ākt-nǎy] adj. of one act

однобортный [ad-na-bórt-nǎy] adj. single-breasted

одновременный [ad-na-vryé-myen-nǎy] adj. simultaneous

однодневный [ad-na-dnyév-nǎy] adj. ephemeral

однозвучный [ad-na-zvōōch-nǎy] adj. monotonous

однозначащий [ad-na-zna-chā-shchi] adj. synonymous

однокашник [ad-na-kāsh-n'ik] sm. school-mate

одноклассник [ad-na-klās-sn'ik] sm. class-mate

однолетний [ad-na-lyét-ni] adj. annual, yearly

однообразие [ad-na-ab-rā-zye] sn. monotony, sameness

однообразный [ad-na-ab-rāz-nǎy] adj. uniform

однородность [ad-na-ród-nōst] sf. similarity

односложный [ad-na-slózh-nǎy] adj. monosyllabic

одноствольный [ad-na-stvól'-năy] *adj.* single-barrelled

односторонний [ad-na-sta-rón-n'ij] *adj.* unilateral; *fig.* prejudiced

однофамилец [ad-na-fa-m'ē-lyets] *sm.* namesake

одобрение [a-da-bryé-nye] *sm.* approval, favour

одолевать [a-da-lye-vát'] (одолеть) *vt.* to overcome, surmount, conquer

одолжать [a-dal-zhát'] (одолжить) *vt.* to lend, loan; *fig.* to oblige

одолжение [a-dal-zhé-nye] *sm.* favour, kindness, service

одр [ódr] *sm.* sick-bed

одуванчик [a-dŏŏ-ván-chik] *sm.* dandelion

одурелый [a-dŏŏ-ryé-lăy] *adj.* stupid, vacant

одурь [ó-dŏŏr'] *sf.* craziness, stupidity; deadly nightshade

одутловатый [a-dŏŏt-la-vá-tăy] *adj.* bloated, puffy

одушевлять [a-dŏŏ-shev-lyát'] (одушевить) *vt.* to animate, inspire

одышка [a-dásh-ka] *sf.* asthma; panting

ожерелье [a-zhe-ryé-lye] *sm.* necklace

ожесточать [a-zhes-ta-chát'] (ожесточить) *vt.* to embitter, harden

оживать [a-zhi-vát'] (ожить) *vi.* to resuscitate; *fig.* to cheer up

оживлять [a-zhiv-lyát'] (оживить) *vt.* to animate, revive

ожидание [a-zhi-dá-nye] *sm.* expectation, waiting

ожог [a-zhóg] *sm.* burn, scald

озабоченность [a-za-bó-chen-nŏst'] *sf.* anxiety, preoccupation

озарять [a-za-ryát'] (озарить) *vt.* to illuminate; *fig.* to enlighten

озвереть [az-vye-ryét'] *vi.* to become brutal

оздоровление [az-da-rav-lyé-nye] *sm.* sanitation

озеро [ó-zye-rŏ] *sm.* lake

озлобление [az-lab-lyé-nye] *sm.* anger, wrath

означать [az-na-chát'] *vt.* to mean, signify

озноб [az-nób] *sm.* chill, shivering

ознобa [az-nó-ba] *sf.* chilblain

озорник [a-zar-n'ĕk] *sm.* disobedient boy, impudent boy; insolent person

оказывать [a-ká-ză-vat'] (оказать) *vt.* to express, show; to render

оканчивать [a-kán-chi-vat'] (окончить) *vt.* to finish, terminate

окаменелый [a-ka-mye-nyé-lăy] *adj.* petrified

окаянный [a-ka-yán-năy] *adj.* cursed, damned

океан [a-kye-án] *sm.* ocean

окисление [a-kis-lyé-nye] *sm.* oxidation

окислость [a-k'ĕs-lŏst'] *sf.* acidity, sourness

окись [ó-k'is'] *sf.* oxide

оклад [a-klád] *sm.* salary

оклеивать [a-klyé-ivat'] *vt.* to glue, paper, paste

оклик [ok-l'ik] *sm.* call, hail

окно [ak-nó] *sm.* window

око [ó-kŏ] *sn.* eye

оковы [a-kó-vă] *sf. pl.* fetters

около [ó-ka-lŏ] *prep.* about, by, thereabouts; near

околодок [a-ka-ló-dŏk] *sm.* environs, vicinity

окольный [a-kól'-năy] *adj.* devious; roundabout

окончание [a-kan-chá-nye] *sn.* completion, ending; *gram.* inflexion

окончательный [a-kan-chá-tyel'-năy] *adj.* final

окоп [a-kóp] *sm.* mil. em-placement; entrenchment

окорок [ó-ka-rŏk] *sm.* gam-mon, ham; leg of mutton

окостенение [a-kas-tye-né-nye] *sn.* numbness; ossifica-tion; stiffness

окраина [a-krá-i-na] *sf.* out-skirts

окраска [a-krás-ka] *sf.* hue, tint

окрестный [a-kryést-năy] *adj.* neighbouring; suburban

окрошка [a-krósh-ka] *sf.* cold sour soup; *fig.* medley, mixture

округ [ó-krŏŏg] *sm.* circuit; district, region

округлый [a-krŏŏg-láy] *adj.* plump; rounded

окружать [a-krŏŏ-zhát'] (о-кружи́ть) *vt.* to encircle, surround

окружность [a-krŏŏzh-nŏst'] *sf.* circuit; circum-ference

октябрь [ak-tyábr'] *sm.* Oc-tober

окунать [a-kŏŏ-nát'] (окуну́ть) *vt.* to dip, immerse

окунь [ó-kŏŏn'] *sm.* perch (*fish*)

окуривать [a-kŏŏ-rʹi-vat'] (окури́ть) *vt.* to fumigate

оладья [a-lá-dya] *sf.* fritter, pancake

оледенелый [a-lye-dye-nyé-láy] *adj.* frozen, iced

оленина [a-lyé-n'i-na] *sf.* venison; buckskin

олень [a-lyén'] *sm.* deer hart, stag

олицетворение [a-l'i-tsye-tva-ryé-nye] *sn.* embodiment, personification

олово [ó-la-vŏ] *sn.* pewter, tin

олух [ó-lŏŏch] *sm.* clown, simpleton

ольха [ól'-cha] *sf.* alder(-tree)

омар [a-már] *sm.* lobster

омела [a-myé-la] *sf.* mistletoe

омерзение [a-myer-zyé-nye] *sn.* abomination; loathing

омертвелость [a-myer-tvyé-lost'] *sf.* numbness; necrosis

омовение [a-ma-vyé-nye] *sn.* ablution

омолаживать [a-ma-lá-zhi-vat'] *vi.* to rejuvenate

омрачать [am-ra-chát'] (ом-рачи́ть) *vt.* to darken, obscure

омут [ó-mŏŏt] *sm.* pool, slough

он [on] *pron.* he; **она** [a-ná] she; **оно** [a-nó] it; **они** [a-n'é] they

опаздывать [a-pázʹ-dă-vat'] (опозда́ть) *vi.* to be late, to come too late

опала [a-pá-la] *sf.* disgrace

опаливать [a-pá-l'i-vat'] *vt.* to singe

опальный [a-páʹ-năy] *adj.* disgraced, in disgrace

опара [a-pá-ra] *sf.* dough

опасение [a-pa-syé-nye] *sn.* apprehension

опасливый [a-pás-l'i-văy] *adj.* cautious

опасность [a-pás-nŏst'] *sf.* danger, peril

опасный [a-pás-năy] *adj.* dangerous

опека [a-pyé-ka] *sf.* guardian-ship, wardship; trusteeship

опекун [a-pye-kōōn] *sm.* guardian, tutor

опекунский [a-pye-kōōn-ski] *adj.* tutorial

оперативный [a-pye-ra-t'év-nay] *adj.* operative

операция [a-pye-rä-tsya] *sf.* operation

оперный [ó-pyer-nay] *adj.* operatic

опечатка [a-pye-chät-ka] *sf.* erratum, misprint

опечатывать [a-pye-chä-tă-vat'] (опечатать) *vt.* to seal up

опивки [a-p'ēv-ki] *sf. pl.* dregs; leavings

опилки [a-p'ēl-ki] *sf. pl.* sawdust; filings

опираться [a-p'i-rät'-sya] *vi.* to lean against, to recline, to support oneself

описание [a-p'i-sä-nye] *sn.* description, portrayal

описательный [a-p'i-sä-tyel'-nay] *adj.* descriptive

описка [a-p'és-ka] *sf.* a slip of the pen; clerical error

описывать [a-p'ē-sä-vat'] (описать) *vt.* to describe, portray

опись [ó-p'is'] *sf.* inventory; list, schedule

оплакивать [a-plä-k'i-vat'] (оплакать) *vt.i.* to lament, mourn; to deplore

оплата [a-plä-ta] *sf.* pay, payment, remuneration

оплачивать [a-plä-chi-vat'] (оплатить) *vt.* to pay, settle an account

оплодотворение [a-pla-da-tva-ryé-nye] *sn.* fertilization, impregnation

оплот [a-plót] *sm.* stronghold

оплошный [a-plósh-nay] *adj.* inadvertent, negligent

оповещать [a-pa-vye-shchät'] (оповестить) *vt.* to announce, inform

опоздание [a-paz-dä-nye] *sn.* delay

опознание [a-paz-nä-nye] *sn.* identification, recognition

оползень [ó-pal-zyen'] *sm.* landslide

ополченец [a-pal-ché-nyets] *sm.* militiaman

опора [a-pó-ra] *sf.* prop, support

опоражнивать [a-pa-räzh-n'i-vat'] (опорожнить) *vt.* to empty; to evacuate

опорочность [a-pa-róch-nóst'] *sf.* blame, censure, defamation; libel

оправа [a-prä-va] *sf.* mounting, setting *(of jewellery)*

оправдание [a-prav-dä-nye] *sn.* apology, excuse, justification; exoneration

оправдывать [a-prä-vdä-vat'] (оправдать) *vt.* to excuse, justify; to acquit

опрашивать [a-prä-shi-vat'] *vt.* to question

определение [a-prye-dye-lyé-nye] *sn.* definition

определённый [a-prye-dye-lyón-nay] *adj.* certain, definite, specific

определимый [a-prye-dye-l'é-may] *adj.* definable, determinable

опровергать [a-pra-vyer-gät'] (опровергнуть) *vt.* to refute

опрокидывать [a-pra-k'ē-dä-vat'] (опрокинуть) *vt.* to overturn, upset; to capsize

опрос [a-prós] *sm.* test; inquest; **-ный лист** [-năy l'ist] questionnaire

опрощать [a-pra-shchăt'] *vt.* to simplify

опрятный [a-pryăt-năy] *adj.* tidy, neat, orderly

оптик [óp-t'ik] *sm.* optician

оптика [óp-t'i-ka] *sf.* optics

оптический [op-t'é-ches-ki] *adj.* optical

оптовый [ap-tó-văy] *adj.* wholesale

опубликование [a-pōō-bl'i-ka-vă-nye] *sn.* publication

опускать [a-pōōs-kăt'] (опустить) *vt.* to drop; to let down, lower; to droop

опустошение [a-pōōs-ta-shé-nye] *sn.* desolation, devastation

опутывать [a-pōō-tă-vat'] (опутать) *vt.* to entangle; to implicate

опухать [a-pōō-chăt'] (опухнуть) *vi.* to swell

опухоль [ó-pōō-chŏl'] *sf.* swelling, tumour

опухший [a-pōōch-shi] *adj.* puffed, swollen

опушённый [a-pōō-shónnăy] *adj.* trimmed with fur

опушка [a-pōōsh-ka] *sf.* fur trimming

опущение [a-pōō-shché-nye] *sn.* omission

опыление [a-pă-lyé-nye] *sn.* pollination

опыт [ó-păt] *sm.* experiment

опытность [ó-păt-nŏst'] *sf.* experience, proficiency

опытный [ó-păt-năy] *adj.* experienced, expert, proficient

опьянение [a-pya-nyé-nye] *sn.* intoxication

опьянённый [a-pya-nyónnăy] *adj.* drunk, intoxicated

опьянеть [a-pya-nyét'] *vi.* to become drunk

опять [a-pyăt'] *adv.* again

орава [a-rá-va] *sf. coll.* gang, horde, crowd

оракул [a-rá-kōōl] *sm.* oracle

оранжерея [a-ran-zhe-ré-ya] *sf.* conservatory, hothouse

орарь [a-răr'] *sm. eccl.* stole

орать [a-răt'] *vi.* to bawl, shout; to plough, to till

орган [ór-gan] *sm.* organ (*anatomical or literary*)

орган [ar-găn] *sm. mus.* organ

организатор [ar-ga-n'i-ză-tŏr] *sm.* organizer

организованный [ar-ga-n'i-zó-van-năy] *adj.* organized

органический [ar-ga-n'é-ches-ki] *adj.* organic

оргия [ór-gya] *sf.* orgy

орден [ór-dyen] *sm. eccl., etc.* order

ординарец [ar-d'i-nă-ryets] *sm. mil.* orderly

ординарный [or-d'i-năr-năy] *adj.* common, ordinary

орёл [a-ryól] *sm.* eagle

ореол [a-rye-ól] *sm.* halo

орех [a-ryéch] *sm.* nut; **грецкий** [gryéts-ki —] walnut; **кокосовый** [ka-kó-sa-văy —] coconut; **мускатный** [mōōs-kát-năy —] nutmeg; **лесной** [lyes-nóy —] hazel-nut

орешник [a-ryésh-n'ik] *sm.* nut-tree

оригинальность [a-r'i-gi-năl'-nŏst'] *sf.* originality

оригинальный [a-r'i-gi-năl'-năy] *adj.* eccentric, original

ориентировка [a-ryen-t'i-róv-ka] *sf.* orientation

оркестр [ar-kyéstr] *sm.* orchestra; **-овка** [-óv-ka] *sf.* orchestration; scoring

орлиный [ar-l'é-nǎy] *adj.* aquiline

орлянка [ar-lyán-ka] *sf.* toss (*heads or tails*)

орошать [a-ra-shát'] (оросить) *vt.* to irrigate

орошение [a-ra-shé-nye] *sn.* irrigation

орудие [a-rōō-dye] *sn. mil.* weapons; instrument, tool; implement(s)

орудовать [a-rōō-da-vat'] *vi. coll.* to administer, manage

оружейный [a-rōō-zhéy-nǎy] *adj.* arms-, gun-; **-завод** [– za-vód] *sm.* armoury, arsenal; **-мастер** [– más-tyer] *sm.* gunsmith

оружие [a-rōō-zhye] *sn.* arms

оса [a-sá] *sf.* wasp

осада [a-sá-da] *sf.* siege

осадка [a-sád-ka] *sf. naut.* draught; settling, sinking, subsidence

осадок [a-sá-dǒk] *sm.* dregs, sediment

осаживать [a-sá-zhi-vat'] (осадить) *vt.* to back (*go or move backwards*); to precipitate

осанка [a-sán-ka] *sf.* deportment

осанистый [a-sa-n'ěs-tǎy] *adj.* dignified, stately

осваивать [a-svá-i-vat'] (освоить) *vt.* to acclimatize, familiarize; **-ся** [-sya] *vt.* to be familiar with; feel at home

осведомление [a-sve-dam-lyé-nye] *sn.* information

осведомлять [a-svye-dam-lyát'] *vt.* to inform; **-ся** [-sya] *vi.* to inquire, make inquiries

освежать [a-svye-zhát'] (освежить) *vt.* to cool, freshen

освежительный [a-svye-zhě-tyel'-nǎy] *adj.* cooling, refreshing

освещать [a-svye-shchát'] (осветить) *vt.* to illuminate, light-up; to elucidate

освещение [a-svye-shché-nye] *sn.* illumination, lighting

освободитель [a-sva-ba-d'é-tyel'] *sm.* liberator, saviour

освобождать [a-sva-bazh-dát'] (освободить) *vt.* to free, liberate, rescue

освобождение [a-sva-bazh-dyé-nye] *sn.* emancipation; liberation; release

освящать [a-svya-shchát'] (освятить) *vt.* to bless, consecrate, sanctify; to inaugurate

оседать [a-sye-dát'] *vi.* to settle, sink, subside

оседлый [a-syéd-lǎy] *adj.* sedentary; settled

осёл [a-syól] *sm.* ass, donkey

оселок [a-sye-lók] *sm.* hone

осенний [a-syén-n'i] *adj.* autumnal

осень [ó-syen'] *sf.* autumn

осенять [a-sye-nyát'] (осенить) *vt.* to shade, shadow, shield

осётр [a-syótr] *sm.* sturgeon

осиливать [a-s'é-li-vat'] (осилить) *vt.* to prevail, subdue

осина [a-s'é-na] *sf.* asp, aspen-tree

осиплый [a-s'ěp-lǎy] *adj.* hoarse, husky

осиротеть [a-s'i-ra-tyét'] *vi.* to become an orphan

оскал [as-kál] *sm.* grin

осквернение [a-skvyer-nyé-nye] *sn.* desecration, violation

осквернительный [a-skvyer-n'é-tyel'-nǎy] *adj.* profane

осколок [as-kó-lŏk] *sm.* chip, [splinter

оскопление [as-kap-lyé-nye] *sn.* castration

оскорбитель [as-kar-b'é-tyel'] *sm.* offender; **-ный** [-nǎy] *adj.* abusive; offensive

оскорбление [as-kar-blyé-nye] *sn.* insult, offence, outrage

оскорблять [as-kar-blyát'] (оскорбить) *vt.* to insult, offend

оскрёбок [as-kryó-bŏk] *sm.* scraping(s)

оскудение [as-kŏŏ-dyé-nye] *sn.* impoverishment

ослабелый [a-sla-byé-lǎy] *adj.* enfeebled, weakened

ослабление [a-slab-lyé-nye] *sn.* laxity, weakening

ослаблять [a-slab-lyát'] (ослабить) *vt.* to relax

ославить [a-slá-vit'] *vt.* to decry, discredit

ослепительный [a-slye-p'é-tyel'-nǎy] *adj.* blinding, dazzling

ослиный [as-l'é-nǎy] *adj.* asinine

осложнять [as-slazh-nyát'] (осложнить) *vt.* to complicate

ослушание [a-slŏŏ-shá-nye] *sn.* disobedience

ослушный [a-slŏŏsh-nǎy] *adj.* disobedient, insubordinate

осматривать [a-smá-tri-vat'] (осмотреть) *vt.* to examine, inspect; survey; **-ся** [-sya] *vi.* to find one's bearings, to look around

осмеивать [a-smyé-i-vat'] (осмеять) *vt.* to mock, ridicule

осмеяние [a-smye-yá-nye] *sn.* mockery

осмотр [a-smótr] *sm.* inspection, survey; **-щик** [-shchik] *sm.* inspector; surveyor

осмысление [a-smǎs-lyé-nye] *sf.* intelligence, understanding [design

оснастка [as-nást-ka] *sf.* rig-

основа [as-nó-va] *sf.* basis, foundation; *pl.* principles

основатель [as-na-vá-tyel'] *sm.* founder

основательный [as-na-vá-tyel'-nǎy] *adj.* solid, sound, thorough, well-grounded

основной [as-nav-nóy] *adj.* essential, principal

основывать [as-nó-vǎ-vat'] *vt.* to establish

особа [a-só-ba] *sf.* individual, person

особенный [a-só-byen-nǎy] *adj.* particular, special; peculiar

осознавать [a-saz-na-vát'] *vt.* to perceive, realize

осока [a-só-ka] *sf.* sedge

осокорь [ó-sa-kŏr'] *sf.* poplar

оспа [ó-spa] *sf.* small-pox; **ветряная** — [vyé-trya-na-ya —] chicken-pox

оспаривать [as-pá-ri-vat'] (оспорить) *vt.* to contend, dispute

осрамление [as-ram-lyé-nye] *sn.* disgrace, shame

оставаться [as-ta-vát'-sya] (остаться) *vi.* to remain, stay

оставлять [as-tav-lyát'] (оста́вить) vt. to abandon, forsake, desert; to leave (employment, etc.)

остально́й [as-tal'-nóy] adj. remaining

остана́вливать [as-ta-náv-l'i-vat'] (останови́ть) to pull up, stop; to check

оста́нки [a-stán-ki] sm. pl. relics, remains

остано́вка [a-sta-nóv-ka] sf. stop, stopping place; station; check; intermission

оста́ток [a-stá-tòk] sm. remainder, surplus; balance (of account)

оста́тки [a-stát-ki] sm. pl. leavings

остерега́ние [as-tye-rye-gá-nye] sn. admonition, warning

остерега́ть [as-tye-rye-gát'] (остере́чь) vt. to caution, warn; -ся [-sya] vi. to beware

осто́в [ós-tòv] sm. framework, skeleton

остолбене́ние [as-tal-bye-nyé-nye] sn. stupor

осторо́жный [as-ta-rózh-này] adj. careful, discreet

остра́стка [as-trás-tka] sf. caution

острига́ть [as-tr'i-gát'] (остри́чь) vt. to clip, crop, shear, shingle

остри́ть [as-tr'ét'] vt. to sharpen; vi. to joke

о́стров [ós-tròv] sm. island; -итя́нин [-i-tyá-n'in] sm. islander; -но́й [-nóy] adj. insular; -ок [-ók] sm. islet

острога́ [as-tra-gá] sf. harpoon

острота́ [as-tra-tá] sf. sharpness; shrewdness

остроу́мный [astra-óóm-

náy] adj. ingenious, smart, witty

о́стрый [ós-tràu] adj. acrid, pungent; acute; sharp

остря́к [as-tryák] sm. coll. a witty person

оступа́ться [as-tōō-pát'-sya] vi. to stumble

остыва́ть [as-tà-vát'] vi. to get cool (as cooked food, hot tea, etc.)

осужда́ть [a-sōōzh-dát'] (осуди́ть) vt. to blame, censure; to condemn, convict, sentence

осужде́ние [a-sōōzh-dyé-nye] sn. blame, censure; conviction

осуждённый [a-sōōzh-dyón-này] adj. condemned; sm. condemned person

осуше́ние [a-sōō-shé-nye] sn. drainage

осуществи́мый [a-sōō-shches-tv'é-màu] adj. feasible, practical

ось [os'] sf. axis, axle, spindle

осяза́емость [a-sya-zá-ye-mòst'] sf. tangibility

осяза́ние [a-sya-zá-nye] sn. feeling, sense of touch

от [òt], **ото** [ò-tò] prep. from, of

ота́ва [a-tá-va] sf. aftermath

ота́пливать [a-táp-l'i-vat'] (отопи́ть) vt. to heat, warm

ота́ра [a-tá-ra] sf. flock (of sheep)

отба́вка [at-báv-ka] sf. diminution

отбива́ть [at-b'i-vát'] (отби́ть) vt. to parry, repel

отбира́ть [at-b'i-rát'] (отобра́ть) vt. to confiscate; to take away; to choose, select

о́тблеск [ót-blyesk] sm. gleam, reflection

отбой [at-bóy] *sm. mil.* retreat; —! cease fire! дать — [dǎt' —] to ring off ('phone)

отбор [at-bór] *sm.* choice, selection; **-ный** [-nǎy] first-class, select

отбрасывать [at-brǎ-să-vat'] (отбросить) *vt.* to reject; to throw away, throw down, throw off

отбросы [at-bró-să] *sm. pl.* refuse, scraps, waste

отбывать [at-bǎ-vát'] (отбыть) *vi.* to depart, set out; to serve (*duty, time*)

отбытие [at-bǎ-tye] *sn.* departure (*of train, etc.*)

отвага [at-vǎ-gǎ] *sf.* audacity; courage, daring

отважный [at-vǎzh-năy] *adj.* bold, fearless

отвал [at-vǎl] *sm.* unmooring; dump

отвар [at-vǎr] *sm.* decoction; broth

отвергать [at-vyer-gǎt'] (отвергнуть) *vt.* to reject, repudiate

отверженец [at-vyér-zhe-nyets] *sm.* outcast

отверстие [at-vyér-stye] *sn.* aperture, opening

отвёртывать [at-vyór-tă-vat'] (отвернуть) *vt.* to unscrew a (*stopper, etc.*)

отвёртка [at-vyórt-kă] *sf.* screwdriver

отвес [at-vyés] *sm.* plummet; **-ный** [-năy] *adj.* vertical

ответ [at-vyét] *sm.* answer, reply, response; **-ный** [-năy] *adj.* responsive

ответственный [at-vyét-stven-năy] *adj.* responsible

отвечать [at-vye-chǎt'] (ответить) *vt.i.* to answer, reply

отвинчивать [at-v'ĕn-chi-vat'] (отвинтить) *vt.* to unscrew

отвислый [at-v'ĕs-lăy] *adj.* baggy, loose

отвлекать [at-vlye-kǎt'] (отвлечь) *vt.* to distract; to divert; **-ся** [-sya] *vi.* to digress

отвлечение [at-vlye-ché-nye] *n.* abstraction; diversion

отвод [at-vód] *sm.* challenge

отводить [at-va-d'ĕt'] (отвести) *vt.* to divert, draw aside, lead away

отвозить [at-va-z'ĕt'] (отвезти) *vt.* to transport

отворачиваться [at-va-rǎ-chi-vat'-sya] *vi.* to turn away

отворот [at-va-rót] *sm.* facing, lapel; boot-top(s)

отворять [at-va-ryǎt'] (отворить) *vt.* to open

отвратительный [at-vra-t'ĕ-tyel'-năy] *adj.* abominable, disgusting, loathsome

отвращать [at-vra-shchǎt'] (отвратить) *vt.* to avert, ward off

отвязывать [at-vyǎ-ză-vat'] (отвязать) *vt.* to unfasten, untie; **-ся** [-sya] *vi.* to become loose, unfastened

отгадка [at-gǎd-ka] *sf.* solution of a riddle

отговаривать [at-ga-vǎ-ři-vat'] (отговорить) *vt.* to dissuade

отговорка [at-ga-vór-ka] *sf.* pretence, pretext

отгонять [at-ga-nyǎt'] (отогнать) *vt.* to disperse, drive away

отгородка [at-ga-ród-ka] *sf.* fencing, partition

отдавать [at-da-vǎt'] (отдать) *vt.* to restore, return

отдаление [at-da-lyé-nye] *sn.* aloofness, remoteness

отдалённый [at-da-lyón-nay] *adj.* distant, far-off

отдалять [at-da-lyát'] (отдалить) *vt.* to estrange; -ся [-sya] *vi.* to keep away from, move off

отдача [at-dá-cha] *sf.* payment; recoil; surrender

отдел [at-dyél] *sm.* department, section

отделение [at-dye-lyé-nye] *sn.* division, partition; chapter; compartment

отделимый [at-dye-lʹé-may] *adj.* separable

отделка [at-dyél-ka] *sf.* finish(ing); trimming

отделывать [at-dyé-lă-vat'] (отделать) *vt.* to trim

отдельный [at-dyélʹ-năy] *adj.* individual, separate

отделять [at-dye-lyát'] (отделить) *vt.* to separate, sever

отдушина [at-dōō-shi-na] *sf.* air-hole, ventilator

отдых [ót-dăch] *sm.* relaxation, repose, rest

отдыхать [at-dă-chát'] (отдохнуть) *vi.* to rest

отёк [a-tyók] *sm.* inflation

отекать [a-tye-kát'] *vi.* to inflate, swell

отец [a-tyéts] *sm.* father

отечество [a-tyé-chest-vŏ] *sn.* fatherland, native country

отживший [at-zhív-shi] *adj.* obsolete

отжиг [ót-zhig] *sm. tech.* tempering

отзвук [ót-zvŏŏk] *sm.* echo

отзыв [ót-zăv] *sm.* reference, testimonial

отзывать [at-ză-vát'] (отозвать) *vt.* to recall, withdraw

отзывчивый [at-zắv-chi-văy] *adj.* appreciative, responsive, sympathetic

отказ [at-káz] *sm.* denial, refusal, rejection

отказывать [at-ká-ză-vat'] (отказать) *vt.* to refuse; -ся [-sya] *vi.* to renounce

откапывать [at-ká-pă-vat'] (откапать) *vt.* to dig up, exhume, unearth

откат [at-kát] *sm.* rebound, recoil

откидной [at-kid-nóy] *adj.* reversible

откладывать [at-klá-dă-vat'] (отложить) *vt.* to put by; to put on one side; to delay, postpone

отклик [ót-kl'ik] *sm.* response

отклонение [at-kla-nyé-nye] *sn.* deflection, deviation

отклонять [at-kla-nyát'] *vt.* to decline; to divert

откос [at-kós] *sm.* declivity

откровение [at-kra-vyé-nye] *sn.* revelation

откровенность [at-kra-vyén-nŏst'] *sf.* frankness

откручивать [at-krōō-chi-vat'] (открутить) *vt.* to untwine, untwist

открывать [at-kră-vát'] (открыть) *vt.* to open, reveal

открытие [at-krá-tye] *sn.* discovery, opening; unveiling

открытка [at-krát-ka] *sf.* post-card

открытый [at-krắ-tăy] *adj.* open; outspoken

откуда [at-kōō-da] *adv.* whence; **—нибудь** [—n'i-bōōd'] from some place or other

откуп [ót-kŏŏp] *sm.* lease

откупировка [at-kŏŏ-p'i-rŏv-ka] *sf.* uncorking

отлагательство [at-la-gá-tyel'-stvŏ] *sn.* delay; procrastination

отлёт [at-lyót] *sm.* flying away

отлив [at-l'ĕv] *sm.* ebb, low tide

отливать [at-l'i-vát] *vt.* to

отливка [at-l'ĕv-ka] *sf.* cast, mould; casting, founding

отличать [at-l'i-chát] (отличить) *vt.* to discern, discriminate; -ся [-sya] *vi.* to differ, to excel

отличие [at-l'ĕ-chye] *sn.* difference, distinction

отличительный [at-l'i-chĕ-tyel'-nǎy] *adj.* characteristic, distinctive

отличный [at-l'ĕch-nǎy] *adj.* excellent, perfect; – от [– at] different, distinct from

отложение [at-la-zhé-nye] *sn.* deflection

отлучать [at-lŏŏ-chát] *vt.* to exclude; to excommunicate

отлынивание [at-lá-n'i-va-nye] *sn.* elusion, shirking

отмель [at-myél'] *sf.* sandbank, shoal

отмена [at-myé-na] *sf.* abolition, abrogation; reprieve

отменный [at-myén-nǎy] *adj.* exquisite

отменять [at-mye-nyát] (отменить) *vt.* to abolish, cancel, revoke

отместка [at-myést-ka] *sf.* vengeance

отметать [at-mye-tát] (отмести) *vt.* to sweep away

отметка [at-myét-ka] *sf.* mark, note, tick

отмечать [at-mye-chát] (отметить) *vt.* to mark, note

отмораживать [at-ma-rá-zhi-vat] (отморозить) *vt.* to freeze up

отмороженный [at-ma-ró-zhen-nǎy] *adj.* frost-bitten

отмститель [atm-st'ĕ-tyel] *sm.* avenger

отмщать [atm-shchát] (отмстить) *vi.* to avenge

отмывать [at-mǎ-vát] (отмыть) *vt.* to wash out

отмыкать [at-mǎ-kát] *vt.* to unlock [master-key

отмычка [at-mǎch-ka] *sf.*

отрицание [at-r'i-ká-va-nye] *sn.* denial, refusal

отнимать [at-n'i-mát] (отнять) *vt.* to take away

относительный [at-na-s'ĕ-tyel'-nǎy] *adj.* concerning, relative

относительность [at-na-s'ĕ-tyel'-nŏst] *sf.* relativity

относить [at-na-s'ĕt] (отнести) *vt.* to carry, deliver; to refer

отношение [at-na-shé-nye] *sn.* attitude; ratio

отныне [at-ná-nye] *adv.* henceforth

отнюдь [at-nyŏŏd'] *adv.* by no means

отнятие [at-nyá-tye] *sn.* amputation

отовсюду [at-a-vsyŏŏ-dŏŏ] *adv.* from everywhere

отодвигание [a-ta-dv'ĕ-ga-nye] *sn.* moving away, removing

отождествление [a-ta-zhdyest-vlyé-nye] *sn.* identification

отопление [a-tap-lyé-nye] *sn.* heating

отпаривание [at-pá-r'i-va-nye] *sn.* steaming

отпарывать [at-pā-rǎ-vat'] *vt.* to rip

отпевание [at-pye-vā-nye] *sn.* funeral service

отпечаток [at-pye-chā-tŏk] *sm.* impression; imprint

отпирать [at-p'i-rāt'] (отпереть) *vt.* to unbolt, unlock

отплата [at-plā-ta] *sf.* repayment

отплачивать [at-plā-chi-vat'] (отплатить) *vt.* to repay; to reward

отповедь [ót-pa-vyed] *sf.* rebuke, retort

отпор [at-pór] *sm.* rebuff, repulse; resistance

отправка [at-práv-ka] *sf.* forwarding, dispatching; shipment

отправлять [at-prav-lyát'] (отправить) *vt.* to forward, dispatch, to send off

отпрыск [ót-prǎsk] *sm.* offshoot, sprout

отпуск [ót-pŏŏsk] *sm.* holiday, leave, vacation

отпускать [at-pŏŏs-kāt'] (отпустить) *vt.* to let go, release

отрава [at-rā-va] *sf.* poison

отравление [at-ra-vlyé-nye] *sn.* poisoning

отрада [at-rā-da] *sf.* comfort, consolation

отражать [at-ra-zhāt'] (отразить) *vt.* to reflect; to repulse

отражение [at-ra-zhé-nye] *sn.* reflection; refutation; percussion

отрасль [ót-rasl] *sf.* branch (*of commerce, science, industry*)

отрез [at-ryéz] *sm.* cut, a part cut off; length of material; plough-share; **-ок** [-ŏk] *sm.* small piece cut off, snippet

отрезвление [at-ryez-vlyé-nye] *sn.* sobering

отрекаться [at-rye-kāt'-sya] (отречься) *vi.* to abdicate; to deny, disown

отрепье [at-ryé-pye] *sn. pl.* rags, tatters

отречение [at-rye-ché-nye] *sn.* abdication; renunciation

отрешать [at-rye-shāt'] (отрешить) *vt.* to dismiss; to interdict

отрицание [at-r'i-tsā-nye] *sn.* denial, negation

отрицательный [at-r'i-tsā-tyel'-nǎy] *adj.* negative

отрицать [at-r'i-tsāt] *vt.* to deny, negate

отросток [at-rós-tŏk] *sm.* shoot, sprig; (*med.*) appendix

отрочество [at-ró-chest-vŏ] *sn.* boyhood, girlhood

отруб [ót-rŏŏb] *sm.* holding (*of land*)

отруби [ót-rŏŏ-bi] *sf. pl.* bran; offal

отрывать [at-rǎ-vāt'] (оторвать) *vt.* to tear away; (отрыть) to dig up, unearth

отрывок [at-rǎ-vŏk] *sm.* fragment, piece; excerpt

отрывочный [at-rǎ-vach-nǎy] *adj.* desultory, snatchy

отряд [at-ryād] *sm.* detachment; detail (*special duties*)

отсадка [at-sād-ka] *sf.* transplanting

отсадок [at-sā-dŏk] *sm.* layer

отсев [at-syév] *sm.* sifting

отсекать [at-sye-kāt'] (отсечь) *vt.* to chop off, to hew

отслойка [at-slóy-ka] *sf.* exfoliation

отсрочивать [at-sró-chi-vat'] (отсрочить) *vt.* to defer

отсрочка [at-sróch-ka] *sf.* adjournment, postponement

отсрочки [at-sróch-ki] *sf. pl.* days of grace; respite

отставать [at-sta-vát'] (отстáть) *vi.* to lag; to lose, be slow (*of watch*)

отставка [at-stáv-ka] *sf.* retirement; **в отставке** [vat-stáv-kye] retired, in retirement; **отставной** [at-stav-nóy] a retired person

отсталый [at-stá-läy] *adj.* backward; in arrears

отстой [at-stóy] *sm.* deposit, sediment

отстройка [at-stróy-ka] *sf.* tuning (*radio*)

отступать [at-stöo-pát'] *vi.* to recede; to retreat; *coll.* to back out

отступничество [at-stöop-n'i-chest-vö] *sn.* apostasy

отсутствие [at-sǎ-lát'stvye] *sn.* absence

отсылать [at-sǎ-lát'] (отослáть) *vt.* to dispatch, to post; to remit

отсылка [at-sǎl-ka] *sf.* dispatch; reference

отсюда [at-syōō-da] *adv.* from here; hence

оттаивать [at-tā-i-vat'] (оттáять) *vt.* to thaw

отталкивающий [at-tál-ki-va-yōō-shchi] *adj.* repulsive

оттенок [at-tyé-nök] *sm.* hue, tinge

оттиск [ót-t'isk] *sm.* impression, print; copy

оттого [at-ta-vó] *adv.* therefore

отторгнутый [at-tórg-nōō-täy] *adj.* torn away

оттуда [at-tōō-da] *adv.* from there

отупевший [a-tōō-pyév-shi] *adj.* dull, sluggish, torpid

отход [at-chód] *sm.* departure

отходная [at-chód-na-ya] *sf.* prayer for the dying

отцепка [at-tsýep-ka] *sf.* uncoupling

отцеплять [at-tsye-plyát'] (отцепить) *vt.* to unhook

отцовский [at-tsóv-ski] *adj.* paternal

отчаиваться [at-chá-i-vat'-sya] (отчáяться) *vi.* to despair; to be disheartened

отчасти [at-chás-t'i] *adv.* partly

отчаяние [at-chá-ya-nye] *sn.* despondency

отчаянный [at-chá-yan-näy] *adj.* desperate, reckless

отчего [at-che-vó] *adv.* wherefore, why

отчество [ót-chest-vö] *sn.* patronymic

отчёт [at-chót] *sm.* account, report

отчётливый [at-chót-l'i-väy] *adj.* clear, distinct

отчим [ót-chim] *sm.* stepfather

отчищать [at-chi-shchát'] (отчистить) *vt.* to clean out

отчуждать [at-chōōzh-dát'] *vt.* to alienate

отшельник [at-shél'-n'ik] *sm.* hermit

отшествие [at-shést-vye] *sn.* departure

отщепенец [at-shche-pyé-nyets] *sm.* heretic; renegade

отъезд [at-yézd] *sm.* departure (*by train, etc.*)

отъезжать [at-yez-zhát'] (отъéхать) *vi.* to depart, leave (*by train, etc.*), to drive away (*in car, etc.*)

отъявленный [at-yáv-lyen-näy] *adj.* arrant, thorough; acknowledged

отыгрыш [a-tă-grăsh] *sm.* money won back (*betting*)

отыскивать [a-tăc-k'i-vat'] (отыскáть) *vt.* to find out, look for, search

отягощение [a-tya-ga-shché-nye] *sn.* oppression, overburdening

офицер [a-f'i-tsyér] *sm.* officer

официальный [a-f'i-tsiäl'-näy] *adj.* formal, official

официант [a-f'i-tsyánt] *sm.* hotel waiter

охапка [a-chăp-ka] *sf.* armful

охать [ó-chat] *vi.* to moan, sigh

охват [ach-vát] *sm.* scope; *mil.* envelopment

охладительный [a-chla-d'ě-tyel'-näy] *adj.* cooling

охлаждение [a-chlazh-dyé-nye] *sn.* cooling, coolness

охота [a-chó-ta] *sf.* hunt, hunting, shooting (*sport*); inclination, liking

охотник [a-chót-n'ik] *sm.* hunter, sportsman; amateur, volunteer

охотно [a-chót-nŏ] *adv.* willingly

охрана [a-chrá-na] *sf.* bodyguard, escort

охранение [a-chra-nyé-nye] *sn.* preservation, protection

охранять [a-chra-nyát'] (охранить) *vt.* to guard, preserve

охриплый [a-chrép-läy] *adj.* hoarse, husky

оценивать [a-tsyé-n'i-vat'] (оценить) *vt.* to estimate, evaluate

оценка [a-tsyén-ka] *sf.* appraisal, estimation, valuation

оценщик [a-tsyén-shchik] *sm.* valuer

очаг [a-chág] *sm.* hearth

очарование [a-cha-ra-vá-nye] *sn.* charm, fascination

очаровательный [a-cha-ra-vá-tyel'-näy] *adj.* attractive, charming, enchanting

очевидец [a-che-v'ě-dyets] *sm.* eye-witness

очевидный [a-che-v'ěd-näy] *adj.* manifest, obvious

очень [ó-chen'] *adv.* exceedingly, much, very

очередь [ó-che-ryed'] *sf.* queue, line, turn

очерк [ó-cherk] *sm.* essay, sketch [slander

очернить [a-cher-n'ět'] *vt.* to

очертание [a-cher-tá-nye] *sn.* contour, outline

очерчивать [a-chér-chi-vat'] (очертить) *vt.* to sketch, trace

очёски [a-chós-ki] *sf. pl.* combings; flocks

очистка [a-chěst-ka] *sf.* cleaning, cleansing; clearance, purification

очищать [a-chi-shchắt'] (очистить) *vt.* to clean, cleanse, purify, refine; to clear

очищенный [a-chě-shchen-näy] *adj.* clarified, purified

очки [ach-kē] *sn. pl.* eyeglasses, spectacles

очко [ach-kó] *sn.* pip (on cards, dice, etc.); point (in games); small hole; fig, dust, speck

очной [ach-nóy] *adj.* eye-, ocular

очнуться [ach-nōŏt'-sya] *vi.* to come to, recover, regain consciousness

очути́ться [a-chōō-t'ĕt'-sya] *vi.* to appear suddenly, find oneself (*somewhere unexpectedly*)

оше́йник [a-shéy-n'ik] *sm.* dog's collar

ошеломля́ть [a-she-lam-lyát'] (ошеломи́ть) *vt.* to stun, stupefy

ошиба́ться [a-shi-bát'-sya] *vi.* to err, blunder, miscount

оши́бка [a-shíb-ka] *sf.* mistake, oversight; fault

оши́бочный [a-shí-bach-nǎy] *adj.* erroneous, faulty, wrong

ошпа́ривание [ash-pā-r'i-va-nye] *sn.* scalding

ощи́пывать [a-shchí-pă-vat'] (ощипа́ть) *vt.* to pluck

ощу́пывать [a-shchōō-pă-vat'] (ощупа́ть) *vt.* to feel, grope, touch

о́щупь [ó-shchōōp'] *sf.* fumbling, groping

ощуща́ть [a-shchōō-shchát'] (ощути́ть) *vt.* to apprehend, notice, perceive

ощуще́ние [a-shchōō-shché-nye] *sn.* perception, sensation

П

павли́н [pāv-l'in] *sm.* peacock

па́губа [pā-gōō-ba] *sf.* destruction, ruin

па́губный [pā-gōō-bnǎy] *adj.* baneful, destructive, pernicious

па́далица [pa-dā-l'i-tsa] *sf.* windfall

па́даль [pā-dal'] *sf.* carrion; fallen fruit

па́дать [pā-dat'] (пасть) *vi.* to drop, fall

паде́ж [pa-dyézh] *sm. gram.* case

падёж [pa-dyózh] *sm.* murrain

паде́ние [pa-dyé-nye] *sn.* downfall; slump

паду́б [pā-dōōb] *sm.* holly

па́дчерица [pād-che-r'i-tsa] *sf.* step-daughter

паёк [pa-yók] *sm.* allowance, ration, share

паз [pāz] *sm.* groove, mortise

па́зуха [pā-zōō-cha] *sf.* bosom

пай [pāy] *sm.* share; **-щик** [-shchik] *sm.* shareholder

па́йка [pāy-ka] *sf.* soldering

паке́т [pa-kyét] *sm.* packet, parcel

пакова́ть [pa-ka-vát'] (y-) *vt.* to pack

па́костник [pa-kast-n'ik] *sm.* mischief-maker, nasty person

па́кость [pā-kŏst'] *sf.* filth; trash

пала́та [pa-lá-ta] *sf.* chamber, tribunal; hospital ward; **торго́вая —** [tar-gŏ-va-ya —] Chamber of Commerce

палата́льный [pa-la-tāl'-nǎy] *adj.* palatal

пала́тка [pa-lát-ka] *sf.* marquee, tent

пала́ч [pa-lách] *sm.* executioner; *fig.* butcher

па́левый [pā-lye-vǎy] *adj.* straw-coloured

па́лец [pā-lyets] *sm.* finger, toe

палиса́дник [pa-l'i-sád-n'ik] *sm.* small front garden

пали́тра [pa-l'ét-ra] *sf.* palette

палить [pa-l'ět'] (с-) *vt.* to burn, scorch, singe; to fire; **пали!** pa-l'ě] (*mil.* command) fire!

палка [pál-ka] *sf.* cane, stick, walking stick

паломник [pa-lóm-n'ik] *sm.* pilgrim

паломничество [pa-lóm-n'i-chest-vǒ] *sn.* pilgrimage

палочка [pa-lach-ka] *sf.* baton, small stick, wand; stick (of rock, etc.)

палтус [pál-tōōs] *sm.* halibut, turbot

палуба [pá-lōō-ba] *sf.* deck (of ship)

палый [pá-lǎy] *adj.* perished

пальба [pāl'-ba] *sf.* gunnery

пальма [pál'-ma] *sf.* palm-tree

пальто [pal'-tó] *sn.* overcoat

памятливый [pā-myat-l'i-vǎy] *adj.* retentive (of memory)

памятник [pā-myat-n'ik] *sm.* memorial, monument

памятный [pā-myat-nǎy] *adj.* memorable

память [pā-myat'] *sf.* memory

панель [pa-nyél'] *sf.* footpath; panel; wainscotting

панихида [pa-n'i-chě-da] *sf.* dirge, requiem

пансион [pan-sión] *sm.* boarding-house; boarding-school; **-ер** [-yér] *sm.*, **-ерка** [-yérka] *sf.* boarder

панталоны [pan-ta-ló-nǎ] *sm. pl.* trousers

панцырь [pan-tsár'] *sm.* armour

папа [pā-pa] *sm.* daddy, papa; pope

папильота [pa-p'i-lyó-ta] *sf.* paper-bag

папильотка [pa-p'i-lyót-ka] *sf.* curling-paper

папироса [pa-p'i-ró-sa] *sf.* cigarette

папка [pāp-ka] *sf.* portfolio

папоротник [pā-pa-rat-n'ik] *sm.* bracken, fern

папский [pāp-ski] *adj.* papal, pontifical

папство [pāp-stvǒ] *sn.* papacy

пар [pār] *sm.* steam, vapour; fallow

пара [pā-ra] *sf.* couple, pair; brace

парадный [pa-rād-nǎy] *adj.* gala-; — **ход** [— chod] main entrance

паразит [pa-ra-z'ět] *sm.* parasite; sponger

паралич [pa-ra-l'ěch] *sm.* paralysis

параллельный [pa-ra-lyel'-nǎy] *adj.* parallel

парение [pā-rye-nye] *sm.* steaming, stewing

парение [pa-ryé-nye] *sm.* hovering, soaring

парень [pā-ryen'] *sm. coll.* chap, fellow

пари [pa-rě] *sn.* bet, wager; **держать** — [dyer-zhát' —] to back, bet

парижанин [pa-r'i-zhā-n'in] *sm.* Parisian

парижский [pa-r'ízh-ski] *adj.* Parisian

парик [pa-r'ěk] *sm.* wig; **-махер** [-mā-cher] *sm.* hairdresser; **-махерская** [-mā-cher-ska-ya] *sf.* hairdressing saloon

парить [pā-r'it'] *vt.* to steam, stew; **парить** [pa-r'ět'] *vi.* to hover, soar

парламент [par-lā-myent] *sm.* parliament

парник [par-n'ёk] *sm.* hotbed

паровик [pa-ra-v'ёk] *sm.* boiler; steam-engine

паровоз [pa-ra-vóz] *sm.* locomotive

пароль [pa-ról'] *sm.* password

паром [pa-róm] *sm.* ferry, ferry-boat, ferry-bridge; **-щик** [-shchik] *sm.* ferryman

парообразный [pa-ra-a-bráz-nǎy] *adj.* vaporous

пароход [pa-ra-chód] *sm.* steamboat, steamer; **-ство** [-stvŏ] *sn.* steam-navigation

парта [pār-ta] *sf.* school-desk

партитура [par-t'i-tōō-ra] *sf. mus.* score

партия [pār-tya] *sf.* party; *mus.* part

партнёр [part-nyór] *sm.* partner

парус [pā-rōōs] *sm.* sail

парусина [pa-rōō-s'ē-na] *sf.* canvas; duck; tarpaulin

парусник [pā-rōōs-n'ik] *sm.* windjammer; sail-maker

пасека [pā-sye-ka] *sf.* apiary

пасечник [pā-syech-n'ik] *sm.* bee-keeper

пасквиль [pās-kv'il'] *sm.* lampoon; libel; **-ный** [-nǎy] *adj.* libellous

пасмурный [pās-mōōr-nǎy] *adj.* dismal, gloomy

пассажир [pa-ssa-zhír] *sm.* passenger

пассив [pas-s'ёv] *sm. com.* liabilities

пассивный [pass-s'ёv-nǎy] *adj.* passive

паста [pās-ta] *sf.* paste

пастбище [pāst-b'i-shche] *sn.* pasture

паства [pāst-va] *sf.* flock, herd

пастель [pas-tyél'] *sf.* crayon; pastel

пастернак [pa-styer-nāk] *sm.* parsnip

пасти [pas-t'ё] *vt.* to graze; to tend

пастух [pas-tōōch] *sm.* herdsman, shepherd

пастушеский [pas-tōō-shes-ki] *adj.* pastoral

пастырь [pas-tǎr'] *sm.* shepherd; pastor

пасть [pāst'] *sf.* mouth (*of animal*); trap: *pl.* jaws; *vi.* to fall, sink

Пасха [pās-cha] *sf.* Easter; Passover

пасынок [pā-sǎ-nŏk] *sm.* stepson

патока [pā-ta-ka] *sf.* treacle; syrup

патрон [pa-trón] *sm.* cartridge; pattern; patron

патруль [pa-trōōl'] *sm.* patrol

пауза [pāōō-za] *sf. mus.* pause, rest

паук [pa-ōōk] *sm.* spider

паутина [pa-ōō-t'ē-na] *sf.* cobweb

пах [pāch] *sm.* groin; **-овой** [-a-vóy] *adj.* inguinal

пахарь [pa-chār'] *sm.* ploughman [plough, till

пахать [pā-chat'] (вс-) *vt.* to

пахнуть [pāch-nōōt'] *vt.* to smell; to savour; *fig.* to imply; [pach-nōōt'] *vi.* to emit smoke

пахота [pa-cha-tā] *sf.* ploughing, tillage

пахотный [pā-chat-nǎy] *adj.* arable

пачка [pāch-ka] *sf.* batch, bundle, parcel; pack (*cards*)

пачкать [pāch-kat'] (за-вы-) *vt.* to blot, smirch, stain

пачкотня [pach-kat-nyá] *sf.* daubing, scrawling; mess

пашня [pásh-nya] *sf.* arable land; field

паяльник [pa-yál'-n'ik] *sm.* soldering-iron

паяльщик [pa-yál'-shchik] *sm.* tinsmith

паять [pa-yát'] (за-) *vt.* to solder

паяц [pa-yáts] *sm.* clown

певец [pye-vyéts] *sm.*, **певица** [pye-v'é-tsa] *sf.* singer, vocalist

певун [pye-vóon] *sm.* songster; **-ья** [-ya] *sf.* songstress

педаль [pe-dál'] *sf.* pedal; treadle

пейзаж [pey-zázh] *sm.* landscape

пекарня [pye-kár-nya] *sf.* bakery

пекарь [pýe-kar'] *sm.* baker

пелена [pye-lye-ná] *sf.* shroud; **алтарная** – [al-tár-na-ya –] altar-cloth

пеленать [pye-lye-nát'] (за-) *vt.* to swaddle; to swathe

пелёнка [pye-lyón-ka] *sf.* napkin

пелёнки [pye-lyón-ki] *sf. pl.* baby-linen

пелеринка [pye-lye-r'én-ka] *sf.* cape

пемза [pyém-za] *sf.* pumice

пена [pýe-na] *sf.* foam, froth

пение [pýe-nye] *sn.* singing

пенсия [pyén-sya] *sf.* pension

пень [pyén'] *sm.* stub, stump

пенять [pye-nyát'] *vi.* to reproach

пепел [pýe-pyel] *sm.* ash(es), cinder(s)

пепельница [pye-pyel'-n'í-tsa] *sf.* ash-tray

первенец [pyér-vye-nyets] *sm.* first-born

первенство [pyer-vyen-stvó] *sn.* priority

первичный [pyer-v'éch-nắy] *adj.* initial, primary, primitive

первобытность [pyer-va-bắt-nŏst'] *sf.* primitiveness

первоначальный [pyer-va-na-chál'-nắy] *adj.* elementary

первоцвет [pyer-va-tsvyét] *sm.* primrose

первый [pyér-vắy] *adj.* chief; *num.* first

пергамент [pyer-gá-myent] *sm.* parchment

перебегать [pye-rye-bye-gát'] (перебежать) *vi.* to run across (*street, etc.*)

перебирать [pye-rye-b'í-rát'] (перебрáть) *vt.* to examine, sift, sort out; *typ.* to reset; **-ся** [-sya] *vi.* to move, remove

перебой [pye-rye-bóy] *sm. med.* intermission; jam (*in machinery, etc.*); interruption

переборка [pye-rye-bór-ka] *sf.* sorting; *typ.* resetting

перебранка [pye-rye-brán-ka] *sf.* quarrel

перевал [pye-rye-vál] *sm.* mountain pass

перевалка [pye-rye-vál-ka] *sf.* waddle; transfer

перевёрнутый [pye-rye-vyór-nŏo-tắy] *adj.* reverse, upset; upside-down

перевёрстка [pye-rye-vyórst-ka] *sf. typ.* reimposition

перевёртывать [pye-rye-vyór-tắ-vat'] (перевернýть) *vt.* to reverse; to turn over; to upset

перевес [pye-rye-vyés] *sm.* overweight; preponderance

перевод [pye-rye-vód] *sm.* transfer; translation; **-чик** [-chik] *sm.* translator

переводить [pye-rye-va-d'ět'] (перевести) *vt.* to transfer; to translate

перевоз [pye-rye-vóz] *sm.* transport, ferry; **-ка,** *sf.* conveyance, transportation; **-чик** [-chik] *sm.* ferryman

переворот [pye-rye-va-rót] *sm.* overturn, upheaval

перевязка [pye-rye-vyáz-ka] *sf.* binding; bandage; dressing (*wounds*)

перевязывать [pye-rye-vyá-ză-vat'] (перевязать) *vt.* to bind, tie up; to bandage, dress

перевязь [pyé-rye-vyaz'] *sf.* bandoleer, belt

переговорный [pye-rye-ga-vór-năy] *adj.* negotiable

переговоры [pye-rye-ga-vó-ră] *sm. pl.* negotiations

перегон [pye-rye-gón] *sm.* stage (*distance between 'bus stops, etc.*); cattle driving (*cattle*); outstripping; distillation; **-щик** [-shchik] *sm.* distiller

перегонять [pye-rye-ga-nyát'] (перегнать) *vt.* to drive (*cattle*); to outstrip; to distil

перегорать [pye-rye-ga-rat'] (перегореть) *vi.* to burn out, burn through

перегородка [pye-rye-ga-ród-ka] *sf.* partition, screen

перегрузка [pye-rye-grooz-ka] *sf.* overloading; transhipment

перед [pyé-ryed] *prep.* before, in front of

перёд [pye-ryód] *sm.* fore-part, front

передавать [pye-rye-da-vat'] (передать) *vt.* to deliver, hand over, pass on, transmit

передаточный [pye-rye-dá-tach-năy] *adj.* transferable

передача [pye-rye-dá-cha] *sf.* transmission

передвигать [pye-rye-dv'i-gát'] (передвинуть) *vt.* to move, shift

передвижение [pye-rye-dv'i-zhé-nye] *sn.* locomotion; removal, travel

передел [pye-rye-dyél] *sm.* repartition

переделка [pye-rye-dyél-ka] *sf.* alteration, repairs

переделывать [pye-rye-dyé-lă-vat'] (переделать) *vt.* to alter, remake

передёргивать [pye-rye-dyór-gi-vat'] (передёрнуть) to cheat, smuggle, swindle; to pull over

передний [pye-ryéd-n'i] *adj.* anterior

передник [pye-ryéd-n'ik] *sm.* apron, overall

передняя [pye-ryéd-nya-ya] *sf.* ante-room, entrance hall; vestibule

передовица [pye-rye-da-v'é-tsa] *sf.* leading article; editorial

передовой [pye-rye-da-vóy] *adj.* leading, foremost

передок [pye-rye-dók] *sm.* upper, vamp (*of shoe*); limber

передроглый [pye-rye-dróg-lăy] *adj.* chilled through and through

передряга [pye-rye-dryá-ga] *sf.* commotion; *coll.* row

передышка [pye-rye-dăsh-ka] *sf.* respite

переезд [pye-rye-yézd] *sm.* crossing (*over water*); passage, transit; level-crossing

переживать [pye-rye-zhi-vát'] (пережить) *vi.* to outlive, survive; to endure

переживание [pye-rye-zhi-vá-nye] *sn.* experience

пережиток [pye-rye-zhí-tŏk] *sm.* survival

переимчивость [pye-rye-ĕm-chi-vŏst'] *sf.* imitation, mimicry

переимчивый [pye-rye-ĕm-chi-văy] *adj.* appropriate; imitative

перекат [pye-rye-kát] *sm.* sandbank; thunderclap

перекись [pye-rye-kĕs'] *sf.* peroxide

перекладина [pye-rye-klá-di-na] *sf.* beam, joist

перекладывать [pye-rye-klá-dă-vat'] (переклáсть) *vt.* to interlay, interleave; to put off

перекличка [pye-rye-kl'ĕch-ka] *sf.* roll-call; inter-region broadcast

переключатель [pye-rye-klyŏŏ-chá-tyel'] *sm.* switch

перекоп [pye-rye-kóp] *sm.* canal

перекос [pye-rye-kós] *sm.* bending, curving

перекупщик [pye-rye-kŏŏp-shchik] *sm.* second-hand dealer

перекусывать [pye-rye-kŏŏ-să-vat'] (перекусить) *vt.* to bite through; to have a snack

перелагать [pye-rye-la-gát'] (переложить) *vt. mus.* to transpose

переламывать [pye-rye-lă-mă-vat'] (переломить) *vt.* to fracture; break in two, crash

перелесок [pye-rye-lyé-sŏk] *sm.* copse, thicket

перелёт [pye-rye-lyót] *sm.* flight, passage

перелив [pye-rye-l'ĕv] *sm.* modulation

переливание [pye-rye-l'i-vá-nye] *sn.* decanting; transfusion

переливаться [pye-rye-l'i-vát'-sya] *vi.* to overflow, run over

перелог [pye-rye-lóg] *sm.* fallow

переложение [pye-rye-la-zhé-nye] *sn. mus.* scoring, transposition

перелом [pye-rye-lóm] *sm.* breakage; crisis (*in illness*); fracture; rupture

переманивать [pye-rye-mă-n'i-vat'] (переманить) *vt.* to entice, win over

перемежающийся [pye-rye-mye-zhă-yŏŏ-shchi-sya] *adj.* intermittent

перемена [pye-rye-myé-na] *sf.* alteration, change

переменный [pye-rye-myén-năy] *adj.* changeable, variable

переменчивый [pye-rye-myén-chi-văy] *adj.* fickle, inconstant

переменять [pye-rye-mye-nyát'] (переменить) *vt.* to alter, change, vary

перемёт [pye-rye-myót] *sm.* fishing-net

перемешивать [pye-rye-myé-shi-vat'] (перемешáть) *vt.* to intermix, jumble up; to intersperse

перемещение [pye-rye-mye-shché-nye] *sn.* shuffle; transference

переминать [pye-rye-m'i-nát'] (перемя́ть) *vt.* to knead

перемирие [pye-rye-m'é-rye] *sn.* armistice, truce

перемол [pye-rye-mól] *sm.* grist

перемычка [pye-rye-mǎch-ka] *sf.* crosspiece; spandrel

перенимать [pye-rye-n'i-mát'] (переня́ть) *vt.* to intercept; to adopt; to imitate

перенос [pye-rye-nós] *sm.* carrying forward; division (*of words*); transfer

переносный [pye-rye-nós-nǎy] *adj.* portable; transferable; figurative

переодеваться [pye-rye-a-dye-vát'-sya] (переоде́ться) *vi.* to change one's clothes

переоценка [pye-rye-a-tsyén-ka] *sf.* revaluation

перепаивать [pye-rye-pá-i-vat'] (перепая́ть) *vt.* to resolder; (перепои́ть) *vt.* to intoxicate

перепалка [pye-rye-pál-ka] *sf.* firing; *fig.* skirmish

перепёлка [pye-rye-pyól-ka] *sf.* quail

перепелятник [pye-rye-pye-lyát-n'ik] *sm.* sparrow hawk

перепечатка [pye-rye-pye-chát-ka] *sf.* reprint

перепечатывать [pye-rye-pye-chá-tǎ-vat'] (перепеча́тать) *vt.* to reprint

перепиваться [pye-rye-p'i-vát'-sya] *vi.* to become intoxicated

переписка [pye-rye-p'és-ka] *sf.* copying; typing; correspondence

переписчик [pye-rye-p'és-chik] *sm.* copyist; typist

переписывать [pye-rye-p'é-sǎ-vat'] (переписа́ть) *vt.* to copy, rewrite; **-ся** [-sya] *vi.* to correspond with someone

перепись [pyé-rye-p'is'] *sf.* census; inventory

переплата [pyé-rye-plá-ta] *sf.* overpayment, surplus payment

переплёт [pye-rye-plyót] *sm.* binding; book cover; **-ная** [-na-ya] *sf.* bindery; **-чик** [-chik] *sm.* bookbinder

переплетать [pye-rye-plye-tát'] (переплести́) *vt.* to bind (*books*); to cane (*chairs*)

переполох [pye-rye-pa-lóch] *sm.* alarm, uproar

переполошить [pye-rye-pa-la-sh'ét'] *vt.* to raise an alarm

перепонка [pye-rye-pón-ka] *sf.* cere (*of birds*); membrane; web (*of bat*)

перепончатый [pye-rye-pón-cha-tǎy] *adj.* membranous, webbed; web-footed

перепрягать [pye-rye-prya-gát'] *vt.* to change (*horses*)

перепутывать [pye-rye-pǒǒ-tǎ-vat'] (перепу́тать) *vt.* to confuse; entangle

перепутье [pye-rye-pǒǒ-tye] *sn.* cross-roads

перерастать [pye-rye-ras-tát'] *vi.* to outgrow, overgrow

перерасход [pye-rye-ras-chód] *sm.* over-spending; overdraft

перерез [pye-rye-ryéz] *sm.* cross-cut; cross-section

перерешать [pye-rye-rye-shát'] vi. to change one's mind

перерождение [pye-rye-razh-dyé-nye] sn. regeneration; revival

перерыв [pye-rye-rív] sm. break, interruption; interval

пересадка [pye-rye-sád-ka] sf. transplanting; change, transfer (trains, etc.)

пересаживать [pye-rye-sázhi-vat'] (пересадить) vt. to graft; to transplant; **-ся** [-sya] vi. to change one's seat, shift from one place to another (in theatre, train, etc.)

пересдавать [pye-rye-zdavát'] (пересдать) vt. to sublet

пересекать [pye-rye-syekát'] (пересечь) vt. to intersect; to traverse

переселенец [pye-rye-syelyé-nyets] sm. colonist, settler

переселение [pye-rye-syelyé-nye] sn. emigration, immigration; transmigration

пересиливать [pye-rye-sýe-li-vat'] (пересилить) vt. to overpower

переслушивать [pye-rye-slóo-shi-vat'] vt. to hear again (as a repeat performance, etc.)

пересматривать [pye-rye-smá-tri-vat'] (пересмотреть) vt. to look over, revise; to review

пересмотр [pye-rye-smótr] sm. review; revision

перестановка [pye-rye-stanóv-ka] sf. permutation; rearrangement; transposition

переступать [pye-rye-stóo-pat'] (переступить) vt. to cross over; to transgress

пересуды [pye-rye-sóo-dǎ] sm. pl. gossip

пересылка [pye-rye-sál-ka] sf. forwarding; remittance

перетягивать [pye-rye-tyá-gi-vat'] (перетянуть) vt. to outweigh, overbalance

перетяжка [pye-rye-tyázh-ka] sf. intake; strap

переулок [pye-rye-óo-lŏk] sm. alley, lane, sidestreet

переутомление [pye-rye-óo-tam-lyé-nye] sn. overfatigue, overstrain

перехват [pye-rye-chvát] sm. intake; waist (of dress)

перехватывать [pye-rye-chvá-tǎ-vat'] (перехватить) vt. to intercept; to snatch up

переход [pye-rye-chód] sm. passage; transition; mus. transposition

переходить [pye-rye-cha-dét'] (перейти) vt.i. to pass over, traverse

переходный [pye-rye-chód-nǎy] adj. transitional; gram. transitive

перец [pyé-ryets] sm. pepper

перечень [pyé-rye-chen'] sm. list, schedule; enumeration

перечёт [pye-rye-chót] sm. surplus

перечислять [pye-rye-chis-lyát'] (перечислить) vt. to enumerate; to rehearse

перечить [pye-rye-chit'] vi. to contradict

перечница [pyé-ryech-n'i-tsa] sf. pepper-box

перешеек [pye-rye-shé-yek] sm. isthmus

перешиб [pye-rye-shíb] sm. fracture

перешивка [pye-rye-shív-ka] sf. alteration (of dress, etc.)

перещеголять [pye-rye-shche-ga-lyát'] *vt.i.* to excel

перила [pye-r'é-la] *sf.* hand-rail, railing; banisters

перина [pye-r'é-na] *sf.* feather bed

период [pe-ryód] *sm.* period, phase

периодика [pe-ry-ó-d'i-ka] *sf.* periodical (*journal*)

периодический [pe-ri-a-d'é-cheski] *adj.* periodical

перламутр [per-la-mōōtr] *sm.* mother-of-pearl

перлюстрация [per-lyōō-strá-tsya] *sf.* censoring

пернатый [pyer-ná-tǎy] *adj.* feathered, feathery

перо [pye-ró] *sn.* feather, plume; pen; quill

перочинный ножик [pye-ra-chén-nǎy nó-zhik] *sm.* penknife

перочистка [pyé-ra-chést-ka] *sf.* penwiper

персидский [pyer-s'éd-ski] *adj.* Persian

персик [pyér-s'ik] *sm.* peach

перстень [pyér-styen'] *sm.* signet-ring

перхота [pyer-chó-ta] *sf.* slight cough

перхоть [pyer chót'] *sf.* scurf

перчатка [pyer-chát-ka] *sf.* glove

перчаточник [pyer-chá-tach-n'ik] *sm.* glover

перчинка [pyer-chén-ka] *sf.* peppercorn

першить [pyer-shét'] *vi.* to tickle (*in throat*)

пёс [pyós] *sm.* dog

песенник [pyé-syen-n'ik] *sm.* album of folk-tunes

пескарь [pyes-kár'] *sm.* gudgeon

песнь [pyésn'] *sf.* chant; canto

песня [pyés-nya] *sf.* song

песок [pye-sók] *sm.* gravel; sand

песочный [pye-sóch-nǎy] *adj.* sandy

пестик [pyés-t'ik] *sm.* pestle

пестрота [pyes-tra-tá] *sf.* motley, variety of colours

пёстрый [pyós-trǎy] *adj.* multi-coloured, variegated

петит [ptět] *sm. typ.* brevier

петлица [pyet-l'é-tsa] *sf.* buttonhole; frog (*for sword*)

петля [pyét-lya] *sf.* eye (*hook and eye*), loop

петрушка [pye-trōōsh-ka] *sf.* parsley; Punch

петух [pye-tōōch] *sm.* cock

петушок [pye-tōō-shók] *sm.* cockerel

петь [pyét'] (спеть) *vi.* to sing

пехота [pye-chó-ta] *sf.* infantry

пехотинец [pye-cha-t'é-nyets] *sm.* infantryman

печалить [pye-chá-l'it'] *vi.* to grieve

печаль [pye-chál'] *sf.* grief, sorrow

печальный [pye-chál'-nǎy] *adj.* mournful, sad

печатать [pye-chá-tat'] (на-) *vt.* to print

печатня [pye-chát-nya] *sf.* printing-works

печать [pye-chát'] *sf.* seal, stamp; press; print

печень [pyé'-chen] *sf.* liver

печенье [pye-ché-nye] *sn.* baking; pastry

печь [pyéch'] *sf.* oven, stove; furnace, kiln; *vt.* to bake, roast

пешеход [pye-she-<u>ch</u>ód] *sm.* pedestrian

пешка [pyésh-ka] *sf.* pawn (*in chess*)

пешком [pyesh-kóm] *adv.* on foot

пещера [pye-shché-ra] *sf.* cave, den, grotto

пианино [pia-n'é-nŏ] *sn.* pianoforte

пивная [p'iv-ná-ya] *sf.* public-house (*licensed to sell beer only*)

пиво [p'évŏ] *sn.* beer

пивовар [p'i-va-vár] *sm.* brewer

пивоварение [p'i-va-va-ryé-nye] *sn.* brewing

пивоварня [p'i-va-vár-nya] *sf.* brewery

пиджак [p'id-<u>zh</u>ák] *sm.* sailor's jacket

пика [p'é-ka] *sf.* lance, spear

пикание [p'é-ka-nye] *sn.* chirping

пикантный [p'i-kánt-nǎy] *adj.* savoury

пики [p'é-ki] *sf. pl.* spades (*cards*)

пиковка [p'i-kóv-ka] *sf.* spade (*card*)

пила [p'i-lá] *sf.* file; saw

пилав [p'i-láf] *sm.* Russian rice pudding (*a sweet made from cooked rice mixed with mince-meat and baked till brown*)

пилить [p'i-l'ét'] *vt.* to saw; to file

пилюля [p'i-lyŏŏ-lya] *sf.* pill

пинать [p'i-nát'] *vt.* to spurn

пинцет [p'in-tsyét] *sm.* pincers

пир [p'ĕr] *sm.* banquet, feast

пирование [p'i-ra-vá-nye] *sn.* feasting, revelling

пировать [p'i-ra-vát'] *vi.* to carouse, feast

пирог [p'i-róg] *sm.* pasty, pie, tart

пирожник [p'i-ró<u>zh</u>-n'ik] *sm.* pastry-cook

пирожное [p'i-ró<u>zh</u>-na-ye] *sn.* fancy cake

пиршественный [p'ér-shest-vven-nǎy] *adj.* convivial, festive

писака [p'i-sá-ka] *sm.* scribbler

писание [p'i-sá-nye] *sn.* writing; scripture

писарь [p'é-sar'] *sm.* clerk, writer

писатель [p'i-sá-tyel'] *sm.* author, man of letters; **-ница** [-n'i-tsa] *sf.* authoress

писать [p'i-sát'] (на-) *vt.* to write; **- красками** [- krás-ka-mi] to paint

писец [p'i-syéts] *sm.* calligrapher

писклявый [p'i-skl'é-vǎy] *adj.* squeaky

пискун [p'is-kŏŏn] *sm.* squeaker

письменный [p'és-myen-nǎy] *adj.* writing-, written

письмо [p'is'-mó] *sn.* letter; **-вник** [-v-n'ik] *sm.* ABC copy-book, **-водство** [-vódstvŏ] *sn.* secretarial work

питание [p'i-tá-nye] *sn.* nourishment, nutrition

питательный [p'i-tǎ-tyel'nǎy] *adj.* nourishing, nutritive

питать [p'i-tát'] *vt.* to feed, nourish

питомец [p'i-tó-myets] *sm.* foster-son; **питомица** [p'i-tó-m'i-tsa] *sf.* foster-daughter

питомник [p'i-tóm-n'ik] *sm.* nursery (*for plants*)

пить [p'ĕt'] (вы-) *vt.* to drink

питьё [p'i-tyó] *sn.* beverage, drink

пихание [p'i-chá-nye] *sn.* pushing

пихта [p'ĕch-ta] *sf.* fir-tree

пишущая машина [p'e-shŏŏ-shcha-ya ma-shē-na] *sf.* typewriter

пища [p'ĕ-shcha] *sf.* food

пищать [p'i-shchát'] *vi.* to scream, squeal; to creak; to whine

пищеварение [p'i-shche-va-ryé-nye] *sn.* digestion

пищеварительный [p'i-shche-va-r'ē-tyel'-năy] *adj.* digestive

пищевод [p'i-shche-vód] *sm.* gullet

пищевой [p'i-shche-vóy] *adj.* alimentary, food-

пиявка [pi-yáv-ka] *sf.* leech

плаванье [plá-va-nye] *sn.* swimming; sailing

плавать [plá-vat'] *vi.* to swim; to float; to navigate

плавить [plá-v'it'] (рас-) *vt.* to smelt

плавка [pláv-ka] *sf.* fusion

плавник [pláv-n'ik] *sm.* fin

плавный [pláv-năy] *adj.* smooth; liquid (*speech, sound*)

плакат [pla-kát] *sm.* bill, placard, poster; *typ.* broad-sheet

плакать [plá-kat'] (за-) *vi.* to cry, weep; **-ся** [-sya] *vi.* to complain, lament

пламенеть [pla-mye-nyét'] *vi.* to blaze

пламенный [plá-myen-năy] *adj.* flaming; *fig.* ardent, passionate

пламя [plá-mya] *sn.* blaze, flame

план [plán] *sm.* design, plan, scheme

планёр [pla-nyór] *sm.* glider

планета [pla-nyé-ta] *sf.* planet

планетный [pla-nyét-năy] *adj.* planetary

плановый [plá-na-văy] *adj.* systematic

планшетка [plan-shét-ka] *sf.* husk

пласт [plást] *sm.* layer; stratum

пластинка [plas-t'ĕn-ka] *sf.* plate, sheet (*of metal*); gramophone record; lamina; *typ.* stereo

пластичный [plas-t'ĕch-năy] *adj.* plastic

пластырь [plás-tăr'] *sm.* plaster

плата [plá-ta] *sf.* charge; pay; wages

платёж [pla-tyózh] *sm.* payment

платежеспособность [pla-tye-zhe-spa-sób-nŏst'] *sf.* solvency

платить [pla-t'ĕt'] (за-) *vt.* to pay

платок [pla-tók] *sm.* neckerchief, shawl; **носовой** – [na-sa-vóy –] handkerchief

платье [plá-tye] *sn.* dress; clothes

плаха [plá-cha] *sf.* block, log

плацдарм [pláts-darm] *sm.* play-ground

плацкарта [plats-kár-ta] *sf.* reserved seat

плач [plách] *sm.* lamentation; weeping

плачевный [pla-chév-năy] *adj.* deplorable; woeful

плашкот [plash-kót] *sm.* lighter, pontoon

плащ [pläshch] *sm.* cloak, mantle; дождевой – [dazh-dye-vóy –] raincoat

плащаница [pla-shcha-nʹé-tsa] *sf.* shroud

плева [plye-vä́] *sf.* film, membrane

плевательница [plye-vä́-tyelʹ-nʹi-tsa] *sf.* spittoon

плевать [plye-vä́tʹ] (на-) *vi.* to spit

плевел [plye-vyel] *sm.* weed

плевок [plye-vók] *sm.* saliva, spittle; sputum

плеврит [plye-vrё́t] *sm.* pleurisy

плед [plyéd] *sm.* plaid

племя [plyé-mya] *sn.* race, tribe; breed, pedigree

племенной [plye-myen-nóy] *adj.* racial; – скот [– skot] pedigree cattle

племянник [plye-myǎn-nʹik] *sm.* nephew

племянница [plye-myǎn-nʹi-tsa] *sf.* niece

плен [plyén] *sm.* captivity

пленение [plye-nyé-nye] *sn.* capture

пленительный [plye-nʹé-tyelʹ-näy] *adj.* captivating, fascinating

плёнка [plyón-ka] *sf.* pellicle

пленник [plyén-nʹik] *sm.*, **пленница** [plyén-nʹi-tsa] *sf.* captive, prisoner

пленять [plye-nyä́tʹ] (пле-нить) *vt.* to charm

плёс [plyós] *sm.* reach (of river)

плесень [plyé-syenʹ] *sf.* mustiness

плеск [plyésk] *sm.* splash; lap

плескать [plyes-kätʹ] (плес-нуть) *vi.* to splash

плести [plyes-tʹё́] *vt.* to braid, plait; to twine; to weave

плетёнка [plye-tyón-ka] *sf.* network

плетень [plye-tyénʹ] *sm.* wicker-hurdle

плетенье [plye-tyé-nye] *sn.* braiding, netting, weaving; basket-work

плечо [plye-chó] *sn.* shoulder

плешивый [plye-shё́-väy] *adj.* bald

плешь [plyéshʹ] *sf.* bald patch

плинтус [plʹё́n-tŏŏs] *sm.* plinth; skirting-board

плис [plʹés] *sm.* plush

плита [plʹi-tä́] *sf.* cooking-range; flagstone; gravestone

плитка [plʹё́t-ka] *sf.* slab, tile; bar (of chocolate)

плитолотня [plʹi-ta-lót-nya] *sf.* quarry

пловец [pla-vyéts] *sm.* swimmer

пловучий [pla-vŏŏ-chi] *adj.* floating

пловучесть [pla-vŏŏ-chestʹ] *sf.* buoyancy

плод [plod] *sm.* fruit

плодовитость [pla-da-vʹё́-tŏstʹ] *sf.* fertility

плодовитый [pla-da-vʹё́-täy] *adj.* fruitful; productive

плодородный [pla-da-ród-näy] *adj.* fertile

пломба [plóm-ba] *sf.* filling (dental)

пломбир [plom-bʹёr] *sm.* iced gateau

пломбировать [plom-bʹё-ra-vätʹ] *vt.* to fill, stop (teeth)

плоский [plós-ki] *adj.* flat; fig. trivial

плоскогубцы [plos-ka-gŏŏb-tsá] *sm. pl.* pliers

плоскодонка [plos-ko-dón-ka] *sf.* flat boat

плоскость [plós-kŏst'] *sf.* flatness; plain

плотва [plat-vá] *sf.* roach

плотина [pla-t'é-na] *sf.* dam, dike, weir

плотник [plót-n'ik] *sm.* carpenter

плотничество [plót-n'i-chest-vŏ] *sn.* carpentry

плотность [plót-nŏst'] *sf.* compactness; density

плотоядный [pla-ta-yád-näy] *adj.* carnivorous

плотский [plót-ski] *adj.* carnal

плоть [plot'] *sf.* flesh

плохо [pló-chŏ] *adv.* badly, poorly

плохой [pla-chóy] *adj.* bad, nasty, poor

площадка [pla-shchád-ka] *sf.* platform; landing place; pleasure-ground

площадь [pló-shchad'] *sf.* area, square; esplanade

плуг [plŏŏg] *sm.* plough

плут [plŏŏt] *sm.* impostor, rogue

плутня [plŏŏt-nyä] *sf.* swindle, trick

плутовство [plŏŏ-tav-stvó] *sn.* cheating, fake, trickery

плыть [pl't'] *vi.* to sail; to navigate

плюс [plyŏŏs] *sm.* plus (+)

плюш [plyŏŏsh] *sm.* velvet

плющ [plyŏŏshch] *sm.* ivy

плющить [plyŏŏ-shchét'] (c-) *vt.* to flatten, laminate

пляж [plyäzh] *sm.* beach

плясание [plya-sä-nye] *sn.* dancing

плясать [plya-sät'] (по-) *vi.* to dance

по [pŏ] *prep.* at, by, in, on, to, up to

побаиваться [pa-bä-i-vat'-sya] *vi.* to be rather afraid

побег [pa-byég] *sm.* desertion; escape; elopement

победа [pa-byé-da] *sf.* victory

победитель [pa-bye-d'é-tyel'] *sm.* conqueror, victor

победоносный [pa-bye-da-nós-näy] *adj.* triumphant, victorious

побеждать [pa-byezh-dát'] (победить) *vt.* to conquer, defeat, win (*a battle*)

побережный [pa-bye-ryézh-näy] *adj.* littoral

побережье [pa-bye-ryé-zhye] *sn.* coast, shore

поблажка [pa-blázh-ka] *sf.* connivance

поблизости [pa-bl'é-zas-t'i] *adv.* in the neighbourhood, near-by

побои [pa-bó-i] *sm. pl.* beating, blows, thrashing

побоище [pa-bó-i-shche] *sn.* bloodshed, slaughter

побольше [pa-ból'-she] *adv.* rather more

побор [pa-bór] *sm.* requisition

поборник [pa-bór-n'ik] *sm.* champion, supporter

побочный [pa-bóch-näy] *adj.* accessory; collateral; **ребёнок** [- rye-byó-nŏk] illegitimate child

по-братски [pa-brät-ski] *adv.* brotherly

побрезговать [pa-bryéz-ga-vat'] *vi.* to disdain, dislike

побрякушка [pa-brya-kōōsh-ka] sf. child's rattle

побудитель [pa-bōō-d'ē-tyel'] sm. instigator

побуждать [pa-bōōzh-dât'] (побудить) vt. to instigate, rouse, stir

побуждение [pa-bōōzh-dyé-nye] sn. incentive, motive

побывать [pa-bǎ-vât'] vi. to visit occasionally

побыть [pa-bǎt'] vi. to stay (for a little time)

повадка [pa-vâd-ka] sf. habit

повалить [pa-va-l'ēt'] vt. to overthrow; to throng

повальный [pa-vâl'-nǎy] adj. general, without exception

повар [pó-var] sm. chef, cook

поваренный [pa-va-ryen-nǎy] adj. culinary

поведать [pa-vye-dât'] vt. to relate, to tell

поведение [pa-vye-dyé-nye] sn. behaviour, conduct

повелевать [pa-vye-le-vât'] (повелеть) vt. to command, order

повелительный [pa-vye-l'ē-tyel'-nǎy] adj. dictatorial, imperative

повергать [pa-vyer-gât'] (повергнуть) vt. to plunge, precipitate, throw down

поверка [pa-vyér-ka] sf. check, control; verification; proof

поверочный [pa-vyé-rach-nǎy] adj. checked, verified

повёртывать [pa-vyór-tǎ-vat'] vt. to turn round

поверх [pa-vyérch] prep. above, over

поверхностный [pa-vyérch-nast-nǎy] adj. superficial; fig. shallow

поверхность [pa-vyerch-nŏst'] sf. surface

поверье [pa-vyé-rye] sn. superstition

поверять [pa-vye-ryât'] (поверить) vt. to confide, impart; to check, verify

повеса [pa-vyé-sa] sf., m. madcap, tomboy, rascal

повеселиться [pa-vyes-n'i-chā-nye] sn. dissipation

повесничать [pa-vyés-n'i-chat'] vi. to be uncouth

повествование [pa-vyest-va-vâ-nye] sn. narration, narrative; recital

повествовать [pa-vyést-va-vat'] vt. to narrate, relate, tell

повестка [pa-vyést-ka] sf. notice, notification; writ; – дня [– dnyá] agenda; судебная – [sōō-dyéb-na-ya –] summons

повесть [pó-vyest] sf. novel, tale

поветрие [pa-vyét-rye] sn. epidemic

повещать [pa-vye-shchât'] (повестить) vt. to announce, inform

повивать [pa-v'i-vât'] vt. to swathe; to twine

повивальщица [pa-v'i-vâl'-shchi-tsa] sf. midwife

по-видимому [pa-v'ē-d'i-ma-mōō] adv. apparently, seemingly

повиниться [pa-v'i-n'ēt'-sya] vi. to plead guilty

повинная [pa-v'ēn-na-ya] sf. confession

повинность [pa-v'ēn-nŏst'] sf. duty, obligation; service; воинская – [va-ēn-ska-ya –] compulsory military service

повинный [pa-v'ēn-nay] *adj.* guilty

повиноваться [pa-v'i-na-vát'sya] *vt.i.* to obey

повиновение [pa-v'i-na-vyé-nye] *sn.* obedience, submission

повлечь [pa-vlyéch'] *vt.* to involve, necessitate

повод [pó-vŏd] *sm.* bridle, halter; motive; occasion; reason; **по -у** [pa -ŏ̄d] *as regards, in connection with*

повозка [pa-vŏz-ka] *sf.* cart, vehicle

поворот [pa-va-rót] *sm.* bend, turn, turning, winding; reversal

поворотливость [pa-va-rót-l'i-vŏst'] *sf.* agility, nimbleness

поворотливый [pa-va-rót-l'i-vay] *adj.* active, agile, nimble, quick

повреждать [pa-vryezh-dát'] (повредить) *vt.* to damage, spoil; to injure; *fig.* to harm

повреждение [pa-vryezh-dyé-nye] *sn.* damage, injury

повременный [pa-vrye-myén-nay] *adj.* now and then, periodical

повседневный [pa-vsye-dnyév-nay] *adj.* daily

повсеместный [pa-vsye-myést-nay] *adj.* general, universal

повсечасно [pa-vsye-chás-nŏ] *adv.* hourly

повстанец [pa-vstá-nyets] *sm.* insurgent, rebel

повсюду [pa-vsyŏ̄-dŏ̄] *adv.* everywhere, throughout

повторение [paf-ta-ré-nye] *sn.* reiteration, repetition

повторительный [paf-ta-r'é-tyel'-nay] *adj.* repetitive

повторять [paf-ta-ryát'] (повторить) *vt.* to repeat

повышать [pa-vă-shát'] (повысить) *vt.* to heighten, raise; to promote

повышение [pa-vă-shé-nye] *sn.* advancement, elevation, promotion

повязка [pa-vyáz-ka] *sf.* bandage; headband

повязывать [pa-vyá-ză-vat'] (повязать) *vt.* to bind, tie, wrap

поганка [pa-găn-ka] *sf.* toadstool; sheldrake

поганый [pa-gă-nay] *adj.* foul, unclean

погань [pó-gan'] *sf.* filth

погашать [pa-ga-shát'] (погасить) *vt.* to extinguish, to put out; to cancel

погашение [pa-ga-shé-nye] *sn.* extinction; liquidation; suppression

погибать [pa-gi-bát'] (погибнуть) *vi.* to perish

погибель [pa-gé-byel'] *sf.* destruction, doom, ruin

погибший [pa-gĕb-shi] *adj.* lost; perished

поглощать [pa-gla-shchát'] (поглотить) *vt.* to absorb; to devour; to engulf

поглощение [pa-gla-shché-nye] *sn.* absorption, swallowing up

поговаривать [pa-ga-vă-r'i-vat'] (поговорить) to chat, to speak

поговорка [pa-ga-vór-ka] *sf.* proverb, a saying

погода [pa-gó-da] *sf.* weather

погонщик [pa-gón-shchik] *sm.* driver (*of cattle, etc.*)

погоня [pa-gó-nya] *sf.* chase, pursuit

погонять [pa-ga-nyát'] (погнать) *vt.* to drive, spur, urge

погорелец [pa-ga-ryé-lyets] *sm.* one left destitute after a fire

погорелый [pa-ga-ryé-lǎy] *adj.* somewhat burnt

погост [pa-góst] *sm.* churchyard

погреб [pó-gryeb] *sm.* cellar; **-альный** [-ál'-nǎy] *adj.* funereal

погребать [pa-gre-bát'] *vt.* to bury

погребальщик [pa-gre-bál'-shchik] *sm.* grave-digger

погребение [pa-gre-byé-nye] *sn.* burial, interment

погреться [pa-gryét'-sya] *vi.* to warm oneself

погрешать [pa-gre-shát'] *vi.* to err; to sin

погрозить [pa-gra-z'ёt'] *vt.* to threaten

погружение [pa-grōō-zhé-nye] *sn.* immersion, sinking

погрузка [pa-grōōz-ka] *sf.* loading, shipment

под [pŏd] *prep.* under; towards; *sm.* hearth

подавать [pa-da-vát'] (подáть) *vt.* to give, present; to serve (*at dinner, in tennis*); to submit; **-ся** [-sya] *vi.* to yield

подавленный [pa-dáv-lyennǎy] *adj.* despondent

подавлять [pa-dav-lyát'] (подавить) *vt.* to crush, stamp out, suppress

подагра [pa-dág-ra] *sf.* gout

подарок [pa-dá-rŏk] *sm.* gift, present; gratuity

податель [pa-dá-tyel'] *sm.* bearer; petitioner

податливость [pa-dát-l'ivŏst'] *sf.* complaisance

податливый [pa-dát-l'ivǎy] *adj.* compliant; yielding

подача [pa-dá-cha] *sf.* giving, presenting, serving

подаяние [pa-da-yá-nye] *sn.* alms, charity; dole

подбавлять [pad-bav-lyát'] (подбáвить) *vt.* to add

подбадривать [pad-bád-ri-vat'] *vi.* to encourage, hearten

подбегать [pad-bye-gát'] *vi.* to run up towards

подбивать [pad-b'i-vát'] (подбить) *vt.* to line (*garments*); to instigate

подбивка [pad-b'ёv-ka] *sf.* lining

подбирать [pad-b'i-rát'] *vt.* to gather, pick up; to assort, match, select

подблюдник [pad-blyōōd-n'ik] *sm.* protective table mat

подболтка [pad-bólt-ka] *sf.* thickening

подбор [pad-bór] *sm.* assortment, selection

подбородок [pad-ba-ró-dŏk] *sm.* chin

подвал [pad-vál] *sm.* basement, cellar

подведомственный [pad-vyé-dam-stvyen-nǎy] *adj.* dependent

подвергать [pad-vyer-gát'] (подвéргнуть) *vt.* to expose, inflict, subject; **-ся** [-sya] *vi.* to undergo

подвержение [pad-vyer-zhé-nye] *sn.* subjection

подверженность [pad-vyér-zhen-nŏst'] *sf.* liability

подвёртывание [pad-vyŏr-tǎ-va-nye] *sn.* screwing; spraining; wricking

подвеска [pad-vyés-ka] *sf.* suspension

подвесок [pad-vyé-sŏk] *sm.* pendant

подветренный [pad-vyét-ren-nǎy] *adj.* leeward

подвешивание [pad-vyé-shi-va-nye] *sn.* hanging, suspension

подвиг [pód-vig] *sm.* deed, exploit, feat

подвигать [pad-vi-gǎt'] (подвинуть) *vt.* to advance, push on

подвижный [pad-v'ēzh-nǎy] *adj.* mobile, volatile

подвластный [pad-vlǎst-nǎy] *adj.* meek, submissive

подвода [pad-vó-da] *sf.* cart-and-horse

подводить [pad-va-d'ét'] (подвести) *vt.* to lead up to; to introduce (*a subject, etc.*)

подводный [pad-vód-nǎy] *adj.* submerged; under water; **подводная лодка** [pad-vód-na-ya lót-ka] *sf.* submarine

подвоз [pad-vóz] *sm.* transport

подвозить [pad-va-z'ét'] (подвезти) *vt.* to bring; to convey; to supply

подворный [pad-dvór-nǎy] *adj.* farmstead-, of farmstead

подвох [pad-vóch] *sm.* plot, trap; *coll.* dirty trick

подвязка [pad-vyáz-ka] *sf.* garter, suspender

подглядывание [pad-glyá-dǎ-va-nye] *sn.* peeping, peering

подговор [pad-ga-vór] *sm.* instigation; persuasion

подгородный [pad-ga-ród-nǎy] *adj.* suburban

подгорье [pad-gó-rye] *sn.* lowland

подготовлять [pad-ga-tav-lyǎt'] (подготовить) *vt.* to prepare; to get ready

подготовка [pad-ga-tóv-ka] *sf.* preparation; **военная –** [va-yén-na-ya –] military drill

поддавать [pad-da-vát'] (поддать) *vt.* to add, increase; **-ся** [-sya] *vi.* to give in, give way

подданный [pód-dan-nǎy] *adj. as sm.*, subject (*as British subject, etc.*)

подданство [pód-dan-stvŏ] *sn.* citizenship, nationality

подделка [pad-dyél-ka] *sf.* counterfeit; forgery; imitation

подделывание [pad-dyé-lǎ-va-nye] *sn.* artificiality, falsification

поддельный [pad-dyél'-nǎy] *adj.* artificial, false; sham

поддерживать [pad-dyér-zhi-vat'] (поддержать) *vt.* to maintain, support, uphold

поддержка [pa-dyér-zhka] *sf.* assistance; maintenance; support

поддонник [pad-dón-n'ik] *sm.* saucer

подействовать [pa-dyéy-stva-vat'] *vi.* to have an effect, to operate, work (*as medicine*)

подённый [pa-dyón-nǎy] *adj.* daily

подёнщик [pa-dyón-shchik] *sm.* day-worker; journeyman

подёнщица [pa-dyón-shchi-tsa] *sf.* charwoman

подёргивание [pa-dyór-gi-va-nye] *sn.* jerk, twitch, twitching

подержанный [pa-dyér-zhan-nǎy] adj. second-hand, used, worn

поджаривание [pad-zhā-ri-va-nye] sn. frying, roasting, toasting

поджарый [pad-zhā-rǎy] adj., coll. lean, meagre; stingy

подживать [pad-zhi-vát] (поджить) vt.i. to heal

поджигательство [pad-zhi-gā-tyel'-stvǒ] sn. incendiarism

поджигать [pad-zhi-gát] (поджечь) vt. to set on fire; to burn

поджидание [pad-zhi-dā-nye] sn. expectation, waiting

поджог [pad-zhóg] sm. arson

подзаголовок [pad-zā-ga-la-vǒk] sm. subheading, subtitle

подземелье [pad-zye-myé-lye] sn. cave, vault

подземка [pad-zyém-ka] sf. subway, underground (tube)

подземный [pad-zyém-nǎy] adj. subterranean

подивиться [pad-d'i-v'ét'-sya] vt.i. to admire, be surprised, wonder at

подирать [pa-d'i-rát] vt. to pull, tear

подкалывать [pad-kā-la-vat] vt. to cleave, split; to tuck

подкапывать [pad-kā-pǎ-vat] (подкапáть) vt. to dig, undermine

подкашивать [pad-kā-shi-vat] (подкосить) vt. to cut, mow

подкладка [pad-klād-ka] sf. lining

подкладывать [pad-klā-dǎ-vat] (подложить) vt. to line, pad, underlay

подклейка [pad-klyéy-ka] sf. glueing, pasting

подкова [pad-kó-va] sf. horse-shoe

подкованный [pad-kó-van-nǎy] adj. shod (of horse)

подкожный [pad-kózh-nǎy] adj. hypodermic

подкоп [pad-kóp] sm. mine; sap; undermining

подкрашивать [pad-krā-shi-vat] (подкрáсить) vt. to colour, paint; to touch up; to dye

подкрепление [pad-krye-plyé-nye] sn. fortifying; reinforcement; confirmation

подкуп [pód-kōōp] sm. bribe, bribery, corruption

подкупать [pad-kōō-pát] (подкупить) vt. to bribe, buy over, corrupt

подле [pód-lye] prep. beside, by, near

подлежащее [pad-lye-zhā-shche-ye] adj.gram. nominative (case); sn. subject

подлец [pad-lyéts] sm. scoundrel, villain

подливка [pad-l'ēv-ka] sf. gravy, sauce

подлинник [pad-l'ēn-n'ik] sm. original

подлинный [pad-l'ēn-nǎy] adj. authentic, original

подложный [pad-lózh-nǎy] adj. false, spurious; supposititious

подлость [pód-lǒst] sf. baseness

подлый [pód-lǎy] adj. despicable, mean, villainous

подмен(а) [pad-myén(a)] sm., sf. exchange, substitution

подметание [pad-mye-tā-nye] sn. sweeping

подмётка [pad-myót-ka] *sf.* sole (of shoe)

подмётывать [pad-myó-tä-vat'] (подметать) *vt.* to baste, tack

подмечать [pad-mye-chät'] (подметить) *vt.* to notice, observe

подмешивать [pad-myé-shi-vat'] (подмешать) *vt.* to mix

подмога [pad-mó-ga] *sf. coll.* aid, help; **итти на подмогу** [i-t'é na pad-mó-gōō] lend a hand

подмостки [pad-móst-ki] *sm. pl.* scaffolding, trestles; *theat.* platform, stage

подначальный [pad-na-chäl'-näy] *adj.* subordinate

поднебесный [pad-nye-byés-näy] *adj.* terrestrial

поднебесная [pad-nye-byés-na-ya] *sf.* the earth, the universe, the world

поднебесье [pad-nye-byé-sye] *sn.* air, atmosphere; the heavens

подневольный [pad-nye-vól'-näy] *adj.* subjected

поднимать [pad-n'i-mät'] (поднять) *vt.* to hoist, lift, raise; to pick up; **-ся** [-sya] *vi.* to ascend, go up, rise

подновление [pad-nav-lyé-nye] *sn.* renovation

подновлять [pad-nav-lyät'] (подновить) *vt.* to freshen up, renew, renovate

подножие [pad-nó-zhye] *sn.* base, foot; foot-stool; pedestal

подножка [pad-nózh-ka] *sf.* footboard; step

поднос [pad-nós] *sm.* salver, tray

подносить [pad-na-s'ét'] (поднести) *vt.* to bring, offer, present

подношение [pad-na-shé-nye] *sn.* presentation, tribute

поднятие [pad-nyä-tye] *sn.* lift, rise; upheaval

подобие [pa-dó-bye] *sn.* likeness, similarity

подобный [pa-dób-näy] *adj.* equal; like, similar

подобострастный [pa-da-ba-sträst-näy] *adj.* humble, servile

подогревание [pa-da-grye-vä-nye] *sn.* warming up

подождать [pa-dazh-dät'] *vi.* to wait awhile

подозревание [pa-da-zrye-vä-nye] *sn.* distrust, suspicion

подозрительный [pa-da-zr'è-tyel'-näy] *adj.* suspicious

подойник [pa-dóy-n'ik] *sm.* milking-pail

подоконник [pad-a-kón-n'ik] *sm.* window-sill

подол [pa-dól] *sm.* hem, train (of gown)

подольщаться [pa-dal'-shchät'-sya] (подольститься) *vi.* cajole

по-домашнему [pa-da-mäsh-nye-mōō] *adv.* homely, simply, unceremoniously

подонки [pa-dón-ki] *sm. pl.* dregs, offal, sediment; *fig.* scum (people)

подорожать [pa-da-ra-zhät'] *vi.* to become expensive

подошва [pa-dósh-va] *sf.* sole (of foot, boot); foot (of hill)

подпирать [pad-p'i-rät'] (подпереть) *vt.* to prop up, support

подписание [pad-p'i-sá-nye] *sn.* signing

подписка [pad-p'ĕs-ka] *sf.* subscription; written document

подписчик [pad-p'ĕs-chik] *sm.* subscriber

подписывать [pad-p'ĕ-sá-vat'] (подписать) *vt.* to sign, subscribe; -ся [-sya] *vi.* to sign one's name

подпись [pód-p'is'] *sf.* signature

подполковник [pad-pal-kóv-n'ik] *sm.* lieutenant-colonel

подполье [pad-pó-lye] *sn.* cellar; *fig.* illegal (or secret, or underground) activity

подпольный [pad-pól'-nǎy] *adj.* under the floor; *fig.* illegal, secret, underground

подпольщик [pad-pól'-shchik] *sm.* member of a secret organization

подпорка [pad-pór-ka] *sf.* prop, support

подпоручик [pad-pa-róo-chik] *sm.* second lieutenant

подпочва [pad-póch-va] *sf.* subsoil

подражать [pa-dra-zhát'] *vi.* to copy, imitate, mimic

подражатель [pa-dra-zhá-tyel'] *sm.* impersonator, mimic

подразумевать [pad-ra-zōō-mye-vat'] *vt.* to imply, mean

подробность [pa-drób-nŏst'] *sf.* detail

подробный [pa-drób-nǎy] *adj.* detailed, particular

подросток [pad-rós-tŏk] *sm.* youth

подруга [pa-drōō-ga] *sf.* friend (*girl*)

по-дружески [pa-drōō-zhes-ki] *adv.* amicably, friendly

подружиться [pad-rōō-zhit'sya] *vi.* to make friends, become friendly

подручный [pad-rōōch-nǎy] *adj.* adaptable, handy; *as sm.* assistant

подрыв [pa-drάv] *sm.* detriment, harm, injury

подрывать [pa-drά-vát'] (подрыть) *vt.* to blow up, undermine; to hurt, wrong

подряд [pad-ryád] *sm.* contract; *adv.* in succession

подрядчик [pad-ryád-chik] *sm.* contractor

подряжать [pad-rya-zhát'] (подрядить) *vt.* to contract, engage, hire

подсвечник [pad-svyéch-n'ik] *sm.* candlestick

подсказывание [pad-ská-zǎ-va-nye] *sn.* prompting

подслащать [pad-sla-shchát'] (подсластить) *vt.* to sweeten

подслушивание [pad-slōō-shi-va-nye] *sn.* eavesdropping

подслушивать [pad-slōō-shi-vat'] (подслушать) *vt.* to overhear; to listen, spy

подсмеиваться [pad-smyé-i-vat'-sya] *vi.* to laugh at, ridicule, tease

подснежник [pad-snyézh-n'ik] *sm.* snowdrop

подсолнечник [pad-sól-nyech-n'ik] *sm.* sunflower

подставка [pad-stáv-ka] *sf.* stand

подстановка [pad-sta-nóv-ka] *sf.* substitution

подстилка [pad-stěl-ka] *sf.* bedding, litter *(for animals)*

подстрекание [pad-strye-ká-nye] *sn.* instigation; stimulation

подстригать [pad-stri-gát'] (подстричь) *vt.* to clip, crop; to shear; to trim; to prune

подстриженный [pad-strĕ-zhen-năy] *adj.* bobbed, cut short, shingled

подступ [pód-stŏŏp] *sm.* approach, advance

подсудимый [pad-sŏŏ-d'é-măy] *adj.* accused; *as sm.* the accused, prisoner at the bar

подсудный [pad-sŏŏd-năy] *adj.* authoritative, jurisdictional

подтверждать [pad-tvyer-zhdát'] (подтвердить) *vt.* to affirm, confirm, corroborate

подтекать [pad-tyé-kát'] (подтечь) *vi.* to leak

подтрунивание [pad-trŏŏ-n'i-va-nye] *sn.* chaffing, teasing

подтягивать [pad-tyá-gi-vat'] (подтянуть) *vt.* to draw, pull; to tighten

подтяжки [pad-tyázh-ki] *sf. pl.* braces

подумать [pa-dŏŏ-mat'] *vi.* to consider, reflect

подушка [pa-dŏŏsh-ka] *sf.* cushion, pillow

подход [pad-chód] *sm.* manner, mode, way

подходить [pad-cha-d'ét'] (подойти) *vi.* to approach; to draw near

подходящий [pad-cha-dyá-shchi] *adj.* advantageous, fitting, suitable

подчас [pad-chás] *adv.* occasionally

подчёркивать [pad-chór-ki-vat'] (подчеркнуть) *vt.* to stress, underline

подчинение [pad-chi-nyé-nye] *sn.* dependence, subordination

подчиняться [pad-chi-nyát'-sya] *vi.* to obey, submit

подчищать [pad-chi-shchát'] (подчистить) *vt.* to clean up, tidy up

подшипник [pad-ship-n'ik] *sm. tech.* bearing(s)

подштанники [pad-shtán-n'i-ki] *sm. pl.* drawers, pants

подштопывать [pad-shtó-pă-vat'] (подштопать) *vt.* to darn

подъезд [pad-yézd] *sm.* entrance, porch; private drive

подъезжать [pad-yez-zhát'] (подъехать) *vi.* to drive up *(from gates to house)*

подъём [pad-yóm] *sm.* instep; lift; lever; **-ник** [-n'ik] *sm.* elevator; **-ный** [-năy] *adj.* elevating, lifting; **-ный мост** [-năy most] *sm.* drawbridge; **-ные деньги** [-nă-ye dyén'-gi] *pl.* travelling expenses

поезд [pó-yezd] *sm.* train

поездка [pa-yézd-ka] *sf.* journey, trip; voyage; outing

поёмный [pa-yóm-năy] *adj.* inundated

пожалуй [pa-zhá-lŏŏy] *adv.* maybe, most likely, possibly

пожалуйста [pa-zhál-sta] *expression,* be so kind, if you please, please; sorry!

пожар [pa-zhár] *sm.* conflagration, fire; **-ище** [-ish-che] *sn. tech.* after-site *(after a fire)*; **-ная команда** [-na-ya ka-mán-da] fire brigade

пожарный [pa-zhár-nǎy] *adj.* fire-; *as sm.* fireman

пожатие [pa-zhá-tye] *sn.* pressing, squeezing; clasp, shake (*of the hand*)

по-женски [pa-zhén-ski] *adv.* womanly

пожертвование [pa-zhértva-a-nye] *sn.* offering, sacrifice

пожилой [pa-zhi-lóy] *adj.* elderly

пожитки [pa-zhít-ki] *sm. pl.* belongings, effects, property

поза [pó-za] *sf.* attitude, pose, posture

позавчера [pa-za-fche-rá] *adv.* the day before yesterday

позади [pa-za-d'é] *adv.* further back; to the rear; *prep.* behind

по-зверски [pa-zvyér-ski] *adv.* beastly, brutally

позволение [paz-va-lyé-nye] *sn.* permission

позволительный [paz-val'é-tyel'-nǎy] *adj.* permissible

позволять [paz-va-lyát'] (позволить) *vt.* to allow, oblige, permit

позвонок [pa-zvó-nŏk] *sm.* vertebra

поздний [pózd-ni] *adj.* late, tardy; backward

поздравлять [paz-drav-lyát'] (поздравить) *vt.* to congratulate

позём [pa-zyóm] *sm.* manure

поземельный [pa-zye-myél'-nǎy] *adj.* agrarian; territorial

позёмка [pa-zyóm-ka] *sf.* snowdrift

позиция [pa-z'é-tsya] *sf.* attitude, position

познаваемый [pa-zna-vá-ye-mǎy] *adj.* knowledgeable

познавать [paz-na-vát'] (познать) *vt.* to know, perceive

познакомиться [pa-zna-kó-m'it'-sya] *vi.* to get acquainted

позолотить [pa-za-la-t'ét'] *vt.* to gild [shame

позор [pa-zór] *sm.* infamy,

позыв [pó-zǎv] *sm.* inclination; longing

поимка [pa-ém-ka] *sf.* capture, seizure

поиски [pó-is-ki] *sm. pl.* quest, search

поистине [pa-ēs-t'i-nye] *adv.* indeed, verily

поить [pa-ét'] (на-) *vt.* to water (*horses*)

пойло [póy-lŏ] *sn.* mash, swill; trough

поймать [pay-mát'] *vt.* to catch

пойти [pay-t'é] *vi.* to go; **– в солдаты** [– vsal-dá-tǎ] to enlist; **– сюда** [– syoō-dá] to come here

пока [pa-ká] *adv.* meanwhile, until, whilst; for the present

показ [pa-káz] *sm.* show; **на –** [na –] for exhibition, for viewing

показание [pa-ka-zá-nye] *sn.* affidavit, evidence, testimony

показатель [pa-ka-zá-tyel'] *sm.* index; exponent

показательный [pa-ka-zá-tyel'-nǎy] *adj.* exemplary, typel'; significant

показывать [pa-ká-zǎ-vat'] (показать) *vt.* to display, exhibit, show; **-ся** [-sya] *vi.* to appear, seem; to show off

покаместь [pa-kā-myest']
adv. in the meantime

покатый [pa-kā-tăy] *adj.*
declivous, sloping

покаяние [pa-ka-yā-nye] *sn.*
penitence, repentance

покаяться [pa-ka-yāt'-sya]
vi. to repent

покидать [pa-k'i-dāt'] (по-
кинуть) *vt.* to abandon,
desert, vacate

покинутый [pa-k'ē-nōō-tăy]
adj. desolate, forlorn

поклажа [pa-klā-zha] *sf.*
cargo

поклёп [pa-klyóp] *sm.* calumny, slander

поклон [pa-klón] *sm.* greeting, salute; **низкий –**
[n'ḗz-ki –] curtsy

поклонение [pa-kla-nyé-
nye] *sn.* adoration, worship

поклонник [pa-klón-n'ik]
sm. admirer, worshipper

покланяться [pa-kla-nyāt'-
sya] (поклониться) *vi.* to
greet, salute; to adore, worship

покой [pa-kóy] *sm.* peace,
repose, quiet

покойник [pa-kóy-n'ik] *sm.*
deceased

покойницкая [pa-kóy-n'íts-
ka-ya] *sm.* mortuary

покойный [pa-kóy-năy] *adj.*
calm, restful; deceased, late

поколебаться [pa-ka-lye-
bāt'-sya] *vi.* to hesitate

поколение [pa-ka-lyé-nye]
sn. generation

покорение [pa-ka-ryé-nye]
sn. subjugation

покорность [pa-kór'-nŏst']
sf. acquiescence, submission

покорный [pa-kór'-năy] *adj.*
humble, obedient

покорять [pa-ka-ryāt'] (по-
корить) *vt.* to subdue, sub-
jugate; **-ся** [-sya] *vi.* to give
in, submit

покос [pa-kós] *sm.* meadow;
mowing, **второй –** [fta-
róy –] aftermath

покража [pa-krā-zha] *sf.*
theft; *pl.* stolen articles

покраснеть [pa-kras-nyét']
vi. to blush; to become red

покров [pa-króv] *sm.* cover;
shelter

покровитель [pa-kra-v'ē-
tyel'] *sm.* patron, supporter;
-ство [-stvŏ] *sn.* patronage,
protection

покрой [pa-króy] *sm.* cut,
shape; style

покромка [pa-króm-ka] *sf.*
selvage

покрывало [pa-krǎ-vā-lŏ] *sn.*
bedspread, counterpane; veil

покрывать [pa-krǎ-vāt']
(покрыть) *vt.* to cover,
spread over

покрышка [pa-krǎsh-ka] *sf.*
lid

покупатель [pa-kōō-pā-
tyel'] *sm.* buyer, customer

покупать [pa-kōō-pāt'] *vt.*
to buy, purchase

покупка [pa-kōōp-ka] *sf.*
buying, purchase; **делать
покупки** [dyé-lat' pa-kōōp-
ki] to go shopping

покушаться [pa-kōō-shat'-
sya] *vt.t.* to attempt, try

покушение [pa-kōō-shé-
nye] *sn.* attempt, endeavour

пол [pol] *sm.* floor, ground;
sex; *adj.* female-, half-, semi-

пола [pa-la] *sf.* flap, skirt

полагать [pa-la-gāt'] *vt.* to
deem, suppose; **-ся** [-sya]
vi. to rely

полгода [pol-gó-da] *sm.* half-year

полдень [pól-dyen'] *sm.* mid-day

полдюжина [pal-dyōō-zhi-na] *sf.* half a dozen

поле [pó-lye] *sn.* field, open country; margin (*in book*)

полеводство [pa-lye-vód-stvŏ] *sn.* husbandry

полегоньку [pa-lye-gón'-kŏŏ] *adv.* easily, steadily

полезный [pa-lyéz-năy] *adj.* beneficial, useful, utilitarian

полемика [pa-lyé-mi-ka] *sf.* controversy

полено [pa-lyé-nŏ] *sn.* chunk of wood, log

полёт [pa-lyót] *sm.* flight

ползать [pal-zăt'] (поползти) *vi.* to crawl, creep

поливать [pa-li-vát'] (полить) *vt.* to water (*flowers, etc.*)

поливка [pa-l'ĕv-ka] *sf.* watering

полирование [pa-l'i-ra-vá-nye] *sn.* burnishing, polishing

полировка [pa-l'i-róv-ka] *sf.* gloss, polish

полировщик [pa-l'i-róv-shchik] *sm.* polisher

политика [pa-l'ĕ-ti-ka] *sf.* politics

политипаж [pa-l'i-t'i-pázh] *sm.* woodcut

политический [pa-l'i-t'ĕ-ches-ki] *adj.* political

политура [pa-l'i-tōō-ra] *sf.* polish, varnish

полицейский [pa-l'i-tsyéy-ski] *adj.* police-; *sm.* policeman

полиция [pa-l'ĕ-tsya] *sf.* constabulary

полк [polk] *sm.* regiment

полка [pól-ka] *sf.* rack, shelf; weeding

полковник [pal-kóv'n'ik] *sm.* colonel

полковой [pal-ka-vóy] *adj.* regimental

полнеть [pal-nét'] (по-) *vi.* to grow stout, put on weight

полно [pól-nŏ] *adv.* completely; full to the brim; -! *interj.* enough !

полновластный [pal-na-vlăst-năy] *adj.* sovereign, supreme

полнокровный [pal-na-króv-năy] *adj.* full-blooded

полнолицый [pal-na-l'ĕ-tsăy] *adj.* full-faced

полнолуние [pal-na-lōō-nye] *sn.* full moon

полномочный [pal-na-móch-năy] *adj.* authorized, empowered; *as sm.* envoy

полноправный [pal-na-práv-năy] *adj.* competent

полнота [pal-na-tă] *sf.* corpulence; fullness

полночь [pól-nŏch'] *sf.* midnight

полный [pól-năy] *adj.* full

половик [pa-la-v'ĕk] *sm.* strip of carpet

половина [pa-la-v'ĕ-na] *sf.* half

половой [pa-la-vóy] *adj.* sexual; **половая зрелость** [pa-la-vá-ya zryé-lŏst'] *sf.* puberty

полный [pól-năy] *adj.* complete, full

положение [pa-la-zhé-nye] *sn.* position, situation; circumstance, state

положительный [pa-la-zhi-tyel'-năy] *adj.* affirmative, positive; sedate (*of character*)

полольник [pa-lól'-n'ik] *sm.* hoe

полоса [pa-la-sá] *sf.* bar, strip

полосатый [pa-la-sá-tăy] *adj.* striped, streaky

полоска [pa-lós-ka] *sf.* band, slip, strip

полоскание [pa-la-skă-nye] *sn.* gargle; mouth-wash; rinsing

полость [pó-lŏst] *sf.* cavity

полотенце [pa-la-tyén-tse] *sn.* towel

полотно [pa-lat-nó] *sn.* linen; cloth; железнодорожное – [zhe-lyez-na-da-rózh-na-ye –] permanent way

полоть [pa-lót'] (выполоть) *vt.* to weed

полоумный [pa-la-ōŏm-năy] *adj.* crazy, halfwitted

полсотни [pal-sót-n'i] *num.* fifty ('half-hundred')

полтора [pal-ta-rá] *num.* one and a half

полтораста [pal-ta-rás-ta] *num.* hundred and fifty

полугласный [pa-lŏŏ-glás-năy] *adj. as s.* semi-vowel

полуостров [pa-lŏŏ-óst-rŏv] *sm.* peninsula

полупансионер [pa-lŏŏ-pan-sio-nyér] *sm.* day-boarder

полусвет [pa-lŏŏ-svyét] *sm.* twilight

полутон [pa-lŏŏ-tón] *sm. mus.* semitone

получатель [pa-lŏŏ-chă-tyel'] *sm.* recipient

получать [pa-lŏŏ-chăt'] (получить) *vt.* to get, obtain, receive

полушарие [pa-lŏŏ-shă-rye] *sn.* hemisphere

полый [pó-lăy] *adj.* hollow; bare, uncovered

полынь [pa-lǎn'] *sf.* wormwood

польза [pól'-za] *sf.* advantage, benefit, use

пользовать [pól'-za-vat'] *vt.* to attend, treat; -ся [-sya] *vi.* to take advantage, make use of

полька [pól'-ka] *sf.* polka; Polish woman

польский [pól'-ski] *adj.* Polish

по-людски [pa-lyŏŏd-ski] *adv.* humanly

полюс [pó-lyŏŏs] *sm.* pole; -ный [-năy] *adj.* polar

поляк [pa-lyǎk] *sm.* Pole

полянка [pa-lyăn-ka] *sf.* glade

помазание [pa-mă-za-nye] *sn.* annointing; unction

помарка [pa-măr-ka] *sf.* blot; blur; *typ.* cancel

померанец [pa-mye-ră-nyets] *sm.* Seville orange

поместительный [pa-myes-t'ê-tyel'-năy] *adj.* roomy, spacious

поместный [pa-myést-năy] *adj.* local

поместье [pa-myés-tye] *sn.* estate; manor

помесь [pa-myes'] *sf.* crossbreed, hybrid

помёт [pa-myót] *sm.* dung, manure; litter, farrow

пометка [pa-myét-ka] *sf.* note; notice

помеха [pa-myé-cha] *sf.* hindrance, impediment, obstacle

помеченный [pa-myé-chen-năy] *adj.* dated, marked, noted

помешанный [pa-myé-shan-năy] *adj.* insane; *as sm.* maniac

помещать [pa-mye-shchát'] (поместить) vt. to place, put; to invest; to locate

помещение [pa-mye-shchénye] sn. investment; premises; insertion

помещик [pa-myé-shchik] sm. landowner

помидор [pa-m'i-dór] sm. tomato

помилование [pa-m'i-lavâ-nye] sn. forgiveness, pardon, remission

помимо [pa-m'ē-mŏ] prep. apart, besides, but, moreover

поминальный [pa-m'inâl'-năy] adj. memorial

поминать [pa-m'i-nât'] (помянуть) vt. to mention, remember; to say Mass for the dead

поминовение [pa-m'i-navyé-nye] sn. commemoration (at church services)

поминутно [pa-m'i-nŏŏt-nŏ] adv. every minute, minute by minute

помнить [póm-n'it'] (вс-) vt. to remember

помногу [pa-mnó-gŏŏ] adv. in large quantities; often

помножать [pa-mna-zhât'] (помножить) vt. to multiply

помогать [pa-ma-gât'] (помочь) vi. to aid, help

по-моему [pa-mó-ye-mŏ] adv. to my mind; in my own way

помои [pa-mó-i] sm. pl. dish-water, slops

помойка [pa-móy-ka] sf. kitchen sink

помолвка [pa-mólv-ka] sf. betrothal, engagement

помолодевший [pa-mala-dyév-shi] adj. rejuvenated

по-молодецки [pa-ma-ladyéts-ki] adv. bravely, daringly, sportingly

поморье [pa-mó-rye] sn. sea-coast, seaside

помост [pa-móst] sm. dais

помощник [pa-móshch-n'ik] sm. assistant, help, servant

помощь [pó-mŏshch] sf. assistance, help

помпа [póm-pa] sf. pump; pomp

помрачать [pa-mra-chât'] (помрачить) vt. to darken, obscure

помысел [pó-mă-syel] sm. idea, notion, thought

помышлять [pa-mă-shlyât'] (помыслить) vi. to ponder, think

понапрасну [pa-na-prâsnŏ] adv. in vain

по-настоящему [pa-nas-ta-yâ-shche-mŏŏ] adv. in earnest, really, truly

по-нашему [pa-nâ-she-mŏŏ] adv. according to us; to our mind

поневоле [pa-nye-vó-lye] adv. necessarily; perforce; 'Hobson's choice'

понедельник [pa-nye-dyél'n'ik] sm. Monday

понемногу [pa-nye-mnógŏŏ] adv. by degrees, a little at a time

понижать [pa-n'i-zhât'] (понизить) vt. to abate, lower, reduce; to debase

понижение [pa-n'i-zhénye] sn. fall, falling, reduction

поникать [pa-n'i-kât'] (поникнуть) vi. to droop, wither

понимание [pa-n'i-mâ-nye] sn. comprehension, intelligence

понимать [pa-n'i-mát'] (по-ня́ть) *vt.* to understand

пономарь [pa-na-már'] *sm.* sexton

понос [pa-nós] *sm.* diarrhoea

поносить [pa-na-s'ét'] *vt.* to abuse, slander

поношение [pa-na-shé-nye] *sn.* defamation, slander

поношенный [pa-nó-shen-nǎy] *adj.* old, worn

понтировка [pan-t'i-róv-ka] *sf.* punting

понудительный [pa-nŏŏ-d'é-tyel'-nǎy] *adj.* coercive, impellent

понуждение [pa-nŏŏzh-dyé-nye] *sn.* compulsion

по-нутру [pa-nŏŏ-trŏŏ] *adv.* agreeable, to one's taste

пончик [pón-chik] *sm.* dumpling

понятие [pa-nyá-tye] *sn.* conception, understanding

понятливый [pa-nyát-l'i-vǎy] *adj.* bright, intelligent

понятно [pa-nyát-nŏ] *adv.* clearly, plainly; naturally, of course

поодиночке [pa-a-d'i-nóch-ke] *adv.* singly

по-отцовски [pa-at-tsóv-ski] *adv.* fatherly

по-очереди [pa-ó-che-rye-d'i] *adv.* alternately, in turn

поощрение [pa-a-shchryé-nye] *sn.* encouragement, incentive

поп [pop] *sm.* priest

попарёк [pa-pye-ryók] *adv.* crosswise

поперечник [pa-pye-ryéch-n'ik] *sm.* diameter; girth

поперечный [pa-pye-ryéch-nǎy] *adj.* diametrical, transverse

попечение [pa-pye-ché-nye] *sn.* care; solicitude

попечитель [pa-pye-ché-tyel'] *sm.* guardian, trustee

поплавок [pa-plá-vŏk] *sm.* float

поповник [pa-póv-n'ik] *sm.* daisy

попойка [pa-póy-ka] *sf.* carouse, spree

пополам [pa-pa-lám] *adv.* in half, in two

поползновение [pa-pal-zna-vyé-nye] *sn.* inclination

пополнение [pa-pal-nyé-nye] *sn.* addition, supplement; reinforcement

пополнять [pa-pal-nyát'] (пополнить) *vt.* to fill up, replenish, supplement

пополудни [pa-pa-lŏŏ-dn'i] *adv.* post meridiem

пополуночи [pa-pa-lŏŏ-na-chi] *adv.* ante meridiem

попона [pa-pó-naj *sf.* trappings

поправимый [pa-pra-v'é-mǎy] *adj.* reparable, remediable; corrigible

поправка [pa-práv-ka] *sf.* correction; recovery; repair

поправлять [pa-prav-lyát'] (поправить) *vt.* to mend, repair; to correct, -ся [-sya] *vi.* to get better, pick up, recover (*from illness*); to correct oneself (*error in speech, etc.*)

по-прежнему [pa-pryézh-nye-mŏŏ] *adv.* as formerly

попрёк [pa-pryók] *sm.* reproach, reproof

попрекать [pa-prye-kát'] (попрекнуть) *vt.* to blame, scold rebuke

поприще [pó-pri-shche] *sm.* career, profession; *fig.* field, sphere (*of activity*)

по-приятельски [pa-pri-yá-tyel'-ski] *adv.* friendly (*disposition, manner*)

попросту [pó-pras-tŏŏ] *adv.* simply, unceremoniously

попугай [pa-pŏŏ-gáy] *sm.* parrot

популярный [po-pŏŏ-lyár-nǎy] *adj.* popular

попутный [pa-pŏŏt-nǎy] *adj.* fair, favourable

попутчик [pa-pŏŏt-chik] *sm.* fellow-traveller

попытка [pa-pắt-ka] *sf.* attempt, trial, venture

попятный [pa-pắt-nǎy] *adj.* retrograde

пора [pa-rǎ] *sf.* time, while; **давно – [davnó –] it's high time; порою [pa-ró-yŏŏ] *adv.* occasionally

пора [pó-ra] *sf.* pore

поработать [pa-ra-bó-tat'] *vi.* to work (*intermittently*)

порабощать [pa-ra-ba-shchát'] (поработить) *vt.* to enslave

порабощение [pa-ra-ba-shché-nye] *sn.* enslavement, subjugation

поражать [pa-ra-zhát'] (поразить) *vt.* to astonish, surprise; to defeat, rout; to deliver a blow; **-ся** [-sya] *vi.* to be startled, surprised, thunderstruck

поражение [pa-ra-zhé-nye] *sn.* blow, defeat; disease

поразительный [pa-ra-z'ế-tyel'-nǎy] *adj.* astounding, striking

по-ребячески [pa-rye-byá-ches-ki] *adv.* childishly

порез [pa-ryéz] *sm.* cut, gash

порезаться [pa-ryé-zat'-sya] *vi.* to cut oneself

порей [pa-ryéy] *sm.* leek

поречный [pa-ryéch-nǎy] *adj.* riverside

поречье [pa-ryé-chye] *sn.* river country

пористый [pa-r'ěs-tǎy] *adj.* porous

порицать [pa-r'i-tsát'] *vt.* to censure

порка [pór-ka] *sf.* flogging, whipping; unpicking, unstitching of *clothing, etc.*

поровну [pó-rav-nŏŏ] *adv.* equally

порог [pa-róg] *sm.* threshold

пороги [pa-ró-gi] *sm. pl.* rapids, waterfall

порода [pa-ró-da] *sf.* breed, species, stock

породистый [pa-ró-d'i-stǎy] *adj.* thoroughbred

порожний [pa-rózh-ni] *adj.* empty

порознь [pó-rŏzn'] *adv.* separately

порок [pa-rók] *sm.* defect; vice

поросёнок [pa-ra-syó-nŏk] *sm.* porkling, sucking-pig

поросль [pó-rŏsl'] *sf.* shoots, verdure

поросятина [pa-ra-syá-t'i-na] *sf.* (young) pork

пороть [pa-rót'] (распороть) *vt.* to rip, unpick; to whip

порох [pó-rŏch] *sm.* gunpowder

порочный [pa-róch-nǎy] *adj.* imperfect; depraved, vicious

пороша [pa-ró-sha] *sf.* first fall of snow

порошинка [pa-ra-shín-ka] *sf.* speck of dust, grain of powder

порошок [pa-ra-shók] *sm.* cleaning *or* dusting powder

порт [port] *sm.* harbour, port

портить [pór-t'it'] (ис-) *vt.* to damage, spoil; to corrupt

портниха [part-n'ē-cha] *sf.* dressmaker

портной [part-nóy] *sm.* tailor

портняжничество [part-nyázh-n'i-chest-vŏ] *sn.* tailoring

портплед [port-plyéd] *sm.* hold-all

портрет [par-tryét] *sm.* portrait; **-ист** [-ĕst] *sm.* portrait-painter; **-ная живопись** [-na-ya zhí-va-p'is'] portraiture

портсигар [port-si-gár] *sm.* cigarette-case

португалец [por-tŏŏ-gá-lyets] *sm.* Portuguese

португальский [por-tŏŏ-gäl'-ski] *adj.* Portuguese

портфель [part-fýel'] *sm.* portfolio

поругание [pa-rŏŏ-gá-nye] *sn.* insult, outrage

порука [pa-rŏŏ-ka] *sf.* bail, surety

поручать [pa-rŏŏ-chát'] (поручить) *vt.* to commission, entrust

поручение [pa-rŏŏ-ché-nye] *sn.* errand; verbal message; mission

поручень [pa-rŏŏ-chen'] *sm.* hand-rail; handcuff; railing

поручитель [pa-rŏŏ-che-tyel'] *sm.* guarantor

порфира [par-f'ē-ra] *sf.* purple

порхать [par-chát'] (порхнуть) *vi.* to flit, flutter

порция [pór-tsya] *sf.* portion

порцион [par-tsyón] *sm.* ration; **-ный** [-näy] *adj.* à la carte

порча [pór-cha] *sf.* deterioration, spoiling

поршень [pór-shen'] *sm.* piston

порыв [pa-rǎv] *sm.* impulse; passion; gust; **-истый** [-ĕs-täy] *adj.* impetuous, vehement

порывать [pa-rǎ-vát'] (порвать) *vt.* to tear asunder

порыжелый [pa-rǎ-zhé-läy] *adj.* rusty

порядковый [pa-ryād-ka-väy] *adj.* ordinal

порядок [pa-ryā-dŏk] *sm.* form, order; arrangement, sequence

порядочный [pa-ryā-dach-näy] *adj.* decent, honest, respectable

посадка [pa-sád-ka] *sf.* embarkation; planting; alighting, landing; seat

по-светски [pa-svyét-ski] *adv.* worldly

посвящение [pa-svye-shché-nye] *sn.* dedication; devotion; ordination

по-своему [pa-svó-ye-mŏŏ] *adv.* in one's own way

посвящать [pa-svya-shchát'] (посвятить) *vt.* to consecrate, dedicate, devote; to ordain

посев [pa-syév] *sm.* sowing

поселенец [pa-sye-lyé-nyets] *sm.* colonist, settler

поселение [pa-sye-lyé-nye] *sn.* colony, settlement; **ссылка на -** [sǎl-ka na -] *sf.* deportation

поселок [pa-syó-lok] *sm.* hamlet; settlement

посетитель [pa-sye-t'ĕ-tyel'] *sm.* caller, visitor

посещать [pa-sye-shchát'] (посетить) *vt.* to call on, frequent, visit

посещение [pa-sye-shché-nye] *sn.* visit

поскольку [pa-skól'-kŏŏ] *conj.* so far as; since

послабление [pa-slab-lyé-nye] *sn.* indulgence

посланец [pa-slá-nyets] *sm.* envoy; messenger

послание [pa-slá-nye] *sn.* epistle; message

посланник [pa-slán-n'ik] *sm.* envoy, minister

после [pó-slye] *prep.* after; *adv.* afterwards, later on

последки [pa-slyéd-ki] *sm. pl.* leavings, remainder

последний [pa-slyéd-ni] *adj.* final, last; latter

последование [pa-slye-da-vá-nye] *sn.* following

последователь [pa-slyé-da-va-tyel'] *sm.* disciple, follower, partisan

последовательный [pa-slyé-da-va-tyel'-năy] *adj.* successive

последствие [pa-slyéd-stvye] *sn.* consequence, sequel

последующий [pa-slyé-dŏŏ-yŏŏ-shchi] *adj.* following, subsequent

послесловие [pa-slye-sló-vye] *sn.* epilogue

пословица [pa-sló-vi-tsa] *sf.* adage, proverb

послужной [pa-slŏŏzh-nóy] *adj.* serviceable

послушание [pa-slŏŏ-shá-nye] *sn.* docility, obedience; **исполнять** — [is-pal-nyát'–] to do penance

послушать [pa-slŏŏ-shat'] *vi.* to listen

послушник [pa-slŏŏsh-n'ik] *sm.* novice; lay brother

послушный [pa-slŏŏsh-năy] *adj.* docile, obedient

посмеиваться [pa-smyé-i-vat'-sya] *vi.* to chuckle, mock, to ridicule

посменно [pa-smyén-nŏ] *adv.* in shifts

посмертный [pa-smyért-năy] *adj.* posthumous

посмеяние [pa-smye-yá-nye] *sn.* mockery, ridicule

пособие [pa-só-bye] *sn.* assistance, help; relief (*monetary*); appliance

посол [pa-sól] *sm.* ambassador

посольство [pa-sól'-stvŏ] *sn.* embassy; legation

посох [pó-sŏch] *sm.* shepherd's crook; crozier; staff

поспевать [pa-spye-vát'] (поспеть) *vi.* to ripen; to arrive in time; to be ready

поспешность [pa-spyésh-nŏst'] *sf.* haste; promptness

поспешный [pa-spyésh-năy] *adj.* hasty, hurried; prompt

посрамлять [pa-sram-lyát'] (посрамить) *vt.* to humiliate, shame

посреди [pa-srye-d'ĕ] *prep.* among; amid, amidst

посредник [pa-sryéd-n'ik] *sm.* intermediary, middleman; negotiator

посреднический [pa-sryéd-n'i-ches-ki] *adj.* arbitral, pleading

посредственность [pa-sryéd-stvyen-nŏst'] *sf.* mediocrity

посредственный [pa-sryéd-stvyen-nǎy] adj. impartial, indifferent, second-rate

посредство [pa-sryéd-stvŏ] sn. agency, means; -м, by means of, through

пост [post] sm. fast; **Великий** – [vye-l'ě-ki –] Lent; halt, standing-place; mil. post

постав [pa-stǎv] sm. loom; set of millstones

поставить [pa-stǎ-v'it'] vt. to place, put; to set up

поставлять [pas-tav-l'yǎt'] vt. to cater, furnish, purvey, supply

поставщик [pas-tav-shchĭk] sm. caterer, contractor, purveyor; outfitter

постановка [pas-ta-nóv-ka] sf. erection, putting-up; staging; training

постановление [pas-ta-nav-lyé-nye] sn. decision; decree, enactment

постарелый [pa-sta-ryé-lay] adj. aged

по-старому [pa-stǎ-ra-mŏŏ] adv. as before, as of old

постель [pa-styél'] sf. bed, bedding

постепенный [pas-tye-ryén-nǎy] adj. gradual

постигать [pa-st'i-gǎt'] (постигнуть) vt. to grasp, understand; to befall

постижение [pas-t'i-zhé-nye] sn. comprehension

постилать [pa-st'i-lǎt'] (постлать) vt. to lay, spread; – постель [– pa-styél'] to make the bed; – пол [– pol] to cover the floor

постилка [pa-st'ĕl-ka] sf. litter (for animals)

постой [pa-stóy] sm. mili-

tary quarters; billet; –! halt!

постольку [pa-stól'-kŏŏ] adv. in as much as

посторонний [pas-ta-rón-n'iĭ] adj. accessory, foreign; extraneous; sm. outsider, stranger

постоялец [pa-sta-yǎ-lyets] sm. lodger, tenant

постоянный [pa-sta-yǎn-nǎy] adj. constant, invariable, lasting, perpetual

постригать [pa-stri-gǎt'] (постричь) vt. to cut the hair

пострижение [pa-stri-zhé-nye] sn. taking monastic vows, taking the veil

построение [pa-stra-yé-nye] sn. construction, structure

постройка [pa-stróy-ka] sf. building, structure

постромка [pa-stróm-ka] sf. trace (of vehicle)

поступательный [pa-stŏŏ-pǎ-tyel'-nǎy] adj. progressive

поступать [pa-stŏŏ-pǎt'] (поступить) vi. to act, to deal; to behave, comport; to enter (a school, etc.); to enlist

поступок [pa-stŏŏ-pŏk] sm. conduct, step

постыдный [pa-stǎd-nǎy] adj. repelling, shameful

посуда [pa-sŏŏ-da] sf. crockery, kitchen utensils

посудина [pa-sŏŏ-d'i-na] sf. dish, jar, vessel

посудить [pa-sŏŏ-d'ĕt'] vt. to consider; to judge

посылать [pa-sǎ-lǎt'] (послать) vt. to dispatch, send

посылка [pa-sǎl-ka] sf. parcel; sending

посягательство [pa-sya-gǎ-tyel'-stvŏ] sn. attempt; infringement

пот [pot] *sm.* perspiration, sweat

потакание [pa-ta-kā-nye] *sn.* connivance, indulgence

потворствовать [pa-tvór-stva-vat'] *vi.* to connive, indulge; to spoil

потёмки [pa-tyóm-ki] *sf. pl.* darkness

потемнение [pa-tyem-nyé-nye] *sn.* dimness; dullness

потение [pa-tyé-nye] *sn.* perspiring

потенциальность [pa-tyen-tsiâl'-nöst] *sf.* potentiality

потёртый [pa-tyór-tāy] *adj.* shabby, threadbare

потеря [pa-tyé-rya] *sf.* bereavement; loss

потеть [pa-tyét'] *vi.* to sweat

потеха [pa-tyé-cha] *sf.* amusement, diversion, fun

потешный [pa-tyésh-nāy] *adj.* amusing, funny

потир [pa-t'ēr] *sm.* chalice

потирать [pa-t'i-rāt'] (потереть) *vt.* to rub lightly

потихоньку [pa-t'i-chón-kōō] *adv.* gently, noiselessly, silently

поток [pa-tók] *sm.* flow, stream

потолок [pa-ta-lók] *sm.* ceiling

потом [pa-tóm] *adv.* after, afterwards, then

потомки [pa-tóm-ki] *sm. pl.* progeny

потомок [pa-tó-mŏk] *sm.* descendant

потомственный [pa-tóm-stvyen-nāy] *adj.* hereditary

потомство [pa-tóm-stvŏ] *sn.* posterity

потому [pa-ta-mōō] *adv.*

for, in consequence of; that's why; *conj.* **-что** [-shto] because

потоп [pa-tóp] *sm.* deluge, flood

потребитель [pa-trye-b'ē-tyel'] *sm.* consumer; **-ная лавка** [-na-ya lāv-ka] *sf.* co-operative store; **-ское общество** [-ska-ye ób-shchest-vŏ] co-operative society

потреблять [pa-tryeb-lyāt'] (потребить) *vt.* to consume, use

потребный [pa-tryéb-nāy] *adj.* necessary

потрескивание [pa-tryés-ki-va-nye] *sn.* crackling

потроха [pa-tra-châ] *sm. pl.* bowels, entrails, intestines

потрясение [pa-trya-syé-nye] *sn.* shock

потупленный [pa-tōōp-lyen-nāy] *adj.* downcast

потухание [pa-tōō-chā-nye] *sn.* extinction

потчевание [pa-tche-vā-nye] *sn.* regaling

потягивать [pa-tyā-gi-vat'] (потянуть) *vt.* to pull

потянуться [pa-tya-nōōt'-sya] *vr.* to stretch oneself

поучение [pa-ōō-ché-nye] *sn.* instruction, lesson, precept, sermon

похабщина [pa-chāb-shchi-na] *sf.* coarseness, obscenity

похвала [pa-chva-lā] *sf.* eulogy; praise

похвальный [pa-chvāl'-nāy] *adj.* praiseworthy

похваляться [pa-chva-lyāt'-sya] *vi.* to brag

похититель [pa-chi-t'ē-tyel'] *sm.* abductor, kidnapper

похищать [pa-chi-shchát'] (похитить) vt. to abduct, kidnap; to ravish

похлёбка [pa-chlyób-ka] sf. gruel (of the sort served in prisons) [hangover

похмелье [pa-chmyé-lye] sn.

поход [pa-chód] sm. campaign, expedition; cruise; **крестовый** – [kryes-tó-vay –] crusade

походить [pa-cha-d'ét'] vt. to resemble

походка [pa-chód-ka] sf. gait, step

похождение [pa-chazh-dyé-nye] sn. adventure

похожий [pa-chó-zhi] adj. resembling, similar

похороны [pó-cha-ra-nă] sf. pl. burial, funeral

похотливый [pa-chót-l'i-văy] adj. lecherous, wanton

похоть [pó-chŏt'] sf. desire, lust

поцелуй [pa-tse-lóŏy] sm. kiss

почасно [pa-chás-nŏ] adv. hourly

почасту [pa-chás-tŏŏ] adv. frequently

почва [póch-va] sf. earth, ground, land, soil

почём [pa-chóm] adv. how much? – знать? [– znăt'] who knows?

почему [pa-che-móŏ] adv. why; **-то** [-tŏ] for some reason or other

почерк [pó-cherk] sm. handwriting

почернеть [pa-cher-nyét'] vi. to become black

почернить [pa-cher-n'ét'] vt. to blacken

почесть [pó-chest'] sf. distinction, esteem, honour

почёт [pa-chót] sm. esteem, respect

почётный [pa-chót-năy] adj. honorary; honourable

почечник [pa-chéch-n'ik] sm. jade

почечный [pó-chech-năy] adj. nephritic; **-камень** [-kă-myen'] sm. gall-stone

почивать [pa-chi-vát'] (почить) vi. to rest, sleep awhile

починка [pa-chён-ka] sf. darn(ing); mend(ing); repair(ing)

почитать [pa-chi-tát'] (почтить) vt. to honour, respect; to read occasionally

почка [póch-ka] sf. bot. bud; anat. kidney

почта [póch-ta] sf. mail; post, post-office

почтальон [pach-ta-l'ón] sm. postman

почтение [pach-tyé-nye] sn. consideration, esteem, veneration

почтенный [pach-tyén-năy] adj. honourable, respectable

почти [pach-t'é] adv. almost, nearly

почтительный [pach-t'é-tyel'-năy] adj. deferential, respectful

почтовый [pach-tó-văy] adj. postal; **почтовая марка** [pach-tó-va-ya măr-ka] sf. postage stamp

пошиб [pa-shéb] sm. manner

пошлина [pósh-l'i-na] sf. customs, duty, tax

пошлый [pósh-lăy] adj. banal, commonplace, trivial

поштучно [pa-shtóŏch-nŏ] adv. piecemeal

пощада [pa-shchá-da] sf. mercy, pardon

пощёлкивание [pa-shchól-ki-va-nye] *sn.* clicking, snapping

пощёчина [pa-shchó-chi-na] *sf.* slap, smack (*on the cheek*)

поэзия [pa-é-zya] *sf.* poetry

поэма [pa-é-ma] *sf.* poem

поэт [pa-ét] *sm.* poet; **-ический** [-t-é-ches-ki] *adj.* poetic(al)

поэтому [pa-é-ta-mŏŏ] *conj.* therefore

появление [pa-ya-vlyé-nye] *sn.* apparition; appearance

появляться [pa-ya-vlyát'-sya] (появиться) *vi.* to emerge, make one's appearance

поярковый [pa-yár-ka-väy] *adj.* of felt, of lamb's wool

поярок [pa-yâ-rok] *sm.* felt, lamb's wool

пояс [pó-yas] *sm.* belt, girdle, sash; zone

пояснение [pa-yas-nyé-nye] *sn.* elucidation

пояснительный [pa-yas-n'é-tyel'-näy] *adj.* explanatory

пояснять [pa-yas-nyát'] (пояснить) *vt.* to elucidate, explain, illustrate

прабабушка [pra-bä-bŏŏsh-ka] *sf.* great-grandmother

правда [práv-da] *sf.* truth; *adv.* certainly; indeed?

правдивый [prav-d'é-väy] *adj.* reliable, truthful

правдоподобие [pra-vda-pa-dó-bye] *sn.* likelihood, probability

праведность [prä-vyed-nŏst'] *sf.* righteousness

правило [prä-vi-lŏ] *sn.* principle, regulation, rule

правило [pra-v'é-lŏ] *sn.* helm, rudder; guide-rod

правильный [prä-vil'-näy] *adj.* accurate, correct; normal, proper

правитель [pra-v'é-tyel'] *sm.* administrator, manager

правительство [pra-v'é-tyel'-stvŏ] *sn.* government

править [prä-v'it'] *vt.* to govern, direct, rule; to correct; to strop

правка [práv-ka] *sf. typ.* galley-proof; reading and correcting

правление [prav-lyé-nye] *sn.* government; administration, direction; board of directors

правнук [práv-nŏŏk] *sm.* great-grandson

правнучка [práv-nŏŏch-ka] *sf.* great-grand-daughter

право [prä-vŏ] *sn.* law, right; claim; *adv.* really, truly

правоведение [pra-va-vyé-dye-nye] *sn.* jurisprudence

правоверность [pra-va-vyér-nŏst'] *sf.* orthodoxy

правонарушение [pra-va-na-rŏŏ-shé-nye] *sn.* transgression

правописание [pra-va-p'i-sä-nye] *sn.* orthography

православие [pra-va-slä-vye] *sn.* orthodoxy (*Greek Church*)

правосудие [pra-va-sŏŏ-dye] *sn.* justice

правота [pra-va-tä] *sf.* equity; integrity

правый [prä-väy] *adj.* right (*direction*); just, right, upright

прадедушка [pra-dyé-dŏŏsh-ka] *sm.* great-grandfather

празднество [práz-dnyest-vŏ] *sn.* festival

праздник [prázd-n'ik] *sm.* holiday

праздничный [prázd-n'ich-năy] *adj.* festive, holiday-

праздновать [prázd-na-vat'] *vt.* to celebrate

праздный [prázd-năy] *adj.* empty, idle

практик [prăk-t'ik] *sm.* practical person; practitioner

практика [prăk-t'i-ka] *sf.* practice

практичный [prak-t'ĕch-năy] *adj.* practical

прародитель [pra-ra-d'é-tyel'] *sm.* ancestor, forefather

прасол [prá-sol] *sm.* cattle-dealer

прах [prách] *sm.* ashes; dust

прачечная [prá-chech-na-ya] *sf.* laundry, wash-house

прачка [prách-ka] *sf.* laundress

праща [pra-shchá] *sf.* sling

преблаженный [pre-bla-zhén-năy] *adj.* most holy

пребывать [prye-bă-vát'] (пребыть) *vi.* to reside, sojourn stay

превозмогать [prye-vaz-ma-gát'] (превозмочь) *vt.* to master, surmount

превозношение [prye-vaz-na-shé-nye] *sn.* exaltation

превосходительство [prye-vas-cha-d'é-tyel'-stvŏ] *sn.* (title) excellency

превосходный [prye-vas-chód-năy] *adj.* capital, excellent; *gram.* superlative

превратный [prye-vrát-năy] *adj.* inconstant; unpleasant

превращать [prye-vra-shchát'] (превратить) *vt.* to convert, change, transform

превращение [prye-vra-shché-nye] *sn.* transformation

превышать [prye-vă-shát'] *vt.* to exceed, surpass

преграда [prye-grá-da] *sf.* barrier, obstacle

предавать [prye-da-vát'] (предать) *vt.* to betray

предание [prye-dá-nye] *sn.* legend, tradition

преданный [pryé-dannăy] *adj.* attached, devoted

предатель [prye-dá-tyel'] *sm.* traitor; **-ский** [-ski] *adj.* treacherous; **-ство** [-stvŏ] *sn.* betrayal, treachery, treason

предварение [prye-dva-ryé-nye] *sn.* premonition; precedence

предварительный [pryed-va-r'ĕ-tyel'-năy] *adj.* preliminary

предварять [pred-va-ryát'] (предварить) *vt.* to warn; to anticipate; to precede

предвестие [pryed-vyés-tye] *sn.* omen, portent, presage

предвестник [pryed-vyest-n'ik] *sm.* forerunner

предвечность [pryed-vyéch-nŏst'] *sf.* eternity

предвзятый [pryed-vzyá-tăy] *adj.* pre-conceived

предвидеть [pryed-v'é-dyet'] *vt.* to forecast, foresee

предводительство [pryed-va-d'é-tyel'-stvŏ] *sn.* leadership

преддверие [pryed-dvyé-rye] *sn.* beginning, eve; vestibule

предел [prye-dyél] *sm.* boundary, landmark, limit; term

предисловие [prye-d'i-sló-vye] *sn.* preface, introduction

предки [pryéd-ki] *sm. pl.* ancestry

предлагать [pryed-la-gát'] (предложить) *vt.* to offer; to propose

предлог [pryed-lóg] *sm.* preposition; pretence

предложение [pryed-la-zhé-nye] *sn.* offer, proposal; suggestion

предместье [pryed-myés-tye] *sn.* outskirts

предмет [pryed-myét] *sm.* article; object; subject; topic; *com.* article

предназначать [pryed-naz-na-chát'] (предназначить) *vt.* to destine, to foreordain

предназначение [pryed-na-zna-ché-nye] *sn.* predestination

преднамеренный [pryed-na-myé-ryen-năy] *adj.* premeditated

предоставлять [prye-da-stav-lyát'] (предоставить) *vt.* to allow, let

предостережение [prye-da-stye-rye-zhé-nye] *sn.* caution, premonition, warning

предосторожность [prye-da-sta-rózh-nöst'] *sf.* precaution, safeguard

предосудительный [prye-da-sŏŏ-d'é-tyel'-năy] *adj.* reprehensible

предотвращать [prye-dat-vra-shchát'] (предотвратить) *vt.* to obviate, prevent, ward off

предохранение [pryed-a-chra-nyé-nye] *sn.* preservation, protection

предписание [pryed-p'i-sá-nye] *sn.* injunction; prescription

предполагать [pryed-pa-la-gát'] (предположить) *vt.* to conjecture, surmise

предположение [pryed-pa-la-zhé-nye] *sn.* assumption, conjecture, supposition

предпоследний [pryed-pa-slyéd-n'i] *adj.* penultimate

предпосылка [pryed-pa-săl-ka] *sf.* premise; *fig.* ground, reason

предпочтение [pryed-pach-tyé-nye] *sn.* preference

предприимчивость [pryed-pr'i-ĕm-chi-vöst'] *sf.* enterprise, undertaking

предпринимать [pryed-pr'i-n'i-mát'] (предпринять) *vt.* to undertake (*an expedition, a task, etc.*)

предприятие [pryed-pr'i-yá-tye] *sn.* business, concern, project; adventure, venture

предрасположение [pryed-ras-pa-la-zhé-nye] *sn.* predisposition; diathesis

предрассудок [pryed-ras-sŏŏ-dŏk] *sm.* prejudice

председатель [pryed-sye-dá-tyel'] *sm.* chairman, president, speaker; **-ство** [-stvŏ] chairmanship

предсказание [pryed-ska-zá-nye] *sn.* prediction, prophecy

представитель [pryed-sta-v'é-tyel'] *sm.* representative; spokesman; **-ный** [-năy] *adj.* imposing, portly; *polit.* representative; **-ство** [-stvŏ] *sn.* representation

представление [pryed-stav-lyé-nye] *sn.* theatrical performance, presentation

представлять [pryed-stav-lyát'] (представить) *vt.* to introduce, present (*in a social sense*); to represent; **-ся** [-sya] (представиться) to occur, present itself, seem

предтеча [pryed-tyé-cha] *sf.* forerunner, precursor

предубеждение [pryed-ōō-byezh-dyé-nye] *sn.* bias, prejudice

предупредительный [pryed-ōō-prye-d'ē-tyel'-năy] *adj.* precautionary, preventive; anticipating

предупреждать [pryed-ōō-pryezh-dát'] (предупредить) *vt.* to anticipate; to forestall, prevent; to forewarn

предусмотрительный [pryed-ōō-sma-tr'ē-tyel'-năy] *adj.* provident, prudent

предчувствие [pryed-chōōv-stvye] *sn.* foreboding, presentiment

предшественник [pryed-shést-vyen-n'ik] *sm.* predecessor

предъявлять [pryed-yav-lyát'] (предъявить) *vt.* to exhibit, produce (*a document, etc.*); to institute (*proceedings, etc.*); to prefer (*a charge, etc.*)

предыдущий [prye-dá-dōō-shchi] *adj.* preceding

преемник [prye-yém-n'ik] *sm.* successor

преемственный [prye-yém-stvyen-năy] *adj.* successive

прежде [pryézh-dye] *adv.* before, formerly, previously

преждевременный [pryezh-dye-vryé-myen-năy] *adj.* premature, untimely; precocious

прежний [pryézh-ni] *adj.* former, previous

презирать [prye-z'i-rát'] *vt.* to despise, scorn

презрение [prye-zryé-nye] *sn.* contempt, disdain

преимущество [prye-i-mōō-shchest-vŏ] *sn.* advantage, privilege; preference

прейскурант [preys-kōō-ránt] *sm.* price-list

преклонение [prye-kla-nyé-nye] *sn.* inclination; bowing

прекословие [prye-ka-sló-vye] *sn.* contradiction

прекрасный [prye-krás-năy] *adj.* beautiful, excellent, fine, handsome

прекращать [prye-kra-shchát'] (прекратить) *vt.* to cease, discontinue, leave off

прекращение [prye-kra-shché-nye] *sn.* cessation, discontinuance, stoppage

прелестный [prye-lyést-năy] *adj.* charming, delightful

прелесть [prye-lyest'] *sf.* charm, fascination

прельщение [pryel'-shché-nye] *sn.* captivation, fascination

прелюбодеяние [prye-lyŏbo-ba-dye-yá-nye] *sn.* adultery

премия [pryé-mya] *sf.* premium; prize

премудрый [pryé-mōōd-răy] *adj.* sagacious, very wise

пренебрегать [prye-nye-bre-gát'] *vt.* to disregard, neglect

пренебрежение [prye-nye-bre-zhé-nye] *sn.* contempt, disregard, neglect

преобладание [prye-ab-la-dá-nye] *sn.* predominance, prevalence

преображение [prye-a-bra-zhé-nye] *sn.* transfiguration, transformation

преобразование [prye-a-bra-za-vá-nye] *sn.* reform, reorganization

преодоление [prye-a-da-lýé-nye] *sn.* mastering, surmounting

преосвященный [prye-a-svya-shchén-năy] *adj.* Right Reverend

преосвященство [prye-a-svya-shchén-stvŏ] *sn.* Eminence, Grace, Lordship

преподавание [prye-pa-da-vá-nye] *sn.* teaching

преподавать [prye-pa-da-vát'] *vt.* to instruct, teach

преподношение [prye-pad-na-shé-nye] *sn.* offering, presentation

преподобие [prye-pa-dó-bye] *sn.* Reverence

преподобный [prye-pa-dób-năy] *adj.* reverend

препона [prye-pó-na] *sf.* impediment, obstacle

препровождение [prye-pra-vazh-dyé-nye] *sn.* despatching, forwarding

препятствие [prye-pyát-stvye] *sn.* hindrance, obstruction

пререкание [prye-rye-ká-nye] *sn.* dispute, quarrel

прерывание [prye-ră-vá-nye] *sn.* interruption

пресечение [prye-sye-ché-nye] *sn.* suppression

преследовать [prye-slyé-da-vat'] *vt.* to chase, pursue; to persecute

пресный [pryés-năy] *adj.* fresh; unleavened

пресса [prés-sa] *sf.* the Press

престол [prye-stól] *sm.* altar; throne

преступать [prye-stŏŏ-p'át'] (преступи́ть) *vt.* to overstep, transgress, violate

преступление [prye-stŏŏp-lyé-nye] *sn.* crime, offence; transgression; treason

преступник [prye-stŏŏp-n'ik] *sm.* criminal, delinquent, offender

пресыщение [prye-să-shché-nye] *sn.* satiation

претерпевание [prye-tyer-pye-vá-nye] *sn.* endurance, suffering [repel

претить [prye-t'ět'] *vt.* to

преувеличение [prye-ŏŏ-vye-l'i-ché-nye] *sn.* exaggeration, overstatement

преуменьшение [prye-ŏŏ-myen'-shé-nye] *sn.* understatement

преуспевание [prye-ŏŏs-pye-vá-nye] *sn.* advancement, prosperity, success

при [pr'ē] *prep.* at, by, during, in, near; in the time of

прибавление [pr'i-bav-lyé-nye] *sn.* addition, increase, supplement

прибежище [pr'i-bye-zhi-shche] *sn.* asylum, refuge

прибирать [pr'i-b'i-rát'] (прибра́ть) *vt.* to arrange, put in order, tidy up

приближать [pr'i-bl'i-zhát'] (прибли́зить) *vt.* to approximate; to draw nearer

приближение [pr'i-bl'i-zhé-nye] *sn.* approach; approximation

приблизительно [pr'i-bl'i-zĕ-tyel'-nŏ] *adv.* approximately

прибой [pr'i-bóy] *sm.* breakers, surf, wash

прибор [pr'i-bór] *sm.* apparatus, gear, instruments; set (*as tea-set, etc.*)

прибрежный [pr'i-bryézh-nǎy] *adj.* littoral

прибывать [pr'i-bǎ-vát'] (прибыть) *vi.* to arrive, come; to rise, swell (*of water*)

прибыль [pr'é-bǎl'] *sf.* gain, profit, return

прибытие [pr'i-bá-tye] *sn.* arrival

привал [pr'i-vál] *sm.* halt

приведение [pr'i-vye-dyé-nye] *sn.* adduction; bringing

привередливый [pr'i-vye-ryéd-l'i-vǎy] *adj.* fastidious, squeamish

приверженец [pr'i-vyér-zhe-nyets] *sm.* adherent, partisan

привет [pr'i-vyét] *sm.* greeting, reception, welcome; regards; —! hail! **-ливость** [-l'i-vǒst'] *sf.* affability; **-ливый** [-l'i-vǎy] *adj.* courteous; **-ствие** [-stvye] *sn.* salutation

привнвание [pr'i-v'i-vá-nye] *sn.* grafting; inoculation, vaccination

привнвок [pr'i-v'é-vǒk] *sm.* graft

привидение [pr'i-v'i-dyé-nye] *sn.* apparition

привкус [pr'iv-kōōs] *sm.* flavour, tang

привлекательный [pr'i-vlye-kǎ-tyel'-nǎy] *adj.* attractive, engaging

привлекать [pr'i-vlye-kát'] (привлечь) *vt.* to attract

привод [pr'i-vód] *sm.* bringing; drive, gear, transmission

приводить [pr'i-va-d'ét'] (привести) *vt.* to bring, lead up; to bring forward, lead

приводка [pr'i-vód-ka] *sf. typ.* register

привоз [pr'i-vóz] *sm.* import, importation

приволье [pr'i-vó-lye] *sn.* abundance; good living

привольный [pr'i-vól'-nǎy] *adj.* comfortable (*of circumstances*); plentiful

привратник [pr'i-vrát-n'ik] *sm.* doorkeeper, porter

привычка [pr'i-vách-ka] *sf.* custom, habit

привязчивый [pr'i-vyáz-chi-vǎy] *adj.* affectionate, loving

приглашение [pr'i-gla-shé-nye] *sn.* invitation

приговор [pr'i-ga-vór] *sm.* award; judgment, sentence

пригодный [pr'i-gód-nǎy] *adj.* fit, suitable

пригожий [pr'i-gó-zhi] *adj.* comely, good-looking, pretty

пригородный [pr'ē-ga-rad-nǎy] *adj.* suburban

пригорок [pr'i-gó-rok] *sm.* hillock

приготовительный [pr'i-ga-ta-v'ē-tyel'-nǎy] *adj.* preparatory

приготовлять [pr'i-ga-ta-vlyát'] (приготовить) *vt.* to prepare

придавать [pr'i-da-vát'] (придать) *vt.* to add, give; to attach

приданое [pr'i-dá-na-ye] *sn.* dowry; trousseau

придаток [pr'i-dá-tǒk] *sm.* appendage

придаточный [pr'i-dá-tach-nǎy] *adj.* additional, supplementary

придача [pr'i-dā-cha] *sf.* addition, increase; **в придачу** [vpr'i-dā-chōō] into the bargain

придворный [pr'i-dvór-nǎy] *adj.* court, royal; *sm.* official of the court; courtier; – **поэт** [– pa-ét] poet laureate

придел [pr'i-dyél] *sm.* chapel, side-altar

приделывать [pr'i-dyé-lǎ-vat'] (приделать) *vt.* to attach, fasten, fix

придерживать [pr'i-dyér-zhi-vat'] (придержать) *vt.* to detain; to hold on, stick to

придира [pr'i-d'ē-ra] *sf.* nagger

придираться [pr'i-d'i-rāt'-sya] *vi.* to cavil, nag, quibble

придирка [pr'i-d'ēr-ka] *sf.* nagging, sophistry

придирчивый [pr'i-d'ēr-chi-vǎy] *adj.* captious, quarrelsome

придорожный [pr'i-da-rózh-nǎy] *adj.* roadside, wayside

придумывать [pr'i-dōō-mǎ-vat'] (придумать) *vt.* to contrive, devise; imagine; to meditate

придурь [pr'ē-dōōr'] *sf.* eccentricity; foolishness

придушить [pr'i-dōō-shět'] *vt.* to choke, smother, strangle

придыхание [pr'i-dǎ-chā-nye] *sn.* aspiration, breathing

придыхательный [pr'i-dǎ-chā-tyel'-nǎy] *adj.* aspirate

приезд [pr'i-yézd] *sm.* arrival

приезжать [pr'i-yez-zhāt'] (приехать) *vi.* to come, arrive (*not on foot*)

приезжий [pr'i-yéz-zhi] *sm.* newcomer, stranger; *adj.* non-resident, visiting

приём [pr'i-yóm] *sm.* method, mode, way; reception (*social*); dose (*of medicine*); enrolment

приёмная [pr'i-yóm-na-ya] *sf.* drawing-room, guest-room, reception hall

приёмник [pr'i-yóm-n'ik] *sm.* receiver; recipient

приёмный [pr'i-yóm-nǎy] *adj.* receiving; reception; adopted, foster

приёмыш [pr'i-yó-mǎsh] *sm.* adopted child

приживальщик [pr'i-zhi-vāl'-shchik] *sm.*, **приживалка** [pr'i-zhi-vāl-ka] *sf.* hanger-on, sponger

прижигать [pr'i-zhi-gāt'] (прижечь) *vt.* to cauterize, scorch

прижимание [pr'i-zhi-mā-nye] *sn.* pressing, squeezing

приз [pr'ēz] *sm.* prize; *naut.* capture, prize

призадумываться [pr'i-za-dōō-mǎ-vat'-sya] *vi.* to become pensive

призвание [pr'i-zvā-nye] *sn.* calling, vocation

приземистый [pr'i-zyé-m'is-tǎy] *adj.* stocky

признавать [pr'i-zna-vāt'] (признать) *vt.* to acknowledge, admit, recognize

признак [pr'ē-znak] *sm.* indication, sign, token; symptom

признание [pr'i-znā-nye] *sn.* acknowledgment; confession

признательный [pr'i-znā-tyel'-nǎy] *adj.* grateful, thankful

призор [pr'i-zór] *sm.* care, protection

призрак [pr'ĕ-zrak] *sm.* apparition, vision

призрачный [pr'ĕ-zrach-năy] *adj.* illusory, unreal

призрение [pr'i-zryé-nye] *sn.* care, caring, charity; **дом призрения** [dom pr'i-zryé-nya] alms-house

призыв [pr'ĕ-zăv] *sm.* appeal, call, enrolment; conscription; levy

призывать [pr'i-ză-vát'] (призвать) *vt.* to call; to call up; to invoke

прииск [pr'ĕ-isk] *sm.* mine

приискание [pr'i-is-ká-nye] *sn.* searching

приказ [pr'i-káz] *sm.* command, injunction, order

приказчик [pr'i-káz-chik] *sm.*, shop-assistant; steward

приказывать [pr'i-ká-ză-vat'] (приказáть) *vt.* to bid, command

прикалывать [pr'i-ká-lă-vat'] (приколóть) *vt.* to fasten with pins

приканчивать [pr'i-kán-chi-vat'] *vt.* to finish off; to kill

прикасаться [pr'i-ka-sát'-sya] *vi.* to brush against

приклад [pr'i-klád] *sm.* butt (*of rifle*); accessories (*for dresses, etc.*)

прикладной [pr'i-klad-nóy] *adj.* applied

прикладывать [pr'i-klá-dă-vat'] (приложить) *vt.* to apply (*a coat of paint, etc.*); to affix, set; to enclose

приклеивать [pr'i-klyé-i-vat'] (приклéить) *vt.* to glue, paste, stick

приключение [pr'i-klyŏŏ-ché-nye] *sn.* adventure

приковывать [pr'i-kó-vă-vat'] (прикова́ть) *vt.* to chain; to forge; to rivet

прикоплять [pr'i-ka-plyát'] *vt.* to accumulate

прикорм [pr'i-kórm] *sm.* bait; lure

прикосновенный [pr'i-kas-na-vyén-năy] *adj.* implicated

прикраса [pr'i-krá-sa] *sf.* embellishment

прикрашивать [pr'i-krá-shi-vat'] (прикрáсить) *vt.* to adorn, embellish, ornament

прикрытие [pr'i-krá-tye] *sn.* covering; escort

прилавок [pr'i-lá-vŏk] *sm.* counter (*of shop*)

прилаживание [pr'i-lá-zhi-va-nye] *sn.* adaptation, adjustment, fitting

приласкать [pr'i-las-kát'] *vt.* to caress, pat, stroke

прилегающий [pr'i-lye-gá-yŏŏ-shchi] *adj.* adjacent

прилежание [pr'i-lye-zhá-nye] *sn.* application, diligence, industry

прилежный [pr'i-lyézh-năy] *adj.* diligent, painstaking

прилёт [pr'i-lyót] *sm.* arrival, flight (*of birds*); **-ный** [-năy] *adj.* migratory

прилечь [pr'i-lyéch'] *vi.* to lie down for a while

прилив [pr'i-l'ĕv] *sm.* flow, influx; tide; **волна -а** [val-ná -a] tidal wave

прилипание [pr'i-l'i-pá-nye] *sn.* adhesion, sticking

прилипчивый [pr'i-l'ĕp-chi-văy] *adj.* contagious

приличие [pr'i-l'ĕ-chye] sn. decency, propriety

приличный [pr'i-l'ĕch-năy] adj. decent, proper

приложение [pr'i-la-zhé-nye] sn. application; apposition; appendix, supplement

прильнуть [pr'il'-nōōt'] vi. to cling; to nestle up to

примачивать [pr'i-má-chi-vat'] (примочить) vt. to foment; moisten

применимый [pr'i-mye-n'ĕ-măy] adj. applicable

пример [pr'i-myér] sn. example, instance; **-ный** [-năy] adj. exemplary

примесь [pr'ĕ-myes] sf. admixture; tinge

примета [pr'i-myé-ta] sf. sign, token

приметливый [pr'i-myét-l'i-văy] adj. observant

приметный [pr'i-myét-năy] adj. perceptible, visible

примечание [pr'i-mye-chá-nye] sn. note, comment; footnote

примечательный [pr'i-mye-chá-tyel'-năy] adj. notable, noteworthy

примирение [pr'i-m'i-ryé-nye] sn. reconciliation

примирительный [pr'i-m'i-r'ĕ-tyel'-năy] adj. conciliatory

примиряться [pr'i-m'i-ryát'-sya] (примириться) vi. to make it up (with someone), to reconcile oneself with, to resign oneself to

приморский [pr'i-mór-ski] adj. maritime; littoral, seaside (as seaside town, etc.)

приморье [pr'i-mó-rye] sn. seaside

примочка [pr'i-móch-ka] sf. lotion, wash; fomentation

примыкать [pr'i-mă-kát'] (примкнуть) vt. to abut, adjoin; to fix, join

принадлежать [pr'i-nad-lye-zhát'] vi. to appertain, belong

принадлежность [pr'i-nad-lyézh-nŏst'] sf. appurtenance, belonging(s), possession

приниженный [pr'i-n'ĕ-zhen-năy] adj. humble, servile

принимать [pr'i-n'i-mát'] (принять) vt. to accept; to assume; to receive; to take

приноравливаться [pr'i-na-ráv-l'i-vat'-sya] vi. to adapt oneself to; to accommodate oneself; to conform

приносить [pr'i-na-s'ét'] (принести) vt. to bring, fetch

приношение [pr'i-na-shé-nye] sn. offering

принуждать [pr'i-nōōzh-dát'] (принудить) vt. to compel, force

принуждение [pr'i-nōōzh-dyé-nye] sn. compulsion, constraint; coercion

принцип [prin-ts'ĕp] sm. principle

принятие [pr'i-nyá-tye] sn. acceptance, admission, assumption

приобретать [pr'i-a-brye-tát'] (приобрести) vt. to acquire, gain

приобретение [pr'i-a-brye-tyé-nye] sn. acquisition

приобщать [pr'i-ab-shchát'] (приобщить) vt. to aggregate, join, unite; eccl. to administer

приор [pr'ē-ŏr] sm. eccl. prior; -итет [-i-tyét] sm. priority

приостановка [pr'i-a-sta-nóv-ka] sf. respite, stopping, suspension

припадок [pr'i-pā-dŏk] sm. attack, fit, paroxysm

припарка [pr'i-pār-ka] sf. poultice

припас [pr'i-pās] sm. provision, stock, supply, -ы [-ă] sm. pl. food, provisions

припев [pr'i-pyév] sm. mus. accompaniment, refrain

припевать [pr'i-pye-vāt'] vt. to harmonize vocally; to join singing with someone

приписка [pr'i-p'ēs-ka] sf. postscript; rider

приписывать [pr'i-p'ē-să-vat'] (приписáть) vt. to add (in writing); to attach, register; to ascribe

приплата [pr'i-plā-ta] sf. additional payment

приплод [pr'i-plód] sm. issue, offspring

приподняться [pr'i-pad-nyát'-sya] vi. to get up, raise oneself; to tip-toe

припоминать [pr'i-pa-m'i-nāt'] (припóмнить) vt. to recall, recollect, remember

приправа [pr'i-prā-va] sf. condiment, flavouring, relish, seasoning

приправка [pr'i-prāv-ka] sf. preparation; dressing (culinary); make-ready

припутывать [pr'i-pōō-tă-vat'] (припýтать) vt. to entangle, implicate

приработок [pr'i-ra-bó-tŏk] sm. extra earnings

приравнивать [pr'i-rāv-n'i-vat'] (приравнить) vt. to level

приращение [pr'i-ra-shché-nye] sn. augmentation, increase, increment

природа [pr'i-ró-da] sf. nature

природный [pr'i-ród-năy] adj. innate; native; natural

прирост [pr'i-róst] sm. growth

приручение [pr'i-rŏŏ-ché-nye] sn. domestication; taming

присваивать [pr'i-svā-i-vat'] vt. to appropriate, embezzle

присвоение [pr'i-sva-yé-nye] sn. appropriation, embezzlement

приседать [pr'i-sye-dāt'] (присéсть) vi. to squat; to curtsy

присест [pr'i-syést] sm. sitting; session

прискорбие [pr'i-skór-bye] sn. affliction, sorrow

прислуга [pr'i-slŏŏ-ga] sf. maid; pl. domestics, servants

прислуживать [pr'i-slŏŏ-zhi-vat'] vt.i. to attend, serve, wait upon

прислужник [pr'i-slŏŏzh-n'ik] sm. attendant

прислушиваться [pr'i-slŏŏ-shi-vat'-sya] vi. to listen

присматриваться [pr'i-smā-tri-vat'-sya] vi. to examine minutely; to scrutinize

присмотр [pr'i-smótr] sm. attendance; superintendence, supervision

приспособление [pr'i-spa-sa-blyé-nye] sn. adaptation; device

приспособлять [pr'i-spa-sa-blyát'] (приспособить) *vt.* to accommodate, adapt, adjust, fit

приставать [pr'i-sta-vát'] (пристáть) *vi.* to adhere, stick [*prefix*]

приставка [pr'i-stáv-ka] *sf.*

пристанище [pr'i-stá-n'i-shche] *sn.* refuge, shelter

пристань [pr'ē-stan'] *sf.* harbour, pier, quay, wharf

пристёгивать [pr'i-styó-gi-vat'] (пристегнуть) *vt.* to button; to tack on; *coll.* to implicate

пристойный [pr'i-stóy-nǎy] *adj.* decorous

пристрастие [pr'i-strá-stye] *sn.* partiality, predilection

пристрастный [pr'i-strást-nǎy] *adj.* partial, prejudiced

пристращать [pr'i-stra-shchát'] (пристрастить) *vt.* to intimidate

пристройка [pr'i-stróy-ka] *sf.* annex, outhouse

пристукивать [pr'i-stóō-ki-vat'] *vi.* to click (*with one's heels*)

приступ [pr'ē-stōōp] *sm.* assault, storming; attack, fit

приступать [pr'i-stōō-pát'] (приступить) *vi.* to approach; to begin, enter upon, set to

приступок [pr'i-stōō-pŏk] *sm.* step

присуждать [pr'i-sōōzh-dát'] (присудить) *vt.* to award; to condemn, sentence; to confer

присуждение [pr'i-sōōzh-dyé-nye] *sn.* adjudication, condemnation

присутствие [pr'i-sōōt-stvye] *sn.* presence

присутствовать [pr'i-sōōt-stva-vat'] *vi.* to attend; to be present

присяга [pr'i-syá-ga] *sf.* oath

присягать [pr'i-sya-gát'] (присягнуть) *vi.* to take the oath, swear

присяжный [pr'i-syázh-nǎy] *adj.* juryman; **суд присяжных** [sōōd pr'i-syázh-nǎch] jury

притаивать [pr'i-tá-i-vat'] (притаить) *vt.* to conceal, hide, secrete; – **дыхание** [–dǎ-chá-nye] to hold one's breath

притаскивать [pr'i-tás-ki-vat'] (притащить) *vt.* to drag, trail

притвор [pr'i-tvór] *sm.* porch, portico

притворность [pr'i-tvór-nŏst] *sf.* hypocrisy

притворный [pr'i-tvór-nǎy] *adj.* affected, feigned, hypocritical

притворяться [pr'i-tva-ryát'-sya] *vi.* to pretend

притеснение [pr'i-tyes-nyé-nye] *sn.* oppression, persecution

притирание [pr'i-t'i-rá-nye] *sn.* grinding, rubbing; cosmetic(s), paint, rouge

притихать [pr'i-t'i-chát'] (притихнуть) *vi.* to become quiet, still; to lower one's voice

приток [pr'i-tók] *sm.* tributary; influx

притом [pr'i-tóm] *adv.* besides

притон [pr'i-tón] *sm.* den, haunt

приторный [pr'i-tór-nǎy] *adj.* luscious; sugary (*of smile*); insipid (*of perfume, etc.*); mealy-mouthed

притуплять [pr'i-tŏŏp-lyát'] (**притупить**) *vt.* to blunt, deaden

притча [pr'ĕt-cha] *sf.* parable

притягательный [pr'i-tya-gá-tyel'-nǎy] *adj.* attractive

притяжательный [pr'i-tya-zhá-tyel'-nǎy] *adj. gram.* possessive

притязание [pr'i-tya-zá-nye] *sn.* claim, pretension

притязательный [pr'i-tya-zá-tyel'-nǎy] *adj.* contentious: exacting, exigent

приурочивать [pr'i-ŏŏ-ró-chi-vat'] (**приурочить**) *vt.* to fix a date; to appoint a time

приучать [pr'i-ŏŏ-chát'] (**приучить**) *vt.* to accustom, school, train

приход [pr'i-chód] *sm.* arrival; income; parish; **-ский** [-ski] *adj.* parochial

приходить [pr'i-cha-d'ét'] (**притти**) *vi.* to arrive, come

прихожанин [pr'i-cha-zhá-n'in] *sm.* parishioner

прихожая [pr'i-chó-zha-ya] *sf.* lobby

прихотливый [pr'i-chót-l'i-vǎy] *adj.* capricious, fastidious

прихоть [pr'i-ĕ-chót'] *sf.* caprice, fancy, whim

прихрамывание [pr'i-chrá-mǎ-va-nye] *sn.* limping

прицел [pr'i-tsýel] *sm.* aim; sight (*of rifle*)

прицеливаться [pr'i-tsýe-l'i-vat'-sya] (**прицелиться**) *vi.* to aim

прицеп [pri-tsýep] *sm.* trailer

прицепка [pr'i-tsýep-ka] *sf.* coupling, hitching, hooking; tendril

причаливание [pr'i-chá-l'i-va-nye] *sn.* mooring

причастие [pr'i-chás-tye] *sn. gram.* participle; Communion

причастник [pr'i-chást'n'ik] *sm.* Communicant

причастный [pr'i-chást-nǎy] *adj.* concerned, participating

причащение [pr'i-cha-shché-nye] *sn.* administering of Holy Communion

причёска [pr'i-chós-ka] *sf.* coiffure

причёсывать [pr'i-chó-sǎ-vat'] (**причесать**) *vt.* to brush, comb, dress (*hair*)

причётник [pr'i-chét-n'ik] *sm.* clerk, lay reader

причина [pr'i-chē-na] *sf.* cause, reason

причинять [pr'i-chi-nyát'] (**причинить**) *vt.* to cause

причислять [pr'i-chi-slyát'] (**причислить**) *vt.* to number, reckon; to add; to attach

причитание [pr'i-chi-tá-nye] *sn.* lament, lamentation

причт [pr'ēcht] *sm.* clergy; church retinue

причуда [pr'i-chŏŏ-da] *sf.* fancy, oddity, whim

причудливый [pr'i-chŏŏd-l'i-vǎy] *adj.* fanciful, fantastic, queer

пришелец [pr'i-shé-lyets] *sm.* new-comer, stranger

пришепётывание [pr'i-she-pyó-tǎ-va-nye] *sn.* lisping

пришествие [pr'i-shést-vye] *sn.* advent, coming

пришлый [pr'ĕ-shlăy] *adj.* alien, foreign, strange; newly arrived

пришивать [pr'i-shi-văt'] (пришить) *vt.* to sew on (*as* button, etc.)

прищемление [pr'i-shchem-lyé-nye] *sn.* nipping, pinching

прищуривать [pr'i-shchōŏr'i-vat'] (прищурить) *vt.i.* to blink, wink

приют [pr'i-yōōt] *sm.* refuge, shelter; детский – [dyét-ski –] orphanage

приязненный [pr'i-yáznyen-năy] *adj.* amicable, benevolent, friendly

приязнь [pr'i-yázn'] *sf.* benevolence, good-will

приятель [pr'i-yă-tyel'] *sm.* friend

приятный [pr'i-yát-năy] *adj.* agreeable, nice, pleasant

про [prŏ] *prep.* about, of

проба [prŏ-ba] *sf.* test, trial; assay, standard; hall-mark; sample

пробавляться [pra-ba-vlyăt'-sya] *vi.* to subsist

пробалтывать [pra-băltă-vat'] (проболтать) *vt.* to chatter, mutter, talk idly

пробел [pra-byél] *sm. typ.* blank, quad, space, white; gap

пробивать [pra-b'i-văt'] (пробить) *vt.* to breach, pierce, punch

пробитие [pra-b'ĕ-tye] *sn.* breaching

пробка [prŏb-ka] *sf.* cork; plug; stopper

проблеск [prŏb-lyesk] *sm.* gleam, ray of light, spark

пробовать [prŏ-ba-vat'] (по–) *vt.* to attempt, try; to sample, taste

пробочник [prŏ-bach-n'ik] *sm.* cork-screw

пробуждать [pra-bōōzhdăt'] *vt.* (пробудить) to arouse, awake

пробуравливание [prabōō-răv-l'i-va-nye] *sn.* boring, perforation

пробывать [pra-bă-văt'] (пробыть) *vt.* to remain, stay

провал [pra-văl] *sm.* downfall; failure

проваливаться [pra-vă-l'ivat'-sya] *vi.* to collapse; to fail

провевать [pra-vye-văt'] *vt.* to blow; to winnow

проведение [pra-vye-dyé-nye] *sn.* conducting, leading; passing

проверка [pra-vyér-ka] *sf.* checking, verification; – счётов [– schŏ-tŏv] audit

проверять [pra-vye-ryat'] (проверить) *vt.* to check, examine; to audit

проветривать [pra-vyé-tri-vat'] (проветрить) *vt.* to air

провидение [pra-v'i-dyé-nye] *sn.* providence

провинциальный [pra-v'intsyăl'-năy] *adj.* provincial

провод [pro-vŏd] *sm. electr.* cable, conductor, wire

проводить [pra-va-d'ĕt'] (провести) *vt.* to convey, lead; to pass (*as* time)

проводник [pra-vŏd-n'ik] *sm.* conductor, guard, guide

провожать [pra-va-zhăt'] (проводить) *vt.* to escort, see one home

провоз [pra-vŏz] *sm.* carriage, conveying, transport

провозвещение [pra-vaz-vye-shché-nye] *sn.* prediction; prophecy; proclamation

провозглашать [pra-vaz-gla-shăt'] (провозгла́сить) *vt.* to announce, proclaim

провозить [pra-va-z'ět'] (провезти́) *vt.* to carry, convey, transport

проволока [pró-va-la-ka] *sf.* wire; **колю́чая** — [ka-lyŏŏ-cha-ya -] barbed wire

проволочка [pra-va-lóch-ka] *sf.* protraction

проворный [pra-vór-năy] *adj.* agile, nimble, quick

проворство [pra-vór-stvŏ] *sn.* alertness, promptness

прогалина [pra-gă-l'i-na] *sf.* glade

проглатывание [pra-glă-tă-va-nye] *sn.* swallowing; voracity

проглядывать [pra-glyă-dă-vat'] (проглядеть) *vt.* to miss, overlook; — [-] (проглянуть) *vi.* to appear, get through

прогневать [pra-gnye-vat'] *vt.* to anger, displease

проговориться [pra-ga-va-r'i-vat'-sya] (проговори́ться) *vt.* to blab; to divulge

проголодаться [pra-ga-la-dăt'-sya] *vi.* to feel hungry

прогонять [pra-ga-nyăt'] (прогна́ть) *vt.* to dismiss; to drive away, turn away; to dispel

прогорелый [pra-ga-ryé-lăy] *adj.* burnt through

прогорклый [pra-górk-lăy] *adj.* bitter, rancid

прогрессивный [pra-gryes-s'ěv-năy] *adj.* progressive

прогу́ливаться [pra-gŏŏ-l'i-vat'-sya] *vi.* to go for a stroll

прогулка [pra-gŏŏl-ka] *sf.* ramble, short walk

прогу́льщик [pra-gŏŏl'-shchik] *sm.* shirker

продавать [pra-da-văt'] (прода́ть) *vt.* to sell

продавец [pra-dă-vyets] *sm.* vendor; shop assistant

продавщица [pra-dav-shché-tsa] *sf.* saleswoman

продажа [pra-dă-zha] *sf.* sale, selling

продвигать [pra-dv'i-găt'] (продви́нуть) *vi.* to move forward; *fig.* to advance, promote

проделка [pra-dyél-ka] *sf.* escapade, prank, trick

продерживать [pra-dyér-zhi-vat'] (продержа́ть) *vt.* to detain, keep

продирать [pra-d'i-răt'] (продра́ть) *vt.* to tear up, wear out

продление [pra-dlyé-nye] *sn.* lengthening, prolongation

продолговатый [pra-dal-ga-vă-tăy] *adj.* longish; oblong

продолжать [pra-dal-zhăt'] (продолжи́ть) *vt.* to continue, proceed; to resume

продолжение [pra-dal-zhé-nye] *sn.* continuation; sequel; — **следует** [- slyé-dŏŏ-yet] to be continued

продольный [pră-dól'-năy] *adj.* longitudinal

продувать [pra-dŏŏ-văt'] (проду́ть) *vt.* to blow through

продуктивный [pra-dŏŏk-t'ěv-năy] *adj.* productive

продукция [pra-dŏŏk-tsya] *sf.* output, production

продумывать [pra-dōō-mă-vat'] (продумать) vt. to reason out, think out

продушина [pra-dōō-shi-na] sf. air-hole

проедать [pra-ye-dát'] (проесть) vt. to corrode; to spend excessively on food

проезд [pra-yézd] sm. passage, thoroughfare

проезжать [pra-yez-zhát'] (проехать) vi. to drive, pass by

проезжий [pra-yéz-zhi] sm. passer-by, traveller

проект [pra-yékt] sm. plan, project, scheme

проекция [pra-yék-tsya] sf. projection

прожёвывать [pra-zhó-vă-vat'] (прожевать) vt. to masticate

проживать [pra-zhi-vát'] (прожить) vi. to live, reside; to sojourn, stay (for a time)

прожилка [pra-zhíl-ka] sf. vein

прожорливый [pra-zhór-li-văy] adj. greedy, ravenous

прозорливость [pra-zór-l'i-vŏst'] sf. insight, penetration, sagacity

прозрачность [pra-zrách-nŏst'] sf. transparency

прозывать [pra-ză-vát'] (прозвать) vt. to name, nickname

прозябание [pra-zya-bá-nye] sn. sprouting, vegetating, vegetation

проигрывать [pra-ĕ-grá-vat'] (проиграть) vt. to lose (in gambling)

проигрыш [pró-i-grăsh] sm. gambling losses

произведение [pra-iz-vye-dyé-nye] sn. composition, production, work; лучшее – [lōōch-sheye –] masterpiece

производитель [pra-iz-va-d'é-tyel'] sm. producer; -ный [-năy] adj. productive

производить [pra-iz-va-d'ét'] (произвести) to produce

производный [pra-iz-vód-năy] adj. derivative

производственный [pra-iz-vód-stvyen-năy] adj. industrial

производство [pra-iz-vód-stvŏ] sn. manufacture, production; derivation; promotion

произвольный [pra-iz-vól'-năy] adj. arbitrary

произнесение [pra-iz-nye-syé-nye] sn. pronouncing, uttering

произносить [pra-iz-na-s'ét'] (произнести) vt. to enunciate, pronounce

произношение [pra-iz-na-shé-nye] sn. pronunciation

происки [pró-is-ki] sm. pl. intrigues, machinations, plotting

проистекать [pra-is-tye-kát'] (проистечь) to emanate, result, spring from

происхождение [pra-is-chazh-dyé-nye] sn. descent, extraction, lineage; origin

происшествие [pra-is-shést-vye] sn. event, incident, occurrence

пройма [próy-ma] sf. aperture, hole, opening; slit (in dress)

прок [prok] sm. benefit, use

прокажённый [pra-ka-zhón-nay] *adj.* leprous; *sm.* leper

проказа [pra-ká-za] *sf.* leprosy

проказы [pra-ká-ză] *sf. pl.* frolic, mischief, spree

прокат [pra-kát] *sm.* hire; *tech.* rolling; rolled metal

прокатывать [pra-ká-ti-vat'] (прокатáть) *vt.* to flatten, roll; (прокати́ть) to take for a drive

прокладка [pra-klád-ka] *sf.* padding, stuffing; washer; *typ.* lead(s)

прокладывать [pra-klá-di-vat'] *vt.* to interlay, interleave; to lay

проклинать [pra-kl'i-nát'] (прокля́сть) *vt.* to curse, damn

проклинающий [pra-kl'i-ná-yŏŏ-shchi] *adj.* maledictory

проклятия [pra-klyá-tya] *sn. pl.* obscene language

проклятый [pra-klyá-tăy] *adj.* cursed, damned

прокол [pra-kól] *sm.* puncture

прокорм [pra-kórm] *sm.* nourishment, sustenance

прокурор [pra-kŏŏ-rór] *sm.* public prosecutor

прокучивать [pra-kŏŏ-chi-vat'] (прокути́ть) *vt.* to squander, waste

пролаза [pra-lá-za] *sm., f.* dodger, sneak

проламывать [pra-lá-mi-vat'] (проломáть) *vt.* to break (*ice, stone, wall*); to cut open; to fracture

пролежень [pró-lye-zhen'] *sm.* bedsore

пролесок [pra-lyé-sŏk] *sm.* glade; vista

пролёт [pra-lyót] *sm.* flight of stairs; span of bridge

пролетарий [pra-lye-tá-ri] *sm.* proletarian

пролетать [pra-lye-tát'] (пролетéть) *vi.* to fly past, fly through

пролив [pra-l'ĕv] *sm.* sound, strait(s)

проливать [pra-l'i-vát'] (проли́ть) *vt.* to shed, spill

пролитие [pra-l'ĕ-tye] *sn.* effusion, shedding

пролом [pra-lóm] *sm.* breach, gap; fracture (*of skull*)

проматывать [pra-má-ta-vat'] (промотáть) *vt.* to dissipate

промах [pró-mach] *sm.* blunder, fault; miss

промачивать [pra-má-chi-vat'] (промочи́ть) *vt.* to drench, soak

промедление [pra-myed-lyé-nye] *sn.* retardation

промежуток [pra-mye-zhŏŏ-tŏk] *sm.* interval, space

промежуточный [pra-mye-zhŏŏ-tach-năy] *adj.* intermediate; intervening

промен [pra-myén] *sm.* barter, exchange

променивать [pra-myé-n'i-vat'] (променя́ть) *vt.* to barter, exchange; to change (*a job, etc.*)

промер [pra-myér] *sm.* measurement; sounding; error (*in measuring*)

промеривать [pra-myé-r'i-vat'] (промéрить) *vt.* to measure, sound; to ascertain correct measurement

промозглый [pra-mózg-lǎy] *adj.* foul, mouldy

промокать [pra-ma-kát'] (промокнуть) *vi.* to get soaked, wet; **промокательная бумага** [pra-ma-ká-tyel'-na-ya bōō-mā-ga] *sf.* blotting-paper

промывание [pra-mǎ-vā-nye] *sn.* irrigation; washing out

промывать [pra-mǎ-vat'] (промыть) *vt.* to rinse out, wash out; to syringe

промысел [pró-mǎ-syel] *sm.* business, craft, trade

промышленник [pra-másh-lyen-n'ik] *sm.* manufacturer, trader

промышленность [pra-másh-lyen-nǒst'] *sf.* industry

промышленный [pra-másh-lyen-nǎy] *adj.* industrial

пронзать [pran-zát'] (пронзить) *vt.* to bore through, pierce; to spear

пронзение [pran-zé-nye] *sn.* piercing

пронзительный [pran-z'í-tyel'-nǎy] *adj.* acute, penetrating, sharp, shrill

проникание [pra-n'i-ká-nye] *sn.* filtering, percolation, permeation

проницаемый [pra-n'i-tsá-ye-mǎy] *adj.* pervious

проницательность [pra-n'i-tsá-tyel'-nǒst'] *sf.* astuteness; shrewdness

проныра [pra-ná-ra] *sf.* intriguer, intruder

пронырство [pra-nár-stvǒ] *sn.* slyness

прообраз [pra-ób-raz] *sm.* prototype, symbol

пропадать [pra-pa-dát'] (пропасть) *vi.* to be lost; to disappear, vanish; to perish

пропажа [pra-pā-zha] *sf.* loss

пропасть [pró-past'] *sf.* abyss, precipice

промашка [pra-másh-ka] *sf.* ploughing

промашник [pra-másh-n'ik] *sm.* cultivator

пропащий [pra-pā-shchi] *adj.* lost, ruined

прописка [pra-p'és-ka] *sf.* visa

прописной [pra-p'is-nóy] *adj.* **прописная буква** [pra-p'is-nā-ya bōōk-va] capital letter

прописывать [pra-p'é-sǎ-vat'] (прописать) *vt.* to prescribe

пропитание [pra-p'i-tā-nye] *sn.* living, subsistence

пропитывать [pra-p'é-tǎ-vat'] (пропитать) *vt.* to pregnate, transfuse; to saturate; to swamp

пропитанный [pra-p'é-tan-nǎy] *adj.* imbued, impregnated

проповедник [pra-pa-vyéd-n'ik] *sm.* preacher

проповедовать [pra-pa-vyé-da-vat'] *vt.* to preach, propagate, sermonize

проповедь [pró-pa-vyed'] *sf.* sermon

пропойца [pra-póy-tsa] *sm. coll.* drunkard

пропорция [pra-pór-tsya] *sf.* proportion, ratio

пропуск [pró-pōōsk] *sm.* pass, permit; lapse, omission; blank, gap пропускать [pra-pōōs-kāt'] (пропустить) vt. to pass; to permit passing through; to omit, skip; to filtrate

прорастание [pra-ras-tā-nye] sn. germination

прорез [pra-ryéz] sm. slot; notch

прорицание [pra-r'i-tsā-nye] sn. oracle

пророк [pra-rók] sm. prophet

пророчество [pra-ró-chest-vŏ] sn. prophecy

прорубь [pró-rōōb'] sf. ice-hole

прорывать [pra-ră-vāt'] (прорвать) vt. to break through; to pierce; to cut open

просаливать [pra-sā-l'i-vat'] (просолить) vt. to grease; to pickle, preserve in salt

просвет [pra-svyét] sm. clear space, chink; light shining through

просвечивание [pra-svyé-chi-va-nye] sn. radioscopy; X-raying

просвещение [pra-svye-shché-nye] sn. enlightenment, instruction; civilization [Host

просвира [pra-sv'ē-ra] sf.

просеивать [pra-syé-i-vat'] vt. to riddle, sift

просека [pra-syé-ka] sf. vista

посёлок [pra-syó-lŏk] sm. country lane

просиживание [pra-s'ē-zhi-va-nye] sn. sitting up (late into the night)

проситель [pra-s'ē-tyel] sm. applicant, petitioner

просить [pra-s'ét'] (по-) to ask, beg; beseech; solicit

просиять [pra-s'i-yāt'] vi. to brighten up, irradiate; to shine through

проскомидия [pras-ka-m'ē-dya] sf. oblation

проскурняк [pras-kōōr-nyāk] sm. marshmallow

прославление [pra-slav-lyé-nye] sn. celebration, glorification

прославлять [pra-slav-lyāt'] (прославить) vt. to extol, glorify

прослеживать [pra-slyé-zhi-vat'] vt. to follow, trace, track

просматривать [pra-smā-tr'i-vat'] (просмотреть) vt. to glance over, look through; to overlook, omit

просмотр [pra-smótr] sm. recession; survey; blunder; oversight

просо [pró-sŏ] sn. millet

просроченный [pra-sró-chen-nǎy] adj. overdue

просрочка [pra-sróch-ka] sf. expiration of time-limit

простак [pra-stāk] sm. simpleton

простенок [pra-styé-nŏk] sm. pier (between windows); partition

простирать [pra-st'i-rāt'] (простереть) vt. to extend, reach, stretch

простительный [pra-st'i-tyel'-nǎy] adj. excusable, justifiable, pardonable

просто [pró-stŏ] adv. plainly, simply; merely

простоватый [pra-sta-vā-tǎy] adj. plain, silly, simple

простодушив [pra-sta-dōō-shye] sn. artless, frank, innocent, naïve

простой [pra-stóy] *adj.* common, ordinary, simple; *sm.* demurrage

простокваша [pra-sta-kvá-sha] *sf.* clotted milk

простолюдин [pra-sta-lyōō-d'ĕn] *sm.* plebeian

простонародье [pra-sta-na-ró-dye] *sn.* the people, populace

простор [pra-stór] *sm.* scope, spaciousness; elbow-room

просторечие [pra-sta-ryé-chye] *sn.* colloquial language, country speech

просторный [pra-stór-nǎy] *adj.* ample, capacious, roomy

простосердечие [pra-sta-syer-dyé-chye] *sn.* candour, frankness, simple-heartedness

простота [pra-sta-tá] *sf.* simplicity

пространство [pra-stránstvǒ] *sn.* expanse, scope, space

прострел [pra-stryél] *sm.* lumbago

простуда [pra-stōō-da] *sf.* chill, cold

простудный [pra-stōōdnǎy] *adj.* catarrhal

проступок [pra-stōō-pŏk] *sm.* delinquency, offence, misdemeanour

простыня [pra-stǎ-nya] *sf.* linen sheet

просушка [pra-sōōsh-ka] *sf.* thorough drying

просчёт [pras-chót] *sm.* error in counting; checking figures

просыпать [pra-sǎ-pát'] (проспать) *vi.* to oversleep; **-ся** [-sya] *vi.* to wake

просыпать [pra-sǎ-pat'] *vt.* to spill

просьба [prós'-ba] *sf.* request, solicitation; application, petition

проталкивание [pra-tǎlp'i-va-nye] *-n.* heating

протаскивать [pra-tás-k'ivat'] (протащить) to drag, trail

протекать [pra-tye-kát'] (протечь) *vi.* to flow by; to leak; to elapse, fly (*of time*)

протекция [pra-tyék-tsya] *sf.* protection

протёртый [pra-tyór-tǎy] *adj.* threadbare, worn

против [pró-t'iv] *prep.* against; contrary; opposite; versus [grid

противень [pró-t'i-veyn'] *sm.*

противиться [pra-t'ē-v'it'sya] *vi.* to oppose, resist

противник [pra-t'ĕv-n'ik] *sm.* adversary, opponent

противный [pra-t'ĕv-nǎy] *adj.* contrary, opposed; foul; loathsome, repugnant

противо- [pra-t'ĕ-vǒ] *prefix,* anti-, un-

противоборство [pra-t'iva-bór-stvǒ] *sn.* antagonism

противогазовый [pra-t'iva-gã-za-vǎy] *adj.* gasproof

противодействие [pra-t'iva-dyéy-stvye] *sn.* counteraction; reaction

противоестественный [pra-t'i-va-yes-tyést-vyennǎy] *adj.* unnatural

противозаконный [pra-t'iva-za-kón-nǎy] *adj.* illegal

противоположность [pra-t'i-va-pa-lózh-nǒst'] *sf.* contrast, opposition

противоречивый [pra-t'iva-rye-chē-vǎy] *adj.* contradictory

противостоять [pra-t'i-va-sta-yát'] *vi.* to confront; to resist, withstand

противоядие [pra-t'i-va-yá-dye] *sn.* antidote

протирать [pra-t'i-rát'] (протереть) *vt.* to fray; to rub; to wipe

протодиакон [pra-ta-dyá-kŏn] *sm.* archdeacon

протоиерей [pra-ta-ye-ryéy] *sm.* dean

проток [pra-tók] *sm.* canal; channel; duct

протокол [pra-ta-kól] *sm.* minutes, proceedings; protocol; record; transactions

проторжка [pra-tórzh-ka] *sf.* damage(s), expense(s); loss(es)

проточный [pra-tóch-năy] *adj.* flowing, running (*water*)

протрава [pra-trá-va] *sf.* chem. mordant

протягивать [pra-tyá-gi-vat'] (протянуть) *vt.* to extend, reach out, stretch; to prolong, spin out

протяжение [pra-tya-zhé-nye] *sn.* extent; spread

профессиональный [pra-fyes-sia-nál'-năy] *adj.* professional

профессия [pra-fyés-sya] *sf.* profession; calling; function

прохвост [pra-chvóst] *sm.* blackguard, scoundrel

прохлада [pra-chlá-da] *sf.* coolness, freshness

прохладный [pra-chlád-năy] *adj.* breezy, cool

проход [pra-chód] *sm.* avenue, passage, throughfare; aperture; gangway

проходимость [pra-cha-ďe-mŏst'] *sf.* practicability; permeability

проходить [pra-cha-ďět'] (пройти) *vi.* to go, to pass along, walk about

прохожий [pra-chó-zhi] *sm.* passer-by

процветание [pra-tsvye-tá-nye] *sn.* flourishing; prosperity

процветать [pra-tsvye-tát'] *vi.* to prosper, thrive

процедура [pra-tsye-dōō-ra] *sf.* procedure

процеживать [pra-tsyé-zhi-vat'] (процедить) *vt.* to filter, percolate

процент [pra-tsyént] *sm.* percentage

процессия [pra-tsés-sya] *sf.* procession

прочёсывать [pra-chó-să-vat'] (прочесать) *vt.* to comb thoroughly; to hackle thoroughly

прочий [pró-chi] *adj.* other; **и прочее** (и пр.) [i pró-cheye] etc.; **между прочим** [myézh-dōō pró-chim] by the way

прочитывать [pra-chě-tă-vat'] (прочитать) *vt.* to peruse thoroughly

прочищать [pra-chi-shchát'] (прочистить) *vt.* to cleanse; to purge; to scour

прочность [próch-nŏst'] *sf.* firmness, stability

прочный [próch-năy] *adj.* durable, tough; stable, substantial; fast (*of colour*)

прочтение [prach-tyé-nye] *sn.* perusal, reading

прочувствованный [pra-chōōv-stvo-van-năy] *adj.* extremely emotional

прочь [proch'] *adv.* away! be off! clear out!

прошедший [pra-shéd-shi] *adj.* past, bygone

прошение [pra-shé-nye] *sn.* application, petition

прошивать [pra-shi-vát'] (прошить) *vt.* to hem, stitch

прошлое [prósh-lŏye] *adj.* as *sn.* the past

прошлый [prósh-lǎy] *adj.* bygone, past; former

прощальный [pra-shchál'-nǎy] *adj.* farewell, parting, valedictory

прощание [pra-shchá-nye] *sn.* farewell, goodbye, leave-taking, parting

прощать [pra-shchát'] (простить) *vt.* to forgive, pardon; to excuse

прощение [pra-shché-nye] *sn.* forgiveness; remission

проявлять [pra-yav-lyát'] (проявить) *vt.* to manifest; to develop (*photograph*)

проявление [pra-yav-lyé-nye] *sn.* display, show; manifestation

пруд [prŏod] *sm.* pond

пружина [prŏo-zhí-na] *sf.* spring (*metal*)

пружинный [prŏo-zhín-nǎy] *adj.* spring-, springy

прусак [prŏo-sák] *sm.* cockroach

прут [prŏot] *sm.* rod, twig

прыгать [prá-gat'] (прыгнуть) *vi.* to hop, jump, leap

прыжок [prǎ-zhók] *sm.* jump, leap; caper

прыскать [prís-kat'] (прыснуть) *vt.* to spray

прыткий [prát-ki] *adj.* nimble, quick, swift

прыть [prăt'] *sf.* rapid pace, speed; *fig.* energy, initiative

прыщик [prǎ-shchik] *sm.* pimple, pustule

прядение [prya-dyé-nye] *sn.* spinning

прядильный [prya-d'él'nǎy] *adj.* spinning-; – станок [– sta-nók] *sm.* loom; – орган [– ór-gan] *sm.* spinneret

прядильщик [prya-d'él'-shchik] *sm.* spinner

прядь [pryăd'] *sf.* strand; ply

пряжа [pryā-zha] *sf.* thread, yarn

пряжка [pryāzh-ka] *sf.* buckle; clasp

прялка [pryāl-ka] *sf.* distaff; spinning-wheel

прямизна [prya-m'iz-ná] *sf.* straightness

прямиком [prya-m'i-kóm] *adv.* across-country; point-blank; straight on

прямить [prya-m'ét'] *vt.* to straighten

прямо [pryā-mŏ] *adv.* straight(ly), upright(ly)

прямодушие [prya-ma-dŏō-shye] *sn.* frankness, straight-forwardness

прямой [prya-móy] *adj.* direct; erect; straight, upright

прямолинейный [prya-ma-l'i-nyéy-nǎy] *adj.* rectilinear

прямота [prya-ma-tá] *sf.* rectitude; *fig.* bluntness

прямоугольник [prya-ma-ŏō-gól'-n'ik] *adj.* rectangle

пряник [pryā-n'ik] *sm.* gingerbread, treacle-cake

пряный [pryā-nǎy] *adj.* gingery, rich, spicy

прясть [pryäst'] *vt.* to spin

прятать [pryä-tat'] (с-) *vt.* to conceal, hide

прятки [pryät-ki] *sf. pl.* 'hide-and-seek'

пряха [pryä-cha] *sf.* spinner

псалмопение [psal-ma-pyénye] *sn.* psalmody

псалом [psa-lóm] *sm.* psalm

псалтырь [psal-tår'] *sf.* Psalter

псарня [psär-nya] *sf.* kennel

псевдо- [psyév-dŏ] *prefix* pseudo-

псинка [ps'ĕn-ka] *sf.* nightshade

псовый [psŏ-väy] *adj.* canine

птица [pt'ĕ-tsa] *sf.* bird; **домашняя** – [da-mäshnya-ya –] poultry

птицевод [pt'i-tse-vód] *sm.* bird-fancier; **-ство** [-stvŏ] *sn.* bird-fancier's business; poultry farming

птичий [pt'ĕ-chi] *adj.* avian; bird's, poultry-; **вид с птичьего полёта** [v'id spt'ĕ-chye-vŏ pa-lyŏ-ta] bird's-eye-view

птичник [pt'ĕch-n'ik] *sm.* aviary; poultry-yard; bird-dealer

публика [pŏŏb-l'i-ka] *sf.* [audience, public

публикация [pŏŏb-l'i-kä-tsya] *sf.* advertisement, publication

публиковать [pŏŏb-l'i-ka-vät'] *vt.* to announce; to publish; to advertise

публичный [pŏŏb-l'ĕch-näy] *adj.* public

пугало [pŏŏ-ga-lŏ] *sn.* scarecrow [crow

пугать [pŏŏ-gät'] (ис-) *vt.* to frighten, scare; **-ся** [-sya] *vi.* to be frightened, scared, startled; to shy (*horse*)

пугливый [pŏŏg-l'ĕ-väy] *adj.* fearful, timid, timorous; shy (*horse*)

пуговица [pŏŏ-ga-v'i-tsa] *sf.* button

пуд [pŏŏd] *sm.* pood, = 36 English pounds (*weight*)

пудра [pŏŏd-ra] *sf.* powder

пудреница [pŏŏd-rye-n'i-tsa] *sf.* powder-box

пудрить [pŏŏd-r'it'] (на-) *vt.* to powder

пузо [pŏŏ-zŏ] *sn.* paunch

пузырёк [pŏŏ-zä-ryók] *sm.* phial

пузырь [pŏŏ-zår'] *sm.* blister, bubble; bladder; cyst; **жёлчный** – [zhólch-näy –] gall

пук [pŏŏk] *sm.* bunch; truss; tuft

пулемёт [pŏŏ-lye-myót] *sm.* machine-gun; **-чик** [-chik] *sm.* gunner

пульпа [pŏŏl'-pa] *sf.* pulp

пульс [pŏŏl's] *sm.* pulse

пульт [pŏŏl't] *sm.* desk, stand

пуля [pŏŏ-lya] *sf.* bullet, shot; pellet; slug

пункт [pŏŏnkt] *sm.* point; spot; item

пунктир [pŏŏnk-t'ĕr] *sm.* dotted line, stipple; **-овка** [-óv-ka] *sf.* dotting, stippling

пунктуальность [pŏŏnk-tŏŏ-äl'-nòst'] *sf.* accuracy, punctuality

пунктуальный [pŏŏnk-tŏŏ-äl'-näy] *adj.* precise, punctual

пунктуация [pŏŏnk-tŏŏ-ä-tsya] *sf.* punctuation

пунцовый [pŏŏn-tsó-väy] *adj.* crimson

пунш [pŏŏnsh] *sm.* punch; **-евая чаша** [-ye-vä-ya chä-sha] *sf.* punch-bowl пуп [pōōp] *sm.* navel

пурга [pōōr-gā] *sf.* snow-storm

пурпур [pōōr-pōōr] *sm.* purple; -овый [-a-våy] *adj.* purplish

пускать [pōōs-kāt'] (пустить) *vt.* to allow, let, permit

пустеть [pōōs-tyét'] (o-) *vi.* to become empty, deserted

пустой [pōōs-tóy] *adj.* empty, void; hollow; idle; vacant

пустомеля [pōōs-ta-myé-lya] *sm., f.* babbler, chatterbox

пустословие [pōōs-ta-slóvye] *sn.* idle talk

пустота [pōōs-ta-tā] *sf.* blankness; emptiness; frivolity

пустынник [pōōs-tăn-n'ik] *sm.* hermit; recluse

пустынь [pōōs-tắn'] *sf.* hermitage

пустыня [pōōs-tắ-nya] *sf.* desert, waste; wilderness

пустырь [pōōs-tắr'] *sm.* vacant building plot

пустышка [pōōs-tắsh-ka] *sf.* blank (*lottery*); dummy (*baby's*); *fig.* shallow person

пустяки [pōōs-tya-kē] *sm. pl.* nonsense

пустячный [pōōs-tyāch-năy] *adj.* paltry, petty, trivial

путаница [pōō-ta-n'i-tsa] *sf.* confusion, tangle

путать [pōō-tat'] (на-) *vt.* to confuse, mix up

путеводитель [pōō-tye-va-d'ē-tyel'] *sm.* guide, guide-book, itinerary

путепровод [pōō-tye-pra-vód] *sm.* viaduct

путешественник [pōō-tye-shést-vyen-n'ik] *sm.* traveller, tourist

путешествие [pōō-tye-shést-vye] *sn.* journey; voyage

путешествовать [pōō-tye-shést-va-vat'] *vi.* to travel, voyage [farer

путник [pōōt-n'ik] *sm.* way-

путный [pōōt-năy] *adj.* decent; sensible

путы [pōō-tă] *sf. pl.* fetters, shackles

путь [pōōt'] *sm.* course, path, road, way

пух [pōōch] *sm.* down; fluff

пухлый [pōōch-lăy] *adj.* chubby, plump

пухнуть [pōōch-nōōt'] (рас-) *vi.* to swell up

пуховик [pōō-cha-v'ĕk] *sm.* featherbed

пуховка [pōō-chóv-ka] *sf.* powder-puff

пучеглазый [pōō-che-glā-zăy] *adj.* goggle-eyed

пучина [pōō-chē-na] *sf.* chasm; gulf

пучок [pōō-chók] *sm.* cluster; tuft; wisp

пучковатый [pōōch-ka-vā-tăy] *adj.* fascicular

пушинка [pōō-shín-ka] *sf.* single particle of fluff; flake; снежная – [snyézh-na-ya –] snowflake

пушка [pōōsh-ka] *sf.* cannon; gun

пушной [pōōsh-nóy] *adj.* furry

пуща [pōō-shcha] *sf.* dense forest

пчела [pche-lā] *sf.* bee

пчеловод [pche-la-vód] *sm.* beekeeper; -ство [-stvó] *sn.* apiculture

пчельник [pchél'-n'ik] *sm.* apiary

пшеница [pshe-n'ḗ-tsa] *sf.* wheat

пшено [pshe-nó] *sn.* millet

пыж [pázh] *sm.* wad

пыл [pál] *sm.* blaze, flame; *fig.* fervour, glow, passion; **-ание** [-ā-nye] *sn.* blazing, flaming

пылесос [pá-lye-sós] *sm.* vacuum cleaner

пылинка [pă-l'ēn-ka] *sf.* speck of dust

пылить [pă-l'ět'] *vi.* to dust

пылкий [pál-k'i] *adj.* ardent, impetuous, passionate

пыль [pál'] *sf.* dust

пыльник [pál'-n'ik] *sm.* dustcloak; duster; *bot.* anther

пыльный [pál'-năy] *adj.* dusty; **пыльная тряпка** [pál'-na-ya tryáp-ka] *sf.* duster

пыльца [păl'-tsā] *sf.* pollen

пырять [pă-ryāt'] (пырнуть) *vt.* to butt, jab, thrust

пытать [pă-tāt'] *vt.* to torment

пытаться [pă-tāt'-sya] *vi.* to endeavour, try; to sound

пытка [pát-ka] *sf.* torture

пытливый [pát-l'ē-văy] *adj.* keen, searching; inquisitive

пыхтение [păh-tyé-nye] *sn.* panting; snorting

пыхтеть [păch-tyét'] *vi.* to pant, puff

пышка [pásh-ka] *sf.* doughnut

пышный [pásh-năy] *adj.* exuberant, pompous; costly, luxurious, rich

пышность [pásh-nŏst'] *sf.* splendour

пьеса [pyé-sa] *sf. theat.* piece, play

пьяница [pyā-n'i-tsa] *sm., f.* drunkard

пьянство [pyăn-stvŏ] *sn.* drunkenness, intoxication; **-вать** [-vat'] *vi.* to lead a drunkard's life

пьяный [pyā-năy] *adj.* drunk

пюпитр [pyŏŏ-p'ĕtr] *sm.* desk; reading-stand

пядь [pyăd'] *sf.* span

пяление [pya-lyé-nye] *sn.* stretching

пялить [pya-l'ĕt'] (pac-) *vt.* to stretch; **– глаза** [– gla-zā] to stare

пяльцы [pyāl'-tsā] *sm. pl.* tambour; lace-frame

пята [pya-tā] *sf.* heel; *arch.* spandrel

пятидесятница [pya-t'i-dye-syāt-n'i-tsa] *sf.* Whitsuntide

пятидневка [pya-t'i-dnyév-ka] *sf.* five-day week

пятикнижие [pya-t'i-kn'ḗ-zhye] *sn.* Pentateuch

пятить [pya-t'ĕt'] *vt.* to back, move back; **-ся** [-sya] *vi.* to jib, move backwards

пятнадцать [pyat-nād-tsat'] *num.* fifteen

пятница [pyāt-n'i-tsa] *sf.* Friday

пятно [pyat-nó] *sn.* blot, spot, stain

пятый [pyā-tăy] *num.* fifth

пять [pyăt'] *num.* five

пятьдесят [pyat'-dye-syāt] *num.* fifty

пятьсот [pyat-sót] *num.* five hundred

Р

раб [răb] *sm.* slave; **-ский** [-ski] *adj.* servile

раболепие [ra-ba-lyé-pye] *sn.* servility

раболепный [ra-ba-lyép-nǎy] *adj.* servile, slavish; cringing; *fig.* slimy

работа [ra-bó-ta] *sf.* labour, task, work; job

работать [ra-bó-tat'] (по-) *vt.i.* to toil, work

работник [ra-bót-n'ik] *sm.* worker

работоспособность [ra-bo-ta-spa-sób-nǒst'] *sf.* efficiency, skill

работящий [ra-ba-tyá-shchi] *adj.* laborious, industrious, painstaking

рабочий [ra-bó-chi] *adj.* labouring, operating, working; *sm.* artisan, operator, workman; **рабочая сила** [ra-bó-cha-ya s'ё-la] *sf.* man-power

раввин [ra-v'ёn] *sm.* rabbi

равендук [ra-vyen-dóok] *sm.* canvas, duck

равенство [rá-vyen-stvǒ] *sn.* equality, parity

равнение [rav-nyé-nye] *sn.* equalization, levelling; — **направо** [— na-prá-vǒ] *mil.* eyes right!

равнина [rav-n'ё-na] *sf.* plain, tract of level ground

равно [rav-nó] *adv.* alike, equally

равновесие [rav-na-vyé-sye] *sn.* balance, equilibrium

равновременный [rav-na-vryé-myen-nǎy] *adj.* isochronous, of equal time

равноденствие [rav-na-dyén-stvye] *sn.* equinox

равнодушный [rav-na-dóosh-nǎy] *adj.* indifferent, unconcerned

равнозначащий [rav-na-znǎ-cha-shchi] *adj.* equivalent, synonymous

равномерный [rav-na-myér-nǎy] *adj.* proportional

равноправие [rav-na-prá-vye] *sn.* (equal) rights

равносторонний [rav-na-sta-rón-ni] *adj.* equilateral

равный [rǎv-nǎy] *adj.* equal, similar

равнять [rav-nyǎt'] (по-) *vt.* to equalize, even, level

рад [rǎd] *adj.* glad, pleased; **— не** [— nye] willy-nilly

радение [ra-dyé-nye] *sn.* vigilance, zeal

ради [rá-d'i] *prep.* for the sake of

радиальный [ra-d'i-ál'-nǎy] *adj.* radial

радиация [ra-d'i-á-tsya] *sf.* radiation

радио [rá-d'iǒ] *sn.* radio, wireless

радиовещание [ra-d'ia-vye-shchǎ-nye] *sn.* broadcasting

радиопередатчик [ra-d'ia-pye-rye-dát-chik] *sm.* transmitter

радовать [rá-da-vat'] (об-) *vt.i.* to gladden, rejoice; **-ся** [-sya] *vi.* to be delighted, jubilate

радостный [rá-dast-nǎy] *adj.* joyful

радость [rá-dǒst'] *sf.* delight, gladness, joy

радуга [rá-dōо-ga] *sf.* rainbow

радужный [rá-dōоzh-nǎy] *adj.* iridescent

радушие [ra-dōо-shye] *sn.* cordiality

радушный [ra-dōоsh-nǎy] *adj.* affable, genial

раёк [ra-yók] *sm. theat.* gallery

ражий [rá-zhi] *adj.* corpulent; robust

раз [ráz] *sm.* time (*as every time, this time*); *adv.* once, one day; **два** (**три,** *etc.*) **раза** [dva [trē] rá-za] twice (three, *etc.*) times; *conj.* since

разбавлять [raz-bav-lyát'] (**разбáвить**) *vt.* to dilute

разбалтывать [raz-bál-tă-vat'] (**разболтáть**) *vt.* to stir up; to blurt out, divulge

разбег [raz-byég] *sm.* run, start; **-áться** [-át'-sya] *vi.* to disperse; to start running

разбередить [raz-bye-rye-d'ét'] *vt.* to irritate

разбивáть [raz-b'i-vát'] (**разбить**) *vt.* to break, smash; to stave

разбивка [raz-b'év-ka] *sf.* breaking (*into pieces*); laying out (*garden,* etc.); **в разбивку** (vraz-b'év-kŏŏ) separately, haphazardly; piece by piece

разбирáтельство [raz-b'i-rá-tyel'-stvŏ] *sn.* discussion, examination; *leg.* court-examination; trial

разбирáть [raz-b'i-rát'] (**разобрáть**) *vt.* to disjoint, dismantle, take to pieces; to decipher; to sort out; **-дело** [- dyé-lŏ] to try a case; **-ся** [-sya] *vi.* to discriminate

разбитнóй [raz-b'it-nóy] *adj.* bright, smart, sprightly

разбитость [raz-b'é-tŏst'] *sf.* breakdown, collapse

разбогатевший [raz-ba-ga-tyév-shi] *adj.*, *sm.* newly-rich

разбогатеть [raz-ba-ga-tyét'] *vi.* to acquire wealth

разбой [raz-bóy] *sm.* bri-

gandage, robbery; **-ник** [-n'ik] *sm.* bandit; outlaw; **-ничество** [-n'i-chest-vŏ] *sn.* pillage, piracy

разбор [raz-bór] *sm.* choice, selection; distinction

разборный [raz-bór-năy] *adj.* collapsible

разборчивый [raz-bór-chi-văy] *adj.* cautious; fastidious; clear, legible, plain

разбранить [raz-bra-n'ét'] *vt.* to abuse, scold; *coll.* to fly at someone; **-ся** [-sya] *vi.* to have a row, start a quarrel

разбрасывать [raz-brá-să-vat'] (**разбросáть**) *vt.* to scatter, throw about

разбросанный [raz-bró-san-năy] *adj.* disconnected, dispersed

разбудить [raz-bŏŏ-d'ét'] *vt.* to awaken, rouse

разбухать [raz-bŏŏ-chát'] (**разбýхнуть**) *vi.* to tend to fly at someone; **-ся** [-sya] *vi.* inflate, swell

развал [raz-vál] *sm.* collapse, disorganization; downfall

развалина [raz-vá-l'i-na] *sf.* debris, ruin, wreck

разве [ráz-vye] *adv.* if, unless; perhaps; **-?** is that so?

разведение [raz-vye-dyé-nye] *sn.* disunion, parting; stock-raising

разведённый [raz-vye-dyón-năy] *adj.*, *sm.* divorced (*husband*)

разведка [raz-vyéd-ka] *sf.* exploration, search; reconnaissance; prospecting

разведчик [raz-vyéd-chik] *sm. mil.* scout; *nav.* patrol plane

развенчивать [raz-vyén-chi-vat'] (**развенчáть**) *vt.* to dethrone

развёртывать [raz-vyór-tă-vat'] (развернуть) vt. to unfold, unroll, unwrap

развес [raz-vyés] sm. weighing

развеселять [raz-vye-sye-lyát'] (развеселить) vi. to amuse, cheer up

разветвление [raz-vyet-vlyé-nye] sn. ramification

развешивать [raz-vyé-shi-vat'] (развешать) vt. to hang out, suspend; – (развесить) vt. to weigh out

развивать [raz-v'i-vát'] (развить) vt. to evolve; to develop; to untwist

развилина [raz-v'ē-l'i-na] sf. bifurcation, forking

развинчивать [raz-v'ēn-chi-vat'] (развинтить) vt. to unscrew

развитие [raz-v'ē-tye] sn. development, progress

развлечение [raz-vlye-ché-nye] sn. amusement, diversion; recreation

развод [raz-vód] sm. divorce; mil. parade

разводить [raz-va-d'ét'] (развести) vt. to divorce; to separate; to propagate

разводка [raz-vód-ka] sf. divorced wife; tech. saw-set

развозка [raz-vóz-ka] sf. carrying, conveying, transport

разволноваться [raz-val-na-vát'-sya] vi. to become agitated, stirred

разврат [raz-vrát] sm. corruption, perversity

развратничать [raz-vrát-n'i-chat'] vi. to lead a dissipated life

развязка [raz-vyáz-ka] sf. issue, outcome; dénouement

развязно [raz-vyáz-nŏ] adv. free and easy

разгадка [raz-gád-ka] sf. answer, key, solution; clue

разгадчик [raz-gád-chik] sm. diviner

разгар [raz-gár] sm. culmination; fig. climax; in full swing

разгибать [raz-gi-bát'] (разогнуть) vt. to straighten, unbend

разглаживание [raz-glá-zhi-va-nye] sn. ironing, pressing; smoothing

разглашать [raz-gla-shát'] (разгласить) vt. to proclaim, publish, spread

разглядывать [raz-glyá-dă-vat'] (разглядеть) vt. to consider, scrutinize, view

разговаривать [raz-ga-vá-r'i-vat'] vi. to converse; to discourse; to talk

разговор [raz-ga-vór] sm. conversation; **-ный** [-năy] adj. colloquial; spoken; **-чивый** [-chi-văy] adj. talkative

разгонять [raz-ga-nyát'] (разогнать) vt. to dispel, drive away

разграбление [raz-grab-lyé-nye] sn. plundering

разгром [raz-gróm] sm. destruction, havoc; rout; devastation

разгул [raz-gōōl] sm. revelry; drinking-bout

разгульный [raz-gōōl'-năy] adj. dissolute

раздавание [raz-da-vá-nye] sn. distribution

раздавать [raz-da-vát'] (раздать) vt. to deal out

раздача [raz-dā-cha] *sf.* allotment; delivery; presentation

раздевалка [raz-dye-vāl-ka] *sf.* cloak-room

раздевание [raz-dye-vā-nye] *sn.* undressing

раздевать [raz-dye-vāt'] (раздеть) *vt.* to undress

раздел [raz-dyél] *sm.* division, section

разделение [raz-dye-lyé-nye] *sn.* division, separation; *gram.* syllabication

разделительный [raz-dye-l'ē-tyel'-năy] *adj. gram.* partitive

раздельный [raz-dyél'-năy] *adj.* separate

разделять [raz-dye-lyāt'] *vt.* to divide, part, separate; to share

раздирать [raz-d'i-rāt'] (разодрать) *vt.* to lacerate, tear; to wrench; *fig.* to distress

раздолье [raz-dó-lye] *sn.* comfort, ease, freedom, abundance, expanse

раздор [raz-dór] *sm.* discord, dissension; яблоко -а [yā-bla-kŏ -a] bone of contention

раздражать [raz-dra-zhāt'] (раздражить) *vt.* to annoy, irritate; to exasperate; -ся [-sya] *vi.* to fret, lose one's temper

раздражительный [raz-dra-zhē-tyel'-năy] *adj.* irritable, peevish, touchy

раздроблять [raz-drab-lyāt'] (раздробить) *vt.* to break up into small particles; to dismember; to splinter; *math.* turn into

раздувать [raz-doō-vāt']

(раздуть) *vt.* to blow; to disperse; to fan

раздумывать [raz-doō-mă-vat'] (раздумать) *vt.* to change one's mind; to hesitate, waver

раздумывание [raz-doō-mă-va-nye] *sn.* doubt, meditation, uncertainty

раздумье [raz-doō-mye] *sn.* hesitation, wavering; reflection

разевать [ra-zye-vāt'] (разинуть) *vi.* to gape

разжалобиться [raz-zhā-la-b'it'-sya] *vi.* to be moved with compassion

разжалование [raz-zhā-la-va-nye] *sn.* degradation

разжаловаться [raz-zhā-la-va-vat'-sya] *vi.* to have a grievance

разжёвывать [raz-zhó-vă-vat'] (разжевать) *vt.* to chew, masticate; *fig.* to reiterate

разжива [raz-zhē-va] *sf.* gain, profit

разжигать [raz-zhi-gāt'] (разжечь) *vt.* to kindle; *fig.* to excite, stimulate

разжижение [raz-zhi-zhé-nye] *sn.* dilution; rarefaction

разительный [ra-z'ē-tyel'-năy] *adj.* impressive, striking

разлагать [raz-la-gāt'] (разложить) *vt.* to analyse, decompose, resolve; -ся [-sya] *vi.* to decay, putrefy

разлад [raz-lād] *sm.* disagreement

разлениваться [raz-lyé-n'i-vat'-sya] *vi.* to become lazy, succumb to idleness

разлив [raz-l'ĕv] *sm.* overflow

разливать [raz-l'i-vát'] (разлить) vt. to draw off, pour out; to bottle

разливка [raz-l'év-ka] sf. bottling

различение [raz-l'i-ché-nye] sn. discrimination, distinction

различие [raz-l'é-chye] sn. difference, diversity

различительный [raz-l'i-ché-tyel'-năy] adj. distinctive

различный [raz-l'éch-năy] adj. different

разложение [raz-la-zhé-nye] sn. analysis, resolution; decomposition

разлом [raz-lóm] sm. break, fracture

разлука [raz-lōō-ka] sf. separation

разлучаться [raz-lōō-chát'-sya] vi. to part, separate; to sever

разлучение [raz-lōō-ché-nye] sn. severance

размазня [raz-maz-nyá] sf. thin, or poor gruel; fig. listless person

разматывать [raz-má-tá-vat'] (размотать) vt. to uncoil, unwind; to waste (money)

размах [raz-mách] sm. range (of activities); sweep, swing; span

размахивать [raz-má-chi-vat'] (размахнуть) vt. to brandish; to flap; to wave; — руками [— rōō-ká-mi] to gesticulate

размачивать [raz-má-chi-vat'] (размочить) vt. to saturate, soak, steep

размен [raz-myén] sm. change, exchange

размер [raz-myér] sm. dimension; rate; size; extent

размеривать [raz-mye-r'í-vat'] (размерить) vt. to measure off

размешивать [raz-myé-shi-vat'] (размешать) to knead; to stir

размещать [raz-mye-shchát'] (разместить) vt. to allocate; to dispose; to billet; —ся [-sya] vi. to take seats

разминать [raz-m'i-nát'] (размять) vt. to crumble; to mash

разминуться [raz-m'i-nōōt'-sya] vi. to cross, pass one another

размножать [raz-mna-zhát'] (размножить) vt. to multiply

размол [raz-mól] sm. grinding, grist

размолвка [raz-mólv-ka] sf. misunderstanding, variance; tiff

размывать [raz-má-vát'] (размыть) vt. to scoop out, wash off

размыкать [raz-má-kát'] vt. to unfasten, unlock; to disconnect (in electricity)

размыкать [raz-má-kat'] vt. to shake off

размышление [raz-má-shlyé-nye] sn. consideration, reflection

размягчение [raz-myach-ché-nye] sn. mollification, softening

размякать [raz-mya-kát'] (размякнуть) vi. to become mellow, tender; fig. to get sentimental

разниться [ráz-n'it'-sya] vi. to differ

разница [ráz-n'i-tsa] *sf.* contrast; difference; inequality

разновидность [raz-na-v'ĕd-nŏst'] *sf.* variety

разновидный [raz-na-v'ĕd-nǎy] *adj.* diverse, varied; variant

разновременный [raz-na-vryé-myen-nǎy] *adj.* alternative

разногласие [raz-na-glá-sye] *sn.* discord; dissonance

разномыслие [raz-na-mǎs-lye] *sn.* dissidence

разнообразие [raz-na-a-brá-zye] *sn.* diversity

разнородный [raz-na-ród-nǎy] *adj.* heterogeneous

разноска [raz-nós-ka] *sf.* hawking, peddling; delivery (*of letters, etc.*)

разносчик [raz-nós-chik] *sm.* hawker, pedlar

разный [ráz-nǎy] *adj.* different, various

разоблачать [ra-za-bla-chát'] (разоблачить) *vt.* to disrobe, divest; to undress; *fig.* to expose

разобщение [ra-zab-shché-nye] *sn.* isolation; insulation

разорение [ra-za-ryé-nye] *sn.* ravage, ruin

разоружать [ra-za-rŏŏ-zhát'] *vt.* to disarm; to dismantle

разоружение [ra-za-rŏŏ-zhé-nye] *sn.* disarmament; dismantling

разорять [ra-za-ryát'] (разорить) *vt.* to destroy, spoil, waste

разочарование [ra-za-cha-ra-vá-nye] *sn.* disappointment, disillusionment

разрабатывать [raz-ra-bá-tǎ-vat'] (разработать) *vt.* to develop, work out

разработка [raz-ra-bót-ka] *sf.* treatment; cultivation

разражаться [raz-ra-zhát'-sya] (разразиться) *vi.* to burst, explode

разрез [raz-ryéz] *sm.* cut, rift; gash, slash; slit

разрешать [raz-rye-shát'] (разрешить) *vt.* to authorize; to permit; to solve; to grant; to resolve

разрешение [raz-rye-shé-nye] *sn.* permission; licence; solution; dispensation

разруха [raz-rŏŏ-cha] *sf.* disorder

разрушение [raz-rŏŏ-shé-nye] *sn.* destruction; downfall

разрыв [raz-rǎv] *sm.* break, rupture, severance; explosion

разрывать [raz-rǎ-vát'] (разорвать) *vt.* to disrupt, lacerate, tear; – (разрыть) *vt.* to dig up; *fig.* to ransack

разряд [raz-ryád] *sm.* category, class, rank; discharge (*of gun, etc.*)

разрядка [raz-ryád-ka] *sf. typ.* spacing

разуверять [ra-zŏŏ-vye-ryát'] *vt.* to dissuade

разум [rȃ-zŏŏm] *sm.* intelligence, mind, reason

разуметь [ra-zŏŏ-myét'] *vt.* to comprehend

разумный [ra-zŏŏm-nǎy] *adj.* intelligent, reasonable, sensible

разучивать [ra-zŏŏ-chi-vat'] (разучить) *vt.* to learn, study; to practise

разъедать [raz-ye-dãt'] (разъесть) *vt.* to eat into; to erode

разъедение [raz-ye-dyé-nye] *sn.* canker, erosion

разъединять [raz-ye-d'i-nyãt'] *vt.* to disconnect, disjoint, unlink

разъезд [raz-yézd] *sm.* departure, setting-out; siding (*railway*); cavalry patrol

разъезжаться [raz-yez-zhãt'-sya] *vt.* to break up, separate(*a travelling party*); to lose sight of someone; to fray

разъярённый [raz-ya-ryón-nãy] *adj.* furious; *coll.* in a rage, mad

разъяснение [raz-yas-nyé-nye] *sn.* elucidation, explanation; *fig.* key to a solution; explanatory note

разъяснять [raz-yas-nyãt'] (разъяснить) *vt.* to explain, expound, illuminate

разыгрывание [ra-zã-grã-va-nye] *sn.*, *theat.*, *mus.* performance, execution

разыскивание[ra-zãs-ki-va-nye] *sn.* discovering, finding, investigation, search; inquiry

рай [rãy] *sm.* heaven, paradise; **-ский** [-ski] *adj.* heavenly

район [ra-yón] *sm.* area, district, quarter; field (*of activity*); *mil.* zone

рак [rãk] *sm.* crab, crayfish, lobster; Cancer, Crab; *med.* cancer

рака [rã-ka] *sf.* shrine

ракета [ra-kyé-ta] *sf.* battledore; (*tennis*) racket; rocket

ракита [ra-k'é-ta] *sf.* willow

раковидный[ra-ka-v'éd-nãy] *adj.* crustacean; cancerous

раковина [rã-ka-v'i-na] *sf.* blister; shell; **ушная** - [ōōsh-nã-ya –] helix

рама [rã-ma] *sf.* frame

рампа [rãm-pa] *sf.* footlights

рана [rã-na] *sf.* wound

раненько [rã-nyen'-kõ] *adv.* rather early

ранец [rã-nyets] *sm.* kit, knapsack, pack, satchel

ранить [rã-n'it'] *vt.* to wound

ранний [rãn-n'i] *adj.* early

рано [rã-nõ] *adv.* early

рант [rant] *sm.* welt; brim, edge

рань [rãn'] *sf.* early hour(s)

раньше [rãn'-she] *adv.* formerly; earlier, sooner

рапира [ra-p'é-ra] *sf.* foil, rapier

раса [rã-sa] *sf.* breed, race

расовый [rã-sa-vãy] *adj.* racial

раскаиваться [ras-kã-i-vat'-sya] (раскáяться) *vi.* to regret, repent

раскалённый [ras-ka-lyón-nãy] *adj.* incandescent

раскалывать [ras-kã-lã-vat'] (расколóть) *vt.* to cleave, chop, split; to crack (*china, etc.*)

раскат [ras-kãt] *sm.* peal, roll

раскачивание [ras-kã-chi-va-nye] *sn.* swaying, swinging

раскаяние [ras-kã-ya-nye] *sn.* remorse, repentance

расквасить [ras-kvã-s'it'] *vt.* to crush, squash

раскладывать [ras-klã-dã-vat'] (разложить) *vt.* to spread out; to unpack

расклеивать [ras-klyé-i-vat'] (расклéить) *vt.* to unstick; to bill (*posters on hoardings*)

раскол [ras-kól] *sm.* cleft, crack; split (*in pol. party*); schism, sect

раскольник [ras-kól'-n'ik] *sm.* sectarian

раскопка [ras-kóp-ka] *sf.* digging, excavation

раскосый [ras-ko-sǎy] *adj.* cross-eyed

раскошеливаться [raz-kashé-l'i-vat'-sya] (раскошелиться) *vi.* to be generous, liberal; to disburse, pay up

раскрадывание [ras-krá-dǎ-na-ye] *sn.* pilfering, stealing, thieving

раскраснеться [ras-krasnyét'-sya] *vi.* to blush, colour, redden

раскрашивание [ras-kráshi-va-nye] *sn.* graining, marbling, painting

раскрашивать [ras-kráshi-vat'] (раскрасить) *vt.* to colour, paint

раскручивать [ras-kroochi-vat'] (раскрутить) *vt.* to disentangle, untwine, untwist

раскрывать [ras-krǎ-vát'] (раскрыть) *vt.* to open, uncover; to disclose; to unfurl

раскрытый [ras-krǎ-tǎy] *adj.* disclosed, exposed, open

раскупать [ras-koo-pát'] *vt.* to buy up

распад [ras-pád] *sm.* break-up, disintegration; *chem.* decay

распадаться [ras-pa-dát'-sya] *vi.* to disintegrate, fall to pieces

распаковка [ras-pa-kóv-ka] *sf.* unpacking

распаривать [ras-pá-r'i-vat'] (ras-pá-r'it) *vt.* to steam, stew

распарывать [ras-pá-rǎvat'] (распороть) *vt.* to rip up, unpick

распахивать [ras-pá-chivat'] (распахать) to plough up, till; to break up fresh ground; – (распахнуть) to throw open

распев [ras-pyév] *sm.* drawl

распечатывать [ras-pyechá-tǎ-vat'] (распечатать) *vt.* to unseal

распивать [ras-p'i-vát'] (распить) *vt.* to drink up

распивочная [ras-p'é-vachna-ya] *adj. as sf.* tap-room

распинание [ras-p'i-ná-nye] *sn.* crucifixion

распинать [ras-p'i-nát'] (распять) *vt.* to crucify

расписание [ras-p'i-sá-nye] *sn.* schedule, time-table

расписка [ras-p'és-ka] *sf.* receipt; voucher; painting (*decorator's*)

расписывать [ras-p'é-sǎvat'] (расписать) *vt.* to depict, describe

расплакаться [ras-plá-kat'-sya] *vi.* to burst into tears

расплата [ras-plá-ta] *sf.* payment

расплачиваться [ras-plá-chi-vat'-sya] (расплатиться) *vi.* to settle an account

распознавать [ras-pa-znavát'] (распознать) *vt.* to discern, distinguish

располагать [ras-pa-la-gát'] (расположить) *vt.* to dispose, place, set; to grade

расположение [ras-pa-la-zhé-nye] *sn.* disposition; situation; inclination

распорка [ras-pór-ka] *sf.* cross-bar; strut

распорядитель [ras-pa-rya-d'é-tyel'] *sm.* director, manager; master of ceremonies; organiser; **-ный** [-nǎy] *adj.* active, efficient

распоряжение [ras-pa-rya-zhé-nye] *sn.* arrangement, disposition, order; decree; by-law

расправа [ras-prā-va] *sf.* court, tribunal; justice; punishment

расправлять [ras-prav-lyát'] (расправить) to redress; to smooth, straighten

распределение [ras-prye-dye-lyé-nye] *sn.* allocation, assignment, distribution

распродажа [ras-pra-dā-zha] *sf.* clearance sale

распространять [ras-pra-stra-nyát'] *vt.* to broadcast, circulate; to diffuse; to propagate

распря [rās-prya] *sf.* conflict

распускание [ras-pōos-kā-nye] *sn.* *chem.* solution; blossoming

распускать [ras-pōos-kāt'] (распустить) *vt.* to dissolve; to melt; to dismiss

распутный [ras-pōot-nǎy] *adj.* dissolute, wanton

распутывание [ras-pōo-tǎ-va-nye] *sn.* disentanglement

распутывать [ras-pōo-tǎ-vat'] (распутать) *vt.* to unravel

распутье [ras-pōo-tye] *sn.* crossroad

распухать [ras-pōo-chat'] (распухнуть) *vi.* to bulge, swell

распухание [ras-pōo-chā-nye] *sn.* inflation, swelling

распылитель [ras-pǎ-l'é-tyel'] *sm.* atomizer, pulverizer

рассада [ras-sā-da] *sf.* shoot, sprout; seedling

рассадка [ras-sād-ka] *sf.* planting, transplanting

рассадник [ras-sād-n'ik] *sm.* hotbed, nursery

рассаживать [ras-sā-zhi-vat'] (рассажать) *vt.* to transplant; to seat; to place (*in class*)

рассаривать [ras-sā-r'i-vat'] *vi.* to litter; to squander

рассвет [ras-svyét] *sm.* dawn

рассев [ras-syév] *sm.* sowing

рассеивать [ras-syé-i-vat'] *vt.* to sow; to dispel, disperse

расселина [ras-syé-l'i-na] *sf.* cleft, rift

расселять [ras-syé-lyat'] (расселить) *vt.* to settle displaced persons

рассеяние [ras-syé-ya-nye] *sn.* dispersion

рассеянный [ras-séy-yan-nǎy] *adj.* absent-minded; distracted

рассказ [ras-skāz] *sm.* story, tale

рассказчик [ras-skāz-chik] *sm.* narrator, story-teller

рассказывать [ras-skā-zǎ-vat'] (рассказать) *vt.* to narrate, relate, tell

расслабление [ras-slab-lyé-nye] *sn.* enfeeblement, weakening; depression

расслаблять [ras-slab-lyát'] (расслабить) *vi.* to become feeble, weaken

расследование [ras-slyé-da-va-nye] *sn.* investigation; inquiry

рассматривать [ras-smá-tri-vat'] (рассмотре́ть) vt. to examine, inspect, look through, scrutinize

рассмеяться [ras-smye-yát'-sya] vi. to burst into laughter

расснастка [ras-snást-ka] sf. naut. dismantling, un-rigging

рассол [ras-sól] sm. brine; pickle

рассо́риться [ras-só-r'it'-sya] vi. to fall out, to quarrel

расспра́шивание [ras-sprá-shi-va-nye] sn. inquiry; questioning

рассро́чка [ras-sróch-ka] sf. instalment

расставля́ть [ras-stá-vlyat'] (расста́вить) vt. to arrange, dispose, place; to put in order

расстано́вка [ras-sta-nóv-ka] sf. arrangement, order

расстёгивать [ras-styó-gi-vat'] (расстегну́ть) vt. to un-button, unfasten, undo

расстоя́ние [ras-sta-yá-nye] sn. distance; space

расстра́ивать [ras-strá-i-vat'] (расстро́ить) vt. to dis-concert, perturb, upset

расстре́л [ras-stryél] sm. mil. execution

расстри́га [ras-strě-ga] sf. degraded, unfrocked priest

расстрига́ть [ras-stri-gát'] (расстри́чь) vt. to degrade; to unfrock

расстриже́ние [ras-stri-zhé-nye] sn. degradation

расстро́енный [ras-stró-yen-nåy] adj. disturbed, upset

рассуди́тельность [ras-sŏŏ-d'ě-tyel'-nåst'] sf. consideration, judiciousness, sagacity, sense

рассу́док [ras-sŏŏ-dŏk] sm. mind, reason, sense, under-standing

рассужда́ть [ras-sŏŏzh-dát'] (рассуди́ть) vt. to argue, debate, reason

рассчи́тывать [ras-schě-tå-vat'] (рассчита́ть) to calcu-late, compute, figure out; to discharge, dismiss, pay off

рассы́льный [ras-sál'-nåy] adj. as sm. errand-boy

рассыпа́ть [ras-să-pát'] (рассы́пать) vt. to scatter, spill; to intersperse

рассы́пка [ras-sáp-ka] sf. scattering, strewing

рассы́пчатый [ras-sáp-chå-tåy] adj. crumbly, powdery

раста́пливать [ras-táp-l'i-vat'] (растопи́ть) vt. to heat; to kindle, light; to melt, thaw

раста́птывать [ras-táp-tå-vat'] (растопта́ть) vt. to crunch; to crush; to trample

раста́скивать [ras-tás-ki-vat'] (растаска́ть, рас-тащи́ть) vt. to drag, pull, pull away

раство́р [ras-tvór] sm. open-ing; chem. solution; **-имый** [-ě-måy] adj. soluble

растворя́ть [ras-tva-ryát'] vt. to dissolve; to liquefy; to open

расте́ние [ras-tyé-nye] sn. plant

растеря́нный [ras-tyé-ryan-nåy] adj. confused, embar-rassed, perplexed

растеряться [ras-tye-ryát'-syal] *vi.* to be at a loss; *fig.* to lose one's head

растеряха [ras-tye-ryá-cha] *sm., f.* careless, untidy person

расти [ras-t'é] *vi.* to grow, shoot up; to thrive

растирать [ras-t'i-rát'] (растереть) *vt.* to rub; to massage

растительность [ras-t'ě-tyel'-nöst'] *sf.* vegetation, verdure

растить [ras-t'ět'] *vt.* to cultivate (*plants*), to grow, raise

растлевать [ras-tlye-vát'] (растлить) *vt.* to contaminate; corrupt, deprave

расталковывание [ras-tal-kó-vă-va-nye] *sn.* explication, interpretation

растолочь [ras-ta-lóch'] *vt.* to grind, pound, pulverize

растопка [ras-tóp-ka] *sf.* firelighter; melting; smelting

растопленный [ras-tóp-lyen-năy] *adj.* molten

расторжение [ras-tar-zhé-nye] *sn.* breach, break, rupture; dissolution

расторопный [ras-ta-róp-năy] *adj.* expeditious; prompt, smart

расточать [ras-ta-chát'] *vt.* to dissipate, squander; to lavish

расточитель [ras-ta-chě-tyel'] *sm.* profligate, spendthrift, wastrel

растравливание [ras-tráv-l'i-va-nye] *sn.* irritation (of skin, wound)

растрата [ras-trá-ta] *sf.* embezzlement

растревожить [ras-trye-vó-zhit'] *vi.* to alarm, disquiet, fret

растрёпанный [ras-tryó-pan-năy] *adj.* dishevelled, ruffled, rumpled

растрогивать [ras-tró-gi-vat'] (растрогать) *vt.* to affect, move, touch; **-ся** [-sya] *vi.* to be deeply moved

раструб [ras-trŏŏb] *sm.* funnel-shaped opening; bell

растягивать [ras-tyá-gi-vat'] (растянуть) *vt.* to dilate; to lengthen, spin out

растяжение [ras-tya-zhé-nye] *sn.* expansion, extension; sprain

расформирование [ras-far-m'ě-ra-va-nye] *sn. mil.* disbandment

расфрантиться [ras-fran-t'ět'-sya] *vi.* to array oneself, dress up, overdress

расхаживать [ras-chá-zhi-vat'-sya] *vi.* to stroll along aimlessly; to walk about

расхват [ras-chvát] *sm.* grabbing, snatching

расхищение [ras-chi-shché-nye] *sn.* depredation, pillage, plunder

расхлябанный [ras-chlyá-ban-năy] *adj.* loose, relaxed, slack

расход [ras-chód] *sm.* disbursement, expenditure, expense; накладные — [na-klad-nóy —] overhead expenses

расходиться [ras-cha-d'ět'-sya] (разойтись) *vi.* to part, separate; to differ, disagree, fall out; to diverge; to break up (*a meeting, etc.*)

расходовать [ras-chó-da-vat'] (из-) *vt.* to lay out, spend, use up

расхождение [ras-chazh-dýé-nye] *sn.* divergence

расхолаживать [ras-cha-lá-zhi-vat'] (расхолодить) *vt.* to chill, cool; *fig.* to damp one's feelings

расцвет [ras-tsvyét] *sm.* bloom, blossoming

расцеловать [ras-tsye-la-vát'] *vt.* to kiss repeatedly, smother with kisses; **-ся** [-sya] *vi.* to exchange kisses

расценивать [ras-tsyé-ni-vat'] (расценить) *vt.* to assess; to estimate

расценка [ras-tsyén-ka] *sf.* rate, tariff

расцепление [ras-tsye-plyé-nye] *sn.* uncoupling, unhooking

расчёсывание [ras-chó-să-va-nye] *sn.* combing out; carding

расчёт [ras-chót] *sm.* account, calculation, computation; *mil.* crew; detachment

расчётливый [ras-chót-li-văy] *adj.* economical, thrifty; calculating, careful; **– день** [– dyén'] *sm.* pay-day

расчисление [ras-chi-slyé-nye] *sn.* reckoning

расчистка [ras-chést-ka] *sf.* clearing

расчищать [ras-chi-shchát'] (расчистить) *vt.* to clear away

расчленять [ras-chlye-nyát'] (расчленить) *vt.* to dismember, dissect; to analyse; to partition

расшатанность [ras-shá-tan-nŏst'] *sf.* instability

расшевеливать [ras-she-vyé-l'i-vat'] (расшевелить) *vt.* to move, stir; *coll.* to jog (one's memory)

расшивать [ras-shi-vát'] (расшить) *vt.* to embroider, to adorn with fancy stitches

расширение [ras-shi-ryé-nye] *sn.* enlargement, expansion, widening

расшифровывать [ras-shif-ró-vă-vat'] (расшифровать) *vt.* to decipher, decode

расщелина [ras-shché-l'i-na] *sf.* chink, cleft, crevice

расщепление [ras-shche-plyé-nye] *sn.* splintering

ратовать [rá-ta-vat'] *vi.* to declaim

ратуша [rá-tōō-sha] *sf.* guildhall, town hall

рафинад [ra-fi-nád] *sm.* lump sugar; refined sugar; **-ный завод** [-năy za-vód] sugar refinery

рациональный [ra-tsyo-nál'-năy] *adj.* rational

рашкуль [rash-kōōl'] *sm.* charcoal-crayon

рашпиль [răsh-pil'] *sm.* rasp

рвань [rvăn'] *sf.* rags; *tech.* clamp; *fig.* ragamuffin, scamp

рвать [rvát'] (разорвáть) *vt.* to rip, tear; to pick, pluck

рвение [rvyé-nye] *sn.* eagerness, zeal

рвота [rvó-ta] *sf.* vomiting; flaw

рвотный [rvót-năy] *adj.* emetic

pe [re] *sn. mus.* D

реакционер [re-ak-tsio-nyér] *sm.* reactionary

реал [rẹ-ál] *sm. typ.* frame, rack

реальность [rẹ-ál'-nŏst'] *sf.* reality

реальный [rẹ-ál'-năy] *adj.* real, tangible

ребёнок [rye-byó-nŏk] *sm.* child

ребро [rye-bró] *sn.* rib; brink, edge, verge

ребята [rye-byá-ta] *sm. pl.* children; boys, lads

ребяческий [rye-byá-ches-ki] *adj.* childish

ребячество [rye-byá-chest-vŏ] *sn.* puerility

рёв [ryóv] *sm.* bellowing, roar

реванш [re-vánsh] *sm. sport.* return match

ревень [re-vyén'] *sm.* rhubarb

реверанс [re-ve-ráns] *sm.* curtsy

реветь [rye-vyét'] *vi.* to bellow, roar, squall

ревизия [re-vē-zya] *sf.* audit; examination, inspection

ревматический [rev-ma-t'é-ches-ki] *adj.* rheumatic

ревизор [re-v'i-zór] *sm.* auditor, inspector

ревнивец [ryev-n'é-vyets] *sm.* jealous man

ревнивый [ryev-n'é-văy] *adj.* jealous

ревность [ryév-nŏst'] *sf.* jealousy, zeal

революционер [re-va-lyōō-tsia-nyér] *sm.* revolutionary

революционный [re-va-lyōō-tsión-năy] *adj.* revolutionary

революция [re-va-lyōō-tsya] *sf.* revolution

регистр [re-gēstr] *sm.* refer-

ence book; official list; *mus.* register

регистратор [re-gi-strá-tŏr] *sm.* actuary, recorder, registrar

регламент [re-gla-mýent] *sm.* regulation, rule, statute

регулировать [re-gōō-l'ē-ra-vat'] *vt.* to control, regulate

регулы [re-gōō-lă] *sf. pl.* menstruation, periods

регулярный [rye-gōō-lyár-năy] *adj.* regular

регулятор [re-gōō-lyá-tŏr] *sm. tech.* regulator, governor

редактор [rye-dák-tŏr] *sm.* editor

редакционный [rye-dak-tsión-năy] *adj.* editorial

редакция [rye-dák-tsya] *sf.* editorship; editorial office

редеть [rye-dyét'] (по-) *vi.* to become sparse

редиска [rye-d'ēs-ka] *sf.* radish

редкий [ryéd-k'i] *adj.* rare, uncommon; infrequent; sparse

редко [ryéd-ko] *adv.* far-between; seldom

редкость [ryéd-kŏst'] *sf.* rarity; scarcity

редька [ryéd'-ka] *sf.* horse radish

режим [rye-zhém] *sm.* regime; *med.* regimen

режиссёр [rye-zhis-syór] *sm.* producer, stage-manager

резак [rye-zák] *sm.* chopping-knife, cleaver; ploughshare

резальщик [rye-zál'-shchik] *sm.* carver, cutter

резать [rye-zat'] *vt.* to carve, cut; to slice

резвый [ryéz-văy] *adj.* game, playful; high-spirited

резервный [rye-zyér̄v-năy] *adj. mil.* reserve

резец [rye-zyéts] *sm.* engraver's chisel, cutter; incisor

резиденция [rye-zi-dyén-tsya] *sf.* residence

резина [rye-z'ĕ-na] *sf.* india-rubber; elastic

резиновый [rye-z'ĕ-na-văy] *adj.* rubber

резкий [ryéz-ki] *adj.* crude, hard, harsh; rough; sharp

резкость [ryéz-kŏst'] *sf.* keenness, sharpness

резник [ryéz-n'ik] *sm.* butcher

резня [ryez-nyä] *sf.* butchery, slaughter

резолюция [rye-za-lyŏŏ-tsya] *sf.* resolution

результат [rye-zŏŏl'-tät] *sm.* consequence, result

резчик [ryéz-chik] *sm.* carver, engraver; sculptor

резь [ryéz'] *sf.* colic, gripe, stitch

резьба [ryez'-bä] *sf.* fretwork

резюме [rye-zyŏŏ-mé] *sn.* résumé, summary

резюмировать [rye-zyŏŏ-m'ē-ra-vat'] *vt.* to recapitulate, sum up

рейка [rýéy-ka] *sf.* lath

река [rye-kä] *sf.* river

реквизировать [re-kvi-z'ē-ra-vat'] *vt.* to requisition

реквизит [re̦-kvi-zĕt] *sm. theat.* properties

реклама [re̦-klä-ma] *sf.* advertisement

рекогносцировка [re-ka-gnas-tsi-róv-ka] *sf.* reconnaissance, reconnoitring, scouting

рекомендация [re̦-ka-myen-dä-tsya] *sf.* introduction, recommendation; reference

ректор [ré̦k-tŏr] *sm.* principal, provost, rector

религиозный [re-l'i-gióznăy] *adj.* religious

религия [re̦-l'ē-gya] *sf.* religion

реликвия [re̦-l'ĕk-vya] *sf.* relic

рельс [re̦l's] *sm.* rail; **-овый путь** [-óvăy pŏŏt'] railway track

ремень [ryé-myen'] *sm.* belt, strap

ремесленник [rye-myéslyen-n'ik] *sm.* artisan, craftsman

ремесло [rye-mye-sló] *sn.* handicraft, trade

ремесса [re̦-myés-sa] *sf.* remittance

ремешок [rye-mye-shók] *sm.* narrow leather strap

ремонт [re̦-mónt] *sm.* overhaul, repair

ремонтировать [re̦-mant'ē-ra-vat'] *vt.* to erect, put up, recondition

ренклод [ryen-klód] *sm.* greengage

рента [ryén-ta] *sf.* annuity, rent

рентгенизация [re̦nt-ge̦n'i-zä-tsya] *sf.* X-raying

реорганизовать [re̦-ar-ga-n'i-za-vät'] *vt.* to reorganize

репа [rye-pa] *sf.* turnip

репетиция [re̦-pe̦-t'ē-tsya] *sf.* rehearsal

реплика [ryé-pl'i-ka] *sf.* cue, hint

реполов [rye-pa-lóv] *sm.* robin redbreast

репортаж [re̦-por-tâz̄h] *sm.* reporting

репортёр [rȩ-por-tyór] *sm.* newspaperman, reporter

репрессалия [rȩ-prȩs-sá-lya] *sf.* reprisal

репрессия [rȩ-prȩ́s-sya] *sf.* repression

рептилия [rȩp-t'ḗ-lya] *sf.* reptile

репутация [rȩ-pŏŏ-tā-tsya] *sf.* character, fame, reputation, repute

реконтро [rȩs-kón-tro] *sn.* ledger

рескрипт [rȩs-krȩ́pt] *sm.* mandate, order

ресница [ryes-n'ḗ-tsa] *sf.* eyelash

республика [ryes-pŏŏb-l'i-ka] *sf.* republic; **-нец** [-nyets] *sm.* republican

рессора [rȩs-só-ra] *sf.* spring (*metal*)

реставрация [rȩ-sta-vrā-tsya] *sf.* restoration

ресторан [rȩ-sta-rán] *sm.* restaurant

ретивый [rye-t'ḗ-vǎy] *adj.* eager, zealous

ретирада [rȩ-ti-ráda] *sf.* W.C., toilet; *mil.* retreat

ретировка [rye-t'i-róv-ka] *sf.* retreat, withdrawal

ретуширование [re-tŏŏ-shi-ra-va-nye] *sn.* retouching

реферат [re-fe-rát] *sm.* essay, paper; review

референт [re-fe-rént] *sm.* reader, reviewer

реформа [re-fór-ma] *sf.* amendment, reform

реформация [re-for-mā-tsya] *sf.* The Reformation

рецензия [re-tsén-zya] *sf.* critique, review

рецепт [re-tsyépt] *sm.* prescription; recipe

рецептивный [re-tsyep-t'ēv-nǎy] *adj.* receptive

рецидив [re-tsi-d'ēv] *sm.* relapse, setback

речка [rýech-ka] *sf.* brook, rivulet, stream

речной [rȩech-nóy] *adj.* fluvial, riverain

речь [rýech'] *sf.* oration, speech

решать [rye-shát'] (**pe-шить**) *vt.* to decide, determine; to resolve

решающий [rye-shā-yŏŏ-shchi] *adj.* conclusive, decisive

решение [rye-shé-nye] *sn.* decision, resolution; solution

решётка [rye-shót-ka] *sf.* fender; fire-guard; grate; lattice; trellis

решето [rye-she-tó] *sn.* sieve; screen

решимость [rye-shē-mŏst'] *sf.* determination, firmness, resoluteness

решительный [rye-shē-tyel'-nǎy] *adj.* categorical, resolved

решка [rýesh-ka] *sf.* 'tail' (of coin)

реять [rýe-yat'] (**рúнуть**) *vi.* to float; to soar; to hover

ржа [rzhá] *sf.* rust; mildew; **-вый** [-vǎy] *adj.* rusty

ржавчина [rzháv-chi-na] *sf.* rust

ржать [rzhát'] *vi.* to neigh

рига [r'ē-ga] *sf.* barn; corn-kiln

риза [r'ē-za] *sf.* chasuble

ризница [r'ēz-n'i-tsa] *sf.* vestry

ринуться [r'ē-nŏŏt'-sya] *vi.* to fly at, rush

РИС 273 РОДСТВЕННИК

рис [ris] *sm.* rice

риск [risk] *sm.* risk

рисковать [ris-ka-vāt'] (рискнуть) *vt.* to hazard, venture

рисовальщик [ri-sa-vāl'-shchik] *sm.* designer, draughtsman

рисование [ri-sa-vā-nye] *sn.* drawing, painting; depicting, describing

рисовать [ri-sa-vāt'] (на-) *vt.* to draw, sketch

рисунок [ri-sōō-nŏk] *sm.* drawing, illustration, picture

ритм [ritm] *sm.* rhythm

ритмический [rit-mē-ches-ki] *adj.* rhythmical

риторика [ri-tó-ri-ka] *sf.* rhetoric

ритуальный [ri-tōō-āl'-nǎy] *adj.* ritual

риф [rēf] *sm.* reef (of sail); ledge, reef

рифма [rēf-ma] *sf.* rhyme

рифмовать [rif-ma-vāt'] *vi.* to rhyme

рициновое масло [ri-tsē-na-va-ye mā-slō] *sn.* castor oil

роба [ró-ba] *sf.* gown, robe

робеть [ra-byét'] *vi.* to flinch, shrink; to be shy

робкий [rób-ki] *adj.* bashful, shy, timid

робость [ró-bŏst'] *sf.* diffidence, timidity

ров [rov] *sm.* ditch, trench

ровность [róv-nŏst'] *sf.* evenness, flatness; smoothness

ровный [róv-nǎy] *adj.* even, flat; level, plane; smooth

рог [rog] *sm.* horn; bugle

рогатка [ra-gāt-ka] *sf.* turnpike; chevaux-de-frise

рогатый [ra-gā-tǎy] *adj.* horned

рогожа [ra-gó-zha] *sf.* bast, matting

рогоза [ra-gó-za] *sf.* bulrush; reed-mace

род [rod] *sm.* kind, gender; generation

родильница [ra-d'ēl'-ni-tsa] *sf.* nursing mother

родильня [ra-d'ēl'-nya] *sf.* maternity home

родимый [ra-d'ē-mǎy] *adj.* native

родина [ró-d'i-na] *sf.* homeland

родинка [ró-d'in-ka] *sf.* birth-mark; mole

родины [ra-d'ē-nǎ] *sf. pl.* confinement, delivery

родители [ra-d'ē-tye-l'i] *sm. pl.* parents

родитель [ra-d'ē-tyel'] *sm.* parent

родительный [ra-d'ē-tyel'-nǎy] *adj. gram.* genitive, possessive

родительский [ra-d'ē-tyel'-ski] *adj.* parental

родник [rad-n'ēk] *sm.* source, spring [own

родной [rad-nóy] *adj.* natal, native

родня [rad-nyā] *sf.* relative(s)

родовой [ra-da-vóy] *adj.* ancestral, racial

родом [ró-dŏm] *adv.* by birth, by origin

родоначальник [ra-da-na-chāl'-n'ik] *sm.* progenitor

родословие [ra-da-sló-vye] *sn.* genealogy, pedigree

родословный [ra-da-slóv-nǎy] *adj.* genealogical; **родословная книга** [ra-da-slóv-na-ya kn'ē-ga] *sf.* studbook

родственник [ród-stvyen-n'ik] *sm.* relation, relative

родственный [ród-stvyen-năy] *adj.* related

родство [rad-stvó] *sn.* relationship

роды [ró-dǎ] *sm. pl.* childbirth

роение [ra-yé-nye] *sn.* swarming (bees)

рожа [ró-zha] *sf.* ugly face; *med.* erysipelas

рождаемость [razh-dā-yemŏst'] *sf.* birth-rate

рождение [razh-dyé-nye] *sn.* birth, delivery

Рождество [razh-dyest-vó] *sn.* Christmas

рожки [rózh-ki] *sm. pl.* antennae, feelers

рожь [rozh'] *sf.* rye

роза [ró-za] *sf.* rose

розарий [ra-zā-ri] *sm.* rosary

розга [róz-ga] *sf.* birch twig

роздых [róz-dǎch] *sm.* repose, rest; *mil.* halt

розетка [ra-zyét-ka] *sf.* rosette; rose-window

розмарин [raz-ma-r'ěn] *sm.* rosemary

розница [róz-n'i-tsa] *sf.* retail **розничный** [róz-n'ich-nǎy] *adj.* retail

розный [róz-nǎy] *adj.* incomplete, odd, unmatched **рознь** [rózn'] *sf.* difference, diversity

розовый [ró-za-vǎy] *adj.* pink, rose-coloured

розыгрыш [ró-zǎ-grǎsh] *sm.* draw, drawn game

розыск [ró-zǎsk] *sm.* inquest, inquiry, search

рой [róy] *sm.* cluster, swarm

рок [rok] *sm.* destiny, fate lot; злой – [zlóy –] doom

роковой [ra-ka-vóy] *adj.* fatal, fateful

рокот [ró-kŏt] *sm.* roar, roll

роль [rol'] *sf. theat.* character, part, rôle

ром [rom] *sm.* rum

роман [ra-mán] *sm.* novel; **-нист** [-n'ěst] *sm.* novelist

романс [ra-máns] *sm.* ballad

ромашка [ra-másh-ka] *sf.* daisy

ромб [romb] *sm.* rhombus; diamond; lozenge; **-ический** [-ě-ches-ki] *adj.* rhombic

ронять [ra-nyát'] (уронить) *vt.* to drop; to moult; to shed

ропот [ró-pŏt] *sm.* murmur, muttering

роптать [rap-tát'] *vi.* to complain, grumble; to murmur

роса [ra-sá] *sf.* dew

росинка [ra-s'ěn-ka] *sf.* dewdrop

роскошный [ras-kósh-nǎy] *adj.* luxurious, sumptuous

роскошь [rós-kŏsh'] *sf.* luxury, splendour

рослый [rós-lǎy] *adj.* grown up, tall

роспись [rós-p'is'] *sf.* inventory, list; fresco

роспуск [rós-pŏŏsk] *sm.* breaking up, dismissal; disbandment; dissolution

россыпь [rós-sǎp'] *sf. geol.* deposit

рост [rost] *sm.* height, stature

ростовщик [ras-tav-shchík] *sm.* money-lender, pawnbroker

ростовщичество [ras-tav-shchě-chest-vŏ] *sn.* usury

росток [ras-tók] *sm.* shoot, sprout

росчерк [rós-cherk] *sm.* flourish, scroll

рот [rot] *sm.* mouth

рота [ró-ta] *sf. mil.* company

ротационный [ra-ta-tsión-nǎy] *adj.* rotary

ротозей [ra-ta-zyéy] *sm.* loafer [grove

роща [ró-shcha] *sf.* coppice,

рояль [ra-yál'] *sm.* pianoforte, concert grand

ртуть [rtóot'] *sf.* mercury

рубанок [rōō-bā-nŏk] *sm.* plane *(tool)*

рубаха [rōō-bā-cha] *sf.* shirt

рубашка [rōō-bāsh-ka] *sf.* shirt; chemise

рубеж [rōō-byézh] *sm.* border, limit, verge

рубец [rōō-byéts] *sm.* hem, rib, seam; fluting; *anat.* paunch; chitterling; tripe *(food)*

рубильник [rōō-b'ěl'-n'ik] *sm.* chopper

рубин [rōō-b'ēn] *sm.* ruby

рубить [rōō-b'ět'] (на−) *vt.* to chop, cut, hack; to fell

рубище [rōō-b'i-shche] *sn.* rags, tatters

рубка [rōōb-ka] *sf.* chopping, hewing; deck-cabin

рубрика [rōōb-r'i-ka] *sf.* heading, rubric

рубчатый [rōōb-chā-tǎy] *adj.* seamed

ругань [rōō-gan'] *sf.* abuse; swearing

ругательный [rōō-gā-tyel'-nǎy] *adj.* abusive

ругать [rōō-gāt'] *vi.* abuse, curse, rail, scold, swear

руда [rōō-dā] *sf.* ore

рудник [rōōd-n'ik] *sm.* mine

рудокоп [rōō-da-kŏp] *sm.* miner, pitman

ружьё [rōō-zhyó] *sn.* gun, rifle

рука [rōō-kā] *sf.* hand; arm, forearm

рукав [rōō-kāv] *sm.* sleeve; arm, estuary, firth; **пожарный −** [ra-zhār-nǎy −] hose *(for watering)*

рукавица [rōō-ka-v'ě-tsa] *sf.* mitten; gauntlet

рукавчик [rōō-kāv-chik] *sm.* cuff

руководитель [rōō-ka-va-d'ē-tyel'] *sm.* guide, instructor, leader, supervisor

руководить [rōō-ka-va-d'ět'] *vt.* to guide, direct, lead

руководство [rōō-ka-vód-stvŏ] *sn.* guidance, leadership; textbook, manual

рукоделие [rōō-ka-dyé-lye] *sn.* needlework; fancy-work; manual work

рукодельный [rōō-ka-dyél'-nǎy] *adj.* hand-made, manual

рукомойник [rōō-ka-móy-n'ik] *sm.* wash-basin

рукопашный [rōō-ka-pāsh-nǎy] *adj.* hand-to-hand

рукопись [rōō-ka-p'is'] *sf.* manuscript

рукоплескать [rōō-ka-plyes-kāt'] *vi.* to applaud, clap

рукопожатие [rōō-ka-pa-zhā-tye] *sn.* hand-clasp

рукополагать [rōō-ka-pa-la-gāt'] (рукоположить) *vt.* to ordain

рукоположение [rōō-ka-pa-la-zhé-nye] *sn.* ordination

рукотворный [rōō-ka-tvór-nǎy] *adj.* artificial

рукоятка [rōō-ka-yāt-ka] *sf.* handle; haft; hilt

рулевой [rōō-lye-vóy] *adj.* as *sm.* helmsman, pilot, steersman; **рулевое колесо** [rōō-lye-vó-ye ka-lye-só] helm

рулетка [rōō-lyét-ka] *sf.* roulette; tape-measure

руль [rōōl'] *sm.* rudder; **сила руля** [s'ē-la rōō-lyá] steerage

румын [rōō-mǎn] *sm.* ; **-ка**, *sf.* Rumanian

румынский [rōō-mǎn-ski] *adj.* Rumanian

румяна [rōō-myā-na] *sf.* rouge

румянец [rōō-myā-nyets] *sm.* natural complexion

румянить [rōō-mya-n'ět'] *vt.* to rouge; to paint red

румяный [rōō-myān-nǎy] *adj.* rosy, ruddy

рундук [rōōn-dōōk] *sm.* locker

руно [rōō-nó] *sn.* fleece, wool; shoal

рунный [rōōn-nǎy] *adj.* fleecy

рупор [rōō-pŏr] *sm.* megaphone, speaking tube

русак [rōō-sǎk] *sm.* grey hare

русалка [rōō-sǎl-ka] *sf.* water-nymph

русло [rōō-sló] *sn.* bed (*of river*); channel; waterway

русский [rōōs-ski] *sm.*, **русская** [rōōs-ska-ya] *sf.* Russian; *adj.* Russian

русый [rōō-sǎy] *adj.* blond, fair

рутина [rōō-t'ē-na] *sf.* routine; groove

рухлядь [rōōch-lyǎd'] *sf.* lumber

рухнуть [rōōch-nōōt'] *vi.* to crash, tumble; to destroy, thwart

ручательство [rōō-chā-tyel'-stvŏ] *sn.* bail, guaranty, voucher, warrant

ручаться [rōō-chāt'-sya]

(поручиться) *vt.i.* to guarantee, pledge, warrant

ручей [rōō-chéy] *sm.* brook, stream

ручища [rōō-chē-shcha] *sf.* heavy (*huge*) hand

ручка [rōōch-ka] *sf.* tiny hand; handle, knob; chair arm; penholder

ручной [rōōch-nóy] *adj.* hand-made; manual; domesticated, tame

рушиться [rōō-shět'-sya] *vi.* to crumble, fall in; to collapse

рыба [rǎ-ba] *sf.* fish

рыбак [rǎ-bǎk] *sm.* fishmonger [torial]

рыбный [rǎb-nǎy] *adj.* piscatorial

рыбоводство [rǎ-ba-vód-stvŏ] *sn.* pisciculture

рыболов [rǎ-ba-lóv] *sm.* angler; fisherman; **-ство** [-stvŏ] *sn.* fishery

рыгать [rǎ-gǎt'] (рыгнуть) *vi.* to belch

рыдать [rǎ-dǎt'] *vi.* to sob

рыжеватый [rǎ-zhe-vǎ-tǎy] *adj.* somewhat gingery (*of hair, complexion*)

рыжеть [rǎ-zhét'] *vi.* to become rust-coloured

рыжий [rǎ-zhi] *adj.* gingery, red-haired

рыжик [rǎzhik] *sm.* brown mushroom

рыкать [rǎ-kǎt'] (рыкнуть) *vi.* to roar

рыло [rǎ-la] *sn.* snout

рыльце [rǎl'-tsyé] *sn.* spout; *bot.* stigma

рынок [rǎ-nók] *sm.* market, market-place

рысак [rǎ-sǎk] *sm.* trotter

рысистый [rǎ-s'ēs-tǎy] *adj.* fleet, rapid

рысь [răs] *sf.* lynx; trot

рытвина [rắt-v'i-na] *sf.* groove, ravine, rut

рыть [rắt'] (по-) *vt.* to burrow, hollow out; to ransack

рыхлый [rắch-lăy] *adj.* crumbly, mellow; pasty (*of complexion*)

рыцарство [rắ-tsar-stvŏ] *sn.* knighthood

рыцарь [rắ-tsar'] *sm.* knight

рычаг [ră-chăg] *sm.* jack; lever

рычать [ră-chăt'] *vi.* to growl, snarl

рюмка [ryōōm-ka] *sf.* liqueur glass

рюшь [ryōōsh] *sf.* quilling, ruche

рябина [rya-b'ē-na] *sf.* mountain-ash

рябить [rya-b'ĕt'] *vt.* to curl, ruffle

рябой [rya-bóy] *adj.* speckled, spotted

рябчик [ryăb-chik] *sm.* wood-grouse

рябь [ryab'] *sf.* ripple, rippling

ряд [ryăd] *sm.* file, line, range, row; rank; **-ами** [ā-mi] in rows, in sets; **торговые ряды** [tar-gó-vă-ye ă] market stalls

рядить [rya-d'ēt'] *vt.* to engage, hire; to dress up

рядовой [rya-da-vóy] *adj.* common-place, ordinary; *as sm. mil.* private; **рядовые солдаты** [rya-da-vă-ye sal-dă-tă] rank and file

рядом [ryā-dŏm] *adv.* a-breast, alongside; side by side

ряса [ryā-sa] *sf.* cassock

C

с, со [s, sŏ] *prep.* with; from, since

сабля [săb-lya] *sf.* sabre, sword

саботировать [sa-ba-t'ē-ra-vat'] *vt.* to sabotage

сабур [sa-bōōr] *sm.* aloes

саван [sa-văn] *sm.* shroud

саванна [sa-văn-na] *sf.* prairie

саго [să-gŏ] *sn.* sago

сад [săd] *sm.* garden; **-ик** [-'ik] *sm.* small garden

садить [sa-d'ĕt] (по-) *vt.* to plant, put, set; **-ся** [-sya] *vi.* to sit down; to mount (*a horse, etc.*); to shrink (*of material*); to settle (*of dust, etc.*); to set, sink (*of sun*)

садка [săd-ka] *sf.* planting, plantation

садовник [sa-dóv-n'ik] *sm.* gardener

садовый [sa-da-vód] *sm.* horticulturist; **-ство** [-stvŏ] *sn.* gardening, horticulture

садок [sa-dók] *sm.* fish-pond; oyster-bank; warren

сажа [să-zha] *sf.* smut, soot

сажать [sa-zhăt'] *vt.* to seat; to set

сазан [sa-zăn] *sm.* carp

сайга [săy-ga] *sf.* antelope

сак [săk] *sm.* bag

саквояж [sak-va-yăzh] *sm.* handbag, travelling-bag

салазки [sa-lăz-ki] *sf. pl.* toboggan; small sleigh

салака [sa-lă-ka] *sf.* sprat

салат [sa-lăt] *sm.* lettuce; salad

салатник [sa-lãt-n'ik] *sm.* salad-bowl

сало [sã-lõ] *sn.* fat, grease; lard; suet; tallow

салон [sa-lõn] *sm.* drawing-room

салфетка [sal-fyét-ka] *sf.* napkin, serviette

сальный [sãl'-năy] *adj.* greasy; *fig.* obscene

сам [sãm] *sm.* self, himself

самец [să-myets] *sm.* male; самка [sãm-ka] *sf.* female (*of animals*)

самобытный [sa-ma-bãt-năy] *adj.* original

само- [să-mõ-] *prefix*, auto-, self-, *etc.*

самовар [sa-ma-vãr] *sm.* Russian tea-urn ('self-boiler')

самовластный [sa-ma-vlãst-năy] *adj.* absolute, autocratic, despotic

самовнушение [sa-ma-vnŏŏ-shé-nye] *sn.* autosuggestion

самовольный [sa-ma-võl'-năy] *adj.* arbitrary; wilful

самовосхваление [sa-ma-vos-chva-lyé-nye] *sn.* boasting, vainglory

самодействующий [sa-ma-dyéy-stvŏŏ-yŏŏ-shchi] *adj.* automatic

самодельщина [sa-ma-dyél'-shchi-na] *sf.* roughly-made goods

самодержавие [sa-ma-dyer-zhã-vye] *sn.* autocracy

самодовольный [sa-ma-da-võl'-năy] *adj.* conceited, self-satisfied; smug; *coll.* swollen-headed

самодурство [sa-ma-dŏŏr-stvõ] *sn.* stubbornness, wilfulness.

самозащита [sa-ma-za-shchế-ta] *sf.* self-defence

самозванец [sa-ma-zvã-nyets] *sm.* impostor, usurper

самокат [sa-ma-kãt] *sm.* bicycle

самолёт [sa-ma-lyót] *sm.* aeroplane

самолично [sa-ma-l'êch-nŏ] *adv.* personally

самолюбие [sa-ma-lyŏŏ-bye] *sn.* self-esteem, pride

самомнение [sa-ma-mnyé-nye] *sn.* conceit

самонадеянность [sa-ma-na-dyé-yan-nŏst'] *sf.* presumption; self-confidence

самообожание [sa-ma-aba-zhã-nye] *sn.* self-adoration

самообразование [sa-ma-abra-za-vã-nye] *sn.* self-education

самоотверженность [sa-ma-at-vyér-zhen-nŏst'] *sf.* abnegation, self-denial

самоотверженный [sa-ma-at-vyér-zhen-năy] *adj.* unselfish

самоотречение [sa-ma-at-rye-ché-nye] *sn.* renunciation

самоохрана [sa-ma-a-chrã-na] *sf.* self-preservation

самопомощь [sa-ma-pŏ-mŏshch'] *sf.* self-help

самопроизвольно [sa-ma-pra-iz-võl'-nŏ] *adv.* spontaneously; voluntarily

самопрялка [sa-ma-pryãl-ka] *sf.* spinning-wheel

самородный [sa-ma-rŏd-năy] *adj.* native, virgin (*ore*)

самостоятельный [sa-ma-sta-yã-tyel'-năy] *adj.* independent

самоубийство [sa-ma-ŏŏ-bêst-vŏ] *sn.* suicide

самоуважение [sa-ma-oō-va-zhé-nye] sn. self-respect

самоуверенный [sa-ma-oō-vye-ren-nǎy] adj. assured, self-reliant; coll. bumptious

самоуправление [sa-ma-oō-prav-lyé-nye] sn. self-government; pol. Home Rule

самоучитель [sa-ma-oō-chē-tyel'] sm. self-instructor (book)

самоучка [sa-ma-oōch-ka] sm., f. self-taught person

самохвал [sa-ma-chvál] sm. braggart

самый [sá-mǎy] pron. same; most; adv. very

сан [sǎn] sm. relig. order; dignity

сани [sá-n'i] sf. pl. sledge, sleigh

санитар [sa-n'i-tár] sm. male nurse, orderly

санитарный [sa-n'i-tár-nǎy] adj. sanitary

санкция [sǎnk-tsya] sf. assent, sanction

сановитый [sa-na-v'ē-tǎy] adj. majestic, stately

сановник [sa-nóv-n'ik] sm. dignitary

сапёр [sa-pyór] sm. sapper

сапог [sa-póg] sm. boot

сапожник [sa-pōzh-n'ik] sm. bootmaker

сапожничество [sa-pōzh-n'i-chest-vó] sn. bootmaking

сапфир [sap-fēr] sm. sapphire

сарай [sa-rǎy] sm. shed; **товарный –** [ta-vár-nǎy –] goods-yard

саранча [sa-ran-chá] sf. grasshopper

сардинка [sar-d'ēn-ka] sf. sardine

саржа [sár-zha] sf. serge

сатанинский [sa-ta-n'ēn-ski] adj. satanic

сатира [sa-tē-ra] sf. satire

сахар [sá-char] sm. sugar; **-ный** [-nǎy] adj. sugar-, sugary

сахарница [sá-char-n'i-tsa] sf. sugar-basin

сачок [sa-chók] sm. fishing-net

сбавка [zbáv-ka] sf. abatement, cut, reduction

сбавлять [zbav-lyát'] (сбавить) vt. to decrease, lower, reduce

сбегать [zbye-gát'] (сбежáть) vi. to run along; to elope; to run away

сбегать [zbyé-gat'] vi. to hasten

сбежаться [zbye-zhát'-sya] vi. to come running; to crowd, flock

сберегать [zbye-re-gát'] (сберéчь) vt. to conserve, to reserve, to save

сбережения [zbye-re-zhé-nya] sn. pl. savings

сбивать [zbi-vát'] (сбить) vt. to knock down; to knock off; to churn

сбивка [zb'ēv-ka] sf. churning, whipping

сбивчивый [zb'ēv-chi-vǎy] adj. confused, indistinct

сближать [zbl'i-zhát'] (сблизить) vt. to bind, connect; to draw together; to compare; **-ся** [-sya] vi. to become friendly

сближение [zbl'i-zhé-nye] sn. accord; reconciliation

сбоку [zbó-koō] adv. sideways

сбор [zbor] sm. assemblage, gathering; collection; yield

сборище [zbó-ri-shche] *sn.* jumble; medley; reduction

сборка [zbór-ka] *sf.* assembling, fitting; fold, tuck

сборник [zbor'n'ik] *sm.* collection *of articles, cuttings, literary works)*

сборный [zbór-năy] *adj.* miscellaneous

сборщик [zbór-shchik] *sm.* collector; fitter; roundsman

сбрасывать [zbrá-sa-vat'] (сбросить) *vt.* to discard, throw down

сбривать [zbr'i-vát'] (сбрить) *vt.* to shave off

сброд [zbrod] *sm.* rabble; gang of ruffians

сбруя [zbroo-ya] *sf.* harness

сбывать [zbá-vat'] (сбыть) *vt.* to dispose, sell off

сбыт [zbăt] *sm.* market, sale

сбыточный [zbá-tach-năy] *adj.* feasible, probable

свадебный [svá-dyeb-năy] *adj.* bridal, marriage-, nuptial

свадьба [svád'-ba] *sf.* marriage, wedding

сваебойная машина [sva-ye-bóy-na-ya ma-shé-na] *sf.* pile-driver

сваливать [svá-l'i-vat'] (свалить) *vt.* to hurl, **-ся** [-sya] *vi.* to fall off, tumble down

свалка [svál-ka] *sf.* scramble

сварка [svár-ka] *sf.* weld

сварливый [svar-l'é-văy]*adj.* cantankerous; **сварливая женщина** [svar-l'é-va-ya zhén-shchi-na] *sf.* shrew

сват [svát] *sm.* match-maker; *(the father of one's son-or daughter-in-law is called* сват)

сватовство [sva-tav-stvó] *sn.* courting, match-making

свая [svá-ya] *sf.* pile, stake

сведение [svyé-dye-nye] *sn.* information; knowledge

сведение [svye-dyé-nye] *sn.* contraction, cramp; reduction

сведущий [svyé-dŏo-shchi] *adj.* adept, conversant, versed

свежевать [svye-zhe-vát'] *vt.* to dress, flay, skin

свежесть [svyé-zhest'] *sf.* coolness; freshness

свежеть [svye-zhét'] *vi.* to freshen

свежий [svyé-zhi] *adj.* breezy, cool, crisp; fresh *(of food)*; recent *(of news)*

свёкла [svyók-la] *sf.* beetroot

свёкор [svyó-kŏr] *sm.* father-in-law *(husband's father)*

свекровь [svye-króv'] *sf.* mother-in-law *(husband's mother)* [itch

свербеть [svyer-byét'] *vi.* to

свербёж [svyer-byózh] *sm.* itching

свергать [svyer-gát'] (свергнуть) *vt.* to cast down; overthrow; to precipitate

сверка [svyér-ka] *sf.* collation, revise; verification

сверкание [svyer-ká-nye] *sn.* glitter, sparkle

сверление [svyer-lyé-nye] *sn.* boring, drilling

свёрток [svyór-tŏk] *sm.* package, packet, roll

свёртывать [svyór-tă-vat'] (свернуть) *vt.* to roll, wrap up

сверх [svyérch] *prep.* above, beyond, over

сверху [svyér-chŏo] *adv.* at the top, from above, uppermost сверхурочный [svyerch-ōō-róch-năy] *adj.* overtime

сверхштатный [svyerch-shtát-năy] *adj.* supernumerary

сверхъестественный [svyerch-yes-tyést-vyen-năy] *adj.* supernatural

сверчок [svyer-chók] *sm.* cricket (*insect*)

свершать [svyer-shát] (свершить) *vt.* to accomplish, achieve, complete

свершилось! [svyer-shē-los] it is accomplished! it is done! it has occurred!

сверять [svye-ryát] (сверить) *vt.* to adjust; to compare; to regulate

свет [svyet] *sm.* daylight, light; world

светать [svyetát] *vi.* to dawn

светёлка [svye-tyól-ka] *sf.* attic

светик [svye-t'ik] *sm. coll.* darling, pet

светило [svye-t'ĕ-lŏ] *sn.* luminary

светильня [svye-t'ĕl'-nya] *sf.* wick

светить [svye-t'ĕt'] *vi.* to shine

светлый [svyét-lăy] *adj.* bright, light, luminous; clear, lucid

светляк [svyet-lyák] *sm.* glow-worm

светосила [svyeta-s'ĕla] *sf.* candle-power

светотени [svye-ta-tyé-n'i] *sf. pl.* light and shade

светоч [svye-tóch] *sm.* torch

светский [svyét-ski] *adj.* lay, secular, temporal; mundane; fashionable

свечение [svye-ché-nye] *sn.* glint, shimmer(ing)

свечка [svyéch-ka] *sf.* candle; запальная – [za-pál'-na-ya –] sparking-plug

свешивать [svye-shi-vat'] (свесить) *vt.* to weigh; to hang down

свивать [sv'i-vát] (свить) *vt.* to coil, wind; to wreathe

свидание [sv'i-dá-nye] *sn.* appointment, meeting; до свидания [da-sv'i-dá-nya] au revoir, goodbye

свидетель [sv'i-dyé-tyel'] *sm.* witness

свидетельство [sv'i-dyé-tyel'-stvŏ] *sn.* evidence, testimony; certificate, testimonial

свидетельствовать [sv'i-dyé-tyel'-stva-vat'] *vt.* to attest; to testify; to witness

свинарник [sv'i-nár-n'ik] *sm.* pigsty

свинец [sv'i-nyéts] *sm.* lead

свинина [sv'i-n'ĕ-na] *sf.* pork

свинка [sv'ĕn-ka] *sf.* mumps; pig (*iron*); морская – [mar-ská-ya –] guinea-pig

свиноводство [sv'i-na-vód-stvŏ] *sn.* pig-keeping

свинский [sv'ĕn-ski] *adj.* piggish

свинство [sv'ĕn-stvŏ] *sn.* piggishness; dirt, filth

свинцовка [sv'in-tsóv-ka] *sf.* plumbago

свинчивать [sv'in-chi-vat'] (свинтить) *vt.* to fasten with screws

свинья [sv'i-nyá] *sf.* hog, pig, sow, swine

свирель [sv'i-ryél'] *sf.* reed-pipe

свирепость [sv'i-ryé-pŏst'] *sf.* fierceness, violence

свирепый [sv'i-ryé-pǎy] *adj.* ferocious, truculent

свисать [sv'i-sát'] (свис-нуть) *vi.* to dangle, hang down; to slouch; to trail (*as plants*)

свислый [sv'ēs-lǎy] *adj.* drooping, hanging

свист [sv'ēst] *sm.* whistle, whistling

свистать [sv'is-tát'] (свис-теть) *vi.* to whistle; to pipe (*of birds*); to sing (*of wind*)

свисток [sv'is-tók] *sm.* whistle (*instrument*)

свистулька [sv'is-tōōl'-ka] *sf.* tin-whistle

свистун [sv'is-tōōn] *sm.* whistler

свистящий [sv'i-styǎ-shchi] *adj.* sibilant

свита [sv'ē-ta] *sf.* escort, retinue, suite

свиток [sv'ē-tŏk] *sm.* roll, scroll

свихнуть [sv'ich-nōōt'] *vt.* to dislocate, sprain

свищ [sv'ēshch] *sm.* fistula

свобода [sva-bō-da] *sf.* freedom, liberty

свободный [sva-bód-nǎy] *adj.* free; exempt

свободомыслие [sva-ba-da-mǎs-lye] *sn.* free-think-ing; liberalism

свободомыслящий [sva-ba-da-mǎs-lyǎ-shchi] *adj.* liberal (*views, etc.*); *as sm.* free-thinker

свод [svod] *sm.* arch, cove, vault; code; **небесное** – [nye-byés-nay –] firmament

сводить [sva-d'ēt'] *vt.* to pay off, square up; to get together

сводка [svód-ka] *sf.* summary; *typ.* revise [curer

сводник [svód-n'ik] *sm.* procurer

сводничать [svód-n'i-chat'] *vi.* to procure

сводный [svód-nǎy] *adj.* combined, compound; – **брат** [–brát] *sm.* step-brother

своевольный [sva-ye-vól'-nǎy] *adj.* headstrong, high-handed, wilful

своевременный [sva-ye-vryé-myen-nǎy] *adj.* opportune, timely; seasonable

своекорыстие [sva-ye-ka-rǎs-tye] *sn.* cupidity

своенравие [sva-ye-nrá-vye] *sn.* wilfulness

своеобразие [sva-ye-a-brá-zye] *sn.* eccentricity, originality

свозить [sva-z'ēt'] (свезти) *vt.* to carry, convey

свозка [svóz-ka] *sf.* carting, conveying, removal

свой [svóy] *pron.* one's own

свойственник [svóy-stven-n'ik] *sm.* relation; relative (*by marriage*)

свойство [svóy-stvó] *sn.* attribute, virtue; **целебное** – [tsye-lyéb-na-ye –] healing property

свойство [svay-stvó] *sn.* affinity, relationship (*by marriage*)

сволочь [svó-lach'] *sf.* rogue, villain; mob, rabble

свора [svó-ra] *sf.* leash; pack (*dogs*)

сворачивать [sva-rá-chi-vat'] (своротить) *vt.* to dislodge, remove; to shunt

сворить [svó-r'it'] *vt.* to leash

свояк [sva-yák] *sm.* brother-in-law

свояченица [sva-yā-che-n'i-tsa] *sf.* sister-in-law

свыкаться [svă-kát-sya] (свыкнуться) *vi.* to become accustomed, get used to

свысока [svă-sa-ká] *adv.* from above; condescendingly

свыше [své-she] *adv.* above, beyond, upwards

связанный [svyā-zan-năy] *adj.* bound, linked, tied

связка [svyáz-ka] *sf.* bundle, pack, sheaf; ligament; *gram.* copula

связный [svyáz-năy] *adj.* coherent, connected

связывать [svyā-ză-vat'] (связать) *vt.* to bind, tie

связь [svyáz'] *sf.* bond, junction, tie; communication; liaison

святилище [svya-t'ē-l'i-shche] *sn.* sanctuary

святитель [svya-t'ē-tyel'] *sm.* prelate

святить [svya-t'ét] (o-) *vt.* to consecrate; to sanctify

святки [svyát-ki] *sf. pl.* Yuletide

святой [svya-tóy] *adj.* holy, sacred, saintly; *sm.* saint

святотатство [svya-ta-tát-stvó] *sn.* sacrilege

святоша [svya-tó-sha] *sm., f.* hypocrite, sanctimonious individual

святцы [svyát-tsă] *sm. pl.* ecclesiastical calendar

святыня [svya-tă-nya] *sf.* holy object; shrine

священник [svya-shchén-n'ik] *sm.* clergyman, priest; chaplain

священнодействие [svya-shchen-na-dyéy-stvye] *sn.* celebration of divine service

священный [svya-shchén-năy] *adj.* consecrated, holy

священство [svya-shchen-stvó] *sn.* clergy; priesthood

сгиб [zgib] *sm.* curve, bend; flexion

сгибать [zgi-bát'] (согнуть) *vt.* to bend, curve

сгинуть [zgē-nōōt'] *vi.* to disappear, vanish

сглаживать [zglā-zhi-vat'] (сгладить) *vt.* to level out, press, smooth

сглупить [zglōō-p'ét'] *vi.* to blunder; to act foolishly

сгнивать [zgn'i-vát'] (сгнить) *vi.* to putrefy, rot

сговариваться [zga-vā-r'i-vat'-sya] *vi.* to conspire; to concert; to make arrangements

сговор [zgó-vŏr] *sm.* betrothal; agreement; engagement

сговорчивый [zga-vór-chi-văy] *adj.* accommodating, compliant, willing

сгонять [zga-nyát'] (согнать) *vt.* to chase, drive away, round up

сгораемый [zga-rā-ye-măy] *adj.* combustible, inflammable

сгорание [zga-rā-nye] *sn.* combustion

сгорать [zga-rāt'] (сгореть) *vi.* to burn out; to be consumed

сгорбиться [zgar-b'ét'-sya] *vi.* to slouch, stoop

сгоряча [zga-rya-chā] *adv.* angrily; passionately; rashly

сгребание [zgrye-bā-nye] *sn.* raking

сгружать [zgrōō-zhāt'] (сгрузить) *vt.* to unload

сгуститель [zgōō-st'ē-tyel'] *sm.* condenser

сгусток [zgōōs-tŏk] *sm.* clot

сгущать [zgōō-shchāt'] (сгустить) *vt.* to condense, thicken; to compress

сгущение [zgōō-shchē-nye] *sn.* coagulation, condensation; compression

сдабривать [zdā-br'i-vat'] (сдобрить) *vt.* to improve the taste, enrich a dish or pastry; to season

сдавать [zda-vāt'] (сдать) *vt.* to check (luggage); to deal (cards); to give up; to lease; to rent (house); -ся [-sya] *vi.* to surrender, yield

сдавливать [zdā-vl'i-vat'] (сдавить) *vt.* to press, squash, squeeze

сдача [zdā-cha] *sf.* small change; *mil.* cession, surrender

сдваивать [zdvā-i-vat'] *vt.* to double

сдвиг [zdv'ĕg] *sm.* dislocation, displacement; *fig.* upheaval (social)

сдвигать [zdv'i-gāt'] (сдвинуть) *vt.* to displace, move, remove; to close up

сделать [zdē-lat'] *vt.* to do, make, manufacture

сделка [zdyél-ka] *sf.* agreement, settlement, transaction; *coll.* bargain, deal

сдельщик [zdyél'-shchik] *sm.* piece-worker

сдёргивать [zdyór-gi-vat'] (сдёрнуть) *vt.* to pull down, tear off

сдержанный [zdyér-zhan-nāy] *adj.* demure, modest, reserved

сдерживать [zdyér-zhi-vat'] (сдержать) *vt.* to check, restrain; *fig.* to curb, repress

сдирать [zd'i-rāt'] (содрать) *vt.* to flay, skin, strip

сдружиться [zdrōō-zhēt'-sya] *vi.* to strike up a friendship

сдувать [zdōō-vāt'] (сдуть) *vt.* to blow away; to foist

сдурить [zdōō-r'ēt'] *vi.* to act stupidly

сдуру [zdōō-rōō] *adv.* foolishly

себя [sye-byā] *pron.* oneself; myself, himself, *etc.*

себялюбие [sye-bya-lyōō-bye] *sn.* egoism

себялюбивый [sye-bya-lyōō-b'ĕ-vāy] *adj.* egoistic, selfish

сев [syév] *sm.* sowing

север [syé-vyer] *sm.* north; **-ный** [-nāy] *adj.* northern; **-янин** [-yä-n'in] *sm.* northerner

севрюга [sye-vryōō-ga] *sf.* sturgeon

сегодня [sye-vód-nya] *adv.* today; **-шний** [-shn'i] *adj.* today's, present

седалище [sye-dā-l'i-shche] *sn.* seat

седалищный [sye-dā-l'ishch-nāy] *adj.* sciatic

седёлка [sye-dyól-ka] *sf.* saddle-strap

седельник [sye-dyél'-n'ik] *sm.* saddler

седеть [sye-dyét'] (по-) *vi.* to turn grey

седина [sye-d'i-nā] *sf.* grey hair

седлать [syed-lát'] vt. to saddle

седло [syed-ló] sn. saddle

седой [sye-dóy] adj. grey (of hair)

седок [sye-dók] sm. horseman, rider; passenger

седьмой [syed'-móy] num. seventh

сезон [sye-zón] sm. season; -ный [-náy] adj. seasonal

сей [syéy] pron. this

сейчас [syey-chás] adv. immediately, now

секрет [sye-krét] sm. secret; -ный [-náy] adj. confidential, secret

секретарство [sye-kre-tár-stvŏ] sn. secretaryship

секретарь [sye-kre-tár'] sm. secretary

секретка [sye-krét-ka] sf. letter-card

секунда [sye-kŏón-da] sf. second

секундомер [sye-kŏón-da-myér] sm. stop-watch

секция [syék-tsya] sf. section

селёдка [sye-lyód-ka] sf. herring; копчёная – [kap-chó-na-ya –] bloater, red herring

селезёнка [sye-lye-zyón-ka] sf. anat. spleen

селезень [syé-lye-zyen'] sm. drake [selection

селекция [sye-lyék-tsya] sf.

селение [sye-lyé-nye] sn. settlement; village

селитра [sye-l'ét-ra] sf. saltpetre

селить [sye-l'ét'] vt. to colonize, settle

село [sye-ló] sn. village

сельдерей [syel'-dye-réy] sm. celery

сельдь [syel'd'] sf. herring

сельский [syél'-ski] adj. rural

сельскохозяйственный [syel'-ska-cha-zyáy-stvyen-náy] adj. agricultural, farming

сельцо [syel'-tsó] sn. hamlet

сёмга [syóm-ga] sf. salmon

семейный [sye-myéy-náy] adj. domestic, of household

семейство [sye-myéy-stvŏ] sn. family, household

семестр [sye-myéstr] sm. term (school, etc.)

семинария [sye-mi-ná-rya] sf. seminary

семнадцатый [syem-nád-tsa-táy] num. seventeenth

семнадцать [syem-nád-tsat'] num. seventeen

семь [syem] num. seven

семьдесят [syem'-dye-syät] num. seventy

семьсот [syem'-sót] num. seven-hundred

семья [sye-myá] sf. family, household

семьянин [sye-mya-n'én] sm. family man

семя [syé-mya] sn. grain, seed

сенник [syen-n'ék] sm. straw mattress

сено [syé-nŏ] sn. hay

сеновал [sye-na-vál] sm. hayloft

сенокос [sye-na-kós] sm. mowing

сенокосилка [sye-na-ka-s'ól-ka] sf. mower

сентябрь [syen-tyábr] sm. September

сень [syén'] sf. canopy; fig. protection, shelter

сера [syé-ra] sf. brimstone, sulphur

серб [syérb] *sm.* Serb; **-ский** [-ski] *adj.* Serbian

сервиз [syer-v'éz] *sm.* set, service (*dinner, tea, etc.*)

сердечник [syer-dyéch-n'ik] *sm.* core

сердечность [syer-dyéch-nŏst'] *sf.* cordiality, friendliness

сердечный [syer-dyéch-näy] *adj.* cordial, hearty; cardiac

сердитый [syer-d'é-täy] *adj.* angry, cross

сердить [syer-d'ét] (рас-) *vt.* to anger, irritate, vex; **-ся** [-sya] *vi.* to become angry, take offence

сердоболие [syer-da-bó-lye] *sn.* compassion, pity

сердце [syérd-tse] *sn.* heart

сердцебиение [syerd-tse-b'i-yé-nye] *sn.* palpitation

сердцевидный [syerd-tse-v'éd-näy] *adj.* heart-shaped

сердцевина [syerd-tse-v'é-na] *sf.* core, heart; pith

серебрение [sye-re-bré-nye] *sn.* silver-plating

серебристый [sye-re-brés-täy] *adj.* silvery

серебрить [sye-re-br'ét] (по-) *vt.* to silver

серебро [sye-re-bró] *sn.* silver

серебряный [sye-ré-brya-näy] *adj.* silvery, of silver

середина [sye-re-d'é-na] *sf.* middle, midst; centre

серёжка [sye-ryózh-ka] *sf.* earring; catkin; wattle

сереть [sye-ryét] (по-) *vi.* to become grey

серия [sé-rya] *sf.* series, set

сермяжина [syer-myá-zhi-na] *sf.* drab, rough material; smock-frock

серна [syér-na] *sf.* chamois

сернистый [syer-n'és-täy] *adj.* sulphureous

серобурый [sye-ra-bōō-räy] *adj.* greyish-brown

сероватый [sye-ra-vá-täy] *adj.* greyish

серопегий [sye-ra-pyé-gi] *adj.* piebald

серость [sýe-rast'] *sf.* greyness

серп [syérp] *sm.* sickle; reaping-hook

серповидный [syer-pa-v'éd-näy] *adj.* crescent-shaped

серсо [syer-só] *sn.* hoop

серый [sýe-räy] *adj.* grey; *fig.* coarse, ignorant

серьёзность [sye-ryóz-nŏst'] *sf.* gravity, seriousness

серьёзный [sye-ryóz-näy] *adj.* earnest, serious

сессия [syés-sya] *sf.* session, sitting

сестра [syes-trá] *sf.* sister; **двоюродная —** [dva-yōō-rad-na-ya —] cousin; **—милосердия** [— m'i-la-syér-dya] trained nurse

сетка [syét-ka] *sf.* net; rack; **калильная —** [ka-l'él'-na-ya —] gas-mantle

сетовать [sye-ta-vát'] *vi.* to complain; to deplore; to grieve

сеть [syet'] *sf.* net, netting; mesh

сеча [sýe-cha] *sf.* slaughter

сечение [sye-ché-nye] *sn.* thrashing, whipping; cutting up; section

сечка [sýech-ka] *sf.* chopper, cleaver; chaff

сечь [syéch'] (вы-) *vt.* to beat, flog, thrash; to chop, mince; **-ся** [-sya] *vi.* to cut, split

сеялка [syé-yal-ka] *sf.* drill; seed-sowing machine

сеятель [syé-ya-tyel'] *sm.* sower

сеять [syé-yat'] (по-) *vt.* to drill; to sow

сжалиться [zzhā-l'it'-sya] *vt.* to pity; to have compassion on

сжатие [zzhā-tye] *sn.* compression, condensation; grasp, grip; jamming; shrinkage; tightening

сжатость [zzhā-tóst'] *sf.* conciseness

сживаться [zzhi-vāt'-sya] *vi.* to get used to; to make oneself at home

сжигание [zzhi-gā-nye] *sn.* burning up; cremation; incineration

сжигать [zzhi-gāt'] (сжечь) *vt.* to burn up, consume

сжимать [zzhi-māt'] (сжать) *vt.* to contract, press, squeeze

сзади [zzā-d'i] *adv.* behind, from behind; at the rear

си [sē] *sn. mus.* B

сибирский [s'i-bēr-ski] *adj.* Siberian

сибиряк [s'i-b'i-ryāk] *sm.* Siberian

сигара [s'i-gā-ra] *sf.* cigar

сигаретка [s'i-ga-ryét-ka] *sf.* cigarette

сигарочница [s'i-gā-rach-n'i-tsa] *sf.* cigar-case

сигнатура [sig-na-tōō-ra] *sf. typ.* signature

сиделец [s'i-dyé-lyets] *sm.* barman, tapster

сиделка [s'i-dyél-ka] *sf.* sick-nurse

сиденье [s'i-dyé-nye] *sn.* folding chair, seat; pillion

сидеть [s'i-dyét'] *vi.* to sit

сидр [s'ēdr] *sm.* cider

сидячий [si-dyā-chi] *adj.* sedentary

сизый [sē-zǎy] *adj.* greyish-blue

сила [s'ē-la] *sf.* force, strength, vigour

силач [s'i-lāch] *sm.* strong man; athlete

силиться [s'ē-l'it'-sya] *vi.* to strive, try; to endeavour

силовая станция [s'i-la-vā-ya stān-tsya] *sf.* power-station

силок [s'i-lók] *sm.* noose, snare, trap

силуэт [si-lōō-et] *sm.* silhouette

сильный [s'ēl'-nǎy] *adj.* powerful, strong, vigorous; keen; severe, violent

символ [s'ēm-vól] *sm.* emblem, symbol

симметрия [s'im-mé-trya] *sf.* symmetry

симпатический [s'im-pa-t'ē-ches-ki] *adj.* sympathetic

симпатичный [s'im-pa-t'ēch-nǎy] *adj.* genial, kind, likeable

синдикат [s'in-d'i-kāt] *sm.* syndicate

синеватый [s'i-nye-vā-tǎy] *adj.* bluish

синий [s'ē-n'i] *adj.* dark blue

синить [s'i-n'ēt'] *vt.* to blue

синица [s'i-n'ē-tsa] *sf.* tomtit

синь [s'ēn'] *sf.* blue colour **-ка** *sf.* blu(e)ing; blueprint

синяк [s'i-nyāk] *sm.* bruise; wale, weal

сип [s'ēp] *sm.* griffin; hoarseness

сиплый [s'ēp-lǎy] *adj.* hoarse, husky

сирена [s'i-ryé-na] *sf.* hooter, siren; mermaid

сирень [s'i-ryén'] *sf.* lilac

сироп [s'i-róp] *sm.* syrup

сирота [s'i-ra-tá] *sf., sm.* orphan

система [s'is-tyé-ma] *sf.* method, system

систематический [s'is-tye-ma-t'é-ches-ki] *adj.* systematic

ситец [s'é-tyets] *sm.* calico; chintz; cotton

ситник [s'ét-n'ik] *sm.* bulrush; coarse bread

сито [s'é-tŏ] *sn.* sieve

сияние [s'i-yá-nye] *sn.* brightness, radiance

сиятельный [s'i-yá-tyel'-năy] *adj.* illustrious

сиять [s'i-yát'] (за-) *vi.* to gleam, shine, sparkle

сияющий [s'i-yă-yŏŏ-shchi] *adj.* beaming, radiant

скабрёзный [ska-bryóz-năy] *adj.* obscene

сказание [ska-zá-nye] *sn.* legend, narrative, story

сказать [ska-zát'] *vt.* to tell, say

сказка [skáz-ka] *sf.* fairy tale, short story

сказочник [ská-zach-n'ik] *sm.* raconteur, story-teller

сказочный [ská-zach-năy] *adj.* fantastic, legendary

сказуемое [ska-zŏŏ-ye-ma-ye] *adj. as sn.* predicate

сказывать [ská-ză-vat'] (сказа́ть) *vt.* to narrate, tell

скакалка [ska-kál-ka] *sf.* skipping-rope

скакание [ska-ká-nye] *sn.* hopping, skipping

скакать [ska-kát'] *vi.* to hop, jump, skip

скакун [ska-kŏŏn] *sm.* jumper, leaper

скала [ska-lá] *sf.* cliff, crag, rock

скала [ská-la] *sf.* barometric graduation; *mus.* scale

скалистый [ska-l'és-tăy] *adj.* craggy, rocky

скалка [skál-ka] *sf.* rolling-pin

скалывать [ska-lă-vat'] (сколо́ть) *vt.* to cleave, split; to trace, transfer; to pin

скамейка [ska-myéy-ka] *sf.* bench, long seat

скамеечка [ska-myé-yech-ka] *sf.* footstool

скамья [ska-myá] *sf.* bench, form

скандальный [skan-dál'-năy] *adj.* scandalous

скандирование [skan-d'é-ra-va-nye] *sn.* scansion

скапливать [ska-pl'i-vat'] *vt.* to collect, hoard

скарб [skárb] *sm.* household goods; *fig.* goods and chattels

скаредный [ska-ryed-năy] *adj.* grudging; stingy; odious

скат [skát] *sm.* skate (*fish*); declivity, slope

скатерть [ska-tyert'] *sf.* table-cloth

скатывать [ska-tă-vat'] (скати́ть) *vt.* to roll, slide

скачка [skách-ka] *sf.* horse-race

скачок [ska-chók] *sm.* jump, leap, spring

скашивать [ska-shi-vat'] *vt.* to mow down; to bevel, slope

скважина [skvá-zhi-na] *sf.* chink, slit; key-hole

скважистый [skvá-zhis-tăy] *adj.* porous

скверный [skvyér-năy] *adj.* bad, nasty

сквернословие [skvyer-na-sló-vye] *sn.* bad language, swearing

сквозной [skvaz-nóy] *adj.* transparent; – **ветер** [– vyé-tyer] *sm.* draught; – **поезд** [– pó-yezd] *sm.* through train

сквозь [skvoz'] *prep.* through

скворец [skva-ryéts] *sm.* starling

скелет [ske-lyét] *sm.* skeleton

скептический [skyep-t'é-ches-ki] *adj.* sceptical

скидка [sk'ěd-ka] *sf.* abatement, allowance, discount, rebate

скидывать [sk'ě-dă-vat'] (скидать) *vt.* to take off, throw off; to deduct, reduce

скиния [skē-nya] *sf.* tabernacle

скипидар [ski-p'i-dār] *sm.* turpentine

скирда [skir-dā] *sf.* hayrick, haystack

скисать [sk'i-sāt'] *vt.* to curdle, turn sour; *fig.* to be off colour

скит [sk'ět] *sm.* hermitage

скиталец [sk'i-tā-lyets] *sm.* rover, vagabond, wanderer

скитание [sk'i-tā-nye] *sn.* roaming, wandering

скитник [sk'ět-n'ik] *sm.* hermit, recluse

склад [sklād] *sm.* storeroom; warehouse; – **ума** [– ōō-mā] mentality

складка [sklād-ka] *sf.* crease, fold, tuck; wrinkle

складный [sklād-năy] *adj.* coherent, harmonious

складчина [sklād-chi-na] *sf.* contribution; pooling

складывать [sklā-dă-vat'] (сложить) *vt.* to double up; to put together; to pile up; to cancel; to furl

склеивать [sklyé-i-vat'] *vt.* to glue, paste together; -**ся** [-sya] *vi.* to stick

склеп [sklyép] *sm.* crypt; tomb; vault

склёпка [sklyóp-ka] *sf.* fastening, riveting

склёпывать [sklyó-pă-vat'] *vt.* to clench, rivet

склизкий [skl'ěz-ki] *adj.* slimy

скликать [sklē-kat'] (скликнуть) *vt.* to call together

склон [sklon] *sm.* side, slope; decline

склонение [skla-nyé-nye] *sn.* inclination; *gram.* declension

склонность [sklón-nŏst'] *sf.* inclination, proclivity, propensity, leaning; relish

склонный [sklón-năy] *adj.* disposed, inclined, prone

склоняемый [skla-nyā-ye-măy] *adj. gram.* declinable

склонять [skla-nyāt'] (склонить) *vt.* to bend, bow, incline, stoop; *gram.* to decline

склянка [sklyān-ka] *sf.* medicine bottle, flask, phial

скобка [skŏb-ka] *sf.* brace, clamp; boot-scraper; *typ.* bracket, parenthesis

скоблить [skab-l'ít'] *vt.* to file, scrape; to scarify

скобяные товары [ska-byā-nă-ye ta-vā-rĭ] *sm. pl.* ironware

сковка [skóv-ka] *sf.* welding

сковорода [ska-va-ra-dā] *sf.* frying pan

сковывать [skó-vă-vat'] (сковать) *vt.* to forge, weld

скок [skok] *sm.* jump, leap; **-ом** [-öm] by leaps and bounds

сколачивать [ska-lā-chi-vat'] (**сколотить**) *vt.* to join; to amass

сколок [skó-lŏk] *sm.* copy; facsimile, pattern

скольжение [skal'-zhé-nye] *sn.* gliding, sliding; skidding, slipping

скользить [skal'-z'ét'] (**скользнуть**) *vi.* to slide, slip, slither

скользкий [skól'-zki] *adj.* slippery

сколько [skól'-kŏ] *adv.* how much, how many; **-нибудь** [-n'i-bōōd'] just a little, slightly

скоморох [ska-ma-róch] *sm.* buffoon, clown

скоморошество [ska-ma-ró-shest-vŏ] *sn.* buffoonery, clowning

сконфузиться [skan-fōō-z'it'-sya] *vi.* to be confused; to lose one's bearings

скончаться [skan-chāt'-sya] *vi.* to die, expire

скоп [skop] *sm.* savings

скопец [ska-pyéts] *sm.* eunuch

скопидом [ska-p'i-dóm] *sm.* hoarder, miser

скопидомство [ska-p'i-dóm-stvŏ] *sn.* avarice, miserliness

скопище [skó-p'i-shche] *sn.* crowd, horde, mob

скопление [skap-lyé-nye] *sn.* accumulation; multitude; afflux

скорбеть [skar-byét'] *vi.* to deplore; grieve, mourn

скорбный [skórb-nāy] *adj.* afflicted, sorrowful; **- лист** [- l'ést] death-roll

скорбь [skorb'] *sf.* sorrow

скорлупа [skor-lōō-pā] *sf.* shell (of egg, nut, etc.)

скорняк [skar-nyāk] *sm.* furrier

скоро [skó-rŏ] *adv.* quickly, rapidly

скороговорка [sko-ro-ga-vór-ka] *sf.* patter

скоропалительный [sko-ro-pa-l'é-tyel'-nāy] *adj.* rash

скороспелый [sko-ro-spyé-lāy] *adj.* early, forward (of growth)

скорость [skó-rŏst'] *sf.* rapidity, speed; velocity

скоротечный [sko-ro-tyéch-nāy] *adj.* transient

скорый [skó-rāy] *adj.* fast, rapid, swift

скос [skos] *sm.* bevel; splay

скот [skot] *sm.* cattle, live stock

скотина [ska-t'é-na] *sf.* beast, brute

скотник [skót-n'ik] *sm.* cowherd, drover

скотобойня [ska-ta-bóy-nya] *sf.* slaughter-house

скотовод [ska-ta-vód] *sm.* cattle-breeder

скотоводство [ska-ta-vód-stvŏ] *sn.* cattle-raising

скотский [skót-ski] *adj.* bestial, brutal

скрадывать [skrā-dā-vat'] (**скрасть**) *vt.* to conceal

скрашивать [skrā-shi-vat'] (**скрасить**) *vt.* to adorn, embellish

скребница [skryeb-n'é-tsa] *sf.* currycomb

скребок [skrye-bók] *sm.* scraper; trowel

скрежет [skryé-zhet] *sm.* gnashing, grinding, gritting

скрепа [skryé-pa] *sf.* clamp, tie

скрепка [skryép-ka] *sf.* paper clip, fastener

скрепление [skryep-lyé-nye] *sn.* fastening, tightening; countersigning

скреплять [skryep-lyát'] (скрепить) *vt.* to consolidate, strengthen; to clamp, splice; to bolt

скрести [skryes-t'ē] *vt.* to scrape, scrub; to claw, scratch

скрестить [skryes-t'ēt'] *vt.* to cross; -руки [-rōō-k'i] to fold one's arms

скрещение [skrye-shché-nye] *sn.* crossing, interbreeding

скривить [skr'i-v'ēt'] *vt.* to bend, crook, twist

скрип [skrēp] *sm.* creak; scratch (*with pen*); crunch

скрипач [skri-pách] *sm.* violinist

скрипеть [skri-pyét'] *vi.* to creak, crunch, grate

скрипичный [skri-p'éch-nāy] *adj. mus.* of violin, of treble

скрипка [skríp-ka] *sf.* violin

скрипучий [skri-pōō-chi] *adj.* creaky, grinding, scratchy

скромный [skróm-nāy] *adj.* demure, discreet, modest

скромность [skróm-nŏst'] *sf.* discretion, modesty

скручивать [skrōō-chi-vat'] (скрутить) *vt.* to contort, roll up, twist

скрывание [skrŭ-vā-nye] *sn.* concealment

скрывать [skrŭ-vāt'] (скрыть) *vt.* to conceal, hide,

secrete; to disguise (*an intention, etc.*); **-ся** [-sya] *vi.* to disappear, hide oneself, vanish

скрытный [skrŭt-nāy] *adj.* dissimulative, furtive, secretive

скрытый [skrŭ-tāy] *adj.* concealed, hidden, surreptitious; cryptic

скрючиваться [skryōō-chi-vat'-sya] *vi.* to bend, crook; **- от боли** [- at bó-l'i] to writhe in pain

скряга [skryā-ga] *sf.*, *m.* miser, niggard

скряжничать [skryāzh-n'i-chat'] *vi.* to be miserly, stingy

скудель [skōō-dyél'] *sf.* clay; **-ник** [-n'ik] *sm.* potter; **-ный** [-nāy] *adj.* earthen; *fig.* feeble, frail

скудность [skōōd-nŏst'] *sf.* bareness; sparseness; scantiness

скудный [skōōd-nāy] *adj.* meagre, poor, slender

скудоумный [skōō-da-ōōm-nāy] *adj.* stupid, dull

скука [skōō-ka] *sf.* boredom, listlessness

скула [skōō-lā] *sf.* cheekbone, **-стый** [-stāy] *adj.* of prominent cheek-bones

скульптура [skōōl'-ptōō-ra] *sf.* sculpture

скульптурный [skōōl'p-tōōr-nāy] *adj.* sculptural, statuary

скумбрия [skōōm-brē-ya] *sf.* mackerel

скунс [skōōns] *sm.* skunk

скупать [skōō-pāt'] (скупить) *vt.* to buy up; to forestall

скуфейка [skŏŏ-fýéy-ka] sf. skull-cap

скучать [skŏŏ-chát'] (по-) vi. to be bored; to feel lonely; to be weary

скученность [skŏŏ-chen-nòst'] sf. congestion, density; overcrowding

скученный [skŏŏ-chen-năy] adj. boxed-up, closely-packed, huddled together

скучивать [skŏŏ-chi-vat'] vt. to heap, pile; to crowd

скучный [skŏŏch-năy] adj. boring, tedious, wearisome; dull

скушать [skŏŏ-shat'] vt. to eat up

слабеть [sla-byét'] (осла-беть) vi. to weaken; to waste away

слабить [slá-b'it'] vi. med. to purge

слабодушие [sla-ba-dŏŏ-shye] sn. cowardice, timidity

слабоумие [sla-ba-ŏŏ-mye] sn. idiocy

слабый [slá-băy] adj. feeble, delicate, weak

слава [slá-va] sf. fame, glory, repute

славить [slá-v'it'] (про-) vt. to celebrate, glorify, praise

славный [sláv-năy] adj. famous, renowned; decent, fine, good, splendid

славословить [sla-va-slŏ-v'it'] vt. to eulogize, glorify

славянин [sla-vya-n'ēn] sm. Slav

славянский [sla-vyăn-ski] adj. Slav, Slavonic

слагать [sla-gát'] (сложить) vt. to clasp, fold up, join, put together

сладкий [slád-ki] adj. sugary,

sweet; honeyed; сладкое блюдо [slád-ka-ye blyŏŏ-dŏ] sn. sweet (as a course); сладкое мясо [- myă-sŏ] sn. sweetbread

сладкозвучный [slad-ka-zvŏŏch-năy] adj. melodious

сладкоречивый [slad-ka-rye-chē-văy] adj. glib

сладостный [slá-dast-năy] adj. delightful; suave; sweet

сладострастие [sla-da-strás-tye] sn. lust, sensuality

сладострастный [sla-da-strást-năy] adj. lustful, voluptuous

сладость [slá-dŏst'] sf. sweetness; fig. charm, delight, loveliness

слаживать [slá-zhi-vat'] (сладить) vt. to arrange, settle

сламывать [slá-mă-vat'] (сломить) vt. to break, demolish; to pull down

сланец [slá-nyets] sm. slate; schist

сласти [slás-t'i] sf. pl. confection, sweetmeats

сластить [slas-t'ét'] vt. to sweeten

сластолюбивый [slas-ta-lyŏŏ-b'ē-văy] adj. lewd, sensual

слева [slyé-va] adv. from the left, to the left

слегка [slyech-ká] adv. slightly; superficially

след [slyed] sm. mark, trace

следить [slye-d'ét'] vt. to follow, shadow, spy, watch

следование [slyé-da-va-nye] sn. following; sequence

следовательно [slye-da-va-tyel'-nŏ] adv. consequently, hence, therefore

следовать [slyé-da-vat'] (по-) vi. to follow; to succeed

следствие [slyéd-stvye] sn. consequence, deduction, effect, result

следующий [slyé-dōō-yōō-shchi] ad. following, next

слёживаться [slyó-zhi-vat'-sya] (слежаться) vi. to deteriorate

слеза [slye-zā] sf. tear; **слёзы** [slyó-za] pl. tears

слезать [slye-zāt'] (слезть) vi. to alight, dismount; to descend

слезливый [slyez-l'ē-väy] adj. tearful

слезоточивый газ [slye-za-ta-chē-väy gāz] adj. tear-gas

слепень [slye-pyén'] sm. horsefly; breeze

слепец [slye-pyéts] sm. blind man

слепой [slye-póy] adj. blind; as sm. blind person

слепок [slyé-pŏk] sm. cast, mould, stamp

слепота [slye-pa-tā] sf. blindness

слесарня [slye-sār-nya] sf. locksmith's workshop

слесарь [slyé-sar'] sm. locksmith

слёт [slyót] sm. flight (of birds); assembly, gathering (of people)

слетать [slye-tāt'] (слететь) vi. to fly down

слива [sl'ē-va] sf. plum

сливать [sl'i-vāt'] (сл'ёт) vt. to pour off; -ся [-sya] vt. to combine, fuse, merge

сливки [sl'ēv-ki] sf. pl. cream

сливочник [sl'ē-vach-n'ik] sm. cream-jug

слизень [sl'ē-zyen'] sm. slug

слизистый [sl'ē-zis-täy] adj. slimy

слизкий [sl'ēz-ki] adj. slimy, slippery

слизняк [sl'iz-nyāk] sm. snail

слизь [sl'ēz'] sf. mucus, phlegm

слинять [sl'i-nyāt'] vi. to fade

слипаться [sl'i-pāt'-sya] (слипнуться) vi. to cling together, to stick to

слитный [sl'ēt-näy] adj. coalescent, fused, united

слиток [sl'ē-tŏk] sm. bullion; ingot

сличать [sl'i-chāt'] (сличить) vt. to compare; to collate

сличение [sl'i-ché-nye] sn. collation

слишком [sl'ēsh-kŏm] adv. too; too many, too much; over

слияние [sl'i-yā-nye] sn. blending; confluence; merging

слобода [sla-ba-dā] sf. large village; suburb

словарь [sla-vār'] sm. dictionary, vocabulary; glossary

словесник [sla-vyés-n'ik] sm. man of letters

словесный [sla-vyés-näy] adj. oral, verbal

словесность [sla-vyés-nŏst'] sf. literature

словно [slov-nŏ] adv. as, as if, as though; like

слово [sló-vŏ] sn. word; speech, term; – в – [– v –] verbatim

словолитня [sla-va-l'ēt-nya] sf. typefoundry

словолитчик [sla-va-l'ēt-chik] sm. type-founder

словом [sló-vŏm] *adv.* in short

словоохотливый [sla-va-a-chót-l'i-văy] *adj.* talkative, verbose

словопрение [sla-va-pryé-nye] *sn.* controversy, dispute

словопроизводство [slo-vo-pra-iz-vód-stvŏ] *sn.* etymology

словоударение [sla-va-ōō-da-ryé-nye] *sn.* accentuation, stress

словцо [slav-tsó] *sn.* jest; witty saying

слог [slog] *sm.* syllable; style (*literary*)

сложение [sla-zhé-nye] *sn.* addition, constitution, physique

сложеный [sló-zhe-năy] *adj.* folded; **хорошо –** [cha-ra-shó –] trim, well-built

сложность [slózh-nŏst'] *sf.* complexity, intricacy

сложный [slózh-năy] *adj.* complex, complicated; compound

слоистый, [sla-ĕs-tăy] *adj.* flaky, stratiform

слоиться [sla-ĕt'-sya] *vi.* to peel off, scale

слой [sloy] *sm.* layer, stratum; lamina; foil

слойка [slóy-ka] *sf.* flaky paste

слом [slom] *sm.* breaking; demolition; pulling down

слон [slon] *sm.* elephant; bishop (chess)

слонёнок [sla-nyó-nŏk] *sm.* elephant calf

слониха [sla-n'ē-cha] *sf.* cow-elephant

слоновый [sla-nó-văy] *adj.* elephantine; **слоновая**

кость [sla-nó-va-ya kost'] *sf.* ivory

слоняться [sla-nyát'-sya] *vi.* to ramble, saunter; *coll.* to mooch about

слуга [slōō-gá] *sm.* man-servant

служанка [slōō-zhán-ka] *sf.* maid, house-maid, maid-servant

служащий [slōō-zha-shchi] *adj.* serving; *as sm.* employee

служба [slōō-zh-ba] *sf.* service; duty, job, work; employment

служебник [slōō-zhéb-n'ik] *sm.* missal

служебный [slōō-zhéb-năy] *adj.* official; subordinate

служение [slōō-zhé-nye] *sn.* ministry; service

служитель [slōō-zhé-tyel'] *sm.* attendant; orderly

служить [slōō-zhét'] (про-) *vi.* to serve, work; to be employed

слух [slōōch] *sm.* hearing; **хороший –** [cha-ró-shi –] good ear; news, report, rumour

слуховой [slōō-cha-vóy] *adj.* acoustic, auditory

случай [slōō-chay] *sm.* chance, circumstance, occurrence

случайность [slōō-chăy-nŏst'] *sf.* accident, chance; fluke; hazard

случайный [slōō-chăy-năy] *adj.* accidental, casual

случать [slōō-chát'] (случить) *vt.* to couple, pair; **–ся** [-sya] *vi.* to happen; to turn up

случка [slōōch-ka] *sf.* copulation; coupling

слушание [sloo-sha-nye] *sn.* audition; hearing

слушатели [sloo-sha-tye-l'i] *sm. pl.* audience

слушатель [sloo-sha-tyel'] *sm.* hearer, listener; university student

слушать [sloo-shat] (по-) *vt.* to listen; **-ся** [-sya] *vi.* to follow, take note, pay attention; to obey [to hear

слыхать [slá-chat] (y-) *vi.* to hear [audible

слышать [slá-shat] *vt.i.* to hear

слышный [slásh-náy] *adj.*

слюда [slyoo-dá] *sf.* mica

слюна [slyoo-ná] *sf.* saliva, spittle

слякоть [slyá-kót'] *sf.* mire; slush

смазка [smáz-ka] *sf.* lubricant; lubrication

смазливый [sma-zl'ē-vǎy] *adj.* good-looking, pretty; prepossessing

смазчик [smáz-chik] *sm.* lubricator

смазывать [smá-zǎ-vat'] (смáзать) *vt.* to grease, lubricate, oil; *fig.* to bribe

смакование [sma-ka-vá-nye] *sn.* gusto, relish

смалу [smá-lōō] *adv.* since childhood

сманивать [sma-n'i-vat'] (сманить) *vt.* to entice, lure

смарагд [sma-rágd] *sm.* emerald

сматывать [smá-tǎ-vat'] (смотáть) *vt.* to reel, wind

смахивать [smá-chi-vat'] (смахнýть) *vt.* to brush aside; *coll.* to resemble

смачивать [smá-chi-vat'] (смочить) *vt.* to moisten, soak, wet

смачный [smách-nǎy] *adj.* savoury, tasty

смежный [smyézh-nǎy] *adj.* adjacent, neighbouring, proximate

смекалка [smye-kál-ka] *sf.* good sense, perception

смелость [smye-lóst] *sf.* bravery

смелый [smye-lǎy] *adj.* bold, daring, plucky

смельчак [smyel'-chák] *sm.* daredevil

смена [smye-na] *sf.* change, relay, replacement; shift

сменный [smyén-nǎy] *adj.* changeable

сменяемый [smye-nyā-ye-mǎy] *adj.* removable

сменять [smye-nyát'] (сменить) *vt.* to change, remove, replace; to relay; to relieve

смеркаться [smyer-kát'-sya] (смеркнýться) *vi.* to become dusk

смертельный [smyer-tyél'-nǎy] *adj.* deadly, mortal; fatal

смертник [smyért-n'ik] *sm.* prisoner condemned to death

смертность [smyért-nóst'] *sf.* mortality

смертоносный [smyer-ta-nós-nǎy] *adj.* murderous

смертоубийство [smyer-ta-ōō-b'ēst-vǒ] *sn.* homicide, murder

смерть [smyert'] *sf.* death

смерч [smyerch] *sm.* waterspout; whirlwind

смесь [smyes'] *sf.* concoction; medley; mixture; miscellany

смета [smye-ta] *sf.* calculation, estimate

сметана [smye-tá-na] *sf.* sour cream

сметать [smye-tát'] (сместú) *vt.* to dust; to sweep

сметка [smyót-ka] *sf.* sagacity, shrewdness

сметливый [smyé-tl'i-văy] *adj.* resourceful, sagacious

сметывать [smyó-tă-văt'] (сметáть) *vt.* to baste, tack; to fling

сметь [smyet'] (по-) *vi.* to dare, risk, venture

смех [smyech] *sm.* laughter

смехотворный [smye-cha-tvór-năy] *adj.* laughable, ridiculous

смешанный [smyé-shan-năy] *adj.* composite, mixed

смешение [smye-shé-nye] *sn.* blending, mixture

смешивание [smyé-shi-va-nye] *sn.* mixing

смешивать [smyé-shi-vat'] (смешáть) *vt.* to blend, combine, mingle, mix up; to disarrange; -ся [-sya] *vi.* to get mixed up, intermingle; *fig.* to become confused, perplexed

смешить [smye-shét'] (на-) *vi.* to make one laugh

смешливый [smye-shl'é-văy] *adj.* risible

смешной [smye-shnóy] *adj.* amusing, comical, funny

смещать [smye-shchát'] (сместúть) *vt.* to dislodge, dismiss, remove; -ся [-sya] *vi.* to heave, rise and fall

смещение [smye-shché-nye] *sn.* displacement; removal; dislocation, upheaval

смеяться [smye-yát'-sya] (за-) *vi.* to laugh

смиловаться [sm'ĕ-la-vát'-**sya** *vi.* to take pity on

смирение [sm'i-ryé-nye] *sn.* humility, submissiveness

смиренный [sm'i-ryén-năy] *adj.* lowly, meek

смирный [sm'ér-năy] *adj.* gentle, quiet, tame

смирять [sm'i-ryát'] (смирúть) *vt.* to appease, to humble, subdue

смоква [smók-va] *sf.* fig; home-made marmalade

смоковница [sma-kóv-n'i-tsa] *sf.* fig-tree; sycamore

смола [sma-lá] *sf.* pitch, tar; resin

смолистый [sma-l'ēs-tăy] *adj.* resinous

смолить [sma-l'ĕt'] *vt.* to resin, tar

смолкать [smal-kát'] (смолкнуть) *vi.* to become silent

смолоду [smó-la-dŏŏ] *adv.* since one's youth

смолокурня [sma-la-kŏŏr-nya] *sf.* tarworks

сморкаться [smar-kát'-sya] (сморкнуться) *vi.* to blow one's nose

смородина [sma-ró-d'i-na] *sf.* currant

сморщиться [smar-shchĕt'-sya] *vi.* to crumple, shrink; to crinkle, wrinkle

смотр [smotr] *sm.* inspection; parade, review

смотреть [sma-tryét'] (по-) *vi.* to contemplate, look; to eye, view; **смотри!** [sma-trĕ] behold!; **смотря** [sma-tryá] according

смрад [smrăd] *sm.* stench

смуглый [smŏŏg-lăy] *adj.* swarthy, tawny

смуглянка [smŏŏg-lyán-ka] *sf.* brunette

смута [smōō-ta] *sf.* alarm; disturbance; sedition

смутный [smōōt-năy] *adj.* indistinct; confused, vague

смущать [smōō-shchát] (смутить) *vt.* to bewilder, embarrass, perplex

смущение [smōō-shché-nye] *sn.* confusion, perplexity

смущённый [smōō-shchón-năy] *adj.* abashed, agitated, embarrassed

смысл [smăsl] *sm.* meaning, purport, sense

смычок [smă-chók] *sm. mus.* bow; leash

смышлённый [smăsh-lyón-năy] *adj.* bright, intelligent; smart

смягчать [smyach-chát] (смягчить) *vt.* to mollify, to tone down, soothe; to commute

смягчающий [smyach-chá-yōō-shchi] *adj.* emollient

смятение [smya-tyé-nye] *sn.* commotion, consternation

смять [smyat] *vt.* to crumple ruffle

снабжать [snab-zhát] (снабдить) *vt.* to furnish, provide, supply; to cater

снабжение [snab-zhé-nye] *sn.* catering; provision, supply

снадобье [snă-do-bye] *sn.* condiment, ingredient; drug

снаружи [sna-rōō-zhi] *adv.* externally, outwardly

снаряд [sna-ryád] *sm.* missile, projectile, shell; equipment

снаряжать [sna-rya-zhát] (снарядить) *vt.* to equip, furnish

снаряжение [sna-rya-zhé-nye] *sn.* equipment, outfit

снасть [snast'] *sf.* implement, tool; rigging, tackle

сначала [sna-chá-la] *adv.* firstly, primarily

снашивать [sna-shi-vat'] (сносить) *vt.* to wear out

снег [snyég] *sm.* snow

снегирь [snye-gĕr'] *sm.* bullfinch

снегоочиститель [snye-ga-a-chis-t'é-tyel] *sm.* snow-plough

снегурочка [snye-gōō-rach-ka] *sf.* snow-maiden

снежинка [snye-zhén-ka] *sf.* snow-flake

снежный [snyézh-năy] *adj.* snowy

снежок [snye-zhók] *sm.* snowball

снесение [snye-syé-nye] *sn.* pulling down; tearing away

снижать [sn'i-zhát] (снизить) *vt.* to bring down, lower, mark down, reduce, sink

снизу [sn'ézōō] *adv.* from below, underneath

снимать [sn'i-mát'] (снять) *vt.* to draw off, take off; to skim; to take (*a photograph*)

снимок [sn'é-mŏk] *sm.* copy, print; photo

снисходительность [sn'is-cha-d'é-tyel'-nŏst'] *sf.* forbearance, indulgence

снисходительный [sn'is-cha-d'é-tyel'-năy] *adj.* condescending, lenient

снисходить [sn'is-cha-d'ĕt'] (снизойти) *vi.* to condescend

снисхождение [sn'is-chazh-dyé-nye] *sn.* condescension leniency

сниться [sn'ĕt'-sya] *vi.* to dream

снова [snó-va] *adv.* afresh, anew

сновать [sna-vát'] *vt.* to warp; to scurry

сновидение [sna-v'i-dyé-nye] *sn.* dream, vision

сновидец [sna-v'ĕ-dyets] *sm.* dreamer

сноп [snop] *sm.* sheaf

сноровка [sna-róv-ka] *sf.* ability, knack, skill

снос [snos] *sm.* demolition, taking away

сносить [sna-s'ĕt'] (снести́) *vt.* to carry, take; to pull down; *fig.* to bear, suffer; to deduct, reduce; **-ся** [-sya] *vi.* to confer, negotiate

сноска [snós-ka] *sf.* footnote, reference

сносный [snós-nǎy] *adj.* bearable, endurable

снотворный [sna-tvór-nǎy] *adj.* narcotic, somniferous

сноха [sna-chá] *sf.* daughter-in-law

сношение [sna-shé-nye] *sn.* intercourse; connection, dealings, relation

со [so] *prep.* with; from; since

собака [sa-bá-ka] *sf.* dog, hound

собачий [sa-bá-chi] *adj.* canine, dog's

собачка [sa-bách-ka] *sf.* puppy; small dog

собачник [sa-bách-n'ik] *sm.* dog-fancier

собачонка [sa-ba-chón-ka] *sf.* mongrel

собеседование [sa-bye-syé-da-va-nye] *sn.* colloquy, conversation

собеседовать [sa-bye-syé-da-vat'] *vi.* to converse

собирание [sa-b'i-rá-nye] *sn.* gathering, collecting, collection

собирательный [sa-b'i-rá-tyel'-nǎy] *adj.* collective

собирать [sa-b'i-rát'] (собра́ть) *vt.* to collect, gather; to assemble; to convene; **-ся** [-sya] *vi.* to get ready; to congregate

соблазн [sa-blázn] *sm.* temptation

соблазнительный [sa-blaz-n'ĕ-tyel'-nǎy] *adj.* alluring; suggestive; tempting

соблазнять [sa-blaz-nyát'] (соблазни́ть) *vt.* to entice, tempt; to corrupt

соблюдать [sa-blyŏŏ-dát'] (соблюсти́) *vt.* to maintain, observe, stick to

соблюдение [sa-blyŏŏ-dyé-nye] *sn.* fulfilment, observance

соболезновать [sa-ba-lyéz-na-vat'] *vi.* to commiserate, condole, sympathize

соболь [só-bŏl'] *sm.* sable

собор [sa-bór] *sm.* cathedral; council; synod

собрание [sa-brá-nye] *sn.* assembly, gathering; conference, meeting, session

собрат [sa-brát] *sm.* colleague

собственник [sób-stvyen-n'ik] *sm.* owner, proprietor

собственно [sób-stvyen-nŏ] *adv.* really, truthfully; properly, strictly

собственность [sób-stvyen-nŏst'] *sf.* possessions, property

собственный [sób-stvyen-nǎy] *adj.* own, proper

событие [sa-bá-tye] *sn.* event, occurrence

сова [sa-vá] *sf.* owl

совать [sa-vát'] (сунуть) *vt.* to poke, shove, thrust; **-ся** [-sya] *vi.* to butt in, intrude

совершать [sa-vyer-shát'] (совершить) *vt.* to accomplish, achieve

совершение [sa-vyer-shé-nye] *sn.* accomplishment, completion; perpetration

совершенно [sa-vyer-shén-nŏ] *adv.* entirely, fully, wholly

совершеннолетие [sa-vyer-shen-nŏ-lyé-tye] *sn.* majority (in age)

совершенный [sa-vyer-shén-năy] *adj.* perfect, thorough

совестливый [só-vyest-l'i-văy] *adj.* conscientious, scrupulous

совесть [só-vyest'] *sf.* conscience

совет [sa-vyét] *sm.* council; advice, counsel; opinion

советник [sa-vyét-n'ik] *sm.* counsellor, guide

советовать [sa-vyé-ta-vat'] *vt.* to advise

совещание [sa-vye-shchá-nye] *sn.* counsel; consultation

совещаться [sa-vye-shchát'-sya] *vi.* to confer, seek advice

совиновный [sa-v'i-nóv-năy] *sm.* accomplice

совладать [sa-vla-dát'] *vt.* to overcome, master

совладелец [sa-vla-dyé-lyets] *sm.* copartner, joint owner

совместимый [sa-vmyest'-ĕ-măy] *adj.* compatible

совместность [sa-vmyést-nŏst'] *sf.* compatibility

совместный [sa-vmyést-năy] *adj.* joint; **совместная работа** [sa-vmyést-na-ya ra-bó-ta] team-work

совмещать [sa-vmye-shchát'] (совместить) *vt.* to combine; to join

совокупление [sa-va-kŏŏ-plyé-nye] *sn.* coalition; union

совокупный [sa-va-kŏŏp-năy] *adj.* collective, joint

совпадать [sav-pa-dát'] (совпасть) *vi.* to coincide, tally

совпадение [sav-pa-dyé-nye] *sn.* coincidence, concurrence

совращать [sa-vra-shchát'] (совратить) *vt.* to corrupt, mislead

современник [sa-vryé-myen-n'ik] *sm.* contemporary

современный [sa-vryé-myen-năy] *adj.* contemporaneous

совсем [sa-vsyém] *adv.* absolutely, entirely; altogether; quite

согласие [sa-glá-sye] *sn.* acquiescence, assent; accord, harmony

согласно [sa-glás-nŏ] *adj.* in compliance with

согласный [sa-glás-năy] *adj.* conforming, harmonious; **согласная буква** [sa-glás-na-ya bŏŏk-va] *sf.* gram. consonant

согласование [sa-gla-sa-vá-nye] *sn.* concordance; concord

согласовать [sa-gla-sa-vát'] *vt.* to conciliate, conform; **-ся** [-sya] *vi.* to agree, consent

соглашательство [sa-gla-shä-tyel'-stvǒ] *sn.* agreement; conciliation

соглашаться [sa-gla-shät'-sya] *vi.* to acquiesce, consent

соглашение [sa-gla-shé-nye] *sn.* agreement, understanding

согражданин [sa-grazh-da-n'ën] *sm.* fellow-citizen

согревать [sa-grye-vät'] (согреть) *vt.* to heat, warm

согрешать [sa-grye-shät'] (согрешить) *vi.* to sin, trespass

содействие [sa-dyéy-stvye] *sn.* co-operation

содействовать [sa-dyéy-stva-vat'] *vi.* to assist, cooperate

содержание [sa-dyer-zhä-nye] *sn.* allowance, maintenance; contents

содержатель [sa-dyer-zhä-tyel'] *sm.* landlord, owner

содержать [sa-dyer-zhät'] *vt.* to keep, maintain; support; to contain, include

содержимость [sa-dyer-zhé-mǒst'] *sf.* capacity, volume

содрогание [sa-dra-gä-nye] *sn.* shiver, shudder

содрогаться [sa-dra-gät'-sya] *vi.* to shiver, tremble

содружество [sa-drǒǒ-zhest-vǒ] *sn.* concord, co-operation; friendship (*of nations*)

соединение [sa-ye-d'i-ṇyé-nye] *sn.* combination; juncture, union

соединять [sa-ye-d'i-nyät'] *vt.* to connect, join, unite

сожаление [sa-zha-lyé-nye] *sn.* regret; repentance; compassion, pity

сожалеть [sa-zha-lyét'] *vi.* to deplore, regret; to be sorry

сожитель [sa-zhé-tyel'] *sm.* companion, partner, roommate

сожительство [sa-zhi-tyel'-stvǒ] **сожитие** [sa-zhi-tye] *sn.* cohabitation

созвездие [sa-zvyëz-dye] *sn.* constellation

созвучие [sa-zvǒǒ-chye] *sn.* harmony

создавать [saz-da-vät'] (создать) *vt.* to create, make; to form, frame, set up

создание [saz-dä-nye] *sn.* creation; creature

созерцание [sa-zyer-tsä-nye] *sn.* contemplation

созерцать [sa-zyer-tsät'] *vt.* to contemplate, ponder

созидательный [sa-z'i-dä-tyel'-näy] *adj.* constructive, creative

сознавать [za-zna-vät'] (сознать) *vt.* to acknowledge, recognize; **-ся** [-sya] *vi.* to confess

сознание [sa-znä-nye] *sn.* acknowledgment, confession; conscience

сознательность [sa-znä-tyel'-nǒst'] *sf.* consciousness

созревать [sa-zrye-vät'] (созреть) *vi.* to mature, ripen

созыв [sa-záv] *sm.* convocation, summons; rally

соизволение [sa-iz-va-lyé-nye] *sn.* approbation, assent; sanction

соизмеримый [sa-iz-mye-r'ē-mäy] *adj.* commensurable

сойка [sóy-ka] *sf.* jay

сок [sok] *sm.* juice, sap

сокол [só-kǒl] *sm.* falcon, hawk

сокращать [sa-kra-shchát'] (сократи́ть) vt. to abbreviate, reduce, shorten

сокращение [sa-kra-shché-nye] sn. abbreviation, abridgment

сокровенность [sa-kra-vyén-nŏst'] sf. secrecy

сокровище [sa-kró-v'i-shche] sn. treasure

сокровищница [sa-kró-v'i-shchn'i-tsa] sf. treasury

сокрушать [sa-kroŏ-shát'] (сокруши́ть) vt. to demolish, shatter, smash

сокрушение [sa-kroŏ-shé-nye] sn. destruction; contrition

сокрытие [sa-krǎ-tye] sn. concealment

солдат [sal-dát] sm. soldier

солдатчина [sal-dát-chi-na] sf. soldiering; conscription

соление [sa-lyé-nye] sn. pickling, salting

соленье [sa-lyé-nye] sn. pickled and salted foods

солидарность [sa-l'i-dár-nŏst'] sf. solidarity

солидный [sa-l'ĕd-năy] adj. firm, sound

солить [sa-l'ĕt'] (по-) vt. to pickle, salt

солнечный [sól-nyech-năy] adj. solar; sunny

солнце [són-tse] sn. sun

солнцестояние [son-tse-sta-yă-nye] sn. solstice

солист [sa-l'ĕst] sm. soloist

соловей [sa-la-vyéy] sm. nightingale

соловый [sa-ló-văy] adj. fallow

солод [só-lŏd] sm. malt

солодовник [sa-la-dóv-n'ik] sm. maltster

солодовня [sa-la-dóv-nya] sf. malt-house

солома [sa-ló-ma] sf. straw; **крыть соломой** [krăt' sa-ló-mŏy] to thatch

соломорезка [sa-la-ma-ryéz-ka] sf. chaff-cutter

солонина [sa-la-n'é-na] sf. corned beef; junk, salt-beef

солонка [sa-lón-ka] sf. salt-cellar

солоноватый [sa-la-na-vă-tăy] adj. brackish, saltish

солончак [sa-lan-chák] sm. salt-marsh

соль [sol'] sf. salt; **английская –** [an-gl'ĕ-ska-ya –] Epsom salt(s); mus. G

солянка [sa-lyán-ka] sf. Russian cabbage-dish

сом [som] sm. catfish

сомневаться [sam-nye-vát'-sya] vt.i. to doubt, to be uncertain

сомнение [sam-nyé-nye] sn. doubt, misgiving, suspicion

сомнительный [sam-n'ĕtyel'-năy] adj. doubtful, dubious, questionable

сомон [sa-món] adj. salmon, pinkish

сон [son] sm. dream; sleep

сонливый [san-l'ĕ-văy] adj. drowsy, sleepy; fig. indolent

сонный [són-năy] adj. sleepy

соня [só-nya] sf. dormouse; coll. sleepy-head

соображать [sa-a-bra-zhát'] (сообрази́ть) vt. to consider, take into account

соображение [sa-a-bra-zhé-nye] sn. consideration

сообразительный [sa-a-bra-z'ĕ-tyel'-năy] adj. discriminative, shrewd

сообразно [sa-a-bráz-nŏ] *adv.* accordingly, in compliance with

сообразный [sa-a-bráz-nǎy] *adj.* conformable; consistent; suitable

сообща [sa-ab-shchá] *adv.* conjointly

сообщать [sa-ab-shchát'] (сообщи́ть) *vt.* to communicate, impart, inform

сообщение [sa-ab-shché-nye] *sn.* communication, message, notification

сообщество [sa-ób-shche-stvŏ] *sn.* association, corporation, fellowship

сообщительный [sa-ab-shché-tyel-nǎy] *adj.* communicative, talkative

сообщник [sa-ób-shchn'ik] *sm.* associate, partner; accomplice

сообщничество [sa-obshchn'é-chest-vŏ] *sn.* complicity; participation

сооружать [sa-a-rŏŏ-zhát'] (сооруди́ть) *vt.* to build, erect

сооружение [sa-a-rŏŏ-zhé-nye] *sn.* construction, erection; edifice

соответственность [sa-at-vyét-stvyen-nŏst'] *sf.* conformity, suitability

соответственный [sa-at-vyét-stvyen-nǎy] *adj.* corresponding, expedient, suitable

соответствовать [sa-at-vyét-stva-vat'] *vi.* to fit, match, suit, tally

соответствующий [sa-at-vyét-stvŏŏ-yŏŏ-shchi] *adj.* appropriate, becoming

соответчик [sa-at-vyét-chik] *sm.* co-respondent

соотечественник [sa-a-tyé-chest-vyen-n'ik] *sm.* compatriot, countryman

соотносительный [sa-at-na-s'é-tyel'-nǎy] *adj.* correlative (rival

соперник [sa-pyér-n'ik] *sm.* (rival

соперничество [sa-pyér-n'i-chest-vŏ] *sn.* competition, contest, rivalry

сопеть [sa-pyét'] (за-) *vi.* to sniff, wheeze

сопка [sóp-ka] *sf.* small volcano; hill, mound

соплеменник [sa-plye-myén-n'ik] *sm.* kinsman, tribesman

сопло [sóp-lŏ] *sn.* nozzle

сопоставление [sa-pas-ta-vlyé-nye] *sn.* juxtaposition

сопревать [sa-prye-vát'] *vi.* to fester

сопредельный [sa-prye-dyél'-nǎy] *adj.* adjacent, adjoining

соприкосновение [sa-pr'i-kas-na-vyé-nye] *sn.* contact, touch; osculation

сопроводительный [sa-pra-va-d'é-tyel'-nǎy] *adj.* accompanying, concomitant

сопровождать [sa-pra-vazh-dát'] (сопроводи́ть) *vt.* to accompany, attend; to escort

сопротивление [sa-pra-t'iv-lyé-nye] *sn.* opposition; resistance

сопротивляться [sa-pra-t'i-vlyát'-sya] (сопроти́виться) *vi.* to oppose, resist

сопряжение [sa-prya-zhé-nye] *sn.* junction, union

сор [sor] *sm.* litter, rubbish

соразмерный [sa-raz-myér-nǎy] *adj.* proportionate

сорванец [sar-va-nyéts] *sm.* madcap; tomboy

соревнование [sa-ryev-na-vá-nye] *sn.* contention, emulation

сорить [sa-r'ét'] (на-) *vt.i.* to litter; to squander

сорный [sór-nǎy] *adj.* dirty, filthy; weedy

сорок [só-rók] *num.* forty

сорока [sa-ró-ka] *sf.* magpie

сороковой [sa-ra-ka-vóy] *num.* fortieth

сороконожка [sa-ra-ka-nózh-ka] *sf.* centipede

сорочка [sa-róch-ka] *sf.* chemise, shirt

сорт [sort] *sm.* class, kind, quality, sort

сортировать [sar-t'ē-ra-vat'] (рас-) *vt.* to assort, match, sort

сортировка [sar-t'i-róv-ka] *sf.* assortment, sorting

сортировщик [sar-t'i-róv-shchik] *sm.* sorter

сосать [sa-sát'] *vt.* to suck

сосватать [sa-svá-tā-vat'] (сосватать) *vt.* to betroth

сосед [sa-syéd] *sm.* neighbour

соседний [sa-syéd-ni] *adj.* adjoining, neighbouring

сосиска [sa-s'ës-ka] *sf.* sausage

соска [sós-ka] *sf.* feeding-bottle; dummy, soother

соскабливать [sas-ká-bli-vat'] (соскаблить) *vt.* to erase, scrape, scratch; to grain

соскучиваться [sas-kõõ-chi-vat'-sya] (соскучиться) *vi.* to become melancholy, to be bored

сослагательный [sa-sla-gá-tyel'-nǎy] *adj. gram.* subjunctive

сосланный [só-slan-nǎy] *adj.* banished, exiled; *as sm.* exile

сословие [sa-sló-vye] *sn.* estate

сослуживец [sa-slōō-zhē-vyets] *sm.* colleague

сосна [sas-ná] *sf.* pine, pine-tree

соснуть [sas-nōōt'] *vi.* to take a nap

сосняк [sas-nyák] *sm.* pine-forest

сосок [sa-sók] *sm.* nipple, teat

сосредоточивать [so-sryeda-tó-chi-vat'] (сосредоточить) *vt.* to concentrate; to focus

состав [sas-táv] *sm.* body; composition; staff

составитель [sas-ta-v'ē-tyel'] *sm.* arranger, compiler

составлять [sas-tav-lyát'] (составить) *vt.* to assemble put together; to compose, form, work out; to compile

состариться [sas-ta-r'ét'-sya] *vi.* to age, grow old

состояние [sas-ta-yā-nye] *sn.* condition, state, status; fortune

состоятельность [sas-ta-yā-tyel'-nóst'] *sf.* competence; solvency

состоятельный [sas-ta-yā-tyel'-nǎy] *adj.* comfortable, well-off; solvent

состоять [sas-ta-yát'] *vi.* to be composed, to be made of; to consist; **-ся** [-sya] *vi.* to happen, to be realized, to take place

сострадание [sas-tra-dā-nye] *sn.* commiseration, compassion, pity, sympathy

сострадательный [sas-tra-dā-tyel'-năy] *adj.* compassionate, pitiful

состязание [sas-tya-zā-nye] *sn.* contest; dispute; match (*sport*)

сосуд [sa-sŏŏd] *sm.* container; vessel; *anat.* vessel

сосудистый [sa-sŏŏ-d'ēs-tăy] *adj.* vascular

сосулька [sa-sŏŏl-ka] *sf.* icicle

сосун [sa-sŏŏn] *sm.*, **-ья** [-nya] *sf.* suckling

сосчитывать [sas-chē-tă-vat'] (сосчитáть) *vt.* to calculate, count

сот [sot] *sm.* honeycomb

сотворение [sa-tva-ryé-nye] *sn.* creating; making; fabrication (*also ironically*)

сотворять [sat-va-ryăt'] (сотворить) *vt.* to fabricate, make

сотрудник [sa-trŏŏd-n'ik] *sm.* collaborator, contributor

сотрудничать [sa-trŏŏd-n'i-chat'] *vi.* to collaborate, cooperate

сотрясение [sa-trya-syé-nye] *sn.* commotion, disturbance, stir; -- мозга [- maz-gã] concussion

сотый [só-tăy] *num.* hundredth

соумышленник [sa-ŏŏ-măsh-lyen-n'ik] *sm.* accomplice

соусник [só-ŏŏs-n'ik] *sm.* gravy-boat

соучаствовать [sa-ŏŏ-chăst-va-vat'] *vi.* to participate

соучастник [sa-ŏŏ-chăst-n'ik] *sm.* associate, participant

соученик [sa-ŏŏ-che-n'ĕk] *sm.* fellow-student

сохнуть [sóch-nŏŏt'] *vi.* to dry, parch; *fig.* to pine

сохранение [sa-chra-nyé-nye] *sn.* conservation, preservation; custody

сохранный [sa-chrān-năy] *adj.* intact, safe, secure

сохранять [sa-chra-nyăt'] (сохранить) *vt.* to conserve, keep, maintain, preserve

социальный [sa-tsyăl'-năy] *adj.* social

сочельник [sa-chél'-n'ik] *sm.* Christmas Eve

сочетать [sa-che-ta-văt'] (сочетáть) *vt.* to combine, connect, unite

сочетание [sa-che-tă-nye] *sn.* combination; union

сочинение [sa-chi-nyé-nye] *sn.* composition, treatise, work

сочинять [sa-chi-nyăt'] (сочинить) *vi.* to compose, write

сочиться [sa-chēt'-sya] *vi.* to dribble, ooze out, trickle

сочный [sóch-năy] *adj.* juicy, succulent; mellow

сочувствие [sa-chŏŏv-stvye] *sn.* feeling, sympathy

сочувствовать [sa-chŏŏv-stva-vat'] *vi.* to condole, sympathize

сошествие [sa-shést-vye] *sn.* descent

сошка [sósh-ka] *sf.* share (of plough); gun-rack; мелкая -- [myél-ka-ya --] *fig.* small fry

сошник [sósh-n'ik] *sm.* coulter

союз [sa-yŏŏz] *sm.* alliance; league, union

союзник [sa-yŏŏz-n'ik] *sm.* ally, confederate

союзный [sa-yōōz-năy] *adj.* allied, union-

спадать [spa-dát'] (спасть) *vt.* to abate, diminish, lower

спаивать [spa-i-vat'] (спаять) *vt.* to solder, weld; to intoxicate

спай [spáy] *sm.* joint

спайка [spáy-ka] *sf.* soldering, welding

спалить [spa-l'ēt'] *vt.* to singe

спальня [spál'-nya] *sf.* bedroom

спаньё [spa-nyó] *sn. coll.* sleep, sleeping

спаржа [spár-zha] *sf.* asparagus

спас [spás] *sm.* Saviour

спасание [spa-sá-nye] *sm.* rescue; salvage; salvation

спасать [spa-sát'] (спасти́) *vt.* to rescue, save; to redeem

спасибо [spa-s'ē-bŏ] *int.* thanks, thank you

спаситель [spa-s'ē-tyel'] *sm.* rescuer, saviour; Redeemer, Saviour

спасительный [spa-s'ē-tyel'-năy] *adj.* salutary

спасовать [spa-sa-vát'] *vi.* to pass (*in games*)

спать [spát'] *vi.* to sleep, to be asleep

спевка [spyév-ka] *sf.* choir practice

спектакль [spyek-tákl'] *sm.* exhibition, performance, play

спекулянт [spye-kōō-lyánt] *sm.* speculator

спелый [spyé-lăy] *adj.* mature, ripe

сперва [spyer-vá] *adv.* firstly

спереди [spe-rye-d'ē] *adv.* in front

спёртый [spyór-tăy] *adj.* close, stuffy

спесивый [spye-s'ē-văy] *adj.* haughty, supercilious

спесь [spyés'] *sf.* arrogance, pride

спеть [spyét'] (по-) *vi.* to ripen

спех [spyéch] *sm.* haste

специальный [spye-tsyál'-năy] *adj.* particular, special

специальность [spye-tsyál'-nŏst'] *sf.* speciality

спешивать [spyé-shi-vat'] (спешить) *vt.* to dismount

спешить [spye-shét'] (по-) *vi.* to hasten, hurry, press on

спешный [spyésh-năy] *adj.* hasty, urgent

спина [spi-ná] *sf. anat.* back

спинка [sp-ēn-ka] *sf.* back (of chair, etc.)

спинной [spin-nóy] *adj.* spinal

спиральный [spi-rál'-năy] *adj.* helical

спирт [spért] *sm.* alcohol spirits

спиртовка [spir-tóv-ka] *sf.* spirit-lamp

список [sp'ē-sŏk] *sm.* list, register, roll

списывать [sp'ē-să-vat'] (списать) *vt.* to copy, transcribe

спица [sp'ē-tsa] *sf.* spoke; knitting needle

спичечница [sp'ē-chech-n'i-tsa] *sf.* match-box

спичка [sp'ēch-ka] *sf.* match

сплав [splắv] *sm.* alloy; fusion

сплавлять [splav-lyát'] (сплавить) *vt.* to raft; to alloy, fuse

сплавной [splav-nóy] *adj.* floatable

сплавщик [splâv-shchik] *sm.* rafter; smelter

сплачивать [splá-chi-vat'] (сплотить) *vt.* to clamp, join; to rally

сплеснивать [splyés-ni-vat'] (сплеснить) *vt.* to splice

сплетать [splye-tát'] (сплести) *vt.* to interlace; to plait

сплетение [splye-tyé-nye] *sn.* entanglement; plexus

сплетник [splyét-n'ik] *sm.* scandalmonger

сплетничать [splyét-n'i-chat'] (на-) *vi.* to gossip

сплетня [splyét-nya] *sf.* gossip, tattle

сплочение [spla-ché-nye] *sn.* firmness, solidarity

сплошной [splash-nóy] *adj.* compact, dense; uninterrupted

сплошь [splosh'] *adv.* continuously

сплывать(ся) [splä-vát'(sya] (сплыть) *vi.* to blend, merge; to drift

сплющенный [splyōō-shchen-näy] *adj.* flattened out

сподручный [spad-rōōch-näy] *adj.* convenient, handy; as *sm.* assistant, helper

спозаранку [spa-za-rän-kōō] *adv.* in good time, very early

спокойный [spa-kóy-näy] *adj.* calm, tranquil; sedate; sober, subdued; **спокойной ночи** [spa-kóy-nŏy nó-chi] good night!

спокойствие [spa-kóy-stvye] *sn.* peacefulness, quietude

сполна [spal-ná] *adv* completely, entirely, fully

сполошить [spa-la-shĕt'] *vt.* to alarm, perturb

спор [spor] *sm.* controversy; discussion, dispute

спорить [spó-rit'] (по-) *vi.* to argue, debate

спорный [spór-näy] *adj.* contestable, questionable

спортсменство [sports-myén-stvŏ] *sn.* sportsmanship

спорый [spó-räy] *adj.* advantageous, profitable

способ [spó-sŏb] *sm.* manner, means, method

способность [spa-sób-nŏst] *sf.* ability, talent; faculty

способный [spa-sób-näy] *adj.* capable, gifted; *coll.* cute

способствовать [spa-sób-stva-vat'] *vi.* to assist, contribute, help

спотыкаться [spa-tä-kät'-sya] (споткнуться) *vi.* to stumble, trip

спохватываться [spa-chvä-tä-vat'-sya] (спохватиться) *vi.* to recollect

справа [sprä-va] *adv.* from the right

справедливость [spra-vye-dl'ĕ-vŏst'] *sf.* fairness, justice, right

справедливый [spra-vye-dl'ĕ-väy] *adj.* equitable, fair; righteous

справка [sprâv-ka] *sf.* information, inquiry, investigation

справлять [sprav-lyät'] (справить) *vt.* to celebrate; to repair; **-ся** [-sya] *vi.* to consult, make inquiries; to manage, master

справочник [sprä-vach-n'ik] *sm.* gazetteer, guide, reference book

спрашивать [sprä-shi-vat'] [спросить] vt. to ask, interrogate

спрос [spros] sm. leave, permission; demand, request

спроста [spras-tä] adv. naïvely, simply, unaffectedly

спрут [sprōōt] sm. octopus

спрыгивание [sprä-gi-va-nye] sn. jumping, springing

спрыскивание [spräs-ki-va-nye] sn. sprinkling

спрягать [sprya-gät'] vt. gram. to conjugate

спряжение [sprya-zhé-nye] sn. gram. conjugation

спугивать [spōō-gi-vat'] (спугнуть) vt. to frighten away

спуск [spōōsk] sm. descent, slope; launching

спускать [spōōs-kät'] (спустить) vt. to lower; to watch, -ся [-sya] vi. to come down

спустя [spōōs-tyä] prep. after, later on

спутанный [spōō-tan-näy] adj. entangled

спутник [spōōt-n'ik] sm. fellow-traveller; astron. satellite

спутывать [spōō-tä-vat'] (спутать) vt. to entangle, mix up; to embarrass

спячка [spyäch-ka] sf. sleepiness; hibernation

сравнение [srav-nyé-nye] sn. comparison

сравнивание [srâv-n'i-va-nye] sn. comparing; levelling

сравнивать [srâv-ni-vat'] (сравнить) vt. to compare; – (сравнять) to balance; to level, smooth

сравнительный [srav-n'é-

tyel'-näy] adj. comparative, relative, respective

сражать [sra-zhät'] (сразить) vt. to overwhelm; -ся [-sya] vi. to combat, fight, struggle

сражение [sra-zhé-nye] sn. battle, combat, engagement

сразу [srä-zōō] adv. at once

срам [sräm] sm. shame

срамный [srâm-näy] adj. disgraceful, shameful

срастание [sras-tä-nye] sn. coalescence; inosculation

сребролюбивый [sryc-bra-lyōō-b'é-väy] adj. avaricious, greedy

сребролюбие [sryc-bra-lyōō-bye] sn. avarice

среда [srye-dä] sf. Wednesday; surroundings; environment

среди [srye-d'é] prep. amid(st), among(st)

средина [srye-d'é-na] sf. centre, middle

средневековый [sryed-nye-vye-kó-väy] adj. medieval

средневековье [sryed-nye-vye-kó-vye] sn. Middle Ages

средний [sryéd-ni] adj. middle; gram. neuter

средоточие [srye-da-tó-chye] sn. centre-point; focus

средство [sryéd-stvó] sn. expedient, means; remedy

срез [sryez] sm. cut, incision

срезывать [sryé-zä-vat'] (срезать) vt. to cut off

сродный [sród-näy] adj. innate, natural

сродство [sród-stvó] sn. kinship, relationship

срок [srok] sm. term, time

срочный [sróch-näy] adj. pressing, urgent

сруб [srōōb] sm. framework

срубать [sroō-bāt'] (сру-бить) *vt.* to cut down, fell

срыв [srẁv] *sm.* disruption, tearing off

срывать [srā-vāt'] (сорвáть) *vt.* to pick, pluck, snatch, tear off

срытие [srá-tye] *sn.* razing to the ground

сряду [sryā-doō] *adv.* consecutively, successively; continuously

ссадина [ssā-d'i-na] *sf.* abrasion, hack, scratch

ссаживать [ssā-zhi-vat'] (ссадить) *vt.* to alight, dismount; to land; to chafe; to graze (skin, etc.)

ссек [ssyék] *sm.* sirloin

ссора [ssó-ra] *sf.* quarrel, squabble

ссориться [ssó-rit'-sya] *vi.* to quarrel

ссуда [ssoō-da] *sf.* loan (money)

ссужать [ssoō-zhāt'] (ссудить) *vt.* to advance, lend, loan

ссылать [ssā-lāt'] (сослáть) *vt.* to banish, deport; to send away; **-ся** [-sya] *vi.* to allude; to cite, quote; to be exiled

ссылка [ssál-ka] *sf.* reference; banishment, deportation

ссыльнопоселенец [ssál'-na-pa-sye-lyé-nyets] *sm.* deportee; displaced person

ссыльный [ssál'-nay] *adj.* as *sm.* convict, exile, outlaw

ссыхаться [ssā-chāt'-sya] *vi.* to dry up, shrink

ставень [stā-vyen'] *sm.* shutter

ставить [stā-v'it'] (по-) *vt.* to place, put, set

ставка [stāv-ka] *sf.* placing,

putting, setting; rate, rating-stake

ставленник [stāv-lyen-n'ik] *sm.* henchman; protégé

стадион [stā-dión] *sm.* stadium

стадный [stād-nay] *adj.* gregarious

стадо [stā-dö] *sn.* flock, herd, shoal; mob

стажёр [sta-zhyór] *sm.* probationer

стажирование [sta-zhé-ra-va-nye] *sn.* probation

ставать [stā-i-vat'] (стáять) *vi.* to melt away; to thaw

стакан [sta-kān] *sm.* glass, tumbler

сталкивать [stāl-ki-vat'] (столкáть) *vt.* to push, shove; **-ся** [-sya] *vi.* to collide, encounter, stumble; to clash

сталь [stāl'] *sf.* steel

стамеска [sta-myés-ka] *sf.* chisel; **круглая —** [kroōg-la-ya —] gouge

стан [stān] *sm.* stature; camp; mill

станноль [sta-niól'] *sm.* tinfoil

становиться [sta-na-v'ét'-sya] (стать) *vi.* to become, get; to stand (as in a queue); **становись!** [sta-na-v'és'] fall in!

станок [sta-nók] *sm.* bench, frame, stand

станция [stān-tsya] *sf.* station; **узловая —** [oōz-la-vā-ya —] junction

стапель [stā-pyel'] *sf.* dockyard

сталивать [stā-pli-vat'] (стопить) *vt.* to fuse, melt

стаптывать [stāp-tă-vat'] (стоптáть) *vt.* to trample; **to wear out** (shoes)

старание [sta-rá-nye] *sn.* diligence, effort, endeavour

старательный [sta-rá-tyel'-nǎy] *adj.* assiduous, painstaking; efficient; studious

стараться [sta-rát'-sya] (по-) *vt.i.* to endeavour, strive, try; *vi.* to exert oneself, to strain; to do one's best

старейшина [sta-réy-shi-na] *sm.* elder; syndic

стареть [sta-ryét'] *vi.* to age, grow old

старец [stá-ryets] *sm.* elder, aged person; monk

старик [sta-r'ĕk] *sm.* old man

старина [sta-ri-ná] *sf.* antiquity; *coll.* the good old days; *sm. coll.* old fellow, old man

старинный [sta-r'ĕn-nǎy] *adj.* ancient; old-fashioned

старобытный [sta-ra-bắt-nay] *adj.* archaic

староватый [sta-ra-vá-tǎy] *adj.* oldish

стародавний [sta-ra-dáv-n'i] *adj.* ancient

старожил [sta-ra-zhíl] *sm.* old inhabitant

старозаконный [sta-ra-za-kón-nǎy] *adj.* of the Old Testament

старомодный [sta-ra-mód-nǎy] *adj.* quaint

старообразный [sta-ra-ab-ráz-nǎy] *adj.* antique

староста [stá-ras-ta] *sm.* bailiff; elder; church-warden

старость [stá-rŏst] *sf.* old age, senility

старуха [sta-rōō-cha] *sf.* old woman

старческий [stár-ches-ki] *adj.* senile

старший [stár-sh'i] *adj.* elder; eldest, oldest; senior

старшина [star-shi-ná] *sm.* foreman; *mil.* sergeant-major; warrant officer

старшинство [star-shin-stvó] *sn.* seniority

старый [stá-rǎy] *adj.* old

старьё [sta-ryó] *sn.* old clothing; rubbish

стаскивать [stás-ki-vat'] (стаскáть) *vt.* to drag, pulldown

статейка [sta-tyéy-ka] *sf.* short article (*in newspaper*)

статика [stá-t'i-ka] *sf.* statics

статист [sta-t'ĕst] *sm. theat.* supernumerary; non-speaking performer

статистик [sta-t'ĕs-t'ik] *sm.* statistician

статистика [sta-t'ĕs-t'i-ka] *sf.* statistics

статный [stát-nǎy] *adj.* shapely, stately

статский [stát-ski] *adj.* civic, civil

статуя [sta-tōō-ya] *sf.* statue

стать [stát'] *vt.i.* to begin; to take to; она стáла говорить, she began to speak; он стал пить, he took to drinking

статья [sta-tyá] *sf.* article (*in newspaper, etc.*)

стачка [stách-ka] *sf.* connivance, plot; strike

стая [stá-ya] *sf.* bevy, flock, shoal

ствол [stvol] *sm.* trunk (*of tree*); shaft; barrel (*of gun*)

створка [stvór-ka] *sf.* fold

створчатый [stvar-chá-tǎy] *adj.* folding (*as door, etc.*)

стебель [styé-byel'] *sm.* stalk, stem

стёганый [styó-ga-nǎy] *adj.* quilted

стега́ть [stye-gǎt'] (co-) vt. to quilt; – (стегну́ть) to lash, whip; to flick

стёжка [styózh-ka] sf. quilting

стежо́к [stye-zhók] sm. stitch

стека́ть [stye-kǎt'] (сте́чь) vi. to trickle

стекло́ [styek-ló] sn. glass

стекло́видный [styek-la-vʼĕd-nǎy] adj. vitreous

стекля́нный [styek-lyǎn-nǎy] adj. glass-, glassy

стеко́льщик [stye-kólʼ-shchik] sm. glazier

стели́ть [stye-lʼĕt'] (стла́ть) vt. to make the bed; to spread

сте́лька [styélʼ-ka] sf. inner sole, shoe-sock

сте́льная [styelʼ-nǎ-ya] adj. with calf (of cow)

стена́ [stye-nǎ] sf. wall

стена́ть [stye-nǎt'] (за-) vi. to groan, moan

стенно́й [styen-nóy] adj. mural

сте́ньга [styén-ga] sf. top-mast

степе́нный [stye-pyén-nǎy] adj. demure, sedate

сте́пень [styé-pyen'] sf. degree, grade

степь [styépʼ] sf. steppe, veldt

степня́к [styep-nyǎk] sm. inhabitant of the steppe

сте́рва [styér-va] sf. carcass, carrion

стереже́ние [stye-rye-zhé-nye] sn. custody, guard(ing), watch(ing)

стере́чь [stye-ryéch'] vt. to guard, watch over; to take care of someone

сте́ржень [styér-zhen'] sm. rod; shank; plug

стери́льный [stye-rʼĕlʼ-nǎy] adj. sterile, sterilized

стерпе́ть [styer-pyét'] vt. to endure, tolerate

стесне́ние [styes-nyé-nye] sn. constraint

стеснённый [styes-nyón-nǎy] adj. cramped, pinched

стесни́тельный [styes-nʼĕ-tyelʼ-nǎy] adj. cumbrous, inconvenient; troublesome

стесня́ть [stye-snyǎt'] (стесни́ть) vt. to constrain, embarrass, hamper; –ся [-sya] vi. to feel shy; to be ashamed

стече́ние [stye-ché-nye] sn. confluence; coincidence

стиль [stʼĕlʼ] sm. style; –ный [-nǎy] adj. stylish

стира́лка [stʼi-rǎl-ka] sf. dishcloth; scrubber

стира́ть [stʼi-rǎt'] (вы́-) vt. to launder, wash; to dust, rub off, wipe

сти́рка [stʼér-ka] sf. wash(ing)

сти́скивать [stʼés-ki-vat'] (сти́снуть) vt. to clench; to hug; to squeeze

стих [stʼĕch] sm. verse; –и [-ĕ] sm. pl. poems, poetry

стиха́ть [stʼi-chǎt'] (стиха́-нуть) vi. to abate; to calm down; to become speechless

стихи́йный [stʼi-chĕ-nǎy] adj. elemental

стихи́я [stʼi-chĕ-ya] sf. element

стихосложе́ние [stʼi-cha-sla-zhé-nye] sn. versification; prosody (science)

стихотворе́ние [stʼi-cha-tva-ryé-nye] sn. poem

стихотво́рец [stʼi-cha-tvó-ryets] sm. poet

стихотво́рный [stʼi-cha-tvór-nǎy] adj. poetical

стихотворство [st'i-cha-tvór-stvó] *sn.* poetry

сто [sto] *num.* hundred

стог [stog] *sm.* haystack; mow, rick

стоимость [stó-i-möst'] *sf.* cost, value, worth

стоить [stó-it'] *vi.* to cost, to be worth

стойка [stóy-ka] *sf.* bar, counter; prop, support

стойкий [stóy-ki] *adj.* firm, staunch; stedfast

стойло [stóy-lö] *sn.* horse-box, pen, stall

стоймя [stoy-myä] *adv.* erect, upright

сток [stok] *sm.* drip, flow; drain, sewer

стократный [sta-krät-näy] *adj.* centuple

стол [stol] *sm.* table; board, meal, repast; **со -ом** [sa -óm] with board

столб [stolb] *sm.* column, pillar, post; **-ец** [-yéts] newspaper column

столбенеть [stalb-bye-nyét'] (о-) *vi.* to be dumbfounded

столбняк [stalb-nyäk] *sm.* stupor; tetanus

столетие [sta-lyé-tye] *sn.* age, century; centenary

столетний [sta-lyét-n'i] *adj.* centennial

столица [sta-l'ē-tsa] *sf.* capital, metropolis

столичный [sta-l'ēch-näy] *adj.* metropolitan

столкновение [stal-kna-vyé-nye] *sn.* collision, impact

столоваться [sta-la-vät'-sya] *vi.* to board, to feed

столовая [sta-ló-va-ya] *sf.* dining-room, mess-room, refectory

столочь [sta-lóch'] *vt.* to grind, pound

столпиться [stal-p'ét'-sya] *vi.* to crowd, throng

столпотворение [stal-pa-tva-ryé-nye] *sn.* chaos, crowding, disorder

столько [stol'-kö] *adv.* so many, so much

столяр [sta-lyär] *sm.* carpenter, joiner; cabinet-maker

столярня [sta-lyär-nya] *sf.* carpenter's workshop

стонать [sta-nät'] (за-) *vi.* to moan; to sigh

стопа [sta-pä] *sf.* foot, sole; footprint; foot (*measure*); ream (*of paper*)

стопор [stó-pör] *sm.* catch, plug

сторговаться [star-ga-vät'-sya] *vi.* to conclude a bargain; to come to an understanding

сторож [stó-rözh] *sm.* caretaker, watchman; keeper; warder

сторожить [sta-ra-zhét'] *vt.* to guard, watch

сторожка [sta-rózh-ka] *sf.* lodge; sentry-box

сторона [sta-ra-nä] *sf.* side

сторониться [sta-ra-n'ét'-sya] (по-) *vi.* to avoid, shun, withdraw; to stand aside

сторонний [sta-rón-n'i] *adj.* irrelevant

сторонник [sta-rón-n'ik] *sm.* adherent, partisan, supporter

стоялый [sta-yä-läy] *adj.* stale

стояние [sta-yä-nye] *sn.* bearing, deportment; standing

стоянка [sta-yän-ka] *sf.* stand; billet, quarters

стоять [sta-yát'] (по-) *vi.* to stand; to stay

стоячий [sta-yā-chi] *adj.* stagnant; standing, upright

стравливать [stráv-l'i-vat'] (стравить) *vt.* to trample (on grass); to incite

страда [strā-dá] *sf.* coll. harvest-time

страдалец [stra-dā-lyets] *sm.* martyr; sufferer

страдание [stra-dā-nye] distress, suffering

страдательный [stra-dā-tyel'-nǎy] *adj.* gram. passive

страдать [stra-dát'] (по-) *vi.* to bear, endure, suffer

страдающий [stra-dā-yōō-shchi] *adj.* distressed

стража [strázha] *sf.* guard, watch

страна [stra-ná] *sf.* country, land, region

страница [stra-n'ē-tsa] *sf.* leaf, page

странник [strān-n'ik] *sm.* pilgrim, traveller, wanderer

странничество [stran-n'ē-chest-vŏ] *sn.* pilgrimage

странность [strān-nŏst'] *sf.* quaintness; strangeness

странный [strān-nǎy] *adj.* odd, peculiar, queer, strange

странствование [strān-stva-va-nye] *sn.* roaming, wandering

странствующий [strān-stvŏō-yōō-shchi] *adj.* ambulant; — **актёр** [- ak-tyór] *sm.* strolling player; — **музыкант** [- mŏō-zā-kánt] *sm.* minstrel; — **рыцарь** [- rā-tsar'] *sm.* knight-errant

страстишка [stras-t'ēsh-ka] *sf.* addiction

страстный [strāst-nǎy] *adj.* passionate; **страстная неделя** [strāst-na-ya nye-dyé-lya] *sf.* Holy Week

страсть [strāst'] *sf.* passion; craving; lust; *adv.* awfully

страус [strāōōs] *sm.* ostrich

страх [strāch] *sm.* fear, scare, terror, trepidation; *adv.* dreadfully, terribly

страхование [stra-cha-vā-nye] *sn.* insurance

страховать [stra-cha-vát'] (за-) *vt.* to insure

страшилище [stra-shí-l'i-shche] *sn.* fright; scarecrow

страшить [stra-shit'] (y-) *vt.* to alarm, frighten, terrify; **-ся** [-sya] *vi.* to be afraid

страшный [strāsh-nǎy] *adj.* dreadful, ghastly, terrible; — **суд** [- sŏōd] *sm.* doomsday

стращание [stra-shchā-nye] *sn.* intimidation

стрекало [strye-kā-lŏ] *sn.* goad

стрекоза [strye-kŏ-za] *sf.* dragon-fly; *coll.* madcap

стрекотать [strye-ka-tát'] (стрекотнуть) *vi.* to chirp, jabber

стрела [strye-lá] *sf.* arrow, bolt; dart

стрелец [strye-lyéts] *sm.* archer; marksman; musketeer

стрелка [stryél-ka] *sf.* hand, needle, pointer

стрелок [strye-lók] *sm.* rifle-man

стрелочник [stryé-lach-n'ik] *sm.* signalman

стрельба [stryel'-bā] *sf.* firing, shooting; cannonade

стрельбище [stryél'-bi-shche] *sn.* rifle-range

стрелять [strye-lyát'] (стрельнуть) *vi.* to fire, shoot

стремглав [stryem-gláv] *adv.* headlong, rashly

стремительный [strye-mé-tyel'-năy] *adj.* impetuous, violent

стремиться [strye-mét'-sya] *vi.* to aspire; to crave, long

стремление [stryem-lyé-nye] *sn.* ardour, vehemence; aspiration, inclination, yearning

стремнина [stryem-n'ē-na] *sf.* rapid(s); cliff, precipice

стремя [stryé-mya] *sn.* stirrup

стремянка [strye-myán-ka] *sf.* step-ladder

стреноживание [strye-nó-zhi-va-nye] *sn.* hobbling

стриж [strézh] *sm.* martin

стрижка [strézh-ka] *sf.* haircutting; shearing

стричь [str'ēch'] (по-) *vt.* to cut; to clip, shear

строгало [stra-gá-lŏ] *sn.* plane (tool)

строгать [stra-gát'] (вы-) *vt.* to plane, shave

строгий [stró-gi] *adj.* severe, strict; stringent

строевой [stra-ye-vóy] *adj.* front-line

строение [stra-yé-nye] *sn.* building, construction, edifice; texture; tuning

строитель [stra-ē-tyel'] *sm.* builder

строить [stró-it'] (по-) *vt.* to build, construct; *mus.* to tune; *mil.* to draw up, line up; **стройся!** [stróy-sya] fall in!

строй [stróy] *sm.* arrangement, order, régime; *mus.* tune; *mil.* formation, front, line

стройка [stróy-ka] *sf.* building, construction

стройный [stróy-năy] *adj.* harmonious, in tune; proportionate, shapely

строка [stra-ká] *sf.* line; **красная –** [krás-na-ya –] new paragraph

стропило [stra-p'ē-lŏ] *sn.* rafter, truss

строптивый [strap-t'ē-văy] *adj.* contrary, disobedient, obstinate

строчить [stra-chét'] (на-) *vt.* to scribble; to back stitch

строчка [stróch-ka] *sf.* hemstitch; short printed or written line

строчной [strach-nóy] *adj.* linear; small; **строчная буква** [strach-nă-ya bŏŏk-va] *sf.* small letter; *typ.* lower-case

струбцинка [strŏŏb-ts'ēn-ka] *sf.* cramp-iron

струг [strŏŏg] *sm. tech.* plane, scraper

стружка [strŏŏzh-ka] *sf.* planing; chip, shaving(s)

струистый [strŏŏ-és-tăy] *adj.* undulating, wavy

струиться [strŏŏ-ēt'-sya] *vi.* to flow, ripple

структурный [strŏŏk-tŏŏr-năy] *adj.* structural

струна [strŏŏ-ná] *sf.* string (gut or wire)

струп [strŏŏp] *sm.* scab

стручковый [strŏŏch-kó-văy] *adj.* leguminous

стручок [strŏŏ-chók] *sm.* pod; silica

струя [strŏŏ-yá] *sf.* current, stream; ray; jet, spout

стряпать [stryá-pat'] *vt.* to dress, concoct, cook

стряпня [stryap-nyä] *sf.* cooking, dressing (*culinary*)

стряпчий [stryáp-chi] *adj. as sm.* counsel, lawyer, notary

стрястись [strya-st'ěs'] *vi.* to befall, happen, occur

стряхивать [strya-chi-vat'] (стряхнуть) *vt.* to shake down, shake off

студенеть [stoo-dye-nyét'] *vi.* to get cold, cool down

студенистый [stoo-dye-n'ís-täy] *adj.* gelatinous

студент [stoo-dyént] *sm.* student, undergraduate

студень [stoo-dyen'] *sm.* brawn; jelly

студить [stoo-d'ět'] *vt.* to chill, cool, refrigerate

студия [stoo-dya] *sf.* studio

стужа [stoo-zha] *sf.* cold, frost

стук [stook] *sm.* knock, rap, tap; clatter, patter

стукальце [stoo-käl'-tsye] *sn.* knocker

стул [stool] *sm.* chair, seat

стульчак [stool'-chäk] *sm.* stool

ступа [stoo-pä] *sf.* mortar (*vessel*)

ступать [stoo-pät'] (ступить) *vi.* to step, stride, tread

ступень [stoo-pyén'] *sf.* rung, step; phase

ступица [stoo-p'ě-tsa] *sf.* hub, nave

ступня [stoop-nyä] *sf.* sole (of foot)

стучать [stoo-chät'] (стукнуть) *vi.* to hammer, knock

стыд [städ] *sm.* disgrace, shame

стыдить [stä-d'ět'] *vt.* to shame; -ся [-sya] *vi.* to be ashamed

стыдливый [städ-l'ě-väy] *adj.* bashful, modest, shy

стык [stäk] *sm.* abutment, butt; joint, splice

стынуть [stä-nöot'] *vi.* to cool, tepefy

стычка [stäch-ka] *sf.* dispute, quarrel

стягивать [styä-gi-vat'] (стянуть) *vt.* to tighten; to lace, strap

стяжание [stya-zhá-nye] *sn.* acquisition

стяжательный [stya-zhá-tyel'-näy] *adj.* covetous, greedy

стяжать [stya-zhát'] *vt.* to acquire, obtain

суббота [sōōb-bó-ta] *sf.* Saturday

субъект [sōō-byékt] *sm.* subject

субъективный [sōō-byek-t'ěv-näy] *adj.* subjective

сугроб [sōō-grób] *sm.* snow-drift

сугубый [sōō-góo-bäy] *adj.* especial, particular; individual, own, personal (as one's opinion)

суд [sōōd] *sm.* court, tribunal; **военный** – [va-yén-näy –] court martial; **третейский** – [trye-tyéy-ski –] Court of Referees

судак [sōō-däk] *sm.* pike (*fish*)

сударыня [sōō-dä-rä-nya] *sf.* lady, madam

сударь [sōō-dar'] *sm.* master

судебник [sōō-dyéb-n'ik] *sm.* code of law

судебный [sōō-dyéb-näy] *adj.* legal

судейский [sōō-dyéy-ski] *adj.* judicial

судимость [sōō-d'ě-möst'] *sf.* conviction

судить [soo-d'ět'] *vt.* to judge, try

судно [soo̅d-nŏ] *sn.* boat, ship, vessel

судовладелец [soo-da-vla-dyé-lyets] *sm.* shipowner

судовой [soo-da-vóy] *adj.* naval, ship's

судоговорение [soo-da-ga-va-ryé-nye] *sn.* pleading, proceedings

судок [soo-dók] *sm.* castor, cruet; set of dishes

судомойка [soo-da-móy-ka] *sf.* scullery-maid; dish-washer; scullery

судопроизводство [soo-pra-iz-vód-stvŏ] *sn.* legal procedure

судорога [soo-da-ra-ga] *sf.* convulsion, cramp

судорожный [soo-da-razh-nǎy] *adj.* spasmodic

судостроение [soo-da-stra-yé-nye] *sn.* shipbuilding

судоустройство [soo-da-oo-stróy-stvŏ] *sn.* judicial system

судоходный [soo-da-chód-nǎy] *adj.* navigable

судоходство [soo-da-chód-stvŏ] *sn.* navigation

судьба [soo̅d'-bā] *sf.* destiny, fate

судья [soo-dyā] *sm.* judge; **мировой –** [m'i-ra-vóy –] Justice of the Peace

суеверие [soo-ye-vyé-rye] *sn.* superstition

суеверный [soo-ye-vyér-nǎy] *adj.* superstitious

суета [soo-ye-tā] *sf.* fuss; *fig.* vanity

суетиться [soo-ye-t'ět'-sya] *vi.* to bustle, fidget, fuss

суетливый [soo-yet-l'ě-vǎy] *adj.* anxious, restless; fussy

суетный [soo-yet-nǎy] *adj.* idle, vain

суждение [soo̅zh-dyé-nye] *sn.* judgment, sentence

сужение [soo-zhé-nye] *sn.* contraction, narrowing

сук [sook] *sm.* bough, branch

сука [soo-ka] *sf.* bitch

сукно [sook-nó] *sn.* cloth

суконный [soo-kón-nǎy] *adj.* of cloth; **– товар** – [ta-vár] *sm.* clothing

суконщик [soo-kón-shchik] *sm.* clothier, draper

сумасброд [soo-ma-zbród] *sm.* extravagant person

сумасбродничать [soo-ma-zbród-n'i-chat'] *vi.* to behave extravagantly

сумасбродный [soo-ma-zbród-nǎy] *adj.* crazy, extravagant, wild

сумасшедший [soo-mas-shéd-shi] *adj.* insane, mad; *as sm.* lunatic

сумасшествие [soo-mas-shé-stvye] *sn.* lunacy, madness

суматоха [soo-ma-tó-cha] *sf.* disorder, turmoil

сумерки [soo-myer-ki] *sf. pl.* dusk, twilight

сумка [soom-ka] *sf.* handbag; satchel; wallet; soldier's pack; follicle, pouch

сумма [soom-ma] *sf.* amount, sum, sum total

сумрак [soom-rak] *sm.* darkness, obscurity; *fig.* gloom

сумрачный [soom-rach-nǎy] *adj.* cloudy, overcast; gloomy

сумчатый [soom-chā-tǎy] *adj.* marsupial

сундук [soon-dook] *sm.* box, chest, trunk; coffer

суп [sōōp] *sm.* soup; **-ник** [-n'ik] *sm.* tureen

супонь [sōō-pón'] *sf.* collar, thong (*of harness*)

супруг [sōōp-rōōg] *sm.* husband; **-а**, *sf.* wife

супружеский [sōōp-rōō-zhes-ki] *adj.* conjugal, marital

супружество [sōōp-rōō-zhest-vŏ] *sn.* marriage, matrimony

сургуч [sōōr-gōōch] *sm.* sealing-wax

сурдинка [sōōr-d'ĕn-ka] *sf. mus.* mute

сурик [sōō-r'ik] *sm.* red lead

суровость [sōō-ró-vŏst'] *sf.* austerity, sternness; harshness, severity

суровый [sōō-ró-văy] *adj.* austere, rigorous; coarse; grim; unbleached

сурок [sōō-rók] *sm.* marmot

суррогат [sōōr-ra-gắt] *sm.* substitute

сурьмить [sōōr'-m'ĕt'] *vt.* to blacken, darken (*eyebrows*)

сусаль [sōō-sắl'] *sf.* tinsel

сустав [sōōs-tắv] *sm.* articulation, joint; **-ный** [-năy] *adj.* articulate

сутки [sōōt-ki] *sf. pl.* day and night (24 *hours*)

суточный [sōō-tach-năy] *adj.* daily, diurnal

сутулиться [sōō-tōō-l'it'-sya] *vi.* to stoop

сутуловатый [sōō-tōō-la-vă-tăy] *adj.* round-shouldered

суть [sōōt'] *sf.* essential(s), substance; gist

сутяга [sōō-tyắ-ga] *sm., f.* pettifogger, plotter

сутяжничать [sōō-tyắzh-

n'i-chat'] *vi.* to cheat; to quibble

суфлёр [sōōf-lyór] *sm. theat.* prompter

суфлировать [sōōf-l'ḗ-ra-vat'] *vi. theat.* to prompt

суффикс [sōōf-fiks] *sm.* suffix

сухарь [sōō-chár'] *sm.* rusk

сухарница [sōō-chár-n'i-tsa] *sf.* biscuit-tin

суховатый [sōō-cha-vă-tăy] *adj.* rather dry

сухожильный [sōō-cha-zhél'-năy] *adj.* sinewy

сухой [sōō-chóy] *adj.* dry, lean, parched

сухомятка [sōō-cha-myắt-ka] *sf.* dry *or* solid food

сухопарый [sōō-cha-pă-răy] *sm.* lanky, lean, scraggy

сухопутный [sōō-cha-pōōt-năy] *adj.* of dry land; terrestrial

сухость [sōō-chŏst'] *sf.* aridity, dryness

сухотка [sōō-chót-ka] *sf.* emaciation

сухощавый [sōō-cha-shchá-văy] *adj.* emaciated, meagre

сучильщик [sōō-chél'-shchik] *sm.* spinner

сучить [sōō-chét'] (с-) *vt.* to roll up, spin, twist

сучковатый [sōōch-ka-vă-tăy] *adj.* knotty

сучок [sōō-chók] *sm.* knot (*in trunk of tree*)

суша [sōō-sha] *sf.* dry land

сушение [sōō-shé-nye] *sn.* desiccation, drying

сушилка [sōō-shil-ka] *sf.* drying apparatus

сушить [sōō-shét'] (вы́-) *vt.* to air, dry

сушильня [sōō-shél'-nya] *sf.* desiccator, drying-room

сушь [sōosh'] *sf.* dryness; dry weather

существенный [sŏŏ-shchést-vyen-nǎy] *adj.* essential; substantial

существительное [sŏŏ-shchest-v'ē-tyel'-nǎy] *adj.* substantive; not subsidiary

имя существительное [ē-mya sŏŏ-shchest-v'ē-tyel'-na-ye] *sn. gram.* noun, substantive

существо [sŏŏ-shchest-vó] *sn.* being, creature; essence, nature

существование [sŏŏ-shchest-va-vǎ-nye] *sn.* existence, subsistence

существовать [sŏŏ-shchest-va-vát'] *vi.* to be, exist, live

сущий [sōō-shchi] *adj.* existing; real, true

сущность [sōō-shchnŏst'] *sf.* essence, nature, substance

сфера [sfyé-ra] *sf.* realm, scope, sphere

сферический [sfye-rē-ches-ki] *adj.* spherical

схватка [schvát-ka] *sf.* conflict, scuffle; encounter, skirmish

схватывать [schvá-tǎ-vat'] (схватить) *vt.* to grasp, seize

схема [schyé-ma] *sf.* project, scheme

схлынуть [schlǎ-nōōt'] *vi.* to abate, recede

сход [schod] *sm.* descending, descent; meeting

сходить [scha-d'ēt'] (сойти́) *vi.* to alight, descend, go down; **-ся** [-sya] (сойти́сь) *vi.* to come together, join in, meet

сходка [schód-ka] *sf.* assemblage, gathering

сходни [schód-n'i] *sf. pl.* gangway

сходный [schód-nǎy] *adj.* analogous, similar; reasonable

сходство [schód-stvŏ] *sn.* likeness, similarity

сцеживать [stsyé-zhi-vat'] (сцеди́ть) *vt.* to decant, draw off, strain

сцена [stsé-na] *sf.* scene; stage

сцеп [stsyep] *sm.* chain, hook, link

сцепка [stsyép-ka] *sf.* coupling

сцепление [stsye-plyé-nye] *sn.* adhesion; cohesion; clutch

сцеплять [stsyep-lyát'] (сцепи́ть) *vt.* to chain, couple, link together; **-ся** [-sya] *vi.* to grapple with; to catch (on something)

счалка [schál-ka] *sf.* hawser

счастливец [schast-l'ē-vyets] *sm.* lucky man

счастливый [schast-l'ē-vǎy] *adj.* fortunate, happy, lucky

счастье [schás-tye] *sn.* happiness; good fortune

счерпывать [schér-pǎ-vat'] (счерпнуть) *vi.* to scoop

счерчивать [schér-chi-vat'] (счерти́ть) *vt.* to copy, trace; to draw, sketch

счёсывать [schó-sǎ-vat'] (счеса́ть) *vt.* to comb out; to card off

счёт [schót] *sm.* account; bill; score

счётный [schót-nǎy] *adj.* account-, of account; **-ная линейка** [schót-na-ya l'i-nyéy-ka] slide-rule; **-машина** [– ma-shē-na] *sf.* calculating machine

счетовод [sche-ta-vód] *sm.* book-keeper; **-ство** [-stvŏ] *sn.* book-keeping

счётчик [schót-chik] *sm.* counter; meter, register; teller

счёты [schó-tŭ] *sm. pl.* abacus

счисление [schis-lyé-nye] *sn.* calculation, numeration, reckoning

считать (schi-tát') (счесть) *vt.* to compute, count up; to reckon, score

счищать [schi-shchát'] (счистить) *vt.* to clean, cleanse

сшибать [sshi-bát'] (сшибить) *vt.* to cast off, strike down

сшивать [sshi-vát' (сшить) *vt.* to sew up; to patch

сшивка [sshёv-ka] *sf.* sewing, tacking

съедать [sye-dát'] (съесть) *vt.* to devour, eat up

съедобный [sye-dób-nǎy] *adj.* edible

съёживаться [syó-zhi-vat'-sya] *vi.* to contract, shrink, shrivel up; to cower

съезд [syezd] *sm.* conference, congress, convention

съезжать [syez-zhát'] (съехать) *vi.* to run down, slide down; to descend (*in a vehicle*)

съёмка [syóm-ka] *sf.* plan, survey; cut (*at cards*)

сыворотка [să-va-rat-ka] *sf.* buttermilk; whey; *med.* serum

сыграться [să-grát'-sya] *vi.* to practise, rehearse

сын [săn] *sm.* son

сыновний [să-nóv-ni] *adj.* filial

сынок [să-nók] *sm.* sonny

сыпать [să-pat'] (по-) *vt.* to pour, scatter, strew

сыпучий [să-pŏŏ-chi] *adj.* friable

сыпь [săp] *sf.* eruption, rash

сыр [săr] *sm.* cheese

сыреть [să-rýét'] (о-) *vi.* to get damp, moist

сырец [să-rýéts] *sm.* raw silk

сырник [săr-n'ik] *sm.* cheese-cake

сыроварня [să-ra-vár-nya] *sf.* cheese dairy

сыроватый [să-ra-vá-tǎy] *adj.* dampish

сырой [să-róy] *adj.* damp, raw, sodden

сыромятник [să-ra-myát-n'ik] *sm.* tanner

сыромятня [să-ra-myát-nya] *sf.* tannery

сырость [să-rŏst'] *sf.* humidity, moisture

сырьё [să-ryó] *sm.* raw material

сыск [săsk] *sm.* pursuit, search

сыскной [săsk-nóy] *adj.* detective, investigating

ситный [săt-nǎy] *adj.* nutritive, satisfying

сытый [să-tǎy] *adj.* replete, satisfied

сыщик [să-shchik] *sm.* detective, inquiry agent

сюда [syŏŏ-dá] *adv.* here, hither

сюжет [syŏŏ-zhét] *sm.* subject; theme

сюртук [syŏŏr-tŏŏk] *sm.* frock-coat

сюсюкание [syŏŏ-syŏŏ-ka-nye] *sn.* lisping

сяк [syák] *adv.* **так и сяк** [tăk i syák] this way and that

сям [syám] *adv.* **там и сям** [tăm i syám] here and there

T

та [tā] *f. pron.* that

табак [ta-bāk] *sm.* tobacco, tobacco plant; plug (*for chewing*): **нюхательный —** [nyōō-cha-tyel'-năy —] snuff

табакерка [ta-ba-kyér-ka] *sf.* snuff-box; tobacco pouch

табачник [ta-bāch-n'ik] *sm.* tobacconist; heavy smoker; habitual snuff-taker

табачок [ta-ba-chók] *sm.* pinch of snuff

табель [ta-byél'] *sf.* list, roll, table

таблетка [ta-blyét-ka] *sf.* lozenge, tablet, tabloid

таблица [ta-bl'ē-tsa] *sf.* table (*as multiplication table, etc.*)

табличный [ta-bl'ēch-năy] *adj.* tabular

табор [tā-bŏr] *sm.* encampment; a gipsies' camp

табун [ta-bōōn] *sm.* stud (*horses*)

табуретка [ta-bŏō-ryét-ka] *sf.* stool

тавро [ta-vró] *sn.* brand, mark, stamp

таган [ta-gān] *sm.* trivet

таз [tāz] *sm.* basin; pelvis; **-овый** [-ó-văy] *adj.* pelvic

таинственность [ta-ēn-stvyen-nŏst'] *sf.* secrecy; mysteriousness

таинственный [ta-ēn-stvyen-năy] *adj.* mysterious, secret; sacramental

таинство [tā-in-stvŏ] *sn.* sacrament; mystery

таить [ta-ēt'] *vt.* to conceal, hide, secrete

тайком [tay-kóm] *adv.* secretly, surreptitiously

тайна [táy-na] *sf.* secret; privacy

тайник [táy-n'ik] *sm.* secret hiding place

тайный [táy-năy] *adj.* cryptic, mysterious, secret; **— Совет** [- să-vyét] Privy Council

так [tāk] *adv.* so, thus

такать [tā-kat] *vi. coll.* to affirm; to be a yes-man

такелаж [ta-kye-lāzh] *sm.* rigging, tackle

также [tak-zhe] *adv.* also, likewise, too

таков, таковой, таковский, такой [ta-kóv, ta-ka-vóy, tă-kov-ski, ta-kóy] *adj.* such; **таким образом** [ta'k'ēm ób-ra-sŏm] in such a manner

такса [tāk-sa] *sf.* fixed rate, tariff; basset; dachshund

таксировать [tak-s'ē-ra-vat'] *vt.* to fix prices, to tax

такт [tākt] *sm.* tact; *mus.* beat, measure, time; tact

тактик [tāk-t'ik] *sm.* tactician; **-а,** *sf.* tactic(s)

тактичный [tak-t'ēch-năy] *adj.* tactful

талант [ta-lănt] *sm.* gift, talent; **-ливый** [-l'ē-văy] *adj.* gifted, talented

талия [tā-lya] *sf.* waist; deal (*cards*)

талон [ta-lón] *sm.* coupon; money-order

тальк [tāl'k] *sm.* talc

там [tām] *adv.* there, yonder; **-ошний** [-ash-n'i] *adj.* from that place

тамбур [tam-bōōr] *sm.* drum; embroidery frame; platform (*of railway carriage*); **-ное шитьё** [-na-ye shı-tyó] *sn.* embroidery

таможня [ta-mózh-nya] *sf.* custom-house

танец [tā-nyets] *sm.* dance

тантьема [tan-tyé-ma] *sf.* bonus

танцовать [tan-tsa-vát'] (по-) *vt.* to dance

танцовщик [tan-tsóv-shchik] *sm.* dancer

танцор [tan-tsór] *sm.* trained dancer

тапёр [ta-pyór] *sm.* dance-pianist

тапочка [tā-pach-ka] *sf.* gym shoe, slipper

тара [tā-ra] *sf.* tare

тарабарский [ta-ra-bār-ski] *adj.* incomprehensible, obscure

таракан [ta-ra-kān] *sm.* blackbeetle; cockroach

таран [ta-rān] *sm.* battering-ram; *tech.* ram

тарань [ta-rān'] *sf.* carp

таращить [ta-ra-shchēt'] (вы-) *vt.* to gape, stare

тарелка [ta-ryél-ka] *sf.* plate; *sf. pl.* cymbals

тартинка [tar-t'ēn-ka] *sf.* sandwich

таскать [tas-kāt'] (вы-) *vt.* to drag, draw, lug

тасовать [ta-sa-vát'] (с-) *vt.* to shuffle (*cards*)

тасовка [ta-sóv-ka] *sf.* shuffling (*cards*)

тачка [tāch-ka] *sf.* wheel-barrow

тащить [ta-shchēt'] (по-) *vt.* to haul, tow; to trail

таять [tā-yat'] (рас-) *vi.* to melt, thaw; *fig.* to waste away

тварь [tvar'] *sf.* creature, thing; *fig.* подлая – [pódla-ya –] *sf.* vermin

твердеть [tvyer-dyét'] *vi.* to harden; to become solid, become tough

твердить [tvyer-d'ēt'] *vt.* to memorize; to reiterate

твёрдость [tvyór-dŏst] *sf.* solidity, toughness; *fig.* firmness, hardness; grit

твёрдый [tvyór-dăy] *adj.* firm, hard, solid; *fig.* resolved, steadfast

твердыня [tvyer-dǎ-nya] *sf.* citadel, stronghold

твой [tvóy] *pron.* thy, thine

творение [tva-ryé-nye] *sn.* creation; creative work

творец [tva-ryéts] *sm.* author; creator

творительный [tva-r'ē-tyel'-năy] *adj. gram.* ablative, instrumental

творить [tva-r'ēt'] (со-) *vt.* to create, make, produce

творог [tva-róg] *sm.* curd(s)

творческий [tvór-ches-ki] *adj.* creative

театр [tye-ātr] *sm.* theatre

театральный [tye-a-trāl'-năy] *adj.* scenic, theatrical

тёзка [tyóz-ka] *sf.* namesake

текстильный [tyek-stēl'-năy] *adj.* textile

текучий [tye-kōō-chi] *adj.* flowing, running, streaming

текущий [tye-kōō-shchi] *adj.* current, present

телега [tye-lyé-ga] *sf.* cart, truck

телеграфировать [tye-lye-gra-f'ē-ra-vat'] *vt.* to telegraph, wire

телеграфный [tye-lye-grāf-năy] *adj.* telegraphic

тележка [tye-lyézh-ka] *sf.* barrow, trolley

телёнок [tye-lyó-nŏk] *sm.* calf (*animal*)

телесный [tye-lyés-năy] *adj.* corporeal

телефонировать [tye-lye-fa-n'ě-ra-vat'] *vi.* to telephone

тёлка [tyól-ka] *sf.* heifer

тело [tyé-lŏ] *sn.* body; substance

телогрейка [tye-la-gryéy-ka] *sf.* cardigan

телодвижение [tye-la-dv'i-zhé-nye] *sn.* physical exercise

телосложение [tye-la-sla-zhé-nye] *sn.* build, physique

тельце [tyél'-tse] *sn.* corpuscle

телятина [tye-lyă-t'i-na] *sf.* veal

тема [tyé-ma] *sf.* theme; subject, topic

темнеть [tyem-nyét'] (за-) *vi.* to get dark

темница [tyem-n'ě-tsa] *sf.* jail, prison

темноватый [tyem-na-vă-tăy] *adj.* somewhat dark

темнота [tyem-na-tă] *sf.* darkness, obscurity

тёмный [tyóm-năy] *adj.* dark, obscure; drab, gloomy

темя [tyé-mya] *sn.* crown of head, sinciput; peak, summit

тенёта [tye-nyó-ta] *sn.* net, snare

тенистый [tye-n'és-tăy] *adj.* shaded, shady

тень [tyén'] *sf.* shade, shadow

теория [tye-ó-rya] *sf.* theory

теперешний [tye-pyé-resh-nij] *adj.* actual, of the present time

теперь [tye-pyér'] *adv.* now

теплеть [tye-plyét'] (по-) *vi.* to get warm

теплица [tye-pl'ě-tsa] *sf.* conservatory, greenhouse

тепло [tye-pló] *sn.* heat, warmth; mildness (*weather*); *adv.* warmly; *fig.* heartily; it is warm

тепловатый [tye-pla-vă-tăy] *adj.* lukewarm, tepid

тепловой [tye-pla-vóy] *adj.* thermal

теплоёмкость [tye-pla-yóm-kŏst'] *sf.* specific heat

теплокровный [tye-pla-króv-năy] *adj.* warm-blooded

тепломер [tye-pla-myér] *sm.* thermometer

теплопроводный [tye-pla-pra-vód-năy] *adj.* heat-conducting

теплородный [tye-pla-ród-năy] *adj.* calorific

теплота [tye-pla-tă] *sf.* warmth

тёплый [tyó-plăy] *adj.* mild; tepid, warm

терапевтический [tye-rav-pye-t'ě-ches-ki] *adj.* therapeutic

теребить [tye-rye-b'ět'] (pac-) *vt.* to pluck

тереть [tye-ryét'] (по-) *vt.* to chafe, grate, scrape

терзание [tyer-ză-nye] *sn.* agony, torment

терзать [tyer-zăt'] (ис-, pac-) *vt.* to lacerate, tear to pieces; to tease, torment, worry

тёрка [tyór-ka] *sf.* grater

термин [tyér-min] *sm.* expression, term

терминология [tyer-m'i-na-ló-gya] *sf.* nomenclature, terminology

тёрн [tyórn] *sm.* sloe

тернистый [tyer-n'és-tăy] *adj.* prickly, thorny

терновник [tyer-nóv-n'ik] *sm.* brier, gorse

терпеливость [tyer-pye-lé-vŏst'] *sf.* patience, toleration

терпеливый [tyer-pye-lé-vǎy] *adj.* forbearing, patient, tolerant

терпеть [tyer-pyét'] (по-) *vt.* to bear, endure, suffer

терпимый [tyer-p'é-mǎy] *adj.* bearable, tolerable

терпкий [tyérp-ki] *adj.* acrid, bitter, tart

терпуг [tyer-pōŏg] *sm.* rasp

терраса [tyer-rá-sa] *sf.* balcony, terrace

терция [tyér-tsya] *sf.* third (*musical interval*); *typ.* great primer; tierce (*cards*)

терять [tye-ryát'] (по-) *vt.* to forfeit, lose; to waste (*time*); **-ся** [-sya] *vi.* to get lost, lose oneself; to disappear

тесак [tye-sák] *sm.* cutlass

тесать [tye-sát'] (с-) *vt.* to hew

тесёмка [tye-syóm-ka] *sf.* braid, tape

теснина [tye-sn'é-na] *sf.* gorge, narrow pass

теснить [tye-sn'ét'] *vt.* to cram, press; **-ся** [-sya] *vi.* to crowd, hustle, squeeze in

тесноватый [tyes-na-vá-tǎy] *adj.* crowded, crushed

теснота [tyes-na-tá] *sf.* closeness; tightness; crush

тесный [tyés-nǎy] *adj.* narrow, tight; *fig.* intimate

тесто [tyés-tŏ] *sn.* dough, paste

тесть [tyést'] *sm.* father-in-law (*wife's father*)

тётка [tyót-ka] *sf.* auntie (*endearing*)

тетрадь [tye-trád'] *sf.* exercise book

тётя [tyó-tya] *sf.* aunt

техник [tyéch-n'ik] *sm.* mechanic; technician

техника [tyéch-n'i-ka] *sf.* technique

техникум [tyéch-n'i-kōŏm] *sm.* technical college

технический [tyech-n'é-ches-ki] *adj.* technical

технология [tyech-na-ló-gya] *sf.* technology

течение [tye-ché-nye] *sn.* course, current, track

течка [tyéch-ka] *sf.* heat, rut

течь [tyéch'] (по-) *vi.* to flow; to leak; to fly, pass (*time*); *sf.* leakage

тешить [tye-shét'] (у-) *vt.* to gratify, please

тёща [tyó-shcha] *sf.* mother-in-law (*wife's mother*)

тигель [t'é-gel'] *sm.* crucible

тигр [t'ĕgr] *sm.* tiger

тик [t'ĕk] *sm.* fustian, ticking; *med.* tic; *bot.* teak

тиканье [t'é-ka-nye] *sn.* tick, ticking (*of clock, etc.*)

тикать [t'é-kat'] *vi.* to tick

тимиан [t'i-mián] *sm.* thyme

тимпан [t'im-pán] *sm.* kettledrum; tympanum

тина [t'é-na] *sf.* mire, mud, slime

тинистый [t'i-n'és-tǎy] *adj.* muddy, slimy

тип [t'ĕp] *sm.* figure, kind, type

типичный [t'i-p'éch-nǎy] *adj.* typical

типограф [t'i-pó-graf] *sm.* printer

типография [t'i-pa-grá-fya] *sf.* printing works

тир [t'ĕr] *sm.* shooting range

тирада [t'i-rá-da] *sf.* tirade

тираж [t'i-rázh] *sm.* draw (*of lottery, etc.*); circulation (*of newspapers, etc.*)

тиран [t'i-rán] sm. tyrant

тиранство [t'i-rán-stvŏ] sn. tyranny

тире [t'i-rýé] sn. dash, hyphen

тис [t'ĕs] sm. yew(-tree)

тискать [t'ĕs-kat'] (стиснýть) vt. to squeeze; to print, stamp

тиски [t'is-kĕ] sm. pl. press, vice

титул [t'ē-tŏŏl] sm. title

тиф [t'ĕf] sm. typhus; **-озный** [-óz-năy] adj. typhoid

тихий [t'ē-chi] adj. calm, quiet, still

тишина [t'i-shi-ná] sf. silence, tranquility

ткань [tkăn'] sf. cloth, fabric, stuff; tissue, web

тканьё [tka-nyó] sn. weaving

ткать [kăt'] vt. to weave

ткацкий [tkăts-ki] adj. weaver's, woven; **- станок** [- sta-nók] loom

ткач [tkăch] sm. weaver

тление [tlyé-nye] sn. smouldering

тленный [tlyén-năy] adj. frail; perishable

тлетворный [tlye-tvór-năy] adj. baneful

то [to] pron. that; adv. then

товар [ta-vár] sm. merchandise, goods, wares

товарищ [ta-vă-rishch] sm. comrade, mate

товарищество [ta-vă-ri-shchest-vŏ] sn. association, company, society

тогда [tag-dä] adv. at that time, then; **-шний** [-shni] adj. of that time, bygone

то есть [tó yest'] adv. that is to say; **т.е.** = i.e.

тождественный [tazh-dyést-vyen-năy] adj. identical

тоже [tó-zhe] adv. also, too

ток [tok] sm. current (air, electric); threshing floor; pairing time (of birds)

токарный [ta-kăr-năy] adj. turner's, turning; **- станок** [- sta-nók] sm. lathe; **токарная бабка** [ta-kăr-na-ya băb-ka] sf. mandrel

токарня [ta-kăr-nya] sf. turnery

токарь [ta-kăr'] sm. turner

толк [tolk] sm. meaning, sense; doctrine, sect; rumour

толкать [tal-kăt'] (толкнýть) vt. to jostle, push, shove; to nudge

толкач [tal-kăch] sm. pestle, pounder; pusher

толкование [tal-ka-vă-nye] sn. commentary, interpretation

толкователь [tal-ka-vă-tyel'] sm. commentator

толковать [tal-ka-vät'] vt. to comment, explain, interpret; (по-) vi. to converse, discuss, talk

толкотня [tal-ka-tnyă] sf. crush, throng

толмач [tal-măch] sm. interpreter

толочь [ta-lóch] (ис-) vt. to crush, pound, powder

толпа [tal-pá] sf. crowd, mob

толстеть [tal-styét'] (пас-) vi. to become stout

толстокожий [tal-sta-kó-zhi] adj. thick skinned

толстый [tól-stăy] adj. corpulent, fat, stout

толстяк [tal-styăk] sm. fat little man, squab

толчок [tal-chók] sm. jerk, jolt; impulse

толщина [tal-shchi-ná] sf. thickness; corpulence

только [tól'-kŏ] *adv.* merely, only, solely

том [tom] *sm.* tome, volume

томбуй [tam-bŏŏy] *sm.* buoy

томительный [ta-m'é-tyel'-nǎy] *adj.* tiresome, wearisome

томить [ta-m'ét'] (y-) *vt.* to fatigue, harass, weary; **-ся** [-sya] *vi.* to languish, tire; to be oppressed

томление [tam-lyé-nye] *sn.* depression, fatigue, languor

томность [tóm-nŏst'] *sf.* lassitude

тон [ton] *sm.* intonation, tone; *mus.* key

тоника [tó-n'i-ka] *sf. mus.* tonic; keynote

тонический [ta-n'é-ches-ki] *adj.* tonic

тонкий [tón-ki] *adj.* fine, thin; delicate, slender

тонкость [tón-kŏst'] *sf.* acuteness, sharpness, subtlety; thinness

тонна [tón-na] *sf.* ton

тоннаж [tan-názh] *sm.* tonnage

тонуть [ta-nŏŏt'] (по-) *vi.* to drown, to sink

тоня [tó-nya] *sf.* fishery, fishing-place; haul

топать [tó-pat'] *vi.* to stamp *(with foot)*

топить [ta-p'ét'] (за-) *vt.* to heat; to smelt; to founder; to scuttle, sink

топический [ta-p'é-ches-ki] *adj.* topical

топка [tóp-ka] *sf.* furnace; heating; melting

топкий [tóp-ki] *adj.* marshy, muddy, swampy

топливо [tap-l'é-vŏ] *sn.* fuel

тополь [tó-pŏl'] *sm.* poplar

топор [ta-pór] *sm.* axe

топорик [ta-pó-r'ik] *sm.* hatchet

топорный [ta-pór-nǎy] *adj.* coarse, rough

топтать [tap-tát'] (за-) *vt.* to trample

топчак [tap-chák] *sm.* treadmill

топь [top'] *sf.* fen, marsh, swamp

торба [tór-ba] *sf.* nose-bag

торг [torg] *sm.* commerce, trade; bargain, bargaining

торги [tor-gé] *sm. pl.* auction

торговать [tar-ga-vát'] *vt.* to deal in, trade; to negotiate; to peddle; **-ся** [-sya] *vi.* to bargain

торговец [tar-gó-vyets] *sm.* dealer, merchant; shopkeeper

торговля [tar-góv-lya] *sf.* commerce, trade

торговый [tar-gó-vǎy] *adj.* commercial, trading

торжественность [tar-zhést-vyen-nŏst'] *sf.* solemnity

торжественный [tar-zhést-vyen-nǎy] *adj.* pompous, solemn, triumphal

торжество [tar-zhest-vó] *sn.* celebration

торжествующий [tar-zhest-vŏŏ-yōō-shchi] *adj.* exultant, triumphant

тормоз [tór-mŏz] *sm.* brake, check

тормозить [tar-ma-z'ét'] *vt.* to brake, put the brake on

тормошить [tar-ma-shét'] *vt.* to harass, to tease, worry

торопить [ta-ra-p'ét'] (по-) *vt.* to hasten, hurry; to urge; **-ся** [-sya] *vi.* to make haste, be in a hurry

торопливость [ta-ra-pl'ē-vŏst'] sf. haste, speed

торчать [tar-chát'] vi. to protrude, stick out

торчком [tar-chkóm] adv. erectly, on end, uprightly, vertically

тоска [tas-kā] sf. anguish, distress, grief

тоскливый [tas-kl'ē-vǎy] adj. anxious, melancholy, miserable; dull (of mood or weather)

тот [tot] pron. that

тотчас [tót-chas] adv. immediately, instantly

точение [ta-ché-nye] sn. grinding, sharpening, turning

точёный [ta-chó-nǎy] adj. chiselled, well shaped

точилка [ta-chēl-ka] sf. grindstone

точильный [ta-chēl'-nǎy] adj. grinding; — **ремень** [– rye-myén'] sm. razor-strap; – **камень** [– kā-myen'] sm. hone

точильня [ta-chēl'-nya] sf. grinder's workshop

точильщик [ta-chēl'-shchik] sm. grinder

точить [ta-chēt'] vt. to sharpen; to gnaw, wear away; to turn (on lathe)

точка [tóch-ka] sf. dot; full stop; point; stropping; whetting

точно [tóch-nŏ] adv. accurately, exactly; as if; like

точность [tóch-nŏst'] sf. accuracy, exactitude

точный [tóch-nǎy] adj. precise, punctual

тошнить [tash-n'ēt'] vi. to feel sick; to vomit

тошнота [tash-na-tā] sf. nausea, sickness

тошный [tósh-nǎy] adj. nauseating; fig. disgusting, loathsome

тощать [ta-shchāt'] vi. to lose weight; to pine, waste away

тощий [tó-shchi] adj. emaciated, lean, meagre

трава [tra-vā] sf. grass, herb

травинка [tra-v'ēn-ka] sf. blade (of grass)

травить [tra-v'ēt'] vt. to hunt, persecute; to exterminate, poison; to damage; to trample down; to ease, slack

трагедия [tra-gé-dya] sf. tragedy

трагический [tra-gē-cheski] adj. tragic

традиция [tra-d'ē-tsya] sf. tradition

тракт [trakt] sm. highway

трактат [trak-tāt] sm. treatise; treaty

трактир [trak-t'ĕr] sm. inn, public-house

трактирщик [trak-t'ĕr-shchik] sm. innkeeper, publican

трактирщица [trak-t'ĕr-shchi-tsa] sf. hostess

трактовка [trak-tóv-ka] sf. interpretation, treatment

тралить [tra-l'ēt'] vt. to trawl

тральщик [tral'-shchik] sm. trawler; mine-sweeper

транжирить [tran-zhē-rit'] (рас-) vt. to dissipate, squander

транскрипция [tran-skrēp-tsya] sf. transcription

транспортировать [tran-spar-t'ē-ra-vat'] vt. to convey, transport

траншея [tran-shé-ya] sf. dug-out, trench

трапезная [tra-pyéz-na-ya] sf. refectory

трапеция [tra-pyé-tsya] sf. trapeze

трата [trá-ta] sf. expenditure

тратить [trá-t'it'] (по-) vt. to spend; to disburse

тратта [trát-ta] sf. draft, bill of exchange

траур [trá-ōōr] sm. mourning; **-ный** [-nǎy] adj. funereal, mournful, mourning

трафарет [tra-fa-ryét] sm. stencil

треба [tryé-ba] sf. religious ceremony

требник [tryéb-n'ik] sm. breviary; missal; prayer-book

требование [tryé-ba-va-nye] sn. claim, demand, request

требовательный [tryé-ba-va-tyel'-nǎy] adj. exacting, fastidious, particular

требовать [tryé-ba-vat'] (по-) vt. to claim, demand, exact, require

требуемый [tryé-bōō-ye-mǎy] adj. requisite

требуха [trye-bōō-chá] sf. entrails; offal; fig. rubbish

тревога [trye-vó-ga] sf. anxiety, concern, trouble

тревожить [trye-vó-zhit'] (вс-) vt. to alarm, disturb, harass

трегубый [trye-gōō-bǎy] adj. hare-lipped

трезвенник [tryéz-vyen-n'ik] sm. abstainer, teetotaller

трезвон [tryez-vón] sm. chime, peal

трезвонить [tryez-vó-n'it'] vi. to ring a peal

трезвость [tryéz-vŏst'] sf. soberness, temperance

трезвучие [trye-zvōō-chye] sn. mus. triad

трезвый [tryéz-vǎy] adj. sober, temperate; judicious, sound

трезубец [trye-zōō-byets] sm. trident

трель [tryél'] sf. mus. shake, [trill

трельяж [trye-lyázh] sm. lattice-work, trellis

трение [tryé-nye] sn. friction, rubbing

тренировать [trye-n'é-ra-vat'] vt. to train

треножить [trye-nó-zhit'] vt. to fetter; to hobble

треножник [trye-nózh-n'ik] sm. tripod

трепак [trye-pák] sm. Russian dance

трепать [trye-pát'] vt. to beat; to swingle (flax)

трепет [tryé-pet] sm. palpitation, tremble

трепетать [trye-pye-tát'] (за-) vi. to pant, shake, throb

треск [tryésk] sm. crack(ing), crackling

трескаться [tryes-kát-sya] (рас-) vi. to chap, crack

трескотня [tryes-kat-nyá] sf. clatter, rattle

треснуть [tryes-nōōt'] vt. to burst, split

трест [trest] sm. trust

третейский [trye-tyéy-ski] adj. arbitrary

третий [tryé-t'i] num. third

треугольник [trye-ōō-gól'-n'ik] sm. triangle

треугольный [trye-ōō-gól'-nǎy] adj. three-cornered

трефы [tryé-fǎ] sf. pl. clubs (cards)

трёхлетие [tryoch-lyé-tye] *sn.* triennial

трёхмесячный [tryóch-myé-syach-nǎy] *adj.* quarterly, trimestral

трещать [trye-shchát'] (за-) *vi.* to crackle, rattle; to creak; to chirp; to burst, split

трещина [trye-shché-na] *sf.* chink, cleft, crevice, flaw

три [trē] *num.* three

тридцать [tréd-tsat'] *num.* thirty

трико [tri-kó] *sn.* tricot; tights; stockinet

трикотаж [tri-ka-tázh] *sm.* hosiery

трилистник [tri-l'ést-n'ik] *sm.* trefoil; clover; shamrock

тринадцать [tri-nád-tsat'] *num.* thirteen

триста [trís-ta] *num.* three hundred

трогательный [tró-ga-tyel'-nǎy] *adj.* moving, pathetic, touching

трогать [tró-gat'] (тró-нуть) *vt.* to handle, touch

троица [tró-i-tsa] *sf.* Trinity

тройка [tóy-ka] *sf.* troika (*vehicle drawn by three horses abreast*); three (*cards*)

тройной [tray-nóy] *adj.* triple, triplicate; treble

тройня [tróy-nya] *sf.* triplet(s)

трон [tron] *sm.* throne

тропа [tra-pá] *sf.* footpath, path; track

тропики [tró-p'i-ki] *sm. pl.* the tropics

тропический [tra-p'é-ches-ki] *adj.* tropical

тростинка [tras-t'én-ka] *sf.* reed

тростник [trast-n'ék] *sm.* cane; reed; rush

тростить [tras-t'ět'] *vt.* to splice, twist

тростник [trast-n'ěk] *sm.* cane, reed, bush, sedge

трость [tróst'] *sf.* cane, walking-stick

тростянка [tras-tyän-ka] *sf.* reed pipe

тротуар [tra-tōōár] *sm.* pavement

троякий [tra-yä-ki] *adj.* threefold

труба [trōō-bá] *sf.* pipe, tube; funnel; trumpet

трубач [trōō-bách] *sm.* trumpeter; trumpet-player

трубить [trōō-b'ět'] *vi.* to blow, play (*a wind instrument*)

трубка [trōōb-ka] *sf.* smoker's pipe; scroll; tube

трубочист [trōō-ba-chést] *sm.* chimney-sweep

трубчатый [trōōb-chä-tǎy] *adj.* tubular

груд [trōōd] *sm.* labour, toil, work; difficulty, trouble

трудиться [trōō-d'ět'-sya] (по-) *vi.* to work hard

трудновато [trōōd-na-vä-tó] *adv.* rather difficult

трудность [trōōd-nǒst'] *sf.* difficulty

трудный [trōōd-nǎy] *adj.* difficult, hard; laborious

трудовик [trōō-da-v'ěk] *sm.* member of Labour Party

трудолюбивый [trōō-da-lyōō-b'ě-vǎy] *adj.* industrious

трудоспособный [trōō-da-spa-sób-nǎy] *adj.* efficient

трудящиеся [trōō-dyä-shchi-ye-sya] *adj. as s. pl.* working-class

труженик [trōō-zhe-n'ik] *sm.* hard-working man

труп [troŏp] *sm.* corpse

труппа [troŏ-pa] *sf.* troupe

трус [troŏs] *sm.* coward; timid person; sneak

трусики [troŏ-s'i-ki] *sm. pl.* shorts

трусить [troŏ-s'ēt'] (pac-) *vt.* to powder, scatter, sprinkle; to jog along (of horses)

трусить [troŏ-s'it'] *vi.* to be afraid; to dread, fear

трусливый [troŏs-l'ē-văy] *adj.* cowardly, timorous

трут [troŏt] *sm.* tinder

трутень [troŏ-tyen'] *sm.* drone; *fig.* humdrum

трухлявый [troŏch-lyă-văy] *adj.* decayed

трущоба [troŏ-shchó-ba] *sf.* slum; thicket *[ship]*

трюм [tryŏm] *sm.* hold (in

тряпичник [trya-p'ēch-n'ik] *sm.* ragman

тряпка [tryăp-ka] *sf.* rag

трясение [trya-syé-nye] *sn.* shivering, trembling

трясина [trya-s'ē-na] *sf.* bog, marsh, quagmire

тряска [tryăs-ka] *sf.* bumping, jolting

тряский [tryăs-ki] *adj.* shaky; rough, uneven

трясти [tryas-t'ē] (тряхнӳть) *vt.* to jolt, shake, wag

туберкулёз [toŏ-ber-koŏ-lyóz] *sm.* tuberculosis

туго [toŏ-gó] *adv.* stiffly, tightly

тугой [toŏ-góy] *adj.* stiff, tight; dull; stingy

тугоплавкий [toŏ-ga-plắv-ki] *adj.* refractory

туда [toŏ-dắ] *adv.* there, thither

тужурка [toŏ-zhoŏr-ka] *sf.* Norfolk jacket

туз [toŏz] *sm.* ace (cards); dinghy; *fig.* bigwig, nob

туземец [toŏ-zyé-myets] *sm.* aborigine

туземный [toŏ-zyém-năy] *adj.* indigenous, native

туки [toŏki] *sm. pl.* manure

туловище [toŏ-ló-v'i-shche] *sn.* body, trunk

тулья [toŏ-lyă] *sf.* crown of hat

тумак [toŏ-mắk] *sm.* blow, punch

туман [toŏ-mắn] *sm.* fog, haze, mist

туманный [toŏ-mắn-năy] *adj.* foggy, misty, overcast

тумба [toŏm-ba] *sf.* curbstone; pedestal; *fig.* clumsy person

тунец [toŏ-nyéts] *sm.* tunny

тунеядство [toŏ-nye-yắd-stvŏ] *sn.* idleness, parasitism

туннель [toŏn-nyél'] *sm.* subway, tunnel

тупеть [toŏ-pyét'] (за-) *vi.* to become blunt

тупик [toŏ-p'ēk] *sm.* cul-de-sac

тупица [toŏ-p'ē-tsa] *sm., f.* dunce

тупой [toŏ-póy] *adj.* blunt, dull

тур [toŏr] *sm.* round; turn; gabion

тура [toŏ-ra] *sf.* castle, rook (in chess)

турецкий [toŏ-ryéts-ki] *adj.* Turkish

турнепс [toŏr-nyéps] *sm.* swede, turnip

турникет [toŏr-n'i-kyét] *sm.* turnstile

турнир [toŏr-n'ēr] *sm.* tournament

турок [toŏ-rŏk] *sm.*, **турчанка** *sf.* Turk

турусы [too-roo-sä] *sm. pl.* nonsense, rubbish

тусклый [toosk-läy] *adj.* dim; dull; tarnished

тускнеть [toosk-nyét'] *vi.* to become dull; to wane

тут [toot] *adv.* here

тутовая ягода [too-tó-va-ya yä-ga-da] *sf.* mulberry

туфля [toof-lya] *sf.* slipper

тухлый [tooch-läy] *adj.* putrefied, tainted

тухнуть [tooch-noot'] (про-) *vi.* to be extinguished, go out; to become putrefied, spoiled; tainted

туча [too-chä] *sf.* cloud

тучный [tooch-näy] *adj.* corpulent, stout

туш [toosh] *sm. mus.* flourish

тушевать [too-she-vät'] (на-) *vt.* to shade (*in drawing*)

тушение [too-shé-nye] *sn.* extinguishing; stewing

тушить [too-shět'] (по-) *vt.* to blow out, put out; to braise, jug

тушь [toosh'] *sf.* Indian ink

тщательный [tshchä-tyel'-näy] *adj.* elaborate, thorough

тщедушие [tshche-doo-shye] *sn.* debility, infirmity

тщедушный [tshche-doosh-näy] *adj.* feeble, puny, weak

тщеславие [tshche-slä-vye] *sn.* conceit, pride, vainglory

тщеславный [tshche-släv-näy] *adj.* vain

тщетно [tshchét-nö] *adv.* vainly

тщетность [tshchet-nöst'] *sf.* frustration; futility; vanity

ты [tä] *pron.* thou; (*the second*

person singular is extensively used in the USSR)

тыкать [tä-kat'] (ткнуть) *vt.* to poke, thrust; to say "thou" to one, to be familiar

тыква [täk-va] *sf.* pumpkin; marrow; gourd

тыл [täl] *sm.* back, rear; reverse

тын [tän] *sm.* fence, paling

тысяча [tä-sya-cha] *sf., adj.* thousand

тысячелетний [tä-sya-che-lyét-n'i] *adj.* millenial

тысячный [tä-syach-näy] *num.* thousandth

тычина [tä-chē-na] *sf.* prop, stake

тычинка [tä-chēn-ka] *sf.* stamen

тьма [t'mä] *sf.* darkness; *coll.* a multitude; thousands

тюк [tyook] *sm.* bale, package

тюлень [tyoo-lyén'] *sm.* seal, sea-calf, sea-dog; *fig.* lout

тюль [tyool'] *sm.* tulle

тюльпан [tyool'-pän] *sm.* tulip

тюремщик [tyoo-ryém-shchik] *sm.* jailer; warder

тюрьма [tyoor'-mä] *sf.* prison

тюфяк [tyoo-fyäk] *sm.* mattress

тявкать [tyäv-kat'] (тявкнуть) *vi.* to bark, yelp

тяга [tyä-ga] *sf.* draught; current; pull; connecting rod

тягание [tya-gä-nye] *sn.* litigation

тягостный [tyä-gast-näy] *adj.* distressing, oppressive, troublesome, weighty

тягость [tyä-göst'] *sf.* burden, load; heaviness, weight

тяготение [tya-ga-tyé-nye] *sn.* attraction, gravitation

тяготеть [tya-ga-tyét'] *vi.* to gravitate; to be attracted by

тяготить [tya-ga-t'ét'] *vt.* to overburden, overload, overwhelm; to hang heavily (*upon one's mind*)

тягучий [tya-ɡōō-chi] *adj.* flexible, malleable, tensile

тяжеловесный [tya-zhe-la-vyés-nay] *adj.* ponderous

тяжёлый [tya-zhó-lay] *adj.* heavy, weighty; difficult, hard; close; stodgy

тяжесть [tyā-zhest'] *sf.* weight; gravity

тянуть [tya-nōōt'] (по-) *vt.* to drag, pull, stretch, tug; -ся [-sya] *vi.* to extend, lengthen; to hold out, linger; to strive

тяпать [tyā-pat'] (тяпнуть) *vt.* to chop, hack; to snatch

тяпка [tyāp-ka] *sf.* chopper, cleaver

тятенька [tyā-tyen'-ka] *sm.* dad, daddy

У

у [ōō] *prep.* at, by, to; close by, close to, near; **у меня . . .** [ōō mye-nyā] I have . . .

убавка [ōō-bāv-ka] *sf.* curtailment, decrease, reduction

убавлять [ōō-ba-vlyát'] (убавить) *vt.* to diminish, lessen, reduce, shorten; to deduct (*from wages, etc.*)

убаюкивать [ōō-ba-yōō-ki-vat'] (убаюкать) *vt.* to lull, still; to rock to sleep

убегать [ōō-bye-gát'] (убежать) *vi.* to desert, flee, run away; to escape; to elope

убедительный [ōō-bye-d'ē-tyel'-nay] *adj.* convincing, demonstrative, persuasive

убеждать [ōō-byezh-dát'] (убедить) *vt.* to convince, persuade; to induce, prevail

убеждение [ōō-byezh-dyé-nye] *sn.* conviction, persuasion

убежище [ōō-byé-zhi-shche] *sn.* asylum; refuge, retreat, shelter

уберегать [ōō-bye-rye-gát'] (уберечь) *vt.* to guard, preserve, protect; -ся [-sya] *vi.* to protect oneself

убивать [ōō-b'i-vát'] (убить) *vt.* to kill, murder

убийственный [ōō-b'ēst-vyen-nay] *adj.* deadly, mortal

убийство [ōō-b'ēst-vō] *sn.* assassination, murder

убийца [ōō-b'ē-tsa] *sm.* assassin, murderer

убирать [ōō-b'i-rát'] (у-брать) *vt.* to remove, take off; to store; to decorate, tidy, trim

ублажать [ōō-bla-zhát'] (ублажить) *vt.* to entreat; to pamper, pet

ублюдок [ōō-blyōō-dōk] *sm.* mongrel; hybrid

убогий [ōō-bó-gi] *adj.* miserable, wretched; -um beggar, wretch

убожество [ōō-bó-zhest-vō] *sn.* poverty, squalor

убой [ōō-bóy] *sm.* slaughter

убор [ōō-bór] *sm.* attire, dress, finery, set of jewels

убористый [ŏŏ-ba-r'ĕs-tāy] *adj.* close, compact

уборка [ŏŏ-bór-ka] *sf.* arranging, decoration, putting in order, trimming

уборная [ŏŏ-bór-na-ya] *sf.* cloak-room, dressing-room, toilet

уборщик [ŏŏ-bór-shchik] *sm.* cloak-room attendant

убывать [ŏŏ-bă-vát'] (убыть) *vi.* to decrease, diminish; to decline, wane

убыль [ŏŏ-băl'] *sf.* decrease, fall; subsidence; *mil.* losses

убыток [ŏŏ-bă-tŏk] *sm.* damage, loss; detriment, disadvantage

убыточный [ŏŏ-bă-tach-năy] *adj.* detrimental; ruinous, wasteful

уважаемый [ŏŏ-va-zhá-ye-măy] *adj.* estimable, respectful

уважать [ŏŏ-va-zhát'] (уважить) *vt.* to consider, esteem, respect

уважение [ŏŏ-va-zhé-nye] *sm.* appreciation; esteem, regard, respect; consideration

уваривать [ŏŏ-vă-r'i-vat'] (уварить) *vt.* to boil away, stew

уведомительный [ŏŏ-vye-da-m'ĕ-tyel'-năy] *adj.* advisory, informative

уведомление [ŏŏ-vye-dam-lyé-nye] *sn.* information, intimation

уведомлять [ŏŏ-vye-dam-lyát'] (уведомить) *vt.* to advise, inform, notify

увековечивать [ŏŏ-vye-ka-vyé-chi-vat'] (увековечить) *vt.* to commemorate

увеличение [ŏŏ-vye-li-ché-nye] *sn.* augmentation, enlargement, increase; magnification

увеличивать [ŏŏ-vye-l'ĕ-chi-vat'] (увеличить) *vt.* to enlarge, increase; to magnify

увенчивать [ŏŏ-vyén-chi-vat'] (увенчать) *vt.* to crown

уверение [ŏŏ-vye-ryé-nye] *sn.* assertion, assurance

уверенный [ŏŏ-vyé-ren-năy] *adj.* confident, sure

увёртка [ŏŏ-vyórt-ka] *sf.* evasion

увёртливый [ŏŏ-vyórt-l'i-văy] *adj.* elusive, evasive

увёртывать [ŏŏ-vyór-tă-vat'] *vt.* to wrap up; **-ся** [-sya] *vi.* to dodge, evade; to shirk

увертюра [ŏŏ-vyer-tyó-ra] *sf. mus.* overture

уверять [ŏŏ-vye-ryát'] (уверить) *vt.* to assure, convince; **-ся** [-sya] *vi.* to ascertain, make sure

увеселение [ŏŏ-vye-sye-lyé-nye] *sn.* amusement, enjoyment; diversion

увеселять [ŏŏ-vye-sye-lyát'] (увеселить) *vt.* to amuse, enliven, entertain

увечить [ŏŏ-vyé-chit'] (из-) *vt.* to cripple, maim, mutilate

увечный [ŏŏ-vyéch-năy] *adj.* lame, crippled; *sm.* cripple

увечье [ŏŏ-vyé-chye] *sn.* injury, lameness, mutilation

увешивать [ŏŏ-vyé-shi-vat'] (увешать) *vt.* to hang up, put up (*pictures, ornaments*)

увещание [ŏŏ-vye-shchá-nye] *sn.* admonition, exhortation

увещевать [ŏŏ-vye-shche-vät'] (увещáть) vt. to admonish, exhort

увивать [ŏŏ-v'i-vät'] (увúть) vt. to entwine, wrap round

увидать [ŏŏ-v'i-dät'] (увúдеть) vt. to behold, espy; perceive

увиливать [ŏŏ-v'ē-l'i-vat'] (увильнýть) vi. to elude, evade

увлажнять [ŏŏ-vlazh-nyät'] (увлажнúть) vt. to damp, moisten

увлекательность [ŏŏ-vlye-kä-tyel'-nóst'] sf. attractiveness, charm

увлекательный [ŏŏ-vlye-kä-tyel'-näy] adj. captivating

увлекать [ŏŏ-vlye-kät'] (увлéчь) vt. to carry away; fig. to captivate, fascinate

увлечение [ŏŏ-vlye-ché-nye] sn. enthusiasm, impulse

увод [ŏŏ-vód] sm. leading away; abduction; theft (of live-stock)

уводить [ŏŏ-va-d'ēt'] (увести́) vt. to lead away, march off; to steal (cattle)

увоз [ŏŏ-vóz] sm. carrying off

увольнять [ŏŏ-val'-nyät'] (увóлить) vt. to cashier, dismiss, turn away

увы [ŏŏ-vä] interj. alas!

увядание [ŏŏ-vya-dä-nye] sn. fading, withering

увядать [ŏŏ-vya-dät'] (увя́нуть) vi. to droop, fade; to waste away

увязка [ŏŏ-vyäz-ka] sf. tying up; fig. agreement, concordance

увязывать [ŏŏ-vyä-zä-vat']

(увязáть) vt. to pack up, tie up, truss; fig. to bring into concord

угадывание [ŏŏ-gä-dä-va-nye] sn. guessing

угадывать [ŏŏ-gä-dä-vat'] (угадáть) vt. to divine; to foresee; to guess

угасать [ŏŏ-ga-sät'] (угáснуть) vi. to put out, be extinguished; to become extinct

угашать [ŏŏ-ga-shät'] (угасúть) vt. to extinguish, quench; fig. to stifle

углаживать [ŏŏ-glä-zhi-vat'] (углáдить) vt. to smooth out

углекоп [ŏŏ-glye-kóp] sm. collier

углепромышленность [ŏŏ-glye-pra-mäsh-lyen-nóst'] sf. coal-mining industry

углерод [ŏŏ-glye-ród] sm. carbon

угловатый [ŏŏ-gla-vä-täy] adj. angular

угловой [ŏŏ-gla-vóy] adj. angulous, corner-; — дом [—dom] corner house

углубление [ŏŏ-glŏŏb-lyé-nye] sn. deepening; cavity, hollow, recess

углублять [ŏŏ-glŏŏb-lyät'] (углубúть) vt. to deepen

углядывать [ŏŏ-glyä-dä-vat'] (углядéть) vt. to behold, perceive; vi. to take care of

угнетатель [ŏŏ-gnye-tä-tyel'] sm. oppressor

угнетать [ŏŏ-gnye-tät'] (угнéсть) vt. to compress, press down; to oppress

угнетение [ŏŏ-gnye-tyé-nye] sn. compression; oppression

уговаривать [ŏŏ-ga-vă-r'i-vat'] (уговори́ть) vt. to exhort, urge; to induce, persuade

уговор [ŏŏ-ga-vór] sm. agreement, settlement; **с -ом** [s -ŏm] on condition

угода [ŏŏ-gó-da] sf. gratification; **в угоду** [vŏŏ-gó-dŏŏ] to oblige, please

угодливый [ŏŏ-gód-l'i-văy] adj. officious

угодничать [ŏŏ-gód-n'i-chat'] vi. to be obliging

угодный [ŏŏ-gód-năy] adj. agreeable, pleasing; suitable

угождать [ŏŏ-gazh-dăt'] (угоди́ть) vt. to gratify, humour

угождение [ŏŏ-gazh-dýé-nye] sn. compliance

угол [ŏŏ-gŏl] sm. angle; corner; nook

уголовный [ŏŏ-ga-lóv-năy] adj. penal

уголовщина [ŏŏ-ga-lóv-shchi-na] sf. criminal act

уголь [ŏŏ-gŏl'] sm. coal

угольник [ŏŏ-gŏl'-n'ik] sm. set-square

угольный [ŏŏ-gól'-năy] adj. angular; corner-

угольный [ŏŏ-gŏl'-năy] adj. coal-

угольщик [ŏŏ-gŏl'-shchik] sm. coal-ship, collier; charcoal dealer, coal-merchant

угонять [ŏŏ-ga-nyăt'] (угна́ть) vt. to drive away; -ся [-sya] vi. to catch up, overtake

угорать [ŏŏ-ga-răt'] (угоре́ть) vi. to be poisoned by coal-gas

угорелый [ŏŏ-ga-ryé-lăy] adj. asphyxiated; fig. frenzied

угорь [ŏŏ-gŏr'] sm. blackhead, pimple; pustule; eel

уготовление [ŏŏ-ga-tav-lýé-nye] sn. preparation

уготовлять [ŏŏ-ga-tav-lyăt'] (угото́вить) vt. to get ready; make ready, prepare

угощать [ŏŏ-ga-shchăt'] (угости́ть) vt. to entertain, treat

угощение [ŏŏ-ga-shché-nye] sn. entertaining, reception, treating

угреватый [ŏŏ-grye-vă-tăy] adj. blotchy, pimply

угрожать [ŏŏ-gra-zhăt'] (угрози́ть) vt. to menace, threaten

угроза [ŏŏ-gró-za] sf. menace, threat

угрюмость [ŏŏ-gryŏŏ-mŏst'] sf. peevishness, surliness

угрюмый [ŏŏ-gryŏŏ-măy] adj. gloomy, morose

удав [ŏŏ-dăv] sm. boa, boa-constrictor

удаваться [ŏŏ-da-vắt'-sya] (уда́ться) vi. to get on, succeed

удавить [ŏŏ-da-v'ĕt'] vt. to strangle, throttle

удавление [ŏŏ-dav-lýé-nye] sn. strangling

удаление [ŏŏ-da-lyé-nye] sn. recession, removal, withdrawal

удалый [ŏŏ-dă-lăy] adj. audacious, bold, daring

удалять [ŏŏ-da-lyăt'] (удали́ть) vt. to banish, expel, remove

удар [ŏŏ-dăr] sm. blow, hit, knock; impact; shock

ударение [ŏŏ-da-ryé-nye] sn. emphasis; stress; accent (as acute, grave, etc.)

ударник [ōō-dár-n'ik] *sm.* pellet

ударный [ōō-dár-năy] *adj.* percussive; shock; accented; stressed

ударять [ōō-da-ryát'] (ударить) *vt.* to hit, strike; to kick

удача [ōō-dá-cha] *sf.* chance, luck, success

удачный [ōō-dách-năy] *adj.* fortunate, successful

удваивать [ōō-dvá-i-vat'] (удвоить) *vt.* to double, duplicate

удел [ōō-dyél] *sm.* lot, share; fate; apanage

удельный [ōō-dyél'-năy] *adj.* apportioned; – вес [– vyés] specific gravity

уделять [ōō-dye-lyát'] (уделить) *vt.* to allot, share out

удержание [ōō-dyer-zhá-nye] *sn.* keeping back retaining

удерживать [ōō-dyér-zhi-vat'] (удержать) *vt.* to hold back, retain, withhold; to deter, restrain, -ся [-sya] *vi.* to abstain, check oneself

удешевлять [ōō-dye-shev-lyát'] (удешевить) to cheapen, reduce the price

удивительный [ōō-d'i-v'í-tyel'-năy] *adj.* amazing, astonishing, surprising, wonderful

удивление [ōō-d'iv-lyé-nye] *sn.* mazement, wonder

удивлять [ōō-d'iv-lyát'] (удивить) *vt.* to amaze, surprise

удилище [ōō-d'é-li-shche] *sn.* fishing-rod [bit

удило [ōō-d'é-lŏ] *sn.* bridle-

удильщик [ōō-d'él'-shchik] *sm.* angler

удить [ōō-d'ét'] *vt.* to fish

удлинение [ōō-dl'i-nyé-nye] *sn.* lengthening, prolongation; elongation

удлинять [ōō-dl'i-nyát'] (удлинить) *vt.* to lengthen, prolong, stretch out

удобный [ōō-dób-năy] *adj.* comfortable, convenient, favourable; handy

удобоваримый [ōō-da-ba-va-ré-măy] *adj.* digestible

удобрение [ōō-da-bryé-nye] *sn.* fertilization, manuring

удобство [ōō-dób-stvŏ] *sn.* comfort, convenience; accommodation

удовлетворительный [ōō-da-vlye-tva-r'é-tyel'-năy] *adj.* satisfactory

удовлетворять [ōō-da-vlye-tva-nyát'] (удовлетворить) *vt.* to gratify, satisfy

удовольствие [ōō-da-vól'-stvye] *sn.* enjoyment, joy, pleasure

удой [ōō-dóy] *sm.* milking

удорожать [ōō-da-ra-zhát'] (удорожить) *vt.* to raise (cost, prices)

удостаивать [ōō-da-stá-i-vat'] *vt.* to deign, vouchsafe; to bestow, confer

удостоверение [ōō-das-ta-vye-ryé-nye] *sn.* attestation; certificate

удостоверитель [ōō-das-ta-vye-r'é-tyel'] *sm.* attestor, witness

удостоверять [ōō-das-ta-vye-ryát'] (удостоверить) *vt.* to attest, certify, testify

удочка [ōō-dach-ka] *sf.* fishing-rod

удружить [ōō-drōō-zhét'] *vt.* to befriend; to oblige a friend

удручать [ŏŏ-drŏŏ-chát'] (удручи́ть) *vt.* to deject, dispirit

удушать [ŏŏ-dŏŏ-shát'] (удуши́ть) *vt.* to stifle, suffocate; to smother, strangle

удушливый [ŏŏ-dŏŏ-shl'ĕ-văy] *adj.* choking, stifling

удушье [ŏŏ-dŏŏ-shye] *sn.* asthma

уединение [ŏŏ-ye-d'i-nyé-nye] *sn.* retirement, seclusion, solitude

уединённый [ŏŏ-ye-d'i-nyón-năy] *adj.* lonely, solitary

уезд [ŏŏ-yézd] *sm.* district

уезжать [ŏŏ-yez-zhát'] (уе́хать) *vi.* to depart go away, leave (*not on foot*)

уж [ŏŏzh] *sm.* grass-snake; *adv.* already

ужаление [ŏŏ-zha-lyé-nye] *sn.* sting

ужас [ŏŏ-zhas] *sm.* dismay, horror, terror

ужасать [ŏŏ-zha-sát'] (у-жасну́ть) *vt.* to horrify, shock, terrify

ужасно [ŏŏ-zhas-nŏ] *adv.* awfully, frightfully, horribly

ужасный [ŏŏ-zhás-năy] *adj.* dreadful, ghastly, horrid

уже [ŏŏ-zhé] *adj.* narrower (*comp. of* у́зкий)

уже [ŏŏ-zhé] *adv.* already; **-не** [-nye] no longer

ужение [ŏŏ-zhé-nye] *sn.* angling

уживчивый [ŏŏ-zhiv-chi-văy] *adj.* good tempered, easy to live with, sociable

уживчивость [ŏŏ-zhiv-chi-vŏst'] *sf.* good disposition; amicability

ужимка [ŏŏ-zhím-ka] *sf.* grimace

ужин [ŏŏ-zhin] *sm.* supper

ужинать [ŏŏ-zhi-nat'] (по-) *vi* to sup, sit down to supper

узаконять [ŏŏ-za-ka-nyát'] (узакони́ть) *vt.* to decree; to legalize, to ordain

узда [ŏŏz-dá] *sf* bridle; *fig.* check, restraint

узел [ŏŏ-zyel] *sm.* knot; node, bundle, pack

узкий [ŏŏz-ki] *adj* narrow; tight (*as clothing*)

узловатый [ŏŏ-zla-vá-tăy] *adj.* knotty, nodulous

узнавать [ŏŏ-sna-vát'] (узна́ть) *vt.* to identify, recognize, to find out

узник [ŏŏz-n'ik] *sm.* captive, convict, slave

узор [ŏŏ-zór] *sm.* design, figure, pattern

узорчатый [ŏŏ-zar-chá-tăy] *adj* figured, flowered, ornamented

узы [ŏŏ-zí] *sf. pl.* bonds, ties, shackles

указ [ŏŏ-káz] *sm.* act, decree, edict, ukase

указание [ŏŏ-ka-zá-nye] *sn.* direction, indication; information

указатель [ŏŏ-ka-zá-tyel'] *sm.* guide, index; indicator; signpost

указывать [ŏŏ-ká-ză-vat'] (указа́ть) *vt.* to indicate, point out

укалывать [ŏŏ-ká-lă-vat'] (уколо́ть) *vt.* to prick; **-ся** [-syaj *vr.* to prick oneself

укатывать [ŏŏ-ká-tă-vat'] (уката́ть) *vt.* to roll, smooth out; (укати́ть) to roll away

укачивать [oo-kā-chi-vat'] (укачать) *vt.* to rock to sleep; *vi.* to be sea-sick

уклад [oo-klād] *sm.* tenor, usage

укладка [oo-klād-ka] *sf.* packing, stowage; laying down; stacking

укладчик [oo-klād-chik] *sm.* packer

укладывать [oo-klā-dă-vat'] (уложить) *vt.* to pack, pack up, stow away; to arrange, place, set up

уклон [oo-klón] *sm.* declivity, slope; gradient

уклонение [oo-kla-nyé-nye] *sn.* deviation; evasion

уклончивый [oo-klón-chi-văy] *adj.* evasive

уклоняться [oo-kla-nyát'-sya] *vi.* to deviate, evade, shirk, shun; to wriggle out

укол [oo-kól] *sm.* prick; injection; sting

укор [oo-kór] *sm.* blame, reproach

укорачивать [oo-ka-rā-chi-vat'] (укратить) *vt.* to shorten

укоризненный [oo-ka-r'ēz-nyen-năy] *adj.* reproachful

украдкой [oo-krād-koy] *adv.* furtively, stealthily

украшать [oo-kra-shāt'] (украсить) *vt.* to adorn, decorate, embellish

украшение [oo-kra-shé-nye] *sn.* ornamentation; ornament

укрепление [oo-krye-plyé-nye] *sn.* fortifying, strengthening; fort, fortification

укреплять [oo-krye-plyāt'] (укрепить) *vt.* to consolidate, reinforce; to fortify, make secure

укрепляющий [oo-krye-plyā-yoo-shchi] *adj.* bracing, invigorating; restorative

укромность [oo-króm-nŏst'] *sf.* retirement, seclusion

укромный [oo-króm-năy] *adj.* cosy, isolated, quiet

укротитель [oo-kra-t'í-tyel'] *sm.* tamer

укрощать [oo-kra-shchāt'] (укротить) *vt.* to subdue, tame; to break in, curb; to appease, calm, pacify

укрывание [oo-krā-vā-nye] *sn.* concealment

укрывать [oo-krā-vāt'] (укрыть) *vt.* to cover, protect; to conceal, screen; to harbour

укрытие [oo-krā-tye] *sn.* concealment *mil.* cover, shelter

уксус [ook-sŏos] *sm.* vinegar

уксусница [ook-sŏos-n'í-tsa] vinegar cruet

уксусный [ook-sŏos-năy] *adj.* acetic, vinegary

укус [oo-kŏos] *sm.* bite, biting

укутываться [oo-kŏo-tă-vat'-sya] (укутаться) *vi.* to wrap oneself up well

улавливать [oo-lāv-l'i-vat'] (уловить) *vt.* to catch; to detect, discern

улаживать [oo-lā-zhi-vat'] (уладить) *vt.* to make up, reconcile

улей [oo-lyéy] *sm.* bee-hive

улёт [oo-lyót] *sm.* flight, migration

улетать [oo-lye-tāt'] (улететь) *vi.* to fly away, hurry away

улика [oo-l'ĕ-ka] *sf.* evidence, proof

улитка [oo-l'ĕt-ka] *sf.* snail; helix

улица [ōō-l'i-tsa] *sf.* street; **на улице** [na ōō-l'i-tsye] outside

уличать [ōō-l'i-chāt'] (уличи́ть) *vt.* to convict; to detect; to catch in the act

уличение [ōō-l'i-ché-nye] *sn.* conviction; detection

уличный [ōō-l'ich-nǎy] *adj.* street

улов [ōō-lóv] *sm.* catch (of fish, etc.)

уловимый [ōō-la-v'é-mǎy] *adj.* perceptible

уловка [ōō-lóv-ka] *sf.* dodge, ruse, trick

уложение [ōō-la-zhé-nye] *sn.* code; statute

улучшать [ōō-lōōch-shāt'] (улучши́ть) *vt.* to amend, better, improve

улучшение [ōō-lōōch-shé-nye] *sn.* amelioration, improvement

улыбаться [ōō-lǎ-bāt'-sya] (улыбну́ться) *vi.* to smile

улыбка [ōō-láb-ka] *sf.* smile

ум [ōōm] *sm.* intellect, mind

умаление [ōō-ma-lyé-nye] *sn.* belittling; diminution; disparagement

умаливание [ōō-mā-l'i-va-nye] *sn.* supplication

умалишённый [ōō-ma-l'i-shón-nǎy] *adj.* insane, mad; *sm.* lunatic, mental defective

умалчивание [ōō-māl-chi-va-nye] *sn.* suppression; pretermission

умалять [ōō-ma-lyāt'] (умали́ть) *vt.* to diminish, lessen; to belittle, disparage

умасливать [ōō-mās-l'i-vat'] (умасли́ть) *vt.* to grease, oil; *fig.* to grease someone's palm

умащать [ōō-ma-shchāt'] (умасти́ть) *vt.* to anoint

умелый [ōō-myé-lǎy] *adj.* expert, skilful

уменье [ōō-myé-nye] *sn.* ability, dexterity, skill

уменьшать [ōō-myen'-shāt'] (уменьши́ть) *vt.* to decrease, reduce; to cut down (expenses); to alleviate (pain)

уменьшение [ōō-myen'-shé-nye] *sn.* abatement, reduction; extenuation

уменьшительный [ōō-myen'-shē-tyel'-nǎy] *adj.* diminutive

умерение [ōō-mye-ryé-nye] *sn.* moderation; restraint

умеренный [ōō-myé-ryen-nǎy] *adj.* moderate, temperate; abstemious

умеренность [ōō-myé-ryen-nóst'] *sf.* temperance; saneness, sobriety

умерший [ōō-myer-shi] *adj.* defunct; deceased; **умершие** [ōō-myer-shi-ye] *sm. pl.* the dead

умерщвлять [ōō-myer-shchvlyāt'] (умертви́ть) *vt.* to put to death; to mortify

умерять [ōō-mye-ryāt'] (умери́ть) *vt.* to moderate, to mitigate

уместительный [ōō-myes-t'é-tyel'-nǎy] *adj.* roomy, spacious; commodious

уместный [ōō-myést-nǎy] *adj.* appropriate, relevant, well-timed

умёт [ōō-myót] *sm. mil.* post, trench; refuse

уметь [ōō-myét'] (с-) *vt.* to be able, know how (to do things)

умиление [ōō-m'i-lyé-nye] *sn.* emotion, tenderness

умилостивление [ōō-m'i-la-st'iv-lyé-nye] *sn.* appeasement, propitiation

умильный [ōō-m'ĕl'-năy] *adj.* imploring, suppliant

умирать [ōō-m'i-rát'] (умереть) *vi.* to die

умирающий [ōō-m'i-rá-yōō-shchi] *adj.* dying

умиротворять [ōō-m'i-ra-tva-ryát'] (умиротворить) *vt.* to conciliate, pacify

умник [ōōm-n'ik] *sm.* clever person, wise man

умница [ōōm-n'i-tsa] *sf.* clever and good girl; very clever man

умножать [ōōm-na-zhát'] (умножить) *vt.* to augment, increase; *math.* to multiply

умножение [ōōm-na-zhé-nye] *sn.* multiplication

умный [ōōm-năy] *adj.* intelligent, sensible, wise

умовение [ōō-ma-vyé-nye] *sn.* ablution, washing

умозрение [ōō-ma-zryé-nye] *sn.* speculation

умол [ōō-mól] *sm.* grinding

умолачивать [ōō-ma-lá-chi-vat'](умолотить) *vt.* to thresh

умолкать [ōō-mal-kát'] (умолкнуть) *vi.* to become silent, to subside

умолот [ōō-ma-lót] *sm.* yield (of farming produce)

умолять [ōō-ma-lyát'] (умолить) *vi.* to beseech, implore, supplicate

уморительный [ōō-ma-r'é-tyel'-năy] *adj.* amusing, droll, funny

умственный [ōōm-stvyen-năy] *adj.* brainy, intellectual

умствовать [ōōm-stva-vat'] *vi.* to reason

умывальник [ōō-mă-văl'-n'ik] *sm.* wash-stand

умывание [ōō-mă-vá-nye] *sn.* wash; washing; lotion

умывать [ōō-mă-vát'] (умыть) *vt.* to wash; **-ся** [-sya] *vr.* to wash oneself

умысел [ōō-mă-syel] *sm.* design, intention, purpose

умышленный [ōō-máshlyen-năy] *adj.* deliberate, intentional

умышлять [ōō-măsh-lyát'] (умыслить) *vt.* to contrive, plot, premeditate, scheme

умягчать [ōō-myach-chát'] (умягчить) *vt.* to alleviate, to mollify, soften

универсальный [ōō-n'i-vyer-sál'-năy] *adj.* universal

университет [ōō-n'i-vyer-s'i-tyét] *sm.* university

унижать [ōō-n'i-zhát'] (унизить) *vt.* to lower; to degrade, humiliate; to underrate

унижение [ōō-n'i-zhé-nye] *sn.* abasement, degradation, humiliation

униженный [ōō-n'i-zhón-năy] *adj.* humble, lowly

унимать [ōō-n'i-mát'] (унять) *vt.* to abate, repress, soothe

уничтожать [ōō-n'i-chta-zhát'] (уничтожить) *vt.* to annihilate, destroy; to abolish, suppress

уничтожение [ōō-n'i-chta-zhé-nye] *sn.* annihilation, destruction

уносить [ōō-na-s'ét'] (унести) *vt.* to carry off

унылый [ōō-ná-lăy] *adj.* despondent, downcast

унынiе [ōō-nū́-nye] *sn.* dejection, melancholy

упадок [ōō-pā́-dŏk] *sm.* decay; decline; decadence

упаковщик [ōō-pa-kóv-shchik] *sm.* packer

упаковывать [ōō-pa-kó-vȧ-vat'] (упаковáть) *vt.* to pack up

упасáть [ōō-pa-sāt'] (упастú) *vt.* to preserve, save

упивáться [ōō-p'i-vāt'-sya] (упíться) *vi.* to get drunk

упирáться [ōō-p'i-rāt'-sya] *vi.* to lean, recline; to oppose, resist

уплáта [ōō-plā́-ta] *sf.* paying, payment

уплáчивать [ōō-plā́-chi-vat'] (уплатíть) *vt.* to pay up; to discharge a debt

уплотнять [ōō-plat-nyāt'] (уплотнúть) *vt.* to condense, thicken

уплотненiе [ōō-plat-nyé-nye] *sn.* condensation

упованiе [ōō-pa-vā́-nye] *sn.* confidence, trust

уподобленiе [ōō-pa-dab-lyé-nye] *sn.* assimilation; comparison

упоенiе [ōō-pa-yé-nye] *sn.* ecstasy, rapture

упоительный [ōō-pa-ḗ-tyel'-năy] *adj.* delightful, intoxicating, ravishing

упокоенiе [ōō-pa-ka-yé-nye] *sn.* repose, rest; peace of mind

уполномоченный [ōō-pal-na-mó-chen-năy] *adj. as sm.* delegate, representative; agent, proxy

уполномочивать [ōō-pal-na-mó-chi-vat'] (уполномóчить) *vt.* to authorize, empower

упоминáть [ōō-pa-m'i-nāt'] (упомянýть) *vt.* to mention, refer to; to cite

упомнить [ōō-póm-n'it'] *vi.* to remember, retain

упор [ōō-pór] *sm.* rest, support; resistance

упорность [ōō-pór-nŏst'] *sf.* obstinacy, tenacity

употребительный [ōō-pa-trye-b'é-tyel'-năy] *adj.* customary, usual

употребленiе [ōō-pa-trye-blyé-nye] *sn.* application, use, usage

употреблять [ōō-pa-trye-blyāt'] (употребíть) to apply, employ, use

управа [ōō-prā́-va] *sf.* administration; management; satisfaction, justice; городская — [ga-rad-skā́-ya —] town council

управлять [ōō-prav-lyāt'] (упрáвить) *vt.* to control, govern

управляющий [ōō-prav-lyā́-yōō-shchi] *adj.* governing, managing; *as sm.* director, manager

упражненiе [ōō-prazh-nyé-nye] *sn.* exercise, practice

упражнять [ōō-prazh-nyāt'] *vt.* to drill, instruct; **-ся** [-sya] *vi.* to exercise, practise

упрáшивать [ōō-prā́-shi-vat'] (упросíть) *vt.* to beg, entreat

упрёк [ōō-pryók] *sm.* rebuke, reproach

упрекáть [ōō-prye-kāt'] (упрекнýть) *vt.* to rebuke, scold, upbraid

упроченiе [ōō-pra-ché-nye] *sn.* consolidation, strengthening

упрочивать [ŏŏ-pró-chi-vat'] (упрóчить) vt. to secure; to make durable; to consolidate; **-ся** [sya] to strengthen, gain strength

упрощать [ŏŏ-pra-shchát'] (упростить) vt. to simplify

упругий [ŏŏ-prŏŏ-gi] adj. elastic, resilient

упругость [ŏŏ-prŏŏ-gŏst'] sf. elasticity, resilience; stiffness

упряжка [ŏŏ-pryázh-ka] sf. team (dogs, horses, etc.)

упряжь [ŏŏ-pryazh'] sf. gear, harness

упрямство [ŏŏ-pryám-stvŏ] sn. obstinacy, stubbornness

упрямый [ŏŏ-pryá-mäy] adj. headstrong, obstinate

упускать [ŏŏ-pŏŏs-kát'] (упустить) vt. to omit; to escape (one's mind, notice); to miss (an opportunity, etc.)

упущение [ŏŏ-pŏŏ-shché-nye] sn. neglect, omission, shortcoming

упырь [ŏŏ-pár'] sm. vampire

уравнивать [ŏŏ-ráv-n'i-vat'] (уравнять) vt. to even, equalize, level

уравновешенный [ŏŏ-rav-na-vyé-shen-näy] adj. well-balanced; equable, steady

ураган [ŏŏ-ra-gán] sm. hurricane, tornado

уразумение [ŏŏ-ra-zŏŏ-mye-nye] sn. comprehension, understanding

урезка [ŏŏ-ryéz-ka] sf. curtailment, abridgment

урезывать [ŏŏ-ryé-zä-vat'] (урéзать) vt. to curtail, cut down, reduce [urinal

урильник [ŏŏ-r'él'-nik] sm.

урина [ŏŏ-r'é-na] sf. urine

урна [ŏŏr-na] sf. urn; box

уровень [ŏŏ-ra-vyen'] sm. level, standard

уродина [ŏŏ-ró-d'i-na] sf. abortion; freak, monster

уродливость [ŏŏ-ród-l'i-vŏst'] sf. abnormity, deformity, ugliness

уродливый [ŏŏ-ród-l'i-väy] adj. abnormal, deformed, ugly

урожай [ŏŏ-ra-zháy] sm. crop, harvest, yield

урожайный [ŏŏ-ra-zháy-näy] adj. abundant, fruitful, rich

урождённая [ŏŏ-razh-dyón-na-ya] adj. born (nee)

урок [ŏŏ-rók] sm. lesson; task; наглядный — [na-glyád-näy –] object lesson; давать -и [da-vát' -i] to teach

урон [ŏŏ-rón] sm. loss; damage, harm

урочный [ŏŏ-róch-näy] adj. determined, fixed

урчать [ŏŏr-chát'] vi. to rumble

урывать [ŏŏ-rä-vát'] (урвáть) vt. to seize, snatch

ус [ŏŏs] sm. moustache; beard (of corn); antenna; shoot

усадьба [ŏŏ-sád'-ba] sf. farmstead, homestead, manor

усаживать [ŏŏ-sá-zhi-vat'] (усадить) vt. to place, seat, settle; to conduct one to a seat; **-ся** [-sya] vi. to sit down, take a seat

усатый [ŏŏ-sá-täy] adj. bewhiskered

усваивать [ŏŏ-svá-i-vat'] (усвóить) vt. to acquire, adopt; to assimilate

усвоение [ŏŏ-sva-yé-nye] sn. adoption; assimilation; mastering

усердие [oo-syér-dye] sn. diligence, zeal

усердный [oo-syérd-nay] adj. ardent, eager, enthusiastic, industrious

усидчивый [oo-s'éd-chi-vay] adj. assiduous, persevering

усик [oo-s'ik] sm. tendril

усиление [oo-s'i-lyé-nye] sn. intensification, reinforcement, strengthening

усиливать [oo-s'é-l'i-vat'] (усилить) vt. to intensify, reinforce; to aggravate (pain)

усилие [oo-s'é-lye] sn. effort, exertion

ускакивать [oo-ská-k'i-vat'] (ускакать) vi. to gallop away

ускользать [oo-skal'-zát] (ускользнуть) vi. to slip away

ускорение [oo-ska-ryé-nye] sn. acceleration, hastening

ускоритель [oo-ska-r'é-tyel'] sm. accelerator

ускорять [oo-ska-ryát'] vt. to hasten, precipitate, quicken

услада [oo-slá-da] sf. delight, joy

усладительный [oo-sla-d'é-tyel'-nay] adj. agreeable, delightful, refreshing

услаждать [oo-slazh-dát'] (усладить) vt. to charm, cheer, delight, solace

услащать [oo-sla-shchát'] (усластить) vt. to sweeten

условие [oo-sló-vye] sn. condition, stipulation, clause, proviso; contract

условный [oo-slóv-nay] adj. conditional, conventional, probational

усложнять [oo-slazh-nyát'] vt. to complicate, entangle

услуга [oo-slóo-ga] sf. service; к вашим -м [kvá-shim -m] at your service

услуживать [oo-slóo-zhi-vat'] (услужить) vi. to render a service, to wait upon

услужливый [oo-slóozh-l'i-vay] adj. complaisant, obliging

усматривать [oo-smá-tri-vat'] (усмотреть) vt. do discern, observe

усмирение [oo-sm'i-ryé-nye] sn. pacification

уснащать [oo-sna-shchát'] (уснастить) vt. to garnish

усобица [oo-só-b'i-tsa] sf. dissension

усовершенствование [oo-sa-vyer-shén-stva-va-nye] sn. improvement; perfection

усовещивать [oo-só-vye-shchi-vat'] (усовестить) vt. to admonish; vi. to have scruples

усопший [oo-sóp-shi] adj. dead, late; sm. deceased

успевать [oo-spye-vát'] (успеть) vi. to be successful, to make progress

Успение [oo-spyé-nye] sn. Assumption

успех [oo-spyéch] sm. advancement, progress, success

успешный [oo-spyésh-nay] adj. successful

успокоивать [oo-spa-kā-i-vat'] (успокоить) vt. to calm, reassure, soothe

устав [oo-stáv] sm. regulation, statute; article(s), by-law(s), rule(s)

уставать [oo-sta-vát'] (устать) vi. to get tired, to tire; to be fatigued, to be weary

уставлять [ŏŏ-stav-lyát'] (уста́вить) vt. to fix, place in order, set up

устаивать [ŏŏ-stá-i-vat'] (устоя́ть) vi. to resist, withstand; **-ся** [-sya] vi. to filter; to settle (scum, sediment)

усталость [ŏŏ-stá-lŏst'] sf. fatigue, lassitude

усталый [ŏŏ-stá-lăy] adj. tired, weary, worn out; languid

устанавливать [ŏŏ-stanáv-l'i-vat'] (установи́ть) vt. to determine, establish; to find out; to arrange, range; to mount (a gun)

установка [ŏŏ-sta-nóv-ka] sf. placing, setting; mounting; aim, purpose

устарелый [ŏŏ-sta-ryé-lăy] adj. aged, elderly; antiquated, obsolete

устилать [ŏŏ-st'i-lát'] (устла́ть) vt. to pave; to spread over; to cover (a floor)

устный [ŏŏst-năy] adj. oral, verbal, viva voce

устой [ŏŏ-stóy] sm. abutment; basis; coll. cream; нра́вственный – [nráv-stvyen-năy –] moral principle

устойчивость [ŏŏ-stóy-chi-vŏst'] sf. firmness, stability

устойчивый [ŏŏ-stóy-chi-văy] adj. firm, stable, steady

устраивать [ŏŏ-strá-i-vat'] (устро́ить) vt. to arrange, make arrangements, organize; **-ся** [-sya] vi. to establish oneself, settle one's affairs, settle down

устранять [ŏŏ-stra-nyát'] (устрани́ть) vt. to alienate, divert, set aside; to obviate;

-ся [-sya] vi. to keep at a distance, withdraw

устрашать [ŏŏ-stra-shát'] (устраши́ть) vt. to intimidate, scare

устрашающий [ŏŏ-strashá-yŏŏ-shchi] adj. formidable

устрашение [ŏŏ-stra-shé-nye] sn. frightening, terrorizing; intimidation

устремление [ŏŏ-stryemlyé-nye] sn. tendency

устрица [ŏŏ-str'í-tsa] sf. oyster

устройство [ŏŏ-stróy-stvŏ] sn. arrangement, organization; order

уступ [ŏŏ-stŏŏp] sm. ledge, step; terrace; projection; mil. echelon

уступать [ŏŏ-stŏŏ-pát'] (уступи́ть) vt. to give in, submit, yield; to give up, resign; to relinquish

уступка [ŏŏ-stŏŏp-ka] sf. discount, deduction; concession; cession

уступчивый [ŏŏ-stŏŏp-chivăy] adj. accommodating, compliant

устье [ŏŏ-stye] sn. aperture; estuary; orifice

усугублять [ŏŏ-sŏŏ-gŏŏblyát'] (усугуби́ть) vt. to aggravate, worsen

усы [ŏŏ-să] sm. pl. moustache(s)

усылать [ŏŏ-să-lát'] (усла́ть) vt. to send away

усыновление [ŏŏ-să-navlyé-nye] sn. adoption, affiliation

усыпальница [ŏŏ-să-pál'n'i-tsa] sf. mausoleum, sepulchre, tomb

усыпление [ōō-să-plyé-nye] *sn.* lulling to sleep; stupefaction

усыхание [ōō-să-chá-nye] *sn.* drying, shrinkage

утайка [ōō-tắy-ka] *sf.* concealment; embezzlement

утварь [ōōt-var'] *sf.* implements, utensils

утвердительный [ōō-tvyer-d'ē-tyel'-năy] *adj.* affirmative, assertive, dogmatic

утверждать [ōō-tvyer-zhdắt'] (утвердить) *vt.* to affirm, assert, maintain; to approve, confirm; to consolidate

утверждение [ōō-tvyer-zhdyé-nye] *sn.* assertion; approval; ratification

утекать [ōō-tye-kắt'] (утечь) *vi.* to escape (as gas, etc.)

утёнок [ōō-työ́-nŏk] *sm.* duckling

утепление [ōō-tye-plyé-nye] *sn.* warming

утеривать [ōō-tyé-r'i-vat'] (утерять) *vt.* to forfeit

утёс [ōō-työ́s] *sm.* cliff, crag, rock

утеха [ōō-tyé-cha] *sf.* diversion; solace

утечка [ōō-tyéch-ka] *sf.* leakage

утешать [ōō-tye-shắt'] (утешить) *vt.* to comfort, console

утешение [ōō-tye-shé-nye] *sn.* consolation, solace

утиральник [ōō-t'i-rāl'-nik] *sm.* towel

утирание [ōō-t'i-rắ-nye] *sn.* wiping

утирать [ōō-t'i-rắt'] (утереть) *vt.* to wipe

утихать [ōō-t'i-chắt'] (утихнуть) *vi.* to abate, to subside; to alleviate; to calm

утка [ōōt-ka] *sf.* duck; *fig.* canard; scare; *naut.* cleat

уток [ōō-tók] *sm.* weft, woof

утолщение [ōō-tal-shché-nye] *sn.* thickening

утолять [ōō-ta-lyắt'] (утолить) *vt.* to assuage, quench, satisfy

утомительный [ōō-ta-m'é-tyel'-năy] *adj.* fatiguing, tiresome, wearisome; exhausting

утомлять [ōō-tam-lyắt'] (утомить) *vt.* to exhaust, tire

утончать [ōō-tan-chắt'] (утончить) *vt.* to thin; to rarify, refine

утончённый [ōō-tan-chón-năy] *adj.* delicate, fine, refined, subtle

утопать [ōō-ta-pắt'] (утонуть) *vi.* to drown

утрамбовка [ōō-tram-bóv-ka] *sf.* ramming, stamping

утрате [ōō-trắ-ta] *sf.* loss

утренний [ōō-tryen-n'i] *adj.* early, matutinal

утренник [ōō-tryen-n'ik] *sm.* matinée; early morning frost

утро [ōō-trŏ] *sn.* morning; -м, *adv.* in the morning

утроба [ōō-tró-ba] *sf.* belly, maw; womb

утроение [ōō-tra-yé-nye] *sn.* trebling; triplication

утруждать [ōō-trōōzh-dắt'] (утрудить) *vt.* to hinder, inconvenience, trouble

утюг [ōō-tyōōg] *sm.* flat-iron

утюжить [ōō-tyōō-zhit'] *vt.* to iron

утюжка [ōō-tyōōsh-ka] *sf.* ironing; iron-holder

утягивать [ōō-tyă-gi-vat'] (утянуть) *vt.* to bind, tie; to drag along; *fig.* to haggle

ухаб [oō-cháb] *sm.* hole, pit

ухабистый [oō-chá-b'ís-tảy] *adj.* bumpy (*of road*)

ухаживание [oō-chá-zhi-va-nye] *sn.* nursing, tending; courting, courtship, wooing

ухаживатель [oō-chá-zhi-va-tyel'] *sm.* admirer, suitor

ухаживать [oō-chá-zhi-vat'] *vi.* to nurse, tend; to take care; to court

ухватка [oō-chvát-ka] *sf.* knack, manner; trick

ухватывать [oō-chvá-tă-vat'] (ухватить) *vt.* to grasp, grip, seize

ухищрение [oō-chi-shchryé-nye] *sn.* artifice, contrivance, dodge

ухо [oō-chó] *sn.* ear; *pl.* уши

уховёртка [oō-cha-vyórt-ka] *sf.* earwig

уход [oō-chód] *sm.* departure, leaving; attendance, care

уходить [oō-cha-d'ét'] (уйти) *vi.* to go away, leave

ухудшать [oō-chōod-shát'] *vt.* to deteriorate

участвовать [oō-chast-va-vat'] *vi.* to participate; to be involved

участие [oō-chás-tye] *sn.* partaking, participation, share; complicity

участливость [oō-chást-l'i-vŏst'] *sf.* compassion, solicitude

участник [oō-chást-n'ik] *sm.* participant, partner; competitor

участок [oō-chás-tŏk] *sm.* district, region; plot, strip; section; police-station

учебник [oō-chéb-n'ik] *sm.* manual, class-book, text-book

учебный [oō-chéb-năy] *adj.* class-, school- (*as books, room, etc.*)

учение [oō-ché-nye] *sn.* instruction, teaching, tuition; learning, study; apprenticeship; doctrine; *mil.* drill, exercise

ученик [oō-che-n'ĕk] *sm.* pupil, scholar; apprentice; **старший** – [stár-shi-] monitor, prefect

ученический [oō-che-n'é-ches-ki] *adj.* pupillary

учёный [oō-chó-năy] *adj.* academic, learned, scholarly; *sm.* scholar, scientist

учёт [oō-chót] *sm.* calculation, counting; discount; registration

училище [oō-chē-l'i-shche] *sn.* school

учинять [oō-chi-nyát'] (учинить) *vt.* to commit, perpetrate

учитель [oō-chē-tyel'] *sm.* master, teacher, tutor; **-ский** [-ski] *adj.* tutorial

учить [oō-chit'] (на-) *vt.* to instruct, teach, train; to learn, study; to drill; **-ся** [-sya] *vi.* to learn, study, swot

учредитель [oō-chre-d'í-tyel'] *sm.* founder

учреждать [oō-chrezh-dát'] (учредить) *vt.* to establish, found, set up; to institute

учтивый [oōch-t'é-văy] *adj.* courteous, polite

ушат [oō-shát] *sm.* cowl, tucket, tub

ушиб [oō-shíb] *sm.* bruise; contusion; injury

ушибание [oō-shi-bá-nye] *sn.* bruising

ушко [ōōsh-kó] *sn*. eye (of *needle*); handle; tab, tag

ушной [ōōsh-nóy] *adj*. auricular

ущелье [ōō-shché-lye] *sn*. gorge; pass; ravine; canyon

ущемлять [ōō-shchem-lyât'] (ущемить) *vt*. to jam, nip

ущерб [ōō-shchérb] *sm*. damage, harm; wane; prejudice

ущипывать [ōō-shchē-pă-vat'] (ущипнуть) *vt*. to nip, pinch, squeeze

уютный [ōō-yōōt-năy] *adj*. comfy, cosy, snug

уязвимый [ōō-yaz-v'ē-măy] *adj*. vulnerable

уяснение [ōō-yas-nyé-nye] *sn*. elucidation

Ф

фа [fā] *mus*. F

фабрика [fā-bri-ka] *sf*. factory, manufactory, mill, works

фабрикант [fa-bri-kánt] *sm*. manufacturer

фабрикат [fa-bri-kât] *sm*. manufactured product

фабричный [fa-brēch-năy] *adj*. factory-, manufacturing; **фабричная марка** [fa-brích-na-ya mâr-ka] *sf*. trade-mark; *as sm*. factory employer

фагот [fa-gót] *sm. mus*. bassoon

фаза [fā-za] *sf*. phase

фазан [fa-zán] *sm*. pheasant

факел [fā-kyel] *sm*. torch

факельщик [fā-kyel'-shchik] *sm*. torch-bearer

фактический [fak-t'ē-ches-

ki] *adj*. actual, based upon fact

фактор [fâk-tŏr] *sm*. factor; *typ*. overseer

фактура [fak-tōō-ra] *sf*. bill, invoice; technique

факультет [fa-kōōl'-tyét] *sm*. faculty

факция [fâk-tsya] *sf*. faction

фалбала [fal-bā-la] *sf*. flounce

фальсификация [fal'-si-fi-kā-tsya] *sf*. falsification

фальцет [fal'-tsyét] *sm. mus*. falsetto

фальшивить [fal'-shē-v'it'] *vi*. to cheat, to be false; to sing out of tune

фальшивка [fal'-shēv-ka] *sf*. forged document

фальшивый [fal'-shē-văy] *adj*. false; incorrect; counterfeit

фальшь [fāl'-sh'] *sf*. fabrication, falsehood

фамилия [fa-m'ē-lya] *sf*. surname

фамильярный [fa-m'ilyār-năy] *adj*. familiar, unceremonious

фанаберия [fa-na-bé-rya] *sf*. arrogance; snobbishness

фанера [fa-nyé-ra] *sf*. plywood; veneer

фанза [fān-za] *sf*. foulard

фант [fant] *sm*. forfeit

фантазёр [fan-ta-zyór] *sm*. dreamer

фантазия [fan-tā-zya] *sf*. fancy, fantasy; *mus*. fantasia

фантастичный [fan-tast'ēch-năy] *adj*. fantastic, fanciful, imaginary

фанфара [fan-fā-ra] *sf*. fanfare; flourish

фара [fā-ra] *sf*. head-light

фармацевтика [far-ma-tsyév-t'i-ka] *sf.* pharmaceutics

фармация [far-mā-tsya] *sf.* pharmacy

фартук [fār-tŏŏk] *sm.* apron

фарфор [far-fór] *sm.* china, porcelain

фарш [fārsh] *sm.* stuffing; force-meat, sausage-meat

фаршировать [far-shē-ra-vat'] *vt.* to stuff

фасоль [fa-sól'] *sf.* haricot bean, kidney bean

фасон [fa-són] *sm.* cut, fashion, style

фатоватый [fa-ta-vā-tǎy] *adj.* foppish

фатум [fa-tŏŏm] *sm.* fate

фашина [fa-shē-na] *sf.* faggot

фашинник [fa-shēn-n'ik] *sm.* brushwood

февраль [fye-vrāl'] *sm.* February

федерация [fye-dye-rā-tsya] *sf.* federation

фееричный [fye-ye-rēch-nǎy] *adj.* fairy, magical

фельдмаршал [fyel'd-mār-shal] *sm.* field-marshal

фельдфебель [fyel'd-fyé-byel'] *sm.* sergeant-major

фельдшер [fyél'd-sher] *sm.* medical assistant; hospital orderly

феномен [fye-nó-myen] *sm.* phenomenon

ферзь [fyérz'] *sf.* queen (*chess*)

ферма [fyér-ma] *sf.* farm;

фермер [fér-myer] *sm.* farmer

фермерство [fér-myer-stvŏ] *sn.* farming

фетр [fyetr] *sm.* felt

фехтовальщик [fyech-to-vāl'-shchik] *sm.* fencing master

фехтовать [fyech-ta-vāt'] *vi.* to fence (*sword*)

фея [fyé-ya] *sf.* fairy

фиалка [fi-āl-ka] *sf.* violet

фибра [fē-bra] *sf.* fibre

фига [f'ē-ga] *sf.* fig

фигляр [f'i-glyār] *sm.* mountebank

фиглярство [f'i-glyār-stvŏ] *sn.* buffoonery

фигура [f'i-gŏŏ-ra] *sf.* figure; form, shape; picture-card (*playing cards*)

фигурка [f'i-gŏŏr-ka] *sf.* statuette

фигурный [f'i-gŏŏr-nǎy] *adj.* figured, ornamented with figures

физик [f'ē-zik] *sm.* physicist

физика [f'ē-zika] *sf.* physics

физиология [f'i-zi-a-ló-gya] *sf.* physiology

физический [f'i-z'ē-ches-ki] *adj.* physical; – труд [– trŏŏd] manual labour

физкультура [f'iz-kŏŏl'-tŏŏ-ra] *sf.* physical culture; gymnastics

фиктивный [f'ik-t'ēv-nǎy] *adj.* fictitious

фикция [f'ĕk-tsya] *sf.* fiction

филей [f'i-lyéy] *sm.* fillet, sirloin

филёнка [f'i-lyón-ka] *sf.* panel

филёнчатый [f'i-lyón-cha-tǎy] *adj.* panelled

филин [f'i-l'ĕn] *sm.* eagle-owl

филолог [f'i-la-lóg] *sm.* philologist

филология [f'i-la-ló-gya] *sf.* philology

философ [f'i-la-sóf] *sm.* philosopher

философия [f'i-la-só-fya] *sf.* philosophy

фильм [f'él'm] *sm.* film

фильтр [f'él'tr] *sm.* filter, strainer

фильтрация [f'il'-trā-tsya] *sf.* filtration

фимиам [f'i-miám] *sm.* incense

финал [f'i-nāl] *sm. mus.* finale; final (*sport*)

финансовый [f'i-nān-sa-văy] *adj.* financial

финансы [fi-nān-să] *sm. pl.* finance(s)

финик [f'ē-n'ik] *sm.* date (*fruit*)

финифть [f'i-n'ēft'] *sf.* enamel

финн [f'ēn] *sm.* native of Finnland, Finn

финский [f'ēn-ski] *adj.* Finnish

финтить [f'in-t'ēt'] (*c-*) to shuffle

финтифлюшка [f'in-t'i-flōōsh-ka] *sf.* bagatelle, bauble

фиолетовый [f'i-a-lyé-ta-văy] *adj.* violet (*colour*)

фирма [f'ēr-ma] *sf.* firm, business house

фисташка [f'is-tāsh-ka] *sf.* pistachio

фитиль [f'i-t'ēl] *sm.* wick

фитюлька [f'i-tyōōl'-ka] *sf.* dwarf; whipper-snapper

флаг [flāg] *sm.* banner, flag; ensign; **флагманское судно** [flag-mān-ska-ye sōōd-nŏ] *sn.* flagship; **флагшток** [flag-shtók] *sm.* flagstaff

флакон [fla-kón] *sm.* small bottle, flask

фламандец [fla-mān-dyets] *sm.* Fleming

фламандский [fla-mānd-ski] *adj.* Flemish

фланг [flāng] *sm.* flank, wing

фланель [fla-nyél'] *sf.* flannel

фланёр [fla-nyór] *sm.* idler, lounger

фланец [flā-nyets] *sm.* flange

фланкировка [flan-k'i-róv-ka] *sf.* flanking

флегма [flyég-ma] *sf.* phlegm

флейта [flyéy-ta] *sf.* flute

флейтист [flyey-t'ēst] *sm.* flautist

флексия [flyék-sya] *sf.* flexion, inflexion

флёр [flyór] *sm.* crape, crêpe

флигель [f'ē-gyel] *sm. arch.* wing; outbuilding

флигель-адъютант [f'ē-gyel'-a-dyŏō-tānt] *sm.* aide-de-camp

флот [flot] *sm.* fleet; **военный** — [va-yén-năy -] navy; **воздушный** — [vaz-dōōsh-năy -] air-force; **торговый** — [tar-gó-văy -] mercantile marine

флотский [flót-ski] *adj.* naval

флюгер [flyōō-ger] *sm.* weather-cock

флюс [flyōōs] *sm.* gumboil; flux

фляжка [flyāzh-ka] *sf.* flask

фок [fok] *sm.* foresail; — **мачта** [—māch-ta] *sf.* foremast

фокус [fō-kŏōs] *sm.* trick; freak, whim

фокусник [fó-kŏōs-n'ik] *sm.* conjuror, juggler

фокусный [fó-kŏōs-năy] *adj.* focal

фолиант [fo-liānt] *sm.* folio, volume

фольга [fól'-ga] *sf.* tinfoil

фон [fon] *sm.* background

фона́рь [fa-när'] *sm.* lantern, street-lamp

фона́рщик [fa-när-shchik] *sm.* lamp-lighter

фо́нды [fóndä] *sm. pl.* public funds; stocks; **фо́ндовая би́ржа** [fan-dó-va-ya bёr-zha] *sf.* stock exchange

фоне́тика [fa-nyé-t'i-ka] *sf.* phonetics

форе́ль [fa-ryél'] *sf.* trout

форза́ц [fór-zats] *sm. typ.* fly-leaf

фо́рма [fór-ma] *sf.* form, shape; cast, mould

форма́льность [far-mäl'-nöst'] *sf.* formality

форма́льный [far-mäl'-näy] *adj.* formal

форма́т [far-mät] *sm. typ.* format, size

форма́ция [far-mä-tsya] *sf.* formation

фо́рменный [fór-myen-näy] *adj.* formal; positive; regular; **фо́рменная оде́жда** [fór-myen-na-ya a-dyézh-da] *sf.* uniform (*dress*)

формирова́ть [far-m'ē-ra-vat'] *vt. mil.* to form

формиро́вка [far-m'i-róv-ka] *sf. mil.* formation

формова́ть [far-ma-vät'] (с-) *vt.* to cast, mould

формо́вка [far-móv-ka] *sf.* casting, moulding

формо́вщик [far-móv-shchik] *sm.* moulder

форпо́ст [far-póst] *sm.* outpost

форсу́нка [far-sōōn-ka] *sf.* sprayer

форто́чка [fór-tach-ka] *sf.* casement window; sky-light

форшла́г [fór-shlag] *sm. mus.* grace-note

фосфори́стый [fas-fa-r'ēs-täy] *adj.* phosphorous

фото́граф [fa-tó-graf] *sm.* photographer

фотографи́ческий [fa-ta-gra-f'ē-ches-ki] *adj.* photographic

фотогра́фия [fa-ta-grä-fya] *sf.* photography

фра́за [frä-za] *sf.* phrase, sentence ('tails')

фрак [fräk] *sm.* frock-coat

фра́кция [fräk-tsya] *sf.* faction, group

франки́ровать [fran-k'ē-ra-vat'] *vt.* to prepay

франки́ровка [fran-k'i-róv-ka] *sf.* prepayment

франкмасо́н [frank-ma-són] *sm.* freemason; **-ство** [-stvö] *sn.* freemasonry

фра́нко [frän-kö] *adv.* paid, prepaid

франт [fränt] *sm.* dandy, fop, swank

франти́ха [fran-t'ē-cha] *sf.* smart woman

францу́женка [fran-tsōō-zhen-ka] *sf.* Frenchwoman

францу́з [fran-tsōōz] *sm.* Frenchman

францу́зский [fran-tsōōz-ski] *adj.* French

фрахт [frächt] *sm.* freight

фрахто́вщик [frach-tóv-shchik] *sm.* freighter

фрега́т [frye-gät] *sm.* frigate

фре́за [fryé-za] *sf. tech.* cutter

фре́йлина [fryey-l'ē-na] *sf.* maid of honour

фриз [frēz] *sm.* frieze

фрикцио́нный [fr'ik-tsión-näy] *adj.* frictional

фришева́ть [fr'i-she-vät'] *vt.* to refine

фронтон [fran-tón] *sm.* pediment

фрукт [frōōkt] *sm.* fruit; **-овый сад** [-ó-vǎy sad] *sm.* orchard; **-овщик** [-óv-shchik] *sm.* fruiterer

фуга [fōō-ga] *sf. mus.* fugue

фуганок [fōō-gâ-nŏk] *sm.* joiner's plane

фукс [fōōks] *sm.* fluke (*billiards*)

фуксово стекло [fōōk-só-vŏ styek-ló] *sn.* water-glass

фуляр [fōō-lyâr] *sm.* foulard; scarf

фундамент [fōōn-dá-myent] *sm.* foundation, groundwork

фундаментальный [fōōn-da-myen-tál'-nǎy] *adj.* fundamental; substantial

функция [fōōnk-tsya] *sf.* function

фунт [fōōnt] *sm.* pound, lb., *f.*

фура [fōō-ra] *sf.* cart, van, waggon

фураж [fōō-rázh] *sm.* fodder, forage

фуражка [fōō-rázh-ka] *sf.* peak-cap; *mil.* service cap

фут [fōōt] *sm.* foot (12″); **указный –** [ōō-kâz-nǎy –] foot-rule

футболист [fōōt-ba-l'ist] *sm.* footballer

футляр [fōōt-lyâr] *sm.* box, case, sheath

футлярщик [fōōt-lyâr-shchik] *sm.* case-maker

фуфайка [fōō-fây-ka] *sf.* jersey, sweater

фыркать [fár-kat'] (фы́ркнуть) *vi.* to snort (*as a horse*); to spit (*as a cat*); to burst out laughing

X

халат [cha-lát] *sm.* dressing-gown

халатный [cha-lát-nǎy] *adj.* careless, negligent, remiss

хам [chǎm] *sm.* cad

хамоватый [cha-ma-vá-tǎy] *adj.* rather caddish

хамский [chǎm-ski] *adj.* impudent

хандра [chǎn-dra] *sf.* moroseness, spleen

хандрить [chan-dr'ēt'] *vi.* to be in the dumps, to feel melancholy

ханжа [chan-zhá] *sm., f.* hypocrite

ханжество [chan-zhest-vó] *sn.* bigotry, hypocrisy

хаос [cha-ós] *sm.* chaos

хаотический [cha-at'ē-ches-ki] *adj.* chaotic

характер [cha-rák-tyer] *sm.* character, disposition

характерный [cha-rák-tyer-nǎy] *adj.* characteristic

харкать [chár-kat'] (хáркнуть) *vi.* to expectorate

хартия [chár-tya] *sf.* charter; **великая –** [vye-l'ē-ka-ya –] Magna Charta

харчевня [char-chév-nya] *sf.* eating-house, tavern; cook-shop

харчевник [char-chév-n'ik] *sm.* proprietor of an eating-house

харчи [char-chē] *sm. pl.* victuals

хата [chá-ta] *sf.* hut, peasant's cottage

хаять [chá-yat'] (за-) *vt.* to criticize, find fault

хвала [chva-lá] *sf.* eulogy, praise

хвалебный [chva-lyéb-nǎy] *adj.* laudatory

хвалить [chva-l'ét'] (по-) *vt.* to commend, flatter, praise

хвальба [chval'-bá] *sf.* boasting, showing off; ostentation

хвастаться [chvás-tat'sya] *vi.* to boast, brag, swagger

хвастливый [chvast-l'é-vǎy] *adj.* vainglorious

хвастун [chvas-tóōn] *sm.* braggart

хватать [chva-tát'] (схва-тить) *vt.* to seize, snatch; *vi.* (хватить) to suffice; **хватит!** [chvá-t'it] that will do!

хватка [chvát-kǎ] *sf.* grasp, grip

хвойный [chvóy-nǎy] *adj.* coniferous

хворать [chva-rát'] *vi.* to be indisposed

хворост [chvó-rǒst] *sm.* twig(s)

хворый [chvó-rǎy] *adj.* ailing, sickly

хворь [chvor'] *sf.* sickliness

хвост [chvost] *sm.* tail; queue

херес [chyé-res] *sm.* sherry

херить [chye-r'ét'] *vt.* to cancel, cross out

херувим [chye-rōō-v'ém] *sm.* cherub

хибарка [ch'i-bár-kǎ] *sf.* hut, hovel, shanty

хижина [ch'é-zhi-na] *sf.* cabin

хилый [ch'é-lǎy] *adj.* infirm, sick

химик [ch'é-m'ik] *sm.* chemist (*expert in chemistry*)

химический [ch'i-m'é-ches-ki] *adj.* chemical

химия [ch'é-mya] *sf.* chemistry

хинин [ch'i-n'én] *sm.* quinine

хиромант [ch'i-ra-mánt] *sm.* palmist

хиромантия [ch'i-ra-mán-tya] *sf.* palmistry

хирург [ch'i-rōórg] *sm.* surgeon

хирургический [ch'i-rōōr-g'é-ches-ki] *adj.* surgical

хирургия [ch'i-rōōr-gya] *sf.* surgery

хитрец [ch'i-tryéts] *sm.* crafty individual

хитрость [ch'é-trǒst] *sf.* artfulness, cunning

хитрый [ch'é-trǎy] *adj.* astute, crafty, wily

хихикать [ch'i-ch'é-kat] (хихикнуть) *vi.* to giggle, snigger

хищение [ch'i-shché-nye] *sn.* plundering

хищник [ch'é-shchn'ik] *sm.* plunderer, robber

хищный [ch'é-shchnǎy] *adj.* rapacious; **хищные птицы** [ch'éshch-ná-ye pt'é-tsǎ] birds of prey

хладнокровие [chlad-na-kró-vye] *sn.* composure, coolness

хладнокровный [chlad-na-króv-nǎy] *adj.* calm, collected, cool

хлам [chlám] *sm.* rubbish, trash

хлеб [chlyéb] *sm.* bread; loaf; corn

хлебать [chlye-bát'] (по-) *vt.* to sip; *vt.* to eat with a spoon

хлебец [chlyé-byets] *sm.* small loaf

хлебок [chlye-bók] *sm.* mouthful, sip, spoonful

хлебопашество [chlye-ba-pä-shest-vŏ] sn. agriculture, husbandry

хлебопашец [chlye-ba-pä-shets] sm. farmer, peasant, ploughman

хлебопекарня [chlye-ba-pye-kär-nya] sf. bakery, bakehouse

хлебопечение [chlye-ba-pye-ché-nye] sn. bread baking

хлебосольный [chlye-ba-sŏl'-näy] adj. hospitable

хлеботорговец [chlye-ba-tar-gó-vyets] sm. corn-merchant

хлев [chlyév] sm. cow-shed

хлестать [chlye-stät'] (хлестнуть) vt. to lash, slash, whip

хлёсткий [chlyóst-kı] adj. biting, trenchant

хлопание [chló-pa-nye] sn. banging, slamming

хлопать [chló-pat'] vi. to bang, slam; to pop

хлопководство [chlap-ka-vŏd-stvŏ] sn. cotton-growing

хлопок [chló-pŏk] sm. cotton

хлопотать [chla-pa-tät'] (по-) vi. to bustle, make a fuss, stir

хлопотливость [chla-pa-tl'ě-vŏst'] sf. commotion, fussiness

хлопотливый [chla-pa-tl'ě-väy] adj. fussy, troublesome

хлопоты [chla-pŏ-tă] sf. pl. ado, bustle, fuss, trouble

хлопчатобумажный [chlap-cha-ta-bŏŏ-mázh-näy] adj. cottony, downy

хлопья [chló-pya] sm. pl. snowflakes; wool flocks

хлор [chlor] sm. chlorine

хлористый [chla-r'ěs-täy] adj. chloride

хлынуть [chlắ-nŏŏt'] vi. to gush out; to pour in torrents; to rush

хлыст [chlăst] sm. horsewhip

хлябь [chlyab'] sf. abyss

хмара [chmä-ra] sf. cloud, mist: darkness

хмелеводство [chmye-lye-vŏd-stvŏ] sn. the cultivation of hops

хмелеть [chmye-l'yét] vi. to become intoxicated

хмель [chmyél] sm. hop(s)

хмельник [chmyél'-n'ik] sm. hop garden

хмельной [chmyel'-nóy] adj. heady, tipsy

хмуриться [chmŏŏ-r'ět'-sya] vi. to frown, scowl

хмурый [chmŏŏ-räy] adj. gloomy, sullen

хныкать [chnắ-kat'] vi. to snivel, whimper, whine

хобот [chó-bŏt] sm. elephant's trunk; proboscis

ход [chod] sm. course, march; motion, movement; speed; move (in chess, etc.)

ходатай [cha-dä-tay] sm. intercessor, mediator

ходатайство [cha-dä-tay-stvŏ] sn. intercession, petition, solicitation

ходатайствовать [cha-dä-tay-stva-vat'] (по-) vi. to intercede, plead

ходить [cha-dět'] (с-) vi. to go, walk; to ply; to tend

ходкий [chód-ki] adj. marketable, saleable; goes easily, turns easily

ходок [cha-dók] sm. walker; foot-messenger

ходули [cha-dōō-l'i] *sf. pl.* stilts

ходьба [chad'-bā] *sf.* pacing to and fro; walking

ходячий [cha-dyā-chi] *adj.* walking; current (*money, etc.*)

хождение [chazh-dyé-nye] *sn.* going, pacing, walking

хозяин [cha-zyā-in] *sm.* master, owner, proprietor; landlord

хозяйка [cha-zyáy-ka] *sf.* hostess, landlady

хозяйничать [cha-zyáy-n'i-chat'] *vi.* to manage a household; *coll.* to domineer, to run the show

хозяйственный [cha-zyáy-stvyen-nǎy] *adj.* economical, thrifty

хозяйство [cha-zyáy-stvŏ] *sn.* economy; house-keeping, housewifery

холение [cha-lyé-nye] *sn.* cherishing, tending

холеный [chó-lye-nǎy] *adj.* well-groomed

холить [chó-l'it'] (по-) *vt.* to cherish, tend

холка [chól-ka] *sf.* withers

холм [cholm] *sm.* hillock, mound

холмистый [chal-m'ĕs-tǎy] *adj.* hilly

холод [chó-lod] *sm.* coldness, cold weather

холодеть [cha-la-dyét'] *vi.* to get cold, to chill

холодильник [cha-la-d'ĕl'-n'ik] *sm.* refrigerator

холодить [cha-la-d'ĕt'] *vt.* to cool, refrigerate

холодноватый [cha-la-dna-vá-tǎy] *adj.* chilly

холодный [cha-lód-nǎy] *adj.* cold, frigid, wintry

холопство [cha-lóp-stvŏ] *sn.* bondage, serfdom

холостить [cha-la-st'ét'] (вы-) *vt.* to castrate, geld

холостой [cha-la-stóy] *adj.* celibate, unmarried, single; – патрон [– pa-trón] *sm.* blank cartridge

холостяк [cha-la-styák] *sm.* bachelor

холощение [cha-la-shché-nye] *sn.* emasculation

холст [cholst] *sm.* canvas, sackcloth; клееный – [klyé-ye-nǎy –] buckram

холстинка [chal-st'ĕn-ka] *sf.* gingham

холя [chó-lya] *sf.* neatness, tidiness; – рук [– rōōk] manicure

хомут [cha-mōōt] *sm.* horse's collar, *fig.* yoke

хомяк [cha-myák] *sm.* hamster; *fig.* sluggard

хор [chor] *sm.* choir, chorus

хорёк [cha-ryók] *sm.* polecat

хорист [cha-r'ĕst] *sm.* -ка, *sf.* chorister

хормейстер [char-méy-str] *sm.* chorus master

хоромы [cha-ró-mǎ] *sf. pl.* dwelling house, mansion

хоронить [cha-ra-n'ĕt'] (по-) *vt.* to bury, to inter

хорошенький [cha-rón-shen'-ki] *adj.* rather good-looking, pretty

хороший [cha-ró-shi] *adj.* fine, nice; good

хорошо [cha-ra-shó] *adv.* all right! very well!

хоругвь [cha-rōōgv'] *sf.* religious banner, standard

хотеть [cha-tyét'] (за-) *vt.* to desire, want, wish

хоть [chŏt'] **хотя** [cha-tyâ] *conj.* although, though; **-бы** [-bă] even, if only

хохлатый [cha-chlá-tăy] *adj.* crested, tufted

хохол [cha-chól] *sm.* crest, tuft

хохот [chó-chŏt] *sm.* hearty laughter

хохотать [cha-cha-tát'] *vi.* to laugh boisterously

храбреть [chrab-ryét'] (по-) *vi.* to become brave

храбрец [chrab-ryéts] *sm.* brave, courageous man

храбриться [chrab-r'ĕt'-sya] *vi.* to pretend bravery; to brag

храбрость [chráb-rŏst'] *sf.* bravery, courage, valour

храбрый [chráb-răy] *adj.* brave, gallant, valiant

храм [chrâm] *sm.* temple

хранение [chra-nyé-nye] *sn.* custody, safe-keeping; storage; conservation

хранилище [chra-n'ĕ-lí-shche] *sn.* repository, storehouse

хранитель [chra-n'ĕ-tyel'] *sm.* custodian, guardian, keeper; curator

хранить [chra-n'ĕt'] (co-) *vt.* to guard, keep, preserve

храпеть [chra-pyét'] *vi.* to snore; to snort

хребет [chre-byét] *sm.* backbone, spine; mountain-range, ridge of mountain

хрен [chryén] *sm.* horseradish

хрестоматия [chryes-ta-má-tya] *sf.* reader (book), anthology

хрипение [chri-pyé-nye] *sn.* crepitation, rattle

хриплый [chríp-lăy] *adj.* hoarse, husky, throaty, raucous

хрипнуть [chrip-nŏŏt'] *vi.* to become hoarse

хрипота [chri-pa-tá] *sf.* hoarseness

хцистианин [chris-tya-n'ênj] *sm.* **христианка** [chris-tyân-ka] *sf.* Christian

христианский [chris-tyân-ski] *adj.* Christian, christianly

христианство [chris-tyân-stvŏ] *sn.* Christianity

Христос [chris-tós] *sm.* Christ

христосоваться [chris-ta-sa-vát'-sya] *vi.* to kiss one another at Easter

хром [chrom] *sm.* chrome; chromium

хроматизм [chra-ma-t'êzm] *sm.* chromatics

хроматический [chra-ma-t'ê-ches-ki] *adj. mus.* chromatic

хромать [chra-mât'] *vi.* to hobble, limp

хромой [chra-móy] *adj.* lame, limping

хромоножка [chra-ma-nózh-ka] *sf.* cripple

хромота [chra-ma-tá] *sf.* lameness

хроника [chró-n'i-ka] *sf.* chronicle

хроникёр [chra-n'i-kyór] *sm.* chronicler, reporter

хронологический [chra-na-la-g'ê-ches-ki] *adj.* chronological

хрупкий [chrŏŏp-ki] *adj.* brittle, fragile, frail

хруст [chrŏŏst] *sm.* crunch, crunching

хрусталь [chrŏŏ-stâl'] *sm.* crystal, cut-glass

хрустальный [chrōō-stál'-nǎy] *adj.* crystalline

хрустеть [chrōō-styét'] (хрустнуть) *vi.* to crack, crackle, crunch

хрущ [chrōōshch] *sm.* cockchafer

хрыч [chrách] *sm.* greybeard, old fogy

хрычовка [chrǎ-chóv-ka] *sf.* old hag, vixen

хрюкать [chryōō-kat'] (хрюкнуть) *vi.* to grunt

хрящ [chryashch] *sm.* cartilage, gristle; gravel, grit

худеть [chōō-dyét'] (по-) *vi.* to lose weight

худо [chōō-dǒ] *sn.* evil, harm, wrong; *adv.* badly; **мне –** [mnyé –] I am not feeling well

худоба [chōō-da-bǎ] *sf.* leanness, meagreness

художественный [chōō-dózhest-vyen-nǎy] *adj.* artistic

художество [chōō-dó-zhest-vǒ] *sn.* art; the fine arts

художник [chōō-dózh-n'ik] *sm.* artist, painter

худой [chōō-dóy] *adj.* bad, ill, inferior; lean, meagre, thin

хула [chōō-lǎ] *sf.* blame, censure

хулить [chōō-l'ét'] (по-) *vt.* to blame, censure, reproach

хутор [chōō-tǒr] *sm.* farm, farmhouse

Ц

цапать [tsǎ-pat'] (цапнуть) *vt.* to clutch, grasp; to snap, snatch

цапля [tsǎp-lya] *sf.* heron; **белая –** [byé-la-ya –] egret

цапфа [tsǎp-fa] *sf.* journal, pin; trunnion

царапать [tsa-rǎ-pat'] (царапнуть) *vt.* to claw, scratch; to scrawl, scribble

царапина [tsa-rǎ-p'i-na] *sf.* scratch

царевич [tsa-rvé-v'ich] *sm.* son of a tsar, prince

царевна [tsa-ryév-na] *sf.* daughter of a tsar, princess

царедворец [tsa-rye-dvó-ryets] *sm.* courtier

цареубийство [tsa-rye-ōō-b'ést-vǒ] *sn.* regicide

царить [tsa-r'ét'] *vi.* to reign, rule

царица [tsa-r'é-tsa] *sf.* empress, queen

царский [tsǎr-ski] *adj.* regal, royal

царство [tsǎr-stvǒ] *sn.* empire, kingdom

царствовать [tsǎr-stva-vat'] *vi.* to reign, rule

царь [tsar'] *sm.* emperor, king, tsar

цвель [tsvyel'] *sf.* mouldiness, mustiness

цвести [tsvve-st'é] *vi.* to blossom, flower; *fig.* to flourish

цвет [tsvvét] *sm.* colour, tint; *sn.* bloom, flower

цветение [tsvve-tyé-nye] *sn.* flowering; florescence

цветистый [tsvve-t'és-tǎy] *adj.* florid; flamboyant; **– стиль** [– st'él'] *sn.* exuberant style

цветник [tsvyet-n'ék] *sm.* flower-bed, flower garden

цветной [tsvyet-nóy] *adj.* coloured, floral, tinged; **цветная капуста** [tsvvetná-ya ka-pōōs-ta] *sf.* cauliflower

цветовод [tsyve-ta-vód] *sm.* florist; **-ство** [-stvó] *sn.* floriculture

цветок [tsyve-tók] *sm.* little flower

цветочница [tsyve-tóch-n'i-tsa] *sf.* flower-girl

цветочный [tsyve-tóch-nǎy] *adj.* floral; **– покров** [pa-króv] *sm.* perianth

цветущий [tsyve-tōō-shchi] *adj.* blossoming, flowering

цевка [tsyév-ka] *sf.* bobbin, reel, spool

цедилка [tsye-d'él-ka] *sf.* filter, strainer

цедить [tsye-d'ět'] (про-) *vt.* to filter, strain

цедра [tsye-dra] *sf.* shred of lemon peel

цежение [tsye-zhé-nye] *sn.* filtering, straining

целебность [tsye-lyéb-nǒst'] *sf.* salubrity

целебный [tsye-lyéb-nǎy] *adj.* curative, healing, medicinal; salubrious, sanitary

целесообразность [tsye-lye-sa-ab-rǎz-nǒst'] expediency

целесообразный [tsye-lye-sa-ab-rǎz-nǎy] *adj.* expedient

целеустремлённый [tsye-lye-ōō-stryem-lyón-nǎy] *adj.* purposeful

целибат [tsye-l'i-bǎt] *sm.* celibacy

целиком [tsye-l'i-kóm] *adv.* entirely, totally, wholly

целина [tsye-l'i-nǎ] *sf.* virgin soil

целитель [tsye-l'í-tyel'] *sm.* healer

целительный [tsye-l'í-tyel'-nǎy] *adj.* curative, healthgiving

целить [tsye-l'it'] *vi.* to aim, point; *fig.* to allude to

целлюлярный [tsyel-lyōō-lyǎr-nǎy] *adj.* cellular

целование [tsye-la-vǎ-nye] *sn.* kissing

целовать [tsye-la-vǎt'] (по-) *vt.* to kiss; **-ся** [-sya] to kiss each other

целомудренный [tsye-la-mōō-dryen-nǎy] *adj.* chaste, pure

целомудрие [tsye-la-mōō-drye] *sn.* chastity; virtue

целостный [tsyé-last-nǎy] *adj.* complete, entire, whole; intact

целость [tsyé-lǒst'] *sf.* entirety, wholeness; integrity

целый [tsyé-lǎy] *adj.* entire, whole; intact, unbroken

цель [tsyěl'] *sf.* mark, target; aim; purpose; intention; object

цельный [tsyél'-nǎy] *adj.* integral, total

цемент [tsye-myént] *sm.* cement

цена [tsye-nǎ] *sf.* charge, cost, price, value; **любой**

ценой [lyōō-bóy tsye-nóy] at any price; **скидка цены** [sk'ĕd-ka tsye-nǎ] discount

ценз [tsyénz] *sm.* qualification, right

цензор [tsyén-zǒr] *sm.* censor

цензорство [tsyén-zar-stvǒ] *sn.* censorship

цензура [tsyen-zōō-ra] *sf.* censoring

цензурный [tsyen-zōōr-nǎy] *adj.* censorial

ценитель [tsye-n'í-tyel'] *sm.* connoisseur, judge

ценить [tsye-n'ět'] (о-) *vt.* to estimate, rate, value

ценность [tsyén-nŏst'] *sf.* price, value, worth

ценный [tsyén-năy] *adj.* costly, dear, valuable

центр [tsyentr] *sm.* centre

центральный [tsyen-trál'-năy] *adj.* central

центробежный [tsye-tra-byĕzh-năy] *adj.* centrifugal

центростремительный [tsyen-tra-strye-m'ĕ-tyel'-năy] *adj.* centripetal

цеп [tsyep] *sm.* flail

цепенелый [tsye-pye-nyé-lăy] *adj.* numb, torpid

цепенеть [tsye-pye-nyét'] (о-) *vi.* to become numb, torpid

цепкий [tsyép-ki] *adj.* scansorial; tenacious; adhesive, cohesive

цепляться [tsye-plyát'-sya] *vi.* to cling

цепочка [tsyé-pach-ka] *sf.* small chain, watch-chain

цепь [tsyép'] *sf.* chain; **горная** – [gór-na-ya –] range of mountains

церва [tsyér-va] *sf.* woad, blue dye

перемониться [tsye-rye-mó-n'it'-sya] (по-) *vi.* to stand on ceremony, to make a fuss

церемонный [tsye-rye-món-năy] *adj.* ceremonious

церковник [tsyer-kóv-n'ik] *sm.* churchman, sexton

церковный [tsyer-kóv-năy] *adj.* churchy, ecclesiastical; **– приход** [– pri-chód] parish

церковь [tsyer-kóv'] *sf.* church; **домовая** – [da-ma-vá-ya –] chapel

цесаревич [tsye-sa-ryé-vich] *sm.* heir to the Russian throne

цесарка [tsye-sár-ka] *sf.* guinea-fowl

цивилизация [ts'i-v'i-l'i-zá-tsya] *sf.* civilization

цивилизованный [ts'i-v'i-l'i-zó-van-năy] *adj.* civilized

цивильный [ts'i-v'ĕl'-năy] *adj.* civil (*non-military*)

цикл [tsikl] *sm.* cycle, round

циклист [tsi-kl'ĕst] *sm.* cyclist

циклон [tsi-klón] *sm.* cyclone

цикорий [tsi-kó-ri] *sm.* chicory

цикута [tsi-kóo-ta] *sf.* hemlock

цилиндр [tsi-l'ĕndr] *sm.* cylinder; roller; top hat

цилиндрический [tsi-l'in-dr'ĕ-ches-ki] *adj.* cylindrical

цинический [ts'i-n'ĕ-ches-ki] *adj.* cynical

цинк [tsink] *sm.* zinc; com. spelter; **листовый** – [l'is-tō-văy –] galvanized iron

цирк [tsirk] *sm.* circus

циркуль [tsir-kōōl'] *sm.* compass(es)

циркуляр [tsir-kōō-lyär] *sm.* circular, hand-bill

циркулярный [tsir-kōō-lyär-năy] *adj.* circular

циркуляция [tsír-kōō-lyä-tsya] *sf.* circulation

цирюльник [tsi-ryōōl'-nik] *sm.* barber

цирюльня [tsi-ryōōl'-nya] *sf.* hair-dressing saloon

цистерна [tsis-tyér-na] *sf.* cistern; water cart

цитадель [tsi-ta-dyél'] *sf.* citadel, fort; stronghold

цитата [tsi-tä-ta] *sf.* citation; quotation

цитировать [tsi-t'ĕ-ra-vat'] *vt.* to cite, quote

цитра [tsʼē-tra] *sf.* zither

цитрон [tsi-trón] *sm.* citron

циферблат [tsi-fer-blát] *sm.* dial, index

цифра [tsíf-ra] *sf.* cipher, figure, numeral

цицеро [tsí-tse-rŏ] *sn.* typ. pica

цоколь [tsó-kŏlʼ] *sm.* plinth, socle

цукат [tsŏŏ-kát] *sm.* candied peel

цыбик [tsă-bʼik] *sm.* Russian tea-chest

цыбуля [tsă-bŏŏ-lya] *sf.* spring-onion

цыган [tsă-gán] *sm.*, **цыганка** [tsă-gán-ka] *sf.* gipsy

цыганский [tsă-gán-ski] *adj.* gipsy-like, tsigane

цыкать [tsă-katʼ] *vi.* to hush

цынга [tsăn-gá] *sf.* scurvy

цынготный [tsăn-gót-năy] *adj.* scorbutic

цыновка [tsă-nóv-ka] *sf.* mat

цыплёнок [tsă-plyó-nŏk] *sm.* chick, chicken

Ч

чабан [cha-bán] *sm.* shepherd

чабёр [cha-byór] *sm.* savory

чавкать [cháv-katʼ] (-ав-кнуть) *vi.* to champ, eat noisily

чад [chád] *sm.* smoke; steam; smell of cooking

чадить [cha-dʼítʼ] (на-) *vt.* to smell of burning, cooking; to smoke, steam

чадо [chā-dŏ] *sm. coll.* child

чадолюбивый [cha-da-lyŏŏ-bʼē-văy] *adj.* philoprogenitive

чаевые [chā-ye-va-ye] *sm. pl.* gratuity, tip

чаепитие [cha-ye-pʼē-tye] *sn.* tea-drinking

чай [cháy] *sm.* tea

чай [cháy] *adv. coll.* apparently, possibly

чайка [cháy-ka] *sf.* seagull

чайник [cháy-nʼik] *sm.* tea-pot; tea-urn; kettle

чайница [cháy-nʼi-tsa] *sf.* tea-canister

чайный [cháy-năy] *adj.* tea-
— **магазин** [— ma-ga-zʼēn] tea-shop; — **стол** [— stol] tea-table

чал [chal] *sm.* hawser

чалма [chal-má] *sf.* turban

чалый [chā-lăy] *adj.* roan

чалопегий [cha-la-pʼé-gi] *adj.* skewbald

чан [chān] *sm.* tub, vat; tun

чаровать [cha-ra-vátʼ] (o-) *vi.* to bewitch, charm, enchant

чародей [cha-ra-dʼéy] *sm.* magician, sorcerer, wizard

чародейка [cha-ra-dʼéy-ka] *sf.* enchantress, witch

чары [chā-ră] *sf. pl.* magic, sorcery, witchcraft

час [chās] *sm.* hour; — **обеда** [— a-byé-da] dinner-time; **в добрый** — [vdó-brăy —] good luck! **который** —? [ka-tó-răy —] what is the time?

часовня [cha-sóv-nya] *sf.* chapel

часовой [cha-sa-vóy] *adj.* hour's, of an hour; pertaining to a watch; *sm.* sentinel, sentry

часовщик [cha-sav-shchík] *sm.* watchmaker

часослов [cha-sa-slóv] *sm.* breviary, prayer-book

частица [chas-t'ē-tsa] *sf.* particle; fraction

частичный [chas-t'ēch-năy] *adj.* partial

частность [chāst-nŏst'] *sf.* particularity; **в частности** [vchāst-nas-t'i] in particular

частный [chāst-năy] *adj.* particular; private; special; confidential

часто [chās-tŏ] *adv.* frequently, often; densely, thickly

частокол [chas-ta-kól] *sm.* paling, palisade

частота [chas-ta-tā] *sf.* frequency; closeness, thickness

частушка [chas-tōōsh-ka] *sf.* topical ditty

частый [chās-tăy] *adj.* habitual; frequent; repeated; close, thick; **– гребень** [– gryé-byen'] tooth-comb; **– лес** [– lyés] thick wood; **частая ткань** [chās-ta-ya tkān'] close fabric

часть [chāst'] *sf.* part, portion, share

часы [cha-să] *sm. pl.* clock, watch

чахлый [chāch-lăy] *adj.* emaciated, ill-looking

чахнуть [chāch-nŏŏt'] *vi.* to pine away, waste away

чахотка [cha-chót-ka] *sf.* tuberculosis

чахоточный [cha-chó-tach-năy] *adj.* consumptive

чаша [chā-sha] *sf.* beaker, bowl

чашечка [chā-shech-ka] *sf.* coffee-cup; calyx

чашка [chāsh-ka] *sf.* cup; cupful

чаща [chā-shcha] *sf.* brushwood, thicket

чаяние [chā-ya-nye] *sn.* anticipation, expectation

чаять [chā-yat'] *vt.* to expect, hope

чванливый [chvan-l'ē-văy] *adj.* conceited

чебак [che-bāk] *sm.* bream

чей [chyéy] *pron.* whose; to whom

чека [che-kā] *sf.* linchpin

чекан [che-kān] *sm.* coinage; die, stamp; punch

чеканить [che-kā-n'it'] (вы-) *vt.* to mint; to chase, emboss

чеканщик [che-kān-shchik] *sm.* medallist and minter

чёлка [chól-ka] *sf.* forelock, fringe

чёлн [choḷn] *sm.* canoe, skiff; shuttle, quill

чело [che-ló] *sn.* brow, forehead

челобитная [che-la-b'ēt-na-ya] *sf.* petition

человек [che-la-vyék] *sm.* creature, human being, individual, person

человеколюбие [che-la-vye-ka-lyōō-bye] *sn.* humanity, philanthropy

человекообразный [che-la-vye-ka-ab-rāz-năy] *adj.* manlike

человекоубийство [che-la-vye-ka-ōō-b'é-stvŏ] *sn.* homicide

человечек [che-la-vyé-chek] *sm.* dwarf, manikin

человеческий [che-la-vyé-ches-ki] *adj.* human

человечество [che-la-vyé-ches-tvŏ] *sn.* mankind, universe

человечность [che-la-vyéch-nöst'] *sf.* humanity

человечный [che-la-vyéch-näy] *adj.* compassionate, humane, kind

челюстной [che-lyööst-nóy] *adj.* maxillary; **челюстная судорога** [ché-lyööst-na-ya sōō-da-ra-ga] lock-jaw

челюсть [ché-lyöost'] *sf.* jaw, jowl; chaps (of animals)

челядь [ché-lyad'] *sf.* domestic staff, servants

чем [chem] *pron.* with what, by what; **уйти ни с** — [ōöy-t'é n'is —] go away unrewarded, *conj.* than; at; **. . . тем** [-. . . tyem] the . . . the

чемодан [che-ma-dän] *sm.* portmanteau; suit-case; small trunk

чемпионат [chem-pio-nät] *sm.* championship

чепец [che-péts] *sm.* cap; woman's mob-cap

чепуха [che-pöö-chä] *sf.* nonsense

червеобразный [cher-vye-ab-räz-näy] *adj.* vermiform

червивый [cher-v'é-väy] *adj.* maggoty, worm-eaten

червлёный [cher-vlyó-näy] *adj.* scarlet

червоточина [cher-va-tó-chi-na] *sf.* dry rot, worm-hole

червы [chér-vä] *sf. pl.* hearts (playing cards)

червь [cherv'] *sm.* worm; **шелковичный** — [shel-ka-v'éch-näy —] silkworm; **светящийся червяк** [svye-tyä-shchi-sya cher-vyäk] glow-worm

чердак [cher-däk] *sm.* attic, garret, loft

черёд [che-ryód] *sm.* order, turn

чередоваться [che-rye-da-vät'-sya] *vi.* to alternate, take turns

через [ché-ryez] *prep.* across, over; by; through; — **год** [— god] in a year's time; — **Лондон** [— lón-dön] via London

черемуха [che-rye-mōō-cha] *sf.* black alder

черенок [che-rye-nók] *sm.* graft; scion

череп [ché-ryep] *sm.* cranium, skull

черепаха [che-rye-pä-cha] *sf.* tortoise, turtle

черепица [che-rye-p'é-tsa] *sf.* tile

черепной [cheryep-nóy] *adj.* cranial

черепокожный [che-rye-pa-kózh-näy] *adj.* testaceous

чересчур [che-ryes-chöör] *adv.* too, too many, too much; exceedingly

черешня [che-ryésh-nya] *sf.* cherry

черкать [cher-kät'] (**черкнуть**) *vt.* to scrawl, scribble; to write a line or two

чернеть [cher-nyét'] *vi.* to become black

черника [cher-n'é-ka] *sf.* bilberry

чернила [cher-n'é-la] *sn. pl.* [ink

чернильница [cher-n'él'-n'i-tsa] *sf.* inkstand

чернить [cher-n'ét'] *vt.* to blacken; fig. to defame

черноватый [cher-na-vä-täy] *adj.* blackish

черновик [cher-na-v'ék] *sm.* rough copy, unprepared manuscript

черноклён [cher-na-klyón] *sm.* maple

чернокнижие [cher-na-kn'ē-zhye] *sn.* necromancy

чернокнижник [cher-na-kn'ēzh-n'ik] *sm.* necromancer; wizard

чернокожий [cher-na-kózhi] *adj.* black-skinned; as *sm.* blackamoor

чернолесье [cher-na-lyésye] *sn.* deciduous woods

черномазый [cher-na-mázăy] *adj.* swarthy

чернорабочий [cher-na-ra-bó-chi] *sm.* unskilled workman

чернослив [cher-na-sl'ĕv] *sm.* prune(s)

чернота [cher-na-tã] *sf.* blackness

чёрный [chór-năy] *adj.* black; dirty; soiled; **– день** [– dyén'] evil (fatal) day

чернь [chern'] *sf.* rabble; niello (*on metals*)

черпалка [cher-pál-ka] *sf.* scoop

черпать [chér-pat'] (черпнýть) *vt.* to draw up, ladle out; to ship water

черстветь [cher-stvyét'] (за-) *vi.* to become stale (*as bread, etc.*); *fig.* to harden, become merciless

чёрствый [chór-stvăy] *adj.* dry, hard, stale; cruel

черта [cher-tã] *sf.* line; feature; trait

чертёж [cher-tyózh] *sm.* diagram, drawing, plan, sketch

чертёжник [cher-tyózhn'ik] *sm.* draughtsman

чертёнок [cher-tyó-nŏk] *sm.* imp

чертить [cher-t'ĕt'] (на-) *vt.* to draw, sketch

чертовский [cher-tóv-ski] *adj.* devilish

чертовщина [cher-tóvshchi-na] *sf.* devilment

чертог [cher-tóg] *sm.* apartment, hall, state-room; **-и** [-i] *sm. pl.* palace

чертополох [cher-ta-palóch] *sm.* thistle

черчение [cher-ché-nye] *sn.* designing, drawing, sketching

чесалка [che-sál-ka] *sf.* hemp comb; hackle

чесальщик [che-sál'-shchik] *sm.* carder

чесание [che-sã-nye] *sn.* carding, hackling

чесать [che-sát'] (по-) *vt.* to card, hackle; to scratch; (при-) to comb, dress (*the hair*); **-ся** [-sya] *vi.* to itch

чёска [chós-ka] *sf.* combing

чеснок [ches-nók] *sm.* garlic

чесотка [che-sót-ka] *sf.* itch, rash; mange

чесоточный [che-só-tachnăy] *adj.* scabby; mangy

чествование [chést-va-a-nye] *sn.* honouring; religious respect; church celebration

чествовать [chést-va-vat'] *vt.* to celebrate, honour, respect

честить [ches-t'ĕt'] *vt.* to honour; *fig.* to abuse, scold

честность [chést-nŏst'] *sf.* honesty, integrity

честный [chést-năy] *adj.* fair, honest, upright; **быть честным** [băt' chést-năm] to be straightforward; ‘ play the game ’

честолюбие [chesta-lyōō-bye] *sn.* ambition, aspiration

честолюбивый [ches-ta-lyōō-b'é-vǎy] *adj.* ambitious

честь [chest'] *sf.* honour

чёт [chot] *sm.* even number; pair

чета [che-tā] *sf.* couple, pair

четверг [che-tvyérg] *sm.* Thursday

четвёрка [che-tvyór-ka] *sf.* the four (*of cards*); carriage and four; team of four horses

четвероногий [che-tvye-ra-nó-gi] *adj.* quadruped

четвёртый [che-tvyór-tǎy] *num.* fourth

четвероякий [che-tvye-ra-yā-ki] *adj.* fourfold

четвертичный [che-tvyer-t'éch-nǎy] *adj.* quaternary

четверть [ché-tvyert'] *sf.* quarter; *mus.* fourth

чётки [chót-ki] *sf. pl.* beads, rosary

чёткий [chót-ki] *adj.* clear, legible

чёткость [chót-kŏst'] *sf.* clearness, legibility

чётный [chót-nǎy] *adj.* even (*number*)

четыре [che-tǎ-rye] *num.* four

четыредесятница [che-tǎ-rye-dye-syāt-n'i-tsa] *sf.* Lent

четыреста [che-tǎ-ryes-ta] *num.* four hundred

четырёхсторонний [che-tǎ-ryoch-sta-rón-n'i] *adj.* quadrilateral

четырёхугольник [che-tǎ-ryoch-ōō-gól'-n'ik] *sm.* quadrangle

четырнадцать [che-tǎr-nad-tsat'] *num.* fourteen

чех [chech] *sm.* Czech

чехарда [che-chār-da] *sf.* leap-frog

чехол [che-chól] *sm.* case, cover

чехословацкий [che-cha-sla-vāts-ki] *adj.* Czechoslovak

чечевица [che-che-v'é-tsa] *sf.* lentil

чечётка [che-chót-ka] *sf.* linnet

чешка [chésh-ka] *sf.* Czech woman

чешский [chésh-ski] *adj.* Czech

чешуекрылый [che-shōō-ye-krā-lǎy] *adj.* lepidopterous

чешуя [che-shōō-ya] *sf.* scale (*of fish*)

чижик [chí-zhik] *sm.* chaffinch, siskin; tipcat (*a game*)

чикание [chi-kā-nye] *sn.* clipping; snapping (*as a photograph*)

чикать [chí-kat'] (**чикнуть**) *vi.* to clip, snap; to chirp

чин [chin] *sm.* grade, rank

чинить [chi-n'ét'] *vt.* to mend, patch, repair; to point, sharpen (*a pencil*)

чинность [chin-nŏst'] *sf.* decorum

чинный [chin-nǎy] *adj.* decorous, sedate

чиновник [chi-nóv-n'ik] *sm.* clerk, official

чиновный [chi-nóv-nǎy] *adj.* high-ranking

чиноначалие [chi-na-na-chā-lye] *sn.* subordination

чиноположение [chi-na-pa-la-zhé-nye] *sn.* ritual

чинопроизводство [chi-na-pra-iz-vód-stvŏ] *sn.* promotion

чирей [chí-ryey] *sm.* boil, furuncle

чирикать [chi-r'ē-kat'] *vi.* to twitter

чирок [chi-rók] *sm.* teal

численность [chí-slyen-nöst'] *sf.* number, quantity

численный [chi-slyen-näy] *adj.* numeral

числитель [chi-sl'é-tyel'] *sm.* numerator

числить [chi-sl'ét'] *vt.* to count

число [chi-sló] *sn.* number; quantity; **единственное –** [ye-d'ēn-stvyen-na-ye –] singular; **множественное –** [mnó-zhest-vyen-na-ye –] plural; date

чистилище [chis-t'ē-l'i-shche] *sn.* purgatory

чистильщик [chis-t'ēl'-shchik] *sm.* cleaner; shoeblack

чистить [chís-t'it'] (вы-) *vt.* to clean, cleanse; **-ся** [-sya] *vr.* to brush oneself, clean oneself

чистка [chíst-ka] *sf.* cleaning, cleansing

чистовик [chis-ta-v'ék] *sm.* fair copy, prepared manuscript

чистоган [chis-ta-gän] *sm.* ready cash

чистокровный [chis-ta-króv-näy] *adj.* thoroughbred; full-blooded

чистописание [chis-ta-p'i-sä-nye] *sn.* calligraphy

чистоплотный [chis-ta-plót-näy] *adj.* adroit, dexterous, neat

чистосердечный [chis-ta-syer-dyéch-näy] *adj.* candid, sincere

чистота [chis-tatá] *sf.* cleanliness; clarity, clearness; purity

чистотел [chis-ta-tyél] *sm.* celandine

чистоуст [chis-ta-ōōst] *sm.* flowering fern

чистый [chís-täy] *adj.* clean, neat, pure; **– голос** [– gó-lös] *sm.* clear voice; **чистая правда** [chís-ta-ya práv-da] *sf.* gospel truth

читальня [chi-tál'-nya] *sf.* reading-room

читатель [chi-tä-tyel'] *sm.* reader

читать [chi-tät'] (по-) *vi.* to read

читка [chít-ka] *sf. theat.* play-reading; preliminary rehearsal

чиханье [chi-chä-nye] *sn.* sneezing

чихать [chi-chät'] (чихнуть) *vi.* to sneeze

член [chlyen] *sm.* member; fellow; limb; *gram.* article

членовредительство [chlye-na-vrye-d'ē-tyel'-stvö] *sn.* maiming, mutilation

членораздельный [chlye-na-raz-dyél'-näy] *adj.* articulate, distinct

членство [chlén-stvö] *sn.* membership

чмокать [chmó-kat'] (чмокнуть) *vi.* to smack one's lips

чокаться [chó-kat'-sya] (чокнуться) *vi.* to clink glasses

чопорный [chó-par-näy] *adj.* prim, prudish, stiff

чорт [chort] *sm.* devil; **– возьми!** [– vaz -mé] dash it!

чреватый [chrye-vä-täy] *adj.* fraught with, pregnant with

чревовещание [chre-va-vye-shchá-nye] sn. ventriloquism

чревовещатель [chre-va-vye-shchá-tyel] sm. ventriloquist

чревоугодник [chre-va-oō-gód-n'ik] sm. glutton

чрезвычайный [chrez-vvý-cháy-nay] adj. extraordinary, extreme

чрезмерный [chrez-myér-nay] adj. excessive, exorbitant

чтение [chtyé-nye] sn. perusal, reading

чтец [chtyéts] sm. reciter

чтить [chtēt] vt. to respect, revere

что [shto] pron. how, what; **что-то** [shtó-tŏ] something; **на –?** [na –] what for ?

чтобы [shtó-bǎ] conj. in order to, so that

чуб [choōb] sm. tuft of hair

чубарый [choōb-bá-rǎy] adj. mottled, speckled

чувственный [choōv-stvyen-nǎy] adj. sensual, voluptuous

чувствительность [choōv-stv'ē-tyel'-nŏst'] sf. sensibility, sensitiveness

чувствительный [choōv-stv'ē-tyel'-nǎy] adj. sensitive, sentimental, susceptible, tender; painful

чувство [choōv-stvŏ] sn. feeling, sensation; sense

чувствовать [choōv-stva-vat'] (по–) vt. to experience, feel

чугун [choō-goōn] sm. cast iron; **белый –** [byé-lǎy –] pig iron

чугунка [choō-goōn-ka] sf. coll. portable iron stove

чугунный [choō-goōn-nǎy] adj. cast-iron

чудак [choō-dák] sm.; crank; eccentric person

чудачество [choō-dá-chest-vŏ] sn. eccentricity; extravagance; oddity

чудеса [choō-dye-sá] sm. pl. miracles; **семь чудес света** [syem' choō-dyés svyéta] seven wonders of the world

чудесный [choō-dyés-nǎy] adj. wonderful; miraculous; beautiful, lovely

чудиться [choō-d'ēt'-sya] vi. to seem; to wonder

чудной [choōd-nóy] adj. comical, strange

чудный [choōd-nǎy] adj. beautiful, marvellous

чудо [choō-dŏ] sn. miracle, wonder; **– красоты** [– kra-sa-tál] paragon

чудовище [choō-dó-v'ishche] sn. monster

чудовищность [choō-dó-v'ishch-nŏst'] sf. enormity, monstrosity

чудовищный [choō-dó-v'ishch-nǎy] adj. monstrous

чудотворный [choō-da-vór-nǎy] adj. thaumaturgic

чужак [choō-zhák] sm. alien, stranger

чужбина [choōzh-b'ē-na] sf. foreign country

чуждаться [choōzh-dát'-sya] vi. to become estranged; to avoid, keep away, shun

чуждый [choōzh-dǎy] adj. foreign, strange; hostile

чужеземец [choō-zhe-zyé-myets] sm. foreigner, stranger

чужеядный [choō-zhe-yád-nǎy] adj. parasitic(al)

чужой [choō-zhóy] *adj.* foreign, strange; another's; **чужая жена** [choō-zhá-ya zhe-ná] wife of another; *as sm.* stranger

чулан [choō-lán] *sm.* larder; lumber-room, store-room

чулок [choō-lók] *sm.* stocking; sock

чулочник [choō-lóch-n'ik] *sm.* stocking-knitter

чулочный [choō-lóch-năy] *adj.* hosiery (*department, etc.*)

чума [choō-má] *sf.* pestilence; plague

чумазый [choō-má-zăy] *adj.* filthy, nasty; slovenly

чумичка [choō-m'ĕch-ka] *sf.* untidy woman

чумный [choōm-năy] *adj.* pestilential, plague-stricken

чураться [choō-rát'-sya] *vi.* to hold back, stand aloof

чурбан [choōr-bán] *sm.* block, log, junk

чуткий [choōt-ki] *adj.* considerate, sensitive, tactful

чуткость [choōt-kŏst'] *sf.* sensitiveness; tact; sharpness (*of hearing*); lightness (*of sleep*)

чуть [choōt] *adv.* hardly; **-не** [-nye] almost, nearly; **—,** very little, tiny bit

чутьё [choōt-tyó] *sn.* instinct; flair; scent

чучело [choō-che-lo] *sn.* dummy, stuffed animal; scarecrow

чучельщик [choō-chél'-shchik] *sm.* taxidermist

чушь [choōsh] *sf.* stuff and nonsense

чуять [choō-yat'] *vt.* to scent; to feel; to understand

Ш

шабаш [sha-básh] *sm.* respite, rest; *interj.* that will do!

шабашить [sha-bá-shit'] *vi.* to leave off (*work*)

шаблон [sha-blón] *sm.* mould, pattern

шаг [shåg] *sm.* pace, step, stride; **- за шагом** [- za shå-gŏm] step by step

шагать [sha-gát'] (шагнуть) *vi.* to pace, step, stride; **шажком** [shåzh-kŏm] at a slow pace

шайба [shåy-ba] *sf.* ring, washer

шайка [shåy-ka] *sf.* band, gang; small water pail, tub

шакал [sha-kál] *sm.* jackal

шаланда [sha-lán-da] *sf.* wherry

шалаш [sha-lásh] *sm.* hut, tent

шалеть [sha-lyét'] (о-) *vi.* to be off one's head; to run amuck

шалить [sha-l'ét'] (по-) *vi.* to play pranks; to be mischievous (*of children*)

шаловливый [sha-la-vl'é-văy] *adj.* frolicsome, playful

шалость [shå-lŏst'] *sf.* prank, trick

шалун [sha-loōn] *sm.* mischievous child, playful child; scamp

шалунья [sha-loō-nya] *sf.* tomboy (*of girl*)

шалфей [shal-fyéy] *sm.* sage (*herb*)

шаль [shål] *sf.* shawl

шальной [shal'-nóy] *adj.* crazy, foolish; **шальная**

пуля [shal'-nā-ya pŏō-lya] stray bullet

шампанское [sham-pān-ska-ye] sn. champagne

шандаль [shan-dāl] sm. candlestick [hound

шандра [shān-dra] sf. horehound

шанец [shā-nyets] sm. entrenchment, trench

шантаж [shan-tāzh] sm. blackmail [hood

шапка [shāp-ka] sf. cap,

шаповал [sha-pa-vāl] sm. fuller (clay)

шапочка [shā-pach-ka] sf. child's cap; Красная Шапочка [krās-na-ya –] Little Red Riding Hood

шапочник [shā-pach-n'ik] sm. hatter

шар [shār] sm. ball, globe, sphere; воздушный – [vaz-dōōsh-nǎy –] balloon

шарабан [sha-ra-bān] sm. gig

шарада [sha-rā-da] sf. charade

шарахаться [sha-rāch-tat'-sya] (шарáхнуться) vi. to bolt, shy

шарик [shā-r'ik] sm. globule, corpuscle

шарить [sha-r'ēt'] (об–) vi. to rummage, ransack

шаркать [shār-kat'] (шáркнуть) vi. to scrape one's feet

шарлатан [shar-la-tān] sm. charlatan, impostor, quack

шарлатанство [shar-la-tān-stvŏ] sn. quackery

шарлот [shar-lót] sm. shallot

шарлах [shar-lāch] sm. scarlet

шарманка [shar-mān-ka] sf. barrel-organ, hurdy-gurdy

шарманщик [sha-mān-shchik] sm. organ-grinder

шаровидный [sha-ra-v'ēd-nǎy] adj. globular, spherical

шарф [shārf] sm. comforter, scarf

шатать [sha-tāt'] (шатнýть) vt. to shake, sway; –ся [-sya] vi. to stagger, totter; to work loose (as a nail, screw, etc.)

шатёр [sha-tyór] sm. marquee

шаткий [shāt-ki] adj. faltering, unsteady

шатун [sha-tōōn] sm. tramp; connecting-rod [man

шафер [shā-fyer] sm. best

шафран [shaf-rān] sm. crocus; saffron

шах [shāch] sm. shah; check (in chess)

шахматы [shāch-ma-tä] sm. pl. chess (the game)

шахта [shāch-ta] sf. shaft

шашечница [shā-she-chr'ī-tsa] sf. draught-board, chess-board

шашка [shāsh-ka] sf. sabre, sword; draught piece

шашни [shāsh-n'i] sf. pl. intrigues; pranks, tricks

швабра [shvāb-ra] sf. mop; swab

швальня [shvāl'-nya] sf. tailor's workroom

швед [shvyed] sm. Swede

шведский [shvyéd-ski] adj. Swedish [sewing

швейный [shvyéy-nǎy] adj.

швейцар [shvyéy-tsār] sm. door-keeper, hall-porter

швейцарец [shvyéy-tsā-ryets] sm. Swiss

швейцарский [shvyey-tsār-ski] adj. Swiss

швея [shvye-yā] sf. needlewoman, seamstress

швырять [shvä-ryāt'] vt. to fling, hurl; vi. – деньгами

[– dyen'–gä-mi] to be lavish with money

шевелить [she-vye-l'ét'] *vi.* to move about, stir

шейка [shéy-ka] *sf.* neck of stringed instruments; slender neck   [jugular

шейный [shéy-nåy] *adj.*

шелест [shé-lyest] *sm.* rustle, rustling   [*vi.* to rustle

шелестить [she-lyes-t'ét']

шёлк [sholk] *sm.* silk

шелковина [shel-ka-v'é-na] *sf.* silk thread

шелковистый [shel-ka-v'és-tåy] *adj.* silky

шелковица [shel-ka-v'é-tsa] *sf.* mulberry

шелководство [shel-ka-vód-stvö] *sn.* sericulture

шёлковый [shól-ka-våy] *adj.* of silk-, silky

шелкопряд [shel-ka-pryäd] *sm.* silkworm

шелуха [she-lŏŏ-chä] *sf.* husk, pod, shell, skin

шелушить [she-lŏŏ-shét'] *vt.* to hull, peel, shell

шепелявить [she-pe-lyä-v'ít'] *vi.* to lisp

шепелявый [she-pe-lyä-våy] *adj.* lisping

шёпот [shó-pöt] *sm.* whisper; **шёпотом** [shó-pa-töm] *adv.* in a whisper

шептала [shep-tä-la] *sf.* dried apricot, dried peach

шептать [shep-tät'] *vi.* to whisper

шероховатый [she-ra-cha-vä-tåy] *adj.* rough, rugged

шерстистый [shers-t'és-tåy] *adj.* fleecy, woolly

шерсть [sherst'] *sf.* wool

шерстяной [sher-stya-nóy] *adj.* woollen

шершень [shér-shen'] *sm.* hornet   [staff

шест [shest] *sm.* perch, pole,

шествие [shést-vye] *sn.* procession, train

шестерня [shes-tyer-nyä] *sf.* driving-wheel, pinion

шестнадцать [shest-näd-tsat'] *num.* sixteen

шесток [shes-tók] *sm.* hearth

шестой [she-stóy] *num.* sixth

шесть [shest'] *num.* six

шестьдесят [shest'-dye-syät] *num.* sixty

шея [shé-ya] *sf.* neck

шибкий [shib-ki] *adj.* fast, rapid, swift

шикарный [shi-kär-nåy] *adj.* elegant, stylish

шило [shē-lö] *sn.* awl, brad-awl   [splint

шина [shē-na] *sf.* hoop; tyre;

шинель [shi-nyél'] *sf.* cloak, greatcoat

шинковать [shin-ka-vät'] *vt.* to mince, shred

шип [ship] *sm.* prickle, thorn; calk; crampon; small sturgeon

шипеть [shi-pyét'] (**шип-нуть**) *vi.* to hiss; to sizzle; to spit (*as cat*); to sputter

шиповник [shi-póv-n'ik] *sm.* wild rose

шипучи [shi-pŏŏ-chi] *adj.* sparkling

ширина [shi-ri-nä] *sf.* breadth, width

ширить [shi-r'ét'] (*рас-*) *vt.* to enlarge, widen

ширма [shír-ma] *sf.* screen

широкий [shi-ró-ki] *adj.* broad, wide

широковещание [shi-ra-kve-shchä-nye] *sn.* broadcasting

широта [shi-ra-tä] *sf.* latitude

шить [shit'] (с-) *vt.* to sew

шитьё [shi-tyó] *sn.* sewing

шифр [shífr] *sm.* code, secret cipher; библистечный – [bi-bl'i-a-tyéch-näy –] pressmark

шишак [shi-shäk] *sm.* helmet

шишка [shish-ka] *sf.* bump, lump; boss, knob; cone

шишконосный [shish-ka-nós-näy] *adj.* coniferous

шкап, шкаф [shkäp, shkäf] *sm.* cupboard, dresser; wardrobe [casket

шкатулка [shka-tōōl-ka] *sf.*

шквал [shkväl] *sm.* squall; tornado

шкив [shk'ëv] *sm.* pulley

школа [shkó-la] *sf.* school

школьник [shkól'-n'ik] *sm.* schoolboy

школьница [shkól'-n'i-tsa] *sf.* schoolgirl [skin

шкура [shkōō-ra] *sf.* hide,

шлагбаум [shlag-bäōōm] *sm.* barrier; turnpike

шлак [shläk] *sm.* dross, slag

шлейф [shlyéyf] *sm.* train (*of dress*)

шлёпать [shlyó-pat'] (шлёпнуть) *vi.* to slap, smack, spank; splash; – ногами [– na-gä-mi] to drag one's feet; to shuffle, -ся [-sya] *vi.* to fall down, tumble

шлея [shlye-yä] *sf.* breeching (*of harness*)

шлифовальня [shl'i-fa-väl'-nya] *sf.* polisher's workshop

шлифовальщик [shl'i-fa-väl'-shchik] *sm.* polisher

шли|довать [shl'i-fa-vät'] (от -) *vt.* to polish [ters

шлифы [shl'ë-fä] *sm. pl.* gar-

шлюз [shlyōōz] *sm.* lock, sluice

шлюзник [shlyōōz-n'ik] *sm.* locksman

шлюп [shlyōōp] *sm.* sloop

шляпа [shlyä-pa] *sf.* hat

шляпка [shlyäp-ka] *sf.* bonnet, lady's hat

шляпник [shlyäp-n'ik] *sm.* hat-box

шляпница [shlyäp-n'i-tsa] *sf.* milliner

шляпочник [shlyä-pach-n'ik] *sm.* hatter

шляться [shlyät'-sya] (по-) *vi.* to roam, wander

шмель [shmyél'] *sm.* drone, bumble-bee [string

шнур [shnōōr] *sm.* cord,

шнуровать [shnōō-ra-vät'] *vt.* to lace up

шов [shov] *sm.* seam; joint, junction; commissure; suture

шоколад [sha-ka-läd] *sm.* chocolate

шопот [shó-pŏt] *sm.* whisper, whispering [dler

шорник [shór-n'ik] *sm.* sad-

шоры [shó-rä] *sf. pl.* blinkers

шотландец [shot-län-dyets] *sm.* Scotsman; шотландка [shot-länd-ka] *sf.* Scotswoman

шотландский [shot-länd-ski] *adj.* Scotch, Scottish

шофёр [sho-fyór] *sm.* chauffeur

шпага [shpä-ga] *sf.* sword

шпагат [shpa-gät] *sm.* cord, string

шпажник [shpazh-n'ik] *sm.* flag, gladiolus

шпаклёвка [shpa-klyóv-ka] *sf.* puttying

шпала [shpä-la] *sf.* sleeper (*railway*)

шпация [shpä-tsya] sf. typ. space

шпик [shp'ĕk] sm. salted fat of pig; coll. sleuth [pin

шпилить [shp'ĕ-l'it'] vt. to

шпиль [shp'ĕl'] sm. capstan, spindle; spire, steeple

шпилька [shp'ĕl'-ka] sf. hairpin; tack; pivot

шпинат [shp'i-nät] sm. spinach

шпион [shpión] sm. spy

шпионаж [shpio-näzh] sm. espionage

шпионство [shpión-stvŏ] sn. spying

шпиц [shp'ĕts] sm. church spire; Pomeranian dog

шпон [shpon] sm. typ. lead; reglet [spur

шпорить [shpó-r'it'] vt. to

шпоры [shpó-rä] sf. pl. spurs

шприц [shprits] sm. syringe

шпулька [shpŏŏl'-ka] sf. bobbin, spool

шрифт [shrift] sm. typ. type; жирный – [zhír-näy –] bold type, clarendon; курсивный – [kŏŏr-s'ĕv-näy –] italics; прямой – [pryamóy –] roman type

штаб [shtäb] sm. mil. staff

штамб [shtamb] sm. trunk; timber

штамп [shtamp] sm. punch, stamp [trousers

штаны [shta-nä] sm. pl.

штат [shtat] sm. State; establishment; штатский [shtät-ski] adj. civil; sm. civilian; штатское платье [shtät-ska-ye plä-tye] sn. mufti

штемпель [shtém-pyel] sm. stamp; почтовый – [pach-tó-väy –] postmark

штопать [shtó-pat'] (за-) vt. to darn, mend

штопор [shtó-pŏr] sm. cork-screw [shutter(s)

штора [shtó-ra] sf. blind,

шторм [shtorm] sm. tempest

штоф [shtof] sm. material, stuff [penalty

штраф [shträf] sm. fine,

штрих [shtr'ĕch] sm. stroke (of the pen); trait

штудировать [shtŏŏ-d'ĕ-ra-vat'] vi. to study

штука [shtŏŏ-ka] sf. piece; head (of cattle)

штукатур [shtŏŏ-ka-tŏŏr] sm. plasterer

штукатурка [shtŏŏ-ka-tŏŏr-ka] sf. stucco

штурман [shtŏŏr-man] sm. pilot, steersman

штурмовать [shtŏŏr-ma-vät'] vt. mil. to attack, storm

штык [shtäk] sm. bayonet

шуба [shŏŏ-ba] sf. fur coat

шулерство [shŏŏ-lyer-stvŏ] sn. card-sharping; foul play; trickery

шум [shŏŏm] sm. clamour, noise, riot

шуметь [shŏŏ-myét'] vi. to make a noise

шумиха [shŏŏ-m'ĕ-cha] sf. uproar

шумливый [shŏŏm-l'ĕ-väy] adj. boisterous, clamorous

шумный [shŏŏm-näy] adj. loud, noisy

шурин [shŏŏ-r'in] sm. brother-in-law

шуршать [shŏŏr-shät'] vi. to rustle [jester

шут [shŏŏt] sm. buffoon,

шутить [shŏŏ-t'ĕt'] (по-) vi. to jest, joke; шутя [shŏŏ-tyä] by way of a

joke; for fun; **не шутя**
[nye shoo-tyä] in earnest,
seriously

шутиха [shoo-t'ě-cha] sf.
cracker (*fireworks*)

шутка [shoot-ka] sf. banter,
joke, lark, pleasantry

шутливый [shoot-l'ě-văy]
adj. farcical, funny, playful

шутник [shoot-n'ik] sm.
comic, jester

шуточный [shoo-toch-năy]
adj. comic, facetious

шхеры [shchě-ră] sf. pl.
cliffs, rocks; fiords

шхуна [shchoo-na] sf.
schooner

Щ

щавель [shcha-vyěl'] sm.
sorrel

щадить [shcha-d'ět'] (по-)
vi. to have mercy on; to
spare

щебень [shché-byen'] sm.
[rubble

щебетать [shche-bye-tät']
vi. to chirp

щебетливый [shche-bye-
tl'ě-văy] adj. talkative

щебрец [shche-bryéts] sm.
thyme

щеглёнок [shche-glyó-nŏk]
sm. goldfinch

щеголеватый [shche-ga-
lye-vă-tăy] adj. dashing, elegant, spruce

щеголиха [shche-ga-l'ě-
cha] sf. fashionable lady,
smart woman

щеголять [shche-ga-lyät']
vi. to boast, show off

щедрость [shché-drŏst'] sf.
generosity, munificence

щедрый [shché-drăy] adj.
generous, liberal

щека [shche-kä] sf. anat.
cheek

щекотание [shche-ka-tä-
nye] sn. tickling

щекотать [shche-ka-tät'] vt.
to tickle

щекотливый [shche-ka-
tl'ě-văy] adj. ticklish; fig.
sensitive, touchy

щёлкать [shchól-kat']
(щёлкнуть) vi. to click, crack;
to pop; to chatter (*as teeth*)

щелчок [shchel-chók] sm.
fillip

щель [shchel] sf. chink, cleft,
crevice; flaw, split; peep-
hole; **голосовая –** [ga-la-
sa-vä-ya –] glottis

щемить [shche-m'ět'] (за-)
vt. to nip, pinch

щенок [shche-nók] sm. cub,
puppy, whelp [splinter

щепа [shche-pä] sf. chip,

щепание [shche-pä-nye] sn.
cleaving, splintering, splitting

щепать [shche-pät'] (рас-)
vt. to chip, splinter

щепетильный [shche-pye-
t'ěl'-năy] adj. punctilious,
scrupulous

щербина [shcher-b'ě-na] sf.
chink, crevice

щетина [shche-t'ě-na] sf.
bristle

щетинистый [shche-t'i-
n'ěs-tăy] adj. bristly, stubbly

щётка [shchót-ka] sf. brush;
fetlock

щёточник [shchó-tach-n'ik]
sm. brush-maker, brush-
vendor

щи [shchi] sf. pl. cabbage
soup

щиколка [shchí-kal-ka] *sf.*
щиколотка [shchí-ka-lat-ka] ankle

щипать [shchi-pát'] (щип-нýть) *vt.* to nip, pinch; to browse; to pluck

щипец [shchi-pyéts] *sm.* gable

щипком [shchip-kóm] *adv. mus.* pizzicato (*pluck strings*)

щипцы [shchip-tsá] *sm. pl.* nippers, pincers, tweezers; forceps [wind-screen

щит [shchit] *sm.* shield

щитовидный [shchi-ta-ví̆ed-nǎy] *adj.* thyroid

щиток [shchi-tók] *sm.* cyme; thorax; mudguard

щука [shchōō-ka] *sf.* pike; garfish

щупальце [shchōō-pǎl'-tse] *sn.* feeler, tentacle

щупать [shchōō-pat'] (по-) *vt.* to feel, handle, touch

щуплый [shchōō-lǎy] *adj.* puny, undersized

щур [shchōōr] *sm.* martin

щурить [shchōō-r'ĕt'] (за-) *vt.* to blink, wink

Э

эбеновый [e-byé-na-vǎy] *adj.* of ebony

эбонит [e-ba-n'ĕt] *sm.* ebony, ebonite

эвакуация [e-va-kōō-á-tsya] *sf.* evacuation

эвакуировать [e-va-kōō-é-ra-vat'] *vt.* to evacuate

эвапорация [e-va-pa-rá-tsya] *sf.* evaporation

эвкалипт [ev-ka-l'ĕpt] *sm.* eucalyptus

эволюция [e-va-lyōō-tsya] *sf.* evolution [phony

эвфония [ev-fó-nya] *sf.* eu-

эгоизм [e-ga-ézm] *sm.* egoism, selfishness

эгоист [e-ga-ést] *sm.* egoist

эгрет [e-grét] *sm.* egret; osprey; egret plume

эдельвейс [é-dyel'-veys] *sm.* Alpine plant

Эдем [e-dyém] *sm.* Eden

эй [ey] *interj.* I say!

экватор [e-kvá-tor] *sm.* equator

эквилибр [e-kv'i-l'ĕbr] *sm.* equilibrium

экзальтированный [ek-zal'-t'ĕ-ra-van-nǎy] *adj.* exultant

экзамен [ek-zá-myen] *sm.* examination; держащий – [dyer-zhá-shchi –] examinee

экзаминатор [ek-za-mi-ná-tŏr] *sm.* -ша [-sha] *sf.* examiner [ma

экзема [ek-zyé-ma] *sf.* ecze-

экземпляр [ek-zyem-plyár] *sm.* copy; specimen

экзотический [ek-za-t'é-ches-ki] *adj.* exotic

экипировка [e-k'i-p'i-róv-ka] *sf.* accoutrement, equipment

эконом [e-ka-nóm] *sm.* steward; -ка, *sf.* housekeeper; stewardess

экономика [e-ka-nó-m'i-ka] *sf.* economics

экономить [e-ka-nó-m'it'] *vi.* to economize, save

экономия [e-ka-nó-mya] *sf.* economy

экономный [e-ka-nóm-nǎy] *adj.* economical, thrifty; frugal

экран [e-krán] *sm.* screen (*fire, cinema*); shade

экскавация [ẹks-ka-vá-tsya] *sf.* excavation

экскурс [ẹks-kóors] *sm.* excursion; *fig.* digression

экскурсия [ẹks-kóor-sya] *sf.* excursion, trip

экспансивный [ẹks-pan-s'ẹv-nǎy] *adj.* effusive, gushing; **не-** [nye-] undemonstrative

экспедировать [ẹks-pye-d'ẹ-ra-vat'] *vt.* to expedite

экспедиция [ẹks-pye-d'ẹ-tsya] *sf.* expedition

экспедиционный [ẹks-pye-d'i-tsión-nǎy] *adj.* expeditionary

экспериментальный [ẹks-pye-r'i-myen-tál'-nǎy] *adj.* experimental

эксплуатация [ẹks-plóoa-tá-tsya] *sf.* exploitation

эксплуатировать [ẹks-plóoa-t'ẹ-ra-vat'] *vt.* to exploit

экспозиция [ẹks-pa-z'ẹ-tsya] *sf.* exposition; exposure; display [exporter

экспортёр [ẹks-por-tyór] *sm.*

экспромт [ẹks-prómt] *sm.* impromptu; **-ом** [-ŏm] *adv.* extempore, without preparation

экстаз [ẹk-stáz] *sm.* ecstasy

экстерн [ẹk-stérn] *sm.* outsider

экстракция [ẹks-strák-tsya] *sf.* extraction

экстренный [ẹks-stryén-nǎy] *adj.* extra, special; **- выпуск** [- vǎ-póosk] extra-special edition (*newspaper, etc.*)

эксцентричный [ẹks-tsyen-tr'ẹch-nǎy] *adj.* eccentric, odd, queer

эластичный [ẹlas-t'ẹch-nǎy] *adj.* elastic, resilient

элегантный [ẹ-lye-gánt-nǎy] *adj.* elegant, smart

элегия [ẹ-lyé-gya] *sf.* elegy, lament

электризовать [ẹ-lyek-tr'i-za-vát'] *vt.* to electrify

электрик [ẹ-lyék-tr'ik] *sm.* electrician

электрик [ẹ-lyek-tr'ẹk] *sm.* steel-blue

электрический [ẹ-lyek-tr'ẹ-ches-ki] *adj.* electric(al)

электричество [ẹ-lyek-tr'ẹ-chest-vŏ] *sn.* electricity

электротехник [ẹ-lyek-tra-tyéch-n'ik] *sm.* electrical engineer

элементарный [ẹ-lye-myen-tár-nǎy] *adj.* elementary, rudimentary, simple

элизия [ẹ-l'ẹ-zya] *sf.* elision, omission of a vowel

эльф [ẹl'f] *sm.* elf; sprite

эмалевый [ẹ-má-lye-vǎy] *adj.* of enamel, enamelled

эмаль [ẹ-mál'] *sf.* enamel

эмансипировать [ẹ-man-s'i-p'ẹ-ra-vat'] *vt.* to emancipate

эмблема [ẹm-blyé-ma] *sf.* emblem, ensign

эмигрировать [ẹ-m'i-gr'ẹ-ra-vat'] *vi.* to emigrate

эмиссар [ẹ-m'is-sár] *sm.* emissary

эмульсия [ẹ-móol'-sya] *sf.* emulsion

эмфаз [ẹm-fáz] *sm.* emphasis

энергичный [ẹ-nyer-g'ẹch-nǎy] *adj.* energetic

энергия [ẹ-nyér-gya] *sf.* energy; power

энциклопедия [ẹn-tsi-kla-pyé-dya] *sf.* encyclopaedia

эпидемия [e-p'i-dyé-mya] *sf.* epidemic

эпоха [e-pó-cha] *sf.* age, epoch

эра [é-ra] *sf.* era

эрозия [e-ró-zya] *sf.* erosion

эрцгерцог [erts-gér-tsŏg] *sm.* archduke

эскадра [es-kád-ra] *sf.* nav. squadron

эскадрилья [es-ka-dr'ē-lya] *sf.* flying squadron

эскадрон [es-ka-drón] *sm.* mil. squadron, troop

эскамотаж [es-ka-ma-tắzh] *sm.* dexterity, sleight of hand

эскиз [es-k'ēz] *sm.* outline, sketch

эссенция [es-sén-tsya] *sf.* essence

эстакада [es-ta-kā-da] *sf.* boom (of harbour); scaffold, stockade

эстамп [es-támp] *sm.* engraving, plate, print

эстафета [es-ta-fyé-ta] *sf.* relay race

эстетика [es-tyé-t'i-ka] *sf.* esthetics

эстрагон [es-tra-gón] *sm.* tarragon

эстрада [es-trā-da] *sf.* platform, stage

этаж [e-tắzh] *sm.* floor, storey; **нижний –** [n'ézh-ni –] ground floor

этажерка [e-ta-zhér-ka] *sf.* book-shelves

этакий [é-ta-ki] *adj.* such

этап [e-tắp] *sm.* stage, stop

этика [é-t'i-ka] *sf.* ethics

этикет [e-t'i-kyét] *sm.* etiquette, conventional manners

этикетка [e-t'i-kyét-ka] *sf.* label, tag

этичный [e-t'ēch-năy] *adj.* ethical

этот [é-tŏt] *pron.* this

этюд [e-tyŏŏd] *sm.* exercise, study; mus. étude

эфемериды [e-fye-mye-r'ē-dă] *sf. pl.* ephemerides

эфемерный [e-fye-myér-năy] *adj.* ephemeral, short-lived, transitory

эфес [e-fyés] *sm.* hilt

эфир [e-f'ēr] *sm.* ether

эфирный [e-f'ēr-năy] *adj.* ethereal

эффективный [ef-fyekt'-ēv-năy] *adj.* efficacious

эффектный [ef-fyékt-năy] *adj.* effective

эхо [é-chŏ] *sn.* echo

эшафот [e-sha-fót] *sm.* scaffold

Ю

юбилей [yŏŏ-b'i-lyéy] *sm.* jubilee

юбилейный [yŏŏ-b'i-lyéy-năy] *adj.* jubilee

юбиляр [yŏŏ-b'i-lyär] *sm.* person celebrating his jubilee

юбка [yŏŏb-ka] *sf.* petticoat, skirt

ювелир [yŏŏ-vye-l'ēr] *sm.* jeweller

юг [yŏŏg] *sm.* south

южанин [yŏŏ-zhā-n'in] *sm.* southerner

южный [yŏŏzh-năy] *adj.* south, southern

юла [yŏŏ-lá] *sf.* wood-lark; whirligig; fig. fidgety person

юлить [yŏŏ-l'ēt'] *vi.* to wheedle; to cajole

юмор [yŏŏ-mŏr] *sm.* humour

юморист [yŏŏ-ma-r'ēst] *sm.* humorist

юмористический [yŏŏ-ma-r'is-t'ē-ches-ki] *adj.* humorous

юнга [yŏŏn-ga] *sm.* cabin-boy

юнеть [yŏŏ-nyét'] *vi.* to rejuvenate

юнкер [yōŏn-ker] *sm.* cadet

юность [yōŏ-nŏst'] *sf.* adolescence, youth, youthfulness

юноша [yōŏ-na-sha] *sm.* adolescent, youth

юношеский [yōŏ-na-shes-ki] *adj.* juvenile, youthful

юрисдикция [yōŏ-r'is-d'ĕk-tsya] *sf.* jurisdiction

юрист [yōŏ-r'ist] *sm.* law student; jurist, lawyer

юркий [yōŏr-ki] *adj.* brisk, nimble

юркнуть [yōŏr-knōŏt'] *vi.* to disappear suddenly

юркость [yōŏr-kŏst'] *sf.* agility, swiftness

юродивый [yōŏ-ra-d'ĕ-vǎy] *adj.* of unbalanced mind

юстиция [yōŏ-st'ĕ-tsya] *sf.* justice

ют [yōŏt] *sm.* stern of ship

ютиться [yōŏ-t'ĕt'-sya] (при–) *vi.* to nestle, roost

Я

я [yā] *pron.* I

яблоко [yā-bla-kŏ] *sn.* apple; dapple (*of horse*); глазное – [glāz-na-ye –] eyeball; дикое – [d'ĕ-ka-ye –] crab-apple

яблоня [ya-blŏ-nya] *sf.* apple-tree

яблочный [yā-blach-nǎy] *adj.* of apple; – пирог – [– p'i-róg] apple-pie

явка [yāv-ka] *sf.* appearance, presence

явление [yav-lyé-nye] *sn.* apparition, appearance; – природы [– pr'i-ró-dǎ] phenomenon

являть [yav-lyāt'] (явить) *vt.* to exhibit, display, show;

–ся [-sya] *vi.* to make an appearance

явность [yāv-nŏst'] *sf.* evidence, obviousness

явный [yāv-nǎy] *adj.* evident, manifest, obvious, plain

явственность [yāv-stvyen-nŏst'] *sf.* distinctness

явственный [yāv-stvyen-nǎy] *adj.* clear, distinct

явствовать [yāv-stva-vat'] *vi.* to be apparent, obvious

ягв [yāv'] *sf.* reality [lamb

ягнёнок [ya-gnyó-nŏk] *sm.*

ягнёночек [ya-gnyó-na-chek] *sm.* lambkin

ягода [yā-ga-da] *sf.* berry

ягодица [ya-ga-d'i-tsa] *sf.* buttock

яд [yād] *sm.* poison, venom

ядовитость [ya-da-v'ĕ-tŏst'] *sf.* malignity, virulence; *fig.* malice

ядовитый [ya-da-v'ĕ-tǎy] *adj.* poisonous, virulent

ядрёный [ya-dryó-nǎy] *adj.* juicy, succulent

ядро [ya-dró] *sn.* kernel; nucleus; testicle; *fig.* gist

язва [yāz-va] *sf.* ulcer

язвительность [yaz-v'ĕ-tyel'-nŏst'] *sf.* sarcasm

язвительный [yaz-v'ĕ-tyel'-nǎy] *adj.* caustic, venomous; *fig.* spiteful

язвить [yaz-v'ĕt'] *vt.* to hurt, taunt [language

язык [ya-zák] *sm.* tongue;

языковед [ya-zǎ-ka-vyéd] *sm.* linguist; philologist

языковедение [ya-zǎ-ka-vye-dyé-nye] *sn.* linguistics

языкознание [ya-zǎ-ka-znā-nye] *sn.* philology

языческий [ya-zǎ-ches-ki] *adj.* pagan

язычество [ya-zǎ-chest-vŏ] *sn.* heathenism

язычник [ya-zǎch-n'ik] *sm.* heathen

язычок [ya-zǎ-chók] *sm.* uvula; *mus.* reed

янчко [ya-éch-kŏ] *sn.* small egg; testicle

янчик [ya-éch-n'ik] *sm.* ovary; egg-dealer

янчница [ya-éch-n'i-tsa] *sf.* fried egg(s), scrambled egg(s)

яйцевидный [yay-tsye-v'ĕd-näy] *adj.* oval

яйцо [yay-tsó] *sn.* egg; ovum

якорь [yä-kor'] *sm.* anchor

ялик [yä-l'ik] *sm.* wherry

яличник [yä-l'ich-n'ik] *sm.* boatman, wherryman

яловый [yä-la-väy] *adj.* barren, dry, sterile

яма [yä-ma] *sf.* pit

ямб [yämb] *sm.* iambus, metrical foot

ямочка [yä-mach-ka] *sf.* small pit; hole (*golf*); dimple

ямщик [yäm-shchik] *sm.* coachman

январь [yan-vär'] *sm.* January

янтарь [yan-tär'] *sm.* amber

японец [ya-pó-nyets] *sm.* Japanese [Japanese

японский [ya-pón-skí] *adj.*

яр [yär] *sm.* steep bank; heat (*in animals*) [jugular

яремный [ya-ryém-näy] *adj.*

яркий [yär-ki] *adj.* bright, brilliant, clear, dazzling; rich (*in colour*)

ярлык [yar-lǎk] *sm.* label

ярлычок [yar-lä-chók] *sm.* tie-on-label, tag

ярмарка [yär-mar-ka] *sf.* amusement fair, fair

ярмо [yar-mó] *sn.* yoke; *fig.* burden, load

яровой [ya-ra-vóy] *adj.* spring-; — **уражай** [—ŏŏ-ra-zhäy] spring crops

яростный [yä-rast-näy] *adj.* furious, violent

ярость [yä-rŏst'] *sf.* fury, passion, rage

ярус [yä-rŏŏs] *sm. theat.* circle; tier; layer, stratum

ярый [yä-räy] *adj.* violent, eager, zealous

ярь [yär'] *sf.* verdigris

ясеневый [ya-sye-nye-väy] *adj.* ashen

ясень [yä-syen'] *sm.* ash (*tree*)

ясли [yä-sl'i] *sm. pl.* crib, manger; — **для детей** [— dlya dye-tyéy] crèche

яснеть [yas-nyét'] (*pro-*) *vi.* to brighten, clear up (*weather*)

ясновидение [yas-na-v'i-dyé-nye] *sn.* clairvoyance

ясновидец [yas-na-v'é-dyets] *sm.* clairvoyant

ясность [yäs-nŏst'] *sf.* clarity; lucidity

ясный [yäs-näy] *adj.* bright, clear; distinct; lucid

ястреб [yä-stryeb] *sm.* hawk

яхонт [yä-chönt] *sm.* gem; **красный** — [kräs-näy —] ruby; **синий** — [s'é-ni —] sapphire

яхта [yäch-ta] *sf.* yacht

ячейка [ya-chéy-ka] *sf. biol.* cell

ячмень [yach-myén'] *sm.* barley; *med.* sty

яшма [yäsh-ma] *sf.* jasper

ящерица [yä-shche-r'i-tsa] *sf.* lizard, newt

ящик [yä-shchik] *sm.* box; drawer; till; **мусорный** — [mŏŏ-sór-näy —] dust-bin

ящур [yä-shchŏŏr] *sm.* foot-and-mouth disease

GEOGRAPHICAL NAMES

(Some names which are a transliteration of one language into the other, with hardly a change in pronunciation, are not included here.)

Аахен [ā-chen] Aix-la-Chapelle

Абиссиния [a-bi-sē-nya] Abyssinia

Австралазия [av-stra-lā-zya] Australasia

Австралия [av-strā-lya] Australia

Австрия [āv-strya] Austria

Адриатическое море [a-dr'i-a-t'ē-ches-ka-ye mó-rye] Adriatic Sea

Азия [ā-zya] Asia

Азорские острова [a-zór-ski-ye a-stra-vá] Azores

Албания [al-bā-nya] Albania

Алжир [al-zhēr] Algiers

Алжирия [al-zhē-rya] Algeria

Альпы [āl'-pǎ] the Alps

Аляска [a-lyās-ka] Alaska

Амазонка [a-ma-zón-ka] the Amazon

Америка [a-myé-r'i-ka] America

Англия [ān-glya] England

Анды [ān-dǎ] Andes

Анкара [an-ka-rá] Ankara

Антверпен [an-tvér-pǎn] Antwerp

Антарктика [an-tārk-t'i-ka] Antarctic

Арктика [ārk-t'i-ka] Arctic

Армения [ar-myé-nya] Armenia

Аравия [a-rā-vya] Arabia

Аргентина [ar-gyen-t'ē-na] Argentine

Архангельск [ar-chān-gyel'sk] Archangel

Атлантический Океан [a-tlan-t'ē-ches-ki a-kye-ān] the Atlantic Ocean

Афины [a-f'ē-nǎ] Athens

Африка [ā-fri-ka] Africa

Бавария [ba-vā-rya] Bavaria

Байрейт [bay-réyt] Bayreuth (Germany)

Балканский полуостров [bal-kān-ski pa-lōō-óst-rŏv] Balkan Peninsula

Балканы [bal-kā-nǎ] Balkans

Балтийское море [bal-t'ēs-ka-ye mó-rye] Baltic Sea

Баренцово море [bā-ryen-tsa-va mó-rye] Barents Sea

Бейрут [bey-rōōt] Beirut (Lebanon)

Белград [byel-grād] Belgrade

Бельгия [byél'-gya] Belgium

Бенгалия [ben-gā-lya] Bengal

Берингов пролив [byé-rin-gav pra-lév] Bering Strait

Берлин [ber-l'ēn] Berlin

Бирма [b'ēr-ma] Burma

Бискайский залив [b'is-kāy-ski za-l'ēv] the Bay of Biscay

Богемия [ba-gyé-mya] Bohemia

Болгария [bal-gā-rya] Bulgaria

Боливия [ba-l'ē-vya] Bolivia

Босфор [bas-fór] Bosphorus

Бразилия [bra-z'ē-lya] Brazil

Бретань [brye-tān'] Brittany

Британия [br'i-tā-nya] Britain

375

Брюссель [bryŏŏs-syél'] Brussels

Будапешт [bŏŏ-da-pésht] [Budapest]

Бухарест [bŏŏ-cha-rést] Bucharest

Варшава [var-shā-va] Warsaw

Вашингтон [vă-shing-tŏn] Washington

Везувий [vye-zŏŏ-vi] Mount Vesuvius

Великобритания [vye-l'i-ka-br'i-tā-nya] Great Britain

Вена [vyé-na] Vienna

Венгрия [vyén-grya] Hungary

Венесуэла [vye-ne-sŏŏ-éla] Venezuela

Вьетнам [vyet-nām] Vietnam

Гавр [găvr] Havre

Гаага [gā-ga] The Hague

Гватемала [gva-te-mā-la] Guatemala

Гвиана [gv'i-ā-na] Guiana

Гвинея [gv'i-nyé-ya] Guinea

Гебридские острова [ge-br'ĕd-ski-ye as-tra-vā] The Hebrides

Гент [gent] Ghent

Германия [ger-mā-nya] Germany

Глазго [glāz-gŏ] Glasgow

Голландия [gal-lān-dya] Holland

Греция [gryé-tsya] Greece

Грузия [grŏŏ-zya] Georgia (U.S.S.R.)

Гудзонов залив [gŏŏd-zó-nŏv za-l'ĕv] Hudson Bay

Дания [dā-nya] Denmark

Дарданелы [dar-da-nyé-lă] Dardanelles

Двина [dv'ĕ-na] the Dvina (river)

Дели [dyé-l'i] Delhi

Джорджия [dzhór-dzhya] Georgia (U.S.A.)

Днепр [dnyépr] the Dnieper (river)

Днестр [dnyé-str] the Dniester (river)

Дублин [dŏŏb-l'in] Dublin

Дунай [dŏŏ-náy] Danube

Европа [ye-vró-pa] Europe

Евфрат [ye-frāt] the Euphrates

Египет [ye-g'ĕ-pyet] Egypt

Женева [zhe-nyé-va] Geneva

Золотой Берег [za-la-tóy byé-rĕg] the Gold Coast

Иерусалим [ye-rŏŏ-sa-l'ĕm] Jerusalem

Израиль [i-zrā-il'] Israel

Индийский Океан [in-d'ĕ-ski a-kye-ān] the Indian Ocean

Индия [ín-dya] India

Индо-Китай [in-da-ki-tāy] Indo-China

Иордан [yar-dān] Jordan

Ирак [i-rāk] Irak

Иран [i-rān] Iran

Ирландия [ir-lān-dya] Ireland

Испания [is-pā-nya] Spain

Италия [i-tā-lya] Italy

Кавказ [kav-kāz] the Caucasus

Каир [ka-ĕr] Cairo

Кале [ka-lyé] Calais

Калькута [kal'-kŏŏ-tă] Calcutta

Канада [kā-na-da] Canada

Канарские острова [ka-nār-ski-ye astra-vā] the Canary Islands

Капштадт [kap-shtät] Cape Town

Карабское море [ka-ra-ēb-ska-ye mó-rye] Caribbean Sea

Карпаты [kar-pā-tä] the Carpathians

Каспийское море [kas-pēs-ka-ye mó-rye] Caspian Sea

Кипр [k'ēpr] Cyprus

Китай [k'i-tāy] China

Копенгаген [ko-pen-gā-gen] Copenhagen

Корея [ka-ré-ya] Korea

Корсика [kór-s'i-ka] Corsica

Красное море [krās-na-ye mó-rye] the Red Sea

Крит [krit] Crete

Крым [krǎm] Crimea

Ламанш [la-mänsh] the English Channel

Лапландия [lap-lān-dya] Lapland

Латвия [lät-vya] Latvia

Ледовитый Океан [lye-da-v'ē-tǎy a-kye-ān] the Arctic Ocean

Ливан [l'i-vän] Lebanon

Ливийская пустыня [l'i-v'ēs-ka-ya pŏŏ-stǎ-nya] the Libyan Desert

Лиссабон [l'i-sa-bón] Lisbon

Литва [l'ēt-va] Lithuania

Люксембург [lyŏŏk-sem-bŏŏrg] Luxemburg

Люттих [lyŏŏ-t ich] Liège

Македония [ma-ke-dó-nya] Macedonia

Малая Азия [mā-la-ya ā-zya] Asia Minor

Марокко [ma-rók-kŏ] Morocco [Mexico

Мексика [myé-ks'i-ka]

Монблан [mon-blän] Mont Blanc

Москва [mask-vā] Moscow

Мраморное море [mrā-mar-na-ye mó-rye] the Sea of Marmora

Мыс Горн [mǎs gorn] Cape Horn

Мыс Доброй Надежды [mǎs dób-rŏy na-dyézh-dä] the Cape of Good Hope

Немецкое море [nye-myéts-ka-ye mó-rye] the North Sea

Нигерия [ni-gé-ri-ya] Nigeria

Нидерланды [n'i-dyer-län-dä] the Netherlands

Нил [n'ēl] the Nile

Новая Гвинея [nó-va-ya gv'i-nyé-ya] New Guinea

Новая Зеландия [nó-va-ya zye-län-dya] New Zealand

Норвегия [nar-vyé-gya] Norway

Нью Йорк [nyŏŏ-yórk] New York

Осло [ós-lŏ] Oslo

Па-де-Кале [pā-de-ka-lé] Strait of Dover

Палестина [pa-lyes-t'ē-na] Palestine [guay

Парагвай [pa-ra-gvāy] Para-

Париж [pa-rēʐh] Paris

Пекин [pye-k'ēn] Peking

Персия [pyér-sya] Persia

Пиренеи [p'i-rye-nyé-i] the Pyrenees

Польша [pól'-sha] Poland

Португалия [por-tŏŏ-gā-lya] Portugal

Прага [prā-ga] Prague

Рейн [réyn] Rhine

Рим [r'ĕm] Rome

Родезия [ra-dýe-sya] Rhodesia

Россия [ras-s'ĕ-ya] Russia

Р.С.Ф.С.Р. [er-es-ef-es-er] the Russian Soviet Federal Socialist Republic

Румыния [rōō-mắ-nya] Rumania

С.А.С.Ш. [es-ā-es-shā] the United States of America

Сахара [sa-chā́-ra] the Sahara

Сена [syé-na] the Seine

Сибирь [s'i-b'ĕr'] Siberia

Сингапур [s'in-ga-pōōr] Singapore

Сицилия [s'i-ts'ē-lya] Sicily

Скалистые горы [ska-l'ĕ-stă-ye gó-ră] the Rocky Mountains

Скандинавия [skan-d'i-nā́-vya] Scandinavia

София [só-fya] Sofia

Средиземное море [sryed-i-zyém-na-ye mó-rye] the Mediterranean Sea

С.С.С.Р. [es-es-es-er] the Union of Soviet Socialist Republics

Стокгольм [stók-gŏl'm] Stockholm

Суэцкий Канал [sōō-ét-ski ka-nāl] Suez Canal

Тегеран [tye-gye-rān] Teheran

Темза [tyém-za] the Thames

Тибр [t'ĕ-br] the Tiber

Тигр [t'ĕ-gr] the Tigris

Тихий Океан [t'ĕ-chi a-kye-ān] the Pacific Ocean

Токио [tó-kyo] Tokio

Турция [tōōr-tsya] Turkey

Уругвай [ōō-rōō-gvāy] Uruguay

Уэльс [ōō-él's] Wales

Финляндия [f'in-lyān-dya] Finland

Франция [frān-tsya] France

Хиросима [chi-ró-si-ma] Hiroshima

Хорватия [char-vā-tya] Croatia

Цюрих [tsyōō-rich] Zurich

Чёрное море [chór-na-ye mó-rye] The Black Sea

Чехословакия [che-cha-sla-vă-kya] Czechoslovakia

Чили [ch'ē-l'i] Chile

Швейцария [shvyey-tsā-rya] Switzerland

Швеция [shvyé-tsya] Sweden

Шотландия [shat-lān-dya] Scotland

Эгейское море [e-gyéy-ska-ye mó-rye] Aegean Sea

Эльба [él'-ba] the Elbe

Эстония [es-tó-nya] Estonia

Эфиопия [e-f'i-ō-pya] Ethiopia

Югославия [yōō-ga-slā-vya] Yugoslavia

Южный Ледовитый Океан [yōōzh-năy lye-da-v'ē-tăy a-kye-ān] the Antarctic Ocean

Ялта [yāl-ta] Yalta

Ямайка [ya-māy-ka] Jamaica

Япония [ya-pó-nya] Japan

THE INFINITIVE AND FIRST PERSON SINGULAR OF SOME IRREGULAR AND ANOMALOUS VERBS

беречь – берегу
бить – бью
брать – беру
брить – брею
будить – бужу
везти – везу
видеть – вижу
висеть – вишу
вставать – встаю
воевать – воюю
гнать – гоню
гореть – горю
готовить – готовлю
давать – даю
двигать – движу
держать – держу
есть – ем
ехать – еду
ждать – жду
жить – живу
заходить – захожу
знакомить – знакомлю
идти – иду
искать – ищу

класть – кладу
кричать – кричу
лгать – лгу
лежать – лежу
лететь – лечу
любить – люблю
мыть – мою
носить – ношу
отставать – отстаю
приносить – приношу
просить – прошу
рвать – рву
резать – режу
рисовать – рисую
сидеть – сижу
слышать – слышу
сойти – сойду
торговать – торгую
тратить – трачу
ходить – хожу
хотеть – хочу
целовать – целую
шить – шью
чистить – чищу

CARDINAL NUMBERS

КОЛИЧЕСТВЕННЫЕ ЧИСЛИТЕЛЬНЫЕ

1 один [a-d'ĕn]; one [ўăн]
2 два [dvā]; two [тў]
3 три [tri]; three [θρi]
4 четыре [che-tắ-rye] four [фȯр̌]
5 пять [ruăt']; five [фа́йв]
6 шесть [shest]; six [cĭкc]
7 семь [syem]; seven [cé-вăн]
8 восемь [vó-syem]; eight [эйт]
9 девять [dyé-vyat']; nine [на́йн]
10 десять [dyé-syat']; ten [тĕн]
11 одиннадцать [a-d'ĕn-nad-tsat']; eleven [i-лé-вăн]
12 двенадцать [dvye-nād-tsat']; twelve [тўĕлв]
13 тринадцать [tri-nād-tsat']; thirteen [θȯǝр-ти́н]
14 четырнадцать [che-tắr-nad-tsat']; fourteen [фȯр̌-тин]
15 пятнадцать [pyat-nād-tsat']; fifteen [фĭф-тин]
16 шестнадцать [shest-nād-tsat']; sixteen ¡cĭкc-тин]
17 семнадцать [syem-nād-tsat']; seventeen [cé-вăн-тин]
18 восемнадцать [va-syem-nād-tsat']; eighteen [эй-тин]
19 девятнадцать [dye-vyat-nād-tsat']; nineteen [на́йн-тин]
20 двадцать [dvād-tsat']; twenty [тўĕн-ти]
21 двадцать один [dvād-tsat' a-d'ĕn]; twenty-one [тўĕн-ти-ўăн]
22 двадцать два [dvād-tsat' dva]; twenty-two [тўĕн-ти-тў]
30 тридцать [trĭd-tsat']; thirty [θǝ̌р-ти]
40 сорок [só-rȯk]; forty [фȯр̌-ти]
50 пятьдесят [pyat'-dye-syāt]; fifty [фĭф-ти]
60 шестьдесят [shest'-dye-syāt]; sixty [cĭкc-ти]
70 семьдесят [syem'-dye-syắt]; seventy [cé-вăн-ти]
80 восемьдесят [vó-syem'-dye-syat]; eighty [эй-ти]
90 девяносто [dye-vya-nós-tŏ]; ninety [на́йн-ти]
100 сто [sto]; one hundred [ўăн хăн-дрăд]
200 двести [dvyé-st'i], two hundred [тў хăн-дрăд]
300 триста [tri-sta]; three hundred [θρi-хăн-дрăд]
400 четыреста [che-tắ-ryes-ta], four hundred [фȯр̌-хăн-дрăд]
500 пятьсот [pyat'-sót], five hundred [фа́йв хăн-дрăд]
600 шестьсот [shest'-sót]; six hundred [cĭкc хăн-дрăд]
700 семьсот [syem'-sót]; seven hundred [cé-вăн хăн-дрăд]
800 восемьсот [va-syem'-sót]; eight hundred [эйт хăн-дрăд]
900 девятьсот [dye-vyat'-sót]; nine hundred [на́йн хăн-дрăд]

1,000   тысяча [tắ-sya-cha] ; one thousand [ўán θáў-zănd]

2,000   две тысячи [dvye tắ-sya-chi] ; two thousand [тў θáў-zănd]

5,000   пять тысяч [pyat' tắ-syach] ; five thousand [файв θáў-zănd]

100,000   сто тысяч [sto tắ-syach] ; one hundred thousand [ўán hán-drădd θáў-zănd]

1,000,000   миллион [m'il-lión] ; one million [ўán míl-liăn]

ORDINAL NUMBERS
ПОРЯДКОВЫЕ ЧИСЛИТЕЛЬНЫЕ

1-ый первый [pyér-văy] ; **1st** first [фœрст]

2-ой второй [fta-róy] ; **2nd** second [cé-кăнд]

3-ий третий [tryé-t'i] ; **3rd** third [θœрд]

4-ый четвёртый [che-tvyór-tăy] ; **4th** fourth [фōрθ]

5-ый пятый [pyă-tăy] ; **5th** fifth [фифθ]

6-ой шестой [she-stóy] ; **6th** sixth [сíксθ]

7-ой седьмой [syed'-móy] ; **7th** seventh [cé-вăнθ]

8-ой восьмой [vas'-móy] ; **8th** eighth [эйтθ]

9-ый девятый [dye-vyă-tăy] ; **9th** ninth [найнθ]

10-ый десятый [dye-syă-tăy] ; **10th** tenth [тєнθ]

11-ый одиннадцатый [a-d'ĕn-nad-tsa-tăy] ; **11th** eleventh [i-лé-вăнθ]

12-ый двенадцатый [dvye-năd-tsa-tăy] ; **12th** twelfth [тўєлфθ]

20-ый двадцатый [dvad-tsă-tăy] ; **20th** twentieth [тўéн-ti-ăθ]

21-ый двадцать первый [dvăd-tsat' pyér-văy] ; **21st** twenty-first [тўéн-ti фœрст]

30-ый тридцатый [trid-tsă-tăy] ; **30th** thirtieth [θœр-ri-ăθ]

40-ой сороковой [sa-ra-ka-vóy] ; **40th** fortieth [фōр-ti-ăθ]

50-ый пятидесятый [pya-t'i-dye-syă-tăy] ; **50th** fiftieth [фíфti-ăθ]

100-ый сотый [só-tăy] ; **100th** hundredth [хắн-drădθ]

200-ый двухсотый [dvōōch-só-tăy] ; **200th** two-hundredth [ту хắн-drădθ]

300-ый трёхсотый [tryoch-só-tăy] ; **300th** three-hundredth [θри хăн-drădθ]

1000-ный тысячный [tắ-syach-năy] ; **1000th** one-thousandth [ўán θáў-zăндθ]

1,000,000-ый миллионный [m'il-lion-năy] ; **1,000,000th** one millionth [ўán míl-liăнθ]

ВСТУПИТЕЛЬНОЕ ПРИМЕЧАНИЕ

Неоспоримо известно что в данное время многие молодые люди в Англии усердно изучают язык русского народа.

С этим познанием в виду, издатели уполномочили меня составить и подготовить к печати настоящий русско-английский и англо-русский словарь.

С помощью студенткой фонетики Лондонского Университета, Елена Фэрбанк (Miss Helen Fairbank), и моего коллега А. Н. Уилкинсона (Mr. A. N. Wilkinson), удалось произвести совершенно новую фонетическую систему.

Я надеюсь, что потребители словаря найдут систему удовлетворительной для сносного произношения русских и английских слов.

В. М. ШАПИРО

ГРАММАТИЧЕСКИЕ ЗАМЕТКИ

ЧАСТИ РЕЧИ (*Parts of Speech*)

1. Имя существительное (the Noun)
2. Имя прилагательное (the Adjective)
3. Имя числительное (the Numeral)
4. Местоимение (the Pronoun)
5. Глагол (the Verb)
6. Наречие (the Adverb)
7. Предлог (the Preposition)
8. Союз (the Conjunction)
9. Междометие (the Interjection)
10. Артикль, член (the Article)

Имена существительные имеют два падежа; общий —*man, town*; притяжательный—*man's, town's*.

Имеются два рода существительных: собственные—(*Proper nouns*), всегда пишутся с прописной буквы, а нарицательные—(*Common nouns*) со строчной буквы.

Число (*Number*): в английском языке имеются два числа: **единственное** (*singular*) и **множественное** (*plural*); обыкновенное образование множественного числа добывается путём прибавления буквы 's' (с) к форме единственного числа; после звонких согласных и гласных произносится как **'z'** (з), а после глухих согласных как **'s'** (с).

Слова, оканчивающиеся на буквы **-s** и **-x**, и **-ch**, **-sh**, **-ss** (свистящие и шипящие звуки), образуют множественное число добавлением буквами **-es**.

Слова, оканчивающиеся на **-y** с предшествующей согласной, следует переменить **y** на **-ies**, но если перед буквой **y** стоит гласная, множественное число образуется по общему правилу; другие исключения: **-fe** становится **-ves**; **-ef**—**efs**; **oo** в середине слова—**ee**; **ou** иногда—**i**; **a**—**e** и т.д.

Род (*Gender*): все одушевлённые существительные принадлежат к мужскому или женскому роду согласно их пола; к среднему роду принадлежат все неодушевлённые предметы.

Прилагательные имена (*Adjectives*) не меняются ни по родам, ни по числам, ни по падежам.

Простые называются те прилагательные не имеющие ни префикса ни суффикса; к производным добавляются префикс или суффикс.

Местоимения (*Pronouns*) делятся на следующие группы: (1) **личные** (*personal*), я (*I*) и т.д.; (2) **притяжательные** (*possessive*), мой (*my*) и т.д.; (3) **возвратные** (*reflexive*) (а) -ся, -сь присоединяющиеся к русским глаголам; (б) себе (*myself*) и т.д.; (4) **взаимные** (*reciprocal*), друг друга, один другого (*each other, one another*); (5) **указательными** (*demonstrative*), этот, тот и т.д. (*this, that*); (6) **вопросительные** (*interrogative*), кто, что, который (*who, what, which*); (7) **относительные** (*relative*), кто, что, который (8) **неопределённые** (*indefinite*) какой-нибудь, несколько, никакой, всякий, всё (*some, many, none, each, all*) и т.д.

Глаголы (*Verbs*) бывают **простые** (*common*)—неимеющие ни префиксов ни суффиксы, или **производные**—имеющие префиксы и суффиксы. **Переходные** глаголы (*transitive*) называются такие которые могут иметь при себе прямое дополнение, а **непереходные**, которые не могут иметь при себе прямого дополнения. **Вспомогательные** глаголы (*auxiliary*), называются таковыми, так как при их помощи образуются различные сложные формы глагола.

По способу образования прошедшего неопределённого времени, глаголы делятся на **правильные** (*regular*) и **неправильные** (*irregular*). (см. стр. 765).

Наречия (*Adverbs*): по своему значению наречия делятся на следующие группы: (1) наречие места (*place*); (2) наречие меры и степени (*quantity, degree*); (3) наречие образа действия (*manner*); (4) наречие времени (*time*). **Простые** наречия (*common*); **производные наречия** (*derivative*)—к этой группе относятся наречия образуемые при помощи суффикса **-ly**.

Предлоги (*Prepositions*); в, во, с, со, над, под (*in, with, above, under*) и т.д.—те-же как на русском языке.

Союзы (*Conjunctions*), **простые** (*simple*): а, и, но, если, что (*but, and, if, that*) и т.д.; **составные** (*compound*): также как, чтобы.

Междометия (*Interjections*): ах!, ну!, увы! (*oh!, well!, alas!*)

Артикли, члены (*Articles*): имеются два рода членов: определённый (*definite*) и неопределённый (*indefinite*); форма неопределённого артикля **a** употребляется перед словами начинающимися с согласного звука, вторая форма **an** употребляется перед словами начинающимися с гласного звука. Определённый артикль **'the'** произносится [əð] перед согласными буквами и [əi] перед гласными буквами.

РУКОВОДСТВО К ПРОИЗНОШЕНИЮ АНГЛИЙСКИХ СЛОВ

Английский алфавит	символ	английские примеры	произносится как в слове
A a	а	plant [плант]	давать
	ä	car [кäр]	каждый
	ă	afraid [ă-фрэйд]	круто
	æ	bat [бæт]	это (более 'открытый' звук)
	эй	cane [кэйн]	гейша
	о	ball [бол]	боб
ai	э̄	air [э̄р]	эра
B b	б	band [бæнд]	бант
C c	с	cider [сай-дăр]	сидр
	к	cake [кэйк]	кекс
ch	ч	check [чек]	чай

384

Английский алфавит	символ	английские примеры	произносится как в слове
D d	д	dark [да̄рк]	дать
E e	э	get [гэт]	шест
	э	bell [бэл]	этаж
	и	me [ми]	английский
	œ	berth [бœр̄þ]	cœur (в французском слове, но немного 'шире')
ei	э̄	heir [э̄р]	эра
F f	ф	for [фо̄р]	форма
	в	of [ов]	во
G g	дж	general [джé-нă-рăл]	джут
	г	gate [гэйт]	город
gh	ф	rough [раф]	граф
		bough [баў]	—
H h	х̌	hand [х̌æнд]	халат (без гортонного звука)
	—	hour [áў-ăр̌]	
I i	и	infant [ин-фăнт]	индус
	ай	side [сайд]	май
	œ	fir [фœр]	cœur (см. 'е')
J j	дж	jump [джамп]	джин
K k	к	key [ки]	кот
L l	л	elbow [éл-боў]	алмаз
M m	м	much [мач]	марка
N n	н	entrance [éн-трăнс]	нап
	н̃	sing [син̃]	назальный звук буквы 'н'
O o	о	office [ó-фис]	опера
	оў	old [оўлд]	—
	о̄	or [о̄р]	орган
oo	ȳ (long)	moon [мȳн]	тут
	ў	book [бўк]	рука
ou	áў	out [áўт]	аукцион
oa	óў	boat [бóўт]	—
P p	п	pin [пин]	палка
Q q	к	quite [кўáйт]	квадрат
quo	кўó	quota [кўó-та]	
qua	кўó	quadrant [кўó-дрăнт]	

Английский алфавит	символ	английские примеры	произносится как в слове
R r	р	**r**ip [рип]	**р**ис
	р̧	fa**r** [фӓр̧]	ско́(р)ость
S s	с	**s**on [сан]	**с**ын
	ж	divi**s**ion [ди-ви́-жăн]	а**ж**ур
	ш	pen**s**ion [пе́н-шăн]	**ш**аль
sh	ш	fre**sh** [фреш]	**ш**ашка
T t	т	**t**ea [ти]	**т**ак
th	θ	**th**e [θă]	(вроде греческой буквы θ)
	δ̄	**th**in [δ̄ин]	(то же, но немно́го 'то́ньше')
U u	ю	**u**nion [ю́-ни-ăн]	**ю**г
	а	b**u**t [бат]	**ба**ржа
	œ	f**u**r [фœр̧]	'**cœur**' (см. 'е')
	ў	f**u**ll [фўл]	уда́р
V v	в	**v**oice [войс]	**в**олос
W w	ў		
wa	ўо́	**wa**r	
woo	ўу	**woo**d [ўуд]	
wo	ўœ̈	**wo**rk [ўœ̈рк]	=
we	ўэ́	**we**t [ўэ́т]	
wi	ўа́й	**wi**ne [ўа́йн]	
X x	кс	e**x**claim [экс-клэ́йм]	**кс**тати
	гз	e**x**ample [игз-зе́мпл]	э(к)**з**амен
Y y	и	m**a**ny [ме́-ни]	м**и**нута
	ай	m**y** [май]	с**ай**ка
ye	е	**ye**s [ес]	**е**го́
yi	й	**yi**eld [йилд]	к**и**й
Z z	з	**z**ero [зи́-ро]	**з**аря

АНГЛО-РУССКИЙ
СЛОВАРЬ

a [эй, а] *gram.* неопределённый член (*none in Russian*);
adj. один, некоторый; *mus.*
ля

aback [ă-бэ́к] *adv.* назад,
сза́ди; **to take** – [ту тэйк –]
смутить; застать врасплох

abaft [ă-ба́фт] *adv. naut.* с
кормы; *prep.* сзади

abandon [ă-бэ́н-дăн] *vt.* ос-
тавля́ть, покида́ть; *vi.* от-
ка́зываться; *sn.* небре́жная
свобо́да

abandoned [ă-бэ́н-дăнд] *adj.*
забро́шенный, покинутый;
распутный

abandonment [ă-бэ́н-дăн-
мăнт] *sn.* забро́шенность;
оставле́ние; непринуждён-
ность

abase [ă-бэ́йс] *vt.* укроща́ть,
унижа́ть

abasement [ă-бэ́йс-мăнт] *sn.*
сниже́ние; униже́ние

abash [ă-бэ́ш] *vt.* пристыжа́ть,
сконфузить, смуща́ть

abate [ă-бэ́йт] *vt.* ослабля́ть,
уменьша́ть; *vi.* стиха́ть,
уменьша́ться

abatement [ă-бэ́йт-мăнт] *sn.*
сба́вка; уменьше́ние

abattoir [а-ба-туа́р] *sn.* ското-
бо́йня

abbey [э́-би] *sn.* абба́тство,
ла́вра, монасты́рь, *m.*

abbot [э́-бот] *sn.* абба́т, игу́-
мен

abbreviate [ă-бри-ви-эйт] *vt.*
сокраща́ть

abbreviation [ă-бри-ви-э́й-
шăн] *sn.* сокраще́ние

abdicate [э́б-ди-кэйт] *vt.*
уступа́ть; *vi.* отрека́ться

abdication [э́б-ди-кэ́й-шăн]
sn. абдика́ция, отрече́ние

abdomen [э́б-дă-мăн] *sn.*
брюхо, живот

abdominal [ăб-до́-ми-нăл]
adj. брюшно́й

abduct [ăб-да́кт] *vt.* отво-
ди́ть, похища́ть, увози́ть

abduction [ăб-да́к-шăн] *sn.*
отво́д, похище́ние

aberration [ă-бă-ра́й-шăн]
sn. аберра́ция; заблуж-
де́ние, отклоне́ние

abet [ă-бе́т] *vt.* подстрека́ть

abettor [ă-бе́-тор] *sn.* под-
стрека́тель, соуча́стник

abeyance [ă-бэ́й-ăнс] *sn.*
отсро́чка, приостано́вка; **in**
– [ин –] в ожида́нии

abhor [ăб-хо́р] *vt.* гнуша́ть-
ся, пита́ть отвраще́ние

abhorrent [ăб-хо́-рăнт] *adj.*
гну́сный; отврати́тельный

abide [ă-ба́йд] *vt.i.* ждать;
остава́ться; выноси́ть, тер-
пе́ть; – **by** . . . [– бай] дер-
жа́ться (чего-либо)

abiding [ă-бáй-дiй] *adj.* постоянный, продолжительный

ability [ă-бí-лi-тi] *sn.* лóвкость; способность; умéнье

abject [ǽб-джект] *adj.* жáлкий; унижённый

abjection [ăб-джéк-шăн] *sn.* нíзость; униженіе; пóдлость

ablative [ǽб-лă-тiв] *adj. gram.* творительный

ablaze [ă-блэ́йз] *adv.* в огнé; *adj.* пылáющий

able [эйбл] *adj.* способный, умéющий; **to be – to** [тý би – ту] быть в состоянiи; **to be – to** [тý би эйбл] *vi.* мочь, умéть

ablution [ă-блý-шăн] *sn.* омовéніе, промывка

ably [эй-бли] *adv.* искусно, умéло

abnormal [ǽб-нóр-мăл] *adj.* ненормáльный, непрáвильный; урóдливый (*deformed*)

abnormality [ǽб-нор-мǽли-тi] *sn.* непрáвильность, урóдство

abnormity [ǽб-нóр-мi-тi] *sn.* урóдливость, чудóвищность

aboard [ă-бóрд] *adv.* на кораблé

abode [ă-бóуд] *sn.* жилище, местопребывáніе

abolish [ă-бó-лiш] *vt.* отменять, уничтожáть

abolition [ǽб-ă-лi-шăн] *sn.* отмéна, разрушéніе, уничтоженіе

abominable [ă-бó-мi-нăбл] *adj.* отвратительный

abominate [ă-бó-мi-нэйт] *vt.* питáть отвращéніе, презирáть

abomination [ă-бо-мi-нэ́йшăн] *sn.* мéрзость, отвращéніе

aboriginal [ǽ-бо-рí-джi-нăл] *adj.* кореннóй, первобытный, тузéмный

aborigines [ǽ-бо-рí-джi-низ] *s. pl.* аборигéны, тузéмцы

abort [ă-бóрт] *vi.* выкидывать

abortion [ă-бóр-шăн] *sn.* абóрт, выкидыш; преждеврéменные рóды; *fig.* неудáча

abortive [ă-бóр-тiв] *adj.* преждеврéменный (о рóдах); бесплóдный; зачáточный

abound [ă-бáунд] *vi.* изобиловать; быть богáтым; кишéть

about [ă-бáут] *adv.* кругóм; касáтельно, приблизительно; *prep.* о, об, по; **round – way** [рáунд – уэ́й] окружный путь; **– turn!** [– тёрн] *mil.* кругóм!

above [ă-бáв] *adv.* вы́ше; *prep.* над, свы́ше; **– all** [– óл] глáвным образом, прéжде всегó; *adv.* наверхý, сверх

abrasion [ă-брэ́й-жăн] *sn.* перетирáніе; ссáдина (*wound*); *geol.* абрáзія; *tech.* шлифóвка

abreast [ă-брéст] *adv.* в ряд, рядом; *naut.* против

abridge [ă-брíдж] *vt.* сокращáть, убавлять

abridgment [ă-брíдж-мăнт] *sn.* сокращéніе

abroad [ă-брóд] *adv.* вне дóма, на дворé, снарýжи (*outside*); за границей (*over-seas*)

abrogate [áb-рă-гэйт] vt. отменять; аннулировать

abrogation [áб-рă-гэй-шăн] sm. отмена, уничтожение

abrupt [áб-рáпт] adj. обрывистый (brusque); крутой (steep); внезапный (sudden); резкий (hasty)

abruptness [áб-рáпт-нĕс] s. отрывистость; внезапность (suddenness); крутизна (steepness); резкость (brusqueness)

abscess [áб-сĕс] sn. нарыв, чирей

abscond [аб-сконд] vi. убегать; прятаться; скрываться (from justice; from persecution)

absence [áб-сăнс] sn. отлучка, отсутствие; — of mind [— ов майнд] рассеянность

absent [áб-сăнт] adj. отсутствующий; —minded [—майн-дĭд] рассеянный; [áб-сéнт] vt. отсутствовать

absentee [áб-сăн-ти] sm. отсутствующий

absolute [áб-сă-лут] adj. абсолютный; безусловный (unconditional)

absolutely [áб-сă-лут-ли] adv. абсолютно, совершенно, совсем

absolution [áб-сă-лу-шăн] sn. прощение; разрешение

absolve [áб-золв] vt. прощать; освобождать

absorb [áб-зорб] vt. всасывать; поглощать

absorbent [áб-зор-бăнт] adj. всасывающий, поглощающий

absorbing [áб-зор-бĭй] adj. захватывающий, увлекательный

abstain [аб-стéйн] vi. воздерживаться

abstainer [аб-стéй-нăр] sm. воздерживающийся; трезвенник (from alcohol)

abstemious [áб-сти-ми-ăс] adj. воздержный, умеренный

abstinence [áб-сти-нăнс] sn. умеренность; трезвенность

abstract [áб-стрăкт] sn. конспект, краткое содержание, суть; adj. отвлеченный; абстрактный

abstract [áб-стрáкт] vt. влекать, отнимать

abstruse [áб-струс] adj. непонятный, неясный (not clear)

absurd [áб-сăрд] adj. абсурдный, нелепый, несуразный

absurdity [áб-сăр-ди-ти] sn. вздор, нелепость, чепуха

abundance [ă-бáн-дăнс] sn. достаток, изобилие, наплыв. обилие

abundant [ă-бáн-дăнт] adj. избыточный, изобильный

abuse [ă-бюс] sn. злоупотребление (maltreatment); оскорбление (offence); брань, ругань; [ă-бюз] vt. бранить, злоупотреблять, ругать

abusive [ă-бю-сив] adj. оскорбительный, ругательный

abysmal [ă-биз-мăл] adj. бездонный

abyss [ă-бис] sn. бездна, пропасть; naut. пучина

Abyssinian [æ-бис-си-ни-ан] sm. абиссинец; adj. абиссинский

academy [ă-kắ-dă-mĭ] *sn.* академия

academic [ӕ-kă-dĕ́-mĭk] *adj.* академический

accede [ăk-sĭd] *vi.* вступать, допускать; соглашаться (*to agree*)

accelerate [ăk-sĕ-lă-рэйт] *vt.* ускорять

acceleration [ăk-sĕ-lă-рэ́й-шăн] *sn.* ускорение

accelerator [ăk-sĕ-lă-рэ́й-тăр] *sn.* ускоритель; *tech.* акселератор

accent [ăk-сăнт] *sn.* акцент; ударение (*stress*); [ăk-сĕ́нт] *vt.* делать ударение; ставить знак ударения

accept [ăk-сĕ́пт] *vt.* принимать

acceptable [ăk-сĕ́п-тăбл] *adj.* приемлемый

acceptance [ăk-сĕ́п-тăнс] *sn.* принятие, согласие

access [ăk-сĕс] *sn.* доступ, приближение

accessary [ăk-сĕ́-са-рĭ] *sm.* соучастник

accessible [ăk-сĕ́-сĭбл] *adj.* доступный, проходной

accession [ăk-сĕ́-шăн] *sn.* прирост (*increment*); прибавление, дополнение (*addition*); восшествие, вступление (*to a throne*); **-s** [-з] *pl.* добавочный каталог

accessory [ăk-сĕ́-са-рĭ] *sn.* добавление, побочность (*additional item*); принадлежность (*appurtenance*); *adj.* добавочный (*additional*); соучастный (*aiding*)

accident [ăk-сĭ-дănт] *sn.* случай, случайность; ошибка (*error*)

accidental [ăk-сĭ-дĕ́н-тăл]

adj. случайный; второстепенный

acclaim [ă-клэ́йм] *sn.* шумное приветствие; *vt.* провозглашать

acclamation [ăk-кла-мэ́й-шăн] *sn.* громкое одобрение

accommodate [ă-кóм-мă-дэйт] *vt.* приспособлять; снабжать (*equip, provide*)

accommodating [ă-кóм-мă-дэй-тĭй] *adj.* уживчивый, услужливый

accommodation [ă-кăм-мă-дэ́й-шăн] *sn.* приспособление; удобство; *leg.* соглашение

accompaniment [ă-кăм-нĭ-мăнт] *sn.* сопровождение; *mus.* аккомпанемент

accompanist [ă-кăм-пă-нĭст] *sm. mus.* аккомпаниатор

accompany [ă-кăм-пă-нĭ] *vt.* провожать, сопровождать; *mus.* аккомпанировать

accomplice [ă-кóм-плĭс] *sm.* сообщник, соучастник

accomplish [ă-кóм-плĭш] *vt.* выполнять, совершать

accomplished [ă-кóм-плĭшд] *adj.* законченный

accomplishment [ă-кóм-плĭш-мăнт] *sn.* выполнение, завершение; достижение (*achievement*); *pl.* образование

accord [ă-кóрд] *sn.* согласие, созвучие; *vt.i.* согласовать(ся) (*grant*)

accordance [ă-кóр-дăнс] *sn.* согласие; **in** – [ĭн –] в соответствии

accordingly [ă-кóр-дĭй-лĭ] *adv.* соответственно, таким образом

accost [ă-kóst] *vt.* подходи́ть, приступа́ть

account [ă-ка́унт] *sn.* отчёт, расчёт, счёт; *vi.* дава́ть отчёт, счита́ть; объясни́ть (*explain*)

accountable [ă-ка́ун-тăбл] *adj.* отве́тственный; объясни́мый (*explicable*)

accountant [ă-ка́ун-тăнт] *sm.* бухга́лтер, счетово́д

accrue [ă-кру́] *vi.* накопля́ться; нараста́ть (*interest, etc.*)

accumulate [ă-кю-мю-лэ́йт] *vt.* нака́пливать, собира́ть

accumulation [ă-кю-мю-лэ́й-шăн] *sn.* накопле́ние

accumulative [ă-кю-мю-ла́-тïв] *adj.* накопля́ющий, собира́тельный

accumulator [ă-кю-мю-лэ́й-тăр] *sm.* аккумуля́тор

accuracy [а́к-кю-рӑ-сï] *sn.* пра́вильность, то́чность

accurate [а́к-кю-рӑт] *adj.* аккура́тный, ве́рный, пра́вильный

accursed [ă-ке́р-сïд] *adj.* прокля́тый

accusation [ӑ-кю-зэ́й-шăн] *sn.* изобличе́ние, обвине́ние

accusative [ă-кю́-зӑ-тïв] *adj. gram.* вини́тельный

accuse [ă-кю́з] *vt.* доноси́ть, обвиня́ть, облича́ть

accustom [ă-кăс-та́м] *vt.* привыка́ть, приуча́ть

ace [эйс] *sn.* туз (*cards*); очко́ (*dot or point on dice, etc.*)

acetic [ă-сè-тïк] *adj.* у́ксусный

ache [эйк] *sn.* боль; *vi.* страда́ть (*suffer pain*)

achieve [ă-чи́в] *vt.* выполня́ть, достига́ть, соверша́ть

achievement [ă-чи́в-мӑнт] *sn.* достиже́ние

aching [эй-кïй] *adj.* боле́зненный

acid [ắ-сïд] *sn.* кислота́; *adj.* ки́слый

acidity [æ-сï-дï-тï] *sn. chem.* ки́слость

acknowledge [æк-но́-лïдж] *vt.* допуска́ть, признава́ть (*admit*); удостоверя́ть (*attest*)

acknowledgment [æк-но́-лïдж-мӑнт] *sn.* призна́ние; благода́рность (*thanks*)

acorn [эй-ко́рн] *sn.* жёлудь

acoustic [ă-ку́с-тïк] *adj.* акусти́ческий, слухово́й; **-s** [-с] *s.pl.* акусти́ка

acquaint [ă-кўэ́йнт] *vt.* знако́мить

acquaintance [ă-кўэ́йн-тӑнс] *sn.* знако́мство; знако́мый (*person*)

acquiesce [æ-кўï-éс] *vi.* покоря́ться, соглаша́ться

acquiescence [æ-кўï-éс-сăнс] *s.* поко́рность, соглаше́ние

acquire [ă-кўа́й-ăр] *vt.* добыва́ть, приобрета́ть, усва́ивать (*adopt*)

acquisition [æ-кўï-зï-шăн] *sn.* стяжа́ние

acquit [ă-кўи́т] *vt.* оправды́вать, освобожда́ть

acquittal [ă-кўи́-тăл] *sn.* оправда́ние

acre [эй-кăр] *sn.* акр

acreage [эй-кă-рïдж] *sn.* простра́нство земли́

acrid [æк-рïд] *adj.* е́дкий, о́стрый; ре́зкий, язви́тельный (*harsh*)

acrimonious [æ-крï-мо́у-нï-ăс] *adj.* жёлчный, ко́лкий

acrimony [ǽ-кри-мă-ни] *sn.* е́дкость, острота́, язви́тельность

across [ă-кро́с] *adv.* попере́к; **to come –** [тў кам –] встре́тить; *prep.* сквозь, че́рез

act [æкт] *sn.* акт; де́йствие, де́ло, посту́пок; зако́н (*law*); *vt.i.* де́йствовать; *theat.* игра́ть, представля́ть

acting [ǽк-тиŋ] *adj.* де́йствующий; игра́ющий

action [ǽк-шăн] *sn.* де́йствие, де́ло, посту́пок; иск (*suit, claim*)

active [ǽк-тив] *adj.* де́ятельный, прово́рный; **– service** [– сœ́р-вíс] акти́вная вое́нная слу́жба; *gram.* де́йстви́тельный

activity [æк-ти́-ви-ти] *sn.* акти́вность, де́ятельность

actor [ǽк-тăр] *sm.* актёр

actress [ǽк-трíс] *sf.* актри́са

actual [ǽк-тю-ăл] *adj.* де́йстви́тельный, суще́ственный (*real*); настоя́щий (*current, present*)

actually [ǽк-тю-ăл-ли] *adv.* действи́тельно

actuary [ǽк-тю-ă-ри] *sm.* актуа́риус

actuate [ǽк-тю-эйт] *vt.* возбужда́ть, оживля́ть

acumen [ă-кю́-мэн] *sn.* прони́ца́тельность

acute [ă-кю́т] *adj.* о́стрый (*sharp*); пронзи́тельный

acuteness [ă-кю́т-нíс] *sn.* острота́, пронзи́тельность, то́нкость

adage [ǽ-диджъ] *sn.* погово́рка, посло́вица

adamant [ǽ-дă-мăнт] *adj.* несокруши́мый

Adam's apple [ǽ-дăмз æпл] *sn.* кады́к

adapt [ă-дǽпт] *vt.* приспособля́ть; переде́лывать (*alter, adjust*); **to – oneself** [ту – ўăн-се́лф] прилажи́ваться

adaptability [ă-дǽп-тă-би́-ли-ти] *sn.* примени́мость

adaptation [ă-дǽп-тэ́йшăн] *sn.* примене́ние, приспособле́ние; обрабо́тка (*of literary work*)

add [æд] *vt.* прибавля́ть, присоединя́ть; добавля́ть (*append*); **– up** [– ап] сосчи́тывать

addendum [ă-де́н-дăм] *sn.* приложе́ние; дополне́ние (*in book*)

adder [ă-дǽр] *sm.* гадю́ка, ехи́дна

addiction [ă-ди́к-шăн] *sn.* скло́нность

addition [ă-ди́-шăн] *sn.* дополне́ние, прибавле́ние; *arith.* сложе́ние

additional [ă-ди́шă-нăл] *adj.* доба́вочный, дополни́тельный

address [ă-дре́с] *sn.* а́дрес (*postal*); обраще́ние (*oral*); **to pay -es to** [тў пэ́й -из тў] уха́живание; *vt.* адресова́ть (*postal*); направля́ть (*direct*)

addressee [æд-дрес-си́] *sn.* адреса́т

adduce [ă-дю́с] *vt.* цити́ровать (*to cite*); приводи́ть (доказа́тельства) (*to furnish proof*)

adept [ă-де́пт] *sm.* знато́к; *adj.* зна́ющий, све́дущий

adequate [ǽ-ди-кўăт] *adj.* доста́точный, соотве́тствующий

adhere [ăд-хи́р] *vi.* прилипа́ть, приставать

adherence [ăд-хи́-рăнс] *sn.* приве́рженность

adherent [ăд-хи́-рăнт] *sm.* единомы́шленник, приве́рженец

adhesion [ăд-хи́-жăн] *sn.* привя́занность, прилипа́ние, связь

adhesive [ăд-хи́-сів] *adj.* ли́пкий, кле́йкий

adjacent [ă-дже́к-сăнт] *adj.* близлежа́щий

adjective [а́д-джек-тів] *sn.* и́мя прилага́тельное

adjoining [ă-джо́й-ніŋ] *adj.* сме́жный, сосе́дний

adjourn [ă-джŏ́рн] *vt.* откла́дывать, отсро́чивать

adjournment [ă-джŏ́рн-мăнт] *sn.* отсро́чка, переры́в

adjudicate [ă-джю́-ді-койт] *vt.* выноси́ть реше́ние, присужда́ть

adjudication [ă-джю́-ді-кŏй-шăн] *sn.* присужде́ние, реше́ние

adjudicator [ă-джю́-ді-кŏй-тăр] *sm.* присуди́тель

adjust [ă-джа́ст] *vt.* прила́живать, сверя́ть; *tech.* регули́ровать

adjustment [ă-джа́ст-мăнт] *sn.* приспособле́ние, све́рка

adjutant [а́д-джю-тăнт] *sm. mil.* адъюта́нт

administer [ăд-мі-ні-стăр] *vt.* управля́ть (*manage*); раздава́ть (*dispense*); дава́ть (*give*)

administration [ăд-мі-ні-стре́й-шăн] *sn.* администра́ция, правле́ние, управле́ние

administrative [ăд-мі-ні-

стра́-тів] *adj.* администрати́вный, исполни́тельный

administrator [ăд-мі-ні-стре́й-тăр] *sm.* заве́дующий, управля́ющий

admirable [ăд-мі-рăбл] *adj.* замеча́тельный, превосхо́дный

admiral [а́д-мі-рăл] *sm.* адмира́л; **- of the fleet** [- ов ǝǝ флит] по́лный адмира́л

Admiralty [а́д-мі-рăл-ті] *sn.* адмиралте́йство

admiration [ăд-мі-рǝ́й-шăн] *sn.* восто́рг, восхище́ние

admire [ăд-ма́й-ăр] *vt.* восхища́ться, любова́ться

admirer [ăд-ма́й-рăр] *sm.* покло́нник, почита́тель

admissible [ăд-мі́с-сібл] *adj.* допусти́мый, прие́млемый

admission [ăд-мі́-шăн] *sn.* допуще́ние, вход (*entry*), усту́пка (*concession*)

admit [ăд-мі́т] *vt.* допуска́ть; позволя́ть (*allow*); признава́ть (*acknowledge*)

admittance [ăд-мі́т-тăнс] *sn.* впуск, до́ступ

admonish [ăд-мо́-ніш] *vt.* увеща́ть, предостерега́ть (*caution, warn*)

admonition [ăд-мо-ні́-шăн] *sn.* увеща́ние

ado [ă-ду́] *sn.* хло́поты (*fuss, trouble*); шум (*noise*)

adolescence [æ-до-ле́с-сăнс] *sn.* о́трочество, ю́ность

adolescent [æ-до-ле́с-сăнт] *sm.* отро́к, ю́ноша; *adj.* отро́ческий, ю́ношеский

adopt [ă-до́пт] *vt.* усва́ивать; усыновля́ть (*a child*)

adoption [ă-до́п-шăн] *sn.* приня́тие, усвое́ние; усыновле́ние (*of child*)

adorable [ă-до́-рăбл] *adj.* обожа́емый; восхити́тельный

adoration [æ-до-рэ́й-шăн *sn.* обожа́ние, поклоне́ние; восхище́ние (*rapture*)

adore [ă-до́р] *vt.* обожа́ть; поклоня́ться

adorn [ă-до́рн] *vt.* украша́ть

adornment [ă-до́рн-мăнт] *sn.* прикра́са, украше́ние

adrift [ă-дри́фт] *adv.* по тече́нию

adroit [ăдро́йт] *adv.* нахо́дчивый, прово́рный

adult [ă-да́лт] *sm., sf., adj.* взро́слый

adulterate [ă-да́л-тă-рэйт] *vt.* подде́лывать, подме́шивать

adultery [ă-да́л-тă-рǐ] *sn.* прелюбодея́ние

advance [ăд-ва́нс] *sn.* по́дступ, продвиже́ние; ссу́да (*loan*); *vt.i.* дви́гаться вперёд, подвига́ть; де́лать успе́хи, улучша́ться (*make progress, improve*)

advancement [ăд-ва́нс-мăнт] *sn.* повыше́ние

advantage [ăд-ва́н-тǐдж] *sn.* вы́года, преиму́щество; **to – [ту –] к по́льзе; to take –** [ту тэйк –] воспо́льзоваться

advantageous [æд-ван-тǎй-джǎс] *adj.* вы́годный, спо́рый

Advent [а́д-вěнт] *sn.* Прише́ствие

adventure [ăд-вěн-чǎр] *sn.* похожде́ние, приключе́ние

adventurer [ăд-вěн-чǎ-рăр] *sm.* авантюри́ст

adventurous [ăд-вěн-чǎ-рǎс] *adj.* отва́жный, сме́лый (*brave*); преприи́мчивый (*enterprising*)

adverb [а́д-вěрб] *sn.* наре́чие

adversary [а́д-вǒěр-сǎ-рǐ] *sm.* проти́вник

adverse [ăд-вǒěрс] *adj.* вражде́бный, неприя́зненный

adversity [ăд-вǒěр-сǐ-тǐ] *sn.* невзго́да

advertisement [ăд-вǒěр-ти́с-мǎнт] *sn.* объявле́ние, рекла́ма

advertiser [æд-вǎр-тай-зǎр] *sm.* объяви́тель; лицо́, помеща́ющее рекла́му

advertize [æд-вǎр-тайз] *vt.* объявля́ть, публикова́ть, реклами́ровать

advice [ăд-ва́йс] *sm.* сове́т; извеще́ние (*notice*)

advisable [ăд-ва́й-зǎбл] *adj.* целесообра́зный

advise [ăд-ва́йз] *vt.* сове́товать; извеща́ть

advisory [ăд-ва́й-зǎ-рǐ] *adj.* совеща́тельный

advocate [æд-вǎ-кǐт] *sm.* адвока́т; защи́тник; [æд-вǎ-кэйт] *vt.* защища́ть

aerate [э́-рэйт] *vt.* прове́тривать (*air, ventilate*); газирова́ть (*charge with carbonic acid gas*)

aerial [э́-рǐǎл] *sn.* анте́нна; *adj.* возду́шный

aerodrome [э́-рǎ-дро́ум] *sn.* аэродро́м

aeronautics [э́-рǎ-но́-тǐкс] *sn.* аэрона́втика

aeroplane [э́-рǎ-плэ́йн] *sn.* аэропла́н, самолёт

aesthetic [ес-ōé̇-тĭк] *adj.* эстети́ческий; **-s** *sn.* эсте́тика

afar [ă-фа́р] *adv.* далеко́

affability [æ-фăб́і-лі-ті] *sn.* благоскло́нность, приве́тливость

affable [ắ-фăбл] *adj.* благоскло́нный, досту́пный, ла́сковый

affair [ă-фа́р] *sn.* де́ло

affect [ă-фе́кт] *vt.* возде́йствовать; растро́гивать; *vi.* притворя́ться (*feign*)

affectation [æ-фĕк-тэ́й-шăн] *sn.* притво́рство; жема́нство (*fastidiousness*)

affected [ă-фĕ́к-тĭд] *adj.* притво́рный (*pretended*); тро́нутый (*touchy*); пора́жённый (*by illness*)

affection [ă-фĕк-шăн] *sn.* любо́вь (*love*); привя́занность (*attachment*)

affiance [ă-фа́й-ăнс] *vt.* обруча́ть, помолви́ть

affidavit [æ-фі-дэ́й-віт] *sn.* показа́ние под прися́гой

affiliate [ă-фі́-лі-эйт] *vt.* присоединя́ть (*to join with*)

affiliation [ă-фі-лі-э́й-шăн] *sn.* приня́тие в чле́ны (*acceptance of membership*); связь (*bond, tie*); присоедине́ние (*connection*)

affinity [ă-фí-ні-ті] *sn.* родство́ (*kinship*)

affirm [ă-фё́рм] *vt.* подтвержда́ть, утвержда́ть

affirmation [æ-фĕр-мэ́й-шăн] *sn.* увере́ние

affirmative [ă-фё́р-мă-тĭв] *adj.* положи́тельный, утверди́тельный

affix [ă-фі́кс] прикла́дывать, прикрепля́ть

afflict [ă-флі́кт] *vt.* огорча́ть, опеча́ливать

affliction [ă-флі́к-шăн] *sn.* кручи́на, скорбь; беда́ (*adversity*)

affluence [ǽ-флу-ăнс] *sn.* изоби́лие (*abundance*); прито́к (*influx*)

affluent [æф-флу-ắнт] *adj.* изоби́льный; *sn.* прито́к

afford [ă-фо́рд] *vt.* дава́ть, доставля́ть, приноси́ть (*provide*); име́ть сре́дства

affray [ă-фрэ́й] *sn.* дра́ка, сканда́л

affront [ă-фра́нт] *sn.* оскорбле́ние; *vt.* оскорбля́ть

aflame [ă-флэ́йм] *adv.* в огне́

afloat [ă-фло́ӯт] *adv.* на воде́

aforesaid [ă-фо́р-сĕд] *adj.* вышеска́занный

afraid [ă-фрэ́йд] *adj.* боязли́вый, испу́ганный; *vi.* **to be** – [ту би –] боя́ться

afresh [ă-фре́ш] *adv.* сно́ва

African [ǽ-фрі-кăн] *sn.* африка́нец; *adj.* африка́нский

aft [ăфт] *adv. naut.* в корме́

after [ắф-тăр] *adv.* зате́м, пото́м; *prep.* за, по, по́сле; *adj.* после́дующий; **to look** – [ту лук –] уха́живать

aftermath [ắф-тăр-мæ̇] *sn.* второ́й поко́с; ота́ва

afternoon [ăф-тăр-ну́н] *sn.* пополу́дни, по́сле обе́да

afterwards [ắф-тăр-ӯăдз] *adv.* впосле́дствии

again [ă-гэ́йн] *adv.* опя́ть, сно́ва; **now and –** [ту áнд –] иногда́; **as much –** [аз мач –] вдво́е бо́лее

against [ă-гэ́йнст] *prep.* про́тив; о́коло (*near*)

age [эйдж] *sn.* во́зраст (*of person*); поколе́ние (*generation*); век, го́ды, эпо́ха (*period*); **to be of** – [ту би ов –] быть соверше́ннолетним; *vi.* старе́ть, устаре́ть

aged [эй-джид] *adj.* пожило́й, ста́рый (*old*)

agency [эй-джăн-си] *sn.* аге́нтство (*office*); посре́дство (*means*)

agenda [ă-джéн-дă] *sn.* пове́стка (поря́док) дня

agent [эй-джăнт] *sn.* аге́нт, посре́дник, представи́тель

aggravate [ǽ-грă-вэйт] *vt.* обостря́ть, ухудша́ть; *coll.* раздража́ть (*annoy*)

aggravation [ǽ-грă-вэ́й-шăн] *sn.* отягоще́ние, ухудше́ние

aggregate [ǽ-гри-гăт] *sn.* совоку́пность; *adj.* о́бщий, совоку́пный; [ǽг-гри-гэйт]; *vt.* приобща́ть, собира́ть

aggression [ă-грé-шăн] *sn.* нападе́ние, посяга́тельство

aggressive [ă-грé-сив] *adj.* вражде́бный, наступа́тельный

aggressor [ă-грé-сăр] *sn.* напада́ющий, зачи́нщик

aghast [ă-га́ст] *adj.* ошеломлённый, поражённый

agile [ǽ-джайл] *adj.* ги́бкий, ло́вкий, прово́рный

agility [ă-джи́-ли-ти] *sn.* ло́вкость, прово́рство, ю́ркость

agitate [ǽ-джи-тэйт] *vt.* возмуща́ть, волнова́ть; расстра́ивать (*disturb*); агити-

agitation [ǽ-джи-тэ́й-шăн] *sn.* волне́ние, трево́га; агита́ция (*propaganda*)

agitator [ǽ-джи-тэ́й-тăр] *sn.* агита́тор

aglow [ă-гло́у] *adv.*, *adj.* пыла́ющий

ago [ă-го́у] *adv.* тому́ наза́д; **long** – [ло́н –] уже́ давно́

agony [ǽ-го-ни] *sn.* муче́ние, сильне́йшая боль, душе́вное страда́ние

agree [ă-гри́] *vi.* соглаша́ться (*with*); сгова́риваться (*about*); усла́вливаться (*on, upon*)

agreeable [ă-гри́-ăбл] *adj.* ми́лый, прия́тный, уго́дный (*pleasant*)

agreement [ă-гри́-мăнт] *sn.* догово́р, контра́кт, усло́вие; соглаше́ние (*accord*); *gram.* согласова́ние

agricultural [ǽ-гри-ка́л-чă-рăл] *adj.* земледе́льческий, сельскохозя́йственный

agriculture [ǽ-гри-кал-чăр] *sn.* земледе́лие, се́льское хозя́йство

aground [ă-гра́унд] *adv.* на мели́

ahead [ă-хэ́д] *adv.* вперёд, впереди́

aid [эйд] *sn.* по́мощь; посо́бие (*relief*); *vt.* помога́ть, спосо́бствовать

ail [эйл] *vt.* боле́ть

ailing [эй-лин] *adj.* нездоро́вый

ailment [эйл-мăнт] *sn.* нездоро́вье, нéмочь

aim [эйм] *sn.* му́шка, прице́л; наме́рение, цель (*design, purpose*); *vi.* це́лить; стреми́ться (*aspire*)

air [эр] *sn.* во́здух; дунове́ние (*breath*); вид (*bearing*); поднебе́сье (*atmosphere*); а́рия, пе́сня (*song*); **-s** [эрз] *pl.* ва́жничанье; *vt.* прове́тривать

aircraft [эр-кра́фт] *sn.* возду́шное су́дно; — carrier [- кэ́-риэр] авиама́тка, авианосец

air-hole [эр-хо́ул] *sn.* проду́шина, фо́рточка

airing [э́-рин] *sn.* прове́тривание; прогу́лка (*walk*)

airman [э́р-мэн] *sm.* авиа́тор, лётчик

air-pocket [э́р-по-кит] *sn.* возду́шная я́ма

air-raid [э́р-рэйд] *sn.* возду́шная ата́ка

air-tight [э́р-тайт] *adj.* непроница́емый для во́здуха

airy [э́-ри] *adj.* возду́шный; ве́треный

aisle [айл] *sn.* прохо́д (*passage*); *eccl.* боково́й приде́л хра́ма, крыло́ хра́ма

ajar [а-джа́р] *adv.* полуотво́ренный

akin [а-кин] *adj.* бли́зкий, ро́дственный

alacrity [а-лэ́-кри-ти] *sn.* весёлость, жи́вость; гото́вность (*readiness*)

alarm [а-ла́рм] *sn.* смяте́ние, трево́га; сигна́л; *vt.* волнова́ть, смуща́ть

alarm-clock [а-ла́рм клок] *sn.* буди́льник

alarming [а-ла́р-мин] *adj.* трево́жный

alas [а-лэ́с] *interj.* увы́!

alcohol [э́л-ка-хол] *sn.* алкого́ль, спирт

alcove [э́л-ко́ув] *sn.* алько́в, ни́ша

alderman [о́л-дар-мэн] *sm.* альдерма́н, старшина́ городско́го управле́ния

ale [эйл] *sn.* пи́во, эль

ale-house [эйл-ха́ус] *sn.* каба́к

alert [а-лёрт] *adj.* бди́тельный, прово́рный; **on the** — [он эн —] насторо́же; *sn.* сигна́л трево́ги (*air-raid warning*)

alertness [а-лёрт-нис] *sn.* бо́йкость, прово́рство

algebra [э́л-джи-бра] *sn.* а́лгебра

Algerian [эл-джи́-рян] *sm.* алжи́рец; *adj.* алжи́рский

alias [эй-ли-а́с] *sn.* вы́мышленное и́мя; *adv.* ина́че

alibi [а́-ли-бай] *sn.* али́би

alien [эй-лиэн] *sn.* чужезе́мец, чужестра́нец; *adj.* чу́ждый, чужо́й

alienate [эй-ли-а-нэйт] *vt.* отчужда́ть

alight [а-ла́йт] *vi.* слеза́ть; спе́шиваться, сходи́ть; *adj.* зажжённый; освещённый

align [а-ла́йн] *vt.* выра́внивать, ста́вить в ряд; *vi.* выра́вниваться

alignment [а-ла́йн-мэнт] *sn.* выра́внивание, расстано́вка

alike [а-ла́йк] *adj.* подо́бный, похо́жий; *adv.* одина́ково, схо́дно

aliment [э́-ли-мэнт] *sn.* пи́ща

alimentary [э-ли-ме́н-та-ри] *adj.* пита́тельный, пищево́й; **— canal** [— ка-нэ́л] пищево́д

alive [ă-ла́йв] *adj.* живо́й; бо́дрый (*brisk*); восприи́мчивый (*susceptible*); киша́щий (*swarming with*)

all [ōл] *adj.* весь; це́лый (*complete, full*); *adv.* вполне́, всеце́ло, соверше́нно; – **right** [– ра́йт] ла́дно, хорошо́; *s.* все (*everyone*); всё (*everything*)

allay [ă-ла́й] *vt.* успока́ивать; облегча́ть (*pain*); утоля́ть (*thirst*)

allegation [æ-лі-ґа́й-шăн] *sn.* утвержде́ние

allege [ă-ле́дж] *vt.* ссыла́ться; утвержда́ть (*affirm*)

allegiance [ă-лі́-джănс] *sn.* ве́рность, пре́данность

allegory [ǽ-лі-ві́-ейі] *sn.* иносказа́ние

alleviate [ă-лі́-ві-эйт] *vt.* облегча́ть, смягча́ть

alleviation [ă-лі-ві-эй́-шăн] *sn.* облегче́ние, успокое́ние

alley [ǽ-лі] *sn.* алле́я, переу́лок; **skittle** – [скітл –] ке́гельбан; **blind** – [бла́йнд –] тупи́к

alliance [ă-ла́й-ănс] *sn.* сою́з (*union*); сочета́ние (*marriage*); родство́ (*affinity*)

allied [ă-ла́йд] *adj.* сою́зный, бли́зкий, схо́дный (*near, similar*)

alligator [ǽ-лі-ґэй-тăр] *sn.* аллига́тор, кайма́н

allocate [ǽ-лă-кэйт] *vt.* назнача́ть, распределя́ть

allocation [æ-лă-кэй́-шăн] *sn.* назначе́ние, распределе́ние [раздава́ть]

allot [ă-ло́т] *vt.* определя́ть, надели́ть (*plot of land*)

allotment [ă-ло́т-мăнт] *sn.* до́ля (*share*); наде́л (*plot of land*)

allow [ă-ла́у] *vt.* допуска́ть, позволя́ть, разреша́ть

allowance [ă-ла́у-ănс] *sn.* дозволе́ние, допуще́ние (*permission*); ски́дка (*abatement*); дово́льствие (*grant*); паёк (*ration*)

alloy [ǽ-лой] *sn.* при́месь (*admixture*); сплав (*metal*)

allude [ă-лу́д] *vi.* намека́ть

allure [ă-лю́р] *vt.* завлека́ть, зама́нивать

alluring [ă-лю́-рі́н] *adj.* прима́нчивый, соблазни́тельный

allusion [ă-лу́-жăн] *sn.* намёк

ally [ǽ-лай] *sm.* сою́зник; [ă-ла́й] *vt.* соединя́ть

almanac [о́л-мă-нæк] *sn.* календа́рь, *m.*

almighty [ōл-ма́й-ті] *adj.* всемогу́щий

almond [а́-мăнд] *sn.* минда́ль, *m.*

almost [о́л-моуст] *adv.* почти́, чуть не

alms [āмз] *sn.* ми́лостыня; **–house** [—ха́ус] бога́тельня

aloft [ă-ло́фт] *adv.* наверху́

alone [ă-ло́ун] *adj.* оди́н, одино́кий; *adv.* то́лько

along [ă-ло́н] *adv.* в длину́; **– with** [– уі́e] вме́сте; **come** – [кам –] идёмте; *prep.* вдоль

alongside [ă-ло́н-сайд] *adv.* ря́дом

aloof [ă-лу́ф] *adv.* в стороне́, поо́даль

aloofness [ă-лу́ф-ніс] *sn.* отдале́ние, отчуждённость

aloud [ă-ла́уд] *adv.* вслух, гро́мко (*loudly*)

alphabet [ǽл-фă-біт] *sn.* а́збука, алфави́т

alphabetical [æл-фа-бе́-ти-кǎл] *adj.* алфави́тный

already [ōл-рé-ди] *adv.* уже́

Alsatian [æл-сэ́й-шǎн] *sm.* эльза́сец; *sf.* неме́цкая овча́рка (dog)

also [о́л-соу] *adv.* та́кже, то́же

altar [о́л-тǎр] *sn.* алта́рь, *m.*, престо́л (communion table)

alter [о́л-тǎр] *vt.* изменя́ть, переде́лать

alteration [ōл-та-рэ́й-шǎн] *sn.* измене́ние, переде́лка, переме́на

altercation [ōл-тǎр-кэ́й-шǎн] *sn.* перебра́нка, ссо́ра

alternate [о́л-тǎр-нэйт] *vt.* чередова́ть; [о́л-тǎр-нит] *adj.* перемежа́ющийся, чередую́щийся

alternating [о́л-тǎр-нэ́й-тǐн] *adj.* переме́нный

alternation [ōл-тǎр-нэ́й-шǎн] *sn.* чередова́ние

alternative [ōл-тǎр-нǎ-тǐв] *sn.* альтернати́ва; *adj.* взаи́мно исключа́ющий

although [ōл-ðо́у] *conj.* е́сли бы, да́же, хоть, хотя́

altitude [æл-тǐ-тю̄д] *sn.* высота́; возвы́шенность (elevation)

alto [æл-тоу] *sn. mus.* альт

altogether [ōл-тǎ-гé-ðǎр] *adv.* вполне́, всецело́

alum [æ-лǎм] *sn.* квасцы́, *pl.*

aluminium [æ-лю-мǐ-нǐǎм] *sn.* алюми́ний

always [о́л-уэйз] *adv.* всегда́

amalgamate [ǎ-мæл-гǎ-мэйт] *vt.* амальгами́ровать, соединя́ть

amalgamation [ǎ-мæл-гǎ-мэ́й-шǎн] *sn.* амальгама́ция, смеше́ние (mixing); соеди-

нéние (combining, uniting)

amass [ǎ-мǽс] *vt.* накопля́ть, собира́ть

amateur [æ-мǎ-тǒр] *sm.* люби́тель; – **dramatics** [-дра-мǎ-тǐкс] люби́тельский спекта́кль

amateurish [æ-мǎ-тǒ-рǐш] *adj.* люби́тельский, непрофессиона́льный

amaze [ǎ-мэ́йз] *vt.* изумля́ть, удивля́ть

amazement [ǎ-мэ́йз-мǎнт] *sn.* изумле́ние, удивле́ние

amazing [ǎ-мэ́й-зǐн] *adj.* изуми́тельный

ambassador [æм-бǎ́-сǎ-дǎр] *sm.* посо́л

amber [æм-бǎр] *sn.* а́мбра, янта́рь

ambidexterous [æм-бǐ-де́кс-трǎс] *adj.* двору́чный

ambiguity [æм-бǐ-гю́-ǐ-тǐ] *sn.* двусмы́сленность

ambiguous [æм-бǐ-гю-ǎс] *adj.* двусмы́сленный; двоя́кий

ambition [æм-бǐ-шǎн] *sn.* самолю́бие, честолю́бие

ambitious [æм-бǐ-шǎс] *adj.* властолюби́вый, тщесла́вный

ambulance [æм-бю-лǎнс] *sn.* амбулато́рия, полевой лазаре́т

ambuscade [æм-бюс-кэ́йд] *sn.* заса́да

ambush [æм-бу́ш] *sn.* заса́да; ко́зни (snares)

amelioration [ǎ-ми-лиǎ-рэ́й-шǎн] *sn.* улучше́ние

amen [эй-ме́н] *interj.* ами́нь

amenable [ǎ-ми́-нǎбл] *adj.* отве́тственный (responsible); пода́тливый (compliant); послу́шный (subjected)

amend [ă-мέнд] *vt.* исправля́ть; *vi.* улучша́ться

amendment [ă-мέнд-мăнт] *sn.* исправле́ние; попра́вка (*rectification*)

amends [ă-мέндз] *sn.pl.* возмеще́ние

amenity [ă-мú-нĭ-тĭ] *sn.* любе́зность, прия́тность

American [ă-мέ-рĭ-кăн] *sn.* америка́нец; *adj.* америка́нский

amiable [эй-мĭ-ăбл] *adj.* ми́лый, любе́зный

amicable [ă-мĭ-кăбл] *adj.* дру́жеский

amid [ă-мúд] *prep.* ме́жду, посреди́, среди́

amidst [ă-мúдст] *prep.* среди́

amiss [ă-мúс] *adv.* некста́ти; **take** – [тэйк –] обижа́ться, оскорбля́ться

amity [ắ-мĭ-тĭ] *sn.* дру́жба, согла́сие

ammonia [ă-мó-нĭă] *sn.* аммиа́к; **liquid** – [лú-кўĭд –] наша́тырный спирт

ammunition [ă-мю-нú-шăн] *sn.* амуни́ция; боевы́е припа́сы (*military supplies*)

amnesty [ắм-нăс-тĭ] *sn.* амни́стия; всепроще́ние

among(st) [ă-мáн, ă-мáнгст] *prep.* ме́жду, посреди́; из числа́

amorous [ắ-мă-рăс] *adj.* влюблённый; влюбчивый (*of amorous disposition*)

amount [ă-ма́унт] *sn.* ито́г, су́мма, коли́чество (*quantity*); *vi.* доходи́ть, составля́ть; равня́ться (*to equal to*)

amphibious [ăм-фú-бĭăс] *adj.* земново́дный

ample [ăмпл] *adj.* доста́точный (*sufficient*); обильный

(*abundant*); просто́рный (*spacious*)

amplification [ăм-плĭ-фĭ-кέй-шăн] *sn.* расшире́ние, увеличе́ние, усиле́ние

amplifier [ắм-плĭ-фай-ăр] *sn.* усили́тель

amplify [ắм-плĭ-фай] *vt.* распространя́ть, увели́чивать

amputate [ắм-пю-тэйт] *vt.* ампути́ровать

amputation [ăм-пю-тέй-шăн] *sn.* ампута́ция

amuse [ă-мю́з] *vt.* забавля́ть, развесели́ть, развлека́ть

amusement [ă-мю́з-мăнт] *sn.* поте́ха, развлече́ние, увеселе́ние

amusing [ă-мю́-зĭн] *adj.* заба́вный, смешно́й

an [эн] *indef. art.* (*none in Russian*); *adj.* оди́н; не́который

anæmia [ă-нú-мĭă] *sn.* анэ́мия, бескро́вие, малокро́вие

anæmic [ă-нú-мĭк] *adj.* малокро́вный

analogous [ă-нắ-лă-гăс] *adj.* аналоги́чный

analogy [ă-нắ-лă-джĭ] *sn.* анало́гия, схо́дство

analyse [ắ-нă-лайз] *vt.* анализи́ровать, разлага́ть

analysis [ă-нắ-лĭ-сĭс] *sn.* ана́лиз, разбо́р, разложе́ние

anatomical [ăм-нă-тó-мĭкăл] *adj.* анатоми́ческий

anatomy [ă-нắ-тă-мĭ] *sn.* анато́мия

ancestor [ắн-сĕс-тăр] *sm.* пре́док

ancestral [ăн-сĕс-трăл] *adj.* насле́дственный, родово́й

ancestry [ǽn-сєс-трі] *sn.* происхождение (*descent*); предки (*ancestors*)

anchor [ǽн-кǒр] *sn.* якорь, *m.*; *vi.* стать на якорь

anchorage [ǽн-ка-рідж] *sn.* якорная стоянка

anchovy [ǽн-чо́ў-ві] *sn.* анчоус

ancient [э́йн-шǎнт] *adj.* античный, древний

ancillary [ǽн-сй-лǎ-рі] *adj.* подчинённый, служебный

and [ǽнд] *conj.* и; а

anew [а́-нйу] *adv.* снова

angel [э́йн-джǎл] *sn.* ангел; **guardian** − [гǎ́р-дǐăн −] ангел-хранитель

angelic [эн-джє-лік] *adj.* ангельский

angelus [ǽн-джє-лǎс] *sn.* набожное упражнение

anger [ǽн-гǎр] *sn.* гнев; *vt.* разгневать, раздражать

angina [ǽн-джǎй-нǎ] *sn.* ангина; − **pectoris** [− пєк-то́-ріс] грудная жаба

angle [ǽнгл] *sn.* угол (*corner*); удочка (*fish-hook*); *vi.* удить

angler [ǽн-глǎр] *sn.* рыболов, удильщик

angling [ǽн-глйн] *sn.* ужение

angry [ǽн-грі] *adj.* раздражённый, сердитый

anguish [ǽн-гўйш] *sn.* мука, тоска

angular [ǽн-гю-лǎр] *adj.* угловой, угольный

animadversion [ǽ-ні-мǎд-вǒр-жǎн] *sn.* порицание

animal [ǽ-ні-мǎл] *sn.* животное; *adj.* животный, скотский

animate [ǽ-ні-мэйт] *vt.* воодушевлять, оживлять;

[ǽ-ні-мǎт] *adj.* живой, оживлённый

animation [ǽ-ні-мэ́й-шǎн] *sn.* живость, оживление

animosity [ǽ-ні-мо́-сі-ті] *sn.* враждебность, неприязнь

ankle [ǽнкл] *sn.* лодыжка

annalist [ǽн-ǎ-ліст] *sm.* летописец

annals [ǽн-ǎлз] *sn. pl.* анналы, летопись

anneal [а-ні́л] *vt.* отжигать, прокаливать

annex [ǽ-нє́кс] *vt.* присовокуплять, присоединять

annexation [ǽ-нє-ксǎ́й-шǎн] *sn.* аннексия, присоединение

annexe [ǽн-єкс] *sn.* крыло, прибавка, пристройка

annihilate [ǎ-нǎй-і-лэйт] *vt.* истреблять, уничтожать

annihilation [ǎ-нǎй-і-лǎ́й-шǎн] *sn.* истребление, уничтожение

anniversary [ǽ-ні-вǒр-сǎ-рі] *sn.* годовщина

annotate [ǽ-но-тэйт] *vt.* аннотировать, отмечать

annotation [ǽ-но-тǎ́й-шǎн] *sn.* отметка

announce [ǎ-нǎ́унс] *vt.* извещать (*inform*); объявлять (*advertise*); заявлять (*declare*)

announcement [ǎ-нǎ́унс-мǎнт] *sn.* извещение; объявление; заявление

announcer [ǎ-нǎ́ун-сǎр] *sm.* объявитель

annoy [ǎ-нǒй] *vt.* надоедать (*tease, worry*); раздражать (*irritate*)

annoyance [ǎ-нǒй-ǎнс] *sn.* досада, раздражение

annoying [ǎ-нǒй-ій] *adj.* докучливый

annual [ǽ-ню-ǝл] *sn.* ежегóдник (*journal*); *adj.* годúчный, ежегóдный

annuity [ǎ-ню́-i-ti] *sn.* ежегóдный дохóд, рéнта

annul [ǎ-нáл] *vt.* аннулúровать, уничтожáть

annunciation [ǎ-нан-сi-éй-шǎн] *sn.* возвещéние; *eccl.* Благовéщение

anointment [ǎ-нóйнт-мǎнт] *sn.* помáзание

anomaly [ǎ-нó-мǎ-лi] *sn.* аномáлия, нерегуля́рность

anonymous [ǎ-нó-нi-мǎс] *adj.* анонúмный, безымéнный

another [ǎ-нá-θǎр] *adj.* ещё одúн (*additional*); другóй (*different*)

answer [áн-сǎр] *sn.* возражéние (*retort*); отвéт (*reply*); решéние (*solution*); *vt.i.* возражáть (*retort*); отвечáть (*reply*); ручáться (*be responsible*); – **back** [– бǽк] возражáть

answerable [áн-сǎ-рǎбл] *adj.* отвéтственный

ant [энт] *sn.* муравéй; **white** – [уáйт –] термúт; – **hill** [– хiл] муравéйник

antagonism [æн-тǽ-гǎ-нiзм] *sn.* антагонúзм, противобóрство, сопротивлéние (*resistance*)

antagonist [æн-тǽ-го-нiст] *sn.* протúвник, сопéрник

antecedence [æн-тi-сú-дǎнс] *sn.* пéрвенство, предшéствование

antecedent [æн-тi-сú-дǎнт] *adj.* предполагáемый (*presumptive*); предшéствующий (*previous*) [тилóпа

antelope [æн-тi-лóуп] *s.* ан-

antenna [æн-тéн-нǎ] *sn.* ан-

тéнна (*radio*); *zool.* рожóк, у́сики

anterior [æн-тú-рiǎр] *adj.* передний (*place*); прéжний (*time*)

anthem [æн-θǎм] *sn.* антифóн

anthology [æн-θó-лǎ-джi] *sn.* антолóгия

anthropology [æн-θрǎ-пó-лǎ-джi] *sn.* антрополóгия

antic [æн-тíк] *sn.* гротéскная пóза, движéние, шýтка; *pl.* ужúмки, шутóвство; *adj.* причýдливый

anticipate [æн-тi-сi-пэ́йт] *vt.* предвúдеть (*foresee*); предваря́ть (*forestall*); предвкушáть (*look forward to*)

anticipation [æн-тi-сi-пэ́йшǎн] *sn.* ожидáние, предварéние (*expectation*); **in** – [iн –] зарáнее, в ожидáнии (*чего-либо*)

antidote [æн-тi-доу́т] *sn.* противоя́дие

antipathy [æн-тí-пǎ-θi] *sn.* антипáтия, нерасположéние (*repugnance*); отвращéние (*aversion*)

antiquarian [æн-тi-кýэ́-рi-ǎн] *sn.* антиквáрий; *adj.* антиквáрный

antiquated [æн-тi-кýэ́й-тiд] *adj.* устарéлый

antique [æн-тúк] *sn.* старúнная вещь; *adj.* антúчный, дрéвний

antiquity [æн-тí-кýi-тi] *sn.* дрéвность, старинá

antiseptic [æн-тi-сéп-тiк] *sn.* антисептúческое срéдство; *adj.* противогнилостный

antler [æн́т-лǎр] *sn.* олéний рог

antonym [ӓн-тӑ-нім] *sn.* антóним, слóво противополóжное по значéнию

anvil [ӓн-віл] *sn.* наковáльня

anxiety [ӓнг-зáй-ӑті] *sn.* беспокóйство, забóта, тревóга

anxious [ӓнк-шӑс] *adj.* беспокóящийся, заботлúвый; сúльно желáющий (*earnestly desirous*)

any [э-ні] *adj.* любóй; вся́кий (*every*); *adv.* нéсколько, скóлько-нибудь; *pron.* ктó-нибудь (*person*); какóй-нибудь (*thing*)

anybody [энí-бодí] *sm.* ктó-нибудь; вся́кий

anyhow [энí-хáу] *adv.* кáк-нибудь, кóе-как

anyone [энí-ýан] *sm.* ктó-нибудь

anything [энí-бíн] *sn.* чтó-нибудь; – **but** [– бӑт] далекó не, совсéм не

anyway [энí-ýэй] *adv.* всё таки

anywhere [энí-ýэӗр] *adv.* гдé-нибудь, где угóдно

apart [ӑ-пáрт] *adv.* в стóрону (*aside*); пóрознь (*separately*); – **from** [– фром] не считáтся

apartment [ӑ-пáрт-мӑнт] *sn.* одéжда, кóмната, -s [-с] квартúра

apathetic [ӓ-пӑ-бé-тік] *adj.* равнодýшный; безразлúчный (*indifferent*)

apathy [ӓ-пӑ-бí] *sn.* безразлúчие, бестрáстие

ape [эйп] *sn.* обезья́на; *fig.* подражáтель; *vt.* подражáть (*imitate*)

aperient [ӑ-пí-ріӑнт] *sn.* слабúтельное

aperture [ӓ-пӑр-тюр] *sn.* отвéрстие, прóйма, просвéт; сквáжина (*chink*); *opt.* апертýра

apex [эй-пекс] *sn.* верхýшка, вершúна

apiarist [эй-піӑ-ріст] *sm.* пчеловóд

apiary [эй-піӑ-рі] *sn.* пáсека, пчéльник

apiculture [эй-пі-кал-чӑр] *sn.* пчеловóдство

apish [эй-піш] *adj.* обезья́ний; смешнóй (*droll*)

apologetic [ӑ-по-лӑ-джé-тік] *adj.* защитúтельный

apologize [ӑ-пó-ло-джайз] *vi.* извиня́ться

apology [ӑ-пó-ло-джі] *sn.* извинéние (*excuse*); защúта (*vindication*)

apoplexy [ӓ-по-плéк-сі] *sn.* паралúч, удáр

apostle [ӑ-пóсл] *sm.* апóстол

apostrophe [ӑ-пóс-трӑ-фі] *sn.* обращéние (*exclamatory address*); апóстроф, знак сокращéния (')

appal [ӑ-пóл] *vt.* пугáть (*frighten*); ужасáть (*terrify*)

appalling [ӑ-пóл-ін] *adj.* ужáсный

apparatus [ӓп-ӑ-рэй-тӑс] *sn.* прибóр

apparel [ӑ-пӑ-рӑл] *sn.* одéжда, плáтье (*attire*, *dress*)

apparent [ӑ-пӑ-рӑнт] *adj.* очевúдный (*palpable*); несомнéнный (*indubitable*); кáжущийся (*seeming*)

apparently [ӑ-пӑ-рӑнт-лí] *adv.* повúдимому

apparition [ӓп-ӑ-рí-шӑн] *sn.* появлéние (*appearance*); привидéние, прúзрак (*ghost*); *astron.* вúдимость

appeal [ă-пи́л] *sn.* призы́в; про́сьба (*request*); *vi.* апелли́ровать, взыва́ть

appear [ă-пи́р] *vi.* появля́ться; выходи́ть (*to be issued*); каза́ться (*seem*)

appearance [ă-пи́-ра́нс] *sn.* вне́шний вид (*aspect*); появле́ние (*apparition*)

appease [ă-пи́з] *vt.* облегча́ть (*pain, sorrow*), успока́ивать (*calm, soothe*)

appeasement [ă-пи́з-мăнт] *sn.* облегче́ние; умиротворе́ние (*pacification*)

appellant [ă-пе́л-ăнт] *sm.* апелля́нт; *adj.* жа́лующийся

appellation [ă-пе-ля́й-шăн] *sn.* и́мя, назва́ние; обозначе́ние (*designation*)

append [ă-пе́нд] *vt.* прибавля́ть, приве́шивать

appendage [ă-пе́н-дѝдж] *sn.* прида́ток

appendicitis [ă-пен-ди-са́й-тіс] *sn.* аппендици́т

appendix [ă-пе́н-дікс] *sn.* добавле́ние, приложе́ние; *anat.* отро́сток

appertain [ă-пăр-те́йн] *vi.* каса́ться, относи́ться

appetite [ă-пи-тайт] *sn.* аппети́т; вожделе́ние (*longing*)

applaud [ă-пло́д] *vt.* аплоди́ровать; одобря́ть (*approve*)

applause [ă-пло́з] *sn.* аплодисме́нты

apple [ăпл] *sn.* я́блоко; – **of the eye** [– ов ei ай] *fig.* зени́ца о́ка (*cherished object*); – **-tree** [– три] *sn.* я́блоня

appliance [ă-пла́й-ăнс] *sn.* примене́ние (*use*); прибо́р (*instrument, device*)

applicable [ă-пли-кăбл] *adj.* примени́мый

applicant [ă-пли-кăнт] *sm.* кандида́т; проси́тель

application [ă-пли-ко́й-шăн] *sn.* приложе́ние; прилежа́ние (*diligence*); заявле́ние, про́сьба (*request*); употребле́ние (*use*)

applied [ă-пла́йд] *adj.* прикладно́й, приложи́мый

apply [ă-пла́й] *vt.* прилага́ть, употребля́ть; *vi.* обраща́ться (*address*); относи́ться (*have reference*)

appoint [ă-по́йнт] *vt.* назнача́ть, определя́ть

appointment [ă-по́йнт-мăнт] *sn.* назначе́ние, определе́ние (*to a post*); до́лжность (*situation*); свида́ние (*rendez-vous*); *sn. pl.* снаряже́ние

apportion [ă-по́р-шăн] *vt.* наделя́ть, уделя́ть

apposite [ă-по-зайт] *adj.* подходя́щий, соотве́тственный

appraise [ă-прэ́йз] *vt.* оце́нивать, расце́нивать

appreciable [ă-при́-ши-ăбл] *adj.* заме́тный (*perceptible*); цени́мый (*capable of being estimated*)

appreciate [ă-при́-ши-эйт] *vt.* оце́нивать; уважа́ть (*esteem*)

appreciation [ă-при́-си-э́й-шăн] *sn.* оце́нка; уваже́ние (*regard*)

apprehend [æ-при-хэ́нд] *vt.* понима́ть (*understand*); опаса́ться (*fear*); схва́тывать (*seize*)

apprehension [æ-при-хэ́н-шăн] *sn.* понима́ние; боя́знь, опасе́ние (*dread, fear*)

apprehensive [æ-пpи-хéнсив] *adj.* боязли́вый, озабо́ченный

apprentice [ă-прéн-тис] *sn.* подма́стерье, учени́к в ремесле́; *vt.* отдава́ть в уче́ние (*novice*)

apprenticeship [ă-прéн-тисшип] *sn.* срок уче́ния

approach [ă-про́уч] *sn.* до́ступ (*access*); приближе́ние (*drawing near*); *vt.* подходи́ть, приступа́ть; *vi.* приближа́ться

approachable [ă-про́учăбл] *adj.* достижи́мый, досту́пный

approbation [æ-про-бэ́йшăн] *sn.* одобре́ние

appropriate [ă-про́-при-ăт] *adj.* подходя́щий, уме́стный; [ă-про́-при-эйт] *vt.* присва́ивать, усва́ивать

appropriation [ă-про-приэ́й-шăн] *sn.* присвое́ние

approval [ă-пру́-вăл] *sn.* одобре́ние, согла́сие; **on** — [он —] на про́бу

approve [ă-пру́в] *vt.* одобря́ть; проявля́ть (*manifest*)

approximate [ă-про́-ксимăт] *adj.* приблизи́тельный; [ă-про́-кси-мэйт] *vt.* бли́зить, приближа́ть; *vi.* приближа́ться, сближа́ться

approximation [ă-про-ксимэ́й-шăн] *sn.* приближе́ние, сближе́ние

appurtenance [ă-пёр-тинăнс] *sn.* принадле́жность

apricot [эй-при-кăт] *sn.* абрико́с

April [эй-прил] *sn.* апре́ль

apron [эй-прăн] *sn.* пере́дник, фа́ртук

apt [æпт] *adj.* подходя́щий; скло́нный

aptitude [æп-ти-тюд] *sn.* скло́нность, спосо́бность

aquarium [ă-куэ́-риўм] *sn.* аква́риум

aquatic [ă-кўǽ-тик] *adj.* водяно́й; **-s** [-с] *sn. pl.* во́дный спорт

aqueduct [æ-кўи-дакт] *sn.* акведу́к, водопрово́д

aquiline [æ-кўи-лайн] *adj.* орли́ный

Arab [æ-ра́б] *sn.* ара́б; *adj.* ара́бский

Arabic [æ-ра́-бик] *sn.* ара́бский язы́к; *adj.* ара́бский

arable [æ-рăбл] *sn.* па́шня; *adj.* па́хотный

arbiter [а́р-би-тăр] *sn.* трете́йский судья́

arbitrary [а́р-би-трă-ри] *adj.* произво́льный (*discretionary*); непостоя́нный (*inconstant*)

arbitrate [а́р-би-трэйт] *vt.i.* суди́ть

arbitration [ар-би-трэ́й-шăн] *sn.* арбитра́ж; до́лжность (*function*)

arbitrator [а́р-би-трэй-тăр] *sn.* арби́тр

arbour [а́р-бăр] *sn.* бесе́дка (из зе́лени)

arc [а́рк] *sn.* а́рка, дуга́

arcade [ар-кэ́йд] *sn.* арка́да; пасса́ж с магази́нами

arch [а́рч] *sn.* а́рка, свод; *vt.i.* выводи́ть сво́дом; изгиба́ться; *adj.* лука́вый, хи́трый

archeology [а́р-ке-о́-лăджи] *sn.* археоло́гия

archaic [ар-ке́-ик] *adj.* архаи́ческий, первобы́тный

archangel [а́рк-эйн-джăл] *s.* арха́нгел

archbishop [ắрч-бі-шăп] *sm.* архиепи́скоп, архиере́й

archer [а́р-чăр] *sm.* стрело́к из лу́ка

archery [а́р-чă-рі] *sn.* стрельба́ из лу́ка

archipelago [а́р-кі-пе́-ла-го] *sn.* архипела́г, гру́ппа острово́в

architect [а́р-кі-тєкт] *sm.* архите́ктор

architecture [а́р-кі-тєк-чăр] *sn.* архитекту́ра

archives [а́р-кайвз] *sn. pl.* архи́в

archivist [а́р-кай-віст] *sm.* архива́риус

arctic [а́рк-тік] *adj.* аркти́ческий, поля́рный

ardent [а́р-дăнт] *adj.* горя́чий (*burning*); пы́лкий (*fervent*)

ardour [а́р-дăр] *sn.* жар, пыл

arduous [а́р-дю-ăс] *adj.* трудолюби́вый (*laborious*); напряжённый (*strenuous*)

area [э́-піă] *sn.* пло́щадь, райо́н

arena [ă-рі-нă] *sn.* аре́на, по́прище

argue [а́р-гю] *vi.* дискути́ровать, спо́рить; *vt.* доказа́зывать, убежда́ть (*prove*)

argument [а́р-гю-мăнт] *sn.* аргуме́нт, до́вод; вы́вод (*inference*)

argumentative [а́р-гю-мĕн-тă-тів] *adj.* доказа́тельный; лю́бящий спо́ры (*fond of disputes*)

arid [э́-рід] *adj.* беспло́дный, сухо́й (*parched*); ску́чный (*dull*)

arise [ă-ра́йз] *vi.* возника́ть, происходи́ть, явля́ться; поднима́ться (*rise*)

aristocracy [æ-ріс-то́-крă-сі] *sn.* аристокра́тия

arithmetic [ă-ріθ-мă-тік] *sn.* арифме́тика

ark [а́рк] *sn.* я́щик (*wooden coffer*); ковче́г (Noah's)

arm [а́рм] *sn.* рука́ (*limb*); локо́тник, ру́чка (*of armchair*); *sn. pl.* ору́жие; **to –l** к ору́жию; *vt.i.* вооружа́ть

armament [а́р-мă-мăнт] *sn.* вооруже́ние

armature [а́р-мă-тю̈р] *sn.* вое́нные снаря́ды (*arms*); *tech.* армату́ра; *electr.* я́корь мото́ра

armchair [а́рм-чӭр] *sn.* кре́сло

armful [а́рм-фӱл] *sn.* оха́пка

armhole [а́рм-хӧул] *sn.* про́йма

armistice [а́р-міс-тіс] *sn.* переми́рие

armlet [а́рм-лет] *sn.* нару́ка́вник

armorial [а́р-мо́-ріăл] *adj.* геральди́ческий, гербо́вый

armour [а́р-мăр] *sn.* броня́, па́нцырь, *m.*

armoury [а́р-мă-рі] *sn.* арсена́л, склад ору́жия

armpit [а́рм-піт] *sn.* подмы́шка

army [а́р-мі] *sn.* а́рмия, во́йско

aroma [ă-ро́-мă] *sn.* арома́т

aromatic [æ-ро-ма́-тік] *adj.* благово́нный

around [ă-ра́унд] *adv.* всю́ду, круго́м; *prep.* вокру́г, по

arouse [ă-ра́уз] *vt.* буди́ть (*wake*); вызыва́ть, пробужда́ть (*provoke*)

arraign [ă-ре́йн] *vt.* доноси́ть (*denounce*); обвиня́ть (*accuse*)

arrange [ă-рэ́йндж] *vt.* у-стра́ивать; приводи́ть (в поря́док (*set in order*); ула́живать (*settle*); *vi.* сгова́риваться, усло́вливаться (*make arrangements*)

arrangement [ă-рэ́йндж-мăнт] *sn.* устро́йство; поря́док (*order*); *sn. pl.* пла́ны

arrant [ǽ-рăнт] *adj.* отъя́вленный

array [ă-рэ́й] *sn.* пы́шное облаче́ние (*rich vestments*); наря́д (*smart attire*); боево́й поря́док (*martial order*); *vt.* наряжа́ть, одева́ть (*dress*)

arrear [ă-ри́р] *sn.* отста́лость (*backwardness*); *sn. pl.* недо́имка; долги́ (*debts*)

arrest [ă-ре́ст] *sn.* аре́ст, задержа́ние; *vt.* арестова́ть, заде́рживать; остана́вливать (*halt*)

arrival [ă-ра́й-вăл] *sn.* прибы́тие (*act of arriving*); прие́зд (*by vehicle*); прилёт (*by air, as birds*); прихо́д (*on foot*); **new —** [ню —] новоприбы́вший

arrive [ă-ра́йв] *vi.* прибыва́ть, приходи́ть; случа́ться (*of events*); **— at** [— ǽт] дости́гнуть

arrogance [ǽ-пă-гăнс] *sn.* высокоме́рие, надме́нность

arrogant [ǽ-пă-гăнт] *adj.* высокоме́рный, де́рзкий

arrow [ǽ-роў] *sn.* стрела́; *mil.* флешь

arrowroot [ǽ-ро-рут] *sn.* аропру́т, стре́льный ко́рень

arsenal [а́р-сă-нăл] *sn.* арсена́л, цейхга́уз

arsenic [а́р-сни́к] *sn.* мышья́к; *adj.* [ар-се́-ни́к] мышьяко́вый

arson [а́р-сăн] *sn.* поджо́г

art [а́рт] *sn.* иску́сство, худо́жество; ло́вкость (*dexterity*); **fine arts** [фа́йн а́ртс] *sn. pl.* изя́щные иску́сства

arterial [ар-ти́-ри́ăл] *adj.* артериа́льный; разветвля́ющий (*ramified*)

artful [а́рт-фу́л] *adj.* ло́вкий; хи́трый (*cunning*); обма́нный (*deceitful*)

arthritis [ар-эра́й-тис] *sn.* артри́т; пода́гра (*gout*)

artichoke [а́р-ти-чо́ук] *sn.* артишо́к

article [а́р-тикл] *sn.* вещь, изде́лие, предме́т (*particular thing*); статья́ (*literary*); *gram.* член

articled [а́р-ти-кăлд] *adj.* уста́вный

articulate [ар-ти́-кю-лэ́йт] *vt.* выгова́ривать, я́вственно произноси́ть; *adj.* [ар-ти́-кю-лăт] коленча́тый, я́сный; членоразде́льный (*distinct*)

articulation [ар-ти-кю-лэ́йшăн] *sn.* произноше́ние (*pronunciation*); сочлене́ние (*jointing*); суста́в (*joint*)

artifice [а́р-ти-фи́с] *sn.* иску́сная проде́лка (*device, contrivance*); хи́трость (*trickery*)

artificer [ар-ти́-фи-сăр] *sm.* реме́сленник

artificial [ар-ти-фи́-шăл] *adj.* иску́сственный, подде́льный (*imitated*); притво́рный (*feigned*)

artillery [ар-ти́-лă-ри] *sn.* артилле́рия

artisan [а́р-ти-зăн] *sm.* рабо́чий, реме́сленник

artist [а́р-тíст] *sm.* худо́жник

artistic [а̄р-тíс-тìк] *adj.* артисти́ческий, худо́жественный

as [æз] *adv., conj., pron.* в виду́, дабы, и́бо, как, так же, так как, также как (*as . . . as*); – **far** – [– фа̄р́ –] насто́лько; – **good** – [– гӯд –] в су́щности; – **though** [– ѳо̄у] как бу́дто

asbestos [æз-бéс-тǎс] асбе́ст, го́рный лён

ascend [ǎ-сéнд] *vt.i.* восходи́ть, поднима́ться

ascendancy [ǎ-сéн-дǎн-сì] *sm.* влия́ние

ascendant [ǎ-сéн-дǎнт] *adj.* госпо́дствующий [*predominant*]; восходя́щий (*rising*)

ascension [ǎ-сéн-шǎн] *sm.* восхожде́ние, восше́ствие; **Ascension Day** [– дэй] *sm.* Вознесе́ние

ascent [ǎ-сéнт] *sm.* подня́тие, подъём; крутизна́ (*steepness*)

ascertain [æ-сǎр-тэ́йн] *vt.* удостове́рить, установи́ть

ascetic [ǎ-сé-тìк] *adj.* воздержанный, *sm.* отше́льник

ascribe [ǎс-кра́йб] *vt.* припи́сывать

ash [æш] *sn.* я́сень, *m.* (*tree*); зола́, пе́пел (*powdery residue*); прах (*dust, ashes*); **Ash Wednesday** [– у́э́нзэ-дэй] Среда́ Вели́кого По́ста

ashamed [ǎ-шэ́ймд] *adj.* пристыжённый

ashen [æ-шǎн] *adj.* ясе́невый; пе́пельного цве́та (*colour*); бле́дный (*pale*)

ashore [ǎ-шо́р] *adv.* к бе́регу, на берегу́

ash-pan [æш-пæн] *sn.* зо́льник

ash-tray [æш-трэй] *sn.* пе́пельница

Asiatic [эй-ши-ǽ-тìк] *adj.* азиа́тский

aside [ǎ-са́йд] *adv.* в сто́рону

ask [а́ск] *vt.* спра́шивать; проси́ть (*beg*); приглаша́ть (*invite*)

askance [ǎс-кǎ́нс] *adv.* и́скоса, ко́со; **look – at** [лу́к – æт] сомни́тельно осма́тривать

askew [ǎс-кю́] *adv.* ко́со, набо́к, накло́нно

asleep [ǎ-слúп] *adv., adj.* спя́щий; затёкший (*benumbed*)

asparagus [ǎс-пǎ́-рǎ-гǎс] *sm.* спа́ржа

aspect [ǽс-пèкт] *sn.* вид (*view*); взгляд (*look*)

aspen [æс-пǎн] *sn.* оси́на; *adj.* оси́новый

aspersion [ǎс-пёр́-шǎн] *sn.* клевета́, поноше́ние

asphalt [æс-фǎлт] *sn.* асфа́льт, го́рная смола́

asphyxia [æс-фí-ксìǎ] *sn.* удуше́ние

asphyxiate [æс-фí-кси-эйт] *vt.* задуши́ть

aspirant [ǽ-сп-рǎнт] *sm.* иска́тель, кандида́т, прете́нде́нт; стремя́щийся

aspirate [ǽс-пǐ-ра́т] *sn.* придыха́тельный звук; *adj.* приды́ха́тельный; *vt.* [æс-пǐ-рэ́йт] приды́ха́ть

aspiration [æс-пǐ-рэ́й-шǎн] *sn.* си́льное жела́ние (*strong desire*); стремле́ние (*longing*); домога́тельство (*ambition*); *phon.* придыха́ние

aspire [ăs-пáйр] *vi.* домогáться, стремиться

ass [æс] *sm.* осёл; *sf.* ослица; болвáн, глупéц (*stupid fellow*)

assail [ă-сéйл] *vt.* нападáть, наступáть

assailant [ă-сéй-лянт] *sm.* нападáющий, противник

assassin [ă-сáе-сiн] *sm.* наёмный убийца

assassinate [ă-сáе-сi-нэйт] *vt.* убивáть

assassination [æ-сæ-сi-нэй-шäн] *sn.* убийство

assault [ă-сóлт] *sn.* атáка, приступ, штурм; *vt.* нападáть, штурмовáть

assay [æ-сéй] *sn.* испытáние, прóба (метáллов); *vt.* испытывать, прóбовать

assemble [ă-сéмбл] *vt.* собирáть, созывáть; *tech.* монтировать

assembly [ă-сéм-бли] *sn.* ассамблéя, общество, собрáние

assent [ă-сéнт] *sn.* соглáсие; разрешéние (*permission*); *vi.* соглашáться

assert [ă-сéрт] *vt.* заявлять (*declare*); утверждáть (*affirm*)

assertion [ă-сéр-шäн] *sn.* утверждéние

assess [ă-сéс] *vt.* расцéнивать

assessment [ă-сéс-мянт] *sn.* обложéние, оцéнка

assessor [ă-сéс-сóр] *sm.* податнóй чинóвник; помóщник судьи (*adviser to judge*); оцéнщик (*valuer*)

assets [æ-сэтс] *sn. pl.* активы; налѝчное имýщество; **— and liabilities** [— æнд

лай-ă-бí-ли-тíз] активы и пассив

assiduous [ă-сí-дю-ăс] *adj.* прилéжный

assign [ă-сáйн] *vt.* назначáть, определять; ассигновáть (*grant*); передавáть (*make over to*)

assignable [ă-сáйн-äбл] *adj.* передáточный

assignation [æ-сiг-нэй-шäн] *sn.* назначéние; передáча; свидáние (*appointment*)

assignment [ă-сáйн-мянт] *sn.* ассигновáние; назначéние; передáча имýщества (*make over property, etc.*)

assimilate [ă-сí-ми-лэйт] *vt.* ассимилировать, прирáвнивать, уподоблять

assimilation [ă-сi-ми-лэй-шäн] *sn.* ассимиляция, уподоблéние; усвоéние

assist [ă-сíст] *vt.* помогáть

assistance [ă-сíс-тäнс] *sn.* пóмощь (*help*); содéйствие (*co-operation*)

assistant [ă-сíс-тäнт] *sm.* помóщник

assize [ă-сáйз] *sn.* заседáние, судéбная сéссия; постановлéние; **Grand Assizes** (грæнд —с) Великий трибунáл; *sn. pl.* периодические судéбные сéссии в Áнглии

associate [ă-сó-ши-эйт] *sm.* сою́зник, соучáстник, товáрищ; член товáрищества (*member of an association*); *vt.* принимáть, соединять; *vi. com.* имéть сношéния, общáться; объединяться, соединяться (*join, unite*); *adj.* [ă-сó-шiат] присоединѝтельный, сою́зный

association [ă-co-ciǽй-шăн] *sn.* ассоциа́ция, о́бщество, сою́з; связь (*bond, tie*); обхожде́ние (*intercourse*)

assortment [ă-cópт-мăнт] *sn.* ассортиме́нт, вы́бор, подбо́р

assuage [ă-cýǝйдж] *vt.* смягча́ть, успока́ивать, утоля́ть

assume [ă-сю́м] *vt.* принима́ть на себя́ (*take upon oneself*); симули́ровать (*pretend*); присва́ивать (*usurp*); допуска́ть, предполага́ть (*take for granted*)

assumption [ă-cắмп-шăн] *sn.* предположе́ние (*taking for granted*); высокоме́рие (*arrogance*); *eccl.* Успе́ние

assurance [ă-шу́-рăнc] *sn.* завере́ние, увере́ние, утвержде́ние (*affirmation*); уве́ренность, утверждённость (*feeling certain*); страхова́ние (*insurance*)

assure [ă-шу́р] *vt.* уверя́ть, утвержда́ть (*affirm*); гаранти́ровать, обеспе́чивать (*make sure*); страхова́ть (*insure*)

asterisk [ǽc-тĕ-ри́ск] *sn. typ.* астери́ск, звёздочка

astern [ă-стĕ́рн] *adv.* за кормо́й; сза́ди (*behind*)

asthma [ǽc-мă] *sn.* а́стма, оды́шка

asthmatical [ǽc-мĕ́-ти-кăл] *adj.* астмати́ческий, страда́ющий уду́шьем

astir [ă-стĕ́р] *adv.* в движе́нии

astonish [ăc-то́-ниш] *vt.* изумля́ть, удивля́ть

astonishment [ăc-то́-ниш-мăнт] *sn.* изумле́ние, удивле́ние

astound [ăc-тǻунд] *vt.* поража́ть, удивля́ть

astral [ǽc-трăл] *adj.* астра́льный, звёздный

astray [ă-стрǽй] *adv.* в заблужде́нии; **to go** - [тǝ́ гǒу -] сбива́ться

astride [ă-стра́йд] *adv.*, *prep.* верхо́м; расста́вив но́ги (*legs apart*)

astringent [ăc-три́н-джăнт] *sn.* вя́жущее сре́дство; *adj.* вя́жущий

astrology [ă-стро́-лǎ-джǐ] *sn.* астроло́гия

astronomy [ăc-тро́-нǎ-мǐ] *sn.* астроно́мия

astute [ăc-тю́т] *adj.* проница́тельный (*shrewd*); хи́трый (*crafty*)

asunder [ă-cắн-дǎр] *adv.* отде́льно, по́рознь; попола́м (*in two*)

asylum [ă-са́й-лăм] *sn.* прию́т, убе́жище

at [ǽт] *prep.* в, за, на, по, при, у; - **home** [- хǒ́ум] до́ма; - **last** [- лǎст] наконе́ц; - **once** [- ýăнc] вдруг, сра́зу

atheism [э́й-θǐизм] *sn.* атеи́зм, безбо́жие

atheist [э́й-θǐист] *sm.* безбо́жник

athlete [ǽθ-лит] *sm.* атле́т; боре́ц, сила́ч (*strong man*)

athletic [ǽθ-лĕ́-тǐк] *adj.* атлети́ческий, си́льный; *sn. pl.* атле́тика

at-home [ǽт-хǒ́ум] *sn.* журфи́кс

atlas [ǽт-лǎc] *sn.* а́тлас

atmosphere [ǽт-мос-фир] *sn.* атмосфе́ра; настрое́ние (*mood*); окружа́ющая обстано́вка (*environment*)

atomic [ă-tó-mĭk] *adj.* атóмный

atone [ă-tóун] *vi.* возмещáть, заглáживать

atonement [ă-tóун-мăнт] *sn.* заглáживание, искуплéние

atrocious [ă-тróу-шăс] *adj.* звéрский, лю́тый (*brutal, cruel*); гнýсный, ужáсный (*heinous*); отврати́тельный (*abominable*)

atrocity [ă-тró-сĭ-ті] *sn.* звéрство, жестóкость, ýжас

attach [ă-тéч] *vt.* прикрепля́ть (*adhere, fasten*)

attached [ă-тéчт] *adj.* принадлежáщий (*belonging to*); привя́занный, прéданный (*devoted*)

attachment [ă-тéч-мăнт] *sn.* прéданность (*devotion*); прикреплéние (*fastening*)

attack [ă-тéк] *sn.* атáка, нападéние (*onset*); при́ступ (*of illness*); *vt.* атаковáть, нападáть

attain [ă-тéйн] *vt.* достигáть

attainable [ă-тéй-нăбл] *adj.* достижи́мый

attempt [ă-тéмпт] *sn.* попы́тка, прóба; покушéние (*on someone's life*); *vt.* предпринимáть, прóбовать; покушáться

attend [ă-тéнд] *vt.* посещáть (*lectures, etc.*); обращáть внимáние (*pay attention*); присýтствовать (*be present*); исполня́ть (*carry out*)

attendance [ă-тéн-дăнс] *sn.* сопровождéние (*escort*); услýга, услужéние (*service*); присýтствие (*presence*); **to**

be in [ту би ін —] дежýрить

attendant [ă-тéн-дăнт] *sm.* дежýрный, служи́тель

attention [ă-тéн-шăн] *sn.* внимáние; внимáтельность (*attentiveness*); *interj.* mil. сми́рно!

attentive [ă-тéн-тĭв] *adj.* внимáтельный; забóтливый (*thoughtful*); вéжливый (*polite*)

attenuate [ă-тé-ню-эйт] *vt.* истощáть (*wear out*); ослабля́ть (*weaken*); разжижáть (*to rarefy, thin*); *adj.* [ă-тé-ню-ăт] исхудáвший (*emaciated, slender*); разжи́женный (*rarefied*)

attest [ă-тéст] *vt.* свидéтельствовать (*witness*); удостоверя́ть (*testify*); приводи́ть к прися́ге (*put on oath*)

attestation [æ-тĕс-тэ́й-шăн] *sn.* аттестáт, свидéтельство; показáние (*testimony*)

attestor [æ-тéс-тăр] *sm.* свидéтель

attic [æ-тĭк] *sn.* мансáрда, чердáк

attire [ă-тáй-ăр] *sn.* наря́д, одея́ние, плáтье; *vt.* одевáть, украшáть

attitude [æ-тĭ-тюд] *sn.* осáнка, пóза; отношéние (*regard*)

attorney [ă-тóр-ні] *sm.* повéренный; **— general** [— дже-не-рáл] генерáльный прокурóр

attract [ă-трéкт] *vt.* прельщáть, привлекáть; притя́гивать (*draw to oneself*)

attraction [ă-трéк-шăн] *sn.* привлекáтельность; притяжéние (*act of attracting*)

attractive [ă-трáк-тĭв] *adj.* привлекáтельный

attribute [ǽ-трĭ-бют] *sn.* атрибýт, свóйство; *vt.* [ǽ-трĭ-бют] припи́сывать

attribution [æ-трĭ-бю́-шăн] *sn.* припи́сывание

attributive [ă-трĭ-бю-тĭв] *adj.* атрибути́вный, припи́сываемый

attune [ă-тю́н] *vt.* приводи́ть в созвýчие

auburn [ó-бăрн] *adj.* каштáнового цвéта

auction [óк-шăн] *sn.* аукцио́н; распродáжа; *vt.* распродавáть (с молоткá)

auctioneer [ок-шă-ни́р] *sm.* аукцио́нщик

auctioneering [ок-шă-ни́-рĭн] *sn.* профéссия аукциони́ста

audacious [ō-дéй-шăс] *adj.* смéлый (*daring*); дéрзкий (*impertinent*)

audacity [ō-дǽ-сĭ-тĭ] *sn.* смéлость (*boldness*); дéрзость (*impudence*)

audible [ó-дĭбл] *adj.* внятный, слышный

audience [ó-дĭăнс] *sn.* аудитóрия, пýблика, слýшатели

audit [ó-дĭт] *sn.* ревизия, провéрка (счéтов); *vt.* проверять (счéты)

audition [о-ди́-шăн] *sn.* слýшание

auditor [ó-дĭ-тăр] *sm.* контролёр, ревизóр

auditorium [ō-дĭ-тó-рĭăм] *sn.* аудитóрия, зри́тельный зал (*ли́чивать*

augment [ог-мéнт] *vt.* увеличивать

augmentation [ōг-мăн-тэ́й-шăн] *sn.* прирóст, увеличéние

augur [ó-гăр] *sm.* авгýр, прорицáтель; *vt.i.* гадáть, предвещáть, предскáзывать

augury [ó-гю-рĭ] *sn.* предвещáние, предзнаменовáние

august [ō-гáст] *adj.* величéственный (*majestic*); почтённый (*venerable*); внуши́тельный (*imposing*)

August [ó-гăст] *sn.* áвгуст

aunt [ӓнт] *sf.* тётка, тётя

aural [ó-рăл] *adj.* ушнóй

auriferous [о-ри́-фă-рăс] *adj.* золотонóсный

aurora [ō-рó-рă] *sn.* ýтренняя заря́; **- australis** [- о-стрá-лĭс] ю́жное сия́ние; **- borealis** [- бо-рĭ-á-лĭс] сéверное сия́ние

auspice [óс-пĭс] *sn.* предзнаменовáние, **-s** [-ăс] *pl.* покрови́тельство

auspicious [ос-пи́-шăс] *adj.* благоприятный

austere [ос-ти́р] *adj.* стрóгий (*strict*); сурóвый (*grim, stern*); тéрпкий (*of flavour*)

austerity [ос-тé-рĭ-тĭ] *sn.* воздéржность; стрóгость; сурóвость

austral [ós-трăл] *adj.* ю́жный

Australian [ос-трéй-лĭăн] *sm.* австралиец; *adj.* австрали́йский

Austrian [óс-трĭăн] *sm.* австриец; *adj.* австри́йский

authentic [ō-фéн-тĭк] *adj.* достовéрный, подли́нный

author [ō-ēáр] *sm.* áвтор, писáтель, *m.*

authoritative [ō-ōó-рĭ-тă-тĭв] *adj.* авторитéтный, повели́тельный

authority [ŏ-ŏó-ṛi-ṭi] *sn.* авторите́т; власть (*power*); разреше́ние (*permission*)

authorize [ŏ-ŏá-райз] *vt.* дозволя́ть, уполномо́чивать

autobiography [ŏ-тă-бай-ŏ-гра́-фи] *sn.* автобиогра́фия

autocracy [ŏ-тó-крă-си] *sn.* самодержа́вие

autograph [ŏ-тă-граф] *sn.* авто́граф, оригина́л ру́кописи

automatic [ŏ-тă-ма́-тик] *adj.* автомати́ческий, маши́нный

autonomous [ŏ-тó-нă-мăс] *adj.* автоно́мный

autonomy [ŏ-тó-нă-ми] *sn.* автоно́мия

autumn [ó-тăм] *sn.* о́сень

autumnal [ŏ-тăм-нăл] *adj.* осе́нний

auxiliary [ŏгзі-ліă-ṛi] *adj.* вспомога́тельный

avail [ă-вэ́йл] *sn.* по́льза (*use*); вы́года (*profit*); **of no** – [ов нóу –] бесполе́зный; *vt.i.* быть поле́зным, помога́ть

available [ă-вэ́й-лăбл] *adj.* достижи́мый, досту́пный

avarice [ǽ-вă-рис] *sn.* ску́пость; жа́дность (*cupidity*)

avaricious [ǽ-вă-рі-шăс] *adj.* скупо́й

avenge [ă-ве́ндж] *vt.* мстить

avengeful [ă-ве́ндж-фул] *adj.* мсти́тельный

avenue [ǽ-ві-ню] *sn.* алле́я, прохо́д

average [ǽв-ридж] *sn.* сре́днее число́; сре́дний вы́вод; *adj.* сре́дний

averse [ă-вǿрс] *adj.* нерасполо́женный, нескло́нный

aversion [ă-вǿр-шăн] *sn.* антипа́тия, отвраще́ние

avert [ă-вǿрт] *vt.* отвраща́ть, отдаля́ть

aviary [эй-віă-ṛi] *sn.* пти́чник

aviation [эй-ві-эй-шăн] *sn.* авиа́ция

avid [ǽ-вид] *adj.* а́лчный, жа́дный

avoid [ă-во́йд] *vt.* избега́ть; *vi.* сторони́ться; уничтожа́ть (*destroy, quash*)

avoidance [ă-во́йд-ăнс] *sn.* избежа́ние

avow [ă-ва́у] *vt.* признава́ть; испове́дывать (*confess*)

avowal [ă-ва́у-ăл] *sn.* призна́ние

await [ă-у̌éйт] *vt.* ждать; ожида́ть

awake [ă-у̌éйк] *vt.* буди́ть; *vi.* просыпа́ться; **wide** – [у̌áйд –] *fig.* я́сно понима́ть; *adj.* бди́тельный, бо́дрствующий

award [ă-у̌о́рд] *sn.* пригово́р, реше́ние (*decision*); награ́да (*thing awarded*); *vt.* присужда́ть

aware [ă-у̌éр] *adj.* зна́ющий, осведомлённый, сознаю́щий

awareness [ă-у̌éр-ніс] *sn.* созна́ние

away [ă-у̌éй] *adv.* в отсу́тствии; –! прочь!

awe [ŏ] *sn.* страх (*dread*); благогове́ние (*veneration*); – **struck** [– страк] прони́кнутый благогове́нием

awful [ŏ-фул] *adj.* ужа́сный

awfully [ŏ-фу́-лі] *adv.* стра́шно; чрезвыча́йно (*extremely*)

awhile [ă-ўáйл] *adv.* ненадóлго

awkward [óк-ўă̆рд] *adj.* нелóвкий, неудóбный, неуклю́жий

awkwardness [óк-ўă̆рд-нис] *sn.* нелóвкость, неуклю́жесть

awl [ōл] *sn.* ши́ло

awn [ōн] *sn.* ость (колóса)

awning [ōн-инг] *sn.* паруси́новая кры́ша палубы (*canvas roof of deck*); навéс (*shed*)

awry [ă-рáй] *adv.* кóсо, кри́во (*crookedly*); ху́до (*a-miss*)

axe [экс] *sn.* топóр

axial [ă-ксíăл] *adj.* осевóй

axis [áк-сіс] *sn.* ось; воображáемая центрáльная ли́ния

axle [эксл] *sn.* ось (колесá)

azure [ă-жă̆р] *sn.* лазу́рь; я́сное нéбо (*clear sky*); *adj.* голубóй, лазу́рный

B

B [би] *mus.* си

babble [бэбл] *sn.* болтовня́ (*idle talk*); журчáние (*murmur, ripple*); *vt.i.* бормотáть, лепетáть; журчáть

baboon [бă-бу́н] *sm.* павиáн

baby [бэ́й-би] *sn.* младéнец, малю́тка

babyhood [бэ́й-би-худ] *sn.* младéнчество

babyish [бэ́й-би-иш] *adj.* дéтский, младéнческий, ребя́ческий

bachelor [бэ́-члă̆р] *sm.* холостя́к (*single*); баккалáвр (*person having a degree*)

back [бэк] *sn.* спинá (*person's back*); спи́нка (*chair-*

back); хребéт (*spine*); корешóк (*of book*); *adj.* зáдний; запоздáлый (*belated*); *adv.* назáд; *vt.i.* поддéрживать (*support*); осáживать, стáвить (*bet*); — **out** [— ăўт] уклоня́ться

backbone [бэк-бóун] *sn.* спиннóй хребéт; постоя́нство, твёрдость (*firmness*)

background [бэк-грáунд] *sn.* зáдний план; фон

backward [бэк-ўă̆рд] *adj.* отстáлый (*slow*); тупóй (*dull*); застéнчивый (*shy*)

backward(s) [бэк-ўă̆рд(з)] *adv.* назáд, обрáтно

backwater [бэк-ўо-тă̆р] *sn.* завóдь, застóй

bacon [бэ́й-кăн] *sn.* копчёная груди́нка

bad [бэд] *adj.* дурнóй, плохóй, скве́рный; испóрченный (*defective*)

badge [бэдж] *sn.* значóк; отличи́тельный знак

badger [бэ́-джă̆р] *sm.* барсу́к; *vt.* надоедáть (*tease*)

baffle [бэфл] *vt.* препя́тствовать (*impede*); расстрáивать (*disconcert*); стáвить втупи́к (*perplex*)

bag [бэг] *sn.* мешóк; су́мка (*lady's*); *vt.* класть в мешóк; *coll.* завладéвать (*take possession of*); *vi.* оттопы́риваться (*bulge, hang loosely*)

baggage [бэ́-гідж] *sn.* багáж; *mil.* обóз

bagpipe [бэ́г-пайп] *sn.* волы́нка

bail [бэйл] *sn.* залóг, поручи́тельство; **on** — [он —] на пору́ки; *vt.* брать на пору́ки, поручи́ться; вычéрпывать вóду (*throw out water*)

bailiff [бэ́й-ліф] *sn.* ста́роста, судебный прис́тав

bait [бэйт] *sn.* искушение; приманка (*allurement*); наживка (*food to entice prey*); *vt.* прикармливать (*lure by food*); приманивать (*entice*)

baize [бэйз] *sn.* байка

bake [бэйк] *vt.i.* печь; обжигать (*harden by heat*)

bakehouse [бэ́й-хаўс] *sn.* пека́рня

baker [бэ́й-кăр] *sm.* бу́лочник, пе́карь

bakery [бэ́й-кă-рі] *sn.* пека́рня; бу́лочная; ремесло́ пека́ря (*trade*)

balance [бэ́-лăнс] *sn.* равнове́сие; ве́сы (*weighing apparatus*); ма́ятник (часо́в) (*of clock*); оста́ток (*remainder*); *vt.i.* держа́ть в равнове́сии; взве́шивать (*weigh*)

balcony [бэ́л-кă-ні] *sn.* балко́н

bald [бôлд] *adj.* лы́сый; убо́гий (*meagre*, *pitiable*); обнажённый (*bare*)

baldness [бôлд-ніс] *sn.* плеши́вость; убо́гость

bale [бэйл] *sn.* ки́па, тюк

baleful [бэ́йл-фўл] *adj.* гро́зный, печа́льный; па́губный (*pernicious*); зло́бный (*malignant*)

balk, baulk [бôк] *sn.* ба́лка; бревно́; препя́тствие (*hindrance*); *vt.i.* расстра́ивать (*thwart*); меша́ть (*hinder*)

ball [бôл] *sn.* шар (*sphere*); мяч (*for games*); бал (*dance*); − of the eye [− ов ôй ай] глазно́е я́блоко

ballad [бэ́-лăд] *sn.* балла́да, пе́сня

ballast [бэ́-лăст] *sn.* бал-

ласт; ще́бень (*slag*, *etc. for road making*); *vt.* грузи́ть балла́стом

ball-bearing [бôл-бэ́-рін] *sn.* ша́риковый подши́пник

ballet [ба́-лэ] *sn.* бале́т

balloon [ба-лу́н] *sn.* возду́шный шар

ballot [бэ́-лăт] *sn.* баллоти́ровка; та́йное голосова́ние (*secret voting*); *vi.* баллоти́ровать; тяну́ть жре́бий (*draw lots*)

ballot-box [бэ́-лăт-бокс] *sn.* избира́тельная у́рна

balm [бам] *sn.* бальза́м; болеутоля́ющее сре́дство (*soothing medium*)

balmy [ба́-мі] *adj.* бальза́мный; души́стый (*fragrant*); успока́ивающий (*soothing*); мя́гкий (*soft*)

balustrade [бэ́-лă-стрэйд] *sn.* балюстра́да, пери́ла

bamboo [бэм-бу́] *sn.* бамбу́к

ban [бэн] *sn.* запреще́ние (*prohibition*); *vt.* запреща́ть

banal [бэй-нăл] *adj.* бана́льный; по́шлый

band [бэнд] *sn.* завя́зка (*string*, *tie*); полоса́ (*strip*); о́бруч (*iron*); сою́з (*bond of union*); орке́стр (духово́й) (*of men*); *vt.* составля́ть ба́нду, ша́йку

bandage [бэ́н-дідж] *sn.* бинт, банда́ж, повя́зка; *vt.* бинтова́ть, перевя́зывать

bandit [бэ́н-діт] *sn.* банди́т, разбо́йник

bandmaster [бэнд-ма́с-тăр] *sn.* капельме́йстер

bandsman [бэ́ндз-мăн] *sm.* музыка́нт (орке́стра)

baneful [бэ́йн-фўл] *adj.* ядови́тый; ги́бельный

bang [бӕн] *sn.* удáр (*blow*); хлóпанье (*slapping*); взрыв (*explosion*); *vt.i.* удáрить; хлóпать

bangle [бӕнгл] *sn.* запя́стие

banish [бӕ-ниш] *vt.* высылáть, изгоня́ть

banishment [бӕ-ниш-мӓнт] *sn.* вы́сылка, изгнáние

banister [бӕ-нис-тӓр] *sn.* перила

bank [бӕнк] *sn.* нáсыпь (*embankment*); плóский бéрег (*of river*); бáнка, отмéль (*shallow*); *com.* банк; – **holiday** [– хó-ли-дэй] общéственный прáздник (*holiday*); *vt.* окружáть вáлом (*heap up*); *com.* класть в банк

banker [бӕн-кӓр] *sm.* банки́р; банкомёт (*in games*)

bankrupt [бӕнк-рапт] *sm.* банкрóт; *adj.* несостоя́тельный

bankruptcy [бӕнк-рапт-сi] *sn.* банкрóтство

banner [бӕ-нӓр] *sn.* знáмя, флаг

banns [бӕнз] *sn. pl.* церкóвное оглашéние; **publish the** – [пáб-лиш ðа –] оглашáть о брáке

banquet [бӕн-кэт] *sn.* банкéт, пир, угощéние; *vt.* угощáть; *vi.* пировáть

bantam [бӕн-там] *sm., f.* мáленькая кýрица (*fowl*)

banter [бӕн-тӓр] *sn.* насмéшка, шýтка; *vi.* подшýчивать

baptism [бӕп-тiзм] *sn.* крести́ны, крещéние

baptismal [бӕп-тiз-мал] *adj.* крéстный

baptize [бӕп-тáйз] *vt.* крести́ть

bar [бáр] *sn.* полосá (*дéрева, желéза, мы́ла и пр.*), (*of wood, iron, soap, etc.*); плитка (*slab*); сли́ток (*ingot*); *mus.* такт; буфéт (*in hotel, etc.*); препя́тствие (*hindrance, obstacle*); *leg.* адвокатýра (*fasten*); преграждáть (*obstruct*); исключáть (*exclude*)

barbarian [бáр-бӓ-риӓн] *sm.* вáрвар; *adj.* вáрварский

barbaric [бáр-бӕ-рik] *adj.* жестóкий, инозéмный

barbarity [бáр-бӕ-рi-тi] *sn.* бесчеловéчность, грýбость

barber [бáр-бӓр] *sm.* парикмáхер, цырю́льник

bard [бáрд] *sm.* кéльтский менестрéль; поэт

bare [бэр] *adj.* гóлый (*naked*); обнажённый (*unclothed, uncovered*); скýдный (*scanty*)

barefaced [бэр-фэйсд] *adj.* бессты́дный, нáглый

barely [бэр-лi] *adv.* едвá (*scarcely*); тóлько (*only*)

bareness [бэр-нiс] *sn.* наготá, неприкры́тость; бéдность (*poorness*)

bargain [бáр-гiн] *sn.* сдéлка, торг; вы́годная покýпка (*profitable purchase*); *vi.* торговáться

barge [бáрдж] *sn.* бáржа, шлю́пка

bargee [бáр-джи] *sm.* лóдочник

bark [бáрк] *sn.* корá (*дéрева*); лай (*of dog*); бáрка (*vessel*); *vt.* ошкýривать (*a tree*); обдирáть (*skin*); дуби́ть (*tan*); ля́ть (*dog*)

barley [бáр-лi] *sn.* ячмéнь

barmaid [ба́р-мэйд] *sf.* буфе́тчица

barn [ба́рн] *sn.* амба́р, жи́тница, сара́й

barometer [бæ-ро́-ми-тăр] *sn.* баро́метр

baron [бæ-рăн] *sm.* баро́н

baronetsy [бæ-рă-нęт-сі] *sn.* зва́ние бароне́та

barrack [бǽ-рăк] *sn.* бара́к; *pl. mil.* каза́рма

barrage [бǽ-рăж] *sn.* плоти́на (*barrier*); *mil.* огнева́я заве́са (*dam*)

barrel [бǽ-рăл] *sn.* бочо́нок (*wooden vessel*); ствол (*of rifle*)

barrel-organ [бǽ-рăл-о́р-гăн] *sn.* шарма́нка

barren [бǽ-рăн] *adj.* бесплодный; бесто́лковый, тупо́й (*dull*)

barricade [бæ-рі-кэ́йд] *sn.* баррика́да, прегра́да; *vt.* загроможда́ть

barrier [бǽ-ріăр] *sn.* барье́р, заста́ва, шла́гбаум

barrister [бǽ-ріс-тăр] *sn.* адвока́т

barrow [бǽ-роў] *sn.* курга́н (*tumulus*); та́чка (*wheelbarrow*); носи́лки (*hand-cart*)

barter [ба́р-тăр] *vt.* меня́ть, обме́нивать

base [бэйс] *sn.* ба́зис, осно́ва (*foundation*); пьедеста́л, цо́коль (*pedestal, plinth*); *chem.* основа́ние; *adj.* неблагоро́дный (*despicable, ignoble*)

baseless [бэ́йс-лıс] *adj.* необосно́ванный, неоснова́тельный

basement [бэ́йс-мăнт] *sn.* основа́ние, фунда́мент; подва́льное помеще́ние (*storey below ground level*)

baseness [бэ́йс-ніс] *sn.* ни́зость, по́длость

bashful [бǽш-фул] *adj.* засте́нчивый, ро́бкий (*sheepish*)

basic [бэ́й-сık] *adj.* основно́й

basin [бэ́й-сın] *sn.* ми́ска, таз (*vessel*); резервуа́р (*vessel*); бу́хта, док (*bay, dock, harbour*); бассе́йн (*of river*)

basis [бэ́й-сıс] *sn.* ба́зис, основа́ние

bask [бăск] *vi.* гре́ться (на со́лнце, у огня́, и пр.)

basket [ба́с-кіт] *sn.* корзи́на; **—maker** [—мэ́й-кăр] *sn.* корзи́нщик

basketry [ба́с-кіт-рі] *sn.* корзи́ночное произво́дство (*industry*); плетёные изде́лия (*basket-work*)

bass [бэйс] *s. mus.* бас; *adj.* ба́совый, ни́зкий (*of voice*)

bassinet [бæ-сı-нęт] *sn.* колыбе́ль

bassoon [бă-су́н] *sn. mus.* фаго́т

bastard [ба́с-тăрд] *sn.* внебра́чный ребёнок (*child*); подде́лка (*thing*); ублю́док (*mongrel*); *adj.* внебра́чный (*out of wedlock*); подде́льный (*counterfeit*)

baste [бэйст] *vt.* смётывать (*tack*); полива́ть жарко́е на ве́ртеле (*in cooking*); па́лкой (*cudgel, thrash*)

bat [бæт] *s.* лету́чая мышь (*animal*); дуби́на, жезл (*wooden implement*); бита́ (*cricket*); *vt.i.* игра́ть бито́й

batch [бæч] *sn.* ку́чка, сорт

bate [бэйт] *vt.i.* оставля́ть, убавля́ть, уступа́ть

bath [ба́θ] *sn.* ва́нна (*vessel*); ба́ня (*room*); мытьё, умыва́ние 'wash, washing)

bathe [бэйѳ] *sn.* купанье; *vt.* обмывать, окунать; *vi.* купаться

bather [бэй-ѳəр] *sm.* купальщик

bathing [бэй-ѳий] *sn.* купанье

baton [бэ-тэн] *sn.* жезл (*rod, staff*); дирижёрская палочка (*conductor's*)

batsman [бэтс-мэн] *m.* игрок, отбиватель

batter [бэ-тəр] *sn.* взбитое тесто; *tvp.* сбитый шрифт; *vt.* повторительно бить (*strike repeatedly*); ломать (*break*)

battery [бэ-тə-рі] *sn.* батарея

battle [бэтл] *sn.* битва, бой, сражение; *vi.* бороться, сражаться

battlement [бэтл-мэнт] *sn.* зубчатые стены

battleship [бэтл-шіп] *sn.* броненосец, линейный корабль

bawl [бол] *vi.* кричать, орать

bay [бэй] *sn.* лавровое дерево (*tree*); бухта, залив (*creek, gulf*); ниша (*recess*); выступ (*of window*); гнедая лошадь (*horse*); *adj.* гнедой, каштановый (*colour*)

bayonet [бэй-ə-нэт] *sn.* штык

bazaar [бə-зар] *sn.* восточный базар (*oriental*); рынок (*market*)

be [би] *vi.* быть; существовать (*exist*)

beach [бич] *sn.* взморье, пляж; *vt.* вытащить на берег

beachcomber [бич-коу-мəр] *sm.* расточитель

beacon [би-кəн] *sn.* маяк (*lighthouse*); сигнальный огонь (*signal-fire*)

bead [бид] *sn.* бисерина, шарик; *pl.* чётки

beak [бик] *sn.* клюв (*bird's*); носик сосуда (*spout*); крючковатый нос (*nose*)

beaker [би-кəр] *sn.* кубок, большая чаша

beam [бим] *sn.* балка, перекладина (*timber*); луч (*ray*); *vt.i.* сиять (*shine*); светить (*light*)

bean [бин] *sn.* боб; фасоль (*haricot*)

bear [бэр] *sm.* медведь; грубиян (*person*); *vt.i.* носить (*carry*); выдержать (*sustain*); выдерживать (*support*); терпеть (*suffer*); **testimony** [– тэ-сті-мə-ні] свидетельствовать

bearable [бэ-рəбл] *adj.* сносный

beard [бирд] *sn.* борода; *bot.* ость

bearer [бэ-рəр] *sm.* носитель; *com.* податель, предъявитель

bearing [бэ-рій] *sn.* ношение (*carriage*); терпение (*patience*); поведение (*behaviour*); отношение (*aspect, relation*); *pl. tech.* подшипники

beast [бист] *s.* зверь, *m.*; скотина (*also fig.*)

beastly [бист-лі] *adj.* отвратительный (*disgusting*); досадный (*annoying*); грубый (*rude, unmannered*)

beat [бит] *sn.* удар (*stroke, as on drum*); биение (*throbbing*); дозор, обход (*round*); *mus.* такт; *vt.* бить, ударять; *mus.* отбивать (такт)

beaten [би-тән] *adj.* би́тый, изби́тый

beating [би-тий] *sn.* битьё, побо́и

beatitude [бі-ǽ-ті-тюд] *sn.* блаже́нство

beautiful [бю́-ті-фул] *adj.* краси́вый, прекра́сный; превосхо́дный (*excellent*)

beauty [бю́-ті] *sn.* красота́ (*thing*); *sf.* краса́вица

beaver [би́-вăр] *s.* бобр (*rodent*); бобро́вый мех (*fur*)

because [бі-ко́з] *conj.* потому́ что, ра́ди того́; *prep.* – of [– ов] из-за, ра́ди

beck [бек] *sn.* знак (*nod*); манове́ние (*gesture*)

beckon [бе́-кăн] *vt.* кива́ть, мани́ть

become [бі-ка́м] *vt.i.* станови́ться, стать; годи́ться (*suit*)

becoming [бі-ка́-мій] *adj.* прили́чный, соотве́тствующий

bed [бед] *sn.* посте́ль (*clothes*); гряда́ клу́мба, цветни́к (*of flowers*); дно, ру́сло (*of river*); слой, пласт (*layer*); основа́ние (*base*); **go to –** [го́у ту –] ложи́ться спать

bedding [бе́-дій] *sn.* посте́льные принадле́жности

bedeck [бі-де́к] *vt.* украша́ть

bedroom [бе́д-рум] *sn.* спа́льня

bedside [бе́д-сайд] *sn.* у посте́ли больно́го

bedspread [бе́д-спред] *sn.* покрыва́ло

bedstead [бе́д-стед] *sn.* крова́ть

bedtime [бе́д-тайм] *sn.* вре́мя итти́ спать

bee [би] *s.* пчела́

beech [бич] *sn.* бук; *adj.* буко́вый

beef [биф] *sn.* говя́дина

beehive [би́-хайв] *sn.* у́лей

beer [бир] *sn.* пи́во

beeswax [би́з-уǽкс] *sn.* воск

beet [бит] *sn.* бе́лая свёкла, са́харная свекло́вица

beetle [битл] *s.* жук (*insect*); *tech.* ба́бка (*chuck*); *vt.* трамбова́ть; *vi.* нави́сать (*overhang*)

beetroot [би́т-рут] *sn.* кра́сная свёкла

befall [бі-фо́л] *vt.i.* происходи́ть, случа́ться

before [бі-фо́р] *adv.* вы́ше, впереди́, ра́ньше, уже́; *prep.* до, пе́ред; *conj.* пре́жде чем; скоре́е чем

beforehand [бі-фо́р-хǽнд] *adv.* вперёд, зара́нее

befriend [бі-фре́нд] *vt.* относи́ться дру́жески; покрови́тельствовать (*patronize, protect*); помога́ть (*help*)

beggar [бе́-гăр] *sm.* ни́щий, бедня́га (*penniless person*)

beggarly [бе́-гăр-лі] *adj.* бе́дный; ни́щенский

begging [бе́-гій] *sn.* ни́щенство

begin [бі-гі́н] *vt.* начина́ть

beginner [бі-гі́-нăр] *sm.* начина́ющий, новичо́к

beginning [бі-гі́-ній] *sn.* нача́ло

beguile [бі-гайл] *vt.* обма́нывать (*cheat*); развлека́ть (*charm, amuse*)

begrudge [бі-гра́дж] *vt.* зави́довать

behalf [бі-χáф] *sn.* вы́года, интере́с, по́льза; **on – of** [он – ов] от и́мени кого́-либо

behave [бі-χэ́йв] *vi.* поступа́ть; вести́ себя́; **– yourself!** [– юр-сéлф] веди́те себя́ прили́чно

behaviour [бі-χэ́й-віăр] *sn.* мане́ры, поведе́ние; **good – ** [гуд –] благонра́вие

behind [бі-χáйнд] *sn.* зад; *prep.* за; *prep., adv.* позади́, по́сле, сза́ди; с опозда́нием (*in arrear*); отста́лый, устаре́лый (*times*)

behold [бі-χóулд] *vt.* ви́деть, замеча́ть; *interj.* вот!, смотри́!

behove [бі-χóув] *vt.* подоба́ть, прили́чествовать

being [би́-ій] *s.* существо́ (*creature*); бытьё, существова́ние (*existence*)

belated [бі-лэ́й-тăд] *adj.* запозда́лый

belch [бэлч] *sn.* рыга́ние, отры́жка (*eructation*); *vi.* рыга́ть; изверга́ть (*emit fire*)

beleaguer [бі-ли́-ґăр] *vt.* окружа́ть, осажда́ть

belfry [бэ́л-фрі] *sn.* коло́-ко́льня

Belgian [бэ́л-джăн] *sm.* бельги́ец; *adj.* бельги́й-ский

belief [бі-ли́ф] *sn.* дове́рие (*confidence, trust*); вероиспове́дание (*religion*); убежде́ние (*conviction*); мне́ние (*opinion*); ве́ра (*faith*)

believe [бі-ли́в] *vt.* ве́рить (*accept as truth*); ду́мать, полага́ть (*think, suppose*)

believer [бі-ли́-вăр] *sm.* ве́рующий

bell [бэл] *sn.* ко́локол; коло́кольчик (*small bell*); звоно́к (*on door*)

belligerent [бі-лі́-джă-рăнт] *adj.* вои́нствующий, вою́ющий

bellow [бэ́-лоу] *sn.* мыча́ние, рев; *vi.* мыча́ть, реве́ть

bellows [бэ́-лоуз] *sn. pl.* разду́вальные мехи́

belly [бэ́-лі] *sn.* брю́хо, живо́т

belong [бі-ло́ŋ] *vi.* принадлежа́ть; относи́ться (*pertain*)

belongings [бі-ло́ŋ-інґз] *sn. pl.* ве́щи, принадле́жности

beloved [бі-ла́-вăд] *s., adj.* возлю́бленный, люби́мый; [бі-лавд] **to be – ** [ту би –] быть люби́мым

below [бі-ло́у] *adv., prep.* под, ни́же

belt [бэлт] *sn.* по́яс; реме́нь (*strap*)

bench [бэнч] *sn.* скаме́йка, скамья́ (*seat*); верста́к, стано́к (*worker's*); суд (*judge's*)

bend [бэнд] *sn.* изги́б, сгиб, поворо́т (*turn*); *vt.* гнуть, сгиба́ть (*inflect*); преклоня́ть (*bow*)

beneath [бі-ни́θ] *adv.* внизу́; *prep.* ни́же, под

benediction [бэ́-ні-ді́к-шăн] *sn.* благослове́ние

benefactor [бэ́-ні-фэ́к-тăр] *sm.* благоде́тель, жертвова́тель

beneficence [бі-не́-фі-сăнс] *sn.* благоде́тельность, благотвори́тельность

beneficial [бэ́-ні-фі́-шăл] *adj.* вы́годный, поле́зный; целе́бный (*salubrious*)

benefit [бé-ні-фіт] *sn.* вы́года, по́льза (*advantage*); при́быль (*increment*); theat. бенефи́с; *vt.i.* помога́ть (*help*); извлека́ть по́льзу (*derive profit*)

benevolence [бі-нé-вă-лăнс] *sn.* благоскло́нность, милосе́рдие

benevolent [бі-нé-вă-лăнт] *adj.* благожела́тельный

benign [бі-на́йн] *adj.* до́брый (*kind*); кро́ткий (*gentle*); снисходи́тельный (*condescending*)

bent [бент] *sn.* накло́нность, скло́нность

bequeath [бі-кўи́θ] *vt.* завеща́ть

bequest [бі-кўéст] *sn.* завеща́ние

bereave [бі-ри́в] *vt.* лиша́ть, отнима́ть

bereavement [бі-ри́в-мăнт] *sn.* лише́ние, поте́ря

berry [бé-рі] *sn.* я́года

berth [бăрθ] *sn.* ко́йка

beseech [бі-си́ч] *vt.* проси́ть, умоля́ть

beside [бі-са́йд] *prep.* во́зле, по́дле, ря́дом; по сравне́нию (*compared with*); — **self** [- ўăн-сéлф] вне себя́

besides [- бі-са́йдз] *adv.* вдоба́вок, прито́м, та́кже; *prep.* кро́ме того́

besiege [бі-сі́дж] *vt.* напада́ть, осажда́ть

best [бест] *adj.* (наи)лу́чший; *adv.* лу́чше всего́

bestial [бéс-тіăл] *adj.* ско́тский; развра́тный (*person*)

bestow [біс-то́ў] *vt.* дава́ть (*give*); одаря́ть (*confer*)

bet [бет] *sn.* пари́; ста́вка (*stake*); *vt.i.* держа́ть пари́

betray [бі-тре́й] *vt.* предава́ть; обма́нывать, обнару́живать (*reveal treacherously*)

betrayal [бі-тре́й-ăл] *sn.* преда́тельство

betroth [бі-тро́ўθ] *vt.* обручи́ть, помолви́ть

betrothal [бі-тро́ў-θăл] *sn.* обруче́ние, помо́лвка

better [бé-тăр] *adj.* лу́чший; *adv.* лу́чше; *vt.i.* улучша́ть; превосходи́ть (*surpass*)

between [бі-тўи́н] *adv.*, *prep.* ме́жду

bevel [бé-вăл] *sn.* ма́лка, науго́льник (*tool*); скос (*slope from the right-angle*); *vt.i.* коси́ть, коси́ться

beverage [бé-вă-рідж] *sn.* напи́ток, питьё

bevy [бé-ві] *sn.* ста́я (*flock, shoal etc.*); о́бщество, собра́ние (*of people*)

bewail [бі-ўэ́йл] *vt.* опла́кивать; *vi.* сокруша́ться

beware [бі-ўэ́р] *vi.* бере́чься, остерега́ться

bewilder [бі-ўі́л-дăр] *vt.* запу́тывать, пу́тать; смуща́ть (*perplex*)

bewitch [бі-ўі́ч] *vt.* околдо́вывать; очаро́вывать (*captivate*)

beyond [бі-йо́нд] *sn.* бу́дущая жизнь; неизве́стность; *adv.* вдали́, на расстоя́нии; *prep.* вне, за, пода́ль, све́рху, све́рх

bias [ба́й-ăс] *sn.* укло́н (*declivity*); предубежде́ние (*prejudice*); скло́нность (*propensity*); *vt.* влия́ть (*influence*); наклоня́ть (*incline*)

bib [біб] *sn.* де́тский нагру́дник

Bible [ба́йбл] *sn.* би́блия

biblical [бі-блі-кăл] *adj.* библейский

bibliographical [бі-блио-грă-фі-кăл] *adj.* библиографический

bibliography [бі-блі-ó-грă-фі] *sn.* библиография

biceps [бáй-сепс] *sn.* бицепс, двуглавая мышца

bicker [бі-кăр] *vi.* спорить, ссориться

bicycle [бáй-сікл] *sn.* велосипед

bid [бід] *sn.* предложение цены; надбавка; *vt.i.* надбавлять, предлагать цену; велеть (*command*)

biennial [бай-é-ніăл] *adj.* двухлетний

bier [бир] *sn.* катафалк; *pl.* носилки

big [біг] *adj.* большой, обширный; важный (*important*)

bigamist [бí-гă-міст] *sn.* двоеженец; *sf.* двоемужница

bigamy [бí-гă-мі] *sn.* бигамия, двоебрачие

bigoted [бí-гă-тід] *adj.* безрассудный, фанатический

bigotry [бí-гăт-рі] *sn.* слепая приверженность, ханжество

bilateral [бай-лáт-рăл] *adj.* двусторонний

bile [байл] *sn.* жёлчь (*fluid*); болезнь печени (*illness*)

bilious [бí-ліăс] *adj.* жёлчный

bill [біл] *sn.* клюв (*beak*); узкий мыс (*narrow promontory*); амбар (*halberd*); билль, законопроект (*act of Parliament*); счёт (*account*); афиша, плакат (*pos-*

ter); – of exchange [– ов экс-чэйндж] вексель; – of lading [– ов лэй-дій] коносамент; *vt.* объявлять на плакатах; расклеивать афиши

billet [бí-літ] *sn. mil.* билет для постоя; помещение для постоя (*building where troops are lodged*); *vt.* расквартировать

billiards [бі-ліăрдз] *sn. pl.* бильярд

billow [бí-лоу] *sn.* большая волна, вал; *vi.* вздыматься, волноваться

bin [бін] *sn.* бункер, ящик

bind [байнд] *vt.* вязать, перевязывать; переплетать (*book*); обязывать (*implying obligation*)

binder [бáйн-дăр] *sm.* переплётчик; *sn.* сноповязалка

bindery [бáйн-дă-рі] *sn.* переплётная мастерская

binding [бáйн-дій] *sn.* переплёт (*book-cover*); завязка (*band*); *adj.* обязательный (*obligatory*); скрепляющий (*tightening*)

biography [бай-ó-грă-фі] *sn.* биография

biology [бай-ó-ло-джі] *sn.* биология

birch [бöрч] *sn.* берёза (*tree*); розга (*twig*); *vt.* пороть (*flog*)

bird [бöрд] *sn.* птица; – of prey [– ов прэй] хищная птица

birth [бöрθ] *sn.* рождение (*being born*); роды (*childbirth*); источник, начало (*origin, beginning*); происхождение (*descent, lineage*)

birthday [бёрθ-дэй] *sn.* день рождения

birthmark [бёрθ-мáрк] *sn.* родинка

birth-place [бёрθ-плэйс] *sn.* месторождение

biscuit [бíс-кіт] *sn.* бисквит; сухарь, *m.* (*rusk*)

bisect [бай-сéкт] *vt.* разделять (разрезать) пополам

bisection [бай-сéк-шäн] *sn.* деление пополам

bishop [бí-шäп] *sm.* епископ; *sn.* слон (*chess*)

bit [бíт] *sn.* кусочек (*small piece*); немножко (*small quantity*); удила (*bridle-bit*); пёрка (*drilling-piece*); мундштук (*bridle mouth-piece*)

bitch [біч] *sf.* сука (*dog*); самка (*other animals*)

bite [байт] *sn.* укус; кусочек (*morsel*); клёв, приманка (*for fishing*); *vt.* кусать; клевать (*fishing*)

biting [бáй-тіŋ] *adj.* ёдкий (*caustic*); острый (*sharp*); резкий (*harsh*); язвительный (*scathing*)

bitter [бí-тäр] *sn.* горькое пиво (*beer*); *adj.* горький (*taste*); озлоблённый (*angry, vexed*); мучительный (*painful, poignant*)

bitterness [бí-тäр-ніс] *sn.* горечь

black [бläк] *adj.* чёрный (*colour*); тёмный (*dark*); мрачный (*gloomy*); *vt.* чернить

blackbeetle [бläк-бíтл] *sn.* таракан

blackberry [бläк-бе-рі] *sn.* ежевика, черника

blackbird [бläк-бёрд] *s.* чёрный дрозд

blackboard [бläк-бóрд] *sn.* классная доска

blacken [бläк-кäн] *vt.* чернить; позорить (*defame*)

blackguard [бläк-гáрд] *sm.* мерзавец, подлец, прохвост

blacking [бläк-кіŋ] *sn.* вакса

blackish [бläк-кіш] *adj.* черноватый

blacklead [бläк-лед] *sn.* графит

blackmail [бläк-мэйл] *sn.* вымогательство

blackness [бläк-ніс] *sn.* темнота, чернота

blacksmith [бläк-сміθ] *sm.* кузнец

bladder [блä-дäр] *sn.* пузырь, *m.*

blade [блэйд] *sn.* клинок, лёзвие (*steel*); былинка, лист, травинка (*grass*); лопасть (*oar*)

blame [блэйм] *sn.* порицание, упрёк (*reproof*); вина (*guilt*)

blameless [блэйм-ліс] *adj.* безупречный

blanch [блäнч] *vt.* белить

blandishment [блäн-діш-мäнт] *sn.* ласкательство, обольщение

blank [бläнк] *sn.* бланк, пробел; *adj.* пустой (*void*); — **verse** [— вёрс] бéлые стихи

blanket [бläн-кіт] *sn.* шерстяное одеяло

blare [блэр] *sn.* рёв, шум; *vt.i.* громко трубить

blaspheme [блäс-фíм] *vt.i.* богохульствовать

blasphemy [бläс-фі-мі] *sn.* богохульство

blast [бläст] *sn.* дуновение (*puff, waft*); порыв (*gust*); взрыв (*explosion*); *vt.* губить, разрушать; взрывать

blast-furnace [бла́ст-фœрніс] *sn.* до́менная печь

blatant [бле́й-та̀нт] *adj.* на́глый (*of lie*); крикли́вый (*vociferous*)

blaze [блэйз] *sn.* пла́мя (*flame*); блеск (*glare*); *vi.* горе́ть, пыла́ть

blazer [бле́й-за́р] *sn.* спорти́вная ку́ртка

bleach [блич] *vt.* подбе́ливать

bleak [блик] *adj.* откры́тый (*bare, open*); незащищённый от ве́тра (*windswept*); мра́чный (*dreary*)

bleating [блі́-тӣн] *sn.* бле́яние

bleed [блид] *vi.* кровоточи́ть; сочи́ться (*of trees*); вымога́ть (*extort*)

bleeding [блі́-дӣн] *sn.* кровотече́ние

blemish [бле́-мӣш] *sn.* недоста́ток (*flaw*); пятно́ (*stain*); поро́к (*defect*)

blench [бленч] *vt.i.* отступа́ть

blend [бленд] *sn.* смесь, смеше́ние; *vt.i.* сме́шивать, сме́шаться, соединя́ть

bless [блес] *vt.* благословля́ть, освяща́ть; призыва́ть (*invoke*)

blessed [бле́-сід] *adj.* блаже́нный (*blissful*); счастли́вый (*fortunate*); чти́тельный (*revered*)

blessing [бле́-сӣн] *sn.* благоде́ние, благослове́ние

blight [блайт] *sn.* ржа; *vt.* губи́ть; по́ртить

blind [блайнд] *sn.* нагла́зник, шо́ры (*blinker(s)*); што́ра (*window*); отгово́рка, предло́г (*pretext*); тупи́к

(*alley*); *adj.* слепо́й (*without sight*); безрассу́дный (*devoid of insight*); *vt.* ослепля́ть, затемня́ть (*obscure*)

blindness [бла́йнд-ніс] *sn.* ослепле́ние, слепота́

blink [блінк] *sn.* мерца́ние; взгляд (*gleam*); *vt.i.* мига́ть, щу́риться (*move eyelids*); мерца́ть (*twinkle*)

blinkers [блі́н-ка́рз] *sn. pl.* нагла́зники, шо́ры

bliss [бліс] *sn.* блаже́нство, дово́льствие (*gladness*); благополу́чие (*happiness*)

blister [блі́с-та́р] *sn.* волды́рь, *m.*; пузы́рь, *m.*; *vt.i.* покрыва́ться волдыря́ми

blithe [блайθ] *adj.* весёлый, ра́достный

blizzard [блі-за́рд] *sn.* мете́ль, снежна́я бу́ря

bloated [бло́у-тід] *adj.* разду́тый

bloater [бло́у-та́р] *s.* копчёная селёдка

blob [блоб] *sn.* ка́пля (*drop of liquid*); кля́кса (*ink*)

block [блок] *sn.* чурба́н (*log*); болва́нка (*mould*); фо́рма (*for hats*); ряд (*of houses*); заде́ржка (*jam in traffic*); зато́р (*obstruction*); *vt.* загора́живать (*enclose, fence, jam, obstruct*); заде́лывать (*stop up*); формова́ть (*hats*)

blockade [бло-ке́йд] *sn.* блока́да, обложе́ние; *vt.* блоки́ровать

blockhead [бло́к-хѐд] *sn.* болва́н, дура́к

blond(e) [блонд] *sm.* блонди́н; *sf.* блонди́нка; *adj.* белоку́рый, ру́сый

blood [блад] *sn.* кровь

bloodhound [блád-хӑунд] s. ищéйка; fig. сы́щик (detective)

bloodless [блáд-лíс] adj. бескрóвный (pale)

bloodshed [блáд-шéд] sn. кровопролúтие

bloodshot [блáд-шот] adj. налúтый крóвью (о глазáх)

bloodthirsty [блáд-θер-стí] adj. кровожáдный

blood-vessel [блáд-ве-сăл] sn. кровенóсный сосýд

bloody [блá-дí] adj. кровáвый, окровавлённый

bloom [блум] sn. цветóк (flower); расцвéт (blossoming); цветéние (florescence); румя́нец (flush); vi. цвестú

bloomers [блу-мăрз] sn. pl. жéнские панталóны

blooming [блу-мíн] adj. цветýщий

blossom [блó-сăм] sn. цвет, цветéние; vi. цвестú; распускáться (fig. blossom out)

blot [блот] sn. пятнó (stain); кля́кса (of ink); vt. пáчкать; **- out** [- áут] вычёркивать; изглáживать (efface); высýшивать (dry with blotting paper)

blotch [блоч] sn. прыщ (on skin); кля́кса (ink)

blotting-pad [блó-тíн-пæд] sn. бювáр

blotting-paper [блó-тíн пéй-пăр] sn. промокáтельная бумáга

blouse [блауз] sn. блýза

blow [блóу] sn. удáр (hard stroke); fig. бéдствие (disaster); потрясéние, шок (shock); vt.i. вéять, дуть; звучáть (wind instrument); **- out** [- áут] тушúть; **- up**

[- ап] раздувáть; взрывáть (explode)

blowfly [блóу-флай] s. мя́сная мýха

blowpipe [блóу-пайп] sn. пая́льная трýбка

blubber [блá-бăр] sn. ворвáнь; плач (weeping); vt.i. грóмко плáкать, ревéть (sob)

bludgeon [блá-джăн] sn. дубúнка, кистéнь

blue [блю] sn. сúняя крáска (colour); (launderer's); adj. голубóй, сúний (colour); vt. синúть

bluebell [блю-бéл] sn. колокóльчик

bluebottle [блю-ботл] sn. василёк

bluff [блаф] sn. обмáн (delusion); запýгивание (intimidation); adj. грýбый, неотёсанный (clumsy, uncouth)

bluish [блю-иш] adj. синевáтый

blunder [блáн-дăр] sn. грýбая ошúбка; vi. ошибáться

blunt [блант] adj. тупóй (not sharp); прямóй, рéзкий (plain-spoken); vt. притупля́ть

bluntness [блáнт-нíс] sn. тýпость; грýбость (roughness); прямотá (directness)

blur [блер] sn. смýтность (dimness); помáрка (smear); vt. замарáть, запáчкать; дéлать нея́сным, потускнéть (make dim)

blurt [блерт] vt. сболтнýть; **- out** [- áут] вы́палить

blush [блаш] sn. взгляд, вид (glance); мелькáние (glimpse); румя́нец (rosy glow); vi. краснéть; застыдúться (redress with shame)

blushing [блá-шiй] *adj.* краснéющий, румяный

bluster [блáс-тäр] *sn.* шум (*noise*); бушевáние (*wind*); *vi.* бурлúть; шумéть

boa [бóў-ä] *s.* удáв (*snake*); бóа, горжéтка (*wrap*)

boar [бôр] *sm.* бóров, кабáн; **wild** — [уáйлд —] *s.* вепрь

board [бôрд] *sn.* доскá, плáнка, картóн (*cardboard*); совéт (*council*); борт (*of ship*); *pl.* подмóстки (*of stage*); **— of directors** [— ов дäй-рéк-тäрз] правлéние; **— of trade** [— ов трэйд] торгóвая палáта; *vt.i.* настилáть доскáми (*cover with boards*); столовáться (*be provided with meals*); сесть на корáбль (*embark*)

boarder [бôр-дäр] *sm.* пансионéр

boarding-house [бôр-дúнхäўс] *sn.* пансиóн

boarding-school [бôр-дúнскўл] *sn.* учéбное заведéние с пансиóном

boast [бóуст] *sn.* спесь, хвастовствó; *vi.* хвáстаться

boastful [бóуст-фўл] *adj.* хвастлúвый

boat [бóут] *sn.* лóдка; парохóд (*steamer*)

boatman [бóут-мäн] *sm.* лóдочник

bobbin [бó-бiн] *sn.* катýшка, коклюшка, шпýлька

bob-sleigh [бóб-слэй] *sn.* спортúвные сáни

bode [бóуд] *vt.i.* предвещáть (*foretell*); предчýвствовать (*presage*)

bodice [бó-дiс] *sn.* корсáж, лифчик

bodily [бó-дi-лi] *adj.* телéсный; *adv.* всецéло, целикóм

body [бó-дi] *sn.* плоть, тéло; кóрпус, остóв (*carcass*); человéк (*human being*); тулóвище (*trunk*); сýщность (*substance*)

bodyguard [бó-дi-гäрд] *sm.* телохранúтель; *sn.* охрáна (*retinue*)

bog [бог] *sn.* болóто, топь, трясúна

bogus [бóў-рäс] *adj.* поддéльный, фальшúвый

bogy [бóў-гi] *sm.* дьявол (*devil*); дýхи (*goblins*); пугáло (*bugbear*)

boil [бóйл] *sn.* фурýнкул, чирéй; *vt.i.* варúть, кипятúть; кипéть; сердúться (*be agitated*)

boiler [бóй-лäр] *sn.* котéл

boisterous [бóй-стрäс] *adj.* бýрный, шумлúвый

bold [бóулд] *adj.* дéрзкий (*audacious*); смéлый (*brave*); отчётливый (*handwriting type*)

boldness [бóулд-нiс] *sn.* дéрзость; смéлость

bolster [бóул-стäр] *sn.* изголóвье; *vt.i.* подпирáть вáликом; **to — up** [ту — ап] поддéрживать

bolt [бóулт] *sn.* болт; засóв; удáр мóлнии (*thunderbolt*); *adv.* прямо (*upright*); *vt.i.* запирáть на засóв; скреплять болтáми, исчезáть, убегáть (*vanish, run away*); понестú (*of horse*); плóхо разжёвывать, проглáтывать (*food*)

bomb [бом] *sn.* бóмба; *vt.i.* бомбардúровать; сбрáсывать бóмбы

bombardment [бом-ба́рд-мӑнт] *sn.* бомбардиро́вка

bombastic [бом-ба́с-тік] *adj.* наду́тый, напы́щенный

bomber [бо́-мӑр] *sn.* бомбо-мета́тель; *sm.* бомбардиро́в-щик

bond [бонд] *sn.* связь, у́зы; обяза́тельство (*obligation*); *pl.* око́вы (*fetters*)

bondage [бо́н-дідж] *sn.* ра́б-ство, крепостна́я зави́си-мость, заточе́ние (*incarcera-tion*); обяза́тельство (*pledge*)

bone [бо́ун] *sn.* кость; *vt.* снима́ть мя́со с косте́й; − **dry** [− драй] иссо́хший

bonfire [бо́н-фай-ӑр] *sn.* кос-тёр

bonnet [бо́-ніт] *sn.* да́мская шля́па; че́пчик

bonny [бо́-ні] *adj.* весёлый, здоро́вый, краси́вый

bonus [бо́у-нӑс] *sn.* пре́мия, танте́ма; доба́вочное воз-награжде́ние

bony [бо́у-ні] *adj.* кости́-стый, костля́вый

book [бук] *sn.* кни́га; *vt.* вноси́ть, впи́сывать (в кни́гу); зара́нее зака́зы-вать места́ (*for theatre, etc.*)

bookbinder [бу́к-байн-дӑр] *sm.* переплётчик

bookbinding [бу́к-байн-дій] *sn.* переплётное де́ло

bookcase [бу́к-кэйс] *sn.* кни́жный шкаф

booking-office [бу́-кін-о-фіс] *sn.* биле́тная ка́сса

book-keeper [бу́к-ки-пӑр] *sm.* бухга́лтер, счетово́д

book-keeping [бу́к-ки-пій] *sn.* счетово́дство

booklet [бу́к-літ] *sn.* кни́-жечка

bookmark [бу́к-мӑрк] *sn.* закла́дка

bookseller [бу́к-сӗ-лӑр] *sm.* книгопрода́вец

bookshop [бу́к-шоп] *sn.* кни́жный магази́н

bookstall [бу́к-стол] *sn.* кни́жный ларёк

boom [бу́м] *sn.* бревно́ (*float-ing barrier*); багор (*spar*); гул (*resonant sound*); *com.* бум; *vi.* производи́ть гул; *com.* шу́мно реклами́ровать

boon [бу́н] *sn.* про́сьба (*re-quest*); ми́лость, благодея́-ние (*favour*)

boot [бу́т] *sn.* сапо́г

bootee [бу́-ти́] *sn.* зи́мний боти́нок для дам и дете́й

booth [бу́с] *sn.* бу́дка

boot-tree [бу́т-три] *sn.* са-по́жная коло́дка

boots [бу́тс] *sm.* коридо́р-ный (*in hotel*); чисти́льщик сапо́г (*boot-cleaner*)

booty [бу́-ті] *sn.* добы́ча

booze [бу́з] *sn.* пья́ная пи-ру́шка (*drinking-bout*); пи́-во, во́дка, и пр. (*beer, spirits, etc.*); *vi.* напива́ться

border [бо́р-дӑр] *sn.* бор-дю́р, кайма́; грани́ца (*boundary*); *vt.* обши́вать; окаймля́ть

borderland [бо́р-дӑр-лэнд] *sn.* пограни́чная полоса́

bore [бо́р] *sn.* дыра́, отве́р-стие (*hole*); ствола́, кали́бр (*of gun*); прили́в (*of river*); ску́ка (*ennui*); ску́чный че-лове́к (*person*); *vt.i.* бура́-вить, сверли́ть (*hollow out*); надоеда́ть (*bother, tire*)

boredom [бо́р-дӑм] *sn.* ску́-ка, тоска́

boring [бо́-рій] *sn.* сверле́ние

born [борн] *adj.* рождён-
ный

borough [ба́-рǎ] *sn.* го́род с
самоуправле́нием; о́круг

borrow [бо́-роу] *vt.i.* зани-
ма́ть; заимствовать

borrower [бо́-ро-ǎр] *sm.*
заёмщик

borzoi [бор-зо́й] *s.* борза́я
(*Russian wolfhound*)

bosom [бу́-зǎм] *sn.* грудь,
па́зуха

boss [бос] *sn.* ши́шка; вы́-
пуклое украше́ние (*convex
ornament*); *sm.* хозя́ин

botany [бо́-тǎ-ни] *sn.* бота́-
ника

both [боуθ] *adj., pron.* о́ба

bother [бо́-θǎр] *sn.* беспо-
ко́йствие, хло́поты; *vt.* бе-
споко́ить, надоеда́ть; *vi.*
суети́ться

bottle [ботл] *sn.* буты́лка;
vt. разлива́ть (в буты́лку);
сде́рживать (в себе́ чу́в-
ства) (*bottle up feelings*)

bottom [бо́-тǎм] *sn.* дно,
низ; ни́жняя часть (*lowest
part*); основа́ние (*foundation*); *adj.* ни́жний

bough [бау] *sn.* ветвь, сук

boulder [бо́ул-дǎр] *sn.* ва-
лу́н

bounce [баунс] *sn.* отска́ки-
вание, прыжо́к; *vt.i.* отска́-
кивать подпры́гивать; *adv.*
вдруг, встрепя́но

bouncing [ба́ун-сиŋ] *adj.*
кру́пный и си́льный

bound [баунд] *sn.* преде́л
(*limit*); скачо́к (*leap*); *vi.*
пры́гать, скака́ть; *vt.* огра-
ни́чивать; – **for** [– фор]
направля́ющийся

boundary [ба́ун-дри] *sn.*
грани́ца

boundless [ба́унд-лǐс] *adj.*
безграни́чный

bountiful [ба́ун-ти-фǔл] *adj.*
ще́дрый; расточи́тельный
(*profuse*)

bounty [ба́ун-ти] *sn.* ще́д-
рость; да́ртвенный акт
(*special grant*)

bouquet [бу-ке́] *sn.* буке́т;
fig. арома́т (*aroma*)

bourse [бурс] *sn.* би́ржа

bout [баут] *sn.* схва́тка (*conflict*); раз, черед (*turn*)

bow [бау] *sn.* покло́н (*greeting, salute*); нос корабля́ (*of
ship*); *vt.i.* кла́няться (*bend
or kneel down*); нагиба́ться
(*stoop*)

bow [боу] *sn.* лук (*weapon*);
mus. смычо́к; бант (*ribbon*)

bowel [бау-ǎл] *sn.* ки́шка

bowl [боул] *sn.* ку́бок, ча́ша;
по́лая часть (*hollow of
spoon, etc.*); шар (*wooden ball*);
pl. игра́ в ша́ры (*game*)

bow-legged [боу́-лĕ-гĭд]
adj. кривоно́гий

bowling [бо́у-лиŋ] *sn.* игра́ в
ша́ры; **-green** [-грин] *sn.*
лужа́йка (для игры́)

box [бокс] *sn.* коро́бка,
сундӯк, я́щик; ко́злы
(*drivers seat*); *theat.* ло́жа;
tech. бу́кса, втӯлка; *vi.* бить
кулако́м; боксировать

boxing [бо́к-сиŋ] *sn.* бокс,
кула́чный бой

box-office [бо́кс-о́фис] *sn.*
биле́тная ка́сса

boy [бой] *sn.* ма́льчик

boycott [бо́й-кот] *sn.* бой-
ко́т; *vt.* бойкоти́ровать

boyhood [бо́й-хӯд] *sn.* о́т-
ро́чество

boyish [бо́й-иш] *adj.* маль-
чи́шеский

brace [брэйс] *sn.* связь (*clasp*); скреп (*clamp*); пара (*pair*); *typ.* скобка; *pl.* подтяжки; **– and bit** [– æнд бiт] *vt.* связывать, скреплять

bracelet [брэйс-лiт] *sn.* браслет

bracken [брǽ-кǝн] *sn.* папоротник

bracket [брǽ-кiт] *sn.* подпорка, подставка (*support on wall*); рожок (*for gas light, etc.*); *typ.* скобка; *vt.* ставить в скобки (*enclose in brackets*)

brackish [брǽ-кiш] *adj.* солоноватый

brad [брǽд] *sn.* штифтик

bradawl [брǽд-бл] *sn.* шило

brag [брǽг] *sn.* хвастовство; *vi.* хвастаться

braid [брэйд] *sn.* шнурок, тесьма; коса (*hair*); *vt.* плести

braille [брэйл] *sn.* печать для слепых

brain [брэйн] *sn.* мозг; *fig.* понимание, ум (*understanding*); рассудок (*reason*); *pl.* умственные способности

brainy [брэй-нi] *adj.* остроумный

braise [брэйз] *vt.* тушить (*мясо*)

brake [брэйк] *sn. tech.* тормоз; *bot.* папоротник (*bracken*); кустарник, чаща (*brushwood*); *v.i.* тормозить

bramble [брǽмбл] *sn.* терновник

bran [брǽн] *sn.* отруби

branch [брǽнч] *sn.* ветка; ветвь, сук; отрасль (*of science, etc.*); отделение, филиал (*of bank, business,*

etc.); линия (*of family, etc.*); рукав (*of river*); *vi.* разветвляться

brand [брǽнд] *sn.* головня (*burning wood, etc.*); клеймо, марка (*trade-mark*); выженное тавро (*stigma*); *vt.* клеймить, выжигать тавро

brandish [брǽн-дiш] *vt.* махать, размахивать

brandy [брǽн-дi] *sn.* коньяк

brass [брǎс] *sn.* жёлтая медь, латунь; духовые инструменты (*wind instruments*); **– band** [– бǽнд] духовой оркестр

brassy [брǎ-сi] *adj.* медный

brat [брǽт] *sn.* мальчишка (*презрительно*)

brave [брэйв] *adj.* смелый, храбрый; *vt.* бравировать, смело встречать

bravery [брэйв-рi] *sn.* храбрость

brawl [брбл] *sn.* ссора; *vi.* ссориться

brawn [брбн] *sn.* мускул; мясной студень (*culinary*)

bray [брэй] *sn.* крик осла; *vi.* кричать, реветь; толочь (*pound*)

braze [брэйз] *vt.* делать твёрдым (*harden*); сваривать, спаивать (*solder*)

brazen [брэй-зǝн] *adj.* сделанный из меди; бесстыдный (*shameless*)

brazier [брэй-жiǝр] *sn.* жаровня; *sm.* медник

Brazilian [брǝ-зi-лiǝн] *sm.* бразилец; *adj.* бразильский

breach [брiч] *sn.* нарушение (*infringement*); пролом (*gap*); расторжение (*rupture*)

bread [брэд] *sn.* хлеб

breadth [брэдθ] *sn.* ширина́; полотни́ще

breadwinner [брэ́д-ўи̯-на́р] *sm.* корми́лец

break [брэ́йк] *sn.* отве́рстие (*gap*); разло́м (*fracture*); па́уза (*rest*); переры́в (*interruption*) билья́рдный счёт (*score in billiards*); *vt.* лома́ть, разбива́ть, разруша́ть; наруша́ть (*rules, etc.*); объезжа́ть (*horse*)

breakage [брэ́й-кидж] *sn.* ло́мка

breakdown [брэ́йк-да́ун] *sn.* поте́ря здоро́вья (*of health*); *tech.* поло́мка меха́низма; ава́рия (*damage*)

breakfast [брэ́к-фа́ст] *sn.* (у́тренний) за́втрак; *vi.* за́втракать

breast [брэст] *sn.* грудь

breath [брэθ] *sn.* дыха́ние; вздох (*sigh*); дунове́ние (*puff, whiff*); переды́шка (*respite*)

breathe [бриð] *vi.* дыша́ть; произноси́ть ти́хо (*utter softly*)

breather [бри́-ðа́р] *sn.* о́тдых

breathing [бри́-ðиη] *sn.* дыха́ние; *phon.* придыха́ние

breathless [брэ́ð-лі́с] *adj.* задыха́ющийся, запыха́вшийся; безве́тренный (*windless*)

breech [брич] *sn.* казённая часть (*орудия*); **-es**, *pl.* бри́джи, штаны́

breed [брид] *sn.* поро́да (*strain*); пото́мство (*race*); *vt.i.* порожда́ть

breeder [бри́-да́р] *sm.* производи́тель

breeding [бри́-диη] *sn.* рожде́ние, разведе́ние; воспита́ние (*manners*)

breeze [бриз] *sn.* бриз, лёгкий ветеро́к (*gentle wind*)

breezy [бри́-зі] *adj.* прохла́дный, све́жий; весёлый, живо́й (*lively*)

brethren [брэ́-ðрэн] *sm. pl.* собра́тья

breve [брив] *sn. mus.* бе́лая но́та

breviary [бри́-ві-а́рі] *sn.* моли́твенник, тре́бник

brevier [бра́-ви́р] *sn. typ.* пети́т

brevity [брэ́-ві-ті] *sn.* кра́ткость

brew [бру́] *sn.* насто́йка (*decoction*); ва́рка (*concoction*); *vt.* вари́ть (*пи́во*); сме́шивать, приготовля́ть (*mix, prepare*)

brewery [бру́-а̯-рі] *sn.* пивова́рня

bribe [брайб] *sn.* взя́тка, по́дкуп; *vt.* подкупа́ть

bribery [брай-ба́-рі] *sn.* взя́точничество

brick [брик] *sn.* кирпи́ч

brick-kiln [брик-килн] *sn.* печь (*для обжига́ния кирпича́*)

brick-layer [брик-лэ́й-а́р] *sm.* ка́менщик

bridal [брай-да́л] *adj.* сва́дебный

bride [брайд] *sf.* неве́ста; новобра́чная

bridegroom [брайд-гру́м] *sm.* жени́х, новобра́чный

bridesmaid [брайдс-мэ́йд] *sf.* подру́жка (*неве́сты*)

bridge [бридж] *sn.* мост; *anat.* перено́сица; кобы́лка (*of violin, etc.*); бридж (*game*); *vt.* мости́ть; соединя́ть мо́стом

bridle [брайдл] *sn.* по́вод, узда́; *vt.* взну́здывать, сде́рживать

brief [бриф] *sn. leg.* кра́ткое изложе́ние, суде́бное предписа́ние; *adj.* коро́ткий, кра́ткий; сжа́тый (*concise*)

brief-case [бриф-кэйс] *sn.* ручно́й ко́жаный чемода́нчик

briefly [бриф-ли] *adv.* вкра́тце

brier, briar [брай-а́р] *sn. bot.* ве́реск, терно́вник; тру́бка из ко́рня ве́реска (*pipe*); шипо́вник (*sweet briar*)

brigade [бри-гэ́йд] *sn.* брига́да

brigandage [бри-ган-ди́дж] *sn.* разбо́й

bright [брайт] *adj.* све́тлый, я́сный; блестя́щий (*brilliant*); весёлый (*cheerful*)

brighten [брай-тэн] *vt.i.* освеща́ть (*lighten*); развеселя́ть (*enliven*)

brightness [брайт-нис] *sn.* я́ркость; блеск (*glitter*)

brilliance [бри-лиа́нс] *sn.* блиста́тельность

brilliant [бри-лиа́нт] *sn.* бриллиа́нт, *adj.* блестя́щий

brim [брим] *sn.* край (*of cup, etc.*); по́ле (*of hat*)

brine [брайн] *sn.* рассо́л; соли́ть

bring [бриң] *vt.* достава́ть, приноси́ть; – **about** [– а́-ба́ут] осуществля́ть; – **forth** [– форθ] производи́ть; – **up** – ап] воспи́тывать; вска́рмливать (*nurture*)

brink [бриңк] *sn.* край

briny [брай-ни] *adj.* солёный, солонова́тый

brisk [бриск] *adj.* живо́й, прово́рный

brisket [брис-кит] *sn.* груди́нка

bristle [брисл] *sn.* щети́на; *vi.* подыма́ться ды́бом, щети́ниться

British [бри-тиш] *adj.* брита́нский

brittle [бри-тэл] *adj.* ло́мкий, хру́пкий

brittleness [бри-тэл-нис] *sn.* хру́пкость

broach [броуч] *sn.* верте́л; *tech.* сверло́; *vt.* пробура́вить; – **a subject** [– э са́бджикт] подня́ть вопро́с

broad [брод] *adj.* обши́рный, широ́кий; простра́нный (*extensive*); гру́бый (*coarse*)

broadcast [брод-каст] *sn.* радиопереда́ча; сев в разбро́с (*throwing seed*); *vt.* передава́ть по ра́дио

broadcasting [брод-кас-тиң] *sn.* радиовеща́ние

broaden [бро-дэн] *vt.i.* расширя́ть

broadly [брод-ли] *adv.* откры́то, широко́

brocade [бро-кэйд] *sn.* броке́т, па́рча

brochure [бро-шю́р] *sn.* брошю́ра, кни́жка

brogue [броуг] *sn.* 'гру́бый' башма́к; непромока́тельный гама́ш; заме́тное наре́чие (*dialect*)

broil [бройл] *sn.* волне́ние, ссо́ра, шум; *vt.* жа́рить; пе́чься на со́лнце (*in the sun*)

broken [бро́у-кэн] *adj.* изло́манный, разби́тый

broker [бро́у-ка́р] *sm.* ма́клер, оце́нщик

bronchitis [брон-кáй-тіс] *sn.* бронхíт

bronze [брóнз] *sn.* брóнза; *vt.* бронзíрувати

brooch [брóуч] *sn.* брóшь

brood [брýд] *sn.* вивóдок; *vt.* висúджувати; размышлять (*meditate*); *vi.* сидíть на яйцах (*sit on eggs*)

brook [брýк] *sn.* ручéй

broom [брýм] *sn. bot.* дрок; вéник, метлá (*brush*)

broth [брóѳ] *sn.* бульóн, суп

brother [брá-ѳăр] *sm.* брат

brotherhood [брá-ѳăр-хýд] *sn.* брáтство

brother-in-law [брá-ѳăр-ін-лó] *sm.*шýрин (*wife's brother*); дéверь (*husband's brother*); зять (*sister's husband*)

brotherly [брá-ѳăр-лі] *adj.* брáтский; *adv.* по-брáтски

brow [брáу] *sn.* бровь; лоб, челó (*forehead*); край (*edge*); вúступ (*summit*)

brown [брáун] *sn* корúчневая крáска; *adj.* бýрый, корúчневый; загорéлый, смýглый (*dark-skinned*); - **paper** [– пéй-пăр] обёрточная бумáга

bruise [брýз] *sn.* кровоподтёк, синяк, ушúб; *vt.* избивáть, ушибáть; толóчь (*pound*)

brunt [брант] *sn.* атáка, глáвный удáр, нáтиск

brush [браш] *sn.* кисть, щётка; *vt.* чúстить щёткой; причёсывать (*hair*); – **up** [– ап] чúстить(ся) (*clean, clean oneself*); освежáть, подновлять (*subject, knowledge*)

brushwood [браш-ýуд] *sn.* кустáрник, чáща

brutal [брý-тăл] *adj.* жестóкий, звéрский

brutality [бру-тǽ-лі-ті] *sn.* жестóкость, звéрство

brute [брýт] *s.* живóтное (*animal*); скотúна (*person*)

bubble [бабл] *sn.* пузýрь, *m.*; химéра (*unreal conception*); *vi.* клокотáть, пузýриться

buck [бак] *sm.* сáмец; *sn.* брыкáнье

bucket [бá-кіт] *sn.* ведрó (*pail*); ковш (*scoop*); *vt.i.* черпáть

buckle [бакл] *sn.* пряжка; *vt.* застёгивать; сгибáть (*bend*)

bud [бад] *sn.* пóчка, росток

budge [баджж] *vt.i.* пошевельнýть, шевелúться

budget [бá-джіт] *sn.* бюджéт

buff [баф] *adj.* буро-жёлтый

buffalo [бá-фă-лоу] *s.* бýйвол

buffer [бá-фăр] *sn.* бýфер

buffet [бá-фіт] *sn.* буфéт (*side-board*); буфéтная стóйка (*bar*); *vt.i.* борóться

buffoon [бă-фýн] *sm.* скоморóх, шут

buffoonery [бă-фý-нă-рі] *sn.* шутóвствó

bug [баг] *s.* клоп

bugbear [бáг-бэр] *sn.* бýка, пýгало

bugle [бюгл] *sn.* горн, охотнúчий рог, трубá

bugler [бю-глáр] *sm.* горнúст

build [білд] *sn.* конструкция, фóрма; телослóжéние (*human proportions*); *vt.* создáвáть, стрóить

builder [бíл-дăр] *sm.* строúтель; подрядчик (*contractor*)

building [бíл-дiн] *sn.* здáние; сооружéние; строéние; (*construction, erection*)

bulb [балб] *sn. bot.* клýбень, *m.*; лýковица; шíшка (*cone*); *elect.* лáмпочка

bulbous [бáл-бǎс] *adj.* лýковичный

Bulgarian [бал-гǎ-рiǎн] *sm.* болгáрин; *adj.* болгáрский

bulge [балдж] *sn.* выпуклость; *vi.* вытягиваться

bulgy [бáл-джi] *adj.* распухший; на выкате (*of eyes*)

bulk [балк] *sn.* мáсса (*mass*); объём (*volume*); груз (*ship's cargo*)

bulky [бáл-кi] *adj.* большóй, объёмистый; громóздкий (*unwieldy*)

bull [бул] *sm.* бык

bull-calf [бýл-кáф] *sm.* бычóк

bullet [бý-лiт] *sn.* пýля

bullion [бý-лiǎн] *sn.* слiток; плóтное зóлото (или) серебрó

bullock [бý-лǎк] *sm.* вол

bull's-eye [бýлз-ай] *sn.* центр мишéни (*centre of target*)

bully [бý-лi] *sm.* буян (*ruffian*); задира (*quarrelsome person*); *vt.i.* задирáть

bulwark [бýл-уǎрк] *sn.* оплóт (*rampart*); бóльверк; *naut.* фáльшборт; защита (*protection*)

bumble-bee [бáмбл-бi] *s.* шмель

bump [бамп] *sn.* óпухоль, шíшка (*swelling*); *vt.* ударять; нагонять (*in boat-race*)

bumper [бáм-пǎр] *sn.* пóлный бокáл (*brimming glass*)

bumptious [бáмп-шǎс] *adj.*

надмéнный, самоувéренный

bumpy [бáм-пi] *adj.* ухáбистый

bun [бан] *sn.* бýлочка

bunch [банч] *sn.* связка; гроздь (*cluster*); кисть (*of grapes*)

bundle [бандл] *sn.* связка, узел; *vt.i.* связывать в узел

bung [банг] *sn.* затычка, втýлка; *vt.* затыкáть

bungalow [бáн-гǎ-ло] *sn.* бýнгало (одноэтáжный дóмик)

bungle [бáнгл] *sn.* прóмах; *vt.i.* рабóтать неумéло, пóртить

bunk [банк] *sn.* кóйка

bunker [бáн-кǎр] *sn. naut.* угóльная яма; *tech.* бýнкер; *fig.* препятствие

bunkum [бáн-кǎм] *sn.* болтовня, вздор

bunny [бá-нi] *s.* крóлик

bunting [бáн-тiн] *sn.* флáги; матéрия для флáгов; овсянка, просянка (*bird*)

buoy [бой] *sn.* бáкен, буй, вéха

buoyancy [бóй-ǎн-сi] *sn.* плавýчесть

buoyant [бóй-ǎнт] *adj.* плавýчий; жизнерáдостный (*light-hearted*)

burden [бǎр-дǎн] *sn.* брéмя, вьюк, нóша (*load*); гóре (*grief*); *vt.* обременять

burdensome [бǎр-дǎн-сǎм] *adj.* обремениtельный; беспокóйный (*troublesome*)

bureau [бю-рó] *sn.* контóрка (*desk*); контóра (*office*)

burglar [бǎр-глáр] *sn.* ворвзлóмщик

burglary [бёр-гла-ри] *sn.* взлом, воровство

burial [бе́-риэл] *sn.* похороны.

burial-ground [бе́-риэл-граунд] *sn.* кладбище

burlesque [бёр-ле́ск] *sn.* пародия, шутовство

burly [бёр-ли] *adj.* дородный, дюжий

burn [бёрн] *sn.* клеймо, ожог (*mark*); *vt.i.* гореть, жечь, обжигать

burner [бёр-нёр] *sn.* горелка

burnish [бёр-ниш] *vt.* воронить, полировать

burr [бёр] *sn.* картавость; *vi.* картавить

burrow [ба́-роу] *sn.* нора; *vt.i.* рыть нору; рыться

bursar [бёр-са́р] *sm.* казначей

bursary [бёр-са́-ри] *sn.* стипендия

burst [бёрст] *sn.* вспышка, разрыв; *vt.* разрывать; *vi.* взорваться, лопнуть

bury [бе́-ри] *vt.* хоронить, прятать (*hide*)

bush [буш] *sn.* куст, кустарник; *tech.* втулка, подшипник

bushel [бу́-шэл] *sn.* бушель

bushy [бу́-ши] *adj.* кустистый, густой (*eye-brows*)

business [би́з-нис] *sn.* дело, занятие

businesslike [би́з-нис-лайк] *adj.* деловой, практический

bust [баст] *sn.* бюст; *coll.* разрыв (*burst*)

bustle [басл] *sn.* суета, суматоха; турнюр (*skirt padding*); *vt.* торопить; суетиться, торопиться

busy [би́-зи] *adj.* деятельный (*active, diligent*); оживлённый (*animated*)

but [бат] *adv.* только; *prep.* кроме; *conj.* а, но, однако

butcher [бу́-чёр] *sm.* мясник; *fig.* палач; *vt.* убивать

butchery [бу́-чё-ри] *sn.* бойня, резня

butler [бат-лёр] *sm.* буфетчик; дворецкий (*chief steward*)

butt [бат] *sn.* большая бочка (*large cask*); цель (*target*); приклад (*of rifle*); *vt.* бодать, ударять

butter [ба́-тёр] *sn.* масло; *vt.* намазывать маслом

buttercup [ба́-тёр-кап] *sn.* лютик

butterfly [ба́-тёр-флай] *sn.* бабочка

buttermilk [ба́-тёр-милк] *sn.* пахтанье

buttery [ба́-тё-ри] *sn.* кладовая; *adj.* масляный

buttock [ба́-ток] *sn.* задница

button [ба́-тэн] *sn.* кнопка, пуговица; *vt.* застёгивать

buttonhole [ба́-тэн-хоул] *sn.* петля; бутоньерка (*flower*); *vt.* прометывать (*петли*)

buttress [ба́-трис] *sn.* контрфорс, подпора; *vt.* поддерживать

buxom [ба́-ксэм] *adj.* бодрый, здоровый (*особенно о женщинах*)

buy [бай] *vt.* купить, покупать

buyer [ба́й-ёр] *sn.* покупатель, *m.*

buying [ба́й-ин] *sn.* покупание (*act of*); покупка (*purchase*)

buzz [баз] *sn.* жужжа́нье; *vi.* гуде́ть, жужжа́ть

buzzer [ба́-зәр] *sn.* гудо́к; зу́ммер (*radio*)

by [бай] *adv.* бли́зко, ми́мо, ря́дом; – **and** – [– æнд –] вско́ре; – **the way** [– ðә уэ́й] ме́жду про́чим, мимохо́дом; *prep.* о́коло, по, при, у (*near*); – **heart** [– ха́рт] наизу́сть

bygone [ба́й-гон] *adj.* про́шлый

by-law [ба́й-ло̄] *sn.* уста́в, постановле́ние

by-pass [ба́й-па̄с] *sn.* обхо́д (*roundabout way*); обво́дный кана́л (*pipe*)

by-road [ба́й-ро́уд] *sn.* просёлок; малопроézжая доро́га

bystander [ба́й-стæн-дәр] *sn.* зри́тель, свиде́тель

by-way [ба́й-уэй] *sn.* уеди-нённая доро́га

byword [ба́й-у̇әрд] *sn.* пого-во́рка

C

C [си] *mus.* до

cab [кæб] *sn.* кэб, наёмный экипа́ж

cabbage [кæ-би́дж] *sn.* ка-пу́ста; – **head** [– хæд] коча́н (капу́сты)

cabin [кæ-би́н] *sn.* ка́морка, каю́та (*room*); хи́жина (*hut*); бу́дка (*of locomotive, etc.*)

cabin-boy [кæ-би́н-бой] *sn.* ю́нга

cabinet [кæ-би-ни́т] *sn.* каби-не́т, комо́д (*furniture*); сове́т мини́стров (*council of ministers*)

cabinet-maker [кæ-би-нит-мэ́й-кәр] *sn.* ме́бельщик, столя́р

cable [кэ́йбл] *sn.* ка́бель; кана́т; каблогра́мма (*tele-graphic*); *naut.* ка́бельтов (100 *fathoms*); *vt.i.* теле-графи́ровать

cabman [кǽб-мæн] *sm.* ку́-чер

cab-stand [кæб-стæнд] *sn.* изво́зчичья би́ржа

cackle [кæкл] *sn.* гогота́нье, куда́хтанье; *vi.* гогота́ть, куда́хтать

cad [кæд] *sm.* плут, подле́ц, пройдо́ха

caddie [кǽ-ди] *sm.* ма́льчик, сопровожда́ющий игрока́ в го́льф

caddish [кǽ-диш] *adj.* мép-зкий, по́длый

caddy [кǽ-ди] *sn.* ча́йница

cadge [кадж] *vt.* попроша́й-ничать

cadre [ка́др] *sn. mil.* ка́дры, штат

café [ка́-фе] *sn.* кафе́, ко-фе́йня

cage [кэйдж] *sn.* кле́тка; клеть (*in mines, etc.*); *vt.* сажа́ть в кле́тку

cajole [ка-джо́ул] *vt.* подоль-ща́ться; обха́живать (*de-ceive*)

cake [кэйк] *sn.* лепёшка, пиро́жное; пли́тка, табле́т-ка (*flat piece*); *vt.i.* затверде-ва́ть, сгуща́ться (*harden*); спека́ться (*coagulate*)

calamity [ка-лǽ-ми-ти] *sn.* бе́дствие, несча́стие, па́гу-ба

calculate [кǽл-кю-лэйт] *vt.* вычисля́ть, исчисля́ть; рассчи́тывать (*figure out*)

calculating [кál-кю-лэй-тiй] *adj.* расчётливый;
— **machine** [- мă-шíн] *sn.* арифмометр

calculation [кал-кю-лэ́й-шăн] *sn.* калькуляция, вычисление

calculator [кál-кю-лэй-тăр] *sn.* вычислитель

calendar [кá-лiн-дăр] *sn.* календарь, *m.*; опись (*list, schedule*); указатель (*indicator*)

calender [кá-лiн-дăр] *sn.* лощильный пресс; *vt.* лощить

calf [кáф] *s.* телёнок (*animal*); икра (*of leg*); **with** — [уïе -] стельная

call [кôл] *sn.* зов, призыв (*summons*); вызов (*on telephone*); посещение (*visit*); *vt.i.* звать, называть (*name*); заходить (*visit*); — **up** — [ап] призывать (*service*); вызывать (*on phone*)

caller [кô-лăр] *sm., f.* гость, посетитель

calling [кô-лïй] *sn.* призвание (*vocation*); профессия (*profession*)

callous [кá-лăс] *adj.* мозолистый (*skin*); бессердечный, неотзывчивый (*people*)

callow [кá-лоу] *adj.* неоперившийся (*unfledged*); *fig.* неопытный (*raw, inexperienced*)

calm [кáм] *sn.* тишина; *naut.* штиль, *m.*; *adj.* безветренный (*windless*); спокойный (*tranquil*); *vt.* успокаивать

calmness [кáм-нîс] *sn.* покой, спокойствие

calorific [кă-лă-рí-фîк] *adj.* теплородный

calumny [кá-лăм-нi] *sn.* клевета

Calvary [кál-вă-рi] *sn.* Голгофа

calve [кáв] *vi.* телиться

cam [кáм] *sn. tech.* кулак, палец

camber [кáм-бăр] *sn.* изгиб

camel [кá-мăл] *s.* верблюд

camera [кá-мă-рă] *sn.* фотографический аппарат; камера

camisole [кá-мi-соул] *sn.* кофта

camouflage [кá-му-флäж] *sn. mil.* маскировка; *vt.* маскировать

camp [кáмп] *sn.* лагерь, *m.*; место привала, стоянка; *vt.i.* бивакировать; расположить лагерем; — **out** — [аут] ночевать на воздухе

campaign [кăм-пэ́йн] *sn. polit.* кампания; *mil.* военный поход; *vi.* совершать кампанию; участвовать в походе

camp-bed [кáмп-бéд] *sn.* походная кровать

camphor [кáм-фăр] *sn.* камфора

cam-shaft [кáм-шäфт] *sn.* распределительный вал

can [кáн] *sn.* бидон, лейка; жестяная коробка; *vt.* консервировать; *aux. v.* мочь; **I —** [ай -] я могу

Canadian [кă-нэ́й-дiăн] *sm.* канадец; *adj.* канадский

canal [кă-нáл] *sn.* канал; *anat.* проток, проход; **alimentary —** [ǽли-мéн-тă-рi -] пищевод

canary [кă-нэ́-рi] *s.* канарейка; *adj.* светложёлтый (*colour*)

cancel [кэн-сэ́л] *sn.* аннули́ровка; *vt.* аннули́ровать, уничтожа́ть; вычёркивать (*strike out*)

cancellation [кэн-си-лэ́й-шэн] *sn.* аннули́рование; вычёркивание

cancer [кэн-сэ́р] *sn. med.* рак; *astron.* созве́здие Ра́ка

cancerous [кэн-сэ́-рэс] *adj.* ра́ковый

candid [кэн-ди́д] *adj.* и́скренний, открове́нный

candidate [кэн-ди-дэйт] *sn.* кандида́т

candied [кэн-дид] *adj.* заса́харенный

candle [кэндл] *sn.* свеча́, све́чка

candlestick [кэндл-сти́к] *sn.* подсве́чник

candour [кэн-дэ́р] *sn.* и́скренность, прямота́, чистосерде́чие

candy [кэн-ди] *sn.* ледене́ц

cane [кэйн] *sn. bot.* камы́ш, тростни́к; па́лка (*stick*); *vt.* бить па́лкой; плести́ из камыша́ (*weave*)

canine [кэ-найн] *sn.* клык (*tooth*); *adj.* соба́чий

canister [кэ-ни́с-тэр] *sn.* металли́ческая ча́йница (*for tea*); жестя́нка (*container*)

canker [кэн-кэ́р] *sn.* я́зва, червото́чина (*dry-rot*); *med.* гангре́на

cankerous [кэн-кэ́-рэс] *adj.* губи́тельный, разъеда́ющий

cannon [кэ-нэн] *sn. mil.* ору́дие, пу́шка; карамбо́ль (*billiards*); *vi.* столкну́ться

cannon-ball [кэ-нэн-бол] *sn.* ядро́

canoe [кэ-ну́] *sn.* байда́рка, пиро́га, чёлн

canon [кэ-нэн] *sn.* кано́н, крите́рий (*criterion*); кано́ник (*person*); пра́вила (*rules*)

canopy [кэ-нэ-пи́] *sn.* балдахи́н, поло́г; наве́с (*awning*)

cant [кэнт] *sn.* скос (*tilted position*); жарго́н (*lingo*); лицеме́рие (*hypocrisy*); *v.i.* криви́ться

cantankerous [кэн-тэ́й-кэ́рэс] *adj.* сварли́вый (*cross-grained*); спорли́вый (*quarrelsome*)

canteen [кэн-ти́н] *sn. mil.* ла́вка в войсково́й ча́сти (*provision store*); солда́тский буфе́т (*soldiers' bar*); кру́жка, мане́рка (*mess-tin*); похо́дный я́щик (*box of cooking utensils*)

canter [кэн-тэ́р] *sn.* лёгкий гало́п, рысь; *vt.i.* пусти́ть ло́шадь лёгким гало́пом

canvas [кэн-вэс] *sn.* ка́нва, паруси́на, холст; **under –** [эн-дэ́р –] в пала́тках

canvass [кэн-вэс] *sn.* собира́ние голосо́в (*canvassing*); *vt.i.* собира́ть голоса́; домога́ться зака́зов (*solicit custom*)

cap [кэп] *sn.* ке́пка, фура́жка; чепе́ц (*indoor*); *tech.* колпачо́к, капсю́ля (*vt.* покрыва́ть (*cover*)

capability [кэй-пэ-би́-ли-ти] *sn.* спосо́бность

capable [кэй-пэбл] *adj.* поня́тливый, спосо́бный; правомо́чный (*competent*)

capacious [кэ-пэ́й-шэс] *adj.* объёмистый, просто́рный

capacity [кэ-пэ́-си-ти] *sn.* вмести́мость, ёмкость, объём; спосо́бность (*competency*); мо́щность (*force, power*)

cape [кэйп] sn. пелери́на, плащ (garment); мыс (promontory)

caper [кэй-пӓр] sn. прыжо́к, скачо́к (jump); vi. де́лать прыжки́; **cut -s** [кат -з] дура́читься

capital [кэ-пи-тăл] sn. столи́ца (town); прописна́я бу́ква (letter); капита́л (money); adj. гла́вный (principal); превосхо́дный (excellent); **- punishment** [- пă-ни́ш-мăнт] сме́ртная казнь; **-ship** [- шип] дредно́ут; лине́йный кора́бль, m.

capitation [кэ-пи-тэ́й-шăн] sn. поду́шная пода́ть; поголо́вное исчисле́ние

capitulate [кă-пи́-тю-лэйт] vi. капитули́ровать

caprice [кă-при́с] sn. капри́з, причу́да

capricious [кă-при́-шăс] adj. капри́зный, непостоя́нный, причу́дливый

capsize [кэп-са́йз] vt.i. опроки́дывать(ся), опроки́нуть(ся)

capsule [кэп-сюл] sn. ка́псюля, ка́псюля; bot. семенна́я коро́бочка; tech. ти́гель, m.

captain [кэп-тин] sn. капита́н; полково́дец (commander); шки́пер (master, skipper)

caption [кэп-шăн] sn. заголо́вок; на́дпись

captivate [кэп-ти-вэйт] vt. очаро́вывать; пленя́ть

captive [кэп-тив] sm. пле́нник; adj. пле́нный

captivity [кэп-ти́-ви-ти] sn. плен

capture [кэп-чăр] sn. захва́т, пои́мка; добы́ча (booty); приз (prize)

car [кар] sn. автомоби́ль, m.; трамва́й; пово́зка (vehicle)

caraway [кэ-рă-у́эй] sn. тмин

carbon [кар-бăн] sn. угле-ро́д; у́гольный электро́д (electrical charcoal pencil)

carbon-paper [кар-бăн-пэй-пăр] sn. копирова́льная бума́га

carbuncle [кар-байнкл] sn. карбу́нкул, чире́й

carcass [кар-кăс] sn. труп (human); ту́ша (animal)

card [кард] sn. биле́т (ticket); ка́рта (playing); ка́рточка (visiting); ка́рда, чеса́лка (textile); vt. чеса́ть

cardboard [кард-бо́рд] sn. карто́н

cardiac [кар-диӓк] adj. серде́чный

cardigan [кар-ди-гăн] sn. вя́заная жаке́тка

cardinal [кар-ди-нăл] sm. Кардина́л; adj. гла́вный (chief); основно́й (principal); нача́льный (first, initial)

care [кэр] sn. забо́та (anxiety); попече́ние (solicitude); осторо́жность (caution); vi. забо́титься (be anxious); бере́чь (take care of); уха́живать (look after)

career [кă-ри́ăр] sn. карье́ра; бы́строе движе́ние (rapid progression); vi. бы́стро дви́гаться

careful [кэр-фул] adj. осторо́жный

careless [кэр-лис] adj. беззабо́тный (unconcerned); небре́жный (untidy)

caress [кă-ре́с] sn. ла́ска; vt. гла́дить, ласка́ть

caretaker [кэр-тэй-кăр] sm. дво́рник, сто́рож

cargo [ка́р-гоу] *sn.* груз (корабля́)

caricature [ка́-ри-ка-тю́р] *sn.* карикату́ра

carnage [ка́р-нидж] *sn.* резня́, сеча

carnal [ка́р-нäл] *adj.* пло́тский (*fleshly*); полово́й (*sexual*); све́тский (*worldly*)

carnation [кар-нэ́й-шäн] *sn.* кра́сная гвозди́ка; теле́сный цвет (*colour*); *adj.* а́лый (*colour*)

carnivorous [кар-ни́-врäс] *adj.* плотоя́дный

carol [кä-рäл] *sn.* весёлая песнь (*joyous song*); коля́да (*Christmas hymn*); *vi.* воспева́ть, коля́довать, сла́вить

carouse [ка-ра́уз] *sn.* пиру́шка, попо́йка; *vi.* пирова́ть

carp [ка́рп] *s.* саза́н (*fish*); *vi.* придира́ться

carpenter [ка́р-пин-тäр] *sm.* пло́тник

carpentry [ка́р-пин-три] *s.* пло́тничество

carpet [ка́р-пит] *sn.* ковёр; *vi.* покрыва́ть ковра́ми

carriage [кä-ридж] *sn.* каре́та, экипа́ж (*horse-drawn*); ваго́н (*railway*); перево́з, прово́з (*carrying*); оса́нка (*deportment*)

carrier [кä-риäр] *sm.* во́зчик, носи́льщик; носи́тель (*germ*)

carrot [кä-рäт] *sn.* морко́вь

carry [кä-ри] *vt.i.* нести́, носи́ть, перевози́ть; держа́ться (*oneself*); — **off** [— оф] похища́ть; — **on** [— он] продолжа́ть (*continue*)

cart [ка́рт] *sn.* двуко́лка, теле́га; арба́ (*covered*); та́чка (*hand*); *vt.i.* везти́ в теле́ге

cartage [ка́р-тидж] *sn.* перево́зка (в теле́ге); сто́имость (перево́зки) (*cost*)

carter [ка́р-тäр] *sm.* во́зчик

cart-horse [ка́рт-хо́рс] *s.* ломова́я ло́шадь

cartilage [ка́р-ти-лидж] *sn.* хрящ

carton [ка́р-тäн] *sn.* карто́н; карто́нка (*box*)

cartoon [ка́р-ту́н] *sn.* шарж (*grotesque*); карикату́ра

cartoonist [ка́р-ту́-нист] *sm.* карикатури́ст

cartridge [ка́р-тридж] *sn.* картю́з (*artillery*); патро́н (*rifle*); рисова́льная бума́га (*paper*)

carve [ка́рв] *vt.* ре́зать (*cut*); вы́резать (*cut out*); нареза́ть (*cut up*); высека́ть (*stone*)

carver [ка́р-вäр] *sm.* ре́зчик; *sn.* реза́к (*knife*)

carving [ка́р-вiй] *sn.* резьба́

cascade [кäс-кэ́йд] *sn.* небольшо́й водопа́д

case [кэ́йс] *sn.* обстоя́тельство, слу́чай (*event*); коро́бка, я́щик (*box, crate*); футля́р, чехо́л (*cover, sheath*); *gram.* паде́ж; *jur.* ка́сса

casement [кэ́йс-мäнт] *sn.* око́нница

cash [кäш] *sn.* де́ньги (*money*); нали́чные де́ньги, чистога́н (*ready money*); *vt.* инкасси́ровать

cashier [кä-ши́р] *sm.* касси́р; *vi.* увольня́ть со слу́жбы

cask [ка́ск] *sn.* бочо́нок

casket [ка́с-кит] *sn.* шкату́лка

casserole [кä-сä-ро́ул] *sn.* кухо́нная гли́няная посу́да

cassock [кӗ́-сӗк] *sn.* ря́са

cast [кāст] *sn.* слёпок (*mould*); *i.еаt.* соста́в; косогла́зие (*squint*); бро́сок (*throw*), *vt.i.* броса́ть, кида́ть (*throw*); сбра́сывать (*discard*); роня́ть (*shed*); отлива́ть (*metals*); *theat.* распределя́ть ро́ли

castaway [кāст-ӗ-уӗ́й] *sm.* отве́рженный (*reprobate*); потерпе́вший кораблекруше́ние (*shipwrecked person*)

caste [кāст] *sn.* ка́ста, ранг

castigate [кӗ́с-ти-гӗйт] *vt.* нака́зывать

casting [кāс-тиӊ] *sn.* литьё, отли́вка

cast-iron [кāст-ай-ӗн] *sn.* чугу́н; *adj.* чугу́нный

castle [кāсл] *sn.* за́мок; *chess.* ба́шня, ладья́, ту́ра

castor [кāс-тӗр] *sn.* колёсико, ро́лик (*wheel*); пе́речница (*for pepper*); – **sugar** [– шу́-гӗр] са́харная пу́дра

casual [кӗ́-жу-ӗл] *adj.* непреднаме́ренный, случа́йный

casualty [кӗ́-жу-ӗл-ти] *sn.* несча́стный слу́чай

cat [кāт] *sm.* кот; *sf.* ко́шка

catalogue [кӗ́-тӗ-лог] *sn.* катало́г; *vt.* вноси́ть в катало́г, каталогизи́ровать

cataract [кӗ́-тӗ-рӗкт] *sn.* водопа́д; *med.* катара́кта

catarrh [кӗ-тāр] *sn.* ката́р

catastrophe [кӗ-тӗ́-стрӗ-фи] *sn.* ги́бель, катастро́фа; *theat.* развя́зка

catch [кӗч] *sn.* добы́ча, уло́в; *tech.* защёлка; *vt.* лови́ть; заста́ть (*train, etc.*); зарази́ться (*illness*); – **cold** [– ко́улд] простужи́ваться;

– **fire** [– фа́й-ӗр] загора́ться

catching [кӗ́-чиӊ] *adj.* заразительный (*infectious*)

catchword [кӗч-уӗ́рд] *sn.* ло́зунг [катехи́зис

catechism [кӗ́-ти-кизм] *sn.*

categorical [кӗ-ти-гó-ри-кӗл] *adj.* безусло́вный (*unconditional*); реши́тельный (*resolute*)

category [кӗ́-ти-гӗ-ри] *sn.* катего́рия

cater [кӗй-тӗр] *vi.* поставля́ть, снабжа́ть

caterer [кӗй-тӗ-рӗр] *sm.* поставщи́к

caterpillar [кӗ-тӗр-пи-лӗр] *s.* гу́сеница; *adj. tech.* гу́сеничный

catgut [кӗт-гат] *sn.* ки́шки живо́тных

cathedral [кӗ-ӫи-дрӗл] *sn.* собо́р

catholic [кӗ́-ӫӗ-лик] *sm.* като́лик; *adj.* католи́ческий

cattle [кӗтл] *sn. pl.* кру́пный рога́тый скот

Caucasian [кō-кӗ́й-зиӗн] *sm.* кавка́зец; *adj.* кавка́зский

cauliflower [кó-ли-флау́-ӗр] *sn.* цветна́я капу́ста

cause [кōз] *sn.* причи́на, по́вод (*ground*); *vt.* заставля́ть, причиня́ть

causeway [кṓз-уӗ́й] *sn.* да́мба, мостова́я, шоссе́

caustic [кóс-тик] *sn.* е́дкость, язви́тельность; *adj.* е́дкий, жгу́чий, язви́тельный

cauterize [кó-тӗ-райз] *vt.* прижига́ть

caution [кó-шӗн] *sn.* осторо́жность (*discretion*); предостереже́ние (*warning*); *vt.* предостерега́ть

cautious [кǒ-шǎс] *adj.* осторо́жный

cavalry [кǽ-вǎл-ри] *sn.* кавале́рия

cave [кэйв] *sn.* пеще́ра, подземе́лье; *vt.* вда́вливать; обва́ливаться; – **in**, прова́ливаться

caviare [кæ-виǎр] *sn.* икра́

cavity [кǽ-ви-ти] *sn.* впади́на, по́лость

caw [кǒ] *vi.* ка́ркать

cease [сис] *vt.* перестава́ть, прекраща́ть

ceaseless [сис-лес] *adj.* непреры́вный; непреста́нный

cedar [си-дǎр] *sn.* кедр

cede [сид] *vt.* сдава́ть, уступа́ть

ceiling [си-лiн] *sn.* потоло́к

celebrate [сǝ-лi-брэйт] *vt.* пра́здновать; *eccl.* прославля́ть

celebrated [сǝ-лi-брэй-тǝд] *adj.* знамени́тый

celebration [сǝ-лi-брэй-шǝн] *sn.* пра́зднование; *pl.* торжества́

celebrity [си-лǝ-бри-ти] *sn.* знамени́тость (*eminence*); изве́стность (*fame*); зна́тный челове́к (*person*)

celery [сǝ-лǝ-ри] *sn.* сельдере́й

celestial [си-лес-тiǎл] *adj.* небе́сный

celibacy [сǝ-лi-бǎ-си] *sn.* безбра́чие

celibate [сǝ-лi-бǎт] *sm.* холостя́к; *adj.* безбра́чный

cell [сел] *sn.* ке́лья (*monk's*); яче́йка (*bee's*); ка́мера (*prison's*); *biol.* кле́точка; *elec.* элеме́нт

cellar [сǝ-лǎр] *sn.* по́греб

cement [сi-ме́нт] *sn.* цеме́нт; *vt.* цементи́ровать

cemetery [сǝ-ми-тǎ-ри] *sn.* кла́дбище

censor [сен-сǎр] *sm.* надзира́тель осужде́ний; це́нзор; *vt.* цензурова́ть

censorship [сен-сǎр-шiп] *sn.* цензо́рство, цензу́ра; до́лжность це́нзора (*function*)

censure [сен-шǎр] *sn.* осужде́ние, порица́ние; *vt.* порица́ть

census [сен-сǎс] *sn.* пе́репись

centenarian [сен-ти-нǝ́-рiǎн] *sm.* челове́к ста лет; *adj.* столе́тний

centenary [сен-ти-нǎ-ри] *sn.* столе́тие

centipede [сен-ти-пiд] *s.* многоно́жка

central [сен-трǎл] *adj.* центра́льный

centralize [сен-трǎ-лайз] *vt.i.* централизова́ть

centre [сентр] *sn.* центр; середи́на (*middle*); *vt.i.* сосредото́чивать

centrifugal [сен-трi-фю́-гǎл] *adj.* центробе́жный

century [сен-чǝ-ри] *sn.* век, столе́тие; со́тня (*a hundred*)

ceramic [сi-рǽ-мiк] *adj.* гонча́рный; *sn. pl.* кера́мика

cereal [сi-рiǎл] *adj.* зерново́й; *sn. pl.* зла́ки

cerebral [сǝ-рi-брǎл] *adj.* мозгово́й

ceremonial [сǝ-рi-мо́-нiǎд] *adj.* обря́довый, форма́льный

ceremonious [сǝ-рi-мо́-нiǎс] *adj.* церемо́нный

ceremony [cĕ-rí-mă-ní] *sn.* обря́д, форма́льность, церемо́ния

certain [cĕр-тăн] *adj.* уве́ренный (*sure*); определённый (*settled*); не́кий, не́который, оди́н (*one, some*)

certainly [cĕр-тăн-лī] *adv.* коне́чно; непреме́нно (*without fail*)

certainty [cĕр-тăн-тī] *sn.* несомне́нный факт; уве́ренность

certificate [cĕр-тí-фĭ-кīт] *sn.* свиде́тельство, удостовере́ние (*attestation*)

certify [cĕр-тĭ-фай] *vt.* удостоверя́ть (*attest*); руча́ться (*guarantee*); оповеща́ть (*inform*)

cessation [cĕ-cĕй-шăн] *sn.* остано́вка (*stopping*); прекраще́ние (*discontinuance*)

cesspool [cĕc-пӯл] *sn.* выгребна́я я́ма

chafe [чэйф] *sn.* волне́ние, раздраже́ние; сса́дина (*abrasion*); *vt.i.* растира́ть, тере́ть; горячи́ться

chaff [чăф] *sn.* мяки́на (*husks*); мя́кая соло́ма (*chopped straw*); отбро́сы (*waste*); подтру́нивание (*banter*); насмеха́ться (*laugh at*)

chagrin [шă-гри́н] *sn.* доса́да, огорче́ние

chain [чэйн] *sn.* цепь; цепо́чка (*watch, etc*); *naut.* кана́т; *pl.* око́вы, у́зы; *vt.* ско́вывать, скрепля́ть (*це́пью*)

chair [чэр] *sn.* стул; ка́федра (*university*); кре́сло (*arm*)

chairman [чэ́р-мăн] *sm.* председа́тель

chalk [чōк] *sn.* мел

chalky [чṓ-кī] *adj.* мелово́й

challenge [чэ́-лĭнджǝ] *sn.* вы́зов; о́крик (*sentry's*); *vt.* вызыва́ть (*defy*); *mil.* оклика́ть; оспа́ривать (*impugn*)

chamber [чэйм-бăр] *sn.* спа́льня (*bedroom*); пала́та (*assembly*); патро́нник (*in revolver*); **– of Commerce** [– ов ко́-мăрс] Торго́вая пала́та

chamberlain [чэйм-бăр-лĭн] *sm.* камерге́р

chambermaid [чэйм-бăр-мэйд] *sf.* го́рничная

chamois [шă-мўắ] *s. zool.* се́рна; за́мша (*leather*)

champion [чэ́м-пĭăн] *sm.* победи́тель, побо́рник, чемпио́н; защи́тник (*defender*); *vt.* защища́ть

championship [чэ́м-пĭăн-шĭп] *sn.* чемпио́нство; побо́рничество (*advocacy, support*)

chance [чăнс] *sn.* слу́чай, случа́йность; **by –** [бай –] случа́йно; *vt.i.* случа́ться (*happen*); рискну́ть (*risk*)

chancel [чăн-сăл] *sn.* алта́рь, *m.*

chancellery [чăн-сă-лă-рī] *sn.* канцеля́рия

chancellor [чăн-сă-лăр] *sm.* ка́нцлер; глава́ университе́та (*of university*)

chancery [чăн-сă-рī] *sn.* суд ло́рда-ка́нцлера, канцеля́рия

chandelier [шэн-дĭ-ли́р] *sn.* канделя́бр, лю́стра

change [чэйндж] *sn.* измене́ние, переме́на (*alteration*); ме́лочь, сда́ча (*money*); *vt.* переменя́ть (*alter*); обме́нивать (*substitute*)

changeable [чэйн-джібл] *adj.* непостоя́нный

channel [чэ-нэл] *sn.* кана́л; источник, путь (*passage*)

chant [чант] *sn.* пе́ние; *vt.i.* петь

chaos [кэй-ác] *sn.* хаос

chaotic [кэй-ó-тік] *adj.* хаоти́ческий

chapel [чэ-пэл] *sn.* часо́вня

chaperon [шэ-пэ-ран] *sf.* дуэнья

chaplain [чэп-лін] *sm.* капелла́н

chapter [чэп-тэр] *sn.* глава́ (*of book*); *eccl.* собра́ние кано́ников

char [чар] *vt.i.* обжига́ть, обу́гливать

character [кэ-рік-тэр] *sn.* хара́ктер; репута́ция; ли́чность (*person*); *typ.* бу́ква

characteristic [ка-ра-ктэ-ріс-тík] *adj.* характе́рный

charcoal [чар-ко́ул] *sn.* древе́сный у́голь

charge [чарджь] *sn.* ата́ка, нападе́ние (*attack*); заря́д (*load*), счёт, цена́ (*account, price*); обвине́ние (*accusation*); обя́занность (*duty*); охра́на, попече́ние (*custody*); *vt.i.* вверя́ть, поруча́ть (*entrust*); заряжа́ть (*load*); напада́ть (*attack*)

charitable [чэ-рі-тэбл] *adj.* благотвори́тельный, сострада́тельный

charity [чэ-рі-ті] *sn.* благотвори́тельность, ми́лостыня, милосе́рдие (*clemency, mercy*)

charm [чарм] *sn.* обая́ние, пре́лесть; ча́ры (*spell*); амуле́т (*trinket*); *vt.* очаро́вывать, прельща́ть

charming [чар-мін] *adj.* обая́тельный, преле́стный

chart [чарт] *sn.* *naut.* ка́рта, диагра́мма

charter [чар-тэр] *sn.* ха́ртия; *vt.* зафрахтова́ть су́дно (*ship*)

charwoman [чар-уу́-мэн] *sf.* подённая убо́рщица

chary [чэ-рі] *adj.* бере́жливый, осторо́жный

chase [чэйс] *sn.* ло́вля (*catching*); охо́та (*hunting*); пресле́дование (*pursuing*); *vt.* гоня́ть (*pursue*); чека́нить (*engrave*)

chasm [кэзм] *sn.* бе́здна, пучи́на

chaste [чэйст] *adj.* целому́дренный; стро́гий, чи́стый (*of style, taste*); скро́мный (*demure*)

chasten [чэй-сэн] *vt.* дисциплини́ровать, сде́рживать; очища́ть (*refine*)

chastise [час-та́йз] *vt.* бить, кара́ть, нака́зывать

chastity [чэс-ті-ті] *sn.* целому́дрие; де́вственность (*virginity*)

chat [чэт] *sn.* дру́жеский разгово́р; *vi.* болта́ть

chattels [чэ-тэлс] *sn. pl.* име́ние

chatter [чэ-тэр] *sn.* болтли́вость (*human*); щебета́ние (*bird's*); *vt.i.* болта́ть, щебета́ть

chatterbox [чэ-тэр-бокс] *sm.* болту́н

cheap [чип] *adj.* дешёвый

cheapness [чип-нэс] *sn.* дешеви́зна

cheat [чит] *sm.* обма́нщик, плут; *sn.* обма́н, уло́вка; *vt.* обма́нывать

check [чек] *sn.* шах (*chess*); препятствие (*obstacle*); задержка (*delay*); проверять (*verify*) : квитанция (*token*)

checkmate [чек-мэйт] *sn.* шах и мат

cheek [чик] *sn.* щека; *coll.* наглость, самоуверенность

cheek-bone [чик-боун] *sn.* скула

cheeky [чи-кі] *adj. coll.* нахальный

cheer [чир] *sn.* одобрительное восклицание; *vt.* ободрять (*hearten*); поощрять (*spur on*); **to – up** [ту – ап] утешать

cheerful [чир-фўл] *adj.* бодрый, весёлый

cheese [чиз] *sn.* сыр

chef [шеф] *sm.* главный повар

chemical [ке-мі-кăл] *adj.* химический; *pl.* химические продукты

chemise [ші-мîз] *sn.* женская сорочка

chemist [ке-міст] *sn.* аптекарь (*dealer*); химик (*scientist*)

chemistry [ке-міс-трі] *sn.* химия

cheque [чек] *sn.* чек; **cash a –** [кеш ă –] инкассировать

cherish [че-ріш] *vt.* выращивать, лелеять

cherry [че-рі] *sn.* вишня; *adj.* вишнёвый

cherub [че-рăб] *s.* ангелочек, херувим

chess [чес] *sn.* шахматы

chess-board [чес-борд] *sn.* шашечница

chest [чест] *sn.* сундук (*box, coffer*); **– of drawers** [– ов дрö-ăрз] комод; *anat.* грудь

chestnut [чест-нат] *sn.* каштан (*fruit*); бббка (*horse*); каштановый цвет (*colour*); *adj.* каштановый; бурый, рыжий (*horse*)

chew [чў] *sn.* жвачка; *vt.* жевать

chicanery [ші-кей-нă-рі] *sn.* обход закона (*elusion of law*); интрига

chicken [чі-кĕн] *s.* курёнок, цыплёнок

chicken-pox [чі-кĕн-покс] *sn.* ветряная оспа

chicory [чі-кă-рі] *sn.* цикорий

chief [чиф] *sn.* глава, руководитель; *adj.* главный

chilblain [чіл-блэйн] *sn.* отмороженное место

child [чайлд] *sn.* дитя, ребёнок

child-birth [чайлд-бöрθ] *sn.* роды

childhood [чайлд-хўд] *sn.* детство

childish [чайл-діш] *adj.* детский, ребяческий; глупый (*silly*)

chill [чіл] *sn.* холод; озноб; *med.* простуда; *vt.* охлаждать, холодить

chilly [чі-лі] *adj.* зябкий, холодноватый

chime [чайм] *sn.* куранты, подбор колоколов; *vi.* выбивать мелодию, звонить

chimney [чім-ні] *sn.* дымоход; ламповое стекло (*glass*)

chimney-sweep [чім-ні-сўіп] *sn.* трубочист

chin [чін] *sn.* подбородок

china [чай-нă] *sn.* фарфор

Chinese [чай-нîз] *sm.* китаец; *adj.* китайский

chink [чінк] *sn.* звон (*sound of glasses, etc.*); трещи́на, щель (*slit*)

chip [чіп] *sn.* оско́лок, ще́пка; стру́жка (*shaving(s)*); *pl.* жа́реный карто́фель (*edible*); *vt.i.* отёсывать, струга́ть; обла́мывать (*break off*)

chirp [чёрп] *sn.* чири́канье; *vi.* чири́кать, щебета́ть

chisel [чі-зäл] *sn.* долото́, зуби́ло; *vt.* вая́ть, долби́ть, высека́ть (*stone, etc.*)

chivalrous [ші-вäл-рäс] *adj.* ры́царский

chivalry [ші-вäл-рі] *sn.* ры́царство

chock [чок] *sn.* клин (*wedge*); --full [--фул] битко́м наби́тый

chocolate [чо-кä-літ] *sn.* шокола́д; *adj.* шокола́дный

choice [чойс] *sn.* вы́бор, отбо́р; *adj.* лу́чший (*best*); отбо́рный (*excellent*); разбо́рчивый (*distinct, particular*)

choir [куä-йäр] *sn.* хор; алта́рная часть це́ркви (*chancel*)

choke [чо̆ук] *vt.* души́ть, заглуша́ть (*suppress*); *vi.* дави́ться (*with coughing*); задыха́ться (*with anger*); --down [— да́ун] прогла́тывать (*food*)

choose [чуз] *vt.* выбира́ть, предпочита́ть (*prefer*)

chop [чоп] *sn.* уда́р (*stroke*); отбивна́я котле́та (*meat*); *vt.i.* наре́зать (*cut*); кроши́ть (*mince*)

chopper [чо́-пäр] *sn.* коса́рь, *m.*, се́чка

chopstick [чоп-стік] *sn.* кита́йская па́лочка (*вилка*)

choral [ко́-räл] *adj.* хорово́й

chord [ко̄рд] *sn.* струна́ (*string, etc.*); *mus.* акко́рд

chorister [ко́-ріс-тäр] *sm.* хори́ст

chorus [ко̄-рäс] *sn.* хор

Christ [крайст] Христо́с

christen [крі-сäн] *vt.* крести́ть (*baptize*); дава́ть и́мя (*give name*)

Christendom [крі-сäн-дäм] *sn.* христиа́нский мир

christening [кріс-нін] *sn.* креще́ние

Christian [кріс-чäн] *sm.* христиани́н; *adj.* христиа́нский

Christianity [кріс-тіä-ні-ті] *sn.* христиа́нство

Christmas [кріс-мäс] *sn.* Рождество́; --eve [-- і́в] Соче́льник; -- tree [-- три] ёлка

chromatic [кро-мä-тік] *adj.* цветно́й; *mus.* хромати́ческий

chrome [кро̆ум] *sn.* пигме́нт, кра́ска

chromium [кро̆у-мі-äм] *sn.* хром

chronic [кро́-нік] *adj.* хрони́ческий; застаре́лый (*of illness*)

chronicle [кро́-нікл] *sn.* ле́топись, хро́ника

chrysanthemum [крі-сä́н-ёі-мäм] *sn.* златоцве́т, ризанте́ма

chubby [ча́-бі] *adj.* круголи́цый, полнощёкий, пу́хлый

chuckle [чакл] *sn.* хихи́канье; *vi.* клохта́ть

chum [чам] *sm.* прия́тель, това́рищ

chunk [чанк] *sn. coll.* кусо́к

church [чёрч] *sn.* це́рковь

churchwarden [чœрч-уŏ́р-дăн] *sm.* церко́вный ста́роста

churchyard [чœрч-я́рд] *sn.* кла́дбище

churn [чœрн] *sn.* маслобо́йка (*for butter making*); бито́н для молока́ (*milk*); *vt.* сбива́ть

chute [шут] *sn.* стремни́на; *tech.* спуск

cider [сай-дăр] *sn.* сидр

cigar [сі-га́р] *sn.* сига́ра

cigarette [сі-гă-ре́т] *sn.* папиро́са

cigar-holder [сі-га́р-хŏ́улдăр] *sn.* мундшту́к

cinder [сі́н-дăр] *sn.* пе́пел (*ash*); шлак (*slag*); *pl.* зола́

Cinderella [сін-дă-ре́-лă] *sf.* Зо́лушка

cinema [сі́-ні-мă] *sn.* кинемато́граф, кино́

cinerary [сі́-нă-рă-рі] *adj.* пе́пельный

cinnamon [сі́-нă-мăн] *sn.* кори́ца; *adj.* кори́чневый

cipher [сай-фăр] *sn.* ноль (*nought*); цифр (*figure*); шифр (*secret writing*); *vt.i.* писа́ть ци́фры; шифрова́ть

circle [сœркл] *sn.* круг, окру́жность; кружо́к (*of people*); балко́н, я́рус (*in theatre*); *vt.i.* кружи́ть

circuit [сœр-кіт] *sn.* кругова́я пое́здка (*journey*); кругооборо́т (*circular course*); о́круг (*judge's*); цепь то́ка (*of current*)

circular [сœр-кю-лăр] *sn.* циркуля́р; *adj.* кругово́й, циркуля́рный

circulate [сœр-кю-лэ́йт] *vt.* враща́ться, циркули́ровать

circulation [сœр-кю-лэ́йшăн] *sn.* кровообраще́ние (*of blood*); кругообраще́ние (*rotation*)

circumference [сœр-ка́мфă-рăнс] *sn.* окру́жность, перифе́рия

circumlocution [сœр-кăмло-кю-ша́н] *sn.* многоре́чивость, околи́чность

circumspection [сœр-кăмспе́к-шăн] *sn.* осторо́жность

circumstance [сœр-кăмстăнс] *sn.* обстоя́тельство

circumstantial [сœр-кăмстăн-шăл] *adj.* обстоя́тельный

circumvent [сœр-кăм-ве́нт] *vt.* обману́ть, обойти́

circus [сœр-кăс] *sn.* цирк; кру́глая пло́щадь (*place in town*)

cistern [сіс-тăрн] *sn.* бак, цисте́рна

citadel [сі́-тă-дел] *sn.* кре́пость, цитаде́ль

citation [сай-тэ́й-шăн] *sn.* вы́зов; ссы́лка, цита́та

cite [сайт] *vt.* вызыва́ть (*summon*); цити́ровать

citizen [сі́-ті-зăн] *sm.* граждани́н

citric acid [сі́-трік э́сід] *sn.* лимо́нная кислота́

citron [сі́-трăн] *sn.* цитро́н

city [сі́-ті] *sn.* (большо́й) го́род; **the —** [ə̄ —] комме́рческая и фина́нсовая часть Ло́ндона; *adj.* городско́й

civic [сі́-вік] *adj.* гражда́нский

civil [сі́-віл] *adj.* шта́тский; ве́жливый, любе́зный (*polite*); **— servant** [— сœрвắнт] чино́вник

civilian [сi-ві-ліäн] *sm.*, *adj.* штатский

civility [сi-ві-лі-ті] *sn.* вéжливость, любéзность, учтивость

civilization [сi-ві-лай-зäй-шäн] *sn.* цивилизáция

claim [клэйм] *sn.* трéбование; иск (*suit*); заявка (*statement*); *vt.* трéбовать

claimant [клэй-мäнт] *sm.* истéц

clamber [клäм-бäр] *vi.* карáбкаться

clammy [клä-мі] *adj.* клéйкий, лíпкий; сырóй (*damp*)

clamour [клä-мäр] *sn.* шум; *pl.* крíки; *vi.* кричáть

clamp [клäмп] *sn.* зажúм, скóба, скрéпа

clandestine [клäн-дéс-тін] *adj.* тáйный

clap [клäп] *sn.* удáр (*thunder*); хлопáнье; хлопóк (*hands*); *vt.* рукоплескáть (*hands*); хлóпать

clarify [клä-рi-фай] *vt.* прочищáть, проясня́ть

clarity [клä-рi-ті] *sn.* чистотá, я́сность

clash [клäш] *sn.* столкновéние (*collision*); стук (*bang*); противорéчие (*conflict*); *vi.* стáлкиваться

clasp [к'läсп] *sn.* застёжка, пря́жка; пожáтие (*grip*); объя́тие (*embrace*); *vt.* застéгивать (*fasten*); сжимáть (*grip*); обнимáть (*embrace*)

class [кläс] *sn.* класс; *adj.* классóвый

classic(al) [клä-сiк-(äл)] *adj.* класси́ческий

classify [клä-сi-фай] *vt.* классифицúровать

clatter [клä-тäр] *sn.* стук

(*knock*); шýмная болтовня́ (*noisy talk*); *vi.* стучáть; болтáть

clause [клōз] *sn.* пункт, услóвие; *gram.* предложéние

claw [клō] *sn.* кóготь (*nail*); клешня́ (*crab's*); *tech.* клéщи; *vt.* терзáть, царáпать

clay [клэй] *sn.* гли́на; *adj.* гли́нистый

clean [клин] *adj.* чистоплóтный, чи́стый; *vt.* чи́стить

cleanliness [клéн-лі-нäс] *sn.* чистоплóтность, чистотá

cleanse [кленз] *vt.* очищáть

cleansing [клéн-зій] *sn.* убóрка, чи́стка

clear [клíр] *adj.* свéтлый, чёткий, я́сный; поня́тный (*intelligible*); *vt.i.* очищáть, расчищáть; – **away** – á-уэ́й] убирáть; – **off!** [– оф] убирáйтесь!

clearance [клí-рäнс] *sn.* устранéние (препя́тствий)

clearly [клíр-лі] *adv.* очеви́дно, я́сно

cleavage [клí-ві-дж] *sn.* расхождéние (*divergence*); расщеплéние (*splintering*); раскóл (*split*)

cleave [клив] *vt.* скáлывать

clef [клеф] *sn. mus.* ключ

cleft [клефт] *sn.* трещи́на (*split*)

clemency [клé-мäн-сі] *sn.* милосéрдие, снисходи́тельность

clench [кленч] *sn.* сжимáние; *tech.* заклёпывание; *vt.* сжимáть, сти́скивать

clergy [клéр-джі] *sn.* духовéнство

clergyman [клэ́р-джи-мән] *sm.* поп, свяще́нник

cleric [клэ́-рік] *sm.* духо́вное лицо́

clerical [клэ́-рі-кäл] *adj. eccl.* духо́вный; *com.* канцеля́рский

clerk [кля́рк] *sm.* конто́рский слу́жащий, конто́рщик

clever [клэ́-вäр] *adj.* у́мный; иску́сный, спосо́бный (*skilful, capable*)

cleverness [клэ́-вäр-ніс] *sn.* ло́вкость, спосо́бность

click [клік] *sn.* щёлкание; *vi.* щёлкать

client [клáй-änт] *sm.* клие́нт

clientele [клі-äн-тэ́л] *sn.* клиенту́ра

cliff [кліф] *sn.* круто́й обры́в, скала́

climate [клáй-міт] *sn.* кли́мат

climatic [клай-мä́-тік] *adj.* климати́ческий

climax [клáй-мäкс] *sn.* апоге́й, вы́сшая то́чка

climb [клайм] *sn.* восхожде́ние; подъём горы́; *vt.i.* влеза́ть, ла́зить; кара́бкаться, поднима́ться; ви́ться (*of plants*)

climbing [клáй-мій] *sn.* ла́зание

cling [клій] *vi.* держа́ться, цепля́ться; льнуть

clinic [клі-нік] *sn.* кли́ника

clink [клінк] *sn.* звон; *vt.i.* звуча́ть; чо́каться (*glasses*)

clip [кліп] *sn.* зажи́м, скре́пка; стри́жка (*haircut*); *vt.* сжима́ть; стричь (*hair*)

clipping [клі-пій] *sn.* вы́резка

clique [клик] *sn.* кли́ка

cloak [клоўк] *sn.* плащ; предло́г (*pretext*)

cloak-room [клоўк-ру́м] *sn.* гардеро́б (*clothes*); бага́жная ка́сса (*luggage*)

clock [клок] *sn.* часы́ (не карма́нные)

clockwise [клок-ўáйз] *adv.* по часово́й стре́лке

clockwork [клок-ўэ́рк] *sn.* часово́й механи́зм

clod [клод] *sn.* глы́ба, ком

clog [клог] *sn.* пу́ты; деревя́нный башма́к (*shoe*); *vt.* меша́ть, обременя́ть (*impede*); застопо́ривать (*choke up*)

cloister [клóй-стäр] *sn.* монасты́рь, *m.*

close [клоўс] *adj.* ду́шный, удуши́вый (*stuffy*); бли́зкий (*near*)

close [клоўз] *vt.* закрыва́ть

closeness [клоўс-ніс] *sn.* духота́, бли́зость (*nearness*)

closure [клó-жäр] *sn.* закры́тие; прекраще́ние пре́ний (*parliamentary*)

clot [клот] *sn.* комо́к, сгу́сток; *med.* тромб; *vt.i.* сгуща́ться

cloth [клоθ] *sn.* сукно́, ткань (*stuff*); ска́терть (*table*)

clothe [клоўз] *vt.* одева́ть; облека́ться (*oneself*)

clothes [клоўзз, клоз] *pl.* пла́тье

clothier [клó-θіäр] *sm.* суко́нщик

clothing [клó-θій] *sn.* оде́жда; оде́ние

cloud [клáўд] *sn.* о́блако, ту́ча; *vt.i.* омрача́ть; завола́киваться

cloudless [клаўд-ліс] *adj.* безо́блачный

cloudy [клáу-ді] *adj.* óблачный; непрозрáчный (*liquids*)

clove [клóув] *sn.* гвоздíка

clover [клóу-вǎр] *sn.* клéвер; **in** — в изобилии

clown [клáун] *sm.* клóун, шут

club [клаб] *sn.* клуб; дубúнка (*stick*); трéфа (*card*); *vt.i.* бить дубúной (*strike*)

cluck [клак] *sn.* кудáхтанье; *vi.* клóхтать, кудáхтать

clue [клý] *sn.* путевóдная нить

clump [кламп] *sn.* грýппа; глы́ба (*of earth, ice*)

clumsy [клáм-зі] *adj.* бестáктный (*tactless*); неуклю́жий (*awkward*)

cluster [клáс-тǎр] *sn.* гроздь, кисть, пучóк (*bunch*); грýппа (*of trees, etc.*); рай (*swarm*)

clutch [клач] *sn.* сжáтие (*grasp*); *tech.* зажúм; *vt.* хватáть

clutter [клá-тǎр] *sn.* суматóха; *vt.i.* суетúться

coach [кóуч] *sn.* карéта, экипáж (*carriage*); *sm.* инстрýктор, тренирóвщик; *vt.* учúть (*teach*); тренировáть (*train*)

coachman [кóуч-мǎн] *sm.* кýчер

coagulate [коу-á-гю-лэйт] *vt.* сгущáть

coal [кóул] *sn.* кáменный ýголь

coalesce [коу-ǎ-лéс] *vi.* соединя́ться

coalescence [коу-ǎ-лé-сǎнс] *sn.* соединéние; сращéние (*fusion*)

coalition [коу-ǎ-лí-шǎн] *sn.* коалúция, сою́з

coal-miner [кóул-май-нǎр] *sm.* углекóп

coal-pit [кóул-пíт] *sn.* шáхта

coarse [кóрс] *adj.* грýбый; невéжливый (*of people*); необрабóтанный, сырóй (*of material*)

coarseness [кóрс-нíс] *sn.* грýбость, непристóйность

coast [кóуст] *sn.* побéрежье

coastguard [кóуст-гǎрд] *sn.* береговáя стрáжа

coat [кóут] *sn.* вéрхнее плáтье, пальтó; мех, шерсть, плащ; слой (*of paint, etc.*); — **of arms** — св áрмз гербóвый щит

coax [кóукс] *vt.* задáбривать, угов áривать

cobble [кобл] *sn.* булы́жник; *vt.* чинúть (*mend*)

cobbler [кóб-лǎр] *sm.* бащмáчник, сапóжник (*shoe repairer*)

cobra [кóб-рǎ] *sn.* очкóвая змея́

cobweb [кóб-уэб] *sn.* паутúна

cock [кок] *sm.* петýх (*fowl*); стог (*heap of hay*); кран (*tap*); курóк (*of gun*)

cockade [ко-кэ́йд] *sn.* кокáрда

cockatoo [ко-кǎ-тý] *s.* какадý

cockerel [кóк-рǎл] *sm.* петýшóк

cockle [кокл] *sn.* съедóбный моллюскоотдéщик

cockpit [кóк-піт] *sn.* кабúна; *naut.* кýбрик

cockroach [кóк-рóуч] *s.* таракáн

cocoa [кóу-коу] *s.* какáо

coco-nut [кó-кǎ-нат] *sn.* кокóс

cocoon [ко-ку́н] *sn.* коко́н

cod [код] *s.* треска́

coddle [кодл] *vt.* изне́живать

code [ко́уд] *sn.* ко́декс; шифр; уложе́ние (*law*)

cod-liver oil [код-ли́вăр ойл] *sn.* ры́бий жир

coefficient [ко-и́-фи́-шăнт] *sn.* содéйствующий фа́ктор; *math.* коэффицие́нт

coerce [ко-ăрс] *vt.* принужда́ть

coercion [ко-ăр-шăн] *sn.* наси́лие, принужде́ние

coercive [ко-ăр-сив] *adj.* принуди́тельный

coffee [ко́-фи] *sn.* ко́фе

coffee-pot [ко́-фи-пот] *sn.* кофе́йник

coffer [ко́-фăр] *sn.* сунду́к, я́щик

coffin [ко́-фин] *sn.* гроб

cog [ког] *sn. tech.* зубе́ц, кула́к

cogent [ко́у-джăнт] *adj.* неоспори́мый, убеди́тельный

cogitate [ко́-джи-тэ́йт] *vi.* обду́мывать, размышля́ть

cognate [ког-нэ́йт] *adj.* ро́дственный, схо́дный

cognizance [ко́г-ни-зăнс] *sn.* зна́ние (*knowledge*); *leg.* подсу́дность (*competence, right*); эмбле́ма (*badge*); **take – of** [тэ́йк – ов] заме́тить

cognizant [ко́г-ни-зăнт] *adj.* зна́ющий, уведомлённый

cohabitation [ко-хă-би-тэ́й-шăн] *sn.* сожи́тельство

coherent [ко́у-хи́-рăнт] *adj.* свя́зный; после́довательный (*consistent*)

cohesion [ко́у-хи́-жăн] *sn.* сцепле́ние

coiffure [кўа-фю́р] *sn.* причёска

coil [койл] *sn.* свёрток верёвки; *elect.* кату́шка; *naut.* бу́хта; *vt.i.* дви́гаться изги́бами, свёртывать

coin [койн] *sn.* моне́та; *vt.i.* чека́нить (*mint*); вымышля́ть (*devise*)

coinage [ко́й-нидж] *sn.* чека́нка; моне́тная систе́ма

coincide [ко́у-ин-са́йд] *vi.* совпада́ть

coincidence [ко́у-и́н-си-дăнс] *sn.* совпаде́ние, стече́ние

coke [ко́ук] *sn.* кокс

cold [ко́улд] *sn.* хо́лод; *med.* просту́да; **– in the head** [– ин θă хед] на́сморк; *adj.* холо́дный; безуча́стный (*indifferent*)

coldness [ко́улд-нис] *sn.* хо́лод; равноду́шие (*indifference*)

collaborate [кă-лắ-бă-рэ́йт] *vi.* сотру́дничать

collaborator [кă-лắ-бă-рей-тăр] *sn.* сотру́дник

collapse [кă-лăпс] *sn.* изнеможе́ние; *vi.* изнемога́ть, ослабева́ть

collar [ко́-лăр] *sn.* воротни́к; оше́йник (*dog's*); хому́т (*horse's*)

collarbone [ко́-лăр-бо́ун] *sn.* ключи́ца

collate [ко-лэ́йт] *vt.* слича́ть

collateral [ко-лắт-рăл] *adj.* побо́чный

colleague [ко́-лиг] *sm.* колле́га, сослужи́вец

collect [кă-лéкт] *vt.* собира́ть

collected [кă-лéк-тид] *adj.* споко́йный, хладнокро́вный (*calm*)

collection [ко-лéк-шăн] *sn.* коллéкция; сбóрник; скоплéние (*multitude*); сбор (*assemblage*)

collective [ко-лéк-тив] *adj.* коллектйвный; совокýпный (*cumulative*)

collector [ко-лéк-тăр] *sn.* коллекционéр; сбóрщик

college [кó-лидж] *sn.* кóлледж; срéдняя шкóла

collide [кă-лáйд] *vi.* стáлкиваться

collier [кó-лйăр] *sn.* углекóп; *sn.* ýгольщик (*ship*)

colliery [кó-лйă-ри] *sn.* ýгольная копь

collision [кă-лú-жăн] *sn.* столкновéние; противорéчие (*conflict*)

colloquial [ко-лóу-кўй-ăл] *adj.* разговóрный

colloquialism [ко-лóу-кўй-ă-лизм] *sn.* разговóрный стиль

colon [кóу-лăн] *sn.* двоетóчие; *anat.* тóлстая кишкá

colonel [кă-нăл] *sm.* полкóвник

colonial [кă-лóу-нйăл] *adj.* колониáльный

colonize [кó-лă-найз] *vt.i.* колонизйровать; поселять

colony [кó-лă-ни] *sn.* колóния

coloration [ка-лă-рéй-шăн] *sn.* раскрáска

colossal [кă-лó-сăл] *adj.* колоссáльный

colour [кá-лăр] *sn.* крáска (*paint, etc.*), цвет (*hue*); румя́нец (*complexion*); *vt.* крáсить; *vi.* краснéть (*blush*)

colouring [кá-лă-рйн] *sn.* колорйт, раскрáска

colourless [кá-лăр-лис] *adj.* бесцвéтный

colt [кóулт] *s.* жеребёнок

column [кó-лăм] *sn.* колóнна, столб (*pillar*); графá, столбéц (*of newspaper*)

comb [кóум] *sn.* грéбень, *m.*; *vt.* расчёсывать; — **out** вычёсывать

combat [кóм-бăт] *sn.* бой, сражéние; *vi.* сражáться

combatant [кóм-бă-тăнт] *sn.* сражáющийся

combination [ком-би-нéй-шăн] *sn.* соединéние, сочетáние

combine [кóм-байн] *sn.* кóмбайн (*harvester*); комбинáт, трест (*syndicate*); *vt.i.* комбинúровать, объединя́ться

combustible [кăм-бáс-тибл] *adj.* горю́чий

combustion [кăм-бáс-чăн] *sn.* сгорáние

come [кам] *vi.* прибывáть, приходйть; — **across** [— ă-крóс] встречáться; — **down** [— дáун] спускáться; — **in** [— ин] входйть; — **out** [— áут] выходйть

comedian [кă-мú-дйăн] *sm.* комедиáнт

comedy [кó-мú-ди] *sn.* комéдия

comely [кáм-ли] *adj.* благообрáзный, миловйдный

comestibles [кă-мéс-тиблс] *sn. pl.* съестны́е припáсы

comet [кó-мйт] *sn.* комéта

comfort [кáм-фăрт] *sn.* комфóрт, удóбство; *vt.* успокáивать, утешáть

comfortable [кáм-фăр-тăбл] *adj.* удóбный, ую́тный; спокóйный (*at ease*)

comical [кó-ми-кăл] *adj.* забáвный, смешнóй

comma [ко́-мǎ] *sn.* запята́я

command [кǎ-ма́нд] *sn.* командова́ние; *mil.* кома́нда; прика́з (*order*); *vt.* веле́ть, прика́зывать (*order*); нача́льствовать, управля́ть (*have authority, control*)

commandeer [кǎ-мǎн-ди́р] *vt. mil.* принуди́тельно набира́ть; реквизи́ровать

commander [кǎ-ма́н-дǎр] *sm.* команди́р

commanding [кǎ-ма́н-дин̇] *adj.* внуши́тельный (*impressive*); повели́тельный (*authoritative*)

commandment [кǎ-ма́нд-мǎнт] *sn.* за́поведь

commemorate [кǎ-ме́-мǎ-рэйт] *vt.* увекове́чивать; отмеча́ть (*record*); пра́здновать (*celebrate*)

commence [кǎ-ме́нс] *vt.* начина́ть

commencement [кǎ-ме́нс-мǎнт] *sn.* нача́ло

commend [кǎ-ме́нд] *vt.* хвали́ть

commendable [кǎ-ме́н-дǎбл] *adj.* похва́льный

commensurate [кǎ-ме́н-шǎ-рǐт] *adj.* пропорциона́льный, соразме́рный

comment [ко́-мǎнт] *sn.* коммента́рий; *vi.* комменти́ровать, толкова́ть

commentary [ко́-мǎн-тǎ-рǐ] *sn.* коммента́рий, толкова́ние

commentator [ко́-мǎн-тэй-тǎр] *sm.* коммента́тор

commerce [ко́-мǎрс] *sn.* торго́вля

commercial [кǎ-ме́р-шǎл] *adj.* комме́рческий, торго́-

вый; – **traveller** [– трǎ́-вǎ-лǎр] *sn.* коммивояжёр

commiserate [кǎ-ми́-зǎ-рэйт] *vt.* сожале́ть, сочу́вствовать

commiseration [кǎ-ми́-зǎ-рэ́й-шǎн] *sn.* сочу́вствие

commissary [ко́-ми-сǎ-рǐ] *sm.* интенда́нт

commission [кǎ-ми́-шǎн] *sn.* коми́ссия (*board*); полномо́чие (*warrant*); поруче́ние (*errand*); *mil.* офице́рский чин; *vt.* поруча́ть

commissioner [кǎ-ми́-шǎ-нǎр] *sm.* комисса́р

commit [кǎ-ми́т] *vt.* соверша́ть (*crime, etc.*); доверя́ть, поруча́ть (*entrust*)

commitment [кǎ-ми́т-мǎнт] *sn.* обяза́тельство, соверше́ние

committee [кǎ-ми́-тǐ] *sn.* комите́т

commode [кǎ-мо́уд] *sn.* комо́д

commodious [кǎ-мо́-диǎс] *adj.* удо́бный (*comfortable*); просто́рный (*roomy*)

commodity [кǎ-мо́-ди-тǐ] *sn.* проду́кты, това́р

common [ко́-мǎн] *sn.* вы́гон, общи́нная земля́; па́стбище (*pasture land*); *adj.* о́бщий (*general*); обще́ственный, публи́чный (*public*); обыкнове́нный, просто́й (*ordinary*)

commonplace [ко́-мǎн-плэйс] *sn.* изби́тый цита́т; *adj.* бана́льный

commotion [кǎ-мо́у-шǎн] *sn.* кутерьма́; смяте́ние (*confusion*)

communal [ко́-мю-нǎл] *adj.* общи́нный

communicate [кӑ-мю́-ни-кэйт] vt. передавать, сообщать; vi. сноситься

communication [кӑ-мю-ни-кэ́й-шӑн] sn. сообщение

communion [кӑ-мю́-ниӑн] sn. общение; eccl. причастие

community [кӑ-мю́-ни-ти] sn. общество, община

commute [кӑ-мют] vt. менять, обменивать; смягчать, уменьшать (diminish penalty)

compact [ко́м-пӑкт] sn. договор (agreement); прессованная пудра (powder); adj. компактный, плотный; vt. сжимать

companion [кӑм-пӑ́-ниӑн] sn. товарищ; спутник (fellow traveller)

companionship [кӑм-пӑ́-ниӑн-шип] sn. общение; товарищество

company [кӑ́м-пӑ-ни] sn. компания; общество; товарищество; mil. рота

comparable [ко́м-пӑ-рӑбл] adj. сравнимый

comparative [кӑм-пӑ́-рӑ-тив] adj. сравнительный

compare [кӑм-пӑ́р] vt. сравнивать, уподоблять

comparison [кӑм-пӑ́-ри-сӑн] sn. сравнение

compartment [кӑм-пӑ́рт-мӑнт] sn. отделение; купе (in train)

compass [кӑм-пӑс] sn. объхват, объём (extent, area, etc.); окружность (circuit); компас (instrument); диапазон (of voice); pl. циркуль

compassion [кӑм-пӑ́-шӑн] sn. жалость, сострадание

compassionate [кӑм-пӑ́-шӑ-нӗт] adj. жалостливый, сострадательный

compatible [кӑм-пӑ́-тибл] adj. совместный

compatriot [кӑм-пӑ́-три-ӑт] sn. соотечественник

compel [кӑм-пе́л] vt. заставлять, принуждать

compensate [ко́м-пӑн-сэйт] vt.i. возмещать, вознаграждать

compensation [ком-пӑн-сэ́й-шӑн] sn. возмещение, вознаграждение

compete [кӑм-пи́т] vi. конкурировать, состязаться

competence [ко́м-пи-тӑнс] sn. достаток, состоятельность

competent [ко́м-пи-тӑнт] adj. полноправный

competition [кӑм-пи-ти́-шӑн] sn. конкуренция; соревнование

competitive [кӑм-пе́-ти-тив] adj. конкурирующий

competitor [кӑм-пе́-ти-тӑр] sn. конкурент; соперник (rival)

compile [кӑм-па́йл] vt. компилировать, составлять

complacency [кӑм-плэ́й-сӑн-си] sn. самодовольство; благодушие (placidity)

complacent [кӑм-плэ́й-сӑнт] adj. благодушный; самодовольный

complain [кӑм-плэ́йн] vi. жаловаться; выражать недовольство (express discontent)

complaint [кӑм-плэ́йнт] sn. жалоба, недовольство

complaisant [кӑм-плэ́й-зӑнт] adj. услужливый; уступчивый

complement [ко́м-пли-мэнт] *sn.* дополне́ние

complementary [кам-пли-мéн-тə-ри] *adj.* дополни́тельный

complete [кам-плı́т] *adj.* зако́нченный (*finished*); по́лный (*entire*); *vt.* доде́лывать, зака́нчивать

completion [кам-плı́-шəн] *sn.* заверше́ние, исполне́ние, оконча́ние

complex [ко́м-плекс] *adj.* пу́таный (*confused*); сло́жный (*complicated*)

complexion [кам-плéк-шəн] *sn.* вид (*aspect*); цвет лица́ (*of face*)

complexity [кам-плéк-си-ти] *sn.* сло́жность

compliance [кам-плáй-əнс] *sn.* усту́пчивость; согла́сие (*consent*)

complicate [ко́м-пли-кэйт] *vt.* усложня́ть

complicated [ко́м-пли-кэй-тıд] *adj.* запу́танный, сло́жный

complication [кам-пли-кэй-шəн] *sn.* запу́танность, сло́жность; *med.* осложне́ние

complicity [кам-плı́-си-ти] *sn.* соуча́стие

compliment [ко́м-пли-мэнт] *sn.* похвала́; *pl.* поздравле́ние, покло́н, приве́т; *vt.* приве́тствовать, поздравля́ть

complimentary [кам-пли-мéн-тə-ри] *adj.* поздрави́тельный; ле́стный (*flattering*)

comply [кам-плáй] *vt.* исполня́ть, уступа́ть; *vi.* соглаша́ться

component [кəм-поу́-нəнт] *sn.* компоне́нт; составна́я часть, составно́й элеме́нт; *adj.* составно́й

compose [кəм-поу́з] *vt.* составля́ть, сочиня́ть; *mus.* компони́ровать; успока́ивать (*calm*) *typ.*; набира́ть

composed [кəм-поу́зд] *adj.* сде́ржанный, споко́йный; хладнокро́вный (*cool*)

composer [кəм-поу́-зəр] *sn.* компози́тор

composite [ко́м-пə-зıт] *adj.* сло́жный, составно́й

composition [ком-пə-зı́-шəн] *sn. mus.* компози́ция; сочине́ние (*school*); *typ.* набо́р

compositor [кəм-по́-зи-тəр] *sn. typ.* набо́рщик

composure [кəм-поу́-жəр] *sn.* споко́йствие, хладнокро́вие

compound [ко́м-паунд] *sn.* смесь (*mixture*); соста́в; компа́унд (*enclosure*); *adj.* сло́жный, составно́й; [ком-па́унд] *vt.* сме́шивать

comprehend [ком-прı-хéнд] *vt.* понима́ть, разуме́ть; схвати́ть (*grasp*)

comprehension [ком-прı-хéн-шəн] *sn.* понима́ние, разуме́ние

comprehensive [ком-прı-хéн-сıв] *adj.* объемля́ющий (*embracing much*); исче́рпывающий (*exhaustive*)

compress [ком-прéс] *sn. med.* ко́мпресс; *vt.* [кəм-прéс] сда́вливать, сжима́ть

comprise [кəм-прáйз] *vt.* вмеща́ть, заключа́ть, охва́тывать

compromise [ко́м-пра-майз] *sn.* компроми́сс; *vt.* компромети́ровать

compulsion [кам-па́л-шан] *sn.* принужде́ние

compulsory [кам-па́л-са-ри] *adj.* обяза́тельный, прину́дительный

compunction [кам-па́нк-шан] *sn.* угрызе́ние

computation [ком-пю-тэ́й-шан] *sn.* вы́кладка, вычисле́ние

compute [кăм-пю́т] *vt.* вычисля́ть, подсчи́тывать

comrade [ко́м-ри́д] *sm.* това́рищ

comradeship [ко́м-ри́д-шип] *sn.* това́рищеские отноше́ния

concave [ко́н-кэйв] *adj.* во́гнутый

conceal [кăн-си́л] *vt.* скрыва́ть

concealment [кăн-си́л-мăнт] *sn.* скрыва́ние; та́йное убе́жище (*secret retreat*)

concede [кăн-си́д] *vt.* уступа́ть; допуска́ть (*grant*)

conceit [кăн-си́т] *sn.* самомне́ние, тщесла́вие

conceivable [кăн-си́-вăбл] *adj.* возмо́жный, мысли́мый, постижи́мый

conceive [кăн-си́в] *vt.i.* возыме́ть (*idea*); зача́ть (*child*); представля́ть себе́ (*imagine*)

concentrate [ко́н-сăн-трэйт] *vt.* сосредото́чивать; *chem.* выпа́ривать, сгуща́ть

concentration [ко́н-сăн-трэ́й-шан] *sn.* концентра́ция; сосредото́чение

concept [ко́н-сэпт] *sn.* мысль, поня́тие

conception [кăн-сэ́п-шан] *sn.* конце́пция; поня́тие; зача́тие (*conceiving*)

concern [кăн-сёрн] *sn.* де́ло, предприя́тие (*business*); забо́та, трево́га (*anxiety*); *vi.* каса́ться

concerning [кăн-сёр-ни́н] *prep.* относи́тельно

concert [ко́н-сёрт] *sn.* конце́рт; согла́сие (*unison*); *vi.* [кăн-сёрт] сгова́риваться

concession [кăн-сэ́-шăн] *sn.* конце́ссия (*grant*); усту́пка (*abatement*)

conciliate [кăн-си́-ли-эйт] *vt.* примиря́ть, согласо́вывать

conciliation [кăн-си-ли-э́й-шăн] *sn.* примире́ние

concise [кăн-сайс] *adj.* кра́ткий, сжа́тый

conclave [ко́н-клэйв] *sn.* та́йное совеща́ние; *eccl.* конкла́в

conclude [кăн-клю́д] *vt.i.* зака́нчивать, заключа́ть; выводи́ть (*deduct*)

conclusion [кăн-клю́-жăн] *sn.* заключе́ние, оконча́ние

conclusive [кăн-клю́-сив] *adj.* доказа́тельный, убеди́тельный (*proved*); заключи́тельный (*final*)

concoct [кăн-ко́кт] *vt.* замышля́ть, приду́мывать (*devise*); стряпа́ть (*cook, prepare*)

concoction [кăн-ко́к-шăн] *sn.* вы́мысел, стряпня́ (*food*)

concord [ко́н-кóрд] *sn.* лад, согла́сие; *gram.* согласова́ние

concourse [ко́н-кóрс] *sn.* стече́ние (наро́да), толпа́

concrete [кон-крит] *sn.* бетóн; *adj.* бетóнный; конкрéтный

concur [кан-кéр] *vi.* совпадáть, соглашáться, сходиться

concurrence [кан-кá-ранс] *sn.* совпадéние, соглáсие, стечéние

concussion [кан-кá-шан] *sn.* сотрясéние

condemn [кан-дéм] *vt.* осуждáть; браковáть (*goods*)

condemnation [кан-дем-нэй-шан] *sn.* осуждéние; приговóр

condensation [кан-ден-сэй-шан] *sn.* конденсáция, сгущéние

condense [кан-дéнс] *vt.i.* конденсировать, сгущáть, сжимáть (*make denser*); сокращáть (*make briefer*)

condescend [кан-ди-сéнд] *vi.* снисходить; удостáивать (*deign*)

condiment [кóн-ди-мант] *sn.* приправа

condition [кан-ди-шан] *sn.* обстоя́тельство (*circumstance*); положéние, состоя́ние (*state*); услóвие (*stipulation*); *vt.* услóвливать

conditional [кан-ди-шан-ал] *adj.* услóвный

condole [кан-дóул] *vi.* соболéзновать, сочýвствовать

condolence [кан-дóул-анс] *sn.* соболéзнование

condone [кан-дóун] *vt.* прощáть

conducive [кан-дю-сив] *adj.* способствующий

conduct [кóн-дакт] *sn.* поведéние; *vt.* [кан-дáкт] вести, сопровождáть; руководить (*business*); *mus.* дирижировать

conductor [кан-дáк-тар] *sn.* кондýктор; *mus.* дирижёр; *phys.* проводник; *elect.* прóвод; **lightning —** [лайтнинг —] громоотвóд

cone [кóун] *sn.* кóнус; *bot.* шишка

confection [кан-фéк-шан] *sn.* слáсти

confectioner [кан-фéкшă-нăр] *sn.* кондитер

confectionery [кан-фéкшăн-ăри] *sn.* кондитерская (*shop*); слáдости (*sweets*)

confederate [кан-фé-дарэйт] *sm.* соучáстник, союзник; *adj.* союзный, федеративный

confederation [кан-фе-дарэй-шан] *sn.* союз

confer [кан-фéр] *vt.* даровáть; *vi.* совещáться

conference [кóн-фă-ранс] *sn.* конферéнция, совещáние

confess [кан-фéс] *vt.i.* *eccl.* исповéдывать; признавáть (*acknowledge*)

confession [кан-фé-шан] *sn.* *eccl.* исповедь; признáние

confide [кан-фáйд] *vt.i.* доверя́ть, полагáться, ввéрять (*trust*)

confidence [кóн-фи-данс] *sn.* довéрие (*reliance*), увéренность (*assuredness*); смéлость (*pluck*)

confident [кóн-фи-дант] *adj.* довéрчивый

confidential [кон-фи-дéншан] *adj.* доверительный, конфиденциáльный, секрéтный

confine [кăн-фа́йн] *vt.* заключа́ть (*imprison*); ограни́чивать (*limit*)

confinement [кăн-фа́йнмăнт] *sn.* заключе́ние, заточе́ние (*imprisonment*); ро́ды, *m.pl.* (*child-birth*); уедине́ние (*solitude*)

confirm [кăн-фё́рм] *vt.* подтвержда́ть, утвержда́ть

confirmation [кăн-фăрмэ́й-шăн] *sn.* подтвержде́ние, утвержде́ние; *eccl.* конфирма́ция

confiscate [ко́н-фı̆с-кэйт] *vt.* конфискова́ть

confiscation [кон-фı̆с-кэ́й-шăн] *sn.* конфиска́ция

conflagration [кон-флă-грэ́й-шăн] *sn.* большо́й пожа́р

conflict [ко́н-флı̆кт] *sn.* борьба́ (*struggle*); конфли́кт; столкнове́ние (*collision*); [кăн-флı̆кт] *vi.* ста́лкиваться

conflicting [кăн-флı̆к-тı̆й] *adj.* противополо́жный, противоречи́вый

conform [кăн-фо́рм] *vt.i.* согласова́ться; сообразова́ться (*comply with*); подчини́ться (*submit*); приспособля́ться (*adapt*)

conformity [кăн-фо́р-мı̆-тı̆] *sn.* сообра́зность, соотве́тствие

confound [кăн-фа́унд] *vt.* сме́шивать, спу́тывать

confraternity [кон-фрă-тё́р-нı̆-тı̆] *sn.* бра́тство

confront [кăн-фра́нт] *vt.* сопоставля́ть

confuse [кăн-фю́з] *vt.* смуща́ть; спу́тывать (*entangle*)

confusion [кăн-фю́-жăн] *sn.* смуще́ние; пу́таница; беспоря́док (*disorder*)

confute [кăн-фю́т] *vt.* опроверга́ть

congeal [кăн-джı̆л] *vt.i.* замерза́ть; замора́живать; застыва́ть

congenial [кăн-джı̆-нı̆ăл] *adj.* подходя́щий; симпати́чный

congenital [кăн-дже́-нı̆-тăл] *adj.* прирождённый

congestion [кăн-дже́с-чăн] *sn.* скопле́ние, ску́ченность; *med.* прили́в кро́ви

congratulate [кăн-грă-тю-лэйт] *vt.* поздравля́ть

congratulation [кăн-грă-тю-лэ́й-шăн] *sn.* поздравле́ние

congregate [ко́н-грı̆-гэйт] *vi.* собира́ться

congress [ко́н-грес] *sn.* конгре́сс, съезд

congruous [ко́н-гру-ăс] *adj.* гармони́рующий, соотве́тствующий

conical [ко́-нı̆-кăл] *adj.* конусообра́зный

conifer [ко́у-нı̆-фăр] *sn.* хво́йное де́рево

coniferous [ко́у-нı̆-фă-рăс] *adj.* хво́йный, шишконо́сный

conjecture [кăн-дже́к-чăр] *sn.* дога́дка, предположе́ние; *vt.i.* гада́ть, предполага́ть

conjoin [кăн-джо́йн] *vt.i.* совокупля́ть, соединя́ть

conjugal [ко́н-джу-гăл] *adj.* бра́чный, супру́жеский

conjugate [ко́н-джў-гэйт] *vt. gram.* спряга́ть

conjugation [ко́н-джу-гэ́й-шăн] *sn.* спряже́ние

conjunction [кăн-джăнк-шăн] *sn.* связь, соединение; сочетание (*union*); *gram.* союз

conjunctive [кăн-джăнк-тĭв] *adj.* связывающий (*connective*); *physiol.* соединительный; *gram.* сослагательный

conjuncture [кăн-джăнк-чăр] *sn.* стечение обстоятельств

conjure [кăн-джўр] *vt.* умолять (*entreat*); заклинать (*charm*); [кăн-джăр] *vt.i.* фокусничать (*juggle*); **to — up** [ту – ап] вызывать в воображении

conjurer [кăн-джă-рăр] *sm.* фокусник

connect [кă-нĕкт] *vt.* соединять

connected [кă-нĕк-тĭд] *adj.* связный

connection, connexion [кă-нĕк-шăн] *sn.* связь; сношение (*relation*)

connivance [кă-най-вăнс] *sn.* поблажка, потворство

connive [кă-найв] *vt.* мирволить, потворствовать

connubial [кă-ню-бĭăл] *adj.* брачный, супружеский

conquer [кóн-кăр] *vt.i.* завоёвывать

conqueror [кóн-кăр-ăр] *sm.* завоеватель, победитель

conquest [кóн-кўэст] *sn.* завоевание, покорение

conscience [кóн-шăнс] *sn.* совесть

conscientious [кăн-шĭ-ĕн-шăс] *adj.* добросовестный, совестливый

conscious [кóн-шăс] *adj.* сознательный, сознающий

consciousness [кóн-шăс-нĭс] *sn.* сознание, сознательность

conscript [кóн-скрĭпт] *sm.* призывник

conscription [кăн-скрĭп-шăн] *sn.* призыв; войнская повинность (*military service*)

consecrate [кóн-сĭ-крэйт] *vt.* освящать (*sanctify*); посвящать (*dedicate, ordain*)

consecration [кóн-сĭ-крэй-шăн] *sn.* освящение; посвящение

consecutive [кăн-сĕ-кютĭв] *adj.* последовательный

consent [кăн-сĕнт] *sn.* согласие; *vi.* соглашаться

consequence [кóн-сĭ-кўэнс] *sn.* вывод, заключение; следствие; важность (*importance*)

consequent [кóн-сĭ-кўэнт] *adj.* последовательный

consequently [кóн-сĭ-кўэнт-лĭ] *adv.* вследствие, следовательно

conservation [кăн-сăр-вэй-шăн] *sn.* сохранение

conservative [кăн-сăр-вă-тĭв] *adj.* консервативный

conservatoire [кăн-сăр-вă-тўăр] *sn.* консерватория

conservatory [кăн-сăр-вă-тă-рĭ] *sn.* оранжерея, теплица

conserve [кăн-сăрв] *vt.* сохранять; сберегать; консервировать (*food*)

consider [кăн-сĭ-дăр] *vt.i.* обсуждать, размышлять, рассуждать

considerable [кăн-сĭ-дăр-ăбл] *adj.* значительный

considerate [кăн-сĭ-дă-рĭт] *adj.* внимательный к другим

consideration [кăн-си-дă-рэ́й-шăн] *sn.* размышле́ние (*reflection*); уваже́ние (*regard*)

consign [кăн-са́йн] *vt.* отправля́ть, посыла́ть (*send away, send*); поруча́ть (*commission*)

consignee [кон-сай-ни́] *sm.* товарополуча́тель

consignment [кăн-са́йнмăнт] *sn.* отпра́вка; накладна́я (*bill of lading*)

consist [кăн-си́ст] *vi.* состоя́ть

consistence [кăн-си́с-тăнс] *sn.* консисте́нция; сте́пень пло́тности (*degree of density*)

consistency [кăн-си́с-тăн-си] *sn.* после́довательность

consistent [кăн-си́с-тăнт] *adj.* после́довательный (*constant*); сообра́зный (*compatible*); пло́тный (*solid*)

consolation [кăн-сă-лэ́й-шăн] *sn.* утеше́ние

console [кăн-со́ул] *vt.* утеша́ть

consolidate [кăн-со́-ли-дэ́йт] *vt.* закрепля́ть, укрепля́ть, утвержда́ть

consolidation [кăн-со-ли-дэ́й-шăн] *sn.* утвержде́ние; консолида́ция

consonance [кон-сă-нăнс] *sn.* созву́чие

consonant [кон-сă-нăнт] *sn.* (*let-gram.* согла́сная бу́ква (*letter*); согла́сный звук (*sound*); *adj.* согла́сный

conspicuous [кăн-спи́-кю-ăс] *adj.* ви́дный, заме́тный

conspiracy [кăн-спи́-рă-си] *sn.* за́говор

conspirator [кăн-спи́-рă-тăр] *sm.* загово́рщик

conspire [кăн-спа́й-ăр] *vi.* составля́ть за́говор

constable [кăн-стăбл] *sm.* городово́й, полице́йский

constabulary [кăн-стắ-бю-лă-ри] *sn.* поли́ция

constant [кон-стăнт] *sn. math.* постоя́нная (величина́); *adj.* постоя́нный

constellation [кăн-стĕ-лэ́й-шăн] *sn.* созве́здие

consternation [кон-стăрнэ́й-шăн] *sn.* изумле́ние, смуще́ние, смяте́ние

constipation [кăн-сти-пэ́й-шăн] *sn.* запо́р

constituency [кăн-сти́-тю-ăн-си] *sn.* избира́тельный о́круг

constitute [кон-сти́-тют] *vt.* осно́вывать, составля́ть

constitution [кăн-сти-тю́-шăн] *sn. med., polit.* конститу́ция; составле́ние, учрежде́ние

constitutional [кăн-сти-тю́-шăн-ăл] *adj. med.* органи́ческий; *polit.* конституцио́нный

constraint [кăн-стрэ́йнт] *sn.* принужде́ние; стесне́ние

construct [кăн-стра́кт] *vt.* стро́ить; *gram.* составля́ть

construction [кăн-стра́кшăн] *sn.* констру́кция; строе́ние, строи́тельство

constructive [кăн-стра́к-тив] *adj.* конструкти́вный; тво́рческий (*creative*)

constructor [кăн-стра́к-тăр] *sm.* строи́тель

consulate [кон-сю-лит] *sn.* ко́нсульство

consult [кăн-са́лт] *vt.i.* сове́товаться, совеща́ться, справля́ться

consultant [кăн-сáл-тăнт] *sm.* консультáнт

consultation [кон-сăл-тэ́й-шăн] *sn.* совещáние (*conference*); *med.* консилиум

consume [кăн-сю́м] *vt.* потребля́ть, расхóдовать; сжигáть (*fire*)

consumer [кăн-сю́-мăр] *sm.* потреби́тель

consummate [кăн-сá-мĭт] *adj.* вы́сший, совершéнный; *vt.* [кóн-са-мэйт] завершáть, совершéнствовать

consumption [кăн-сáмп-шăн] *sn.* потреблéние (*use*); расхóд (*amount consumed*); *med.* чахóтка

consumptive [кăн-сáмп-тĭв] *adj.* туберкулёзный, чахóточный

contact [кóн-тæкт] *sm.* контáкт; соприкосновéние

contagious [кăн-тэ́й-джĭ-ăс] *adj.* заразúтельный, зарáзный

contain [кăн-тэ́йн] *vt.* вмещáть, содержáть; – **oneself** [– ўăн-сéлф] сдéрживаться

container [кăн-тэ́й-нăр] *sn.* вмести́лище, сосу́д

contaminate [кăн-тǽ-мĭ-нэйт] *vt.* загрязня́ть, оскверня́ть

contemplate [кóн-тĕм-плэйт] *vt.i.* обду́мывать (*think over*); созерцáть (*meditate*); намéреваться (*intend*)

contemplation [кон-тĕм-плэ́й-шăн] *sn.* размышлéние, созерцáние; **in –** [ĭн –] имéть в виду́

contemporary [кăн-тĕм-пă-рă-рĭ] *sm.* современник; *adj.* совремéнный

contempt [кăн-тĕмпт] *sn.* презрéние; **– of court** [– ов кóрт] неповинéние; нея́вка в суд

contemptible [кăн-тĕмп-тĭбл] *adj.* презрéнный

content [кóн-тĕнт] *sn.* содержáние; объём (*capacity*); довóльствие, удовóльствие (*state of being content*); *adj.* [кăн-тĕнт] довóльный

contention [кăн-тĕн-шăн] *sn.* борьбá, спор, ссóра (*quarrel*); соревновáние (*emulation*)

contentment [кăн-тĕнт-мăнт] *sn.* довóльство (*ease*); удовлетворённость (*satisfaction*)

contest [кóн-тĕст] *sn.* сопéрничество; соревновáние; *vt.* [кăн-тĕст] опровергáть, оспáривать

continence [кóн-тĭ-нăнс] *sn.* воздержáние; сдéржанность

continent [кóн-тĭ-нăнт] *sn.* материк

continental [кон-тĭ-нéн-тăл] *adj.* континентáльный

contingency [кăн-тĭн-джăн-сĭ] *sn.* случáйность

continual [кăн-тĭ-ню-ăл] *adj.* беспрерывный, беспрестáнный

continuation [кăн-тĭ-ню-эй-шăн] *sn.* продолжéние

continue [кăн-тĭ-ню] *vt.i.* остáваться, продолжáть

continuous [кăн-тĭ-ню-ăс] *adj.* непрерывный; сплошнóй; постоя́нный

contortion [кăн-тóр-шăн] *sn.* искривлéние

contour [кóн-тýр] sn. контýр; – map [– мэп] немáя кáрта

contraband [кóн-трă-бæнд] sn. контрабáнда

contraceptive [кон-трă-сéп-тів] adj. противозачáточный

contract [кóн-трæкт] sn. договóр, контрáкт; vt.i. [кăн-трæкт] сжимáть, сýживать (shrink); подрядáть (undertake)

contraction [кăн-трǽк-шăн] sn. сжáтие; сýживание

contractor [кóн-трǽк-тăр] sm. подрядчик

contradict [кăн-трă-дíкт] vt. противорéчить

contradiction [кăн-трă-дíк-шăн] sn. противорéчие

contradictory [кăн-трă-дíк-тă-рі] adj. противорéчивый

contrary [кóн-трă-рі] adj. противополóжный, противорéчивый; adv. вопрекú, противно; on the – [он ђă –] напрóтив; [кăн-трé-рі] adj. несговóрчивый, упрямый

contrast [кóн-траст] sn. противополóжность, противополóжность; vt. [кăн-трáст] противополагáть, сопоставлять

contravention [кóн-трă-вéн-шăн] sn. нарушéние

contribute [кăн-трí-бют] vt.i. вносúть, жéртвовать (money); отдавáть (time)

contribution [кăн-трí-бю-шăн] sn. вклад, уплáта (money); контрибýция; пожéртвование (donation)

contributor [кăн-трí-бю-тăр] sm. сотрýдник, учáстник

contrivance [кăн-трáй-вăнс] sn. придýмывание (concoction); изобретéние (invention); приспособлéние (device)

contrive [кăн-трáйв] vt.i. выдýмывать; замышлять

control [кăн-трóул] sn. руковóдство, управлéние; власть (authority); провéрка, контрóль, надзóр (check); обуздáние (restraint); vt. контролúровать; сдéрживать (restrain)

controller [кăн-трóу-лăр] sm. контролёр, ревизóр

controversial [кон-трă-вёр-шăл] adj. спóрный

controversy [кóн-трă-вёр-сі] sn. полéмика, словопрéние, спор

conundrum [кă-нáн-дрăм] sn. головолóмка, загáдка

convalescence [кон-вă-лéсăнс] sn. выздоровлéние

convalescent [кон-вă-лéсăнт] sm., adj. выздорáвливающий [вăть

convene [кăн-вúн] vt. созывáть

convenience [кăн-ви-ні-ăнс] sn. выгода, удóбство

convenient [кăн-вú-ніăнт] adj. гóдный, удóбный

convent [кóн-вăнт] sn. жéнский монастырь

convention [кăн-вéн-шăн] sn. договóр, соглашéние; собрáние, съезд (assembly)

conventional [кăн-вéншăн-ăл] adj. обуслóвленный, услóвный

converge [кăн-вёрдж] vi. приближáться, сходúться

convergence [кăн-вёрджăнс] sn. сходúмость, схождéние

conversant [кăн-вăр-сăнт] *adj.* сведущий

conversation [кон-вăр-сейшăн] *sn.* беседа, разговор

converse [кăн-вăрс] *vi.* беседовать, разговаривать; [кон-вăрс] *adj.* обратный, перевёрнутый

conversion [кăн-вăр-шăн] *sn.* обращение, превращение; *fin.* конверсия

convert [кон-вăрт] *sm.* обращённый; *vt.* переменять (*change into*); превращать (*transform*)

convertible [кăн-вăр-тибл] *adj.* обратимый, превратимый

convex [кон-вĕкс] *adj.* выгнутый, выпуклый

convey [кăн-вей] *vt.* возить, перевозить; выражать (*express*); сообщать (*impart*)

conveyance [кăн-вей-ăнс] *sn.* отправка, перевозка (*carrying*); наёмный экипаж, повозка (*vehicle*)

convict [кон-викт] *sm.* каторжник, осуждённый, преступник; *vt.* [кăн-викт] изобличать, уличать

conviction [кăн-вик-шăн] *sn.* убеждение (*belief*); *leg.* осуждение

convince [кăн-вĭнс] *vt.* убеждать

convivial [кăн-вĭ-вĭ-ăл] *adj.* весёлый, общительный; праздничный (*festive*)

convocation [кăн-во-кей-шăн] *sn.* собрание, созыв

convoy [кон-вой] *sn.* сопровождение (*escorting*); конвой; *naut.* конвоир; *mil.* обоз; *vt.* конвоировать, сопровождать

convulsion [кăн-вăл-шăн] *sn.* конвульсия, судорога, потрясение (*shock*)

cook [кул] *sm.* повар; *sf.* кухарка; *vt.* варить, стряпать

cookery [ку-кă-рĭ] *sn.* кулинария, стряпня

cooker [ку-кăр] *sm.* печь (для электричества или газа)

cool [кул] *adj.* прохладный, свежий (*fresh*); *fig.* невозмутимый, равнодушный (*of drink, food*)

coolness [кул-нĭс] *sn.* прохлада, холодок; *fig.* хладнокровие

coop [куп] *sn.* клетка для птиц (*for birds*); курятник (*for hens*)

cooper [ку-пăр] *sm.* бондарь

co-operate [коŭ-о-пă-рейт] *vi.* содействовать, сотрудничать

co-operation [коŭ-о-пă-рейшăн] *sn.* кооперация, сотрудничество

co-operative [коŭ-о-пă-рăтĭв] *adj.* кооперативный; совместный, объединённый; -- **society** [-- со-сайăтĭ] потребительское общество

co-ordinate [коŭ-ŏр-дĭ-нĭт] *adj.* координированный, одинаковый, соответствующий; *vt.* [коŭ-ŏр-дĭ-нейт] координировать, устанавливать правильное соотношение

cope [коŭп] *vi.* состязаться (*contend*); справляться (*manage*)

copious [коŭ-пĭ-ăс] *adj.* обильный; -- **style** -- стайл] пышный стиль

copper [ко-пăр] *sn.* медь; ме́дные де́ньги (*coins*); котёл (*cauldron*); *adj.* ме́дный

copperplate [ко-пăр-плэйт] *sn.* купфершти́тс; ме́дная гравирова́льная доска́

copy [ко-пi] *sn.* ко́пия (*duplicate*); образе́ц (*specimen*); ру́копись (*manuscript*); тип. о́ттиск; экземпля́р (*of a book*); *vt.* копи́ровать (*duplicate*); подража́ть (*imitate*)

copy-book [ко-пi-бу́к] *sn.* тетра́дь

copyist [ко-пi-iст] *sm.* перепи́счик

copyright [ко-пi-райт] *sn.* а́вторское пра́во

coquette [ко-ке́т] *sf.* коке́тка

coral [ко́-рăл] *sn.* кора́лл; *adj.* кора́лловый

cord [ко́рд] *sn.* верёвка (*rope*); шнуро́к (*twine*); струна́ (*string*); *vt.* свя́зывать

cordial [ко́р-дi-ăл] *sn.* ободря́ющее влия́ние (*heartening influence*); напи́ток (*drink*); *adj.* и́скренний, серде́чный

cordiality [кор-дi-ǽ-лi-тi] *sn.* раду́шие, серде́чность

cordon [ко́р-дăн] *sn.* кордо́н; о́рденская ле́нта (*ribbon*)

corduroy [ко́р-дю-рой] *sn.* рубча́тый плис; *pl.* брю́ки

core [ко́р] *sn.* сердцеви́на (*of fruit, etc.*); вну́тренность (*interior*); ядро́ (*kernel*); *tech.* суть (*gist*); *vt.* вырыва́ть сердцеви́ну

co-respondent [ко́у-рiс-по́н-дăнт] *sm.* соотве́тчик

cork [ко́рк] *sn.* про́бка; по-плаво́к (*float*); луб (*inner bark*); *vt.* затыка́ть про́бкой; заку́поривать

corkscrew [ко́рк-скрю] *sn.* про́бочник; што́пор

corn [ко́рн] *sn.* жи́то, пшени́ца; зерно́ (*cereal*); мозо́ль (*on foot*)

corned [ко́рнд] *adj.* солёный; – beef [– биф] солони́на

corner [ко́р-нăр] *sn.* у́гол, уголо́к; *vt.* загоня́ть в у́гол

cornet [ко́р-нiт] *sn. mus.* рожо́к, корне́т-а-писто́н; *mil.* корне́т

cornflour [ко́рн-флау-ăр] *sn.* кукуру́зная мука́

cornflower [ко́рн-флау-ăр] *sn.* василёк

corollary [кă-ро́-лă-рi] *sn.* вы́вод, заключе́ние

coroner [ко́-рă-нăр] *sm.* коро́нер; суде́бный сле́дователь

corporal [ко́р-пă-рăл] *sm.* капра́л; *adj.* теле́сный

corporate [ко́р-пă-рiт] *adj.* корпорати́вный, о́бщий

corporation [кор-пă-ре́йшăн] *sn.* корпора́ция

corps [ко́р] *sn. mil.* ко́рпус

corpse [ко́рпс] *sn.* труп

corpulence [ко́р-пю-лăнс] *sn.* доро́дность, ту́чность

corpuscle [ко́р-пасл] *sn.* а́том, те́льце, электро́н, части́ца

correct [кă-ре́кт] *adj.* ве́рный, пра́вильный, то́чный; корре́ктный (*complying with etiquette*); *vt.* корректи́ровать; увещева́ть (*admonish*); *typ.* корректи́ровать, исправля́ть (*amend*)

correction [кă-ре́к-шăн] *sn.* исправле́ние, попра́вка

correctness [кă-рéкт-нĭс] sn. прáвильность

corrector [кă-рéк-тăр] sm. исправи́тель, корре́ктор

correspond [кă-рĭс-пóнд] vi. соотвéтствовать, согласо́ва́ться (agree with); перепи́сываться (exchange letters)

correspondence [кö-рĭс-пóн-дăнс] sn. соотвéтствие, соотноше́ние (relation between things); анало́гия, корреспонде́нция, перепи́ска (exchange of letters)

correspondent [кö-рĭс-пóн-дăнт] sm. корреспонде́нт

corridor [кó-рĭ-дăр] sn. кори́дор

corroborate [кă-ро́-бă-рэ́йт] vt. подтвержда́ть

corrode [кă-ро́уд] vt. вытравля́ть, разъеда́ть

corrosion [кă-ро́у-жăн] sn. корро́зия, разъеда́ние

corrosive [кă-ро́у-зĭв] adj. éдкий, разъеда́ющий

corrugate [кó-рă-гэйт] vt.i. смо́рщивать; **-d iron** [-ĭд а́й-ăн] волни́стое желе́зо

corrupt [кă-ра́пт] adj. развращённый (depraved); прода́жный (venal); vt. развраща́ть (deprave)

corruption [кă-ра́п-шăн] sn. по́рча; разложе́ние (decay); растле́ние (depravity)

corsair [кóр-сэ́р] sm. пира́т

corset [кóр-сĭт] sn. корсе́т

cosmopolitan [коз-мо-по́-лĭ-тăн] sm. космополи́т; adj. космополити́ческий

Cossack [кó-сăк] sm. каза́к; adj. каза́цкий

cost [кост] sn. сто́имость; pl. изде́ржки; **- price** [- прайс] себесто́имость; vi.

сто́ить; расце́нивать (assess)

costermonger [кó-стăр-ма́н-гăр] sm. у́личный разно́счик

costly [кóст-лĭ] adj. дорого́й, дорого сто́ящий

costume [кóс-тю́м] sn. костю́м; же́нское пла́тье

cosy [кóу-зĭ] sn. покры́шка (для ча́йника); adj. ую́тный

cot [кот] sn. де́тская крова́ть, лю́лька

cottage [кó-тĭдж] sn. дереве́нский до́мик; **- hospital** [- хо́с-пĭ-тăл] се́льская больни́ца

cotton [кó-тăн] sn. хлопча́тая ткань; **- wool** [- у́ул] ва́та; **- mill** [- мĭл] бума́гопряди́льня

couch [ка́уч] sn. куше́тка

cough [коф] sn. ка́шель; vi. ка́шлять

council [ка́ун-сĭл] sn. сове́т

councillor [ка́ун-сĭ-лăр] sm., f. член муниципалите́та

counsel [ка́ун-сăл] sn. сове́т; обсужде́ние, совеща́ние (deliberation); мне́ние, сове́т, уведомле́ние (advice); sm. адвока́т (barrister); vt. сове́товать

counsellor [ка́ун-сă-лăр] sm. адвока́т, сове́тник

count [ка́унт] sn. счёт; sm. граф (title); vt. рассчи́тывать, счита́ть

countenance [ка́ун-тĭ-нăнс] sn. выраже́ние лица́ (expression); лицо́ (face); vt. поощря́ть

counter [ка́ун-тăр] sn. прила́вок, сто́йка (in shop); би́рка, фи́шка (disc, token, etc.); adj. противополо́жный; adv. обра́тно; vt.i. отпари́ровать

counterfeit [ка́ун-тăр-фит] *sn.* подде́лка; *sm.* обма́нщик; *adj.* подде́льный, подло́жный, фальши́вый; *vt.* подде́лывать; подража́ть (*imitate*)

counterfoil [ка́ун-тăр-фойл] *sn.* корешо́к (че́ка или квита́нции)

counterpane [ка́ун-тăр-пэйн] *sn.* покрыва́ло (на крова́ти)

countess [ка́ун-тіс] *sf.* графи́ня

counting-house [ка́ун-тіñха́ус] *sn.* конто́ра, бухгалте́рия

countless [ка́унт-ліс] *adj.* бесчи́сленный, несчётный

country [ка́н-трі] *sn.* страна́ (*nation*); ме́стность (*territory*); дере́вня (*rural*)

countryman [ка́н-трі-мăн] *sm.* земля́к, соо́течественник; крестья́нин (*peasant*)

countryside [ка́н-трі-сайд] *sn.* се́льская ме́стность

countrywoman [ка́н-трі-ўў-мăн] *sf.* земля́чка; крестья́нка

county [ка́ун-ті] *sn.* гра́фство, о́круг

couple [капл] *sn.* па́ра; *vt.* соединя́ть; сцепля́ть (*railway*)

coupling [ка́-плій] *sn.* сцепле́ние (*connecting*); *tech.* му́фта, сце́пка

courage [ка́-рідж] *sn.* сме́лость, хра́брость (*bravery*); му́жество (*manliness*)

courageous [кă-рэ́й-джăс] *adj.* отва́жный, сме́лый, хра́брый

course [ко́рс] *sn.* путь, тече́ние, ход (*track*); курс (*of*

lectures); блю́до (*of meal*); **in the - of** [ін ɵ̆ - ов] по хо́ду веще́й; **of - ** [оф -] коне́чно; *v.t.i.* бе́гать, скака́ть (*run, jump*); гна́ться (*pursue*)

court [ко́рт] *sn.* двор (*yard*); суд (*of justice*); дворе́ц (*palace*); *vt.* уха́живать; **- martial** [- ма́р-шăл] вое́нный суд

courteous [ке́р-ті-ăс] *adj.* ве́жливый, учти́вый

courtesy [ке́р-ті-сі] *sn.* ве́жливость, учти́вость; **by - ** [бай -] из любе́зности

courtship [ко́рт-шіп] *sn.* сватовство́, уха́живание

courtyard [ко́рт-ярд] *sn.* двор

cousin [ка́-зăн] *sm.* двою́родный брат; *sf.* двою́родная сестра́

cove [ко́ув] *sn.* бу́хта, зали́в; убе́жище (*sheltered nook*) *arch.* свод

cover [ка́-вăр] *sn.* покро́в, кры́шка (*lid*); обёртка (*wrapper*); чехо́л (*case*); обло́жка (*of book*); прикры́тие, ши́рма (*screen*); *vt.* покрыва́ть, прикрыва́ть

covet [ка́-віт] *vt.* зави́довать (*envy*)

covetous [ка́-ві-тăс] *adj.* а́лчный, жа́дный

cow [ка́у] *sf.* коро́ва; *vt.* запу́гивать (*intimidate*)

coward [ка́у-ăрд] *sm.* трус

cowardice [ка́у-ăр-діс] *sn.* тру́сость; по́длость (*baseness*)

cower [ка́у-ăр] *vi.* робе́ть, съёживаться

cowl [ка́ул] *sn.* капюшо́н (*hood*); колпа́к (*of chimney*)

coxswain [ко́кс-сўэйн] *sn.* рулево́й

coy [кой] *adj.* засте́нчивый, скро́мный

crab [кра́б] *sn.* ди́кое я́блоко, кисли́ца (*apple*); краб, рак (*crustacean*); созве́здие рака (*Crab*)

crack [крæк] *sn.* тре́щина (*fracture*); треск (*sharp noise*); *vt.i.* производи́ть шум, тре́скаться (*chap*); лома́ться (*of voice*)

cracker [крǽ-кăр] *sn.* то́нкий сухо́й би́сквит (*biscuit*); шути́ха (*firework*)

crackle [крæкл] *sn.* потре́скивание, хруст; *vi.* треща́ть, хрусте́ть

cradle [крэ́йдл] *sn.* колыбе́ль, лю́лька; *tech.* лото́к; *fig.* нача́ло (*beginning*); *vt.* кача́ть, класть в лю́льку

craft [крâфт] *sn.* *collect.* ло́дки, суда́; иску́сство, ло́вкость, сноро́вка (*art, skill, ability, etc.*); ремесло́ (*trade*)

craftsman [крâфтс-мăн] *sm.* ма́стер, реме́сленник

craftsmanship [крâфтс-мăн-шип] *sn.* мастерство́

crafty [крâф-ти] *adj.* иску́сный, ло́вкий (*dexterous, ingenious*); лука́вый, хи́трый (*sly, cunning*)

crag [крæг] *sn.* скала́, утёс

cram [крæм] *vt.* перепо́лнить (*fill*); пи́чкать (*stuff*); зубри́ть (*swot*)

cramp [крæмп] *sn.* су́дорога; *tech.* зажи́м (*clamp*); струбци́нка (*frame*); *vt.* стесня́ть, су́живать

crane [крэйн] *sn.* жура́вль *m.* (*bird*); *tech.* подъёмный кран; *vt.i.* вытя́гивать (ше́ю) (*stretch neck*); поднима́ть кра́ном (*lift*)

cranial [крэ́й-ниăл] *adj.* черепно́й

cranium [крэ́й-ниăм] *sn.* че́реп

crank [крæнк] *sm.* причу́дник, чуда́к (*eccentric*); *sn.* при́хоть, причу́да (*fad, whim*); *tech.* кривоши́п, мо́тыль

crape [крэйп] *sn.* креп, флёр

crash [крæш] *sm.* крах (*failure*); гро́хот, треск (*noise*); суро́вое полотно́ (*coarse linen*); *vi.* ру́шиться с гро́хотом

crate [крэйт] *sn.* кле́тка, корзи́на

crater [крэ́й-тăр] *sn.* жерло́, кра́тер

crave [крэйв] *vt.i.* стра́стно жела́ть (*desire vehemently*); жа́ждать (*thirst for*); проси́ть (*entreat*)

craving [крэ́й-вий] *sn.* стра́стное жела́ние

craw [крô] *sn.* зоб (пти́чий)

crawl [крôл] *sn.* пресмыка́ние, ползание; *vi.* ползать; тащи́ться (*trail*)

crayfish [крэ́й-фиш] *s.* речно́й рак

crayon [крэ́й-ăн] *sn.* пасте́ль, цветно́й каранда́ш

craze [крэйз] *sn.* ма́ния

crazy [крэ́й-зи] *adj.* безу́мный, слабоу́мный; ша́ткий (*precarious*)

creak [крик] *sn.* скрип; *vi.* скрипе́ть

cream [крим] *sn.* крем, сли́вки; *fig.* отбо́рное; *adj.* кре́мового цве́та (*colour*)

creamery [кри́-мă-ри] *sn.* моло́чная, маслобо́йня

creamy [кри́-ми] *adj.* кре́мовый, сли́вочный

crease [крис] *sn.* морщи́на, скла́дка; *vt.i.* мять, скла́дывать

create [кри-э́йт] *vt.* создава́ть, твори́ть; *coll.* суети́ться, хлопота́ть

creation [кри-э́й-шäн] *sn.* созда́ние, творе́ние

creative [кри-э́й-тив] *adj.* изобрета́тельный, тво́рческий

creator [кри-э́й-тäр] *sm.* а́втор, созда́тель; Бог, Творе́ц (*God*)

creature [кри́-чäр] *sm.* существо́; тварь; челове́к (*human being*)

crèche [крэйш] *sn.* я́сли

credence [кри́-дäнс] *sn.* ве́ра (*belief*); дове́рие (*trust*)

credential [кри-де́н-шäл] *sn.* манда́т, полномо́чие; *pl.* вери́тельные гра́моты

credible [кре́-дäбл] *adj.* ве́роятный

credit [кре́-дäт] *sn.* похвала́, честь (*honour*); креди́т; долг (*debt*); **letter of ~** [ле́-тäр ~] — аккредити́в; **on ~** [он ~] — в долг; *vt.* ве́рить, доверя́ть; кредитова́ть

creditor [кре́-ди-тäр] *sm.* кредито́р

credulity [кри-дю́-ли-ти] *sn.* дове́рчивость, легкове́рность

credulous [кре́-дю-läс] *adj.* легкове́рный

creed [крид] *sn.* вероуче́ние

creek [крик] *sn.* бу́хта, зали́в

creep [крип] *vi.* по́лзать, таищи́ться; кра́сться (*prowl*)

creepy [кри́-пи] *adj.* вызыва́ющий страх; ползу́чий

cremation [кри-мэ́й-шäн] *sn.* крема́ция

crematorium [кре-мä-то́-риäм] *sn.* кремато́рий

crescent [кре́-сäнт] *sn.* полуме́сяц; *adj.* возраста́ющий, расту́щий; серпови́дный (*shape*)

cress [крес] *sn.* кресс, ре́жуха

crest [крест] *sn.* гребешо́к, хохоло́к (*of bird*); гре́бень (*of mountains, waves*); гри́ва (*of horse*)

cretaceous [кри-тэ́й-шäс] *adj.* мелово́й

crevasse [кри-вäс] *sn.* тре́щина в леднике́ (*in glacier*)

crevice [кре́-вäс] *sn.* расще́лина, щель (*split in wood, stone*)

crew [крý] *sn.* судова́я кома́нда, экипа́ж

cricket [кри́-кäт] *sn.* кри́кет (*игра́*); сверчо́к (*insect*)

crime [крайм] *sn.* преступле́ние; злодея́ние (*wicked act*)

criminal [кри́-ми-нäл] *sm.* престу́пник; *adj.* кримина́льный, престу́пный

crimson [кри́м-зäн] *sn.* румя́нец (*colour*); *adj.* мали́новый

cringe [криндж] *vi.* подслу́живание; *vi.* съёживаться (*cower*); подли́зываться (*be servile*)

crinkle [кри́нкл] *sn.* изги́б, скла́дка; *vt.i.* изгиба́ть

cripple [крипл] *sm., f.* кале́ка; *vt.* кале́чить

crisis [кра́й-сис] *sn.* кри́зис; перело́м (*of illness*)

crisp [крисп] *adj.* хру́пкий (*brittle*); рассы́пчатый (*crusty*)

critical [кри́-ти-кäл] *adj.* крити́ческий

criticism [крí-ти-сізм] *sn.* критика

criticize [крí-ти-сайз] *vt.* критиковать

croak [кróўк] *sn.* кáрканье; квáканье (*frog*); *vi.* кáркать, квáкать

crockery [крó-кă-рĭ] *sn.* посýда

crook [крўк] *sm. coll.* обмáнщик, плут; *sn.* крюк, пóсох (*staff*)

crooked [крý-кĭд] *adj.* искривлённый, кривóй, согнýтый; *fig.* нечéстный

crop [кроп] *sn.* жáтва, урожáй (*yield*); зоб (*of birds*); *vt.* обрéзать, подстригáть

cross [крос] *sn.* крест; *biol.* скрéщивание, смешéние; пóмес, соединéние (*breed*); *adj.* поперéчный, перекрéстный [*transverse*]; взаи́мный (*reciprocal*); грýбый, злой, сердитый (*angry*); *v.i.* пересекáть, скрéщивать (*intersect*); креститься (*make sign of*); переходи́ть (*traverse*); перечёркивать (*cheque*); – out [– аўт] вычёркивать

crossbar [крóс-бáр] *sn.* поперечина, распóрка

crossing [крó-сĭн] *sn.* скрéщивание (*interbreeding*); перекрёсток (*road*); пересечéние (*intersection*); переéзд (*voyage*)

cross-roads [крос-рóўдз] *sn. pl.* перепýтье

crotchet [крó-чĭт] *sn. mus.* четвертнáя нóта

crouch [крáўч] *vi.* приседáть, сгибáться

crow [кróў] *s.* ворóна (*bird*); пéнье петухá (*of cock*); -'s nest [-з нест] марс; *vi.* кричáть кукарéку; грóмко ликовáть (*exult*)

crowbar [кróў-бáр] *sn.* желéзный лом

crowd [крáўд] *sn.* толпá; *coll.* пáртия, компáния; *vi.* толпи́ться

crowded [крáў-дĭд] *adj.* переполненный

crown [крáўн] *sn.* венéц, корóна; макýшка, тéмя (*of head*); тýлья (*of hat*); корóнка (*of tooth*); крóна (*coin*); госудáрство, верхóвная власть (*in monarchy*); *vt.* венчáть, коронова́ть

crucial [крý-шăл] *adj.* крити́ческий, реши́тельный (*decisive*); испытýющий (*searching*)

crucible [крý-сĭбл] *sn.* плави́льник, ти́гель. *m.*

crucifixion [крý-сĭ-фíк-шăн] *sn.* распя́тие

crucify [крý-сĭ-фай] *vt.* распинáть

crude [крўд] *adj.* незрéлый, сырóй (*raw*); грýбый, рéзкий (*rough*)

cruel [крý-ăл] *adj.* жестóкий, мучи́тельный

cruelty [крý-ăл-тĭ] *sn.* жестóкость

cruet [крý-ĭт] *sn.* бутылочка для ýксуса или мáсла

cruet-stand [крý-ĭт-стæнд] *sn.* судóк

cruise [крўз] *sn.* морскóе путешéствие; *vi.* крейси́ровать, путешéствовать

cruiser [крý-зăр] *sn.* крéйсер

crumb [крам] *sn.* кро́шка, кро́ха (*small fragment*), ки́ш (*soft part of loaf*); *fig.* части́ца, пох́од; *vt.i.* кроши́ть; распада́ться

crumble [крамбл] *vt.i.* кроши́ть; раздробля́ться

crumple [крампл] *vt.i.* морщи́ть, мять; смо́рщиваться

crunch [кранч] *sn.* скрип, треск, хруст; *vt.i.* грызть; хрустеть

crusade [кру-сэ́йд] *sn. hist.* крестовый похо́д; *fig.* кампа́ния, похо́д; *vi.* выступа́ть похо́дом

crusader [кру-сэ́й-дэр] *sm.* крестоно́сец

crush [краш] *sn.* разда́вливание; да́вка (*throng*); *vt.* разда́вливать; уничтожа́ть (*destroy, ruin*)

crust [краст] *sn.* ко́рка (*of bread*); кора́ (*rind*); оса́док (*of wine*); *vt.i.* покрыва́ть ко́ркой

crusty [кра́с-ти] *adj.* покры́тый ко́рой

crutch [крач] *sn.* косты́ль, *m.*; раздво́енная подпо́рка (*forked support*)

crux [кракс] *sn.* затрудне́ние, тру́дный вопро́с

cry [край] *sn.* крик (*shout*); мольба́ (*supplication*); плач (*weeping*); *vi.* восклица́ть (*ejaculate*); крича́ть (*shout*); пла́кать (*weep*)

crying [кра́й-ий] *adj.* крича́щий; плачущий

crypt [крипт] *sn.* склеп

cryptic [крип-тик] *adj.* зага́дочный, тайнственный

crystal [крис-тэл] *sn.* хру́сталь, *m.*, *tech.* криста́лл; *adj.* хруста́льный; кри-

стальный; чи́стый (*clear*); прозра́чный (*transparent*)

cub [каб] *s.* детёныш

cube [кюб] *sn.* куб

cubic [кю-бик] *adj.* куби́ческий

cubicle [кю-бикл] *sn.* кубик; кро́шечное ме́сто (*tiny compartment*)

cuckoo [ку́-ку́] *s.* куку́шка

cucumber [кю-кам-бӓр] *s.* огуре́ц

cud [кад] *sn.* жва́чка

cuddle [кадл] *sn.* те́сные объя́тия, *pl.*; *vt.i.* прижа́ться (*nestle together*); обнима́ть (*embrace*)

cudgel [ка́-джэл] *sn.* дуби́на

cue [кю] *sn.* кий (*for billiards*); *theat.* ре́плика; намёк (*hint*)

cuff [каф] *sn.* манже́та, обшла́г; уда́р кулако́м (*blow*); *vt.* бить кулако́м, колоти́ть

culinary [кю-ли-нӓ-ри] *adj.* кулина́рный, ку́хонный

culminate [кал-ми-нэйт] *vi.* достига́ть вы́сшей сте́пени чего́-либо; *astrol.* кульми́нировать

culmination [кал-ми-нэ́й-шӓн] *sn.* кульминацио́нный пункт; *astrol.* кульмина́ция

culpable [кал-пӓбл] *adj.* вино́вный

culprit [кал-прит] *sn.* обвиня́емый (*guilty of offence*); *sm.* престу́пник (*offender*)

cult [калт] *sn.* культ

cultivate [кал-ти-вэйт] *vt.* возде́лывать, обраба́тывать (*ploughing, planting, etc.*); культиви́ровать, развива́ть (*develop*)

cultivation [кал-ти-вэ́й-шăн] n. возде́лывание (of land); культу́ра, разведе́ние (of plants, etc.); разви́тие (development)

cultural [кăл-чă-рăл] adj. культу́рный [ту́ра

culture [кăл-чăр] sn. куль-

cumbrous [кăм-брăс] adj. громо́здкий, затрудни́тельный

cumulative [кю́-мю-лă-тив] adj. нако́пленный, совоку́пный

cunning [кă-ниŋ] adj. ло́вкий; хи́трый

cup [кап] sn. ча́ша, ча́шка; vt. med. ста́вить ба́нки

cupboard [кă-бăрд] sn. шкаф

cupidity [кю-пи́-ди-ти] sn. а́лчность, жа́дность

cur [кăр] sn. грубия́н, дворня́жка, m.; пёс (dog)

curable [кю́-рăбл] adj. излечи́мый [ка́рство

curacy [кю́-рă-си] sn. ви-

curate [кю́-рит] sm. помо́щник прихо́дского свяще́нника

curative [кю́-рă-тив] adj. целе́бный, цели́тельный

curator [кю-ре́й-тăр] sn. храни́тель (музе́я); член университе́тского правле́ния (of university)

curb [кăрб] sn. цепо́чка (ре́мень) (horse's); fig. обузда́ние, узда́; бордю́рный ка́мень (kerb); vt. обузда́ть

curd [кăрд] sn. сверну́вшееся молоко́; pl. творо́г; vt.i. свёртывать, сгуща́ть

curdle [кăрдл] vt. свёртываться, сгуща́ться

cure [кюр] sn. лече́ние; ле́карство, сре́дство (remedy); vt. med. выле́чивать, исцеля́ть; консерви́ровать, сохраня́ть (preserve); копти́ть (smoke); соли́ть (salt)

curfew [кăр-фю] sn. вече́рний звон

curio [кю́-риоў] sn. (худо́жественная) ре́дкость

curiosity [кю-ри-о́-си-ти] sn. любопы́тство; ре́дкость (rarity)

curious [кю́-ри-ăс] adj. любопы́тный (inquisitive); любозна́тельный (eager to learn); курьёзный, стра́нный (strange)

curl [кăрл] sn. бу́кля, ло́кон (of hair); зави́вка, изви́лина (spiral form); vt.i. завива́ть

currant [кă-рăнт] sn. сморо́дина; кори́нка (dried)

currency [кă-рăн-си] sn. де́нежное обраще́ние; употреби́тельность (of words, expressions, etc.); валю́та (exchange, value); де́ньги (money)

current [кă-рăнт] sn. пото́к, струя́ (of air, water); тече́ние, ход (of events); electr. ток; **alternating** – [о́л-тăр-нэй́-тиŋ–] переме́нный ток; **direct** – [дай́-рект–] постоя́нный ток; adj. ходя́чий (of money); теку́щий (time)

curriculum [кă-ри-кю-лăм] sn. уче́бный курс

currier [кă-ри-ăр] sm. коже́вник

curse [кăрс] sn. руга́тельство (oath); прокля́тие (perdition); vt.i. проклина́ть; руга́ть; клясть, руга́ться

cursed [кёр-сід] *adj.* отвратительный (*abominable*); проклятый (*damned*)

cursive [кёр-сів] *sn. typ.* рукописный шрифт; скоропись

cursory [кёр-сă-рі] *adj.* беглый, поверхностный

curt [кёрт] *adj.* краткий, сжатый (*of style*)

curtail [кöр-тэйл] *vt.* обрезывать, сокращать

curtailment [кöр-тэйлмäнт] *sn.* сокращение, урезывание

curtain [кёр-тін] *sn.* занавеска; *theat.* занавес; *mil.* завеса; *vt.* занавешивать

curtsy [кёрт-сі] *sn.* приседание, реверанс; *vi.* приседать

curvature [кöр-вä-чäр] *sn.* кривизна

curve [кёрв] *sn.* кривая; *vt.i.* гнуть, изгибать, искривлять

cushion [ку-шăн] *sn.* диванная подушка; борт (*billiards*)

custodian [кас-тóу-ді-äн] *sm.* сторож, хранитель, опекун (*guardian*)

custody [кас-тă-ді] *sn.* охрана, хранение

custom [кас-тäм] *sn.* привычка (*habit*); обычай (*use*); *pl.* таможенные пошлины

customary [кас-тă-мă-рі] *adj.* обычный

customer [кас-тă-мäр] *sm.* клиент, покупатель

custom-house [кас-тäмхäус] *sn.* таможня

cut [кат] *sn.* разрезывание, разрубание, порез, разрез (*incision*); отрезок (*slice*)

покрой (*style*); *vt.* отрезать, резать; вырезывать (*cut out*); срезать (*flowers*); рубить (*hack*); кроить (*garment*)

cutaneous [кю-тэй-ні-ăс] *adj. med.* накожный

cute [кют] *adj.* остроумный

cutlery [кăт-лă-рі] *sn.* ножовый товар

cutlet [кăт-літ] *sn.* котлета

cutter [кă-тäр] *sn.* резак, резец, сечка; *naut.* катер; *sm.* закройщик (*tailor's*)

cutting [кă-тій] *sn.* резание; вырезка (*newspaper*); *adj. fig.* резкий

cycle [сайкл] *sn.* цикл, велосипед (*bicycle*), *tech.* круговой процесс; *vi.* ездить (на велосипеде)

cyclist [сай-кліст] *sm.* велосипедист

cyclone [сай-клоун] *sm.* циклон

cygnet [сіг-ніт] *s.* молодой лебедь

cylinder [сі-лін-дăр] *sn.* цилиндр; цилиндрический вал (*roller*)

cylindrical [сі-лін-дрі-кăл] *adj.* цилиндрический

cymbals [сім-бăлз] *sn. pl. mus.* тарелки, цымбалы

cynic [сі-нік] *sm.* циник

cynical [сі-ні-кăл] *adj.* бесстыдный (*shameless*); циничный

Cyrillic [сі-рі-лік] *adj.* - **alphabet** [- äл-фă-біт] кириллица; - **type** (*printer's*) [- тайп] гражданский шрифт

cyst [сіст] *sn. biol.* пузырь, *m.*; *med.* киста

Czech [чек] *sm.* чех; *sf.* чешка; *adj.* чешский

D

D [ді] *sn. mus.* ре

dab [дэб] *sn.* лёгкий удар (*light tap*); мазок (*spot*); камбала (*fish*); *vt.i.* ударять слегка; намазывать (*smear*)

dad(dy) [дэд(і)] *sn.* папа

daffodil [дэ-фā-діл] *sn.* жёлтый нарцисс

daft [дāфт] *adj.* безумный

dagger [дэ-гāр] *sn.* кинжал; *typ.* крестик

daily [дэй-лі] *adj.* ежедневный; суточный (*of allowance*); – **bread** [– брэд] насущный хлеб; *adv.* ежедневно

dainty [дэйн-ті] *sn.* лакомство, лакомый кусок; *adj.* вкусный (*tasty*); лакомый (*choice*); нежный (*delicate*)

dairy [дэ-рі] *sn.* молочная

dairying [дэ-рі-ій] *sn.* молочное хозяйство

dairymaid [дэ-рі-мэйд] *sf.* доярка, молочница

dairyman [дэ-рі-мāн] *sm.* молочник

dais [дэ-іс] *sn.* возвышение, помост, эстрада

daisy [дэй-зі] *sn.* маргаритка

dale [дэйл] *sn.* долина

dally [дэ-лі] *vi.* медлить

dam [дэм] *sn.* дамба, запруда, плотина; *sf.* матка (*of animals*); *vt.* запруживать

damage [дэ-мідж] *sn.* вред (*harm*); убыток (*loss*); *pl.* (*deterioration*); *vt.* повреждать (*harm*); портить (*spoil*)

damn [дэм] *vt.* проклинать (*curse*); осуждать (*condemn*)

damnation [дэм-нэй-шан] *sn.* проклятие

damp [дэмп] *sn.* влажность, сырость; *adj.* влажный, сырой; *vt.* смачивать; угнетать (*depress*); обескураживать (*discourage*)

damp-proof [дэмп-пруф] *adj.* непроницаемый для сырости

damson [дэм-зан] *sn.* дамасская слива

dance [дāнс] *sn.* танец; *vt.i.* плясать, танцовать

dancer [дāн-сāр] *sm.* танцовщик, танцор; *sf.* танцорка

dancing [дāн-сій] *sn.* танцование

Dane [дэйн] *sm.* датчанин

danger [дэйн-джāр] *sn.* опасность

dangerous [дэйн-джā-рāс] *adj.* опасный

dangle [дэйнгл] *vt.i.* болтаться, качаться, помахивать, размахивать

Danish [дэй-ніш] *adj.* датский

Danubian [дэ-ню-бі-āн] *adj.* дунайский

dare [дэр] *vt.* сметь

daring [дэ-рій] *sn.* смелость; *adj.* смелый

dark [дāрк] *sn.* темнота, тьма; *adj.* тёмный; мрачный (*gloomy*); смуглый (*of person*); – **ages** [– эй-джіз] средние века, средневековье

darken [дāр-кāн] *vt.* затемнять

darkness [дāрк-ніс] *sn.* мрак, темнота

darling [дāр-лій] *sm.* любимец; *sf.* любимая

darn [дāрн] *sn.* штопка; *vt.* штопать

darning [да́р-ній] *sn.* по-чи́нка, што́панье

dart [да́рт] *sn.* дро́тик; жа́ло (*sting*); *vt.i.* мета́ть (*throw*); броса́ть (*glance*)

dash [дэш] *sn.* тур. тире́; поры́в (*rush*); толчо́к (*impulse*); *vt.i.* броса́ться, разбива́ться

dashing [да́-шін] *adj.* бо́йкий, лихо́й

dastardly [дэ́с-тэ́рд-лі] *adj.* по́длый; трусли́вый

date [дэйт] *sn.* фи́ник (*fruit*); да́та, число́ (*time*); срок (*term*); **out of** – [а́ут ов –] устаре́вший; **up to** – [ап ту –] до сего́дняшнего дня, мо́дный, совреме́нный; *vt.* дати́ровать

dative [дэ́й-тів] *sn., adj., gram.* да́тельный (паде́ж)

daub [до́б] *sn.* пачкотня́ (*smear*); *vt.* ма́зать, па́чкать

daughter [до́-тэр] *sf.* дочь

daughter-in-law [до́-тэр-ін-ло́] *sf.* сноха́

daunt [до́нт] *vt.* устраша́ть

dauntless [до́нт-ліс] *adj.* неустраши́мый, отва́жный

dawdle [до́дл] *vi.* безде́льничать, ме́длить

dawn [до́н] *sn.* заря́, рассве́т; *vi.* рассвета́ть; *fig.* пробужда́ться

day [дэй] *sn.* день, *m.*; су́тки (*24 hours*); дневно́й свет (*daylight*); **by** – [бай –] днём

daybook [дэ́й-бу́к] *sn.* журна́л

daybreak [дэ́й-брэйк] *sn.* рассве́т, у́тренняя заря́

daylight [дэ́й-лайт] *sn.* дневно́й свет; гла́сность (*publicity*)

daze [дэйз] *vt.* удивля́ть, изумля́ть

dazzle [дэзл] *vt.* ослепля́ть; прельща́ть (*tempt*)

dazzling [дэз-лін] *adj.* ослепи́тельный

dead [дэд] *adj.* мёртвый; безжи́зненный (*lifeless*); бесси́льный (*devoid of force*); вя́лый (*spiritless*); до́хлый (*of animals*)

deaden [дэ́-дэн] *vt.* притупля́ть

deadly [дэ́д-лі] *adj.* смерте́льный

deaf [дэф] *adj.* глухо́й; – **mute** [– мют] глухонемо́й

deafen [дэ́-фэн] *vt.* оглуша́ть

deafness [дэ́ф-ніс] *sn.* глухота́

deal [дил] *sn.* до́ля (*amount*); сда́ча (*cards*); коли́чество (*quantity*); ело́вое де́рево (*wood*); *vt.* раздава́ть (*portion out*); сдава́ть (*cards*)

dealer [ди-лэр] *sm.* торго́вец

dealings [ди́-лінз] *sn. pl.* поведе́ние, посту́пки (*conduct*); com. сде́лка, сноше́ние

dear [дир] *adj.* ми́лый; дорого́й, це́нный (*costly*); *adv.* до́рого

dearest [ди́-рест] *sm.* люби́мый; *sf.* люби́мая

dearth [дэрθ] *sn.* недоста́ток (*scarcity*); несостоя́тельность (*failure*)

death [дэθ] *sn.* смерть

deathly [дэ́θ-лі] *adv.* мёртвенный, смерте́льный

debar [ді-ба́р] *vt.* воспреща́ть (*forbid*); препя́тствовать (*hinder*); лиша́ть (*deprive*)

debase [дi-бэ́йс] *vt.* понижа́ть; унижа́ть

debatable [дi-бэ́й-табл] *adj.* спо́рный

debate [дi-бэ́йт] *sn.* диску́ссия; пре́ния; *vt.i.* дискути́ровать, обсужда́ть (*discuss*); спо́рить (*argue*)

debauch [дi-бóч] *sn.* разврат, распу́тство; *vt.* искажа́ть (*vitiate*); обольща́ть (*seduce*); развраща́ть (*corrupt*)

debauchery [дi-бó-чǝ-ри] *sn.* развра́тность, распу́щенность

debenture [дi-бéн-чǝр] *sn.* долгово́е обяза́тельство

debility [дi-бi-лi-тi] *sn.* сла́бость, тщеду́шность

debit [дé-бiт] *sn.* де́бет, прихо́д; *vt.* дебетова́ть, вноси́ть в де́бет

debris [дé-бри] *sn.* оско́лки, *sf. pl.* (*fragments*); разва́лины, *sf. pl.* (*wreckage*)

debt [дет] *sn.* долг

debtor [дé-тǝр] *sm.* должни́к

decade [дé-кǝд] *sn.* дека́да, десятиле́тие; деся́ток (*set of ten*)

decadence [дé-кǝ-дǝнс] *sn.* упа́док

decadent [дé-кǝ-дǝнт] *adj.* декаде́нтский, упа́дочный

decanter [дi-кǽн-тǝр] *sn.* графи́н

decapitate [дi-кǽ-пi-тэйт] *vt.* обезгла́вливать

decay [дi-кэ́й] *sn.* разруше́ние (*collapse*); упа́док (*decline*) гние́ние (*rot*); *vi.* гнить, разлага́ть

decease [дi-си́с] *sn.* кончи́на, смерть; *vi.* умира́ть

deceased [дi-си́сд] *sm.* поко́йный

deceit [дi-си́т] *sn.* обма́н

deceitful [дi-си́т-фул] *adj.* обма́нчивый

deceive [дi-си́в] *vt.* обма́нывать; вводи́ть в заблужде́ние

December [дi-сéм-бǝр] *sn.* дека́брь, *m.*

decency [ди́-сǝн-си] *sn.* благопристо́йность, прили́чие

decent [ди́-сǝнт] *adj.* поря́дочный (*respectable*); прили́чный (*decorous*)

deception [дi-сéп-шǝн] *sn.* ложь, обма́н, обольще́ние

deceptive [дi-сéп-тiв] *adj.* обма́нчивый

decide [дi-са́йд] *vt.i.* реша́ть

decimal [дé-сi-мǝл] *sn. math.* десяти́чная дробь; *adj.* десяти́чный

decipher [дi-са́й-фǝр] *vt.* разбира́ть (*make out meaning*); расшифро́вывать (*turn into clear writing*)

decision [дi-сí-жǝн] *sn.* реше́ние (*resolve*); реши́мость (*resoluteness*)

decisive [дi-са́й-сiв] *adj.* реши́тельный; реша́ющий

deck [дек] *sn.* па́луба; *vt.* настила́ть, покрыва́ть (*cover*); убра́ть, украша́ть (*adorn*)

declaim [дi-клэ́йм] *vt.i.* деклами́ровать; ратова́ть (*inveigh against*)

declamation [дe-клǝ-мэ́й-шǝн] *sn.* деклама́ция

declaration [дe-клǝ-рэ́й-шǝн] *sn.* заявле́ние (*statement*); деклара́ция (*customs*)

declare [дi-клэ́р] *vt.i.* заявля́ть, объявля́ть; предъявля́ть (*produce*)

declension [ді-кле́н-шăн] *sn. gram.* склоне́ние

declination [де-клі-нэ́й-шăн] *sn. astron.* склоне́ние, уклоне́ние

decline [ді-кла́йн] *sn.* упа́док (*loss*); ухудше́ние (*deterioration*); зака́т (*setting*); *vt.i. gram.* склоня́ть; отка́зывать (*refuse*)

decompose [ди-кăм-по́уз] *vt.i.* гнить (*rot*); разлага́ть

decorate [де́-кă-рэйт] *vt.* украша́ть; награжда́ть о́рденом (*invest person*)

decoration [де-кă-рэ́й-шăн] *sn.* декора́ция; украше́ние; знак отли́чия, о́рден

decorative [де́-кă-рă-тів] *adj.* декорати́вный, украша́ющий

decorator [де́-кă-рэй-тăр] *sm.* декора́тор; маля́р (*painter*); обо́йщик (*paper-hanger*)

decorous [де́-кă-рăс] *adj.* прили́чный, присто́йный

decoy [ді-ко́й] *sn.* прима́нка; западня́ (*bait*); *vt.* завлека́ть, зама́нивать

decrease [ді-кри́с] *sn.* у́быль, уменьше́ние; [ді-кри́с] *vt.i.* убыва́ть, уменьша́ть

decree [ді-кри́] *sn.* декре́т, прика́з, ука́з; постановле́ние (*judicial decision*); *vt.* декрети́ровать, предпи́сывать, прика́зывать

decrepit [ді-кре́-піт] *adj.* дря́хлый

decry [ді-кра́й] *vt.* порица́ть

dedicate [де́-ді-кэйт] *vt.* посвяща́ть

dedication [де-ді-ке́й-шăн] *sn.* посвяще́ние

deduce [ді-дю́с] *vt.* выводи́ть

deduct [ді-да́кт] *vt.* вычита́ть, отнима́ть

deduction [ді-да́к-шăн] *sn.* вычита́ние, вы́вод, заключе́ние (*inference*); ски́дка (*abatement*)

deed [дид] *sn.* де́йствие, де́ло, посту́пок (*action*); по́двиг (*exploit*); *leg.* акт, докуме́нт

deem [дим] *vt.* полага́ть, счита́ть

deep [дип] *sn.* бе́здна, про́пасть; *adj.* глубо́кий (*profound*); ни́зкий (*of tone*)

deepen [ди́-пăн] *vt.i.* углубля́ть

deer [дир] *sm.* оле́нь; *sf.* лань

deface [ді-фэ́йс] *vt.* обезобра́живать, уро́довать

defamation [де-фă-ме́й-шăн] *sn.* клевета́, поноше́ние

default [ді-фо́лт] *sn.* недоста́ток (*shortage*); погре́шность (*error*); *leg.* нея́вка; *vi.* преступа́ть

defaulter [ді-фо́л-тăр] *sm.* вино́вный, наруши́тель

defeat [ді-фи́т] *sn.* пораже́ние; *vt.* поража́ть, разбива́ть; побежда́ть (*vanquish*)

defect [ді-фе́кт] *sn.* дефе́кт, недочёт; недоста́ток

defective [ді-фе́к-тів] *adj.* непо́лный, повреждённый

defence [ді-фе́нс] *sn.* защи́та, охране́ние; *mil. pl.* укрепле́ния

defend [ді-фе́нд] *vt.* защища́ть, обороня́ть

defendant [ді-фе́н-дăнт] *sm.* отве́тчик

defender [ді-фéн-дăр] *sm.* защитник

defensive [ді-фéн-сів] *adj.* защитительный, охранительный

defer [ді-фéр] *vt.* отлагáть, отсрóчивать (*postpone*); уступáть (*give way*)

deferential [де-фă-рéн-шăл] *adj.* почтительный

defiance [діфáй-ăнс] *sn.* вызов (*challenge*); отказ починяться (*refusal to submit*)

defiant [ді-фáй-ăнт] *adj.* вызывáющий, дéрзкий

deficiency [ді-фі-шăн-сі] *sn.* недостáток, нехвáтка

deficient [ді-фі-шăнт] *adj.* недостáточный, непóлный

deficit [дé-фі-сіт] *sn.* дефицит, недостáток, недочёт

defile [ді-фáйл] *vt.* загрязнять (*make dirty*); осквернять (*profane*); развращáть (*deprave*); *vi. mil.* дефилировáть; *sn. mil.* ущéлье

define [ді-фáйн] *vt.* обозначáть, определять

definite [дé-фі-ніт] *adj.* определённый (*determinate*); тóчный (*exact*); ясный (*clear*)

definition [де-фі-ні-шăн] *sn.* определéние

deflate [ді-флéйт] *vt.* выкáчивать, выпускáть (вóздух из шины и пр.)

deflation [ді-флéй-шăн] *sn.* дефляция [ніть]

deflect [ді-флéкт] *vt.* отклонять

deform [ді-фóрм] *vt.* уродовать; обезобрáживать (*mutilate*)

deformity [ді-фóр-мі-ті] *sn.* урóдливость

defraud [ді-фрóд] *vt.* надувáть, обмáнывать

defray [ді-фрéй] *vt.* оплáчивать, распла́чивать

deft [дефт] *adj.* лóвкий, провóрный

defunct [ді-фáнкт] *adj.* окончáвшийся, умéрший

defy [ді-фáй] *vt.* вызывáть

degenerate [ді-джé-нă-ріт] *sm.* выродок; *adj.* вырождáющийся; [ді-джé-нă-рéйт] *vi.* вырождáться

degrade [ді-грéйд] *vt.* понижáть, разжáловать, унижáть

degrading [ді-грéй-дій] *adj.* унизительный

degree [ді-грí] *sn.* стéпень, ступéнь (*grade*); грáдус (*measure*); звáние (*rank*); *gram.* стéпень сравнéния; **by -s** [бай -з] постепéнно

deify [дé-і-фай] *vt.* боготворить

deign [дэйн] *vi.* соизволить

deity [дé-і-ті] *sn.* бóжество

dejected [ді-джéк-тід] *adj.* унылый

delay [ді-лéй] *sn.* задéржка, отлагáтельство; *vt.i.* задéрживать, мéдлить

delegate [дé-лі-гăт] *sm.* представитель, делегáт; [дé-лі-гéйт] *vt.* делегировать

delegation [де-лі-гéй-шăн] *sn.* делегáция

delete [ді-лит] *vt.* вычёркивать

deletion [ді-ли-шăн] *sn.* вычёркивание

deliberate [ді-лі-бă-рăт] *adj.* намéренный, обдуманный, умышленный; [ді-лі-бă-рéйт] *vi.* обсуждáть, совещáться

deliberation [ді-лі-бă-рéй-шăн] *sn.* обдумывание, совещáние

delicacy [дэ́-лі-кă-сі] *sn.* деликатность; нежность (*tenderness*); чувствительность (*sensitiveness*)

delicate [дэ́-лі-кіт] *adj.* нежный, тонкий (*tender*); изящный (*luxurious*); утонченный (*fine*)

delicious [ді-лі-шăс] *adj.* восхитительный (*delightful*); вкусный (*tasty*)

delight [ді-лайт] *sn.* восторг, восхищение; *vt.i.* наслаждать, услаждать

delightful [ді-лайт-фӯл] *adj.* восхитительный, приятный

delineate [ді-лі-ні-эйт] *vt.* обрисовать, описывать, очерчивать

delinquency [ді-лій-кўäн-сі] *sn.* виновность, проступок

delinquent [ді-лій-кўäнт] *sm.* правонарушитель, преступник; *adj.* виновный

delirious [ді-лі-рі-ăс] *adj.* бредящий; в экстазе (*ecstatic*)

deliver [ді-лі-вăр] *vt.* вручать, доставлять, разносить (*convey, supply*); произносить (*utter*); выражать (*express*)

deliverance [ді-лі-вă-рăнс] *sn.* избавление, освобождение; выражение, произнесение (*utterance*)

delivery [ді-лі-вă-рі] *sn.* доставка, раздача

dell [дел] *sn.* долина, лощина

delude [ді-люд] *vt.* вводить в заблуждение

deluge [дэ́-людж] *sn.* наводнение, потоп; *vt.* наводнять, потоплять

delusion [ді-лю́-жăн] *sn.* заблуждение

delve [делв] *vt.i.* копать (*dig*); *fig.* рыться (*burrow*)

demand [ді-ма́нд] *sn.* требование (*claim*); прошение (*application*); *com.* спрос; *vt.* спрашивать (*ask*); требовать (*claim*)

demeanour [ді-мі-нáр] *sn.* манеры, обращение, поведение

demented [ді-мéн-тід] *adj.* безумный, сумасшедший

demi- [дэ́-мі] *prefix.* полу-

demise [ді-майз] *vt.* сдавать в аренду

demobilization [ді-моу-бі-лай-зэ́й-шăн] *sn.* демобилизация

democracy [ді-мó-крă-сі] *sn.* демократия

demolish [ді-мó-ліш] *vt.* разрушать, сламывать

demolition [де-мо-лі-шăн] *sn.* разрушение, сломка

demon [ди́-мăн] *sm.* бес, демон

demonstrate [дэ́-мăн-стрэйт] *vt.i.* демонстрировать; доказывать (*give proof*)

demonstration [дэ-мăн-стрэ́й-шăн] *sn.* демонстрация, демонстрирование; доказательство (*proof*)

demonstrative [ді-мóн-стрă-тів] *adj.* доказательный, убедительный; демонстративный; *gram.* указательный

demonstrator [дэ́-мăн-стрэй-тăр] *sn.* демонстратор

demoralize [ді-мó-рă-лайз] *vt.* деморализовать, развращать

demur [дi-мёр] *vi.* представля́ть возраже́ния (*raise objections*); колеба́ться (*hesitate*)

demure [дi-мю́р] *adj.* сде́ржанный, скро́мный (*undemonstrative*); засте́нчивый (*shy*)

den [дэн] *sn.* берло́га, ло́говище; прито́н (*of thieves*); ли́чная ко́мнатка (*private room*)

denial [дi-на́й-ăл] *sn.* отрече́ние, отрица́ние (*negation*); отка́з (*refusal*)

denomination [дi-но-ми-нэ́й-шăн] *sn.* назва́ние; наименова́ние; *eccl.* вероиспове́дание

denominator [дi-но́-ми-нэй-тăр] *sn. math.* знамена́тель, *m.*; дели́тель, *m.* (*divisor*)

denote [дi-но́ут] *vt.* обознача́ть

denounce [дi-на́унс] *vt.* взыва́ть, призыва́ть (*invoke*); доноси́ть (*inform*)

dense [дэнс] *adj.* густо́й; пло́тный (*compact*); глу́пый, тупо́й (*of person*)

density [дэ́н-сi-тi] *sn.* густота́; пло́тность (*compactness*)

dent [дэнт] *sn.* вы́емка, углубле́ние; *vt.* вда́вливать

dental [дэ́н-тăл] *adj.* зубно́й

dentifrice [дэ́н-тi-фрiс] *sn.* зубно́й порошо́к (*powder*); па́ста (для зубо́в) (*paste*)

dentist [дэ́н-тiст] *sm.* зубно́й врач

denture [дэ́н-чăр] *sn.* ряд зубо́в

denunciation [дi-нăн-сi-

эй-шăн] *sn.* доно́с, огово́р; угро́за (*threat*)

deny [дi-на́й] *vt.* отрица́ть

depart [дi-па́рт] *vi.* уезжа́ть (*in vehicle*); уходи́ть (*on foot*); отправля́ться (*set off*)

department [дi-па́рт-мăнт] *sn.* ве́домство, департа́мент; отде́л (*section*)

departmental [дi-па́рт-мéн-тăл] *adj.* ве́домственный

departure [дi-па́р-чăр] *sn.* отбы́тие, отъе́зд, ухо́д

depend [дi-пе́нд] *vi.* зави́сеть (*be contingent*); полага́ться, рассчи́тывать на (*rely on*)

dependab!e [дi-пе́н-дăбл] *adj.* благонаде́жный

dependant [дi-пе́н-дăнт] *sm.* иждиве́нец

dependence [дi-пе́н-дăнс] *sn.* зави́симость; опо́ра (*reliance*); подчине́ние (*subjugation*)

depict [дi-пи́кт] *vt.* изобража́ть; опи́сывать (*describe*)

deplete [дi-пли́т] *vt.* истоща́ть, исче́рпывать

deplorable [дi-пло́-рăбл] *adj.* жа́лкий, плаче́вный

deplore [дi-пло́р] *vt.* опла́кивать, сожале́ть

deploy [дi-пло́й] *vt.i. mil.* развёртывать строй

deport [дi-по́рт] *vt.* высыла́ть, ссыла́ть; вести́ себя́, держа́ться (*conduct oneself*)

deportation [дi-пор-тэ́й-шăн] *sn.* высы́лка, ссы́лка

deportment [дi-по́рт-мăнт] *sn.* мане́ры (*manners*); вид, оса́нка (*carriage*); поведе́ние (*behaviour*)

depose [ді-по́уз] *vt.i.* сверга́ть, смеща́ть

deposit [ді-по́-зіт] *sn.* взнос (*in bank*); задаток (*part payment*); зало́г (*guarantee, security*); оса́док (*sediment*); *vt.* класть, положи́ть

depositor [ді-по́-зі-та̊р] *sm.* вкла́дчик

depository [ді-по́-зі-та̊-рі] *sn.* склад, храни́лище

depraved [ді-прэ́йвд] *adj.* испо́рченный (*corrupt*); развра́тный (*perverse*)

depravity [ді-прǽ-ві-ті] *sn.* развра́тность

depreciate [ді-прі́-ші-эйт] *vt.* обесце́нивать (*sink in value*); унижа́ть (*lower*); умаля́ть (*belittle*)

depreciation [ді-прі-ші-э́й-шă н] *sn.* обесце́нивание; умале́ние

depredation [ді-прі-дэ́й-шă н] *sn.* грабёж, расхище́ние; *pl.* опустоше́ние

depression [ді-прэ́-шă н] *sn.* уны́ние (*low spirits*); пониже́ние (*fall, reduction*); депре́ссия, засто́й, упа́док (*economic*)

deprivation [де-прі-вэ́й-шă н] *sn.* лише́ние, поте́ря

deprive [ді-пра́йв] *vt.* лиша́ть

depth [депθ] *sn.* глубина́, глубь, густота́ (*of colour, paint*); пучина́ (*of water*)

deputation [де-пю-тэ́й-шă н] *sn.* делега́ция, депута́ция

depute [ді-пю́т] *vt.* делеги́ровать, назнача́ть замести́теля

deputize [де́-пю-тайз] *vi.* замеща́ть

deputy [де́-пю-ті] *sm.* вы́борный, делега́т, уполномо́ченный (*delegate*); замести́тель, наме́стник (*substitute*)

derailment [ді-рэ́йл-мант] *sn.* сход с ре́льсов

deranged [ді-рэ́йнджд] *adj.* поме́шанный (*of mind*)

derangement [ді-рэ́йндж-ма́нт] *sn.* беспоря́док, расстро́йство (*disorder*); умопомеша́тельство (*insanity*)

derelict [де́-рі-лікт] *sn. naut.* поки́нутый кора́бль; *adj.* беспризо́рный, оста́вленный, поки́нутый

deride [ді-ра́йд] *vt.* осме́ивать [ме́яние

derision [ді-рі́-жăн] *sn.* ос

derisive [ді-ра́й-сів] *adj.* насме́шливый

derivation [де-рі-вэ́й-шăн] *sn.* исто́чник, происхожде́ние

derivative [ді-рі́-ва-тів] *sn.* дерива́т; *gram.* произво́дное сло́во; *adj.* произво́дный

derive [ді-ра́йв] *vt.* извлека́ть, производи́ть, происходи́ть

derogatory [ді-ро́-гăт-рі] *adj.* поврежда́ющий; унизи́тельный

descend [ді-сэ́нд] *vt.i.* спуска́ться (*go down*); налете́ть, обру́шиться (*swoop down*)

descendant [ді-сэ́н-дăнт] *sm.* пото́мок

descent [ді-сэ́нт] *sn.* нападе́ние, наше́ствие (*attack, swoop*); происхожде́ние (*lineage*); пото́мство (*progeny*); склон, спуск (*slope*); сход (*act of descending*)

describe [дíс-крáйб] *vt.* опи́сывать

description [дíс-крíп-шăн] *sn.* описáние; вид, род (*sort*)

descriptive [дíс-крíп-тíв] *adj.* нагля́дный, изобразительный, описáтельный

desecrate [дé-сí-крэйт] *vt.* оскверня́ть

desert [дé-зăрт] *sn.* пусты́ня; *adj.* необитáемый, пусты́нный [дí-зăрт] *v.t.* оставля́ть, покидáть

deserter [дí-зăр-тăр] *sm.* дезертúр

desertion [дí-зăр-шăн] *sn.* покидáние; дезертúрство

deserve [дí-зăрв] *vt.* заслу́живать

deserving [дí-зăр-вíн] *adj.* досто́йный, заслу́женный

desiccate [дé-сí-кэйт] *vt.* высу́шивать, сушúть

design [дí-зáйн] *sn.* план, узо́р, чертёж; намéрение, ýмысел, умышлéние (*intention, purpose*); *vt.* проектúровать; замышля́ть, намéреваться (*intend*)

designate [дé-зíг-нэйт] *vt.* назначáть (*appoint*); обозначáть (*denote*); *adj.* назнáченный

designation [дé-зíг-нэ́й-шăн] *sn.* назначéние, обозначéние, указáние

designer [дí-зáй-нăр] *sm.* рисовáльщик, чертёжник (*draughtsman*)

desirable [дí-зáй-рăбл] *adj.* желáнный, желáтельный

desire [дí-зáй-ăр] *sn.* желáние; *vt.* желáть

desirous [дí-зáй-рăс] *adj.* желáющий

desist [дí-зíст] *vi.* отступáть, перестáть

desk [дęск] *sn.* конто́рка, пúсьменный стол; пáрта (*scholar's*)

desolate [дé-со-лăт] *adj.* забро́шенный, покúнутый

desolation [дé-со-лэ́й-шăн] *sn.* опустошéние, разорéние

despair [дíс-пăр] *sn.* отчáяние; *vi.* отчáиваться

despatch [дíс-пęч] *sn.* отпрáвка; *vt.* отправля́ть

desperate [дéс-пă-рíт] *adj.* безнадёжный (*hopeless*); отчáянный (*reckless*); отчáянный (*dangerous*)

desperation [дęс-пă-рэ́й-шăн] *sn.* отчáяние

despicable [дęс-пí-кăбл] *adj.* презрéнный; нúзкий, по́длый (*vile*)

despise [дíс-пáйз] *vt.* презирáть

despite [дíс-пáйт] *prep.* вопрекú

despondent [дíс-по́н-дăнт] *adj.* подáвленный, пáвший ду́хом

despot [дéс-пот] *sm.* дéспот, тирáн

despotism [дéс-пă-тíзм] *sn.* деспотúзм, самовлáстие

dessert [дí-зăрт] *sn.* десéрт

destination [дéс-стí-нэ́й-шăн] *sn.* мéсто назначéния

destiny [дéс-тí-ні] *sn.* рок, судьбá, удéл, учáсть

destitute [дéс-тí-тют] *adj.* лишённый, нуждáющийся

destroy [дíс-тро́й] *vt.* истребля́ть, уничтожáть

destroyer [дíс-тро́й-ăр] *sm.* истребúтель, разрушúтель; *naut.* эскáдренный миноно́сец

destruction [діс-трáк-шăн] *sn.* разрушéние, сокрушéние

destructive [діс-трáк-тів] *adj.* разруши́тельный; па́губный (*pernicious*)

desultory [дé-сал-трі] *adj.* несвя́зный, отры́вочный

detach [ді-тéч] *vt.* отделя́ть; *mil.* отряжа́ть

detachment [ді-тéч-мăнт] *sn.* отделéние; *mil.* комáнда, отря́д

detail [ди-тéйл] *sn.* детáль, подрóбность; **in** – [ін –] обстоя́тельно; [ді-тéйл] *vt.* подрóбно расскáзывать; *mil.* назначáть, отряжáть

detain [ді-тэ́йн] *vt.* задéрживать, удéрживать

detect [ді-тéкт] *vt.* обнарýживать

detection [ді-тéк-шăн] *sn.* обнарýжение, откры́тие

detective [ді-тéк-тів] *sm.* детекти́в, сы́щик; *adj.* детекти́вный, сыскнóй

detention [ді-тéн-шăн] *sn.* задержáние, удержáние; *mil.* áрест

deter [ді-тéр] *vt.* отговáривать, удéрживать

detergent [ді-тéр-джănт] *adj.* очищáющий

deteriorate [ді-ті́-рiă-рэйт] *vt.i.* пóртиться (*become spoilt*); ухудшáть (*worsen*)

deterioration [ді-ті-рiă-рэ́й-шăн] *sn.* пóрча; ухудшéние

determinate [ді-тéр-мі-ніт] *adj.* определённый

determination [ді-тăр-мі-нáй-шăн] *sn.* решéние (*resolution*); реши́тельность (*firmness*)

determine [ді-тéр-мін] *vt.i.* определя́ть; решáть (*decide*)

deterrent [ді-тĕ́-рănт] *adj.* удéрживающий

detest [ді-тéст] *vt.* ненави́деть

detestable [ді-тéст-ăбл] *adj.* отврати́тельный

detonate [дé-то-нэйт] *vt.i.* взрывáть, детони́ровать

detour [ді-тýр] *sn.* объéзд, окóльный путь

detract [ді-трáкт] *vt.i.* унижáть

detriment [дé-трі-мăнт] *sn.* вред, ущéрб

detrimental [де-трі-мéн-тăл] *adj.* врéдный, убы́точный

deuce [дюс] *sn.* двóйка (*the two in cards and dice*); дьюс (*in tennis*); чорт (*devil*)

devastation [де-вăс-тóй-шăн] *sn.* опустошéние, разорéние

develop [ді-вé-лăп] *vt.i.* развивáть; *phot.* проявля́ть

development [ді-вé-лăп-мăнт] *sn.* развитие; рост (*growth*); *phot.* проявлéние

deviate [ді-ві-эйт] *vi.* отклоня́ться (*digress*); заблуждáться (*stray*)

deviation [ди-ві-э́й-шăн] *sn.* отклонéние; *naut.* девиáция

device [ді-вáйс] *sn.* вы́думка (*contrivance*); изобретéние (*invention*); спóсоб (*method*); деви́з, эмблéма (*motto, emblem*)

devil [дé-віл] *sm.* бес, дья́вол, чорт

devilish [дé-ві-ліш] *adj.* дья́вольский

devilment [дé-віл-мăнт] *sn.* шáлость

devious [ді-ві-ăс] *adj.* обхо́дный (*round about*); уклоня́ющийся (*erring*)

devise [ді-ва́йз] *vt.* выду́мывать, измышля́ть (*contrive*); завеща́ть (*assign*)

devoid [ді-во́йд] *adj.* лишённый (*lacking*); свобо́дный (*free from*)

devolve [ді-во́лв] *vt.i.* достава́ться, передава́ть

devote [ді-во́ут] *vt.* обрека́ть, посвяща́ть

devoted [ді-во́у-тід] *adj.* пре́данный (*loyal*); обречённый (*doomed*)

devotion [ді-во́у-шăн] *sn.* набо́жность (*sanctiousness*); пре́данность (*attachment*); благоче́стие (*piety*); *pl.* моли́твы (*prayers*); религио́зные обря́ды (*religious exercises*)

devotional [ді-во́у-шăн-ăл] *adj.* благоче́стный, набо́жный

devour [ді-ва́у-ăр] *vt.* поглоща́ть, пожира́ть

devout [ді-ва́ут] *adj.* благогове́йный (*reverent*); благочести́вый (*pious*)

dew [дю] *sn.* роса́

dew-drop [дю́-дроп] *sn.* роси́нка

dexterity [дєкс-тé-рі-ті] *sn.* иску́сность, прово́рство

dexterous [дєкс-трăс] *adj.* ло́вкий, прово́рный

diabolical [дай-ă-бó-лі-кăл] *adj.* дья́вольский

diaeresis [дай-ĕ-рі-сіс] *sn.* знак разделе́ния(''), разре́з

diagnose [дай-ă-гно́уз] *vt.* определя́ть боле́знь ста́вить диагно́з

diagnosis [дай-ă-гно́у-сіс] *sn.* диагно́з

diagonal [дай-ǽ-гă-нăл] *sn.* диагона́ль; *adj.* диагона́льный

diagram [дай-ă-грǽм] *sn.* диагра́мма, схе́ма

dial [дай-ăл] *sn.* цифербла́т; *vt.* ука́зывать на цифербла́те); набира́ть но́мер (*telephone*)

dialect [дай-ă-лєкт] *sn.* диале́кт, наре́чие

dialogue [дай-ă-лог] *sn.* диало́г

diameter [дай-ǽ-мі-тăр] *sn.* диа́метр

diamond [дай-ă-мăнд] *sn.* алма́з (*stone*); бу́бна (*cards*); *geom.* ромб; – **cutter** [– кă-тăр] *sn.* грани́льщик

diaper [дай-ă-păр] *sn.* пелёнка

diarrhoea [дай-ă-рі́ă] *sn.* поно́с

diary [дай-ă-рі] *sn.* дневни́к

dice [дайс] *sn. pl.* игра́льные ко́сти

dictate [дік-тэ́йт] *vt.i.* диктова́ть; предпи́сать (*prescribe*)

dictates [дік-тэ́йтс] *sn. pl.* веле́ние (*decree*); предписа́ние (*injunction*)

dictation [дік-тэ́й-шăн] *sn.* дикто́вка

dictatorial [дік-тă-тó-рі-ăл] *adj.* повели́тельный, диктато́рский

diction [дік-шăн] *sn.* ди́кция (спо́соб выраже́ния)

dictionary [дік-шă-нă-рі] *sn.* слова́рь, *m.*

die [дай] *sn.* чека́н, штамп; *arch.* цо́коль (*plinth*); *vi.* умира́ть; издо́хнуть (*of animals*)

diet [дай-ăт] *sn.* диэ́та; собра́ние (*assembly*); пи́ща, стол (*food*)

differ [ді-фăр] *vi.* отлича́ться, различа́ться (*be unlike*); расходи́ться (*disagree*)

difference [діф-рăнс] *sn.* разли́чие, ра́зница

different [ді-фрăнт] *adj.* разли́чный, ра́зный

differentiate [ді-фă-рĕн-ши-эйт] *vt.i.* распознава́ть

difficult [ді-фи-кăлт] *adj.* тру́дный

difficulty [ді-фи-кăл-ті] *sn.* затрудне́ние (*perplexity*); тру́дность (*hardship*); препя́тствие (*obstacle*)

diffidence [ді-фи-дăнс] *sn.* ро́бость

diffuse [ді-фю́з] *adj.* многосло́вный (*loquacious*); рассе́янный (*of light*); *vt.* распространя́ть

diffusion [ді-фю́-жăн] *sn.* распростране́ние, рассе́яние; диффу́зия

dig [діг] *vt.* копа́ть, рыть; – in [– ін] зарыва́ть; – up [– ăп] вспа́хать, вы́рыть

digest [дай-джĕст] *sn.* компе́ндий, кра́ткое изложе́ние; [ді-джĕст] *vt.i.* перева́ривать (*food*)

digestible [ді-джĕс-тібл] *adj.* перевари́мый, удобовари́мый

digestion [ді-джĕс-чăн] *sn.* пищеваре́ние

digestive [дай-джĕс-тів] *adj.* пищевари́тельный

digit [ді-джіт] *sn.* едини́ца, ци́фра (*figure*); па́лец (*finger*)

dignified [діг-ні-файд] *adj.* благоро́дный, досто́йный

dignify [діг-ні-фай] *vt.* об-

лагора́живать, удоста́ивать

dignitary [діг-ні-тă-рі] *sm.* сано́вник

dignity [діг-ні-ті] *sn.* благоро́дство, досто́инство

digress [дай-грĕс] *vi.* отвлека́ться, отступа́ть

digression [дай-грĕ-шăн] *sn.* отступле́ние

dike [дайк] *sn.* да́мба, плоти́на; ров (*ditch*)

dilapidated [ді-лă-пі-дэй-тід] *adj.* обветша́лый, полуразру́шенный, разва́ливающийся

dilate [дай-лэ́йт] *vt.i.* расширя́ть; *fig.* распространя́ться

dilatory [ді-лă-тă-рі] *adj.* замедля́ющий, медли́тельный

diligence [ді-лі-джăнс] *sn.* прилежа́ние, усе́рдие

diligent [ді-лі-джăнт] *adj.* приле́жный, стара́тельный

dilute [дай-лю́т] *vt.* разбавля́ть, разжижа́ть

dilution [дай-лю́-шăн] *sn.* разжиже́ние, растворе́ние

dim [дім] *adj.* ма́товый, ту́склый

dimension [ді-мĕн-шăн] *sn.* измере́ние, разме́р; *pl.* величина́, объём

diminish [ді-мі-ніш] *vt.i.* уменьша́ть

diminutive [ді-мі-ню-тів] *adj.* ма́ленький, миниатю́рный; *gram.* уменьши́тельный

dimple [дімпл] *sn.* я́мочка (на щеке́, и т.п.)

din [дін] *sn.* гро́хот, шум

dine [дайн] *vt.i.* обе́дать

diner [дай-нăр] *sm.* обеда́ющий

dinghy [ді́н-гі] *sn.* туз, шлю́пка

dingy [ді́н-джі] *adj.* гря́зный (*dirty*); ту́склый (*dull*)

dining-room [да́й-нін-ру́м] *sn.* столо́вая

dinner [ді́-нăр] *sn.* обе́д

dint [дінт] *sn.* след, отпеча́ток

diocesan [дай-о́-сă-зăн] *sm.* епархиа́льный епи́скоп; *adj.* епархиа́льный

diocese [да́й-ă-сіс] *sn.* епа́рхия

dip [діп] *sn.* отко́с, укло́н (*slope*); погруже́ние (*immersion*); *v.t.* окуна́ть (*plunge*); опуска́ть (*lower*); погружа́ть (*immerse*)

diphthong [ді́ф-ѳон] *sn.* двугла́сная бу́ква, дифто́нг

diploma [ді-пло́у-мă] *sn.* дипло́м; свиде́тельство (*certificate*)

diplomacy [ді-пло́у-мă-сі] *sn.* диплома́тия

diplomat [ді-пло́у-мăт] *sm.* диплома́т

diplomatic [ді-пло́у-мắ-тік] *adj.* дипломати́ческий

dire [да́й-ăр] *adj.* стра́шный, ужа́сный

direct [дай-ре́кт] *adj.* прямо́й (*straight*); откры́тый (*frank*); *v.t.i.* направля́ть (*aim at*); руководи́ть (*manage*); ука́зывать (*guide*)

direction [дай-ре́к-шăн] *sn.* направле́ние (*trend*); правле́ние, управле́ние (*management*); *pl.* предписа́ние (*injunction*); приказа́ние (*orders*); директи́вы (*instructions*)

directly [дай-ре́кт-лі] *adv.* неме́дленно, непосре́д-

ственно, тотча́с (*at once*); пря́мо (*point-blank*); *coll.* как то́лько (*as soon as*)

director [дай-ре́к-тăр] *sm.* дире́ктор, нача́льник, управля́ющий

directory [дай-ре́к-тă-рі] *sn.* а́дресная кни́га

dirge [дöрдж] *sn.* панихи́да, погреба́льное пе́ние

dirt [дöрт] *sn.* грязь

dirty [дöр-ті] *adj.* гря́зный, запа́чканный; бессты́дный, непристо́йный (*obscene*)

disability [ді-сă-бі-лі-ті] *sn.* бесси́лие, неспосо́бность

disable [діс-э́йбл] *vt.* обесси́ливать (*weaken*); изуве́чивать, кале́чить (*maim*)

disabled [діс-э́й-балд] *adj.* искале́ченный

disadvantage [діс-ăд-ва́н-тідж] *sn.* невы́года

disagree [діс-ă-грі́] *vi.* не соглаша́ться, расходи́ться в мне́ниях (*differ*); ссо́риться (*quarrel*)

disagreeable [діс-ă-грі́-ăбл] *adj.* неприя́тный (*unpleasant*); проти́вный (*repugnant*)

disagreement [діс-ă-грі́-мăнт] *sn.* несогла́сие, разла́д

disallow [діс-ă-ла́у] *vt.* запреща́ть (*forbid*); не позволя́ть (*not allow*)

disappear [діс-ă-пі́р] *vi.* исчеза́ть

disappearance [діс-ă-пі́-рăнс] *sn.* исчезнове́ние

disappoint [діс-ă-по́йнт] *vt.* разочаро́вать

disappointment [діс-ă-по́йнт-мăнт] *sn.* доса́да, разочарова́ние

disapprove [дíс-æ-прýв] vt. неодобрять, осуждать

disarmament [дíс-áр-мáмант] sn. разоружение

disaster [ді-зáс-тáр] sn. бедствие, катастрофа, несчастье

disastrous [ді-зáс-трáс] adj. бедственный, гибельный, несчастный

disband [дíс-бǽнд] vt.i. разойтись, распускать; mil. расформировать

disbelieve [дíс-бі-лíв] vt. не верить

disburse [дíс-бё́рс] vt.i. платить, раскошеливаться, расплачиваться

disbursement [дíс-бё́рсмант] sn. трата, расходование, уплата

discard [дíс-кáрд] vt. отметать, оставлять, увольнять

discern [ді-зё́рн] vt. различать, распознавать

discerning [ді-зё́р-нін] adj. распознающий

discharge [дíс-чáрдж] sn. выстрел (of gun); увольнение (dismissal); med. вытекание; освобождение (liberation); vt. разгружать (unload); увольнять (dismiss)

disciple [ді-сáйпл] sm. последователь (follower); ученик (pupil)

discipline [дí-сі-плін] sn. благочиние, дисциплина; vt. дисциплинировать

disclose [дíс-клóуз] vt. обнаруживать, разоблачать

disclosure [дíс-клóу-жáр] sn. открытие

discolour [дíс-кá-лáр] vt. обесцвечивать

discomfiture [дíс-кáм-фі-чáр] sn. поражение, смущение

discomfort [дíс-кáм-фáрт] sn. неловкость, неудобство

disconcert [дíс-кáн-сё́рт] vt. расстраивать (upset); смущать (embarrass)

disconnect [дíс-кá-нéкт] vt. разобщать, разъединять

disconsolate [дíс-кóн-сáліт] adj. неутешимый

discontent [дíс-кáн-тéнт] sn. досада, недовольство

discontinue [дíс-кáн-тí-ню] vt. прекращать, прерывать

discord [дíс-кóрд] sn. разлад, разногласие (variance); mus. диссонанс

discordant [дíс-кóр-дáнт] adj. несогласный, противоречивый; mus. нестройный

discount [дíс-каунт] sn. дисконт, скидка, учёт; [дíс-кáунт] vt. учитывать

discourage [дíс-ká-рíдж] vt. обескураживать, отбивать настроение

discourse [дíс-кóрс] sn. речь, рассуждение; vi. разговаривать

discover [дíс-ká-вáр] vt. обнаруживать, отыскивать, раскрывать

discovery [дíс-ká-вá-рі] sn. обнаружение, открытие

discredit [дíс-крé-діт] sn. бесчестие, позор; vt. лишать доверия, позорить

discreet [дíс-крíт] adj. осторожный (careful); осмотрительный (cautious)

discrepancy [дíс-крé-пáнсі] sn. неувязка, различие

discretion [дíс-крé-шáн] sn. осторожность; осмотрительность

discriminate [дíс-крí-мі-нэйт] *vt.i.* отличáть, различáть

discrimination [дíс-крі-мі-нэ́й-шăн] *sn.* отлíчие, различéние

discuss [дíс-кáс] *vt.* обсуждáть, рассуждáть; дискутíровать

discussion [дíс-кá-шăн] *sn.* обсуждéние, прéния; дискýссия

disdain [дíс-дэ́йн] *vt.* презрéние, пренебрежéние; *vt.* презирáть, пренебрегáть

disease [ді-зíз] *sn.* болéзнь

disembark [дíс-ім-бáрк] *vt.i.* выгружáть, высáживать

disengage [дíс-ін-гэ́йдж] *vt.* выпýтывать, отвязывать

disengaged [дíс-ін-гэ́йджд] *adj.* свобóдный (free)

disentangle [дíс-ін-тáнгл] *vt.* распýтывать

disfigure [дíс-фí-гăр] *vt.* обезобрáживать, урóдовать

disgorge [дíс-гóрдж] *vt.* извергáть, изрыгáть; вытекáть (of river)

disgrace [діс-грэ́йс] *sn.* бесчéстие; *vt.* позóрить

disgraceful [діс-грэ́йс-фўл] *adj.* бесчéстный, позóрный; *coll.* возмутíтельный

disguise [діз-гáйз] *sn.* маскирóвка, переодевáние; *vt.* замаскирóвать

disgust [діс-гáст] *sn.* омерзéние, отвращéние; *vt.* внушáть отвращéние

disgusting [діс-гáс-тíй] *adj.* отвратíтельный

dish [дíш] *sn.* блю́до, мíска (vessel); блю́до, кýшанье (food)

dishearten [дíс-хáр-тăн] *vt.*

обескурáживать, приводíть в унние

dishonest [дíс-ó-ніст] *adj.* бесчéстный

dishonour [дíс-ó-нăр] *sn.* бесчéстие, позóр; *vt.* бесчéстить, позóрить

dishonourable [дíс-ó-нă-рăбл] *adj.* бесчéстный, позóрный

disillusion [дíс-і-лю́-жăн] *vt.* разочарóвывать

disinfect [дíс-ін-фéкт] *vt.* дезинфицíровать

disinfectant [дíс-ін-фéк-тăнт] *adj.* дезинфицíрующий

disinherit [дíс-ін-хé-ріт] *vt.* лишáть наслéдства

disintegrate [дíс-íн-тíгрэйт] *vt.* раздроблáть, разлагáть

disintegration [дíс-ін-тíгрй-шăн] *sn.* разложéние, распáд

disinterested [дíс-íн-тăрéс-тíд] *adj.* бескорыстный, беспристрáстный

dislike [діс-лáйк] *sn.* нелюбóвь, отвращéние; *vt.* не любíть

dislocate [дíс-ло-кэ́йт] *vt.* вывихнуть, *fig.* нарушáть, расстрóить

dislocation [дíс-ло-кэ́йшăн] *sn.* вывих, *geol.* сдвиг

dislodge [діс-лóдж] *vt.* смещáть; *mil.* выбивáть, вытеснять

disloyal [діс-лóй-ăл] *adj.* веролóмный, предáтельский

dismal [діз-мăл] *adj.* заунывный, пáсмурный

dismantle [діс-мáнтл] *vt.* расснáщивать

dismay [діс-мэ́й] *sn.* испу́г, у́жас; *vt.* ужаса́ть

dismiss [діс-мі́с] *sn.* mil. во́льно! *vt.* отпуска́ть, отреша́ть; увольня́ть (*cashier*)

dismissal [діс-мі́-сăл] *sn.* отста́вка, увольне́ние

dismount [діс-ма́унт] *vt.i.* сбра́сывать, слеза́ть, спе́шивать (*from horse*); разнима́ть, разбира́ть (*take to pieces*); снима́ть (*gun*)

disobedience [діс-о-бі́-діăнс] *sn.* неповинове́ние, непослуша́ние

disobedient [діс-о-бі́-діăнт] *adj.* непослу́шный, ослу́шливый

disobey [діс-о-бэ́й] *vt.i.* ослу́шиваться

disorder [діс-о́р-дăр] *sn.* беспоря́док, расстро́йство

disorderly [діс-о́р-дăр-лі] *adj.* беспоря́дочный, неопря́тный

disown [діс-о́ун] *vt.* отверга́ть, отка́зываться (от)

disparage [діс-пэ́-ріджк] *vt.* уничижа́ть

disparity [діс-пэ́-рі-ті] *sn.* нера́венство, несоразме́рность

dispatch [діс-пэ́ч] *sn.* отпра́вка, посыла́ние (*sending*); поспе́шность (*promptness*); депе́ша (*message*); *vt.* отправля́ть, посыла́ть

dispel [діс-пэ́л] *vt.* разгоня́ть, рассе́ивать

dispensary [діс-пэ́н-сă-рі] *sn.* апте́ка

dispensation [діс-пен-сэ́й-шăн] *sn.* разда́ча; *eccl.* разреше́ние, диспенса́ция

dispense [діс-пэ́нс] *vt.* раздава́ть, наделя́ть, распреде-

ля́ть (*distribute*); med. приготовля́ть (лека́рство); **to with** [ту — йіз́] обходи́ться без

dispenser [діс-пе́н-сăр] *sm.* фармаце́вт

dispersal [діс-пăр-сăл] *sn.* рассе́ивание, рассыла́ние

disperse [діс-пăрс] *vt.i.* разгоня́ть, рассе́ивать; разбега́ться, расходи́ться (*depart*)

displace [діс-плэ́йс] *vt.* перемеща́ть, смеща́ть

displacement [діс-плэ́йсмăнт] *sn.* перемеще́ние, смеще́ние; водоизмеще́ние (*of water*)

display [діс-плэ́й] *sn.* проявле́ние (*manifestation*); вы́ставка, пока́з (*exhibition*)

displease [діс-плі́з] *vt.* не нра́виться

disposal [діс-по́у-зăл] *sn.* распоряже́ние; удале́ние (*removal*)

dispose [діс-по́уз] *vt.* располага́ть, расставля́ть

disposition [діс-пă-зі́-шăн] *sn.* диспози́ция, расположе́ние; скло́нность (*inclination*); нрав (*character*)

dispossess [діс-пă-зе́с] *vt.* лиша́ть со́бственности

disproportionate [діс-прăпо́р-шă-ніт] *adj.* непропорциона́льный

disprove [діс-пру́в] *vt.* опрове́ргать

disputable [діс-пю́-тăбл] *adj.* спо́рный

dispute [діс-пю́т] *sn.* ди́спут; поле́мика, спор; *vi.* обсужда́ть, оспа́ривать

disqualification [діс-кўо́-лі-фі-кэ́й-шăн] *sn.* непра-

disqualify [діс-кўо́-лі-фай] vt. де́лать непригодным; дисквалифици́ровать

disquiet [діс-кўа́й-ăт] sn. беспоко́йство, волне́ние, трево́га

disregard [діс-рі-га́рд] sn. невнима́ние, пренебреже́ние

disreputable [діс-ре́-пю-тăбл] adj. побо́рный, посты́дный

disrespect [діс-рі-пе́кт] sn. непочти́тельность

disrespectful [діс-рі-пе́кт-фул] adj. неучти́вый

disrupt [діс-ра́пт] vt. разрыва́ть [разры́в

disruption [діс-ра́п-шăн] sn.

dissatisfaction [діс-сă-тіс-фăк-шăн] sn. неудово́льствие

dissect [ді-се́кт] vt. расчленя́ть· fig. анализи́ровать

dissection [ді-се́к-шăн] sn. расчлене́ние; anat. вскры́тие

dissemble [ді-се́мбл] vt.i. лицеме́рить, притворя́ться

disseminate [ді-се́-мі-нэйт] vt. распространя́ть, рассе́ивать

dissension [ді-се́н-шăн] sn. разла́д, раздо́р, разногла́сие

dissent [ді-се́нт] sn. несогла́сие; vi. расходи́ться, не соглаша́ться

dissertation [ді-сœр-те́йшăн] sn. диссерта́ция

disservice [діс-сœр-віс] sn. вред, уще́рб; **do a –** [ду ă –] оказа́ть плоху́ю услу́гу

dissipate [ді-сі-пэйт] vt.i. разгоня́ть, рассе́ивать; прома́тывать (squander); coll. кути́ть

dissipated [ді-сі-пэй-тід] adj. беспу́тный, распу́щенный

dissoluble [ді-со́-любл] adj. раствори́мый

dissolute [ді-сă-лют] adj. развра́тный, распу́тный

dissolution [ді-сă-лю́-шăн] sn. chem. разложе́ние, растворе́ние; расторже́ние (breach); pol. ро́спуск

dissolve [ді-зо́лв] vt. chem. разлага́ть, растворя́ть; растога́ть (marriage); распуска́ть (parliament)

dissonant [ді-со-нăнт] adj. mus. нестро́йный; противоречи́вый (views, etc.)

dissuade [ді-сўэ́йд] vt. отгова́ривать, отсове́товать

distance [діс-тăнс] sn. расстоя́ние; даль; да́льность; **in the –** [ін еă –] вдали́, и́здали

distant [діс-тăнт] adj. да́льний, отдалённый; сде́ржанный (reserved)

distasteful [діс-те́йст-фул] adj. неприя́тный, проти́вный

distemper [діс-те́м-пăр] sn. соба́чья чума́ (dog's), клеева́я кра́ска (paint); vt. окра́шивать кра́ской

distend [діс-те́нд] vt. надува́ть, раздува́ть; растя́гивать (stretch)

distil [діс-ті́л] vt. дистилли́ровать; ка́пать (trickle); fig. очища́ть

distillation [діс-ті-ле́й-шăн] sn. дистилля́ция, перего́нка

distiller [діс-ті-ля́р] sn. виноку́р, перего́нщик

distillery [діс-ті-лă-рі] sn. виноку́ренный заво́д

distinct [діс-тíŋкт] adj. отчётливый, я́сный (clear); определённый (specific); различный (separate)

distinction [діс-тíŋк-шăн] sn. отли́чие, разли́чие (difference); почёт (esteem); возвы́шенность (eminence)

distinctive [діс-тíŋк-тів] adj. отличи́тельный, сво́йственный

distinguish [діс-тíŋ-ґўіш] vt. отлича́ть, различа́ть

distinguished [діс-тíŋ-ґўішд] adj. выдаю́щийся, зна́тный

distort [діс-тóрт] vt. криви́ть (twist), искажа́ть (mutilate)

distortion [діс-тóр-шăн] sn. искривле́ние, искаже́ние

distract [діс-трáкт] vt. отвлека́ть

distracted [діс-трáк-тід] adj. в отча́янии, поме́шанный

distraction [діс-трáк-шăн] sn. развлече́ние (diversion); отча́яние (desperation); безу́мие (frenzy)

distress [діс-трéс] sn. бе́дствие, го́ре; vt. огорча́ть, терза́ть; истоща́ть (exhaust)

distribute [діс-трí-бют] vt. раздава́ть, распределя́ть

distribution [діс-трі-бю́-шăн] sn. раздава́ние, разда́ча, распределе́ние

distributive [діс-трí-бю-тів] adj. распредели́тельный, gram. раздели́тельный

district [діс-трíкт] sn. о́круг, райо́н

distrustful [діс-трáст-фул] adj. недове́рчивый

disturb [діс-тóрб] vt. беспоко́ить, смуща́ть

disturbance [діс-тóр-бăнс] sn. беспоко́йство, трево́га (unrest); смяте́ние (confusion); pl. беспоря́дки, волне́ния

disunite [діс-ю-на́йт] vt. разобща́ть, разъединя́ть

disuse [діс-ю́с] sn. неупотребле́ние; [діс-ю́з] vt. отвыка́ть; выводи́ть из употребле́ния

disyllabic [ді-сі-лǽ-бік] adj. двусло́жный

ditch [діч] sn. кана́ва, ров; vt.i. ока́пывать; осуша́ть (drain)

dive [дайв] sn. ныря́ние; vi. ныря́ть; пики́ровать (in flight)

diver [дай-вăр] sm. водола́з; ныро́к (bird)

diverge [дай-вǽрдж] vi. отклоня́ться, расходи́ться

divergence [дай-вǽр-джăнс] sn. расхожде́ние

diverse [дай-вǽрс] adj. отли́чный, разли́чный, ра́зный

diversion [дай-вǽр-жăн] sn. отвлече́ние, отклоне́ние (deviation); заба́ва, развлече́ние (amusement)

divert [дай-вǽрт] vt. отвлека́ть, отклоня́ть; заба́влять, развлека́ть, увеселя́ть (amuse, entertain)

divest [дай-вéст] vt. раздева́ть (strip, unclothe); лиша́ть (deprive)

divide [ді-вáйд] vt.i. дели́ть, разделя́ть

dividend [ді-ві-дéнд] sn. com. дивиде́нд; math. дели́мое

divination [di-vi-néj-šän] *sn.* предсказа́ние, уга́дывание (*prediction*); гада́ние, прорица́ние (*oracle*)

divine [di-vájn] *s.* богосло́в; *adj.* боже́ственный; *vt.i.* предска́зывать, уга́дывать

diving [дай-вій] *sn.* ныря́ние

divinity [di-vi-ni-ti] *sn.* боже́ственность; бо́жество (*deity*); богосло́вие (*theology*)

divisible [di-ví-zibl] *adj.* дели́мый

division [di-ví-жän] *sn.* боже́ние, разделе́ние; отде́л, отделе́ние, разде́л, часть (*section*); *mil.* диви́зия

divisional [di-vi-жän-äl] *adj.* разделя́ющий; *mil.* дивизио́нный

divorce [di-vórs] *sn.* разво́д; разъедине́ние (*of things*); *vt.* расторга́ть брак; отделя́ть, разъединя́ть

divulge [di-válдж] *vt.* разглаша́ть

dizziness [dí-zi-nis] *sn.* головокруже́ние

dizzy [dí-zi] *adj.* головокружи́тельный, ошеломля́ющий

do [dý] *vt.i.* де́лать (*make, perform*), исполня́ть (*fulfil*); производи́ть (*produce*); де́йствовать (*function*); that will —! [әәt ýil —] дово́льно!; how – you – ? [ҳа̄у – ю –] как пожива́ете?

docile [дó̱у-сайл] *adj.* поко́рный, послу́шный

dock [док] *sn.* верфь, док (*basin*); *bot.* ща́вель; *m.*; *naut.* ста́вить су́дно (в док)

dock-yard [до̄к-я̄рд] *sn.* ста́пель

docker [до́-кäр] *sm.* до́кер, портово́й рабо́чий

docket [до́-кит] *sn.* пе́речень, *m.* (*list, inventory, catalogue*); ярлы́к (*label*); *vt.* вноси́ть (в ро́спись)

doctor [до́к-тäр] *sm.* врач, до́ктор

doctorate [до́к-тä-рэйт] *sn.* доктора́т, до́кторская сте́пень, до́кторство

document [до́-кю-мäнт] *sn.* докуме́нт, свиде́тельство

documentary [до-кю-ме́н-тä-ри] *adj.* документа́льный

dodge [додж] *sn.* уве́ртка, уло́вка; *vt.i.* избега́ть (*elude*); увёртываться, уви́ливать (*shirk*)

doe [до́у] *sf.* лань; са́мка за́йца, кро́лика (*female of hare or rabbit*)

doe-skin [до́у-скін] *sn.* оле́нья ко́жа, за́мша

dog [дог] *sm.* пёс, соба́ка

dogged [до́-гід] *adj.* упо́рный, упря́мый

dogma [до́г-мä] *sn.* до́гмат

doily [до́й-ли] *sn.* салфе́точка

dole [до́ул] *sn.* посо́бие (по безрабо́тице); вспомоществова́ние (*relief*); подая́ние (*alms*)

doll [дол] *sn.* ку́кла

dolly [до́-ли] *sn.* ку́колка

dolorous [до́-лä-рäс] *adj.* гру́стный, печа́льный

dolt [долт] *sm.* болва́н, дура́к, о́лух

domain [до-ме́йн] *sn.* владе́ние, име́ние; о́бласть, сфе́ра (*province, sphere*)

dome [до́ум] *sn.* ку́пол

domestic [до-мéс-тiк] *sm., f.* домáшняя рабóтница, прислýга, слугá; *adj.* домáшний

domesticate [до-мéс-тiкэйт] *vt.* приручáть

domicile [дó-мi-сайл] *sm.* постоя́нное местожи́тельство

dominant [дó-мi-нэнт] *adj.* госпóдствующий, преоблада́ющий

dominate [дó-мi-нэйт] *vt.* госпóдствовать, преоблада́ть

domination [до-мi-нэ́й-шэн] *sn.* власть, влия́ние, преоблада́ние

domineer [до-мi-нú́р] *vi.* госпóдствовать, наси́ливать, тирáнить

dominion [до-мú́-нiэн] *sn.* владьı́чество

donation [доý-нэ́й-шэн] *sn.* дар, пожéртвование

donkey [дóн-кi] *sm.* осёл

doom [дýм] *sn.* рок, судьбá; *vt.* обрекáть, осуждáть

doomsday [дýмз-дэй] *sn.* сýдный день

door [дóр] *sn.* дверь; **in-s** [iн-з] дóма; **out of -s** [аýт ов -з] вне дóма, на свéжем вóздухе

door-keeper [дóр-кú-пáр] *sm.* привра́тник, стóрож, швейцáр

door-mat [дóр-мэт] *sn.* половúк

dope [дóуп] *sn.* наркотúческое снáдобье; *vt.i.* одурмáнивать

dormant [дóр-мэнт] *adj.* бездéйствующий (*not in action*); спя́щий (*sleeping*)

dormitory [дóр-мi-тá-pi] *sn.* дортуáр, óбщая спáльня

dormouse [дóр-мауc] *s.* сóня

dose [дóуc] *sn.* дóза, приём; *vt.* дозúровать

dot [дот] *sn.* тóчка; *vt.* пунктúровать, стáвить тóчку

dotage [дóý-тiдж] *sn.* стáрческое слабоýмие, тупоýмие

double [дабл] *sn.* двóйник; изгúб (*of river*); *adj.* двойнóй, двóйственный; *adv.* вдвóе, двáжды; *vt.i.* склáдывать вдвóе (*fold*); удвáивать (*multiply*); *naut.* обогнýть; **- up** [- ап] скрю́чиваться; **- entry** [- éн-трi] *com.* двойнáя бухгалтéрия

double-bass [дабл-бэ́йc] *sn. mus.* контрабáс

doubt [дáут] *sn.* сомнéние; *vt.i.* недоверя́ть, сомневáться

doubtful [дáут-фýл] *adj.* недостовéрный, сомнúтельный

doubtless [дáут-лic] *adv.* вероя́тно, несомнéнно

douche [дýш] *sn.* душ, облива́ние водóй; *med.* промывáние

dough [дóý] *sn.* тéсто

dove [дав] *s.* гóлубь, *m.*

dovecot [дáв-кэт] *sn.* голубя́тня

dovetail [дáв-тэйл] *sn. tech.* лáсточкин хвост; *vt.i.* плóтно прилáживать, скрепля́ть

down [дáун] *sn.* безлéсная возвьı́шенность (*open high land*); пух (*fluff*); *adv.* внизý

downcast [дáун-каст] *adj.* потуплённый (*of eyes*); уны́лый (*of person*)

downfall [дáун-фол] *sn.* падéние, упáдок

downpour [дáун-пóр] *sn.* ли́вень, *m.*, наводне́ние

downright [дáун-райт] *adj.* открове́нный, я́вный

downstairs [-стэ́рз] внизу́

downward(s) [дáун-уǎрд(з)] *adj.* понижáющийся; вниз, внизу́, ни́зом

dowry [дáу-ри] *sn.* придáное

doze [дóуз] *sn.* дремотá, корóткий сон; *vi.* дремáть, спать уры́вками

dozen [дá-зэн] *sn.* дю́жина

drab [дрǽб] *sn.* тусклокори́чневый цвет (*colour*); моното́нность, однообрáзие (*monotony*); *adj.* тёмного цвéта (*of colour*); однообрáзный, ску́чный (*dull*)

draft [дрǎфт] *sn.* набро́сок, план, чертёж (*plan, drawing, etc.*); *mil.* отря́д; *com* трáтта, чек; черновик (*copy*); *vt.* набрáсывать, составля́ть; отряжáть

draftsman [дрǎфтс-мǎн] *sm.* составитель (докумéнтов и т.п.)

drag [дрǽг] *sn.* дрáга (*dredge*); то́рмоз (*brake*); я́корь, *m.* (*grapnel*); *vt.i.* воло́чить, тащи́ть; **– in** [– ин] втáскивать; **– on** [– он] тяну́ться; **– out** [– áут] выти́гивать

dragon [дрǽ-гǎн] *sm.* дракóн

dragonfly [дрǽ-гǎн-флай] *s.* стрекозá

drain [дрэйн] *sn.* дренáжная трубá (*pipe*); постоя́нная утéчка (*constant outlet*); *vt.i.* дрени́ровать, осушáть

drainage [дрэ́й-нидж] *sn.* дренáж, осушéние

drake [дрэйк] *s.* сéлезень, *m.*

dramatic [дрǎ-мǽ-тик] *adj.* драмати́ческий

dramatist [дрǽ-мǎ-тист] *sm.* драмату́рг

dramatize [дрǽ-мǎ-тайз] *vt.* драматизи́ровать

drape [дрэйп] *vt.* драпи́ровать, украшáть матéрией

draper [дрэ́й-пǎр] *sm.* торго́вец мануфакту́рой

drapery [дрэ́й-пǎ-ри] *sn.* мануфакту́рный товáр (*goods*); драпиро́вка (*hangings*)

drastic [дрǽс-тик] *adj.* си́льно дéйствующий (*strongly operative*); суро́вый (*stern*)

draught [дрǎфт] *sn.* сквозня́к (*current of air*); тя́га (*traction*); глото́к (*dose*); *naut.* осáдка; чертёж, эски́з, чернови́к (*rough copy of document, etc.*); *pl.* шáшки (*game*)

draught-board [дрǎфт-бóрд] *sn.* шáшечная доскá

draughtsman [дрǎфтс-мǎн] *sm.* рисовáльщик, чертёжник

draw [дрó] *sn.* тя́га (*pull*); примáнка (*lure*); ничья́ (*in games*); *vt.i.* воло́чить, тащи́ть, тяну́ть (*drag, pull*); притя́гивать (*attract*); рисовáть, черти́ть (*design*)

drawback [дро́-бǽк] *sn.* недостáток

drawer [дро́-ǎр] *sn.* выдвижно́й я́щик; *pl.* кальсóны, панталóны; **chest of -s** [чест óв –з] комóд

drawing [дро́-иň] *sn.* рисовáние, черчéние (*sketching*); рису́нок (*design, sketch*)

drawing-room *sn.* [дро́-иň-ру́м] гости́ная

drawl [дрóл] *sn.* распéв

dray [дрэй] *sn.* ломовáя подвóда

dread [дред] *sn.* боя́знь, страх; *adj.* грóзный; *vt.* боя́ться, страши́ться

dreadful [дрéд-фул] *adj.* страшный, ужáсный

dream [дрим] *sn.* сновидéние, сон; мечтá (*reverie*); *vt.i.* сни́ться

dreamy [дри́-ми] *adj.* сонли́вый

dreamer [дри́-мăр] *sm.* мечтáтель

dreary [дри́-ри] *adj.* мрáчный, скýчный

dredge [дредж] *sn.* дрáга, землечерпáлка; *vt.i.* вычéрпывать, очищáть

dregs [дрегз] *sn. pl.* осáдок, отбрóсы

drench [дренч] *vt.* промáчивать насквóзь, смáчивать

dress [дрес] *sn.* одéжда, плáтье; **– coat** [– кóут] фрак; **– circle** [– сĕркл] *theat.* пéрвый я́рус; **– full –** [– фул] парáдная фóрма; *vt.i.* наряжáть, одевáть; украшáть (*adorn*); причёсывать (*hair*); выдéлывать (*skin, etc.*); приправля́ть (*food*); перевя́зывать (*wound*); **– up –** [– ап] выряжáться

dresser [дрé-сăр] *sn.* кýхонный шкаф

dressing [дрé-сѝн] *sn.* одевáние; перевя́зка (*bandage*); приправа (*salad, etc.*); **– down –** [– дáун] головомóйка (*reprimand*)

dressing-gown [дрé-сѝн-гáун] *sn.* халáт

dressmaker [дрéс-мэйкăр] *sf.* портни́ха

dribble [дрибл] *vt.i.* кáпать

drift [дрифт] *sn.* направлéние, стремлéние (*tendency*); нанóс, сугрóб (*of snow*); *naut.* дрейф; *vi.* дрейфовáть

drill [дрил] *sn.* обучéние; *mil.* муштрóвка; дрель, сверлó (*tool*); тик (*material*); *vt.* обучáть (*train*), сверли́ть (*bore*)

drink [дри́нк] *sn.* напи́ток, питьё; *vt.i.* пить

drip [дрип] *sn.* кáпание; *vi.* кáпать

drive [драйв] *sn.* катáнье, въéзд (*road*); *tech.* привóд, передáча; *vt.i.* гнать, понимáть (*chase*); éхать (*in carriage*)

drivel [дри́-вăл] *sn.* болтовня́, пустословие (*silly talk*); слю́ни (*saliva*); *vi.* распускáть слю́ни; нести́ чепухý (*talk nonsense*)

driver [драй-вăр] *sm.* кýчер, шофёр; вагоновожáтый (*of trams, etc.*)

drizzle [дризл] *sn.* мéлкий дождь, *m.*; *vi.* мороси́ть

droll [дрол] *adj.* забáвный (*amusing*); стрáнный (*odd, queer*)

drollery [дрó-лă-ри] *sn.* шутовствó

drone [дрóун] *sn.* гудéние, жужжáние (*deep hum*); трýтень, *m.* (*bee*); *vi.* гудéть, жужжáть

droop [друп] *sn.* понимáние; *vi.* понимáть, увядáть; опускáть (*eyes*)

drooping [дрý-пѝн] *adj.* сви́слый

drop [дроп] sn. ка́пля; пониже́ние (in price, temperature, etc.); vt. ка́пать, па́дать, урони́ть (fall); понижа́ть (of voice); **– in** [– iн] загляну́ть; **– out** [– áут] выра́нивать

droppings [дро́-пiнз] sn. pl. помёт (животных)

dross [дрос] sn. ока́лина, шлак; отбро́сы (refuse)

drought [дра́ут] sn. за́суха

drove [дро́ув] sn. гурт, ста́до

drover [дро́у-вăр] sm. гуртовщи́к; скотопромы́шленник (dealer)

drown [дра́ун] vt.i. тону́ть, топи́ться

drowsiness [дра́у-зi-нiс] sn. дремота́, сонли́вость

drowsy [дра́у-зi] adj. дремлю́щий, со́нный

drudge [драдж] vi. исполня́ть ну́дную рабо́ту; sm. тру́женик

drudgery [дра́-джă-рi] sn. ну́дная чёрная рабо́та

drug [драг] sn. снадо́бье; vt. одурма́нивать (stupefy)

druggist [дра́-гiст] sm. апте́карь, m., дроги́ст

drum [драм] sn. бараба́н; vt.i. бараба́нить

drummer [дра́-мăр] sm. бараба́нщик

drunk [дранк] adj. пья́ный

drunkard [дра́н-кăрд] sm., f. пья́ница

drunkenness [дра́н-кăн-нiс] sn. пья́нство

dry [дра́й] adj. сухо́й; несла́дкий (of wine) vt.i. со́хнуть, суши́ть; **– up** [– ап] высыха́ть

dryness [дра́й-нiс] sn.

су́хость; за́суха (of weather)

dry-nurse [дра́й-нăрс] sf. ня́ня

dry-rot [дра́й-рот] sn. труха́

dual [дю́-ăл] sn. gram. дво́йственное число́; adj. дво́йственный

dubious [дю́-бi-ăс] adj. подозри́тельный, сомни́тельный

ducal [дю́-кăл] adj. ге́рцогский

duchess [да́-чiс] sf. герцоги́ня

duchy [да́-чi] sn. ге́рцогство

duck [дак] sf. у́тка; coll. ду́шка; паруси́на (material); vt.i. ныря́ть, окуна́ться; нагиба́ть го́лову (of one's head)

duckling [да́к-лiй] s. утёнок

duct [дакт] sn. кана́л, прото́к

ductility [дак-тí-лi-тi] sn. тягу́честь; ко́вкость; податли́вость

due [дю] sn. до́лжное; pl. нало́ги, по́шлины; adj. до́лжный, сле́дуемый; **in course** [iн – кóрс] в своё вре́мя; adv. то́чно

duel [дю́-ăл] sn. дуэ́ль

duet [дю́-éт] sn. дуэ́т

dug-out [да́г-áут] sn. убе́жище (shelter); земля́нка (hut)

duke [дюк] sm. ге́рцог

dull [дал] adj. тупо́й (blunt); па́смурный, ту́склый (gloomy); ску́чный (lifeless); вя́лый (of business)

duly [дю́-лi] adv. надлежа́щим о́бразом

dumb [дам] adj. немо́й, беззву́чный (silent)

dumb-bells [дам-бэлз] sn. pl. гантели, гимнастические гири

dumbfound [дам-фа́унд] vt. ошеломить, поразить

dummy [да́-мі] sn. болван (in whist); манекен (figure); theat. макет (model); соска (baby's)

dump [дамп] sn. груда хлима, mil. временный склад; vt. сбрасывать

dumpy [дам-пі] adj. коренастый

dunce [данс] sn. глупец

dune [дюн] sn. дюна

dung [дай] sn. навоз

dungeon [дан-джэн] sn. подземная тюрьма

dunghill [дай-хіл] sn. куча навоза

dupe [дюп] sn. обманутый человек; vt. надувать, обманывать

duple [дюпл] adj. двойной

duplex [дю-плэкс] adj. двусторонний

duplicate [дю-плі-кіт] sn. дубликат, копия; adj. удвоенный; [дю-плі-кэйт] vt. размножать, удваивать

duplication [дю-плі-кэй-шэн] sn. удваивание

duplicity [дю-плі-сі-ті] sn. двуличность, двойственность

durability [дю-ра-бі-лі-ті] sn. длительность, долговременность (long lasting); прочность (solidity)

durable [дю-рабл] adj. длительный; прочный

duration [дю-рэй-шэн] sn. продолжительность

duress [дю-рес] sn. заключение, заточение (imprison-ment); принуждение (compulsion)

during [дю-рій] prep. во время, в течение

dusk [даск] sn. сумерки

dust [даст] sn. прах, пыль; vt. осыпать, пылить (sprinkle); вытирать пыль (clean); выколачивать (beat out)

dustbin [даст-бін] sn. мусорный закром

duster [дас-тэр] sn. метёлка

dustman [даст-ман] sm. мусорщик

dustpan [даст-пэн] sn. совок

dusty [дас-ті] adj. пыльный

Dutch [дач] adj. голландский

Dutchman [дач-ман] sm. голландец

dutiful [дю-ті-фул] adj. послушный, почтительный

duty [дю-ті] sn. долг, обязанность (obligation); дежурство, должность, служба (service); пошлина (tax); naut. вахта

dwarf [дуорф] sm. карлик

dwell [дуэл] vi. жить, пребывать (live); созерцать (contemplate)

dweller [дуэ-лэр] sm. житель, m., обитатель, m.

dwelling [дуэ-лій] sn. дом, жилище

dwindle [дуіндл] vi. сокращаться, умаляться

dye [дай] sn. краска; vt. красить

dyer [дай-эр] sm. красильщик

dying [дай-ій] adj. умирающий

dynamic [дай-нэ-мік] adj. динамический; sn. pl. динамика

Е

E [и] *mus.* ми

each [ич] *adj., pron.* ка́ждый; **– other** [э–а́-ээр] друг дру́га

eager [и́-гэр] *adj.* пы́лкий; нетерпели́вый (*impatient*); стремя́щийся (*aspiring*)

eagerness [и́-гэр-нис] *sn.* пыл, рве́ние

eagle [и́гл] *s.* орёл

ear [иэр] *sn.* у́хо; слух (*faculty*); ко́лос (*of corn*)

earl [оэрл] *sm.* граф

early [о́р-ли] *adj.* ра́нний; *adv.* ра́но

earmark [и́р-марк] *vt.* отмеча́ть

earn [оэрн] *vt.* зараба́тывать (*as wages, etc.*); заслу́живать (*deserve*)

earnings [о́р-нийз] *sn. pl.* за́работок

earnest [о́р-нист] *adj.* серьёзный (*serious*); ре́вностный (*ardent*); **in –** [–] серьёзно

ear-ring [и́р-рий] *sn.* серёжка, серьга́

earshot [и́р-шот] *sn.* слы́шное расстоя́ние

earth [оэрс] *sn.* земля́, по́чва; земно́й шар (*globe*); *electr.* заземле́ние; *vt.* зары́ва́ть (*inter*); загоня́ть (*run to –*)

earthenware [о́р-эан-уэр] *sn.* гли́няная посу́да

earthly [о́рс-ли] *adj.* земно́й; **no – use** [но́у – ю́с] соверше́нно бесполе́зно

earthquake [о́рс-куэйк] *sn.* землетрясе́ние

earwig [и́р-уйг] *s.* уховёртка

ease [из] *sn.* дово́льство (*contentment*); лёгкость (*facility*); непринуждённость (*informality*); поко́й (*repose*); **ill at –** [ил эт –] нело́вко; *mil.* **stand at –** [стэнд эт –] стоя́ть во́льно!; *vt.* облегча́ть

easel [и́-зэл] *sn.* мольбе́рт, стано́к

east [ист] *sn.* восто́к; *adj.* восто́чный; *adv.* к восто́ку

Easter [и́с-тэр] *sn.* па́сха

easterly [и́с-тэр-ли] *adj.* восто́чный (лежа́щий на восто́к)

eastern [и́с-тэрн] *adj.* восто́чный

eastward [и́ст-уэ́рд] *adj.* к восто́ку, **-s** [-з] *adv.* на восто́к

easy [и́-зи] *adj.* лёгкий, удо́бный; **– chair** [– чэ́р] *sn.* кре́сло

eat [ит] *vt./i.* есть, ку́шать

eatable [и́т-а́бл] *adj.* съедо́бный; **-s** [-з] *sn. pl.* съестны́е припа́сы; пи́ща (*food*)

eavesdropping [и́вз-дро-пий] *sn.* подслу́шивание

ebb [эб] *sn.* морско́й отли́в (*of tide*); у́быль, упа́док (*decline*); *vi.* отлива́ть, убыва́ть (*of tide*); уменьша́ться (*lessen*)

ebony [э́-ба́-ни] *sn.* эбе́новое (чёрное) де́рево

eccentric [эк-сэ́н-трик] *sn.* *tech.* эксцентри́к; *adj.* эксцентри́чный

ecclesiastic [э-кли́-зи-э́с-тик] *sm.* духо́вное лицо́, свяще́нник

ecclesiastical [э-кли́-зи-э́с-ти-кэл] *adj.* духо́вный, церко́вный

echo [э-ко́у] *sn.* э́хо; отголо́сок *vt.i.* отдава́ть (*return*); повторя́ться (*repeat*)

eclipse [и-кли́пс] *sn.* затме́ние; *vt.* затмева́ть, помрача́ться

economic [е-ка-но́-мик] *adj.* экономи́ческий

economical [е-ка-но́-ми-кăл] *adj.* эконо́мный

economics [и-ка-но́-микс] *sn. pl.* эконо́мика; экономи́ческая нау́ка (*science*)

economize [е-ко́-нă-майз] *vt.i.* эконо́мить

economy [и-ко́-нă-ми] *sn.* эконо́мия; бережли́вость (*thrift*); хозя́йство (*housekeeping*)

ecstasy [эк-стă-си] *sn.* экста́з

edge [эдж] *sn.* край (*brink*); ле́звие (*of blade*); кро́мка (*selvedge*); *vt.i.* заостря́ть, точи́ть (*sharpen*); обре́зывать (*cut off*)

edging [э́дж-ий] *sn.* кайма́, край

edible [е́-дибл] *adj.* съедо́бный

edification [е-ди-фи-ке́й-шăн] *sn.* назида́ние

edifice [е́-ди-фис] *sn.* зда́ние (*building*); сооруже́ние (*construction, erection*)

edify [е́-ди-фай] *vt.* назида́ть, наставля́ть

edit [е́-дит] *vt.* редакти́ровать

edition [е-ди́-шăн] *sn.* изда́ние

editor [е́-ди-тăр] *sn.* реда́ктор

editorial [е-ди-то́-ри-ăл] *sn.* передови́ца, передова́я статья́; *adj.* реда́кторский, редакцио́нный

educate [е́-дю-кэйт] *vt.* воспи́тывать, образова́ть

education [е-дю-кэ́й-шăн] *sn.* воспита́ние, образова́ние; обуче́ние (*training*)

educational [е-дю-кэ́й-шă-нăл] *adj.* воспита́тельный, просвети́тельный

eel [ил] *s.* уго́рь, *m.*

eerie [й-ри] *adj.* стра́нный

efface [и-фэ́йс] *vt.* изгла́живать

effect [и-фе́кт] *sn.* сле́дствие, эффе́кт; *pl.* иму́щество; **carry into —** [кэ́-ри и́н-ту —] осуществля́ть; *vt.* выполня́ть, соверша́ть

effective [и-фе́к-тив] *adj.* действи́тельный, эффекти́вный

effeminate [е-фе́-ми-нит] *adj.* женоподо́бный, изне́женный

effervescence [е-фăр-ве́-сăнс] *sn.* вскипа́ние, шипе́ние

effervescent [е-фăр-ве́-сăнт] *adj.* кипу́чий; шипу́чий

efficacious [е-фи-кэ́й-шăс] *adj.* де́йствующий, приводя́щий к результа́ту

efficiency [е-фи́-шăн-си] *sn.* де́йствие; спосо́бность (*capacity*)

efficient [е-фи́-шăнт] *adj.* де́йственный; уме́лый (*skilful*)

effigy [е́-фи-джи] *sn.* изображе́ние

effort [е́-фăрт] *sn.* попы́тка, уси́лие

effrontery [е-фра́н-тă-ри] *sn.* бессты́дство, на́глость

effuse [е-фю́з] *vt.* излива́ть

effusive [е-фю́-зив] *adj.* излива́ющий

egg [эг] *sn.* яйцо́; *vt.* подзадо́ривать (*incite*)

egg-cup [э́г-кап] *sn.* рю́мка для яи́ц

egg-plant [э́г-плэнт] *sn.* баклажа́н

egoistic [э-гоу́-ѝс-тік] *adj.* эгоисти́чный

Egyptian [і-джи́п-шан] *sn.* египтя́нин; *adj.* еги́петский

eider [ай-дăр] *s.* га́га; **—down** [–да́ун] гага́чий пух (*feathers*); пухо́вое одея́ло (*quilt*)

eight [эйт] *num.* во́семь

eighteen [эй-тѝн] *num.* восемна́дцать

eighth [эйтθ] *num.* восьмо́й

eighty [э́й-ті] *num.* во́семьдесят

either [а́й-ѳăр] *adj.* ка́ждый, тот или друго́й, оди́н из двух; *pron.* любо́й; *adv.* или

ejaculate [і-джэ́-кю-лэйт] *vt.* воскли́кнуть, восклица́ть

eject [і-джэ́кт] *vt.* выгоня́ть, удаля́ть (*expel*); изверга́ть (*emit*)

ejection [і-джэ́к-шан] *sn.* выселе́ние, изгна́ние

elaborate [і-лэ́-бă-рìт] *adj.* сло́жный, тща́тельный; [і-лэ́-бă-рэйт] *vt.* выраба́тывать; дета́льно разраба́тывать (*work out in detail*)

elapse [і-лэ́пс] *vi.* истека́ть (о вре́мени)

elastic [і-лэ́с-тік] *sn.* ла́стик, рези́нка; *adj.* эласти́чный

elasticity [і-лэс-тѝ-сі-ті] *sn.* упру́гость, эласти́чность

elated [і-лэ́й-тід] *adj.* возгорди́вшийся, надме́нный

elbow [э́л-боу] *sn.* ло́коть,

m.; **—room** [– ру́м] просто́р; *vt.* толка́ть локтя́ми

elder [э́л-дăр] *sn. bot.* бузина́; *sm.* стари́к (*aged person*); *adj.* ста́рший (*senior*)

elderly [э́л-дăр-лі] *adj.* пожило́й

elect [і-лэ́кт] *vt.* выбира́ть, избра́ть; *adj.* и́збранный

election [і-лэ́к-шан] *sn.* избра́ние

electioneering [і-лек-шă-ни́р-ій] *sn.* предвы́борная кампа́ния

elector [і-лэ́к-тăр] *sm.* избира́тель

electorate [і-лэ́к-тă-рìт] *sn.* избира́тели, соста́в избира́телей

electrical [і-лэ́к-трі-кăл] *adj.* электри́ческий

electrician [е-лек-трі́-шăн] *sm.* эле́ктрик, электроте́хник

electricity [е-лек-трі́-сі-ті] *sn.* электри́чество

elegance [э́-лі-гăнс] *sn.* изя́щество, элега́нтность

elegant [э́-лі-гăнт] *adj.* изя́щный, элега́нтный

elegy [э́-лі-джі] *sn.* эле́гия

element [э́-лі-мăнт] *sn.* элеме́нт (*also chem.*); *pl.* стихи́я; осно́вы (*rudiments*)

elementary [э-лі-мэ́н-тă-рі] *adj.* первонача́льный, элемента́рный

elephant [э́-лі-фăнт] *s.* слон

elevate [э́-лі-вэйт] *vt.* возвыша́ть, поднима́ть

elevation [е-лі-вэ́й-шăн] *sn.* возвыше́ние, подъём; высота́ (*height*); *tech.* вертика́льный разре́з

elevator [э́-лі-вэ́й-тăр] *sn.* подъёмник, элева́тор

eleven [i-лĕ-вăн] *num.* одúн-
надцать

elf [елф] *s.* кáрлик, эльф

elicit [i-лú-сіт] *vt.* вытя́ги-
вать, извлекáть

eligible [ĕ-лі-джíбл] *adj.*
подходя́щий, соотвéтству-
ющий

eliminate [i-лí-мі-нэйт] *vt.*
исключáть, устраня́ть

elimination [i-лі-мі-нэ́й-
шăн] *sn.* исключéние, удалéние

elk [елк] *sn.* лось, *m.*

elm [елм] *sn.* вяз

elocution [ĕ-ла-кю́-шăн] *sn.*
дúкция

elongate [и́-лон-гэйт] *vt.*
растя́гивать, удлиня́ть

elongation [и-лон-гэ́й-шăн]
sn. удлинéние

elope [i-лóуп] *vi.* сбегáть

elopement [i-лóуп-мăнт] *sn.*
побéг

eloquence [ĕ-ло-кўáнс] *sn.*
краснорéчие

eloquent [ĕ-ло-кўáнт] *adj.*
краснорéчивый

else [елс] *adv.* ещё, крóме
(*besides*); инáче (*otherwise*)

elsewhere [елс-ўэ́р] *adv.* в
другóм мéсте

elucidate [i-лю́-сі-дэйт] *vt.*
освещáть, разъясня́ть

elude [e-лю́д] *vt.* избегáть,
обходúть

elusion [e-лю́-жăн] *sn.* у-
вёртка, хúтрость

elusive [e-лю́-сів] *adj.* неу-
ловúмый, уклóнчивый

emaciate [i-мэ́й-ши-эйт] *vt.*
изнуря́ть, истощáть

emanate [ĕ-мă-нэйт] *vi.* ис-
ходúть, происхекáть

emancipate [i-мéн-сі-пэйт] *vt.* эмансипúровать; осво-

бождáть (*set free*)

embalm [i-бáм] *vt.* баль-
замúровать; наполня́ть бла-
гоухáнием (*make fragrant*)

embankment [im-бéнк-
мăнт] *sn.* дáмба, нáсыпь

embark [im-бáрк] *vt.i.* гру-
зúть (*goods*); садúться на
парохóд (*go on board*)

embarkation [im-бар-кэ́й-
шăн] *sn.* погрýзка, посáдка

embarrass [im-бé-рăс] *vt.*
смущáть, стесня́ть (*perplex*);
затрудня́ть (*hamper*)

embarrassment [im-бé-
рăс-мăнт] *sn.* замешáтель-
ство; затруднéние

embassy [ĕм-бă-сі] *sn.* по-
сóльство

embed [im-бéд] *vt.* внедря́ть

embellish [im-бĕ-лíш] *vt.*
украшáть

embellishment [im-бĕ-лíш-
мăнт] *sn.* украшéние

ember [ĕм-бăр] *sn.* горя́чая
золá (*in fire*); — **days** —
дэйз] пóстные и молúтвен-
ные дни

embezzle [im-бéзл] *vt.* при-
свáивать, растрáтить

embezzlement [im-бéзл-
мăнт] *sn.* присвоéние, рас-
трáта

embodiment [im-бó-ді-
мăнт] *sn.* воплощéние

embody [im-бó-ді] *vt.* вопло-
щáть; олицетворя́ть (*personify*)

emboss [im-бóс] *vt.* чекá-
нить

embrace [im-брэ́йс] *sn.* объ-
я́тие; *vt.i.* восприня́ть, об-
хватúть (*take in with eye or
mind*); обнимáться (*one
another*)

embrocation [ем-бро-кэ́й-шăн] *sn.* натира́ние, примо́чка, припа́рка

embroider [им-брóй-дăр] *vt.* вышива́ть, расшива́ть

embroidery [им-брóй-дă-ри] вышива́ние вы́шивка

embroil [им-брóйл] *vt.* запу́тывать (дела́ и пр.); ссо́рить (*involve in quarrel*)

embryo [éм-бри-оў] *sn.* заро́дыш, эмбрио́н; *adj.* зача́точный

emend [і-мéнд] *vt.* исправля́ть

emerald [é-мă-рăлд] *sn.* изумру́д; изумру́дный цвет (*colour*)

emerge [і-мёрдж] *vi.* появля́ться

emergency [і-мёр-джăн-сі] *sn.* кра́йняя необходи́мость, на́добность; – **exit** [– é-кзіт] запа́сный вы́ход

emersion [і-мёр-шăн] *sn.* появле́ние; всплыва́ние

emery [é-мă-рі] *sn.* нажда́к; – **cloth** [– клоθ] нажда́чная бума́га

emetic [і-мé-тік] *sn.* рво́тное сре́дство; *adj.* рво́тный

emigrant [é-мі-грăнт] *sm.* переселе́нец, эмигра́нт; *adj.* эмигри́рующий

emigration [е-мі-грэ́й-шăн] *sn.* переселе́ние, эмигра́ция

eminence [é-мі-нăнс] *sn.* высо́кое положе́ние (*high position*); возвы́шенность (*height*); знамени́тость (*celebrity*)

eminent [é-мі-нăнт] *adj.* выдаю́щийся, замеча́тельный (*remarkable*); знамени́тый (*celebrated*)

emissary [é-мі-сă-рі] *sm.*

emissar [émissár]; *mil.* лазу́тчик

emission [і-мі-шăн] *sn.* выпуска́ние, распростране́ние; *phys.* излуче́ние; *fin.* эми́ссия

emit [і-мі́т] *vt.* издава́ть, испуска́ть; *fin.* выпуска́ть

emollient [і-мó-лі-ăнт] *sn.* мягчи́тельное сре́дство; *adj.* смягча́ющий

emolument [і-мó-лю-мăнт] *sn.* дохо́д (*profit from employment*); жа́лование (*wages*); вознагражде́ние (*reward*)

emotion [і-мóў-шăн] *sn.* волне́ние, эмо́ция

emperor [éм-пă-рăр] *sm.* импера́тор

emphasis [éм-фă-сіс] *sn.* значи́тельность, ударе́ние, эмфа́з

emphasize [éм-фă-сайз] *v.* де́лать ударе́ние (*stress*); *fig.* подчёркивать (*underline*)

emphatic [ем-фǽ-тік] *adj.* вырази́тельный, насто́йчивый, эмфати́ческий

empire [éм-пайр] *sn.* импе́рия; влады́чество

employ [им-плóй] *vt.* нанима́ть (*engage*); испо́льзовать, употребля́ть (*use*)

employee [им-плóй-й] *sn.* рабо́тающий, служа́щий

employer [им-плóй-ăр] *sn.* нанима́тель, работода́тель

employment [им-плóй-мăнт] *sn.* употребле́ние (*usage*); заня́тие, рабо́та, слу́жба (*work*)

empower [им-па́ў-ăр] *vt.* уполномо́чивать

empress [éм-пріс] *sf.* императри́ца

emptiness [éм-ті-ніс] *sn.* пустота́

empty [ém-ti] *adj.* бессодержа́тельный, порожний, пусто́й; *vt.* опоро́жнить

emulate [é-мю-лэйт] *vt.* соревнова́ть (*compete*); сопе́рничать (*try to excel*); подража́ть (*initiate*)

emulation [э-мю-лэй-шăн] *sn.* соревнова́ние; сопе́рничество; подража́ние

enact [i-нэ́кт] *vt.* предпи́сывать, устана́вливать

enamel [ін-нэ́-мăл] *sn.* финифть, эма́ль

encampment [ін-кэ́мп-мăнт] *sn.* ла́герь, ста́н

enceinte [ăй-сэ́нт] *adj.* бере́менная

enchant [ін-ча́нт] *vt.* очаро́вывать

enchantment [ін-ча́нт-мăнт] *sn.* очарова́ние

enchantress [ін-ча́нт-рíс] *sf.* чароде́йка

encircle [ін-сéркл] *vt.* окружа́ть

enclose [ін-кло́уз] *vt.* содержа́ть (*contain*); вкла́дывать (*in envelope*); огора́живать (*surround*)

enclosure [ін-кло́у-жăр] *sn.* вложе́ние (*in letter*); огра́да (*fence*); содержи́мое (*contents*)

encounter [ін-ка́ун-тăр] *sn.* встре́ча (*meeting*); столкнове́ние (*impact*); *vt.* встреча́ть

encouragement [ін-ка́-рідж-мăнт] *sn.* ободре́ние, поощре́ние

encroachment [ін-кро́уч-мăнт] *sn.* вторже́ние

encumbrance [ін-ка́м-брăнс] *sn.* затрудне́ние (*difficulty*); препя́тствие

hrance); бре́мя (*burden*)

end [энд] *sn.* коне́ц; преде́л (*limit*); наме́рение, цель (*object*); *vt.i.* заключа́ть, конча́ть

endanger [ін-дэ́йн-джăр] *vt.* подверга́ть опа́сности

endeavour [ін-дé-вăр] *sn.* насто́йчивая попы́тка, стара́ние, уси́лие; *vt.i.* пыта́ться, стара́ться

endless [éн-длíс] *adj.* бесконе́чный, непрекраща́ющийся

endorse [ін-до́рс] *vt.* одобря́ть, подтвержда́ть; *com.* индосси́ровать

endorsement [ін-до́рс-мăнт] *sn.* индоссаме́нт

endow [ін-да́й] *vt.* завеща́ть, награжда́ть; облека́ть (*with power*); наделя́ть (*with qualities*)

endowment [ін-да́у-мăнт] *sn.* вклад, наде́л

endurance [ін-дю́-рăнс] *sn.* выно́сливость, терпе́ние (*grit*); продолжи́тельность (*continuance*)

endure [ін-дю́р] *vt.* выде́рживать, терпе́ть; дли́ться (*last*)

enemy [é-ні-мí] *sn.* враг, неприя́тель, *m.*, проти́вник

energetic [э-нăр-дже́-тік] *adj.* энерги́чный

energy [é-нăр-джі] *sn.* эне́ргия

enfold [ін-фо́улд] *vt.* заку́тать (*wrap*); обхвати́ть, обня́ть (*embrace*)

enforce [ін-фо́рс] *vt.* заставля́ть, принужда́ть

engage [ін-гэ́йдж] *vt.i.* нанима́ть (*hire*); обяза́ться (*pledge*); *tech.* зацепля́ть

engagement [ін-гэ́йдж-мăнт] *sn.* дѣло, заня́тіе, до́лжность, мѣсто, (*job, occupation*); обяза́тельство (*obligation*); помо́лвка (*betrothal*); *mil.* бой, сты́чка

engaging [ін-гэ́й-джінг] *adj.* привлека́тельный, чару́ющій (*attractive*)

engine [е́н-джін] *sn.* дви́гатель, локомоти́въ, маши́на

engine-driver [е́н-джін-дра́й-вăр] *sm.* маши́ни́стъ

engineer [ен-джи-ні́р] *sm.* инжене́ръ; *vt.i.* сооружа́ть; *coll.* затѣва́ть, устра́ивать

engineering [ен-джи-ни-рі́н] *sn.* инжене́рное иску́сство

English [ін-глі́ш] *sn.* англі́йскій языкъ (*language*); —**man** [—мăн] *sm.* англича́нинъ, —**woman** [—уу́-мăн] *sf.* англича́нка; *adj.* англі́йскій

engrave [ін-грэ́йв] *vt.* грави́ровать

engraver [ін-грэ́й-вăр] *sm.* гравёръ

engraving [ін-грэ́й-він] *sn.* грави́рованіе; гравю́ра (*product*)

engross [ін-гро́ус] *vt.* завладѣва́ть (*monopolize*); поглоща́ть (*absorb*)

enhance [ін-ха́нс] *vt.* повыша́ть (*quality, etc.*); увели́чивать (*increase*)

enjoy [ін-джо́й] *vt.* наслажда́ться; облада́ть, по́льзоваться (*have the use of*)

enjoyment [ін-джо́й-мăнт] *sn.* наслажде́ніе, удово́льствіе

enlarge [ін-ла́рдж] *vt.i.* расширя́ть; увели́чивать

enlightenment [ін-лай-тăн-мăнт] *sn.* просвѣще́ніе

enlist [ін-лі́ст] *vt.* вербова́ть

enliven [ін-лай-вăн] *vt.* воодушевля́ть, оживля́ть

enmity [е́н-мі-ті] *sn.* вражда́, непрія́знь

enormity [і-но́р-мі-ті] *sn.* гну́сность, чудо́вищность

enormous [і-но́р-мăс] *adj.* грома́дный

enough [і-на́ф] *adj.* доста́точный; *adv.* дово́льно, доста́точно; —l ба́ста! по́лно!

enquire [ін-куа́й-ăр] *vt.i.* освѣдомля́ться, справля́ться (*consult*); спра́шивать (*ask*)

enrage [ін-рэ́йдж] *vt.* бѣси́ть, разъяря́ть

enrich [ен-рі́ч] *vt.* обогаща́ть, пополня́ть; удобря́ть (*improve land*); украша́ть (*adorn*)

enrol [ін-ро́ул] *vt.* вноси́ть въ спи́сокъ; регистри́ровать

enshrine [ін-шра́йн] *vt.* запира́ть, храни́ть

ensign [ен-са́йн] *sn.* значо́къ, эмбле́ма; зна́мя (*flag*); [—са́н] *naut.* кормово́й флагъ

enslave [ін-слэ́йв] *vt.* порабоща́ть

ensue [ін-сю́] *vi.* вытека́ть, слѣдовать

ensuing [ін-сю́-ін] *adj.* бу́дущій, слѣ́дующій; вытека́ющій

ensure [ін-шу́р] *vt.* страхова́ть; обезпе́чивать (*guarantee*)

entail [ін-тэ́йл] *vt.* завеща́ть; дѣлать необходи́мымъ (*necessitate*)

entangle [ін-тэ́нгл] *vt.* запу́тывать

enter [е́н-тăр] *vt.* входи́ть; поступа́ть (*into university, etc.*); вноси́ть (*in book, etc.*)

enterprise [ён-тăр-прайз] *sn.* предприя́тие (*undertaking*); предприи́мчивость (*disposition*)

enterprising [ён-тăр-прай-зйн] *adj.* предприи́мчивый

entertain [ён-тăр-тэ́йн] *vt.* забавля́ть, развлека́ть (*amuse*); подде́рживать (*idea, offer, etc.*)

entertainment [ён-тăр-тэ́йн-мăнт] *sn.* заба́ва, развлече́ние дивертисме́нт (*public show*)

enthral [ин-ѳрôл] *vt.* порабоща́ть (*enslave*); очаро́вывать (*captivate*)

enthusiasm [ин-ѳю́-зиăзм] *sn.* восто́рг, энтузиа́зм

enthusiastic [ин-ѳю-зиа́стик] *adj.* восто́рженный

entice [ин-та́йс] *vt.* перема́нивать, соблазня́ть

entire [ин-та́й-ăр] *adj.* сплошно́й, це́лый, це́льный

entirety [ин-та́й-ăр-тĭ] *sn.* полнота́, це́льность

entitle [ин-та́йтл] *vt.* дава́ть пра́во (*claim*); озагла́вливать (*give title to book, etc.*)

entity [ён-тĭ-тĭ] *sn.* су́щее, существо́

entomb [ęн-ту́м] *vt.* погреба́ть

entrails [ён-трэйлз] *sn. pl.* вну́тренности, кишки́, по́трохи, не́дра (*of earth*)

entrance [ęн-тра́нс] *vt.* приводи́ть в восто́рг

entrance [ęн-транс] *sn.* вход (*admission*); прохо́д (*door, passage, etc. for entrance*)

entreat [ин-три́т] *vt.* умоля́ть

entreaty [ин-три́-тĭ] *sn.*

мольба́, про́сьба

entrust [ин-тра́ст] *vt.* вверя́ть, поруча́ть

entry [ęн-трĭ] *sn.* вход (*admission*); вступле́ние (*entering*); *com.* вно́ска, за́пись

entwine [ин-тўа́йн] *vt.* обвива́ть, вплета́ть

enumerate [і-ню́-мă-рэйт] *vt.* перечисля́ть

enunciate [і-нăн-сі-эйт] *vt.* объявля́ть, провозглаша́ть (*proclaim*); произноси́ть (*pronounce*)

envelop [ин-вḝ-лăп] *vt.* обёртывать, оку́тывать; *mil.* окружа́ть

envelope [ęн-ві-лоўп] *sn.* конве́рт

enviable [ęн-ві-ăбл] *adj.* зави́дный

envious [ęн-ві-ăс] *adj.* зави́стливый

environment [ин-ва́й-рăн-мăнт] *sn.* окружа́ющая обста́новка, среда́

environs [ин-ва́й-рăнз] *sn. pl.* окре́стности

envisage [ин-ві́-зидж] *vt.* рассма́тривать

envoy [ęн-вой] *sm.* посла́нник

envy [ęн-ві] *sn.* за́висть; *vt.* зави́довать

enwrap [ин-рæп] *vt.* завёртывать

ephemeral [е-фḝ-мă-рăл] *adj.* преходя́щий, эфеме́рный

epic [ę́-пік] *sn.* эпи́ческая поэ́ма; *adj.* эпи́ческий

epidemic [е-пі-дḝ-мік] *sn.* эпиде́мия; *adj.* эпидеми́ческий

epilogue [ę́-пі-лог] *sn.* послесло́вие, эпило́г

episode [é-pī-zoŭd] *sn.* происшествие, случай

epistle [e-пísl] *sn.* послание; *coll.* письмо (*letter*)

epitaph [é-пī-тāф] *sn.* надгробная надпись, эпитафия

epitome [e-пī-тā-мı] *sn.* извлечение, конспект (*abstract*); краткое изложение (*summary*)

epoch [й-пок] *sn.* эпоха

equal [й-кўāл] *adj.* одинаковый, равный; *vt.* равняться

equality [i-кўó-лı-тı] *sn.* равенство, равность

equalize [й-кўā-лāйз] *vt.* уравнивать

equanimity [e-кўā-нı́-мı-тı] *sn.* уравновешенность, хладнокровие

equation [i-кўэ́й-шāн] *sn.* уравнение

equator [i-кўэ́й-тāр] *sn.* экватор

equestrian [i-кў-é-стрı-āн] *sn.* всадник, наездник; *adj.* конный

equilibrium [е-кўı-лı́-брı-āм] *sn.* равновесие

equine [е-кўāйн] *adj.* конский, лошадиный

equip [i-кўíп] *vt.* снаряжать

equipment [i-кўíп-мāнт] *sn. mil.* обмундирование; снаряжение (*also general*)

equitable [é-кўı-тāбл] *adj.* беспристрастный, справедливый

equity [é-кўı-тı] *sn.* справедливость

equivalent [i-кўí-вā-лāнт] *sn.* эквивалент; *adj.* равнозначащий, эквивалентный

equivocal [i-кўí-вā-кāл] *adj.* двусмысленный

era [и́-рā] *sn.* эра

eradicate [i-рǽ-дı-кэйт] *vt.* искоренять

erase [i-рэйз] *vt.* соскабливать, стирать

eraser [i-рэй-зāр] *sn.* резинка

erect [i-рéкт] *vt.* воздвигать, сооружать; устанавливать (*mount*); *adj.* прямой

erection [i-рéк-шāн] *sn.* строение (*building*); постановка (*raising*)

ermine [ǽр-мин] *sn.* горностай

erosion [i-роў-жāн] *sn.* вытравливание, разъедание

erosive [i-роў-сив] *adj.* разъедающий; эрозионный

err [œр] *vi.* ошибаться

errand [é-рāнд] *sn.* поручение

errant [é-рāнт] *adj.* странствующий

erratic [i-рǽ-тīк] *adj.* переменчивый

erroneous [i-роў-нı-āс] *adj.* ошибочный

error [é-рāр] *sn.* ошибка

eruption [i-рáп-шāн] *sn.* извержение; *med.* сыпь

escalator [éс-кā-лэй-тāр] *sn.* движущаяся лестница

escapade [ес-кā-пэйд] *sn.* выходка, проделка

escape [ıс-кэйп] *sn.* бегство, побег (*flight*); утечка (*leakage*); *v.i.* избегать, убегать; улетучиваться (*of gas, etc.*)

escort [éс-корт] *sn.* конвой, охрана, свита; [ıс-кóрт] *vt.* провожать (*accompany*); *mil.* конвойровать

eschew [ıс-чу́] *vt.* остерегаться (*shun*); воздерживаться (*abstain*)

espionage [éс-пıā-нāж] *sn.* шпионство

esplanade [ес-плӓ-нэ́йд] *sn.* пло́щадь, проспе́кт, эсплана́да

essay [е-сэ́й] *sn.* попы́тка (*attempt*); сочине́ние (*school composition*); о́черк; рефера́т (*paper*); *vt.* [е-сэ́й] испы́тывать, про́бовать

essence [е́-сáнс] *sn.* существо́, су́щность; эссе́нция (*extract*)

essential [і-сéн-шäл] *adj.* суще́ственный

establish [іс-тӓб-ли́ш] *vt.* осно́вывать, учрежда́ть (*found*); устана́вливать (*settle*)

establishment [іс-тӓб-ли́шмäнт] *sn.* заведе́ние, учрежде́ние

estate [іс-тэ́йт] *sn.* име́ние, поме́стье; **real** — [рил —] недви́жимое иму́щество

esteem [іс-ти́м] *sn.* уваже́ние; *vt.* почита́ть, уважа́ть

estimable [е́с-ти-мäбл] *adj.* досто́йный уваже́ния

estimate [е́с-ти-міт] *sn.* оце́нка; [е́с-ті-мэ́йт] *vt.* оце́нивать, составля́ть сме́ту

estimation [ес-ті-мэ́й-шäн] *sn.* мне́ние, сужде́ние; уваже́ние (*esteem*)

estimator [е́с-ті-мэ́й-тäр] *sm.* оце́нщик

estrangement [іс-трэ́йнджкмäнт] *sn.* отчужде́нность

estuary [е́с-тюä-рі] *sn.* лима́н, у́стье

etch [еч] *vt.i.* гравирова́ть

etching [е-чи́н] *sn.* гравирова́ние; гравю́ра, офо́рт

eternal [і-тäр-näл] *adj.* ве́чный

eternity [і-тäр-ні-ті] *sn.* ве́чность

ether [и́-ӫӓр] *sn.* эфи́р

ethic(al) [е́-ӫі-кäл] *adj.* эти́ческий

ethics [е́-ӫікс] *sn. pl.* э́тика

Ethiopian [и-ӫі-о́у-пі-äн] *sm.* эфио́п; *adj.* эфио́пский

eulogy [ю́-лä-джі] *sn.* похвала́

euphony [ю́-фä-ні] *sn.* благозву́чие

European [ю-рä-пи́-äн] *sm.* европе́ец; *adj.* европе́йский

evacuate [і-вӓ-кю-эйт] *vt.* опорожня́ть; эвакуи́ровать

evacuation [і-вӓ-кю-э́йшäн] *sn.* испражне́ние; эвакуа́ция

evade [і-вэ́йд] *vt.* избега́ть, ускольза́ть; *vi.* уклоня́ться (*deviate*)

evaluate [і-вӓ-лю-эйт] *vt.* оце́нивать

evaluation [і-вӓ-лю-э́йшäн] *sn.* оце́нка

evaporate [і-вӓ-пä-рэйт] *vt.i.* испаря́ть

evaporation [і-вӓ-пä-рэ́йшäн] *sn.* испаре́ние

evasion [і-вэ́й-жäн] *sn.* обхо́д, уклоне́ние (*of laws, etc.*); уве́ртка (*dodge*)

evasive [і-вэ́й-сів] *adj.* уклончи́вый

eve [ив] *sn.* кану́н

even [и́-вäн] *adj.* гла́дкий, ро́вный (*smooth*); ра́вный (*equal*); одина́ковый (*identical*); чётный (*of numbers*); *vt.* ура́внивать; *adv.* да́же

evening [и́в-нін] *sn.* ве́чер

event [і-вэ́нт] *sn.* происше́ствие, слу́чай, собы́тие; исхо́д (*outcome*)

eventful [і-вэ́нт-фӱл] *adj.* по́лный собы́тиями

eventual [i-вén-чўǎл] *adj.* возмóжный; конéчный

eventuality [i-вен-чўǽ-ли-ти] *sn.* возмóжность, стечéние обстоя́тельств

ever [é-вǎр] *adv.* когдá-либо (*some time*); всегдá (*always*); **for** – [фор –] навсегдá

everlasting [é-вǎр-лǎст-иñ] *adj.* вéчный

every [é-ври] *adj.* вся́кий, кáждый

everybody [é-ври-бо-ди] *sm.* кáждый (человéк); все (*all*)

everyday [é-ври-дэй] *adj.* ежеднéвный, повседнéвный

everyone [é-ври-ўан] *pron.* кáждый

everything [é-ври-θиñ] *pron.* всё

everywhere [é-ври-ўэ̄р] *adv.* вездé, всю́ду

eviction [i-вíк-шäн] *sn.* выселéние

evidence [é-ви-дäнс] *sn.* доказáтельство, при́знак, свидéтельство; ули́ка (*proof*)

evident [é-ви-дäнт] *adj.* очеви́дный, я́вный

evil [и́-вǎл] *sn.* вред, зло; *adj.* дурнóй

evoke [i-вóўк] *vt.* вызывáть

evolution [i-вǎ-лю́-шäн] *sn.* эволю́ция; *math.* извлечéние кóрня; *mil.* передвижéние

evolve [i-вóлв] *vt.i.* развёртывать, развивáть

ewe [ю] *sf.* овцá

exact [iгз-ǽкт] *adj.* испрáвный, тóчный; *vt.* взы́скивать, вымогáть

exacting [iгз-ǽкт-иñ] *adj.* взыскáтельный, требовáтельный

exactitude [iгз-ǽк-ти-тюд] *sn.* тóчность

exactly [iгз-ǽкт-ли] *adv.* и́менно так, тóчно

exaggerate [iгз-ǽ-джǎ-рэйт] *vt.* преувели́чивать

exaggeration [iгз-ǽ-джǎ-рéй-шäн] *sn.* преувеличéние

exalt [iгз-óлт] *vt.* возвышáть (*raise*); превозноси́ть (*praise*)

exaltation [iгз-ол-тéй-шäн] *sn.* возвы́шенность (*elation*); востóрг (*rapture*)

examination [iгз-ǽ-ми-нéй-шäн] *sn.* осмóтр (*survey*); экзáмен (*test*); *leg.* допрóс

examine [iгз-ǽ-мин] *vt.* опрáшивать (*question*); исслéдовать (*investigate*); осмáтривать (*inspect*); экзаменовáть (*test*)

examiner [iгз-ǽ-ми-нǎр] *sn.* экзаминáтор

example [iгз-ǽмпл] *sn.* примéр; образéц (*specimen*); **for** – [фор –] напримéр

exasperate [iгз-ǽс-пä-рэйт] *vt.* раздражáть

excavate [éкс-кä-вэйт] *vt.* выдáлбливать, выкáпывать

excavation [éкс-кä-вэ́й-шäн] *sn.* выкáпывание; раскóпки, *pl.*; экскавáция

excavator [éкс-кä-вэ́й-тǎр] *sn.* землекóп, экскавáтор

exceed [ек-сид] *vt.* превышáть

exceedingly [ек-си́-дин-ли] *adv.* чрезвычáйно

excel [ек-сéл] *vt.* превосходи́ть; *vi.* отличáться

excellence [éкс-ä-лäнс] *sn.* высóкое достóинство, превосхóдство

excellency [éks-ă-lăn-si] *sm.* превосходи́тельство

excellent [éks-ă-lănt] *adj.* отли́чный, превосхо́дный

except [ik-sépt] *vt.* исключа́ть; *prep.* исключа́я, кро́ме

exception [ik-sép-шăn] *sn.* исключе́ние; возраже́ние (*objection*)

exceptional [ik-sép-шăn-ăl] *adj.* исключи́тельный

excerpt [ék-сœрпт] *sn.* вы́бор, вы́держка, отры́вок

excess [ik-сéс] *sn.* изли́шек

excessive [ik-сé-сив] *adj.* чрезме́рный

exchange [iks-чэйндж] *sn.* обме́н (*process*); разме́н (*money*); би́ржа (*building*); *vt.* обме́нивать, переменя́ть

exchequer [éks-чé-кăр] *sn.* казначе́йство; казна́ (*treasury*); **Chancellor of the** — [ча́н-сă-лăр ов ei —] мини́стр фина́нсов

excise [ek-сáйз] *sn.* акци́з

excitable [ik-сáй-тăбл] *adj.* возбуди́мый [дать

excite [ik-сáйт] *vt.* возбужда́ть

excitement [iks-сáйт-мăнт] *sn.* возбужде́ние

exclaim [iks-клэ́йм] *vt.i.* восклица́ть

exclamation [éks-клă-мэ́йшăн] *sn.* восклица́ние; **note of** — [но́ут ов —] восклица́тельный знак

exclude [iks-клу́д] *vt.* исключа́ть

exclusion [iks-клу́-жăн] *sn.* исключе́ние

exclusive [iks-клу́-сив] *adj.* исключи́тельный; отбо́рный (*select*)

excrement [éks-кри-мăнт] *sn.* испражне́ние, кал

excretion [ксс-кри́-шăн] *sn.* выделе́ние

excruciating [iks-кру́-ши-эй-тǐй] *adj.* мучи́тельный

excursion [iks-кǒр-шăн] *sn.* пое́здка, экску́рсия

excuse [iks-кю́з] *sn.* извине́ние; оправда́ние (*justification*)

execute [éкс-i-кют] *vt.* выполня́ть, исполня́ть; казни́ть (*put to death*)

execution [éks-i-кю́-шăн] *sn.* исполне́ние; казнь

executive [igз-é-кю-тив] *adj.* исполни́тельный

exemplary [igз-éм-плă-pi] *adj.* образцо́вый

exempt [igз-éмпт] *adj.* изъя́тый, освобождённый; *vt.* изъя́ть, увольня́ть

exemption [igз-éмп-шăн] *sn.* изъя́тие, льго́та (*advantage*); освобожде́ние (*freedom from*)

exercise [éкс-ăр-сайз] *sn.* упражне́ние; *vt.i.* применя́ть, упражня́ться

exert [igз-éрт] *vt.* напряга́ть, ока́зывать

exertion [igз-éр-шăн] *sn.* стара́ние, уси́лие; напряже́ние (*strain*)

exhale [eкс-хэ́йл] *vt.* испуска́ть (*fumes, etc.*); выдыха́ть (*breathe out*)

exhaust [igз-о́ст] *sn.* исхо́д па́ра (и т. п.); *vt.* истоща́ть, исче́рпывать

exhaustion [igз-о́с-чăн] *sn.* истоще́ние

exhibit [igз-i-бит] *sn.* пока́з, экспона́т; *vt.* выставля́ть, пока́зывать [вы́ставка

exhibition [ikз-i-би́-шăн] *sn.* выставка

exhibitor [igз-i-би́-тăр] *sm.* экспоне́нт

exhilarate [егз-і-лă-рэйт] *vt.* веселить, оживлять, развеселять

exhort [ігз-о́рт] *vt.* увещевать

exhume [екс-хю́м] *vt.* выкапывать

exigency [екс-і-джăн-сі] *sn.* крайняя надобность

exile [е́кс-айл] *sm.* изгнанник (*person*); *sn.* изгнание, ссылка; *vt.* ссылать

exist [ігз-і́ст] *vi.* быть (*to be*); жить (*live*); существовать (*subsist*)

existence [ігз-і́ст-ăнс] *sn.* существование

existing [ігз-і́ст-ій] *adj.* живущий, существующий

exit [е́кс-іт] *sn.* выход; *theat.* уход

exonerate [ігз-о́-нă-рэйт] *vt.* оправдывать

exorbitant [ігз-о́р-бі-тăнт] *adj.* непомерный, чрезмерный

exorcize [е́кс-ор-сайз] *vt.* заклинать

exotic [ікз-о́-тік] *adj.* иноземный, экзотический

expand [ікс-пæнд] *vt.* і. распространяться (*spread out*), расширяться (*dilate*)

expanse [ікс-пæнс] *sn.* пространство, протяжение

expansion [ікс-пæн-шăн] *sn.* растягивание, расширение

expansive [ікс-пæн-сів] *adj.* обширный (*extensive*); способный распространяться (*able to expand*)

expatriate [ікс-пǽ-трі-эйт] *vt.* высылать, изгонять

expect [ікс-пéкт] *vt.* ожидать; предполагать (*suppose*)

expectant [ікс-пéк-тăнт] *adj.* ожидающий

expectation [ікс-пек-тэ́йшăн] *sn.* ожидание; упование (*hope*)

expedience [ікс-пи́-ді-ăнс] *sn.* целесообразность; пригодность (*fitness*)

expedient [ікс-пи́-ді-ăнт] *adj.* выгодный, целесообразный; подходящий (*suitable*); *sn.* удобное средство, уловка

expedite [е́кс-пі-дайт] *vt.* отправлять (*dispatch*); содействовать (*help on*); ускорять (*accelerate*)

expedition [екс-пі-ді́-шăн] *sn.* отправка, экспедиция

expeditious [екс-пі-ді́-шăс] *adj.* быстрый, проворный

expel [ікс-пéл] *vt.* выгонять, исключать

expend [ікс-пéнд] *vt.* расходовать, тратить

expenditure [ікс-пéн-ді-чăр] *sn.* расход, трата

expense [ікс-пéнс] *sn.* стоимость; *pl.* издержки

expensive [ікс-пéн-сів] *adj.* дорого стоющий, дорогой

experience [ікс-пи́-рі-ăнс] *sn.* испытание, опытность, переживание; *vt.* испытывать

experiment [ікс-пé-рі-мăнт] *sn.* опыт, эксперимент; *vt.* производить опыты, экспериментировать

experimental [ікс-пе-рі-мéн-тăл] *adj.* опытный

expert [ікс-пéрт] *sm.* знаток; [éкспăрт] *adj.* искусный

expiate [е́кс-пі-эйт] *vt.* искупать

expiration [екс-пі-рэ́й-шän] *sn.* истече́ние (of period); оконча́ние (end); выдыха́ние (breathing out)

expire [екс-па́й-äр] *vi.* истека́ть (of time); выдыха́ть (breathe out); умира́ть (die)

explain [ікс-плэ́йн] *vt.* объясня́ть

explanation [екс-плä-нэ́й-шän] *sn.* объясне́ние

explanatory [екс-плä́-нä-тä-рі] *adj.* объясни́тельный

explicit [ікс-плі́-сіт] *adj.* определённый

explode [ікс-пло́уд] *vt.i.* взрыва́ть, разража́ться

exploit [екс-плойт] *sn.* по́двиг; [ікс-плойт] *vt.* разраба́тывать, эксплоати́ровать

exploitation [екс-плой-тэ́й-шän] *sn.* эксплоата́ция

exploration [екс-пло-рэ́й-шän] *sn.* иссле́дование

explore [ікс-пло́р] *vt.* иссле́довать, рассле́довать

explosion [ікс-пло́у-жän] *sn.* взрыв; вспы́шка (outburst)

explosive [ікс-пло́у-сів] *sn.* взрывча́тое вещество́; *adj.* взрывча́тый; *phon.* взрывно́й

exponent [ікс-по́у-нäнт] *sm.* вырази́тель; экспоне́нт

export [е́кс-порт] *sn.* вы́воз, э́кспорт; [ікс-по́рт] *vt.* вывози́ть, экспорти́ровать

expose [ікс-по́уз] *vt.* выявля́ть, выдерга́ть; разоблача́ть (disclose); *photo.* экспони́ровать

exposed [ікс-по́узд] *adj.* раскры́тый

exposure [ікс-по́у-жäр] *sn.* разоблаче́ние (disclosure);

выст⁓вле́ние, подверга́ние (statement of facts); *photo.* экспози́ция

expound [ікс-па́унд] *vt.* изъясня́ть, толкова́ть

express [ікс-пре́с] *sn.* экспре́сс (train); курье́р, наро́чный (messenger); *adj.* специа́льный (special); наро́чный (intentional); *vt.* выража́ть

expression [ікс-пре́-шän] *sn.* выраже́ние

expressive [ікс-пре́-сів] *adj.* вырази́тельный

expropriate [екс-про́у-прі-эйт] *vt.* экспроприи́ровать

expulsion [ікс-па́л-шän] *sn.* изгна́ние, исключе́ние

exquisite [екс-кýі-зіт] *adj.* изы́сканный

extemporize [екс-те́м-пä-райз] *vt.i.* импровизи́ровать

extend [ікс-те́нд] *vt.i.* простира́ться, тяну́ться; *mil.* растя́гивать; удлиня́ть (prolong time)

extension [ікс-те́н-шän] *sn.* вытя́гивание, растяже́ние; доба́вление (addition); расшире́ние (enlargement)

extensive [ікс-те́н-сів] *adj.* обши́рный, простра́нный

extent [ікс-те́нт] *sn.* разме́р (dimension); протяже́ние (spread)

extenuate [ікс-те́-ню-эйт] *vt.* осла́бить, смягча́ть, уменьша́ть

exterior [ікс-ті́-рі-äр] *sn.* вне́шность, нару́жность; *adj.* нару́жный

exterminate [ікс-тäр-мі-нэйт] *vt.* искореня́ть, требля́ть

external [экс-тœр-нăл] *adj.* внéшний, нарýжный

extinct [икс-тинкт] *adj.* потýхший, угáсший; вымéрший (*obsolete, dead*)

extinction [икс-тинк-шăн] *sn.* потухáние, угасáние; вымирáние (*extermination*)

extinguish [икс-тин-гўйш] *vt.* гасить, погашáть (*сйть*); (*dead*) *vt.* превозмочь

extol [икс-тóл] *vt.* превозносить

extort [икс-тóрт] *vt.* вымогáть, выпытывать

extortion [икс-тóр-шăн] *sn.* вымогáтельство, лихоимство

extra [éкс-трă] *sn.* добáвка; *adj.* особый (*special*); добáвочный, дополнительный (*additional*); *adv.* дополнительно, особо

extract [éкс-трæкт] *sn.* экстрáкт (*preparation*); выдержка, извлечéние (*passage from book, etc.*); [икс-трǽкт] *vt.* выжимáть, вырывáть (*by pressure*); извлекáть (*from book*)

extraction [икс-трǽк-шăн] *sn.* извлечéние; происхождéние (*lineage*)

extradition [екс-трă-ди-шăн] *sn.* выдача (престýпника)

extraordinary [екс-трǽ-óр-ди-нă-ри] *adj.* удивительный (*striking*); чрезвычáйный (*extreme*)

extravagance [икс-трǽ-вǎ-гăнс] *sn.* расточительность, сумасбрóдство

extravagant [икс-трǽ-вǎ-гăнт] *adj.* непомéрный, сумасбрóдный

extreme [икс-трим] *adj.* крáйний, чрезмéрный

extremity [икс-трé-ми-ти] *sn.* крáйность, чрезмéрность; конéц, край (*end*); *pl.* конéчности

extricate [éкс-три-кэйт] *vt.* выпýтывать, высвобождáть

exuberance [игз-ю-бǎ-рăнс] *sn.* избыток, изли́шество; изобилие (*abundance*); рóскошь (*luxury*)

exuberant [игз-ю-бǎ-рăнт] *adj.* пышный, роскóшный

exude [игз-юд] *vi.* просáчиваться (*ooze out*); выделять (*dampness, moisture*); выпотеть (*sweat*)

exult [игз-áлт] *vi.* торжествовáть

exultation [игз-ал-тэй-шăн] *sn.* ликовáние

eye [ай] *sn.* глаз; ушкó (*of needle*); *bot.* глазóк (*of*); *vt.* рассмáтривать, соблюдáть

eyeball [áй-бôл] *sn.* глазнóе яблоко

eyebrow [áй-брау] *sn.* бровь

eyeglass [áй-глǎс] *sn.* линзá; лорнéт, окуляр

eyelash [áй-лæш] *sn.* ресница

eyelet [áй-лит] *sn.* дырочка, глазóк

eyelid [áй-лид] *sn.* вéко

eyesight [áй-сайт] *sn.* зрéние

eyewitness [áй-уит-нис] *sn.* очевидец

F

F [эф] *mus.* фа

fable [фэйбл] *sn.* бáсня, скáзка, выдумка

fabric [фǽб-рик] *sn.* ткань (*material*); постройка (*structure*)

fabricate [фэ́б-ри-кэйт] *vt.* сооружа́ть (*build, make*); изобрета́ть (*invent*); выду́мывать (*think out*); подде́лывать (*forge*)

fabrication [фэб-ри-кэ́й-шэн] *sn.* сооруже́ние; вы́думка, ложь (*lie*)

fabulous [фэ́-бю-лэс] *adj.* баснословный; невероя́тный (*incredible*)

face [фэйс] *sn.* лицо́, физионо́мия; выраже́ние, грима́са (*expression*); пове́рхность (*surface*); цифербла́т (*dial*); *vt.i.* встреча́ть сто́йко (*meet firmly*); отде́лывать (*garment*)

facetious [фэ-си́-шэс] *adj.* шутли́вый

facial [фэ́й-шэл] *adj.* лицево́й

facilitate [фэ-си́-ли-тэйт] *vt.* облегча́ть, упроща́ть

facility [фэ-си́-ли-ти] *sn.* лёгкость, пла́вность; *pl.* сре́дства, удо́бства

facing [фэ́й-син] *sn.* лицева́я отде́лка, облицо́вка; *adv.* напро́тив

fact [фэкт] *sn.* факт; и́стина (*truth*), действи́тельность (*reality*); **as a matter of — ** [эз ǎ мэ́-тǎр ов —] по пра́вде; **in — ** [ин —] в су́щности, действи́тельно

faction [фэ́к-шэн] *sn.* раздо́р, разногла́сие; агё́нт, комиссионе́р

factor [фэ́к-тǎр] *sn.* фа́ктор (*element in result*); *math.* мно́житель, *m.*; аге́нт, комиссионе́р

factory [фэ́к-тǎ-ри] *sn.* заво́д, фа́брика

faculty [фэ́-кǎл-ти] *sn.* дарова́ние (*talent*); спосо́бность

(*aptitude*); факульте́т (*branch of art, etc.*)

fad [фэд] *sn.* при́хоть, причу́да

fade [фэйд] *vi.* бле́кнуть, увяда́ть

fag [фэг] *sn.* тяжёлая рабо́та (*drudgery*); изнуре́ние, истоще́ние (*exhaustion*)

faggot [фэ́-гǎт] *sn.* вяза́нка, оха́пка, пук (хво́роста) (*bundle of sticks*); котле́ты (из печёнки) (*edible*)

fail [фэйл] *sn.* упуще́ние; **without — ** [уǐ-оа́ут —] безусло́вно, непреме́нно; *vt.i.* недостава́ть, недостига́ть (*be deficient*); ошиба́ться (*err*); обанкро́титься (*be broke, bankrupt*); прова́ливаться (*at exams., etc.*)

failing [фэ́й-лин] *sn.* недоста́ток (*deficiency*); сла́бость (*foible*)

failure [фэ́й-лиǎр] *sn.* несостоя́тельность (*insolvency*); неуда́ча, прова́л (*downfall*); неуда́чник (*of person*)

faint [фэйнт] *sn.* о́бморок; *adj.* сла́бый (*feeble*); бле́дный (*pale*); ту́склый (*dim*); *vi.* лиша́ться чувств, па́дать в о́бморок

fair [фэр] *sn.* я́рмарка; *adj.* белоку́рый, ру́сый (*of skin, blond*); справедли́вый (*just*); благоприя́тный (*of weather*); **— play —** [— плэй] справедли́вые усло́вия

fairly [фэ́р-ли] *adv.* дово́льно (*rather*); че́стно (*justly*)

fairy [фэ́-ри] *sf.* фе́я; *adj.* волше́бный, ска́зочный

faith [фэйθ] *sn.* ве́ра; дове́рие (*trust*); рели́гия (*religion*)

faithful [фэйθ-фул] *adj.* вépный (*true*); чéстный (*loyal*); **yours** **-ly** [юрз -лі] с совершéнным почтéнием

fake [фэйк] *sn.* надувáтельство

fall [фôл] *sn.* падéние, упáдок; *vi.* пáдать; оседáть (*subside*); понижáться (*drop*); рýшиться (*collapse*); **-** **asleep** [- ä-слûп] заснýть; **-** **away** [- ä-уэй] отступáть; **-** **in** [- ін] впáдать; *mil.* становись!, стрóйся!; **-** **in love** [- ін лав] влюбля́ться

fallacious [фä-лэй-шäс] *adj.* лóжный, обмáнчивый

fallacy [фэ́-лä-сі] *sn.* заблуждéние, обмáнчивость

fallow [фэ́-лоу] *adj.* под пáром (*uncultivated*); жёлто-корúчневый (*yellow-brownish*)

false [фôлс] *adj.* лóжный, невéрный; обмáнчивый (*deceitful*)

falsehood [фôлс-хỹд] *sn.* ложь (*lie*); лжúвость (*fallacy, penchant*)

falsify [фôл-сі-фай] *vt.* поддéлывать (*forge*); искажáть (*distort*)

falter [фôл-тäр] *vi.* запинáться (*hesitate, stammer*); колебáться (*waver*)

fame [фэйм] *sn.* извéстность, слáва

familiar [фä-мí-лійр] *adj.* дрýжеский, фамилья́рный; общеизвéстный (*well-known*)

family [фэ́-мі-лі] *sn.* семéйство, семья́; *adj.* семéйный, фамúльный

famine [фэ́-мін] *sn.* гóлод

famish [фэ́-міш] *vt.i.* голодáть, морúть гóлодом

famous [фэй-мäс] *adj.* знаменúтый, извéстный

fan [фэн] *sn.* вéер; вентиля́тор; вéялка (*winnowing machine*); *vt.* вéять; обмáхивать вéером; освежáть (*cool*)

fanciful [фэн-сі-фул] *adj.* воображáемый (*imaginary*); причýдливый (*quaint, whimsical*)

fancier [фэн-сі-äр] *sm.* знатóк, любúтель (собáк, и т.д.)

fancy [фэн-сі] *sn.* воображéние (*imagination*); мечтá (*caprice*); прúхоть (*caprice*); причýда (*whim*); *adj.* воображáемый; причýдливый; *vi.* воображáть; **-** **that!** [- ээт] предстáвь себé!; увлекáться (*take a to*); **-** **work** [- ýöрк] ажýрная рабóта, вышивка

fang [фэн] *sn.* клык (*canine tooth*); ядовúтый зуб (*serpent*); зубéц (*spike*)

fantastic [фэн-тäс-тік] *adj.* причýдливый, фантастúческий

fantasy [фэн-тä-зі] *sn.* воображéние, фантáзия

far [фäр] *adj.* далёкий, дáльний, отдалённый; *adv.* далекó; горáздо, намнóго (*much*) **as - as** [эз - эз] поскóльку

farce [фäрс] *sn.* шýтка, фарс

farcical [фäр-сі-кäл] *adj.* фáрсовый, шутóчный

fare [фэр] *sn.* плáта, стóимость (*cost*); кýшанье, стол (*food*); *vi.* быть, поживáть (*be, get on*)

farewell [фэ̌р-уэ̌л] sn. проща́ние; interj. до свида́ния; проща́йте! adj. проща́льный

farinaceous [фæ-ри-нэ́й-шǎс] adj. мучни́стый

farm [фа̌рм] sn. крестья́нское хозя́йство, фе́рма; vt. обраба́тывать зе́млю

farmer [фа̌р-мǎр] sm. земледе́лец, фе́рмер

farmhouse [фа̌рм-ха̌ус] sn. уса́дьба   [мерство

farming [фа̌р-мǐн] sn. фе́р-

farrier [фæ-ри-ǎр] sm. коно́-вал (horse-doctor); кузне́ц (smith)

farsighted [фа̌р-са́й-тǐд] adj. дальнозо́ркий

farther [фа̌р-ǒǎр] adv. да́лее, да́льше

fascinate [фæ-сǐ-нэ́йт] vt. обвора́живать, очаро́вывать

fascination [фæ-сǐ-нэ́й-шǎн] sn. обая́ние, очарова́ние

fashion [фæ-шǎн] sn. мо́да, фасо́н (cut); обыча́й (custom); vt. отде́лывать, придава́ть вид

fashionable [фæ-шǎн-а̌бл] adj. мо́дный (stylish); све́тский (worldly)

fast [фа̌ст] sn. пост; adj. кре́пкий, твёрдый (firm); про́чный (lasting); ско́рый (speedy); распу́щенный (dissipated); vi. пости́ться

fasten [фа̌-сǎн] vt. запира́ть (lock); привя́зывать (tie up); прикрепля́ть (fix)

fastener [фа̌-снǎр] sn. застёжка

fastidious [фǎ-стǐ-дǐ-ǎс] adj. приве́редливый, разбо́рчивый

fat [фæт] sn. жир, са́ло; adj. жи́рный (greasy); то́лстый (stout)

fatal [фэ́й-тǎл] adj. роково́й; сме́ртельный (deadly)

fatality [фǎ-тæ-лǐ-тǐ] sn. рок; несча́стие (calamity)

fate [фэйт] sn. судьба́, уде́л (destiny); ги́бель (destruction)

fateful [фэйт-фу̌л] adj. роково́й (prophetic); реши́тельный (decisive)

father [фа̌-ǒǎр] sm. оте́ц, роди́тель; ба́тюшка (Rev. Father)

father-in-law [фа̌-ǒǎр-ǐн-ло̌] sm. свёкор (wife's); тесть (husband's)

fatherland [фа̌-ǒǎр-лæнд] sn. оте́чество, ро́дина

fatherly [фа̌-ǒǎр-лǐ] adj. оте́ческий

fathom [фæ-ǒǎм] sn. морска́я са́жень; vt. измеря́ть глубину́ (sound depth); проника́ть (comprehend)

fatigue [фǎ-тǐг] sn. уста́лость, утоми́тельность; mil. внестро́евые наря́ды солда́та; vt. утомля́ть

fatten [фæ-тǎн] vt. отка́рмливать

fatuous [фæ-тю-ǎс] adj. бессмы́сленный, глу́пый

fatty [фæ-тǐ] adj. жи́рный, отко́рмленный

fault [фо̌лт] sn. недоста́ток (defect); про́мах, просту́пок (shortcoming); вина́ (blame)

faultless [фо̌лт-лǐс] adj. безоши́бочный; безупре́чный (blameless)

faulty [фо̌л-тǐ] adj. оши́бочный (erroneous); повреждённый (damaged)

favour [фэ́й-вăр] *sn.* благо-
скло́нность, расположе́ние
(*affability*); одобре́ние (*approval*); ми́лость, одобре́-
ние (*kindness*); **in – of** [ин –
ов] в по́льзу; *vt.* благо-
прия́тствовать; спосо́б-
ствовать (*aid*); быть при-
стра́стным (*be partial*)

favourable [фэ́й-вă-рăбл]
adj. благоскло́нный (*well
disposed*); благоприя́тный
(*propitious*); одобри́тель-
ный (*approving*)

favourite [фэ́й-вă-рит] *sm.*
люби́мец, фавори́т; *adj.*
люби́мый

fawn [фōн] *s.* косу́ля, моло-
до́й оле́нь (*animal*); желто-
ва́то-кори́чневый (*colour*)

fear [фир] *sn.* опасе́ние,
страх; **no –!** [нōу –] ма́ло
вероя́тно; *vt.i.* боя́ться,
опаса́ться

fearful [фир-фул] *adj.*
боязли́вый (*afraid*); пугли́-
вый, ро́бкий (*timid*); ужа́с-
ный (*terrible*)

fearless [фи́р-лис] *adj.*
бесстра́шный

feasible [фи́-зибл] *adj.* воз-
мо́жный, исполни́мый

feast [фист] *sn.* пир (*banquet*); пра́здник, пра́здне-
ство (*festival*); чествова́ние
(*religious anniversary*); *vi.*
пирова́ть; пра́здновать; че-
ствова́ть

feat [фит] *sn.* по́двиг, фо́кус,
шу́тка (*trick*)

feather [фе́-ğăр] *sn.* перо́
(*пти́чье*); опере́ние (*plumage*); **– bed** [– бед] пери́-
на; *vt.i.* опери́ться

feathery [фе́-ğă-ри] *adj.* пер-
на́тый

feature [фи́-чăр] *sn.* вид; *pl.*
черты́ лица́; *vt.* изобра-
жа́ть

February [фе́-брў-ă-ри] *sn.*
февра́ль, *m.*

federal [фе́-дă-рăл] *adj.*
сою́зный, федера́льный

federation [фе-дă-ре́й-шăн]
sn. федера́ция

fee [фи] *sn.* гонора́р, пла́та;
вступи́тельный взнос (*entrance*)

feeble [фибл] *adj.* сла́бый,
хи́лый

feed [фид] *sn.* корм; кормле́-
ние (*feeding*); *tech.* пода́ча;
vt.i. корми́ть; пита́ться;
tech. подава́ть

feeder [фи́-дăр] *sm.* едо́к

feel [фил] *sn.* осяза́ние,
ощуще́ние; *vt.i.* осяза́ть,
ощуща́ть; чу́вствовать
(*emotionally*)

feeling [фи́-лĭй] *sn.* впе-
чатле́ние (*impression*); чу́в-
ство (*physical sensation*);
ощуще́ние (*touch*); на-
строе́ние (*mood*); *adj.* чу́в-
стви́тельный

feign [фе́йн] *vt.i.* притво-
ря́ться, симули́ровать

feint [фе́йнт] *sn.* ло́жная
ата́ка (*sham attack*); лицеме́-
рие, притво́рство (*simula-
tion*)

felicitate [фе-ли́-си-тэйт] *vt.*
поздравля́ть

felicitation [фе-ли-си-тэ́й-
шăн] *n.* поздравле́ние

felicitous [фĭ-ли́-си-тăс] *adj.*
подходя́щий, уда́чный

felicity [фĭ-ли́-си-ти] *sn.* бла-
же́нство, сча́стье; уда́ча
(*success*)

feline [фи́-лайн] *adj.* коша́-
чий

fell [фэл] *sn.* мех, овчи́на, шку́ра (*animal's hide*); гора́, холм (*hill*); *vt.* свали́ть (*strike down*); сруби́ть (*cut down*)

fellow [фэ́-лоу] *sm. coll.* па́рень, ма́лый, челове́к; това́рищ (*comrade*); член учёного о́бщества (*of college, etc.*)

fellowship [фэ́-лоу-шип] *sn.* бра́тство, това́рищество; чле́нство (*of college, etc.*)

felon [фэ́-лён] *sm.* престу́пник (*criminal*); *sn.* нары́в (*small abscess*)

felony [фэ́-лă-нi] *sn.* преступле́ние

felt [фэлт] *sn.* во́йлок, фетр

female [фи́-мэйл] *sf.* же́нщина (*woman*); са́мка (*animal*); *adj.* же́нского по́ла, же́нский

feminine [фэ́-мi-нiн] *adj.* же́нский; *gram.* же́нского ро́да

fen [фэн] *sn.* боло́то, топь

fence [фэнс] *sn.* забо́р, огра́да; *vt.* загора́живать, огражда́ть (*of*); *vi.* фехтова́ть (*sword*)

fencing [фэ́н-сiн] *sn.* огора́живание; фехтова́ние (*sword*)

fend [фэнд] *vt.i.* отвраща́ть, отража́ть

fender [фэн-дăр] *sn.* предохрани́тельная ками́нная решётка

ferment [фăр-мэнт] *sn.* дро́жжи, заква́ска (*leaven*); возбужде́ние; волне́ние (*excitement*); [фăр-мэ́нт] *vi.* броди́ть; волнова́ться

fermentation [фăр-мăн-

тэ́й-шăн] *sn.* броже́ние

fern [фăрн] *sn. bot.* па́поротник

ferocious [фă-ро́у-шăс] *adj.* жесто́кий, свире́пый

ferret [фэ́-рiт] *s. zool.* хорёк; тесьма́ (*tape*); *vt.i.* выи́скивать, разы́скивать

ferry [фэ́-рi] *sn.* паро́м; *vt.i.* перевози́ть, переезжа́ть (в ло́дке)

fertile [фăр-та́йл] *adj.* плодоро́дный

fertility [фăр-тí-лi-тi] *sn.* плодоро́дие

fertilize [фăр-тi-ла́йз] *vt.* оплодотворя́ть, удобря́ть

fertilizer [фăр-тi-ла́й-зăр] *sn.* оплодотвори́тель

fervent [фăр-вăнт] *adj.* пы́лкий; усе́рдный (*intense*)

fervour [фăр-вăр] *sn.* жар (*glow*); пыл (*ardour*); усе́рдие (*zeal*)

fester [фэс-тăр] *vi.* гнои́ться, сопрева́ть

festival [фэс-тi-вăл] *sn.* пра́зднество

festive [фэс-тiв] *adj.* пра́здничный

festivity [фэс-тí-вi-тi] *sn.* весе́лье, пра́зднование; *pl.* торжество́

fetch [фэч] *vt.i.* привести́, принести́, доставля́ть

fetching [фэ́-чiн] *adj. coll.* привлека́тельный (*attractive*)

fête [фэйт] *sn.* весе́лье, развлече́ние; *vt.* пра́здновать

fetter [фэ́-тăр] *sn.* канда́л для ног (*for feet*); ра́бство (*bond*); *sn. pl.* око́вы, пу́ты, у́зы; *vt.* зако́вывать (*bind*); сде́рживать (*restrain*)

feud [фюд] *sn.* вражда́, ссо́ра

feudal [фю́-дǎл] *adj.* феода́льный

fever [фи-вǎр] *sn.* жар, лихора́дка

feverish [фи-вǎ-ри́ш] *adj.* лихора́дочный; возбуждённый (*restless*)

few [фю] *sn.* незначи́тельное число́; *adj.* немно́гие, не́сколько

fiancé [фіа́н-сє] *sm.* жени́х, -е, *sf.* неве́ста

fibre [фа́йбр] *sn.* волокно́, фи́бра

fibrous [фай-брǎс] *adj.* волокни́стый, жили́стый

fickle [фıкл] *adj.* изме́нчивый, непостоя́нный

fiction [фı́к-шǎн] *sn.* вы́мысел, небыли́ца, фи́кция; беллетри́стика (*novels*)

fictitious [фıк-тı́-шǎс] *adj.* фикти́вный

fiddle [фıдл] *sn.* скри́пка; *vt.i.* игра́ть на скри́пке (*play*); безде́льничать (*idling*)

fiddler [фıд-лǎр] *sm.* скрипа́ч

fidelity [фı-де́-ки-ти] *sn.* ве́рность, пре́данность

fidget [фı-джıт] *sm.* беспоко́йный челове́к; *pl.* беспоко́йство; *vi.* суети́ться

fidgety [фı-джи-ти] *adj.* неугомо́нный

field [фıлд] *sn.* по́ле, поля́на

fiend [фıнд] *sn.* бес

fiendish [фıн-дıш] *adj.* дья́вольский, жесто́кий

fierce [фıрс] *adj.* лю́тый, свире́пый

fiery [фа́й-ǎ-р̧і] *adj.* о́гненный, пла́менный (*of intense*

heat); вспы́льчивый, пы́лкий (*vehement*)

fife [файф] *sn.* ду́дка

fifteen [фıф-тı́н] *num.* пятна́дцать

fifth [фıфθ] *num.* пя́тый

fifty [фıф-тı] *num.* пятьдеся́т

fig [фıг] *sn.* фи́га

fight [файт] *sn.* би́тва, бой, сраже́ние; *vt.i.* сража́ться

figurative [фı-гю-рǎ-тıв] *adj.* обра́зный; изобрази́тельный (*descriptive*); живопи́сный (*pictorial*)

figure [фı-гǎр] *sn.* ци́фра (*numeral*); о́браз, фигу́ра (*pattern*); о́блик, о́браз, фо́рма (*form*); рису́нок, черте́ж (*sketch, diagram*); *vt.i.* изобража́ть, фигури́ровать;
— **out** [– а́ут] вычисля́ть

filament [фı-лǎ-мǎнт] *sn.* волокно́, нить

file [файл] *sn.* напи́льник (*tool*); регистра́тор, рее́стр (*for documents, etc.*); *mil.* ряд, строй, шере́нга (*dossier*); *vt.* пили́ть, подпи́ливать (*rasp*); *mil.* итти́ шере́нгой; подши́вать дела́, скрепля́ть бума́ги (*put away papers, etc.*)

filial [фı-ли-ǎл] *adj.* сыно́вний (*of son*); до́черний (*of daughter*)

filings [фа́й-лıнз] *sn. pl.* опи́лки

fill [фıл] *sn.* полнота́ (*fullness*); сы́тость (*satiety*); *vt.i.* надува́ть, наполня́ть; насыща́ться (*satiate*)

fillet [фı-лıт] *sn.* у́зкая поло́ска (*narrow strip*); филе́ (*meat*)

**(thin thread); плёнка (photographic); фильма (cinema); vt.i. делать кино-съёмку

filter [філ-тəр] sn. фильтр; vt.i. процеживать, фильтровать; просачиваться (percolate)

filth [філθ] sn. грязь (dirt); отбросы (garbage, etc.)

filthy [філ-θі] adj. грязный, мерзкий

filtration [філ-трэй-шəн] sn. фильтрация

fin [фін] sn. плавник

final [фай-нəл] adj. конечный, окончательный

finality [фай-нə-лі-ті] sn. законченность, окончательность

finance [фі-нəнс] sn. финансы, pl.; управление финансами (management of money); vt.i. финансировать

finch [фінч] s. зяблик

find [файнд] sn. находка; vt. находить; встречать (come across); — out [— аут] обнаруживать, узнать

finding [файн-діŋ] sn. находка; приговор (of jury); pl. полученные данные

fine [файн] sn. пеня, штраф (penalty); adj. чистый (pure); утончённый (refined); ясный (of weather); тонкий (thin); — arts [— артс] изящные искусства; vt. штрафовать

finery [фай-нə-рі] sn. наряд, убор, украшение

finger [фіŋ-гəр] sn. палец; vt. трогать (touch); ощупы-

fingerstall [фіŋ-гəр-стол] sn. предохранительный резиновый палец

fingertip [фіŋ-гəр-тіп] sn. кончик пальца

finical [фі-ні-кəл] adj. жеманный; разборчивый (fastidious)

finish [фі-ніш] sn. окончание; vt. довершать, кончать

finite [фай-найт] adj. ограниченный; gram. личный

Finn [фін] sm. финн, финляндец; sf. финянка

Finnish [фі-ніш] adj. финский

fir [фəр] sn. ель

fire [фай-əр] sn. жар (heat); огонь (combustion); пожар (conflagration); mil. пальба, стрельба; set on [сəт он] поджигать; — vt. зажигать (kindle); палить, стрелять (shoot)

fire-brigade [фай-əр-брігэйд] sn. пожарная команда

fire-escape [фай-əр-іскэйп] sn. пожарная лестница

firefly [фай-əр-флай] s. светляк

fire-grate [фай-əр-грэйт] sn. колосниковая решётка

fire-guard [фай-əр-гард] sn. каминная решётка

fire-lighter [фай-əр-лайтəр] sn. растопка

fireman [фай-əр-мəн] sm. пожарный (of brigade); кочегар (stoker)

firewood [фа́й-ăр-ўўд] *sn. pl.* дрова́

fireworks [фа́й-ăр-ўэркс] *sn.* фейерве́рк

firing [фа́йă-рiн] *sn.* стрельба́

firm [фĕрм] *sn.* фи́рма; *adj.* кре́пкий, сто́йкий (*strong, sturdy*); усто́йчивый (*stable*)

firmament [фĕр-мă-мăнт] *sn.* небе́сный свод

firmness [фĕрм-нiс] *sn.* кре́пость, твёрдость; усто́йчивость (*steadiness*)

first [фĕрст] *num., adj.* пе́рвый; *adv.* сперва́; **- of all** [- ов бл] пре́жде всего́

first-born [фĕрст-бо́рн] *sn.* пе́рвенец

firstly [фĕрст-лi] *adv.* во-пе́рвых

firth [фĕрθ] *sn.* морско́й зали́в, у́стье реки́

fish [фiш] *s.* ры́ба; *vi.* лови́ть ры́бу

fisherman [фíшăр-мăн] *sm.* рыба́к

fishery [фí-шă-рi] *sn.* рыболо́вство (*business of fishing*); ры́бный про́мысел (*industry*)

fishing [фí-шiн] *sn.* ры́бная ло́вля

fishing-line [фí-шiн-лайн] *sn.* леса́

fishing-rod [фí-шiн-род] *sn.* уди́лище, у́дочка

fishmonger [фiш-ман-гăр] *sm.* ры́бник

fishy [фí-шi] *adj.* ры́бий, ры́бный

illness); о́бморок (*fainting*); поры́в, настрое́ние (*temper, mood*); *adj.* го́дный (*suitable*), соотве́тствующий (*appropriate*); здоро́вый (*healthy*); *vt.i.* годи́ться (*suit*); прила́живать, снаб-жа́ть, снаряжа́ть (*furnish*); приспособля́ть (*adapt*)

fitness [фíт-нiс] *sn.* го́дность; здоро́вье (*health*)

fitter [фí-тăр] *sm.* меха́ник, монтёр

fitting [фí-тiн] *sn.* приго́нка; *adj.* подходя́щий; *sn. pl.* аппара́т, приспособле́ние; армату́ра

five [файв] *num.* пять

fix [фiкс] *sn.* затрудни́тельное положе́ние (*difficult situation*); *vt.* укрепля́ть, устана́вливать

fixed [фiкст] *adj.* неподви́жный, постоя́нный

fixture [фíкс-чăр] *sn.* неподви́жность; *pl.* недви́жимое име́ние

fizz [фiз] *sn.* шипе́ние; *vi.* шипе́ть; *coll.* шампа́нское (*champagne*); шипу́чий напи́ток (*fizzy drink*)

fizzy [фí-зi] *adj.* газиро́ванный

flabby [фла́-бi] *adj.* вя́лый, обви́слый

flag [флэг] *sn.* зна́мя, флаг (*banner*); коса́тик, шпа́жник (*plant*); плита́, плитня́к (*slab of rock*); *vi.* пови́снуть, пони́кнуть (*hang down, droop*); опуска́ться, ослабева́ть (*grow languid*)

flagon [флǽ-гăн] *sn.* буты́ль, фля́га

flagrant [флэ́й-грăнт] *adj.* скандáльный (*scandalous*); я́вный (*glaring*)

flagship [флǽг-шип] *sn.* флагмáнское сýдно

flagstaff [флǽг-стаф] *sn.* флагштóк

flail [флэйл] *sn.* молоти́ло, цеп

flair [флэ́р] *sn.* нюх; *fig.* чутьё

flake [флэйк] *sn.* клочóк, хлóпье; **snow -s** [снóу -с] снежи́нки; *vt.i.* рассла́иваться (*stratify*)

flaky [флэ́й-ки] *adj.* хлопьеви́дный

flamboyant [флэм-бóй-ăнт] *adj.* пы́шный, цвети́стый

flame [флэйм] *sn.* плáмя

flaming [флэ́й-мин] *adj.* пламенéющий

flange [флэ́ндж] *sn.* закрáина, каймá, флáнец

flank [флэ́нк] *sn.* бок, сторонá (*side*); *mil.* фланг; *vt.* укрепля́ть фланг

flannel [флǽ-нăл] *sn.* фланéль; *pl.* фланéлевые штаны́; *adj.* фланéлевый

flap [флэп] *sn.* взмах (*of wings*); шлёпок (*light stroke*); *vt.i.* взмáхивать, махáть, хлóпать

flare [флэ́р] *sn.* мерцáющий свет (*unsteady light*); **- up** [- ап] *vi.* вспы́хивать

flash [флэш] *sn.* вспы́шка, прóблеск; *adj.* кричáщий (*gaudy*); *vt.i.* блеснýть, сверкнýть; мелькнýть (*gleam*)

flask [флэ́ск] *sn.* фля́жка

flat [флэт] *sn.* кварти́ра (*suite*); *mus.* бемóль (♭); *adj.* горизонтáльный, рóвный

flat-iron [флэт-áй-ăн] *sn.* утю́г

flatten [флǽ-тăн] *vt.* вырáвнивать, плю́щить

flatter [флǽ-тăр] *vt.* льстить

flatterer [флǽ-тă-рăр] *sm.* льстец

flattery [флǽ-тă-ри] *sn.* лесть

flatulence [флǽ-тю-лăнс] *sn. med.* вéтры, гáзы

flaunt [флóнт] *vt.i.* вáжничать, щеголя́ть

flavour [флэ́й-вăр] *sn.* вкус, при́вкус; *vt.* приправля́ть

flaw [флó] *sn.* трéщина, щель (*breach, crack*); изъя́н, недостáток (*defect*); *vt.i.* поврeждáть

flax [флэкс] *sn.* лён

flaxen [флǽкс-ăн] *adj.* льняно́й

flay [флэ́й] *vt.* сдирáть кóжу (*skin*); обдирáть кóру (*peel off*)

flea [фли] *s.* блохá

fleck [флек] *sn.* пятнó; крапи́нка (*speck*)

fledge [фледж] *vt.* опери́ть

flee [фли] *vi.* бежáть (*run away*); исчезáть (*vanish*)

fleece [флис] *sn.* рунó; облакá барáшками (*of clouds*); шерсть (*wool*); *vt.* обдирáть (*strip*); *fig.* вымогáть

fleecy [фли-си] *adj.* клочковáтый, шерсти́стый

fleet [флит] *sn.* флот, флоти́лия; *adj.* бы́стрый (*swift*)

Flemish [фле-ми́ш] *adj.* фламáндский

flesh [флеш] *sn.* мя́со (*meat*); плоть, тéло (*body*); мя́коть (*of plants*)

flounce [флаўнс] *sn.* оборка (*of skirt*); резкое движение (*sharp movement*); *vt.* отделывать оборками; *vi.* бросаться, шлёпаться

flounder [флаўн-дăр] *sn.* барахтанье; камбала (*fish*); *vi.* барахтаться, спотыкаться

flour [флăў-ăр] *sn.* мука

flourish [флă-риш] *sn.* завитушка, росчерк (*scroll*); цветистое выражение (*expression*); *vi.* процветать, цвести

flow [флоў] *sn.* поток, течение (*flowing*); изобилие (*copious supply*); *vi.* течь

flower [флăў-ăр] *sn.* цвет, цветок; *vi.* цвести; **—bed** [—бед] *sn.* цветник

flowering [флăў-ăр-иň] *sn.* цветение; *adj.* цветущий

flowing [флоў-иň] *adj.* текучий; плавный (*language*)

fluctuate [флăк-тю-эйт] *vi.* колебаться

fluctuation [флăк-тю-ĕй-шăн] *sn.* неустойчивость

flue [флу] *sn.* дымоход (*smoke-duct*); пушок (*fluff*); *coll.* грипп

fluency [флу-ăн-сі] *sn.* плавность; беглость (*of speech*)

fluent [флу-ăнт] *adj.* плавный; беглый

fluff [флăф] *sn.* пух, пушок

fluffy [флă-фі] *adj.* пушистый

fluid [флу-ід] *sn.* жидкость; *adj.* жидкий, текучий

fluke¹ [флук] *sn.* счастливая случайность

flurry [флă-рі] *sn.* волнение, суматоха; порыв ветра, шквал (*gust, squall*); *vt.* волновать

flush [флăш] *sn.* краска, румянец (*blush*); промывка (*of water*); порыв (*of emotion*); *adj.* изобилующий, обильный (*abundant*); полный (*full*); *vi.* краснеть (*blush*); промывать, хлынуть (*with water*)

fluster [флăс-тăр] *sn.* возбуждение; *vt.* волновать, смущать

flute [флют] *sn.* флейта

flutter [флă-тăр] *sn.* порхание (*fluttering*); трепетание (*tremulous excitement*); оживление (*stir*); *vt.i.* махать (*wings*)

fluvial [флу-ві-ăл] *adj.* речной

flux [флăкс] *sn.* истечение, течение (*outflow*); *med.* понос; прилив (*of tide*); *chem.* плавень, флюс

fly [флай] *s.* муха (*insect*); полёт (*flying*); *vi.* летать, спешить (*hurry*)

flyer [флай-ăр] *sn.* лётчик

flying [флай-иň] *sn.* летание; *adj.* летящий

fly-wheel [флай-ўил] *sn.* маховое колесо

foal [фоўл] *s.* жеребёнок

foam [фоўм] *sn.* пена; мыло (*on horse*); *vi.* пениться; взмыливаться

focal [фоў-кăл] *adj.* фокусный

focus [фоў-кăс] *sn.* средоточие, фокус; *vt.i.* сосредоточивать (*focus*)

fodder [фо-дăр] *sn.* корм, фураж

foe [фоў] *sm.* враг

fog [фог] *sn.* густой туман; *vt.* озадачивать (*perplex*)

foggy [фо-гі] *adj.* туманный; неясный (*dim*)

foible [фойбл] *sn.* слабая струнка (*weak point*); слабость (*weakness*); недостаток (*deficiency*)

foil [фойл] *sn.* фольга, зеркальная наводка (*rolled sheet metal*); рапира (*in fencing*); *vt.* отражать (*reverberate*); *vi.* парировать (*parry*)

foist [фойст] *vt.* всучивать, подбрасывать (*palm off*); ложно приписывать (*attribute falsely*)

fold [фоулд] *sn.* загон, овчарня (*for sheep*); паства (*religious congregation*); складка (*doubling*); *vt.* загонять (*sheep*); складывать (*double*); скрещивать (*arms*)

folder [фоулдăр] *sn.* брошюра (*sta*)

foliage [фоули-ăдж] *sn.* листва (*leaves*)

folk(s) [фоук(с)] *sn.pl.* люди

folk-lore [фоук-лōр] *sn.* фольклор, народные сказания

follow [фо-лоу] *vt.i.* следовать; следить (*grasp*); подражать (*imitate*); – **suit** [–сют] следовать примеру; **as –s** [æз –з] следующим образом

follower [фо-лоу-ăр] *sm.* последователь

following [фо-лоу-иŋ] *adj.* следующий (*next*); последующий (*subsequent*)

folly [фо-ли] *sn.* безрассудство, сумасбродство

foment [фоу-мĕнт] *vt.* примачивать (*bathe*); припаривать (*apply warmth*); подстрекать (*incite*)

fomentation [фоу-мăн-тэйшăн] *sn.* примочка

fond [фонд] *adj.* любящий, нежный

fondle [фондл] *vt.* ласкать

fondness [фонд-нĕс] *sn.* нежение, нежность

font [фонт] *sn. eccl.* купель; водоём (*reservoir*); резервуар лампы (*lamp oil container*)

food [фуд] *sn.* пища, провизия; корм (*animal*)

food-stuffs [фуд-стафс] *sn.pl.* пищевые продукты

fool [фул] *sm.* дурак, глупец; шут (*clown, jester*); *vt.i.* дурачиться, шутить; одурачивать (*someone*)

foolish [фу-лиш] *adj.* глупый

foolishness [фу-лиш-нĕс] *sn.* глупость, дурачество

foot [фут] *sn.* нога; **on –** [он –] пешком; *mil.* пехота; подножие (*base*); фут (*measure*); *vt.* надвязывать

foothold [фут-хоулд] *sn.* опора для ноги

footman [фут-мăн] *sm.* ливрейный лакей

footnote [фут-ноут] *sn.* выноска, подстрочное примечание

footpath [фут-пāθ] *sn.* пешеходная дорожка, тропа

footprint [фут-принт] *sn.* след

footwear [фут-уэр] *sn.* обувь

for [фŏр] *prep.* для (*intended for*); за (*instead of*); ради (*for the sake of*); *conj.* ибо, потому что (*because*); так как (*as*)

forage [фо-ридж] *sn.* корм, фураж; *vi.* фуражировать; опустошать (*ravage*)

forbear [фор-бĕр] *vt.i.* быть терпеливым, воздерживаться

forbearance [фор-бэ́-ранс] *sn.* воздержанность, терпеливость; снисходительность (*leniency*)

forbid [фор-бід] *vt.* запрещать

forbidding [фор-бі-дін] *adj.* непривлекательный (*unattractive*); отталкивающий (*repellent*)

force [фôрс] *sn.* сила (*strength*); насилие (*violence*); *pl.* войска; *vt.* заставлять, принуждать

forceful [фôрс-фул] *adj.* действительный, сильный

forceps [фôр-сепс] *sn.* щипцы

forcible [фôр-сібл] *adj.* насильственный, убедительный (*telling*)

ford [фôрд] *sn.* брод

forearm [фôр-ârм] *sn.* предплечье; [фôр-âрм] *vt.* заранее вооружать

forebode [фор-бôуд] *vt.* предчувствовать (кое-что дурнóе)

foreboding [фор-бôу-дін] *sn.* предзнаменование, предчувствие

forecast [фôр-кâст] *sn.* предсказание; [фôр-кâст] *vt.* предвидеть, предсказывать

forefather [фôр-фâ-ѳэр] *sm.* предок

forefinger [фôр-фін-гэр] *sn.* указательный палец

forego [фор-гôу] *vt.i.* предшествовать

foregoing [фор-гôу-ін] *adj.* вышеупомянутый (*previously mentioned*); предшествующий (*preceding*)

forehead [фôр-рід] *sn.* лоб

foreign [фô-рін] *adj.* иностранный; чуждый, чужой (*strange*)

foreigner [фô-рі-нэр] *sm.* иностранец

foreman [фôр-мэн] *sm.* надсмотрщик, старший рабочий; старшинá присяжных (*principal juror*)

foremost [фôр-мôуст] *adj.* передовой; *adv.* во-первых, прежде всего

forenoon [фôр-нûн] *sn.* время до полудня

forerunner [фор-ра́-нэр] *sn.* предтеча

foresee [фор-сі́] *vt.* предвидеть

foreshadow [фор-шэ́-дôу] *vt.* предзнаменовать

foresight [фôр-сайт] *sn.* предвидение, предусмотрительность

forest [фô-ріст] *sn.* лес; *vt.* засаживать лесом

forestall [фор-стôл] *vt.* предупреждать

forester [фô-ріс-тэр] *sm.* лесник, лесничий; обитатель лесов (*inhabitant*)

forestry [фô-ріс-трі] *sn.* лесоводство

foretell [фор-тéл] *vt.* предсказывать

forewarn [фор-уôрн] *vt.* предостерегать

forewoman [фôр-ўу-мэн] *sf.* надсмотрщица

foreword [фôр-ўœрд] *sn.* предисловие

forfeit [фôр-фіт] *sn.* фант, штраф; *pl.* игра в фанты (*game*); *vt.* лишаться

forfeiture [фôр-фі-чэр] *sn.* конфискация, лишение, потеря, штраф

forge [фо̂рдж] *sn.* ку́зница (*smithy*); *sn.* горн (*furnace*); *vt.* кова́ть (*hammer*); выду́мывать (*invent*); подде́лывать (*falsify*)

forgery [фо́р-джӑ-рі] *sn.* подде́лка

forget [фор-ге́т] *vt.* забыва́ть

forgetful [фор-ге́т-фӯл] *adj.* забы́вчивый

forgive [фор-гі́в] *vt.* проща́ть

forgiveness [фор-гі́в-ніс] *sn.* проще́ние

forgo [фор-го́ў] *vt.* отка́зываться, отрека́ться

fork [фо̂рк] *sn.* ви́лка (*for table*); ви́лы (*implement*); разветвле́ние (*divergence*)

forlorn [фор-ло́рн] *adj.* поки́нутый; несча́стный (*unhappy*); безнадёжный (*hopeless*)

form [фо̂рм] *sn.* вид, о́браз, фо́рма (*shape*); скамья́ (*bench*); анке́та, бланк (*paper*)

formal [фо́р-мӑл] *adj.* форма́льный, церемо́нный

formality [фор-мӑ-лі-ті] *sn.* форма́льность

formation [фор-мэ́й-шӑн] *sn.* образова́ние; *mil.* постро́ение, расположе́ние

former [фо́р-мӑр] *adj.* пре́жний; предше́ствующий (*preceding*)

formerly [фо́р-мӑр-лі] *adv.* не́когда, пре́жде

formidable [фо́р-мі-дӑбл] *adj.* гро́зный

formulate [фо́р-мю-лэйт] *vt.* формули́ровать

forsake [фор-се́йк] *vt.* покида́ть

forthcoming [фо̂рṣ-ка-мін] *adj.* гряду́щий, предстоя́щий

fortification [фо̂р-ті-фі-кэ́й-шӑн] *sn.* фортифика́ция; *pl.* укрепле́ния

fortify [фо́р-ті-фай] *vt.* укрепля́ть

fortitude [фо́р-ті-тюд] *sn.* му́жество, твёрдость

fortnight [фо́рт-найт] *sn.* две неде́ли

fortress [фо́рт-ріс] *sn. mil.* кре́пость

fortunate [фо́р-чӑ-ніт] *adj.* уда́чный

fortune [фо́р-чӑн] *sn.* бога́тство (*wealth*); уда́ча (*luck*)

forty [фо́р-ті] *num.* со́рок

forward [фо́р-ўӑд] *adj.* передово́й (*advanced*); роспе́лый (*approaching maturity*); развя́зный (*pert*); *adv.* да́льше (*farther, onward*); *vt.* отправля́ть, посыла́ть (*send*); спосо́бствовать (*promote*)

fossil [фо́-сіл] *sn.* ископа́емое, окамене́лость; *fig.* допото́пный, старомо́дный (*antiquated*); отупе́вший (*torpid*)

foster [фо́с-тӑр] *vt.* леле́ять, пита́ть (*cherish*); поощря́ть (*stimulate*); благоприя́тствовать (*of circumstances*)

foster-father [фо́с-тӑр-фӑ-ѳӑр] *sn.* приёмный оте́ц

foster-mother [фо́с-тӑр-мӑ-ѳӑр] *sf.* приёмная мать

foul [фа́ул] *sn.* столкнове́ние (*collision*); непра́вильная игра́ (*in games*); вони́чий (*stinking*); гря́зный (*filthy*); непристо́йный (obscene); дурной (of weather); vt.i. замарать (dirty); сталкиваться (collide); запутываться (entangle);

found [фа́унд] vt.i. основывать, учреждать; vt. лить, отливать, плавить (melt, mould, fuse)

foundation [фаун-дэ́й-шн] sn. основание, фундамент; учреждение (establishment)

founder [фа́ун-дәр] sm. основатель, учредитель (of establishment); литейщик, плавильщик (smelter); vt.i. пойти ко дну (of ship); закромать (of horse)

foundling [фа́ун-длӣн] sn. найдёныш

foundry [фа́ун-дрі] sn. литейный завод, плавильня

fount [фа́унт] sn. typ. комплект шрифта, литер; источник (spring)

fountain [фа́ун-тін] sn. фонтан; источник (source)

four [фо́р] num. четыре

fourteen [фо́р-тин] num. четырнадцать

fourth [фо́рθ] num. четвёртый

fowl [фа́ул] s. птица, курица; pl. живность; петухи и куры

fox [фокс] s. лисица; vi. хитрить

foxy [фо́-ксі] adj. лисий (foxlike); хитрый (crafty); краснобурый (colour)

fraction [фра́ек-шн] sn. дробь; частица (part)

fracture [фра́ек-чәр] sn. med. перелом; tech. излом; vt.i. переламывать, ломаться

fragile [фра́е-джайл] adj. ломкий (breakable); хилый (feeble, weak); хрупкий (brittle)

fragment [фра́ег-мәнт] sn. обломок, отрывок

fragrance [фра́эй-грәнс] sn. аромат, благовоние

fragrant [фра́эй-грәнт] adj. ароматический, душистый

frail [фрэйл] sn. корзинка (для фруктов); adj. деликатный; хрупкий

frailty [фрэ́йл-ті] sn. непостоянство (inconstancy); слабосилие (feebleness); слабость (weakness)

frame [фрэйм] sn. остов (shell of building); рама (for picture); tech. каркас; - of mind [- ов майнд] настроение; vt. обрамлять

framework [фрэ́йм-ўӛрк] sn. сруб

franchise [фра́ен-чайз] sn. избирательное право

frank [фра́енк] adj. искренний, откровенный

frankness [фра́енк-ніс] sn. откровенность

frantic [фра́ен-тік] adj. нейстовый (furious); бешеный (wildly excited)

fraternal [фра-тӛ́р-нәл] adj. братский

fraternity [фра-тӛ́р-ні-ті] sn. братство; община (guild, etc.)

fraternize [фра́е-тӛр-найз] vi. брататься; общаться

fraud [фрод] sn. обман; t.i. обманщик (person)

fraudulent [фро́-дю-ләнт] adj. мошеннический, обманный

fray [фрэй] *sn.* дра́ка (*fight*); ссо́ра (*quarrel*); столкнове́ние (*conflict*); *vt.* протира́ть (*wear through by rubbing*); обтрепа́ться (*become ragged*)

freak [фрик] *sn.* при́хоть, причу́да (*vagary*); чудо́вищность, уро́дство (*monstrosity*) [ну́шка

freckle [фрэкл] *sn.* вес-

free [фри] *adj.* во́льный, свобо́дный; ще́дрый (*liberal*); доброво́льный (*voluntary*); беспла́тный (*gratis*); *vt.* освобожда́ть

freedom [фри́-дэм] *sn.* во́льность, свобо́да

freethinker [фри́-θи́н-кэр] *sm.* вольноду́мец

freeze [фриз] *vt.i.* замора́живать, замерза́ть

freezing [фри́-зiн] *sn.* замерза́ние

freight [фрэйт] *sn.* груз, фрахт; *vt.* фрахтова́ть

French [фрэнч] *sn.* францу́зский язы́к (*language*); —**man** [-мэн] *sm.* францу́з; —**woman** [-ўу́-мэн] *sf.* францу́женка; *adj.* францу́зский; **take - leave** [тэйк – лив] уйти́ не прости́сь

frenzy [фрэ́н-зi] *sn.* безу́мие, бе́шенство

frequency [фри́-кўэн-сi] *sn.* частота́

frequent [фри́-кўэнт] *adj.* многокра́тный, ча́стый; [фрi-кўэ́нт] *vt.* ча́сто посеща́ть

fresh [фрэш] *adj.* но́вый (*new*); све́жий *of food*; нео́пытный (*inexperienced*); прохлади́тельный (*cool*); пре́сный (*of water*)

fret [фрэт] *sn.* лад (*of guitar*,

etc.); шабло́н (*pattern*); *vi.* беспоко́иться (*worry oneself*)

fretful [фрэ́т-фул] *adj.* раздражи́тельный

fretsaw [фрэ́т-со́] *sn.* прорезна́я пила́

friable [фра́й-эбл] *adj.* кроша́щийся, ры́хлый

friar [фра́й-эр] *sm.* капуци́н, мона́х [ние

friction [фри́к-шэн] *sn.* тре́-

Friday [фра́й-дi] *sn.* пя́тница; **Good -** [гуд –] вели́кая пя́тница, страстна́я пя́тница

friend [фрэнд] *sm.* друг, прия́тель, това́рищ

friendless [фрэ́нд-лiс] *adj.* одино́кий

friendly [фрэ́нд-лi] *adj.* дру́жеский

friendship [фрэ́нд-шiп] *sn.* дру́жба, дружелю́бие

fright [фрайт] *sn.* испу́г

frighten [фра́й-тэн] *vt.* пуга́ть

frightful [фра́йт-фул] *adj.* стра́шный; *coll.* безобра́зный, га́дкий

frigid [фрi-джид] *adj.* холо́дный; леденя́щий

frill [фрил] *sn.* бры́жи, жабо́, обо́рочка

fringe [фрiндж] *sn.* бахрома́, ка́йма; чёлка (*of hair*); *vt.* окаймля́ть

frisky [фри́с-кi] *adj.* ре́звый

fritter [фри́-тэр] *sn.* ола́дья; *vt.* раздробля́ть; **- away** [-а́-ўэй] растра́чивать по ме́лочам

frivolity [фрi-во́-лi-тi] *sn.* несерьёзность, пустота́

frivolous [фрi-ва́-лэс] *adj.* легкомы́сленный, пусты́й

frock [фрок] sn. платье; ряса (monk's); – **coat** [–кбут] sn. сюртук

frog [фрог] s. zool. лягушка; mil. крючок на поясе; – **in-the-throat** [– ін-ѳѳ-ѳрбут] хрипота

frolic [фрб-лік] sn. веселье, шалость; vi. проказничать, резвиться, шалить

from [фром] prep. из, от, по, с, со

front [франт] sn. mil. фронт; передняя сторона (fore part); фасад (face of building); adj. передний; vt.i. выходить на, глядеть; противостоять (oppose)

frontage [фран-тідж] sn. палисадник, фасад

frontal [фран-тäл] adj. лобный (of forehead); mil. лобовой, фронтальный

frontier [фран-тіäр] sn. граница; adj. пограничный

frost [фрост] sn. мороз

frostbite [фрбст-байт] sn. отмораживание

frosty [фрбс-ті] adj. морозный

froth [фроѳ] sn. пена; vt.i. пенить; пениться; взмыливаться (of horses)

frown [фраун] sn. хмурый взгляд; vi. хмуриться

frozen [фрбу-зäн] adj. замёрзший

frugal [фру-гäл] adj. бережливый, скромный, умеренный

fruit [фрут] sn. плод, фрукт

fruiterer [фру-тä-рäр] sn. фруктовщик

fruitful [фрут-фул] adj. плодовитый, плодородный

fruition [фру-ішäн] sn.

пользование; осуществление (of hopes, etc.)

fruitless [фрут-ліс] adj. бесплодный (not bearing fruit); бесполезный (useless)

frustrate [фра-стрéйт] vt. расстраивать (baffle); противодействовать (counteract); обманывать, разочаровывать (disappoint)

frustration [фрас-трéйшäн] sn. расстройство (of plans, etc.); крушение (of hopes, etc.)

fry [фрай] sn. мелкая рыбёшка, **small** – [смол –] мелюзга; vt. жарить

frying-pan [фрай-ін-пäн] sn. сковорода

fuel [фю-äл] sn. топливо

fugitive [фю-джи-тів] sn. беглец; adj. беглый; мимолётный (transient)

fulfil [фул-філ] vt. исполнять, осуществлять

fulfilment [фул-філ-мäнт] sn. выполнение, исполнение

full [фул] adj. полный; насыщенный (satisfied); – **stop** – [стоп] vt. точка

fullness [фул-ніс] sn. полнота

fully [фу-лі] adv. вполне, совершенно

fumble [фамбл] vi. нащупывать

fume [фюм] sn. пар; испарение (exhalation); vt.i. дымиться (reek); окуривать (fumigate); гневаться, кипятиться (chafe)

fumigate [фю-мі-гéйт] vt. окуривать

fumigation [фю-мі-гéйшäн] sn. курение

fun [фан] *sn.* забава, потеха; времяпрепровождение (*pastime*); **make – of** [мэйк – ов] высмеивать

function [файк-шан] *sn.* назначение, обязанности (*assignment, duties*); призвание (*calling*); *math.* функция; *vi.* действовать, функционировать

fund [фанд] *sn.* капитал; фонд; **sinking – [**сйн-кйн –] фонд для погашения

fundamental [фан-дă-мéн-тăл] *adj.* коренной, основной

funeral [фю́-нă-рăл] *sn.* похороны; *adj.* похоронный

funereal [фю-ни-рі-ăл] *adj.* траурный; мрачный (*dismal*)

fungus [фăн-ґăс] *sn.* гриб; нарост (*excrescence*)

funnel [фă-нăл] *sn.* воронка; дымовая труба (*in engines and ships*)

funny [фă-ни] *adj.* забавный, смешной

fur [фăр] *sn.* мех; шкура (*skin*); *med.* налёт, обложение (языка́); накипь (*scum*); шуба (*coat*)

furbish [фăр-биш] *vt.* подновлять; полировать

furious [фю-ри-ăс] *adj.* взбешённый, неистовый, разъярённый, яростный

furl [фăрл] *vt.* сворачивать, убирать; складывать (*umbrella*)

furlong [фăр-лон] *sn.* восьмая часть мили

furlough [фăр-лоу] *sn.* отпуск

furnace [фăр-нíс] *sn.* горн, гóпка

furnish [фăр-нíш] *vt.* доставлять, снабжать (*supply*); меблировать (*a house, room, etc.*)

furnishings [фăр-ни-шйнз] *sn. pl.* домашняя обстановка

furniture [фăр-ни-чăр] *sn.* мебель, обстановка

furrier [фă-рі-ăр] *sn.* меховщик, скорняк

furrow [фă-роу] *sn.* борозда (*trench*); жёлоб, фальц (*groove*); глубокая морщина (*deep wrinkle*)

further [фăр-ешăр] *adv.* далее, дальше, затем; *adj.* добавочный (*additional*); *vt.* содействовать, способствовать

furthermore [фăр-ешăр-мóр] *adv.* сверх того

furtive [фăр-тив] *adj.* скрытый, тайный

furtively [фăр-тив-ли] *adv.* украдкой

fury [фю-ри] *sn.* бешенство, ярость; фурия (*angry woman*)

fuse [фюз] *sn.* зажигательная трубка, запал; *elect.* предохранитель; *vt.i.* плавить, расславляться

fuselage [фю-зі-лăж] *sn.* корпус аэроплана, фюзеляж

fusillade [фю-зі-лэйд] *sn.* обстрел, стрельба

fusion [фю-жăн] *sn.* плавка; слияние, смешение (*blending*)

fuss [фас] *sn.* суета, суматоха; *vi.* суетиться, хлопотать

fussy [фă-сі] *adj.* суетливый, хлопотливый

fusty [фăс-ти] *adj.* затхлый; устаревший (*antiquated*)

futile [фю-тайл] *adj.* беспо-
ле́зный, тще́тный

futility [фю-ті-лі-ті] *sn.*
пустота́, тще́тность

future [фю-чăр] *sn.* бу́-
дущность; *gram.* бу́дущее
вре́мя; *adj.* бу́дущий; **in
the –** [ін еӑ –] в бу́дущем

fuzzy [фă-зі] *adj.* запу́щен-
ный, сму́тный (confused,
hazy)

G

G [джі] *sn., mus.* соль

gabble [гэбл] *vi.* болта́ть,
бормота́ть

gable [гэйбл] *sn.* щипе́ц;
arch. фронто́н

gad [гэд] *vi.* бодря́жни-
чать, шля́ться

gadget [гэ́-джіт] *sn.* вы́-
думка, приспособле́ние

gag [гэг] *sn.* кляп; прекра-
ще́ние пре́ний (closure, guil-
lotine); отсебя́тина (actor's
interpolation); *vt.* вставля́ть
кляп (insert gag); заста́вить
замолча́ть (force silence)

gage [гэйдж] *sn.* зало́г
(pledge); вы́зов (in duel)

gaiety [гэ́йă-ті] *sn.* весе́-
лость

gaily [гэ́й-лі] *adv.* ве́село

gain [гэйн] *sn.* вы́игрыш
(winning); вы́года, при́быль
(profit); *pl.* дохо́ды; *vt.i.*
выи́грывать (win); получа-
ча́ть, зараба́тывать (earn)

gainsay [гэйн-сэ́й] *vt.* возра-
жа́ть, отрица́ть, противо-
ре́чить

gait [гэйт] *sn.* похо́дка

gaiter [гэй-тăр] *sn.* гама́ша

galaxy [гэ́-лă-ксі] *sn.*

мле́чный путь (*Milky Way*);
fig. блестя́щее собра́ние,
плея́да

gale [гэйл] *sn.* си́льный
ве́тер; *naut.* бу́ря, шторм

gall [гôл] *sn.* жёлчь (bile);
сса́дина (abrasion); *vt.* сса-
ди́ть; раздража́ть (vex)

gallant [гă-лэ́нт] *sm.* све́т-
ский челове́к; [гэ́-лăнт]
adj. гала́нтный (courteous);
велича́вый (stately); хра́брый
(brave)

gallantry [гэ́-лăн-трі] *sn.*
ве́жливость, гала́нтность
(courtliness); хра́брость
(bravery)

gallery [гэ́-лă-рі] *sn.* гал-
лере́я; *theat.* галёрка, раёк

galley [гэ́-лі] *sn. hist.* гале́ра;
typ. гра́нка

gallon [гэ́-лăн] *sn.* галло́н

gallop [гэ́-лăп] *sn.* гало́п;
vi. скака́ть гало́пом

gallows [гэ́-лоуз] *sn.* ви́се-
лица

galore [гă-ло́р] *adv.* в боль-
шо́м коли́честве

galosh [гă-ло́ш] *sn.* гало́ша

gamble [гэмбл] *sn.* риско́-
ванное предприя́тие; *vi.*
игра́ть в аза́ртные и́гры;
fig. рискова́ть

gambler [гэ́м-блăр] *sm.*
аза́ртный игро́к

game [гэйм] *sn.* игра́, па́р-
тия; состяза́ние (contest);
play the – [плэй еӑ –]
поступа́ть благоро́дно, со-
блюда́ть пра́вила; дичь (animals); *adj.* предприи́м-
чивый (spirited); энерги́чный
(energetic); искале́ченный
(crippled)

game-keeper [гэ́йм-ки-пăр]
sm. храни́тель живо́тных

gammon [гǽ-мǝн] *sn.* óкорок; вздор, обмáн (*humbug, deception*)

gander [гǽн-дǝр] *sm.* гусáк

gang [гǽй] *sn.* бáнда, грýппа, шáйка

gangster [гǽн-стǝр] *sm.* бандúт

gangway [гǽйг-ўэй] *sn.* схóдня

gaol [джэйл] *sn.* тюрьмá; *vt.* сажáть в тюрьмý

gaoler [джэй-лǝр] *sm.* тюрéмщик

gap [гǽп] *sn.* брешь, пролóм (*in wall, etc.*); пробéл (*empty space*)

gape [гэйп] *sn.* зевóк (*yawn*); изумлённый взгляд (*open-mouthed stare*); *vi.* зевáть, зиять, разевáть

garage [гǽ-рǽж] *sn.* гарáж

garb [гǽрб] *sn.* костюм, одéжда

garbage [гáр-бǝдж] *sn.* мýсор, отбрóсы, требухá

garden [гáр-дǝн] *sn.* сад; огорóд (*kitchen or market*)

gardener [гáр-днǝр] *sm.* садóвник

gardening [гáр-днѝй] *sn.* садовóдство

gargle [гáргл] *sn.* полоскáние (*gargling*); полоскáтельное (*the liquid*); *vt.* полоскáть

garland [гáр-лǽнд] *sn.* венóк, гирлянда

garlic [гáр-лѝк] *sn.* чеснóк

garment [гáр-мǝнт] *sn.* предмéт одéжды; *pl.* плáтье

garner [гáр-нǝр] *sn.* амбáр, житница

garnish [гáр-нѝш] *sn.* гарнúр, убрáнство; *vt.* гарнúровать, уснащáть

garret [гǽ-рѝт] *sn.* чердáк

garrison [гǽ-рѝ-сǝн] *sn.* гарнизóн; *vt.* стáвить гарнизóн

garrulous [гǽ-рў-лǽс] *adj.* болтлúвый

garter [гáр-тǝр] *sn.* подвязка

gas [гǽс] *sn.* газ; *adj.* гáзовый

gas-burner [гǽс-бǝр-нǝр] *sn.* газóвый рожóк

gaseous [гэй-зѝ-ǝс] *adj.* газообрáзный

gash [гǽш] *sn.* глубóкая рáна (*deep wound*); разрéз, шрам (*cut*)

gasometer [рǽ-сó-мѝ-тǝр] *sn.* газóвый резервуáр, газгóльдер

gasp [гáсп] *sn.* затруднённое дыхáние, судорожный вздох; *vi.* дышáть с трудóм (*for breath*)

gastric [гǽс-трѝк] *adj.* желýдочный

gate [гэйт] *sn.* ворóта, калúтка, прохóд (*passage*)

gather [рǽ-ǒǝр] *vt.i.* собирáть (*collect*); морщúть (*draw together*); нарывáть (*fester*); *sn. pl.* сбóрки

gathering [гǽ-ǒǝр-ѝй] *sn.* собрáние, сбор; *med.* нагноéние, нарыв

gaudy [гó-дѝ] *adj.* безвкýсный, кричáщий

gauge [гэйдж] *sn.* калúбр, масштáб, мéра; колея (*railway*); *vt.* измерять, калибровáть; оцéнивать (*estimate*)

gaunt [гóнт] *adj.* измождённый, сухощáвый; мрáчный (*grim*)

gauntlet [гóнт-лѝт] *sn.* рукавúца; **run the –** [рǎн ǒǝ] прохóдить сквозь строй

gauze [gōz] *sn.* газ (*material*); марля (*cheese-cloth*)

gay [гэй] *adj.* весёлый; пёстрый (*of colours*)

gaze [гэйз] *sn.* внимательный взгляд; *vi.* пристально глядеть

gazette [гӑ-зэ́т] *sn.* официальная правительственная газета

gazetteer [гӑ-зи-ти́р] *sn.* географический справочник

gear [гир] *sn.* прибор (*tackle*); привод, передача (*drive, transmission*); упряж (*harness*); такелаж (*rigging*); *vt.* снабжать приводом

gear-box [гир-бокс] *sn.* коробка скоростей

gem [джэм] *sn.* драгоценность; драгоценный камень, *m.* (*stone*)

Gemini [джэ́-ми-най] *sn.* созвездие Близнецов

gender [джэ́н-дӑр] *sn.* род

genealogical [джи-ни-лóджи-кӑл] *adj.* родословный

general [джэ́-нӑ-рӑл] *sm. mil.* генерал; служанка (*maid*); *adj. mil.* генеральный; главный (*chief, head*); общий (*common*); обычный (*usual*)

generalize [джэ́-нӑ-рӑ-лайз] *vt.* обобщать

generally [джэ́-нӑ-рӑ-ли] *adv.* вообще, обычно

generate [джэ́-нӑ-рэйт] *vt.* порождать, производить

generation [джэ-нӑ-рэ́йшӑн] *sn.* поколение; порождение (*begetting*); произведение (*production*); *tech.* генерация, образование

generosity [джэ-нӑ-рó-сити] *sn.* великодушие (*magnanimity*); щедрость (*munificence*)

generous [джэ́-нӑ-рӑс] *adj.* благородный, великодушный; обильный (*copious*)

genesis [джэ́-ни-сіс] *sn.* происхождение, генезис; книга Бытия (*book of Genesis*)

genial [джи-ни-ӑл] *adj.* умеренный (*of climate*); радушный (*of person*)

genitive [джэ́-ни-тів] *adj. gram. - case* – кэйс] родительный падеж

genius [джи-ни-ӑс] *sm.* гений; дух (*spirit*)

genteel [джэн-ти́л] *adj.* благовоспитанный (*polite, well-bred*); элегантный (*elegant*)

gentle [джэнтл] *adj.* кроткий, мягкий

gentleman [джэ́нтл-мӑн] *sm.* господин, джентльмен

gentleness [джэ́нтл-ніс] *sn.* доброта, мягкость

genuflect [джэ́-ню-флэкт] *vi.* преклонять колени (*при богослужении*)

genuine [джэ́-ню-ін] *adj.* настоящий, неподдельный, подлинный

genus [джи-нӑс] *sn.* класс, род

geography [джи-ó-грӑ-фи] *sn.* география

geology [джи-ó-ло-джи] *sn.* геология

geometry [джи-ó-мӑт-рі] *sn.* геометрия

germ [джэрм] *sn.* зародыш

German [джэ́р-мӑн] *sm.* немец; *sf.* немка *adj.* германский, немецкий

germinate [джэр-ми-нэйт] *vt.i.* прорастать

germination [джӕр-мі-нэ́й-шән] *sn.* прораста́ние

gerund [дже́-рәнд] *sn. gram.* геру́ндий, дееприча́стие

gesticulate [дже-стí-кю-лэйт] *vi.* жестикули́ровать

gesture [дже́с-чәр] *sn.* жест, телодвиже́ние

get [гет] *v.t.i.* достава́ть (*obtain*); получа́ть (*receive*); станови́ться (*become*); **– along** [– ӑ-ло́н] де́лать успе́хи, успева́ть; **– away** [– ӑ-уэ́й] избега́ть, удира́ть; **– down** [– да́ун] спуска́ться; **– out** [– а́ут] выходи́ть; **– up** [– ап] встава́ть (*rise*); поднима́ться (*go up*)

geyser [гі-зәр] *sn.* ге́йзер (*apparatus*); пережима́ющийся горя́чий исто́чник (*spring*)

ghastly [га́с-тлі] *adj.* ме́ртвенно бле́дный (*deathly pale*); ужа́сный (*horrible*)

gherkin [гӕ́р-кін] *sn.* корни́шон, огу́рчик

ghost [го́уст] *sn.* привиде́ние (*apparition*); дух (*spectre, spirit*); тень (*shadow*); истощённый челове́к (*emaciated person*)

ghostly [го́уст-лі] *adj.* духо́вный (*spectral*)

giant [джа́й-әнт] *sm.* велика́н, гига́нт

giblets [джíб-літс] *sn. pl.* пти́чьи потроха́

giddiness [гí-ді-ніс] *sn.* головокруже́ние

giddy [гí-ді] *adj.* головокружи́тельный, ошеломля́ющий, пусти́чный (*frivolous*)

gift [гіфт] *sn.* пода́рок (*present*); дар, тала́нт (*natural endowment*)

gifted [гі́ф-тід] *adj.* дарови́тый, одарённый, тала́нтливый

gigantic [джай-гӕ́н-тік] *adj.* гига́нтский, грома́дный

giggle [гігл] *sn.* хихи́канье; *vi.* хихи́кать

gild [гілд] *vt.* золоти́ть

gill [гіл] *sn. pl.* жа́бры (*of fish*); *anat.* второ́й подборо́док; леси́стый овра́г (*wooded ravine*); че́тверть пи́нты (*measure*)

gilt [гілт] *sn.* позоло́та; *adj.* позоло́ченный

gilt-edged [гілт-е́джд] *adj.* золотообре́зный

gimlet [гíм-літ] *sn.* бура́в

gin [джін] *sn.* род во́дки (*spirit*); джин (*machine*); подъёмная лебёдка (*hoisting apparatus*); за́падня (*snare*)

ginger [джін-джәр] *sn.* имби́рь, *m.*; рети́вость (*mettle*); *adj.* ры́жий (*of hair*)

gingerbread [джін-джәр-бред] *sn.* имби́рный пря́ник, коври́жка

gingerly [джін-джәр-лі] *adv.* осмотри́тельно, осторо́жно

gipsy [джíп-сі] *sm.* цыга́н; *adj.* цыга́нский

giraffe [джі-ра́ф] *s.* жира́ф

girder [гӕ́р-дәр] *sn.* ба́лка, фе́рма

girdle [гӕ́рдл] *sn.* куша́к, по́яс; ско́вородка (*iron plate*); *vt.* кольцева́ть (*tree*); подпоя́сывать (*surround with girdle*)

girl [гәрл] *sf.* де́вочка, де́вушка

girlhood [гәрл-худ] *sn.* деви́чество

girth [гӕрθ] *sn.* подпру́га (*for horse*); попере́чник (*band*); обхва́т (*measurement*)

gist [джіст] *sn.* суть

give [гів] *sn.* уступчивость (*yielding*); эластичность (*elasticity*); *vt.i.* дать, передавать; вручать (*deliver, entrust*); **— in** [— ін] сдаваться, уступать; **— over** [— о́у-ва́р] переставать (*abandon, stop*); **— way** [— уэ́й] подаваться, уступать; **—and-take** [— энд тэйк] взаимная уступка; обмен (*exchange*)

glacier [глэ́-сіа́р] *sn.* ледник

glad [глэд] *adj.* рад (*pleased*); радостный (*joyful*)

gladden [глэ́-дэн] *vt.* радовать

glade [глэйд] *sn.* прогалина

gladly [глэд-лі] *adv.* охотно

gladness [глэд-ніс] *sn.* радость

glamour [глэ-ма́р] *sn.* колдовство, обаяние

glamorous [глэ́-ма́-даб] *adj.* колдовской, обаятельный

glance [гланс] *sn.* взгляд; блеск, сверкание (*flash, gleam*); *vi.* взглядывать, просматривать; блестеть, сверкать

gland [глэнд] *sn.* железа

glandular [глэн-дю-ла́р] *adj.* железистой

glare [глэр] *sn.* блеск, мишура; пристальный взгляд (*fixed look*); *vi.* сверкать, свирепо смотреть (*look fiercely*)

glass [глас] *sn.* стекло; зеркало (*mirror*); стакан (*tumbler*); *pl.* очки (*spectacles*)

glass-house [глас-ха́ус] *sn.* теплица

glassy [гла́-сі] *adj.* гладкий (*smooth*); зеркальный (*like mirror*); стеклянный (*of glass*); тусклый (*dull*); прозрачный (*transparent*)

glaze [глэйз] *sn.* глазурь, глянец, лак; лессировка (*glazing*); *vt.i.* застеклять; муравить, лессировать

glazier [глэ́й-зі-а́р] *sn.* стекольщик

gleam [глим] *sn.* отблеск, проблеск; *vi.* мелькать, сиять

glean [глин] *vt.* подбирать, собирать; приобретать (*pick up facts, etc.*)

glee [гли] *sn.* припев (*unaccompanied composition for voices*); веселье (*gaiety, mirth*); радость (*joy*)

glen [глэн] *sn.* долина

glib [гліб] *adj.* бойкий (*fluent*); болтливый (*talkative*)

glide [глайд] *sn.* планирование (*volplaning*); скольжение (*gliding*); *vi.* планировать; скользать

glimmer [глі-ма́р] *sn.* мерцание

glimpse [глімпс] *sn.* мелькание; краткий взгляд (*brief view*)

glisten [глі-сэн] *vi.* поблёскивать, сиять

glitter [глі-та́р] *vi.* блестеть

gloaming [гло́у-мін] *sn.* сумерки

gloat [гло́ут] *vi.* злорадно смотреть, пожирать глазами

globe [глоуб] *sn.* глобус, шар; земной шар (*the earth*)

globular [гло́-бю-ла́р] *adj.* сферический

globule [глó-бюл] *sn.* пилю́ля (*pill*); ша́рик (*small globe*)

gloom [глӯм] *sn.* мрак, уны́ние

gloomy [глӯ-ми] *adj.* мра́чный, уны́лый, хму́рный

glorification [гло-ри-фи-кэ́й-шăн] *sn.* прославле́ние

glorify [глó-ри-фай] *sn.* прославля́ть

glorious [глó-ри-ăс] *adj.* великоле́пный, сла́вный

glory [глó-ри] *sn.* великоле́пие, сла́ва; *vt.* горди́ться (*be proud*)

gloss [глос] *sn.* блеск, лоск

glossary [глó-сă-ри] *sn.* глосса́рий, толко́вый слова́рь

glossy [глó-си] *adj.* глянцеви́тый, лощёный

glottis [глó-тіс] *sn.* голосова́я щель

glove [глав] *sn.* перча́тка

glow [глóў] *sn.* за́рево, заря́, пыл (*flame, fervour*); *vi.* накаля́ться; румя́неть (*blush, redden*)

glow-worm [глóў-ўœ́рм] *s.* светля́к

glue [глю] *sn.* клей; *vt.* кле́ить

glum [глам] *adj.* па́смурный, угрю́мый, хму́рый

glut [глат] *sn.* насыще́ние, пресыще́ние; *vt.* насыща́ть, пожира́ть

glutton [гла́-тăн] *sm.*, *f.* обжо́ра; росома́ха (*animal*)

gluttony [гла́-тă-ни] *sn.* обжо́рливость

gnash [нæш] *vt.i.* скрежета́ть

gnat [нæт] *s.* кома́р

gnaw [нŏ] *vt.i.* глода́ть, грызть

go [гóў] *sn. coll.* жи́вость; **have a go!** [хæв ă –] попро́буйте! *vi.* итти́, ходи́ть; дви́гаться (*of mechanism*); **– away** [– ă-ўэ́й] уходи́ть; уезжа́ть (*not on foot*); **– in** (*enter*) [– ін] входи́ть; **– out** (*leave*) [– аўт] выходи́ть; га́снуть (*of candle, etc.*)

goad [гóўд] *sn.* боди́ло, стрека́ло; *vt.* подгоня́ть

go-ahead [гóў-ă-ҳед] *adj.* предприи́мчивый

goal [гóўл] *sn.* цель (*aim*); коне́ц, фи́ниш (*end*); ме́сто назначе́ния (*destination*); гол (*in games*)

goat [гóўт] *s.* коза́, козёл

goatherd [гóўт-ҳœрд] *sm.* пасту́х

gobble [гóбл] *vt.* жа́дно прогла́тывать (*of eating*); кулды́кать (*of turkey*)

go-between [гóў-біт-ўін] *sm.* посре́дник

goblet [гóб-літ] *sn.* бока́л, ку́бок

god [год] *s.* бог, божество́; **–child** [–-ча́йлд] *sm.* кре́стник (*son*), *sf.* кре́стница (*daughter*)

goddess [гó-дес] *sf.* боги́ня

godfather [год-фа́-ѳăр] *sm.* крёстный оте́ц

godmother [год-ма-ăр] *sf.* крёстная мать

godsend [год-сенд] *sn.* нахо́дка, неожи́данная уда́ча

goggles [гоглз] *sn. pl.* защи́тные очки́, очки́-консе́рвы

goitre [го́йтр] *sn.* зоб

gold [гóўлд] *sn.* зо́лото, золото́й

golden [гóўл-дăн] *adj.* золоти́стый

goldfinch [góŭld-fínч] s. щеглёнок

goldsmith [góŭld-сміθ] sm. золотых дел мастер

golf [голф] sm. гольф

golfer [гóл-фăр] sm. игрóк в гольф

good [гўд] sn. блáго, добрó; пóльза (profit); adj. дóбрый, хорóший

good-bye [гўд-бáй] sn. прощáние; interj. до свидáния!, прощáйте!

good-natured [гўд-нэ́й-чăрд] adj. добродýшный

goodness [гўд-нíс] sn. блáгость, добротá; добродéтель (virtue)

goods [гўдз] sn. pl. товáр

goodwill [гўд-ýíл] sn. доброжелáтельность

goose [гуз] s. гусь

gooseberry [гýз-бă-рі] sn. крыжóвник

gore [гор] sn. запёкшаяся кровь (blood); клин (wedge); vt. вшивáть клин (shape with gore); прободáть (pierce)

gorge [гóрдж] sn. глóтка (internal throat); ущéлье (pass, ravine); vt. жрать (feed greedily)

gorgeous [гóр-джăс] adj. великолéпный, пышный

gormandize [гóр-мăн-дайз] vi. объедáться

gorse [горс] sn. bot. дрок

gospel [гóс-пăл] sn. евáнгелие

gossamer [гó-сă-мăр] sn. осéнняя паутúна (web); тóнкая ткань (tissue)

gossip [гó-сіп] sn. болтовнú; (idle talk); сплéтня (malicious rumour); vi. болтáть; сплéтничать (spread rumours)

gouge [гаўдж] sn. полукрýглое долотó; vt. выдáлбливать

gourmand [гýр-мăнд] sm. лáкомка; adj. обжóрливый

gout [гаўт] sn. подáгра

govern [гá-вăрн] vt. комáндовать, управлять

governess [гá-вăр-нíс] sf. гувернáнтка

government [гá-вăрн-мăнт] sn. правúтельство

governor [гá-вăр-нăр] sm. губернáтор, правúтель; хозяин (boss); tech. регулятор

gown [гаўн] sn. мáнтия (robe); плáтье (dress)

grab [грэб] sn. захвáт; tech. схват; vt. схвáтывать, хватáть

grace [грэйс] sn. благосклóнность, мúлость (favour); грáция, привлекáтельность (charm); молúтва (prayer); vt. удостóивать (honour); украшáть (adorn)

graceful [грэйс-фýл] adj. грациóзный, изящный

grace-note [грэйс-нóут] sn. mus. фóршлаг

gracious [грэй-шăс] adj. мúлостивый, снисходúтельный; **good — !** [гўд —] interj. бáтюшки!, Бóже мой!

gradation [грă-дэй-шăн] sn. градáция, постéпенность

grade [грэйд] sn. грáдус, стéпень (degree); кáчество, сорт (quality); уклóн (declivity); vt. нивелúровать (level); располагáть по стéпеням (arrange in grades)

gradient [грэй-ді-ăнт] sn. уклóн

gradual [грэ́-джю-ăл] adj. постепéнный

graduate [грǽ-дю-ит] *sm.* имеющий учёную степень; [грǽ-дю-эйт] *vt.i.* кончать университет (*take university degree*); градуировать (*mark out in degrees*)

graft [графт] *sn.* прививка, черенок (*shoot, slit*); *med.* пересаженная живая ткань; *vt.* прививать

grafting [граф-тй] *s.* прививание

grain [грэйн] *sn.* крупинка; жито (*cereal*); зерно (*particle*); гран (*weight*)

grammar [грǽ-мǽр] *sn.* грамматика; **--school** [-скул] *sn.* гимназия

grammarian [гра-мǽ-ри-ǽн] *sm.* грамматик

grammatical [гра-мǽ-тикǽл] *adj.* грамматический

granary [грǽ-нǽ-ри] *sn.* амбар, житница

grand [гранд] *adj.* величественный, грандиозный (*magnificent*); превосходный (*excellent*)

grandad [грǽн-дǽд] *sm. coll.* дедушка

grand-daughter [грǽн-дō-тǽр] *sf.* внучка

grandeur [грǽн-диǽр] *sn.* величие

grandfather [грǽнд-фā-ǽр] *sm.* дед

grandmother [грǽнд-ма-ǽр] *sf.* бабушка

grandson [грǽнд-сан] *sm.* внук

grange [грэйндж] *sn.* мыза, ферма, хутор

granite [грǽ-нит] *sn.* гранит

granny [грǽ-ни] *sf. coll.* бабушка

grant [грант] *sn.* дар, до-

тация; *vt.* даровать, дозволять; уступать (*concede*)

granular [грǽ-ню-лǽр] *adj.* зернистый

granulate [грǽ-ню-лэйт] *vt.i.* зернить

grape [грэйп] *sn.* виноградина; *pl.* виноград

graphic [грǽ-фик] *adj.* графический; наглядный (*descriptive*); образный (*vivid*)

grapple [грапл] *sn. naut.* дрек, крюк; схватка (*conflict*); *vt.i.* схватиться, сцепиться

grasp [грасп] *sn.* зажим (*clutch*); захват (*grip*); овладение (*subject*); *vt.* постигать (*comprehend*); схватывать (*grip*)

grasping [грāс-пий] *adj.* жадный (*avaricious*)

grass [грāс] *sn.* трава (*herb*); мурава (*sward*); пастбище (*pasture land*); **- widow** [- ўй-дōў] соломенная вдова

grasshopper [грāс-хо-пǽр] *s.* кузнечик

grate [грэйт] *sn.* каминная решётка; *vt.* тереть (*rub*); скрипеть (*creak*); раздражать (*irritate*)

grateful [грэйт-фул] *adj.* признательный; благодарный (*thankful*)

grater [грэй-тǽр] *sn.* тёрка

gratification [гра-ти-фи-кэй-шǽн] *sn.* удовольствие; вознаграждение (*recompense*)

gratify [грǽ-ти-фай] *vt.* угождать, удовлетворять; вознаграждать (*recompense*)

grating [грэй-тий] *sn.* решётка; *adj.* резкий, скрипучий (*creaking*)

gratitude [грӕ-ти-тюд] *sn.* благода́рность

gratuitous [грӕ-тю́и-тӕс] *adj.* дарово́й (*free*); доброво́льный (*voluntary*); беспричи́нный (*motiveless*); незаслу́женный (*unmerited*)

gratuity [грӕ-тю́и-ти] *sn.* пода́рок (*gift*); чаевы́е (*tip*)

grave [грэйв] *sn.* моги́ла; *adj.* серьёзный (*serious*); торже́ственный (*dignified*)

grave-digger [грэйв-ди́-гӓр] *sm.* моги́льщик

gravel [грӕ-вӕл] *sn.* гра́вий; *med.* мочевы́е ка́мни; *vt.* посыпа́ть гра́вием

gravestone [грэйв-сто́ун] *sn.* моги́льная плита́, надгро́бный ка́мень

graveyard [грэйв-ярд] *sn.* кла́дбище

gravitation [грӕ-ви-тэ́й-шӕн] *sn.* притяже́ние, тяготе́ние

gravity [грӕ-ви-ти] *sn.* серьёзность (*seriousness*); ве́скость, тя́жесть (*weight*); торже́ственность (*solemnity*); **specific —** [спе-си́-фик —] уде́льный вес

gravy [грэй-ви] *sn.* подли́вка

gray [грэй] *adj.* се́рый (*colour*); седо́й (*hair*)

graze [грэйз] *vt.i.* слегка́ каса́ться (*touch lightly*); натере́ть, содра́ть (*abrade*); пасти́ (*feed*)

grease [грис] *sn.* жир, са́ло (*fat*); сма́зка (*lubricant*); [гриз] *vt.* зама́сливать, сма́зывать

greasy [гри́-зи] *adj.* жи́рный, са́льный; ско́льзкий (*slimy*)

great [грэйт] *adj.* большо́й,

вели́кий; огро́мный (*huge*); знамени́тый (*famous*)

greatcoat [грэйт-ко́ут] *sn.* пальто́, шине́ль

great-grandchild [грэйт-грӕнд-чайлд] *sm.* пра́внук; *sf.* пра́внучка; **—grandfather** [—грӕнд-фӓ-ӓӓр] *sm.* пра́дед; **—grandmother** [—грӕнд-мӓ-ӓӓр] *sf.* пра́бабка

greatly [грэйт-ли] *adv.* о́чень

greatness [грэйт-нис] *sn.* величина́ (*of size*); вели́чие (*grandeur*)

greed [грид] *sn.* а́лчность, жа́дность

Greek [грик] *sm.* грек; *sf.* греча́нка; *adj.* гре́ческий

green [грин] *sn.* зелёный цвет (*colour*); зелёная лужа́йка (*piece of grassy land*); расти́тельность (*vegetation*); *pl.* зе́лень, о́вощи; *adj.* зелёный (*colour*); незре́лый (*unripe*)

greengage [грин-гэйдж] *sn.* ренкло́д

greengrocer [грин-гро́у-сӓр] *sm.* зеленщи́к; фрукто́вщик (*fruiterer*)

greenhouse [грин-ха́ус] *sn.* тепли́ца

greenish [гри́-ниш] *adj.* зеленова́тый

greet [грит] *vt.* кла́няться, приве́тствовать

greeting [гри́-тин] *sn.* покло́н, приве́тствие

grey [грэй] *adj.* се́рый (*of colour*); седо́й (*of hair*); **turn —** [тӧрн —] седе́ть

greyhound [грэй-ха́унд] *s.* борза́я соба́ка

grid [грид] *sn.* решётка; сетка (*radio*)

grief [гриф] *sn.* го́ре, печа́ль; **come to —** [кам тý —] дойти́ до беды́; потерпе́ть неуда́чу (*suffer failure*)

grievance [гри́-вăнс] *sn.* жа́лоба

grieve [грив] *vt.i.* горева́ть, огорча́ть, печа́литься

grievous [гри́-вăс] *adj.* тяжёлый (*oppressive*); мучи́тельный (*painful*); ужа́сный (*heinous*)

grill [грил] *sn.* ра́шпер; *vt.* жа́рить на ра́шпере

grim [грим] *adj.* мра́чный, суро́вый (*stern*); жесто́кий (*stern*)

grimace [гри-мэ́йс] *sn.* грима́са, ужи́мка; *vi.* грима́сничать

grime [грайм] *sn.* вче́вшаяся грязь (*ingrained dirt*)

grin [грин] *sn.* оска́л; *vi.* ска́лить зу́бы (*show teeth*); ухмыля́ться (*smirk*); **— and bear it** [— æнд бэр ит] му́жественно переноси́ть боль

grind [грайнд] *sn.* размалыва́ние (*grinding*); тяжёлая, ску́чная рабо́та (*hard, dull work*); *vt.* моло́ть, толо́чь (*crush*); точи́ть (*sharpen*); шлифова́ть (*smooth*); скрежета́ть (*with teeth*)

grinder [грайн-дăр] *sn.* точи́льщик; *sn.* зубри́ла (*crammer*); **organ —** [о́р-гăн —] *sn.* шарма́нщик

grinding [грайн-дий] *sn.* точе́ние; *adj.* точи́льный; **— machine** [— мă-шии] шлифова́льный стано́к

grindstone [грайнд-сто́ун] *sn.* жёрнов, точи́льный ка́мень

grip [грип] *sn.* сжа́тие; *vt.* сжима́ть, ухва́тывать

gripe [грайп] *sn.* зажима́ние, сжа́тие; *med. pl.* спа́змы, резь; *vt.* притесня́ть (*oppress*); сжима́ть (*grip*)

grist [грист] *sn.* помо́л

gristle [грисл] *sn.* хрящ

grit [грит] *sn.* песчи́нка; *coll.* вы́держка

gritty [гри́-ти] *adj.* песча́ный

groan [гро́ун] *sn.* стон; *vt.i.* стона́ть

groats [гро́утс] *sn. pl.* крупа́

grocer [гро́у-сăр] *sn.* бакале́йщик

groceries [гро́у-сă-риз] *sn. pl.* бакале́йные това́ры

grocery [гро́у-сă-ри] *sn.* бакале́я

groggy [гро́-ги] *adj.* неусто́йчивый; дрожа́щий (*shaky*)

groin [гро́йн] *sn.* пах; *arch.* кресто́вый свод

groom [грум] *sn.* жени́х (*bridegroom*); грум, ко́нюх (*ostler*); *vt.* холи́ть (*curry*)

groove [грув] *sn.* вы́емка, желобо́к, паз, ры́твина (*channel*); привы́чка (*habit*); рути́на (*routine*)

grope [гро́уп] *vi.* ощу́пывать; обы́скивать в потёмках (*search in the dark*)

gross [гро́ус] *sn.* гросс (144); *adj. com.* валово́й, опто́вый; гру́бый (*coarse*); це́льный (*total*); **— weight** [— уэ́йт] вес бру́тто; гу́ртом (*wholesale*)

ground [грайнд] *sn.* земля́, по́чва (*earth*); основа́ние (*foundation, motive*); пол (*surface*); грунт, фон (*in painting*); *pl.* сад при до́ме (*garden attached to house*)

grounding [гра́ун-дий] *sn.* обуче́ние

guide [гайд] *sn.* гид, проводник, руководитель, *m.*; *sn.* путеводитель, *m.*, указатель, *m.*; *vt.* вести, направлять, руководить

guild [гилд] *sn.* гильдия, цех

guildhall [гилд-хол] *sn.* ратуша

guile [гайл] *sn.* коварство, лукавство, обман

guilt [гилт] *sn.* вина, виновность

guinea-pig [ги́-ни-пиг] *s.* морская свинка

guise [гайз] *sn.* обманчивый вид; притворство (*pretence*)

gulf [галф] *sn.* морской залив; бездна, пучина (*abyss*); водоворот (*whirlpool*)

gull [гал] *s.* чайка; *vt.* дурачить (*fool*); обманывать (*deceive*)

gullet [га́-лит] *sn.* глотка (*throat*); пищевод (*food-passage*)

gullible [га́-либл] *adj.* доверчивый

gulp [галп] *sn.* глоток (*mouthful*); *vt.i.* жадно глотать

gum [гам] *sn. anat.* десна; гумми, камедь (*resin*); *vt.* склеивать

gumboil [га́м-бойл] *sn.* флюс

gummy [га́-ми] *adj.* клейкий; опухший, отёкший (*of ankles and legs*)

gun [ган] *sn.* пушка (*cannon*); винтовка, ружьё (*rifle*)

gunboat [га́н-боут] *sn.* канонёрка

guncarriage [ган-кэ-ридж] *sn.* лафет

gunner [га́-нӑр] *sn.* канонир

gunpowder [ган-пау-дӑр] *sn.* порох

gunshot [ган-шот] *sn.* дальность полёта

gunsmith [ган- оружейный ма

gurgle [гӧргл] *vi.* булькать, журчать

gush [гаш] *sn.* внезапный поток; излияние (*effusion*); *vi.* литься потоком, хлынуть

gusset [га́-сит] *sn.* ластовица

gust [гаст] *sn.* порыв

gut [гат] *sn.* кишка; *vt.* потрошить; **gutted** [га́-тид] опустошённый

gutter [га́-тӑр] *sn.* жёлоб, канава, лоток

guttural [га́-тӑ-рӑл] *sn.* гортанный звук; *adj.* горловой, гортанный

guy [гай] *sn.* пугало, чучело

guzzle [газл] *vt.i.* жадно глотать, жадно пить

gymnasium [джим-нё-зиӑм] *sn.* гимнастический зал

gymnastic [джим-нӓс-тик] *adj.* гимнастический; *sn. pl.* гимнастика

gypsum [джип-сӑм] *sn.* гипс

gyrate [джай-рэйт] *vi.* вращаться, кружиться

H

haberdasher [хӓ-бӑр-дӓшӑр] *sm.* торговец галантереей

haberdashery [хӓ-бӑр-дӓ-ши-ри] *sn.* галантерея

habit [хӓ-бит] *sn.* обычай, привычка; **riding -** [райдин́ -] амазонка

habitable [хǽ-би-табл] *adj.* жилой

habitation [хæ-би-тэ́й-шæн] *sn.* жилище, жительство

habitual [хǎ-би́-тю-ǎл] *adj.* обычный, привычный

hack [хæк] *sn.* кирка (*pick*); мотыга (*mattock*); наёмная лошадь (*horse*); *vt.* откалывать, рубить; ссадить (*kick*); кашлять (*cough*)

hackneyed [хǽк-нид] *adj.* банальный, избитый

haddock [хǽ-дǎк] *s.* вахня, пикша

haemorrhage [хǽ-мǎ-ридж] *sn.* кровоизлияние

haft [хафт] *sn.* рукоятка

hag [хæг] *sf.* ведьма, карга, баба-яга (*witch*)

haggard [хǽ-гǎрд] *adj.* измождённый, измученный

hail [хейл] *sn.* град (*pellet*); оклик, приветствие (*greeting*); *interj.* привет!; *vt.* сыпаться градом; окликать (*call*); приветствовать (*greet*)

hailstone [хейл-стоун] *sn.* градина

hair [хэр] *sn.* волос

hairbrush [хэр-браш] *sn.* головная щётка

haircutting [хэр-ка-тиṅ] *sn.* стрижка

hairdresser [хэр-дре-сǎр] *sn.* парикмахер

hairpin [хэр-пин] *sn.* шпилька

hairspring [хэр-сприṅ] *sn.* волосок

hairy [хэ́-ри] *adj.* волосатый, косматый

hale [хейл] *adj.* бодрый, здоровый, крепкий

half [хаф] *sn.* половина; *adj.* половинный; *adv.* наполовину; полу (*in compound words*)

halibut [хǽ-ли-бат] *s.* палтус

hall [хол] *sn.* зал, зала; вестибюль, *m.*, передняя, приёмная (*entrance, vestibule*)

hallmark [хол-марк] *sn.* проба, пробирное клеймо

hallow [хǽ-лоу] *vt.* освящать

halo [хей-лоу] *sn.* ореол; круг (*circle*)

halt [холт] *sn.* остановка, привал; *interj.* стой!; *vt.i.* делать привал; останавливаться

halve [хав] *vt.* делить пополам

ham [хæм] *sn.* ветчина, окорок

hamlet [хǽм-лит] *sn.* посёлок

hammer [хǽ-мǎр] *sn.* молот, молоток; *vt.* вбивать

hammock [хǽ-мǎк] *sn.* гамак, койка

hamper [хǽм-пǎр] *sn.* корзина; *vt.* затруднять (*impede*); препятствовать (*obstruct*)

hand [хæнд] *sn.* рука; стрелка (*of clock*); почерк (*writing*); **at** — [æт —] близко; **by** — [бай —] ручным способом; **out of** — [аут ов —] непокорный; **second** — [сé-кǎнд —] подержанный; *vt.* вручать, передавать

handbill [хæнд-бил] *sn.* афиша, реклама

handbook [хæнд-бук] *sn.* справочник

handcuff [хэ́нд-каф] *sn.* нару́чник

handful [хэ́нд-фул] *sn.* горсть, пригоршня

handicap [хэ́н-ди-кэп] *sn.* гандика́п; поме́ха (*impediment, obstacle*); *vt.* уравнове́шивать си́лы (*in sport*); меша́ть (*hinder*)

handicraft [хэ́н-ди-крафт] *sn.* иску́сство (*skill*); ремесло́ (*trade*)

handkerchief [хэ́нд-ка-чиф] *sn.* носово́й плато́к

handle [хэ́ндл] *sn.* рукоя́тка, ру́чка, черено́к (*of knife*); *vt.* тро́гать (*touch*); держа́ть (*hold*); управля́ть (*manage*)

handle-bar [хэ́ндл-ба́р] *sn.* руль (велосипе́да)

handsome [хэн-са́м] *adj.* краси́вый (*of appearance*); ще́дрый (*generous*)

handwriting [хэ́нд-райтиӊ] *sn.* по́черк

handy [хэ́н-ди] *adj.* ло́вкий (*deft*); удо́бный (*convenient*); сподру́чный (*at hand*)

hang [хэӊ] *vt.i.* ве́шать, подве́шивать; окле́ивать (*decorate*); – **about** [– ӑ-ба́ут] околачиваться

hangar [хэ́н-ар] *sn.* анга́р

hanger [хэ́н-ар] *sn.* ве́шалка, крюк, приве́ска

hangings [хэ́н-иӊз] *sn. pl.* драпиро́вки, портье́ры

hangman [хэ́н-мӑн] *sm.* пала́ч

hank [хэӊк] *sn.* мото́к

hanker [хэ́н-кӑр] *vi.* стра́стно жела́ть

haphazard [хэп-хэ́-зӑрд] *adj.* случа́йный

hapless [хэ́п-лӗс] *adj.* зло-получный, несча́стный

happen [хэ́-пӑн] *vi.* происходи́ть (*come to pass*); случа́ться (*chance, occur*)

happiness [хэ́-пи-нӗс] *sn.* сча́стье

happy [хэ́-пи] *adj.* счастли́вый

harass [хэ́-рӑс] *vt.* беспоко́ить, трево́жить

harbour [ха́р-ба́р] *sn.* га́вань, порт; убе́жище (*shelter*); *vt.i.* приюти́ть; укрыва́ть (*screen*)

harbourage [ха́р-ба́-риджк] *sn.* прию́т

hard [ха́рд] *adj.* жёсткий, твёрдый; тру́дный, тяжёлый (*difficult*)

hard-boiled [ха́рд-бойлд] *adj.* круто́й (*of egg*)

harden [ха́р-дӑн] *vt.i.* зака́ливать; черстве́ть (*become harsh*); де́латься мозоли́стым (*become callous*)

hardly [ха́рд-ли] *adv.* едва́

hardship [ха́рд-шип] *sn.* лише́ние (*deprivation*); нужда́ (*exigence*); тру́дность (*difficulty*)

hardware [ха́рд-уэ́р] *sn.* скобяны́е това́ры

hardy [ха́р-ди] *adj.* отва́жный, сме́лый (*bold*); выно́сливый (*enduring*)

hare [хэр] *s.* за́яц

harelip [хэ́р-лип] *sn.* за́ячья губа́

haricot [хэ́-ри-коу́] *sn.* рагу́ (*of mutton*); – **bean** [– бин] фасо́ль

hark [ха́рк] *interj.* чу! *vi.* слу́шать

harm [ха́рм] *sn.* вред; *vt.* вреди́ть (*damage*); задева́ть (*feelings*); ушиба́ть (*hurt*)

harmful [хáрм-фўл] *adj.* врéдный

harmless [хáрм-ліс] *adj.* безврéдный, невúнный

harmonious [хар-мóў-ні-ăс] *adj.* гармонúчный, стрóйный; дружелюбный (*agreeable*)

harmonize [хáр-мă-найз] *vt.i.* гармонизúровать

harmony [хáр-мă-ні] *sn.* гармóния, созвýчие; соглáсие (*concord*)

harness [хáр-ніс] *sn.* упряжь; *vt.* запрягáть

harp [харп] *sn.* áрфа; *vi.* завестú волынку (*dwell tediously on subject*)

harpoon [хар-пýн] *sn.* гарпýн, острогá

harrow [хă-рóў] *sn.* боронá; *vt.* боронúть

harsh [харш] *adj.* неприя́тный (*unpleasant*); рéзкий (*of sound*); бесчýвственный (*heartless*); жёсткий (*of manner*)

harshness [хáрш-ніс] *sn.* жёсткость, тéрпкость, сýровость

hart [харт] *s.* олéнь

harvest [хáр-віст] *sn.* жáтва, урожáй; *vt.* собирáть урожáй

harvester [хáр-віс-тăр] *sn.* жнец; *sm.* жнéйка, сноповя́зка

hasp [хасп] *sn.* засóв, застёжка

haste [хéйст] *sn.* поспéшность, спех, тороплúвость

hasten [хéй-сăн] *vt.i.* спешúть, тороплúться

hasty [хéй-сті] *adj.* поспéшный, вспыльчúвый (*quick-tempered*)

hat [хæт] *sn.* шля́па; top - [топ -] цилúндр

hatch [хæч] *sn.* люк; *vt.i.* вылупляться, высúживать (*bring forth*); замышля́ть, обдýмывать (*plan, plot*)

hatchet [хæ-чіт] *sn.* топóрик

hate [хéйт] *sn.* нéнависть; *vt.* ненавúдеть

hateful [хéйт-фўл] *adj.* нéнавистный

hatred [хéй-трід] *sn.* нéнависть

hatter [хæ-тăр] *sm.* шля́пник; шля́пный фабрикáнт (*manufacturer*)

haughty [хó-ті] *adj.* надмéнный

haul [хōл] *sn.* волочéние, тя́га; *vt.* тащúть, тяну́ть

haulage [хó-лідж] *sn.* перевóзка, тя́га

haunch [хōнч] *sn.* ля́жка

haunt [хōнт] *sn.* притóн, убéжище; *vt.* преслéдовать (*pursue*)

have [хæв] *vt.* имéть; - to [- ту] быть обя́занным; - on [- он] носúть, быть одéтым

haven [хéй-вăн] *sn.* убéжище

haversack [хæ-вăр-сæк] *sn.* рáнец

havoc [хæ-вăк] *sn.* опустошéние, разгрóм

hawk [хōк] *s.* я́стреб; *vt.* торговáть в разнóс (*carry goods for sale*)

hawker [хó-кăр] *sm.* разнóсчик; ýличный продавéц

hay [хéй] *sn.* сéно

haystack [хéй-стæк] *sn.* стог сéна

hazard [хæ-зáрд] *sn.* опáсность (*danger*); риск, шанс (*risk*); *vt.* рисковáть

hazardous [hǎ-zǎr̃-dǎs] *adj.* опа́сный; риско́ванный

haze [hěiz] *sn.* ды́мка, мгла

hazel [hěi-zǎl] *sn.* лещи́на, оре́шник; оре́х (*nut*); *adj.* ка́рий, светлокори́чневый (*colour*)

hazy [hěi-zi] *adj.* нея́сный, сму́тный

he [hi] *pron.* он

head [hěd] *sn.* голова́; вождь, *m.*, глава́ (*chief*); голо́вка (*of pimple, etc.*); шля́пка (*of nail*); изголо́вье (*of bed*); *adj.* гла́вный, передово́й; *vt.i.* возглавля́ть, озаглавля́ть

headache [hěd-ěik] *sn.* головна́я боль

heading [hě-diñ] *sn.* заго́ловок, на́дпись

headland [hěd-lǎnd] *sn.* мыс

head-light [hěd-lait] *sn.* фар

headlong [hěd-lоñ] *adj.* безуде́ржный, опроме́тчивый; *adv.* опроме́тью

headmaster [hěd-mǎs-tǎr] *sm.* заве́дующий шко́лой

headquarters [hěd-kýǒr̃-tǎr̃z] *sn. pl.* гла́вное управле́ние; *mil.* штаб

headstrong [hěd-strоñ] *adj.* своево́льный, упря́мый

headway [hěd-ýěi] *sn.* продвиже́ние, успе́х

heal [hil] *vt.i.* излечи́вать; зажива́ть (*of wound, etc.*)

healing [hi-liñ] *adj.* целе́бный

health [hělθ] *sn.* здоро́вье; – **resort** [– ri-zǒr̃t] курорт

healthy [hěl-θi] *adj.* здоро́вый

heap [hip] *sn.* во́рох, гру́да,

ку́ча; *coll.* ма́сса; **-s better** [-с бě-тǎr̃] гора́здо лу́чше; *vt.* нава́ливать, нагромож-

hear [hir̃] *vt.i.* выслу́шивать, слы́шать; – –! пра́вильно!

hearer [hi-r̃ǎr̃] *sm.* слу́шатель, *m.*

hearing [hi-riñ] *sn.* слух; слу́шание (*audition*)

hearsay [hir̃-sěi] *sn.* слух

hearse [hǒr̃с] *sn.* похоро́нные дро́ги

heart [hǎr̃t] *sn.* се́рдце; сердцеви́на (*centre, core*); су́щность (*essence, substance*); *pl.* че́рвы (*cards*)

heart-beat [hǎr̃t-bit] *sn.* пульс, пульса́ция

heart-broken [hǎr̃t-brǒǔ-kǎn] *adj.* уби́тый го́рем

heartburn [hǎr̃t-bǒr̃n] *sn.* изжо́га

hearten [hǎr̃-tǎn] *vi.* ободря́ть

hearth [hǎr̃θ] *sn.* дома́шний оча́г

heartily [hǎr̃-ti-li] *adv.* серде́чно

heartless [hǎr̃t-lǐс] *adj.* безжа́лостный, бессерде́чный

hearty [hǎr̃-ti] *adj.* и́скренний, серде́чный (*cordial*)

heat [hit] *sn.* жар, жара́; гнев (*anger*); зае́зд (*in races*); *vt.i.* нагрева́ть, топи́ть

heater [hi-tǎr̃] *sn.* нагрева́тель, *m.*

heath [hiθ] *sn.* степь

heathen [hi-ěǎn] *sm.* язы́чник; *adj.* язы́ческий

heather [hě-ǒǎr̃] *sn.* ве́реск

heating [hi-tiñ] *sn.* нагрева́ние, отопле́ние

heave [хив] *sn.* подъём (*of weight*); вздох (*sigh*); *vt.* поднимать (*lift*); – **a sigh** [– ǎ сай] вздохнуть

heaven [хе́-вǎн] *sn.* небо; *pl.* небеса

heavenly [хе́-вǎн-ли] *adj.* небесный; божественный (*divine*)

heavy [хе́-ви] *adj.* тяжёлый; сильный (*of rain, etc.*); бурный (*of seas*)

Hebrew [хи́-брю] *sm.* еврей; *sn.* древне-еврейский язык (*language*); *adj.* еврейский

hectic [хе́к-тик] *adj.* возбуждённый

hedge [хедж] *sn.* изгородь; ограда (*fence*); *vt.* огораживать

hedgehog [хе́дж-хог] *s.* ёж

heed [хид] *sn.* внимание; *vt.* внимательно следить

heel [хил] *sn.* пятка (*of foot*); каблук (*of shoe*); **down at –** [даун æт –] неряшливый (*of person*); стоптанный (*of shoe*); *vt.* набивать (каблуки); кренить (*list*)

hefty [хе́ф-ти] *adj.* дюжий

heifer [хе́-фǎр] *s.* тёлка

height [хайт] *sn.* высота; возвышенность, вышина (*elevation*); верх (*summit*)

heighten [хай-тǎн] *vt.* повышать; усиливать (*intensify*)

heir [эр] *sm.* наследник; – **apparent** [– ǎ-пе́-рǎнт] законный наследник; – **presumptive** [– при-зǎм-тив] вероятный наследник

heiress [э́-рес] *sf.* наследница

hell [хел] *sn.* ад

hellish [хе́-лиш] *adj.* адский

helm [хелм] *sn.* руль, *m.*

helmet [хе́л-мит] *sn.* каска, шлем

help [хелп] *sn.* помощь

helper [хе́л-пǎр] *sm.* помощник

helpful [хе́лп-фул] *adj.* полезный

helping [хе́л-пин] *sn.* порция

helpless [хе́лп-лес] *adj.* беспомощный

hem [хем] *sn.* рубец; *vt.* подрубать

hemisphere [хе́-ми-сфир] *sn.* полушарие

hemp [хемп] *sn.* конопля, пенька

hemstitch [хе́м-стич] *sn.* ажурная строчка

hen [хен] *sf.* курица

hence [хенс] *adv.* отсюда (*from here*); с этих пор (*from now*); следовательно (*consequently*)

henceforth [хе́нс-фо́рθ] *adv.* впредь, отныне

her [хǎр] *pron.* её, ей

herald [хе́-рǎлд] *sn.* вестник; *vt.* возвещать

herb [хǎрб] *sn.* трава; растение (*plant*)

herbaceous [хǎр-бǎй-шǎс] *adj.* злачный, травянистый

herbage [хǎ́р-бидж] *sn.* зелень, травы

herbalist [хǎ́р-бǎ-лист] *sm.* травовед

herd [хǎрд] *sn.* гурт, стадо

herdsman [хǎ́рдз-мǎн] *sm.* пастух

here [хир] *adv.* здесь, тут; сюда; – **is** [– из] вот! **look** –! [лук –] послушайте!

hereafter [хир-ǎ́ф-тǎр] *sn.* будущее; *adv.* в будущем

hereby [хир-ба́й] *adv.* при сим, таким образом

hereditary [xĭ-rĕ́-dĭ-tă-rĭ] *adj.* наследственный

heredity [xĭ-rĕ́-dĭ-tĭ] *sn.* наследственность

heresy [xĕ́-pă-cĭ] *sn.* ересь

herewith [xĭř-ўĭ̆e] *adv.* при сём

heritage [xĕ́-рĭ-тĭдж] *sn.* наследство

hermit [xĕ́р-мĭт] *sm.* отшельник

hernia [xĕ́р-нĭă] *sn.* грыжа

hero [xĭ-роу́] *sm.* герой

heroic [xĭ-роу́-ĭк] *adj.* геройский

heroine [xĕ́-роу-ĭн] *sf.* героиня

heroism [xĕ́-роу-ĭзм] *sn.* геройзм, доблесть

heron [xĕ́-рăн] *s.* цапля

herring [xĕ́-рĭн] *s.* сельд

herself [xăр-сĕ́лф] *pron.* сама; by – [бай –] одна

hesitate [xĕ́-зĭ-тэйт] *vi.* запинаться (*of actions*); колебаться (*of mind*)

hesitation [xĕ-зĭ-тэ́й-шăн] *sn.* запинка; колебание, нерешительность

hew [xю] *vt.* рубить, тесать

hibernate [xáй-бăр-нэйт] *vi.* зимовать

hiccup [xĭ-кăп] *sn.* икота; *vi.* икать

hidden [xĭ-дăн] *adj.* скрытый

hide [xайд] *sn.* кожа, шкура; *vt.i.* прятать, скрывать; колотить (*flog*)

hideous [xĭ-дĭ-ăс] *adj.* отвратительный, противный, уродливый

hiding [xáй-дĭн] *sn.* побои (*beating*); скрывание (*concealment*); – place [– плэйс] тайник

high [xай] *adj.* высокий; слегка испорченный (*tainted*); дорогой (*of price*); – time [– тайм] пора; – water [– ўŏ-тăр] прилйв

highly [xáй-лĭ] *adv.* óчень, чрезвычайно

Highness [xáй-нĭс] *s.* высочество

highway [xáй-ўэй] *sn.* большая дорога

hike [xайк] *vi. coll.* путешествовать пешком

hilarious [xĭ-лĕ́-рĭ-ăс] *adj.* весёлый

hilarity [xĭ-лắ-рĭ-тĭ] *sn.* весёлость, веселье

hill [xĭл] *sn.* возвышенность (*elevation*); холм (*small mountain*); куча (*heap*)

hillock [xĭ-лăк] *sn.* кочка, пригорок

hilly [xĭ-лĭ] *adj.* холмистый

hilt [xĭлт] *sn.* рукоятка, эфес

him [xĭм] *pron.* егó, емý; о нём (*about him*)

himself [xĭм-сĕ́лф] *pron.* сам, самого себя

hind [xайнд] *adj.* задний

hinder [xĭн-дăр] *vt.* мешать, препятствовать

hindrance [xĭн-дрăнс] *sn.* помéха, препятствие

Hindu [xĭн-дý] *sm.* индýс; *adj.* индýсский

hinge [xĭндж] *sn.* петля, шарнир; *fig.* ось; *vt.i.* привéшивать, прикреплять

hint [xĭнт] *sn.* намёк; *vt.i.* намекать

hip [xĭп] *sn.* бедрó; ягода шипóвника (*of rose*)

hippopotamus [xĭ-пă-пó-тă-мăс] *s.* гиппопотáм

hire [хай-әр] *sn.* наём (*engagement*); прокат (*payment*); **let on** — [лет он —] сдавать внаём; *vt.* нанимать, сдавать напрокат

hireling [хай-әр-лий] *sm.* наёмник, наймит

his [хіз] *pron.* его

hiss [хіс] *sn.* свист, шипение, *vt.i.* свистеть, шипеть; освистывать (*drive off stage, etc.*)

historian [хіс-то́-рі-ән] *sm.* историк

historic [хіс-то́-рік] *adj.* исторический (о значении)

historical [хіс-то́-рі-кәл] *adj.* исторический (о факте)

history [хіс-тә-рі] *sn.* история

histrionic [хіс-трі-о́-нік] *adj.* актёрский, театральный; **-s,** *sn. pl.* театральное искусство, театральность

hit [хіт] *sn.* толчок, удар; удача, успех (*success*); *vt.i.* поражать, ударять

hitch [хіч] *sn.* толчок (*jerk*); задержка (*stoppage*); препятствие (*impediment*); закорючка (*difficulty*); *naut.* петля, узел; *vt.i.* прицеплять (*fasten with hook, etc.*)

hitherto [хі-әр-ту́] *adv.* до сих пор

hive [хайв] *sn.* улей; пчелиный рой (*swarm*); *vt.i.* сажать в улей; роиться

hoar [хор] *sn.* иней; *adj.* седой (*grey*)

hoard [хорд] *sn.* запас, клад; *vt.* запасать, накоплять

hoarding [хор-дий] *sn.* временный забор вокруг стройки; щит для плаката

hoarfrost [хор-фрост] *sn.* иней

hoarse [хорс] *adj.* хриплый

hoax [хоукс] *sn.* мистификация, обман, трюк; шутка (*joke*); *vt.* обманывать; шутить

hob [хоб] *sn.* выступ в камине; гвоздь, крюк (*nail, etc.*); кольшек (*in quoits*)

hobble [хобл] *sn.* прихрамывающая походка, хромота (*gait*); *vi.* ковылять, прихрамывать, хромать

hobby [хо́-бі] *sn.* любимое занятие, увлечение

hobbyhorse [хо́-бі-хорс] *sn.* конь-качалка (*rocking*); лошадка (*child's*)

hobnail [хоб-нэйл] *sn.* сапожный гвоздь, *m.*

hoe [хоу] *sn.* мотыга, полольник; *vt.* мотыжить, разрыхлять

hog [хог] *s.* боров, свинья; *vt.i.* выгибаться, сгибать; подстригать гриву (*cut mane*)

hoist [хойст] *sn.* поднятие (*hoisting*); подъёмник (*elevator, lift*); *vt.* поднимать

hold [хоулд] *sn.* взятие, захват (*grasp*); влияние (*influence*); *naut.* трюм; *vt.* держать (*grasp*); вмещать, содержать (*contain*); владеть (*possess*)

hold-all [хоулд-ол] *sn.* портплед, вещевой мешок

holder [хоул-дәр] *sm.* арендатор, владелец; *n.* оправа (*setting*); ручка (*handle*)

holding [хоул-дий] *sn.* земельное владение; арендованный участок

hole [хо́ул] *sn.* дыра́, отве́рстие; углубле́ние, я́ма (*cavity*); я́мочка (*golf*); *vt.* продыря́вить

holiday [хо́-ли-дэй] *sn.* пра́здник; о́тпуск (*leave*)

hollow [хо́-лоу] *sn.* вы́емка, впа́дина, по́лость; *adj.* впа́лый (*sunken*); глухо́й (*of sound*); пусто́й (*empty*); *vt.* вы́далбливать

holly [хо́-ли] *sn.* остроли́ст, паду́б

holy [хо́у-ли] *adj.* свято́й, свяще́нный

homage [хо́-мидж] *sn.* почте́ние, уваже́ние

home [хо́ум] *sn.* дом, жили́ще; прию́т (*refuge*); ро́дина (*native country*); **at** — [æт—] до́ма; *adj.* дома́шний, родно́й; вну́тренний (*internal, not foreign*); *adv.* домо́й

homeless [хо́ум-лic] *adj.* бездо́мный, беспри́ютный

homely [хо́ум-ли] *adj.* дома́шний, ую́тный; просто́й (*plain*)

homesick [хо́ум-сик] *adj.* тоску́ющий по ро́дине

homespun [хо́ум-спан] *adj.* домотка́нный

homestead [хо́ум-стэд] *sn.* фе́рмерская уса́дьба

homeward [хо́ум-уэ́рд] *adv.* домо́й, к до́му

homicidal [хо-ми-са́й-дэл] *adj.* смертоно́сный, уби́йственный

homicide [хо́-ми-сайд] *sm.* человекоуби́йца; *sn.* человекоуби́йство

homogeneous [хо-мо-джи́-ни́-ис] *adj.* одноро́дный

hone [хоун] *sn.* осело́к, точи́льный ка́мень; *vt.* точи́ть

honest [о́-нист] *adj.* правди́вый, че́стный; ве́рный, прямо́й (*upright*)

honesty [о́-нис-ти] *sn.* че́стность; прямота́

honey [ха́-ни] *sn.* мёд; сла́дость (*sweetness*)

honeycomb [ха́-ни-коум] *sn.* медо́вые со́ты; *tech.* ра́ковина; *vt.* изрешети́ть

honeyed [ха́-нид] *adj.* медо́вый, сла́дкий

honeymoon [ха́-ни-му́н] *sn.* медо́вый ме́сяц

honeysuckle [ха́-ни-сакл] *sn.* жи́молость

honorarium [онā-рэ́-рi-ăм] *sn.* гонора́р

honorary [о́-нă-pă-pi] *adj.* почётный

honour [о́-нăр] *sn.* честь; почёт (*respect*); *pl.* награ́ды, по́чести; **your —!** Ва́ша честь!; *vt.* почита́ть, уважа́ть (*esteem*); удоста́ивать (*grace with*); че́ствовать (*celebrate*)

honourable [о́-нă-рăбл] *adj.* благоро́дный, почте́нный

hood [ху́д] *sn.* капюшо́н, ка́пор; капо́т (*of engine*); ку́зов (*of car*); *vt.* покрыва́ть (капюшо́ном и т.д.)

hoodwink [ху́д-уинк] *vt.* обма́нывать

hoof [ху́ф] *sn.* копы́то

hook [ху́к] *sn.* крюк, крючо́к; серп (*for fishing*); серп (*for reaping*); **by — or by crook** (бай — ор бай крук) во что бы то ни ста́ло; „не мытьём, так ка́таньем"; *vt.* застёгивать, зацепля́ть

hoop [ху́п] *sn.* о́бод, о́бруч (*metal band, child's toy*); кло́ушный ка́шель (*cough*)

hooper [ўў-пăр] *sn.* бондарь, бочăр

hooping-cough [хў-пиĭ-коф] *sn.* коклю́ш

hoot [хўт] *sn.* крик, улюлю́канье; крик совы́ (*of owl*); *vt.i.* крича́ть (*of owl*)

hooter [хў-тăр] *sn.* гудо́к, сире́на

hop [хоп] *sn.* хмель (*plant*); прыжо́к, скачо́к (*spring on one foot*); пры́ганье (*springing*); *vi.* прыга́ть, скака́ть

hope [хо̆уп] *sn.* наде́жда; *vi.* наде́яться, упова́ть

hopeful [хо̆уп-фул] *adj.* наде́ющийся

hopeless [хо̆уп-лĭс] *adj.* безнаде́жный

horde [хо̆рд] *sn.* орда́; ша́йка (*gang*)

horizon [хо-рáй-зăн] *sn.* горизо́нт

horizontal [хо-рĭ-зо́н-тăл] *adj.* горизонта́льный

horn [хо̆рн] *sn.* рог; рожо́к, у́сик (*tentacles, antennae*)

hornet [хо̆р-нĭт] *s.* ше́ршень

hornpipe [хо̆рн-пайп] *sn.* волы́нка; матро́сский та́нец (*dance*)

horrible [хо́-рĭбл] *adj.* проти́вный, стра́шный

horrific [хо-рĭ-фĭк] *adj.* ужаса́ющий

horrify [хо́-рĭ-фай] *vt.* пуга́ть, ужаса́ть, шоки́ровать

horror [хо́-рăр] *sn.* страх, у́жас; отвраще́ние (*intense dislike*)

horse [хо̆рс] *s.* конь, *m.*; ло́шадь; ко́нница (*cavalry*); ко́злы (*trestle*); white -s [уайт -ĭз] бара́шки

horseback [хо̆рс-бăк] *sn.* верхо́м

horse-cloth [хо̆рс-клоθ] *sn.* попо́на

horse-dealer [хо̆рс-ди-лăр] *sn.* бары́шник

horse-fly [хо̆рс-флай] *s.* слепе́нь

horse-flesh [хо̆рс-флеш] *sn.* кони́на

horseman [хо̆рс-мăн] *sn.* вса́дник

horseradish [хо̆рс-рæ-дĭш] *sn.* хрен

horseshoe [хо̆рс-шў] *sn.* подко́ва

horsewhip [хо̆рс-уĭп] *sn.* хлыст; *vt.* хлеста́ть

horticulture [хо̆р-тĭ-кал-чăр] *sn.* садово́дство

hose [хо̆уз] *sn.* ки́пка, шланг; чулки́ (*stockings*); *vt.* полива́ть из шла́нга

hosiery [хо̆у-жă-рĭ] *sn.* чуло́чный това́р

hospitable [хо́с-пĭ-тăбл] *adj.* гостеприи́мный

hospital [хо́с-пĭ-тăл] *sn.* больни́ца, го́спиталь, *m.*

hospitality [хос-пĭ-тá-лĭтĭ] *sn.* гостеприи́мство, раду́шие

host [хо̆уст] *sn.* мно́жество, толпа́ (*multitude*); хозя́ин, тракти́рщик (*landlord of inn*); **- of heaven** [- ов хĕ̆-вăн] небе́сные свети́ла; **Host**, Святы́е Да́ры

hostage [хо́с-тĭдж] *sn.* зало́жник

hostel [хо́с-тăл] *sn.* общежи́тие

hostess [хо̆у-стĭс] *sf.* хозя́йка

hostile [хо̆с-тайл] *adj.* вражде́бный

hostility [хос-тĭ-лĭ-тĭ] *sn.* вражде́бность; *pl.* вое́нные де́йствия

hot [хŏт] *adj.* горя́чий; жа́ркий; о́стрый, пря́ный (*pungent, spicy*)

hotel [хŏў-тéл] *sn.* гости́ница, оте́ль, *m.*

hothouse [хŏт-хáўс] *sn.* тепли́ца

hound [хáўнд] *s.* го́нчая, охо́тничья соба́ка

hour [áў-ăр] *sn.* час; **by the –** [бай ѳі –] по часа́м; **rush –s** [раш –з] часы́-пик

hourly [áў-ăр-ли] *adj.* ежеча́сный

house [хáўс] *sn.* дом; торго́вая фи́рма (*business*); **House of Commons** [– ов кó-мăнз] Пала́та О́бщин; *vt.* приюти́ть

houseboat [хáўс-бóўт] *sn.* ба́ржа для жилья́

housebreaker [хáўс-брéй-кăр] *sm.* взло́мщик

houseful [хáўс-фул] *sn.* по́лный дом

household [хáўс-хóўлд] *sn.* домоча́дцы, семья́; дома́шнее хозя́йство (*domestic establishment*); *adj.* дома́шний, семе́йный

householder [хáўс-хóўл-дăр] *sm.* домохозя́ин, глава́ семьи́

housekeeper [хáўс-ки-пăр] *sm.* эконо́м; *sf.* эконо́мка

housekeeping [хáўс-ки-пій] *sn.* домово́дство

housemaid [хáўс-мéйд] *sf.* го́рничная

housewarming [хáўс-ўӧр-мій] *sn.* пра́зднование новосе́лья

housewife [хáўс-ўайф] *sf.* дома́шняя хозя́йка

housework [хáўс-ўӧрк] *sn.* дома́шняя рабо́та

housing [хáў-зій] *sn.* жи́лищное строи́тельство

hovel [хó-вăл] *sn.* лачу́га, хиба́рка, шала́ш; наве́с (*shed*)

hover [хó-вăр] *vi.* пари́ть (*of birds*); нависа́ть (*threaten*); порха́ть (*of butterfly*)

how [хáў] *adv.* как, каки́м о́бразом; **– far?** [– фăр] доку́да? **– much?** [– мач] ско́лько

however [хаў-ĕ-вăр] *adv.* одна́ко, тем не ме́нее; как бы ни, ско́лько бы ни

howl [хáўл] *sn.* вой, завыва́ние, крик, стон; *vt.i.* выть, завыва́ть, крича́ть, стона́ть

howler [хáў-лăр] *sm.* пла́кальщик; *coll. sn.* грубе́йшая оши́бка

hub [хаб] *sn.* колёсная ступи́ца; вту́лка (*bush*)

hubbub [хá-баб] *sn.* гам, гул, шум

hubby [хá-бі] *sm. coll.* муженёк

huddle [хадл] *sn.* беспоря́док, сумато́ха (*confusion*); гру́да (*heap*); *vi.* съёжи-ваться, толпи́ться

hue [хю] *sn.* отте́нок (*tint*); цвет (*colour*); **– and cry** [– ĕнд край] *sn.* пого́ня (*chase, pursuit*)

huff [хаф] *sn.* вспы́шка гне́ва, припа́док раздраже́ния; *vt.i.* задира́ть, обижа́ться, раздража́ть; фу́кнуть (*at draughts*)

hug [хаг] *sn.* объя́тие, сжима́ние; *vt.* обня́ть, сжима́ть

huge [хюдж] *adj.* грома́дный, огро́мный

hull [хал] *sn.* скорлупа́, шелуха́ (*covering, shell*); ко́рпус (*frame of ship*); *vt.* лущи́ть, шелуши́ть (*remove shell, etc.*)

hum [хам] *sn.* гуде́ние, жужжа́ние; *vt.i.* жужжа́ть, мурлы́кать

human [хю́-мэн] *adj.* людско́й, челове́ческий

humane [хю-ме́йн] *adj.* гума́нный, челове́чный

humanitarian [хю-мӑ-ли-тӗ́-ри-ӑн] *sm.* гумани́ст, филантро́п; *adj.* гуманита́рный, человеколюби́вый

humanity [хю-мӑ́-ни-ти] *sn.* гума́нность, челове́чество

humble [хамбл] *adj.* поко́рный, скро́мный, смире́нный; *vt.* смиря́ть (*make humble*); унижа́ть (*abase*)

humbug [ха́м-баг] *sm.* обма́нщик; *sn.* вздор, обма́н, притво́рство

humdrum [ха́м-драм] *adj.* однообра́зный, ску́чный

humid [хю́-мид] *adj.* вла́жный, сыро́й

humidity [хю-ми́-ди-ти] *sn.* вла́жность, сы́рость

humiliate [хю-ми́-ли-эйт] *vt.* оскорбля́ть, унижа́ть

humiliation [хю-ми-ли-э́й-шӑн] *sn.* униже́ние

humility [хю-ми́-ли-ти] *sn.* поко́рность, смире́ние

hummock [ха́-мӑк] *sn.* хо́лмик

humorous [хю́-мӑ-рӑс] *adj.* заба́вный, юмористи́ческий

humour [хю́-мӑр] *sn.* настрое́ние (*state of mind*); скло́нность (*inclination*); *vt.* балова́ть, угожда́ть

hump [хамп] *sn.* горб

humpback [ха́мп-бӕк] *sm.* горбу́н

hunch [ханч] *sn.* горб; ломо́ть, кусо́к (*slice*); *coll.* подозре́ние (*surmise*); предчу́вствие (*premonition*)

hunchback [ханч-бӕк] *sm.* горбу́н

hundred [ха́н-дрӗд] *sn.* со́тня; *num.* сто

hundredweight [ха́н-дрӗд-уэ́йт] *sn.* це́нтнер

Hungarian [хан-гӗ́-ри-ӑн] *sm.* венге́рец; *adj.* венге́рский

hunger [ха́н-гӑр] *sn.* го́лод; *vt.i.* голода́ть; жа́ждать (*crave*)

hungry [ха́н-гри] *adj.* голо́дный

hunt [хант] *sn.* охо́та; по́иски (*quest*); *vt.i.* гнать, трави́ть; охо́титься

hunter [ха́н-тӑр] *sm.* охо́тник; гу́нтер (*horse*)

hunting [ха́н-тий] *sn.* охо́та; *adj.* охо́тничий

huntsman [ха́нтс-мӑн] *sm.* е́герь

hurl [хӗрл] *sn.* си́льный бросо́к; *vt.* броса́ть, швыря́ть

hurricane [ха́-ри-кӑн] *sn.* бу́ря, урага́н

hurry [ха́-ри] *sn.* спе́шка, торопли́вость; *vt.i.* спеши́ть, торопи́ться

hurt [хӗрт] *sn.* вред, повре́жде́ние (*harm*); ра́на (*wound*); *vt.i.* повреди́ть, ра́нить; задева́ть, обижа́ть (*offend*)

hurtful [хӗ́рт-фӱл] *adj.* вре́дный

husband [ха́з-бӑнд] *sm.* муж

husbandman [хáз-бӑнд-мӑн] *sn.* земледéлец

husbandry [хáз-бӑнд-рi] *sn.* полевóдство, сельскóе хозя́йство

hush [хаш] *sn.* молчáние, тишинá; *vt.i.* замолчáть, утихнуть

husk [хаск] *sn.* кóжица, скорлупá, шелухá; *vt.* лущить, снимáть шелуху́

husky [хáс-ки] *sn.* эскимóс; лáйка (dog); *adj.* сиплый, хриплый (hoarse); сухóй (dry)

hustle [хасл] *sn.* толкотня́; *vt.i.* протáлкиваться, тесниться, толкáть

hut [хат] *sn.* хибáрка, хижина; *mil.* барáк

hutch [хач] *sn.* клéтка, конурá (rabbit's); лачу́га (hut)

hydraulic [хай-дрó-лик] *adj.* гидравлический; **-s** [-с] *sn. pl.* гидрáвлика

hydrogen [хáй-дрӑ-джӑн] *sn.* водорóд

hydrophobia [хай-дро-фóу-бiӑ] *sn.* водобоя́знь; бéшенство (rabies)

hyena [хай-и́-нӑ] *s.* гиéна

hygiene [хáй-джи́н] *sn.* гигиéна

hygienic [хай-джи-ник] *adj.* гигиенический

hymn [хим] *sn.* гимн, церкóвное песнопéние

hymnal [хим-нӑл] *sn.* книга гимнов

hyphen [хáй-фӑн] *sn.* дефис, соединительная чёрточка

hyphenate [хáй-фӑ-нэйт] *vt.* соединя́ть чéрез дефис

hypnotic [хип-нó-тик] *adj.* наркотическое срéдство;

загипнотизи́рованный (человéк, person); *adj.* гипнотический, снотвóрный

hypnotism [хип-нӑ-тизм] *sn.* гипнотизм

hypnotize [хип-нӑ-тайз] *vt.* гипнотизировать

hypocrisy [хи-пó-кри-сi] *sn.* лицемéрие, притвóрность, ханжество

hypocrite [хи-пӑ-крит] *sm.* лицемéр, ханжá

hypocritical [хи-пӑ-кри-ти-кӑл] *adj.* лицемéрный

hysterical [хи-стé-ри-кӑл] *adj.* истерический

hysterics [хис-тé-рикс] *sn. pl.* истéрика

I

I [ай] *pron.* я

ice [айс] *sn.* лёд; морóженое (ice-cream); сáхарная глазу́рь (slabs of sugar); *vt.* заморáживать

ice-breaker [áйс-брэй-кӑр] *sn.* ледокóл

ice-cream [айс-кри́м] *sn.* сливочное морóженое

iced [айсд] *adj.* заморóженный

icicle [áй-сикл] *sn.* сосу́лька

icy [áй-сi] *adj.* ледяной; холóдный (cold)

idea [ай-ди́-ӑ] *sn.* идéя; понятие (conception); мысль (thought)

ideal [ай-ди́-ӑл] *sn.* идеáл; *adj.* идеáльный, совершéнный

identical [ай-дéн-ти-кӑл] *adj.* одинáковый, тóждественный, тот же сáмый

identification [ай-ден-ти-фи-кэ́й-шан] *sn.* отождествле́ние

identify [аи-де́н-ти-фай] *vt.* опознава́ть, отождествля́ть

identity [аи-де́н-ти-ти] *sn.* иденти́чность, тожде́ственность

Ideology [ай-ди-о́-лă-джи] *sn.* идеоло́гия, мировоззре́ние

idiom [и-ди-ăм] *sn.* го́вор, и́диом, наре́чие

idiomatic [и-ди-ă-мǽ-тик] *adj.* идиомати́ческий, ме́стный, разгово́рный

idiot [и-ди-ăт] *sm.* идио́т

idiotic [и-ди-о́-тик] *adj.* идио́тский

idle [айдл] *adj.* лени́вый, пра́здный (*lazy*), незаня́тый (*unoccupied*); *vi.* безде́льничать

idleness [айдл-ни́с] *sn.* лень, пра́здность

idler [ай-длắр] *sm.* безде́льник, ленця́й

idol [ай-дăл] *sn.* и́дол, куми́р

idolatry [ай-до́-лă-три] *sn.* обожа́ние, поклоне́ние

idolize [ай-дă-лайз] *vt.* боготвори́ть, обожа́ть, почита́ть

if [иф] *conj.* е́сли; е́сли бы (*conditional*)

ignite [иг-на́йт] *vt.i.* зажига́ть, раскаля́ться

ignition [иг-ни́-шăн] *sn.* воспламене́ние; прока́ливание

ignoble [иг-но́убл] *adj.* неблагоро́дный, по́длый

ignominy [и́г-нă-ми-ни] *sn.* бесче́стие, позо́р по́длость (*meanness*)

ignorance [и́г-нă-рăнс] *sn.* неве́дение, неве́жество

ignorant [и́г-нă-рăнт] *adj.* неве́жественный

ignore [иг-но́р] *vt.* игнори́ровать; отклоня́ть (*reject*)

ill [ил] *sn.* зло; *pl.* несча́стья; *adj.* больно́й, нездоро́вый; – **fame** [– фэйм] дурна́я сла́ва; **fall** [фōл] – заболе́ть; *adv.* пло́хо

illegal [и-ли́-гăл] *adj.* незако́нный

illegality [и-ли-гǽ-ли-ти] *sn.* незако́нность

illegible [и-ле́-джибл] *adj.* неразбо́рчивый, неудобочита́емый

illegitimate [и-ли-джи́-ти-мăт] *adj.* незаконнорожде́нный

illicit [и-ли́-сит] *adj.* запреще́нный, недозво́ленный

illiteracy [и-ли-тă-дă-си] *sn.* негра́мотность

illiterate [и-ли-тă-рăт] *sm.* неу́ч; *adj.* безгра́мотный, необразо́ванный

ill-natured [ил-нэ́й-чăрд] *adj.* зло́бный

illness [и́л-нис] *sn.* боле́знь

ill-tempered [ил-те́м-пăрд] *adj.* раздражи́тельный

illuminate [и-лю́-ми-нэйт] *vt.* освеща́ть, просвеща́ть; разъясня́ть (*explain*); иллюмини́ровать (*decorate with lights*)

illumination [и-лю-ми-нэ́й-шăн] *sn.* иллюмина́ция, освеще́ние

illusion [и-лю́-жăн] *sn.* иллю́зия, обма́н чувств

illusive [и-лю́-сив] *adj.* обма́нчивый, при́зрачный

illustrate [и-лу́-стрэйт] *vt.* иллюстри́ровать; поясня́ть (*make clear*)

ILLUSTRATION 554 IMMUNE

illustration [i-лӯ-стрэ́й-шăн] *sn.* иллюстра́ция, рису́нок; приме́р (*example*)

illustrious [i-лăс-трі-ăс] *adj.* знамени́тый, изве́стный

image [i-мідж] *sn.* изображе́ние, о́браз; подо́бие (*semblance*)

imaginable [i-мǽ-джі-нǎбл] *adj.* вообрази́мый

imaginary [i-мǽ-джі-нǎрі] *adj.* вообража́емый, мни́мый

imagination [i-мǽ-джі-нэ́й-шǎн] *sn.* воображе́ние, фанта́зия

imagine [i-мǽ-джін] *vt.* вообража́ть, представля́ть себе́; полага́ть (*suppose*); предполага́ть (*suppose*)

imbecile [ім-бі-сил] *sm.* глупе́ц, слабоу́мный

imbibe [ім-ба́йб] *vt.* впи́тывать, вса́сывать (*ideas*); вдыха́ть (*inhale*); поглоща́ть (*absorb*)

imbue [ім-бю́] *vt.* напи́тывать, насыща́ть; вдохнова́ть (*inspire*)

imitate [і-мі-тэ́йт] *vt.* имити́ровать, подража́ть

imitation [і-мі-тэ́й-шǎн] *sn.* имити́рование, подража́ние; имита́ция, подде́лка (*counterfeit*)

immaculate [і-мǽ-кю-лĭт] *adj.* незапя́тнанный, чи́стый; безупре́чный (*irreproachable*)

immaterial [і-мǎ-ти́-рі-ăл] *adj.* бестеле́сный, невеще́ственный (*incorporeal*); нева́жный, несуще́ственный (*unimportant*); **it is - to me** [іт із - тӯ ми] мне э́то безразли́чно

immature [і-мǎ-тю́р] *adj.* незре́лый

immeasurable [і-ме́-жǎ-рǎбл] *adj.* неизмери́мый

immediate [і-мӣ-ді-ǎт] *adj.* неме́дленный; непосре́дственный (*direct*)

immemorial [і-мі-мо́-рі-ăл] *adj.* незапа́мятный

immense [і-ме́нс] *adj.* безме́рный, необъя́тный, огро́мный

immerse [і-мǎ́рс] *vt.* погружа́ть

immersion [і-мǎ́р-шăн] *sn.* погруже́ние

immigrate [і́-мі-грэйт] *vt.і.* иммигри́ровать

immigration [і-мі-гро́й-шăн] *sn.* иммигра́ция

imminent [і-мі-нǎнт] *adj.* грозя́щий, немину́емый

immobile [і-мо́у-байл] *adj.* неподви́жный

immobilize [і-мо́у-бі-лайз] *vt.* де́лать неподви́жным

immodest [і-мо́-діст] *adj.* нескро́мный

immoral [і-мо́-рǎл] *adj.* безнра́вственный

immorality [і-мо-рǽ-лі-ті] *sn.* безнра́вственность

immortal [і-мо́р-тǎл] *adj.* бессме́ртный

immortality [і-мор-тǽ-лі-ті] *sn.* бессме́ртие, ве́чность

immortalize [і-мо́р-тǎлайз] *vt.* увекове́чить

immovable [і-му́-вǎбл] *adj.* недви́жимый, неподви́жный; *sn. pl.* недви́жимое иму́щество

immune [і-мю́н] *adj. med.* имму́нный; невосприи́мчивый

immunity [i-мю́-ни-ти] *sn.
med.* иммуните́т; льго́та

imp [имп] *sm.* чертёнок
(*little devil*); шалу́н (*mischievous child*)

impact [им-пэкт] *sn.* столкнове́ние (*collision*); толчо́к;
уда́р (*striking*)

impair [им-пэ́р] *vt.* по́ртить, ухудша́ть; ослабля́ть
(*weaken*)

impart [им-па́рт] *vt.* наделя́ть (*give share*); сообща́ть
(*inform*)

impartial [им-па́р-шăл] *adj.*
беспристра́стный

impassable [им-па́-сăбл]
adj. непроходи́мый

impasse [им-пас] *sn.* глухо́й
прохо́д, тупи́к; затрудне́ние (*fix, difficulty*)

impatience [им-пэ́й-шăнс]
sn. нетерпе́ние

impatient [им-пэ́й-шăнт]
adj. нетерпели́вый

impeach [им-пи́ч] *vt.* обвиня́ть, порица́ть

impeccable [им-пе́-кăбл]
adj. безупре́чный (*faultless*);
непогреши́мый (*not liable to
sin*)

impede [им-пи́д] *vt.* заде́рживать (*retard*); препя́тствовать (*hinder*)

impediment [им-пе́-димăнт] *sn.* заде́ржка, препя́тствие; *pl.* обо́з, поме́ха

impending [им-пе́н-дий] *adj.*
грозя́щий, немину́емый

impenetrable [им-пе́-нитрăбл] *adj.* непроница́емый

impenitent [им-пе́-ни-тăнт]
adj. нераска́вшийся

imperative [им-пе́-рă-тив]
adj. насто́ятельный (*ur-*
gent); необходи́мый (*necessary*); повели́тельный (*commanding*); *gram.* – **mood**
[– мӯд] повели́тельное наклоне́ние

imperceptible [им-пăрсе́п-тибл] *adj.* незаме́тный;
кро́хотный (*tiny*)

imperfect [им-пăр-фи́кт]
adj. недоста́точный, несоверше́нный; *gram.* проше́дшее

imperfection [им-пăр-фе́кшăн] *sn.* неполнота́, несоверше́нство

imperial [им-пи́-ри-ăл] *adj.*
импе́рский; вели́чественный (*title*)

imperil [им-пе́-рил] *vt.*
подверга́ть опа́сности

imperishable [им-пе́-ришăбл] *adv.* непотря́щийся,
нетле́нный

impermeable [им-пăр-ми́ăбл] *adj.* непроница́емый

impersonal [им-пăр-сăнăл] *adj.* безли́чный

impersonate [им-пăр-сăнэ́йт] *vt.* олицетворя́ть

impertinence [им-пăр-тина́нс] *sn.* де́рзость, на́глость

impertinent [им-пăр-тина́нт] *adj.* де́рзкий, на́глый;
неуме́стный (*irrelevant*)

imperturbable [им-пăртăр́-бăбл] *adj.* невозмути́мый

impervious [им-пăр-ви-ăс]
adj. непроница́емый, непроходи́мый

impetuous [им-пе́-тю-ăс]
adj. порыви́стый, стреми́тельный

impetus [им-пă-тăс] *sn.*
и́мпульс, побужде́ние, си́ла движе́ния

impiety [ім-пáй-ă-ті] *sn.* безбóжність (*ungodliness*); невéріе (*disbelief*); непочтúтельність (*irreverece*)

implacable [ім-плé-кăбл] *adj.* непримирúмый, неумолúмый

implement [ím-плі-мăнт] *sn.* орýдіе (*tool*); домáшняя утвáрь (*utensl*); *vt.* исполнять

implicate [ím-плі-кэйт] *vt.* впýтывать, втягивать

implication [ім-плі-кэйшăн] *sn.* вовлечéніе, подразумевáемое

implicit [ім-плí-сіт] *adj.* безуслóвный; подразумевáемый

implore [ім-плóр] *vt.* умолять, упрáшивать

imply [ім-плáй] *vt.* предполагáть, подразумевáть

import [ім-пóрт] *sn.* вáжность (*importance*); значéние, смысл (*meaning*); вывод (*implication*); *com.* ввоз, úмпорт; [ім-пóрт] *vt.* ввозúть, импортúровать

importance [ім-пóр-тăнс] *sn.* вáжность, значúтельность

important [ім-пóр-тăнт] *adj.* вáжный, значúтельный

impose [ім-пóуз] *vt.* налагáть, облагáть; *typ.* заключáть; – **upon** [– ă-пóн] вынуждáть, обмáнывать

imposing [ім-пóу-зін] *adj.* внушúтельный, импозáнтный

imposition [ім-по-зíшăн] *sn.* налóг, наложéніе; обмáн, плутовствó (*piece of deception*); *typ.* замыкáние

impossibility [ім-по-сі-бí-лі-ті] *sn.* невероятность, невозмóжность

impossible [ім-пó-сібл] *adj.* невероятный, невозмóжный, невыносúмый

impostor [ім-пó-стăр] *sm.* самозвáнец

impotence [ím-поу-тăнс] *sn.* бессúліе

impotent [ím-поу-тăнт] *adj.* бессúльный

impoverish [ім-пó-вă-ріш] *vt.* доводúть до бéдности; истощáть (*of soil*)

impregnable [ім-прéг-нăбл] *adj.* непристýпный

impregnate [ім-прéг-ніт] *adj.* оплодотворённый, пропúтанный (*permeated*); [ім-прéг-нэйт] *vt.* оплодоворять; пропúтывать

impress [ім-прéс] *sn.* отпечáток, óттиск (*mark impressed*); впечатлéніе (*effect on mind*); [ім-прéс] *vt.* испóльзовать (*make use of, in argument etc.*); производúть впечатлéніе (*create impression*); усúливать (*enforce*); внушáть, убеждáть (*influence*); отпечáтывать (*imprint*); штемпелевáть (*stamp*)

impression [ім-прéшăн] *sn.* впечатлéніе (*sensation*); отпечáток, óттиск (*imprint*); отпечáтывание (*print*)

impressionable [ім-прéшăн-ăбл] *adj.* восприúмчивый, впечатлúтельный

impressive [ім-прé-сів] *adj.* выразúтельный, разúтельный, трогáтельный

imprint [ім-прінт] *sn.* отпечáток (*impression*); штамп (*stamp*); выходныя свéдения (*publishers' or printers'*)

imprison [ім-прí-зăн] *vt.* заключа́ть, заса́живать

imprisonment [ім-прí-зăн-мăнт] *sn.* заключе́ние

improbable [ім-про́-бăбл] *adj.* невероя́тный, неправдоподо́бный

impromptu [ім-пром-тю] *sn.* экспро́мт; *mus.* импровиза́ция; *adj., adv.* экспро́мптом

improper [ім-про́-пăр] *adj.* непра́вильный (*inacurate*); неприли́чный (*indecent*)

impropriety [ім-про-пра́й-ă-ті] *sn.* неприго́дность (*unfitness*); неприли́чие (*indecency*)

improve [ім-пру́в] *vt.i.* улучша́ться, усоверше́нствовать

improvement [ім-пру́в-мăнт] *sn.* улучше́ние

improver [ім-пру́-вăр] *sm.* стажёр

improvize [ім-про-вайз] *vt.* импровизи́ровать

imprudent [ім-прю́-дăнт] *adj.* опроме́тчивый

impudence [ім-пю-дăнс] *sn.* бессты́дство, на́глость

impudent [ім-пю-дăнт] *adj.* бессты́дный, на́глый

impulse [ім-палс] *sn.* и́мпульс, побужде́ние

impulsive [ім-пал-сів] *adj.* импульси́вный, побужда́ющий

impunity [ім-пю́-ні-ті] *sn.* безнака́занность

impure [ім-пю́р] *adj.* нечи́стый (*dirty*); подде́льный (*adulterated*)

impurity [ім-пю́-рі-ті] *sn.* нечистота́; подде́лка, при́месь (*adulteration*)

in [ін] *prep.* в, во; *adv.* внутри́, внутрь; **come** —! [кам —] зайди́те! **to come** — [тў кам —] войти́; *prefix* (*отрица́тельная приста́вка*) без-, бес-, не-, и т.п.

inability [ін-ă-бí-лі-ті] *sn.* неспосо́бность

inaccessible [ін-ăк-се́-сĭбл] *adj.* недосту́пный, непристу́пный

inaccuracy [ін-ắ-кю-ră-сі] *sn.* неиспра́вность, нето́чность

inaction [ін-ăк-шăн] *sn.* безде́йствие, ине́ртность

inactive [ін-ăк-тів] *adj.* безде́ятельный, ине́ртный

inactivity [ін-ăк-ті-ві-ті] *sn.* безде́ятельность, пра́здность

inadequacy [ін-ắ-ді-кўă-сі] *sn.* недоста́точность, несоотве́тствие, несоразме́рность

inadequate [ін-ắ-ді-кўіт] *adj.* недоста́точный, несоотве́тственный

inadmissible [ін-ăд-мí-сĭбл] *adj.* недопусти́мый, неприе́млемый

inadvertent [ін-ăд-вắр-тăнт] *adj.* небре́жный, невнима́тельный

inane [і-не́йн] *adj.* бессмы́сленный

inanimate [і-нắ-ні-міт] *adj.* безжи́зненный (*lifeless*); неодушевлённый (*spiritless*)

inapplicable [ін-ă-плí-кăбл] *adj.* непримен́имый

inappropriate [ін-ă-про́-прі-іт] *adj.* неподходя́щий, несоотве́тственный

inapt [ін-ăпт] *adj.* неиску́сный (*unskilful*); неподходя́щий (*unfit*)

inaptitude [ин-а́п-ти-тюд] sn. неспособность

inarticulate [ин-а́р-ти́-кю-лёт] adj. невнятный

inasmuch [ин-эз-ма́ч] adv. поскольку

inattentive [ин-а-тён-тив] adj. невнимательный

inaudible [ин-о́-дибл] adj. неслышный

inaugural [ин-о́-гю-рал] adj. вступительный

inaugurate [ин-о́-гю-рэйт] vt. торжественно открывать; начинать (begin)

inauguration [ин-о-гю-рэ́й-шан] sn. открытие; введение (initiation)

inborn [ин-бо́рн] adj. врождённый, природный

incalculable [ин-кэ́л-кю-лабл] adj. неисчислимый, несметный; неуверенный (uncertain)

incandescent [ин-кэн-дэ́-сант] adj. белокалильный, раскалённый

incapable [ин-кэ́й-пабл] adj. неспособный

incapacitate [ин-ка-пэ́-си-тэйт] vt. сделать непригодным

incendiarism [ин-сэн-диа́-ризм] sn. поджигательство

incendiary [ин-сэ́н-диа́-ри] adj. зажигательный, поджигающий; fig. воспламеняющий (inflammatory)

incense [и́н-сэнс] sn. ладан, фимиам; vt. кадить, курить фимиам; [ин-сэ́нс] гневить, раздражать, сердить (exasperate)

incentive [ин-сэ́н-тив] sn. побуждение; adj. побудительный

inception [ин-сэ́п-шан] sn. начало

incessant [ин-сэ́-сант] adj. непрерывный, постоянный

inch [инч] sn. дюйм; **by -es** [бай и́нчэз] мало-по-малу

incident [ин-си́-дант] sn. нечаянность, случайность; происшествие (event); эпизод

incidental [ин-си-дэ́н-тал] adj. побочный, случайный; сопутствующий (attendant)

incinerate [ин-си́-нä-рэйт] vt. испепелять, сжигать

incinerator [ин-си́-нä-рэй-тäр] sn. сжигательная печь

incision [ин-си́-жан] sn. надрез

incite [ин-са́йт] vt. побуждать, подстрекать

inclement [ин-клэ́-мант] adj. суровый

inclination [ин-кли-нэ́й-шан] sn. наклон, отклонение (slant); расположение, склонность (propensity)

incline [ин-кла́йн] sn. наклон, скат; [ин-кла́йн] vt.i. наклонять, склоняться; располагать (dispose)

inclined [ин-кла́йнд] adj.

include [ин-клю́д] vt. включать, заключать

inclusion [ин-клю́-жан] sn. включение

inclusive [ин-клю́-сив] adj. включающий, содержащий

incoherent [ин-коу́-хи́рäнт] adj. несвязный, непоследовательный

income [ин-ка́м] sn. доход; **– tax** [– тэкс] подоходный налог

incomparable [ін-ко́м-па-рəбл] *adj.* бесподо́бный, несравне́нный

incompatibility [ін-кəм-пæ-тə́-бі-лі-ті] *sn.* несовмести́мость, несообра́зность

incompatible [ін-кəм-пǽ-тібл] *adj.* несовмести́мый

incompetence [ін-ко́м-пі-тінс] *sn.* некомпете́нтность

incompetent [ін-ко́м-пі-тəнт] *adj.* несве́дущий, неспосо́бный

incomplete [ін-кəм-плі́т] *adj.* непо́лный; незако́нченный (*not finished*)

incomprehensible [ін-ком-прі-хе́н-сібл] *adj.* непоня́тный

inconceivable [ін-кəн-сі́-вəбл] *adj.* непостижи́мый

inconsiderate [ін-кəн-сі́-дə-рəт] *adj.* нечу́ткий, поспе́шный

inconsistent [ін-кəн-сі́с-тəнт] *adj.* несообра́зный, неусто́йчивый

inconspicuous [ін-кəн-спи́-кю-əс] *adj.* незаме́тный, непримéтный

inconvenience [ін-кəн-ві́-ні-əнс] *sn.* затрудне́ние; неудо́бство; *vt.* утружда́ть

inconvenient [ін-кəн-ві́-ні-əнт] *adj.* затрудни́тельный, нело́вкий, неудо́бный

incorporate [ін-ко́р-пə-рəйт] *vt.i.* соединя́ть, объединя́ть; [ін-ко́р-пə-ріт] *adj.* присоединённый

incorrigible [ін-ко́-рі-джібл] *adj.* неисправи́мый

increase [ін-крис] *sn.* возраста́ние, увеличе́ние; [ін-кри́с] *vt.i.* возраста́ть, увели́чивать; повыша́ться (*rise*)

incredible [ін-кре́-дібл] *adj.* невероя́тный

incredulity [ін-кре-дю́-лі-ті] *sn.* недове́рчивость

increment [ін-крі-мəнт] *sn.* прираще́ние; при́быль (*profit*)

incriminate [ін-крі-мі-нəйт] *vt.* обвиня́ть (*accuse*); инкримини́ровать (*involve in accusation*)

incubate [ін-кю-бэйт] *vt.i.* выси́живать

incubator [ін-кю-бэй-тəр] *n.* инкуба́тор

incur [ін-ко́р] *vt.* навлека́ть; — **debts** [— дэтс] задолжа́ться; — **losses** [— ло́сіз] терпе́ть убы́тки

incurable [ін-кю́-рəбл] *adj.* неизлечи́мый

incursion [ін-ко́р-шəн] *sn.* вторже́ние, набе́г, наше́ствие

indebted [ін-де́-тід] *adj.* находя́щийся в долгу́ (*owing*); обя́занный (*obliged*)

indebtedness [ін-де́-тід-ніс] *n.* задо́лженность

indecent [ін-ді-сəнт] *adj.* неприли́чный; нескро́мный (*immodest*)

indecision [ін-ді-сі́-жəн] *sn.* нереши́тельность

indecisive [ін-ді-сáй-сів] *adj.* нереши́тельный; колебля́ющийся (*wavering*)

indeclinable [ін-ді-кла́й-нəбл] *adj. gram.* несклоня́емый

indeed [ін-ді́д] *adv.* в са́мом де́ле, действи́тельно; коне́чно (*of course*); —? неуже́ли?

indefinite [ін-дé-фі-ніт] *adj.* неопределённый; неограниченный (*unlimited*)

indelible [ін-дé-лібл] *adj.* несмываемый, нестираемый

indemnify [ін-дéм-ні-фай] *vt.* вознаграждать, вознаграждать; застраховать (*secure*)

indemnity [ін-дéм-ні-ті] *sn.* вознаграждение, компенсация

indent [ін-дéнт] *vt.i.* вырезывать, зазубривать (*cut out, make notches*); *typ.* делать абзац; заказывать товары (*order goods*)

independence [ін-ді-пéн-дянс] *sn.* независимость, самостоятельность

independent [ін-ді-пéн-дянт] *adj.* независимый

indescribable [ін-діс-крáй-бабл] *adj.* неописуемый

indestructible [ін-діс-трáк-тібл] *adj.* неразрушимый

indeterminate [ін-ді-тéр-мі-ніт] *adj.* неопределённый; нерешённый

index [ін-дéкс] *sn.* индекс; алфавитный указатель (*alphabetical list*); указательный палец (*finger*); стрелка (*hand, pointer*)

Indian [ін-діян] *sm.* индеец; *sf.* индианка; *adj.* индейский

indicate [ін-ді-кéйт] *vt.* обозначать, указывать

indication [ін-ді-кéй-шян] *sn.* обозначение, указание

indicative [ін-дí-ка-тів] *adj.* указывающий; *gram.* изъявительный

indicator [ін-ді-кéй-тăр] *sn.* индикатор, указатель

indict [ін-дáйт] *vt.* обвинять

indictment [ін-дáйт-мăнт] *sn.* обвинительный акт

indifference [ін-дí-фă-рăнс] *sn.* равнодушие; маловажность (*unimportance*); безразличие (*apathy*)

indifferent [ін-дí-фă-рăнт] *adj.* равнодушный; незначительный (*trifling*); посредственный (*mediocre*)

indigenous [ін-дí-джă-нăс] *adj.* местный, туземный; природный

indigent [ін-ді-джăнт] *adj.* нуждающийся

indigestible [ін-ді-джéс-тібл] *adj.* неудобоваримый

indigestion [ін-ді-джéс-чăн] *sn.* несварение, расстройство желудка

indignant [ін-дíг-нăнт] *adj.* негодующий

indignation [ін-ді-гнéй-шăн] *sn.* возмущение, негодование

indirect [ін-дай-рéкт] *adj.* непрямой, окольный; уклончивый (*evasive*)

indiscreet [ін-діс-крíт] *adj.* необдуманный, нескромный

indiscretion [ін-діс-крé-шăн] *sn.* бестактность, неосторожность

indiscriminate [ін-діс-крí-мі-ніт] *adj.* неразбирающийся, неразборчивый

indispensable [ін-діс-пéн-сăбл] *adj.* необходимый, непременный, обязательный

indisposition [ін-діс-пă-зí-шăн] *sn.* недомогание, нездоровье; нерасположение (*disinclination*)

indistinct [ін-діс-тíнкт] *adj.* неясный, неотчётливый

individual [ін-ді-ві́-дю-ăл] *sm., f.* индивидуум; *coll.* ли́чность, челове́к; *adj.* индивидуа́льный, ли́чный; отде́льный, ча́стный (*single*)

indolence [ін-до-лăнс] *sn.* беспе́чность, ле́ность

indolent [ін-до-лăнт] *adj.* лени́вый, пра́здный

indomitable [ін-до́-мі-тăбл] *adj.* неукроти́мый

indoor [ін-до́р] *adj.* вну́тренний, ко́мнатный; **-s** [ін-до́рз] *adv.* внутри́ до́ма, в помеще́нии

induce [ін-дю́с] *vt.* заставля́ть, угова́ривать

inducement [ін-дю́с-мăнт] *sn.* побужде́ние, причи́на

indulge [ін-да́лдж] *vt.i.* ба́ловать, потво́рствовать, предава́ться

indulgence [ін-да́л-джăнс] *sn.* послабле́ние, потака́ние; снисходи́тельность (*condescension*); *eccl.* индульге́нция

industrial [ін-да́с-трі-ăл] *adj.* промы́шленный

industrious [ін-да́с-трі-ăс] *adj.* приле́жный, трудолюби́вый

industry [ін-дас-трі] *sn.* инду́стрия, промы́шленность; трудолю́бие (*diligence*)

inedible [ін-е́-дібл] *adj.* несъедо́бный

ineffable [ін-е́-фăбл] *adj.* невырази́мый, неизрече́нный

ineffective [ін-і-фе́к-тів] *adj.* недействи́тельный

inefficient [ін-і-фі́-шăнт] *adj.* него́дный, неспосо́бный

ineligible [ін-е́-лі-джібл] *adj.* неизбира́емый; неподходя́щий (*unsuitable*)

inept [і-не́пт] *adj.* абсу́рдный, (*silly*); неуме́стный (*out of place*)

ineptitude [і-не́п-ті-тюд] *sn.* абсу́рдность; неуме́стность

inequality [ін-і-кю́-лі-ті] *sn.* нера́венство

inert [і-на́рт] *adj.* вя́лый, ине́ртный

inestimable [ін-е́с-ті-мăбл] *adj.* неоцени́мый

inevitable [ін-е́-ві-тăбл] *adj.* неизбе́жный

inexhaustible [ін-егз-о́с-тібл] *adj.* неисчерпа́емый

inexplicable [ін-екс-плі́-кăбл] *adj.* необъясни́мый

infallible [ін-фắ-лібл] *adj.* безоши́бочный (*unerring*); непогреши́мый (*impeccable*)

infamous [ін-фă-мăс] *adj.* позо́рный, посты́дный

infamy [ін-фă-мі] *sn.* бесче́стие, позо́р

infancy [ін-фăн-сі] *sn.* младе́нчество

infant [ін-фăнт] *sn.* младе́нец, ребёнок

infantile [ін-фăн-тайл] *adj.* де́тский, младе́нческий

infantry [ін-фăн-трі] *sn.* пехо́та; **-man** [-мăн] *sm.* пехоти́нец

infatuate [ін-фă-тю-эйт] *vt.* увлека́ть

infatuation [ін-фă-тю-э́й-шăн] *sn.* пристра́стие, увлече́ние

infect [ін-фе́кт] *vt.* зараза́ть

infection [ін-фе́к-шăн] *sn.* заража́ние, зара́за, инфе́кция

infectious [ін-фе́к-шăс] *adj.* зара́зный, инфекцио́нный

infer [ін-фёр] vt. выводи́ть (deduce); заключа́ть (conclude)

inferior [ін-фи́-рі-ăр] adj. ни́зший (of position); плохо́й (of quality)

inferiority [ін-фе-ріо́-рі-ті] sn. ни́зшая сте́пень (low rank); ху́дшее ка́чество (poor quality); – **complex** [– ко́м-плекс] компле́кс неполноце́нности

infernal [ін-фёр-нăл] adj. а́дский

inferno [ін-фёр-ноу] sn. ад

infest [ін-фе́ст] vt. кише́ть; опустоша́ть (ravage)

infidel [ін-фі-дăл] sm., adj. неве́рный, неве́рующий

infiltrate [ін-філ-трэ́йт] vt.i. проника́ть, проса́чиваться

infinite [ін-фі-ніт] adj. безграни́чный (boundless); бесконе́чный (endless); несме́тный (great many); gram. неопределённый

infinitesimal [ін-фі-ні-те́-сі-мăл] adj. мельча́йший

infinitive [ін-фі-ні-тів] sn. gram. инфинити́в (неопределённая фо́рма глаго́ла); adj. неопределённый

infinity [ін-фі́-ні-ті] sn. бесконе́чность

infirm [ін-фёрм] adj. дря́хлый, немощный

infirmity [ін-фёр-мі-ті] sn. дря́хлость, не́мощность; сла́бость (weakness)

infirmary [ін-фёр-мă-рі] sn. больни́ца, лазаре́т

inflame [ін-флэ́йм] vt.i. воспламеня́ть (set ablaze); зажига́ть (catch fire)

inflammable [ін-флэ́-мăбл] adj. воспламеня́ющийся, сгора́емый

inflammation [ін-флă-мэ́й-шăн] sn. воспале́ние

inflate [ін-флэ́йт] vt. надува́ть (distend); разбуха́ть (puff up); вздува́ть (prices)

inflation [ін-флэ́й-шăн] sn. надува́ние, наполне́ние; инфля́ция

inflect [ін-флёкт] vt. гнуть (bend); склоня́ть (curve); gram. склоня́ть, спряга́ть

inflexion [ін-флёк-шăн] sn. сгиба́ние; склоне́ние; gram. фле́ксия; mus. модуля́ция го́лоса

inflict [ін-флікт] vt. налага́ть (punishment); наноси́ть (blow); причиня́ть (cause pain)

influence [ін-флу́-ăнс] sn. влия́ние; vt. влия́ть

influential [ін-флу-е́н-шăл] adj. влия́тельный

influenza [ін-флу-е́н-ză] sn. грипп, инфлуэ́нза

influx [ін-флакс] sn. прито́к, прили́в (of river); на́плыв (of people, etc.)

inform [ін-фо́рм] vt. осведомля́ть, сообща́ть

informal [ін-фо́р-мăл] adj. неформа́льный; непринуждённый (unconstrained)

informant [ін-фо́р-мăнт] sm. осведоми́тель

information [ін-фăр-мэ́й-шăн] sn. информа́ция, сообще́ние (notification); изве́стия, но́вости (news)

informative [ін-фо́р-мă-тів] adj. информацио́нный; поучи́тельный (instructive)

informer [ін-фо́р-мăр] sm. доно́счик

infrequent [ін-фри-кўа́нт] adj. ре́дкий

infringe [ін-фри́ндж] vt. наруша́ть

infringement [ін-фри́нджмянт] sn. наруше́ние

infuriate [ін-фю́-ри-эйт] vt. разъяри́ть

infuse [ін-фю́з] vt. влива́ть (pour into); вселя́ть, внуша́ть (instil); наста́ивать (steep)

ingenious [ін-джи́-ни-ас] adj. изобрета́тельный, остроу́мный

ingenuity [ін-джи-ню́-і-ті] sn. остроу́мие

ingot [ін-га́т] sn. брусо́к (of metal); сли́ток (gold, silver)

ingratiate [ін-гре́й-ши-эйт] vt. заи́скивать

ingratitude [ін-гре́-ті-тюд] sn. неблагода́рность

ingredient [ін-гри́-ди-янт] sn. ингредие́нт, составна́я часть

inhabit [ін-хэ́-біт] vt. жить, обита́ть

inhabitant [ін-хэ́-бі-тянт] sm. жи́тель

inhale [ін-хэ́йл] vt. вдыха́ть

inherent [ін-хи́-рянт] adj. прису́щий

inherit [ін-хэ́-ріт] vt. насле́довать

inheritance [ін-хэ́-рі-тянс] sn. насле́дственность; насле́дие, насле́дство

inhuman [ін-хю́-мян] adj. бесчелове́чный; жесто́кий (brutal)

inimitable [ін-і-мі-тäбл] adj. неподража́емый

iniquity [ін-і-кўі-ті] sn. беззако́ние; бессо́вестность; несправедли́вость

initial [і-ні́-шäл] sn. инициа́л; adj. исхо́дный, первонача́льный; vt. поста́вить инициа́лы

initiate [і-ні́-ши-эйт] vt. ввести́, ознако́мить, принима́ть (introduce)

initiation [і-ні-ши-э́й-шän] sn. посвяще́ние (в та́йну)

initiative [і-ні-ши-ä-тів] sn. инициати́ва

inject [ін-дже́кт] vt. впры́скивать

injection [ін-дже́к-шän] sn. впры́скивание, инъе́кция

injunction [ін-дка́нк-шän] sn. прика́з (order); суде́бное запреще́ние (judicial restraint)

injure [ін-джа́р] vt. вреди́ть, по́ртить (impair); ра́нить, уши́бить (hurt)

injurious [ін-джу́-рі-äс] adj. вре́дный

injury [ін-джä-рі] sn. вред, повреждéние (damage); оби́да, оскорбле́ние (insult)

injustice [ін-джäс-тіс] sn. несправедли́вость

ink [і́нк] sn. черни́ла; vt. ма́зать черни́лами

ink-bottle [і́нк-ботл] sn. черни́льница

ink-stand [і́нк-стэнд] sn. пи́сьменный прибо́р

inland [ін-лэнд] sn. вну́тренность страны́; adv. внутри́; [ін-ла́нд] adj. вну́тренний

inlet [ін-лет] sn. бу́хточка, зали́в

inmate [ін-мэйт] sm. жиле́ц

inmost [ін-мо́уст] adj. глубоча́йший

inn [ін] sn. постоя́лый двор, тракти́р

innate [i-нэ́йт] *adj.* врождённый

inner [i-нăр] *adj.* вну́тренний

innermost [i-нăр-мо́уст] *adj.* сокрове́нный

innkeeper [iн-ки-пăр] *sm.* тракти́рщик

innocence [í-но-сăнс] *sn.* неви́нность

innocent [í-но-сăнт] *adj.* безвре́дный (*harmless*); безгре́шный (*sinless*); неви́нный (*not guilty*)

innovation [i-но-вэ́й-шăн] *sn.* нововведе́ние

innumerable [i-нō-мă-рăбл] *adj.* бесчи́сленный

inoculate [i-нó-кю-лэ́йт] *vt.* привива́ть

inoculation [i-но-кю-лэ́й-шăн] *sn.* приви́вка

inoffensive [i-но-фе́н-сив] *adj.* безоби́дный

inopportune [iн-ó-пăр-тю́н] *adj.* несвоевре́менный, неуме́стный

inordinate [iн-о́р-ди-нит] *adj.* чрезме́рный

inquest [iн-кўэст] *sn.* дозна́ние, сле́дствие, суде́бный допро́с

inquire [iн-кўа́й-ăр] *vt.i.* спра́шивать, справля́ться

inquiry [iн-кўа́й-ри] *sn.* вопро́с (*question*); спра́вка, рассле́дование (*investigation*); **make inquiries** [мэйк -з] осведомля́ться

inquisitive [iн-кўí-зи-тив] *adj.* любопы́тный, пытли́вый (*prying*)

inroad [iн-ро́уд] *sn.* набе́г, наше́ствие; вторже́ние (*encroachment*)

insane [iн-сэ́йн] *adj.* безу́мный

insanity [iн-сǽ-ни-ти] *sn.* безу́мие, умопомеша́тельство

insatiable [iн-сэ́й-ши-ăбл] *adj.* ненасы́тный

inscribe [iн-скра́йб] *vt.* надпи́сывать

inscription [iн-скри́п-шăн] *sn.* на́дпись

insect [í́н-сект] *sn.* насеко́мое

insecure [iн-си-кю́р] *adj.* небезопа́сный

insecurity [iн-си-кю́-ри-ти] *sn.* небезопа́сность

insert [iн-сőрт] *vt.* вставля́ть; помеща́ть (*article, advert*)

insertion [iн-сőр-шăн] *sn.* включе́ние, вста́вка; отде́лка, проши́вка (*in material*)

inset [iн-сет] *sn.* вкла́дка, вкле́йка

inside [iн-са́йд] *sn.* вну́тренняя сторона́, вну́тренность; изна́нка (*reverse*) [iн-сайд] *adj.* вну́тренний; — **out** [—ăут] навы́ворот, наизна́нку; *adv.* внутри́

insidious [iн-сí-ди-ăс] *adj.* кова́рный, преда́тельский

insight [í́н-сайт] *sn.* проникнове́ние, проница́тельность; понима́ние (*understanding*)

insignificant [iн-сиг-ни́-фи-кăнт] *adj.* нева́жный, незначи́тельный, незначи́тельный

insinuate [iн-сí-ню-эйт] *vt.* инсинуи́ровать, намека́ть

insinuation [iн-сi-ню-э́й-шăн] *sn.* вкра́дчивость, инсину́ация

insist [iн-сí́ст] *vi.* наста́ивать; насто́йчиво тре́бовать (*demand persistently*)

insolent [ín-că-лăнт] *adj.*
дéрзкий; нáглый; обúдный
(*offensive*)

insoluble [ін-сó-любл] *adj.*
нерастворúмый

insolvent [ін-сóл-вăнт] *sm.*
банкрóт, дóлжник; *adj.* несостоя́тельный

insomnia [ін-сóм-ниă] *sn.*
бессóнница

inspect [ін-спéкт] *vt.* осмáтривать, рассмáтривать; наблюдáть (*survey*); надзирáть (*oversee*)

inspection [ін-спéк-шăн] *sn.*
инспéкция, осмóтр

inspector [ін-спéк-тăр] *sm.*
инспéктор, контролёр; наблюдáтель

inspiration [ін-спі-рéй-шăн] *sn.* вдохновéние

inspire [ін-спáй-ăр] *vt.* внушáть

instability [ін-стă-бí-лі-ті] *sn.* неустóйчивость

install [ін-стóл] *vt.* водворúть, поместúть

installation [ін-сто-лéй-шăн] *sn.* водворéние, провóдка, устрóйство; устанóвка (*mounting*)

instalment [ін-стóл-мăнт] *sn.* очереднóй взнос (*successive entry*); часть (книги) (*part of book*); рассрóчка (*of payment*)

instance [ін-стáнс] *sn.* примéр; for — [фор —] напримéр; отдéльный слýчай (*particular case*); *leg.* инстáнция

instant [ін-стáнт] *sn.* мгновéние, момéнт; *adj.* немéдленный (*immediate*); текýщий (*current*)

instantaneous [ін-стăн-тóй-

ні-ăс] *adj.* мгновéнный

instantly [ін-стáнт-лі] *adv.*
немéдленно, сейчáс

instead [ін-стéд] *adv.* взамéн, вмéсто

instep [ін-стéп] *sn.* плюснá, подъём

instigate [ín-сті-гéйт] *vt.*
подстрекáть

instigation [ін-сті-гéй-шăн] *sn.* подстрекáтельство

instil [ін-стíл] *vt.* вливáть по кáпле (*by drops*); постепéнно внушáть (*ideas, etc., gradually*)

instinct [ін-стíнкт] *sn.* инстúнкт; побуждéние (*impulse*)

institute [ін-сті-тю́т] *sn.*
институ́т, учреждéние; *vt.*
оснóвывать, учреждáть; назначáть (*appoint*)

institution [ін-сті-тю́-шăн] *sn.* заведéние

instruct [ін-стрáкт] *vt.*
просвещáть, учúть (*teach*); сообщáть свéдения (*give information*)

instruction [ін-стрáк-шăн] *sn.* образовáние (*education*); инстрýкция, указáние (*direction*); предписáние (*order*)

instructive [ін-стрáк-тів] *adj.* поучúтельный

instructor [ін-стрáк-тăр] *sm.*
инстрýктор, руководúтель, учúтель

instrument [ін-стру́-мăнт] *sn.* орýдие (*implement*); *mus.*
инструмéнт; *leg.* юридúческий докумéнт

instrumental [ін-стру́-мéн-тăл] *adj. gram.* творúтельный; употребля́емый как срéдство (*serving*); *mus.*
инструментáльный

insubordination [ін-сă-бор-ді-нĕй-шăн] *sn.* неповиновéние, неподчинéние, непокóрность

insular [ін-сю-лăр] *adj.* островнóй; ýзкий (*of outlook*)

insulate [ін-сю-лэйт] *vt.* образовáть óстров; изолúровать (*isolate*)

insulation [ін-сю-лĕй-шăн] *sn.* изоляция, обособлéние

insulator [ін-сю-лэй-тăр] *sn.* изолятор, непровóдник

insult [ін-салт] *sn.* обúда, оскорблéние, поругáние; [ін-сáлт] *vt.* оскорбля́ть

insuperable [ін-сю-пă-рăбл] *adj.* непреодолúмый

insurance [ін-шý-рăнс] *sn.* страховáние

insure [ін-шýр] *vt.* страховáть

insurgent [ін-сĕр-джăнт] *sn.* повстáнец; *adj.* востáвший, мятéжный

insurrection [ін-сă-рĕк-шăн] *sn.* восстáние

intact [ін-тĕкт] *adj.* неповреждённый, нетрóнутый, цéлый

intake [ін-тэйк] *sn.* впуск

intangible [ін-тĕн-джібл] *adj.* неосязáемый; непостижúмый (*incomprehensible*)

integral [ін-ті-грăл] *sn.* интегрáл; *adj.* пóлный, цéльный

integrity [ін-тĕ-грі-ті] *sn.* правотá, чéстность (*honesty*); неприкосновéнность, цéльность (*entirety*)

intellect [ін-ті-лĕкт] *sn.* рассýдок, ум

intellectual [ін-ті-лĕк-тюăл] *sm.* интеллигéнт; *adj.* мыслящий, ýмственный

intelligence [ін-тé-лі-джăнс] *sn.* понятливость, рáзум, ум; извéстия, свéдения (*news, information*)

intelligent [ін-тé-лі-джăнт] *adj.* разýмный, смышлёный

intelligible [ін-тé-лі-джібл] *adj.* вразумúтельный

intemperance [ін-тĕм-пăрăнс] *sn.* невоздéржанность, неумéренность; необýзданность (*unrestraint*)

intend [ін-тéнд] *vt.* намеревáться, предполагáть

intense [ін-тéнс] *adj.* напряжённый (*tense*); сúльный (*strong, vigorous*), пылкий (*ardent*)

intent [ін-тéнт] *sn.* намéreние, цель; *adj.* намеревáющийся, склóнный

intentional [ін-тéн-шăнăл] *adj.* намéренный, нарóчитый, умышленный

inter [ін-тăр] *vt.* погребáть

intercede [ін-тăр-сúд] *vi.* ходáтайствовать

intercept [ін-тăр-сéпт] *vt.* перехвáтывать; схвáтывать (*seize*); прерывáть (*cut off*)

interception [ін-тăр-сéпшăн] *sn.* перехвáтывание; пресечéние (*interruption*)

intercession [ін-тăр-сé-шăн] *sn.* застýпничество

interchange [ін-тăрчĕйндж] *sn.* обмéн, смéна; череговáние (*alternation*); *vt.* обмéнивать, переменя́ть; череговáть

intercommunication [інтăр-ко-мю-ні-кĕй-шăн] *sn.* сношéние

intercourse [ін-тăр-кóрс] *sn.* общéние, сношéние

interdependent [ін-тăр-ді-пéн-дăнт] *adj.* взаимозависимый

interdict [ín-тăр-дікт] *sn.* запрещéние; *vt.* воспрещáть

interest [ín-трíст] *sn.* интерéс (*concern*); корысть (*gain*, *profit*); процéнты (*money*); *vt.* интересовáть; **to be -ed** [ту би -ід] интересовáться

interesting [ín-трíс-тіñ] *adj.* интерéсный

interfere [ін-тăр-фíр] *vi.* вмéшиваться; стáлкиваться (*clash*)

interference [ін-тăр-фíрăнс] *sn.* вмешáтельство; препя́тствие (*obstacle*); столкновéние (*impact*)

interim [ín-тă-рíм] *sn.* промежýток врéмени; *adj.* врéменный, промежýточный

interior [ін-тú-рі-ăр] *sn.* внýтренность, внýтренняя часть; *adj.* внýтренний

interject [ін-тăр-джéкт] *vt.* вставля́ть замечáние

interjection [ін-тăр-джéкшăн] *sn.* восклицáние (*exclamation*); *gram.* междомéтие

interleave [ін-тăр-лíв] *vt.* проклáдывать бумáгу

interlock [ін-тăр-лóк] *vt.* сцепля́ть

interlocution [ін-тăр-локíō-шăн] *sn.* бесéда, диалóг

interlude [ín-тăр-люд] *sn. theat.* интермéдия; *mus.* интерлю́дия; антрáкт, промежýток (*interval*)

intermediary [ін-тăр-мі-діá-ρі] *sn.* посрéдник; *adj.* посрéднический

intermediate [ін-тăр-мí-

діăт] *adj.* переходнóй, промежýточный

interment [ін-тăр-мăнт] *sn.* погребéние

intermission [ін-тăр-мíшăн] *sn.* останóвка, пáуза, перерыв

intermittent [ін-тăр-мí-тăнт] *adj.* перемежáющийся

intern [ін-тŏ́рн] *vt.* интернировáть

internal [ін-тŏ́р-нăл] *adj.* внýтренний

international [ін-тăр-нǽшăн-ăл] *adj.* интернациональный, междунарóдный

internee [ін-тăр-нí] *sm.* интернированный

internment [ін-тŏ́рнмăнт] *sn.* интернировáние

interpolate [ін-тŏ́р-полéйт] *vt.* дéлать встáвки, интерполировáть

interpret [ін-тŏ́р-пріт] *vt.* толковáть, ýстно переводить

interpretation [ін-тăр-прітéй-шăн] *sn.* интерпретáция, толковáние

interpreter [ін-тŏ́р-прітăр] *sm.* толковáтель, ýстный перевóдчик

interrogate [ін-тé-ро-гéйт] *vt.* опрáшивать

interrogation [ін-тé-рогéй-шăн] *sn.* вопрóс, допрóс; **- mark** [- мáрк] вопросительный знак

interrogative [ін-те-рó-гăтів] *adj.* вопросительный

interrupt [ін-тă-рáпт] *vt.* прерывáть; преграждáть

interruption [ін-тă-рáпшăн] *sn.* перерыв

intersect [ін-тăр-сéкт] *vt.i.* перекрéщивать, пересекáть

intersperse [ін-тăр-спéрс] *vt.* рассыпáть (*scatter*); разнообрáзить (*diversify*)

interval [ін-тăр-вăл] *sn.* пáуза, промежýток; *mus.* интервáл

intervene [ін-тăр-вíн] *vi.* вмéшиваться, вступáть, посрéдничать

intervention [ін-тăр-вéн-шăн] *sn.* вмешáтельство; интервéнция (*mediation*)

interview [ін-тăр-вю] *sn.* встрéча, свидáние (*meeting*); интервью (*between journalist and others*); *vt.* имéть бесéду, интервьюировать

intestate [ін-тéс-тіт] *sm.* умéрший без завещáния

intestinal [ін-тéс-ті-нăл] *adj.* кишéчный

intestine [ін-тéс-тін] *sn.* кишкá; *adj.* внýтренний, междуусóбный

intimacy [ін-ті-мă-сі] *sn.* блúзость, интúмность

intimate [ін-ті-міт] *sm.* блúзкий друг; *adj.* блúзкий, интúмный; [ін-ті-мэйт] *vt.* намекáть, подразумевáть, укáзывать (*hint, imply, state*); стáвить в извéстность (*make known*)

intimation [ін-ті-мэй-шăн] *sn.* намёк (*hint*); указáние (*statement*)

intimidate [ін-тí-мі-дэйт] *vt.* запýгивать, пристращáть, пугáть

intimidation [ін-ті-мі-дэ́й-шăн] *sn.* запýгивание, стращáние

into [ін-тý, ін-тă] *prep.* в, во; из; на; с

intolerable [ін-тó-лă-рăбл] *adj.* невыносúмый, нестерпúмый

intolerance [ін-тó-лă-рăнс] *sn.* нетерпúмость

intolerant [ін-тó-лă-рăнт] *adj.* нетерпúмый

intonation [ін-тоў-нэ́й-шăн] *sn.* интонáция; модуляция; акцéнт

intoxicant [ін-тó-ксі-кăнт] *sn.* опьяняющий напúток; *adj.* опьяняющий

intoxicate [ін-тó-ксі-кэйт] *vt.* опьянять, хмелúть; возбуждáть (*excite*)

intoxication [ін-то-ксі-кэ́й-шăн] *sn.* опьянéние; *fig.* упоéние

intransitive [ін-трáн-зі-тів] *adj. gram.* непереходный

intrepid [ін-трé-під] *adj.* бесстрáшный, неустрашúмый

intricacy [ін-трі-кă-сі] *sn.* затруднúтельность, слóжность

intricate [ін-трі-кіт] *adj.* запýтанный

intrigue [ін-трíг] *sn.* интрúга; *pl.* кóзни, прóиски

intrinsic [ін-трін-сік] *adj.* присýщий (*inherent*); сущéственный (*essential*); — **value** [– вá-лю] úстинная цéнность

introduce [ін-трă-дю́с] *vt.* вводúть, выдвигáть; представлять (*present*)

introduction [ін-трă-дáк-шăн] *sn.* внесéние, представлéние (*presentation*); введéние, предислóвие (*preface*)

introductory [ін-трă-дáк-тă-рі] *adj.* вступúтельный, предварúтельный

introspection [ін-трǎ-спéк-шǎн] *sn.* самонаблюдéние

intrude [ін-трю́д] *vi.* вторгáться (*into*); навя́зываться (*upon*)

intrusion [ін-трю́-жǎн] *sn.* вторжéние; geol. внедрéние

intuition [ін-тю-í-шǎн] *sn.* интуи́ция, проницáтельность

inundate [í-нан-дэйт] *vt.* затопля́ть, наводня́ть

inundation [і-нан-дэ́й-шǎн] *sn.* наводнéние

inure [і-ню́р] *vt.* приучáть

invade [ін-вэ́йд] *vt.* вторгáться; набрáсываться (*assail*); посягáть (*encroach*)

invalid [ін-вá-лід] *sn.* больнóй, инвали́д; *adj.* нетрудоспосóбный; *vt.i.* признавáть негóдным к слýжбе (*prove unfit for service*); [ін-вǎ-лíд] *adj.* неосновáтельный

invaluable [ін-вǎ́-лю-ǎбл] *adj.* неоцени́мый

invariable [ін-вǎ́-рі-ǎбл] *adj.* неизмéнный

invasion [ін-вэ́й-жǎн] *sn.* вторжéние, набéг; захвáт (*encroachment*)

invent [ін-вéнт] *vt.* изобретáть; fig. выдýмывать

invention [ін-вéн-шǎн] *sn.* изобретáтельность, fig. вы́думка

inventor [ін-вéн-тǎр] *sm.* изобретáтель

inventory [ін-вǎн-трі] *sn.* инвентáрь, *m.*, óпись имýщества

inverse [ін-вǎ́рс] *adj.* обрáтный

inversion [ін-вǎ́р-шǎн] *sn.*

инвéрсия, перевёрнутость; gram. перестанóвка

invert [ін-вǎ́рт] *vt.* извращáть, перевёртывать

invest [ін-вéст] *vt.* вклáдывать, помещáть (капитáл); облекáть (*with power, rank, etc.*); облагáть (*lay siege to*)

investigate [ін-вéс-ті-гэйт] *vt.* разузнавáть, расслéдовать

investigation [ін-вес-ті-гǎ́й-шǎн] *sn.* исслéдование

investigator [ін-вéс-ті-гэй-тǎр] *sm.* испытáтель, исслéдователь

investment [ін-вéст-мǎнт] *sn.* вклад, вложéние; капиталовложéние (*capital*)

investor [ін-вéс-тǎр] *sm.* вклáдчик

inveterate [ін-вé-тǎ-ріт] *adj.* закоренéлый, застарéлый, заядлый

invidious [ін-ві-ді-ǎс] *adj.* возмути́тельный, оскорби́тельный

invigorate [ін-ві-гǎ-рэйт] *vt.* бодри́ть, возбуждáть живость

invigorating [ін-ві-гǎ-рэ́й-тін] *adj.* бодря́щий, укрепля́ющий

invincible [ін-вíн-сібл] *adj.* непобеди́мый

invisible [ін-ві́-зібл] *adj.* неви́димый

invitation [ін-ві-тǎ́й-шǎн] *sn.* приглашéние

invite [ін-вáйт] *vt.* звать, приглашáть, проси́ть; вызывáть (*solicit*)

invocation [ін-воǔ-кǎ́й-шǎн] *sn.* при́зыв

invoice [ін-вóйс] *sn.* наклáдная, фактýра

invoke [ін-во́ук] *vt.* заклина́ть, призыва́ть

involuntary [ін-во́-лăн-тă-рі] *adj.* нево́льный

involve [ін-во́лв] *vt.* вовлека́ть, впу́тывать; усложня́ть (*complicate*)

invulnerable [ін-ва́л-нă-рăбл] *adj.* неуязви́мый

inward [ін-ўа́рд] *adj.* вну́тренний; у́мственный (*mental*); духо́вный (*spiritual*); **-s** [з] *adv.* вну́тренно, внутрь

iodine [а́й-ă-дайн] *sn.* ио́д

irate [ай-ре́йт] *adj.* серди́тый

Irish [а́й-ріш] *adj.* ирла́ндский

Irishman [а́й-ріш-мăн] *sm.* ирла́ндец

irksome [фрк-сăм] *adj.* утоми́тельный (*tiresome*); доку́чливый (*tedious*)

iron [а́й-ăн] *sn.* желе́зо; утю́г (*implement*); *pl.* канда́лы, у́зы; **cast** - [ка́ст -] чугу́н; *adj.* желе́зный; *vt.* утю́жить; **- out** - а́ут] *fig.* ула́живать, регули́ровать

ironfoundry [а́й-ăн-фа́ун-дрі] *sn.* чугунолите́йный заво́д

ironical [ай-ро́-ні-кăл] *adj.* ирони́ческий, несмешли́вый

ironmonger [а́й-ăн-ма́н-гăр] *sm.* торго́вец желе́зными изде́лиями

ironmongery [а́й-ăн-ма́н-гă-рі] *sn.* ме́лкий желе́зный това́р

irony [а́й-рă-ні] *sn.* иро́ния

irrational [і-ре́-шă-нăл] *adj.* неразу́мный

irreconcilable [і-ре́-кăн-

сай-лăбл] *adj.* непримири́мый

irredeemable [і-рі-ди́-мăбл] *adj.* невы́купа́емый; безнадёжный (*hopeless*)

irregular [і-ре́-гю-лăр] *adj.* непра́вильный, нерегуля́рный

irregularity [і-ре-гю-лă-рі-ті] *sn.* непра́вильность

irrelevant [і-ре́-лі-вăнт] *adj.* неуме́стный

irreparable [і-ре́-пă-рăбл] *adj.* непоправи́мый

irrepressible [і-рі-пре́-сібл] *adj.* неугомо́нный, неукроти́мый

irreproachable [і-рі-про́у-чăбл] *adj.* безукори́зненный, безупре́чный

irresistible [і-рі-зіс-тібл] *adj.* неотрази́мый, непреодоли́мый

irresolute [і-ре́-зă-лют] *adj.* колебля́ющийся, нереши́тельный

irresponsible [і-ріс-по́н-сібл] *adj.* безотве́тственный

irretrievable [і-рі-три́-вăбл] *adj.* невозврати́мый

irreverent [і-ре́-вă-рăнт] *adj.* непочти́тельный

irrevocable [і-ре́-вă-кăбл] *adj.* безвозвра́тный, неотменя́емый

irrigate [і-рі-ге́йт] *vt.* обводни́ть, ороша́ть; *med.* промыва́ть

irrigation [і-рі-ге́й-шăн] *sn.* ирригация, ороше́ние; *med.* промыва́ние

irritable [і-рі-тăбл] *adj.* раздражи́тельный

irritate [і-рі-те́йт] *vt.* раздража́ть (*excite to anger*); воспламеня́ть (*inflame*)

irritation [і-рі-тэ́й-шăн] *sn.* раздражение

isinglass [áй-зін-глáс] *sn.* рыбий клей

island [áй-лăнд] *sn.* о́стров; *adj.* островно́й

islander [áй-лăн-дăр] *sm.* островитя́нин

isle [áйл] *sn.* о́стров

islet [áй-лăт] *sn.* острово́к

isolate [áй-сă-лэйт] *vt.* изоли́ровать, отделя́ть, уединя́ть; *chem.* выделя́ть, разъединя́ть

isolation [áй-сă-лэ́й-шăн] *sn.* изоли́рование, изоля́ция, уедине́ние

issue [і́-сю, і́-шю] *sn.* вы́ход (*outflow*); исхо́д (*outcome*); вы́пуск (*output of newspaper, etc.*); изда́ние (*edition*); припло́д, пото́мство (*children*); *vt.i.* выходи́ть, вытека́ть (*emerge*); выпуска́ть, издава́ть (*circulate, publish*); происходи́ть (*result*)

isthmus [і́с-мăс] *sn.* переше́ек

it [іт] *pron.* оно́

Italian [і-та́-ліăн] *sm.* италья́нец; *adj.* италья́нский

italics [і-та́-лікс] *sn. pl.* курси́в; курси́вный шрифт (*type*)

itch [іч] *sn.* зуд; чесо́тка (*disease*); *vi.* чеса́ться

item [áй-тăм] *sn.* любо́й предме́т, пункт; но́мер (*of programme, etc.*); статья́ счёта (*entry in account*)

itinerary [і-ті-нă-рă-рі] *sn.* маршру́т (*route*); путеводи́тель (*guide-book*); путевы́е заме́тки (*travel notes*); *adj.* доро́жный (*of roads*); путево́й (*of travelling*)

its [ітс] *adj., pron.* его́

itself [іт-се́лф] *pron.* само́; **by —** [бáй —] само́ собо́й, само́ по себе́

ivory [áй-вă-рі] *sn.* слоно́вая кость; *coll. pl.* игра́льные ко́сти (*dice*); билья́рдные шары́ (*billiard-balls*); кла́виши (*piano-keys*); **— black** [— блэк] слоно́вая чёрная кра́ска

ivy [áй-ві] *sn.* плющ

J

jab [джэб] *sn.* пино́к, толчо́к, уда́р

jabber [джэ́-бăр] *vt.i.* болта́ть, бормота́ть

jack [джэк] *sn. tech.* домкра́т, рыча́г; гюйс; *naut.* гюйс; вале́т (*cards*); щу́ка (*pike*)

jackal [джэ́-кăл] *s.* шака́л

jackass [джэ́к-эс] *sm.* осёл (*male ass*); болва́н (*blockhead*)

jackdaw [джэ́к-до̂] *s.* га́лка

jacket [джэ́-кіт] *sn.* жаке́т, ку́ртка; чехо́л (*outer covering*); кожура́ (*of potato*); обло́жка (*of book*)

jack-knife [джэ́к-найф] *sn.* складно́й карма́нный нож

jade [джэйд] *sn. min.* нефри́т; кля́ча (*horse*); озо́рница (*woman*)

jaded [джэ́й-діdone] *adj.* изнурённый

jag [джэг] *sn.* зубе́ц, о́стрый вы́ступ; *vt.* де́лать зазу́брины

jail [джэйл] *sn.* тюрьма́

jailer [джэ́й-лăр] *sm.* тюре́мщик

jam [джæм] *sn.* варéнье (*conserve*); надáвливание, сжáтие (*squeeze*); дáвка, толчéя (*crush*); затóр (*stoppage*); искажéние (*radio*); *vt.* защемлять, прижимáть; искажáть (*distort*)

janitor [джǽ-ни-тǎр] *sm.* двóрник, приврáтник

January [джǽ-нюǎ-ри] *sn.* янвáрь, *p.*

japan [джǎ-пǽн] *sn.* лак; *vt.* лакировáть

Japanese [джæ-пǎ-ни́з] *sm.* япóнец; *adj.* япóнский

jar [джǎр] *sn.* дребезжáние (*jarring sound*); потрясéние, шок (*shock*); ссóра (*wrangle*); бáнка, кувшин (*vessel*); *vt.i.* дребезжáть; раздражáть (*grate*)

jaundice [джóн-дис] *sn.* желтýха

jaunt [джóнт] *sn.* увеселительная прогýлка; *vi.* прогýливаться

jaw [джō] *sn.* чéлюсть; *pl.* пасть, рот (*mouth*); клещи, тиски (*of vice*)

jealous [джé-лǎс] *adj.* ревнивый

jealousy [джé-лǎ-си] *s.* зáвисть, рéвность

jeer [джир] *sn.* глумлéние (*scoffing*); насмéшка (*mockery*); *vi.* насмехáться

jelly [джé-ли] *sn.* стýдень; *vt.i.* застуживать

jelly-fish [джé-ли-фиш] *s.* медýза

jemmy [джé-ми] *s.* воровскóй лом; барáнья головá (*sheep's head*)

jeopardize [джé-пǎр-дайз] *vt.* подвергáть опáсности, рисковáть

jeopardy [джé-пǎр-ди] *sn.* опáсность, риск

jerk [джёрк] *sn.* рéзкий толчóк, рывóк; *vt.i.* дёргать

jerky [джёр-ки] *adj.* отрывистый

jersey [джёр-зи] *sn.* фуфáйка

jest [джест] *sn.* шýтка, посмéшище (*banter*); *vi.* шутить; насмехáться

jester [джéс-тǎр] *sm.* шут

jet [джет] *sn. min.* агáт, чёрная áмбра; струя (*stream*); соплó, форсýнка (*spout, nozzle*)

jetsam [джéт-сǎм] *sn.* груз сброшенный с корабля

jettison [джé-ти-сǎн] *sn.* сбрáсывание; *vt.* сбрáсывать

jetty [джé-ти] *sn.* дáмба, мол; пристань (*landing-pier*)

Jew [джý] *sm.* еврéй

jewel [джý-ǎл] *sn.* драгоцéнный кáмень (*stone*); драгоцéнность (*precious thing*); сокрóвище (*treasure*)

jeweller [джý-ǎ-лǎр] *sm.* ювелир

jewellery [джý-ǎл-ри] *sn.* драгоцéнности (*precious articles*); ювелирные изделия (*manufactured goods*)

Jewish [джý-иш] *adj.* еврéйский

Jewry [джý-ри] *sn.* еврéи; еврéйство

jib [джиб] *sn. naut.* кливер; *tech.* кронштéйн, укóсина; *vi.* упирáться; *naut.* перевáливаться

jibber [джи-бǎр] *sn.* норовистая лóшадь (*horse*)

jig [джіг] *sn.* джи́га (та́нец и му́зыка к джи́ге); *tech.* подсо́бная маши́на

jilt [джілт] *sf.* коке́тка; *vt.* обма́нывать, покида́ть

jingle [джінгл] *sn.* звя́канье; *vt.i.* звене́ть, звя́кать

job [джоб] *sn.* заня́тие, рабо́та, слу́жба

jockey [джо́-кі] *sm.* жоке́й; *vt.i.* перехитри́ть (*to trick*)

jocular [джо́-кю-ляр] *adj.* игри́вый, шутли́вый

jog [джог] *sn.* встря́ска, толчо́к (*nudge*); ме́дленная ходьба́ (*slow walk*); *vt.* толка́ть, трясти́

join [джойн] *vt.i.* свя́зывать, присоединя́ться, соединя́ть

joiner [джой-на́р] *sm.* столя́р

joinery [джой-на́-рі] *sn.* столя́рная рабо́та

joint [джойнт] *sn.* стык, суста́в; то́чка соедине́ния (*point of joining*); *adj.* совме́стный, соединённый; *vt.* расчленя́ть; **- stock** (- сток) акционе́рный капита́л

jointly [джойнт-лі] *adv.* сово́купно

joist [джойст] *sn.* перекла́дина, стропи́ло

joke [джоук] *sm.* шу́тка; *vi.* шути́ть

joker [джо́у-ка́р] *sm.* шу́тник; джо́кер (*cards*)

jolly [джо́-лі] *adj.* весёлый, оживлённый; *coll.* забавный, преле́стный

jolt [джолт] *sn.* тря́ска; *vt.* трясти́; подбра́сывать (*of vehicle*)

jostle [джосл] *vt.i.* толка́ть, пиха́ться, боро́ться (*struggle*)

jot [джот] *sn.* ничто́жное количество (*small amount*); *vt.* бе́гло очерти́ть, кра́тко запи́сывать

journal [джер-на́л] *sn. tech.* ца́пфа, ше́йка ва́ла; дневни́к (*diary*); журна́л (*periodical*); газе́та (*newspaper*)

journalism [джер-на́-лізм] *sn.* газе́тная рабо́та

journalist [джер-на́-ліст] *sm.* журнали́ст

journey [джер-ні] *sn.* пое́здка, путеше́ствие; *vi.* соверша́ть пое́здку, путеше́ствовать

journeyman [джер-ні-ма́н] *sm.* поденщик

jovial [джо́у-ві-ал] *adj.* весёлый, игри́вый

jowl [джаул] *sn.* че́люстная кость (*goitre*); зоб (*flabby cheek*)

joy [джой] *sn.* ра́дость, удово́льствие

joyful [джой-фу́л] *adj.* до-во́льный, ра́достный

jubilant [джу́-бі-лянт] *adj.* лику́ющий

jubilation [джу-бі-ле́й-шая] *sn.* ликова́ние

jubilee [джу́-бі-лі] *sn.* юбиле́й

judge [джадж] *sm.* судья́; знато́к (*expert*); *vt.i.* суди́ть, заключа́ть (*decide*)

judgment [джадж-мант] *sn.* пригово́р, реше́ние суда́ (*sentence*); мне́ние, сужде́ние (*opinion*)

judicial [джу-ді́-шал] *adj.* суде́бный, суде́йский; беспристра́стный (*impartial*)

judicious [джу-ді́-шас] *adj.* обду́манный, рассуди́тельный

jug [джаг] *sn.* жбан, кувшин; *vt.* тушить (*stew*)

juggle [джагл] *vi.* жонглировать, фокусничать

juggler [джаг-ләр] *sm.* жонглёр, фокусник

juice [джус] *sn.* сок

juicy [джу́-сі] *adj.* сочный

July [джу-лай] *sn.* июль, *m.*

jumble [джамбл] *sn.* куча (*heap*); смятение, суматоха (*muddle*); *vt.i.* перемешиваться, двигаться в беспорядке; – **sale** [– сэйл] продажа дешёвых товаров на базарах

jump [джамп] *sn.* прыжок, скачок; *vi.* прыгать, скакать; пропускать (*miss*)

jumper [джа́м-пәр] *sn.* прыгун, скакун; вязаная куртка (*loose jacket*)

junction [джа́нк-шән] *sn.* соединение (*joint*); узловая станция (*station*)

juncture [джа́нк-чәр] *sn.* соединение, сочленение

June [джун] *sn.* июнь, *m.*

jungle [джангл] *sn.* джунгли

junior [джу́-ні-әр] *sn.* младший; студент младшего курса (*in school*); *adj.* младший

junk [джанк] *sn.* колода, обрубок, чурбан (*chunk*); ломоть (*of bread*); *naut.* солонина; джонка (*vessel*)

junket [джан-кіт] *sn.* сладкий творог (*curdled milk*)

jurisdiction [джу-ріс-дік-шән] *sn.* правосудие

juror [джу́-рәр] *sn., m.* член жюри

jury [джу́-рі] *sn. pl.* присяжные

just [джаст] *adj.* справедливый (*fair*); правильный (*correct, proper*); *adv.* именно, точно (*exactly*); едва (*barely*)

justice [джас-тіс] *sn.* правосудие; справедливость (*fairness*); судья (*judge*); – **of the Peace** [– ов әә піс] мировой судья

justification [джас-ті-фі-кэ́й-шән] *sn.* оправдание

justify [джас-ті-фай] *vt.* оправдывать

jut [джат] *vi.* выступать, выдаваться

juvenile [джу́-ві-найл] *sm.,f.* подросток, юноша; *adj.* юношеский

juxtaposition [джакс-тә-по-зі́-шән] *sn.* смежность, сопоставление

K

kale, kail [кэйл] *sn.* кудрявая капуста

keel [кил] *sn.* киль, *m.*; плоскодонное судно (*vessel*); *vt.* опрокидывать

keen [кин] *adj.* острый (*sharp*); пронзительный (*piercing*); пытливый (*searching*); сильный (*of cold, appetite, etc.*) усердный (*eager*); **be – on** [би – он] стремиться, увлекаться

keenness [кін-ніс] *sn.* резкость

keep [кип] *sn.* прокорм, содержание (*maintenance*); пища (*food*); *vt.* держать (*hold*); сохранять (*preserve*); соблюдать (*observe*); содержа́ть (*support*); – in touch [– ін тач] быть в сноше́нии; – off! [– оф] отойди́те! – on [– он] продолжа́ть; – house [– ха́ус] вести́ дома́шнее хозя́йство

keeper [ки́-пǝр] *sn.* сто́рож, храни́тель

keeping [ки́-піñ] *sn.* охра́на, хране́ние (*custody*); согласова́ние (*congruity*); be in – with [би ін – уіθ] согласова́ться

keepsake [ки́п-сэйк] *sn.* пода́рок на па́мять

keg [кег] *sn.* бочо́нок

kennel [ке́-нǝл] *sn.* соба́чья кону́ра, хиба́рка (*hovel*)

kerb [кǝрб] *sn.* бордю́рный ка́мень (*тротуа́ра*)

kerchief [кǝ́р-чіф] *sn.* головно́й плато́к, косы́нка (*three-cornered*)

kernel [кǝ́р-нǝл] *sn.* зёрнушко, ко́сточка, ядро́; основно́е содержа́ние, суть (*essential part*)

kettle [ке́тл] *sn.* котело́к

kettledrum [ке́тл-драм] *sn.* литавра

key [ки] *sn.* ключ (*instrument*); разъясне́ние, реше́ние (*solution*); кла́виша (*of piano*)

keyboard [ки́-бо́рд] *sn.* клавиату́ра

keyhole [ки́-хо́ул] *sn.* замо́чная сква́жина

keystone [ки́-сто́ун] *sn.* замо́к сво́да; *fig.* основно́й при́нцип

kick [кік] *sn.* пино́к, уда́р ного́й; отда́ча ружья́ (*of gun*); *vt.i.* ляга́ть, удара́ть ного́й; брыка́ться; возра-

жа́ть (*protest*); упира́ться (*resist*)

kid [кід] *s.* козлёнок (*goat*); *coll.* ребёнок (*child*); ла́йка (*leather*); *vt.i.* козли́ться, ягни́ться; *coll.* дразни́ть, надува́ть

kidnap [кі́д-нǝп] *vt.* похища́ть

kidnapper [кі́д-нǝп-ǝр] *sm.* похити́тель

kidney [кі́д-ні] *sn.* по́чка

kill [кіл] *vt.* убива́ть

killer [кі-лǝр] *sm.* уби́йца, *m.*

kiln [кілн] *sn.* кали́льная печь

kilt [кілт] *sn.* шотла́ндская ю́бочка

kin [кін] *sn.* род, семья́; ро́дственник (*relation*)

kind [кайнд] *sn.* разря́д, род, сорт, тип; nothing of the – [на-θіñ ов ǝ́і–] ничего́ подо́бного; *adj.* до́брый, ми́лый, сла́вный

kindle [кіндл] *vt.i.* зажига́ть; загора́ться (*catch fire*; *fig. inspire*)

kindling [кін-дліñ] *sn.* зажига́ние; *pl.* ще́пки

kindness [ка́йнд-ніс] *sn.* доброта́, любе́зность

kindred [кін-дрід] *sn.* кро́вное родство́ (*blood relationship*); ро́дственники (*relations*); схо́дство (*resemblance*); *adj.* ро́дственный, схо́дный

king [кіñ] *sn.* коро́ль, царь

kingdom [кіñ-дǝм] *sn.* короле́вство, ца́рство

kink [кіñк] *sn.* перекру́чивание (*twist*); су́дорога (*mental*); *vt.* свёртывать

kipper [кі-пǝр] *s.* копчёная сельдь

kiss [кіс] *sn.* поцелу́й; *vt.i.* целова́ть

kit [кіт] *sn.* ка́дка (*wooden tub*); ра́нец (*soldier's*); рабо́чий снаря́д (*worker's*)

kit-bag [кіт-бэг] *sn.* вещево́й мешо́к

kitchen [кі-чін] *sn.* ку́хня; – **garden** [– га́р-дăн] огоро́д

kitchener [кі-чі-нăр] *sn.* ку́хонная плита́

kite [кáйт] *sn.* коршу́н (*bird*); бума́жный змей (*of paper*)

kitten [кі-тăн] *s.* котёнок

knack [нæк] *sn.* сноро́вка, уме́нье; ло́вкость (*adroitness*)

knapsack [нæп-сæк] *sn.* рюкза́к

knave [нэйв] *sm.* негодя́й, плут (*rogue*); вале́т (*cards*)

knead [нид] *vt.* валя́ть, меси́ть

kneading-trough [ни-дĭнг-троф] *sn.* квашня́

knee [ни] *sn.* коле́но

knee-cap [ни-кæп] *sn.* коле́нная ча́шка, наколе́нник

kneel [нил] *vi.* станови́ться на коле́ни

kneeling [ни-лĭнг] *adj.* коленопреклонённый

knell [нęл] *sn.* похоро́нный звон; предзнаменова́ние сме́рти (*omen*)

knick-knack [нĭк-нæк] *sn.* безделу́шка; украше́ние (*ornament*)

knife [найф] *sn.* нож

knight [найт] *sm.* ры́царь; кавале́р о́рдена (*title*); конь (*chess*)

knighthood [найт-хўд] *sn.* ры́царство

knit [ніт] *vt.i.* вяза́ть; хму́рить (*brows*); сра́щивать (*join, unite*)

knitting [ні-тĭнг] *sn.* вя́зка, вяза́ние

knob [ноб] *sn.* кно́пка, ши́шка (*boss*); кру́глая ру́чка (*of door*); кусо́к угля́ (*of coal*)

knock [нок] *sn.* стук (*at door*); уда́р (*blow*); *vt.* стуча́ть, ударя́ть; – **down** [– да́ун] сбива́ть с ног; присужда́ть (*at sale*)

knocker [нó-кăр] *sn.* колоту́шка

knock-out [нóк-а́ут] *s.* нока́ут, ногсшиба́тельный уда́р

knot [нот] *sn.* у́зел; бант (*ribbon as ornament*); клубо́к (*tangle*); сучо́к (*in tree*)

knotty [нó-ті] *adj.* узлова́тый; запу́танный (*puzzling*)

know [ноў] *vt.* знать; быть знако́мым (*be acquainted*); отлича́ть (*distinguish*)

knowing [нóў-ĭнг] *adj.* себе́ на уме́ (*wide awake*); хи́трый (*cunning*)

knowingly [нóў-ĭнг-лі] *adv.* созна́тельно

knowledge [нó-лĭдж] *sn.* зна́ние, позна́ние; **to my** – [ту май –] по мои́м све́дениям

knowledgeable [нó-лĭдж-ăбăл] *adj.* разу́мный

knuckle [накл] *sn.* суста́в (*пальца*); *vt.i.* – **down** [– да́ун] поддава́ться, подчиня́ться; – **under** [– áн-дăр] поддава́ться, подчиня́ться

knuckle-bone [нáкл-боўн] *sn.* ба́бка; *pl.* игра́ в ба́бки (*game*)

knuckleduster [на́кл-дас-тăр] *sn.* желе́зная перча́тка; касте́т

L

label [лэйбл] *sn.* этике́тка, ярлы́к; *vt.* накле́ивать (*stick*), привя́зывать (*tie on*) ярлы́к

labial [лэ́й-би-ăл] *adj.* губно́й

laboratory [лă-бо́-рă-тă-ри] *sn.* лаборато́рия

laborious [лă-бо́-ри-ăс] *adj.* трудолюби́вый; труди́тельный (*difficult*); утоми́тельный (*tiring*)

labour [лэ́й-бăр] *sn.* рабо́та, труд; рабо́чие (*workers*); родовы́е му́ки (*pains*); *vi.* труди́ться; стара́ться (*exert oneself*); разраба́тывать (*work out*)

labourer [лэ́й-бă-рăр] *sm.* рабо́чий

lace [лэйс] *sn.* кру́жево (*fabric*); шнуро́к (*cord*); *vt.* шнурова́ть

lacerate [лắ-сă-рэйт] *vt.* раздира́ть, терза́ть

lack [лэк] *sn.* недоста́ток; *vt.i.* нужда́ться

lacquer [лắ-кăр] *sn.* лак; *vt.* лакирова́ть

lactic [лắк-тик] *adj.* моло́чный

lad [лэд] *sm.* ма́льчик (*boy*), ю́ноша (*youth*) па́рень (*young fellow*)

ladder [лắ-дăр] *sn.* ле́стница; *naut.* трап

lading [лэ́й-дин] *sn.* груз, фрахт

ladle [лэйдл] *sn.* ковш, черпа́к; *vt.* черпа́ть

lady [лэ́й-ди] *sf.* да́ма

lady-bird [лэ́й-ди-бăрд] *s.* бо́жья коро́вка

ladylike [лэ́й-ди-лайк] *adj.* же́нственный

lady's-maid [лэ́й-диз-мэйд] *sf.* камери́стка

lag [лэг] *vi.* отстава́ть

lair [лэр] *sn.* берло́га, ло́говище, нора́

laity [лэ́й-и-ти] *sn.* миря́не

lake [лэйк] *sn.* о́зеро; крапла́к (*colour*)

lamb [лэм] *s.* а́гнец, ягнёнок; *vi.* ягни́ться

lambkin [лэ́м-кин] *s.* ягнёночек

lambskin [лэ́м-скин] *sn.* мерлу́шка

lame [лэйм] *adj.* хромо́й; неубеди́тельный (*unconvincing*); *vt.* кале́чить

lameness [лэйм-нис] *sn.* хромота́

lament [лă-ме́нт] *sn.* жа́лоба; *v.t.i.* горева́ть, опла́кивать

lamentable [лă-мắн-тăбл] *adj.* приско́рбный

lamentation [лă-мăн-тэ́й-шăн] *sn.* опла́кивание

lamp [лэмп] *sn.* ла́мпа, свети́льник

lampblack [лэмп-блэк] *sn.* ла́мповая ко́поть

lamp-chimney [лэмп-чи́м-ни] *sn.* ла́мповое стекло́

lamp-holder [лэмп-хо́ул-дăр] *sn.* ламподержа́тель; *elec.* патро́н ла́мпы

lamp-lighter [лэ́мп-лай-тăр] *sm.* фона́рщик

lamp-post [лэмп-по́уст] *sn.* фона́рный столб

lamp-shade [лэмп-шэйд] *sn.* абажу́р

lance [лăнс] *sn.* пи́ка; *vt.*, *surg.* вскрыва́ть ланце́том; **— corporal** [- ко́р-пă-рăл] *sm.* ефре́йтор

land [лэнд] *sn.* земля́, су́ша (*earth*); по́чва (*ground, soil*); страна́ (*country*); *pl.* иму́щество, поме́стья (*estates*); **by —** [бай —] сухи́м путём; *vt.i.* выта́скивать (на бе́рег) (*pull out on shore*); выса́живаться (*alight*); *adj.* земе́льный

landing [лэ́н-дий] *sn.* ме́сто вы́садки, деса́нт; приземле́ние (*for planes*); площа́дка (*of stairs*); *adj.* поса́дочный; **— place** [— плэйс] при́стань

landlady [лэнд-лэй-ди] *sf.* хозя́йка (*квартиры*)

landlord [лэнд-ло́рд] *sm.* домовладе́лец; хозя́ин гости́ницы (*of inn*)

landmark [лэнд-марк] *sn.* ве́ха, межево́й знак

landowner [лэнд-оу-нэр] *sm.* землевладе́лец

landscape [лэнд-скэйп] *sn.* ландша́фт, пейза́ж

landslide [лэнд-слайд] *sn.* обва́л, о́ползень

lane [лэйн] *sn.* доро́жка, тропи́нка; просёлок (*country lane*); переу́лок (*alley*)

language [лэ́н-гуйдж] *sn.* язы́к; **native** [— нэй-тив —] родно́й язы́к

languid [лэ́н-гуйд] *adj.* апати́чный, вя́лый, сла́бый, то́мный

languish [лэ́н-гуйш] *vi.* вя́нуть, тоскова́ть, томи́ться, ча́хнуть

languor [лэ́н-гэр] *sn.* то́мность, уста́лость

lanky [лэ́н-ки] *adj.* долговя́зый

lantern [лэ́н-тэрн] *sn.* фона́рь, *m.*; **magic —** [мэ́джик —] волше́бный фона́рь

lap [лэп] *sn.* ло́но; пола́, фа́лда (*flap, skirt*); круг, раунд (*sport*); *vt.* лака́ть

lapel [лэ-пэл] *sn.* отворо́т

lapse [лэпс] *sn.* про́пуск (*slip of memory, etc.*); промежу́ток (*of time*); отступа́ние (*backsliding*); *vi.* впада́ть (*into despair, etc.*); выходи́ть (из употребле́ния) (*become void*)

larceny [лар-сэ-ни] *sn.* воро́вство

lard [лард] *sn.* свино́е са́ло

larder [лар-дэр] *sn.* кладова́я, чула́н

large [лардж] *adj.* большо́й, кру́пный; **at —** [эт —] на свобо́де, простра́нно

largely [ла́рдж-ли] *adv.* оби́льно, широко́; в значи́тельной ме́ре (*to a great extent*); гла́вным о́бразом (*principally*)

lark [ларк] *s.* жа́воронок (*bird*); *sn.* прока́за, шу́тка (*frolic*); *vi.* забавля́ться

larva [лар-ва] *sn.* личи́нка

larynx [лэ́-ринкс] *sn.* горта́нь

lash [лэш] *sn.* уда́р плётью (*strike with thong*); ресни́ца (*of eye*); бич, плеть (*thong*); *vt.* хлеста́ть

lass [лэс] *sf.* де́вушка

lassitude [лэ́-си-тюд] *sn.* уста́лость

last [ласт] *sn.* коло́дка (*shoemaker's*); ласт (*measure*); *adj.* оконча́тельный, после́дний (*final*); про́шлый (*previous*); **— but one** [— бат уан] предпосле́дний; **at —** [эт —] наконе́ц; *vi.* продолжа́ться (*continue*); сохраня́ться (*be preserved*)

lasting [ла́-стін] adj. постоянный (permanent); прочный (durable)

lastly [ласт-лі] adv. наконец; в заключение (in conclusion)

latch [лэч] sn. затвор, щеколда; задвижка (bar); vt. запирать, защёлкнуть

latchkey [лэ́ч-кі] sn. американский ключ

late [лэйт] adj. запоздалый, поздний (of time); бывший, недавний, прежний (former); покойный, умерший (deceased); **to be** – (ту би –) опаздывать

lately [лэйт-лі] adv. недавно

latent [лэ́й-тэнт] adj. скрытый

lateral [лэ́-тэ-рал] adj. боковой

latest [лэ́й-тіст] adj. последний; новейший (newest)

lath [лаθ] sn. планка, рейка

lathe [лэйθ] sn. токарный станок

lather [ла́-θэр] sn. мыльная пена; vt.i. намыливать, мылиться

Latin [лэ́-тін] sn. латинский язык (language); adj. латинский; романский (people)

latitude [лэ́-ті-тюд] sn. широта

latrine [лэ-трін] sn. mil. отхожее место

latter [лэ́-тэр] adj. недавний (recent); последний (last)

latterly [лэ́-тэр-лі] adv. недавно, под конец

lattice [лэ́-тіс] sn. решётка

laud [лод] vt. превозносить, хвалить

laudable [ло́-дабл] adj. похвальный

laugh [лаф] sn. смех; vi. смеяться; – **at** [– эт] высмеивать

laughable [ла́-фабл] adj. забавный, смешной

laughing [ла́-фін] adj. смеющийся; – **stock** [– сток] посмешище

laughter [ла́ф-тэр] sn. смех, хохот

launch [лонч] sn. баркас, шлюпка; моторная лодка; спуск судна (launching); vt. спускать судно в воду; бросать, метать (send forth); начинать (begin)

laundress [лон-дрес] sf. прачка

laundry [лон-дрі] sn. прачечная

laurel [ло́-рал] sn. лавр

lavatory [лэ́-ва-та-рі] sn. уборная

lavender [лэ́-він-дэр] sn. лаванда; сиреневый цвет (colour)

lavish [лэ́-віш] adj. расточительный (extravagant); обильный, щедрый (generous); vt. расточать

law [ло] sn. закон, право; – **and order** [– энд о́р-дэр] правопорядок; **read** – [рид –] изучать право; **practise** – [прэ́к-тіс –] быть юристом

lawcourt [ло́-корт] sn. суд

lawful [ло́-фул] adj. законный

lawn [лон] sn. батист (material); газон, лужайка (piece of smooth turf)

lawsuit [ло́-сют] sn. судебный процесс

lawyer [ló-ер] *sm.* адвока́т, юри́ст

lax [лэкс] *adj.* вя́лый, сла́бый (*not strict*); небре́жный (*negligent*); неопределённый (*vague*); распу́щенный (*loose*)

laxative [лэкс-ă-тив] *sn.* слаби́тельное; *adj.* слаби́тельный

lay [лэй] *adj.* мирско́й, све́тский (*non-clerical*); не профессиона́льный (*non-professional*); *vt.* класть, положи́ть; – **aside** [– ă-са́йд] откла́дывать; проводи́ть (*pipes, etc.*); – **down arms** [– да́ун а̄рмз] сда́ться; – **the table** [– ей тэйбл] накрыва́ть на стол; – **up** [– ап] укла́дывать в посте́ль

layer [лэй-ăр] *sn.* пласт, слой

layman [лэй-мăн] *sm.* миря́нин

laze [лэйз] *vi. coll.* безде́льничать

laziness [лэй-зи-нiс] *sn.* ле́ность, лень

lazy [лэй-зi] *adj.* лени́вый

lead [лед] *sn.* свине́ц; **red** – [ред –] су́рик; **white** – [уа́йт –] свинцо́вые бели́ла; *pl.* тур. шпо́ны; *adj.* свинцо́вый

lead [лид] *sn.* руково́дство (*guidance*); *elect.* про́вод; ход (*in games*); *vt.i.* вести́, приводи́ть, руководи́ть

leader [ли́дăр] *sm.* вождь, руководи́тель; передова́я статья́ (*in journal, etc.*)

leadership [ли́дăр-шiп] *sn.* води́тельство

leading [ли́-дiн] *adj.* веду́щий; передово́й (*of article*)

leaf [лиф] *sn.* лист; ство́рка (*of table, etc.*); **loose** – [лу́с –] вкладно́й лист

leaflet [ли́ф-лiт] *sn.* листо́вка

league [лиг] *sn.* лье́(*measure*); ли́га, сою́з (*association*)

leak [лик] *sn.* течь; *vi.* пропуска́ть во́ду, течь; – **out** [– а́ут] обнару́жить

leakage [ли́-кiдж] *sn.* уте́чка; обнаруже́ние (*of secret, etc.*)

leaky [ли́-кi] *adj.* име́ющий течь, неплотный

lean [лин] *adj.* то́щий, по́стный (*of meat*); *vt.i.* наклоня́ться, прислоня́ть; – **on** [– он] опира́ться

leap [лип] *sn.* прыжо́к, скачо́к; *vi.* пры́гать, ска-

leap-frog [ли́п-фрог] *sn.* чеха́рда; *vi.* игра́ть в чеха́рду

leap-year [ли́п-ер] *sn.* високо́сный год

learn [лёрн] *vt.i.* учи́ть, учи́ться; узнава́ть (*ascertain*)

learned [лёр-нiд] *adj.* учёный

learner [лёр-нăр] *sm.* новичо́к (*beginner*); учени́к (*pupil*)

learning [лёр-нiн] *sn.* учёность, эруди́ция

lease [лис] *sn.* аре́нда, наём, сда́ча; *vt.* арендова́ть; сдава́ть в аре́нду (*let*); брать в аре́нду (*take*)

leasehold [ли́с-хо́улд] *sn.* аре́ндованная земля́; *adj.* аре́ндованный

leaseholder [ли́с-хо́ул-дăр] *sm.* аренда́тор

leash [лиш] *sn.* свора; *vt.* держать на привязи

least [лист] *adj.* малейший, наименьший; **at - [** эт **-]** по крайней мере; **not in the - [** нот ин эа **-]** ничуть; *adv.* наименее

leather [лé-ðэр] *sn.* кожа; *adj.* кожаный

leave [лив] *sn.* разрешение (*permission*); отпуск (*vacation*); прощание (*farewell*); *vt.* уезжать (*go away by train, etc.*); уходить (*quit*); оставлять (*let remain*); **- off** [- оф] прекращать; **- out** [- аут] пропускать, упустить

leaven [лé-вэн] *sn.* дрожжи, закваска; *vt.* заквашивать

leavings [лú-вингз] *sn. pl.* объедки, остатки

lecherous [лé-чэ-рэс] *adj.* распутный

lecture [лéк-чэр] *sn.* лекция, преподавание

lecturer [лéк-чэ-рэр] *sm.* доцент (*university*); лектор

ledge [ледж] *sn.* выступ

ledger [лé-джэр] *sn.* гроссбух, книга счетов

leech [лич] *s.* пиявка

leek [лик] *sn.* лук-порей

leer [лир] *sn.* злобный взгляд; *vi.* подмигивать, злобно смотреть

leeward [лú-уôрд] *adj.* подветренный

leeway [лú-уэй] *sn.* дрейф

left [лефт] *adj.* левый; *adv.* налево, слева

left-handed [лефт-хэ́н-дид] *adj.* левша

leg [лег] *sn.* нога (от колена до ступни); ножка (*of table, etc.*)

legacy [лé-гэ-си] *sn.* наследство

legal [лú-гэл] *adj.* законный, юридический

legality [лú-гэ-ли-ти] *sn.* законность

legalize [лú-гэ-лайз] *vt.* узаконивать

legate [лé-гит] *sm.* папский посол

legation [лú-гэ́й-шэн] *sn.* иностранная миссия, посольство

legend [лé-джэнд] *sn.* легенда; надпись (*inscription*)

leggings [лé-гингз] *sn. pl.* гамаши

legibility [ле-джи-бú-ли-ти] *sn.* чёткость

legible [лé-джибл] *adj.* разборчивый, чёткий

legion [лú-джэн] *sn.* легион; множество (*great number*)

legislate [лé-джис-лэйт] *vi.* законодательствовать, издавать законы

legislation [ле-джис-лэ́й-шэн] *sn.* законодательство

legislature [лé-джис-лэ-чэр] *sn.* законодательная власть

legitimate [лú-джú-ти-мит] *adj.* законный (*lawful*); правильный (*proper*); законнорождённый (*of child*)

leisure [лэ́-жэр] *sn.* досуг; **at - [** эт **-]** на досуге

leisurely [лэ́-жэр-ли] *adj.* досужий; неторопливый (*unhurried*); *adv.* не спеша, спокойно

lemon [лé-мэн] *sn.* лимон; лимонный цвет (*colour*); *adj.* лимонный; **- squash** [- скýош] лимонный сок

lemonade [ле-мэ-нэ́йд] *sn.* лимонад

lend [ленд] *vt.* дава́ть взаймы́, одолжа́ть; ссужа́ть (*at interest*); **- a hand** [- ă хэнд] помога́ть

lender [лéн-дăр] *sm.* заимода́вец

length [ленθ] *sn.* длина́; долгота́ (*of sound*); **at -** [ăт -] наконе́ц (*at last*); подро́бно (*in detail*)

lengthen [лéн-θăн] *vt.* удлиня́ть

lengthwise [лéнθ-ўайз] *adj.* продо́льный; *adv.* в длину́

lengthy [лéн-θи] *adj.* растя́нутый, удлинённый

lenient [ли́-ни-ăнт] *adj.* мя́гкий, снисходи́тельный

lens [ленз] *sn.* ли́нза

Lent [лент] *sn.* вели́кий пост

lenten [лéн-тăн] *adj.* по́стный

lentil [лéн-тил] *sn.* чечеви́ца

leopard [лéп-ăрд] *s.* леопа́рд

leper [лéп-ăр] *sm.* прокажённый

leprosy [лéп-ря̆-си] *sn.* прока́за

less [лес] *adj.* мéньший; *adv.* мéнее, мéньше; **none the -** [нан θă -] тем не мéнее

lessee [лес-си́] *sm.* съёмщик

lessen [лéс-сăн] *vt.* уменьша́ть

lesson [лéс-сăн] *sn.* уро́к

lest [лест] *conj.* как бы не, что́бы не

let [лет] *vt.* позволя́ть, пуска́ть; сдава́ть в наём (*hire out*); **- in** [- ин] впуска́ть; **- loose** [- лу́с] выпуска́ть, освобожда́ть (*free*); **- us!** [- ăс] дава́йте!

letter [лéт-ăр] *sn.* бу́ква (*symbol*); письмо́ (*written communication*); *pl.* литерату́ра (*literature*); **capital -**

[кă-пи-тăл -] прописна́я бу́ква; **small -** [смôл -] строчна́я бу́ква; **initial -** [и-ни́-шăл -] нача́льная бу́ква; *typ.* ли́тера; **to the -** [ту θă -] буква́льно

letter-box [лé-тăр-бокс] *sn.* почто́вый я́щик

lettuce [лé-тис] *sn.* лату́к, сала́т

level [лé-вăл] *sn.* ва́терпас, нивели́р, у́ровень; равни́на (*plain*); *adj.* гла́дкий, ро́вный; ра́вный (*equal*); *vt.* нивели́ровать, ура́внивать

lever [ли́-вăр] *sn.* рыча́г; лом (*cross-bar*); *vt.* поднима́ть рычаго́м

leverage [ли́-вă-ридж] *sn.* подъёмная си́ла

levity [лé-ви-ти] *sn.* ве́треность, легкомы́слие

levy [лé-ви] *sn.* сбор (*collection of tax*); обложе́ние (*imposition*); *mil.* набо́р; *vt.* взима́ть

lewd [люд] *adj.* бессты́дный, развра́тный

liability [лай-ă-би́-ли-ти] *sn.* отве́тственность, подве́рженность; *pl.* долги́, задо́лженность, обяза́тельства

liable [лай-ăбл] *adj.* обя́занный, подве́рженный

liaison [ли-эй-зо́н] *sn.* связь; *phon.* свя́зывание зву́ков

liar [лай-ăр] *sm.* лгун

libel [лай-бăл] *sn.* диффама́ция, клевета́; *vt.* клевета́ть

libellous [лай-бă-лăс] *adj.* клеветни́ческий, ло́жный

liberal [ли́-бă-рăл] *adj.* великоду́шный, ще́дрый (*generous*); либера́льный, свободоомы́слящий (*open-minded*); оби́льный (*abundant*)

liberate [лі-бǎ-рэйт] *vt.* освобождǎть

liberator [лі-бǎ-рэй-тǎр] *sm.* освободǐтель

liberty [лі-бǎр-ті] *sn.* вóльность, свобóда

librarian [лай-брǎ-рі-ǎн] *sm.* библиотéкарь, *m.*

library [лай-брǎ-рі] *sn.* библиотéка

licence [лǎй-сǎнс] *sn.* ліцéнзия, разрешéние; удостоверéние (*certificate*); распýщенность (*excessive liberty of action*)

license [лǎй-сǎнз] *vt.* давáть патéнт, разрешáть

licensed [лǎй-сǎнсд] *adj.* имéющий разрешéние

licentious [лǎй-сéн-шǎс] *adj.* непристóйный, распýщенный

lick [лік] *sn.* лизáнье, облǐзывание; *vt.* лизáть, облǐзывать

lid [лід] *sn.* крышка, колпáк (*cap, cowl*)

lie [лай] *sn.* ложь, обмáн; to tell a – [ту тел ǎ –] солгáть; *vi.* лгать; лежáть (*recline*); ложǐться (*lie down*); быть располóженным, находǐться (*be situated*)

life [лайф] *sn.* жизнь

lifebelt [лайф-бéлт] *sn.* спасáтельный пояс

lifeless [лайф-ліс] *adj.* безжǐзненный

lifelong [лайф-лон] *adj.* пожǐзненный

lift [ліфт] *sn.* лифт, подъёмная машǐна; give a – [гǐв –] подвезтǐ когó-либо, подсадǐть; *vt.* возвышáть, поднимáть

ligament [лі-гǎ-мǎнт] *sn.* связка

ligature [лі-га-чǎр] *sn. surg.* бинт, перевязка; *typ.* лигатýра

light [лайт] *sn.* освещéние (*lighting*); свет (*brightness*); bring to – [брǐн ту –] выявлять; come to – [кǎм ту –] обнарýживаться; strike a – [стрǎйк ǎ –] зажéчь (спǐчку); огóнь (*flame*); *adj.* свéтлый (*bright*); лёгкий (*easy, light, slight*); *vt.* освещáть (*light up*); зажигáть (*set on fire*)

lighten [лǎй-тǎн] *vt.* облегчáть (*make easier*); смягчáть (*mitigate*); светлéть (*shed light*)

lighter [лǎй-тǎр] *sn.* зажигáлка; лǐхтер (*vessel*)

lighthouse [лǎйт-хǎус] *sn.* маяк

lightning [лǎйт-нǐн] *sn.* мóлния; summer – [сǎ-мǎр –] зарнǐца; – conductor – [кǎн-дǎк-тǎр] громоотвóд

lights [лǎйтс] *sn. pl.* лёгкие (*of animals*)

like [лайк] *sn.* нéчто подóбное; *adj.* одинáковый, подóбный, похóжий; *adv.* так, подóбно, так сказáть; *vt.* любǐть, нрáвиться; хотéть (*desire, wish*)

likelihood [лǎйк-лі-хýд] *sn.* вероятность

likely [лǎйк-лі] *adj.* вероятный; подходящий (*appropriate*)

likeness [лǎйк-ніс] *sn.* подóбие, схóдство

likewise [лǎйк-ўáйз] *adv.* тáкже, тóже

liking [ляй-кiй] *sn.* вкус (*one's taste*); расположе́ние (*disposition towards*); скло́нность (*propensity*)

lilac [ляй-ляк] *sn.* сире́нь; *adj.* сире́невый; лило́вый

lilt [лiлт] *sn.* ритм (*пе́сни*); *vt.* ритми́чески напева́ть

limb [лiм] *sn.* о́рган, член (*те́ла*); ветвь, сук (*bough*)

lime [лайм] *sn.* хи́мический и́звесть; сорт лимо́на (*fruit*); ли́па (*tree*)

limestone [лайм-сто́ун] *sn.* известня́к

limit [лi-мiт] *sn.* грани́ца, преде́л; *vt.* ограни́чивать

limitation [лi-мi-тэ́й-шäн] *sn.* огово́рка, ограниче́ние; *pl.* недоста́тки

limp [лiмп] *sn.* прихра́мывание, хромота́; *adj.* вя́лый, мя́гкий, сла́бый; *vi.* хрома́ть

limpid [лiм-пiд] *adj.* прозра́чный

line [лайн] *sn.* ли́ния; черта́, штрих (*feature*); *typ.* строка́; шнур (*cord*); *vt.i.* линова́ть, проводи́ть ли́нии; наби́ва́ть (*put lining into*)

lineage [лi-нi-iдж] *sn.* происхожде́ние

linear [лi-нi-äр] *adj.* лине́йный

linen [лi-нiн] *sn.* полотно́ (*cloth*); бельё (*underwear, etc.*); *adj.* льняно́й

liner [лай-нäр] *sn.* пассажи́рский парохо́д

linger [лiн-гäр] *vi.* ме́длить, ме́шкать; затя́гиваться (*of illness*); тяну́ться (*of time*)

lingerie [лэ́н-жрi] *sn.* же́нское бельё

linguist [лiн-гуiст] *sn.* лингви́ст, языкове́д

linguistics [лiн-гуíс-тiкс] *sn. pl.* лингви́стика, языкозна́ние

liniment [лi-нi-мäнт] *sn.* мягчи́тельная мазь

lining [лай-нiй] *sn.* подкла́дка (*of garment*); обши́вка (*of box, etc.*)

link [лiйк] *sn.* звено́; связь (*tie*); у́зы (*bonds*); сцеп (*connection*); *vt.* свя́зывать, смыка́ть, сцепля́ть

links [лiйкс] *sn. pl.* по́ле для игры́ в гольф

linseed [лiн-сiд] *sn.* льняно́е се́мя

lint [лiнт] *sn.* ко́рпия

lion [лай-äн] *sn.* лев

lip [лiп] *sn.* губа́; край (*edge*)

liquid [лi-куíд] *sn.* жи́дкость; *adj.* жи́дкий; пла́вный (*of sound*)

liquidate [лi-куi-дэйт] *vt.* выпла́чивать, ликвиди́ровать

liquor [лi-кäр] *sn.* спиртно́й напи́ток

liquorice [лi-кä-рiс] *sn.* лакри́чник

lisp [лiсп] *sn.* шепеля́вость; *vi.* сюсю́кать, шепеля́вить

list [лiст] *sn.* ре́естр, спи́сок; кро́мка (*selvedge*); *vt.* вноси́ть, запи́сывать, пере́числя́ть; крени́ть (*of boat*)

listen [лi-сäн] *vi.* слу́шать; прислу́шиваться (*jor*); **in** – [iн –] слу́шать по ра́дио

listener [лiс-нäр] *sn.* слу́шатель; радиослу́шатель, *m.*

listless [лiст-лiс] *adj.* равноду́шный, уста́лый

literacy [лi-тä-рä-сi] *sn.* гра́мотность

literal [лi-тä-рäл] *adj.* буква́льный, досло́вный

literary [лі́-тă-рă-р̣і] *adj.*
литерату́рный

literate [лі́-тă-ріт] *adj.* гра́-
мотный, учёный

literature [лі́-тă-рă-чăр] *sn.*
литерату́ра

Lithuanian [лі-θ̄ӯ-эй-ні-ăн]
sn. лито́вец; *adj.* лито́вский

litigate [лі́-ті-гэйт] *vt.i.* тя́-
га́ться (*go to law*); оспа́ри-
вать (*contest at law*)

litter [лі́-тăр] *sn.* носи́лки
(*invalid carriage*); беспоря́-
док (*disorder*); сор (*rubbish*);
подсти́лка (*for cattle*); по́-
мёт (*brood*); *vt.* мусо́рить,
разбра́сывать

little [літл] *adj.* ма́ленький;
adv. ма́ло

littoral [лі́-то-рăл] *adj.* при-
бре́жный; *sn.* побере́жье

live [лів] *vi.* жить, суще-
ствова́ть; обита́ть (*inhabit*)

live [лайв] *adj.* живо́й
оживлённый; де́йствую-
щий (*active*); заря́женный
(*charged*)

livelihood [ла́йв-лі-х̌ӯд] *sn.*
пропита́ние

lively [ла́йв-лі] *adj.* живо́й,
оживлённый; весёлый
(*gay*)

liver [лі́-вăр] *sn.* пе́чень;
печёнка (*dish*)

liverish [лі́-вă-рі̣ш] *adj.*
страда́ющий боле́знью пе́-
чени

livery [лі́-вă-рі] *sn.* ливре́я

liveryman [лі́-вă-рі-мăн]
sn. извозопромы́шленник

livestock [ла́йв-сток] *sn.*
дома́шний скот, живо́й
инвента́рь

livid [лі́-від] *adj.* посине́в-
ший

living [лі́-ві̣н] *sn.* сре́дства

существова́ния (*means of
existence*); о́браз жи́зни
(*mode of life*); житьё (*life*);
церко́вный прихо́д (*bene-
fice*); — **room** [— ру́м]
жила́я ко́мната; — **wage**
[— уэ́йдж] прожи́точный ми́-
нимум; *adj.* живо́й, живу́-
щий

lizard [лі́-зăрд] *s.* я́щерица

load [ло́уд] *sn.* бре́мя, груз
(*burden*); воз (*cart-load*);
нагру́зка (*lading*); *vt.* гру-
зи́ть, нагружа́ть (*embark*);
обременя́ть (*burden*); заря-
жа́ть (*charge*)

loading [ло́у-ді̣н] *sn.* по-
гру́зка (*shipment*); заря́дка,
заряжа́ние (*charging*)

loaf [ло́уф] *sn.* буха́нка
хле́ба, карава́й; бу́лка
(*small*); — **sugar** [— шу́-
гăр] рафина́д; *vi.* безде́ль-
ничать (*idle*); — **about** [—
ă-ба́ут] слоня́ться

loan [ло́ун] *sn.* заём; **on** —
[он —] взаймы́; заи́мствова-
ние (*of words, pictures, etc.*);
vt. дава́ть взаймы́; заи́м-
ствовать (*of words, etc.*)

loath [ло́уθ] *adj.* неохо́тный
(*reluctant*); несклонный
(*disinclined*)

loathe [ло́уθ] *vt.* ненави́деть
(*detest*); чу́вствовать отвра-
ще́ние (*regard with disgust*)

lobby [ло́-бі] *sn.* прихо́жая,
кулуа́ры (*in House of Commons*)

lobe [ло́уб] *sn. anat.* мо́чка;
до́ля, ло́пасть (*of leaf*)

lobster [ло́б-стăр] *s.* ома́р

local [ло́-кăл] *adj.* ме́стный

locality [ло-кắ-лі-ті] *sn.*
ме́стность, местоположе́-
ние

locate [лоў-кэйт] *vt.* определя́ть ме́сто

location [лоў-кэй́-шăн] *sn.* местоположе́ние; поселе́ние, размеще́ние (*settlement*)

locative [ло́-кă-тив] *adj. gram.* ме́стный

lock [лок] *sn.* замо́к, запо́р (*fastener*); замо́к (*of gun*); плоти́на, шлюз (*section of canal*); ло́кон (*of hair*); *pl.* во́лосы (*hair*); *vt.* запира́ть (*fasten*); тормози́ть (*jam*); – **in** [– ин] замыка́ть; – **up** [– ап] заключа́ть, запира́ть

locker [ло́-кăр] *sn.* ларь, *m.*, ка́фчик

locket [ло́-кит] *sn.* медальо́н

lockjaw [ло́к-джŏ] *sn.* столбня́к, че́люстна́я су́дорога

lock-out [ло́к-аўт] *sn.* ло́каут (*исключе́ние рабо́чих*)

locksmith [ло́к-сми́θ] *sn.* сле́сарь

locomotion [лоў-кă-мо́ў-шăн] *sn.* передвиже́ние

locomotive [лоў-кă-мо́ў-тив] *sn.* локомоти́в, парово́з; *adj.* дви́жущийся

locust [ло́ў-кăст] *s.* саранча́ (*insect*); бе́лая ака́ция (*tree*)

lodge [лодж] *sn.* до́мик, сторо́жка; ло́жа (*freemasons*); *vt.i.* кварти́ровать (*provide accommodation*); помеща́ть (*establish*); вре́менно находи́ться (*stay for a time*); подава́ть (*a complaint*)

lodger [ло́-джăр] *sn.* жиле́ц

lodging [ло́-джин] *sn.* кварти́ра, помеще́ние

lodging-house [ло́-джин-хăўс] *sn.* меблиро́ванные ко́мнаты (*furnished rooms*);

жили́ще (*dwelling*)

loft [лофт] *sn.* черда́к; сенова́л (*hayloft*)

lofty [лоф-ти] *adj.* высо́кий (*high*); возвы́шенный (*elevated, exalted*)

log [лог] *sn.* бревно́, коло́да; чурба́н; *naut.* лаг; судово́й журна́л (*book*)

logbook [ло́г-бук] *sn. naut.* шканечный журна́л

logic [ло́-джик] *sn.* ло́гика

logical [ло́-джи-кăл] *adj.* логи́ческий; логи́чный, после́довательный (*rightly deducible*)

loin [лойн] *sn.* филе́, филе́йная часть; *pl.* поясни́ца

loiter [лой́-тăр] *vi.* ме́шкать, шата́ться без де́ла

loneliness [ло́ўн-ли-нис] *sn.* одино́кость, одино́чество

lonely [ло́ўн-ли] *adj.* одино́кий, тоскли́вый

long [лон] *adj.* дли́нный (*of length*), до́лгий (*of time*); *adv.* давно́, до́лго; – **before** [– би-фо́р] задо́лго; **as – as** [аз – аз] пока́...; – **live**...! [– лив] да здра́вствует...!; – **to** *vt.* стреми́ться (*aspire*); жа́ждать (*crave*); тоскова́ть (*languish*)

longevity [лон-дже́-ви-ти] *sn.* долгове́чность

longing [ло́н-ин] *sn.* си́льное жела́ние (*extreme craving*); тоска́ (*anguish*)

longitude [ло́н-джи-тюд] *sn.* долгота́

longitudinal [лон-джи-тю́-ди-нăл] *adj.* продо́льный

long-sighted [лон-сай́-тид] *adj.* дальнозо́ркий

long-standing [лон-стэ́н-дин] *adj.* да́внишний

look [лу́к] *sn.* взгляд (*glance*); вид (*aspect*); выраже́ние (*expression*); *vi.* смотре́ть; **- after** [- а́ф-тэ̄р] забо́титься, присма́тривать; **- for** [- фо̄р] иска́ть; **- here!** [- хир] послу́шайте! **- on!** [- он] наблюда́ть! **- out** [- а́ут] быть насторо́же; **-out!** береги́сь!

looking-glass [лу́-кин-гла́с] *sn.* зе́ркало

look-out [лу́к-а́ут] *sn.* наблюда́тельный пост

loom [лу́м] *sn.* тка́цкий стано́к; *vi.* майчи́ть

loop [лу́п] *sn.* пе́тля; мёртвая пе́тля (*in flying*); *vi.* де́лать пе́тлю; **- the -** [- ɵ̆ ə -] проде́лывать мёртвую пе́тлю в во́здухе (*in the air*)

loop-hole [лу́п-хо́ул] *sn.* бойни́ца, лазе́йка; уве́ртка (*dodge*)

loose [лу́с] *adj.* непрекреплённый (*not rigidly fixed*); развя́занный (*not fastened*); просто́рный, широ́кий (*of clothing*); во́льный (*of translation*); небре́жный (*of soil*)

loosen [лу́-сэн] *vt.* развя́зывать, распуска́ть; разрыхля́ть (*of soil*)

loot [лу́т] *sn.* добы́ча, грабёж; *vt.* гра́бить

lop [лоп] *vt.* обкорна́ть, подре́зывать (*cut away*); отруба́ть (*chop off*); **-eared** [--ирд] вислоу́хий; **-sided** [--сай-дид] кривобо́кий

loquacious [ло-куэ́й-шас] *adj.* болтли́вый, говорли́вый

lordly [ло́рд-ли] *adj.* го́рдый, надме́нный

lore [ло́р] *sn.* зна́ние, уче́нье; (преда́ние и фа́кты осо́бого сюже́та); эруди́ция; **folk -** [фоук -] фолькло́р

lorry [ло́-ри] *sn.* грузови́к, грузово́й автомоби́ль

lose [лу́з] *vt.* теря́ть, утра́чивать; прои́грывать (*in games*); упуска́ть (*chance, opportunity*); отступа́ть (*ground*); **- oneself** [- у̀ан-сэ́лф] заблужда́ться

loser [лу́-зэр] *sm.* теря́ющий; прои́гравший

loss [лос] *sn.* поте́ря, утра́та; **be at a -** [би æт ɑ -] быть в замеша́тельстве

lot [лот] *sn.* жре́бий (*fate, chance, share*); до́ля (*portion*); уча́сток земли́ (*allotted piece of land*); большо́е коли́чество, ма́сса, мно́жество (*considerable number*)

lotion [ло́у-шан] *sn.* примо́чка

lottery [ло́-тӑ-ри] *sn.* лотере́я

loud [ла́уд] *adj.* гро́мкий (*strongly audible*); шумли́вый, шу́мный (*noisy*); зву́чный (*sonorous*); *fig.* крича́щий (*of colour, dress, etc.*); *adv.* гро́мко; **- speaker** [- спи́-кӑр] громкоговори́тель, *m.*

lounge [ла́ундж] *sn.* ко́мната для о́тдыха (*room*); удо́бное кре́сло (*easy chair*); *vi.* броди́ть, шата́ться

louse [ла́ус] *s.* вошь

lousy [ла́у-зи] *adj.* вши́вый

love [лав] *sn.* любо́вь; **be in -** [би ин -] быть влюблённый; **fall in -** [фол ин -] влюбля́ться; *vt.* люби́ть

loveliness [ла́в-ли-нис] *sn.* красота́

lovely [ла́в-ли] *adj.* краси́вый, преле́стный, чуде́сный

lover [ла́-вăр] *sm.* любо́вник; люби́тель (*amateur*)

loving [ла́-вињ] *adj.* любя́щий

low [лоу] *adj.* ни́зкий; пода́вленный (*dejected*); вульга́рный (*vulgar*); *vi.* мыча́ть (*of cows*)

lower [ло́у-ăр] *vt.* понижа́ть, снижа́ть

loyal [ло́й-ăл] *adj.* ве́рный (*true*); лойя́льный

loyalty [ло́й-ăл-ти] *sn.* ве́рность, лойя́льность

£ s. d. [эл, эс, ди] *sn.* де́ньги (*money*) (фу́нты, ши́ллинги и пе́нсы)

lubricant [лю́-бри-кăнт] *sn.* сма́зка, сма́зочное вещество́

lubricate [лю́-бри-кэйт] *vt.* сма́зывать

lubrication [лю-бри-кэ́йшăн] *sn.* сма́зка; сма́зывание

lucid [лу́-сид] *adj.* я́сный

luck [лак] *sn.* сча́стье, уда́ча; **bad —** [бэд] *sn.* неуда́ча

lucky [ла́-ки] *adj.* счастли́вый, уда́чный

lucrative [лу́-крă-тив] *adj.* вы́годный, дохо́дный, при́быльный

ludicrous [лу́-ди-крăс] *adj.* абсу́рдный, смешно́й

lug [лаг] *vt.* волочи́ть, тащи́ть

luggage [ла́-гидж] *sn.* бага́ж

lukewarm [лук-уо́рм] *adj.* теплова́тый; равноду́шный (*half-hearted*)

lull [лал] *sn.* вре́менное зати́шье; *vt.i.* убаю́кивать

(*send to sleep*); успока́ивать (*soothe*)

lullaby [ла́-лă-бай] *sn.* колыбе́льная пе́сня

lumbago [лам-бэ́й-гоу] *sn.* простре́л

lumber [ла́м-бăр] *sn.* рухля́дь, хлам; *vt.* загроможда́ть

luminous [лу́-ми-нăс] *adj.* светя́щийся, све́тлый

lump [ламп] *sn.* глы́ба, кусо́к; *vt.i.* сме́шивать (*jumble together*)

lumpy [ла́м-пи] *adj.* комкова́тый

lunacy [лу́-нă-си] *sn.* безу́мие; *fig.* больша́я глу́пость

lunar [лу́-нăр] *adj.* лу́нный

lunatic [лу́-нă-тик] *sn.* сумасше́дший, умали́шённый

lunch [ланч] *sn.* второ́й за́втрак, лёгкая заку́ска; *vi.* за́втракать среди́ дня (вообще́ о́коло оди́ннадцати часо́в), по́лдничать

luncheon [ла́н-чăн] *sn.* ра́нний обе́д

lung [лањг] *sn.* лёгкое

lunge [ландж] *vt.i.* пронза́ть

lure [лю́р] *sn.* прима́нка; *vt.* завлека́ть, зама́нивать

lurid [лю́-рид] *adj.* мра́чный, посине́вший, угрю́мый (*ghastly*, *gloomy*, *etc.*); стра́шный (*terrible*)

lurk [лöрк] *vi.* пря́таться, скрыва́ться

luscious [ла́-шăс] *adj.* приторный, со́чный; перегру́женный (*of style*)

lust [ласт] *sn.* вожделе́ние, по́хоть, стра́стное жела́ние

lustre [ла́с-тăр] *sn.* блеск, гля́нец, лоск, лю́стра

luxuriant [лаг-жю́-ри-а́нт] *adj.* плодоро́дный, оби́льный (*profuse*); бога́тый (*rich*)

luxurious [лаг-жю́-ри-а́с] *adj.* пы́шный, ро́скошный

luxury [лáк-шэ-ри] *sn.* ро́скошь

lye [лай] *sn.* щёлок

lymphatic [лим-фэ́-тик] *adj.* медли́тельный, отви́слый

M

mace [мэйс] *sn.* жезл; *hist.* булава́; муска́т (*nutmeg*)

macerate [мэ́-сэ-рэйт] *vt.* выма́чивать (*become soft by soaking*); изнуря́ть, истоща́ть (*reduce by fasting*)

machination [мэ-ки-нэ́й-шэн] *sn.* интри́га, махина́ция

machine [мэ-ши́н] *sn.* маши́на; механи́зм; – **gun** – [– ган] пулемёт; *vt.* рабо́тать на маши́не

machinery [мэши́-нэ-ри] *sn.* маши́нное обору́дование

mackerel [мэ́-крэл] *s.* макре́ль, скумбрия́

mad [мэд] *adj.* безу́мный, сумасше́дший; бе́шеный (*of animals*); восто́рженный (*madly keen*); сумасбро́дный (*reckless*)

madcap [мэ́д-кэп] *sm. f.* сорви-голова́

madden [мэ́д-дэн] *vt.i.* доводи́ть до бе́шенства, раздража́ть, своди́ть с ума́

madman [мэ́д-мэн] *sm.* сумасше́дший

madness [мэ́д-нӗс] *s.* бе́шенство, сумасше́ствие; я́рость (*fury, rage*)

maelstrom [мэ́л-строум] *sn.* водоворо́т, вихрь, *m.*

magazine [мэ-гэ-зи́н] *sn.* периоди́ческий журна́л (*journal*); склад вое́нных припа́сов (*military store*); *tech.* магази́н

maggot [мэ́-гэт] *s.* личи́нка

maggoty [мэ́-гэ-ти] *adj.* черви́вый

magic [мэ́-джик] *sn.* волшебство́, ма́гия; *adj.* волше́бный

magician [мэ-джи́-шэн] *sm.* волше́бник

magistrate [мэ́-джис-трит] *sm.* мирово́й судья́

magnanimity [мэг-нӗ-ни́-ми-ти] *sn.* великоду́шие

magnesium [мэг-ни́-зиӑм] *sn.* ма́гний

magnet [мэ́г-нит] *sn.* магни́т

magnetic [мэг-нӗ́-тик] *adj.* магни́тный

magnificence [мэг-ни́-фи-сӑнс] *sn.* великоле́пие

magnificent [мэг-ни́-фи-сӑнт] *adj.* великоле́пный, первокла́ссный

magnify [мэ́г-ни-фай] *vt.* увели́чивать; преувели́чивать (*exaggerate*)

magnifying [мэ́г-ни-фай-ий] *adj.* увеличи́тельный; – **glass** – [– глӑс] *sn.* лу́па

magnitude [мэ́г-ни-тюд] *sn.* величина́ (*size*); ва́жность (*importance*)

magpie [мэ́г-пай] *s.* соро́ка; болту́н (*chatterer*)

mahogany [мӑ-хо́-гӑ-ни] *sn.* кра́сное де́рево

maid [мэйд] *sf.* го́рничная, дома́шняя рабо́тница; *coll.* деви́ца, де́вушка

maiden [мэ́й-дӗн] *sf.* деви́ца

mail [мэйл] *sn.* броня́, панцырь, *m.*; по́чта (*post*); *vt.* посыла́ть по́чтой

maim [мэйм] *vt.* кале́чить

main [мэйн] *adj.* гла́вный

mainland [мэйн-лэнд] *sn.* матери́к

mainly [мэйн-ли] *adv.* гла́вным о́бразом

mainspring [мэйн-спри́нг] *sn.* ходова́я пружи́на

mainstay [мэйн-стэй] *sn.* гла́вная подде́ржка

maintain [мэйн-тэйн] *vt.* подде́рживать, содержа́ть; утвержда́ть (*assert*)

maintenance [мэйн-тэ-нэнс] *sn.* подде́ржка, содержа́ние; сре́дства существова́ния (*means of subsistence*)

maize [мэйз] *sn.* кукуру́за, маис

majestic [мэ-джэ́с-тик] *adj.* вели́чественный

majesty [мэ́-джис-ти] *sn.* вели́чественность; вели́чество (*title*)

major [мэй-джэр] *sm. mil.* майо́р; совершенноле́тний (*of age*); *adj.* бо́льший, ста́рший; *mus.* мажо́рный

majority [мэ-джо́-ри-ти] *sn.* большинство́; совершенноле́тие (*age*)

make [мэйк] *vt.* де́лать (*do*); создава́ть (*create*); производи́ть, твори́ть (*produce*); приготовля́ть (*prepare*); заставля́ть (*force*)

make-believe [мэйк-би-лiв] *sn.* притво́рство (*pretence*); воображе́ние (*fancy*)

maker [мэй-кэр] *sm.* созда́тель, творе́ц

makeshift [мэйк-шифт] *sn.* вре́менная заме́на

make-up [мэйк-ап] *sn.* грим; *vi.* гримирова́ться

malady [мэ́-лэ-ди] *sn.* боле́знь, расстро́йство здоро́вья

male [мэйл] *sm.* мужчи́на; саме́ц (*animal*); *adj.* мужско́й

malevolent [мэ-ле-во́-лэнт] *adj.* зло́радный, недоброжела́тельный

malice [мэ́-лис] *sn.* злоба́; престу́пное наме́рение (*evil intention*)

malicious [мэ-ли́-шэс] *adj.* зло́бный; преднаме́ренный (*premeditated*)

malignant [мэ-ли́г-нэнт] *adj.* зло́бный, ядови́тый; злока́чественный (*of illness*)

malleable [мэ-ли-а́бл] *adj.* ко́вкий, податли́вый

mallet [мэ́-лiт] *sn.* деревя́нный молото́к

malnutrition [мэл-ню-три́шэн] *sn.* недоеда́ние

malt [молт] *sn.* со́лод; *vt.* солоди́ть

maltreat [мэл-три́т] *vt.* жесто́ко обраща́ться

maltster [молт-стэр] *sm.* солодо́вник

mammal [мэ́-мэл] *sn.* млекопита́ющее живо́тное

mammoth [мэ́-мэθ] *adj.* грома́дный

man [мэн] *sm.* мужчи́на (*male*); челове́к (*person*); ша́шка (*in games*); ~ **of letters** [~ ов ле́-тэрз] писа́тель, учёный; *vt.* снабжа́ть людьми́

manage [мэ́-нiдж] *vt.* заве́дывать, руководи́ть

management [мэ́-нiдж-мэнт] *sn.* управле́ние

manager [мӓ-ни-джӓр] *sm.*
заве́дующий, прави́тель

managerial [мӓ-нӓ-джи-ри́-
ӓл] *adj.* дире́кторский, отно-
ся́щийся к управле́нию

mandate [мӓн-дэйт] *sn.*
манда́т; прика́з (*instruction*);
предписа́ние (*injunction*)

mane [мэйн] *sn.* гри́ва

manger [мэйн-джӓр] *sn.*
я́сли

mangle [мӓнгл] *sn.* като́к;
vt. ката́ть (*put through
mangle*)

manhood [мӓн-хӯд] *sn.*
му́жественность, му́жество

mania [мэ́й-ни] *sn.* ма́ния

maniac [мэ́й-ни-ӓк] *sm.* без-
у́мец, манья́к; *adj.* поме́-
шанный

manicure [мӓ-ни-кю́р] *sn.*
маникю́р; *vt.* де́лать мани-
кю́р

manifest [мӓ-ни-фе́ст] *adj.*
очеви́дный, я́вный (*obvious,
visible*); несомне́нный (*indubitable*); *vt.* проявля́ть

manifestation [мӓ-ни-фе́с-
тэ́й-шӓн] *sn.* манифеста́ция,
проявле́ние

manifold [мӓ-ни-фо́улд]
adj. многообра́зный, много-
численный, разнообра́з-
ный; *vt.* размножа́ть

manipulate [мӓ-ни́-пю-
лэйт] *vt.* манипули́ровать,
уме́ло обраща́ться

mankind [мӓн-ка́йнд] *sn.*
челове́чество

manly [мӓн-ли] *adj.* му́же-
ственный

mannequin [мӓн-ни-ки́н] *sn.*
манеке́н; *sf.* менеке́нщица

manner [мӓ-нӓр] *sn.* о́браз,
спо́соб; сорт (*sort*); стиль
(*style*); **all – of things** [о̄л –

ов би́йз] вся́чина; *pl.* ма-
не́ры, нра́вы, обы́чаи; **no –s**
[но́у –з] пло́хо воспи́тан

mannerly [мӓ-нӓр-ли] *adj.*
воспи́танный (*well brought
up*); ве́жливый, прили́ч-
ный (*decorous*)

manœuvre [мӓ-ну́вр] *sn.*
мане́вр; *vt.i.* маневри́ро-
вать

man-of-war [мӓн-ов-уо́р]
sn. вое́нное су́дно

manor [мӓ-нӓр] *sn.* по-
ме́стье; **– house** [– ха́ус]
поме́щичий дом

mansion [мӓн-шӓн] *sn.*
большо́й особня́к

manpower [мӓн-пау-ӓр] *sn.*
рабо́чая си́ла; людско́й со-
ста́в (*men available*)

manslaughter [мӓн-сло́-
тӓр] *sn.* непреду́мышлен-
ное уби́йство

mantel [мӓнтл] *sn.* обли-
цо́вка ками́на

mantelpiece [мӓнтл-пис] *sn.*
ками́н

mantle [мӓнтл] *sn.* ма́нтия,
наки́дка, плащ; кали́льная
се́тка (*gas*)

manual [мӓ-ню-ӓл] *sn.* ру-
ково́дство, уче́бник; *adj.*
ручно́й

manufacture [мӓ-ню-фӓ́к-
чӓр] *sn.* произво́дство, фаб-
рика́ция; *vt.* выде́лывать,
фабрикова́ть

manufacturer [мӓ-ню-
фӓ́к-чӓ-рӓр] *sm.* фабри-
ка́нт

manure [мӓ-ню́-ӓр] *sn.* на-
во́з; *vt.* удобря́ть, унава́жи-
вать

manuscript [мӓ-ню-скри́пт]
sn. ру́копись; *adj.* руко-
пи́сный

many [мέ-ни] *sn.* мно́жество (*considerable number*); мно́гие, многочи́сленные; **how –?** [хаў –] ско́лько?; **one too –** [ўан тӯ –] ли́шний

map [мэп] *sn.* географи́ческая ка́рта

maple [мэ́йпл] *sn.* клён

mar [ма̄р] *vt.* по́ртить (*spoil*); повреждáть (*impair*)

marble [ма̄рбл] *sn.* мра́мор; ша́рик (*children's*)

march [ма̄рч] *sn.* марш, похо́д; *vt.i.* марширова́ть

March [ма̄рч] *sn.* март

mare [мэ̄р] *sf.* кобы́ла; **–'s nest** [-з нест] вздор

margin [ма̄р-джин] *sn.* край (*border*); грань (*verge*); *typ.* по́ле

marine [мǎ-ри́н] *sm.* моря́к; *sn.* флот; *adj.* морско́й

marital [мέ-ри-тǎл] *adj.* супру́жеский

maritime [мέ-ри-тайм] *adj.* примо́рский

mark [ма̄рк] *sn.* мише́нь, цель (*target*); знак, отме́тка (*symbol*); ме́тка (*sign*); *vt.* ста́вить знак

market [ма̄р-кит] *sn.* ры́нок

market-place [ма̄р-кит-плэйс] *sn.* база́рная пло́щадь

marksman [ма́ркс-мǎн] *sm.* иску́сный стрело́к

marmalade [ма̄р-мǎ-лэйд] *sn.* мармела́д, апельси́новое варе́нье

maroon [мǎ-ру́н] *sn.* кашта́новый цвет (*colour*); **to be –ed** [ту би́ –д] быть в безлю́дной ме́стности

marquee [ма̄р-ки́] *sn.* пала́тка

marriage [мέ-ридж] *sn.*

брак, жени́тьба; сва́дьба (*wedding*); **– lines** [– лайнз] бра́чное свиде́тельство

married [мέ-рид] *adj.* заму́жняя (*of woman*); жена́тый (*of man*)

marrow [мέ-роў] *sn. bot.* кабачо́к, мозгова́я ты́ква; *anat.* костный мозг; *fig.* су́щность; **to be chilled to the –** [ту би чи́лд ту еǎ́ –] продро́гнуть до мо́зга косте́й

marry [мέ-ри] *vt.i.* венча́ться (*wed*); жени́ться (*of man*); выходи́ть за́муж (*of woman*); жени́ть (*join in marriage*)

marsh [ма̄рш] *sn.* боло́то

marshal [ма̄р-шǎл] *sn. mil.* ма́ршал; (*civic*) церемоний-ме́йстер; *vt.* выстра́ивать, приводи́ть в поря́док

marshland [ма́рш-лэнд] *sn.* боло́тистая ме́стность

mart [ма̄рт] *sn. coll.* торго́вый центр

martial [ма̄р-шǎл] *adj.* вое́нный, вои́нственный; **– law** [– ло̄] вое́нное положе́ние; **court –** [ко̄рт –] полево́й суд

martyr [ма̄р-тǎр] *sm.* му́ченик; *vt.* му́чить

martyrdom [ма́р-тǎр-дǎм] *sn.* му́ченичество

marvel [ма́р-вǎл] *sn.* чу́до; *vi.* изумля́ться, удивля́ться

marvellous [ма́р-вǎ-лǎс] *adj.* изуми́тельный, чуде́сный

masculine [мэ́с-кю-лǐн] *adj.* мужско́й (*of gender*); мужественный (*manly*)

mash [мэш] *sn.* по́йло; *vt.* разда́вливать, размина́ть

mask [ма̄ск] *sn.* ма́ска; *vt.* маскирова́ть

mason [мэй-сан] *sm.* каменщик *(tradesman)*; масон

masonic [ма-со́-нік] *adj.* масо́нский

masonry [мэй-сан-рі] *sn.* ка́менная кла́дка

masquerade [мэс-ка-рэ́йд] *sn.* маскара́д; *vi.* маскирова́ться; *fig.* притворя́ться

mass [мэс] *sn.* гру́да, ку́ча, ма́сса, *(celebration)* ме́сса; *vt.i.* собира́ть в ку́чу; *mil.* концентри́ровать

massacre [мэ́-са-ка́р] *sn.* бо́йня, избие́ние, резня́

massage [мэ-са́ж] *sn.* масса́ж; *vt.* масси́ровать

massive [мэ́-сів] *adj.* масси́вный, соли́дный

mast [мэст] *sn.* naut. ма́чта

master [мэ́с-тар] *sm.* владе́лец *(owner)*; господи́н *(mister)*; хозя́ин *(employer)*; глава́ *(head)*; учи́тель *(teacher)*; худо́жник *(skilled artist)*; *vt.* овладева́ть *(gain proficiency)*; одолева́ть *(overcome)*

masterful [мэ́с-тар-фул] *adj.* вла́стный

masterpiece [мэ́с-тар-пис] *sn.* шеде́вр *(замеча́тельное произведе́ние)*

masticate [мэ́с-ті-кэйт] *vt.* жева́ть, разжёвывать

mastication [мэс-ті-кэ́й-шан] *sn.* жева́ние

mat [мэт] *sn.* половик, цыно́вка, доро́жка *(for table, etc.)*; *adj.* ма́товый, неполиро́ванный *(of surface)*; *vt.* стели́ть цыно́вки

match [мэч] *sn.* спи́чка *(for igniting)*; состяза́ние *(competition)*; па́ра, ро́вня *(resembling)*; *vt.* подбира́ть,

подходи́ть, соотве́тствовать

match-box [мэч-бокс] *sn.* спи́чечница

match-making [мэч-мэ́й-кін] *sn.* сватовство́

mate [мэйт] *sm.* това́рищ, naut. помо́щник; мат *(chess)*; *vt.i.* спа́риваться

material [ма-ті-рі-ал] *sn.* материа́л; мате́рия *(textile)*; *adj.* веще́ственный, материа́льный

materialize [ма-ті-ріа-лайз] *vt.i.* осуществля́ть

maternal [ма-тё́р-нал] *adj.* матери́нский

maternity [ма-тё́р-ні-ті] *sn.* матери́нство; — **home** [— хо́ум] роди́льный дом

mathematics [мэ-ѳа-мэ́-тікс] *sn. pl.* матема́тика

mating [мэ́й-тін] *sn.* спа́ривание

matriculation [ма-трі-кюле́й-шан] *sn.* вступи́тельный экза́мен в университе́т

matrimonial [мэ-трі-мо́у-ні-ал] *adj.* супру́жеский

matrimony [мэ́-трі-ма-ні] *sn.* супру́жество

matron [мэ́й-трэн] *sf.* заму́жняя же́нщина, матро́на; эконо́мка *(of school or establishment)*

matter [мэ́-тар] *sn.* вещество́, мате́рия; предме́т, содержа́ние *(subject)*; де́ло *(affair, concern)*; мед. гной; **as a** — **of fact** [эз а́ — ов фэкт] на са́мом де́ле; **no**— [но́ —] безразли́чно; *vi.* име́ть значе́ние; *med.* гнои́ться

matter-of-fact [мэ́-таров-фэкт] *adj.* обыкнове́нный, прозаи́ческий

matting [мǽ-тiн] *sn.* цынóвка

mattress [мǽ-трiс] *sn.* маттрáц, тюфя́к

mature [мǎ-тю́р] *adj.* зрéлый, спéлый (*ripe*); вполнé рáзвитый (*fully developed*); *vt.i.* созревáть (*ripen*); развиться (*develop*)

maturity [мǽ-тю́-ри-ти] *sn.* зрéлость (*ripeness*); завершéние (*completion*)

maul [мōл] *vt.* вредить, калéчить

mauve [мōув] *sn.*, *adj.* блéдно-пурпу́рный (цвет)

May [мǽй] *sn.* май

may [мǽй] *modal v.* мочь, имéть разрешéние; **it – be** [iт – би] возмóжно, мóжет быть

maybe [мǽй-би] *adv.* мóжет быть

mayor [мǽй-ǎр] *sm.* мэр

mayoralty [мǽр-ǎлти] *sn.* дóлжность мэра

mayoress [мǽр-éс] *sf.* женá мэра

maze [мǽйз] *sn.* лабиринт, пу́таница

me [ми] *pron.* мне, меня́

meadow [мé-доу] *sn.* луг

meagre [мигр] *adj.* худóй (*lean*); скýдный (*scanty*); недостáточный (*insufficient*)

meal [мил] *sn.* мукá крýпного помóла (*flour*); едá, принятие пищи (*repast*)

meal-time [мил-тайм] *sn.* врéмя приня́тия пищи

mean [мин] *sn.* середина; *adj.* низкий, пóдлый, скупóй (*low, stingy*); срéдний (*half-way*); **in the – time** [iн ðǎ – тайм] тем врéменем; *vt.* знáчить (*signify*);

имéть намéрение (*intend*); предполагáть (*surmise*)

meaning [ми́-нiн] *sn.* значéние, смысл; *adj.* значительный

meanness [ми́н-нiс] *sn.* пóдлость

means [минз] *sn. pl.* спóсоб, срéдства; **by all –** [бǎй бл –] во что бы то ни стáло, конéчно; **by no –** [бǎй ноу –] никóим óбразом; отню́дь не; **by – of** [бǎй – ов] посрéдством

meantime, meanwhile [ми́н-тайм, ми́н-уǎйл] мéжду тéм, как, тем врéменем

measles [ми́-зǎлз] *sn. pl.* корь; **German –** [джéр-мǎн –] краснýха

measure [мé-жǎр] *sn.* мéра, мéрка, размéр; *mus.* такт; *math.* дéлитель; **made to –** [мǽйд ту –] сдéланный на закáз; *vt.* измеря́ть

measured [мé-жǎрд] *adj.* обдýманный (*of expressions, etc.*); размéренный, ритми́ческий (*rhythmical*)

measurement [мé-жǎр-мǎнт] *sn.* измерéние; *pl.* размéры

meat [мит] *sn.* мя́со

meaty [ми́-ти] *adj.* мяси́стый; *fig.* содержáтельный

mechanic [мi-кǽ-нiк] *sm.* механик; *pl.* механика

mechanical [мi-кǽ-нi-кǎл] *adj.* маши́нный, механи́ческий; маши́нальный (*automatic*)

mechanism [мé-кǎ-низм] *sn.* констрýкция, механи́зм

mechanize [мé-кǎ-найз] *vt.* механизировать

medal [мé-дǎл] *sn.* медáль

meddle [мέдл] *vi.* вмέши-
ваться

mediate [мú-ди-эйт] *vi.* мири́ть, посрέдничать

mediator [мú-ди-эй-тăр] *sm.* посрέдник

medical [мέ-ди-кăл] *adj.* врачέбный, медицú́нский

medicated [мέ-ди-кэй-тид] *adj.* лекáрственный

medicinal [ме-дú-си-нăл] *adj.* лекáрственный, целέбный

medicine [мέ-ди-си́н] *sn.* лекáрство; медицú́на (*science*)

medieval [мε-дú́-и-вăл] *adj.* средневекóвый

meditate [мέ-ди-тэйт] *vi.* размышля́ть

meditation [ме-ди-тέй-шăн] *sn.* размышлέние

medium [мú-ди-ăм] *sn.* посрέдство, срέдство (*agency*); мέдиум (*intermediary*); *adj.* срέдний

medley [мέд-ли] *sn.* смесь, смешέние (*mixture*); *mus.* попурú

meek [мик] *adj.* крóткий

meekness [мú́к-нис] *sn.* крóтость

meet [мит] *vt.i.* встречáть; испы́тывать, подвергáться (*difficulties, etc.*); собирáться (*gather*)

meeting [мú-тйн] *sn.* заседáние, мú́тинг, собрáние; встрέча (*encounter*)

melancholy [мέ-лăн-ка-ли] *sn.* грусть, меланхóлия, уны́ние; *adj.* грýстный, меланхолú́ческий

mellow [мέ-лоу] *adj.* зрέлый, слáдкий, сóчный (*of fruit*); вы́держанный (*of wine*); мя́гкий (*of voice, colour, etc.*)

melodious [мі-лóу-ди-ăс] *adj.* мелодú́чный

melody [мέ-лă-ди] *sn.* мелóдия; мелодú́чность (*tunefulness*)

melon [мέ-лăн] *sn.* ды́ня; water – [уó-тăр –] арбýз

melt [мелт] *vt.i.* плáвить, растопля́ться (*fuse*); тáять (*thaw*); – away [– ă-уέй] исчезáть (*vanish*)

member [мέм-бăр] *sn.* член

membership [мέм-бăр-шип] *sn.* члέнство; колú́чество члέнов (*number of members*)

membrane [мέм-брэйн] *sn.* оболóчка, перепóнка, плέнка

memento [мă-мέн-тоу] *sn.* напоминáние; сувенú́р

memoir [мέ-мýăр] *sn.* крáткая биогрáфия; *pl.* мемуáры; учέные запú́ски (*record of researches, etc.*)

memorable [мέ-мă-рăбл] *adj.* достопáмятный, незабвέнный

memorial [мε-мó-ри-ăл] *sn.* пáмятник; *adj.* мемориáльный, пáмятный; *pl.* исторú́ческая хрóника

memorize [мέ-мă-райз] *vt.* запоминáть, заýчивать наизýст

memory [мέ-мă-ри] *sn.* воспоминáние, пáмять; **in – of** [ин – ов] в пáмять

menace [мέ-нăс] *sn.* угрóза; *vt.* грозú́ть, угрожáть

menacing [мέ-на-сйн] *adj.* угрожáющий

menagerie [мă-нáє-джă-ри] *sn.* зверú́нец

mend [мэнд] *sn.* заштопанная дырка (*mended hole*); заделанная трещина (*mended crack*); **on the** – [он ðə –] на попра́вку; *vt.i.* исправля́ть, чини́ть, што́пать; улучша́ться (*improve*)

menial [ми́-ниэл] *adj.* лаке́йский, рабо́лепный

menstruation [мэн-стру́-эй-шн] *sn.* менструа́ция

mental [мэ́н-тэл] *adj.* мы́сленный, у́мственный; – **affection** [– ǎ-фе́к-шан] душе́вная боле́знь

mentality [мэн-тǎ́-ли-ти] *sn.* мышле́ние

mention [мэ́н-шан] *sn.* упомина́ние; намёк (*allusion*); *vt.* упомина́ть; **don't** – **it** [до́унт – ит] не сто́ит благода́рности (*of thanks*); **not to** – ... [нот ту –] уже́ не говоря́ о ...

mercantile [мǎр-кǎн-тайл] *adj.* комме́рческий, торго́вый; – **marine** [– мǎ-ри́н] торго́вый флот

mercenary [мǎр-си-нǎ-ри] *sm.* наёмник; *adj.* коры́стный (*covetous*); наёмный (*hired*); прода́жный (*corrupt*)

merchandise [мǎр-чǎн-дайз] *sn.* това́р

merchant [мǎр-чǎнт] *sm.* купе́ц, торго́вец

merchantman [мǎр-чǎнт-мǎн] *sn.* торго́вое су́дно

merciful [мǎр-си-фул] *adj.* милосе́рдный; сострада́тельный (*compassionate*)

merciless [мǎр-си-лǐс] *adj.* безжа́лостный

mercury [мǎр-кю-ри] *sn.* ртуть; ртутный препара́т

mercy [мǎр-си] *sn.* милосе́рдие, поща́да; ми́лость, проще́ние (*forgiveness*); **at the** – **of** [æт ðǎ – ов] во вла́сти

mere [мир] *adj.* просто́й, сплошно́й; – **words** [– уǒрдз] одни́ слова́

merely [ми́р-ли] *adv.* про́сто, то́лько

merge [мǎрдж] *vt.i.* поглоща́ть; слива́ться

merger [мǎр-джǎр] *sn.* объедине́ние, поглоще́ние

merit [мэ́-рит] *sn.* досто́инство, ка́чество; *pl.* заслу́ги (*deserts*); *vt.* быть досто́йным, заслу́живать

meritorious [мэ-ри-то́-ри-ǎс] *adj.* похва́льный

mermaid [мǎр-мэйд] *sf.* руса́лка, сире́на

merriment [мэ́-ри-мǎнт] *sn.* весе́лье

merry [мэ́-ри] *adj.* весёлый; **make** – [мэйк –] весели́ться

merry-go-round [мэ́-ри-гоу-ра́унд] *sn.* карусе́ль

mesh [мэш] *sn.* яче́йка се́ти

mess [мэс] *sn.* беспоря́док, пу́таница (*disorder*); грязь (*dirt*); *mil.* о́бщий стол; *vt.* гря́знить, па́чкать (*dirty, soil*); производи́ть беспоря́док (*create confusion*); сда́ть за о́бщим столо́м (*take meals together*)

message [мэ́-сидж] *sn.* обще́ние; поруче́ние (*errand*)

messenger [мэ́-сǐн-джǎр] *sm.* по́сланный, посы́льный; курье́р

metal [мэ́-тǎл] *sn.* мета́лл; ще́бень, *m.* (*stone for road making*); *pl.* ре́льсы (*rails*)

metallic [мє-тǽ-лік] *adj.* металли́ческий

metallurgy [мє-тǽ-лǝр-джі] *sn.* металлу́ргия

meter [ми́-тǝр] *sn.* счётчик (*apparatus*)

method [мé-ѳǝд] *sn.* мéтод, спóсоб; систéма

methodical [мє-ѳó-ді-кǝл] *adj.* методи́ческий, системати́ческий

meticulous [мє-ті́-кю-лǝс] *adj.* дотóшный (*scrupulous*); мéлочный (*petty*)

metre [митр] *sn.* метр

metric [мé-трік] *adj.* метри́ческий

metropolis [мє-трó-пǝ-ліс] *sn.* столи́ца; метропóлия

metropolitan [мє-трǝ-пó-лі-тǝн] *adj.* столи́чный

mettle [мéтл] *sn.* пыл (*fervour*); рети́вость (*zeal*)

mews [мюз] *sn. pl.* конюшня

mica [ма́й-кǝ] *sn.* слюда́

microbe [ма́й-кроуб] *sn.* микрóб

microphone [ма́й-крǝ-фоун] *sn.* микрофóн

microscope [ма́й-крǝ-скоуп] *sn.* микроскóп

mid [мід] *adj.* срéдний

midday [мід-дéй] *sn.* пóлдень, *m.*

middle [мідл] *sn.* середи́на; *adj.* срéдинный, срéдний

middleman [мідл-мǽн] *sn.* посрéдник

middling [мі́-дліñ] *adj.* второсóртный (*second rate*); довóльно снóсно (*fairly well*)

midge [мідж] *s.* мóшка

midget [мі́-джіт] *sn.* кáрлик

midnight [мі́д-найт] *sn.* пóлночь

midst [мідст] *sn.* середи́на; **in our —** [ін ма́уǝр] в нáшей средé, среди́ нас

midsummer [мíд-сǝ-мǝр] *sn.* середи́на лéта

midwife [мíд-уǎйф] *sf.* акушéрка, повивáльная бáбка

midwifery [мíд-ўíф-рі] *sn.* акушéрство

might [майт] *sn.* могу́щество; *modal v.* (прошéдшее от **may**)

mighty [ма́й-ті] *adj.* могу́щественный, мóщный; громáдный, масси́вный (*huge, massive*); *adv. coll.* óчень, совершéнно, чрезвычáйно

migrant [ма́й-грǝнт] *s.* переселéнец

migrate [май-грéйт] *vi.* переселя́ться

migration [май-грéй-шǝн] *sn.* переселéние

milage [ма́й-лідж] *sn.* расстоя́ние в ми́лях

mild [майлд] *adj.* мя́гкий (*of character, climate, etc.*); умéренный (*moderate*); слáбый (*of beer, medicine, etc.*); крóткий (*meek*)

mildew [мíл-дю] *sn.* ми́лдью, плéсень

mildness [ма́йлд-ніс] *sn.* мя́гкость, слáбость

mile [майл] *sn.* ми́ля

milestone [ма́йл-стоун] *sn.* верстовóй столб, ми́льный кáмень; *fig.* вéха в жи́зни

militant [мí-лі-тǝнт] *adj.* войнствующий

military [мí-лі-тǎ-рі] *sn.* **the —** воéнная си́ла, воéнные; *adj.* воéнный, вóинский

milk [мілк] *sn.* молокó; *vt.* дои́ть

milk-float [мілк-флоўт] *sn.* тележка молочницы

milkmaid [мілк-мэйд] *sf.* молочница

milky [мíл-кі] *adj.* молочный; млечный (*lactic*); — **way** [— ўэй] млечный путь

mill [міл] *sn.* мельница; завод, фабрика (*factory*); *vt.i.* молоть, дробить (*crush*); валять (*full*)

millboard [міл-бôрд] *sn.* толстый картон

millenium [мі-лé-ні-ăм] *sn.* тысячелетие; *bibl.* золотой век

miller [мі-лăр] *sm.* мельник

millet [мі-літ] *sn.* просо

milliner [мі-лі-нăр] *sf.* модистка

millinery [мі-лі-нă-рі] *sn.* дамские шляпы

million [міл-ліăн] *num.* миллион

millstone [міл-стоўн] *sn.* жёрнов

milt [мілт] *sn.* молоки (*soft roe*)

mimic [мі-мік] *sm.* имитатор, подражатель; *vt.* подражать

mimicry [мі-мі-крі] *sn.* подражательность

mince [мінс] *vt.* крошить, рубить; говорить жеманно, жеманиться (*restrain one's words*)

mincemeat [мінс-мит] *sn.* фарш

mincing machine [мін-сін мă-шін] *sn.* мясорубка

mind [майнд] *sn.* рассудок, ум (*intellect*); память (*memory*); мнение (*opinion*); сознание (*conscience*); **never —l** [нé-вăр —] ничего!; *vt.*

заботиться, беречь (*take care*); остерегаться (*beware*)

mindful [майнд-фул] *adj.* заботливый

mine [майн] *sn.* рудник, копь; мина (*explosive charge*); шахта (*pit*); **gold** — [гоўлд —] золотой прииск; *fig.* источник; *vt.i.* добывать, копать; минировать; *pron.* мой

minefield [майн-филд] *sn.* минное поле

minelayer [майн-лэй-ăр] *sn.* минный заградитель

miner [май-нăр] *sm.* горнорабочий, горняк

mineral [мі-нă-рăл] *sn.* минерал; *adj.* минеральный

minesweeper [майн-сўі-пăр] *sn.* минный тральщик

mingle [мінгл] *vt.i.* смешивать; вращаться (*with others*)

miniature [мі-ні-ăтюр] *sn.* миниатюра; *adj.* миниатюрный

minim [мí-нім] *sn.* *mus.* полунота; капля (*liquid measure*)

minimize [мі-ні-майз] *vt.* доводить до минимума

mining [май-нін] *sn.* горное дело

minister [мí-ні-стăр] *sm.* министр, посланник; священник (*clergyman*); *vt.i.* прислуживать, служить; *eccl.* совершать богослужение

ministerial [мі-ні-сті-рі-ăл] *adj.* министерский, правительственный

ministry [мí-ні-стрі] *sn.* кабинет, министерство; служение (*service*); *eccl.* священство

minor [ма́й-нăр] *sm.* несовершенноле́тний; *adj.* ма́лый, ме́ньший; *mus.* мино́рный

minority [май-но́-рі-ті] *sn.* меньшинство́

minster [мі́н-стăр] *sm.* кафедра́льный собо́р

minstrel [мі́н-стрăл] *sm.* менестре́ль, *m.*; средневеко́вый певе́ц (*medieval singer*)

mint [мінт] *sn.* моне́тный двор; *bot.* мя́та; *vt.* чека́нить

minus [ма́й-нăс] *adj.* лише́нный (*deprived*), отрица́тельный (*negative, of quantities*); *prep.* без, ми́нус

minute [мі́-ніт] *sn.* мину́та (*time*), заме́тка (*note*); *pl.* протоко́л; [май-нют] *adj.* ме́лкий (*very small*); подро́бный (*detailed*)

minutely [май-нют-лі] *adv.* подро́бно

miracle [мі́-рă-кăл] *sn.* чу́до

miraculous [мі-рэ́-кю-лăс] *adj.* чуде́сный, чудотво́рный

mire [май-ăр] *sn.* грязь (*mud*); тряси́на (*bog*)

mirror [мі́-рăр] *sn.* зе́ркало; *vt.* отража́ть

mirth [мœрθ] *sn.* весе́лье, ра́дость

misapprehension [мі́сăпрі-хĕн-шăн] *sn.* недоразуме́ние, непра́вильное представле́ние

misbehave [мі́с-бі-хэ́йв] *adj.* вести́ себя́ пло́хо

miscalculate [мі́с-кăл-кю-лэ́йт] *vt.i.* ошиба́ться в расчёте, просчита́ться

miscarriage [мі́с-кă-рідж] *sn.* неуда́ча; вы́кидыш (*untimely delivery*)

miscarry [мі́с-кă-рі] *vt.* затеря́ться (*fail to reach destination*); потерпе́ть неуда́чу (*suffer failure*)

miscellaneous [мі-сі-ле́йні-ăс] *adj.* разнообра́зный (*various*); сме́шанный (*mixed*)

miscellany [мі́с-сĕ-лă-ні] *sn.* сбо́рник (*collection*); смесь (*medley*)

mischief [мі́с-чіф] *sn.* вред, зло; де́тские прока́зы (*children's*)

mischievous [мі́с-чі-вăс] *adj.* зло́бный, злонаме́ренный; непослу́шный (*of children*)

misdemeanour [мі́с-ді-мі́нăр] *sn.* просту́пок

miser [ма́й-зăр] *sn.* скря́га

miserable [мі́-зă-рăбл] *adj.* жа́лкий (*pitiable*); несча́стный (*unhappy*), скупо́й (*mean*), скве́рный (*bad*)

misery [мі́-зă-рі] *sn.* несча́стье (*unhappiness*); нищета́ (*poverty*)

misfortune [мі́с-фо́р-чăн] *sn.* бе́дствие, несча́стье

misgiving [мі́с-гі́-віŋ] *sn.* сомне́ние, опасе́ние

mishap [мі́с-хæп] *sn.* злоключе́ние, неуда́ча

mislay [мі́с-лэ́й] *vt.* затеря́ть

mislead [мі́с-лі́д] *vt.* вводи́ть в заблужде́ние

misrepresentation [мі́с-прі-зĕн-тэ́й-шăн] *sn.* искаже́ние

miss [міс] *sf.* ба́рышня, де́вушка (*young lady*); про́мах (*failure, missing*); *vt.i.* промахну́ться, пропусти́ть; скуча́ть, чу́вствовать отсу́тствие (*regret absence*)

missile [мі-сайл] *sn.* снаря́д; *adj.* мета́тельный

missing [мі-сіñ] *adj.* недоста́ющий, отсу́тствующий; пропа́вший (*assumed lost*)

mission [мі́-шäн] *sn.* ми́ссия; призва́ние (*calling*); поруче́ние (*commission*)

missionary [мі́-шä-нä-рі] *sm.* миссионе́р; *adj.* миссионе́рский

mist [міст] *sn.* ды́мка; мгла (*haze*); тума́н (*fog*)

mistake [міс-тэ́йк] *sn.* оши́бка; *vi.* ошиба́ться; не поня́ть (*misunderstand*)

mistaken [міс-тэ́й-кäн] *adj.* оши́бочный

mister [мі́-стäр] *sm.* господи́н; **Mr.**, г-н

mistletoe [мі́сл-тоў] *sn.* оме́ла

mistress [мі́с-тріс] *sf.* хозя́йка (*owner, superior*); учи́тельница (*teacher*); **Mrs.** [мі́-сіс] госпожа́, г-жа

mistrust [міс-тра́ст] *sn.* недове́рие; *vt.* не доверя́ть; подозрева́ть (*doubt, suspect*)

misunderstanding [міс-ан-дäр-ста́н-дін] *sn.* недоразуме́ние

misuse [міс-ю́с] *sn.* злоупотребле́ние; [міс-ю́з] *vt.* злоупотребля́ть

mite [майт] *sn.* zool. клещ, лёпта; ма́ленькое существо́ (*minute thing*); ребёнок (*child*)

mitigate [мі́-ті-гэйт] *vt.* облегча́ть, смягча́ть (*alleviate*); умиротворя́ть (*appease*)

mitten [мі́-тäн] *sn.* ва́режка; рукави́ца (*long*)

mix [мікс] *vt.i.* сме́шивать, обща́ться, сходи́ться (*have social intercourse*)

mixed [мікст] *adj.* сме́шанный

mixer [мі́-ксäр] *tech.* меша́лка, смеси́тель

mixture [мікс-чäр] *sn.* смесь; *med.* миксту́ра

mix-up [мікс-ап] *sn.* неразбери́ха

moan [моўн] *sn.* стон; *vi.* стона́ть; жа́ловаться (*complain*)

moat [моўт] *sn.* ров

mob [моб] *sn.* толпа́; *vt.* напада́ть толпо́й

mobile [мо́ў-байл] *adj.* подви́жной; *mil.* моби́льный

mobility [моў-бі-лі-ті] *sn.* подви́жность; *mil.* моби́льность

mobilization [моў-бі-лай-зэ́й-шäн] *sn.* мобилиза́ция

mock [мок] *adj.* ло́жный, притво́рный; – **trial** – [тра́й-äл] инсцени́рованный проце́сс

mockery [мо́-кä-рі] *sn.* насме́шка

modal [моў-дäл] *adj.* gram. мода́льный

mode [моўд] *sn.* вид, о́браз, спо́соб

model [мо́-дäл] *sn.* моде́ль; образе́ц (*pattern*); нату́рщик (*living model*); приме́р (*example*); *adj.* образцо́вый; *vt.* модели́ровать

moderate [мо́-дä-ріт] *adj.* скро́мный, уме́ренный; посре́дственный, сре́дний (*of quality*); *vt.i.* сде́рживаться; умеря́ть

moderation [мо-дä-рэ́й-шäн] *sn.* уме́ренность

modern [мо́-дäрн] *adj.* совреме́нный

modest [мо́-діст] *adj.* скро́мный

modesty [мо́-дис-ті] *sn.* скро́мность

modification [мо-ді-фі-ке́й-шан] *sn.* видоизмене́ние

modify [мо́-ді-фай] *vt.* изменя́ть, смягча́ть

moist [мойст] *adj.* вла́жный, сыро́й

moisten [мо́й-сăн] *vt.* сма́чивать, увлажня́ть

moisture [мо́йс-чăр] *sn.* вла́жность, сы́рость

mole [моўл] *s.* крот (*animal*); мол (*jetty*); да́мба (*breakwater*); ро́динка (*on skin*)

molest [мо-ле́ст] *vt.* досажда́ть, пристава́ть, трево́жить

molten [мо́ўл-тăн] *adj.* лито́й, распла́вленный

moment [мо́ў-мăнт] *sn.* миг, моме́нт

momentary [мо́ў-мăн-тă-рі] *adj.* мгнове́нный, момента́льный, преходя́щий

momentous [моў-ме́н-тăс] *adj.* ва́жный (*important*); чрева́тый после́дствиями (*pregnant with consequences*)

monarchy [мо́-нăр-кі] *sn.* мона́рхия

monastery [мо́-нăс-трі] *sn.* монасты́рь, *m.*

monastic [ма-на́с-тік] *adj.* монасты́рский

Monday [ма́н-ді] *sn.* понеде́льник

monetary [мо́-ні-тă-рі] *adj.* де́нежный, моне́тный

money [ма́-ні] *sn.* де́ньги

money-box [ма́-ні-бокс] *sn.* копи́лка

money-lender [ма́-ні-лен-дăр] *sn.* ростовщи́к

money-order [ма́-ні-ор-дăр] *sn.* де́нежный перево́д

mongrel [ма́й-грăл] *s.* дворня́га; по́месь (*cross*); *adj.* нечистокро́вный

monitor [мо́-ні-тăр] *sm.* наста́вник (*preceptor*); сове́тчик (*adviser*); ста́рший учени́к (*senior scholar*); *naut.* монито́р

monk [манк] *sm.* мона́х

monkey [ма́н-кі] *s.* обезья́на; *tech.* ба́ба (*pile*); — *vi.* забавля́ться, подшу́чивать; — **wrench** [— рénч] англи́йский ключ

monopoly [мă-но́-пă-лі] *sn.* монопо́лия

monotonous [мă-но́-тă-нăс] *adj.* моното́нный

monotony [мă-но́-тă-ні] *sn.* моното́нность, однообра́зие

monster [мо́н-стăр] *sn.* чудо́вище, уро́д; *adj.* грома́дный (*huge*)

monstrous [мо́н-стрăс] *adj.* уро́дливый, чудо́вищный, исполи́нский (*gigantic*)

month [манθ] *sn.* ме́сяц

monthly [ма́н-θлі] *adj.* ме́сячный; ежеме́сячный (*each month*)

monument [мо́-ню-мăнт] *sn.* па́мятник

monumental [мо-ню-ме́н-тăл] *adj.* монумента́льный; увекове́чивающий (*permanent*)

mood [муд] *sn.* настрое́ние; *gram.* наклоне́ние

moody [му́-ді] *adj.* угрю́мый, хму́рый

moon [мун] *sn.* луна́, ме́сяц; **full** [фул —] полнолу́ние; **half** [хăф —] полулу́ние; **new** [ню —] новолу́ние; **once in a blue** [уăнс ін ă блу —] в ко́и-то ве́ки; броди́ть

moonbeam [мӯн-бим] *sn.* луч луны

moonlight [мӯн-лайт] *sn.* лунный свет

moor [мӯр] *sn.* невозделанные земли; *vt. naut.* причаливать к берегу, швартовать

moorings [мӯ-ри͡ез] *sn. pl.* причалы, стоянка на якоре

moot [мӯт] *adj.* спорный; *vt.* ставить вопрос

mop [моп] *sn.* швабра; *v.* чистить шваброй; – **up** [– ап] вытирать; *mil.* очищать от неприятеля; – **one's brow** [– ýанз брау] утирать пот с лица

mope [мо͡уп] *vi.* хандрить

moral [мó-рǎл] *adj.* нравственный

morale [мǎ-рáл] *sn.* моральное состояние

morality [мǎ-рӓ-ли-ти] *sn.* нравственность

morbid [мóр-бид] *adj.* болезненный

more [мóр] *adj., adv.* более, больше

moreover [мор-óу-вǎр] *adv.* кроме того, сверх того

morning [мóр-ний] *sn.* утро; *adj.* утренний; – **coat** [– кóут] визитка; **good – !** [гуд –] здравствуйте!; – **rose утро**, **in the –** [ин ðǎ –] утром

morose [мǎ-рóус] *adj.* брюзгливый, угрюмый

morsel [мóр-сǎл] *sn.* кусочек

mortal [мóр-тǎл] *adj.* смертельный, смертный

mortality [мор-тӓ-ли-ти] *sn.* смертность

mortar [мóр-тǎр] *sn.* из-

вестковый раствор, мертель (*cement, etc.*); ступка (*vessel*); *mil.* мортира

mortgage [мóр-гидж] *sn.* заклад, ипотека; *vt.* закладывать; ручаться (*pledge*)

mortify [мóр-ти-фай] *vt.i.* досаждать, огорчать, унижать; *med.* гнить, омертветь

mortuary [мóр-тю-ǎри] *sn.* мертвецкая, покойницкая; *adj.* погребальный, похоронный

mosque [моск] *sn.* мечеть

mosquito [мос-кú-то͡у] *s.* комар, москит

moss [мос] *sn.* мох

most [мо͡уст] *adj.* наибольший; *adv.* больше всего, наиболее; **make the – of** [мэйк ðǎ – ов] использовать вовсю

mostly [мо͡уст-ли] *adv.* главным образом; почти всегда (*almost always*)

moth [моθ] *s.* моль, мотылёк

mothball [моθ-бōл] *sn.* нафталиновый шарик

mother [мá-ðǎр] *sf.* мать; – **country** [– кан-три] родина; – **of pearl** [– ов пѐрл] перламутр; – **tongue** [– тан] родной язык

motherhood [мá-ðǎр-худ] *sn.* материнство

mother-in-law [мá-ðǎр-ин-лō] *sf.* тёща (*husband's*); свекровь (*wife's*)

motherly [мá-ðǎр-ли] *adj.* материнский

motion [мó͡у-шǎн] *sn.* движение, ход (*movement*); жест (*gesture*); предложение (*proposition*); *med.* действие, испражнение

motionless [мо́у-шăн-ліс] *adj.* неподви́жный

motive [мо́у-тів] *sn.* моти́в, побужде́ние; *adj.* дви́гательный, дви́жущий

motor [мо́у-тăр] *sn.* дви́гатель, мото́р; – **bicycle** [–ба́й-сікл] мотоцикле́т; *vt.i.* е́хать на автомоби́ле

motor-car [мо́у-тăр-ка̄р] *sn.* автомоби́ль, *m.*

motoring [мо́у-тă-рін] *sn.* автомоби́льная езда́

mottled [мо́-тăлд] *adj.* крапча́тый, пятни́стый

motto [мо́-тоу] *sn.* деви́з, ло́зунг, эпигра́ф

mould [моулд] *sn.* взрыхлённая земля́ (*loose earth*); пле́сень (*fungus*); фо́рма (*shape*); фо́рмочка (*for jellies, etc.*); *vt.* отлива́ть в фо́рму

moult [моулт] *vt.i.* линя́ть

mound [маунд] *sn.* на́сыпь (*heap of earth*); хо́лмик (*hill*)

mount [маунт] *sn.* ло́шадь под седло́м (*horse*); *vt.i.* восходи́ть, поднима́ться (*ascend*); монти́ровать; устана́вливать (*erect machinery, etc.*)

mountain [ма́ун-тін] *sn.* гора́; *adj.* го́рный

mountaineer [маун-ті-ни́р] *sm.* го́рец

mountainous [ма́ун-ті-нăс] *adj.* гори́стый

mourn [мо̄рн] *vt.i.* опла́кивать

mourner [мо̄р-нăр] *sm.* пла́кальщик

mournful [мо̄рн-фул] *adj.* жа́лобный, печа́льный, тра́урный

mourning [мо̄р-нін] *sn.* тра́ур

mouse [мау́с] *s.* мышь

mousetrap [ма́ус-трăп] *sn.* мышело́вка

moustache [мўс-та́ш] *sn.* ус

mouth [мауθ] *sn.* рот; отве́рстие (*opening*); го́рлышко (*of bottle*); у́стье (*of river*)

mouthful [ма́уθ-фул] *sn.* глото́к

mouthpiece [ма́уθ-пис] *sn.* мундшту́к; *fig. m.* вырази́тель

movable [му́-вăбл] *adj.* подви́жно́й; *sn. pl.* дви́жимость, дви́жимое иму́щество

move [мув] *sn.* ход (*chess*); шаг (*step*); **get a – on** [гет ă – он] спеши́ть, торопи́ться; *vt.i.* дви́гать, шевели́ться (*shift*); побужда́ть, тро́гать (*affect, stir, rouse*); – **about** [– ă-ба́ут] дви́гаться

movement [му́в-мăнт] *sn.* движе́ние; *mus.* темп; *tech.* ход

mover [му́-вăр] *sn.* предлага́тель; *sn.* **prime** – [прайм–] исто́чник дви́жущей си́лы

moving [му́-він] *adj.* дви́жущий; волну́ющий, тро́гательный (*emotional*)

mow [моу] *sn.* скирда́, стог; *vt.i.* коси́ть

mower [мо́у-ăр] *sm.* косе́ц; *sn.* коси́лка

mowing [мо́у-ін] *sn.* косьба́, скаши́вание

much [мач] *adj., adv.* мно́го; **as** – [ăз –] сто́лько; **how** – [ха́у –] ско́лько; **too** – [ту́ –] сли́шком мно́го

muck [мак] *sn.* грязь (*dirt*), наво́з (*manure*); *coll.* дрянь, ме́рзость

mucous [мю́-кăс] *adj.* сли́зистый

mucus [мю́-кэс] *sn.* слизь

mud [мад] *sn.* слякоть, тина

muddle [мадл] *sn.* беспоря́док, пу́таница; *vi.* спу́тывать

muddy [ма́-ді] *adj.* гря́зный, тини́стый; му́тный

mudguard [ма́д-гāрд] *sn.* автомоби́льное крыло́, щит от гря́зи

muff [маф] *sn.* му́фта

muffin [ма́-фін] *sn.* кру́глая бу́лочка

muffle [мафл] *vt.* заку́тывать, оку́тывать; заглуша́ть (*deaden sound*)

muffler [ма́ф-лăр] *sn.* кашне́, шарф; *tech.* глуши́тель, *m.*

mug [маг] *sn.* кру́жка

muggy [ма́-гі] *adj.* тёплый и вла́жный; удуши́вый (*oppressive*)

mule [мюл] *sm.* мул

multiple [ма́л-тіпл] *sn.* кра́тное число́; *adj.* многокра́тный, многочи́сленный

multiplication [мал-ті- плі-кэ́й-шăн] *sn.* умноже́ние

multiplier [ма́л-ті-плай-ăр] *sn.* мно́житель, *m.*

multiply [ма́л-ті-плай] *vt.i.* умножа́ть; увели́чиваться (*increase*)

multitude [ма́л-ті-тюд] *sn.* мно́жество; толпа́ (*crowd*)

mumble [мамбл] *sn.* бормота́нье; *vt.i.* бормота́ть; ча́вкать (*when eating*)

mummy [ма́-мі] *sn.* му́мия (*corpse*); ма́ма (*mother*)

mumps [мампс] *sn. pl.* сви́нка

munch [манч] *vt.i.* жева́ть,

municipal [мю-ні-сі-пăл] *adj.* городско́й, муниципа́льный

municipality [мю-ні-сі-па́-лі-ті] *sn.* го́род с самоуправле́нием; муниципалите́т

munitions [мю-ні-шăнс] *sn. pl.* вое́нные запа́сы

mural [мю́-рăл] *adj.* стенно́й

murder [мёр-дăр] *sn.* уби́йство; *vt.* убива́ть

murderer [мёр-дă-рăр] *sm.* уби́йца

murderous [мёр-дă-рăс] *adj.* уби́йственный

murky [мёр-кі] *adj.* мра́чный, тёмный

murmur [мёр-мăр] *sn.* журча́нье, шо́рох; *vi.* журча́ть, ропта́ть

muscle [масл] *sn.* му́скул, мы́шца

muscular [ма́с-кю-лăр] *adj.* му́скулистый, му́скульный

muse [мюз] *vi.* мечта́ть, размышля́ть

museum [мю-зі-ăм] *sn.* музе́й

mushroom [маш-ру́м] *sn.* гриб

music [мю́-зік] *sn.* му́зыка; но́ты (*sheet music*)

musical [мю́-зі-кăл] *adj.* музыка́льный; мелоди́чный (*tuneful*)

musician [мю-зі́-шăн] *sn.* музыка́нт

musket [ма́с-кіт] *sn.* мушке́т

musketry [ма́с-кіт-рі] *sn.* руже́йное упражне́ние

muslin [маз-лі́н] *sn.* кисея́

mussel [масл] *sn.* двуство́рчатая ра́ковина

must [маст] *v. aux.* I – [ай –] я до́лжен; долженствова́ть (*to be obliged*)

mustard [ма́с-тăрд] *sn.* горчи́ца; – **plaster** [– пла́с-тăр] горчи́чник; – **pot** [– пот] горчи́чница

muster [мáс-тăр] sn. o-смóтр, переклúчка, смотр; vt.i. собирáться

musty [мáс-ті] adj. зáтхлый; устарéлый (antiquated)

mutation [мю-тэ́й-шăн] sn. изменéние, перемéна; biol. мутáция

mute [мют] sm. немóй (person); sn. согласный (consonant); mus. сурдúнка; adj. немóй (of person); безглáсный, молчалúвый (soundless, silent)

mutilate [мю́-ті-лэйт] vt. увéчить, искажáть (distort)

mutilation [мю́-ті-лэ́й-шăн] sn. увéчье; искажéние (distortion)

mutineer [мю-ті-нúр] sm. мятéжник

mutiny [мю́-ті-ні] sn. восстáние, мятéж; vi. взбунтовáться (enforce silence)

mutter [мá-тăр] sn. бормотáнье, рóпот; vt.i. бормотáть

mutton [мá-тăн] sm. барáнина; adj. барáний

mutual [мю́-тью-ăл] adj. взаúмный, обоюдный (reciprocal)

muzzle [мăзл] sn. мóрда, ры́ло (snout); дýло, жерлó (of rifle); намóрдник (dog's); vt. затыкáть, надевáть (намóрдник); fig. заставить молчáть (enforce silence)

my [май] pron. мой

myself [май-сéлф] pron. сам, себя

mysterious [міс-тú-рі-ăс] adj. таúнственный

mystery [міс-тă-рі] sn. тáйна; мистéрия (rite); rel. тáинство

mystify [мíс-ті-фай] vt. мистифицировать

myth [міθ] sn. миф

mythical [мí-θі-кăл] adj. мифúческий

N

nab [нæб] vt. coll. поймáть, схватúть; обнарýживать (detect)

nag [нæг] s. coll. лóшадь; vt.i. изводúть, придирáться

nail [нэйл] sn. нóготь (on finger and toe); кóготь (bird's); гвоздь, m. (metal); **hard as -s** [хăрд æз -з] закалённый; **on the -** [он θă -] срáзу, тóтчас-же; vt. прибивáть гвоздями; coll. захватúть, овладéть

nailbrush [нэйл-браш] sn. щётка для ногтéй

naïve [нă-úв] adj. наúвный

naked [нэ́й-кід] adj. гóлый, нагóй; незащищённый (defenceless); обнажённый (bare, exposed)

name [нэйм] sn. úмя, назвáние; фамúлия; слáва (fame); **by -** [бай -] по úмени; vt. звать, назывáть; назначáть (nominate), обозначáть, укáзывать (specify)

nameless [нэ́йм-ліс] adj. безымя́нный

namely [нэ́йм-лі] adv. úменно, то-есть

namesake [нэ́йм-сэйк] sn. тёзка

nanny [нæ-ні] sf. ня́ня

nanny-goat [нæ-ні-гоýт] sf. козá

nap [нæп] *sn.* ворс (*on cloth*); дремо́та (*sleep*); *vi.* вздремну́ть, дрема́ть

nape [нэйп] *sn.* — **of the neck** [— ов ðæ нэк] за́дняя часть ше́и

napkin [нæп-кін] *sn.* салфе́тка (*serviette*); пелён-ка (*sanitary towel*)

narrate [нæ-рэ́йт] *vt.* пове́ствовать, расска́зывать

narration [нæ-рэ́й-шън] *sn.* повествова́ние

narrative [нæ-рǎ-тів] *sn.* по́весть, расска́з

narrator [нæ-рэ́й-тǎр] *sm.* расска́зчик

narrow [нæ-ро́у] *adj.* те́сный, у́зкий; *vt.i.* ограни́чивать, су́живать(ся); *sn. pl.* тесни́на; — **-minded** [—-ма́йн-дід] *с* у́зким кругозо́ром

nasal [нэй-зǎл] *adj.* гнуса́вый, носово́й

nasty [нáс-ті] *adj.* га́дкий, ме́рзкий; отврати́тельный (*of smell, taste*); па́костный (*obscene*); скве́рный, бу́рный (*of weather*)

natal [нэй-тǎл] *adj.* роди́мый

nation [нэй-шǎн] *sn.* на́ция; наро́д (*people*); **United —s** [ю-на́й-тід —з] Объединённые На́ции

national [нæ-шǎ-нǎл] *adj.* наро́дный, национа́льный

nationality [нæ-шǎ-нǎ-лі-ті] *sn.* наро́дность, национа́льность

native [нэй-тів] *sn.* тузе́мец; уроже́нец; *adj.* тузе́мный; — **-country** [— кáн-трі] оте́чество; ме́стный (*indigenous*); саморо́дный (*of metals*)

natural [нæ-чǎ-рǎл] *sn. mus.* бека́р; *adj.* есте́ственный, натура́льный (*normal*); приро́дный (*inborn*); внебра́чный (*illegitimate*)

naturalization [нæ-чǎ-рǎ-лай-зэ́й-шǎн] *sn.* натурализа́ция

naturally [нæ-чǎ-рǎ-лі] *adv.* есте́ственно, конечно

nature [нэй-чǎр] *sn.* приро́да; нату́ра (*character*)

naught [нôт] *sn.* ничто́ (*nothing*); *math.* ноль

naughtiness [нô-ті-ніс] *sn.* непослу́шность; шаловли́вость (*child's*)

naughty [нô-ті] *adj.* непослу́шный, капри́зный, шаловли́вый

nausea [нô-сіǎ] *sn.* тошнота́; отвраще́ние (*loathing*)

nautical [нô-ті-кǎл] *adj.* морско́й

naval [нэй-вǎл] *adj.* кора́бельный, фло́тский

nave [нэйв] *sn.* неф (*of church*); ступи́ца колеса́ (*of wheel*); вту́лка маховика́ (*hub*)

navel [нэй-вǎл] *sn.* пупо́к

navigable [нæ-ві-гǎбл] *adj.* судохо́дный

navigate [нæ-ві-гэйт] *vt.i.* пла́вать (на корабле́) (*sail ship*), лета́ть (на самолёте) (*fly plane*); управля́ть (*direct course, manage ship, etc.*)

navigation [нæ-ві-гэ́й-шǎн] *sn.* пла́вание, судохо́дство; навига́ция (*science*)

navigator [нæ-ві-гэ́й-тǎр] *sm.* морепла́ватель; шту́рман (*pilot*)

navvy [нæ-ві] *sm.* землеко́п; *sn.* землечерпа́лка

navy [нэй-ві] *sn.* военно-морской флот

navy-blue [нэй-ві-блу] *adj.* темносиний

naze [нэйз] *sn.* мыс

near [нир] *adj.* ближний, ближайший, близкий; *adv.* близко, подле, около; вблизи (*in proximity*); *prep.* близ, возле, около; *vt.i.* подходить, приближаться

nearly [нир-лі] *adv.* почти, приблизительно

near-sighted [нир-сай-тід] *adj.* близорукий

neat [нит] *adj.* чистый (*clean*), опрятный (*tidy*); беспримесный (*of drink*); отточенный (*of style, etc.*)

nebulous [нэ-бю-лəс] *adj.* облачный, туманный

necessary [нэ-сі-сэ-рі] *adj.* надобный, необходимый, нужный

necessitate [ні-сэ-сі-тэйт] *vt.* делать необходимым, вынуждать (*compel*)

necessity [ні-сэ-сі-ті] *sn.* необходимость, нужда, потребность

neck [нэк] *sn.* шея; горлышко (*of bottle*); гриф, шейка (*of violin, 'cello, etc.*)

neckband [нэк-бэнд] *sn.* ворот, обшивка (рубашки)

neckerchief [нэ-кəр-чиф] *sn.* шейный платок

necklace [нэк-ліс] *sn.* ожерелье

necklet [нэк-літ] *sn.* меховая горжетка, ошейник

neck-tie [нэк-тай] *sn.* галстук

née [нэй] *adj. f.* урожденная

need [нид] *sn.* надобность, нужда; *vt.i.* иметь надобность; нуждаться

needle [нидл] *sn.* игла, иголка

needless [нид-ліс] *adj.* излишний, ненужный

needlewoman [нидл-уумəн] *sf.* портниха, швея

needlework [нидл-уəəрк] *sn.* вышивание, шитье

needy [ни-ді] *adj.* неимущий, нуждающийся

negate [ні-гэйт] *vt.* отрицать

negation [ні-гэй-шəн] *sn.* отрицание

negative [нэ-гə-тів] *sn.* отрицательное утверждение; *phot.* негатив; *adj.* отрицательный, негативный; *vt.* возражать, отвергать; противоречить (*contradict*)

neglect [ні-глэкт] *sn.* запущение, пренебрежение; *vt.* запускать, пренебрегать

neglectful [ні-глэкт-фул] *adj.* забывчивый, невнимательный

negligence [нэ-глі-джəнс] *sn.* небрежность, нерадивость

negligent [нэ-глі-джəнт] *adj.* небрежный

negligible [нэ-глі-джібл] *adj.* незначительный

negotiable [ні-гоу-ші-əбл] *adj.* могущий быть переступленным (*of cheque, etc.*); доступный, проходимый (*accessible, passable*)

negotiate [ні-гоу-ші-эйт] *vt.i.* вести переговоры, договариваться; торговать (*bargain*)

negotiations [ні-гоу-ші-эй-шəнз] *sn. pl.* переговоры

negotiator [ні-гоу-ші-эй-тəр] *sm.* посредник

Negro [ні-гроў] *sm.* негр; *adj.* негритянский

neigh [нэй] *sn.* ржа́ние; *vi.* ржать

neighbour [нэй-бăр] *sm.* сосе́д

neighbourhood [нэй-бăр-хўд] *sn.* сосе́дство (*people of a district*); окре́стности, окру́га (*district*); бли́зость (*vicinity*)

neighbouring [нэй-бă-рiñ] *adj.* сме́жный, сосе́дний

neighbourly [нэй-бăр-лi] *adj.* добрососе́дний, дру́жеский

neither [на́й-ѕăр] *adj.* ни оди́н, никако́й; *adv.* ни, никто́; *pron.* ни тот ни друго́й; *conj.* ни; **neither ... nor** [- ... нôр] ни ... ни ...

nephew [не́-вю] *sm.* племя́нник

nerve [нŏрв] *sn.* нерв; *bot.* жи́лка; *pl.* не́рвность; не́рвы

nervous [нŏр-вăс] *adj.* не́рвный; ро́бкий (*diffident*); беспоко́йный (*agitated*)

nervousness [нŏр-вăс-ніс] *sn.* не́рвность, раздражи́тельность

nest [нест] *sn.* гнездо́; гнёздышко, ую́тный уголо́к (*snug retreat*); *vi.* гнезди́ться

nestle [несл] *vi.* приюти́ться, устра́иваться

net [нет] *sn.* се́тка, сеть; тенёта (*snare*); *adj. com.* не́тто, чи́стый; – **price** [- прайс] действи́тельная цена́; – **profit** [- прó-фіт] чи́стая при́быль; *vt.i.* ло-ви́ть сетя́ми (*catch with*)

nettle [нетл] *sn. bot.* крапи́ва; *vt.* обжига́ть крапи́вой; – **rash** [– рăш] крапи́вная лихора́дка

network [нéт-ўŏрк] *sn.* сеть (*railways*); плетёная рабо́та

neuralgia [ню-рăл-джiă] *sn.* невралги́я

neuter [ню́-тăр] *sn. gram.* сре́дний род (*gender*); непере-хо́дный глаго́л (*intransitive verb*); *adj.* сре́дний; *bot.* беспо́лый (*asexual*)

neutral [ню́-трăл] *adj.* нейтра́льный; безуча́стный (*impartial*)

neutrality [ню-трă-лi-тi] *sn.* нейтралите́т

neutralize [ню́-трă-лайз] *vt.* нейтрализова́ть, урав-нове́шивать (*counterbalance*)

never [не́-вăр] *adv.* никогда́; – **mind!** [– майнд] ничего́!, пустяки́!

nevertheless [не-вăр-ѕă-ле́с] *adv.* несмотря́ на, тем не ме́нее, одна́ко

new [ню] *adj.* но́вый; све́жий (*fresh*); молодо́й (*of wine, potatoes, etc.*); ра́ний (*of liquid*)

newcomer [ню́-ка-мăр] *sm., f.* вновь прибы́вший

newly [ню́-лi] *adj.* вновь, за́ново (*afresh*); неда́вно, то́лько что (*recently*)

news [нюз] *sn.* изве́стия, но́вости

newsagent [нюз-эй-джăнт] *sm.* газе́тчик

newspaper [ню́с-пэй-пăр] *sn.* газе́та

news-print [ню́з-прінт] *sn.* газе́тная бума́га

news-room [ню́з-рўм] *sn.* газе́тная чита́льня

next [нэкст] *adj.* сле́дующий; ближа́йший, сосе́дний (*nearest*); *adv.* по́сле, пото́м; **what — ?** [уот —] что да́льше? *prep.* ря́дом

nib [ніб] *sn.* остриё пера́

nibble [нібл] *sn.* куса́нье; клев; *vt.i.* грызть, обку́сывать; клева́ть (*as fish*)

nice [найс] *adj.* ми́лый (*kind*); хоро́ший (*good*); прия́тный (*pleasant*)

nicety [най-сі-ті] *sn.* то́чность (*precision*); утончённость (*subtle quality*)

nick [нік] *sn.* зару́бка, отме́тина (*notch*); **in the — of time** [ін оâ — ов тайм] как-раз во́-время; *vt.* де́лать зару́бки (*indent*)

nickname [нік-нэйм] *sn.* прозвище

niece [ніс] *sf.* племя́нница

niggardly [ні-гâрд-лі] *adj.* скаре́дный, скуды́й

nigger [ні-гâр] *sm.* темноко́ричневый цвет (*colour*)

night [найт] *sn.* ночь

nightcap [найт-кэп] *sn.* колпа́к

nightdress [найт-дрес] *sn.* ночна́я соро́чка

nightfall [найт-фôл] *sn.* су́мерки

nightingale [най-тін-гэйл] *s.* солове́й

night-light [найт-лайт] *sn.* ночни́к

nightly [найт-лі] *adj.* ночно́й; *adv.* ежено́щный

nightmare [найт-мэр] *sn.* кошма́р

nil [ніл] *sn.* нуль (*zero*); ничего́ (*nothing*)

nimble [німбл] *adj.* ло́вкий; прово́рный; ги́бкий (*mind*)

nine [найн] *num.* де́вять

nineteen [найн-ті́н] *num.* девятна́дцать

ninety [найн-ті] *num.* девяно́сто

nip [ніп] *sn.* щипо́к; *vt.* сжима́ть, щипа́ть

nippers [ні-пârз] *sn. pl.* щипцы́

nipple [ніпл] *sn.* сосо́к; со́ска (*of feeding bottle*)

no [но́у] *adj.* никако́й; **— one** [— уан] никто́; *adv.* не; *particle*, нет

nobility [но́у-бі-лі-ті] *sn.* дворя́нство

noble [но́убл] *adj.* благоро́дный

nobleman [но́убл-мân] *sm.* дворяни́н

nobody [но́у-бâ-ді] *sn.* ничто́жество; *pron.* никто́

nod [нод] *sn.* киво́к; *vt.i.* кива́ть

noise [нойз] *sn.* гро́хот, шум

noiseless [нойз-лíс] *adj.* бесшу́мный

noisy [но́й-зі] *adj.* шу́мный

nominal [но́-мі-нâл] *adj.* именно́й, номина́льный; нарица́тельный (*of price*); усло́вный (*of sentence*)

nominate [но́-мі-нэйт] *vt.* именова́ть, назнача́ть, называ́ть; выставля́ть (*a candidate*)

nomination [но-мі-нэй-шân] *sn.* назначе́ние (*to a post*); выставле́ние (*for election*)

nominative [но́-мі-нâ-тів] *sn. gram.* имени́тельный паде́ж (*case*); *adj.* имени́тельный

nominee [но-мі-ні́] *sm.* наименно́ванный кандида́т

nonchalance [нóн-ша-лянс] *sn.* беззабóтность, безразлѝчие, бесстрáстность

nonchalant [нóн-ша-лянт] *adj.* беззабóтный, безразлѝчный, бесстрáстный

non-committal [нан-кă-мѝтăл] *adj.* уклóнчивый

none [нан] *adj.* не, ни, никакóй, ни одѝн; *pron.* никто́, ничтó; *adv.* нискóлько, совсѐм не

nonsense [нóн-сăнс] *sn.* бессмы́слица, вздор, ерундá, чепухá

nonsensical [нăн-сѐн-сикăл] *adj.* вздóрный, бессмы́сленный

nook [нӯк] *sn.* закоýлок

noon [нӯн] *sn.* пóлдень, *m.*

noose [нӯс] *sn.* лассó, пѐтля; ловýшка, силóк (*trap*); *vt.* заманѝть в ловýшку

nor [нóр] *conj.* ни

normal [нóр-мăл] *adj.* нормáльный, обыкновѐнный

north [нóрθ] *sn.* сѐвер; *adv.* к сѐверу (*towards*); на сѐвере (*in the*)

northerly [нóр-ðăр-ли] *adj.* напрáвленный к сѐверу; дýющий с сѐвера; *adv.* на сѐвер

northern [нóр-ðăрн] *adj.* сѐверный

Norwegian [нор-уѝ-джăн] *sn.* норвѐжец; *adj.* норвѐжский

nose [нóуз] *sn.* нос

nosebag [нóуз-бæг] *sn.* тóрба

nose-dive [нóуз-дайв] *sn.* ныря́ние, пикѝрование; *vi.* ныря́ть, пикѝровать

nosegay [нóуз-гэй] *sn.* букѐт

nostalgia [нăс-тǽл-джѝă] *sn.* ностальгѝя, тоскá по рóдине

nostril [нóс-трѝл] *sn.* ноздря́

not [нот] *adv.* не; нет; – **at all** [– æт óл] совсѐм нет

notable [нóу-тăбл] *adj.* замечáтельный, значѝтельный; выдаю́щийся (*of person*)

notation [ноу-тѐй-шăн] *sn.* систѐма обозначѐния; *mus.* нóтная зáпись

notch [ноч] *sn.* вы́емка, зарýбка, прорѐз; *vt.* дѐлать вы́емки

note [нóут] *sn.* примечáние, снóска (*comment, footnote*); знак (*mark*); запѝска (*short letter, memo*); *mus.* нóта; *vt.* замечáть; обращáть внимáние (*observe, take note*)

notebook [нóут-бӯк] *sn.* запѝсная книжка

noted [нóу-тѝд] *adj.* знаменѝтый

notepaper [нóут-пѐй-пăр] *sn.* почтóвая бумáга

noteworthy [нóут-ўăр-ðи] *adj.* достопримечáтельный

nothing [нá-ðѝн] *sn.* ничегó, ничтó; *adv.* нискóлько, совсѐм нет

notice [нóу-тѝс] *sn.* извещѐние, уведомлѐние; объявлѐние (*announcement*); **at short** [æт шóрт –] в корóткий срок; **give –** [гѝв –] предупреждáть; *vt.* замечáть, обращáть внимáние; отмечáть

noticeable [нóу-тѝ-сăбл] *adj.* замѐтный, примѐтный

notification [ноу-тѝ-фѝ-кѐйшăн] *sn.* повѐстка, сообщѐние

notify [нóу-тѝ-фай] *vt.* извещáть, осведомля́ть, уведомля́ть

notion [ноу́-шăн] *sn.* взгляд, мне́ние, представле́ние (*concept*); наме́рение, по́мысел (*intention*)

notoriety [ноу-тă-ра́й-ăти] *sn.* гла́сность, изве́стность (*reputation*); дурна́я сла́ва (*ill fame*)

notorious [ноу-то́-ри-ăс] *adj.* изве́стный, пресло́вутый; отъя́вленный (*arch-*)

notwithstanding [нот-уйётстăн-дий] *adv.* одна́ко, тем не ме́нее; *prep.* несмотря́ на; *conj.* хотя́

nought [нот] *sn.* нуль; ничего́ (*nothing*)

noun [на́ун] *sn. gram.* и́мя существи́тельное

nourish [на́-риш] *vt.* корми́ть, пита́ть

nourishing [на́-ри-ший] *adj.* пита́тельный

nourishment [на́-ришмăнт] *sn.* пита́ние (*sustenance*); пи́ща (*food*)

novel [но́-вăл] *sn.* рома́н (*fictitious tale*); по́весть (*narrative, story*); *adj.* но́вый (*new*); неизве́данный (*unknown*)

novelist [но́-вă-лист] *sm.* писа́тель-романи́ст

novelty [но́-вăл-ти] *sn.* новизна́, но́вость

November [но-ве́м-бăр] *sn.* ноя́брь

novice [но́-вис] *sm.* нови́чок; учени́к (*learner*)

novitiate [но-ви́-ши-ăт] *sn.* пери́од учени́чества, иску́с

now [на́у] *sn.* настоя́щее вре́мя; *adv.* сейча́с, тепе́рь; – **and then** [– ăнд ϑ̆ен] иногда́; *conj.* а, же

nowadays [на́у-ă-дэйз] *sn.*

на́ше вре́мя; *adv.* в нынешнем времена́

nowhere [но́у-уэр] *adv.* нигде́

noxious [нок-шăс] *adj.* вре́дный, па́губный

nozzle [нозл] *sn.* но́сик, ры́льце, сопло́

nuclear [нё-кли-ăр] *adj.* я́дерный; а́томный

nucleus [нё-кли-ăс] *sn.* яче́йка (*cell*); заро́дыш (*embryo*)

nude [нюд] *sn.* обнажённая фигу́ра; *adj.* го́лый, наго́й

nudge [надж] *sn.* лёгкий толчо́к; *vt.* подзадо́ривать, подта́лкивать

nudity [нё-ди-ти] *sn.* голизна́, нагота́

nuisance [нё-сăнс] *sn.* доса́да, неприя́тность; надое́дливый челове́к (*person*); **public –** [па́-блик –] наруше́ние обще́ственного поря́дка; **what a –!** [уот ă –] вот доса́да!

null [нал] *adj.* недействи́тельный (*not valid*); невырази́тельный (*expressionless*); несуществу́ющий (*non-existent*); **– and void** [– ăнд войд] недействи́тельный, не име́ющий си́лы (*юриди́ческое выраже́ние*)

numb [нам] *adj.* онеме́лый, оцепене́лый

number [на́м-бăр] *sn.* число́; коли́чество (*quantity*); мно́жество (*multitude*); су́мма (*sum*); но́мер (*of house, periodical, etc.*); *vt.* причисля́ть; нумерова́ть

numbness [на́м-нис] *sn.* онеме́ние, оцепене́ние

numeral [нё-мă-рăл] *sn.* ци́фра; *adj.* числово́й

numeration [ню-мă-рэ́й-шăн] sn. исчисле́ние, нумера́ция

numerator [ню́-мă-рэ́й-тăр] sm. вычисли́тель, нумера́тор; math. числи́тель

numerical [ню-ме́-ри-кăл] adj. чи́сленный

numerous [ню́-мă-рăс] adj. многочи́сленный

nun [нан] sf. мона́хиня

nunnery [на́-нă-ри] sn. же́нский монасты́рь, m.

nuptial [на́п-шăл] adj. бра́чный, сва́дебный

nurse [нэ́рс] sf. корми́лица (wet); ня́ня (dry); сиде́лка (sitter-in); медици́нская сестра́ (hospital); vt. выка́рмливать (suckle); ня́нчить (children); уха́живать (the sick)

nursemaid [нэ́рс-мэйд] sf. ня́ня

nursery [нэ́р-сă-ри] sn. де́тская (children's); пито́мник, расса́дник (for plants); **public – for children** [па́-блик – фор чи́л-дрен] я́сли

nursing-home [нэ́р-сиŋ-хо́ум] sn. ча́стная лече́бница

nurture [нэ́р-чăр] sn. воспита́ние, взра́щивание, обуче́ние; vt. воспи́тывать, выра́щивать; пита́ть (feed)

nut [нат] sn. оре́х; tech. га́йка; pl. ме́лкий у́голь (coal)

nutcracker [на́т-крæ-кăр] sn. оре́шные клещи́цы

nutmeg [на́т-мег] sn. муска́тный оре́х

nutriment [ню́-три-мăнт] sn. пита́тельная пи́ща

nutrition [ню-три́-шăн] sn. пита́ние

nutshell [на́т-шел] sn. оре́ховая скорлупа́; **in a –** [ин ă –] fig. в двух слова́х, кра́тко, сжа́то

nutty [на́-ти] adj. име́ющий вкус оре́ха

nuzzle [назл] vt.i. ню́хать; рыть (burrow)

O

oak [о́ук] sn. дуб; adj. дубо́вый

oar [о́р] sn. весло́; vt. грести́

oarsman [о́рз-мăн] sm. гребе́ц

oasis [оŭ-э́й-сис] sn. оа́зис

oaten [оŭ-тăн] adj. овся́ный

oath [оŭθ] sn. кля́тва, прися́га; **on –** [он –] под прися́гой; бо́жба (swearing); прокля́тие, руга́тельство (curse, cursing)

oatmeal [о́ут-мил] sn. овся́нка

oats [о́утс] sn. pl. овёс

obdurate [о́б-дю-рĭт] adj. закоснéлый; упря́мый

obedience [о-би-ди́-ăнс] sn. повинове́ние, поко́рность, послуша́ние

obedient [о-би́-ди-ăнт] adj. послу́шный

obeisance [о-бе́й-сăнс] sn. почте́ние, уваже́ние; покло́н (bow, curtsy)

obelisk [о́-би-лĭск] sn. обели́ск; typ. знак ссы́лки (reference mark)

obese [оŭ-би́с] adj. по́лный, то́лстый, тучны́й

obesity [оŭ-би́-си-ти] sn. полнота́, ту́чность

obey [oў-бэ́й] *vt.i.* повиноваться, слушаться

obituary [о-би́-тю-а̀ри] *sn.* некролог; *adj.* некрологический

object [об-джи́кт] *sn.* вещь, предмет (*thing*); объект; намерение, цель (*aim*) *gram.* дополнение; [а̀б-джэ́кт] *vt.* возражать, противиться

objection [об-джэ́к-шän] *sn.* возражение, упрёк

objectionable [а̀б-джэ́к-шä-на̀бл] *adj.* нежелательный

objective [а̀б-джэ́к-тив] *sn. gram.* винительный (падёж); объектив; стремление, цель (*aspiration*); *adj.* объективный, предметный

objector [а̀б-джэ́к-тäр] *sn.* возражающий, отказывающийся

obligation [о-бли-гэ́й-шän] *sn.* обязанность

obligatory [ä-бли́-гä-три] *adj.* обязательный, принуждающий

oblige [ä-бла́йдж] *vt.* обязывать (*bind*); заставлять, принуждать (*compel*); делать одолжение, угождать (*gratify*); **much -d** [мач -д] очень обязан

obliging [ä-бла́й-дж] *adj.* любезный, услужливый

oblique [о-бли́к] *adj.* косой, наклонный; *gram.* косвенный; *vi. mil.* продвигаться вкось

obliterate [о-бли́-тä-рэйт] *vt.* вычёркивать

obliteration [о-бли-тä-рэ́й-шän] *sn.* вычёркивание; уничтожение (*annulment*)

oblivion [об-ли́-ви-äн] *sn.*

забвение; пренебрежение (*disregard*); **fall into -** [фол ин-ту -] быть преданным забвению

oblivious [об-ли́-ви-äс] *adj.* забывчивый, непомнящий

oblong [об-ло́нġ] *adj.* продолговатый, удлинённый

obnoxious [об-но́к-шäс] *adj.* несносный, противный

oboe [оў-бо́у] *sn.* гобой

obscene [об-си́н] *adj.* бесстыдный, непристойный

obscenity [об-си́-ни-ти] *sn.* бесстыдство, скабрёзность

obscure [об-скю́р] *adj.* тёмный, тусклый (*dim*); тёмный, непонятный (*indistinct*); скрытый (*hidden*); *vt.* затемнять, помрачать

obscurity [об-скю́-ри-ти] *sn.* мрак, тьма (*darkness*); неясность (*vagueness*)

obsequies [о́б-си-кўиз] *sn. pl.* погребение, похороны

obsequious [об-си́-кўи-äс] *adj.* подобострастный, раболепный

observance [äб-зёр-вäнс] *sn.* соблюдение (закона и пр.); обряд (*ceremonial*)

observant [äб-зёр-вäнт] *adj.* внимательный, наблюдательный

observation [об-зёр-вэ́й-шän] *sn.* высказывание, замечание (*comment*, *remark*); наблюдение (*perception*)

observatory [äб-зёр-вä-тä-ри] *sn.* обсерватория

observe [äб-зёрв] *vt.i.* наблюдать (*watch*); соблюдать (*adhere to*, *keep*); замечать (*perceive*); делать замечания (*comment*, *mark*)

observer [åб-зэ́р-вăр] *sm.* наблюдатель

obsess [åб-сéс] *vt.* завладевать, преследовать

obsession [åб-сé-шăн] *sn.* наваждение (*evil suggestion*); навязчивая идея (*fixed idea*)

obsolete [об-сă-лит] *adj.* вышедший из употребления, устарелый

obstacle [об-стăкл] *sn.* помеха, препятствие

obstinacy [об-сти-нă-си] *sn.* настойчивость, упрямство

obstinate [об-сти-нит] *adj.* упорный, упрямый

obstruct [åб-стрăкт] *vt.* блокировать, загораживать, затруднять проход (*hamper passage*)

obstruction [åб-стрăк-шăн] *sn.* заграждение, обструкция, препятствие

obtain [åб-тэ́йн] *vt.* получать (*receive*); добывать, доставать (*procure*); приобретать (*acquire*)

obtainable [åб-тэ́йн-ăбл] *adj.* достижимый

obtrusive [åб-тру́-сив] *adj.* навязчивый

obtuse [åб-тю́с] *adj.* тупой (*blunt*); бестолковый, неспособный (*of person*);

—angle [— ǽнгл] тупой угол

obverse [об-вэ́рс] *sn.* лицевая сторона

obvious [об-ви-ăс] *adj.* очевидный, явный

occasion [å-кэ́й-жăн] *sn.* случай, обстоятельство, повод, причина (*ground, reason*); событие (*event*);

seize the — [сиз эi —] воспользоваться случаем;

vt. причинять, служить поводом

occasional [å-кэ́й-жăн-ăл] *adj.* по временам, случайный

occasionally [å-кэ́й-жă-нăли] *adv.* время от времени, изредка, подчас

occult [о-кăлт] *adj.* оккультивный, сокровенный, тайный

occupant [о́-кю-пăнт] *sm.* жилец (*of house*); временный владелец (*temporary holder of property*)

occupation [о-кю-пэ́й-шăн] *sn.* занятие, профессия, *mil.* оккупация

occupier [о́-кю-пай-ăр] *sm.* жилец (*of dwelling*); арендатор (*lessee*)

occupy [о́-кю-пай] *vt.* занимать, арендовать; *mil.* оккупировать

occur [å-кăр] *vi.* попадаться, случаться

occurrence [å-кă-рăнс] *sn.* происшествие, случай

ocean [о́у-шăн] *sn.* океан; *fig.* масса, множество (*immense quantity*)

o'clock [о-клóк] *sn.* час; **at one —** [эт уа́н —] в один час

octave [о́к-тив] *sn.* *mus.* октава

October [ок-тó-бăр] *sn.* октябрь, *m.*

ocular [о-кю-лăр] *adj.* глазной, окулярный

odd [од] *adj.* непарный, разрозненный (*unpaired*); нечётный (*not even*); странный (*strange*); лишний (*supernumerary*)

oddment [о́д-мăнт] *sn.* остаток; *pl.* остатки

odds [одз] *sn. pl.* нера́венство (*inequalities*); ра́зница (*difference*); преиму́щество (*balance of advantage*); ша́нсы (*gambling*); держа́ть пари́ (*lay odds*); **– and ends** [– æнд ендз] оста́тки

ode [о́уд] *sn.* о́да

odious [о́у-ді-ăс] *adj.* нена́вистный, отврати́тельный

odour [о́у-дăр] *sn.* арома́т, благоуха́ние (*fragrance*); за́пах (*smell*)

of [ов] *prep.* из, от; **of course** [ов корс] коне́чно

off [оф] *adj.* бо́лее отдалённый (*farther*); *adv.* на расстоя́нии от, прочь (*at a distance*); **it is far –** [ит из фăр –] далеко́; *prep.* на, с со

offal [о́фăл] *sn.* объе́дки (*scraps*); отбро́сы, подо́нки (*waste food*); потроха́ (*intestines, giblets, etc.*)

offence [о-фе́нс] *sn.* оби́да, оскорбле́ние; просту́пок (*misdemeanour*); **no –!** [но́у –!] не обижа́йтесь!

offend [о-фе́нд] *vt.* обижа́ть, оскорбля́ть

offender [о-фе́н-дăр] *sm.* оби́дчик, оскорби́тель; правонаруши́тель, престу́пник (*criminal*)

offensive [о-фе́н-сів] *sn. mil.* наступле́ние; **take the –** [тэйк ѳі –] перейти́ в наступле́ние; *adj. mil.* агресси́вный, наступа́тельный; оскорби́тельный (*insulting*)

offer [о́-фăр] *sn.* предложе́ние; *vt.i.* предлага́ть; приноси́ть (*sacrifice*); явля́ться (*to present*); про́бовать, пыта́ться (*attempt*); случа́ться

offering [о́-фă-рій] *sn.* подноше́ние (*thing offered*); *eccl.* жертвоприноше́ние

off-hand [оф-хе́нд] *adv.* без приготовле́ний, экспро́мтом; *adj.* бесцеремо́нный

office [о́-фіс] *sn.* до́лжность, слу́жба (*function*); бюро́, канцеля́рия, конто́ра (*place of business*); **Foreign –** [фо́рін –] министе́рство иностра́нных дел; **Home –** [хо́ум –] министе́рство вну́тренних дел

officer [о́-фі-сăр] *sm.* офице́р; должностно́е лицо́ (*functionary*); чино́вник (*of government departments*)

official [о-фі́-шăл] *sm.* чино́вник, служа́щий; *adj.* официа́льный, служе́бный

officiate [о-фі́-ші-эйт] *vi.* исполня́ть обя́занности (*carry out duties*); *eccl.* соверша́ть богослуже́ние

offset [о́ф-сет] *sn.* ответвле́ние, отпры́ск; усту́п (*of mountain*); *vt.* возмеща́ть, своди́ть бала́нс; *typ.* литографи́ческий спо́соб печа́ти

offshoot [о́ф-шут] *sn.* отро́г, отро́сток

offspring [о́ф-спрій] *sn.* пото́мок

often [о́-фăн] *adv.* ча́сто, мно́го раз

oil [ойл] *sn.* (минера́льное, расти́тельное) ма́сло; нефть (*mineral oil*); ма́сло (*animal oil*); *vt.* ма́слить, сма́зывать

oilcan [ойл-кен] *s.* ма́слёнка

oilcloth [ойл-кло́ѳ] *sn.* клеёнка

oil-pipe [ойл-пайп] *sn.* нефтепрово́д

oilskin [ойл-скін] *sn.* промасленная ткань; *pl.* клеенчáтый костюм

oil-well [ойл-уэл] *sn.* нефтянáя скважина

oily [ой-лі] *adj.* жирный, масляни́стый

ointment [ойнт-мäнт] *sn.* мазь, помáда

old [оулд] *adj.* стáрый; **the -** [еі -] стари́к; дáвнишний, дрéвний (*antique*); **- age** [- эйдж] стáрость; **- man** [- мäн] стари́к; **- woman** [- ÿÿ-мäн] стару́ха

old-fashioned [оулд-фä-шäнд] *adj.* старомóдный; устарéлый (*antiquated*)

olive [ó-лів] *sn.* масли́на; оли́вковое дéрево (*tree*)

olive-branch [ó-лів-бранч] *sn.* оли́вковая ветвь; *fig.* предложéние примирéния

omen [óу-мäн] *sn.* предзнаменовáние

ominous [ó-мі-нäс] *adj.* зловéщий, угрожáющий

omission [оу-мі-шäн] *sn.* пропуск, упущéние

omit [оу-мі́т] *vt.* опускáть, пропускáть; пренебрегáть (*neglect*)

omnipotent [ом-ні-по-тäнт] *adj.* всемогу́щий

omniscient [ом-ні-сі-äнт] *adj.* всезнáющий

on [он] *prep.* на; *adv.* вперёд, дáльше

once [уäнс] *sn.* оди́н раз; *adv.* однáжды (*formerly*); нéкогда (*in former times*); *conj.* раз; **- for all** [- фор ôл] раз навсегдá; **- more** [- мôр] ещё раз; **at -** [äт -] срáзу; **- upon a time** [- ä-пóн ä тайм] жил был когдá-то

one [ÿáн] *num.* оди́н; *adj.* еди́ный, нéкій, еди́нственный (*only*); *pron.* ктó-то, нéкто; **- and a half** [- äнд ä хäф] полторá

onerous [ó-нä-рäс] *adj.* обремени́тельный

oneself [уäн-сéлф] *pron.* сам, себя́

one-sided [уäн-сáй-дід] *adj.* односторо́нний; пристрáстный (*partial*)

onion [á-ніäн] *sn.* лук; лу́ковица (*bulb*)

onlooker [он-лу́-кäр] *sn.* зри́тель, свидéтель, *m.*

only [óун-лі] *adj.* еди́нственный; *adv.* тóлько

onslaught [он-слôт] *sn.* жестóкая атáка, нападéние, нáтиск

onus [óу-нäс] *sn.* брéмя, отвéтственность (*responsibility*)

onward [он-ÿäрд] *adj.* подвигáющийся; *adv.* вперёд, дáлее

ooze [ÿз] *sn.* жи́дкая грязь, ти́на; просáчивание (*exudation*); *vi.* просáчиваться

opaque [оу-пéйк] *adj.* непрозрáчный; непроницáемый (*impenetrable*)

open [óу-пäн] *adj.* откры́тый; **wide -** [ÿáйд -] нáстежь; и́скренний, открóвенный (*frank*); *vt.i.* открывáть, раскрывáть; обнару́живать (*lay open, disclose*)

opening [óуп-ніŋ] *sn.* отвéрстие (*gap, etc.*); вступлéние, начáло (*beginning*); дебют (*chess*); возмóжность (*opportunity, possibility*); *adj.* начáльный (*initial*)

operate [ó-пă-рэйт] *vt.i.* действовать (*be in action*); приводить в действие; управлять (*work machine, etc.*); *med.* оперировать

operatic [о-пă-рǽ-тĭк] *adj.* оперный

operation [о-пă-рǒ́й-шăн] *sn.* действие (*action*); работа (*working*); *med., mil.,* операция

operative [ó-пă-рă-тĭв] *sm.* рабочий; *adj.* действующий; оперативный

opinion [ă-пí-нйăн] *sn.* мнение

opponent [ă-пóу-нăнт] *sn.* оппонент, противник

opportune [о-пăр-тю́н] *adj.* своевременный (*well-timed*); подходящий (*favourable*)

opportunity [о-пăр-тю́-нĭ-тĭ] *sn.* удобный случай

oppose [ă-пóуз] *vt.* противиться (*put into contrast*); противопоставлять (*place front to front*); сопротивляться (*resist*)

opposite [о-пă-зĭт] *adj.* противоположный; *adv.* напротив, против

opposition [о-пă-зí-шăн] *sn.* противоположность (*contrast*); сопротивление (*resistance*); *parl.* оппозиция

oppress [ă-прéс] *vt.* притеснять, угнетать

oppression [ă-прé-шăн] *sn.* притеснение, угнетение

oppressive [ă-прé-сĭв] *adj.* гнетущий, обременительный; знойный, душный (*of weather*)

oppressor [ă-прé-сăр] *sm.* притеснитель, угнетатель

optical [óп-тĭ-кăл] *adj.* зрительный, оптический

optician [оп-тí-шăн] *sm.* оптик

optimistic [оп-тĭ-мíс-тĭк] *adj.* оптимистический

option [óп-шăн] *sn.* выбор; право замены (*freedom of choice*)

optional [óп-шă-нăл] *adj.* необязательный

or [ǒр] *conj.* или

oral [ó-рăл] *adj.* устный; *anat.* стоматический

orange [ó-рĭндж] *sn.* апельсин; *adj.* оранжевый

oration [о-рǒ́й-шăн] *sn.* речь

orator [ó-рă-тăр] *sm.* оратор

oratory [ó-рă-рĭ] *sn.* ораторство, риторика

orb [ǒрб] *sn.* сфера, шар

orbit [óр-бĭт] *sn.* орбита; глазная впадина (*eye socket*)

orchard [óр-чăрд] *sn.* фруктовый сад

orchestra [óр-кĭс-трă] *sn.* оркестр

orchestral [ор-кéс-трăл] *adj.* оркестровый

orchid [óр-кĭд] *sn.* орхидея

ordain [ор-дǒ́йн] *vt.* предназначать, предписывать (*appoint, destine*); *eccl.* посвящать в духовный сан

ordeal [óр-дĭ-ăл] *sn.* испытание, пытка

order [óр-дăр] *sn.* приказ (*command*); порядок (*arrangement*); *mil.* строй; заказ (*to grocer, for goods*); духовный сан; *civic,* орден; **in — to** [ĭн — тŷ] для того, чтобы; *vt.* велеть, приказывать (*bid*); заказывать (*requisition*); прописывать (*prescribe*)

orderly [ŏр-дăр-лі] *sm. mil.* вестово́й, ордина́рец; сани-та́р (*in hospital*); *adj.* опря́тный; пра́вильный (*correct*)

ordinal [ŏр-ді-нăл] *adj.* поря́дковый

ordinance [ŏр-ді-нăнс] *sn.* декре́т, ука́з (*decree*); *eccl.* обря́д

ordinary [ŏр-ді-нă-рі] *adj.* обыкнове́нный, обы́чный

ordination [ŏр-ді-нэ́й-шăн] *sn.* посвяще́ние в духо́вный сан

ordnance [ŏ́рд-нăнс] *sn.* артиллери́йские ору́дия (*mounted guns, etc.*); склад вое́нных ору́дий

ore [ŏр] *sn.* руда́

organ [ŏр-гăн] *sn. mus.* орга́н; шарма́нка (*barrel-organ*); **mouth –** [мăўð –] гу́бная гармо́ника, *anat.* о́рган; го́лос (*voice*); газе́та (*newspaper, etc.*)

organic [ор-гắ-нік] *adj.* органи́ческий

organism [ŏр-гă-нізм] *sn.* органи́зм

organist [ŏр-гă-ніст] *sn.* органи́ст

organization [ор-гă-ні-зэ́й-шăн] *sn.* организа́ция, устро́йство

organize [ŏр-гă-найз] *vt.i.* организо́вывать, устра́ивать

orgy [ŏр-джі] *sn.* о́ргия, попо́йка, распу́щенная пиру́шка

orient [ŏ-рі́єнт] *sn.* восто́к (*east*); восто́чные стра́ны; *adj.* восто́чный; *vt.* определя́ть местонахожде́ние

oriental [о-рі́єн-тăл] *sm.* жи́тель восто́ка; *adj.* азиа́тский, восто́чный

orientation [о-рі́єн-тэ́й-шăн] *sn.* ориента́ция

orifice [ŏ-рі-фіс] *sn.* отве́рстие, прохо́д

origin [ŏ-рі-джін] *sn.* исто́чник, нача́ло; происхожде́ние (*descent*)

original [ă-рі-джі-нăл] *sn.* оригина́л, по́длинник; *adj.* оригина́льный; первонача́льный (*initial*); самобы́тный (*novel*)

originality [о-рі-джі-нắ-лі-ті] *sn.* оригина́льность; по́длинность (*authenticity*)

originate [ă-рі-джі-нэйт] *vt.i.* дава́ть нача́ло, порожда́ть (*initiate*); происходи́ть (*have origin*)

ornament [ŏр-нă-мăнт] *sn.* украше́ние; [ор-нă-ме́нт] *vt.* украша́ть

ornamental [ор-нă-ме́н-тăл] *adj.* декорати́вный, орнамента́льный

ornate [ор-нэ́йт] *adj.* укра́шенный; витиева́тый (*of style*)

orphan [ŏр-фăн] *sm.*, *f.* сирота́; *adj.* сиро́тский

orphanage [ŏр-фă-ніджъ] *sn.* прию́т для сиро́т, сиро́тский дом

orthodox [ŏр-ðо-докс] *adj.* ортодокса́льный; *eccl.* правосла́вный

orthography [ор-ðо́-гră-фі] *sn.* правописа́ние

oscillate [ŏ-сі-лэйт] *vi.* кача́ться (*swing*); вибри́ровать (*vibrate*); колеба́ться (*waver*)

ostensible [ос-тéн-сібл] *adj.* ка́жущийся, мни́мый, очеви́дный

ostentation [ос-тăн-тэ́й-шăн] *sn.* тщеславие, хвастовство

ostentatious [ос-тăн-тэ́й-ши-ăс] *adj.* показной

ostler [о́с-лăр] *sm.* конюх

ostracize [о́с-трă-са́йз] *vt.* исключать

ostrich [о́с-трич] *s.* страус

other [а́-ơăр] *adj.* другой, иной; *adv.* иначе; *pl.* остальные

otherwise [а́-ơăр-ўайз] *adv.* другим образом, иначе

ounce [а́ўнс] *sn.* унция

our [а́ўр] *adj.*, *pron.* наш

ours [а́ў-ăрз] *pron.* наш

ourselves [а́ўр-сĕлвз] *pron.* мы сами, самих себя

oust [а́ўст] *vt.* выгонять, прогнать

out [а́ўт] *adv.* вон, вне, из, наружу; *adj.* внешний, наружный; *prep.* из

outbreak [а́ўт-брэ́йк] *sn.* внезапное начало

outbuilding [а́ўт-би́л-дий] *sn.* пристройка

outburst [а́ўт-бœрст] *sn.* взрыв, вспышка

outcast [а́ўт-кăст] *sm.* изгнанник, отверженец; *adj.* отверженный; бездомный (*homeless*)

outcome [а́ўт-кам] *sn.* исход (*issue*); последствие (*result*)

outcry [а́ўт-край] *sn.* вопль, крик; шумный протест (*loud protest*)

outdoor [а́ўт-дŏр] *adj.* совершающийся вне дома (*-s*); =**s** [-з] *adv.* на открытом воздухе

outer [а́ў-тăр] *adj.* внешний, наружный

outfit [а́ўт-фи́т] *sn.* снаряжение, экипировка

outfitter [а́ўт-фи́-тăр] *sm.* поставщик снаряжения

outgoing [а́ўт-гоу-ий] *adj.* выходящий; =**s** [-з] *sn. pl.* издержки, расходы

outgrow [а́ўт-гро́у] *vt.* перерастать; отделаться от (*get rid of*)

outhouse [а́ўт-ха́ўс] *sn.* надворное строение

outing [а́ў-тий] *sn.* прогулка

outlandish [а́ўт-лăн-ди́ш] *adj.* чужеземный (*foreign looking*); диковинный, странный (*bizarre*)

outlaw [а́ўт-лŏ] *sn.* человек вне закона; *vt.* лишать законной силы

outlay [а́ўт-лэ́й] *sn.* затраты, издержки

outlet [а́ўт-лĕт] *sn.* выпуск, исход

outline [а́ўт-лайн] *sn.* контур, очертание; *pl.* общие черты; *vt.* описывать, обрисовать; сделать набросок (*sketch*)

outlook [а́ўт-лу́к] *sn.* вид, перспектива, точка зрения

outpost [а́ўт-поуст] *sn.* аванпост, застава

output [а́ўт-пу́т] *sn.* производительность; **coal** — [коул —] выдача угля; продукция (*production*)

outrage [а́ўт-рэ́йдж] *sn.* насильственное нарушение прав; оскорбление (*offence*); *vt.* насиловать, оскорблять

outrageous [а́ўт-рэ́й-джăс] *adj.* жестокий (*cruel*); неистовый (*violent*); оскорбительный (*offensive*)

outright [а́ўт-райт] *adj.* полный, совершенный; *adv.* вполне, совершенно

outset [а́ут-сęт] *sn.* нача́ло; **at the —** [ęт ęi —] *вначале*; **from the —** [фром ęi —] *самого начала*

outside [аут-са́йд] *sn.* нару́жная сторона́ (*external surface*); вне́шняя часть (*outer part*); *adj.* вне́шний, нару́жный; *adv.* снару́жи; *prep.* вне, за преде́лы

outsider [аут-са́й-дăр] *sn.* посторо́нний челове́к

outskirts [а́ут-скęртс] *sn. pl.* окра́ина, предме́стье

outspoken [аут-спо́у-кăн] *adj.* открове́нный

outstanding [аут-стęн-дiй] *adj.* выдаю́щийся; неупла́ченный (*of debt, etc.*)

outstretched [аут-стре́чд] *adj.* протя́нутый, растя́нутый

outward [а́ут-ўăд] *adj.* вне́шний, нару́жный; ви́дный (*apparent, visible*); **-s** [-з] *adv.* нару́жу

oval [о́у-вăл] *sn.* ова́л. *adj.* ова́льный

ovary [о́у-вă-ри] *sn. anat.* яи́чник; *bot.* завя́зь

ovation [о́у-ве́й-шăн] *sn.* ова́ция

oven [á-вăн] *sn.* печь

over [о́у-вăр] *adv.* сли́шком, чересчу́р; (*note: using the prefix "пере" in conjunction with a verb and sometimes a noun, will often correctly translate verbs beginning with "over"*); *prep.* над, через, сверх

overall [о́у-вăр-о́л] *sn.* хала́т; **-s** [-з] рабо́чий костю́м

overboard [о́у-вăр-бо́рд] *adv.* за борт

overcast [о́у-вăр-кęст] *adj.*

па́смурный; *vt.* зашива́ть (*stitch*)

overcoat [о́у-вăр-ко́ут] *sn.* пальто́

overcome [о́у-вăр-кáм] *vt.* поборо́ть, преодоле́ть

overcrowded [о́у-вăр-кра́у-дiд] *adj.* перепо́лненный

overdraft [о́у-вăр-дра́фт] *sn.* превыше́ние креди́та

overdue [о́у-вăр-дю́] *adj.* просро́ченный

overflow [о́у-вăр-флоу́] *sn.* наводне́ние, разли́в; избы́ток (*copiousness*); *vt.i.* залива́ть, перетека́ть

overgrown [о́у-вăр-гро́ун] *adj.* обро́сший

overhang [о́у-вăр-хęй] *vt.i.* выда́ваться, нависа́ть, свешиваться

overhaul [о́у-вăр-хо́л] *sn.* ремо́нт; *vt.* пересма́тривать

overlook [о́у-вăр-лу́к] *vt.* прогля́дывать, надзира́ть (*supervise*)

overpower [о́у-вăр-па́у-ăр] *vt.* переси́ливать

overrun [о́у-вăр-ра́н] *vt.* наводня́ть (*inundate*); опустоша́ть (*devastate*); *typ.* перебира́ть

overseas [о́у-вăр-си́з] *adv.* за́ морем; **— trade** [— трęйд] вне́шняя торго́вля

overseer [о́у-вăр-си́-ăр] *sn.* деся́тник, надзира́тель, надсмо́трщик

oversight [о́у-вăр-са́йт] *sn.* недосмо́тр, опло́шность

oversleep [о́у-вăр-сли́п] *vi.* заспа́ться

overtake [о́у-вăр-те́йк] *vt.* догна́ть, наверста́ть (*catch up*); пости́гнуть (*of sorrow, illness, etc.*)

overthrow [оў-вӑр-ѳро́ў] *vt.* опроки́дывать

overtime [о́ў-вӑр-тайм] *sn.* сверхуро́чное вре́мя; *adv.* сверхуро́чно

overture [о́ў-вӑр-тю́р] *sn.* нача́ло перегово́ров (*opening of negotiations*); форма́льное предложе́ние (*formal proposal*); *mus.* увертю́ра

overturn [о́ў-вӑр-те́рн] *vt.* опроки́дывать

overweight [о́ў-вӑр-уэ́йт] *sn.* переве́с

overwhelm [о́ў-вӑр-хуэ́лм] *vt.* разбива́ть, сокруша́ть (*crush*); сража́ть (*with down*); подавля́ть (*with emotion*)

owe [о́ў] *vt.* быть до́лжным

owing [о́ў-йѓ] *adj.* до́лжный

owl [а́ўл] *s.* сова́

own [о́ўн] *adj.* свой, со́бственный; *vt.* владе́ть, име́ть

owner [о́ў-нӑр] *sm.* владе́лец, со́бственник

ownership [о́ў-нӑр-ши́п] *sn.* со́бственность

ox [окс] *sm.* вол

oxygen [о́кс-и-джӗн] *sn.* кислоро́д

oyster [о́й-стӑр] *s.* у́стрица

P

pace [пэ́йс] *sn.* по́ступь, похо́дка (*gait*); шаг (*step*); ско́рость (*speed*); *vi.* шага́ть; итти́ и́ноходью (*of horse*)

pacific [пӑ-си́-фйк] *adj.* миролюби́вый, споко́йный, тихоокеа́нский (*of Ocean*)

pacify [пӑ-си́-фай] *vt.* уми-

ротворя́ть, усмиря́ть, успока́ивать

pack [пэк] *sn.* ки́па, свя́зка, тюк (*bundle*); коло́да (*of cards*); ста́я (*of wolves*); *mil.* ра́нец, су́мка; сво́ра (*of hounds*); ша́йка (*of thieves*); ма́ссы плаву́чего льда (*of ice*); *vt.i.* укла́дываться (*for journey*); упако́вывать (*wrap up*)

package [пӑ-ки́дж] *sn.* посы́лка, свёрток, у́зел

packet [пӑ-ки́т] *sn.* паке́т; — **boat** — (бо́ут] почто́вый парохо́д; па́чка (*of cigarettes*)

packing [пӑ-ки́ѓ] *sn.* упако́вка (*of*); *tech.* наби́вка, прокла́дка

pact [пэкт] *sn.* догово́р, пакт, усло́вие

pad [пэд] *sn.* мя́гкая прокла́дка (*soft padding*); мя́гкое седло́ (*soft saddle*); ла́па, поду́шечка (*animal's*); блокно́т, бюва́р (*blotting paper*); *vt.* закла́дывать, подкла́дывать

padding [пӑ-ди́ѓ] *sn.* наби́вка; наби́вочный материа́л

paddle [пэдл] *sn.* весло́, гребля́ (*of*); *vt.i.* грести́

paddock [пӑ-до̆к] *sn.* вы́гон, заго́н, лужа́йка

padlock [пӑд-ло́к] *sn.* вися́чий замо́к

pagan [пэ́й-гӑн] *sm.* язы́чник; *adj.* язы́ческий

page [пэ́йдж] *sm.* паж (*boy*); страни́ца (*of book*)

pageant [пӑ-джӗнт] *sn.* карнава́льное ше́ствие, пы́шное зре́лище

pageantry [пӑ-джӗн-три́] *sn.* великоле́пие, пы́шность

paginate [пэ́-джі-нэйт] vt. нумеровать, считать (страницы)

pail [пэйл] sn. ведро

pain [пэйн] sn. боль; страдание (suffering); pl. старания, усилия (endeavours, exertion); **take -s** [тэйк -з] прилагать усилия; vt. причинять боль

painful [пэйн-фул] adj. болезненный

painstaking [пэйнз-тэйкій] adj. прилежный, старательный, усердный

paint [пэйнт] sn. краска, румяна; - **brush** [- браш] кисть; vt.i. красить

painter [пэйн-тар] sm. маляр (decorator); живописец, художник (artist)

painting [пэйн-тій] sn. живопись (art); картина (picture); малярное дело (trade)

pair [пэр] sn. пара, чета; **in -s** [ін -з] парами, по-двое; vt.i. совокупляться, спариваться; подбирать по парам; - **off** [- оф] разделиться по парам

pal [пэл] sm. coll. друг

palace [пэ́-ліс] sn. дворец

palatable [пэ́-лă-табл] adj. вкусный, пикантный

palatal [пэ́-лă-тăл] adj. нёбный; палатальный (of sound)

palate [пэ́-літ] sn. anat. нёбо; вкус (taste)

pale [пэйл] sn. кол (stake); граница, предел (boundary); adj. бледный; vi. бледнеть

paling [пэй-лій] sn. колья, ограда, тын

palisade [пэ-лі-сэйд] sn. забор, палисад, частокол

pall [пôл] sn. покров (coffin

cloth); eccl. мантия, ряса; vi. докучать, надоедать

pallid [пэ́-лід] adj. изможденный

pallor [пэ́-лăр] sn. бледность, изможденность

palm [пâм] sn. ладонь; пальма (tree); - **Sunday** [- сандій] Вербное Воскресенье

palmist [пâ-міст] sm., f. хиромант

palmistry [пâ-міс-трі] sn. хиромантия

palpable [пэл-пăбл] adj. осязаемый, ощутимый; очевидный (obvious)

palpitation [пэл-пі-тэйшăн] sn. биение, трепетание

palsy [пôл-зі] sn. паралич; паралич; паралический дрожание (trembling)

paltry [пôл-трі] adj. незначительный, пустячный

pamper [пэ́м-пăр] vt. баловать, нежить

pamphlet [пэ́м-фліт] sn. брошюра, памфлет

pan [пэн] sn. кастрюля, сковорода

pancake [пэн-кэйк] sn. блин, оладья

pander [пэ́н-дăр] sm. сводник; vi. потворствовать

pane [пэйн] sn. оконное стекло

panel [пэ́-нăл] sn. панель, филёнка; продольная полоса (vertical strip in dress)

pang [пэн] sn. приступ боли; pl. муки, тоски

panic [пэ́-нік] sn. паника; adj. панический

pant [пэнт] vt.i. пыхтеть (breathe heavily); трепетать (throb, of heart); выпаливать (utter breathlessly)

pantry [пэ́н-трі] *sn.* кладова́я, чула́н

pants [пэнтс] *sn. pl.* кальсо́ны

papal [пэ́й-пэл] *adj.* па́пский

paper [пэ́й-пэр] *sn.* бума́га; газе́та (*newspaper*); обо́и (*wall-paper*); *adj.* бума́жный; *vt.* окле́ивать обо́ями; **-hanger** [-хэ́н-эр] *sm.* маля́р, обо́йщик; **-mill** [-міл] бума́жная фа́брика; **-weight** [-уэ́йт] пресспапье́

par [пар] *sn.* номина́льная сто́имость

parable [пэ́-рэбл] *sn.* при́тча

parade [пэ-ро́йд] *sn.* пара́д, пока́з, смотр; обще́ственное гуля́ние (*promenade*); *vt.i. mil.* марширова́ть, стро́иться; выставля́ть напока́з (*display*); прогу́ливаться (*walk leisurely*)

paradise [пэ́-рэ-дайс] *sn.* рай

paraffin [пэ́-рэ-фін] *sn.* парафи́н (*waxy substance*); кероси́н, парафи́новое ма́сло (*oil*)

paragraph [пэ́-рэ-граф] *sn.* пара́граф (*passage in book*); абза́ц, разде́л (*indention*)

parallel [пэ́-рэ-лел] *sn. typ.* спра́вочный знак (||); *sn.* паралле́льная ли́ния (*line on map*); сравне́ние (*comparison*); *adj.* паралле́льный, подо́бный, схо́дный (*corresponding, similar*); *vt.* сра́внивать

paralyse [пэ́-рэ-лайз] *vt.* парализова́ть

paralysis [пэ-рэ́-лі-сіс] *sn.* парали́ч

paramount [пэ́-рэ-ма́унт] *adj.* верхо́вный, вы́сший;

of – importance [ов – ім-по́р-тэнс] велича́йшей ва́жности

parapet [пэ́-рэ-піт] *sn.* парапе́т, пери́ла; *mil.* бру́ствер

paraphrase [пэ́-рэ-фрэйз] *sn.* парафра́з, переска́з, толкова́ние; *vt.* перефрази́ровать

parasite [пэ́-рэ-сайт] *s.* пара́зит, туне́ядец

parasol [пэ́-рэ-сол] *sn.* зо́нтик (от со́лнца)

parcel [пар́-сэл] *sn.* паке́т, посы́лка; *com.* па́ртия; уча́сток земли́ (*piece of land*); *vt.* дели́ть на ча́сти

parch [парч] *vt.i.* высу́шивать (*dry by heat*); поджа́ривать (*roast slightly*); опаля́ть (*of sun*); **-ed lips** [-д ліпс] запёкшиеся гу́бы

parchment [парч-мэнт] *sn.* перга́мент

pardon [пар́-дэн] *sn.* извине́ние (*indulgence*); проще́ние (*forgiveness*); поми́лование (*remission of punishment*); *vt.* извиня́ть; поми́ловать; проща́ть

pare [пэр] *vt.* обреза́ть, среза́ть

parent [пэ́-рэнт] *sm.* роди́тель; *sf.* роди́тельница; *pl.* роди́тели

parentage [пэ́-рэнт-ідж] *sn.* происхожде́ние (*descent*); ли́ния родства́ (*lineage*)

parental [па-ре́н-тэл] *adj.* роди́тельский; отцо́вский (*of father*); матери́нский (*of mother*)

parenthesis [пэ-ре́н-ѳі-сіс] *sn. gram.* вво́дное сложе́ние; кру́глая ско́бка [( )]

parenthetical [пæ–рǎн-ðĕ́-ти-кǎл] *adj.* вводный, вставной

parenthood [пǎ́–рǎнт-хŷд] *sn.* отцовство (*male*); материнство (*female*)

paring [пḗ–рǐ] *sn.* обрёзывание, срезывание; *pl.* обрёзки

parish [пǽ–рǐш] *sn. eccl.* церковный приход; *civil*, гражданский округ; прихожане (*inhabitants*)

parishioner [пǎ–рǐ–шǎ–нǎ́р] *sm.* прихожанин; *sf.* прихожанка

parity [пǽ–рǐ-тǐ] *sn.* паритет, равенство; соответствие (*conformity*)

park [пǎрк] *sn.* парк; огороженное место (*enclosure*); *vt.* поставить на стоянку (*cars*)

parley [пǎ́р–лǐ] *sn.* переговоры, совещание; *vt.i.* вести переговоры, совещаться

parliament [пǎ́р–лǎ–мǎнт] *sn.* парламент

parliamentary [пǎ̄р–лǐǎ–мéн–тǎ–рǐ] *adj.* парламентарный

parlour [пǎ́р–лǎр] *sn.* гостиная, зал; приёмная (*of inn*)

parochial [пǎ–рó́у–кǐ–ǎл] *adj.* приходский; местный (*local*)

parole [пǎ–рóул] *sn.* обещание, честное слово; *mil.* пароль

parrot [пǽ–рǎт] *sn.* попугай; *vt.i.* бессмысленно повторять

parry [пǽ–рǐ] *sn.* отражение, парирование; *vt.* отбивать, отражать, парировать

parse [пǎрз] *vt.* делать грамматический разбор

parsimonious [пǎ̄р–сǐ–мóу́–нǐ–ǎс] *adj.* бережливый, экономный; скупой, скаредный (*mean, stingy*)

parsley [пǎ́р–слǐ] *sn. bot.* петрушка

parsnip [пǎ́р–снǐп] *sn. bot.* пастернак

parson [пǎ́р–сǎн] *sm.* приходский священник

parsonage [пǎ́р–сǎн–ǐдж] *sn.* дом священника, пасторат

part [пǎрт] *sn.* доля, часть (*share*); роль (*role*); сторона (*side*); отдел, *m.* (*section*); *mus.* партия; **take – in** [тэйк – ǐн] принимать участие; *adv.* отчасти, частью; *vt.i.* делить, разделять; **– with** [– ўǐе] расстаться

partake [пǎр–тэ́йк] *vi.* принимать участие

partial [пǎ́р–шǎл] *adj.* неполный, частичный (*incomplete*); неравнодушный, пристрастный (*biased*)

participate [пǎр–тǐ–сǐ–пэ́йт] *vi.* участвовать

participation [пǎр–тǐ–сǐ–пэ́й–шǎн] *sn.* участие

participle [пǎ́р–тǐ–сǐпл] *sn. gram.* причастие

particle [пǎ́р–тǐкл] *sn.* частица; *gram.* префикс, суффикс

particular [пǎр–тǐ́–кю–лǎр] *sn.* деталь, подробность; **in** [ин] особенно; *pl.* подробный отчёт (*detailed account*); подробности (*details*); *adj.* особенный, особый (*singular, special*); отличительный (*distinctive*); требовательный (*exacting*); придирчивый (*fastidious*)

parting [па́р-тиң] *sn.* разлу́ка, расстава́ние; отделе́ние (*division*); **the - of the ways** [ви́з — ов еʌ у́эйз] распу́тье

partisan [па́р-ти-зǽн] *sm.* приве́рженец, сторо́нник

partition [пар-ти́-шǽн] *sn.* перегоро́дка (*structure*); отделе́ние (*in box, drawer, etc.*); разделе́ние (*division*); *vt.* дели́ть, разделя́ть

partitive [па́р-ти-тив] *sn. gram.* раздели́тельное сло́во; *adj.* раздели́тельный

partly [па́рт-ли] *adv.* отча́сти

partner [па́рт-нǽр] *sm.* компаньо́н, уча́стник; партнёр (*dancing, games*); *vt.* быть партнёром

partnership [па́рт-нǽр-шип] *sn.* компа́ния, това́рищество

partridge [па́р-тридж] *s.* куропа́тка

party [па́р-ти] *sn.* па́ртия (*faction*), гру́ппа, отря́д (*detachment*); приём госте́й, ве́чер, вечери́нка (*social reception*); *adj.* парти́йный

pass [пас] *sn.* прохо́д (*avenue*); перева́л, уще́лье (*of mountain*); про́пуск (*permit*); сда́ча экза́мена (*of examination*); *vt.i.* минова́ть, проезжа́ть, проходи́ть; передава́ть (*hand*); **- away** [- ǽ-уэ́й] конча́ться, умере́ть; **- by** [- ба́й] проходи́ть ми́мо

passage [пǽ-сидж] *sn.* прое́зд, прохо́д, перелёт (*of birds*), коридо́р (*in house*)

passenger [пǽ-сǽн-джǽр] *sn.* пассажи́р, пу́тник

passer-by [пǽ-сǽр-ба́й] *sm.* прохо́жий

passion [пǽ-шǽн] *sn.* пыл, страсть; поры́в гне́ва (*outburst of anger*)

passionate [пǽ-шǽ-нịт] *adj.* пы́лкий, стра́стный

passport [пас-по́рт] *sn.* па́спорт

past [паст] *sn.* мину́вшее, проше́дшее; *adj.* про́шлый; *prep.* вне, за (*beyond*); по́сле (*after*); свы́ше (*exceeding*); *adv.* ми́мо

paste [пэйст] *sn.* те́сто (*dough*); кле́йстер (*adhesive mixture*); *vt.* накле́ивать, скле́ивать

pasteboard [пэ́йст-бо́рд] *sn.* карто́н

pastime [пǽс-тайм] *sn.* заба́ва, развлече́ние

pastoral [пǽс-тǽ-рǽл] *adj.* пастора́льный, пасту́шеский

pastry [пэ́й-стри] *sn.* пече́нье, пиро́жное

pastry-cook [пэ́й-стри-ку́к] *sm.* конди́тер

pasture [пǽс-чǽр] *sn.* па́стбище

pat [пǽт] *sn.* лёгкий уда́р, шлёпанье; комо́к (*of butter*); *adj.* подходя́щий, уда́чный; *vt.* похло́пывать

patch [пǽч] *sn.* запла́та (*repair*); пятно́ (*stain*); клочо́к земли́ (*plot*); *vt.* лата́ть, чини́ть; **- up** [- ап] заде́лывать (*repair temporarily*); ула́живать (*quarrel*)

patchy [пǽ-чи] *adj.* разноше́рстный

patent [пэ́й-тǽнт] *sn.* пате́нт; *adj.* патенто́ванный (*pa-*

paternal [пă-тёр́-нăл] *adj.* отéческий, отцóвский

path [пă̄θ] *sn.* дорóжка, тропи́нка

pathetic [пă-θĕ́-тĭк] *adj.* жáлостный, патети́ческий, трóгательный

pathos [пэ́й-θŏс] *sn.* пáфос

pathway [пă̄θ-уэ́й] *sn.* тротуáр

patience [пэ́й-шăнс] *sn.* терпéние; насто́йчивость (*perseverance*)

patient [пэ́й-шăнт] *sm.* пациéнт; *adj.* терпели́вый

patriotic [пэ-три́-ó-тĭк] *adj.* патриоти́ческий

patrol [пă-трóул] *sn.* дозóр, патрýль, *m.*; *vi.* патрули́ровать

patron [пэ́й-трăн] *sm.* покрови́тель

patronage [пĕ́т-рă-нĭдж] *sn.* покрови́тельство

patronize [пĕ́т-рă-найз] *vt.* покрови́тельствовать, поощря́ть

patter [пĕ-тăр́] *sn.* звук дождевы́х капéль (*of rain*); топотáнье (*of child*); скороговóрка (*theat.*); *vi.* барабáнить (*of rain*); топотáть (*of child*); тарато́рить (*talk rapidly*)

pattern [пĕ-тăр́н] *sn.* образéц, модéль (*model*); узóр (*design*); вы́кройка (*of dress*); *tech.* шаблóн

patty [пĕ-ти́] *sn.* пирожóк

paunch [пóнч] *sn.* брю́хо, живóт, пýзо; *vt.* потроши́ть

pauper [пŏ́-пăр] *sm.* бедня́к, ни́щий

pause [пóз] *sn. mus.* пáуза, перед́ышка (*respite*); *vi.*

останá́вливаться (*halt for a while*)

pave [пэ́йв] *vt.* мости́ть (*road*); вы́стилать (*floor*); **– the way** – ой у́эй] прокла́дывать путь

pavement [пэ́йв-мăнт] *sn.* тротуáр

pavilion [пă-ви́-лиăн] *sn.* палáтка, шатёр (*tent, etc.*); павильóн (*building*)

paving [пэ́й-вĭн] *sn.* мостовáя

paw [пŏ] *sn.* лáпа

pawn [пŏ́н] *sn.* заклáд, залóг (*thing as pledge*); пéшка (*chess*); *vt.* заклáдывать (*deposit*)

pawnbroker [пŏ́н-брóу-кăр] *sm.* ростовщи́к

pawnshop [пŏ́н-шóп] *sn.* ломбáрд

pay [пэ́й] *sn.* заработная плáта, жáлованье; посóбие (*dole, relief, strike, etc.*); *vt.* опла́чивать, плати́ть; упла́чивать; распла́чиваться (*settle payment*); оказывать (*attention, compliments, etc.*)

pay-day [пэ́й-дэ́й] *sn.* день платежá

paying [пэ́й-ĭй] *adj.* вы́годный, дохóдный (*profitable*)

paymaster [пэ́й-мáс-тăр] *sm.* казначéй

payment [пэ́й-мăнт] *sn.* платёж, уплáта

pea [пи] *sn.* горóх; **split –** [спли́т –] лущёный горóх; **sweet –** [су́йт –] душистый горóшек

peace [пис] *sn.* мир (*after war*); порядок, споко́йствие (*civil order*); тишинá (*calm*); **at –** [ăт –] в ми́ре

peaceful [пи́с-фŭл] *adj.* ми́рный, споко́йный

peacemaker [пи́с-мэй-кар] *sm.* примири́тель

peach [пич] *sn.* пе́рсик

peacock [пи́-кок] *sm.* павли́н

peak [пик] *sn.* верши́на, пик; козырёк (*of cap*)

peal [пил] *sn.* гро́хот, раска́т (*of thunder*); звон колоко́лов, трезво́н (*chime*); взрыв сме́ха (*of laughter*); *v.t.i.* греме́ть; трезво́нить

peanut [пи́-нат] *sn.* земляно́й оре́х

pear [пэр] *sn.* гру́ша

pearl [пэрл] *sn.* же́мчуг, жемчу́жина

peasant [пе́-зэнт] *sm.* крестья́нин; *adj.* крестья́нский; се́льский (*rural*)

peasantry [пе́-зэн-три] *sn.* крестья́нство

peat [пит] *sn.* торф

pebble [пебл] *sn.* га́лька, го́льш; го́рный хруста́ль (*rock-crystal*); ли́нза (*lens*)

peck [пек] *sn.* че́тверть бу́шеля (*measure*); клево́к (*of bird*); лёгкий поцелу́й (*kiss*); *v.t.i.* долби́ть, клева́ть

peculiar [пи-кю́-ли-ар] *adj.* необы́чный, своеобра́зный, стра́нный (*strange*); своеобра́зный (*eccentric*); осо́бенный, характе́рный (*characteristic*)

peculiarity [пи-кю-лиэ́-ри-ти] *sn.* стра́нность (*strangeness*); своеобра́зность (*eccentricity*); осо́бенность (*singularity*)

pecuniary [пи-кю́-ниэ́-ри] *adj.* де́нежный

pedal [пе́-дэл] *sn.* педа́ль; *adj.* педа́льный; *anat.* ножно́й; *v.t.i.* рабо́тать педа́лями (*work pedals, cycling, etc.*)

pedestal [пе́-дис-тэл] *sn.* подно́жие, подста́вка, пьеде́стал

pedestrian [пи-де́с-три-ан] *sm.* пешехо́д; *adj.* пешехо́дный

pedigree [пе́-ди-гри] *sn.* генеало́гия, родосло́вие; происхожде́ние (*descent*)

pedlar [пе́д-лар] *sm.* разно́счик, у́личный торго́вец

peel [пил] *sn.* ко́жица, шелуха́; candied – [ка́н-дид –] цука́т; *v.t.i.* лупи́ть, лупи́ться, очища́ть; шелуши́ть (*of skin*)

peeling [пи́-лин] *sn.* счи́щенная ко́рка; кожу́ра; potato -s [по-тэ́й-тоу́ -з] картофе́льные очи́стки

peep [пип] *sn.* взгляд украдко́й (*furtive glance*); про́блеск (*of dawn*); *vi.* пища́ть, чири́кать (*chirp, squeak*); – at [– эт] подгля́дывать

peer [пир] *sm.* лорд, пэр (*X*); *vi.* взгля́дываться, всма́триваться

peerage [пи́-ридж] *sn.* зва́ние пэ́ров, пэ́рство

peevish [пи́-виш] *adj.* ворчли́вый, сварли́вый (*cantankerous*); раздражи́тельный (*fretful*); серди́тый (*cross*)

peg [пег] *sn.* ко́лышек, деревя́нный гвоздь; ве́шалка; *mus.* колок; *tech.* вту́лка, затычка; *v.t.i.* забива́ть (ко́лышек и пр.); – away [– а-уэ́й] корпе́ть, си́льно рабо́тать, упо́рствовать

pelican [пе́-ли-кэн] *s.* пелика́н

pellet [пе́-літ] *sn.* ка́тышек, ша́рик (из бума́ги, хле́ба и т.п.)

pell-mell [пел-ме́л] *adv.* вперемѣ́шку

pelt [пелт] *sn.* ко́жа, шку́ра (*animals' skin*); *vt.i.* броса́ть, швыря́ть (ка́мни, грязь и т.п.) (*assail with stones, etc.*)

pen [пен] *sn.* перо́ (*writing implement*); **— and ink** [— ænd iŋк] пи́сьменные принадле́жности; заго́н (*enclosure*); *vt.* писа́ть (*write*); сочиня́ть (*compose*); загоня́ть, запира́ть (*confine, enclose*)

penal [пи́-нäл] *adj.* кара́тельный, ка́торжный, уголо́вный

penalize [пи́-нä-лайз] *vt.* кара́ть

penalty [пе́-нäл-ті] *sn.* ка́ра, наказа́ние; штраф (*in games*)

penance [пе́-нäнс] *sn. eccl.* епитимья́

pencil [пе́н-сіл] *sn.* каранда́ш; *vt.* отмеча́ть (*mark*)

pendant [пе́н-дäнт] *sn.* брело́к, висюлька, подвѣ́ска

pending [пе́н-дін] *adj.* в ожида́нии, ожида́ющий; *prep.* в продолже́ние, до

pendulum [пе́н-дю-läм] *sn.* ма́ятник

penetrate [пе́-ні-трэйт] *vt.* прони́зывать, проника́ть

penetrating [пе́-ні-трэ́йтін] *adj.* пронзи́тельный, проница́тельный

penetration [пе-ні-трэ́й-шäн] *sn.* проникнове́ние, проница́тельность

penholder [пе́н-хōул-дäр] *sn.* ру́чка для пера́

peninsula [пе-ні́н-сю-лä] *sn.* полуо́стров

peninsular [пе-ні́н-сю-лäр] *adj.* полуостровно́й

penitence [пе́-ні-тäнс] *sn.* покая́ние, раская́ние

penitent [пе́-ні-тäнт] *adj.* ка́ющийся

penitentiary [пе-ні-те́н-шä-рі] *sn.* исправи́тельный дом

penknife [пе́н-найф] *sn.* перочи́нный но́жик

pen-name [пе́н-нэйм] *sn.* литерату́рный псевдони́м

pennant [пе́-нäнт] *sn. naut.* вы́мпел

penniless [пе́-ні-ліс] *adj.* безде́нежный; нужда́ющийся (*needy*)

pension [пе́н-шäн] *sn.* пе́нсия; пансио́н (*establishment*); *vt.* назнача́ть пе́нсию

pensioner [пе́н-шä-нäр] *sn.* пенсионе́р

pensive [пе́н-сів] *adj.* заду́мчивый

Pentecost [пе́н-ті-кост] *sn.* пятидеся́тница

penultimate [пі-нäл-ті-мäт] *adj.* предпослѣ́дний

penury [пе́-ню-рі] *sn.* бѣ́дность, нищета́, нужда́

people [пипл] *sn. sing.* на́ция, наро́д; *pl.* жи́тели, ли́ца, лю́ди; **young —** [яŋ —] молодёжь; *vt.* заселя́ть, населя́ть

pepper [пе́-päр] *sn.* пе́рец; *vt.* пе́рчить

pepper-castor [пе́-päр-кäс-тäр] *sn.* пе́речница

peppercorn [пе́-päр-кōрн] *sn.* перчи́нка

peppermint [пе́-päр-мінт] *sn. bot.* пе́речная мя́та; мя́тная лепёшка (*sweet*)

per [пэр] *prep.* по, посредством, через; в, на

perambulator [па́-рэ́м-бю-лэ́й-тэр] *sn.* де́тская коля́ска

perceive [пэр-си́в] *vt.* замеча́ть, познава́ть, уви́дать

percentage [пэр-сэ́н-тидж] *sn.* проце́нт

perceptible [пэр-сэ́п-тибл] *adj.* заме́тный, ощути́мый

perception [пэр-сэ́п-шан] *sn.* восприя́тие, познава́ние, понима́ние

perch *s.* о́кунь (*fish*); жёрдочка, насе́ст (*roost*); шест (*pole*); ме́ра длины́ (о́коло пяти́ ме́тров) (*measure*); *vt.i.* сажа́ть, сади́ться

perchance [пэр-ча́нс] *adv.* возмо́жно, случа́йно

percolate [пэр-ка́-лэйт] *vt.i.* проце́живать, проса́чиваться

percolator [пэр-ка́-лэй-тэр] *sn.* фильтр, цеди́лка; **coffee —** [ко́-фи —] ко́фейник с си́течком

percussion [пэр-ка́-шан] *sn.* вибра́ция, дрожа́ние (*jarring, vibration*); уда́р (*striking*); *mus.* уда́рный инструме́нт

perdition [пэр-ди́-шан] *s.* поги́бель, прокля́тие

peremptory [па-рэ́м-та-ри] *adj.* насто́йчивый, повели́тельный

perennial [па-рэ́-ниал] *adj. bot.* для́щийся (*continuing*); многоле́тний (*of many years*)

perfect [пэр-фи́кт] *adj.* отли́чный, соверше́нный; безоши́бочный (*faultless*)

perfection [пэр-фе́к-шан] *sn.* отли́чность, соверше́н-

ство, усоверше́нствование

perfidious [пэр-фи́-ди-ас] *adj.* вероло́мный, преда́тельский

perfidy [пэ́р-фи-ди] *sn.* вероло́мство, изме́на, преда́тельство

perforate [пэ́р-фа-рэйт] *vt.* пробура́вливать, просве́рливать

perforce [пэр-фо́рс] *adv.* по необходи́мости; во́лей-нево́лей (*willy-nilly*)

perform [пэр-фо́рм] *vt.* выполня́ть, исполня́ть, соверша́ть (*carry into effect*); приводи́ть в исполне́ние (*accomplish*); представля́ть (*act, execute*); разы́грывать (*act, execute*); игра́ть (*on an instrument*)

performance [пэр-фо́р-манс] *sn.* исполне́ние, соверше́ние (*thing accomplished*); *theat.* представле́ние; по́двиг (*deed, feat*)

performer [пэр-фо́р-мэр] *sn.* исполни́тель, актёр (*actor*); *sf.* актри́са (*actress*)

perfume [пэ́р-фюм] *sn.* арома́т, прия́тный за́пах; духи́ (*fluid*); [пэр-фю́м] *vt.* наду́шить

perfunctory [пэр-фа́нк-та-ри] *adj.* небре́жный (*careless*); пове́рхностный (*superficial*)

perhaps [пэр-хэ́пс] *adv.* возмо́жно, мо́жет быть

peril [пе́-рил] *sn.* опа́сность (*danger*); риск (*risk*); угро́за (*menace*)

perilous [пе́-ри-лас] · *adj.* опа́сный, угро́зный

period [пи́-ри-ад] *sn.* пери́од, промежу́ток вре́мени; эпо́ха (*epoch*); то́чка (*full stop*)

periodical [пі-рі́о-ді-кәл] *sn.* журна́л, периоди́ческое изда́ние; *adj.* периоди́ческий

periphery [пә-рі́-фә-рі] *sn.* окру́жность, перифери́я

perish [пé-ріш] *vi.* погиба́ть

perishable [пé-рі-шәбл] *adj.* бре́нный, непро́чный, скоропо́ртящийся

perjury [пé-джә-рі] *sn.* клятвопреступле́ние, лжесвиде́тельство

perky [пéр-кі] *adj.* на́глый (*saucy*); самоуве́ренный (*self-assertive*)

permanence [пéр-мә-нәнс] *sn.* неизме́нность, постоя́нство

permanency [пéр-мә-нән-сі] *sn.* постоя́нная до́лжность

permanent [пéр-мә-нәнт] *adj.* неизме́нный, постоя́нный

permeate [пéр-мі-эйт] *vt.* проника́ть

permission [пәр-мí-шән] *sn.* позволе́ние, разреше́ние

permit [пéр-міт] *sn.* про́пуск; [пәр-міт] *vt.* допуска́ть, позволя́ть

pernicious [пәр-ні́-шәс] *adj.* вре́дный (*injurious*); разруши́тельный (*destructive*)

peroration [пе-ро-ро́й-шән] *sn.* заключе́ние ре́чи

perpendicular [пәр-пән-ді́-кю-ла́р] *adj.* отве́сный

perpetrate [пéр-пі-трэйт] *vt.* соверша́ть

perpetual [пәр-пé-тю-ал] *adj.* бесконе́чный, ве́чный, непреры́вный

perpetuate [пәр-пé-тю-эйт] *vt.* увекове́чивать

perpetuity [пәр-пі-тю́-і-ті] *sn.* ве́чность

perplex [пәр-плéкс] *vt.* смуща́ть; запу́тывать (*puzzle*); усложня́ть (*complicate*)

perplexity [пәр-плéкс-і-ті] *sn.* замеша́тельство, смуще́ние; диле́мма

perquisite [пéр-кўі-зіт] *sn.* побо́чный дохо́д

persecute [пéр-сі-кют] *vt.* пресле́довать, притесня́ть

persecution [пәр-сі-кю́шән] *sn.* гоне́ние, пресле́дование

perseverance [пәр-сі-ві́-рәнс] *sn.* насто́йчивость

persevere [пәр-сі-ві́р] *vi.* быть сто́йким, наста́ивать

Persian [пéр-шән] *sm.* перс; *sf.* персия́нка; *adj.* перси́дский

persist [пәр-сíст] *vi.* упо́рствовать, устоя́ть

persistent [пәр-сíс-тәнт] *adj.* сто́йкий, упо́рный

person [пéр-сән] *sm.,* *f.* лицо́, ли́чность, осо́ба

personage [пéр-сә-ніджә] *sm., theat.* персона́ж

personal [пéр-сә-нәл] *adj.* ли́чный

personality [пер-сә-нá-лі-ті] *sn.* ли́чность; ли́чные сво́йства

personify [пәр-со́-ні-фай] *vt.* олицетворя́ть

personnel [пәр-сә-нéл] *sn.* ли́чный соста́в, персона́л

perspective [пәр-спéк-тів] *sn.* перспекти́ва; *adj.* перспекти́вный

perspicacity [пәр-спі-ка́с-і-ті] *sn.* проница́тельность

perspiration [пәр-спі-рә́-шән] *sn.* испа́рина, пот (*sweat*); поте́ние (*sweating*)

persuade [пар-сўэйд] vt. убежда́ть, угова́ривать

persuasion [пар-сўэй-жан] sn. убежде́ние, уве́ренность

pert [пөрт] adj. де́рзкий, наха́льный; бо́йкий (forward)

pertain [пар-тэйн] vi. относи́ться, принадлежа́ть

pertinacious [пар-ти-нэй-шӑс] adj. насто́йчивый

pertinence [пӧр-ти-нӑнс] sn. приго́дность, соотве́тствие, уме́стность

pertinent [пӧр-ти-нӑнт] adj. относя́щийся к де́лу, подходя́щий, уме́стный

perturb [пар-төрб] vt. волнова́ть, расстра́ивать

perusal [па-рў-зӑл] sn. прочте́ние, внима́тельное чте́ние

peruse [па-рўз] vt. прочи́тывать, рассма́тривать

pervade [пар-вэйд] vt. насыща́ть (satiate); проника́ть (penetrate); пропи́тывать (impregnate)

perverse [пар-вөрс] adj. извращённый, несгово́рчивый, превра́тный; поро́чный (wicked)

perversion [пар-вөр-шӑн] sn. извраще́ние

pervert [пөр-вӑрт] sm. извращённый челове́к; [пар-вӧрт] vt. извраща́ть, совраща́ть

pervious [пӧр-ві-ӑс] adj. проница́емый, пропуска́ющий

pest [пест] sn. моро́вая я́зва, чума́ (plague); бич, вреди́тель, парази́т (of person, animal, thing)

pestilence [пе́с-ти-лӑнс] sn. бубо́нная чума́; поветрие

pestilent [пе́с-ти-лӑнт] adj. вре́дный, ядови́тый; надое́дливый (troublesome)

pet [пет] sm. бало́вень, люби́мец (person); люби́мое живо́тное (animal); vt.i. балова́ть, ласка́ть

petal [пе́-тӑл] sn. лепесто́к

petition [пи-ти-шӑн] sn. пети́ция, проше́ние; про́сьба (request); vt.i. подава́ть пети́цию; умоля́ть (ask humbly)

petitioner [пи-ти-шӑ-нӑр] sm. проси́тель

petrifaction [пе-три-фӑк-шӑн] sn. окамене́ние

petrify [пе́-три-фай] vt. окаменева́ть; парализова́ть у́жасом (paralyse with terror)

petrol [пе́-трӑл] sn. газоли́н

petroleum [пе-тро́-лі-ӑм]sn. нефть

petticoat [пе́-ти-ко́ут] sn. ни́жняя ю́бка

pettifogging [пе́-ти-фо-гій] adj. каве́рзный, ме́лочный, ничто́жный

petty [пе́-ти] adj. малова́жный, пустя́чный

petulant [пе́-тю-лӑнт] adj. нетерпели́вый, прихотли́вый; оби́дчивый (touchy)

pew [пю] sn. скамья́ в це́ркви

phantasy [фӑн-тӑ-зи] sn. воображе́ние, фанта́зия

phantom [фӑн-тӑм] sn. привиде́ние, при́зрак, фанто́м; иллю́зия; adj. ка́жущийся, при́зрачный

pharmaceutical [фар-мӑ-сю́-ти-кӑл] adj. фармацевти́ческий

pharmacy [фа́р-мă-сі] *sn.* аптéка; фармаци́я

pharynx [фǽ-рíнкс] *sn. anat.* глóтка, зев

phase [фэйз] *sn.* період, фáза

pheasant [фе́-зăнт] *s.* фазáн

phenomenal [фі-нó-мі-нăл] *adj.* необычáйный, феноменáльный

phenomenon [фі-нó-мі-нăн] *sn.* фенóмен, явлéние

phial [фай-ăл] *sn.* пузырёк, фля́га

philanthropy [фі-лǽн-ѳрă-пі] *sn.* филантрóпия; человеколю́бие

philately [фі-лǽ-тă-лі] *sn.* филатéлия; коллекциони́рование почтóвых мáрок

philology [фі-лó-лă-джі] *sn.* филолóгия

philosophy [фі-лó-сă-фі] *sn.* филосóфия

phlegm [флем] *sn.* мокрóта, слизь, флéгма

phlegmatic [флег-мǽ-тік] *adj.* флегмати́ческий

phonetic [фо-нé-тік] *adj.* фонети́ческий; *pl.* фонéтика

photograph [фó́у-тă-граф] *sn.* фотографи́ческий снимок

photography [фă-тó-грă-фі] *sn.* фотогрáфия

phrase [фрэйз] *sn.* фрáза; идиомати́ческое выражéние (*idiomatic expression*); словосочетáние (*combination of words*); *mus.* фрáза; *vt.* фрази́ровать

physical [фі́-зі-кăл] *adj.* физи́ческий; материáльный (*material*); телéсный (*bodily*)

physician [фі-зі́-шăн] *sn.* врач, дóктор

physics [фі́-зікс] *sn. pl.* фи́зика

physiognomy [фі-зіó-нă-мі] *sn.* лицó, физионóмия; вид (*appearance*); óблик (*countenance*)

physique [фі-зи́к] *sn.* телосложéние

pianist [пі́-æ-ніст] *sm.* пиани́ст; *sf.* пиани́стка

piano, pianoforte [піа́-ноу, піæ-но-фó́р-ті] *sn.* фортепиáно; **upright** – [áп-райт –] пиани́но; **grand** – [грæнд –] роя́ль, *m.*

piccalilli [пі-кă-лі-лі] *sn.* маринáд

pick [пік] *sn.* кирка́, мотыга (*tool*); выбор, отбóр (*choice*); *vt.* долби́ть, взрывáть (*break up ground*); выбирáть (*select*); собирáть, срывáть (*flowers, fruit*); обирáть (*gather*); клевáть (*peck*); обгла́дывать (*bone*); обворóвывать (*pocket*)

pickaxe [пі́к-æкс] *sn.* кайлá, остроконéчная кирка́

picket [пі́-кіт] *sn.* кол, столб (*peg*); *sm.* пикéт (*pl.*); сторожевáя застáва; *vt.* огорáживать (*set with stakes*); пикети́ровать (*post soldiers, strikers*)

pickings [пі́-кіηз] *sn. pl.* объéдки, остáтки; мéлкая пожи́ва (*small profits*)

pickle [пікл] *sn.* рассóл; *fig.* неприя́тное состоя́ние; *vt.* маринóвать; *pl.* маринóванные óвощи

pickpocket [пі́к-по-кіт] *sm.* вор-карма́нник

picnic [пі́к-нік] *sn.* пикни́к, прия́тное времяпрепровождéние; *vi.* учáствовать в пикни́ке

pictorial [пік-тô-ріäл] *sn.* иллюстрированный журнал; *adj.* иллюстрированный, картинный

picture [пік-чäр] *sn.* картина; изображение (*image*); портрет (*portrait*); *pl.* кино; *vt.* изображать, описывать, представлять; воображать (*imagine*)

picturesque [пік-чä-рéск] *adj.* живописный; графический, яркий (*of language*)

pie [пай] *sn.* пирог (*meat or fruit*); сорока (*bird*)

piebald [пай-бôлд] *s.* пегая лошадь (*horse*); *adj.* пегий, пёстрый (*motley*)

piece [пис] *sn.* кусок, штука; монета (*coin*); образец (*example*); пьеса (*play*) *vt.* добавлять, присоединять

piecemeal [піс-мил] *adv.* кусками, по частям

piece-work [піс-ўзрк] *sn.* сдельная работа

pied [пайд] *adj.* пёстрый

pier [пир] *sn.* дамба, мол; пристань (*landing-stage*); волнорез (*break-water*)

pierce [пирс] *vt.* прокалывать, просверливать

piercing [пир-сін] *adj.* пронзительный (*of noise*); пронизывающий (*of cold, glance*)

piety [пай-ä-ті] *sn.* благочестие, набожность

pig [піг] *sf.* свинья; *tech.* болванка, чушка

pigeon [пі-джін] *s.* голубь, *m.*

pigheaded [піг-хê-дід] *adj.* упрямый

pigment [піг-мänт] *sn.* пигмент

pigsty [піг-стай] *sn.* свинарник

pigtail [піг-тэйл] *sn.* косичка

pike [пайк] *s.* щука (*fish*); копьё, пика (*spear*)

pile [пайл] *sn.* груда, куча (*heap*); свая (*beam*); ворс (*nap*); *pl. med.* геморрой

pilfer [піл-фäр] *vt.i.* воровать, таскать

pilgrim [піл-грім] *sm.* паломник, пилигрим; странник (*wanderer*)

pilgrimage [піл-гри-мідж] *sn.* паломничество, пилигримство; странствование

pill [піл] *sn.* пилюля

pillage [пі-лідж] *sn.* грабёж, мародёрство, расхищение; *vt.* грабить

pillar [пі-лäр] *sn.* колонна, столб; *fig.* опора, столп (*person*)

pillar-box [пі-лäр-бокс] *sn.* почтовый ящик

pillion [пі-ліän] *sn.* седельная подушка (*cushion*); заднее сиденье (*of motor-cycle*)

pillory [пі-лä-рі] *sn.* позорный столб

pillow [пі-лоу] *sn.* постельная подушка

pillow-case [пі-лоу-кэйс] *sn.* наволочка

pilot [пай-лäт] *sm.* лётчик, пилот (*air*); лоцман, рулевой, штурман (*sea*); *vt.* управлять рулём

pimple [пімпл] *sn.* прыщик

pin [пін] *sn.* булавка, шпилька; *tech.* нагель, цапфа, шип; английская булавка (*safety*); *vt.* пришпиливать

pinafore [пі-нä-фôр] *sn.* передник, фартук (*woman's*)

pincers [пíн-сăрз] *sn. pl.* клéщи, цúпчики

pinch [пíнч] *sn.* щипóк (*nip*); щепóтка (*of salt, etc.*); *vt.i.* уципнýть; жать (*of shoes*)

pincushion [пíн-кý-шăн] *sn.* подýшечка для булáвок

pine [пайн] *sn.* соснá; *vi.* иссыхáть, чáхнуть (*pine away*); томúться, тосковáть (*long, languish*)

pine-apple [пáйн-æпл] *sn.* ананáс

pinion [пí-ниăн] *sn.* оконéчность птúчьего крылá (*outer joint of bird's wing*); *poet.* крылó (*wing*); маховóе перó (*flight-feather*); *tech.* зубчáтое колесó, шестерня́

pink [пíнк] *sn. bot.* гвоздúка; рóзовый цвет (*colour*); *adj.* рóзовый

pinnacle [пí-нăкл] *sn.* верхýшка, шпиц

pint [пайнт] *sn.* пúнта (восьмáя часть галлóна)

pioneer [пай-а-нúр] *sn.* пионéр; исслéдователь (*explorer*); *mil.* сапёр; *vi.* быть пионéром

pious [пáй-ăс] *adj.* благочестúвый, набóжный

pip [пíп] *sn.* зёрнышко, кóсточка (*of fruit*); очкó (*on domino, etc.*); звёздочка (*on officer's shoulder*)

pipe [пайп] *sn.* курúтельная трýбка (*smoking*); трубá, трубопровóд (*tube*); *mus.* дýдка, свистóк; *pl.* волынка; *vt.i. mus.* игрáть, свистéть

piper [пáй-пăр] *sn.* дýдочник, игрáющий на волынке

piping [пáй-пиñ] *sn.* трубы;

кант (*on dress*); узóр (*on cake*)

pipe-line [пáйп-лайн] *sn.* трубопровóд

pippin [пí-пин] *sn.* сорт я́блок

piquant [пú-кăнт] *adj.* пикáнтный

pique [пúк] *vt.* задéть, уколóть; возбуждáть (*curiosity*)

piracy [пáй-ра-си] *sn.* пирáтство

pirate [пáй-рăт] *sn.* пирáт; *vt.* занимáться пирáтством, плагиúровать

pistol [пíс-тăл] *sn.* пистолéт, револьвéр

piston [пíс-тăн] *sn.* пóршень (*plug*); клапáн (*of wind instruments*)

pit [пíт] *sn.* впáдина, углублéние, я́ма (*hollow*); копь, шáхта (*mine*); ряби́на (*on skin*); партéр (*floor of theatre auditorium*); лóжечка (*o stomach*); *vt.* рыть я́му; противопоставля́ть (*match person against*)

pitch [пíч] *sn.* дёготь, смолá (*tar product*); стéпень (*degree*); *mus.* диапазóн, тон, уравнéние тóна; часть крúкетного пóля (*cricket*); *vt.* смолúть (*tar*); раски́дывать (*tent, etc.*)

pitcher [пí-чăр] *sn.* кувши́н

piteous [пí-ти-ăс] *adj.* жáлостный

pitfall [пíт-фôл] *sn.* западня́, ловýшка

pith [пíθ] *sn. bot.* сердцеви́на; сýщность (*quintessence*); сúла, энéргия (*vigour*)

pitiable [пí-ти-ăбл] *adj.* достóйный сожалéния

pitiful [пи́-ти-фу́л] *adj.* возбужда́ющий сострада́ние, жа́лостливый

pitiless [пи́-ти-лис] *adj.* безжа́лостный

pittance [пи́-тэнс] *sn.* ничто́жное вспомоществова́ние

pity [пи́-ти] *sn.* жа́лость, сожале́ние; *vt.* жале́ть, соболе́зновать

pivot [пи́-вэт] *sn.* веретено́, шкво́рень, *m.*, шпиль; *vt.i.* верте́ться, враща́ться; устана́вливать сте́ржень, *m.*

placard [пла́-ка́рд] *sn.* афи́ша, плака́т; *vt.* объявля́ть, реклами́ровать

placate [пла-ке́йт] *vt.* примиря́ть, умилостивля́ть

place [плэйс] *sn.* ме́сто, до́лжность (*job, situation*); пло́щадь (*square*); *vt.* класть, помеща́ть, ста́вить

placid [пла́-сид] *adj.* ми́рный, споко́йный

plague [плэйг] *sn.* мор, чума́, огорче́ние (*affliction*)

plain [плэйн] *sn.* равни́на; *pl.* пре́рии, сте́пи; *adj.* поня́тный, я́вный (*clear*); обыкнове́нный, просто́й (*simple*); невзра́чный (*homely*); *adv.* разбо́рчиво, чётко

plaintiff [плэйн-тиф] *sn.* исте́ц; *sf.* исти́ца

plaintive [плэйн-тив] *adj.* жа́лобный, зауны́вный

plait [плэйт] *sn.* коса́ (*hair*); скла́дка (*tuck*); *vt.* плести́

plan [плэн] *sn.* план, чертёж, прое́кт (*project*); *vt.* замышля́ть, плани́ровать

plane [плэйн] *sn.* аэропла́н, самолёт (*aeroplane*); руба́нок, струг (*tool*); пло́скость, у́ровень (*surface*); *vt.* вы-

ра́внивать (*smooth*); строга́ть (*shave wood*)

planet [пла́-нит] *sn.* плане́та

plank [плэнк] *sn.* доска́; *vt.* настила́ть доски́

plant [плэнт] *sn. bot.* расте́ние; заво́д, фа́брика (*factory*); обору́дование (*equipment*); *vt.* вса́живать

plantation [плэн-тэ́й-шэн] *sn.* планта́ция

planter [плэн-тэ́р] *sm.* планта́тор

plaque [плэк] *sn.* металли́ческий диск

plaster [пла́с-тэ́р] *sn. med.* пла́стырь, *m.*; штукату́рка (*for walls*); *vt.* зама́зывать, штукату́рить

plastic [пла́с-тик] *adj.* пласти́ческий

plate [плэйт] *sn.* таре́лка, столо́вое серебро́ (*silver table utensils*); металли́ческая доска́, пласти́нка (*thin sheet of metal*)

plateau [пла́-то́у] *sn.* плато́, плоского́рье

platform [пла́т-фо́рм] *sn.* платфо́рма; сце́на, эстра́да (*stage*); площа́дка (*landing place*)

platinum [пла́-ти-нэм] *sn.* пла́тина

platitude [пла́-ти-тюд] *sn.* по́шлость, тривиа́льность

platoon [пла-ту́н] *sn.* взвод

plausible [пло́-зибл] *adj.* вероя́тный, благови́дный

play [плэй] *sn.* игра́ (*game*), заба́ва, развлече́ние (*amusement*); *theat.* пье́са; *vt.i.* забавля́ться, игра́ть

player [плэ́й-эр] *sm. theat.* актёр; *sport.* игро́к; *mus.* музыка́нт

playful [плэ́й-фўл] *adj.* игри́вый, шаловли́вый, шутли́вый

playmate [плэ́й-мэйт] *sm.* това́рищ по игре́

plaything [плэ́й-ðиŋ] *sn.* игру́шка

playtime [плэ́й-тайм] *sn.* шко́льный о́тдых, вре́мя для забавле́ния

plea [пли] *sn.* оправда́ние (*excuse, justification*); про́сьба (*request*); защи́та (*defence*)

plead [плид] *vt.i.* защища́ть (*defend*); обраща́ться (*address*); отвеча́ть (*answer*); хода́тайствовать (*intercede*); умоля́ть (*appeal*)

pleasant [пле́-зэнт] *adj.* прия́тный

pleasantry [пле́-зэн-трі] *sn.* шутли́вость; шу́тка (*jest*)

please [плиз] *vt.i.* нра́виться; доставля́ть удово́льствие (*give joy or satisfaction*); **if you —** [иф ю —] пожа́луйста!; **be pleased** [би плизд] быть дово́льным

pleasing [пли́-зіŋ] *adj.* нра́вящийся, прия́тный

pleasure [пле́-жăр] *sn.* наслажде́ние (*delight*); удово́льствие (*satisfaction*)

pleat [плит] *sn.* скла́дка

plebeian [плі-бі́-ăн] *adj.* плебе́йский, простонаро́дный

plebiscite [пле́-бі-сіт] *sn.* плебисци́т

pledge [пледж] *sn.* зада́ток, закла́д, зало́г (*deposit*); пору́чительство (*guarantee*); *vt.* закла́дывать, отдава́ть в зало́г (*pawn*); обяза́ться, руча́ться (*solemnly promise*)

plenipotentiary [пле-ні-па́-тєн-шіā-рі] *sm.* по́сланник, полномо́чный представи́тель; *adj.* полномо́чный

plentiful [пле́н-ті-фўл] *adj.* оби́льный, плодоро́дный

plenty [пле́н-ті] *sn.* изоби́лие, оби́лие (*abundance*)

pleurisy [плў-рі-сі] *sn.* плеври́т

pliable [пла́й-ăбл] *adj.* ги́бкий, податли́вый; усту́пчивый (*yielding*)

pliers [пла́й-ăрз] *sn. pl.* плоскогу́бцы, щи́пчики

plight [плайт] *sn.* бе́дственное положе́ние

plimsolls [плі́м-сăлз] *sn. pl.* паруси́новые ту́фли

plinth [плінθ] *sn.* плі́нтус; цо́коль

plod [плод] *vi.* тащи́ться (*trudge*); труди́ться (*toil*)

plodder [пло́-дăр] *sn. coll.* усе́рдный челове́к

plot [плот] *sn.* за́говор; у́мысел (*design*); сюже́т, фа́була (*subject of play*); клочо́к земли́ (*of land*); завя́зка (*plan*); *vt.i.* замышля́ть, интригова́ть

plough [пла́у] *sn.* плуг (*implement*); *vt.* паха́ть; бороди́ть (*waves*)

ploughman [пла́у-мăн] *sm.* па́харь

pluck [плак] *sn.* потроха́ (*of animal*); *coll.* му́жество, сме́лость; *vt.* выде́ргивать, срыва́ть

plucky [пла́-кі] *adj.* отва́жный, сме́лый

plug [плаг] *sn.* вту́лка, заты́чка, про́бка; *electr.* ште́псель, про-

plum [плам] *sn.* сли́ва; изю́м (*currant, raisin*); *adj.* сли́вовый

plumage [плу́-мідж] *sn.* опере́ние

plumb [плам] *sn.* отве́с; грузи́ло (*sounding-lead*); *adj.* вертика́льный, отве́сный; *vt.i.* пая́ть; измеря́ть глубину́ (*measure depth*)

plumber [пла́-мэр] *sm.* водопрово́дчик, пая́льщик

plume [плум] *sn.* перо́ (*feather*); плюма́ж, султа́н (*head ornament*); *vt.* укра́шать перо́м

plump [пламп] *adj.* пу́хлый, по́лный, прямо́й (*of statement*); безусло́вный (*uncompromising*); *vt.i.* толсте́ть (*fatten*); бу́хаться (*down*); *adv.* внеза́пно, неожи́данно (*unexpectedly*)

plunder [пла́н-дэр] *sn.* грабёж (*robbery*); добы́ча (*spoils*); *vt.* гра́бить, расхища́ть

plunge [пландж] *sn.* ныря́ние (*diving, plunging*); погруже́ние (*submersion*); реши́тельный шаг (*decisive step*); *vt.i.* окуна́ть, погружа́ться

plural [плу́-рэл] *adj. gram.* мно́жественный

plus [плас] *prep.* плюс; положи́тельный (*positive*); *sn.* знак плюс (+) (*symbol*)

plush [плаш] *sn.* плюш

ply [плай] *sn.* ордина́рная толщина́ (*strand*), сгиб, скла́дка (*bend, crease*); *vt.i.* усе́рдно рабо́тать (*work vigorously*); уси́ленно угоща́ть (*treat pressingly*); курси́ровать (*of ship, etc.*)

pneumatic [ню-мэ́-тік] *adj.* пневмати́ческий; *pl.* пневма́тика

pneumonia [ню-мо́у-нія] *sn. med.* воспале́ние лёгких, пневмо́ния

poach [по́уч] *vt.* вари́ть я́йца без скорлупы́ (*eggs*); *vt.i.* занима́ться браконье́рством (*take game, etc. illegally*)

poacher [по́у-чэр] *sm.* браконье́р

pocket [по́-кіт] *sn.* карма́н; лу́за (*billiards*); возду́шная я́ма (*air*); *vt.* прикарма́нивать; загоня́ть (*billiards*)

pocket-book [по́-кіт-бу́к] *sn.* бума́жник

pod [под] *sn.* кожура́, стручо́к, шелуха́; *vt.* лущи́ть, шелуши́ть

podgy [по́-джі] *adj. coll.* ни́зенький и то́лстый

poem [по́у-ім] *sn.* поэ́ма, стихотворе́ние

poet [по́у-іт] *sm.* поэ́т; *sf.* поэте́сса

poetical [по́у-ѓ-ті-кал] *adj.* поэти́ческий

poetry [по́у-а-трі] *sn.* поэ́зия, стихи́

poignant [по́й-нэнт] *adj.* о́стрый (*keen*); е́дкий, ко́лкий (*stinging*); ре́зкий (*of pain*); мучи́тельный (*of memories*)

point [пойнт] *sn.* то́чка (*stop*); ме́сто (*place*); пункт (*feature, spot*); моме́нт (*exact moment*); ко́нчик, острие́ (*tip, edge*); очко́ (*in sport*); черта́ (*feature*); ка́чество (*quality*); *pl.* стре́лки (*railway*); ру́мбы (*of compass*); *vt.i.* заостря́ть, чини́ть (*sharpen*); ука́зывать (*indicate*); ста́вить зна́ки препина́ния (*punctuate*)

pointed [по́йн-тід] *adj.* о́стрый (*sharp*); вырази́тельный (*expressive*); подчёркнутый (*emphatic*); эпиграмати́ческий

pointer [по́йн-та̊р] *sn.* стре́лка (*of watch, etc.*); указа́тель *m.* (*indicator*); намёк (*hint*); по́йнтер (*dog*)

poise [по́йз] *sn.* равнове́сие (*equilibrium*); оса́нка (*deportment*); *vt.* взве́шивать, уравнове́шивать; держа́ть го́лову (*carry one's head*)

poison [по́й-за̊н] *sn.* отра́ва, яд; *fig.* ги́бельное влия́ние; *vt.* отравля́ть

poisonous [по́й-за̊-на̊с] *adj.* ядови́тый

poke [по́ук] *sn.* толчо́к, тычо́к; *vt.* сова́ть, толка́ть

poker [по́у-ка̊р] *sn.* кочерга́

polar [по́у-ла̊р] *adj.* поля́рный, по́люсный

pole [по́ул] *sn.* столб, шест (*long piece of wood or metal*); *naut.* без пару́сов; ме́ра длины́ (*около пяти́ ме́тров*) (*measure*); по́люс

Pole [по́ул] *sn.* поля́к

pole-axe [по́ул-æкс] *sn.* реза́к (*butcher's*); бердьі́ш, секи́ра (*halbert*)

polecat [по́ул-кæт] *s.* хорёк

police [по-лі́с] *sn.* поли́ция; **the —** [а̊ᵊ —] поли́це́йские; *vt.* подде́рживать поря́док; **-man** [-ма̊н] *sm.* городово́й, полице́йский

policy [по́-лі-сі] *sn.* поли́тика; о́браз де́йствия (*course of action*); по́лис (*insurance*)

polish [по́-ліш] *sn.* политу́ра (*substance*); лоск (*gloss*); утончённость (*refinement*); *vt.i.* полирова́ть, шлифова́ть

Polish [по́у-ліш] *adj.* по́льский

polite [па-ла́йт] *adj.* ве́жливый, учти́вый

politeness [па-ла́йт-ніс] *sn.* ве́жливость, любе́зность; благовоспи́танность (*good breeding*)

politic [по́-лі-тік] *adj.* обду́манный, расчётливый; сообрази́тельный (*sagacious*)

political [па-лі́-ті-ка̊л] *adj.* полити́ческий

politics [по́-лі-тікс] *sn. pl.* поли́тика

poll [по́ул] *sn.* подсчёт голосо́в (*counting of votes*); голосова́ние (*voting at election*); *vt.i.* баллоти́ровать, голосова́ть

pollen [по́-лін] *sn. bot.* пыльца́

pollination [по-лі-не́й-шан] *sn.* опыле́ние

pollute [па-лю́т] *vt.* оскверня́ть

pollution [па-лю́-шан] *sn.* загрязне́ние; поллю́ция

polony [па-ло́у-ні] *sn.* род соси́ски

polygamy [по-лі́-га-мі] *sn.* многобра́чие, полига́мия

polyglot [по́-лі-глот] *adj.* многоязы́чный

pomegranate [по́мі-грæ-ніт] *sn. bot.* грана́т

pomp [помп] *sn.* по́мпа, пы́шность

pomposity [пом-по́-сі-ті] *sn.* напы́щенность, помпе́зность

pompous [пом-пáс] *adj.* помпéзный, пы́шный

pond [понд] *sn.* пруд

ponder [пóн-дəр] *vt.i.* обдýмывать, размышля́ть

ponderable [пóн-дə-рəбл] *adj.* вéский

ponderous [пóн-дрəс] *adj.* тяжелове́сный (*of style, talk, etc.*); тяжёлый (*heavy*)

pontiff [пóн-тиф] *sn.* Пáпа (*Pope*); архиере́й (*high priest*)

Pontifical [пон-ти́-фи-кəл] *adj.* пáпский; первосвяще́ннический

pontoon [пон-тýн] *sn.* понтóн

pony [пóу-ни] *s.* пóни (*собака*)

poodle [пýдл] *s.* пýдель (*собака*)

pool [пул] *sn.* большáя лýжа, прудóк (*pond*); омýт (*deep water*); **swimming** - [сýи-мин -] бассéйн для плáвания; *com.* пул; *vt.* вноси́ть в общий фонд

poop [пуп] *sn. naut.* кормá, ют

poor [пур] *adj.* бéдный; скýдный (*of soil*); недостáточный (*scanty*); ничтóжный (*insignificant*); жáлкий, несчáстный (*unfortunate*); **the** - [ðā -] *sn.* беднотá, неимýщие

poorly [пýр-ли] *adv.* недостáточно (*insufficiently*); неуспéшно (*with little success*); *adj.* нездорóвый (*unwell*)

Pope [пóуп] *sn.* Пáпа

poplar [пó-плəр] *sn.* тóполь, *m.*

poppy [пó-пи] *sn.* мак; *adj.* мáковый

populace [пó-пю-лəс] *sn.* нарóд, населéние

popular [пó-пю-лəр] *adj.* нарóдный; популя́рный (*generally liked*)

popularity [по-пю-лǽ-ри-ти] *sn.* популя́рность

populate [пó-пю-лэйт] *vt.* заселя́ть, населя́ть

population [по-пю-лэ́йшəн] *sn.* жи́тели, населéние

populous [пó-пю-лəс] *adj.* многолю́дный

porcelain [пóр-сə-лин] *sn.* фарфóр; *adj.* фарфóровый

porch [пóрч] *sn.* крыльцó, пóртик

pore [пóр] *sn.* пóра, сквáжинка; отвéрстие (*opening*); *vi.* сосредотóчиваться

pork [пóрк] *sn.* свинина́

porous [пó-рəс] *adj.* пóристый; проницáемый (*permeable*)

porridge [пó-ри́дж] *sn.* кáша, овся́нка

port [пóрт] *sn.* портвéйн (*wine*); гáвань, порт (*harbour*); *naut.* бортовóе отвéрстие (*of ship*); лéвая сторонá корабля́ (*left of ship*)

portable [пóр-тəбл] *adj.* перенóсный, удобоноси́мый, перенóсный

portal [пóр-тəл] *sn.* глáвный вход, портáл

portend [пóр-тéнд] *vt.* предвещáть

portent [пóр-тəнт] *sn.* предзнаменовáние (*omen*); чýдо

portentous [пóр-тéн-тəс] *adj.* зловéщий; знаменáтельный; чудóвищный (*prodigious*)

porter [пóр-тəр] *sm.* приврáтник (*attendant*); носи́льщик (*railway*); пóртер, чёрное пи́во (*dark beer*)

portfolio [порт-фо́у-лиоў] *sn.* портфе́ль, *m.*

portion [по́р-шан] *sn.* до́ля, часть, удел, уча́сть (*lot, destiny*); *vt.* дели́ть на ча́сти

portly [по́рт-ли] *adj.* оса́нистый (*stately*); доро́дный (*corpulent*); представи́тельный (*dignified*)

portmanteau [по́рт-ма́нтоў] *sn.* чемода́н (*трет*)

portrait [по́р-трет] *sn.* портре́т

portray [пор-тре́й] *vt.* изобража́ть, опи́сывать

portrayal [пор-тре́й-ал] *sn.* изображе́ние, описа́ние

Portuguese [пор-тю-ги́з] *sm.* португа́лец; *sf.* португа́лка; *adj.* португа́льский

pose [по́уз] *sn.* по́за; *vt.i.* пози́ровать; предлага́ть, ста́вить (*propound*)

poser [по́у-зар] *sn.* тру́дный вопро́с (*difficult question*); позёр (*person*)

position [па-зи́-шан] *sn.* положе́ние (*state of affairs*); местоположе́ние (*relative place*); пози́ция (*strategic point*); до́лжность (*post*)

positive [по́-зи-тив] *adj.* поло́жительный (*definite*); утверди́тельный (*affirmative*); безусло́вный (*absolute*)

possess [па-зе́с] *vt.* владе́ть, облада́ть

possession [па-зе́-шан] *sn.* владе́ние, облада́ние; *pl.* иму́щество

possessive [па-зе́-сив] *adj.* име́ющий; *gram.* притяжа́тельный

possibility [по-си-би́-ли-ти] *sn.* возмо́жность

possible [по́-сибл] *adj.* вероя́тный, возмо́жный

post [по́уст] *sn.* столб (*pillar*); по́чта (*conveying of letters, etc.*); до́лжность (*appointment*); *vt.* выве́шивать объявле́ние (*display notice, etc.*); сдава́ть в по́чту (*hand in, drop in letter-box*); *mil.* расставля́ть на места́; *prep.* по́сле; **-office** [-о́фис] по́чта

postage [по́у-стидж] *sn.* пла́та за почто́вую пересы́лку; **- stamp** [- стэмп] почто́вая ма́рка

postal [по́у-стал] *adj.* почто́вый

postcard [по́уст-ка́рд] *sn.* откры́тка (плака́т)

poster [по́у-стар] *sn.* афи́ша

posterior [пост-ти́-ри-ар] *sn.* зад; *adj.* за́дний (*rear*); поздне́йший, после́дующий (*later in time or order*)

posterity [пост-те́-ри-ти] *sn.* пото́мство

posthumous [по́с-тю-мас] *adj.* посме́ртный

postman [по́уст-ман] *sm.* почтальо́н

postmortem [по́уст-мо́ртäм] *sn.* вскры́тие (тру́па) (*autopsy*); *adj.* посме́ртный; *adv.* по́сле сме́рти

postpone [по́уст-по́ун] *vt.* откла́дывать, отсро́чивать

postponement [поуст-по́унмäнт] *sn.* отсро́чка

postscript [по́уст-скрипт] *sn.* припи́ска

postulate [по́с-тю-лэйт] *vt.* постули́ровать

posture [по́с-чар] *sn.* по́за, положе́ние, состоя́ние

posy [по́у-зи] *sn.* буке́т цвето́в

pot [пот] *sn.* горшо́к, коте́лок; *v.t.* сажа́ть (*plant*), консерви́ровать (*preserve*)

potato [пǝ-тэ́й-тоў] *sn.* картóфель, *m.*

potent [пóў-тǝнт] *adj.* могу́щественный; влия́тельный (*influential*)

potentate [пóў-тǝн-тэйт] *sm.* власти́тель, монáрх

potential [пǝ-тéн-шǝл] *adj.* возмóжный, потенциáльный

potion [пóў-шǝн] *sn.* дóза, напи́ток, питьё (*lekárstvo*, яд)

potter [пó-тǝр] *sn.* гончáр; *vi.* лоды́рничать (*idle*); околáчиваться (*dawdle*)

pottery [пó-тǝ-рi] *sn.* гончáрня (*factory*); гли́няная посу́да (*earthenware*)

pouch [пáўч] *sn.* мешóчек, сýмка, *vt.i.* прикармáнивать; висéть мешкóм (*hang like pouch*)

poultice [пóўл-тiс] *sn.* припáрка; *vt.* класть припáрку

poultry [пóўл-трi] *sn.* домáшняя пти́ца, жи́вность

pounce [пáўнс] *sn.* внезáпный спуск; *vi.* бросáться, врывáться, накáдываться

pound [пáўнд] *sn.* фунт (*money*, *weight*); загóн (*enclosure*); *vt.i.* колоти́ть (*thump*); толóчь (*crush*); бомбарди́ровать (*bombard*)

pour [пóр] *vt.i.* впадáть; ли́ться; разливáть (*tea*, *wine*)

pout [пáўт] *sn.* гримáса; минóга (*fish*); *vi.* ду́ться

poverty [пó-вǝр-тi] *sn.* бéдность, нищетá

powder [пáў-дǝр] *sn.* порошóк (*cleaning*, *medicine*); пýдра (*cosmetic*); пыль (*dust*); пóрох (*explosive*)

vt.i. превращáть в порошóк; пýдриться

powder-puff [пóў-дǝр-паф] *sn.* пухóвка

power [пáў-ǝр] *sn.* власть (*authority*, *rule*); держáва (*nation*, *state*); мóщность, си́ла (*force*, *strength*); спосóбность (*ability*); *tech.* энéргия

powerful [пáў-ǝр-фǝл] *adj.* могу́щественный, си́льный

practicable [прǽк-тi-кǝбл] *adj.* исполни́мый, осуществи́мый; проходи́мый (*of road*, *etc.*)

practical [прǽк-тi-кǝл] *adj.* практи́ческий; óпытный (*experienced*)

practically [прǽк-тi-кǝ-лi] *adv.* практи́чески; в сýщности (*virtually*); почти́ (*almost*)

practice [прǽк-тiс] *sn.* прáктика; нáвык, обычáй (*habitual action*); привы́чка (*custom*); упражнéние (*repeated exercise*)

practise [прǽк-тiс] *vt.i.* исполня́ть (*carry out*); практиковáть (*pursue profession*, *etc.*); упражня́ть

practitioner [прǽк-тi-шǝ-нǝр] *sm.* частнопрактику́ющий врач

prairie [прэ́-рǝi] *sn.* прéрия

praise [прэ́йз] *sn.* похвалá восхвалéние (*glorification*); *vt.* хвали́ть

praiseworthy [прэ́йз-ўǝ́р-ǝi] *atj.* похвáльный

pram [прǽм] *sn. coll.* дéтская коля́ска

prance [прǽнс] *sn.* прыжóк, скачóк; *vi.* гарцовáть, станови́ться на дыбы́

prank [præŋk] sn. продёлка, шалость; vt.i. украшать (adorn, deck); наряжаться (show off)

prate [прэйт] sn. пустословие; vi. болтать

prattle [прэтл] sn. лёпет; vi. лепетать

pray [прэй] vt.i. молиться, просить; умолять (ask earnestly)

prayer [прэ-эр] sm. молящийся, проситель; sn. молитва; прóсьба (request)

prayer-book [прэ-эр-бук] sn. молитвенник

preach [прич] vt.i. проповедывать

preacher [при-чэр] sm. проповедник

preamble [при-эмбл] sn. вступление, предисловие

precarious [при-кэ-ри-эс] adj. ненадёжный, неустойчивый (uncertain); опасный (dangerous); рискóванный (risky)

precaution [при-кó-шäн] sn. предосторожность

precede [при-сид] vt. предшествовать

precedent [прé-си-дäнт] sn. прецедент

preceding [при-си-дий] adj. предшествующий

precept [при-сéпт] sn. прáвило, указáние; leg. предписáние; увещевáние (exhortation)

precinct [при-сиňкт] sn. округ, предéл; pl. окрéстность

precious [прé-шäс] adj. драгоцéнный; coll. дорогóй, любимый, милый

precipice [прé-си-пис] sn. прóпасть

precipitate [при-си-пи-тäт] adj. опромéтчивый (rash); стремительный (impetuous); [при-си-пи-тэйт] vt. низвергáть (throw headlong down); ускорять (hasten); chem. осождáть

precipitous [при-си-пи-тäс] adj. обрывистый, отвéсный

precise [при-сáйс] adj. тóчный; тщáтельный (exact); щепетильный (scrupulous)

precision [при-си-жäн] sn. аккурáтность (accuracy); тóчность (exactness)

preclude [при-клюд] vt. предотвращáть; устранить (remove)

precocious [при-кóу-шäс] adj. преждеврéменный, рáнний, скороспéлый

preconceive [при-кон-сив] vt. предвзять зарáнее; судить зарáнее

preconception [при-кäн-сéп-шäн] sn. предвидéние, предубеждéние

precursory [при-кéр-сä-ри] adj. предвещáющий

predatory [прé-дä-тä-ри] adj. грабительский, хищный

predecessor [при-ди-сé-säр] sm. предшéственник

predetermine [при-ди-тéр-мин] vt. предрешáть

predicament [при-ди-кä-мäнт] sn. затруднéние, неприятное положéние

predict [при-дикт] vt. предскáзывать, прорицáть

predominant [при-дó-ми-нäнт] adj. госпóдствующий, преобладáющий

predominate [при-дó-ми-нэйт] vi. преобладáть

pre-eminent [prɪ-émɪ-nänt] *adj.* выдаю́щийся

preface [préfǎс] *sn.* предисло́вие; *vt.* дать предисло́вие

prefect [prɪ́-фе̄кт] *sm. f.* префе́кт; ста́рший учени́к (*school*)

prefer [prɪ-фө̄р] *vt.* предпочита́ть (*like better*); выдвига́ть (*bring forward, submit*)

preference [pré-фǎ-ränc] *sn.* предпочте́ние; преиму́щественное пра́во (*priority*)

preferential [prɪ-фǎ-рéншǎл] *adj.* по́льзующийся предпочте́нием; льго́тный (*of import duties, treatment*)

prefix [прɪ́-фɪкс] *sn.* пре́фикс, приста́вка; [prɪ́-фɪкс] *vt.* приставля́ть пре́фикс; предпосыла́ть

pregnancy [прéг-нǎн-сɪ] *sn.* бере́менность

pregnant [прег-нǎнт] *adj.* бере́менная; чрева́тый (*fruitful in results, with consequences*); содержа́тельный, тво́рческий (*with ideas*)

prejudice [pré-джу́-дɪс] *sn.* предрассу́док, предубежде́ние; уще́рб (*detriment*); *vt.* предубежда́ть; наноси́ть уще́рб; подрыва́ть (*sap*)

prejudicial [pré-джу́-дɪ-шǎл] *adj.* наноси́щий уще́рб, убы́точный

preliminary [prɪ-лɪ́-мɪ-на̄-рɪ] *adj.* предвари́тельный; *pl.* предвари́тельные усло́вия

prelude [pré-лю̄д] *sn.* вступле́ние; *mus.* прелю́дия; *vt.* служи́ть вступле́нием

premature [pré-мǎ-чǎр] *adj.* преждевре́менный (*occurring before time*); скороспе́лый (*done too early*)

premeditated [prɪ-мé-дɪ-тэ̄й-тɪд] *adj.* предумы́шленный

premeditation [prɪ-мé-дɪ-тэ̄й-шǎн] *sn.* преднаме́ренность

premier [pré-мɪǎр] *sm* премье́р-мини́стр; *adj.* пе́рвый; передово́й (*foremost*)

premise [pré-мɪс] *sn.* предпосы́лка; *pl.* дом, помеще́ние; [prɪ-ма́йз] *vt.* предпосыла́ть

premium [прɪ́-мɪ-ǎм] *sn.* награ́да, пре́мия; пла́та

premonition [prɪ-мо-нɪ́-шǎн] *sn.* предостереже́ние, предупрежде́ние (*forewarning*); предчу́вствие (*presentiment*)

preoccupation [прɪ-о-кокю̄пэ́й-шǎн] *sn.* озабо́ченность; рассе́янность (*mental absorption*)

preparation [пре-пǎ-рэ́й-шǎн] *sn.* приготовле́ние; подгото́вка

preparatory [prɪ-пǎ̄-рǎ-та̄-рɪ] *adj.* вступи́тельный, приготови́тельный; *adv.* пре́жде чем

prepare [prɪ-пэ̄р] *vt.* гото́вить, приготовля́ть

preponderance [prɪ-по́н-дǎ-рǎнс] *sn.* переве́с; превосхо́дство (*superiority*)

preponderate [prɪ-по́н-дǎ-рэ̄йт] *vi.* переве́шивать (*be heavier*); превосходи́ть (*be superior*); преоблада́ть (*predominate*)

preposition [пре-пǎ-зɪ́-шǎн] *sn. gram.* предло́г

prepossess [при-па-зе́с] *vt.* внуша́ть (*inspire*); овладева́ть (*take possession*); предрасполага́ть (*produce favourable impression*)

preposterous [прі-по́с-та́-рас] *adj.* неле́пый (*absurd*); превра́тный (*perverse*)

prerogative [прі-ро́-га-тів] *sn.* прерогати́ва

presage [пре́-сідж] *sn.* предсказа́ние, предчу́вствие; *vt.* знаменова́ть, предвеща́ть

prescribe [прі-скра́йб] *vt.i.* предпи́сывать (*lay down course of action*); пропи́сывать (*medicine, treatment*)

prescription [прі-скрі́п-шан] *sn. med.* реце́пт; *leg.* пра́во да́вности; предписа́ние (*prescribing*)

presence [пре́-занс] *sn.* прису́тствие; оса́нка (*appearance*)

present [пре́-зант] *sn.* пода́рок (*gift*); настоя́щее вре́мя (*tense, time*); *adj.* прису́тствующий (*at meeting, etc.*); да́нный, настоя́щий, тепе́решний (*of time*); [прі-зе́нт] *vt.* дари́ть (*offer gift*); представля́ть (*exhibit, show*); *theat.* ста́вить

presentable [прі-зе́н-табл] *adj.* прили́чный, презента́бельный

presentation [пре-зан-тэ́й-шан] *sn.* поднесе́ние (*of gift, etc.*); *theat.* постано́вка; представле́ние (*introduction*)

presentiment [прі-зе́н-ти-мянт] *sn.* предчу́вствие

presently [пре́-зант-лі] *adv.* вско́ре

preservation [пре-зар-ве́й-шан] *sn.* сохране́ние

preservative [прі-зе́р-ва-тів] *sn.* предохрани́тельное сре́дство; *adj.* предохраня́ющий

preserve [прі-зе́рв] *sn.* варе́нье (*jam*); запове́дник (*for birds, etc.*); *vt.* сохраня́ть, уберега́ть, консерви́ровать

preside [прі-за́йд] *vi.* председа́тельствовать

president [пре́-зі-дянт] *sm.* председа́тель, президе́нт

press [прес] *sn.* да́вка (*crowding*); пресс (*machine for pressing*); печа́ть, пре́сса (*printing*); **the –** [ē –] газе́ты; *vt.* сжать, сжима́ть (*squeeze*); сплю́щивать (*flatten*); наста́ивать, нужда́ть (*urge*)

pressman [пре́с-мян] *sm.* газе́тчик, журнали́ст

pressure [пре́-ша́р] *sn.* давле́ние (*pressing*); понужде́ние (*urgency*)

prestige [прес-ті́ж] *sn.* прести́ж

presumably [пре-зю́-мáб-лі] *adv.* повиди́мому

presume [прі-зю́м] *vt.i.* предполага́ть; осме́ливаться (*be impudent*)

presumption [прі-за́мп-шан] *sn.* предположе́ние (*assumption*), самонаде́янность (*over-confidence*); за-но́сивость (*arrogance*)

presumptuous [прі-за́мп-тю-а́с] *adj.* самонаде́янный

presuppose [прі-са́-по́уз] *vt.* предполага́ть

pretence [прі-те́нс] *sn.* притво́рство; отгово́рка (*subterfuge*)

pretend [прі-те́нд] *vi.* притворя́ться

pretension [прі-тéн-шăн] sn. притяза́ние, прете́нзия

pretext [прі-тéкст] sn. предло́г

pretty [прі-ті] adj. хоро́шенький; adv. дово́льно, почти́

prevail [прі-вэ́йл] vi. одолева́ть, преоблада́ть (gain mastery over); достига́ть це́ли (attain object); госпо́дствовать (be predominant); угова́ривать (persuade)

prevalent [прé-вă-лăнт] adj. госпо́дствующий, преоблада́ющий

prevaricate [прі-вǽ-рі-кэйт] vi. виля́ть, говори́ть укло́нчиво

prevarication [прі-вǽ-рі-кэ́й-шăн] sn. лука́вство, плутовство́

prevent [прі-вéнт] vt. предотвраща́ть, препя́тствовать (hinder, stop from doing)

prevention [прі-вéн-шăн] sn. предотвраще́ние; предупрежде́ние

preventive [прі-вéн-тів] sn. предохрани́тельная ме́ра; adj. предотвраща́ющий, предупреди́тельный

previous [прі́-ві-ăс] adj. предыду́щий, пре́жний; adv. ~ to [~ ту] пре́жде, ра́нее

prey [прэй] sn. добы́ча; vi. охо́титься; подта́чивать (afflict)

price [прайс] sn. цена́; cost [кост ~ кост] себесто́имость; vt. назнача́ть це́ну, оце́нивать

priceless [прайс-лéс] adj. бесце́нный; coll. бесподо́бный (second to none); восхити́тельный (delightful)

prick [прік] sn. проко́л, уко́л; vt. прока́лывать

prickle [прікл] sn. колю́чка, шип; vi. уко́лоться

prickly [прік-лі] adj. колю́чий

pride [прайд] sn. го́рдость, спесь

priest [прист] sm. жрец, свяще́нник

priesthood [прист-хýд] sn. духове́нство, свяще́нство

prig [пріг] sm. педа́нт, формали́ст, тщесла́вный челове́к (conceited person)

priggish [прі-гіш] adj. самодово́льный

prim [прім] adj. чо́порный

primacy [прай-мă-сі] sn. пе́рвенство (pre-eminence); прима́т (office)

primary [прай-мă-рі] adj. перви́чный, первонача́льный

primate [прай-міт] sm. архиепи́скоп, прима́с

prime [прайм] adj. гла́вный (chief); ва́жнейший (most important); лу́чший (best); vt. грунтова́ть

primer [прай-мăр] sn. буква́рь, m., нача́льный уче́бник

primeval [прай-мú-вăл] adj. первобы́тный

priming [прай-мíн] sn. грунто́вка

primitive [прі́-мі-тів] adj. примити́вный

primrose [прім-ро́уз] sn. bot. первоцве́т, при́мула; adj. бледножёлтый (colour)

prince [прінс] sm. князь, принц

princess [прін-сéс] sf. княги́ня, принце́сса

principal [прíн-сі-пǎл] *sm.* дирéктор, начáльник (*of school*); главá (*of department*); основнóй капитáл (*capital sum*); *adj.* важнéйший (*first in importance*); глáвный (*main*); ведýщий (*leading*); основнóй (*basic*)

principality [прíн-сі-пǎ-лі-ті] *sn.* княжество

principle [прíн-сіпл] *sn.* закóн, прáвило, принцúп (*moral rule*); первопричúна (*primary source*)

print [прíнт] *sn.* óттиск, печáть (*impression*); гравюра (*engraving*); шрифт (*type*); *vt.* печáтать (*on paper*); набивáть (*on callico*)

printer [прíн-тǎр] *sm.* печáтник, типóграф; набóйщик (*of textiles*)

printing [прíн-тій] *sn.* печáтание

prior [прáй-ǎр] *sm.* аббáт, настоáтель; *adj.* предшéствующий; *adv.* до, прéжде, рáньше

priority [прай-ó-рі-ті] *sn.* очерёдность, первенствó

priory [прáй-ǎ-рі] *sn.* монастырь, *m.*

prism [прíзм] *sn.* прúзма

prison [прí-зǎн] *sn.* тюрьмá

prisoner [прі-зǎ-нǎр] *sm.* заключённый, плéнный

privacy [прáй-вǎ-сі] *sn.* одинóчество, уединéние, уединённость

private [прáй-віт] *sm.* рядовóй, солдáт; *adj.* лúчный, чáстный, секрéтный (*confidential*); уединённый (*secluded*)

privately [прáй-віт-лі] *adv.* наедúне

privateering [прай-ві-тú-рій] *sn.* кáперство

privation [прай-вéй-шǎн] *sn.* лишéние, нуждá

privilege [прí-ві-лєдж *sn.* привилéгия, преимýщество

privy [прí-ві] *adj.* чáстный (*private*); тáйный (*secret*); скрытый (*hidden*); **Privy Council** [-кáýн-сǎл] тáйный совéт

prize [прайз] *sn.* награда, прéмия, приз; выигрыш (*winnings*); *vt.* высокó ценúть (*value highly*); вскрывáть (*force open*)

pro [прóу] *prefix*, для, за, вмéсто

probability [про-бǎ-бí-лі-ті] *sn.* вероятность

probable [прó-бǎбл] *adj.* вероятный, возмóжный, правдоподóбный

probation [прǎ-бéй-шǎн] *sn.* испытáние, стажирóвка; *eccl.* искýс

probe [прóуб] *sn.* зонд; *vt.* зондúровать

probity [прóу-бі-ті] *sn.* неподкýпность (*incorruptibility*); чéстность (*integrity*)

problem [прó-лєм] *sn.* задáча, проблéма

problematical [про-блє-мǎ-ті-кǎл] *adj.* сомнúтельный, проблематúчный

procedure [прǎ-сí-джǎр] *sn.* óбраз дéйствий, процедýра

proceed [прǎ-сíд] *vi.* продолжáть (*continue*); отправлáться (*set off*)

proceeding [прǎ-сí-дій] *sn.* постýпок; *sn. pl.* ведéние дéла; *leg.* судогово́рение, судопроизвóдство

proceeds [próу-сидз] *sn. pl.* выручка, доход

process [пró-сęс] *sn.* процéсс; мéтод, спóсоб (*method*); *leg.* вы́зов, предписáние; *vt.* подвергáть процéссу

procession [прă-сé-шăн] *sn.* процéссия, шéствие

proclaim [прă-клéйм] *vt.* провозглашáть (*herald*); объявля́ть (*announce*)

proclamation [про-клă-мéй-шăн] *sn.* воззвáние, прокламáция; объявлéние (*announcement*)

proclivity [прă-клí-ви-ти] *sn.* склóнность, стремлéние

procrastinate [прă-крǽс-ти-нэйт] *vi.* мéдлить (*tarry*); откла́дывать (*put off*)

procrastination [прă-крǽс-ти-нэй-шăн] *sn.* промедлéние; отлагáтельство

procure [прă-кю́р] *vt.* достáвать, обеспéчивать

prod [прод] *sn.* тычóк; *vt.* ты́кать

prodigal [прó-ди-гăл] *sm.* мот, расточи́тель; *adj.* расточи́тельный; щéдрый (*lavish*)

prodigious [прă-дí-джăс] *adj.* громáдный, огрóмный (*enormous*); необыча́йный, чудéсный (*marvellous*)

prodigy [прó-ди-джи] *sn.* чýдо, *sm., f.* одарённый человéк (*person*)

produce [прă-дю́с] *sn.* продýкт, продýкция; [прǎ-дю́с] *vt.* вырáбатывать, производи́ть; *theat.* постáвить; предъявля́ть (*show ticket, etc.*)

producer [прă-дю́-сăр] *sm.*

производи́тель; *theat.* постанóвщик, режиссёр

product [прó-дăкт] *sn.* издéлие, продýкт

production [прă-дăк-шăн] *sn.* продýкция (*products*); производство (*producing*); вырабóтка (*working out*); *theat.* постанóвка, спектáкль, *m.*

productive [прă-дăк-тив] *adj.* продукти́вный, производя́щий

profane [прă-фэ́йн] *adj.* богохýльный (*outside of the sacred*); свéтский, мирскóй (*secular*); языческий (*heathen*); *vt.* оскверня́ть, профани́ровать

profess [прă-фéс] *vt.* исповéдывать; признавáть (*admit*)

profession [прă-фé-шăн] *sn.* звáние (*calling*); профéссия; признáние (*avowal*); вероисповéдание (*vow of faith*)

professional [прă-фé-шă-нăл] *sm.* профессионáл; *adj.* профессионáльный

professor [прă-фé-сăр] *sm.* профéссор

proffer [прó-фăр] *sn.* предложéние; *vt.* предлагáть

proficiency [прă-фí-шăн-си] *sn.* óпытность, умéлость

profile [прóу-файл] *sn.* прóфиль, *m.*; очертáние (*outline*)

profit [прó-фит] *sn.* вы́года, пóльза (*advantage*); бары́ш, при́быль (*pecuniary gain*); *vt.i.* получáть пóльзу (*bring advantage*); воспóльзоваться (*take advantage*); улучшáться (*improve*)

profitable [прó-фи-тăбл]
adj. вы́годный, дохо́дный,
при́быльный; поле́зный
(useful)

profiteer [прă-фи-ти́р] sm.
спекуля́нт; vi. спекули́ро-
вать

profligate [прóф-ли-гит]
sm. распу́тник; adj. распу́т-
ный; безрассу́дный (reck-
less)

profound [прă-фáунд] adj.
глубо́кий (deep); дально-
ви́дный (of great insight);
му́дрый (of knowledge)

profuse [прă-фью́с] adj.
расточи́тельный (extrava-
gant); оби́льный (copious);
чрезме́рный (excessive)

profusion [прă-фью́-жăн]
sn. избы́ток, оби́лие

progeny [прó-джи-ни] sn.
пото́мство

prognostication [прă-гнос-
ти-кэ́й-шăн] sn. предсказа́-
ние

programme [прóу-грæм]
sn. план, програ́мма

progress [прóу-грес] sn.
продвиже́ние (advance-
ment); прогре́сс, разви́тие
(development); улучше́ние
(improvement); vi. подви-
га́ться, прогресси́ровать

progressive [прă-грé-сив]
adj. поступа́тельный; про-
гресси́вный

prohibit [прă-хи́-бит] vt.
воспреща́ть, запреща́ть

prohibition [прóу-хи-би́-шăн]
sn. запре́т, запреще́ние

project [прó-джект] sn.
за́мысел, план, прое́кт;
[прă-джéкт] vt.i. замыш-
ля́ть, обду́мывать, проекти́-
ровать

projectile [про-джéк-тайл]
sn. снаря́д; [прă-джéк-
тайл] adj. мета́тельный

projection [прă-джéк-шăн]
sn. проекти́рование; вы́-
ступ (protuberance); полёт
(flight)

proletariate [проу-ле-тэ́-
ри-ăт] sn. пролетариа́т

prolific [прă-ли́-фик] adj.
плодоро́дный (of offspring);
плодови́тый (fruitful); из-
оби́льный (plentiful)

prolong [прă-ло́н] vt. затя́-
гивать, продли́ть

promenade [про-мă-на́д]
sn. гуля́нье (walking); про-
гу́лка (stroll, walk); ме́сто
для гуля́нья (place); vt.i.
гуля́ть, прогу́ливаться

prominence [прó-ми-нăнс]
sn. вы́пуклость, вы́ступ (projection); отли́чие (distinction)

prominent [прó-ми-нăнт]
adj. выступа́ющий, вы́-
пуклый (jutting out);
выдаю́щийся (distinguished)

promiscuous [прă-ми́с-кю-
ăс] adj. разноро́дный, сме́-
шанный; неразбо́рчивый
(indiscriminate)

promise [прó-мис] sn.
обеща́ние; vt.i. обеща́ть

promising [прó-ми-син] adj.
подаю́щий наде́жды

promontory [прó-мăн-тă-ри]
sn. мыс

promote [прă-мóут] vt.
выдвига́ть, повыша́ть; спо-
со́бствовать (help forward,
contribute to)

promoter [прă-мóу-тăр] sm.
покрови́тель

promotion [прă-мóу-шăн]
sn. выдвиже́ние, повыше́-
ние

prompt [промпт] *adj.* незамедли́тельный; *vt.* побужда́ть (*invite*); внуша́ть (*inspire*); *theat.* суфли́ровать

prompter [промп-тäр] *sn.* суфлёр

promptitude [промп-ти-тюд] *sn.* быстрота́, прово́рство; аккура́тность (*of payments, etc.*)

promulgate [про́-мäл-гэйт] *vt.* обнаро́довать, опублико́вывать, провозглаша́ть; распространя́ть (*spread*)

prone [проўн] *adj.* накло́нный, скло́нный (*disposed*); лежа́щий ничко́м (*lying face downwards*)

prong [прон] *sn.* вил, зубе́ц

pronoun [про́ў-наун] *sn.* местоиме́ние

pronounce [пра-на́ўнс] *vt.i.* выгова́ривать, произноси́ть; выска́зываться (*speak one's mind*); объявля́ть (*announce*)

pronouncement [пра-на́ўнс-мäнт] *sn.* объявле́ние реше́ния, официа́льное заявле́ние

pronunciation [пра-нан-си-э́й-шän] *sn.* произноше́ние

proof [пруф] *sn.* доказа́тельство; испыта́ние, про́ба (*trial*); *тур.* корректу́ра (*of armour*); непроница́емый (*impervious*)

prop [проп] *sn.* опо́ра, подпо́рка, подста́вка; *vt.* подде́рживать, подпира́ть

propagate [про́-пä-гэйт] *vt.i.* разводи́ть (*disseminate*); размножа́ть (*multiply*); распространя́ться (*spread*)

propel [пра-пе́л] *vt.* приводи́ть в движе́ние, продвига́ть

propeller [пра-пе́-лäр] *sn.* воздушный винт (*air*); гребно́й винт (*sea*)

propensity [пра-пе́н-зи-ти] *sn.* накло́нность, предрасположе́ние

proper [про́-päр] *adj.* настоя́щий (*veritable*); подходя́щий (*fitting*); со́бственный (*own*); пра́вильный (*correct*); прили́чный (*decent*)

properly [про́-päр-ли] *adv.* до́лжным о́бразом; как сле́дует

property [про́-päр-ти] *sn.* достоя́ние, иму́щество, со́бственность (*possessions*); свойство, ка́чество (*attribute*); *pl. theat.* бутафо́рия

prophecy [про́-фи-си] *sn.* проро́чество

prophesy [про́-фи-сай] *vt.i.* предска́зывать, проро́чествовать

prophet [про́-фит] *sm.* проро́к

prophetic [пра-фе́-тик] *adj.* проро́ческий

propitiate [пра-пи́-ши-эйт] *vt.* умилостивля́ть

propitious [пра-пи́-шäс] *adj.* благоприя́тный, благоскло́нный

proportion [пра-по́р-шän] *sn.* коли́чественное отноше́ние; пропо́рция, часть; соразме́рность (*ratio*); соразме́рить

proposal [пра-по́ў-зäл] *sn.* предложе́ние

propose [пра-по́ўз] *vt.i.* предлага́ть; де́лать предложе́ние (*marriage*); намерева́ться (*intend*)

proposition [прэ-пэ-зи́-шэн] sn. предложе́ние; утвержде́ние (assertion)

propound [прэ-па́унд] vt. выдвига́ть (consider); ста́вить на обсужде́ние (put forth for discussion); зага́дывать (riddle)

proprietary [прэ-пра́й-э-тэ-ри] adj. собственни́ческий; патенто́ванный

proprietor [прэ-пра́й-э-тэр] sm. владе́лец, со́бственник; хозя́ин (householder, innkeeper, etc.)

propriety [прэ-пра́й-э-ти] sn. пра́вильность, прили́чие; уме́стность (suitability)

propulsion [прэ-па́л-шэн] sn. движе́ние вперёд

prorogue [прэ-ро́уг] vt.i. отсро́чить; откла́дывать (се́ссию парла́мента)

prosaic [проу-зэ́й-ик] adj. прозаи́ческий; повседне́вный (commonplace)

proscribe [про-скра́йб] vt. изгоня́ть, оглаша́ть

prose [проуз] sn. про́за, vi. говори́ть ну́дно

prosecute [про́-си-кют] vt. пресле́довать

prosecution [про-си-кю́-шэн] sn. веде́ние (pursuing studies, etc.); выполне́ние (carrying out); leg. суде́бное пресле́дование

prospect [про́-спект] sn. вид (view); ожида́ние (expectation); vt.i. иссле́довать

prospective [прэ-спе́к-тив] adj. бу́дущий, ожида́емый

prosper [про́с-пэр] vi. преуспева́ть, процвета́ть

prosperity [про́с-пе́-ри-ти] sn. благоде́нствие, благо-

prosperous [про́с-пэ-рэс] adj. богате́ющий, процвета́ющий

prostitution [про-сти-тю́-шэн] sn. проститу́ция

prostrate [про́-стрэ́т] adj. изможде́нный, обесси́левший, распростёртый; [про-стрэ́йт] vt. истоща́ть, поверга́ть; унижа́ть (reduce to submission)

prostration [прэ-стрэ́й-шэн] sn. изнеможе́ние, истоще́ние, простра́ция

protect [прэ-те́кт] vt. покрови́тельствовать; защища́ть (defend)

protection [прэ-те́к-шэн] sn. покрови́тельство; защи́та

protector [прэ-те́к-тэр] sm. защи́тник, покрови́тель; пре́дохрани́тель (appliance)

protest [про́у-тест] sn. проте́ст; **under –** [а́н-дэр –] наси́льно; [прэ-те́ст] vt. протестова́ть

protestant [про-тис-та́нт] sn. протеста́нт

protestation [про-тес-тэ́й-шэн] sn. возраже́ние, завере́ние

protract [прэ-тра́кт] vt. растя́гивать, тяну́ть

protracted [прэ-тра́к-тид] adj. дли́тельный

protrude [прэ-тру́д] vt.i. выдава́ться, торча́ть

protuberance [прэ-тю́-бэ-рэнс] sn. вы́пуклость; о́пухоль (swelling)

proud [прауд] adj. го́рдый, надме́нный (haughty); высокоме́рный (conscious of) *superiority*); великоле́пный (*of things*); ретивый (*of horse*)

prove [прӯв] *vt.* дока́зывать; удостоверя́ть (*ascertain*); *leg.* утвержда́ть

proverb [про́-вӑрб] *sn.* погово́рка, посло́вица

proverbial [прӑ-вӑ́р-би-ӑл] *adj.* общеизве́стный

provide [прӑ-ва́йд] *vt.* снабжа́ть (*supply*); заготовля́ть, запаса́ть (*make preparation*); предусма́тривать (*take precautions*)

provided [про́-ва́й-дид] *conj.* е́сли то́лько, при усло́вии

providence [про́-ви-дӑнс] *sn.* предусмотри́тельность; *rel.* провиде́ние

provident [про́-ви-дӑнт] *adj.* бере́жливый (*thrifty*); предусмотри́тельный (*showing foresight*)

providential [прӑ-ви-де́н-шӑл] *adj.* предопределённый, провиденциа́льный

province [про́-винс] *sn.* о́бласть, прови́нция

provision [прӑ-ви́-жӑн] *sn.* заготовле́ние, снабже́ние; *leg.* усло́вие; *pl.* прови́зия

provisional [прӑ-ви́-жӑнӑл] *adj.* вре́менный

proviso [прӑ-ва́й-зоӯ] *sn.* усло́вие

provocation [про-вӑ-ке́й-шӑн] *sn.* вы́зов; подстрека́тельство (*instigation*); провока́ция

provocative [прӑ-во́-кӑ-тив] *adj.* возбужда́ющий, вызыва́ющий, раздража́ющий

provoke [прӑ-во́ӯк] *vt.*

вызыва́ть (*rouse*); раздража́ть (*irritate*); серди́ть (*anger*)

prowess [пра́ӯ-ис] *sn.* до́блесть, у́даль

prowl [праӯл] *vi.* броди́ть, кра́сться

proximate [про́-кси-мит] *adj.* ближа́йший

proximity [прӑ-кси́-ми-ти] *sn.* бли́зость

proxy [про́-кси] *sm.* замести́тель; *sn.* дове́ренность (*warrant*)

prudence [прӯ-дӑнс] *sn.* осмотри́тельность, осторо́жность (*discretion*); рассуди́тельность (*sound sense*)

prudent [прӯ-дӑнт] *adj.* благоразу́мный, осторо́жный

prudish [прӯ-диш] *adj.* стыдли́вый, щепети́льный

prune [прӯн] *sn.* черносли́в (сухо́й); *vt.* подреза́ть (ве́тви); сокраща́ть (расхо́ды) (*reduce expenses, etc.*)

pry [пра́й] *vi.* подсма́тривать, ры́ться

pseudonym [сю́-дӑ-ним] *sn.* псевдони́м

psychiatry [сай-ка́й ӑ-три] *sn.* психиатри́я

psychology [сай-ко́-лӑ-джи] *sn.* психоло́гия

public [пӑ-блик] *sn.* пу́блика; *adj.* обще́ственный, публи́чный; - **house** [- ха́ӯс] каба́к, тракти́р

publican [пӑ-бли-кӑн] *sm.* тракти́рщик

publication [пӑ-бли-ке́й-шӑн] *sn.* изда́ние (*edition, published book, etc.*); оглаше́ние, опубликова́ние (*issuing*)

publicity [па-блí-си-ти] sn. публи́чность; гла́сность (notoriety); рекла́ма (advertisement)

publish [па́-блиш] vt. издава́ть, публикова́ть

publisher [па́-бли-шáр] sn. изда́тель

pucker [па́-кáр] sn. морщи́на, скла́дка; vt. морщи́ть

puddle [падл] sn. лу́жица; гли́няная обкла́дка (kind of cement)

puerile [пю́-ă-райл] adj. ребя́ческий

puff [паф] sn. дунове́ние (of wind); дымо́к, клуб (of smoke); powder – [па́у-дáр –] пухо́вка; v.t.i. пыхте́ть (of person); дыми́ть (smoke); надува́ть (inflate)

puffy [па́-фи] adj. одутло́ватый

pugilist [пю́-джи-лист] sn. боксёр

pugnacity [паг-нǽ-си-ти] sn. драгли́вость

pull [пул] sn. натяже́ние, тя́га; гребля́ (spell of rowing); глото́к (gulp); v.t.i. тащи́ть, тяну́ть; дёргать (handle, rope); грести́ (boat); – down [– да́ун] сноси́ть; – up [– ап] сде́рживать, остана́вливаться (stop)

pullet [пу́-лит] sf. ку́рочка

pulley [пу́-ли] sn. блок, шкив

pullover [пул-оу́-вáр] sn. фуфа́йка

pulp [палп] sn. мя́коть (fruit); бума́жная ма́сса (paper); anat. пу́льпа; v.t.i. превраща́ть в мя́гкую ма́ссу

pulpit [пу́л-пит] sn. ка́федра

pulpy [па́л-пи] adj. мяси́стый

pulsate [пал-сэ́йт] vi. би́ться, пульси́ровать

pulse [палс] sn. пульс; бие́ние (beating); вибра́ция (throbbing); bot. стручко́вые о́вощи; vi. пульси́ровать

pummel [па́-мáл] vt. бить кулака́ми, тузи́ть

pump [памп] sn. насо́с; больша́я лакиро́ванная ту́фля (dancing shoe); vt. выка́чивать, кача́ть

pun [пан] sn. каламбу́р; vi. каламбу́рить

punch [панч] sn. уда́р кулако́м (blow with fist); бо́йник (tool); пунш (drink); vt. ударя́ть кулако́м (hit with fist); продыря́вить (make hole); штампова́ть (stamp)

punctilious [пайк-ти́-ли-ăс] adj. щепети́льный

punctual [пайк-тю-ăл] adj. пунктуа́льный, то́чный

punctuate [пайк-тю-эйт] vt. ста́вить зна́ки препина́ния, перемежа́ть (diversify)

punctuation [пайк-тю-эй-шăн] sn. пунктуа́ция

puncture [пайк-чáр] sn. пробо́й, проко́л; vt. пробива́ть, прока́лывать

pungent [па́н-джăнт] adj. е́дкий, о́стрый

punish [па́-ниш] vt. нака́зывать; кара́ть (chastise)

punishment [па́-ниш-мăнт] sn. наказа́ние

punitive [пю́-ни-тив] adj. кара́тельный

punt [пант] sn. плоскодо́нная ло́дка (boat); уда́р ного́й (kick); vt.i. плыть на плоскодо́нке (propel with pole)

puny [пю́-ни] *adj.* ма́ленький, сла́бый, хи́лый

pup [пап] *s.* щено́к; *vt.i.* щени́ться

pupil [пю́-пil] *s.* учени́к (*learner*); воспи́танник (*scholar*); зени́ца, зрачо́к (*of eye*)

puppet [па́-пит] *s.* марионе́тка; *adj.* ку́кольный

puppy [па́-пi] *s.* щено́к

purchase [пёр-чäс] *s.* поку́пка, ку́пленная вещь (*thing bought*); *agr.* годово́й дохо́д; за́жим, захва́т (*grip*); лебёдка (*winch*); *vt.* покупа́ть (*buy*)

pure [пю́р] *adj.* беспри́месный, чи́стый (*unadulterated*); просто́й (*simple*); отчётливый, я́сный (*of tone, sound*); целому́дренный (*chaste*)

purely [пю́р-ли] *adv.* исключи́тельно (*solely*); соверше́нно (*entirely*)

purgative [пёр-гä-тив] *s.* слаби́тельное; *adj.* прочища́ющий, слаби́тельный

purgatory [пёр-гä-тä-рi] *s.* чисти́лище

purge [пёрдж] *s.* очище́ние; чи́стка (*also political*); слаби́тельное (*an aperient*); *vt.* прочища́ть; искупа́ть (*expiate*)

purify [пю́-ри-фай] *vt.* очища́ть

purity [пю́-ри-тi] *s.* чистота́; неви́нность (*innocence*)

purple [пёрпл] *s.* пурпу́р; *adj.* пурпу́рный

purport [пäр-по́рт] *s.* смысл, содержа́ние (*meaning, substance*); наме́рение,

цель (*object*); *vt.* выдава́ть, полага́ть

purpose [пёр-пäс] *s.* у́мысел, целеустремлённость, цель; **on** – [он –] наро́чно; *vt.* име́ть це́лью; *vi.* намерева́ться (*intend*)

purposeful [пёр-пäс-фул] *adj.* умы́шленный (*deliberate*); целеустремлённый (*having a purpose*)

purposeless [пёр-пäс-лиc] *adj.* бесце́льный

purposely [пёр-пäс-лi] *adv.* наро́чно

purr [пёр] *s.* мурлы́канье; *vi.* мурлы́кать

purse [пёрс] *s.* кошелёк, мошна́ (*pouch*); де́ньги (*money*); де́нежный приз (*cash prize*); *vt.i.* мо́рщиться (*wrinkle*)

pursuance [пäр-сю́-äнс] *s.* выполне́ние, исполне́ние

pursue [пäр-сю́] *vt.i.* гна́ться (*overtake*); пресле́довать (*assail*); продолжа́ть (*continue*)

pursuit [пäр-сю́т] *s.* пого́ня (*chase*); пресле́дование (*assailing*); заня́тие (*business, study*)

purulent [пю́-ру-лäнт] *adj.* гно́йный

purvey [пäр-вёй] *vt.* поставля́ть, снабжа́ть

push [пуш] *s.* толчо́к (*shove*); *mil.* си́льная ата́ка; предприи́мчивость (*enterprise*); *vt.i.* толка́ть; прота́лкиваться; – **aside** [– ä-са́йд] устраня́ть; – **away** [– ä-уэ́й] отта́лкивать

push-cart [пу́ш-кäрт] *s.* ручна́я теле́жка

puss [пус] *s.* ко́шечка

put [пу́т] *vt.i.* класть, положи́ть, поста́вить (*place*); выража́ть (*express*); – **aside** [– а́-сайд] откла́дывать; – **on** [– он] надева́ть (*clothing*); – **up** [– ап] приюти́ть (*person*); раскрыва́ть (*umbrella*); воздвига́ть (*building, etc.*); [пат] *vt.* гнать мяч в лу́нку (*golf*)

putrefy [пю́-три-фай] *vi.* гнить

putrid [пю́-трид] *adj.* гнило́й; воню́чий (*stinking*)

putty [па́-ти] *sn.* зама́зка

puzzle [пазл] *sn.* головоло́мка, зага́дка (*problem*); недоуме́ние (*quandary*); *vt.i.* недоумева́ть (*perplex*); запу́тывать (*bewilder*); обду́мывать (*ponder*)

pyjamas [пи́-джа́-маз] *sn. pl.* пижа́ма, спа́льный костю́м

pyramid [пи́-ра́-мид] *sn.* пирами́да

pyre [па́й-а́р] *sn.* костёр

Q

quack [куа́ек] *sn.* кря́канье; *vi.* кря́кать; *sm.* зна́харь, шарлата́н

quadrangle [куо́д-ра́енгл] *sn.* четырёхуго́льник; четырёхуго́льный двор (*court*)

quadrilateral [куо́-дри́-ла́е-та́-рал] *adj.* четырёхсторо́нний

quadruped [куо́-дру́-пед] *sn.* четвероно́гое живо́тное

quadruple [куо́-друпл] *adj.* учетверённое коли́чество;

adj. учетверённый, четверно́й; *vt.i.* учетверя́ть

quagmire [куа́г-май-а́р] *sn.* боло́то, тряси́на

quail [куэ́йл] *s.* пе́репел; *vi.* испуга́ться, струси́ть

quaint [куэ́йнт] *adj.* необы́чный, стра́нный; старомо́дный (*old-fashioned*)

quake [куэ́йк] *vi.* дрожа́ть, трепета́ть

qualification [куо́-ли-фи́-кэ́й-шан] *sn.* квалифика́ция

qualify [куо́-ли-фай] *vt.i.* квалифици́ровать, ограни́чивать (*put limitations on*); видоизменя́ть (*modify*)

quality [куо́-ли-ти] *sn.* ка́чество, досто́инство (*attribute*); тембр (*of voice, sound*)

qualm [куа́м] *sn.* дурнота́, тошнота́; сомне́ние (*doubt*); угрызе́ние со́вести (*scruple of conscience*)

qualmish [куа́-миш] *adj.* неспоко́йный

quandary [куо́н-да́-ри] *sn.* затрудне́ние, недоуме́ние

quantity [куо́н-ти-ти] *sn.* коли́чество; *pl.* большо́е коли́чество, мно́жество

quarantine [куо́-ра́н-тайн] *sn.* каранти́н

quarrel [куо́-рал] *sn.* вражда́, ссо́ра; расхожде́ние (*breach*); *vi.* ссо́риться

quarrelsome [куо́-ра́л-сам] *adj.* задо́рный, приди́рчивый, сварли́вый

quarry [куо́-ри] *sn.* дичь, добы́ча (преднаме́ренная) (*intended prey*); каменоло́мня, карье́р (*excavation*)

quart [куо́рт] *sn.* ква́рта (че́тверть галло́на)

quarter [куо́р-та́р] *sn.* чётверть (*a fourth*); квартёра вёса); квартал (*district*); *pl.* жилище; *vt.* делить на четыре; расквартировывать (*billet*)

quarterly [кўо́р-тэр-ли] *sn.* журнал, выходящий раз в три месяца; *adj.* трёхмесячный; *adv.* раз в три месяца

quartet [кўо́р-тэт] *sn.* квартет

quash [кўош] *vt.* отменять

quaver [кўэ́й-вэр] *sn.* дрожание голоса (*of voice*); трель (*trill*); *mus.* восьмая ноты; *vt.i.* вибрировать, дрожать

quay [ки] *sn.* набережная

queen [кўи́н] *sf.* королёва; *sn.* дама (*cards*); матка (*bee*); ферзь (*chess*)

queer [кўир] *adj.* странный, эксцентричный; подозрительный, сомнительный

quell [кўел] *vt.* подавлять, сокрушать

quench [кўенч] *vt.* утолять (*thirst*); охлаждать (*cool with water*); заглушать, тушить (*extinguish*)

querulous [кўэ́-рў-лас] *adj.* ворчливый

query [кўи́-ри] *sn.* вопрос; вопросительный знак (*mark of interrogation*); *vt.* спрашивать (*ask*)

quest [кўест] *sn.* поиски; *vi.* искать

question [кўес-чан] *sn.* вопрос; проблёма; *vt.* допрашивать, задавать вопросы; подвергать сомнению (*put to the test*); исследовать (*investigate*)

-mark [-марк] *sn.* вопросительный знак

questionable [кўес-ча-набл] *adj.* сомнительный

questionnaire [кўес-тион-нэ́р] *sn.* вопросник

queue [кю] *sn.* коса (*of hair*); очередь (*turn*); *vi.* становиться в очередь

quibble [кўибл] *sn.* игра слов (*play on words*); уклонение (*evasion*); аргумент, довод (*argument*); *vi.* уклоняться от вопроса

quick [кўик] *adj.* быстрый, скорый; живой, проворный (*lively, alert*); находчивый (*resourceful*)

quicken [кўи́-кан] *vt.i.* оживляться, ускорять

quickly [кўи́к-ли] *adv.* быстро, скоро

quid [кўид] *sn.* кусок табаку

quiescent [кўай-é-сант] *adj.* покоящийся

quiet [кўа́й-ат] *sn.* тишина; *adj.* смирный, спокойный, тихий; скромный (*unobtrusive*); *vt.i.* успокаивать

quietness [кўа́й-ат-нис] *sn.* покой, спокойствие, тишина

quill [кўил] *sn.* перо; поплавок удочки (*fishing float*); катушка (*bobbin*); *pl.* иглы дикобраза

quilt [кўилт] *sn.* стёганое одеяло; *vt.* стегать

quince [кўинс] *sn.* айва

quinine [кўи-нин] *sn.* хинин

quinsy [кўи́н-зи] *sn. med.* ангина

quire [кўа́й-ар] *sn.* десть

quit [кўит] *vt.i.* покидать (*abandon*); уезжать (*depart*)

quite [кўайт] *adv.* вполне, совсем

quits [кўитс] квиты

quiver [kŭĭ-văr] *sn.* дрожь, трéпет; колчáн (*case for holding arrows*); *vi.* дрожáть, трепетáть, трястись

quixotic [kŭĭ-ксó-тĭк] *adj.* донкихóтский

quiz [kŭĭз] *sn.* загáдка, шýтка (*puzzle*); *sm.* насмéшник (*person*); *vt.* подшýчивать

quorum [kŭó-рăм] *sn.* квóрум

quota [kŭó-тă] *sn.* дóля, нóрма, квóта

quotation [kŭóу-тéй-шăн] *sn.* цитáта; **– marks** [– мáркс] *sn. pl.* кавы́чки

quote [kŭóўт] *vt.i.* цити́ровать

R

rabbi [рá-бай] *sm.* раввин

rabbit [рá-бĭт] *s.* крóлик

rabble [рáбл] *sn.* сброд, чернь; беспорядочная толпá (*disorderly crowd*)

rabid [рá-бĭд] *adj.* нейстовый, я́ростный; бéшеный (*of dog*)

rabies [рá-бĭз] *sn.* бéшенство; (*canine madness*) водобоязнь (*hydrophobia*)

race [рэйс] *sn.* гóнка, состязáние в скóрости (*speed contest*); путь (*of sun, moon*); потóк, сильное движéние (*strong current*); *pl.* скáчки; рáса (*breed*); потóмство (*posterity*); *vi.* состязáться в скóрости; гнать (*horse*)

racecourse [рэйс-кóрс] *sn.* ипподрóм, скаковóй круг

racehorse [рэйс-хóрс] *s.* скаковáя лóшадь

racial [рэ́й-шăл] *adj.* рáсовый

rack [рэк] *sn.* кормýшка (*for fodder*); вéшалка (*peg, stand*); рáма (*frame*); несýщиеся облачкá (*driving clouds*); *fig.* ги́бель, мучéние, разорéние; *vt.i.* класть на пóлку (*put on rack*); пытáть, мýчить (*inflict pain, torture*)

racket [рá-кĭт] *sn.* ракéтка (*tennis*); гам, шум (*uproar*); лы́жа (*snow-shoe*); *pl.* род тéнниса (*game*)

racy [рэ́й-сĭ] *adj.* живóй, энерги́чный (*vigorous*); характéрный

radiance [рэ́й-дĭ-ăнс] *sn.* лучезáрность, сия́ние

radiant [рэ́й-дĭ-ăнт] *adj.* лучи́стый, сия́ющий

radiate [рэ́й-дĭ-эйт] *vt.i.* излучáть, сия́ть

radiator [рэ́й-дĭ-эй-тăр] *sn.* радиáтор

radical [рá-дĭ-кăл] *adj.* кореннóй, радикáльный

radio [рэ́й-дĭ-оў] *sn.* рáдио; *vt.i.* передавáть по рáдио

radio-active [рэ́й-дĭóу-éктĭв] *adj.* радиоакти́вный

radish [рá-дĭш] *sn.* реди́ска

radius [рэ́й-дĭ-ăс] *sn.* рáдиус

raffle [рэфл] *sn.* лотерéя; *vt.* разы́грывать

raft [рафт] *sn.* плот

rafter [рáф-тăр] *sn.* плотови́щик; *sm. tech.* бáлка, стропи́ло

rag [рэг] *sn.* лоскýт, обры́вок, тря́пка; *pl.* лохмóтья, трапьé; беспорядочное поведéние (*disorderly conduct*)

ragamuffin [рэ-гă-мá-фĭн] *sm.* оборвáнец

rage [рэйдж] *sn.* гнев, я́рость; увлече́ние, вре́менный энтузиа́зм (*temporary enthusiasm*); *vi.* свире́пствовать (*of epidemic, etc.*); разбушева́ться (*rave, storm*); беси́ться (*be mad*)

ragged [рэ́-гид] *adj.* косма́тый (*shaggy*); истрёпанный, обо́рванный (*frayed, torn*)

ragtime [рэг-тайм] *sn. mus.* синкопи́ческая му́зыка

raid [рэйд] *sn.* набе́г, налёт; *mil.* рейд; *v.t.i.* соверша́ть налёт, вторга́ться (*break in*)

rail [рэйл] *sn.* пери́ла (*bar of gate, etc.*); перекла́дина (*of door or window*); рельс (*railway, etc.*); *vi.* руга́ться (*use abusive language*)

railing [рэ́й-лин] *sn.* огра́да, пери́ла

railway [рэйл-уэ́й] *sn.* желе́зная доро́га; *adj.* железнодоро́жный

rain [рэйн] *sn.* дождь, *m.*; *vi.* дожди́ть

rainbow [рэйн-бо́у] *sn.* ра́дуга; *adj.* ра́дужный

raincoat [рэйн-ко́ут] *sn.* непромока́емый плащ

rainfall [рэйн-фо́л] *sn.* коли́чество оса́дков

rainy [рэ́й-ни] *adj.* дождли́вый (*weather*); дождево́й (*clouds*)

raise [рэйз] *vt.* возвыша́ть (*voice*); поднима́ть (*lift*); буди́ть (*rouse*); воспи́тывать (*bring up*); повыша́ть (*increase pay*); возбужда́ть (*excite, provoke*); добыва́ть, извлека́ть (*from soil*); собира́ть (*assemble*)

raisin [рэй-зін] *sn.* изю́м

rake [рэйк] *sn.* гра́бли; *sn.* пове́са, распу́тник (*dissipated man, libertine*); *v.t.i.* загреба́ть, сгреба́ть, собира́ть (*collect, gather up*); равня́ть (*level*); ры́ться в по́исках (*ransack, search*)

rally [рэ́-ли] *sn.* восстановле́ние, объедине́ние; *vi.* объединя́ться, соедини́ться, сплоти́ться

ram [рэм] *sn.* бара́н (*sheep*); *vt.* вкола́чивать

ramble [рэмбл] *sn.* пое́здка, прогу́лка, экску́рсия; *vi.* броди́ть (*walk leisurely*); говори́ть бессвя́зно (*incoherently*)

rambler [рэм-бла́р] *sn.* праздношата́ющийся (*person*); *sn.* род ползу́чей ро́зы (*climbing rose*)

rambling [рэм-блин] *adj.* разбро́санный (*straggling*); бессвя́зный (*of speech*); слоня́ющийся (*wandering*)

ramification [рэ-мі-фи-кэ́й-шэн] *sn.* разветвле́ние

ramp [рэмп] *sn.* скат, укло́н

rampant [рэм-пэнт] *adj.* необу́зданный (*unchecked*); отъя́вленный (*unmitigated*)

rampart [рэм-па́рт] *sn.* крепостно́й вал (*defensive mound*); опло́т (*protection*)

ramshackle [рэм-шэкл] *adj.* ве́тхий, разва́ливающийся

ranch [ранч] *sn.* ра́нчо; америка́нская скотово́дческая фе́рма

rancid [рэн-сід] *adj.* прого́рклый, протухший

rancour [рэн-ка́р] *sn.* вражда́, зло́ба

random [ръ́н-дъм] *adj.* случа́йный; шально́й (*of bullet*); at - [æt -] наобу́м, науга́д

range [рэйндж] *sn.* ли́ния, ряд (*line, row*); цепь, хребе́т (*of mountains*); зо́на, сфе́ра (*scope*); кухо́нная плита́ (*kitchener*); преде́лы (*bound, limits*); *vt.i.* помеща́ть, ста́вить в ряд (*place in row, etc.*); простира́ться (*extend*); *mil.* пристре́ливаться; броди́ть, стра́нствовать (*wander*)

ranger [ръ́йн-джър] *sm.* лесни́чий

rank [рэ́нк] *sn.* ряд (*row*); шере́нга (*file*); зва́ние, положе́ние (*grade, station*); чин (*status*); разря́д (*category*); *vt.i.* распределя́ть (*classify*); счита́ться (*regard as*); *adj.* ро́скошный (*luxuriant*); гру́бый (*coarse*); мёрзкий *loathsome*); прого́рклый (*rancid*)

rankle [рэ́нкл] *vt.* глода́ть, му́чить

ransack [рэ́н-сǽк] *vt.* обы́скивать

ransom [рǽн-съм] *sn.* вы́куп; *vt.* выкупа́ть; искупа́ть (*redeem*)

rant [рэ́нт] *vt.i.* говори́ть напы́щенно (*talk pompously*)

rap [рэ́п] *sn.* лёгкий стук; *vi.* стуча́ть, слегка́ ударя́ть

rapacious [ръ-пэ́й-шъс] *adj.* жа́дный, хи́щный

rape [рэйп] *sn.* изнаси́лование, похище́ние

rapid [рǽ-пид] *sn.* стремни́на; *adj.* бы́стрый, ско́рый; круто́й (*steep*)

rapidity [ръ-пи́-ди-ти] *sn.* быстрота́, ско́рость

rapt [рǽпт] *adj.* восхищённый

rapture [рǽп-чър] *sn.* восто́рг, восхище́ние, упое́ние

rapturous [рǽп-чъ-ръс] *adj.* восто́рженный

rare [рэ́р] *adj.* ре́дкий, ре́дкостный, необы́чный (*uncommon*); исключи́тельный (*exceptional*); не густо́й (*not dense*)

rarefy [рǽ-ри-фай] *vt.i.* разжижа́ть

rarity [рǽ-ри-ти] *sn.* ре́дкость

rascal [рǽс-къл] *sm.* кана́лья, него́дяй

rash [рǽш] *sn.* сыпь; *adj.* безрассу́дный, необду́манный

rasher [рǽ-шър] *sn.* ло́мтик ветчины́

rashness [рǽш-нис] *sn.* стреми́тельность (*impetuosity*); опроме́тчивость (*hastiness*)

rasp [рǽсп] *sn.* ра́шпиль, *m.*; *vt.i.* подпи́ливать; соска́бливать (*scrape off*); раздража́ть (*grate upon feelings*)

raspberry [рǽз-бри] *sn.* мали́на

rat [рǽт] *s.* кры́са; *sm.* перебе́жчик (*turncoat*); *vi.* истребля́ть крыс

ratable [рэ́й-тъбл] *adj.* облага́емый нало́гом

rate [рэйт] *sn.* но́рма (*standard*); расце́нка, тари́ф (*tariff*); ско́рость, темп (*speed*); ме́стный нало́г (*local tax*); сте́пень (*degree*); - of wages - [ов у́эй-джиз] у́ровень пла́ты; *vt.i.* исчисля́ть, оце́нивать (*estimate*); облага́ть нало́гом (*tax*); брани́ть (*scold*)

ratepayer [рэ́йт-пэй-ăр] *sm.* налогоплате́льщик

rather [ра́-ðăр] *adv.* верне́е (*more truly*); скоре́е (*to a great extent*); предпочти́тельно (*preferably*); не́сколько (*somewhat*)

ratify [рэ́-ті-фай] *vt.* подпи́сывать, утвержда́ть

rating [рэ́й-тіŋ] *sn.* оце́нивание; *naut.* зва́ние моряка́; вы́говор, нагоня́й (*angry scolding*)

ratio [рэ́й-ши-оў] *sn.* отноше́ние, пропо́рция

ration [рэ́-шăн] *sn.* паёк; *vt.* выдава́ть пайки́

rational [рэ́-шă-нăл] *adj.* разу́мный, рациона́льный

rattle [рэтл] *sn.* побря́кушка, погрему́шка, трещо́тка (*toy*); *bot.* погремо́к; сумато́ха (*noisy gaiety*); треско́тня (*rattling sound*) *vi.* грохота́ть, треща́ть; болта́ть без у́молку (*talk away senselessly*)

raucous [ро́-кăс] *adj.* хри́плый

ravage [рэ́-відж] *sn.* опустоше́ние (*devastation*); разруши́тельное де́йствие (*destructive effect*); *vt.* опустоша́ть, разоря́ть

rave [рэйв] *vi.* бре́дить; бушева́ть, вы́ть (*of sea, wind*)

ravel [рэ́-вăл] *sn.* пу́таница; *vt.i.* запу́тывать (*entangle*); распу́тывать (*disentangle*)

raven [рэ́й-вăн] *s.* во́рон

ravenous [рэ́-вă-нăс] *adj.* прожо́рливый (*voracious*); изголода́вшийся (*famishing*)

ravine [ра-ви́н] *sn.* лубо́кое уще́лье

ravish [рэ́-віш] *vt.* похища́ть (*carry away by force*); восхища́ть (*enrapture*)

ravishing [рэ́-ві-шіŋ] *adj.* восхити́тельный

raw [ро̂] *adj.* сыро́й (*crude*); недова́ренный (*uncooked*); нео́пытный (*inexperienced*); чувстви́тельный (*sensitive from exposure*)

ray [рэй] *sn.* луч; скат (*fish*)

raze [рэйз] *vt.* разруша́ть до основа́ния; вычёркивать, стира́ть (*wipe out*)

razor [рэ́й-зăр] *sn.* бри́тва

re- [рі] *prefix* за́ново, пере-, сно́ва

reach [рич] *sn.* протя́гивание; уча́сток реки́ (*of river*); *vt.i.* достига́ть, доходи́ть (*attain*); простира́ться (*extend*); протя́гивать (*stretch out*)

react [рі-э́кт] *vi.* реаги́ровать (*respond*); возде́йствовать (*influence*); *chem.* вызыва́ть реа́кцию

reaction [рі-э́к-шăн] *sn.* противоде́йствие, реа́кция

read [рид] *vt.i.* чита́ть

reader [рі́-дăр] *sm.* чита́тель; корре́ктор (*printer's*); *sn.* хрестома́тия (*book*)

readily [рé-ді-лі] *adv.* охо́тно

readiness [рé-ді-ніс] *sn.* гото́вность

reading [рі́-діŋ] *sn.* чте́ние

ready [рé-ді] *adj.* гото́вый, скло́нный; *adv.* зара́нее

real [рил] *adj.* действи́тельный, настоя́щий; по́длинный (*genuine*)

realistic [ri-æ-lís-tik] *adj.* реалистичный

reality [ri-ǽ-li-ti] *sn.* действительность, реальность; подлинная сущность (*genuine thing*)

realize [ri-ā-laiz] *vt.* осуществлять (*accomplish*); реализировать (*convert*); осознавать (*perceive*)

really [rí-li] *adv.* в самом деле, действительно; – ? неужели?

realm [рэлм] *sn.* область, сфера (*region, sphere*); королевство (*kingdom*)

reap [рип] *vt.i.* жать (*cut grain, etc.*); снимать урожай (*make harvest*); пожинать плоды (*reap the fruits of . . .*)

reaper [рú-пăр] *sn.* жнец; *sn.* жатвенная машина, жнейка (*machine*)

rear [рир] *sn.* задняя сторона, тыл; *adj.* задний; *vt.i.* возносить, поднимать (*raise*); воспитывать, выводить (*bring up, educate*); становиться на дыбы (*of horse*)

rearmament [ri-âr-мă-мăнт] *sn.* перевооружение

rearrangement [ri-ă-рэйнджх-мăнт] *sn.* перегруппировка

reason [ри́-зăн] *sn.* довод, причина (*cause*); оправдание (*justification*); разум, рассудок (*intellect*); *vi.* обсуждать, рассуждать

reasonable [ри́-зă-năбл] *adj.* благоразумный (*sound of judgment*); умеренный (*moderate*)

reassure [ри-ă-шýр] *vt.* успокаивать

rebate [рú-бэйт] *sn.* скидка, уступка

rebel [рéбл] *sm.* бунтовщик, мятежник, повстанец; [ри-бéл] *vi.* восставать, протестовать

rebellion [ри-бé-ли-ăн] *sn.* бунт, восстание

rebellious [ри-бé-ли-ăс] *adj.* бунтарский, мятежный

rebound [ри-бáунд] *sn.* отдача, отскок; *vi.* отскакивать

rebuff [ри-бáф] *sn.* отпор; резкий отказ (*sharp refusal*); *vt.* давать отпор

rebuke [ри-бю́к] *sn.* выговор, упрёк; *vt.* упрекать

recalcitrant [ри-кǽл-си-трăнт] *adj.* непокорный, упорствующий

recall [ри-кόл] *sn.* отозвание; *vt.* отзывать (*summon back*); воскрешать (*of memory*); отменять (*cancel*)

recant [ри-кǽнт] *vi.* отрекаться

recapitulate [ри-кă-пú-тю-лэйт] *vt.* резюмировать

recede [ри-сúд] *vi.* отступать, удаляться

receipt [ри-сúт] *sn.* получка, приход; получение (*receiving*); рецепт (*recipe*); *com.* квитанция

receive [ри-сúв] *vt.* получать, принимать

receiver [ри-сú-вăр] *sm. leg.* казначей; укрыватель (*of stolen goods*); получатель (*recipient*); *sn.* приёмник (*radio*)

recension [ри-сéн-шăн] *sn.* пересмотр, проверка

recent [рú-сăнт] *adj.* недавний, современный

receptacle [ри-сéп-тăкл] *sn.* вместилище

reception [pi-cép-шăн] *sn.* получéние, принятие; приём (*of guests*); вечеринка (*party*)

receptive [pi-cép-тĭв] *adj.* восприимчивый

recess [pi-céc] *sn.* каникулы (*vacation*); ниша (*niche, alcove*); углублéние (*cavity*)

recession [pi-cé-шăн] *sn.* удалéние

recipe [ré-ci-пi] *sn.* рецéпт; срéдство (*remedy*)

recipient [pi-cí-пi-ăнт] *sm.* получáтель

reciprocal [pi-cí-прă-кăл] *adj.* взаимный, обоюдный

reciprocate [pi-cí-прă-кэйт] *v.t.* отплáчивать (*make requital*); обмéниваться (*interchange*)

recital [pi-cáй-тăл] *sn.* изложéние, повествовáние; *mus.* концéрт артиста

recitation [ре-ci-тэ́й-шăн] *sn.* деклáмация

recite [pi-cáйт] *vt.* деклами́ровать читáть наизу́сть

reckless [рéк-лĭс] *adj.* беззабóтный, безрассу́дный

reckon [рé-кăн] *vt.i.* подводить итóг, считáть; рассчитываться

reckoning [рé-кă-нĭй] *sn.* счёт

reclaim [pi-клэйм] *vt.* исправля́ть, приручáть

recline [pi-клáйн] *v.t.i.* лежáть (*lie*); опирáться, прислоня́ться (*lean against*)

recluse [рĭк-лу́с] *sm.* затвóрник, отшéльник

recognition [рé-кăг-ни́-шăн] *sn.* опознáние, узнавá-ние; признáние (*acknowledgment*)

recognize [рé-кăг-нáйз] *vt.* признавáть; узнавáть

recoil [pi-кóйл] *sn.* откáт; *vi.* отступáть

recollect [рé-кă-лéкт] *vt.* вспоминáть

recommend [рé-кă-мéнд] *vt.* рекомендовáть

recommendation [рé-кă-мен-дэ́й-шăн] *sn.* рекомендáция

recompense [рé-кăм-пéнс] *sn.* вознаграждéние, компенсáция; *vt.* вознаграждáть отплáчивать

reconcile [рé-кăн-сáйл] *vt.* примиря́ть (*make friendly again*); улáживать (*smooth over*)

recondition [pi-кăн-ди́-шăн] *vt.* производи́ть осмóтр и ремóнт

reconnaissance [pi-кó-ни́-сăнс] *sn.* рекогносциро́вка, развéдка

reconnoitre [pi-кă-нóйтр] *vt.* рекогносци́ровать

reconstruction [pi-кăн-стрáк-шăн] *sn.* перестрóйка

record [рé-кóрд] *sn.* зáпись (*entry*); *leg.* протокóл, свидéтельство (*testimony*); пластинка (*gramophone*); рекóрд (*sport*); [pi-кóрд] *vt.* записывать (*register*)

recount [ри́-кáунт] *sn.* повтóрный подсчéт; [pi-кáунт] *vt.* пересчи́тывать; излагáть подрóбно (*tell in detail*)

recoup [pi-кýп] *v.i.* возмещáть, компенси́ровать

recourse [pi-кóрс] *sn.* обращéние

recover [рі-ка́-вăр] *vt.i.* получа́ть обра́тно; выздора́вливать (*from illness*)

recovery [рі-ка́-вă-рі] *sn.* обра́тное получе́ние (*of thing*); выздоровле́ние (*of health*)

recreate [ре́-крі-эйт] *vt.i.* занима́ть, развлека́ться

recreation [ре-крі-эй́-шăн] *sn.* развлече́ние

recrimination [рі-крі-мі-нэ́й-шăн] *sn.* взаи́мное обвине́ние

recruit [рі-кру́т] *sm.* новобра́нец, рекру́т; *vt.i.* вербова́ть; подкрепля́ть (*replenish*)

rectangular [ре́кт-е́н-гю-лăр] *adj.* прямоуго́льный

rectify [ре́к-ті-фай] *vt.* исправля́ть

rector [ре́к-тăр] *sm.* ре́ктор (*educational*); приходско́й свяще́нник (*parish priest*)

recumbent [рі-ка́м-бăнт] *adj.* лежа́щий, отки́нувшийся

recuperate [рі-кю́-пă-рэйт] *vi.* оправля́ться

recur [рі-кẽ́р] *vi.* повторя́ться (*occur again*); возвраща́ться (*come back*)

recurrence [рі-ка́-рăнс] *sn.* возвраще́ние, повторе́ние

red [ред] *adj.* кра́сный

redbreast [ре́д-брест] *s.* мали́новка

redden [ре́-дăн] *vi.* красне́ть

redeem [рі-ди́м] *vt.* выку́пать (*buy back*); спаса́ть (*save, rescue*); искупа́ть (*sins*); скра́шивать (*make amends*)

redemption [рі-де́мп-шăн] *sn.* вы́куп; искупле́ние

red-handed [ред-хе́н-дід] *adj.* на посту́пле́ние преступле́ния

red-hot [ред-хо́т] *adj.* раскалённый докрасна́; *fig.* взбешённый

redistribution [рі-діс-трі-бю́-шăн] *sn.* перераспределе́ние

redolent [ре́-до-лăнт] *adj.* благоуха́ющий (*of smell*); напомина́ющий (*suggestive of*)

redouble [рі-да́бл] *vt.i.* удва́ивать (*multiply*); увели́чивать (*increase*); уси́ливаться (*intensify*)

redoubtable [рі-да́ут-ăбл] *adj.* гро́зный, устраша́ющий

redress [рі-дре́с] *sn.* возмеще́ние, исправле́ние; *vt.* загла́живать, исправля́ть

reduce [рі-дю́с] *vt.* понижа́ть (*bring down, lower*); ослабля́ть (*weaken*); уменьша́ть (*diminish*)

reduction [рі-да́к-шăн] *sn.* ски́дка, сниже́ние (*of price*); уменьше́ние (*reducing*); уме́ньшенная ко́пия (*of picture, etc.*)

redundant [рі-да́н-дăнт] *adj.* изли́шний, чрезме́рный; многосло́вный (*copious*)

reed [рід] *sn.* тростни́к; *mus.* свире́ль (*pipe*); язычо́к (*in wood instruments*)

reedy [рі́-ді] *adj.* тростни́ковый; скрипу́чий (*of voice*)

reef [ріф] *sn.* риф, скали́стая гряда́; *vt. naut.* брать ри́фы

reefer [рі́-фăр] *sn.* двубо́ртная тужу́рка (*jacket*)

reek [рик] *sn.* вонь (*stench*); пар (*vapour*); испарение (*exhalation*); *vi.* пахнуть (*smell*); дымиться (*of vapour*)

reel [рил] *sn.* катушка, мотовило; барабан (*in machine*); шатание (*staggering motion*); шотландский танец; *vi.* шататься

refectory [ри-фёк-тă-ри] *sn.* столовая (*in schools*); трапезная (*in monasteries*)

refer [ри-фёр] *vt.i.* направлять; касаться, ссылаться

referee [ре-фă-ри] *sm. leg.* третейский судья; *sport.* рефери; *vi.* судить

reference [ре-фă-рăнс] *sn.* справка (*referring*); ссылка (*direction to page, etc.*); рекомендация

refill [ри-фил] *sn.* пополнение; *vt.* пополнять

refine [ри-файн] *vt.i.* очищать, рафинировать; делаться утонченным (*make elegant*)

refinement [ри-файн-мăнт] *sn.* изысканность, утонченность

refinery [ри-фай-нă-ри] *sn.* очистительный завод

reflect [ри-флёкт] *vt.i.* отражать (*light, sound*); размышлять (*meditate, consider*)

reflection [ри-флёк-шăн] *sn.* отражение (*of mirror*); размышление (*thought*); отблеск (*of light, etc.*)

reflexive [ри-флёк-сив] *adj. gram.* возвратный

reform [ри-фőрм] *sn.* реформа, исправление (*amendment*); улучшение (*improvement*); *vt.i.* реформировать, улучшать; исправляться

reformation [ре-фőр-мейшăн] *sn.* преобразование, реформация

reformatory [ри-фőр-мă-тă-ри] *sn.* заведение для малолетних преступников

reformer [ри-фőр-мăр] *sm.* реформатор, сторонник реформ

refractory [ри-фрăк-тă-ри] *adj.* упорный, упрямый

refrain [ри-фрейн] *sn.* припев, рефрен; *vi.* воздерживаться

refresh [ри-фрёш] *vt.* освежать; оживлять (*reinvigorate*)

refreshment [ри-фрёш-мăнт] *sn.* оживление, подкрепление; *pl.* закуски и напитки

refrigerate [ри-фриджă-рейт] *vt.* охлаждать (*make cool or cold*); замораживать (*freeze*)

refrigerator [ри-фриджă-рей-тăр] *sn.* холодильник, комнатный ледник

refuge [ре-фюдж] *sn.* убежище; скрываться от преследования (*shelter from pursuit*)

refugee [ре-фю-джи] *sm.* беженец; полит-эмигрант (*political*)

refund [ри-фанд] *sn.* уплата; [ри-фанд] *vt.i.* возвращать; возмещать (*reimburse*)

refusal [ри-фю-зăл] *sn.* отказ

refuse [ре-фюс] *sn.* отбросы; [ри-фюз] *vt.i.* отказывать

refute [ри-фют] *vt.* опровергать

regain [ри-гейн] *vt.* восходить (*reach again*); получать обратно (*obtain again*)

regal [ри́-гал] *adj.* короле́вский

regale [рі-гэ́йл] *sn.* пи́ршество; *vt.i.* пирова́ть, угоща́ть (*entertain*); услажда́ть (*give delight*)

regard [рі-га́рд] *sn.* взор (*gaze, look*); внима́ние (*heed*); отноше́ние (*relation*); уваже́ние (*esteem*); *pl.* приве́т; *vt.i.* смотре́ть (*observe*); при́стально гляде́ть (*gaze upon*); почита́ть

regardless [рі-га́рд-ліс] *adj.* не счита́ющийся; *adv.* не счита́я

regency [ри́-джэн-сі] *sn.* реге́нтство

regenerate [рі-джэ́-нэ́-рэйт] *vt.i.* возрожда́ть, перерожда́ться

regent [ри́-джэнт] *sn.* реге́нт

regime [ре-жи́м] *sn.* режи́м

regimen [ре́-джи-мэн] *sn.* правле́ние; *med.* режи́м; *gram.* управле́ние

regiment [ре́-джи-мэнт] *sn.* полк

regimental [ре-джи-мэ́н-тэл] *adj.* полково́й; *pl.* полкова́я фо́рма

region [ри́-джэн] *sn.* о́бласть

register [ре́-джи-стар] *sn.* журна́л (*book*); официа́льный спи́сок (*official list*); *mus.* реги́стр; *vt.i.* регистри́ровать; запи́сываться

registration [ре-джи-стрэ́й-шэн] *sn.* регистра́ция

registry [ре́-джис-трі] *sn.* регистрату́ра

regret [рі-гре́т] *sn.* сожале́ние; *vt.* жале́ть, сожале́ть

regrettable [рі-гре́-табл] *adj.* приско́рбный

regular [ре́-гю-лар] *adj.* регуля́рный; пра́вильный (*proper*)

regularity [ре-гю-лǽ-рі-ті] *sn.* регуля́рность

regulate [ре́-гю-лэйт] *vt.* регули́ровать; сообразова́ть (*be consistent*)

regulation [ре-гю-лэ́й-шэн] *sn.* пра́вило (*rule*); регули́рование (*control*); регла́мент (*order*)

rehabilitate [рі-ă-бі-лі-тэйт] *vt.* восстановля́ть в права́х (*restore to rights*); реабилити́ровать

rehearsal [рі-хǽр-сăл] *sn.* репети́ция

rehearse [рі-хǽрс] *vt.i.* репети́ровать, переска́зывать

reign [рэйн] *sn.* госпо́дство; ца́рствование; *vi.* госпо́дствовать; ца́рствовать

rein [рэйн] *sn.* вожжа́; *fig.* сде́рживающее нача́ло; *vt.* сде́рживать (*check*); управля́ть (*manage*)

reindeer [рэ́йн-дир] *s.* се́верный оле́нь

reinforce [ри-ин-фо́рс] *vt.* подкрепля́ть (*support*); уси́ливать (*strengthen*)

reinforcement [ри-ин-фо́рс-мăнт] *sn.* подкрепле́ние; *pl. mil.* доба́вочные солда́ты, ору́дия и т.п.

reinstate [ри-ин-стэ́йт] *vt.* восстана́вливать

reiterate [ри-і-тă-рэйт] *vt.* повторя́ть

reject [рі-дже́кт] *vt.* отверга́ть, отклоня́ть

rejoice [рі-джо́йс] *vt.i.* ра́довать; весели́ться

rejoicings [рі-джо́й-сіҥз] *sn. pl.* весе́лье

rejoin [ri-джо́йн] *vt.i.* возража́ть, отвеча́ть (*retort*); возвраща́ться (*return*)

rejoinder [ri-джо́йн-дăр] *sn.* возраже́ние

rejuvenate [ri-джу́-ви-нэйт] *vt.i.* молоди́ть

relapse [ri-лэ́пс] *sn.* рециди́в (*a falling back*); *med.* возвра́т боле́зни; *vi.* вновь предава́ться (*fall back into worse state*); *med.* сно́ва заболева́ть

relate [ri-лэ́йт] *vt.i.* расска́зывать (*narrate*); приводи́ть в связь (*establish relation*); каса́ться (*concern*)

related [ri-лэ́й-тĭд] *adj.* ро́дственный; свя́занный (*connected*)

relation [ri-лэ́й-шăн] *sn.* отноше́ние (*attitude*); повествова́ние (*narration, telling*); *sm.* ро́дственник (*kinsman*)

relative [ре́-лă-тiв] *sm.* ро́дственник; *adj.* относи́тельный; сравни́тельный (*comparative*)

relax [ri-лэ́кс] *vt.i.* рассла́блять; ослабля́ться; смягча́ться (*become limp*)

relaxation [ри-лэкс-э́й-шăн] *sn.* о́тдых (*rest*); развлече́ние (*recreation, amusement*)

relay [ри́-лэй] *sn.* сме́на (*change*); *tech.* реле́

release [ri-ли́с] *sn.* вы́пуск (*of film, publication, etc.*); освобожде́ние (*liberation from*); *leg.* переда́ча пра́ва; *vt.* выпуска́ть; освобожда́ть, отпуска́ть; *leg.* передава́ть

relegate [ре́-лi-гэйт] *vt.* направля́ть, отсыла́ть

relent [ri-ле́нт] *vi.* смягча́ться

relentless [ri-ле́нт-лĭс] *adj.* безжа́лостный

relevant [ре́-лĭ-вăнт] *adj.* относя́щийся, уме́стный

reliability [ri-лай-ă-би́-лĭ-тĭ] *sn.* надёжность (*confidence*); про́чность (*of goods*)

reliable [ri-ла́й-ăбл] *adj.* надёжный; про́чный

reliance [ri-ла́й-ăнс] *sn.* дове́рие, уве́ренность; опо́ра (*support*)

relic [ре́-лĭк] *sn.* рели́квия, пережи́ток (*survival*); сувени́р (*memento*); *pl.* оста́нки, оста́тки

relief [ri-ли́ф] *sn.* облегче́ние (*alleviation*); посо́бие (*assistance*); подкрепле́ние (*reinforcement*); сме́на (*replacement*); релье́ф (*raised work*)

relieve [ri-ли́в] *vt.* облегча́ть (*ease*); ока́зывать по́мощь (*render assistance*); сменя́ть (*change, replace*)

religion [ri-ли́-джăн] *sn.* рели́гия

religious [ri-ли́-джăс] *adj.* религио́зный

relinquish [ri-ли́нк-ўĭш] *vt.* отка́зываться (*give up*); оставля́ть, покида́ть (*surrender*)

relish [ре́-лĭш] *sn.* вкус, при́вкус; припра́ва (*sauce, etc.*); удово́льствие от еды́ (*enjoyment of food, etc.*); *vt.* приправля́ть, смакова́ть

reluctance [ri-лăк-тăнс] *sn.* нежела́ние, неохо́та

rely [ri-ла́й] *vi.* полага́ться

remain [ri-мэ́йн] *vi.* остава́ться

remainder [рі-мэ́йн-дар] *sn.* остаток (*residue*); остальные (*people*)

remains [рі-мэ́йнз] *sn. pl.* останки; труп (*corpse*)

remark [рі-ма́рк] *sn.* заметка (*note*); замечание (*noticing, comment*); *vt.* замечать, отмечать

remarkable [рі-ма́рк-абл] *adj.* замечательный; удивительный (*striking*)

remedy [ре́-мі-ді] *sn.* излечение (*cure*); лекарство (*medicine*); средство (*means*); *vt.* исправлять

remember [рі-ме́м-бар] *vt.* вспоминать

remembrance [рі-ме́м-бранс] *sn.* воспоминание (*recollection*); память (*memory*); *pl.* привет

remind [рі-ма́йнд] *vt.* напоминать

reminder [рі-ма́йн-дар] *sn.* напоминание

reminiscent [ре-мі-ні-сáнт] *adj.* воспоминающий

remission [рі-мі-шáн] *sn.* нерадивость (*neligence*); ослабление (*lacking energy*)

remit [рі-мíт] *vt.i.* прощать (*pardon*); пересылать (*transmit*); смягчать (*mitigate*)

remittance [рі-мí-тáнс] *sn.* пересылка денег, ремесса

remnant [ре́м-нáнт] *sn.* остаток

remonstrate [рі-мóн-стрэйт] *vi.* протестовать

remorse [рі-мóрс] *sn.* раскаяние, угрызения совести

remorseless [рі-мóрс-лíс] *adj.* безжалостный, несострадательный

remote [рі-мóут] *adj.* от-

далённый; уединённый (*secluded*)

removal [рі-му́-вáл] *sn.* удаление, устранение; перемена квартиры (*местожительства*) (*change house, district*)

remove [рі-му́в] *vt.i.* передвигать (*move elsewhere*); удалять, устранять (*put farther away*); переезжать (*go to another place*)

remunerate [рі-мю́-нáрэйт] *vt.* вознаграждать, оплачивать

remuneration [рі-мю-нáрэ́й-шáн] *sn.* вознаграждение

remunerative [рі-мю-нá-рá-тів] *adj.* вознаграждающий, выгодный (*profitable*)

renaissance [рá-нэй-сáнс]*sn.* возрождение; Ренессанс

rend [ренд] *vt.* рвать, разрывать; раздирать (*lacerate*)

render [ре́н-дáр] *vt.* отдавать (*give in return*); платить (*pay*); оказывать (*service*); изображать (*portray*); исполнять (*execute*)

rendering [ре́н-дá-рін] *sn.* перевод (*translation*); изображение (*portrayal*); *tech.* штукатурка

rendezvous [рáй-дé-ву̃] *sn.* свидание (*meeting*); место свидания (*place*)

renegade [ре́-ні-гэйд] *sn.* ренегат

renew [рі-ню́] *vt.i.* возобновлять, обновлять

renewal [рі-ню́-áл] *sn.* возобновление, обновление; восстановление (*restoration, renovation*)

renounce [ri-náuns] *vt.i.* отка́зывать, отрека́ться

renovation [рҫ-но-вҙ́й-шҙн] *sn.* восстановле́ние

renown [ri-náun] *sn.* изве́стность (*being celebrated*); сла́ва (*fame*)

rent [рҫнт] *sn.* проре́ха (*in clothes*); ре́нта (*payment for house, etc.*); наём (*hire*); нанима́ть (*occupy*); сдава́ть (*let*)

renunciation [ri-нан-сı-ҙ́й-шҙн] *sn.* отка́з, самоотрече́ние

reorganize [ri-о́р-гӑ-найз] *vt.* реорганизова́ть

repair [ri-пэ́р] *sn.* почи́нка, ремо́нт; *vt.* поправля́ть, чини́ть; исправля́ть (*correct*); возмеща́ть (*amend*)

reparation [рҫ-пӑ-ҙ́й-шҙн] *sn.* возмеще́ние (*amends*); репара́ция (*compensation*)

repartee [рҫ-пӑр-ти́] *sn.* нахо́дчивость, остроу́мие

repatriate [ri-пҙ́-три-эйт] *vt.* возвраща́ть на ро́дину

repay [ri-пэ́й] *vt.* отпла́чивать

repayment [ri-пэ́й-мҙнт] *sn.* отпла́та

repeal [ri-пи́л] *sn.* отме́на; *vt.* аннули́ровать, отменя́ть

repeat [ri-пи́т] *sn. mus.* повторе́ние; *vt.* повторя́ть; подража́ть (*imitate*)

repeatedly [ri-пи́-тед-ли] *adv.* не́сколько раз (*several times*); повто́рно (*again and again*)

repel [ri-пе́л] *vt.* отта́лкивать

repent [ri-пе́нт] *vi.* раска́иваться

repentant [ri-пе́н-тӑнт]

adj. ка́ющийся, раска́ивающийся

repercussion [ри-пӑр-ка́-шҙн] *sn.* отда́ча (*после уда́ра*); о́тзвук (*echoing sound*); *fig.* отраже́ние

repetition [рҫ-пı-ти́-шҙн] *sn.* повторе́ние; ко́пия

replace [ri-плэ́йс] *vt.* класть обра́тно (*put back*); заменя́ть, замеща́ть (*substitute*)

replenish [ri-пле́-ниш] *vt.* сно́ва наполня́ть

replica [ре́-пли-ка] *sn.* дублика́т; ко́пия

reply [ri-плáй] *sn.* отве́т; *vt.* отвеча́ть

report [ri-по́рт] *sn.* докла́д, отчёт (*statement*); молва́, слух (*rumour*); звук взры́ва (*sound of explosion*); *vt.i.* докла́дывать, доноси́ть; сообща́ть (*inform*)

reporter [ri-по́р-тӑр] *sm.* докла́дчик; репортёр

repose [ri-по́уз] *sn.* о́тдых (*respite*); поко́й (*tranquility*); сон (*sleep*); *vt.i.* отдыха́ть (*rest*); поко́иться (*be tranquil*)

repository [ri-по́-зı-тӑ-ри] *sn.* вмести́лище, храни́лище

reprehend [рҫ-при-хҙ́нд] *vt.* де́лать вы́говор, порица́ть

represent [рҫ-при-зҙ́нт] *vt.* представля́ть (*introduce*); изобража́ть (*portray*)

representation [рҫ-при-зҙн-тҙ́й-шҙн] *sn.* изображе́ние (*portraying*); представле́ние (*performance*)

representative [рҫ-при-зҙ́н-тӑ-тив] *sn.* представи́тель; *adj.* показа́тельный, представи́тельный, характе́рный

repress [рi-прéс] *vt.* подавлять

repression [рi-прé-шăн] *sn.* подавление, репрессия

reprieve [рi-прйв] *sn.* прощение (*pardon*); отсрочка (*commutation*); *vt.* отсрочивать

reprimand [рé-прi-мăнд] *sn.* выговор; *vt.* делать выговор

reprisal [рi-прáй-зăл] *sn.* возмездие; репрессалия

reproach [рi-прóуч] *sn.* укор, упрёк; *vt.* упрекать

reproduce [рi-прă-дйóс] *vt.* воспроизводить

reproduction [рi-прă-дáк-шăн] *sn.* воспроизведение; репродукция

reproof [рi-прýф] *sn.* выговор, порицание

reprove [рi-прýв] *vt.* бранить, порицать

reptile [рéп-тайл] *s.* рептилия

republic [рi-пáб-лiк] *sn.* республика

repudiate [рi-пйó-дi-эйт] *vt.i.* отвергать; отрекаться

repudiation [рi-пйó-дi-эй-шăн] *sn.* аннулирование, отказ

repugnant [рi-пáг-нăнт] *adj.* отвратительный, противный; несовместимый (*incompatible*)

repulse [рi-пáлс] *sn.* отпор; *vt. mil.* отражать, разбивать; отталкивать (*drive back*)

repulsive [рi-пáл-сiв] *adj.* омерзительный (*loathsome*); отталкивающий

reputation [рé-пю-тéй-шăн] *sn.* репутация

repute [рi-пйóт] *sn.* общее мнение

reputed [рi-пйó-тiд] *adj.* предполагаемый

request [рi-кýэст] *sn.* просьба; *vt.* просить

require [рi-кýáй-ăр] *vt.* требовать (*demand*); нуждаться (*call for*)

requisite [рé-кýi-зiт] *sn.* необходимый предмет (*thing*); необходимое качество (*quality*); *adj.* требуемый

requisition [рe-кýi-зí-шăн] *sn. mil.* реквизиция; официальное требование; *vt.* реквизировать

rescind [рi-сíнд] *vt.* отменять

rescue [рéс-кю] *sn.* спасение; *vt.* избавлять, спасать

research [рi-сáрч] *sn.* научное исследование; тщательные поиски (*thorough search*)

resemblance [рi-зéм-блăнс] *sn.* сходство

resemble [рi-зéмбл] *vt.* походить (*be like*); иметь сходство (*have similarity*)

resent [рi-зéнт] *vt.* негодовать (*be indignant*); обижаться (*take offence*)

resentment [рi-зéнт-мăнт] *sn.* обида, чувство негодования

reservation [рé-зăр-вéй-шăн] *sn.* оговорка

reserve [рi-зёрв] *sn.* запас; *mil.* резерв; скрытность (*reticence*); ограничение (*limitation*); умолчание (*self-restraint*)

reservoir [рé-зăр-вýăр] *sn.* бассейн, резервуар

reside [рі-зáйд] *vi.* прожи-
вáть

residence [рé-зі-дăнс] *sn.*
пребывáние, проживáние;
местожи́тельство (*place*);
резиде́нция

resident [рé-зі-дăнт] *sm.*
жи́тель; резиде́нт; *adj.* жи-
ву́щий, прожива́ющий

residue [рé-зі-дю] *sn.* остáток

resign [рі-зáйн] *vt.i.* покидáть (*relinquish*), уступáть
(*yield*), отказываться (*refuse*); слагáть (*renounce*),
уходи́ть в отстáвку (*from
employment*)

resignation [рé-зіг-нéй-
шăн] *sn.* ухóд с дóлжности
(*from employment*); отстáвка
(*retirement*); покóрность,
смирéние (*submission*)

resigned [рі-зáйнд] *adj.* без-
рóпотный, покóрный

resilient [рі-зí-лі-ăнт] *adj.*
упрýгий

resin [рé-зін] *sn.* кáмедь,
смолá; *vt.* смоли́ть

resist [рі-зíст] *vt.i.* проти-
востоя́ть, сопротивля́ться;
воздéрживаться (*refrain
from*)

resistance [рі-зíст-ăнс] *sn.*
противодéйствие, сопро-
тивлéние

resolute [рé-зă-лют] *adj.*
реши́тельный (*determined*),
усто́йчивый (*firm*)

resolution [рé-зă-лю́-шăн]
sn. резолю́ция; решéние;
разрешéние (*of problem*)

resolve [рі-зóлв] *sn.* решéние; *vt.i.* решáть

resonant [рé-зă-нăнт] *adj.*
звучáщий, резони́рующий

resort [рі-зóрт] *sn.* при-
менéние срéдства (*resorting
to an expedient*); ресýрс;
чáсто посещáемое мéсто
(*frequenting*); курóрт
(*health*); *vi.* прибегáть

resound [рі-зáунд] *vt.i.*
звучáть; оглашáться; про-
изводи́ть сенсáцию (*pro-
duce sensation*); отражáть
звук (*echo*)

resource [рі-сóрс] *sn.* спóсоб, срéдство; изобретá-
тельность, нахóдчивость
(*expedient*)

respect [ріс-пéкт] *sn.* увa-
жéние (*esteem*); *pl.* почтé-
ние; *vt.* уважáть; щади́ть
(*spare*)

respectability [ріс-пек-тă-
бí-лі-ті] *sn.* почтéнность,
респектáбельность

respectable [ріс-пéк-тăбл]
adj. почтéнный (*of social
standing*); поря́дочный (*of
amount*); прили́чный (*decent*)

respective [ріс-пéк-тів]
adj. соотвéтственный

respiration [рéс-пі-рáй-
шăн] *sn.* дыхáние

respite [рéс-піт] *sn.* отсрóч-
ка наказáния (*delay in discharge of penalty*); передышка (*interval of rest or relief*);
vt. давáть отсрóчку

resplendent [ріс-сплéн-дăнт]
adj. блестя́щий, блистá-
тельный

respond [ріс-пóнд] *vi.* отвечáть; отзывáться, реаги́ро-
вать (*react*)

respondent [ріс-пóн-дăнт]
sm. leg. отвéтчик

response [ріс-пóнс] *sn.* отвéт; отвéтное чýвство; óт-
клик

responsibility [ріс-пон-сі-бі-лі-ті] *sn.* обя́занность, отве́тственность

responsible [ріс-пóн-сібл] *adj.* отве́тственный

rest [рéст] *sn.* о́тдых (*resting*); поко́й (*quiet*); сон (*sleep*); опо́ра, подста́вка (*support*); *mus.* па́уза; *vt.i.* поко́иться (*be still*); опи́ра́ться (*lean for support*); полага́ться (*rely*); положи́ть (*place*); отдыха́ть (*repose*)

restaurant [рес-то-ра́й] *sn.* гости́ница, рестора́н

restful [рéст-фýл] *adj.* успоко́йтельный

restitution [рес-ті-тю́-шäн] *sn.* возвраще́ние, восстановле́ние (*restoring*); возмеще́ние убы́тков (*reparation for damage, etc.*)

restoration [рес-то-ро́й-шäн] *sn.* реставра́ция

restorative [ріс-тô-рä-тів] *sn.* укрепля́ющее сре́дство; *adj.* укрепля́ющий

restore [ріс-тốр] *vt.* возвраща́ть (*give back*); восстана́вливать, реставри́ровать (*make restitution*)

restrain [ріс-трэ́йн] *vt.* сде́рживать (*check*); уде́рживать (*hold back*); умеря́ть (*moderate*); подверга́ть зак ючéнию (*imprison*)

restraint [ріс-трэ́йнт] *sn.* обузда́ние; самооблада́ние (*self-control*)

restrict [ріс-трíкт] *vt.* ограни́чивать

restriction [ріс-трíк-шäн] *sn.* ограниче́ние

result [рі-зäлт] *sn.* исхо́д, результа́т; *vi.* происходи́ть, проистека́ть, сле́довать

resume [рі-зю́м] *vt.* возобновля́ть

résumé [рé-зю-мé] *sn.* ито́г (*result, total*); сво́дка (*summary*)

resumption [рі-зä́мп-шäн] *sn.* возобновле́ние

resurrection [ре-зä-рéк-шäн] *sn.* воскресе́ние; воскреще́ние (*revival from disuse*)

retail [рѝ-тэ́йл] *sn.* ро́зничная прода́жа; [рі-тэ́йл] *vt.i.* продава́ть в ро́зницу; переска́зывать (*recount bit by bit*)

retailer [рі-тэ́й-лäр] *sn.* ла́вочник

retain [рі-тэ́йн] *vt.* сохраня́ть, уде́рживать; по́мнить (*remember*); нанима́ть (*secure services*)

retaliate [рі-тä́-лі-эйт] *vt.i.* отомща́ть, отпла́чивать

retaliation [рі-тä́-лі-эй-шäн] *sn.* возме́здие, отпла́та

retard [рі-тấрд] *vt.i.* заде́рживать, замедля́ть

reticence [рé-ті-сäнс] *sn.* молчали́вость (*in speech*); сде́ржанность (*discretion*); скры́тность (*secretive*)

retinue [рé-ті-ню] *sn.* сви́та

retire [рі-тай-äр] *vi.* отступа́ть (*retreat*); удаля́ться (*withdraw*); уединя́ться (*seek seclusion*); ложи́ться спать (*go to bed*); оставля́ть (*leave*)

retired [рі-тай-äрд] *adj.* отставно́й; уединённый (*secluded*)

retirement [рі-тай-äр-мäнт] *sn.* отста́вка; уедине́ние (*solitude*)

retiring [рі-тай-ä-рій] *adj.* засте́нчивый, скро́мный

retort [рі-то́рт] *sn.* возражение, находчивый ответ; *vt.i.* возражать, отпаривовать

retouch [рі-та́ч] *vt.* ретушировать

retract [рі-тра́кт] *vt.i.* втягивать

retreat [рі-три́т] *sn.* отступление; убежище (*asylum, shelter*); *mil.* ретировка; уединение (*seclusion*); *vi.* отступать

retrench [рі-тренч] *vt.i.* сокращать, уменьшать (*reduce*); экономить (*economize*)

retrenchment [рі-тренч-мэ́нт] *sn.* сокращение; *mil.* окоп, ретраншемент

retribution [ре-трі-бю́шэн] *sn.* воздаяние

retrieve [рі-три́в] *vt.i.* снова находить (*regain*); восстанавливать (*restore*); подавать (*of dog*)

retrograde [ре́-троу-грэйд] *adj.* направленный назад (*directed backwards*); реакционный, ретроградный; *vi.* двигаться назад

retrospect [ре́-троу-спект] *sn.* обозрение прошедшего

return [рі-то́рн] *sn.* возвращение (*returning*); отдача (*thing returned*); доход, прибыль (*profit*); отчёт, рапорт (*report*)

reunion [рі-ю́-ніэн] *sn.* воссоединение; *vi.* живать

reveal [рі-ві́л] *vt.* обнаруживать

revel [ре́-вэл] *sn.* пирушка; *vi.* бражничать, пировать

revelation [ре-вэ-лэ́й-шэн] *sn.* откровение, открытие

revelry [ре́-вэл-рі] *sn.* разгул, пиршество

revenge [рі-ве́ндж] *sn.*

месть, мщение, реванш; *vt.i.* отомстить

revenue [ре́-ві-ню) *sn.* доход; *pl.* доходные статьи

reverberate [рі-во́р-бэрэйт] *vt.i.* отражать (чтить

revere [рі-ві́р] *vt.* уважать,

reverence [ре́-вэ-ра́нс] *sn.* благоговение, почитание

reverend [ре́-вэ́-рэнд] *adj.* почтенный; преподобный

reverent [ре́-вэ-рэнт] *adj.* благоговейный, почтительный

reversal [рі-во́р-сэл] *sn.* обратный ход

reverse [рі-во́рс] *sn.* противоположное (*the contrary*); неудача (*defeat*); оборотная сторона (*of coin, etc.*); *adj.* обратный, перевёрнутый; *vt.i.* перевёртывать; отменять (*revoke*)

reversible [ре-во́р-сібл] *adj.* обратимый

revert [рі-во́рт] *vt.i.* возвращаться; оглянуться

review [рі-вю́] *sn.* обозрение (*survey*); пересмотр (*revision*); рецензия (*critique*); *mil.* смотр; журнал (*periodical*); *vt.i.* обозревать; пересматривать; рецензировать

revile [рі-ва́йл] *vt.* оскорблять (*abuse*); бранить, ругать (*rail at*)

revise [рі-ва́йз] *sn.* *тур.* сверка; *vt.* исправлять, пересматривать

revision [ре-ві́-жэн] *sn.* осмотр, пересмотр

revival [рі-ва́й-вэл] *sn.* возрождение

revive [рі-ва́йв] *vt.i.* возрождаться, оживать

revoke [rí-vóŭk] *vt.* отменять

revolt [rí-вóлт] *sn.* восстáние, мятéж; отвращéние (*aversion*); *vi.* восставáть; чýвствовать отвращéние

revolting [rí-вóл-тïн̆] *adj.* возмутительный

revolution [рę-вă-лý-шăн] *sn. tech.* круговóе вращéние; пóлный оборóт (*of machine*); револю́ция (*reversal of conditions*)

revolutionary [рę-вă-лý-шă-нă-рi] *adj.* революциóнный

revolve [рí-вóлв] *vt.i.* вращáться

revolver [рí-вóл-вăр] *sn.* револьвéр

revulsion [рí-вăл-шăн] *sn.* внезáпное рéзкое изменéние чувств; *med.* отвлечéние

reward [рí-уóрд] *sn.* награ́да; *vt.* награждáть

rhapsody [рæп-сă-дï] *sn. mus.* рапсóдия

rhetoric [рę-тă-рïк] *sn.* ритóрика

rheumatic [рў-мǽ-тïк] *adj.* ревматический

rheumatism [рý-мă-тïзм] *sn.* ревматизм

rhinoceros [рай-нó-сă-дăс] *s.* носорóг

rhubarb [рý-бáрб] *sn.* ревéнь, *m.*

rhyme [райм] *sn.* ри́фма; *vt.i.* рифмовáть

rhythm [рïз̆м] *sn.* ритм

rhythmical [рï̆з̆-мï-кăл] *adj.* ритмический

rib [рïб] *sn. anat.* ребрó; *naut.* шпáнгоут

ribald [рí-бăлд] *adj.* непристóйный

ribaldry [рí-бăлд-рï] *sn.* сквернослóвие

ribbed [рïбд] *adj.* ребри́стый

ribbon [рí-бăн] *sn.* лéнта

rice [райс] *sn.* рис

rich [рïч] *adj.* богáтый (*wealthy*); плодорóдный (*fertile*); оби́льный (*ample, abundant*); роскóшный (*elaborate*); жи́рный (*fatty*); *pl.* **-es** [рí-чïз] богáтство

rick [рïк] *sn.* копнá, скирдá, стог

rickety [рí-кă-тï] *adj.* рахитичный; расслáбленный (*weak-jointed*); расшáтанный, шáткий (*tottering*)

rid [рïд] *vt.* избавлять

riddance [рí-дăнс] *sn.* избавлéние, освобождéние

riddle [рïдл] *sn.* загáдка (*puzzle*); решетó (*sieve*); просéивать (*sift*)

ride [райд] *sn.* eздá; *vt.i.* éхать

rider [рай-дăр] *sm.* наéздник; *sn.* дополнéние, попрáвка (*of document*)

ridge [рïдж] *sn.* гóрный кряж, хребéт (*of hills*); конёк (*of roof*); грáдка (*of garden*)

ridicule [рí-дï-кюл] *sn.* осмеяние; *vt.* осмéивать

ridiculous [рí-дï-кю-лăс] *adj.* нелéпый, смехотвóрный

rife [райф] *adj.* изобилýющий (*abundant*); чáстый (*of common occurrence*)

riff-raff [рïф-рæф] *sn.* подóнки óбщества; отбрóсы (*rabble*)

rifle [райфл] *sn.* винтóвка; *vt.* огрáбить (*search and rob*); дéлать нарéзку (*make grooves*)

rift [ріфт] *sn.* трещи́на, щель

rig [ріг] *sn. naut.* осна́стка; вне́шний вид челове́ка (*person's appearance*); проде́лка, уло́вка (*trick, dodge, etc.*); *vt. naut.* оснаща́ть; снаряжа́ть (*fit out*)

rigging [рі́-гің] *sn.* такела́ж

right [райт] *sn.* пра́во (*claim*); справедли́вость (*justice*); *adj.* пра́вый, пра́вильный (*correct*); прямо́й (*straight*); all — [ол —] хорошо́; *vt.i.* выпрямля́ть (*straighten*); исправля́ть (*correct*)

righteous [райт-чәс] *adj.* правди́вый

rightful [райт-фул] *adj.* зако́нный (*legitimate*); пра́вильный (*correct*)

rigid [рі́-джід] *adj.* жёсткий, негну́щийся; ре́зкий (*harsh*); стро́гий (*strict*)

rigidity [рі-джі́-ді-ті] *sn.* стро́гость, суро́вость

rigorous [рі́-гә-рәс] *adj.* стро́гий, суро́вый

rigour [рі-гәр] *sn.* резкость, стро́гость

rim [рім] *sn.* обод (*outer ring*); край (*edge, border*)

rind [райнд] *sn.* кора́, кожура́; ко́рка (*of cheese*)

ring [рің] *sn.* кольцо́, круг (*circle*); опра́ва (*for spectacles*); цирковая аре́на (*of circus*); звон (*sound*); *vt.i.* окружа́ть (*encompass*); звене́ть, звони́ть (*of bell*)

ringleader [рі́ң-лі-дәр] *sm.* зачи́нщик, конова́л

ringlet [рі́ң-літ] *sn.* ло́кон (*of hair*); коле́чко (*small ring*)

ringworm [рі́ң-уәрм] *sn. med.* стригу́щий лиша́й

rink [рі́нк] *sn.* като́к

rinse [рінс] *sn.* полоска́нье; *vt.* полоска́ть

riot [рай-әт] *sn.* бунт (*rebellion*); беспоря́док (*disturbance*) *vi.* поднима́ть шум

riotous [рай-ә-тәс] *adj.* шу́мный, шумли́вый

rip [ріп] *vt.i.* рвать, разре́зывать; — off [— оф] сдира́ть

ripe [райп] *adj.* зре́лый, спе́лый

ripen [рай-пән] *vi.* зреть

ripple [ріпл] *sn.* зыбь, рябь; волни́стость (*of hair*); журча́нье (*hum*); *vt.i.* журча́ть; стру́иться

rise [райз] *sn.* повыше́ние (*upward incline*); происхожде́ние (*origin*); нача́ло (*start*); восхо́д (*of sun*); увеличе́ние (*increase*); *vi.* встава́ть (*get up*); восстава́ть (*revolt*); поднима́ться (*ascend*); восходи́ть (*of sun*); возраста́ть (*increase*)

risk [ріск] *sn.* риск; *vt.* рискова́ть

rite [райт] *sn.* обря́д; церемо́ния

ritual [рі-тю-әл] *sn.* ритуа́л

rival [рай-вәл] *sn.* сопе́рник; *adj.* сопе́рничать

rivalry [рай-вәл-рі] *sn.* сопе́рничество, соревнова́ние

river [рі-вәр] *sn.* река́

rivet [рі-віт] *sn.* заклёпка; *vt.* заклёпывать

rivulet [рі́-вю-лєт] *sn.* ручёй

road [ро́уд] *sn.* доро́га, путь; у́лица (*street*)

roadway [ро́уд-уэй] *sn.* мостовая, шоссе́

roam [роўм] *vt.i.* броди́ть, скита́ться, стра́нствовать

roar [рôр] *sn.* рёв (*of lion, thunder, etc.*); гро́мкий смех (*loud laughter*); *vt.i.* ора́ть, реве́ть; хохота́ть (*laugh*)

roaring [рó-риŋ] *adj.* бу́йный, шу́мный

roast [роўст] *sn.* жарко́е; *adj.* жа́реный; *vt.i.* жа́рить, печь; гре́ться

rob [роб] *vt.* гра́бить, обкра́дывать

robber [ро́-бăр] *sm.* граби́тель, разбо́йник

robbery [ро́-бă-ри] *sn.* грабёж

robe [роўб] *sn.* ма́нтия; ри́са (*of priest*); *vt.i.* облача́ться в ма́нтию

robin [ро́-бин] *s.* малино́вка

robot [ро́-бăт] *sn.* автома́т, ро́бот

robust [ро-ба́ст] *adj.* дю́жий, здоро́вый, си́льный

rock [рок] *sn.* скала́; валу́н (*stone*); кра́шеный леденец (*sweetmeat*); *vt.i.* кача́ть (*oscillate*); убаю́кивать (*in arms, cradle*)

rocket [ро́-кит] *sn.* раке́та (*sn.*); взлета́ть, взмыва́ть (*of birds*)

rocky [ро́-ки] *adj.* камени́стый, скали́стый

rod [род] *sn.* прут (*stick*); у́дочка (*for fishing*); сте́ржень, *m.* (*bar*); ро́зга (*of birch*)

rodent [ро́-дăнт] *s.* *zool.* грызу́н

roe [роў] *sn.* икра́ (*hard*); моло́ки (*soft*); косу́ля (*deer*)

rogue [роўг] *sm.* моше́нник, плут; шалу́н (*mischievous child*)

roguish [ро́-гиш] *adj.* жу́ликова́тый

rôle [роўл] *sn.* роль

roll [роўл] *sn.* свито́к (*cylinder*); кату́шка (*of paper, material, etc.*); развива́лная похо́дка (*gait*); бу́лочка (*small loaf*); спи́сок (*of names*) *vt.i.* верте́ть, враща́ться; ката́ться (*skate*); раска́тывать (*flatten*)

roller [ро́-лăр] *sn.* ро́лик, цили́ндр; вал (*billow*); *printer's*)

rollick [ро́-лик] *vi.* весели́ться

rolling-pin [ро́у-лиŋ-пин] *sn.* ска́лка

Roman [ро́у-мăн] *adj.* ри́мский

romance [ро-мэ́нс] *sn.* рома́н (*book*); романи́ческий эпизо́д (*love affair*)

romantic [ро-мэ́н-тик] *adj.* романти́чный

Romany [ро́у-мă-ни] *sn.* цыга́н; *adj.* цыга́нский

romp [ромп] *vi.* вози́ться

roof [рŷф] *sn.* кры́ша (*of house, etc.*); нёбо (*of mouth*); *vt.* крыть, покрыва́ть

roofing [рŷ-фиŋ] *sn.* кро́вельный материа́л

rook [рўк] *sn.* ту́ра (*in chess*); *sm.* моше́нник, шу́лер (*cheat*); *s.* грач (*bird*); нече́стно игра́ть

room [рŷм] *sn.* ко́мната (*in house*); простра́нство (*space*); ме́сто (*place*); кварти́ра

roomy [рŷ-ми] *adj.* свобо́дный (*free*); просто́рный (*spacious*)

roost [рŷст] *sn.* насе́ст; *vi.* уса́живаться на насе́ст; устра́иваться на ночлёг (*settle for sleep*)

rooster [ру́-тăр] *sm.* пету́х

root [рут] *sn.* ко́рень, *m.*; *fig.* исто́чник, ко́рень (*source*); *vt. i.* вкореня́ть

rooted [ру́-тĭд] *adj.* укорени́вшийся, про́чный (*firm*)

rope [роуп] *sn.* верёвка, кана́т; *vt.* сцепля́ть, привя́зывать (канатом)

rosary [ро́у-зă-ри] *sn.* гря́дка с ро́зами (*bed of roses*); чётки (*beads*); роза́рий

rose [роуз] *sn.* ро́за; си́то на ле́йке (*nozzle*); а́лый цвет (*colour*); *adj.* ро́зовый

rosette [ро́у-зе́т] *sn.* розе́тка

roster [ро́-стăр] *sn. mil.* расписа́ние дежу́рств

rostrum [ро́-стрŭм] *sn.* ка́федра, трибу́на

rosy [ро́у-зи] *adj.* ро́зовый, румя́ный

rot [рот] *sn.* гние́ние, труха́; *vt. i.* гнить, по́ртиться

rota [ро́у-тă] *sn.* чередова́тельный спи́сок

rotary [ро́у-тă-ри] *adj.* враща́тельный, коловра́тный

rotation [ро́у-тэ́й-шăн] *sn.* враще́ние (*revolving*); периоди́ческое повторе́ние (*recurrence*); чередова́ние (*regular succession*)

rotten [ро́-тăн] *adj.* гнило́й, ту́хлый; испо́рченный (*corrupt*)

rotund [роу-та́нд] *adj.* по́лный, то́лстый (*of person*); высокопа́рный (*grandiloquent*); округлённый (*rounded*)

rouble [рубл] *sn.* рубль, *m.*

rouge [руж] *sn.* румя́на; *vi.* румя́ниться

rough [раф] *adj.* гру́бый,

шерша́вый (*coarse*), косма́тый (*hairy*); бу́йный, ре́зкий (*crude, harsh*); бу́рный (*stormy*); неотде́ланный, чернов о́й (*in unfinished state*)

roughen [ра́-фăн] *vt. i.* де́лать шерохова́тым

round [раунд] *sn.* круг (*circle*); кругово́е движе́ние (*revolving motion*); обхо́д (*beat, inspection*); о́чередь (*one's turn*); *adj.* кру́глый, сфери́ческий; *adv.* вокру́г, круго́м; *vt. i.* округля́ть, поворачиваться; окружа́ть

roundabout [ра́унд-ă-баут] *sn.* карусе́ль (*children's*); око́льный путь (*circuitous way*); *adj.* око́льный (*circumlocutory*)

rouse [рауз] *vt. i.* буди́ть (*wake*); просыпа́ться (*wake up*); возбужда́ть воодушевля́ть (*stir*)

rout [раут] *sn.* разгро́м; *vt.* разбива́ть го́лову

route [рут] *sn.* маршру́т; [ра́ут] *mil.* прика́з о выступле́нии

routine [ру-ти́н] *sn.* рути́на

rove [роув] *vi.* блужда́ть, броди́ть, скита́ться

rover [ро́у-вăр] *sm.* скита́лец; пира́т (*pirate*)

row [роу] *sn.* ряд; *vt. i.* грести́ (*propel boat*); [рау] *sn.* спор (*quarrel*); ссо́ра, сумато́ха (*disturbance*); *vt.* де́лать вы́говор, отчи́тывать (*reprimand*)

rowdy [ра́у-ди] *adj.* шу́мный

rowdyism [ра́у-ди-изм] *sn.* хулига́нство

rowing [ро́у-иŋ] *sn.* гре́бля; [ра́у-иŋ] *sn.* упрёки

royal [рóй-ăл] *adj.* корóлевский; величéственный (*splendid*); первоклáссный (*first rate*)

royalty [рóй-ăл-ті] *sn. pl.* члéны корóлевской фамúлии; áвторский гонорáр (*payment to authors*)

rub [раб] *sn.* трéние; *coll.* затруднéние (*difficulty*); *vt.i.* натирáть, терéть; - **off** [-оф] вытирáть, стирáть

rubber [рá-бăр] *sn.* каучýк, резúна; резúнка (*eraser*)

rubbing [рá-біњ] *sn.* трéние

rubbish [рá-біш] *sn.* мýсор, хлам (*litter*); вздор, дребéдень (*nonsense*)

rubble [рабл] *sn.* гáлька (*pebble*); щéбень

rubicund [рý-бі-кăнд] *adj.* румя́ный

ruby [рý-бі] *sn.* рубúн (*stone*); яркокрáсный цвет (*colour*); *adj.* рубúновый; яркокрáсный

rudder [рá-дăр] *sn.* руль

ruddy [рá-ді] *adj.* румя́ный

rude [рýд] *adj.* грýбый; невоспúтанный (*uneducated*)

rudimentary [рý-ді-мéн-тă-рі] *adj.* зачáточный, начáльный, элементáрный

rudiments [рý-ді-мăнтс] *sn. pl.* начáтки, элементáрные прúнципы

rue [рý] *vt.* раскáиваться, сожалéть

rueful [рý-фýл] *adj.* печáльный, уны́лый

ruffian [рá-фĭăн] *sn.* головорéз, хулигáн

ruffle [рафл] *sn.* рябь (*ripple of water*); *vt.* ерошúть (*disturb hair, etc.*); ря́бить (*disturb water*); нарушáть

спокóйствие (*upset tranquillity*)

rug [раг] *sn.* плед (*woollen wrap*); мохнáтый кóврик (*floor-mat*)

rugged [рá-гід] *adj.* неглáдкий (*uneven*); шероховáтый (*rough*); рéзкий (*harsh*)

ruin [рý-ін] *sn.* гúбель, крушéние; *pl.* развáлины; *vt.* губúть, разрушáть

ruinous [рý-і-нăс] *adj.* губúтельный, разорúтельный

rule [рýл] *sn.* власть (*authority*); правлéние (*government*); прáвило (*law*); разрéз (*standard*); линéйка (*measure*); лúния (*thin line*); *vt.i.* прáвить, управля́ть (*govern*); линевáть (*draw lines*); постановля́ть (*establish*)

ruler [рý-лăр] *sn.* правúтель; *sn.* линéйка (*for drawing lines*)

ruling [рý-ліњ] *sn.* постановлéние (*decision*); управлéние (*governing*); *adj.* обладáющий (*prevailing*); цáрствующий (*reigning*)

rum [рам] *sn.* ром

Rumanian [рý-мǽ-ні-ăн] *sn.* румы́нец; *adj.* румы́нский

rumble [рамбл] *sn.* грóхот, раскáты; *vi.* гремéть, грохотáть

ruminate [рý-мі-нэйт] *v.i.* жевáть жвáчку; *fig.* обдýмывать, размышля́ть (*meditate, ponder*)

rummage [рá-мідж] *sn.* пóиски (*search*); остáтки (*odds and ends*); *vt.i.* обы́скивать, ры́ться

rumour [ру́-мӑр] *sn.* молва́, слух; *vt.* разглаша́ть

rump [рамп] *sn.* крестец

rum·ple [рампл] *vt.* мять (*linen, paper*); взъеро́шивать (*hair*)

run [ран] *sn.* бег, пробе́г; огоро́женное ме́сто (*enclosure*); *vt.i.* бе́гать, бежа́ть; ли́ться, течь (*of water*); вести́ (*business*); управля́ть (*manipulate machine, etc.*); – **away** [– ӑ-уэ́й] убега́ть; – **down** [– да́ун] остана́вливаться (*of watch*); утомля́ться (*tire*), – **off** [– оф] удира́ть

runaway [ра́н-ӑ-уэ́й] *sn.* бегле́ц, дезерти́р; *adj.* сбежа́вший

rung [ран] *sn.* ступе́нька, перекла́дина

runner [ра́-нӑр] *sm.* бегу́н

running [ра́-нин] *sn.* бе́ганье; *adj.* бегу́щий; теку́щий (*account*); подстро́чный (*commentary*); слезя́щий (*eye*)

rupture [ра́п-чӑр] *sn. med.* гры́жа, перело́м, расторже́ние (*breach*); *vt.i.* прорыва́ть (*burst*); порыва́ть (*sever*)

rural [ру́-рӑл] *adj.* дереве́нский, се́льский

ruse [руз] *sn.* уло́вка, хи́трость

rush [раш] *sn. bot.* си́тник, тростни́к; *adj.* тростнико́вый; *sn.* на́тиск (*movement*); спе́шка (*haste*); стреми́тельная ата́ка, штурм (*onslaught*); *vt.i.* торопи́ть; увлека́ть стреми́тельно (*impel rapidly*)

russet [ра́-сіт] *sn.* сорт я́блок (*apple*); *adj.* красно-ва́то-кори́чневый (*colour*)

Russian [ра́-шӑн] *sm.* ру́сский; *adj.* росси́йский

rust [раст] *sn.* ржавчина; *bot. sn.* ржаве́ть; *vt.i.* притупля́ться (*deaden, lose quality*)

rustic [ра́с-тік] *sm.* се́льский жи́тель, мужи́к; *adj.* дереве́нский, просто́й

rustle [расл] *sn.* ше́лест, шо́рох (*sound*); *vt.i.* шелесте́ть

rusty [ра́с-ті] *adj.* заржа́вленный; цве́та ржа́вчины (*colour*); запу́щенный (*impaired by neglect*); уста́ревший (*antiquated*)

rut [рат] *sn.* коле́я

ruthless [ру́ѳ-ліс] *adj.* безжа́лостный; жесто́кий

rye [рай] *sn.* рожь

S

sabbath [сӑ́-бӑѳ] *sn. bibl.* суббо́та (*Saturday, Jewish*); воскресе́нье (*Sunday, Christian*)

sable [сэйбл] *s.* со́боль; собо́лий мех (*fur*)

sabotage [сӑ́-бӑ-та́ж] *sn.* сабота́ж; *vi.* саботи́ровать

sabre [сэйбр] *sn.* са́бля; *vt.* рубить са́блей

sack [сӑк] *sn.* куль, мешо́к; увольне́ние (*dismissal*); *vt.* гра́бить (*plunder*); сы́пать в мешо́к (*put into sack*); *coll.* увольня́ть (*dismiss*)

sackcloth [сӑ́к-кло́ѳ] *sn.* дерюга

sacrament [сӑ́-крӑ-мӑнт] *sn.* таи́нство

sacred [сэ́й-крід] *adj.* свято́й

sacrifice [сǽ-кри-файс] *sn.* жертвоприноше́ние; же́ртва (*gift or victim*); *vt.* же́ртвовать

sacrilege [сǽ-кри-лидж] *sn.* святота́тство

sad [сǽд] *adj.* гру́стный, печа́льный

saddle [сǽдл] *sn.* седло́; *vt.i* седла́ть; обременя́ть (*burden*)

saddler [сǽ-дляр̆] *sm.* седе́льный ма́стер, шо́рник

sadness [сǽд-нис] *sn.* грусть, огорче́ние, печа́ль

safe [сэйф] *sn.* сейф; чула́н (*larder*); *adj.* безопа́сный; невреди́мый (*unharmed*)

safe-guard [сэйф-га́рд] *sn.* предосторо́жность; *vt.* защища́ть, охраня́ть

safety [сэ́йф-ти] *sn.* безопа́сность

safety-pin [сэ́йф-ти-пин] *sn.* английская була́вка

sag [сǽг] *vi.* обвиса́ть (*hang sideways*); оседа́ть (*sink*)

sagacious [са-гэ́й-шас] *adj.* смётливый, сообрази́тельный

sagacity [са-гǽ-си-ти] *sn.* проница́тельность

sage [сэйдж] *sm.* мудре́ц; *adj.* му́дрый, рассуди́тельный; *sn. bot.* шалфе́й

sail [сэйл] *sn.* па́рус; *vt.i* итти́ под паруса́ми, плыть

sailor [сэ́й-лор] *sm.* моря́к, матро́с

saint [сэйнт] *sm.* свято́й

sake [сэйк] *sn.* **for the – of** [фор эǎ – ов] ра́ди, для – **for my** – [фор май –] ра́ди меня́

salad [сǽ-ляд] *sn.* сала́т

salary [сǽ-ля-ри] *sn.* жа́лование, окла́д

sale [сэйл] *sn.* прода́жа; распрода́жа (*clearance sale*)

salesman [сэ́йлз-мǎн] *sm.* продаве́ц

salient [сэ́й-ли-ǎнт] *adj.* выдаю́щийся, выступа́ющий

sallow [сǽ-лоу] *adj.* бле́дный, боле́зненный

sally [сǽ-ли] *sn. mil.* вы́лазка; пое́здка, прогу́лка (*excursion*); *vi.* де́лать вы́лазку

salmon [сǽ-мǎн] *s.* лосо́сь, сёмга; желтова́то-ро́зовый цвет (*colour*)

saloon [са-лу́н] *sn.* зал

salt [солт] *sn.* соль; *vt.* соли́ть

salt-cellar [солт-се-ляр̆] *sn.* соло́нка

salubrious [са-лу́-бри-ǎс] *adj.* целе́бный

salutary [сǽ-лю-тǎ-ри] *adj.* благотво́рный

salutation [са-лю-тэ́й-шǎн] *sn.* приве́тствие

salute [са-лю́т] *sn.* покло́н; *mil.* салю́т; *vt.i.* приве́тствовать (*greet*); салютова́ть

salvage [сǽл-видж] *sn.* спасе́ние иму́щества; *vt.* спаса́ть

salvation [сǽл-вэ́й-шǎн] *sn.* спасе́ние

salve [сǎв] *sn.* целе́бная мазь; *vt.* смягча́ть (*soothe*); сма́зывать (*anoint*)

salver [сǎл-вǎр̆] *sn.* подно́с

salvo [сǽл-воу] *sn. mil.* оруди́йный залп

same [сэйм] *adj.* одина́ковый, однор́одный; *pron.* тот же

sample [сǽмпл] *sn.* образе́ц, про́ба; *vt.* испы́тывать, про́бовать

sanctify [sǽnk-tǐ-фай] *vt.* освящáть

sanctimonious [сǽнк-тǐ-мóу-нǐ-ăс] *adj.* хáнжеский

sanction [сǽнк-шăн] *sn.* сáнкция; *vt.i.* санкциони́ровать

sanctity [сǽнк-тǐ-тǐ] *sn.* свя́тость

sanctuary [сǽнк-тю-ă-рǐ] *sn.* святи́лище; убéжище (*retreat*)

sand [сǽнд] *sn.* песóк; *pl.* пески́; песчáный пляж (*at sea-side*)

sandal [сǽндл] *sn.* сандáлия

sandbank [сǽнд-бǽнк] *sn.* мель, óтмель

sand-storm [сǽнд-стóрм] *sn.* самýм

sandwich [сǽнд-уǐч] *sn.* бутербрóд, сáндвич; *vt.* прослáивать

sandy [сǽн-дǐ] *adj.* песóчный; желтовáто-крáсный (*colour*)

sane [сǽйн] *adj.* здрáвый, нормáльный; здравомыслящий (*sound of mind*)

sanguinary [сǽн-гỹǐ-нă-рǐ] *adj.* кровопроли́тный (*attended by bloodshed*); кровожáдный (*bloodthirsty*)

sanguine [сǽн-гỹǐн] *adj.* сангвини́ческий, оптими́стический; багрóвый (*of complexion*)

sanitary [сǽ-нǐ-тă-рǐ] *adj.* гигиени́ческий, санитáрный

sanitation [сǽ-нǐ-тéй-шăн] *sn.* оздоровлéние

sanity [сǽ-нǐ-тǐ] *sn.* нормáльное состоя́ние (*normal condition*); здрáвость, здравомы́слие (*common sense*)

sap [сǽп] *sn.* сок (*of plants*); *fig.* живýчесть; *vt.* извлекáть сок (*drain*); истощáть си́лы (*exhaust vigour*)

sapling [сǽп-лǐн] *sn.* молодóе дерéвцо

sapphire [сǽ-фай-ăр] *sn.* сапфи́р

sarcasm [сáр-кǽзм] *sn.* сар-кáзм; язви́тельное замечáние

sarcastic [сáр-кǽс-тǐк] *adj.* саркасти́ческий

sardine [сáр-ди́н] *s.* сарди́нка

sardonic [сáр-дó-нǐк] *adj.* насмéшливый, сардони́ческий

sash [сǽш] *sn.* пóяс; шарф; окóнная рáма (*window frame*)

satanic [сǽ-тá-нǐк] *adj.* сатани́ческий

satchel [сǽ-чăл] *sn.* рáнец, сýмка

sate [сǽйт] *vt.* насыщáть

satellite [сǽ-тă-лайт] *sm.* послéдователь (*follower*); привéрженец (*adherent, partisan*); *astron.* спýтник

satiate [сóй-шǐ-эйт] *vt.* насыщáть

satin [сǽ-тǐн] *sn.* атлáс

satire [сǽ-тай-ăр] *sn.* сати́ра

satisfaction [сǽ-тǐс-фǽк-шăн] *sn.* удовлетворéние; искуплéние (*expiation*)

satisfactory [сǽ-тǐс-фǽк-тă-рǐ] *adj.* удовлетвори́тельный; снóсный (*adequate*); довóльный (*good enough*)

satisfy [сǽ-тǐс-фай] *vt.* выполня́ть (*fulfil*); удовлетворя́ть (*content*); утоля́ть (*hunger*)

saturate [сă-чă-рэйт] *vt.* пропи́тывать

Saturday [сă-тă̆р-дэй] *sn.* суббо́та

sauce [сŏс] *sn.* со́ус; *coll.* де́рзость, на́глость

saucepan [сŏс-пăн] *sn.* кастрю́ля

saucer [сŏ-сă̆р] *sn.* блю́дце, поддо́нник

saucy [сŏ-сi] *adj.* де́рзкий, наха́льный

saunter [сŏн-тă̆р] *sn.* прогу́лка; *vi.* прогу́ливаться, проха́живаться

sausage [сŏ-сiдж] *sn.* соси́ска; колбаса́ (*cooked with garlic, etc.*)

savage [сă-видж] *sm.* дика́рь; *adj.* ди́кий, свире́пый; *coll.* рассе́рженный

save [сэйв] *vt.i.* сберега́ть (*reserve*), сохраня́ть (*conserve*); спаса́ть (*rescue*) *prep.* кро́ме (*but, except*)

saving [сэй-вiн] *sn.* сбереже́ние; *pl.* сбереже́ния; скоп

saviour [сэй-вi-ă̆р] *sm.* освободи́тель, спаси́тель

savour [сэй-вă̆р] *sn.* вкус, привкус; отличи́тельное сво́йство (*distinctive attribute*); *vt.i.* име́ть вкус; отве́дывать (*taste of*); смакова́ть (*relish*)

savoury [сэй-вă̆-рi] *sn.* о́страя заку́ска; *adj.* вку́сный, пика́нтный

saw [сŏ] *sn.* погово́рка (*maxim*); пила́ (*tool*); *vt.i.* пили́ть, распи́ливать

sawdust [сŏ-даст] *sn.* опи́лки

say [сэй] *sn.* мне́ние (*opinion*); *vt.i.* сказа́ть; говори́ть (*speak*); **that is to** [ðæт iз ту –] то́-есть

saying [сăй-iн] *sn.* погово́рка

scab [скăб] *sn.* струп; парша́ (*skin-disease*)

scabbard [скă-бă̆рд] *sn.* но́жны

scaffold [скă-фолд] *sn.* эшафо́т; помо́ст (*platform*)

scaffolding [скă-фăл-дiн] *sn.* леса́, подмостки

scald [сколд] *sn.* ожо́г; *vt.* обга́ривать, ошпа́ривать; кипяти́ть (*of milk*)

scale [скэйл] *sn.* ча́ша весо́в (*pan of weighing-balance*); *pl.* весы́; шкала́ (*range*); масшта́б (*in measuring*); *mus.* га́мма; чешуя́ (*of fish*); *vt.* взве́шивать (*weigh*); взбира́ться (*climb wall, stairs, etc.*)

scallop [скŏ-лăп] *s.* гребешо́к; ра́ковина (*shell*); *pl.* зу́бцы, фесто́ны

scalp [скăлп] *sn.* скальп; *vt.* скальпи́ровать

scamp [скăмп] *sm.* безде́льник

scamper [скăм-пă̆р] *sn.* гало́п; *vi.* убега́ть, удира́ть

scan [скăн] *vt.i.* рассма́тривать; скандирова́ть

scandal [скăн-дăл] *sn.* клевета́, спле́тня (*malicious gossip*); позо́р, сканда́л

scandalize [скăн-дă-лайз] *vt.* шоки́ровать

scandalous [скăн-дă-лăс] *adj.* возмути́тельный, позо́рный, сканда́льный

Scandinavian [скăн-дi-нэй-вi-ăн] *adj.* скандина́вский

scanty [скăн-тi] *adj.* ску́дный

scapegoat [скэ́йп-гоут] *sn. coll.* козёл отпущения

scar [скáр] *sn.* рубец, шрам (*mark*); утёс (*crag*)

scarce [скэ́рс] *adj.* рéдкий

scarcely [скэ́рс-лі] *adv.* едвá

scarcity [скэ́р-сі-ті] *sn.* недостáток, нехвáтка, рéдкость

scare [скэ́р] *sn.* страх, ýжас; *vt.* пугáть, страшить

scarecrow [скэ́р-кроу] *sn.* пугáло

scarf [скáрф] *sn.* шарф; гáлстук (*necktie*)

scarlet [скáр-літ] *sn.* áлый цвет; *adj.* áлый

scarlet-fever [скáр-літ-фі-вáр] *sn.* скарлатина

scathing [скэ́й-ѳіѳ] *adj.* злой, язвительный

scatter [скэ́-тáр] *vt.i.* разбрáсывать, рассéивать, рассыпáть

scavenger [скэ́-вáн-джáр] *sn.* мýсорщик

scene [син] *sn.* сцéна; зрéлище (*spectacle*); пейзáж (*landscape*)

scenery [си́-нä-рі] *sn. theat.* театрáльные декорáции; вид, пейзáж (*landscape*)

scenic [си́-нік] *adj.* живописный (*picturesque*); *theat.* сценический

scent [сéнт] *sn.* зáпах (*smell*); духи́ (*odour, fragrance*); след (*track*); нюх, чутьё (*sense of smell*)

sceptical [скéп-ті-кäл] *adj.* скептический

sceptre [сéп-тáр] *sn.* скипетр

schedule [шé-дюл] *sn.* опись

scheme [скім] *sn.* проéкт, схéма; зáговор, интрига

(*plot, design*); *vt.i.* составлять плáны; интриговáть

schism [сізм] *sn.* раскóл

scholar [скó-лáр] *sn.* учéник (*pupil*); знатóк, учёный (*learned person*)

scholarship [скó-лáр-шіп] *sn.* учёность, эрудиция; стипéндия

scholastic [ско-лáс-тік] *adj.* схоластический; школьный

school [скул] *sn.* училище, шкóла; стáя (*of fish*); *vt.* обучáть (*instruct*); приучáть (*train*)

schoolboy [скул-бой] *sn.* шкóльник

school-fellow [скул-фé-лоу] *sn.* соучéник

schoolmaster [скул-мáс-тáр] *sn.* учитель

schooner [скý-нáр] *sn.* шхýна

science [сáй-äнс] *sn.* наýка

scientific [сáй-äн-ті-фік] *adj.* наýчный

scientist [сáй-äн-тіст] *sn.* учёный

scintillate [сін-ті-лэйт] *vi.* мерцáть, сверкáть

scissors [сі-зäз] *sn. pl.* нóжницы

scoff [скоф] *sn.* насмéшка, посмешище; *vi.* издевáться, насмехáться

scold [скоулд] *sf.* сварливая жéнщина; *vt.i.* бранить

scolding [скóул-діѳ] *sn.* брань, упрёки

scone [скоун] *sn.* пшени́чная лепёшка

scoop [скýп] *sn.* ковш (*bucket*); совóк (*shovel*); вычéрпывать

scope [скóуп] *sn.* кругозóр, простóр; размáх (*range*)

scorch [скӧрч] *vt.i.* обжигать, опаляться, палить

score [скӧр] *sn.* зарубка, метка (*notch*); счёт (*reckoning*); двадцать (*twenty*); *mus.* партитура; *vt.i.* делать отметки (*mark*); засчитывать (*reckon*); *mus.* оркестровать

scorn [скӧрн] *sn.* презрение; *vt.* презирать

scornful [скӧрн-фул] *adj.* презрительный

Scot [скот] *sm.* шотландец

Scotch [скоч], **Scottish** [скӧтиш] *adj.* шотландский

scoundrel [скаун-дрэл] *sm.* негодяй, подлец

scour [скау-әр] *sn.* прочистка, чистка; *vt.* прочищать, чистить; пробегать (*go along hastily*)

scourge [скэрдж] *sn.* бедствие, бич; *vt.* карать, наказывать

scout [скаут] *sm.* разведчик; скаут; *vi.* разведывать; отвергать (*reject*)

scowl [скаул] *sn.* хмурный вид; *vi.* хмуриться

scraggy [скрæ-гi] *adj.* сухопарый

scramble [скрæмбл] *sn.* схватка (*scrimmage*); *vt.i.* карабкаться, ползти (*climb, crawl*)

scrap [скрæп] *sn.* кусочек, клочок; вырезка (*from newspaper, etc.*); *pl.* остатки, отбросы; *vt.* выбрасывать (*discard*)

scrape [скрэйп] *sn.* беда, затруднение (*predicament*); царапина (*scraping*); *vt.i.* скоблить; тереться (*graze*) пиликать (*on violin*)

scraper [скрэй-пәр] *sn.* скребок

scrap-heap [скрæп-хӣп] *sn.* свалка отбросов

scrappy [скрæ-пi] *adj.* лоскутный; бессвязный (*disconnected*)

scratch [скрæч] *sn.* царапина (*mark*); царапанье (*scratching*); *sport.* стартовая черта; *vt.i.* оцарапать, царапать; чесаться (*itch*); царапаться (*scratch oneself*); *adj.* случайный (*impromptu*)

scratchy [скрæ-чi] *adj.* небрежный, неискусный (*careless, unskilful*); случайно подобранный (*of crew, team*)

scrawl [скрӧл] *sn.* каракули; *vt.i.* писать каракулями

scream [скрим] *sn.* крик; резкий звук (*harsh sound*); *vt.i.* вопить, кричать

screech [скрич] *sn.* визг, пронзительный крик; *vt.i.* визжать

screen [скрин] *sn.* ширма (*piece of furniture*); щит (*protection*); экран (*cinema*); перегородка (*partition*); *vt.* прикрывать, укрывать (*shelter, hide partly*); демонстрировать, показывать (на экране) (*show on screen*); просеивать (*sort*)

screw [скру] *sn.* винт; *vt.* ввинчивать

screwdriver [скру-драй-вәр] *sn.* отвёртка

scribble [скрибл] *vt.i.* писать небрежно, черкать

scrimmage [скрi-мидж] *sn.* стычка, схватка

scripture [скрип-чәр] *sn.* библия, священное писание

scroll [скроўл] *sn.* свиток (*parchment*); легенда (*legend*); завиток (*sculptured*); волюта (*volute*)

scrub [скраб] *sn.* кустарник (*brushwood*); чистка щёткой (*scrubbing*); *vt.* тереть

scrubby [скра́-бі] *adj.* низкоро́слый (*of animal, person*); захуда́лый (*impoverished, shabby*)

scruff [скраф] *sn.* ши́ворот

scruple [скру́пл] *sn.* скру́пул (20 *grains*); со́вестливость (*conscientious objection*); сомне́ние (*doubt*); *vt.* колеба́ться (*hesitate*)

scrupulous [скру́-пю-лас] *adj.* добросо́вестный (*dutiful*); со́вестливый (*conscientious*)

scrutinize [скру́-ті-найз] *vt.* подверга́ть подро́бному рассмотре́нию

scrutiny [скру́-ті-ні] *sn.* рассмотре́ние

scuffle [скафл] *sn.* дра́ка, потасо́вка; *vi.* дра́ться

scull [скал] *sn.* кормово́е весло́; *vt.i.* грести́

scullery [ска-ла́-рі] *sn.* помеще́ние при ку́хне для мытья́ посу́ды и пр.

sculptor [скалп-та́р] *sm.* ску́льптор

sculpture [скалп-ча́р] *sn.* изва́яние, скульпту́ра (*art*); скульпту́рное произведе́ние (*works*); *vt.i.* вая́ть; украша́ть изва́яниями (*adorn with sculpture*)

scum [скам] *sn.* на́кипь, пе́на (*froth*); *fig.* подо́нки (*riff-raff*)

scurf [скёрф] *sn.* пе́рхоть

scurrilous [ска́-рі-лас] *adj.* гру́бый, непристо́йный, оскорби́тельный

scurry [ска́-рі] *sn.* беготня́; суета́ (*bustle*); *vi.* носи́ться

scuttle [скатл] *sn.* ведёрко для у́гля (*coal-scuttle*); *naut.* люк; *vt.i.* пробива́ть ды́ру, удира́ть (*run away*); дезерти́ровать (*desert*)

scythe [сайθ] *sn.* коса́; *vt.* коси́ть

sea [сі] *sn.* мо́ре

sea-borne [си-бо́рн] *adj.* перево́зимый мо́рем

seafaring [си-фэ́-рін] *adj.* морехо́дный

sea-gull [си-гал] *s.* ча́йка

seal [сил] *sn.* печа́ть (*stamp*); *vt.* запеча́тывать, скрепля́ть печа́тью; *s.* тюле́нь, *m.* (*animal*)

sealing-wax [си-лін-ўэкс] *sn.* сургу́ч

seam [сим] *sn.* шов; паз; *geol.* просло́йка; *vt.* сшива́ть

seaman [си-ман] *sm.* моря́к

seamless [сим-ліс] *adj.* без шва

seamstress [сим-стріс] *sf.* швея́

seamy [си-мі] *adj.* со шва́ми; *fig.* непригля́дный

seaplane [си-плэйн] *sn.* гидропла́н

sear [сир] *vt.* опаля́ть, прижига́ть; *fig.* притупля́ть

search [сёрч] *sn.* о́быск; по́иски (*quest*); *vt.i.* обы́скивать, оты́скивать; иска́ть (*look for*); прохва́тывать (*of cold, wind*)

searching [сёр-чін] *adj.* тща́тельный (*thorough*); испыту́ющий (*of look*)

seashore [си-шо́р] *sn.* взмо́рье, побере́жье

seasickness [сӣ-сӣк-нӗс] *sn.* морска́я боле́знь

seaside [сӣ-сайд] *sn.* примо́рье

season [сӣ-зӑн] *sn.* вре́мя го́да, сезо́н; *adj.* сезо́нный; *vt.i.* закаля́ть (*of people, armies*); поспева́ть, созрева́ть (*of fruit, etc.*); высыха́ть, суши́ть (*of wood*); приправля́ть (*flavour with condiments*)

seasonable [сӣ-зӑ-набл] *adj.* подходя́щий, своевре́менный

seasoning [сӣз-нӣӈ] *sn.* припра́ва

seat [сит] *sn.* сиде́нье, стул (*chair*); ме́сто (*place*); местонахожде́ние (*location*); расса́дник (*of illness*); *vt.* сажа́ть, усади́ть; вмеща́ть (*theatre, etc.*)

seaweed [сӣ-ӯид] *sn.* во́доросль

secede [сӣ-сӣд] *vi.* отка́лываться, отступа́ть

seclude [сӣ-клӯд] *vt.* уедини́ть

seclusion [сӣ-клӯ-жӑн] *sn.* удале́ние, уедине́ние

second [сӗ-кӑнд] *sn.* моме́нт, секу́нда; *sm.* секунда́нт (*in duel*); *adj.* второ́й; *vt.* подде́рживать (*support*)

secondary [сӗ-кӑн-дӑ- р̣і] *adj.* втори́чный; второстепе́нный (*of quality*); сре́дний (*of school*)

second-hand [сӗ-кӑнд-ха́нд] *adj.* букинисти́ческий (*of books*); поде́ржанный (*of things*)

secrecy [сӣ-крӑ-сі] *sn.* секре́тность, таи́нственность

secret [сӣ-крӣт] *sn.* секре́т,

та́йна; *adj.* секре́тный, скры́тый, та́йный

secretary [сӗ-крӑ-тӑ- р̣і] *sm.* секрета́рь, *m.*; мини́стр

secrete [сӣ-крӣт] *vt.* пря́тать; *physiol.* выделя́ть

secretion [сӣ-крӣ-шӑн] *sn.* сокры́тие; *physiol.* выделе́ние, секре́ция

sect [сӗкт] *sn.* се́кта

sectarian [сӗк-тэ́-рі-ӑн] *sm.* секта́нт, фана́тик; *adj.* секта́нтский

section [сӗк-шӑн] *sn.* се́кция (*part cut off*); отде́л (*division*); пара́граф; разре́з (*cut*)

secular [сӗ-кю-лӑр̣] *adj.* мирско́й, све́тский

secure [сӣ-кю́р̣] *adj.* безопа́сный, обеспе́ченный; *vt.* обеспе́чивать, страхова́ть

security [сӣ-кю́-рі-ті] *sn.* безопа́сность (*safety*); обеспе́чение (*guarantee*); уве́ренность (*confidence*)

sedate [сӣ-дэ́йт] *adj.* сде́ржанный, степе́нный

sedative [сӗ-дӑ-тів] *sn.* успока́ивающее сре́дство; *adj.* успока́ивающий

sedentary [сӗ-дӗн-тӑ- р̣і] *adj.* осе́длый, сидя́чий

sediment [сӗ-ді-мӑнт] *sn.* оса́док

sedition [сӣ-ді-шӑн] *sn.* сму́та

seditious [сӣ-ді-ша́с] *adj.* бунта́рский, мяте́жный

seduce [сӣ-дю́с] *vt.* обольща́ть, соблазня́ть

See [сӣ] *sn. eccl.* епа́рхия

see [сӣ] *vt.* ви́деть; посмотре́ть (*look at*); понима́ть (*understand*); провожа́ть (*escort*)

seed [сид] *sn.* céмя; *vt.i.* засеять; пойти в семя; очищать от зёрен (*remove from*)

seedling [си́-дли̌н] *sn.* сеянец

seedy [си́-ди] *adj. coll.* жалкий, обносившийся

seek [сик] *vt.i.* искать

seem [сим] *vi.* казаться, представляться

seeming [си́-мий] *adj.* кажущийся

seemly [си́м-ли] *adj.* подходящий; приличный (*decorous*)

seer [сир] *sm.* провидец, пророк

seesaw [си́-со́] *sn.* детские качели; качание (*motion*) *vi.* качаться

seethe [сив] *vt.i.* бурлить, кипеть

segment [сéг-мăнт] *sn.* кусóк, отрéзок; сегмéнт

segregate [сé-грі-гэйт] *vt.* изолировать, отделять

seize [сиз] *vt.i.* схватывать; завладеть (*take possession*)

seizure [си́-жăр] *sn.* конфискáция, захвáт; *med.* припáдок

seldom [сéл-дăм] *adv.* рéдко

select [сі-лéкт] *adj.* избранный (*picked*), отборный (*choice*); *vt.* выбирать, подбирать

selection [сі-лéк-шăн] *sn.* выбор, отбор, подбор

self [сéлф] *s.* сам; лично «я» (I); личность (*personality*); *adj.* однородный, сплошной

self- [сéлф] *prefix*, само-

self-conscious [сéлф-кóн-шăс] *adj.* застéнчивый

selfish [сéл-фіш] *adj.* эгоистичный

selfishness [сéл-фіш-ні́с] *sn.* эгоизм

self-starter [сéлф-стáр-тăр] *sn.* самопуск

sell [сел] *vt.i.* продавáть

seller [сé-лăр] *sm.* продавéц

semi- [сé-мі] *prefix*, полу-

semicolon [сé-мі-кóу-лăн] *sn.* тóчка с запятóй

semifinal [сé-мі-фáй-нăл] *sn.* предпослéдний круг

senate [сé-ніт] *sn.* сенáт; совéт

send [сенд] *vt.i.* отправлять, посылать; — **away** [-ă-уэй] прогонять; — **for** [– фôр] вызывáть

sender [сéн-дăр] *sm.* отправитель

senile [си́-найл] *adj.* старческий

senior [си́-ні-ăр] *adj.* старший

sensation [сен-сэ́й-шăн] *sn.* ощущéние, чувство (*feeling*); впечатлéние (*impression*); сенсáция (*emotional stirring*)

sensational [сен-сэ́й-шă-нăл] *adj.* сенсационный

sense [сенс] *sn.* значéние, смысл (*meaning*); сознáние (*consciousness*); ощущéние, чувство (*faculty*); рáзум (*reason*); *vt.* ощущáть; чувствовать

senseless [сéнс-ліс] *adj.* бессмысленный (*inane*); бесчувственный (*insensible*); бессознáтельный (*unconscious*)

sensible [сéн-сібл] *adj.* разýмный, рассудительный

sensitive [сéн-сі-тів] *adj.* чýткий

sensual [сéн-шў-ăл] *adj.* сладострáстный, чýвственный

sentence [сéн-тăнс] *sn. gram.* изречéние, предложéние, фрáза; *leg.* пригово́р; *vt.* осуждáть, пригова́ривать

sentiment [сéн-ти-мăнт] *sn.* проявлéние чувств; мнéние, отношéние (*opinion, attitude*)

sentimental [сɛн-ти-мéн-тăл] *adj.* сентиментáльный

sentry [сéн-три] *sn.* часово́й; *adj.* дежýрный, карáульный

sentry-box [сéн-три-бокс] *sn.* карáульная бýдка

separate [сé-пă-рĭт] *adj.* отдéльный; самостоя́тельный (*independent*); [сé-пă-рэйт] *vt.i.* отделя́ть, разделя́ть; различáться (*part*)

separation [сɛ-пă-рэ́й-шăн] *sn.* разделéние; разлýка (*parting*); *leg.* развóд

September [сɛп-тéм-бăр] *sn.* сентя́брь, *m.*

septic [сéп-тĭк] *adj.* септи́ческий

sepulchre [сé-пăл-кăр] *sn.* гро́бница, моги́ла

sequel [сí-кўăл] *sn.* послéдствие

sequence [сí-кўăнс] *sn.* послéдовательность; хронологи́ческий разря́д; поря́док

Serbian [сéр-бĭ-ăн] *sn.* серб; *adj.* сéрбский

serenade [сɛ-рĭ-нэ́йд] *sn.* серенáда; *vt.* петь серенáду

serene [сĭ-рíн] *adj.* безмятéжный, споко́йный

serenity [сĭ-рé-ни-тĭ] *sn.* безмятéжность

serf [сɛрф] *sn.* крепостнóй

serfdom [сéрф-дăм] *sn.* крепостнóе состоя́ние, рáбство

sergeant [сáр-джăнт] *sn.* сержáнт; – **major** [– мэ́й-джăр] *sn.* стáрший сержáнт; фельдфéбель

serial [сí-рĭ-ăл] *sn.* продолжáющееся издáние; *adj.* сери́йный

series [сí-рĭз] *sn.* ряд, сéрия

serious [сí-рĭ-ăс] *adj.* серьёзный

seriousness [сí-рĭ-ăс-нĭс] *sn.* серьёзность

serjeant [сáр-джăнт] *sn.* судéбный пристáв

sermon [сéр-мăн] *sn.* про́поведь

serpent [сéр-пăнт] *s.* змей; змей (*snake*)

servant [сéр-вăнт] *s, f.* прислýга, слугá; служáнка (*maid*)

serve [сɛрв] *vt.i.* прислýживать, служи́ть; подавáть (*at table, tennis, etc.*); годи́ться (*be useful*); – **up** [– ап] подáть к столý

service [сéр-вĭс] *sn.* обслýживание, слýжба, служéние (*duty*); пóмощь (*help*); услýга (*good turn*); серви́з (*set of dishes*); подáча (*tennis*)

serviceable [сéр-вĭ-сăбл] *adj.* рóдный, полéзный

serviette [сáр-вĭĕт] *sn.* салфéтка

servile [сéр-вайл] *adj.* зави́симый, прини́женный, рáбский

session [сé-шăн] *sn.* заседáние, сéссия

set [сэт] *sn.* очерта́ние (*form*); ряд, се́рия (*group*); сет (*tennis*); набо́р (*collection*); *adj.* засты́вший (*stationary*); затверде́вший (*of cement*); *vt.i.* ста́вить (*place*, *put*), застыва́ть, тверде́ть (*harden*), заходи́ть, сади́ться (*of sun*); *typ.* набира́ть; – **aside** [– а-са́йд] отстрани́ть; – **on fire** [– он фа́й-а̌р] поджига́ть; – **free** [– фри] освобожда́ть; – **a razor** [– а̌ рэ́й-за̌р] точи́ть бри́тву

set-back [сэт-бэ́к] *sn.* заде́ржка, препя́тствие

set-square [сэт-скуэ́р] *sn.* уго́льник

settee [сэ-ти́] *sn.* дива́н, канапе́, козе́тка

setting [сэ́-тиӊ] *sn.* окружа́ющая обстано́вка (*environment*); опра́ва (*of gem*); захо́д (*of sun*); *theat.* декора́ция и костю́мы; напра́вка (*of blades*, *etc.*)

settle [сэтл] *vt.i.* реша́ть (*decide*); установи́ться (*become established*) колонизи́ровать, поселя́ться (*colonize*); оседа́ть (*subside*); опла́чивать (*account*)

settlement [сэ́тл-ма̌нт] *sn.* посёлок, селе́ние (*of village*); коло́ния, поселе́ние (*colony*); устро́йство (*arrangement*)

settler [сэ́т-ла̌р] *sn.* поселе́нец

seven [сэ́-ва̌н] *num.* семь

seventeen [сэ́-ва̌н-тин] *num.* семна́дцать

seventh [сэ́-ва̌нӭ] *num.* седьмо́й

seventy [сэ́-ва̌н-ти] семьдеся́т

sever [сэ́-ва̌р] *vt.i.* отделя́ть, разъединя́ть

several [сэ́-ва̌-ра̌л] *adj.* мно́гие; отде́льный (*separate*); *pron.* не́которые, не́сколько

severe [сi-ви́р] *adj.* стро́гий (*rigorous*); суро́вый (*of sentence*, *weather*); напряжённый (*arduous*)

severity [сi-ве́-ри-ти] *sn.* стро́гость

sew [соу] *vt.i.* шить; – **on** [– он] пришива́ть; – **up** [– ап] зашива́ть

sewage [сю́-идж] *sn.* сто́чные во́ды

sewer [сю́-а̌р] *sn.* сто́чная труба́

sewerage [сю́-а̌-ридж] *sn.* систе́ма канализа́ции

sex [сэкс] *sn.* пол

sexual [сэ́кс-ю-а̌л] *adj.* полово́й, сексуа́льный

shabby [шэ́-би] *adj.* поно́шенный, потёртый

shackle [шэкл] *vt.* зако́вывать, ско́вывать; *sn. pl.* канда́лы, око́вы

shade [шэйд] *sn.* тень; отте́нок (*tint*); абажу́р (*of lamp*); *vt.i.* заслоня́ть (*from light*)

shadow [шэ́-доу] *sn.* тень; отраже́ние (*reflection*); *vt. fig.* сле́довать по пята́м

shady [шэ́й-ди] *adj.* тени́стый; *fig.* сомни́тельный (*of reputation*)

shaft [шэфт] *sn.* стрела́ (*arrow*); ды́шло (*pole*); *tech.* вал, ось; ша́хта (*mine*)

shaggy [шэ́-ги] *adj.* волоса́тый, косма́тый

shake [шэйк] *sn.* встря́ска, стрясе́ние; *mus.* трель; *vt.i.* трясти́; дрожа́ть (*tremble*); здоро́ваться (*hand*)

shaky [шэй-ки] *adj.* колеблющийся (*wavering*); ненадёжный (*unreliable*)

shallow [шэ-лоу] *sn.* мелково́дье, о́тмель; *adj.* ме́лкий; *fig.* пове́рхностный; *vt.i.* меле́ть, уменьша́ть глубину́

sham [шэм] *sn.* притво́рство; *adj.* притво́рный, фальши́вый (*counterfeit*); *vt.i.* симули́ровать (*feign*); притворя́ться (*pretend to be*)

shamble [шэмбл] *vi.* тащи́ться, ша́ркать; *sn.* pl. бо́йня

shame [шэйм] *sn.* стыд; позо́р, срам, —! сты́дно! *vt.i.* позо́рить, срами́ть, стыди́ться

shameful [шэйм-фул] *adj.* посты́дный, сканда́льный

shamrock [шэм-рок] *sn.* трили́стник (эмбле́ма Ирла́ндии)

shank [шэнк] *sn.* го́лень; сте́ржень, *m.* (*shaft*); веретено́ (*of anchor*); сте́бель (*stem*)

shape [шэйп] *sn.* вид, о́браз, фо́рма; при́зрак (*phantom*); *vt.i.* образо́вывать, придава́ть вид; формирова́ться

shapely [шэйп-ли] *adj.* стро́йный, хорошо́ сло́женный

share [шэр] *sn.* до́ля, часть (*part*); пай (*interest*); com. а́кция; леме́х, со́шник (*of plough*); *vt.i.* дели́ться, разделя́ть; участвовать (*take part*)

shareholder [шэр-хоул-дэр] *sm.* акционе́р

shark [шарк] *s.* аку́ла; *fig.* моше́нник, хи́щник, шу́лер

sharp [шарп] *sn.* mus. дие́з (♯); *adj.* о́стрый; пронизи́тельный (*piercing*); находчивый (*quick-witted*); *adv.* пунктуа́льно, то́чно; ро́вно (*of time*)

sharpen [шар-пэн] *vt.* заостря́ть, точи́ть; чини́ть (*of pencil*)

shatter [шэ-тэр] *vt.i.* разбива́ться; расшата́ть (*health, nerves*); расстра́ивать (*plans, etc.*)

shave [шэйв] *sn.* бритьё; *vt.i.* брить, бри́ться; строга́ть (*wood*)

shavings [шэй-вийз] *sn.* pl. стру́жки

shawl [шол] *sn.* шаль

she [ши] *pron.* она́

sheaf [шиф] *sn.* сноп; вяза́нка (*bundle*)

shears [шиэрз] *sn.* но́жницы

sheath [шиθ] *sn.* но́жны; футля́р (*case*); anat. обо́лочка

shed [шэд] *sn.* наве́с, сара́й; хлев (*cattle-shed*); *vt.* пролива́ть; роня́ть (*of hair*)

sheen [шин] *sn.* блеск, сия́ние

sheep [шип] *s.* бара́н (*ram*); овца́ (*ewe*)

sheep-dog [шип-дог] *s.* овча́рка

sheepskin [шип-скин] *sn.* овчина

sheer [шир] *adj.* просто́й (*mere*); абсолю́тный; безгово́рочный (*unqualified*); отве́сный (*perpendicular*)

sheet [шит] *sn.* простыня́; лист (*paper*)

shelf [шэлф] *sn.* по́лка

shell [шэл] *sn.* ра́ковина, раку́шка; скорлупа́ (*of eggs, nuts, etc.*); *mil.* грана́та, снаря́д; о́стов (*of structure*); *vt.* снима́ть скорлупу́, шелуши́ть; *mil.* бомбарди́ровать

shell-shock [шэл-шок] *sn.* конту́зия

shelter [шэл-тăр] *sn.* прию́т, убе́жище; *vt.i.* приюти́ть, укрыва́ться

shelve [шэлв] *vt.i.* ста́вить на по́лки

shepherd [шэ-пăрд] *sn.* пасту́х; *fig.* пасты́рь; *vt.* пасти́

sherry [шэ-pi] *sn.* хе́рес

shield [шилд] *sn.* щит; *vt.* заслони́ть, защища́ть

shift [шифт] *sn.* рабо́чая сме́на (*relay*); обхо́д, сре́дство (*means*); *vt.i.* меня́ть (*change*); изворо́чиваться (*manage somehow*)

shin [шин] *sn.* го́лень.

shine [шайн] *sn.* свет, сия́ние; со́лнечное сия́ние (*sunshine*); блеск (*lustre*); *vt.i.* блиста́ть, сия́ть; свети́ться

shingle [шингл] *sn.* деревя́нная черепи́ца, дра́нка (*wooden roof-tile*); га́лька, го́льш (*pebble*); *pl. med.* опоя́сывающий лиша́й

shiny [шай-ни] *adj.* блестя́щий, лосня́щийся

ship [шип] *sn.* кора́бль, парохо́д, су́дно; *vt.i.* грузи́ть (*goods*); производи́ть поса́дку (*passengers*)

shipbuilding [шип-бил-дин] *sn.* кораблестрое́ние

shipment [шип-мăнт] *sn.* торго́вый груз (*goods*); отпра́вка, погру́зка (*of goods*)

shipping [ши-пин] *sn.* торго́вый флот (*ships*); отпра

вле́ние грузо́в (*dispatch of goods*)

shipwreck [шип-рэк] *sn.* кораблекруше́ние

shipwright [шип-райт] *sm.* корабе́льный пло́тник, судострои́тель

shipyard [шип-ярд] *sn.* верфь

shirk [шăрк] *vt.i.* отлы́нивать, увиля́ть, уклоня́ться

shirker [шăр-кăр] *sm.* прогу́льщик

shirt [шăрт] *sn.* руба́шка

shiver [ши-вăр] *sn.* обло́мок, оско́лок (*splinter*); дрожь; тре́пет (*momentary shivering*); *vi.* дрожа́ть, трясти́сь

shoal [шоул] *sn.* руно́, стя́я (*of fish*); мель, песча́ная о́тмель (*shallow place, submerged sandbank*); *vi.* меле́ть

shock [шок] *sn.* копна́ (*cornsheaves*); копна́ воло́с (*of hair*); потрясе́ние, шок (*impact*); *vt.* возмуща́ть, шоки́ровать

shocking [шо́-кин] *adj.* возмути́тельный, сканда́льный, шоки́рующий; *adv.* ужа́сно!

shoe [шу] *sn.* башма́к, боти́нок, ту́фля; *vt.* подко́вывать

shoelace [шу-лэйс] *sn.* шнуро́к для боти́нок

shoemaker [шу-мэй-кăр] *sm.* сапо́жник

shoot [шут] *sn. bot.* побе́г, росто́к; вы́стрел (*report, shot*); *vt.i.* промелькну́ть (*go swiftly*); расстреля́ть, стреля́ть (*fire*); дёргать (*of pain*); прораста́ть (*of plant*)

shooting [шý-тін] *sn.* охóта

shop [шоп] *sn.* лáвка, магазúн; мастерскáя (*workshop*); *vt.i.* дéлать покýпки, покупáть

shop-assistant [шóп-ă-сúстăнт] *sm.* продавéц

shopkeeper [шóп-ки-пăр] *sm.* лавóчник

shop-window [шóп-ỹін-доỹ] *sn.* витрúна

shore [шôр] *sn.* бéрег, примóрье

short [шôрт] *adj.* корóткий, крáткий; нúзкого рóста (*stature*); недостáточный (*insufficient*); рассы́пчатый (*of pastry*); запыхáвшийся (*of breath*); *sn. pl.* трýсики

shortage [шôр-тідж] *sn.* недостáток, нехвáтка

shorten [шôр-тăн] *v.t.* сокращáть, укорáчивать

shorthand [шôрт-хæнд] *sn.* стеногрáфия

shortly [шôрт-лі] *adj.* вскóре (*briefly*); незадóлго (*soon*); вкрáтце (*in short*)

short-sighted [шôрт-сáйтід] *adj.* близорýкий; *fig.* недальновúдный

shot [шот] *sn.* вы́стрел; пýля (*bullet*); дробúнка (*pellet*)

shoulder [шôул-дăр] *sn.* плечó; лопáтка (*of meat*); *vt.i.* брать на плéчи, взвáливать на плéчи (*hoist on to*); – arms! [– áрмз] на плечó!

shoulder-blade [шóул-дăр-блéйд] *sn.* плечевáя кость, лопáтка

shout [шáут] *sn.* крик; *vt.i.* кричáть

shovel [шá-вăл] *sn.* лопáта,

show [шоỹ] *sn.* вы́ставка (*exhibition*); внéшний вид (*outward appearance*); *vt.i.* покáзывать; появля́ться (*appear*); проводúть (*conduct*)

shower [шáỹ-ăр] *sn.* лúвень

showery [шáỹ-ă-рі] *adj.* дождлúвый

shrapnel [шрǽп-нăл] *sn.* шрапнéль

shred [шред] *sn.* лоскутóк, клочóк, обрéзок; *vt.i.* кромсáть, раздёргивать

shrew [шрý] *s.* землерóйка; *sf.* сварлúвая жéнщина (*woman*)

shrewd [шрýд] *adj.* проницáтельный (*penetrating*); хúтрый (*astute*)

shriek [шрик] *sn.* визг, крик; *vt.i.* визжáть, кричáть

shrill [шріл] *adj.* пронзúтельный, рéзкий

shrimp [шрімп] *s.* кревéтка

shrine [шрайн] *sn.* рáка, храм

shrink [шрінк] *vt.i.* сжимáть (*contract*); садúться (*of material*); сокращáться (*shorten*)

shrinkage [шрінк-ідж] *sn.* сжáтие, сокращéние

shrivel [шрí-вăл] *vi.* съёживаться

shroud [шрáуд] *sn.* пелена́, покрóв, сáван; *vt.* скрывáть *conceal*

shrub [шраб] *sn.* куст, кустáрник

shrug [шраг] *sn.* пожимáние плечáми; *vi.* пожимáть плечáми

shudder [шá-дăр] *sn.* содрогáние; *vi.* содрогáться

shuffle [шафл] *sn.* шáркающая похóдка (*gait*); тасóвка (*of cards*); *vt.i.* волочи́ть (*of feet*); тасовáть (*cards*)

shun [шан] *vt.* избегáть, остерегáться

shunt [шант] *sn.* замéна; *rail.* перевóд; *vt.i.* переводи́ть; *fig.* откла́дывать

shut [шат] *vt.i.* закрывáть, затворя́ть; **— up** [— ап] заключáть; *coll.* замолчáть

shutter [ша́-тăр] *sn.* стáвень, *m.*

shuttle [шатл] *sn.* челнóк

shy [шай] *adj.* застéнчивый, рóбкий; пугли́вый (*of animal*); *vi.* бросáться в стóрону (*of horse*); швыря́ть (*throw*)

sick [сік] *adj.* больнóй (*ill*); чýвствующий тошнотý (*disposed to vomit*); **be —** [би — ов] пресыщáться

sickle [сікл] *sn.* серп

sickly [сі́к-лі] *adj.* болéзненный (*ill*); тошнотвóрный

sickness [сі́к-ніс] *sn.* болéзнь (*illness*); тошнотá

side [сайд] *sn.* сторонá; бок (*flank*); **— by —** [— бай —] ря́дом; **take —s** [тэйк -з] примкнýть; *adj.* боковóй

sideboard [сайд-бóрд] *sn.* буфéт

sideways [сайд-уэйз] *adv.* бóком, кóсвенно

siding [сай-ді́н] *sn.* запаснóй путь, разъéзд

siege [сідж] *sn.* осáда

sieve [сів] *sn.* решетó, си́то; *vt.* просéивать

sift [сіфт] *vt.* просéивать; тщáтельно рассмáтривать (*scrutinize*); *vi.* посыпáть

sigh [сай] *sn.* вздох; *vt.i.*

вздыхáть; тосковáть (*yearn*)

sight [сайт] *sn.* зрéние (*faculty of vision*); зрéлище (*spectacle*); взгляд (*look*); вид (*view*); пóле зрéния (*range of vision*); прицéл (*of weapon*); **at first —** [æт фёрст —] с пéрвого взгля́да; **in —** [ін —] на видý; **long —** [лон —] дальнозóркость; **short —** [шóрт —] близорýкость; *vt.i.* наблюдáть (*observe*); наводи́ть (*adjust*)

sightseeing [сáйт-си-ін] *sn.* осмáтривание

sign [сайн] *sn.* знак (*mark*); при́знак (*indication*); си́мвол (*symbol*); *vt.i.* отмечáть, стáвить знак (*mark*); подпи́сываться (*affix name*)

signal [сíг-нăл] *sn.* сигнáл; *adj.* сигнáльный; *vt.i.* сигнализи́ровать

signalman [сíг-нăл-мăн] *sn.* сигнáльщик

signatory [сíг-нă-тă-рі] *sn.* сторонá подписáвшая соглашéние; *adj.* подписáвший (догово́р)

signature [сíг-нă-чăр] *sn.* пóдпись, *f.*; *mus.* означéние тонáльности; *typ.* сигнатýра

signboard [сáйн-бóрд] *sn.* вывеска

significance [сіг-ні́-фі-кăнс] *sn.* вáжность, многознáчительность

significant [сіг-ні́-фі-кăнт] *adj.* вáжный, сущéственный

signify [сíг-ні-фай] *vt.i.* знáчить, означáть; предвещáть (*intimate*); сообщáть (*inform*)

signpost [сáйн-пóуст] *sn.* указáтельный столб

silence [сáй-лăнс] *sn.* молчáние; безмóлвие; тишинá (*stillness*); забвéние (*oblivion*); *vt.* заглушáть (*stifle*); замолкáть

silencer [сáй-лăн-сăр] *sn. tech.* глушитель

silent [сáй-лăнт] *adj.* безмóлвный, молчаливый

silk [сілк] *sn.* шёлк; шёлковая матéрия

silken [сíл-кăн] *adj.* шёлковый; мягкий (*soft*)

silky [сíл-кі] *adj.* шелковистый

sill [сіл] *sn.* подокóнник; порóг (*of door*)

silly [сí-лі] *adj.* глýпый

silo [сáй-лоў] *sn.* силос

silt [сілт] *sn.* ил, осáдок

silver [сíл-вăр] *sn.* серебрó; серебряные дéньги (*money*); серéбряная ýтварь (*implements*); *adj.* серéбристый, серéбряный; *vt.i.* серебрить

silversmith [сíл-вăр-сміѳ] *sm.* серéбряных дел мáстер

silverware [сíл-вăр-ўăр] *sn.* серéбряные издéлия

silvery [сíл-вă-рі] *adj.* серéбристый

similar [сí-мі-лăр] *adj.* подóбный, похóжий, схóдный

similarity [сі-мі-лǽ-рі-ті] *sn.* подóбие, схóдство

simmer [сí-мăр] *vt.i.* булькáть, закипáть

simper [сíм-пăр] *vt.i.* глýпо улыбáться

simple [сімпл] *adj.* простóй

simpleton [сíм-пăл-тăн] *sm.* простáк

simplicity [сім-плí-сі-ті] *sn.* простотá, простодýшие

simplify [сíм-плі-фай] *vt.* упрощáть

simulate [сí-мю-лэйт] *vt.* притворяться, симулировать

simultaneous [сі-мăл-тóй-ні-ăс] *adj.* одновремéнный

sin [сін] *sn.* грех; *vi.* согрешáть

since [сінс] *adv.* давнó, с тех пор; *prep.* пóсле, с, со; *conj.* поскóльку, так как

sincere [сін-сíр] *adj.* искренний, чистосердéчный

sincerity [сін-сé-рі-ті] *sn.* искренность

sinew [сí-ню] *sn.* сухожилие; *pl.* мускулатýра; *fig.* двигáтельная сила (*motive power*); **-y** [-і] *adj.* жилистый

sinful [сін-фўл] *adj.* грéшный

sing [сіӈ] *vt.i.* петь, распевáть

singe [сіндж] *vt.i.* обжигáть, опалять, спалить

singer [сíӈ-ăр] *sm.* певéц

singing [сíӈ-іӈ] *sn.* пéние

single [сіӈгл] *adj.* единственный, один (*sole*); холостóй (*unmarried*); отдéльный (*as room, bed, etc.*); одинóкий (*solitary*); *vt.* выбирáть, отбирáть

singly [сíӈ-лі] *adv.* в отдéльности, поодинóчке

singular [сíӈ-гю-лăр] *adj.* необычáйный, стрáнный (*unusual*); *gram.* единственный

sinister [сí-ніс-тăр] *adj.* зловéщий, сквéрный

sink [сіӈк] *sn.* рáковина; *vt.i.* потонýть (*drown*) — погружáться (*immerse*) — in silence, *etc.*); опускáться (*disappear below horizon*); оседáть (*of structure*); рыть (*of well*)

sinking [сі́н-кің] *sn.* погру-
же́ние; вне́запная сла́бость
(*collapse, weakness*)

sinner [сі́н-ар] *sm.* гре́шник

sip [сіп] *sn.* глото́к; *vt.i.*
подтя́гивать, пить ме́лкими
глотка́ми

sir [сœр] *sm.* господи́н, сэр,
су́дарь

sire [са́й-ар] *sm. poet.* оте́ц,
пре́док; саме́ц (*of animals*)

sirloin [сœр-ло́йн] *sn.* филе́й

sister [сі́с-тар] *sf.* сестра́

sister-in-law [сі́с-тар-ін-
ло́] *sf.* неве́стка (*brother's
wife*); золо́вка (*husband's
sister*); своя́ченица (*wife's
sister*)

sit [сіт] *vi.* сиде́ть; заседа́ть
(*be in session*); – **down** [–
да́ун] сади́ться; – **out** [–
а́ут] не уча́ствовать (*as at
a dance, etc.*); – **up** [– ап]
заси́живаться

site [сайт] *sn.* местоположе́-
ние, уча́сток

sitter [сі́-тар] *sm.* нату́р-
щик; *sf.* нату́рщица

sitting [сі́-тің] *sn.* сиде́ние;
заседа́ние (*session*)

sitting-room [сі́-тің-ру́м]
sn. гости́ная

situate [сі́-тю-эйт] *vt.*
размеща́ть, распологáть

situated [сі́-тю-эй-тід] *adj.*
располо́женный

situation [сі-тю-э́й-шан] *sn.*
до́лжность, ме́сто (*post*);
расположе́ние (*location*);
положе́ние (*circumstance*)

six [сікс] *num.* шесть

sixteen [сíкс-тин] *num.*
шестна́дцать

sixth [сіксф] *num.* шесто́й

sixty [сíкс-ті] *num.* шесть-
деся́т

size [сайз] *sn.* ме́ра, объём,
разме́р (*dimension*); фор-
ма́т (*of book*); клей (*paste*);
vt. прокле́ивать (*glaze*)

sizzle [сізл] *sn.* шипе́ние; *vi.*
шипе́ть

skate [скэйт] *s.* скат (*fish*);
конёк (*for skating*); *vi.* ка-
та́ться

skater [скэ́й-тар] *sm.* конь-
кобе́жец

skating [скэ́й-тің] *sn.* ка-
та́нье

skating-rink [скэ́й-тің-
рі́нк] *sn.* като́к

skein [скэйн] *sn.* мото́к,
та́лька

skeleton [скé-лі-тăн] *sn.*
скеле́т; – **key** [– ки] отмы́ч-
ка

sketch [скеч] *sn.* набро́сок,
эски́з (*rough outline*); о́черк
(*essay*); рису́нок (*drawing*);
vt.i. де́лать набро́сок, на-
бра́сывать, черти́ть

sketchy [скé-чі] *adj.* эски́з-
ный

skewer [скю́-ар] *sn.* ве́ртел

ski [ши] *sn.* лы́жа; *vi.*
ходи́ть на лы́жах

skid [скід] *sn.* тормозно́й
башма́к (*brake*); скольже́-
ние колёс (*skidding of
wheels*); *vi.* скользи́ть (*of
wheels*)

skier [ши-ар] *sm.* лы́жник

skilful [скіл-фу́л] *adj.*
иску́сный, уме́лый

skill [скіл] *sn.* ло́вкость,
мастерство́, уме́нье

skim [скім] *vt.i.* снима́ть
(*take off*); скользи́ть по
пове́рхности (*glide over*)

skimp [скімп] *vt.i.* ску́дно
снабжа́ть; скаре́дничать (*be
parsimonious*)

skin [скін] *sn.* кóжа, шкýра; шелухá, кóжица (*peel, rind*); *vt.* сдирáть (кóжу и т.д.).

skinny [скі-ні] *adj.* худóй

skip [скіп] *sn.* прыжóк, скачóк; подпрыгивание (*skipping motion*); *vi.* прыгать, скакáть; перескáкивать (*in conversation*)

skipper [скі-пăр] *sm.* шкúпер

skipping-rope [скі-пíн-роўп] *sn.* скакáлка

skirmish [скǒр-міш] *sn.* стычка, схвáтка; *vi.* сражáться

skirt [скǒрт] *sn.* юбка; полá (*of dress*); край, окрáина (*edge, border*); *vt.i.* иттú вдоль (бéрега и т.д.) (*go along edge*); граничить (*border on*)

skittle [скітл] *sn.* кéгля

skulk [скалк] *vi.* прятаться, скрывáться; крáсться (*move stealthily*)

skull [скал] *sn.* чéреп; **thick –** [ѳік –] *fig.* тяжелодýм

skunk [сканк] *s.* воню́чка, скунс; скунсóвый мех (*skin*)

sky [скай] *sn.* нéбо, небесá (*heaven*)

sky-blue [скай-блю] *sn.* лазýрь; *adj.* лазýрный

sky-lark [скай-лăрк] *s.* жáворонок

skylight [скай-лайт] *sn.* свéтовой люк, фóрточка

skyline [скай-лайн] *sn.* очертáния горизóнта

sky-scraper [скай-скрéйпăр] *sn.* небоскрёб

slab [слæб] *sn.* горбыль (*in building*); ломóть (*of bread*); плитá (*of stone, etc.*)

slack [слæк] *sn.* ýгольная пыль (*of coal*); *adj.* ненатя́нутый (*loose*); расхля́банный (*lax*); медлительный (*slow*); *vt.i.* лоды́рничать, распускáться

slacken [слé-кăн] *vt.* ослабля́ть (*relax*)

slam [слæм] *sn.* шлем (*in card-games*) хлóпанье (*of doors*); *vt.i.* хлóпать

slander [слăн-дăр] *sn.* злослóвие, клеветá; *vt.* клеветáть, сплéтничать

slanderous [слăн-дă-рăс] *adj.* клеветнический

slang [слæн] *sn.* жаргóн, сленг

slant [слăнт] *sn.* уклóн; **on the –** [он ѳă –] вкось; *vt.i.* иттú в кось, имéть наклóн

slanting [слăн-тій] *adj.* косóй, наклóнный

slap [слæп] *sn.* шлепóк; пощёчина (*on cheek*); *vt.* шлёпать

slash [слæш] *sn.* разрéз (*cut*); рéзкий удáр (*slashing stroke*); *vt.i.* рубúть (*with sword*); дéлать разрéзы (*make cuts*); хлестáть (*whip*)

slat [слæт] *sn.* переклáдина, плáнка

slate [слэйт] *sn.* слáнец, шúфер; грúфельная доскá (*for writing on*); *vt.* крыть плúтами (*roof*); дéлать вы́говор (*reprimand*); рéзко критиковáть (*severely criticize*)

slate-pencil [слэйт-пéнсіл] *sn.* грúфель

slaughter [слó-тăр] *sn.* убóй (*of animals*); резня́ (*slaying*); кровопролúтие (*bloodshed*); *vt.* зарéзывать; убивáть (*kill*)

slaughter-house [слó-тăр-хăус] *sn.* бóйня

Slav [слăв] *sm.* славяни́н; *adj.* славя́нский

slave [слэйв] *sm.* невóльник, раб; *vi.* рабóтать как раб

slavery [слэ́й-вă-рĭ] *sn.* рáбство

slavish [слэ́й-вĭш] *adj.* рáбский

Slavonic [слă-вó-нĭк] *adj.* славя́нский

slay [слэй] *vt.* убивáть

sled [след] *sn.* сáни; салáзки (*toboggan*)

sledge [следж] *sn.* сáни; кузнéчный мóлот (*hammer*)

sleek [слик] *adj.* глáдкий и мя́гкий, лосня́щийся (*of hair, skin*); ухóженный, хóленый (*well-fed, well-groomed*)

sleep [слип] *sn.* сон, спя́чка; **go to** – [гóу ту] – засыпáть; *vi.* заснýть, спать

sleeper [сли-пăр] *sm.* спя́щий (человéк); *sm.* шпáла

sleeping [сли-пĭн] *adj.* спáльный; – **draught** – [дрáфт] снотвóрное срéдство

sleepless [слип-лĭс] *adj.* бессóнный

sleepy [сли-пĭ] *adj.* сонли́вый, сóнный

sleet [слит] *sn.* мóкрый снег, снег с дождём

sleeve [слив] *sn.* рукáв; *tech.* втýлка

sleigh [слэй] *sn.* сáни

sleight [слайт] *sn.* провóрство; – **of hand** [– ов хăнд] жонглёрство

slender [слéн-дăр] *adj.* стрóйный, тóнкий; скýдный (*meagre, scanty*)

slice [слайс] *sn.* лóмтик (*piece*); часть (*share*); *vt.i.* рéзать лóмтиками

slide [слайд] *sn.* скольжéние (*act of sliding*); катóк (*track for sliding on*); диапозити́в (*for lantern*); *vt.i.* катáться, скользи́ть

sliding [слáй-дĭн] *adj.* скóльзящий

slight [слайт] *sn.* неуважéние, пренебрежéние (*disrespect, disregard*); *adj.* лёгкий, непрóчный, хрýпкий, незначи́тельный (*insignificant*); *vt.* пренебрегáть (*disregard*)

slim [слим] *adj.* изя́щный, стрóйный

slime [слайм] *sn.* грязь, ил

slimy [слáй-мĭ] *adj.* болоти́стый, сли́зистый

sling [слин] *sn.* прáща; ремéнь, *m.* (*leather strap*); перевя́зь (*support*); *vt.i.* метáть, швыря́ть

slink [слинк] *vi.* идти́ крáдучись, крáсться

slip [слип] *sn.* ýзкая полóса (*of paper, etc.*); *typ.* грáнка; оши́бка, промáх (*casual error*); скольжéние (*act of slipping*); ли́фчик (*underbodice*); нáволочка (*pillowcase*); *vt.i.* поскользнýться, скользи́ть (*skid*); случáйно ошибáться (*make casual mistake*)

slipper [сли-пăр] *sn.* кóмнатная тýфля

slippery [сли-пă-рĭ] *adj.* скóльзкий

slipshod [слип-шод] *adj.* неряшли́вый

slipway [слип-ýэй] *sn.* покáтый спуск

slit [сліт] *sn.* продо́льный разре́з (*cut*); щель (*aperture*); *vt.* раска́лывать, расщепля́ть

slog [слог] *sn.* си́льный уда́р наудачу (*hit*); *vt.i.* уда́рить кулако́м (*hit*); упо́рно рабо́тать (*work*)

slogan [сло́у-ґăн] *sn.* деви́з, ло́зунг

sloop [слӯп] *sn.* одноома́чтовое су́дно, шлюп

slop [слоп] *vt.i.* пролива́ть, распле́скать; *sn. pl.* помо́и; жи́дкая пи́ща (*food*)

slope [слоуп] *sn.* накло́н, отко́с; *vt.i.* опуска́ться; – **arms!** – а́рмз] ружьё на плечо́!

slop-pail [слоп-пэйл] *sn.* помо́йное ведро́

slot [слот] *sn.* проре́з; отве́рстие (в автома́те); оле́ний след (*track*)

slothful [сло́уθ-фǔл] *adj.* беспе́чный, лени́вый

slot-machine [слот-мăши́н] *sn.* автома́т

slouch [слауч] *sn.* суту́лость, тяжёлая по́ступь; неуклю́жесть (*clumsiness*); опу́щенные поля́ (*of hat*); *vt.i.* свиса́ть, суту́литься

slovenly [сла́-вăн-лі] *adj.* неря́шливый

slow [слоу] *adj.* ме́дленный; отстаю́щий (*of watch*)

sludge [сладж] *sn.* густа́я грязь

slug [слаг] *s.* слизня́к (*snail*); самоде́льная ружёйная пу́ля (*bullet*); *тур.* ли́ния шрифта́

sluggish [сла́-ґіш] *adj.* вя́лый

sluice [слӯс] *sn.* кана́л,

шлюз; *vt.i.* залива́ть, ороша́ть

slum [слам] *sn.* трущо́ба

slumber [слăм-бăр] *sn.* забытьё, дремо́та; *vi.* дрема́ть, спать

slump [сламп] *sn.* внеза́пное ре́зкое паде́ние цен; паде́ние спро́са на това́р

slur [слёр] *sn.* пятно́ на репута́ции (*stigma*); прогла́тывание зву́ков (*in pronunciation*); *mus.* знак лега́то (⌢)

slush [слаш] *sn.* та́лый снег (*snow*), грязь, сля́коть (*mud*)

slushy [сла́-ші] *adj.* сля́котный

slut [слат] *sf.* неря́ха

sly [слай] *adj.* лука́вый, проны́рливый; **on the –** [он ей –] тайко́м

smack [смăк] *sn.* вкус, при́вкус (*taste*); при́месь (*spice or dash of something*); смак, рыболо́вное су́дно (*fishing boat*); звук уда́ра (*sound*); шлепо́к (*slap*); *vt.i.* шлёпать (*slap*); щёлкать (*with whip*); чмо́кать (*make noise with lips*)

small [смол] *adj.* ма́ленький, ма́лый; скупо́й (*mean*); – **hours** [– а́ў-ăрз] по́сле полу́ночи

small-arms [смол-а́рмз] *sn. pl.* ручно́е стрелко́вое ору́жие

small-pox [смол-покс] *sn.* о́спа

smart [смăрт] *sn.* жгу́чая боль (*stinging pain*); *adj.* наря́дный, шика́рный (*spruce*); находчивый, остроу́мный (*dexterous, quickwitted*); расторо́пный (*effi-*

cient, prompt); о́стрый, ре́зкий (*sharp*); *vi.* чу́вствовать о́струю боль

smartness [смáрт-нíс] *sn.* бо́йкость; нара́дность

smash [смэш] *sn.* битьё crockery, *etc.*); разгро́м (*destruction*); разло́м (*break, fracture*); разоре́ние (*ruin*); *vt.i.* лома́ть, разбива́ть

smattering [смǽ-тǎ-риǎ] *sn.* пове́рхностное зна́ние

smear [сми́р] *sn.* пятно́; *vt.* запа́чкать, ма́зать

smell [смэл] *sn.* нюх, обоня́ние (*sense*); за́пах (*aroma*); вонь (*stench*); *vt.i.* ню́хать, обоня́ть; па́хнуть, воня́ть; **— a rat** [— ǎ рэт] подозрева́ть недо́брое

smelt [смэлт] *vt.* пла́вить

smile [смайл] *sn.* улы́бка; *vi.* улыба́ться

smirch [смǒрч] *vt.* па́чкать

smite [смайт] *vt.i.* срази́ть

smith [смиθ] *sn.* кузне́ц

smithereens [сми́-ǎ-ри́нз] *sn. pl.* ме́лкие обло́мки, черепки́; **smash into —** [смэш ин-тý —] разбива́ть вдре́безги

smithy [сми́-ǒи] *sn.* кузни́ца

smoke [смо́ук] *sn.* дым; *vt.i.* дыми́ться; копти́ть (*of lamp*); кури́ть (*cigarette, etc.*)

smoker [смо́у-кǎр] *sn.* куря́щий, кури́льщик; отделе́ние для куря́щих (*compartment*)

smoke-screen [смо́ук-скри́н] *sn.* дымова́я заве́са

smoking-room [смо́у-киǎрýм] *sn.* кури́лка

smoky [смо́у-ки] *adj.* дымово́й, дымя́щий; закопчённый (*of lamp, chimney*)

smooth [смýǒ] *adj.* гла́дкий, ро́вный; споко́йный (*of sea*); благополу́чный (*of voyage*); *vt.* де́лать гла́дким; сгла́живать

smoothness [смýǒ-нíс] *sn.* гла́дкость, ро́вность

smother [смá-ǒǎр] *vt.* души́ть; подавля́ть, уде́рживать (*suppress*); притуши́ть (*of fire*)

smoulder [смо́ул-дǎр] *sn.* тле́ющий ого́нь; *vt.i.* тлеть

smudge [смадж] *sn.* гря́зное пятно́; *vt.i.* ста́вить кля́ксу (*blot*); па́чкать (*soil*); запа́чкаться

smug [смаг] *adj.* самодово́льный

smuggle [смагл] *vt.i.* занима́ться контраба́ндой

smut [смат] *sn.* са́жа; непристо́йности (*obscene talk*)

snack [снэк] *sn.* лёгкая заку́ска

snag [снэг] *sn.* вы́ступ (*stump*); *fig.* препя́тствие

snail [снэйл] *s.* ули́тка; *tech.* спира́ль

snake [снэйк] *s.* змея́

snap [снэп] *sn.* щёлканье (*with fingers or whip*); защёлка (*spring fastening*); внеза́пный хо́лод (*of cold weather*); *vt.i.* щёлкать; ца́пать (*snatch*); де́лать сни́мки (*take photograph*)

snapshot [снэ́п-шот] *sn.* момента́льный сни́мок

snare [снэ́р] *sn.* лову́шка, сило́к

snarl [снарл] *sn.* ворча́нье, рыча́ние; *vt.i.* огрыза́ться, рыча́ть

snatch [снэч] *sn.* хвата́нье; *vt.i.* вы́рвать, хвата́ться

snatchy [снё́-чі] *adj.* отры́-
вистый

sneak [сник] *sn.* доно́счик
(*telltale*); ни́зкий челове́к
(*low person*); *vi.* кра́сться

sneaking [сни́-кің] *adj.* ра-
боле́пный

sneer [снир] *sn.* насме́шка,
усме́шка; *vt.i.* высме́ивать,
насмеха́ться

sneeze [сниз] *sn.* чиха́нье;
vi. чиха́ть

sniff [сниф] *sn.* фы́рканье;
vt.i. втя́гивать во́здух (*draw
in air*); фы́ркать (*snort*)

snigger [сні-ға́р] *sn.* хихи́-
канье; *vi.* хихи́кать

snip [сніп] *sn.* отре́з; *vt.*
ре́зать но́жницами

snipe [снайп] *s.* бека́с; *vt.i.*
стреля́ть бека́сов (*go snipe
shooting*); *mil.* стреля́ть из-
под прикры́тия

sniper [снай-пӑр] *sn.* ме́т-
кий стрело́к, снайпер

snivel [сні-вӑл] *vi.* пла́-
каться, хны́кать

snob [сноб] *sn.* сноб

snore [снӧр] *sn.* храп, хра-
пе́ние; *vi.* храпе́ть

snort [снӧрт] *sn.* пыхте́ние;
vi. пыхте́ть

snout [снаут] *sn.* мо́рда,
ры́ло; *tech.* ду́льце, сопло́

snow [сноу] *sn.* снег; белизна́
(*white substance*); *vi.*
покры́ть сне́гом; **it -s** [ит
-з] идёт снег

snowball [сно́у-бо̄л] *sn.* снежо́к

snowbound [сно́у-баунд]
adj. заснежённый

snowdrift [сно́у-дріфт] *sn.*
сне́жный сугро́б

snowdrop [сно́у-дроп] *sn.*
подсне́жник

snowfall [сно́у-фо̄л] *sn.* сне-
гопа́д

snowflake [сно́у-флэ́йк] *sn.*
снежи́нка

snowplough [сно́у-плау] *sn.*
снегоочисти́тель, *m.*

snowstorm [сно́у-сто́рм]
sn. мете́ль

snub [снаб] *sn.* вы́говор; *vt.*
очи́тывать, пробира́ть; *adj.*
курно́сый (*of nose*)

snuff [снаф] *sn.* нага́р на
свече́ (*of candle*); поню́шка
(*powdered tobacco*); *vi.* ню́-
хать таба́к (*take snuff*)

snuff-box [сна́ф-бокс] *sn.*
таба́керка

snug [снаг] *adj.* ую́тный

snuggle [снагл] *vt.i.* при-
жа́ться, приюти́ться

so [соу] *adv.* так, так же,
таки́м о́бразом; *interj.* так;
pron. то, это

soak [соук] *sn.* промока́ние;
vt.i. выма́чивать, промя́чи-
вать; проса́чиваться (*into,
through*)

soap [соуп] *sn.* мы́ло; *vt.i.*
мы́лить, намы́ливать

soap-suds [со́уп-садз] *sn.
pl.* мы́льная пе́на, обмы́лки

soapy [со́у-пі] *adj.* мы́льный

soar [со̄р] *vi.* вспа́рхивать,
пари́ть; поднима́ться ввысь

sob [соб] *sn.* всхли́пывание,
рыда́ние; *vi.* рыда́ть

sober [со́у-бӑр] *adj.* тре́з-
вый; здравомы́сленный
(*sane*); уме́ренный (*moderate*); *vt.i.* вытрезви́ть

sobriety [со-бра́й-ӑ-ті] *sn.*
тре́звость; уме́ренность
(*moderation*)

sociable [со́у-шӑбл] *adj.*
общи́тельный; дру́жеский
(*friendly*)

social [со́у-шəл] *sn.* ве́чер, вечери́нка, собра́ние; *adj.* обще́ственный, социа́льный

socialism [со́у-шə-ли́зм] *sn.* социали́зм

socialization [со́у-шə-лай-зэ́й-шəн] *sn.* обобществле́ние, социализа́ция

society [сə-са́й-ə-ти] *sn.* о́бщество; све́тское о́бщество (,,свет") (*upper classes*)

sock [сок] *sn.* носо́к; стелька (*in shoe*)

socket [со́-кит] *sn.* впа́дина, углубле́ние; *electr.* патро́н

sodden [со́-дəн] *adj.* намо́ченный, пропи́танный; сыро́й (*of bread*)

sofa [со́у-фə] *sn.* дива́н

soft [софт] *adj.* мя́гкий; не́жный (*gentle*); ти́хий (*of sound*); глупова́тый (*silly*); безалкого́льный (*of drinks*)

soften [со-фəн] *vt.i.* смягча́ть

soil [сойл] *sn.* земля́, по́чва; грязно́е пятно́ (*dirty mark*) *vt.i.* грязни́ть; па́чкаться

sojourn [сə-джёрн] *sn.* вре́менное пребыва́ние; *vi.* вре́менно гости́ть, пребыва́ть

solace [со́-лəс] *sn.* утеше́ние; *vt.* облегча́ть, утеша́ть

solar [со́-лəр] *adj.* со́лнечный

solder [со́л-дəр] *sn.* спа́йка; *vt.* пая́ть, спа́ивать

soldier [со́л-джəр] *sm.* солда́т

sole [со́ул] *sn.* подо́шва, подмётка; соль (*fish*); *adj.* еди́нственный, оди́н; исключи́тельный (*exclusive*)

solemn [со́-лəм] *adj.* торже́ственный

solemnity [со-лём-ни-ти] *sn.* торже́ственность

solicit [сə-ли́-сит] *vt.* проси́ть, хода́тайствовать

solicitation [сə-ли-си-тэ́й-шəн] *sn.* про́сьба, хода́тайство

solicitor [сə-ли́-си-тəр] *sm.* адвока́т; хода́тай (*intercessor*)

solicitous [сə-ли́-си-тəс] *adj.* забо́тливый, озабо́ченный

solicitude [сə-ли́-си-тюд] *sn.* забо́тливость

solid [со́-лид] *sn.* твёрдое те́ло; геометри́ческое те́ло; *adj.* твёрдый; кре́пкий (*firm*); про́чный (*durable*); соли́дный

solidarity [со-ли-дə́-ри-ти] *sn.* солида́рность

solidity [со-ли́-ди-ти] *sn.* про́чность, твёрдость

soliloquy [сə-ли́-лə-кўи] *sn.* моноло́г; разгово́р с сами́м собо́й

solitary [со́-ли-тə-ри] *adj.* одино́кий, уединённый

solitude [со́-ли-тюд] *sn.* одино́чество, уедине́ние

solo [со́у-лоу] *sn.* *mus.* со́ло

soloist [со́у-лоу-ист] *sm.* соли́ст

soluble [со́-любл] *adj.* раствори́мый; разреши́мый (*solvable*)

solution [сə-лю́-шəн] *sn.* реше́ние, разреше́ние (*of problem*); *chem.* раство́р, растворе́ние

solve [солв] *vt.* разреша́ть, реша́ть

solvent [со́л-вəнт] *adj.* растворя́ющий; платёжеспосо́бный

sombre [сомбр] *adj.* мра́чный, тёмный

some [сам] *adj.* нéкий, нéкоторый, какóй-нибудь (*certain*); немнóго (*little*); нéсколько (*a few*); óколо (*about*); *pron.* кóе-кто

somebody [сáм-бо-дi] *s.* ктó-нибудь, ктó-то, нéкто

somehow [сáм-ʜау] *adv.* кáк-нибудь, кáк-то

someone [сáм-уан] *pron.* ктó-нибудь

somersault [сá-мäр-сôлт] *sn.* кувыркáнье

something [сáм-ѳiй] *sn.* нéчто, чтó-нибудь

sometime [сáм-тайм] *adj.* бывший, прéжний; *adv.* когдá-то; прéжде; **-s** [-з] *adv.* иногдá, по временáм

somewhere [сáм-уэр] *adv.* гдé-либо, в другóм мéсте

somnolent [сóм-нä-лäнт] *adj.* дрéмлющий, сонлúвый

son [сан] *sm.* сын

song [сон] *sn.* пéсня

songster [сóн̆-стäр] *s.* певýн; *s.* пéвчая птúца (*bird*)

son-in-law [сáн-iн-лô] *sm.* зять

sonnet [сó-нiт] *sn.* сонéт

sonority [сä-нó-рi-тi] *sn.* звýчность, звýчность

sonorous [сä-нó-рäс] *adj.* звýчный; сонóрный

soon [сýн] *adv.* вскóре, вскóром врéмени; рáно (*early*); **as – as** [аз – аз] как тóлько

soot [сýт] *sn.* сáжа

soothe [суз] *vt.* успокáивать, утишáть; облегчáть (*pain*)

soothsayer [сýе-сай-ăр] *sm.* предскáзатель

sooty [сý-тi] *adj.* покрытый кóпотью

sop [соп] *sn.* обмóкнутый кусóчек хлéба

sophisticated [со-фíс-тi-кей-тiд] *adj.* извращéнный, лишéнный простотьı

soppy [сó-пi] *adj.* промóкший

sorcerer [сóр-сä-рäр] *sm.* колдýн

sorcery [сóр-сä-рi] *sn.* волшéбство, колдовствó

sordid [сóр-дiд] *adj.* запýщенный, убóгий (*squalid, mean*); корыстный (*mercenary*)

sore [сôр] *sn.* болячка, я́зва; *adj.* воспалéнный (*of throat, eyes*); болéзненный (*painful*)

sorrel [сó-рäл] *sn.* *bot.* щавéль

sorrow [сó-роу] *sn.* гóре, печáль, скорбь; *vi.* горевáть, скорбéть

sorrowful [сó-роу-фул] *adj.* огорчúтельный, печáльный, прискóрбный

sorry [сó-рi] *adj.* сожалéющий; **I am –** [ай äм –] винóват; мне óчень жаль (*I sympathize*); сострадáтельный (*pitiful*); **– sight** [– сайт] печáльное зрéлище

sort [сôрт] *sn.* вид, класс, род, сорт; *vt.* сортировáть; **– out** [– аут] отбирáть

sortie [сôр-тi] *sn.* *mil.* вылазка

SOS [ес-оу-ес] *sn.* радиосигнáл о бéдствии

soul [сôул] *sn.* душá

sound [сáунд] *sn.* звук; *adj.* здрáвый (*healthy*); прóчный (*firm*); *vt.i.* звучáть; *med.* выстýкивать, выслýшивать

soup [сӯп] *sn.* суп; **– plate** [– плэйт] глубокая тарелка

sour [са́-ӑр] *adj.* ки́слый; раздражи́тельный, серди́тый (*of person*)

source [сӧрс] *sn.* исто́чник

souse [са́ус] *vt.i.* маринова́ть, соли́ть

south [сауӫ] *sn.* юг; *adj.* ю́жный

southern [са́-ӗӑрн] *adj.* ю́жный

southerner [са́-ӗӑр-нӑр] *sm.* южа́нин

southward [са́уӫ-уӑрд] *adj.* обращённый на юг; *adv.* на юг

sovereign [со́-врӏн] *sm.* мона́рх; *sn.* золото́й фунт (£); *adj.* полновла́стный, суверенный

sovereignty [со́-врӑн-тӏ] *sn.* верхо́вная власть, суверенитет

sow [сау] *sf.* свиноматка

sow [соу] *vt.* се́ять

sower [со́-ӑр] *sm.* се́ятель; *sn.* се́ялка (*machine*)

spa [спā] *sn.* куро́рт с минера́льными во́дами

space [спэйс] *sn.* промежу́ток, протяже́ние (*interval between things*); простра́нство (*area*); срок (*period of time*); ме́сто (*place*); *mus.* интерва́л; *vt.* расставля́ть; *typ.* разбива́ть на шпа́ции

spacious [спэ́й-шӑс] *adj.* обши́рный, просто́рный

spade [спэйд] *sn.* лопа́та; **call a – a –** [кол ā – ā –] называ́ть ве́щи свои́ми имена́ми; **– work** [– уӧрк] тща́тельная рабо́та; пи́ка (*playing card*)

span [спэн] *sn.* пядь (9″); пролёт (*of bridge*); разма́х (*of aeroplane wings*); расстоя́ние (*of space*); промежу́ток (*of time*); *vt.* измеря́ть пя́дями (*measure*); покрыва́ть (*cover*); соединя́ть мосто́м (*connect with bridge*)

spangles [спэ́нглз] *sn. pl.* блёстки

Spaniard [спэ́-нӣӑрд] *sm.* испа́нец; *sf.* испа́нка

spaniel [спэ́-нӣӑл] *s.* спаниель

Spanish [спэ́-нӣш] *adj.* испа́нский

spank [спэнк] *vt.i.* шлёпать

spanner [спэ́-нӑр] *sn.* га́ечный ключ

spar [спāр] *sn.* брусо́к, перекла́дина (*pole*); *min.* шпат; *vi.* бокси́ровать; *fig.* препира́ться

spare [спӭр] *sn.* запасна́я часть; *adj.* запасно́й (*reserve*); ли́шний (*superfluous*); свобо́дный (*free*); *vt.i.* щади́ть

spark [спāрк] *sn.* и́скра; про́блеск (*flash*); *vi.* и́скриться

sparking-plug [спā́р-кӣй плаг] *sn.* запа́льная свеча́

sparkle [спāркл] *sn.* сверка́нье; *vi.* и́скриться, сверка́ть

sparrow [спэ́-роу] *s.* воробей

sparse [спāрс] *adj.* разбро́санный, ре́дкий

spasm [спэзм] *sn.* су́дорога

spasmodic [спэз-мо́-дӣк] *adj.* судоро́жный

spats [спэтс] *sn. pl.* башма́чные гётры

spatter [спэ́-тӑр] *vt.* бры́згать

spatula [спа́-тю-ла́] *sn.* шпа́-
тель, *m.*

spawn [спо́н] *sn.* икра́; *bot.*
мице́лий

speak [спик] *vt.i.* говори́ть;
разгова́ривать *(converse)*

speaker [спи́-кяр] *sm.* ора́-
тор; *parl.* спи́кер; **loud —**
[ла́уд —] *sn.* громкоговори́-
тель

spear [спи́р] *sn.* дро́тик,
копьё

special [спе́-шял] *adj.*
осо́бенный, осо́бый

specialist [спе́-шя-лист] *sn.*
специали́ст

speciality [спе-шиа́-ли-ти]
sn. специа́льность

species [спи́-шиз] *sn. sing.*, *pl.*
поро́да, род, тип; *biol.* вид,
разнови́дность

specific [спа-си́-фик] *adj.*
осо́бый, специфи́ческий

specification [спе-си-фи-
ке́й-шян] *sn.* дета́ли *(details)*; специфика́ция

specify [спе́-си-фай] *vt.* опреде-
ля́ть, подро́бно обозна-
ча́ть

specimen [спе́-си-мин] *sn.*
образе́ц, обра́зчик; **-** *sn.*
[- ко́-пи] про́бный экземпля́р

specious [спи́-шяс] *adj.*
правдоподо́бный, благо-
ви́дный

speck [спек] *sn.* крапи́нка,
пя́тнышко; части́чка *(tiny particle)*

speckled [спе́клд] *adj.*
кра́пчатый, пёстрый

spectacle [спе́к-такл] *sn.*
вид, зре́лище; сце́на; *pl.*
очки́

spectacular [спек-та́-кю-
ля́р] *adj.* импоза́нтный

spectator [спек-те́й-та́р] *sm.*
зри́тель; очеви́дец *(witness)*

spectral [спе́к-трял] *adj.*
при́зрачный *(ghost-like)*;
спектра́льный

spectre [спе́ктр] *sm.* приви-
де́ние, при́зрак

spectrum [спе́к-трум] *sn.*
спектр

speculate [спе́-кю-лэ́йт] *vi.*
игра́ть на би́рже, спекули́-
ровать; обду́мывать, раз-
мышля́ть *(indulge in thought)*

speculation [спе-кю-лэ́й-
шян] *sn.* спекуля́ция; раз-
мышле́ние *(reflection)*

speculative [спе́-кю-ла́-
тив] *adj.* спекуляти́вный;
умозри́тельный

speculator [спе́-кю-лэ́й-
та́р] *sm.* биржеви́к, спеку-
ля́нт; мысли́тель

speculum [спе́-кю-лу́м] *sn.*
med. зе́ркало, расшири́тель,
рефле́ктор

speech [спич] *sn.* речь

speech-day [спич-дэ́й] *sn.*
а́ктовый день

speechify [спи́-чи-фай] *vi.*
ора́торствовать

speechless [спи́ч-лис] *adj.*
безмо́лвный

speed [спид] *sn.* быстрота́,
ско́рость; *vt.i.* спеши́ть; **-
up** [- а́п] *vt.* ускоря́ть

speedy [спи́-ди] *adj.* бы́стрый

spell [спел] *sn.* обая́ние,
ча́ры *(charm)*; **under a -**
[ан-да́р а́ -] зачаро́ванный;
вре́мя, промежу́ток вре́-
мени, пери́од *(time)*; *vt.i.*
писа́ть по бу́квам; назы-
ва́ть по бу́квам; чита́ть по
бу́квам; означа́ть *(mean)*

spellbound [спе́л-ба́унд]
adj. очаро́ванный

spelling [спé-лін] *sn.* правописáние

spend [спенд] *vt.i.* расхóдовать, трáтить; проводи́ть *(time)*; исчéрпывать *(energy)*

spendthrift [спéнд-ѳрифт] *sm.* мот, расточи́тель

sperm [спœрм] *sn.* спéрма

sphere [сфир] *sn.* сфéра; глóбус, шар

spherical [сфé-ри-кăл] *adj.* сфери́ческий; шарообрáзный *(shape)*

spice [спайс] *sn.* прáдность, спéция; *vt.* приправля́ть

spicy [спáй-си] *adj.* аромати́чный, пря́ный

spider [спáй-дăр] *s.* паýк; **-'s web** [-з ўэб] паути́на

spidery [спáй-дă-ри] *adj.* тончáйший *(very thin)*; паукообрáзный *(of form)*

spike [спайк] *sn.* костьі́ль, острие́ *(pointed piece of metal)*; гвоздь *(nail)*; шип *(on shoes)*; *bot.* кóлос; *vt.* закрепля́ть, прибивáть *(гвозди́ми и пр.)*

spill [спіл] *sn. coll.* падéние *(fall)*; разбрáзгивание *(of liquid)*; лучи́на *(strip of wood, twisted paper)*; *vt.i.* проливáть *(of liquid)*; вывáливать, сброси́ть *(let fall, upset)*

spin [спін] *sn.* верчéние, кружéние; *vt.i.* вертéть, кружи́ться; вить, плести́, прясть *(twist)*; **- out** [- áут] расти́гивать рассказ *(a tale)*

spinach [спí-ніджк] *sn.* шпинáт

spinal [спáй-нăл] *adj.* спиннóй; **- cord** [- кŏрд] спиннóй мозг

spindle [спíндл] *sn.* веретенó; *tech.* вал маховикá

spine [спайн] *sn.* хребéт; позвонóчный столб *(vertebral column)*; конёк *(of roof)*; корешóк *(of book)*

spineless [спáйн-ліс] *adj.* безпозвонóчный *(lacking character)*

spinner [спí-нăр] *sm.* пряди́льщик

spinney [спí-ні] *sn.* подлéсок, рóщица

spinning [спí-нін] *sn.* прядéние; **- wheel** [- ўіл] *sn.* пря́лка

spinster [спíн-стăр] *sf.* незамýжняя жéнщина; стáрая дéва *(old maid)*

spiny [спáй-ні] *adj.* колю́чий

spiral [спáй-рăл] *adj.* винтовóй, спирáльный

spire [спáй-ăр] *sn.* шпиль, шпиц; виток, спирáль

spirit [спí-ріт] *sn.* дух; мýжество *(courage)*; привидéние *(apparition)*; воодушевлéние *(zeal)*; спирт *(alcohol)*; *pl.* настроéние *(mood)*; спиртны́е напи́тки *(liquor)*; **- of wine** [- ов ўайн] чи́стый спирт

spirited [спí-рі-тід] *adj.* оживлённый *(lively)*; предприи́мчивый *(enterprising)*; горя́чий *(of horse)*

spirit-lamp [спі-рíт-лæмп] *sn.* спиртóвка

spiritless [спí-ріт-ліс] *adj.* безжи́зненный, уны́лый

spiritual [спí-рі-чў-ăл] *adj.* духóвный; одухотворённый

spiritualism [спí-рі-чў-ă-лі́зм] *sn.* спиритуали́зм; спиритизм

spirituous [спí-рі-тю-ăс] *adj.* спиртнóй

spit [спіт] *sn.* вéртел (*for roasting on*); косá (*on sea*); плевóк (*spittle*); *vi.* плевáть; шипéть (*of cat*)

spite [спайт] *sn.* злóба, злость; **in - of** [iн - ов] вопрекú; *vt.* досаждáть

spiteful [спайт-фýл] *adj.* злóбный, язвúтельный

spitfire [спіт-фай-áр] *sm.* вспыльчивый человéк

spittle [спітл] *sn.* слюнá

spittoon [спі-тýн] *sn.* плевáтельница

splash [спляш] *sn.* брызги, плеск; *vt.* брызгать, плескáть

spleen [сплін] *sn. anat.* селезёнка; мрáчное настрoéние, хандрá (*moroseness*)

splendid [сплéн-дід] *adj.* великолéпный, превосхóдный

splendour [сплéн-дáр] *n.* пышность, рóскошь

splice [сплайс] *sn. naut.* скреплéние, сплéсень; *vt.* сплéснивать, срáщивать

splint [сплінт] *sn. med.* лубóк, шúна

splinter [сплín-тáр] *sn.* лучúна, оскóлок, щéпка; *vt.i.* разбивáть, раскáлываться, расщеплять

split [спліт] *sn.* раскóл, щель; *vt.* раздроблять, разрывáть

split-pin [спліт-пíн] *sn.* скрéпка

splitting [сплí-тíй] *adj.* оглушúтельный (*deafening*)

splutter [сплá-тáр] *vi.* говорúть запинáясь

бáловать (*child*); пóртить (*damage*); грáбить, расхищáть (*plunder*)

spoilage [спóй-лíдж] *sn.* пóрча

spoke [споук] *sn.* спúца (*of wheel*); переклáдина, ступéнька (*rung*)

spokesman [спóукс-мáн] *sm.* представúтель

spoliation [споу-лí-эй-шáн] *sn.* грабёж, захвáт имýщества

sponge [спандж] *sn.* гýбка; *vt.i.* мыть гýбкой; жить на чужóй счёт (*live on others*); вымогáть, высáсывать (*money*)

sponger [спáн-джáр] *sm.* паразúт; прижимáльщик

spongy [спáн-джí] *adj.* губчáтый

sponsor [спон-сáр] *sm.* поручúтель; крёстный отéц (*father*); *sf.* крёстная мать (*godmother*); *vi.* ручáться

spontaneity [спон-тá-нí-íтí] *sn.* самопроизвóльность

spontaneous [спон-тéйнí-áс] *adj.* самопроизвóльный, спонтáнный

spool [спул] *sn.* катýшка, шпýлка

spoon [спун] *sn.* лóжка; *vt.i.* черпáть лóжкой

spoon-fed [спýн-фед] *adj.* питáющийся с лóжки; *fig.* искýсственно поддéрживаемый (*of industry*)

spoonful [спýн-фýл] *sn.* пóлная лóжка (как мéра)

sporadic [спо-рá-дík] *adj.* нерегуля́рный, спорадúческий

sport [спóрт] *sn.* спорт, игрá, развлечéние (*play,*

diversion); *pl.* спортивные состязания; *zool.*, *bot.* уклонение от нормального типа

sporting [спо́р-тің] *adj.* спортивный

sportive [спо́р-тів] *adj.* весёлый, игривый, резвый

sportsman [спо́ртс-мән] *sn.* спортсмен

spot [спот] *sn.* место (*place*); пятно (*stain*); прыщик (*pimple*); крапинка (*speck*); *vt.i.* пятнать (*mark with spots*); пачкать (*stain*); *coll.* опознавать, отмечать; — **cash** [— кæш] наличные деньги

spotless [спо́т-ліс] *adj.* совершенно чистый; безупречный (*irreproachable*)

spotty [спо́-ті] *adj.* пёстрый, пятнистый

spouse [спаус] *sm.* супруг, *sf.* супруга; чета (*couple; husband and wife*)

spout [спаут] *sn.* горлышко, носик; жёлоб (*of fountain*); *vt.i.* бить струёй; *coll.* разглагольствовать

sprain [спрэйн] *sn.* вывих, растяжение; *vt.* вывихнуть, растягивать

sprat [спрæт] *s.* килька, шпрота; малыш (*small person*)

sprawl [спрбл] *vt.i.* расползаться, растянуться

spray [спрэй] *sn. bot.* ветка, побег; водяная пыль, брызги (*of water*); *vt.* обрызгивать, прыскать

sprayer [спрэ́й-әр] *sn.* форсунка

spread [спред] *vt.* протягивать, протяжённость (*extent*); распространение (*cir-*

culation); простор (*expanse*); *vt.i.* разглашать (*diffuse*); простирать (*stretch*); распространять (*circulate*)

spree [спри] *sn.* веселье, шалость

sprig [спріг] *sn. bot.* веточка, отросток; штифт (*nail*); *fig.* франт

sprightly [спрайт-лі] *adj.* оживлённый

spring [спрің] *sn.* весна (*season*); источник (*source*); *tech.* рессора, пружина; прыжок (*leap*)

spring-balance [спрің-бǽлянс] *sn.* безмен, пружинные весы

spring-board [спрің-бӧрд] *sn.* трамплин

spring-tide [спрің-тайд] *sn.* сильный весенний прилив (*tide*)

springy [спрі́ң-і] *adj.* упругий

sprinkle [спрінкл] *vt.* брызгать, обрызгивать

sprinkler [спрі́нк-лӓр] *sn.* опрыскиватель, *m.*

sprinkling [спрі́нк-лің] *sn.* кропление, обрызгивание; небольшое количество чего-либо (*little here and there*)

sprint [спрінт] *sn.* короткий бег; *vi.* бежать на скорость

sprinter [спрі́н-тӓр] *sm.* бегун, спринтер

sprout [спраут] *sn.* побег, росток (*shoot*); *pl.* (**Brussels**)-s [брá-сӓлс -с] брюссельская капуста; *vt.i.* расти, производить

spruce [спрюс] *adj.* щеголеватый

spry [спрай] *adj.* живо́й, прово́рный

spud [спад] *sn.* ки́рка (*small spade*); моты́га (*hoe*); *coll.* карто́шка

spur [спɛ́р] *sn.* шпо́ра (*spike, projection on cock's leg*); верши́на, отро́г (*of mountain*); побужде́ние (*incitement*); *vt.i.* пришпо́ривать; подстрека́ть (*incite*)

spurious [спю́-ри-ǎс] *adj.* подде́льный, подло́жный

spurn [спɛ́рн] *vt.* отпи́хнуть

spurt [спɛ́рт] *sn.* струя́; *vt.i.* бить струёй; выбра́сывать

sputter [спа-тǎр] *vt.i.* бры́згать слюно́й; говори́ть бессвя́зно (*speak incoherently*)

sputum [спю-тỳм] *sn. med.* мокро́та, плёвки

spy [спай] *sn.* шпио́н; **- on** [- он] следи́ть за ке́м-либо

spyglass [спай-глас] *sn.* подзо́рная труба́

squab [скуо́б] *s.* неопери́вшийся птене́ц (*bird*); призе́мистый толстя́к (*of person*); *adj.* коро́ткий и то́лстый, призе́мистый

squabble [скуо́бл] *sn.* ссо́ра; *vi.* пререка́ться, ссо́риться

squad [скуо́д] *sn.* отря́д; **- drill** [- дрɪл] обуче́ние новобра́нцев

squadron [скуо́-дрǎн] *sn. mil.* эскадро́н; *naut.* эска́дра

squalid [скуо́-лɪд] *adj.* запу́щенный, убо́гий

squall [скуо́бл] *sn.* визг, писк (*scream*); шквал, шторм (*sudden storm*); *vi.* визжа́ть, пища́ть

squander [скуо́н-дǎр] *vt.i.* расточа́ть

square [скуэ́р] *sn.* квадра́т (*figure*); квадра́тная пло́щадь (*area*); *mil.* карре́; науго́льник (*gauge*); *adj.* квадра́тный; *vt.i.* возводи́ть в квадра́т; обтёсывать (*timber*); сбаланси́ровать (*accounts*); **- root** [- руṫ] квадра́т числа́

squash [скуо́ш] *sn.* су́толока (*crowded state*); lemon (*etc.*) - лɛ́-мǎн (и пр.) - лимо́нная вода́ (*etc.*); *vt.* сжима́ть, расква́сить; *fig.* заста́вить замолча́ть

squat [скуо́т] *vi.* сиде́ть на ко́рточках

squeak [скуик] *sn.* скрип, писк; *vi.* пища́ть, скрипе́ть

squeaky [скуи́-кɪ] *adj.* пискли́вый

squeal [скуил] *sn.* визг; *vi.* визжа́ть

squeamish [скуи́-мɪш] *adj.* щепети́льный (*petty*); разбо́рчивый (*fastidious*)

squeeze [скуиз] *sn.* сжа́тие; теснота́ (*crowded state*); *vt.i.* выжима́ть, сжима́ть; проти́скиваться

squint [скуɪ́нт] *sn.* косогла́зие; взгляд (*glance*); *vi.* коси́ть (глаза́ми); *coll.* щу́риться; *adj.* раско́сый

squire [скуа́й-ǎр] *sn.* поме́щик, сквайр

squirrel [скуɪ́-рǎл] *s.* бе́лка

squirt [скуɛ́рт] *sn.* шприц; *vt.i.* бить струёй, забры́згивать

stab [стǎб] *sn.* уда́р (кинжа́лом и т.п.); внеза́пная о́страя боль (*sudden pain*); *vt.i.* вонза́ть, ра́нить

stability [стǎ-бɪ́-лɪ-тɪ] *sn.* усто́йчивость

stabilize [стэ́й-бі-лайз] vt. стабилизи́ровать

stabilizer [стэ́й-бі-лай-зэр] sn. tech. стабилиза́тор

stable [стэйбл] sn. коню́шня; adj. про́чный, сто́йкий

stack [стэк] sn. скирда́, стог (rick); ки́па (of paper); гру́да, ку́ча (pile); vt. накла́дывать стог

stadium [стэ́й-ді-ăм] sn. стадио́н

staff [стăф] sn. персона́л, штат (personnel); mil. штаб; па́лка, по́сох (stick); naut. флагшто́к; дре́вко (pole); mus. но́тные лине́йки; vt. зачисля́ть в штат

stag [стэг] sm. оле́нь-саме́ц

stage [стэйдж] sn. theat. сце́на; перего́н, перее́зд (distance); перио́д, фа́за (period, phase); остано́вка (stopping place); vt.i. ста́вить пье́су (put on play); — **manager** [— мǎ́-нǎ-джǎр] режиссёр

stager [стэ́й-джǎр] sm. о́пытный челове́к

stagger [стэ́-гǎр] vi. шата́ться

stagnant [стэ́г-нǎнт] adj. засто́йный, стоя́чий (of water); недви́жимый (motionless); безде́ятельный (inert)

stagnate [стэ́г-нэйт] vi. косне́ть

stagnation [стэг-нэ́й-шǎн] sn. засто́й

staid [стэйд] adj. тре́звый

stain [стэйн] sn. пятно́; кра́сящее вещество́ (colouring liquid); vt. кра́сить (colour); мара́ть (daub)

stainless [стэйн-ліс] adj.

незапя́тнанный; безупре́чный (of reputation); нержаве́ющий (of steel)

stair [стэр] sn. ступе́нька; pl. ле́стница; **flight of -s** [флайт ов -з] пролёт ле́стницы

staircase [стэ́р-кэйс] sn. ле́стница

stake [стэйк] sn. кол, столб (stout stick); ста́вка (in games); pl. приз; vt. рискова́ть; огора́живать (mark out)

stale [стэйл] adj. несве́жий, чёрствый; изби́тый, уста́ревший (of joke); спёртый (of air)

stalemate [стэ́йл-мэйт] sn. пат (chess)

stalk [сток] sn. ствол, сте́бель, m.; vt.i. подкра́дываться (make furtive approach); ше́ствовать го́рдо (walk haughtily)

stall [стол] sn. сто́йло (compartment); ларёк, пала́тка (in market); theat. кре́сло в парте́ре; v.i. ста́вить в сто́йло; теря́ть равнове́сие (of plane)

stallion [стэ́-ліǎн] sm. жеребе́ц

stalwart [стол-уǎрт] sm. стра́стный сторо́нник (of party); дю́жий, здоро́вый, сто́йкий

stamen [стэ́й-мǎн] sn. bot. тычи́нка

stamina [стэ́-мі-нǎ] sn. вы́держка, жи́зненные си́лы

stammer [стэ́-мǎр] sn. замка́ние; vi. замка́ться, запина́ться

stammerer [стэ́-мǎ-рǎр] sm. за́ика

stamp [стæмп] *sn.* почто́вая ма́рка (*postage*); штамп, ште́мпель (*impression*); то́панье (*with foot*); *vt.i.* то́пать ного́й (*with foot*); накла́дывать, штамповáть (*impress*); чека́нить (*mint*)

stampede [стæм-пи́д] *sn.* пани́ческое бе́гство; *vt.i.* броса́ться врассыпну́ю

stand [стæнд] *sn.* подста́вка, сто́йка, этаже́рка (*pedestal, rack, etc.*); остано́вка (*stationary position*); сто́йнка (*for taxis, etc.*); кио́ск, трибу́на; *vt.i.* стоя́ть; вы́держивать (*endure*); угоща́ть (*treat*); – **against** [а-гэ́йнст] сопротивля́ться; – **by** [– бай] поддержи́вать (*support*); – **up** [– ап] вставáть

standard [стǽн-дард] *sn.* зна́мя, флаг, штанда́рт (*flag*); но́рма, станда́рт (*degree of quality*); мери́ло (*gauge*); *adj.* ка́чественный, образцо́вый, станда́ртный

standard-bearer [стǽн-дард-бэ́-рар] *sn.* знамено́сец; *fig.* побо́рник

standardize [стǽн-дардайз] *vt.* нормирова́ть

stand-by [стǽнд-бай] *sn.* надёжная опо́ра

standing [стǽн-дий] *sn.* положе́ние (*repute*); продолжи́тельность (*continuance*); *adj.* сто́йчий; постано́вленный, устано́вленный (*constant*); регуля́рный (*regular*)

standpoint [стæнд-по́йнт] *sn.* то́чка зре́ния

standstill [стǽнд-сти́л] *sn.* засто́й, остано́вка

stannary [стǽ-нæ-ри] *sn.* оловя́нные рудники́

staple [стэ́йпл] *sn.* основна́я о́трасль (*of industry*); гла́вный элеме́нт (*chief element*); ка́чество волокна́ (*of wool*); крюк, скоба́, скре́пка (*sharpened metal rod*)

star [ста́р] *sn.* звезда́, звёздочка; *typ.* астери́ск; гла́вный актёр (*chief actor*); украша́ть звёздами (*adorn with*); игра́ть гла́вную роль

starboard [ста́р-ба́рд] *sn. naut.* пра́вый борт, штирбо́рт

starch [ста́рч] *sn.* крахма́л; *fig.* чо́порность; *vt.* крахма́лить

starchy [ста́р-чи] *adj.* накрахма́ленный; *fig.* чо́порный

stare [стэ́р] *sn.* при́стальный взгляд; *vi.* тара́щить, пыли́ть глаза́

staring [стэ́-рий] *adj.* крича́щий, я́ркий

stark [ста́рк] *adj.* засты́вший (*rigid*); по́лный (*entirely, quite*)

starling [ста́р-лий] *s.* скворе́ц

starry [ста́-ри] *adj.* звёздный

start [ста́рт] *sn.* нача́ло (*beginning*); отправле́ние, старт (*of races, etc.*); вска́кивание, скачо́к (*sudden movement*); *vt.i.* начина́ть (*begin*); вскочи́ть (*make sudden movement*); пусти́ть в ход (*put into motion*)

startle [ста́ртл] *vt.* испуга́ть, изуми́ть

starvation [стар-вэ́й-шан] *sn.* го́лод; истоще́ние (*exhaustion*)

starve [старв] *vt.i.* голода́ть; умира́ть с го́лоду (*die from starvation*).

state [стэйт] *sn.* положе́ние, состоя́ние (*condition*); ранг (*rank*); пы́шность (*pomp*); госуда́рство (*country*); штат (*corporation*); *vt.* заявля́ть, формули́ровать

stately [стэйт-ли] *adj.* вели́чавый

statement [стэйт-мэнт] *sn.* заявле́ние, сообще́ние, утвержде́ние

state-room [стэйт-ру́м] *sn.* пара́дный зал

statesman [стэйтс-мэн] *sm.* госуда́рственный де́ятель

station [стэй-шан] *sn.* ме́сто, пост (*place held*); ста́нция (*base, etc.*); вокза́л (*railway*); обще́ственное положе́ние (*of person*); *vt.* располага́ть, ста́вить

stationary [стэй-ша-на-ри] *adj.* неподви́жный, стациона́рный

stationer [стэй-ша-на́р] *sm.* торго́вец канцеля́рскими принадле́жностями

stationery [стэй-ша-на-ри] *sn.* канцеля́рские принадле́жности

station-master [стэй-шан-ма́с-тăр] *sm.* нача́льник вокза́ла

statistical [стă-ти́с-ти-кăл] *adj* статисти́ческий

statistics [стă-ти́с-тикс] *sn. pl.* стати́стика

statuary [стă-тю-ă-ри] *adj.* скульпту́рный

statue [стă-тю] *sn.* ста́туя; изва́яние

stature [стă-ча́р] *sn.* рост; фигу́ра

status [стэй-тăс] *sn.* положе́ние, состоя́ние

statute [стă-тют] *sn.* зако́н, законода́тельный акт, стату́т, уста́в

statutory [стă-тю-тă-ри] *adj.* узако́ненный, устано́вленный зако́ном

staunch [стонч] *adj.* ве́рный, сто́йкий

stave [стэйв] *sn.* бо́ча́рная доска́, клёпка (*of cask, etc.*); строфа́ (*of song, verse*); *mus.* но́тные лине́йки; *vt.* проломи́ть (*break through*); – off [– оф] предотврати́ть

stay [стэй] *sn.* пребыва́ние (*sojourn*); остано́вка (*check, delay*); выно́сливость (*stamina*); *naut.* штаг; *vt.i.* остава́ться (*remain*), остана́вливаться (*at hotel, etc.*); ждать (*wait*); – away [– ă-уэ́й] отсу́тствовать; –! [–] подожди́!

stay-at-home [стэй-æт-хо́ум] *sm.* домосе́д

steadfast [стэд-фăст] *adj.* сто́йкий, твёрдый

steady [стэ́-ди] *adj.* усто́йчивый

steal [стил] *vt.* ворова́ть, красть

stealth [стэлθ] *sn.* by– [бай –] втихомо́лку, укра́дкой

stealthy [стэл-θи] *adj.* скры́тый, та́йный

steam [стим] *sn.* пар; *vt.i.* выпуска́ть пар, па́рить; вари́ть на пару́ (*cook*); парово́й

steamer [сти-мăр] *sn.* парохо́д

steamy [сти-ми] *adj.* парообра́зный; запоте́вший (*dimmed*)

steed [стид] *s.* конь, *m.*

steel [стил] *sn.* сталь; *adj.* стально́й; жёсткий, кре́пкий (*hard*, *tough*); *fig.* неумоли́мый

steep [стип] *adj.* круто́й, отве́сный; *vt.* выма́чивать, пропи́тывать

steeple [стипл] *sn.* шпиль

steeplechase [сти́пл-чэйс] *sn.* ска́чки с препя́тствиями

steeplejack [сти́пл-джэк] *sm.* верхола́з, кро́вельщик

steer [стир] *sm.* молодо́й вол; *vt.* пра́вить рулём, управля́ть

steerage [сти́-ридж] *sn.* рулево́е устро́йство; четвёртый класс (*for passengers*)

steersman [сти́рз-мэн] *sm.* рулево́й, штурма́н (*ный*)

stellar [стэ́-лэр] *adj.* звёздный

stem [стэм] *sm.* ствол (*trunk*), сте́бель (*stalk*); но́жка (*of wineglass*); *gram.* осно́ва; нос (*of ship*); *vt.* сопротивля́ться (*resist*); сде́рживать (*hold back*)

stench [стэнч] *sn.* вонь

stencil [стэ́н-сил] *sn.* трафаре́т, шабло́н; *vt.* раскра́шивать

step [стэп] *sn.* шаг (*pace*); подно́жка, ступе́нька (*stair*); посту́пок (*action taken*); *pl.* стремя́нка; *vt.i.* ступа́ть, шага́ть; де́лать па (*in dancing*); — **down** [—да́ун] спусти́ться; — **into** [— и́н-ту] вступа́ть; — **off** [—оф] сходи́ть; — **over** [— о́у-вэр] переступа́ть, перешагну́ть

stepbrother [стэ́п-бра-ээр] *sm.* сво́дный брат

stepchild [стэп-чайлд] *sn.*

па́сынок (*boy*); па́дчерица (*girl*)

stepdaughter [стэп-до́тэр] *sf.* па́дчерица

stepfather [стэп-фа́-ээр] *sm.* о́тчим

stepmother [стэп-ма-ээр] *sf.* ма́чеха

steppe [стэп] *sn.* степь

stepsister [стэп-си́с-тэр] *sf.* сво́дная сестра́

stepson [стэп-сан] *sm.* па́сынок

stereotype [сти́-ри-а-тайп] *sn.* стереоти́п; *adj.* стереоти́пный

sterile [стэ́-райл] *adj.* беспло́дный; *med.* стери́льный

sterilize [стэ́-ри-лайз] *vt.* стерилизова́ть

sterling [стэ́р-лий] *sn.* сте́рлинг; *adj.* неподде́льный (*genuine*); полноце́нный (*of solid worth*)

stern [стэрн] *sn. naut.* корма́; *adj.* неумоли́мый, стро́гий

stevedore [сти́-ви-дор] *sm.* портово́й гру́зчик

stew [стю] *sn.* тушёное мя́со (*dish*); *vt.* туши́ть; изнемога́ть от жары́ (*welter in heat*)

steward [стю́-ард] *sm.* управи́тель, управля́ющий; эко́ном; *naut.* официа́нт

stewardess [стю́-ар-дес] *sf.* го́рничная; официа́нтка

stewardship [стю́-ард-шип] *sn.* управле́ние

stick [стик] *sn.* па́лка, па́лочка; *vt.i.* втыка́ть (*thrust*); прикле́ивать (*fasten with gum*); приде́рживаться (*remain constant*)

sticky [стʹі-кі] *adj.* клейкий, липкий

stiff [стіф] *adj.* негибкий, тугой; окостеневший (*of limbs*); крепкий (*of drinks*); трудный (*difficult*)

stiffen [стʹі-фән] *vt.* делать тугим; окоченеть (*of limbs*); сгущать (*condense*)

stifle [стайфл] *vt.i.* душить, задыхаться

stifling [стайф-лій] *adj.* удушливый

stigma [стʹіг-мǎ] *sn.* позор, пятно; *bot.* рыльце

stile [стайл] *sn.* ступеньки

still [стіл] *sn.* перегонный куб (*distilling apparatus*); безмолвие, тишина (*quiet*); *adj.* бесшумный, тихий (*noiseless*); неподвижный (*motionless*); *vt.* успокаивать, утихомиривать; *adv.* однако, всё ещё

still-born [стʹіл-бôрн] *adj.* мертворождённый

stillness [стʹіл-ніс] *sn.* тишина; спокойствие (*tranquillity*)

stilt [стілт] *sn.* ходуля; морской кулик (*bird*)

stimulant [стʹі-мю-лǎнт] *adj.* возбуждающий

stimulate [стʹі-мю-лэйт] *vt.* побуждать, стимулировать; поощрять

sting [стій] *sn.* жало; ожог (*nettle*); *vt.i.* жалить; обжигать

stinginess [стʹін-джі-ніс] *sn.* скаредность, скупость

stingy [стʹін-джі] *adj.* скупой

stink [стійк] *sn.* вонь; *vt.i.* вонять

stint [стінт] *sn.* ограниче-

ние; *vt.* скряжничать, скудно снабжать

stipend [стай-пәнд] *sn.* жалованье, плата

stipendiary [стʹі-пән-діǎ-рі] *adj.* оплачиваемый

stipple [стіпл] *sn.* пунктир; *vt.i.* гравировать пунктиром

stipulate [стʹі-пю-лэйт] *vt.i.* обусловливать

stipulation [стʹі-пю-лэ̆й-шǎн] *sn.* соглашение, условие

stir [стэр] *sn.* волнение, суета; оживление (*animation*); *vt.i.* возбуждать, шевелиться; мешивать (*liquid*)

stirrup [стʹі-рǎп] *sn.* стремя

stitch [стіч] *sn.* стежок; колотье (*sharp pain*); *vt.* прошивать

stoat [стоўт] *sn.* горностай

stock [сток] *sn.* запас, фонд; главный ствол (*of tree*); происхождение, род (*origin*); *vt.i.* снабжать, иметь в продаже; *bot.* левкой

stockade [сток-кэ̆йд] *sn.* частокол; *vt.* окружать частоколом

stockbreeder [сток-бри-дǎр] *sn.* животновод

stockbroker [сток-броу-кǎр] *sn.* маклер

stockinet [сто-кі-нэт] *sn.* трико

stocking [сто-кій] *sn.* чулок

stockstill [сток-стіл] *adj.* остолбеневший

stock-taking [сток-тэ̆й-кій] *sn.* проверка инвентаря

stocky [сто-кі] *adj.* приземистый

stodgy [стó-джі] *adj.* тяжёлый (*of food*)

stoke [стóук] *vt.i.* поддёр-
живать огонь

stoker [стóу-кăр] *sm.* кочё-
гáр

stole [стóул] *sn.* орáрь, *m.*

stolid [стó-лід] *adj.* вя́лый,
флегмати́ческий

stomach [стá-мăк] *sn.*
желýдок; живóт (*belly*)

stone [стóун] *sn.* кáмень, *m.*;
зёрнышко, кóсточка (*of
fruit*); *vt.* побивáть кáм-
нями; вынимáть кóсточки
(*fruit*)

stone-mason [стóун-мэй-
сăн] *sm.* кáменщик

stoneware [стóун-ўэ̆р] *sn.*
гли́няная посýда

stonework [стóун-ўэ̆рк] *sn.*
кáменная клáдка

stony [стóу-ні] *adj.* камени́-
стый, кáменный

stool [стýл] *sn.* табурéтка;
скамéечка для ног (*for
feet*); *med.* стул

stoop [стýп] *sn.* сутýлость;
vt.i. нагибáть, наклоня́ть;
сгорби́ться, сутýлиться;
снисходи́ть (*condescend*);
унижáться (*abase oneself*)

stop [стоп] *sn.* задéржка
(*check*); останóвка (*halt*);
тóчка (*point*); *vt.i.* останáв-
ливаться, перестáвать
(*cease*)

stoppage [стó-підж] *sn.*
задéржка, останóвка; *tech.*
засорéние; забастóвка
(*strike*)

stopper [стó-пăр] *sn.*
затычка (*plug*); прóбка
(*cork*)

stopping [стó-пiн] *sn.*
зубнáя плóмба (*dental*)

stopwatch [стóп-ўоч] *sn.*
секундомéр

storage [стó-рiдж] *sn.* хра-
нéние; склáды (*storehouse*)

store [стóр] *sn.* запáс (*stock*);
магази́н (*shop*); склад (*dépôt,
warehouse*); *vt.* запасти́,
откла́дывать

storey [стó-рi] *sn.* этáж

stork [стóрк] *s.* áист

storm [стóрм] *sn.* бýря,
грозá, штурм; *vt.i.* штурмовáть; горячи́ться (*talk
violently*)

stormy [стóр-мi] *adj.*
бýрный

story [стó-рi] *sn.* истóрия,
пóвесть, рассказ; *coll.* вра-
ньё, ложь

story-teller [стó-рi-тĕ-лăр]
sm. расскáзчик

stout [стáут] *sn.* крéпкий
пóртер (*porter*); *adj.* от-
вáжный, реши́тельный, у-
пóрный (*undaunted, reso-
lute*); крéпкий, си́льный
(*strong*); пóлный, тýчный
(*corpulent*)

stove [стóув] *sn.* пéчка,
печь

stow [стóу] *vt.* прятать,
склáдывать, убирáть

stowage [стóу-iдж] *sn.*
склáдывание, уклáдка

stowaway [стóу-ă-ўэй] без-
билéтный пассажи́р

straddle [стрэ́дл] *vt.i.*
широкó расставля́ть нóги;
сидéть верхóм (*sit across
horse*)

straggle [стрэгл] *vi.*
итти́ вразбрóд (*walk separately*); быть разбрóсанным
(*lack compactness*)

straggler [стрэ́г-лăр] *sm.*
отстáвший

straight [стрэйт] *adj.* прямо́й; **put things —** [пут θíнз —] приводи́ть в поря́док; *adv.* прямо; **— away** [- ə-ýэй] сразу

straighten [стрэ́й-тън] *vt.* выпрямля́ть

straightforward [стрэйт-фо́р-уəрд] *adj.* откры́тый, прямоду́шный, че́стный; *adv.* прямо

strain [стрэйн] *sn.* порода (*breed, stock*); напряже́ние, уси́лие (*tension, exertion*); черта́ хара́ктера (*of character*); *pl.* мело́дия; *vt.i.* напряга́ть, натя́гивать; переутомля́ть (*of heart*); проце́живать (*sieve*)

strained [стрэйнд] *adj.* напряжённый, натя́нутый

strainer [стрэ́й-нəр] *sn.* фильтр

strait [стрэйт] *sn.* у́зкий проли́в; *pl.* затрудни́тельное положе́ние, нужда́ (*difficulty, need*); *adj.* стро́гий (*strict*); у́зкий (*narrow*)

strand [стрэнд] *sn.* прядь каната

stranded [стрэ́н-дід] *adj.* сидя́щий на мели́; *fig.* бе́дствующий

strange [стрэйндж] *adj.* стра́нный (*odd, singular*); чу́ждый, чужо́й (*alien*); незнако́м й (*unknown*)

stranger [стрэ́йн-джəр] *sn.* незнако́мец

strangle [стрэ́нгл] *vt.* души́ть, удави́ть

strangulate [стрэ́н-гю-лэйт] *vt.* удуша́ть

strangulation [стрэн-гю-лэ́й-шън] *sn.* удавле́ние, удуше́ние

strap [стрэп] *sn.* ре́мень, *m.*; *tech.* обру́ч, хому́т; *vt.* стя́гивать ремнём; *med.* накла́дывать пла́стырь, *m.*; бить ремнём (*beat*)

strapping [стрэ́-пін] *sn.* ли́пкий пла́стырь в ви́де ле́нты; *adj.* дю́жий, ро́слый

stratagem [стрэ́-тə-джəм] *sn.* вое́нная хи́трость

strategic [стрə-ти́-джік] *adj.* стратеги́ческий

strategy [стрэ́-ті-джі] *sn.* страте́гия; *mil.* операти́вное иску́сство

stratum [стрэ́-тəм] *sn.* слой

stratus [стрэ́-тəс] *sn.* слои́стое облако

straw [стро] *sn.* соло́ма; **the last —** [ə̄ ласт —] после́дняя ка́пля; *adj.* соло́менный

strawberry [стро́-бə-рі] *sn.* земляни́ка (*wild*); клубни́ка (*garden*)

stray [стрэй] *sn.* заблуди́вшееся живо́тное (*animal*), беспризо́рный ребёнок (*child*); *adj.* заблуди́вшийся; шально́й (*bullet*); *vi.* блужда́ть, сбива́ться с пути́

streak [стрик] *sn.* поло́ска, просло́йка; *fig.* черта́ (*of character*); жи́лка (*vein*)

stream [стрим] *sn.* пото́к (*flow*); ручёй (*brook*); *vi.* вылива́ться, струи́ться, течь

street [стрит] *sn.* у́лица; *adj.* у́личный

strength [стреҥθ] *sn.* кре́пость, си́ла; **on the — of** [он θ̄ə — ов] на основа́нии

strengthen [стре́ҥ-θən] *vt.* укрепля́ть, уси́ливать

strenuous [стре́-ню-ăс] *adj.* напряжённый, энерги́чный

stress [стрес] *sn.* напряже́ние, уси́лие; ударе́ние (*accent*); значи́тельность (*emphasis*); *vt.* ока́зывать давле́ние; ста́вить ударе́ние

stretch [стреч] *sn.* вытя́гивание (*act of stretching*); натя́жка (*strained to attention*); протяже́ние (*expanse*); *vt.i.* вытя́гивать, натя́гивать, простира́ться, растя́гиваться; – **out** – [аут] протяну́ть (ру́ку, но́гу)

stretcher [стре́-чăр] *sn.* носи́лки

strew [стрю] *vt.* разбра́сывать, усыпа́ть

stricken [стри́-кăн] *adj.* поражённый

strict [стрикт] *adj.* стро́гий, то́чный (*accurate*); определённый (*precise*)

stricture [стри́к-чăр] *sn.* кри́тика, осужде́ние; *med.* суже́ние

stride [страйд] *sn.* большо́й шаг; *vt.i.* кру́пно шага́ть; перешагну́ть

strident [страй-дăнт] *adj.* пронзи́тельный, ре́зкий

strife [страйф] *sn.* борьба́ (*hostilities*); спор (*quarrels*)

strike [страйк] *sn.* забасто́вка, ста́чка; *vt.i.* бастова́ть (*stop work*); ударя́ть (*hit*); наткну́ться на (come *across, find*); поража́ть (*deal a blow*); бить (*chime*); зажига́ться (*match*); – **out** – [аут] вычёркивать; – **up** – [ап] заигра́ть (*of band, etc.*)

striker [страй-кăр] *sn.* забасто́вщик

striking [страй-кий] *adj.* рази́тельный (*impressive*)

string [стрий] *sn.* верёвка, шнуро́к; *mus.* струна́; the **-s** [зă -з] *mus.* стру́нные инструме́нты; – **of pearls** [– ов пёрлз] ни́тка жемчу́га; *vt.i.* завя́зывать, свя́зывать

stringent [стри́н-джăнт] *adj.* стро́гий

stringy [стри́й-и] *adj.* волокни́стый, жи́листый

strip [стрип] *sn.* лоску́т, поло́ска; *vt.i.* сдира́ть, снима́ть; обнажа́ть (*denude*)

stripe [страйп] *sn.* полоса́; наши́вка (*chevron*)

striped [страйпт] *adj.* полоса́тый

stripling [стри́п-лий] *sm.* подро́сток, ю́ноша

strive [страйв] *vi.* стара́ться

stroke [строук] *sn.* уда́р (*blow*); черта́, штрих (*of pen, etc.*); погла́живание (*act of stroking*); *vt.* гла́дить, погла́живать

stroll [строул] *sn.* прогу́лка; *vi.* броди́ть, прогу́ливаться

stroller [стро́у-лăр] *sn.* стра́нствующий актёр (*actor*)

strong [строй] *adj.* кре́пкий, си́льный; про́чный (*firm*); гро́мкий (*of voice*); **how many –?** [хау ме́ни –?] ско́лько вас?

stronghold [строй-хоулд] *sn.* кре́пость, опло́т

strop [строп] *sn.* бри́твенный реме́нь, *m. наш.* строп; *vt.* пра́вить (бри́тву)

structural [стра́к-чă-рăл] *adj.* конструкти́вный, структу́рный

structure [стрáк-чăр] sn. здáние, постройка, структýра; строй (as social, of society), etc.)

struggle [страгл] sn. борьбá, напряжéние, усилие; vi. бороться, дéлать усилия, старáться

strum [страм] vt.i. бренчáть

strut [страт] sn. подпóрка (of framework); гóрдая пóступь (gait); vt.i. вáжничать, гóрдо выступáть

stub [стаб] sn. пень (stump); облóмок (of tooth); огрызок (of pencil); окýрок (of cigar); vt. выкóрчёвывать

stubble [стабл] sn. жнивьé

stubborn [стá-бăрн] adj. упóрный, упрямый

stud [стад] sn. зáпонка; кóнный завóд (of horses)

student [стю-дănт] sm. студéнт

studio [стю-ди-оў] sn. стýдия

studious [стю-ди-ăс] adj. прилéжный, усéрдный

study [стá-ди] sn. изучéние, кабинéт (room); vt. изучáть, исслéдовать

stuff [стаф] sn. матéрия (textile); вещество, материáл (material); – and nonsense! [– энд нóн-сăнс] вздор! чепухá!; vt.i. заполнять, набивáть (cram into); фаршировáть (in cookery)

stuffing [стá-фин] sn. начинка; фарш

stuffy [стá-фи] adj. дýшный, спёртый

stultify [стáл-ти-фай] vt. дéлать бессмысленным

stumble [стамбл] sn. споты-

кáнье; заминка (hesitation); vi. уступáться, спотыкáться; запинáться (hesitate)

stumbling-block [стáмблин блок] sn. кáмень преткновéния

stump [стамп] sn. кýльтя, обрýбок

stun [стан] vt. оглушáть, ошеломлять

stunning [стá-нин] adj. ошеломляющий

stunt [стант] vt. задéрживать рост (check growth)

stupefy [стю-пи-фай] vt. изумлять, притуплять ум

stupendous [стю-пéн-дăс] adj. изумительный, огрóмный

stupid [стю-пид] adj. глýпый, тупóй

stupidity [стю-пи-ди-ти] sn. глýпость, тýпость

stupor [стю-пăр] sn. med. столбняк; оцепенéние

sturdy [стёр-ди] adj. стóйкий

sturgeon [стёр-джăн] s. осётр

stutter [стá-тăр] sn. заикáние; vi. заикáться

stutterer [стá-тă-рăр] sn. заика

sty [стай] sn. свинóй хлев; ячмéнь (на глазý) (of eye)

style [стайл] sn. стиль; m., фасóн

stylish [стáй-лиш] adj. мóдный, шикáрный, щеголь-скóй

styptic [стип-тик] adj. вяжущий, кровоостанáвливающий

suave [сўэйв] adj. учтивый; мягкий (of flavour)

sub- [саб-] *pref.* под-

subaltern [са́-бăл-тăрн] *sm.* мла́дший офице́р

subconscious [саб-ко́н-шăс] *adj.* подсозна́тельный

subdue [саб-дю́] *vt.* покоря́ть, укроща́ть

subheading [саб-хе́-дiн] *sm.* подзаголо́вок

subject [саб-джiкт] *s.* по́дданный (*of country*); грам. подлежа́щее, субъе́кт; предме́т (*topic*); *adj.* подлежа́щий (*theme*); подчинённый, подчинённый (*theme*); *adj.* подлежа́щий, подчинённый; *adv.* допуска́я, при усло́вии; [саб-дже́кт] *vt.* подверга́ть, покоря́ть

subjection [саб-дже́к-шăн] *sm.* подчине́ние, покоре́ние

subjective [саб-дже́к-тiв] *adj.* субъекти́вный; — **case** [- кэ́йс] грам. имени́тельный паде́ж

subjoin [саб-джо́йн] *vt.* добавля́ть

subjugation [саб-джу́-ге́й-шăн] *sm.* порабоще́ние

subjunctive [саб-джа́нк-тiв] *adj.* сослага́тельный

sublime [сă-бла́йм] *adj.* возвы́шенный

submarine [саб-мă-ри́н] *sm.* подво́дная ло́дка; *adj.* подво́дный

submerge [саб-мăрдж] *vt.i.* затопля́ть

submission [саб-ми́-шăн] *sm.* подобостра́стие

submissive [саб-ми́-сiв] *adj.* поко́рный

submit [саб-ми́т] *vt.* представля́ть, ука́зывать; подчиня́ть, покоря́ться

subordinate [сă-бо́р-дi-нiт] *sm. adj.* подчинё-

ный; *gram.* прида́точный

[са-бо́р-дi-нэйт] *vt.* подчиня́ть

subordination [са-бо́р-дi-нэ́й-шăн] *sm.* подчинённость

subscribe [сăб-скра́йб] *vt.i.* подпи́сывать (*sign*), абони́роваться (*to a journal, etc.*); присоединя́ться (*to a view, opinion, etc.*)

subscriber [сăб-скра́й-бăр] *sm.* подпи́счик

subscription [саб-скри́п-шăн] *sm.* абонеме́нт; подпи́ска

subsequent [сăб-сi-куэ́нт] *adj.* после́дующий

subservient [саб-сăр-вi-ăнт] *adj.* рабо́лепный; соде́йствующий (*instrumental*)

subside [саб-са́йд] *vi.* убыва́ть (*of water*); па́дать (*fall*); умолка́ть, утиха́ть (*abate*); оседа́ть (*settle*)

subsidence [саб-сi-дăнс] *sm.* оседа́ние, паде́ние

subsidiary [саб-сi-дi-ăрi] *adj.* вспомога́тельный

subsidize [саб-сi-да́йз] *vt.* субсиди́ровать

subsidy [саб-сi-дi] *sm.* де́нежная асигно́вка, дота́ция

subsist [сăб-сíст] *vt.i.* корми́ться, пробавля́ться, существова́ть

subsistence [саб-сíс-тăнс] *sm.* пропита́ние

substance [сăб-стăнс] *sm.* вещество́, мате́рия; су́щность (*essence*)

substantial [сăб-стǽн-шăл] *adj.* суще́ственный

substantiate [сăб-стǽн-шi-эйт] *vt.* приводи́ть доказа́тельства

substantive [сăб-стăн-тĭв] *sn. gram.* существительное; *adj.* независимый

substitute [сăб-стĭ-тют] *sn.* заместитель; *sn.* замена; *vt.* заменять (*of thing*); замещать (*of person*)

substitution [сăб-стĭ-тю́-шăн] *sn.* замена; замещение

subterfuge [сăб-тăр-фюдж] *sn.* отговорка, увёртка

subterranean [сăб-тă-рắй-нĭ-ăн] *adj.* подземный

subtle [сатл] *adj.* утончённый; неуловимый (*elusive*)

subtlety [сă-тăл-тĭ] *sn.* нежность, тонкость

subtract [сăб-трăкт] *vt.* вычитать

subtraction [сăб-трăк-шăн] *sn.* вычитание

suburb [сă-бăрб] *sn.* пригород; *pl.* предместья

suburban [сă-бắр-бăн] *adj.* пригородный

subversion [сăб-вắр-шăн] *sn.* ниспровержение

subversive [сăб-вắр-сĭв] *adj.* гибельный, разрушительный

subway [сăб-у́эй] *sn.* тоннель, *m.*

succeed [сăк-сид] *vi.* следовать (*follow*); успевать (*prosper*)

success [сăк-сéс] *sn.* успех

successful [сăк-сéс-фўл] *adj.* преуспевающий, удачный, успешный

succession [сăк-сé́-шăн] *sn.* последовательность; **in** – [ĭн –] подряд

successive [сăк-сé-сĭв] *adj.* последующий

successor [сăк-сé-сăр] *sn.* преемник

succour [сă-кăр] *vt.* помогать

succulent [сă-кю-лăнт] *adj.* сочный

succumb [сă-кáм] *vi.* изнемогать, уступать

such [сач] *adj.* такой; **– as** [– ăз] такой как; *pron.* таковой

suck [сак] *vt.* сосать; впитывать (*imbibe*)

suckling [сăк-лĭй] *s.* грудной ребёнок (*child*)

suction [сăк-шăн] *sn.* всасывание

sudden [сă-дăн] *adj.* внезапный; **all of a** – [ôл ов ă –] вдруг

suds [садз] *sn. pl.* мыльная пена

sue [сю] *vt.i.* преследовать (*prosecute*); просить (*entreat*)

suède [сўэйд] *sn.* замша; *adj.* замшевый

suet [сю́-ĭт] *sn.* говяжье сало

suffer [сă-фăр] *vt.i.* страдать; допускать, терпеть (*permit*)

sufferer [сă-фă-рăр] *sm.* страдалец

suffering [сă-фă-рĭй] *sn.* страдание

suffice [сă-фáйс] *vt.i.* быть достаточным, хватать

sufficient [сă-фĭ́-шăнт] *adj.* достаточный

suffix [сă-фĭкс] *sn.* суффикс

suffocate [сă-фă-кэйт] *vt.i.* душить, удушать; задыхаться

suffocation [сă-фă-кáй-шăн] *sn.* удушение

suffrage [сă-фрĭдж] *sn.* избирательное право, право голоса

suffuse [сă-фю́з] *vt.* залива́ть

sugar [шу́-ğăр] *sn.* cа́хар; *vt.i.* обса́харивать (*sprinkle*); подсла́щивать (*sweeten*); *chem.* сахаро́за

sugar-basin [шу́-ğăр-бэ́й-сĭн] *sn.* cа́харница

sugary [шу́-ğă-рĭ] *adj.* cа́харный, сла́дкий; *fig.* льсти́вый

suggest [сă-дж́ест] *vt.* внуша́ть, наводи́ть (*hint*); предлага́ть (*propose*)

suggestion [сă-джéщи-чăн] *sn.* внуше́ние; предложе́ние

suicide [сю́-и-сайд] *sn.* самоуби́йство

suit [сют] *sn.* костю́м; проше́ние, ходата́йство (*petition*); масть (*cards*); *vt.i.* годи́ться, подходи́ть (*fit*); приспособля́ть (*adapt*)

suitable [сю́-тăбл] *adj.* подходя́щий, приго́дный

suit-case [сю́т-кэ́йс] *sn.* чемода́нчик

suite [суи́т] *sn.* сви́та; ряд ко́мнат (*rooms*); гарниту́р (*furniture*); *mus.* сюи́та

suiting [сю́-тĭн] *sn.* мате́рия (для костю́ма)

suitor [сю́-тăр] *sn.* уха́живатель; *leg.* исте́ц, проси́тель

sulk [салк] *vi.* ду́ться

sulky [сáл-кĭ] *adj.* наду́тый, хму́рый

sullen [сá-лăн] *adj.* за́мкнутый, угрю́мый

sulphate [сáл-фĭт] *sn.* соль се́рной кислоты́

sulphur [сáл-фăр] *sn.* се́ра; зеленова́то-жёлтый цвет (*colour*); *vt.* оку́ривать се́рой

sultry [сáл-трĭ] *adj.* зно́йный

sum [сам] *sn.* cу́мма; ито́г (*total*); арифмети́ческая зада́ча (*problem*); – **up** [– ап] подводи́ть ито́г, сумми́ровать

summarize [сá-мă-райз] *vt.* резюми́ровать

summary [сá-мă-рĭ] *sn.* изложе́ние, резюме́; *adj.* сумма́рный

summer [сá-мăр] *sn.* ле́то; *vt.i.* проводи́ть ле́то; – **lightning** [– лайт-нĭн] зарни́ца; *adj.* ле́тний

summer-house [сá-мăр-хăус] *sn.* бесе́дка

summit [сá-мĭт] *sn.* верши́на; *fig.* верх, преде́л (*of happiness, etc.*)

summon [сá-мăн] *vt.* вызыва́ть, созыва́ть; – **up courage** [– ап кá-рĭдж] собира́ться с ду́хом

summons [сá-мăнз] *sn.* вы́зов, зов

sumptuous [сáмп-тю-ăс] *adj.* пы́шный, роско́шный

sun [сан] *sn.* cо́лнце; *vt.i.* выставля́ть на со́лнце (*expose*); гре́ться на со́лнце (*sunbathe*)

sunbeam [сáн-бим] *sn.* луч со́лнца

sunburn [сáн-бŏрн] *sn.* зага́р

sunburnt [сáн-бŏрнт] *adj.* загоре́лый

Sunday [сáн-дĭ] *sn.* воскресе́нье

sundown [сáн-даýн] *sn.* зака́т

sundries [сáн-дрĭз] *sn. pl.* вся́кая вся́чина

sundry [сáн-дрĭ] *adj.* разли́чный, ра́зный

sunflower [сáн-флаý-ăр] *sn.* подсо́лнечник

sunken [сан-кăн] *adj.* за-то́пленный (*of ship*); опа́вший (*of cheeks*); впа́лый (*of eyes*)

sunlight [сан-лайт] *sn.* со́лнечный цвет

sunny [са́-ні] *adj.* со́лнечный; *fig.* ра́достный

sunrise [сан-райз] *sn.* восхо́д со́лнца

sunset [сан-сэт] *sn.* зака́т со́лнца

sunshade [сан-шэйд] *sn.* зо́нтик (от со́лнца)

sunshine [сан-шайн] *sn.* я́сная пого́да (*weather*); *fig.* весе́лье, ра́дость

sunstroke [сан-стро́ук] *sn.* со́лнечный уда́р

sup [сап] *vi.* у́жинать

super [сю́-пăр] *sm. theat.* стати́ст; *adj.* квадра́тный; *com.* перворкла́ссный

super- [сю-пăр-] *pref.* над, сверх, сли́шком

superannuate [сю-пăр-а́-ню-э́йт] *vt.* увольня́ть по ста́рости

superannuation [сю-пăр-æ-ню-э́й-шăн] *sn.* увольне́ние по ста́рости; пе́нсия (*pension*)

superb [сю-пэ́рб] *adj.* велико-ле́пный, превосхо́дный

supercilious [сю-пăр-сі́-лі-ăс] *adj.* высокоме́рный

superficial [сю-пăр-фі́-шăл] *adj.* пове́рхностный

superfine [сю-пăр-фа́йн] *adj.* тонча́йший; *com.* вы́сшего со́рта

superfluous [сю-пэ́р-флу́-ăс] *adj.* изли́шний

superheat [сю-пăр-хі́т] *vt.* перегрева́ть

superhuman [сю-пăр-хю́-мăн] *adj.* сверхчелове́ческий

superimpose [сю-пăр-ім-по́уз] *vt.* накла́дывать

superintend [сю-прін-тэ́нд] *vt.* контроли́ровать, наблюда́ть, надзира́ть

superintendent [сю-прін-тэ́н-дăнт] *sm.* заве́дующий, надзира́тель; полице́йский инспе́ктор (*of police*)

supernumerary [сю-пăр-ню́-мă-рă-рі] *sm.* сверх-шта́тный рабо́тник; *theat.* стати́ст

superior [сю-пи́-рі-ăр] *sm.* нача́льник, ста́рший; насто́ятель (*of monastery, etc.*); *adj.* лу́чший, вы́сший

superiority [сю-пі-рі́о́-рі-ті] *sn.* превосхо́дство; ста́ршинство

superlative [сю-пăр-лă-тів] *sn. gram.* превосхо́дная сте́пень; *adj.* высоча́йший

supernatural [сю-пăр-нэ́-чă-рăл] *adj.* сверхъесте́ственный

supersede [сю-пăр-си́д] *vt.* заменя́ть, увольня́ть

superstition [сю-пăр-сті́-шăн] *sn.* суеве́рие

superstitious [сю-пăр-сті́-шăс] *adj.* суеве́рный

superstructure [сю-пăр-стра́к-чăр] *sn.* надстро́йка

supervise [сю-пăр-ва́йз] *vt.* наблюда́ть (за чём-либо); надзира́ть

supervision [сю-пăр-ві́-жăн] *sn.* наблюде́ние, надзо́р

supervisor [сю-пăр-ва́й-зăр] *sm.* надзира́тель, надсмо́трщик

supine [сю-пайн] *sn. gram.* супин; [сю-пайн] *adj.* лежачий навзничь; покоящийся (*quiescent*)

supper [са-пăр] *sn.* ýжин

supplant [са-плант] *vt.* выживать, вытеснять

supple [сапл] *adj.* гибкий; находчивый (*adroit*)

supplement [са-плі-мăнт] *sn.* добавление; [са-плă-мéнт] *vt.* пополнять

supplementary [са-плі-мéн-тă-рі] *adj.* дополнительный

suppliant [са-плі-ăнт] *adj.* умоляющий

supplicate [са-плі-кéйт] *vt.* молить, умолять

supplication [са-плі-кéй-шăн] *sn.* мольбá, прóсьба

supply [са-плай] *sn.* снабжéние; запáс (*stock*); *pl.* припáсы; *vt.* снабжáть

support [са-пóрт] *sn.* опóра, поддéржка; *vt.* поддéрживать

supporter [са-пóр-тăр] *sm.* сторóнник

suppose [са-пóуз] *vt.* полагáть, предполагáть

supposition [са-по-зí-шăн] *sn.* предположéние

supposititious [са-по-зі-ті-шăс] *adj.* подлóжный

suppress [са-прéс] *vt.* подавлять (*put an end to*); умáлчивать (*keep secret*)

supremacy [сю-прé-мă-сі] *sn.* верховéнство

supreme [сю-прíм] *adj.* верхóвный, вы́сший

sure [шўр] *adj.* увéренный, вéрный (*true*); несомнéнный (*certain*); *adv.* конéчно, несомнéнно; безуслóвно

surely [шўр-лі] *adv.* навéрно, увéренно

surety [шўр-ті] *sm.* поручи́тель; *sn.* порýка

surf [сăрф] *sn.* бýрун, прибóй

surface [сăр-фіс] *sn.* повéрхность

surfeit [сăр-фіт] *sn.* пресыщéние; *vt.i.* перекáрмливать (*overfeed*); пресыщáться (*be satiated*)

surge [сăрдж] *sn.* волнéние (*surging*); вóлны (*waves*); *vt.* поднимáться

surgeon [сăр-джăн] *sn.* хирýрг

surgery [сăр-джі-рі] *sn.* хирургия; приёмная (*room*)

surly [сăр-лі] *adj.* приветливый, угрюмый

surmise [сăр-майз] *sn.* догáдка (*guess*); подозрéние (*suspicion*); *vt.i.* подозревáть (*suspect*)

surmount [сăр-мáунт] *vt.* преодолевáть

surname [сăр-нэйм] *sn.* фами́лия

surpass [сăр-пáс] *vt.* превосходи́ть, превышáть

surplus [сăр-плáс] *sn.* изли́шек, остáток

surprise [са-прайз] *sn.* сюрпри́з, удивлéние; *vt.* изумлять, удивлять

surrender [са-рéн-дăр] *sn.* сдáча, устýпка; *vt.i.* сдавáть, предавáться

surreptitious [са-рăп-ти́-шăс] *adj.* сдéланный исподти́шка

surround [са-рáунд] *vt.* окружáть

surroundings [са-рáун-дінз] *sn. pl.* окрéстности; средá (*midst*)

survey [сэ́р-вэй] sn. обзор, осмотр; обследование (inspection); съёмка (operation); [сэ́р-вэй] vt. межевать (of land); осматривать (view)

surveyor [сэ́р-вэй-ăр] sm. землемер; топограф

survival [сăр-вай-вăл] sn. переживание; пережиток

survive [сăр-вайв] vt. переживать

susceptibility [сă-сéп-ти-бі-лі-ті] sn. восприимчивость, впечатлительность

susceptible [сă-сéп-тибл] adj. чувствительный

suspect [сáс-пект] sm. подозреваемый (человек); [сăс-пéкт] vt. подозревать

suspend [сăс-пéнд] vt. вешать, подвешивать (hang up); приостанавливать (stop); отрешать (deprive)

suspenders [сăс-пéн-дăрз] sn. pl. подтяжки, помочи

suspense [сăс-пéнс] sn. беспокойствие, состояние неизвестности

suspension [сăс-пéн-шăн] sn. подвешивание; приостановка (stopping); отрешение (temporary dismissal)

suspicion [сăс-пі-шăн] sn. подозрение

sustain [сăс-тэ́йн] vt. выдерживать, выносить, поддерживать

sustenance [сáс-ті-нăнс] sn. питательность, прокорм

swagger [сýă-ґăр] vi. важничать, чваниться; adj. щегольской

swallow [сýо-лоу] s. ласточка (bird); глотка (gullet); глоток (gulp); vt. глотать, проглатывать

swamp [сýомп] sn. болото, топь; vt. наливать, пропитывать, заваливать (overwhelm); подавлять (in numbers, quantity)

swan [сýон] sn. лебедь, m.; adj. лебединый

sward [сýорд] sn. дёрн

swarm [сýорм] sn. рой, стая; толпа (of people); пчелиный рой (of bees); vi. толпиться

swathe [сýэй] sn. бинт, повязка; vt. бинтовать

sway [сýэй] sn. качание, колебание; власть, правление (power, rule); господство (domination); vt.i. качать, колебаться; править, управлять

swear [сýэ́р] vi. клясться; ругаться (curse)

sweat [сýэт] sn. пот; потение (perspiration); coll. тяжёлая работа; vt.i. потеть, трудиться (drudge, toil); припаивать (solder)

Swede [сýид] sm. швед; sn. шведская брюква (turnip)

Swedish [сýи-діш] adj. шведский

sweep [сýип] sm. трубочист (person); sn. размах (motion); vt.i. мести, сметать, очищать (with broom); очищать (clean)

sweepstake [сýип-стэ́йк] sn. пари на скачках

sweet [сýит] sn. конфета; сладкое (as a dish); adj. сладкий

sweeten [сýи-тăн] vt. услаждать

sweetheart [сýит-хăрт] sm. возлюбленный

sweets [сýитс] sn. pl. сласти

swell [суэл] *sn.* возвышёние, выпуклость, надутость; волнёние, зыбь (*of waves*); *vt.i.* надувáться, разбухáть; нарастáть (*of sound*)

swelling [суэ́-лий] *sn.* опухоль

swelter [суэ́л-тăр] *vi.* изнемогáть от зноя

swerve [суэ́рв] *vt.i.* отклонять, уклоняться

swift [суйфт] *adj.* бóрзый, быстрый

swill [суйл] *vt.i.* полоскáть; пить жáдно (*drink greedily*)

swim [суйм] *sn.* плáвание (*spell of swimming*); *vt.i.* плáвать, плыть

swimmer [суй-мăр] *sm.* пловéц

swindle [суйндл] *sn.* мошéнничество; обмáн (*fraud*); *vt.i.* надувáть, обмáнывать

swindler [суйн-дляр] *sm.* мошéнник, обмáнщик

swine [суáйн] *s.* свинья

swing [суйй] *sn.* качáние (*oscillation*); ритм (*rhythm*); качéли (*child's*); *vt.i.* вертéться, качáться; размáхивать (*with stick, etc.*)

swipe [суáйп] *sn.* сильный удáр

swirl [суэрл] *sn.* водоворóт; *vi.* образóвывать воронки

Swiss [суйс] *sm.* швейцáрец; *adj.* швейцáрский

switch [суйч] *sn.* прут (*rod, twig*); накладкá (*of hair*); *electr.* выключáтель, переключáтель, *vt.i.* стегáть прутóм (*lash*); переводить (*transfer*)

swivel [суй-вăл] *sn.* вертлюг

swoon [суýн] *sn.* обмóрок; *vi.* пáдать в обмóрок

swoop [суýп] *sn.* налёт,

нападéние; *vi.* бросáться, налетáть

sword [сôрд] *sn.* сáбля, шпáга

swordsman [сôрдз-мăн] *sm.* фехтовáльщик

syllable [сí-лăбл] *sn.* слог

syllabus [сí-лă-бăс] *sn.* прогрáмма обучéния, расписáние

symbol [сíм-бăл] *sn.* сíмвол, эмблéма

symbolical [сíм-бó-ли-кăл] *adj.* символíческий

symmetrical [сí-мé-три-кăл] *adj.* симметрíческий

sympathize [сíм-пă-ɵайз] *vi.* симпатизíровать, сочýвствовать

sympathy [сíм-пă-ɵи] *sn.* симпáтия, сочýвствие

symphony [сíм-фă-ни] *sn.* симфóния

symptom [сíмп-тăм] *sn.* прíзнак, симптóм

synchronize [сíн-крă-найз] *vt.i.* совпадáть во врéмени, синхронизíровать

syndicate [сíн-ди-кíт] *sn.* синдикáт

synonym [сí-нă-нíм] *sn.* синóним

synopsis [сí-нóп-сíс] *sn.* конспéкт, обзóр

synthetic [сíн-ɵé-тíк] *adj.* синтетíческий

syringe [сí-рíндж] *sn.* спринцóвка (*syringing*); шприц (*surgical*); *vt.* проливáть; промывáть

syrup [сí-рăп] *sn.* сирóп, пáтока (*treacle*)

system [сíс-тăм] *sn.* систéма; строй; формáция

systematic [сíс-тí-мă-тíк] *adj.* систематíческий

TAB 723 TAN

T

tab [тæб] *sn.* пéтелька, ушкó; *mil.* нашивка

table [тэйбл] *sn.* стол; таблица (*list, etc.*)

table-cloth [тэйбл-клоθ] *sn.* скáтерть

tablet [тǽб-лĭт] *sn.* дóщечка, пластинка (*slab*); таблéтка (*lozenge*)

taboo [тă-бý] *sn.* табý; *adj.* запрéтный

tabulate [тǽ-бю-лейт] *vt.* располагáть в виде таблиц

tacit [тǽ-сĭт] *adj.* молчали́вый

tack [тæк] *sn.* кнóпка, корóткий гвоздь (*small nail*); намéтка (*stitch*); *naut.* поворóт, галс; *vt.i.* прикреплять гвóздиками (*nail*); смётывать (*stitch*); *naut.* лави́ровать

tackle [тǽкл] *sn.* принадлéжности, снаряжéние; *naut.* такелáж; *vt.* борóться с (*grapple with*)

tacky [тǽ-кĭ] *adj.* ли́пкий

tact [тæкт] *sn.* такт; такти́чность

tactics [тǽк-тĭкс] *sn. pl.* тáктика

tag [тæг] *sn.* жестянóй кóнчик (*of shoe lace, etc.*); ярлы́к, этикéтка (*label*); наконéчник (*loose end*); ходя́чая фрáза (*stock phrase*); *vt.* приделывать, прицеплять

tail [тэйл] *sn.* хвост; косá (*of hair*)

tailor [тэ́й-лăр] *sm.* портнóй; *vt.i.* быть портны́м (*be a tailor*); портня́жничать

taint [тэйнт] *sn.* порóк (*blemish*); пятнó (*stain*); следы́ гние́ния (*trace of badness*); зарáза (*contamination*); *vt.i.* заражáть, пóртиться

take [тэйк] *vt.i.* брать, взять, принимáть; снимáть (*photograph*); испытывать (*offence*); разрушáть, сноси́ть (*demolish*)

take-off [тэ́йк-оф] *sn.* взлёт, старт

taking [тэ́й-кĭй] *adj.* привлекáтельный (*captivating*); *sn. pl.* бары́ш

tale [тэйл] *sn.* рассказ

talent [тǽ-лăнт] *sn.* талáнт

talk [тōк] *sn.* разговóр (*conversation*); слух (*rumour*); бесéда (*lecture*); *vt.i.* говори́ть, разгова́ривать

talkative [тṓ-кă-тĭв] *adj.* болтли́вый, разговóрчивый

tall [тōл] *adj.* высóкий; высóкого рóста (*of person*); *adv.* преувели́ченно

tallow [тǽ-лоу] *sn.* жир, сáло

tally [тǽ-лĭ] *sn.* би́рка; *vi.* совпадáть, соотвéтствовать

tame [тэйм] *adj.* приручённый, ручнóй (*of animals*); вя́лый (*insipid*); *vt.* приручáть, смиря́ть, укрощáть

tamer [тэ́й-мăр] *sm.* укроти́тель

tamper [тǽм-пăр] *vi.* вмéшиваться, сова́ться

tan [тæн] *sn.* загáр (*sunburn*); толчёная дубóвая корá (*crushed bark of oak*); *adj.* рыжевáто-кори́чневый (*colour*); *vt.i.* загорáть (*become bronzed*)

tandem [тӕн-дӕм] *sn.* упряжка цугом; *adv.* гуськом, цугом

tang [тӕн] *sn.* резкий привкус (*of taste*)

tangible [тӕн-джибл] *adj.* осязаемый

tangle [тӕнгл] *sn.* запутанность

tank [тӕнк] *sn.* бак, водоём, цистерна; *mil.* танк

tankard [тӕн-кӕрд] *sn.* пивная кружка

tanker [тӕн-кӕр] *sn.* нефтеналивное судно

tanner [тӕ-нӕр] *sm.* дубильщик, кожевник

tantalize [тӕн-тӕ-лайз] *vt.* дразнить, мучить

tantamount [тӕн-тӕ-маунт] *adj.* равносильный

tap [тӕп] *sn.* кран; лёгкий удар (*light blow*); вино (или пиво) из бочёнка (*wine or beer*); *vt.* подстукивать (*knock gently*)

tape [тӕйп] *sn.* тесьма; лента

taper [тӕй-пӕр] *sn.* тонкая свечка; слабый свет (*feeble light*); *adj.* конический; *vi.* суживаться

tapestry [тӕ-пі-стрі] *sn.* гобелен, затканная материя

tapeworm [тӕйп-ӱӧрм] *sn.* глист

tar [тӓр] *sn.* дёготь, жидкая смола; *мазать* дёгтем, смолить

tardiness [тӓр-ді-ніс] *sn.* медлительность (*slowness*); опоздание (*delaying*)

target [тӓр-гіт] *sn.* мишень

tariff [тӕ-ріф] *sn.* тариф; таможенная пошлина (*cus-*

tom duty); прейскурант (*price list*)

tarnish [тӓр-ніш] *sn.* тусклость; *vti.* омрачать, тускнеть

tarpaulin [тӓр-пӧ-лін] *sn.* брезент

tarry [тӕ-рі] *adj.* вымазанный смолой; *vi.* оставаться

tart [тӓрт] *sn.* торт, фруктовое пирожное; *adj.* кислый; *fig.* колкий, резкий

task [тӓск] *sn.* задание, задача, работа; урок (*school*)

tassel [тӕ-сӕл] *sn.* кисточка

taste [тӕйст] *sn.* вкус; склонность (*propensity*); *vti.* вкушать (*savour*); испытывать, пробовать (*try*)

tasty [тӕйс-ті] *adj.* вкусный

tattered [тӕ-тӓрд] *adj.* оборванный

tattle [тӕтл] *vi.* сплетничать

tattoo [тӕ-ту́] *sn.* барабанный бой; *vt.* татуировать

taunt [тӧнт] *sn.* насмешка, попрёк, укол; язвительное замечание (*sarcastic remark*); *vt.* говорить колкости, упрекать, язвить

taut [тӧт] *adj. naut.* туго натянутый (*tight*)

tavern [тӕ-вӓрн] *sn.* кабачок, трактир

tawny [тӧ-ні] *adj.* краснобурый

tax [тӕкс] *sn.* налог; бремя (*burden*); напряжение (*strain*); *vt.* облагать налогом; напрягать

taxation [тӕкс-ӧй-шӓн] *sn.* обложение налогом

taxi [тӕ-ксі] *sn.* такси; *vti.* ехать на такси; рулить по земле (*of 'plane*)

tea [ти] *sn.* чай; *adj.* чайный

teach [тич] *vt.i.* преподавать, учить; давать уроки (*give lessons*)

teacher [ти́-чăр] *sn.* преподаватель, учитель

teaching [ти́-чий] *sn.* обучение, учение

team [тим] *sn.* спортивная команда (*side of players*); упряжка (*of animals*); бригада (*of workmen*)

tea-pot [ти́-пот] *sn.* чайник

tear [тэ́р] *sn.* дыра, разрез (*hole, cut*); прореха (*rent*); *vt.i.* отрывать, рвать, разрываться

tear [тиăр] *sn.* слеза

tearful [ти́р-фŭл] *adj.* плачущий (*given to tears*); слезливый

tease [тиз] *sn.* задира (*person*); *vt.* дразнить, надоедать; чесать (*wool*); ворсить, чесать (*cloth*)

teaser [ти́-зăр] *sn.* трудная задача (*hard task*); *sm.* задира, приставала

teaspoonful [ти́-спун-фŭл] *sn.* полная чайная ложка

teat [тит] *sn.* сосок

technical [тĕк-ни-кăл] *adj.* технический

technicality [тĕк-ни-кǽ-ли-ти] *sn.* техническое свойство

technique [тĕк-ни́к] *sn.* техника (*in performance*)

tedious [ти́-ди-ăс] *adj.* скучный, утомительный

teem [тим] *vi.* кишеть

teen-age [ти́н-эйдж] *s.* подросток

teens [тинз] *sn. pl.* возраст от 13 до 19 лет

teething [ти́-ий] *sn.* прорезывание зубов

teetotal [ти́-тоў-тăл] *adj.* трезвенный

telegram [тĕ́-ли-грæм] *sn.* телеграмма

telegraphy [ти-лĕ́-грă-фи] *sn.* телеграфия

telephone [тĕ́-ли-фоўн] *sn.* телефон; *vt.i.* телефонировать

telescope [тĕ́-ли-скоўп] *sn.* телескоп

television [тĕ-ли-ви́-жăн] *sn.* телевидение, фотоэлектрическая передача

tell [тĕл] *vt.i.* рассказывать, сказать (*relate*); доносить, сообщать (*inform*); приказывать (*order*); считать (*count*)

telling [тĕ́-лий] *adj.* многозначительный (*significant*); убедительный (*convincing*)

temerity [ти-мĕ́-ри-ти] *sn.* безрассудство

temper [тĕ́м-пăр] *sn.* нрав, настроение (*mood*); вспышка (*fit of anger*); закал (*of steel*); *vt.* закаливать (*steel*); смягчать (*mitigate*)

temperament [тĕ́м-пă-рă-мăнт] *sn.* темперамент

temperance [тĕ́м-пă-рăнс] *sn.* сдержанность, умеренность

temperate [тĕ́м-пă-рит] *adj.* умеренный

temperature [тĕ́м-пă-рă-чăр] *sn.* температура

tempest [тĕ́м-пист] *sn.* буря

temple [тĕмпл] *sn.* храм; висок (*of head*)

temporal [тĕ́м-пă-рăл] *adj.* светский (*secular*); временный, преходящий (*of time*)

temporary [тĕ́м-пă-рă-ри] *adj.* временный

tempt [тємпт] *vt.* искушáть, соблазнять: прельщáть

temptation [тємп-тэ́й-шăн] *sn.* искушéние, соблáзн

ten [тєн] *num.* дéсять

tenable [тє́-нăбл] *adj.* устóйчивый; *mil.* оборонослосóбный

tenacious [ті-нэ́й-шăс] *adj.* вя́зкий, ли́пкий (*strongly adhesive*); упóрный (*stubborn*)

tenacity [ті-нắ-сі-ті] *sn.* упóрство; цéпкость

tenancy [тє́-нăн-сі] *sn.* арéнда

tenant [тє́-нăнт] *sn.* жилéц, наниматель

tend [тєнд] *vi.* клони́ться, направля́ться (*towards*); *vt.* забóтиться (*look after*)

tendency [тє́-дăн-сі] *sn.* стремлéние, тендéнция

tender [тє́н-дăр] *sn.* тéндер (*of ship, locomotive*); *com.* зая́вка, предложéние, *vt.i.* предлагáть (*offer*); подавáть (*render*); *adj.* нéжный

tenderness [тє́н-дăр-ніс] *sn.* мя́гкость, нéжность

tendon [тє́н-дăн] *sn.* сухожи́лка

tendril [тє́н-дріл] *sn.* у́сик

tenement [тє́-ні-мăнт] *sn.* многокварти́рный дом

tennis [тє́-ніс] *sn.* тéннис

tenor [тє́-нăр] *sn.* уклáд (*course or routine*); óбщее содержáние, смысл (*purport*); *mus.* тéнор

tense [тєнс] *sn. gram.* врéмя; *adj.* напряжённый

tension [тє́н-шăн] *sn.* напряжённость, натя́нутость, растяжéние

tent [тєнт] *sn.* палáтка, шатёр; *med.* тампóн

tentacle [тє́н-тăкл] *sn.* щу́пальце

tentative [тє́н-тă-тів] *adj.* прóбный

tenterhooks [тє́н-тăр-ху́кс] *sn. pl.* натяжны́е крючки́

tenth [тєнθ] *num.* деся́тый

tenure [тє́-нюр] *sn.* владéние (*of property*); занимáние (*of office*)

tepid [тє́-під] *adj.* тепловáтый

term [тœрм] *sn.* срок (*period*); семéстр (*of school*); сéссия (*session*); тéрмин (*expression*); *pl.* договóр, условия

terminal [тœ́р-мі-нăл] *sn.* конéчный пункт; *electr.* зажи́м; *adj.* конéчный, семéстрóвый (*school*)

terminate [тœ́р-мі-нэйт] *vt.i.* закáнчивать, кончáться

termination [тœр-мі-нэ́й-шăн] *sn.* конéц, окончáние

terminus [тœ́р-мі-нăс] *sn.* конéчная стáнция

terrace [тє́-рăс] *sn.* террáса; усту́п (*natural shelf*)

terrain [тă-рэ́йн] *sn.* мéстность

terrestrial [ті-рє́с-трі-ăл] *adj.* земнóй (*of the earth*); сухопу́тный (*of dry land*)

terrible [тє́-рібл] *adj.* стрáшный, ужáсный

terrify [тє́-рі-фай] *vt.* пугáть, устрашáть

territorial [тє-рі-тó́-рі-ăл] *adj.* территориáльный

territory [тє́-рі-тă-рі] *sn.* земля́, террито́рия; *fig.* óбласть, сфéра

terror [тє́-рăр] *sn.* у́жас

terse [тœрс] *adj.* выразительный

test [тéст] *sn.* испытáние, прóба; мери́ло (*standard*); *vt.* испробовать, испытывать

testament [тéс-тă-мăнт] *sn.* завещáние; завéт

testify [тéс-ти-фай] *vt.i.* давáть показáния, свидéтельствовать

testimonial [тес-ти-мóу́-ни-ăл] *sn.* аттестáт, свидéтельство

testimony [тéс-ти-мă-ни] *sn.* торжéственное заявлéние (*solemn declaration*); доказáтельство (*proof*); *leg.* показáние

text [тéкст] *sn.* текст; тéма (*theme*)

textbook [тéкст-бŷк] *sn.* учéбник

textile [тéкс-тайл] *adj.* тексти́льный; *pl.* тексти́льные издéлия (*goods*); ткань (*fabrics*)

texture [тéкс-чăр] *sn.* строéние (*of leather, wood, etc.*); кáчество ткáни (*quality of cloth*)

than [ðăн] *conj.* нéжели, чем

thank [ðăйк] *vt.* благодари́ть; *pl.* благодáрность

that [ðăт] *pron.* тот, *m.*, та *f.*, то, *n.*; *conj.* что, чтóбы; *adv.* так, до такóй стéпени; *relative pron.* котóрый (= *which*)

thatch [ðăч] *sn.* солóменная крыша; *vt.* крыть солóмой

thaw [ðô] *sn.* óттепель, тáяние; *vt.i.* тáять; *fig.* смягчáться

ð как пéред согласным, ӫі пéред глáсным, ӫи под-

ударéнием] *adj.* gram. определённый член; *adv.* **the . . . the,** чем . . . тем

theatre [ðí-ă-тăр] *sn.* теáтр

theatrical [ðі-ă-три́-кăл] *adj.* театрáльный; *fig.* напыщенный; *pl.* люби́тельский спектáкль

theft [ðéфт] *sn.* воровствó, крáжа

their [ðэ-ăр] *adj.* их, свой

theirs [ðэ-ăрз] *pron.* их

theme [ðим] *sn.* тéма; предмéт (*of conversation*)

themselves [ðăм-сéлвз] *pron.* они́ сáми, сáми себя́

then [ðéн] *sn.* то врéмя; *adj.* тогдáшний; *adv.* затéм, потóм, тогдá; в такóм слýчае (*under such circumstances*)

thence [ðéнс] *adv.* отсю́да

theology [ðі-ó-лă-джи] *sn.* богослóвие

theory [ðи́-ă-ри] *sn.* теóрия

there [ðэ́р] *sn.* (пóле предлóгов) до тогó мéста, отту́да; *adv.* там; тудá (*thither*); *interj.* вот, ну

thereby [ðэ́р-бáй] *adv.* посрéдством этого

therefore [ðэ́р-фôр] *adv.* поэтому, слéдовательно

thermometer [ðăр-мố-мǐ-тăр] *sn.* грáдусник, термóметр

these [ðиз] *pron. pl.* э́ти

they [ðéй] *pron. pl.* они́

thick [ðик] *adj.* тóлстый, густóй (*dense*); перепóлненный (*packed*); мýтный, нея́сный (*not clear*); *adv.* хри́пло (*huskily*)

thicken [ðи́-кăн] *vt.i.* густéть, сгущáться

thicket [ðи́-кіт] *sn.* зáросли, чáща

thickness [θĭk-nĭс] *sn.* толщина́; слой (*layer*); густота́ (*density*)

thief [θиф] *sm.* вор

thigh [θай] *sn.* бедро́

thimble [θĭмбл] *sn.* напёрсток

thin [θĭн] *adj.* то́нкий; ре́дкий (*of hair*); худоща́вый (*lean*); поджа́рый (*meagre*); сла́бый (*of voice*); водяни́стый, жи́дкий (*watery*)

thing [θĭнг] *sn.* вещь, предме́т; *pl.* принадле́жности (*belongings*)

think [θĭнк] *vt.i.* ду́мать, мы́слить; полага́ть (*deem*)

thinker [θĭн-кăр] *sm.* мысли́тель

third [θɔ̈рд] *num.* тре́тий

thirst [θɔ̈рст] *sn.* жа́жда; *vi.* жа́ждать

thirsty [θɔ̈р-стĭ] *adj.* жа́ждущий

thirteen [θɔ̈р-тин] *num.* трина́дцать

thirty [θɔ̈р-тĭ] *num.* три́дцать

this [θĭс] *adj., pron.* э́тот, *m.,* э́та, *f.;* э́то, *n.*

thistle [θĭсл] *sn.* тата́рник, чертополо́х

thong [θой] *sn.* реме́нь, *m.;* плеть

thorn [θо̄рн] *sn.* колю́чка, шип

thorough [θá-pă] *adj.* по́лный, соверше́нный

thoroughbred [θá-pă-бред] *adj.* поро́дистый, чистокро́вный

thoroughfare [θá-pă-фăр] *sn.* прое́зд, прохо́д

though [θōу] *adv. coll.* всё-таки, одна́ко-же; *conj.* хотя́

thought [θō̄т] *sn.* мысль; мышле́ние

thoughtful [θō̄т-фŭл] *adj.* заду́мавшийся, мысля́щий; заду́мчивый (*pensive*); забо́тливый (*solicitous*)

thoughtless [θō̄т-лĭс] *adj.* легкомы́сленный, необду́манный

thousand [θáу-зănд] *num.* ты́сяча

thrash [θрæш] *vt.* бить, колоти́ть

thread [θред] *sn.* ни́тка, нить (*filament*); винтова́я наре́зка (*spiral*); *vt.* продева́ть ни́тку; нани́зывать (*beads*)

threadbare [θред-бăр] *adj.* изно́шенный, протёртый; *fig.* изби́тый

threat [θрет] *sn.* угро́за

threaten [θре́-тăн] *vt.* грози́ть, угрожа́ть

three [θри] *num.* три

thresh [θреш] *vt.* молоти́ть

threshold [θреш-оу́лд] *sn.* поро́г; преддве́рие

thrift [θрĭфт] *sn.* бережли́вость, эконо́мия

thrill [θрĭл] *sn.* содрога́ние; тре́пет; *vt.i.* возбужда́ть, испы́тывать; быть возбуждённым

thrive [θрайв] *vi.* процвета́ть, преуспева́ть

throat [θроут] *sn.* го́рло

throb [θроб] *sn.* бие́ние (*beat*); пульса́ция, тре́пет (*palpitation*); *vi.* пульси́ровать, трепета́ть

throes [θроуз] *sn. pl.* му́ки

throne [θроун] *sn.* трон

throng [θройн] *sn.* толпа́, толчея́; *vt.i.* переполня́ть (*fill with numbers*); стека́ться, толпи́ться

throttle [ѳротл] sn. tech. регуляру́ющий клапа́н; vt. подавля́ть, удави́ть; tech. тормози́ть

through [ѳру́] adj. беспереса́дочный (of train); adv. наскво́зь; prep. че́рез; посре́дством (by means of)

throughout [ѳру́-а́ут] adv. наскво́зь, повсю́ду; prep. во весь, по всему́

throw [ѳроу́] sn. броса́ние; бросо́к (hurl); vt.i. броса́ть, кида́ть

thrush [ѳраш] s. дрозд

thrust [ѳраст] sn. толчо́к, уда́р; vt.i. коло́ть, пронза́ть, сова́ть

thud [ѳад] sn. глухо́й стук; vi. глу́хо стуча́ть

thumb [ѳам] sn. большо́й па́лец; vt. пачкать

thump [ѳамп] sn. стук; vt.i. стуча́ть, ударя́ть

thunder [ѳан-да́р] sn. гром; vi. греме́ть

thunderbolt [ѳа́н-дăр-болт] sn. уда́р мо́лнии

thunderstorm [ѳа́н-дăр-сто́рм] sn. гроза́

Thursday [ѳёрз-ді] sn. четве́рг

thus [ѳас] adv. так so); таки́м о́бразом (in such manner); так наприме́р (as an example)

thwart [ѳуо́рт] vt. расстра́ивать

tick [тік] sn. ти́канье; значо́к (✓), отме́тка (mark); клещ (mite); чехо́л (of bolster, etc.); креди́т (credit); vt.i. ти́кать

ticket [ті-кіт] sn. биле́т; ярлы́к (label)

tickle [тікл] vt. щекота́ть; sn. щекота́ние; vt. щекота́ть

tide [тайд] sn. прили́в и отли́в

tidings [та́й-дінз] sn. pl. изве́стия, но́вости

tidy [та́й-ді] adj. опря́тный; vt. приводи́ть в поря́док

tie [тай] sn. га́лстук (necktie); связь (bond, connection); vt. связывать; pl. у́зы

tiff [тіф] sn. размо́лвка

tier [тір] sn. ряд, я́рус

tiger [та́й-гăр] s. тигр

tight [тайт] adj. натя́нутый, туго́й; пло́тный (firm); непроница́емый (impervious)

tighten [та́й-тăн] vt.i. натя́гивать, стя́гиваться

tile [тайл] sn. ка́фель, черепи́ца; vt. крыть черепи́цами

till [тіл] sn. де́нежный я́щик (money-drawer); vt. возде́лывать (cultivate); prep. до; conj. до тех пор, пока не

tillage [ті́-лідж] sn. обрабо́тка земли́; па́шня

tiller [ті́-лăр] sn. земледе́лец; sn. naut. ру́мпель, руль

tilt [тілт] sn. накло́н; vt.i. опроки́дывать, наклоня́ться

timber [ті́м-бăр] sn. лесно́й материа́л (wood as material), строево́й лес (standing trees)

time [тайм] sn. вре́мя; срок (period); what is the —? [уот із ѳă —] кото́рый час?; vt.i. назнача́ть вре́мя

timely [та́йм-лі] adj. совреме́нный

time-table [тайм-тэйбл] sn. расписа́ние

timid [ті́-мід] adj. боязли́вый, ро́бкий

timorous [ті́-мă-рăс] adj. пугли́вый

tin [тін] *sn.* жесть, óлово; жестянка (*container*); *vt.* лудить; консервировать (*conserve*)

tincture [тíнк-чǎр] *sn.* оттéнок (*of colour*); *med.* тинктýра

tinder [тíн-дǎр] *sn.* трут, фитиль, *m.*

tinge [тíндж] *sn.* оттéнок; *vt.* слегкá окрáшивать

tingle [тíнгл] *vi.* испытывать ощущéние колющей бóли

tinker [тíн-кǎр] *sm.* лудильщик, мéдник; *vi.* лудить, починять

tinkle [тíнкл] *sn.* звон колокóльчика; *vi.* звенéть, звякать

tint [тíнт] *sn.* колорит, оттéнок; *vt.* окрáшивать, подцвéчивать

tiny [тáй-ні] *adj.* крóшечный

tip [тíп] *sn.* толчóк (*light push*); кóнчик, наконéчник (*point*); чаевые дéньги (*gratuity*); совéт (*advice*); *vt.* давáть на чай (*give gratuity*); наклонять (*tilt*)

tipsy [тíп-сі] *adj.* подвыпивший

tiptoe [тíп-тоу] on – [он –] *adv.* на цыпочках

tiptop [тíп-топ] *adj.* первоклáссный, превосхóдный

tirade [тай-рéйд] *sn.* тирáда

tire [тай-ǎр] *sn.* óбод колесá (*of wheel*); шина (*rubber*); *v.i.* устáвать, утомляться

tireless [тáй-ǎр-ліс] *adj.* неутомимый

tiresome [тáй-ǎр-сǎм] *adj.* надоéдливый, утомительный

tissue [тí-шю] *sn.* (*textile and anat.*) ткань

titbit [тíт-біт] *sn.* лáкомый кусóчек

tithe [тайθ] *sn.* церкóвная десятина

title [тáйтл] *sn.* заглáвие, заголóвок; титул (*of person*)

titter [тí-тǎр] *sn.* хихиканье; *vi.* хихикать

tittle-tattle [тíтл-тэтл] *sn.* болтовня, сплéтня; *vi.* болтáть, сплéтничать

to [ту] *prep.* к, ко; до, на, у

toad [тоуд] *s.* жáба

toast [тоуст] *sn.* подрумяненный хлеб; гренóк; тост, предложéние тóста (*propose one's health, etc.*); *v.t.i.* подрумянивать, поджáривать (*brown, cook, warm*)

tobacco [тǎ-бǎ-коу] *s.* табáк

tobacconist [тǎ-бǎ-кǎ-ніст] *sn.* табáчник

tobacco-pouch [тǎ-бǎ-коу-пауч] *sn.* кисéт

today [ту-дéй] *sn.* сегóдняшний день; *adv.* сегóдня

toddle [тодл] *sn.* ковыляние; *vi.* ковылять

toe [тоу] *sn.* пáлец на ногé; носóк (*of shoe, sock*); *vt.* касáться носкóм

together [ту-гé-θǎр] *adv.* вмéсте

toil [тойл] *sn.* труд; *vi.* трудиться

toilet [тóй-літ] *sn.* туалéт, убóрная (*cloak-room*); *adj.* туалéтный

token [тóу-кǎн] *sn.* знак, примéта

tolerance [тó-лǎ-рǎнс] *sn.* терпимость

tolerate [тó-лǎ-рéйт] *vt.* выносить, терпéть

toleration [то-лă-рэ́й-шăн] *sn.* веротерпи́мость (*religious*); терпи́мость

toll [тол] *sn.* по́шлина, сбо́р (*money collection*); похоро́нный звон (*death bell*); *vt.i.* звони́ть по уме́ршем; благове́стить

tomato [тă-мắ-тоў] *sn.* помидо́р, тома́т

tomb [тўм] *sn.* гробни́ца, моги́ла; надгро́бный па́мятник (*monument*)

tomboy [то́м-бой] *s.* резву́нья; сорване́ц (*mad-cap*)

tom-cat [то́м-кæт] *sm.* кот

tomfoolery [том-фу́-лă-ри] *sn.* баловство́, шутовство́

tomorrow [тă-мо́-роў] *sn.* за́втрашний день; *adv.* за́втра

ton [тан] *sn.* то́нна

tone [тоўн] *sn. mus.* тон; *med.* то́нус; *vt.i.* настра́ивать (*attune to*); гармони́ровать (*be in tune with*); повыша́ть тон (*raise pitch*)

tongs [тонз] *sn.pl.* кле́щи, щипцы́

tongue [тан] *sn.* язы́к (*various meanings*); язычо́к (*of shoe, musical instruments*)

tonic [то́-ник] *n. med.* укрепля́ющее сре́дство; *adj. med.* укрепля́ющий, тони́ческий

tonight [ту-на́йт] *sn.* наступа́ющая ночь; *adv.* сего́дня но́чью

tonsil [то́н-сіл] *sn.* миндале́видная железа́

too [тў] *adv.* та́кже, то́же (*also*); сли́шком (*overmuch*); чрезвыча́йно (*very much, extremely*)

tool [тўл] *sn.* рабо́чий инструме́нт; ору́дие (*also fig.*); *tech.* ре́зец

tooth [тўθ] *sn.* зуб; зубе́ц (*cog*)

toothache [тўθ-эйк] *sn.* зубна́я боль

toothbrush [тўθ-браш] *sn.* зубна́я щётка

toothed [тўθд] *adj.* зубча́тый

toothpick [тўθ-пік] *sn.* зубочи́стка

top [топ] *sn.* верши́на, верху́шка (*summit*); волчо́к, куба́рь, *m.* (*toy*) *naut.* марс; *adj.* ве́рхний, вы́сший; пе́рвый (*of school*); *vt.i.* превосходи́ть (*surpass*) перева́ливать (*surmount*)

topboots [то́п-бўтс] *sn.pl.* высо́кие сапоги́ с отворо́тами

top-heavy [топ-хэ́-ві] *adj.* неусто́йчивый

topic [то́-пік] *sn.* предме́т, те́ма

topical [то́-пі-кăл] *adj.* злободне́вный, ме́стный

topmost [то́п-моўст] *adj.* наивы́сший, са́мый ве́рхний

topple [топл] *vt.i.* вали́ть, опроки́дываться

topsyturvy [топ-сі-тŏ́р-ві] *adj.* переве́рнутый вверх дном, наоборо́т; *adv.* ши́ворот-навы́ворот

torch [тŏ́рч] *sn.* фа́кел; *electr.* электри́ческий фона́рь

torment [тŏр-ме́нт] *sn.* муче́ние; [тŏр-ме́нт] *vt.* му́чить, раздража́ть

tormentor [тŏр-ме́н-тăр] *sm.* мучи́тель

torpedo [тŏр-пі́-доў] *sn.* ми́на (*mine*); торпе́да; *vt.i.* взрыва́ть ми́ной

torpid [тŏ́р-під] *adj.* вя́лый, онеме́лый

torpidity [tŏr-pĭ-dĭ-tĭ] *sn.* апатия, цепенение

torrent [tŏ-рănт] *sn.* поток

torrential [тŏ-рéн-шăл] *adj.* проливной, стремительный

torrid [тó-рĭд] *adj.* жаркий, знойный

torso [тŏр-соў] *sn.* туловище

tortoise [тŏр-тăс] *s.* черепаха

tortuous [тŏр-тю-ăс] *adj.* извилистый (*winding*); запутанный (*involved*); окольный (*round-about*)

torture [тŏр-чăр] *sn.* пытка; *vt.* мучить, пытать; коверкать (*distort*); искривлять (*twist*)

toss [тос] *sn.* качание, метание; вскидывание (*of head*); жеребьёвка (*of coin*); *vt.i.* качаться метаться; швырять (*of boat*); подбрасывать (*coin*)

total [тóў-тăл] *sn.* итог, общая сумма; *adj.* весь, общий, полный; тотальный (*of war*); *vt.* подсчитывать, суммировать

totter [тó-тăр] *vi.* шататься

touch [тач] *sn.* прикосновение (*contact*); осязание (*sense of touch*); *mus.* туше; *vt.i.* трогать; осязать; затрагивать (*a subject, etc.*); дотрагиваться

touching [тá-чĭй] *adj.* трогательный (*impressive, moving*); *prep.* касательно, о, об, относительно

touchy [тá-чĭ] *adj.* обидчивый

tough [таф] *adj.* крепкий, твёрдый; жёсткий (*of meat, etc.*); выносливый (*hardy*)

tour [тўр] *sn.* поездка, путешествие, турне, экскурсия; *vt.i.* объехать, обходить, путешествовать

tournament [тўр-нă-мănт] *sn.* турнир

tousle [тáўзл] *vt.* растрепать, тормошить

tow [тоў] *vt.* буксировка; *vt.* буксировать, тащить

towards [тў-ўŏрдз] *prep.* к, по направлению; по отношению (*in relation to*)

towel [тáў-ăл] *sn.* полотенце

tower [тáў-ăр] *sn.* башня; крепость (*fortress*); *vi.* парить (*soar*); превосходить ростом (умом) (*be of outstanding height or mind*)

town [таўн] *sn.* город; *adj.* городской; **– hall** [– хŏл] ратуша

toy [той] *sn.* игрушка; *adj.* игрушечный; *vi.* забавляться

trace [трэйс] *sn.* след; оттенок (*tinge*); *vt.* очерчивать (*outline*); прослеживать (*follow*)

track [трæк] *sn.* колея (*of traces*); след (*trail*); тропа (*path*); *sport.* трек; рельсовый путь (*railway*); *vt.* выслеживать

tract [трæкт] *sn.* область, полоса земли; трактат; брошюра (*pamphlet, etc.*) *anat.* тракт

tractable [трæк-тăбл] *adj.* послушный, сговорчивый

tractor [трæк-тăр] *sn.* локомобиль, *m.*, трактор

trade [трэйд] *sn.* торговля; ремесло (*craft*); *vt.i.* торговать

trader [трэй-дəр] *sm.* торговец; промышленник

tradesman [трэйдз-мäн] *sm.*
ла́вочник, торго́вец; ре-
ме́сленник (*craftsman*)

trade-union [трэйд-ю́-
ниäн] *sn.* профсою́з

tradition [трä-ди́-шäн] *sm.*
преда́ние; тради́ция

traffic [трэ́-фік] *sn.* движе́-
ние (*movement*); тра́нспорт,
перево́зки

tragedy [трэ́-джі-ді] *sn.*
траге́дия

tragic [трэ́-джік] *adj.* тра-
ги́ческий

trail [трэйл] *sn.* след; *mil.*
хо́бот лафе́та (*of gun-
carriage*); *bot.* стле́ющиеся по-
бе́ги; *vt.i.* волочи́ть, та-
щи́ть (*draw along*); сви-
са́ть (*of plants*)

train [трэйн] *sn.* по́езд (*railway*); шлейф (*of gown*); ве́-
рени́ца (*string of persons or
animals*); сви́та (*retinue*)
vt.i. обуча́ть, учи́ть (*educate*); трениро́вать (*sport*);
дрессирова́ть (*animals*);
направля́ть рост (*of plants*)

trainer [трэй-нäр] *sm.* тре́-
нёр

training [трэй-нін] *sn.* обу-
че́ние (*education*); трени-
ро́вка (*sport*); дрессиро́вка
(*animals*)

trait [трэйт] *sn.* черта́,
штрих

traitor [трэй-тäр] *sm.* из-
ме́нник, преда́тель

tram [трэм] *sn.* трамва́й

tramp [трэмп] *sm.* бродя́га,
обо́рвыш, стра́нник; *vt.i.*
бродя́жничать

trample [трэмпл] *vt.* топта́ть

trance [транс] *sn.* гранс

tranquil [трэн-ку́іл] *adj.*
споко́йный

transact [трэн-зэ́кт] *vt.* зак-
люча́ть, проводи́ть

transaction [трэн-зэ́к-шäн]
sn. веде́ние де́ла, сде́лка;
pl. протоко́лы, труды́

transcend [трэн-сэ́нд] *vt.*
переходи́ть за преде́лы;
превыша́ть (*soar*); превос-
ходи́ть (*surpass*)

transcribe [трэн-скра́йб]
vt. спи́сывать; *mus.* перела-
га́ть

transfer [транс-фäр] *sn.*
переда́ча, перено́с; пере-
водно́й рису́нок (*design*);
[трэнс-фäр] *vt.* переме-
ща́ть, переноси́ть; переса́-
живаться (*shift*)

transferable [трэнс-фä-
рäбл] *adj.* переводи́мый,
переноси́мый

transfiguration [трэнс-фі-
гю-рэ́й-шäн] *sn.* видоиз-
мене́ние; преобразова́ние

transform [трэнс-фо́рм] *vt.*
превраща́ть

transfusion [трэнс-фю́-
жäн] *sn.* перелива́ние

transgress [трэнс-грéс] *vt.i.*
преступа́ть; наруша́ть (*law*);
провини́ться (*be guilty*)

transit [трэн-зіт] *sn.* пе-
рее́зд; прохожде́ние

transition [трэн-зі-шäн]
sn. перехо́д

transitive [трэн-зі-тів] *adj.*
gram. перехо́дный

translate [трэнс-лэ́йт] *vt.*
переводи́ть; объясня́ть (*explain*); передава́ть (*render*)

translation [трэнс-лэ́й-
шäн] *sn.* перево́д

translator [транс-лэ́й-тäр]
sm. перево́дчик

transmission [трэнс-мі-шйн] *sn.* передача

transmit [трэнс-міт] *vt.* передавать, пересылать

transparent [трэнс-пэ́-рйнт] *adj.* прозрачный; *fig.* очевидный, ясный

transpire [трэнс-па́й-йр] *vt.i.* испаряться (*emit moisture*); обнаруживаться (*emerge*)

transplant [трэнс-плант] *vt.* пересаживать

transport [трэнс-порт] *sn.* перевозка, транспорт; восторг (*rapture*); [трэнс-порт] *vt.* перевозить, транспортировать; увлекать (*captivate*)

transportation [трэнс-пор-тэ́й-шйн] *sn.* перевозка

transpose [трэнс-поуз] *vt.* переставлять; *mus.* перелагать

trap [трэп] *sn.* западня, ловушка; люк (*hatch*); *vt.* поймать в ловушку

trash [трэш] *sn.* вздор, дребедень, дрянь

travel [трэ́-вйл] *sn.* поездка, путешествие; *vi.* ехать, путешествовать

traveller [трэ́-вй-лйр] *sn.* путешественник

traverse [трэ́-вйрс] *sn.* поперечина; *vt.* пересекать; противиться (*oppose*)

travesty [трэ́-віс-ті] *sn.* пародия; *vt.* пародировать

tray [трэй] *sn.* поднос

treacherous [трэ́-чй-рйс] *adj.* вероломный, предательский

treachery [трэ́-чй-рі] *sn.* измена, предательство

treacle [трикл] *sn.* патока

tread [трэд] *sn.* поступь,

походка; ступенька (*of stair*); обод колеса (*of wheel*); *vi.* идти, ступать, топтать

treadle [трэдл] *sn.* педаль, подножка; *vi.* работать педалью

treadmill [трэд-міл] *sn.* топчак

treason [трй-зйн] *sn.* государственная измена; предательство (*betrayal*)

treasure [трэ́-жйр] *sn.* сокровище; *vt.* высоко ценить (*value highly*); хранить (*store*)

treasurer [трэ́-жй-рйр] *sn.* казначей

treasury [трэ́-жй-рі] *sn.* казначейство

treat [трит] *sn.* удовольствие (*pleasure*); *vt.i.* обращаться, обходиться; угощать (*entertain*); лечить (*illness, etc.*)

treatise [трй-тайз] *sn.* трактат

treatment [трит-мйнт] *sn.* хождение, обхождение; обработка (*manipulation*); лечение (*medical*)

treaty [трй-ті] *sn.* договор, соглашение

treble [трэбл] *sn. mus.* дискант; тройное количество (*amount*)

tree [три] *sn.* дерево

trek [трэк] *sn.* переход, поход

trellis [трэ́-ліс] *sn.* решётка, шпалера

tremble [трэмбл] *sn.* дрожь; *vi.* дрожать, трепетать

tremendous [трі-мэ́н-дйс] *adj.* громадный, огромный

tremor [трэ́-мйр] *sn.* трепет

tremulous [тре́-мю-лəс] adj. вибри́рующий, дрожа́щий

trench [тренч] sn. mil. транше́я; желобо́к (groove)

trenchant [трен-чант] adj. о́стрый, ре́жущий; fig. проница́тельный

trend [тренд] sn. о́бщее направле́ние, тенде́нция

trepidation [тре-пи-де́й-шəн] sn. волне́ние, тре́пет

trespass [трес-пəс] sn. наруше́ние грани́ц, просту́пок; vi. наруша́ть грани́цы, злоупотребля́ть

trespasser [трес-па-сəр] sm. наруши́тель

tress [трес] sn. коса́, ло́кон; pl. распу́щенные во́лосы

trestle [тресл] sn. ко́злы, подста́вка

trial [тра́й-əл] sn. испыта́ние (probation); попы́тка (attempt); о́пыт, про́ба (test); leg. суде́бное разбира́тельство

triangle [тра́й-əнгл] sn. треуго́льник

triangular [трай-а́й-гюлəр] adj. треуго́льный

tribe [трайб] sn. пле́мя, род; zool. подотря́д

tribesman [тра́йбз-мəн] sm. член пле́мени

tribulation [три-бю-ле́йшəн] sn. бе́дствие, го́ре

tribunal [трай-бю-нəл] sn. суд, трибуна́л

tribune [три́-бюн] sn. трибу́н; трибу́на (rostrum)

tributary [три́-бю-тə-ри] sm. да́нник; sn. прито́к; adj. платя́щий дань (of paying); вспомога́тельный (auxiliary)

tribute [три́-бют] sn. дань

trice [трайс] vt. naut. подтя́гивать; sn. мгнове́ние; in a – [ин ə –] ми́гом

trick [трик] sn. вы́ходка, ша́лость (prank); обма́н, уло́вка, хи́трость (stratagem); фо́кус (sleight of hand); vt. надува́ть, обма́нывать

trickery [три́-кə-ри] sn. надува́тельство

trickle [трикл] sn. ка́панье; vi. ка́пать

trickster [трик-стəр] sm. обма́нщик, плут

tricky [три́-ки] adj. ло́вкий; хи́трый; щекотли́вый; сло́жный, тру́дный (complicated, difficult)

trifle [трайфл] sn. безде́лица, ме́лочь; пустя́к; сорт пиро́жного (sweet); vi. забавля́ться

trifling [тра́йф-лиŋ] adj. незначи́тельный, пустя́чный

trigger [три́-гəр] sn. защёлка, соба́чка

trill [трил] sn. трель; vt.i. выде́лывать тре́ли

trim [трим] sn. поря́док; adj. аккура́тный, в поря́дке; vt. отде́лывать, приводи́ть в поря́док, убира́ть; подреза́ть (clip)

trimming [три́-миŋ] sn. отде́лка; pl. гарни́р, припра́ва

trinity [три́-ни-ти] s. тро́ица

trinket [три́-нкит] sn. балабо́лка, безде́лушка; брело́к

trio [три́-оу] sn. mus. три́о, тро́е, тро́йка (of persons)

trip [трип] sn. пое́здка, экску́рсия; спотыка́нье (stumble); vi. спотыка́ться

tripe [трайп] sn. рубе́ц, требуха́

triple [трiпл] *adj.* тройный, тройкий

tripod [трай-под] *sn.* треножник

trite [трайт] *adj.* банальный, избитый

triumph [трай-ǎмф] *sn.* торжество, триумф; *vi.* ликовать, торжествовать

triumphal [трай-ǎм-фǎл] *adj.* триумфальный

triumphant [трай-ǎм-фǎнт] *adj.* ликующий, торжествующий; победоносный (*victorious*)

trivial [трi-вi-ǎл] *adj.* будничный, пустячный

trolley [тро-лi] *sn.* вагонетка, дрезина, тележка

troop [трӯп] *sn.* масса, толпа (*of people*); стадо (*of animals*); *pl.* войска

trooper [трӯ-пǎр] *sm.* рядовой кавалерист

trophy [трóу-фi] *sn.* трофей (*prize*); добыча (*spoils*)

tropic [тро-пiк] *sn.* тропик; *pl.* тропики

trot [трот] *sn.* рысь; быстрый ход (*of person*); *vt.i.* бежать рысью

trouble [трабл] *sn.* заботы, хлопоты (*worry, fuss*); беспокойство (*unrest*); волнение, тревога (*anxiety*); горе (*grief*); *vt.i.* надоедать, приставать; беспокоиться, тревожиться

troublesome [трабл-сǎм] *adj.* беспокойный, хлопотливый; назойливый (*tiresome*)

trough [троф] *sn.* кормушка, корыто

trounce [траунс] *vt.* бить, пороть; наказывать (*punish*)

trousers [трáу-зǎрс] *sn. pl.* брюки, панталоны, штаны

trout [траут] *s.* форель

trowel [трáул] *sn.* скребок (*for chipping bricks*); садовый совок (*garden*)

truant [трý-ǎнт] *sm.* прогульщик

truce [трӯс] *sn.* перемирие

truck [трак] *sn.* грузовик, тележка

truculent [трá-кю-лǎнт] *adj.* беспощадный, свирепый

trudge [традж] *vt.* ходить с трудом, тащиться

true [трӯ] *adj.* верный, истинный; преданный (*devoted*)

truly [трý-лi] *adv.* воистину (*with truth*); искренно (*sincerely*); преданно (*devotedly*); действительно (*really*)

trump [трамп] *sn.* козырь, *m.* *vt.i.* крыть козерем, козырять

trumpet [трáм-пiт] *sn. mus.* труба; *vt.i.* трубить; *fig.* возвещать; реветь (*of elephant*)

truncheon [трáн-чǎн] *sn.* жезл; дубинка (*полицейского*)

trundle [трандл] *vt.i.* катиться, тянуть

trunk [транк] *sn.* ствол (*of tree*); хобот (*of elephant*); туловище (*of man and animal*); корпус (*body of structure*); сундук, чемодан (*box, case*)

truss [трас] *sn.* охапка (*bundle of hay*); балка, стропило (*timber tie*); гроздь, пучок (*cluster*); *med.* бандаж; *vt.* связывать, укреплять

trust [траст] *sn.* дове́рие, *com.* трест; *vt.i.* ве́рить, доверя́ться; вверя́ть, поруча́ть (*entrust*); полага́ться (*rely*)

trustee [трас-ти́] *sn.* попечи́тель; опеку́н (*guardian*)

trustworthy [траст-уёр-ѕи] *adj.* заслу́живающий дове́рия, достове́рный

truth [труѕ] *sn.* и́стина, пра́вда; достове́рность, правди́вость (*authenticity*)

truthful [труѕ-фул] *adj.* правди́вый (*of person*); пра́вильный (*of story*, *etc.*)

try [трай] *sn. coll.* попы́тка; *vt.i.* испы́тывать, про́бовать (*test*); суди́ть (*judge*); стара́ться (*attempt, take pains*); — **on** [—он] приме́рить

trying [тра́й-иѕ] *adj.* изнури́тельный, утоми́тельный (*exhausting*); раздража́ющий (*exasperating*)

tub [таб] *sn.* ка́дка, лоха́нка

tubby [та́-би] *adj.* коро́ткий и то́лстый (*of person*)

tube [тюб] *sn.* труба́, тру́бка; тю́бик (*of cream, etc.*); метрополите́н (*railway*)

tubular [тю́-бю-ла́р] *adj.* трубча́тый

tuck [так] *sn.* скла́дка; *vt.* де́лать скла́дки

Tuesday [тю́з-ди] *sn.* вто́рник

tuft [тафт] *sn.* пучо́к, хохоло́к

tug [таг] *sn.* дёрганье (*jerky pull*); букси́р (*boat*); *vt.i.* дёргать, тащи́ть; букси́ровать

tuition [тю-и́-шан] *sn.* обуче́ние, уче́ние

tulip [тю́-лип] *sn.* тюльпа́н

tumble [тамбл] *sn. coll.* паде́ние; *vt.i.* опроки́дываться, па́дать

tumbler [та́м-бла́р] *sn.* стака́н (*glass*); го́лубь-верту́н (*pigeon*); *sm.* акроба́т

tumour [тю́-ма́р] *sn.* о́пухоль

tumult [тю́-малт] *sn.* волне́ние, шум; смяте́ние чувств (*conflict of emotions*)

tumultuous [тю-ма́л-тю-а́с] *adj.* бу́йный, шу́мный

tun [тан] *sn.* бо́чка (*cask*); пивова́рный чан (*vat*)

tune [тюн] *sn.* мело́дия, моти́в; **in** — [ин—] настро́енный (*of piano, etc.*); в тон (*of voice*); *vt.* настра́ивать, *fig.* приспособля́ть (*adapt*)

tuneful [тю́н-фул] *adj.* мелоди́чный

tuner [тю́-на́р] *sm.* настро́йщик

tunic [тю́-ник] *sn.* туни́ка; ки́тель (*soldier's, etc.*)

tunnel [та́-нал] *sn.* тунне́ль, *m.*; *vt.i.* проводи́ть тунне́ль

turbid [тёр-бид] *adj.* му́тный

turbidity [та́р-би́-ди-ти] *sn.* нея́сность, му́тность

turbine [тёр-байн] *sn.* турби́на

turbot [тёр-бат] *s.* па́лтус

turbulence [тёр-бю-ла́нс] *sn.* волне́ние, беспоря́док, шумли́вость, бу́рность (*of wind, waves, etc.*)

turbulent [тёр-бю-ла́нт] *adj.* бу́йный, мяте́жный; бу́рный (*of wind, waves*)

tureen [тю-ри́н] *sn.* супова́я ми́ска

turf [тёрф] *sn.* дёрн; *vt.* выстила́ть дёрном

turgid [тёр-джід] *adj.* напы́-
щенный (*of language, etc.*);
вздутый, опухлый (*inflated*)

Turk [тёрк] *sm.* тýрок; *sf.*
турчáнка

turkey [тёр-кі] *s.* индю́к,
индéйка (*cooked*)

Turkish [тёр-кіш] *adj.* тý-
рéцкий

turmoil [тёр-мойл] *sn.* смя-
тéние, суматóха

turn [тёрн] *sn.* оборóт, поворóт (*turning*); óчередь
(*sequence*); услýга (*service*);
vt.i. вертéть, вращáть, кру-
жи́ться; – **about** [– ă-бáут]
поворáчиваться; – **back**
[– бэк] повернýть обрáтно;
– **down** [– дáун] прикрý-
ти́ть (*as wick of lamp, etc.*);
– **off** [– оф] закрывáть (*tap,
etc.*); – **round** [– рáунд]
повернýться

turner [тёр-нăр] *sm.* тóкарь

turning [тёр-нін] *sn.* перекрёсток, поворóт (*in road*);
токáрное искýсство (*craft*);
кри́зис

turnip [тёр-ніп] *sn.* брю́ква,
рéпа

turnover [тёрн-оў-вăр]
sn. com. óбщий оборóт

turnstile [тёрн-стайл] *sn.*
турникéт

turpentine [тёр-пăн-тайн]
sn. скипидáр

turquoise [тёр-койз] *sn.*
бирюзá

turret [тá-ріт] *sn.* бáшенка

turtle [тёртл] *s.* морскáя
черепáха

turtle-dove [тёртл-дав]
s. гóрлица

tusk [таск] *sn.* клык

tussle [тасл] *sn. coll.* борьбá;
vi. борóться

tutor [тю̄-тăр] *sm.* учи́тель;
преподавáтель (*university*);
опекýн (*guardian*)

tutorial [тю-тō̄-рі-ăл] *adj.*
настáвнический

twang [тўэн] *sn.* звук стру-
ны́ (*of string*); *vt.i.* бренчáть

tweezers [тўӣ-зăз] *sn. pl.*
щи́пчики, пинцéт

twelve [тўелв] *num.* двенáд-
цать

twenty [тўэн-ті] *num.* двáд-
цать

twice [тўайс] *adv.* двáжды

twig [тўіг] *sn.* вéточка,
прýтик

twilight [тўáй-лайт] *sn.* сý-
мерки

twin [тўін] *sm.* близнéц;
пáрная вещь (*thing*); *adj.*
двойнóй

twine [тўáйн] *sn.* бечёвка,
шнурóк, шпагáт; *vt.* вить,
сви́вать

twinge [тўіндж] *sn.* при́ступ
бóли

twinkle [тўíнкл] *sn.* мигáние,
сверкáние; *vi.* мерцáть,
мигáть, сверкáть

twirl [тўёрл] *sn.* верчéние,
кружéние; завитýшка, рóс-
черк (*pen-flourish*); *vt.*
вертéть, кружи́ть

twist [тўіст] *sn.* изги́б,
кривизнá; *vt.i.* крути́ть,
скрýчивать; извивáться

twitch [тўíч] *sn.* дёрганье,
сýдорога; *vt.i.* дрожáть;
искривля́ться

twitter [тўі-тăр] *sn.* щебéт,
чири́канье; *vi.* щебетáть,
чири́кать

two [тў] *num.* два

twofold [тў-фолд] *adj.*
двойнóй, удвóенный; *adv.*
вдвойнé

type [тайп] *sn.* класс, род, тип *(kind)*; *typ.* набор, шрифт; *vt.* писа́ть на маши́нке

typewriter [тайп-рай-тӑр] *sn.* пи́шущая маши́на

typhoon [тай-фӯн] *sn.* тайфу́н

typical [ти́-пи-кӑл] *adj.* типи́чный

typify [ти́-пи-фай] *vt.* служи́ть приме́ром

typist [тай-пист] *sf.* машини́стка

typography [тай-по́-грӑ-фи] *sn.* книгопеча́тание

tyranny [ти́-рӑ-ни] *sn.* жесто́кость, тира́нство

tyrant [тай́-рӑнт] *sm.* тира́н

tyre [тай-ӑр] *sn.* ши́на

U

ubiquity [ю-би́-кўи-ти] *sn.* вездесу́щность

udder [а́-дӑр] *sn.* вы́мя

ugliness [а́-гли-нис] *sn.* некраси́вость *(of features)*; безобра́зие *(of manners, etc.)*

ugly [а́-гли] *adj.* некраси́вый *(of features)*; га́дкий *(bad)*; безобра́зный *(vile)*; угрожа́ющий *(threatening)*

Ukrainian [ю-крӗй-ни-ӑн] *sm.* украи́нец; *adj.* украи́нский

ulcer [а́л-сӑр] *sn.* я́зва

ulterior [ал-ти́-ри-ӑр] *adj.* дальне́йший, после́дующий; пу́тосторо́нний

ultimate [а́л-ти-мит] *adj.* коне́чный, оконча́тельный; основно́й *(fundamental)*; перви́чный *(primary)*

ultimatum [ал-ти-мэ́й-тӑм] *sn.* ультима́тум

umber [а́м-бӑр] *sn.* у́мбра; *adj.* кори́чнево-жёлтый *(colour)*

umbilical [ам-би́-ли-кӑл] *adj.* пупо́чный; *fig.* центра́льный

umbrage [а́м-бридж] *sn.* оби́да, оскорбле́ние

umbrella [ам-брé-лӑ] *sn.* зо́нтик

umpire [а́м-пай-ӑр] *sm.* посре́дник; *leg.* трете́йский судья́; *vt.* быть посре́дником

un- [ан] *prefix,* раз-, рас-; без-, не-

unable [ан-э́йбл] *adj.* не могу́щий, неспосо́бный

unaccustomed [ан-ӑ-ка́с-тӑмд] *adj.* непривы́чный

unaffected [ан-ӑ-фе́к-тид] *adj.* незатро́нутый

unaided [ан-э́й-дид] *adj.* без по́мощи

unalterable [ан-о́л-тӑ-рӑбл] *adj.* неизменя́емый

unanimity [ю-нӑ-ни́-ми-ти] *sn.* единоду́шие

unanimous [ю-нӑ́-ни-мӑс] *adj.* единогла́сный, единоду́шный

unarmed [ан-а́рмд] *adj.* безору́жный, невооружён-ный

unassuming [ан-ӑ-сю́-мин] *adj.* скро́мный

unavoidable [ан-ӑ-во́й-дӑбл] *adj.* неизбе́жный, немину́емый

unaware [ан-ӑ-у́эр] *adj.* незна́ющий, неподозрева́ющий; -s [-з] *adv.* врасплóх, неожи́данно

unbecoming [ан-би-ка́-мин] *adj.* неподходя́щий

unbearable [ан-бэ́-рӑбл] *adj.* невыноси́мый

unbeliever [ан-би-ли́-вӑр] *sm.* неве́рующий

unbiased [ан-ба́й-ӑст] *adj.* непредубеждённый

unbroken [ан-бро́у-кӑн] *adj.* непреры́вный (*uninterrupted*); це́лый (*whole*)

unbutton [ан-ба́-тӑн] *vt.* расстёгивать

uncalled-for [ан-ко́лд-фо́р] *adj.* непро́шенный

uncanny [ан-ка́-ни] *adj.* стра́нный, таи́нственный

unceremonious [ан-сӗ-ри-мо́у-ни-ӑс] *adj.* бесцеремо́нный, фамилья́рный

uncertain [ан-сӗ́р-тӑн] *adj.* неуве́ренный, сомнева́ющийся

uncivil [ан-сı́-вил] *adj.* гру́бый, неве́жливый

uncle [анкл] *sm.* дя́дя

uncomfortable [ан-ка́м-фӑр-тӑбл] *adj.* неудо́бный, неую̀тный

uncommon [ан-ко́-мӑн] *adj.* необыкнове́нный, необы́чный

unconcerned [ан-концсӗ́рнд] *adj.* беззабо́тный

unconditional [ан-кон-ди́-шӑ-нӑл] *adj.* безусло́вный

unconscious [ан-ко́н-шӑс] *adj.* бессозна́тельный

uncouth [ан-ку́ѳ] *adj.* несклáдный, неукло́жий

uncover [ан-ка́-вӑр] *vt.* снимáть (*take off*); разоблачáть, раскрывáть

unction [а́нк-шӑн] *sm.* помáзание, элéйность

uncultivated [ан-ка́л-ти-вей-тıд] *adj.* необрабóтанный

undaunted [ан-дóн-тıд] *adj.* неустрашúмый

undecided [а́н-ди-сай-дıд] *adj.* нерешённый, нерешúтельный (*irresolute*)

undeniable [ан-ди-нáй-ӑбл] *adj.* неоспорúмый

under [а́н-дӑр] *adj.* нúжний; *adv.* внизý, ни́же; в подчинённое положéние (*insubordinate position*); *prep.* под, нúже; мéньше чем (*less than*); *prefix*, нúже-, под-

underclothes [а́н-дӑр-клоуэз] *sm. pl.* нúжнее бельé

undergo [ан-дӑр-гóу] *vt.* подвергáться

undergraduate [ан-дӑр-грǽ-дю-ıт] *sm.* студéнт

underground [ан-дӑр-гра́унд] *sn.* the – [ei –] метрополитéн (*railway*); *adj.* подзéмный

underhand [ан-дӑр-хǽнд] *adj.* закулúсный

underline [ан-дӑр-лайн] *vt.* подчёркивать

underneath [ан-дӑр-нúѳ] *adv., prep.* нúже, под, снúзу

underrate [ан-дӑр-рэ́йт] *vt.* недооцéнивать

understand [ан-дӑр-стǽнд] *vt.* понимáть

understanding [ан-дӑр-стǽн-дıн] *sn.* понимáние, понятлúвость; ум, интеллéкт (*intellect*); проницáтельность (*insight*)

understatement [ан-дӑр-стéйт-мӑнт] *sn.* преуменьшéние

understudy [а́н-дӑр-ста-дı] *sm.* дублёр; *vt.* дублúровать

undertake [ан-дӑр-тэ́йк] *vt.* предпринимáть

undertaker [án-dăр́-тэй-кăр́] *sm.* подря́дчик; гробовщи́к (*funeral*)

underwear [án-дăр́-у́эр́] *sn.* ни́жнее бельё

underworld [án-дăр́-уóэрлд] *sn.* подо́нки о́бщества; престу́пный мир

undesirable [ан-ди-за́йрăбл] *adj.* нежела́тельный

undo [ан-ду́] *vt.* развя́зывать, расстёгивать; раскрыва́ть (*box, packet, etc.*)

undoubtedly [ан-да́у-тидли] *adv.* несомне́нно

undress [ан-дре́с] *vt.i.* раздева́ть; *vr.* раздева́ться

undue [ан-дю́] *adj.* несвоевре́менный, несообра́зный

undulate [án-дю-лэйт] *vi.* волнова́ться, струи́ться

unearned [ан-сёрнд] *adj.* незаслу́женный

unearth [ан-сёр́] *vt.* вы́рыть, отко́пать

unearthly [ан-сёр́-ли] *adj.* незе́мный, сверхъесте́ственный; *fig.* кра́йне неподходя́щий

uneasy [ан-и́-зи] *adj.* встрево́женный

uneducated [ан-é-дю-кэй-тид] *adj.* необразо́ванный

unemployed [ан-им-пло́йд] *adj.* безрабо́тный; неза́нятый (*unoccupied*); **the –** [ей –] безрабо́тные

unemployment [ан-импло́й-мăнт] *sn.* безрабо́тица

unequal [ан-и́-кýăл] *adj.* неро́вный

unerring [ан-сёр́-рий] *adj.* безоши́бочный

uneven [ан-и́-вăн] *adj.* неро́вный

unexpected [ан-икс-пéк-тид] *adj.* неожи́данный

unfailing [ан-фэ́й-лий] *adj.* неистощи́мый

unfair [ан-фэ́р́] *adj.* несправедли́вый

unfasten [ан-фá-сăн] *vt.* отвя́зывать, расстёгивать

unfavourable [ан-фэ́й-рăбл] *adj.* неблагоприя́тный

unfit [ан-фи́т] *adj.* него́дный, неспосо́бный

unfold [ан-фо́улд] *vt.i.* открыва́ть; развёртываться, расстила́ть

unfortunate [ан-фо́р-чăнит] *adj.* несча́стный, неуда́чный

unfriendly [ан-фре́нд-ли] *adj.* недружелю́бный

unfurl [ан-фёрл] *vt.* раскрыва́ть (*umbrella*); развёртывать (*flag, etc.*)

unhappy [ан-хǽ-пи] *adj.* несчастли́вый; гру́стный, печа́льный (*sad*)

unhealthy [ан-хéл-ёи] *adj.* нездоро́вый

unification [ю-ни-фи-кǽй-шăн] *sn.* объедине́ние

uniform [ю́-ни-фóрм] *sn.* мунди́р, фо́рменная оде́жда; *adj.* единообра́зный, однообра́зный

uniformity [ю-ни-фóр-ми-ти] *sn.* одина́ковость, одноро́дность

unify [ю́-ни-фай] *vt.* соединя́ть

unilateral [ю-ни-лǽ-тă-рăл] *adj.* односторо́нний

union [ю́-ни-ăн] *sn.* сою́з; соедине́ние (*uniting*)

unique [ю-ни́к] *adj.* бесподо́бный, еди́нственный

unison [ю-ни-зэн] *sn.* согласие

unit [ю-нiт] *sn.* единица; *mil.* часть

unite [ю-найт] *vt.i.* объединять, соединяться

unity [ю-нi-ти] *sn.* единство

universal [ю-ни-вёр-сэл] *adj.* всеобщий, всемирный, универсальный

universe [ю-ни-вёрс] *sn.* вселенная, мир

university [ю-ни-вёр-си-ти] *sn.* университет

unjust [ан-джаст] *adj.* несправедливый

unkempt [ан-кёмпт] *adj.* нечёсанный; запущенный (*neglected*)

unknown [ан-ноўн] *adj.* неизвестный

unlawful [ан-ло-фул] *adj.* незаконный

unless [ан-лéс] *conj.* если не

unlike [ан-лайк] *adj.* непохожий

unlikely [ан-лайк-ли] *adj.* маловероятный

unload [ан-лоўд] *vt.* выгружать

unlucky [ан-ла-ки] *adj.* несчастливый, неудачный

unmarried [ан-мæ-рiд] *adj.* женатый, холостой

unmask [ан-маск] *vt.* разоблачать

unmoved [ан-мувд] *adj.* равнодушный

unnatural [ан-нæ-чā-рэл] *adj.* неестественный

unnecessary [ан-нé-сi-сā-pi] *adj.* излишний, ненужный

unpin [ан-пiн] *vt.* откалывать

unpleasant [ан-плэ́-зэнт] *adj.* неприятный

unqualified [ан-кўо́-лi-файд] *adj.* безоговорочный

unquestionable [ан-кўэ́сч-чā-нāбл] *adj.* неоспоримый

unravel [ан-рǽвэл] *vt.* распутывать

unreasonable [ан-рi-зā-нāбл] *adj.* безрассудный; непомерный (*excessive*)

unreservedly [ан-рi-зǿр-вiд-лi] *adv.* безоговорочно

unrest [ан-рéст] *sn.* беспокойство, волнение

unruly [ан-ру́-лi] *adj.* непокорный

unsatisfactory [ан-сæ-тiс-фǽк-тā-рi] *adj.* неудовлетворительный

unscrew [ан-скрю́] *vt.* отвинчивать

unscrupulous [ан-скрю́-пю-лāс] *adj.* бессовестный

unseemly [ан-сим-лi] *adj.* непристойный

unseen [ан-сiн] *adj.* невидимый

unselfish [ан-сéл-фiш] *adj.* безкорыстный, самоотвержённый

unsettled [ан-сé-тāлд] *adj.* неустановившийся

unsightly [ан-сайт-лi] *adj.* непривлекательный, уродливый

unskilful [ан-скiл-фул] *adj.* неискусный, неумелый

unskilled [ан-скiлд] *adj.* необученный

unsteady [ан-стé-дi] *adj.* неустойчивый (*not firm*); непостоянный (*changeable, fluctuating*); шаткий (*faltering*); валкий (*shaky, rickety*)

untie [ан-тай] *vt.* отвязывать, развязывать

until [ан-тíл] *prep.* до; *conj.* пока

untimely [ан-тáйм-лì] *adj.* несвоевре́менный

untold [ан-тóлд] *adj.* бесчи́сленный (*beyond count*)

untrue [ан-трý] *adj.* ло́жный

unusual [ан-ю́-жý-ал] *adj.* необыкнове́нный; замеча́тельный (*remarkable*)

unwell [ан-уэ́л] *adj.* нездоро́вый; больно́й (*ill*)

unwilling [ан-уи́-лиṅ] *adj.* неохо́тный, несклóнный

unwise [ан-ṷáйз] *adj.* неблагоразу́мный

unworthy [ан-ṷǝ́р-ѳи] *adj.* недосто́йный

unwrap [ан-рǽп] *vt.* развёртывать

unyielding [ан-ий́л-дин̄] *adj.* неусту́пчивый; твёрдый (*firm*)

up [ап] *adv.* вверх, наверху́

upbraid [ап-брэ́йд] *vt.* брани́ть, укоря́ть

upbringing [áп-бриṅ-иṅ] *sn.* воспита́ние

upheaval [ап-хи́-вǝл] *sn. geol.* сме́щение пласто́в; *fig.* переворо́т; сдвиг (*heaving up*)

uphill [ап-хíл] *adv.* в го́ру

uphold [ап-хóўлд] *vt.* подде́рживать

upholster [ап-хóўл-стǝр] *vt.* меблирова́ть, обива́ть

upholsterer [ап-хóўл-стǝ-рǝр] *sm.* обивщи́к

upkeep [áп-кип] *sn.* ремóнт; стóимость (содержа́ния) (*cost*)

uplift [ап-лíфт] *vt.* возвыша́ть

upon [а-пóн] *prep.* на, при, у

upper [á-пǝр] *adj.* вéрхний, вы́сший; *sn. pl.* передки́ (*of shoe*)

upright [áп-райт] *sn.* подпóрка, стóйка (*support*); *adj.* вертика́льный, прямóй (*vertical, erect*); чéстный (*honest*)

uprising [áп-рай-зин̄] *sn.* восста́ние

uproar [áп-рǝр] *sn.* бу́йство; гам, шум

uproot [ап-рýт] *vt.* искореня́ть

upset [ап-сéт] *sn.* опроки́дывание (*upsetting*); потрясéние (*being upset*); *vt.i.* опроки́дывать (*overturn*); расстра́ивать (*perturb*)

upside-down [ап-сайд-да́ўн] *adj., adv.* вверх дном

upstairs [ап-стǝ́рз] *adj.* в вéрхнем этажé; *adv.* наверху́

upstart [áп-стáрт] *sm.* вы́скочка

upward [áп-ṷǝрд] *adj.* напра́вленный вверх

upwards [áп-ṷǝрдз] *adv.* вверх, кве́рху, свы́ше

urban [ǝ́р-бǎн] *adj.* городскóй

urchin [ǝ́р-чин] *sm.* мальчи́шка (*youngster*); прострéл (*roguish boy*)

urge [ǝ́рдж] *sn.* побуждéние, стремлéние; *vt.* подгоня́ть, понужда́ть; наста́ивать (*persist*)

urgent [ǝ́р-джǎнт] *adj.* безотлага́тельный, срóчный

urgency [ǝ́р-джǎн-си] *sn.* насто́йчивость, спéшность

urine [ю́-рин] *sn.* мочá

urn [ǝ́рн] *sn.* у́рна

ursine [ёр-сайн] *adj.* медвёжий

us [ас] *pron.* нам, нас

usage [ю́-зiдж] *sn.* обхождёние, употреблёние (*manner of using*); обы́чай (*custom*)

use [юс] *sn.* по́льзование, применёние, употреблёние; по́льза (*benefit*); обы́чай, привы́чка (*custom, habit*); [юз] *vt.i.* употребля́ть; обходи́ться (*manage with*)

useful [ю́с-фул] *adj.* поле́зный, пригодный

useless [ю́с-лiс] *adj.* бесполе́зный, никуда́ не го́дный

usher [а́-шэр] *sn.* швейца́р; при́став (*court*); *vt.* вводи́ть

usual [ю́-жу-ал] *adj.* обыкновённый, обы́чный

usurer [ю́-жа-рэр] *sm.* ростовщи́к

usurp [ю-зэ́рп] *vt.* захва́тывать, узурпи́ровать

usury [ю́-жу-рi] *sn.* ростовщи́чество

utensil [ю-тён-сiл] *sn.* у́тварь

utility [ю-тí-лi-тi] *sn.* поле́зность; вы́годность

utilize [ю́-тi-лайз] *vt.* по́льзоваться, утилизи́ровать

utmost [а́т-мо́уст] *adj.* кра́йний (*furthest*); са́мый отдалённый (*extreme*)

utter [а́-тэр] *adj.* по́лный, совершённый; *vt.* выража́ть слова́ми; произноси́ть

utterance [а́-тэ-рэнс] *sn.* выраже́ние, выска́зывание

utterly [а́-тэр-лi] *adv.* кра́йне, чрезвыча́йно

uvula [ю́-вý-ла] *sn.* язычо́к

V

vacancy [вэ́й-кэн-сi] *sn.* вака́нсия (*unoccupied post*); свободное ме́сто (*empty space*); рассе́янность (*distraction*)

vacant [вэ́й-кэнт] *adj.* вака́нтный, свободный; рассе́янный (*absent-minded*); отсу́тствующий (*absent*)

vacate [ва́-кэ́йт] *vt.* оставля́ть, покида́ть

vacation [ва́-кэ́й-шэн] *sn.* кани́кулы, о́тпуск

vaccination [вэ́к-сi-нэ́й-шэн] *sn.* приви́вка; привива́ние

vacillate [вэ́-сi-лэйт] *vi.* колеба́ться

vacuum [вэ́-кю-ỹм] *sn.* пустота́; **– cleaner** [– клú-нэр] *sn.* пылесо́с

vagabond [вэ́-га-бонд] *sm.* бродя́га; *adj.* бродя́чий, стра́нствующий

vagary [вэй-гá-рi] *sn.* причу́да

vagrancy [вэ́й-грэн-сi] *sn.* бродя́жничество, скита́ние

vagrant [вэ́й-грэнт] *sm.* бродя́га, скита́лец; *adj.* стра́нствующий

vague [вэйг] *adj.* неопределённый, сму́тный

vain [вэйн] *adj.* самодово́льный, тщесла́вный (*conceited*); су́етный, тще́тный (*futile*)

vainglorious [вэйн-гло́-рi-ас] *adj.* хвастли́вый

vale [вэйл] *sn.* доли́на

valet [вэ́-лiт] *sm.* камерди́нер

valiant [вǽ-лі-ǎнт] *adj.* дóблестный, мужественный, храбрый

valid [вǽ-лід] *adj.* здрáвый (*sound*); хорошó обоснóванный (*well-grounded*), действительный (*effective*)

validity [вǽ-лі-ді-ті] *sn.* вéскость, основáтельность

valise [вǎ-лíс] *sn.* дорóжная сýмка

valley [вǽ-лі] *sn.* долина

valour [вǽ-лǎр] *sn.* дóблесть, мýжество

valuable [вǽ-лю-ǎбл] *adj.* драгоцéнный, цéнный; *sn. pl.* драгоцéнности

valuation [вǽ-лю-ǝ́й-шǎн] *sn.* оцéнка

value [вǽ-лю] *sn.* стóимость (*cost*); цéнность (*worth*); *vt.* оцéнивать, ценить

valve [вǽлв] *sn.* клáпан

van [вǽн] *sn.* вагóн, фýра; *mil.* авангáрд

vane [вѣйн] *sn.* флюгер; крылó (*of windmill*); лóпасть (*of propeller*)

vanguard [вǽн-гáрд] *sn.* авангáрд

vanish [вǽ-ніш] *vi.* исчезáть, пропадáть

vanity [вǽ-ні-ті] *sn.* суетá, тщеслáвие

vanquish [вǽй-кўіш] *vt.* побеждáть, покорять

vapid [вǽ-під] *adj.* безвкýсный; бессодержáтельный (*lacking content*)

vapour [вѣй-пǎр] *sn.* пар

variable [вǝ́-рі-ǎбл] *adj.* изменчивый, перемéнный

variance [вǝ́-рі-ǎнс] *sn.* несоглáсие, разноглáсие

variation [вǝ́-рі-ǝ́й-шǎн] *sn.* изменéние

variegated [вǝ́-рі-гǝ́й-тід] *adj.* пёстрый, разноцвéтный

variety [вǎ-рáй-ǎ-ті] *sn.* разнообрáзие (*diversity*); варьетэ (*entertainment*)

various [вǝ́-рі-ǎс] *adj.* различный, рáзный

varnish [вáр-ніш] *sn.* лак, политýра; *fig.* внéшний лоск; *vt.* лакировáть

vary [вǝ́-рі] *vt.i.* изменять, менять, отличáться

vase [вáз] *sn.* вáза

vast [вǽст] *adj.* громáдный, обширный

vat [вǽт] *sn.* бак, кáдка, чав

vault [вóлт] *sn.* свод (*arched roof*); пóгреб, подвáл (*cellar*); склеп (*tomb*); прыжóк (*jump*); *vt.i.* прыгать

veal [віл] *sn.* телятина

veer [вір] *vi.* менять направлéние; *fig.* переменить мнéние

vegetable [вé-джі-тǎбл] *sn.* óвощ; *adj.* овощнóй

vegetation [вé-джі-тǝ́й-шǎн] *sn.* растительность

vehemence [ві-і-мǎнс] *sn.* запáльчивость, неистóвство

vehicle [ві-ікл] *sn.* повóзка, экипáж

veil [вѣйл] *sn.* вуáль; покрывáло (*covering*); завéса (*curtain*); *fig.* мáска; *vt.i.* покрывáть вуáлью

vein [вѣйн] *sn. anat.* вéна; *bot., zool.* жилка; настроéние (*mood*)

velocity [ві-лó-сі-ті] *sn.* бéглость, скóрость

velvet [вéл-віт] *sn.* бáрхат; *fig.* кáжущаяся мягкость

vendor [вéн-дǎр] *sm.* продавéц

veneer [вᶒ-нӣр] *sn.* фанᶒра; облицӧвка (*facing*); *vt.* обклᶒивать фанᶒрой

venerable [вᶒ-нӑ-рӑбл] *adj.* почтᶒнный; *eccl.* преподӧбный

veneration [вᶒ-нӑ-рᶒй-шӑн] *sn.* благоговᶒние, почтᶒние

vengeance [вᶒн-джӑнс] *sn.* месть

venial [вӣ-нӣ-ӑл] *adj.* пустячный (*trivial*); простительный (*pardonable*)

venison [вᶒн-зӑн] *sn.* оленина

venom [вᶒ-нӑм] *sn.* яд; *fig.* злӧба

venous [вӣ-нӑс] *adj.* венӧзный; *bot.* жилковатый

vent [вᶒнт] *sn.* отдӱшина (*air-hole*); отвᶒрстие (входнӧе или выходнӧе (*outlet*)

ventilation [вᶒн-ти-лᶒй-шӑн] *sn.* провᶒтривание; обсуждӓть (*exchange opinions*)

venture [вᶒн-чᶒр] *sn.* рискӧванное предприятие; спекуляция; *vt.i.* отвӓживаться, рисковӓть

veracity [вӑ-рᶒ-си-ти] *sn.* правдивость

verb [вᶒрб] *sn.* глагӧл

verbal [вᶒр-бӑл] *adj.* словᶒсный, ӱстный

verbatim [вᶒр-бӓй-тим] *adj.* дословный; *adv.* слово в слово

verbose [вᶒр-бӧус] *adj.* многослӧвный

verdant [вᶒр-дӑнт] *adj.* зелёный

verdict [вᶒр-дӣкт] *sn.* приговӧр

verge [вᶒрдж] *sn.* граница, край; клониться (*incline*)

verify [вᶒ-рӣ-фай] *vt.* проверять; исполнять

veritable [вᶒ-рӣ-тӓбл] *adj.* истинный, настоящий

vermilion [вӑр-мӣ-лӣ-ӑн] *sn.* киновӓрь; *adj.* яркокрасный

vermin [вᶒр-мӣн] *sn.* вредители; паразиты; *fig.* сброд

vernacular [вӑр-нᶒ-кюлӑр] *adj.* мᶒстный (*local*); роднӧй (о языкᶒ) (*native*)

versatile [вᶒр-сӑ-тайл] *adj.* разносторӧнний

verse [вᶒрс] *sn.* стих, строфӓ

versed [вᶒрст] *adj.* ӧпытный, свᶒдущий

version [вᶒр-шӑн] *sn.* вᶒрсия; осӧбый перевӧд (*translation*)

vertical [вᶒр-тӣ-кӑл] *adj.* вертикальный

verve [вᶒрв] *sn.* живость; яркость (*of imagination*)

very [вᶒ-рӣ] *adj.* истинный, сущий (*truly such*); тот самый (*identical*); *adv.* ӧчень, вечӧ́рня

vespers [вᶒс-пӑрз] *sn. pl.* вечᶒ́рня

vessel [вᶒ-сӑл] *sn.* сосӱд (*container*); корабль, *m.*, судно (*ship*)

vest [вᶒст] *sn.* нательная фуфайка; жилет (*waistcoat*)

vestige [вᶒс-тӣдж] *sn.* след (*trace*); признак (*evidence*); малейший остаток (*particle*)

vestment [вᶒст-мӑнт] *sn.* одежда, одеяние; *eccl.* облачение

vestry [вᶒс-трӣ] *sn. eccl.* ризница; собрание прихожан (*meeting of parishioners*)

veteran [вᶒ-тӑ-рӑн] *sn.* ветерӓн; бывалый солдат

veterinary [вé-трі-нǎ-рі] *adj.* ветеринáрный

veto [ві-тоу́] *sn.* вéто, запрещéние; *vt.* налагáть вéто

vex [вęкс] *vt.* досаждáть, раздражáть (*annoy*), огорчáть (*distress*)

vexed [вęкст] *adj.* спóрный

viaduct [вáй-ǎ-дакт] *sn.* виадýк

vibrate [вай-брэ́йт] *vt.i.* вибрúровать, дрожáть

vicar [ві-кǎр] *sm.* викáрий, прихóдский свящéнник

vicarage [ві-кǎ-рíдж] *sn.* дом свящéнника

vice [вайс] *sn.* порóк; недостáток (*failing*), *tech.* тискú; нóров (*in horses*); *pref.* вице-

vicinity [ві-сí-ні-ті] *sn.* блúзость (*nearness*); окрéстности (*neighbourhood*)

vicious [ві-шǎс] *adj.* порóчный; непрáвильный (*faulty*); злóбный (*malicious*); норовúстый (*of horses*)

vicissitude [ві-сí-сі-тюд] *sn.* преврáтность

victim [вíк-тім] *sm.* жéртва

victimization [вíк-ті-майзѝй-шǎн] *sn.* увольнéние рабóчих

victor [вíк-тǎр] *sm.* побеѝдитель

victory [вíк-тǎ-рі] *sn.* побéда

victualler [ві-тǎ-лǎр] *sm.* поставщúк провизии

victuals [ві-тǎлз] *sn.* провиáнт, провизия

vie [вай] *vi.* сопéрничать

view [вю] *sn.* вид (*aspect*) пейзáж (*landscape, scenery*); взгляд, мнéние (*opinion*);

kругозóр (*outlook*); осмóтр (*survey*); *vt.* осмáтривать, рассмáтривать

vigil [ві-джіл] *sn.* бдéние, бóдрствование

vigilance [ві-джі-лǎнс] *sn.* бдúтельность

vigorous [ві-гǎ-рǎс] *adj.* бóдрый, сúльный

vigour [ві-гǎр] *sn.* бóдрость, энéргия

vile [вайл] *adj.* нúзкий, пóдлый; отвратúтельный (*abominable*)

vilify [ві-лі-фай] *vt.* поносúть

villa [ві-лǎ] *sn.* вúлла (*suburban*); дáча (*country residence*)

village [ві-лідж] *sn.* дерéвня, селó

villager [ві-лі-джǎр] *sm.* дерéвенский жúтель

villain [ві-лǎн] *sm.* злодéй, негодя́й

villainy [ві-лǎ-ні] *sn.* злодéйство, пóдлость

vindicate [він-ді-кэ́йт] *vt.* опрáвдывать (*exculpate*); восстанáвливать (*establish truth, justice, etc.*)

vindictive [він-дíк-тів] *adj.* мстúтельный, карáтельный

vine [вайн] *sn.* виногрáдная лозá

vinegar [ві-ні-гǎр] *sn.* ýксус

vineyard [він-ярд] *sn.* виногрáдник

vintage [він-тідж] *sn.* сбор виногрáда; винó определённого гóда (*of particular year*)

viola [віóй-лǎ] *sn.* *mus.* альт; [вай-óу́-лǎ] *sn.* *bot.* фиáлка

violate [вáй-ǎ-лэ́йт] *vt.* нарушáть, преступáть (*transgress*); насúловать (*force*)

violation [вай-ӑ-лӑ́й-шӑн] *sn.* изнаси́лование (*rape*); оскверне́ние (*profanation*)

violent [ва́й-ӑ-лӑнт] *adj.* бу́йный (*tempestuous*); наси́льственный (*forceful*); стра́стный (*passionate*)

violet [ва́й-ӑ-лӗт] *sn. bot.* фиа́лка; *adj.* фиоле́товый (*colour*)

violin [вай-ӑ-ли́н] *sn.* скри́пка

violoncello [вiо-лӑн-че́-лоу] *sn.* виолонче́ль

viper [ва́й-пӑр] *s.* гадю́ка, ехи́дна

virgin [вёр-джин] *sn.* де́ва, де́вственница; **the Virgin**, богоро́дица; *adj.* де́вственный

virile [ві́-райл] *adj.* му́жественный; возмужа́лый (*of a mature man*)

virtual [вёр-тю-ӑл] *adj.* факти́ческий; действи́тельный (*real*)

virtue [вёр-тю] *sn.* доброде́тель; целому́дрие (*chastity*); досто́инство (*merit*)

virtuous [вёр-тю-ӑс] *adj.* доброде́тельный; целому́дренный (*chaste*)

virulent [ви-ру́-лӑнт] *s.* ядови́тый (*of poison*); зло́бный (*of hatred*)

visa [ви-зӑ] *sn.* пропи́ска

visage [ви́-зiджк] *sn.* лицо́

viscount [ва́й-каунт] *sm.* вико́нт

viscountess [ва́й-каун-тiс] *sf.* виконте́сса

viscous [ві́с-кӑс] *adj.* вя́зкий

visibility [ви-зи-би́-лi-тi] *sn.* ви́димость

visible [ві́-зiбл] *adj.* ви́димый; очеви́дный, я́вный

vision [ві́-жӑн] *sn.* виде́ние (*sight*); зре́ние (*faculty*)

visionary [ві́-жӑ-нӑ-рi] *sm.* мечта́тель, ми́стик; *adj.* вообража́емый, при́зрачный

visit [ві́-зiт] *sn.* визи́т, посеще́ние; *vt.* посеща́ть; гости́ть (*call on someone*)

visitor [ві́-зi-тӑр] *sm.* гость, посети́тель

visual [ві́-жу-ӑл] *adj.* зри́тельный

vital [ва́й-тӑл] *adj.* ва́жный, жи́зненный, суще́ственный

vitality [вай-тӑ́-лi-тi] *sn.* жизнеспосо́бность

vitiate [ві́-ши-эйт] *vt.* по́ртить (*spoil*); лиша́ть де́йственности (*deprive of efficacy*)

vituperate [ві-тю́-пӑ-рэйт] *vt.* оскорбля́ть, поноси́ть

vivacity [ві-вӑ́-сi-тi] *sn.* жи́вость, оживлённость

vivid [ві́-вiд] *adj.* я́ркий (*bright*); нагля́дный (*descriptive*)

vixen [ві́кс-ӑн] *sf.* са́мка лиси́цы; ве́дьма, меге́ра (*woman*)

vocabulary [вӑ-кӑ́-бю-лӑ-рi] *sn.* слова́рь, *m.*

vocal [во́у-кӑл] *adj.* вока́льный, голосово́й

vocalist [во́у-кӑ-лiст] *sm.* певе́ц; *sf.* певи́ца

vocation [во-кӑ́й-шӑн] *sn.* призва́ние; профе́ссия (*profession*); ремесло́ (*trade*)

vociferous [во́у-сi-фӑ-рӑс] *adj.* горла́стый, громогла́сный

vogue [во́уг] *sn.* мо́да (*fashion*); популя́рность

voice [войс] *sn.* го́лос; *gram.* зало́г; *vt.* выража́ть

void [войд] *adj.* пусто́й (*empty*); лишённый (*devoid of*); *leg.* де́лать недействи́тельным

volatile [во́-лă-тайл] *adj. chem.* испаря́ющийся, лету́чий; непостоя́нный, рту́тный (*mercurial*)

volcano [вол-кэ́й-ноу] *sn.* вулка́н

volition [воу-ли́-шăн] *sn.* во́ля, хоте́ние

volley [во́-лĭ] *sn.* залп; град, пото́к (*of oaths, questions, etc.*); *vt.i.* стреля́ть за́лпами

volt [волт] *sn. electr.* вольт

voluble [во́-любл] *adj.* красноречи́вый

volume [во́-люм] *sn.* том (*tome*), объём (*size*) простра́нство (*space*)

voluminous [во-лю́-мĭ-нăс] *adj.* многото́мный (*of books*); плодови́тый (*of writers*); обши́рный (*ample*)

voluntary [во́-лăн-тă-рĭ] *adj.* доброво́льный

volunteer [во-лăн-ти́р] *sm.* волонтёр, доброво́лец; *vi.* вызыва́ться; служи́ть доброво́льцем (*serve*); предлага́ть (*offer*)

voluptuous [вă-ла́п-тю-ăс] *adj.* сластолюби́вый

vomit [во́-мĭт] *sn.* рво́та; *vt.i.* изверга́ть

voracious [во-рэ́й-шăс] *adj.* жа́дный, прожо́рливый

vote [во́ут] *sm.* баллотиро́вка, голосова́ние (*poll*); число́ голосо́в (*number*); *vi.* голосова́ть

voter [во́у-тăр] *sm.* избира́тель

vouch [ва́уч] *vi.* руча́ться

voucher [ва́у-чăр] *sn.* поручи́тельство; распи́ска

vouchsafe [ва́уч-сэ́йф] *vi.* удоста́ивать

vow [вау] *sn.* кля́тва, обе́т; *vt.* дава́ть обе́т, кля́сться

vowel [ва́у-ăл] *sn.* гла́сный звук; гла́сная бу́ква

voyage [во́-идж] *sn.* путеше́ствие

vulgar [ва́л-гăр] *adj.* вульга́рный, по́шлый

vulgarity [вал-гă-ри-тĭ] *sn.* вульга́рность, по́шлость

vulnerable [ва́л-нă-рăбл] *adj.* уязви́мый

vulture [ва́л-чăр] *s.* гриф, стервя́тник; *fig.* хи́щник

W

wad [уод] *sn.* клочо́к ва́ты, пыж; *vt.* подбива́ть ва́той

wadding [уо́-дĭн] *sn.* ва́та (*cotton-wool*); материа́л для наби́вки (*material for padding*)

waddle [уодл] *sn.* перева́ливающаяся похо́дка; *vi.* ходи́ть перева́ливаясь

wade [уэ́йд] *vi.* переходи́ть вброд, пробира́ться

wafer [уэ́й-фăр] *sn.* ва́фля (*biscuit, etc.*); обла́тка (*disk*); *eccl.* просви́ра

waft [уэ́фт] *sn.* дунове́ние; *vt.* переноси́ть, рассека́ть

wag [уæг] *sn.* взмах, киво́к; *vt.* маха́ть, трясти́

wage [уэ́йдж] *sn.* жа́лованье, зарабо́тная пла́та; *vt.* вести́ (войну́) (*war*)

wager [уэ́й-джăр] *sn.* пари́; *vt.i.* держа́ть пари́

waggon [уǎ-гǎн] *sn.* повозка, подвода, фургон

waif [уэйф] *sn.* брошенная вещь (*ownerless object*); *sm.* бездомник (*person*); беспризорный ребёнок (*child*)

wail [уэйл] *sn.* вой, вопль, *m.*; причитание (*lamentation*); *vi.* вопить, выть; причитать (*lament*)

waist [уэйст] *sn.* талия; перехват, сужение (*of coat, violin, etc.*); *naut.* шкафут

waistcoat [уэйст-кǎт] *sn.* жилет

wait [уэйт] *sn.* ожидание; постерегание (*watching for*); *vt.i.* ждать; прислуживать (*at table*) [циант

waiter [уэй-тǎр] *sm.* официант

wake [уэйк] *sn.* кильватер (*track on water*); *vt.i.* будить; просыпаться; пробуждаться (*awaken*)

wakeful [уэйк-фул] *adj.* бдительный (*vigilant*); бессонный (*sleepless*)

wale [уэйл] *sn.* рубец от удара кнутом

walk [уǒк] *sn.* прогулка пешком, ходьба; *vi.* гулять; ходить (*go*)

walker [уǒ-кǎр] *sm.* ходок

walking [уǒ-кǐн] *sn.* гуляньe

walking-stick [уǒ-кǐн-стǐк] *sn.* палка, трость

wall [уǒл] *sn.* стена; *vt.* обносить стеной; **— up** [— ап] замуровывать

wallet [уǒ-лǐт] *sn.* бумажник

wallflower [уǒл-флǎу-ǎр] *sn.* жёлтофиоль

wallpaper [уǒл-пэй-пǎр] *sn.* обои

walnut [уǒл-нат] *sn.* грецкий орех

walrus [уǒл-рǎс] *s. zool.* морж

waltz [уǒлс] *sn.* вальс; *vi.* вальсировать

wan [уǒн] *adj.* бледный (*pale*); изможденный (*exhausted*) [пǎлочка

wand [уǒнд] *sn.* жезл;

wander [уǒн-дǎр] *vi.* бродить, странствовать; блуждать (*of thoughts, etc.*); бредить (*be delirious*)

wanderer [уǒн-дǎ-рǎр] *sm.* скиталец, странник

wandering [уǒн-дǎ-рǐн] *sn.* блуждание

wane [уэйн] *sn.* убывание; ущерб (*of moon*); *vi.* убывать

want [уǒнт] *sn.* недостаток (*lack*); нужда (*need*); *vi.* нуждаться; недоставать (*fall short*); хотеть (*wish*)

wanting [уǒн-тǐн] *adj.* недостающий; *prep.* без

wanton [уǒн-тǎн] *sf.* распутная женщина (*woman*); *sm.* шалопай (*person*); *adj.* игривый (*sportive*); капризный (*capricious*)

war [уǒр] *sn.* война

warble [уǒрбл] *vt.i.* щебетать

ward [уǒрд] *sn.* надзор (*control*); опека (*guardianship*); камера (*of prison*); палата (*of hospital*); квартал (*district*)

wardrobe [уǒр-дрǒуб] *sn.* гардероб [товар

ware [уэр] *sn.* изделия; *pl.*

warehouse [уэр-хǎус] *sn.* товарный склад; *sm.* [-ман] кладовщик

warfare [уǒр-фэр] *sn.* война; ведение войны

warlike [уǒр-лайк] *adj.* воинственный

warm [ўо̄рм] adj. тёплый; сердечный (hearty); vt.i. греть

warmer [ўо̄-мӗр] sn. грелка

warmth [ўо̄рмθ] sn. теплота

warn [ўо̄рн] vt. предупреждать (notify in time); предостерегать (caution)

warning [ўо̄р-нӥй] sn. предостережение, предупреждение

warp [ўо̄рп] sn. коробление (of wood); извращение (perversion); vt.i. искривлять, искажаться (be distorted)

warrant [ўо̄-рӑнт] sn. доверенность, полномочие; vt. уполномочивать

warren [ўо̄-рӗн] sn. кроличий садок

warrior [ўо̄-ри-ӑр] sn. боец

warship [ўо̄р-шӥп] sn. военное судно

wart [ўо̄рт] sn. бородавка

wary [ўз̄-ри] adj. осторожный

wash [ўош] sn. мытьё, стирка; умыванье (washing); примочка (lotion); vt.i. отмывать, стирать, смывать; vr. мыться; – up [– ап] мыть посуду

washer [ўо̄-шӗр] sn. прокладка, шайба; –woman [–ўў-мӑн] sf. прачка

washing [ўо̄-шӥй] sn. мытьё, стирка; adj. стирающий

washstand [ўош-стэнд] sn. умывальник

wasp [ўосп] s. оса

wastage [ўэй-стӥдж] sn. потери, утечка

waste [ўэйст] sn. пустыня (barren expanse); отбросы, остатки (scraps); adj. заброшенный (not inhabited or cultivated); ненужный (superfluous); расточать (time, money, etc.); чахнуть (wither)

wasteful [ўэйст-фӱл] adj. расточительный

wastrel [ўэй-стрӑл] sm. расточитель

watch [ўоч] sn. карманные часы (timepiece); бдительность (vigilance); naut. вахта; keep – [кип –] быть настороже; vt.i. бодрствовать; охранять (guard)

watchful [ўоч-фӱл] adj. бдительный

watchmaker [ўоч-мэй-кӑр] sm. часовщик

watchman [ўоч-мӑн] sm. сторож

watchword [ўоч-ўӗрд] sn. лозунг

water [ўо̄-тӑр] sn. вода; vt. орошать, поливать; поить (give drink)

water-closet [ўо̄-тӑр-кло-зӥт] sn. уборная

water-colour [ўо̄-тӑр-ка-лӑр] sn. акварель

watercress [ўо̄-тӑр-крес] sn. водяной крес

waterfall [ўо̄-тӑр-фо̄л] sn. водопад

watering-can [ўо̄-тӑ-рӥй-кӑн] sn. лейка

watering-place [ўо̄-тӑ-рӥй-плэйс] водопой (for animals); морской курорт (seaside); воды (spa)

waterlogged [ўо̄-тӑр-логд] adj. заболоченный

water-melon [ўо̄-тӑр-ме-лӑн] sn. арбуз

waterproof [ўо̄-тӑр-прӯф] непромокаемый плащ (cloak); adj. водонепроницаемый

waterspout [ўŏ-тăр-спáут] *sn.* смерч

water-tower [ўŏ-тăр-таў-ăр] *sn.* водока́чка

waterworks [ўŏ-тăр-ўэ́ркс] водопрово́дная ста́нция

watery [ўŏ-тă-рį] *adj.* водяни́стый

wave [ўэ́йв] *sn.* волна́ (*sea*); вал (*billow*); ма́хание (*of hand*); колеба́ние (*oscillation*); *vt.i.* маха́ть, разма́хивать; колеба́ться

waver [ўэ́й-вăр] *vi.* дро́гнуть (*falter, of troops*); колыха́ться (*flicker*); колеба́ться (*hesitate*)

wavy [ўэ́й-вį] *adj.* волни́стый

wax [ўэкс] *sn.* воск; ушна́я се́ра (*of ear*); sealing – [си́-лйų –] сургу́ч; *adj.* восково́й

waxwork [ўэ́кс-ўэ́рк] *sn.* восково́я фигу́ра

way [ўэй] *sn.* доро́га, путь (*road*); мане́ра (*manner*); спо́соб (*method*); – in – [– ін] вход; by the – [бай ŏá –] кста́ти, ме́жду про́чим; – out [– áут] вы́ход

wayfarer [ўэ́й-фэ́-рăр] *sm.* пу́тник

waylay [ўэй-лэ́й] *vi.* подстерега́ть, устра́ивать заса́ду

wayward [ўэ́й-ўăрд] *adj.* капри́зный, своенра́вный

we [ўį] *pron.* мы

weak [ўįк] *adj.* сла́бый; хи́лый (*feeble, sickly*)

weaken [ўį-кăн] *vt.i.* ослабева́ть, слабе́ть

weakling [ўįк-лįų] *sn.* слабово́льный челове́к

weakness [ўįк-нįс] *sn.* сла́бость

weal [ўįл] *sn.* рубе́ц (от уда́ра кнуто́м); бла́го, благосостоя́ние

wealth [ўэлŏ] *sn.* бога́тство; изоби́лие (*abundance*)

wealthy [ўэ́л-ŏį] *adj.* бога́тый; the – бога́тые лю́ди

wean [ўįн] *vt.* отнима́ть от груди́ (*child*); отвлека́ть, отуча́ть (*of habit, etc.*)

weapon [ўэ́-пăн] *sn.* ору́жие

wear [ўэ́р] *sn.* ноше́ние; оде́жда (*clothes*); – and tear [– æнд тэ́р] изно́с; *vt.i.* носи́ть; изна́шивать (*wear out*); изнуря́ть, истоща́ть (*exhaust*)

weariness [ўį-рį-нįс] *sn.* уста́лость (*tiredness*); ску́ка (*boredom*)

wearisome [ўį-рį-сăм] *adj.* ску́чный (*tedious*); утоми́тельный (*tiresome, fatiguing*)

weary [ўį-рį] *adj.* утомлённый, уста́лый

weasel [ўį-зăл] *s.* ла́ска

weather [ўэ-ŏăр] *sn.* пого́да

weathercock [ўэ-ŏăр-кок] *sn.* флю́гер

weave [ўįв] *vt.i.* ткать; сплета́ть (*story, etc.*)

weaver [ўį-вăр] *sm.* ткач

web [ўэб] *sn.* паути́на (*spider's*); ткань (*fabric*); перепо́нка (*membrane*); *tech.* перемы́чка (*чатый*)

webbed [ўэбд] *adj.* перепо́нчатый

wed [ўэд] *vt.i.* венча́ть, повенча́ться

wedding [ўэ́-дįų] *sn.* сва́дьба

wedge [ўэдж] *sn.* клин (*s.*); *vt.* закрепля́ть кли́ном

wedlock [ўэд-лок] *sn.* брак, супру́жество

Wednesday [ўэн-здį] *sn.* среда́

weed [уйд] sn. сорная трава́, плеве́л; vt. поло́ть; — out [— а́ут] вырыва́ть, удаля́ть

week [уйк] sn. неде́ля

week-day [уйк-дэй] sn. бу́дний день

weekly [уйк-ли] adj. еженеде́льный

weep [уйп] vi. пла́кать

weigh [уэй] vt.i. взве́шивать, ве́сить; влия́ть (influence); размышля́ть (consider); — down [— да́ун] угнета́ть; — upon [— а-по́н] тяготи́ть (important); — anchor [— э́н-кэр] снима́ться с я́коря

weighbridge [уэй-бридж] sn. мостовы́е весы́

weighing-machine [уэй-ин-ма-ши́н] sn. весы́

weight [уэйт] sn. вес, тя́жесть; ги́ря (for weighing with)

weighty [уэй-ти] adj. ве́ский, тяжёлый; fig. ва́жный (important)

weir [уйр] sn. запру́да

weird [уйрд] adj. ве́щий, роково́й (fateful), колдовско́й (magical); сверхъесте́ственный (unearthly); coll. непоня́тный (incomprehensible); стра́нный (strange)

welcome [уэл-кэм] sn. приве́тствие, раду́шный приём; adj. жела́нный

weld [уэлд] sn. сва́рка; vt.i. сва́ривать металлы

welfare [уэл-фэр] sn. благосостоя́ние

well [уэл] sn. коло́дец, m.; скважина (mining); adj. здоро́вый (of person); adv. как сле́дует, хорошо́; interj. —! ну!; —? а что да́льше?; prefix. бла́го-, хорошо́-

well-behaved [уэл-би-хэ́йвд] adj. благонра́вный

well-being [уэл-би-ин] sn. благополу́чие

well-bred [уэл-бред] adj. благовоспи́танный (of person); чистокро́вный (pure)

well-to-do [уэл-ту-ду́] adj. зажи́точный, состоя́тельный

Welsh [уэлш] adj. валли́йский [ский

Welshman [уэлш-мэн] sm. валли́ец

welt [уэлт] sn. рант

welter [уэл-тэр] vi. бара́хтаться, валя́ться

west [уэст] sn. за́пад; adj. за́падный; adv. к за́паду

westerly [уэст-тэр-ли] adj. за́падный

westward(s) [уэст-уэрд(з)] adj., adv. в за́падном направле́нии

wet [уэт] adj. вла́жный, мо́крый; дождли́вый (rainy); vt. мочи́ть, сма́чивать

wet-nurse [уэт-нэрс] sf. корми́лица

whale [уэйл] s. кит

whaler [уэй-лэр] sm. китоло́в; sn. китобо́йное су́дно

wharf [уо́рф] sn. верфь, при́стань

what [уот] adj. како́й; pron. что

whatever [уот-э-вэр] pron. всё что, что бы ни; adj. любо́й, никако́й

wheat [уйт] sn. пшени́ца

wheaten [уй-тэн] adj. пшени́чный

wheedle [уйдл] vt. льстить, прельща́ть

wheel [уйл] n. колесо́; руль, штурва́л (steering); vt.i.

везти́, кати́ть; повора́чи-
ваться (*turn*)

wheelbarrow [ýйл-бǽ-роў]
sn. та́чка

wheelwright [ýйл-райт] *sm.*
коле́сник

wheeze [ýйз] *sn.* сопе́ние;
vi. дыша́ть с присви́стом,
сопе́ть

wheezy [ýи-зі] *adj.* задыха́ю-
щийся

whelp [ýэлп] *s.* детёныш,
щено́к; *vt.i.* щени́ться

when [ýэн] *adv.* когда́

whence [ýэнс] *adv.* отку́да

whenever [ýэн-ĕ-вǎр] *adv.*
когда́ бы ни, как то́лько

where [ýэр] *adv.* где, куда́

whereabouts [ýэр-ǎ-баўтс]
sn. приблизи́тельное место-
расположе́ние

whereas [ýэр-ǽз] *conj.* при-
нима́я во внима́ние; тогда́
как

wherever [ýэр-ĕ-вǎр] *adv.*
где бы ни, куда́ бы ни

wherry [ýέ-рі] *sn.* ло́дка,
я́лик

whet [ýэт] *vt.* точи́ть (*sharpen*); возбужда́ть (*appetite*)

whether [ýǎ-эǎр] *conj.* и́ли,
ли

whetstone [ýэт-стоўн] *sn.*
точи́льный ка́мень

whey [ýэй] *sn.* сы́воротка

which [ýич] *adj.* како́й; *pron.*
кото́рый

whichever [ýич-ĕ-вǎр] *adj.*
како́й бы ни

whiff [ýиф] *sn.* дунове́ние;
глото́к во́здуха (*of air*);лёг-
кий я́лик (*skiff*); клуб (*puff*)

while [ýайл] *sn.* промежу́-
ток вре́мени (*time*); **not
worth** — [нот ýǎрθ —] не
сто́ит труда́; *conj.* в то
вре́мя, во вре́мя, пока́

whilst [ýайлст] *conj.* пока́

whim [ýим] *sn.* при́хоть

whimper [ýим-пǎр] *sn.* хны́-
канье; *vi.* хны́кать

whimsical [ýим-зі-кǎл] *adj.*
причу́дливый

whine [ýайн] *sn.* вой, жа́-
лобный визг; *vi.* скули́ть,
хны́кать

whip [ýип] *sn.* кнут, хлыст;
организа́тор па́ртии (*parliament*); *vt.i.* хлеста́ть; рас-
шевели́вать (*urge*)

whipcord [ýип-кȯ́рд] *sn.*
верёвка

whippet [ýĭ-піт] *s.* го́нчая
соба́ка; *mil.* танке́тка

whirl [ýǎрл] *sn.* враще́ние,
круже́ние; *vt.i.* верте́ть,
кружи́ться

whirlpool [ýǎрл-пȳл] *sn.*
водоворо́т

whirlwind [ýǎрл-ýинд] *sn.*
вихрь, *m.*, урага́н

whisk [ýіск] *sn.* ве́нник,
метёлка; сбива́лка (*implement*); сби́вка (*churning*);
vt.i. сбива́ть (*churn*); смáхи-
вать (*brandish*); помáхивать
(*wave*); ю́ркнуть (*disappear*)

whiskers [ýіс-кǎрз] *sn. pl.*
бакенба́рды; усы́ (*cat's*)

whisper [ýіс-пǎр] *sn.*
шȅ́пот; *vt.* шепта́ть

whistle [ýісл] *sn.* свист,
свисто́к (*instrument*); *vt.i.*
свиста́ть

white [ýайт] *adj.* бе́лый;
бле́дный (*pale*); — **of egg**
[— эг] зг бело́к

whiten [ýай-тǎн] *vt.i.* бе-
ли́ть; беле́ть (*become white*)

whiteness [ýайт-ніс] *sn.*
белизна́

whitewash [ýайт-ýош] *sn.*
побе́лка; *vt.* бели́ть

whiting [уа́й-тіṅ] s. мерла́н (*fish*); мел (*chalk*)

whittle [уітл] vt.i. строга́ть (*wood*); **– away** [– ă-уэ́й] fig. свести́ на-не́т

who [ху́] pron. кото́рый, кто, тот кто

whoever [ху-ȩ́-вăр] pron. кото́рый бы ни

whole [хо́ул] sn. це́лое; adj. весь, це́лый; **on the –** [он ӗ̆ –] вообще́, в о́бщем

wholesale [хо́ул-сэйл] sn. опто́вая торго́вля; adj. опто́вый; adv. о́птом

wholesome [хо́ул-сăм] adj. благотво́рный, здоро́вый

wholly [хо́у-лі] adv. вполне́, целико́м

whom [ху́м] pron. кого́, кому́; **with –** [уіȝ –] с кем

whooping-cough [ху́-піṅ-коф] sn. коклю́ш

whose [ху́з] pron. чей

why [уа́й] adv. почему́

wick [уік] sn. фити́ль

wicked [уі́-кід] adv. злой, поро́чный; безнра́вственный (*immoral*)

wicker [уі́-кăр] sn. и́вовые пру́тья; **– chair** [– чэ́р] плетёный стул

wicket [уі́-кет] sn. кали́тка, воро́тца (*cricket*)

wide [уа́йд] adj. широ́кий

widen [уа́й-дăн] vt.i. расширя́ть

wide-spread [уа́йд-спред] adj. широко́ распространённый

widow [уі́-доу] sf. вдова́

widower [уі́-доу-ăр] sm. вдове́ц

width [уідɵ] sn. ширина́

wield [уі́лд] vt. владе́ть, облада́ть

wife [уа́йф] sf. жена́

wig [уіг] sn. пари́к

wild [уа́йлд] adj. ди́кий; бу́рный (*weather*); взбешённый (*frenzied*)

wilderness [уі́л-дăр-нăс] sn. пусты́ня [ди́кость

wildness [уа́йлд-ніс] sn.

wiles [уа́йлз] sn. pl. про́делка

wilful [уі́л-фӯл] adj. своево́льный, упря́мый; доброво́льный, наме́ренный (*of free choice, intentionally*)

will [уіл] sn. во́ля (*faculty*); завеща́ние (*testament*); **against one's –** [ă-ге́йнст уăнз –] принуди́тельно; **at –** [æт –] по жела́нию; **good –** [гӯд –] благоскло́нность; vt.i. жела́ть, хоте́ть; заста́вить (*compel*); завеща́ть (*bequeath*)

willing [уі́-ліṅ] adj. доброво́льный, охо́тный

will-o'-the-wisp [уіл-о-ĕй уісп] sn. блужда́ющий огонёк (*ignis fatuus*); fig. неулови́мый челове́к

willow [уі́-лоу] sn. и́ва

wilt [уі́лт] vt.i. вя́нуть, пони́кать; погуби́ть (*flowers*)

wily [уа́й-лі] adj. кова́рный, хи́трый

win [уі́н] sn. вы́игрыш; vt.i. выи́грывать

wince [уі́нс] sn. содрога́ние; vi. вздра́гивать, мо́рщиться

winch [уі́нч] sn. вӗ́рот, лебёдка

wind [уінд] sn. ве́тер; дыха́ние (*breath*)

wind [уа́йнд] vt.i. нама́тывать; ви́ться, извива́ться (*twist*); заводи́ть (*watch, etc.*); **– up** [– ап] ликвиди́ровать (*a company, etc.*)

windfall [уи́нд-фōл] *sn.* па́даль, па́данец (*of fruit*); *fig.* неожи́данная уда́ча

winding [уа́йн-дин] *sn.* изги́б; *electr.* обмо́тка

windlass [уи́нд-лāс] *sn. tech.* бра́шпиль, лебёдка

windmill [уи́нд-мӣл] *sn.* ветряна́я ме́льница, ветря́нка

window [уи́н-доу] *sn.* окно́

windy [уи́н-ди] *adj.* ве́треный

wine [уа́йн] *sn.* вино́

wineglass [уа́йн-глāс] *sn.* рю́мка, стака́нчик

wing [уи́н] *sn.* крыло́; *mil.* фланг; *theat. pl.* кули́сы

winged [уи́нгд] *adj.* крыла́тый; *fig.* бы́стрый (*swift*)

wink [уи́нк] *sn.* мига́ние, морга́нье; намёк гла́зом; *vt.i.* мига́ть, морга́ть

winnow [уи́-ноу] *vt.* ве́ять, просе́ивать; *fig.* разбира́ть

winter [уи́н-тāр] *sn.* зима́; *vi.* зимова́ть, проводи́ть зи́му

wintry [уи́н-три] *adj.* зи́мний; холо́дный (*cold*)

wipe [уа́йп] *sn.* вытира́ние; *vt.* вытира́ть, утира́ть; осуша́ть (*wipe dry*); **– out** [– а́ут] уничтожа́ть (*destroy*)

wire [уа́йāр] *sn.* про́волока; *electr.* про́вод; *coll.* телегра́мма (*telegram*); *vt.i.* прокла́дывать про́волоки, соединя́ть провода́ми; телеграфи́ровать

wireless [уа́й-āр-лӣс] *sn.* ра́дио; *adj.* беспрово́лочный

wiry [уа́й-āри] *adj.* выносли́вый (*enduring*); му́скулистый, жи́листый (*sinewy*)

wisdom [уи́з-дāм] *sn.* му́дрость

wise [уа́йз] *adj.* му́дрый;

благоразу́мный (*reasonable*); *suffix,* -обра́зно

wish [уи́ш] *sn.* жела́ние; *vt.* жела́ть; хоте́ть

wishful [уи́ш-фӯл] *adj.* жела́ющий

wisp [уи́сп] *sn.* пучо́к

wistful [уи́ст-фӯл] *adj.* гру́стный, заду́мчивый

wit [уи́т] *sn.* остроу́мие, ра́зум; *sm.* остря́к

witch [уи́ч] *sn.* ве́дьма, колду́нья; чароде́йка

witchcraft [уи́ч-крāфт] *sn.* колдовство́

with [уи́ð] *prep.* с, со

withdraw [уиð-дро́] *vt.i.* брать наза́д (*take back*), отзыва́ть (*recall*); отходи́ть, удаля́ться (*retire, retract*)

withdrawal [уиð-дро́-āл] *sn.* отозва́ние, отхо́д

wither [уи́-ðāр] *vi.* вя́нуть, со́хнуть

withhold [уиð-хōулд] *vt.* уде́рживать

within [уи-ðíн] *prep.* внутри́; **from –** [фром –] изнутри́; **– the law** [– ðā лō] в преде́лах пра́ва

without [уи-ðа́ут] *adv.* вне, снару́жи; *prep.* без

withstand [уиð-стэ́нд] *vt.* противостоя́ть, сопротивля́ться

witness [уи́т-нӣс] *sm.* свиде́тель; **eye –** [ай –] очеви́дец; *sn.* доказа́тельство (*testimony*); *vt.i.* свиде́тельствовать; быть свиде́телем

witty [уи́-ти] *adj.* остроу́мный

wizard [уи́-зāрд] *sm.* колду́н; волше́бник (*magician*); чароде́й (*sorcerer*)

wobble [уо́бл] *vi.* кача́ться, шата́ться

woe [уоу́] sn. го́ре, скорбь; pl. бе́дствия, несча́стия

wolf [уу́лф] s. волк

woman [уу́-ман] sf. же́нщина

womanhood [уу́-ман-ху́д] sn. же́нственность

womb [уу́м] sn. ма́тка

wonder [уа́н-дӑр] sn. удивле́ние, чу́до; vi. диви́ться, удивля́ться

wonderful [уа́н-дӑр-фу́л] adj. удиви́тельный, чуде́сный [ший]

wont [уо́унт] adj. привы́к-

woo [уу́] vt. уха́живать

wood [уу́д] sn. де́рево; лес (forest); дрова́ (fuel); – pulp [– палп] древе́сная ма́сса

woodcut [уу́д-кат] sn. гравю́ра на де́реве

woodcutter [уу́д-ка-тӑр] sm. дровосе́к

wooded [уу́-дид] adj. леси́стый [вя́нный]

wooden [уу́-дан] adj. дере-

woodland [уу́д-ленд] sn. леси́стая ме́стность

woodman [уу́д-ман] sm. лесни́к, лесору́б

woodpecker [уу́д-пе-кӑр] s. дя́тел

woodwind [уу́д-уи́нд] sn. pl. mus. деревя́нные духовы́е инструме́нты

woodwork [уу́д-уа́рк] sn. деревя́нные изде́лия

woody [уу́-ди] adj. дереви́стый

wool [уу́л] sn. шерсть

woollen [уу́-лан] adj. шерстяно́й [стый]

woolly [уу́-ли] adj. шерсти́-

word [уа́рд] sn. сло́во; сообще́ние (communication, message)

work [уа́рк] sn. рабо́та; де́йствие (operation); де́ло (concern); труд (labour); vt.i. рабо́тать; труди́ться (labour); занима́ться (study)

workable [уа́р-кабл] adj. поддаю́щийся обрабо́тке; примени́мый (applicable)

worker [уа́р-кӑр] sm. рабо́тник, рабо́чий

working [уа́р-кий] sn. разрабо́тка; adj. рабо́тающий

workman [уа́рк-ман] sm. рабо́тник, рабо́чий

workmanship [уа́рк-ман-шип] sn. иску́сство, мастерство́

works [уа́ркс] sn. pl. заво́д

workshop [уа́рк-шоп] sn. мастерска́я

world [уа́рлд] sn. мир, свет; челове́чество (mankind)

worldly [уа́рлд-ли] adj. земно́й, мирско́й, све́тский

world-power [уа́рлд-па́уӑр] sn. мирова́я держа́ва

world-wide [уа́рлд-уа́йд] adj. всеми́рно-изве́стный

worm [уа́рм] s. червя́к, червь; незначи́тельный челове́к (insignificant person); vt.i. проника́ть (through); вкра́дываться (into favour)

wormeaten [уа́рм-и́тан] adj. исто́ченный червя́ми; fig. устаре́лый

wormwood [уа́рм-уу́д] sn. полы́нь; fig. исто́чник го́речи

wormy [уа́р-ми] adj. черви́вый

worn-out [уо́рн-а́ут] adj. изно́шенный; fig. истощё́нный

worry [уа́-рі] *sn.* беспоко́йство, трево́га; *vt.i.* надоеда́ть; терза́ть; беспоко́иться; грызть, трепа́ть (*of dog*)

worse [уо́рс] *adj.* ху́дший; *adv.* ху́же

worsen [уо́р-сăн] *vt.i.* ухудша́ть

worship [уо́р-шіп] *sn.* богослуже́ние (*divine service*); обожа́ние, поклоне́ние (*adoration, homage*); your — [юр —] ва́ша ми́лость; *vt.i.* моли́ться (*pray*), обожа́ть, поклоня́ться (*adore, idolize*)

worshipful [уо́р-шіп-фŭл] *adj.* благоро́дный, почте́нный

worshipper [уо́р-ші-пăр] *sm.* покло́нник

worst [уо́рст] *adj.* наиху́дший

worsted [уу́-стід] *sn.* шерстяна́я пря́жа

worth [уо́рѳ] *sn.* сто́имость, цена́, це́нность; *adj.* заслу́живающий (*merited*), сто́ящий (*cost*); — while — [— ўа́йл] име́ющий смысл

worthy [уо́р-еі] *adj.* заслу́живающий, досто́йный

would-be [ўд-бі] *adj., adv.* мни́мый, притво́рный

wound [ўу́нд] *sn.* ра́на, поре́з; *vt.* ра́нить

wrack [рæк] *sn.* bot. водоросль; — and ruin [— æнд ру́-ін] по́лное разоре́ние, разруше́ние

wrangle [ръæнгл] *sn.* переpека́ние, ссо́ра; *vi.* перека́ться, спо́рить

wrap [ръæп] *sn.* плато́к, шаль; *vt.i.* заве́ртывать; заку́тывать (*wrap up*); ку́таться (*oneself up*)

wrapper [ръæ-пăр] *sn.* бандеро́ль, обёртка

wrath [ро́ѳ] *sn.* гнев, я́рость

wreath [ріѳ] *sn.* вено́к; гирля́нда

wreck [рęк] *sn.* круше́ние, ава́рия (*of ship*); разва́лина (*of building or person*); *vt.* разва́ливать, разруша́ть, сокруша́ть

wreckage [рę́-кідж] *sn.* обло́мки круше́ния

wren [рęн] *s.* крапи́вник

wrench [ренч] *sn.* дёрганье, скру́чивание; вы́вих (*of ankle, etc.*); *tech.* га́ечный ключ

wrest [рęст] *vt.* истолко́вывать в свою по́льзу; вырыва́ть (*snatch*); исторга́ть (*extract*)

wrestle [рęсл] *sn.* состяза́ние в борьбе́; схва́тка (*scuffle*); *vi.* боро́ться

wrestler [рę́с-лăр] *sm.* боре́ц

wretch [реч] *sm.* жа́лкий, несча́стный (челове́к) (*pitiable person*); негодя́й (*scoundrel*); poor — [пўр —] бедня́га

wretched [рę́-чід] *adj.* несча́стный (*unhappy*); скве́рный (*bad*); плохо́й (*of health, weather*)

wrick [рік] *sn.* растяже́ние (му́скула); *vt.* растяну́ть

wriggle [рігл] *sn.* изви́в (*of ship*); *vi.* извива́ть, изгиба́ться

wring [ріŋ] *sn.* сти́скивание; *vt.* свёртывать, сти́скивать; выжима́ть (*washing*); — out [— аўт] отжима́ть

wringer [ріŋ-ăр] *sn.* маши́на для выжима́ния белья́

wrinkle [рі́ŋкл] *sn.* морщи́на; *coll.* поле́зное руково́дство (*useful guidance*); *vt.i.* нахму́ривать, морщи́ться

wrist [ріст] *sn.* запя́стье

wristlet [ріст-літ] *sn.* брасле́т; ремешо́к для часо́в (*of watch*) [приказ

writ [ріт] *sn.* предписа́ние,

write [райт] *vt.i.* писа́ть

writer [рай-тăр] *sn.* писа́тель; -'s cramp [-з крæмп] пи́счий спазм

writhe [райз] *vi.* ко́рчиться от бо́ли

writing [рай-тĭн] *sn.* писа́ние

wrong [рон] *sn.* непра́вда, несправедли́вость (*injustice*), оби́да (*offence*); do [ду -] греши́ть; *adj.* непра́вильный, оши́бочный, быть несправедли́вым (*be unjust*); подрыва́ть (*harm*), вреди́ть (*injure*)

wrongful [рон-фŭл] *adj.* незако́нный

wrought-iron [рот-ай-ăн] *sn.* ко́ваное желе́зо

wry [рай] *adj.* криво́й, переко́шенный (*of face*)

X

Xmas [крíс-мăс, сокраще́ние от **Christmas**] *sn.* рождество́

X-rays [экс-ре́йз] *sn. pl.* рентге́новы лучи́; **to be x-rayed** [ту би экс-ре́йд] подверга́ться просве́чиванию

xylophone [зай-лă-фо́ун] *sn. mus.* ксилофо́н

Y

yacht [йот] *sn.* я́хта; *vi.* пла́вать на я́хте

yachting [йо́-тĭн] *sn.* ката́ние на я́хтах

yap [яп] *sn.* тя́вканье; *vi.* тя́вкать

yard [ярд] *sn.* двор (*court*); ярд (=3 фу́та), *naut.* ре́я

yarn [ярн] *sn.* пря́жа, *coll.* расска́з (*story*)

yawl [йол] *sn.* я́блóт

yawn [йон] *sn.* зево́та; *vi.* зева́ть; зия́ть (*gape*)

yeanling [йин-лĭн] *s.* козлёнок (*kid*); ягнёнок (*lamb*)

year [йир] *sn.* год; *pl.* во́зраст (*age*); **getting on in -s** [ге́тĭн он ин -з] пожило́й он

yearbook [е́р-бŭк] *sn.* ежего́дник

yearling [йир-лĭн] *sn.* годова́лое живо́тное, годови́к

yearly [е́р-лі] *adj.* ежего́дный; *adv.* раз в год

yearn [йăрн] *vi.* томи́ться, тоскова́ть

yeast [йист] *sn.* дро́жжи, заква́ски

yell [ел] *sn.* вы́крик, прони́зи́тельный крик; *vi.* крича́ть

yellow [е́-лоу] *adj.* жёлтый; *vt.i.* желте́ть

yellowish [е́-лоу-иш] *adj.* желтова́тый

yelp [елп] *sn.* визг, взви́згивание, лай; *vi.* взви́згивать, ла́ять, тя́вкать

yes [ес] *adv.* да

yesterday [е́-стăр-ді] *sn., adv.* вчера́

yet [ет] *adv.* ещё (*still*);

вдоба́вок (*in addition*); *conj.* одна́ко (*however*); несмотря́ на (*notwithstanding*); уже́ (*already*)

yew [ю] *sn.* ти́совое де́рево

Yiddish [йй-дйш] *sn.* евре́йский язы́к (*language*)

yield [йилд] *sn.* сбор (*of fruit*); урожа́й (*crop*); произво́дительность (*productivity*); *vt.i.* дава́ть, приноси́ть (*provide*); производи́ть (*produce*); уступа́ть (*give way*)

yoke [йо́ук] *sn.* ярмо́ (*wooden neckpiece*); у́зы (*ties*); коромы́сло (*wooden shoulder-piece*); коке́тка (*on dress*); *tech.* закре́па, связь; *vt.i.* впряга́ть в ярмо́

yokel [йо́у-кэл] *sm.* дереве́нщина

yolk [йо́ук] *sn.* желто́к

yonder [йо́н-да̀р] *adv.* там

you [ю] *pron.* вы; ты (*familiar*)

young [ян] *s.* детёныш (*offspring*); *adj.* молодо́й, ю́ный; нео́пытный (*immature*)

youngster [ян-ста́р] *sm.* ма́льчик, подро́сток

your(s) [йо́р(з)] *adj., pron.* ваш; твой (*familiar*)

yourself [йо̀р-се́лф] *pron.* сам, са́ми; **you are not quite** — [ю я̀р нот куа́йт —] вам не по себе́

youth [юё] *sm.* ю́ность; мо́лодёжь (*young people*)

youthful [юё-фул] *adj.* моложа́вый, ю́ный, ю́ношеский

Yugoslav [ю̀-гоу-сла́в] *sm.*

жи́тель Югосла́вии; *adj.* югосла́вский

yule(-tide) [юл(-тайд)] *sn.* свя́тки

Z

zeal [зил] *sn.* рве́ние, усе́рдие

zealous [зэ́-лас] *adj.* рья́ный, усе́рдный

zebra [зи-бра́] *s.* зе́бра

zenith [зэ́-нѝё] *sn.* зени́т

zephyr [зэ́-фа̀р] *sn.* за́падный ве́тер (*west wind*); зефи́р, лёгкий ветеро́к (*light breeze*); ткань (*fabric*); ма́йка (*sporting vest*)

zero [зй-роу́] *sn.* нуль (0); ничто́ (*nil, nought*); *mil.* нача́льный пункт

zest [зэст] *sn.* пика́нтность; *coll.* изю́минка, ре́зкий интере́с

zigzag [зи́г-зэг] *sn.* зигза́г; *adj.* зигзагообра́зный; *vi.* де́лать зигза́ги

zinc [зйнк] *sn.* цинк; *adj.* ци́нковый; *vt.* оцинко́вывать

zip-fastener [зи́п-фа̀с-на̀р] застёжка, „мо́лния"

zither [зи́-эа̀р] *sn. mus.* ци́тра

zone [зо́ун] *sn.* зо́на; о́бласть, полоса́ (*circle, band*); *vt.* опоя́сывать

zoo [зу] *sn. coll.* зоопа́рк

zoological [зу̀-ло́-джи-ка̀л] *adj.* зоологи́ческий

zoologist [зу̀-о́-ла̀-джѝст] *sm.* зоо́лог

zoology [зу̀-о́-ла̀-джи] *sn.* зооло́гия

GEOGRAPHICAL NAMES
ГЕОГРАФИЧЕСКИЕ НАЗВАНИЯ

Adriatic Sea [эй-дри-ѐ-тĭк си] Адриати́ческое мо́ре

Aegean Sea [и-джи́-ан си] Эге́йское мо́ре

Africa [ѐ-фри-кӑ] А́фрика

Aix-la-Chapelle [экс-ла-ша-пе́л] А́ахен

Albania [æл-бѐй-нĭӑ] Алба́ния

Algeria [æл-джи́-рĭӑ] Алжи́рия

Algiers [æл-джи́рз] Алжи́р

Alps, The [ѐi æлпс] А́льпы

Amazon [ѐ-мӑ-зӑн] Амазо́нка

America [ӑ-мѐ-ри-кӑ] Аме́рика

Ankara [ѐн-кӑ-рӑ] Анкара́

Antarctic Ocean [æн-та́рк-тĭк оу́-шӑн] Ю́жный Ледови́тый океа́н

Antwerp [æнт-ўэ́рп] Антве́рпен

Apennines [ѐ-пĕ-найнз] Апенни́ны

Arabia [ӑ-рѐй-бĭӑ] Ара́вия

Arctic Ocean [а́рк-тĭк оу́-шӑн] Ледови́тый океа́н

Argentina [а́р-джĕн-ти́-нӑ] Аргенти́на

Armenia [а́р-ми́-нĭӑ] Арме́ния

Asia [ѐй-шӑ] А́зия

Asia Minor [ѐй-шӑ-ма́й-нӑр] Ма́лая А́зия

Athens [ѐ-θĭнз] Афи́ны

Atlantic Ocean [ӑ-тлѐн-тĭк оу́-шӑн] Атланти́ческий океа́н

Australasia [о-стрӑ-лѐй-зĭӑ] Австрала́зия

Australia [о-стрѐй-лĭӑ] Австра́лия

Austria [о́-стрĭӑ] А́встрия

Balkan Peninsula [ба́л-кӑн пĕ-нĭн-сю-лӑ] Балка́нский полуо́стров

Baltic Sea [бо́л-тĭк си] Балти́йское мо́ре

Bavaria [бӑ-ваѐ́-рĭӑ] Бава́рия

Bayreuth [бай-ро́йт] Байре́йт (Germany)

Beirut [бэй-ру́т] Бейру́т (Lebanon)

Belgium [бѐл-джӑм] Бе́льгия

Belgrade [бĕл-грѐйд] Белгра́д

Berlin [бӑр-лĭ́н] Берли́н

Bessarabia [бĕс-ӑ-рѐй-бĭӑ] Бессара́бия

Bethlehem [бѐθ-лĭ-ӑм] Вифлее́м

Biscay, Bay of [бэй ов бĭ́скэй] Биска́йский зали́в

Black Sea [блæк си] Чёрное мо́ре

Bohemia [бо-хи́-мĭӑ] Боге́мия

Bosphorus [бо́с-фӑ-рӑс] Босфо́р

Brazil [брӑ-зĭ́л] Брази́лия

Britain [брĭ́-тӑн] Брита́ния

Brittany [брĭ́-тӑ-ни] Брета́нь

Brussels [брӑ-сӑлз] Брюссе́ль

Bucharest [бу́-ка-рĕст] Буха́рест

Budapest [бю-да-пе́ст] Будапе́шт

Bulgaria [бăл-гɜ́-риă] Бол-
гáрия

Burma [бɛ́р-мă] Бирма

Cairo [кáй-роу] Каир

Canada [кá-на-дă] Канáда

Canary Islands [кă-нɜ́-рı
áй-лăндз] Канáрские ос-
тровá

Cape Horn [кэйп хȯ́рн]
Мыс Горн

Cape of Good Hope [кэйп
ов гŭд хȯ́уп] Мыс Дóброй
Надéжды

Caribbean Sea [кæ-рı-бú-
ăн сı] Карайбское мóре

Carpathians [кар-пɜ́й-ѳı-
ăнс] Карпáты

Caucasus [кȯ́-кă-сăс] Кав-
кáз

Ceylon [сı-лȯ́н] Цейлóн

China [чáй-нă] Китáй

Chinese People's Republic
[чáй-нıз пú-пăлс рı-пáб-лık]
Китáйская Нарóдная Рес-
пýблика

Copenhagen [кȯ́у-пăн-хɜ́й-
гăн] Копенгáген

Crete [крıт] Крит

Crimea [край-мú-ă] Крым

Croatia [кроу-эй-шă] Кроá-
ция

Cyprus [сáй-прăс] Кипр

Czechoslovakia [чɛ-коу-
сло-вǽ-кıă] Чехословáкия

Danube [дǽ-нюб] Дунáй

Delhi [дɛ́-лı] Дéли

Denmark [дɛ́н-марк] Дáния

Dnieper [днı-пɜ́р] Днепр

Dniester [днı-стɜ́р] Днестр

Dublin [дá-блın] Дýблин

Edinburgh [ɛ́-дın-брǝ]
Эдинбýрг

Egypt [ú-джıпт] Егúпет

Elbe [эл-бǝ] Эльба

England [ıн-глăнд] Áнглия

English Channel [ıн-глıш
чǽ-нăл] Ла-Мáнш

Estonia [эс-тȯ́-нıă] Эстóния

Ethiopia [ı-ѳı-ȯ́у-пıă] Эфиó-
пия, Абиссиния

Europe [ю́-рăп] Еврóпа

Finland [фún-лăнд] Фин-
ля́ндия

France [франс] Фрáнция

Geneva [джı-нú-вă] Женéва

Georgia [джȯ́р-джıă] Грý-
зия (U.S.S.R); Джóрджия
(U.S.A.)

Germany [джɛ́р-мă-нı]
Гермáния

Ghent [гɛнт] Гент

Glasgow [глǽз-гоу] Глáзго

Gold Coast [гȯ́улд кȯуст]
Золотóй бéрег

Great Britain [грэйт брú-
тăн] Великобритáния

Greece [грıс] Грéция

Guatemala [гȳă-тɛ-мǽ-лă]
Гватемáла

Guiana [гı-á-нă] Гвиáна

Guinea [гı́-нı] Гвинéя

Hague, The [ǝǎ хȯ́йг] Гаáга

Hebrides [хɛ́-брı-дız] Ге-
брúдские островá

Himalayas [хı-мă-лɜ́й-ăз]
Гималáи

Hindustan [хın-дȳ-стáн]
Индостáн

Holland [хȯ́-лăнд] Голлáн-
дия

Hudson Bay [хǎд-сăн бэй]
Гудзóнов залúв

Hungary [хáй-гă-рı] Вéн-
грия

Iceland [а́йс-лăнд] Исландия	Монблан
India [и́н-диă] Индия	**Montenegro** [мон-ти-не́г-роў] Черногория
Indian Ocean [и́н-ди-ăн оў-ша́н] Индийский океан	**Morocco** [мă-ро́-коў] Марóко
Indo-China [и́н-до-ча́й-нă] Индокитай	**Moscow** [мóс-коў] Москва́
Ireland [а́й-ăр-лăнд] Ирландия	**Netherlands** [нé-ðăр-лăндз] Нидерланды
Israel [и́з-рэй-ăл] Израиль	**New Guinea** [ню ги́-ни] Новая Гвинея
Italy [и́-тă-ли] Италия	**New-York** [ню-йóрк] Нью Йóрк
Jamaica [джă-мэ́й-кă] Ямайка	**New-Zealand** [ню-зи́-лăнд] Новая Зеландия
Japan [джă-пæн] Япония	**Nigeria** [най-джи́-риă] Нигéрия
Jerusalem [джă-ру́-сă-лăм] Иерусалим	**Nile** [найл] Нил
Jordan [джóр-дăн] Иордан	**North Sea** [нóрθ си] Сéверное мóре
Korea [ко-ри́ă] Корéя	**Norway** [нóр-ўэй] Норвéгия
Lapland [лæп-лăнд] Лапландия	**Oslo** [óз-лоў] Óсло
Lebanon [лé-ба-нăн] Ливан	**Ottawa** [ó-тă-ўă] Оттáва
Latvia [лǽт-виă] Латвия	**Pacific Ocean** [пæ-си́-фик óў-шăн] Тихий океан
Libyan Desert [ли́-би-ăн дé-зăрт] Ливийская пустыня	**Palestine** [пǽ-лис-тайн] Палестина
Liege [ли́ж] Люттих	**Paraguay** [пǽ-рă-гўай] Парагвай
Lisbon [ли́з-бăн] Лиссабóн	**Paris** [пǽ-рис] Париж
Lithuania [ли-θ̆ў-эй-ниă] Литва	**Peking** [пи-ки́н] Пекин
Luxemburg [лáкс-ăм-бœрг] Люксембург	**Persia** [пœ́р-шă] Пéрсия
	Peru [пă-ру́] Пéру
Macedonia [мæ-си-дóў-ниă] Македóния	**Poland** [пóў-лăнд] Пóльша
Marmora, Sea of [си ов мăр́-мă-рă] Мрáморное мóре	**Portugal** [пóр-чă-гăл] Португáлия
Mediterranean Sea [мé-ди-тă-рэй-ни-ăн си] Средизéмное мóре	**Prague** [прāг] Прáга
	Prussia [прá-шă] Прýссия
Mexico [мéкс-и-коў] Мéксика	**Pyrenees** [пи-ри-ни́з] Пиренéй
Mont Blanc [мой блáй]	**Red Sea** [рéд си] Крáсное мóре

Rocky Mountains [ró-кі máўн-тінз] Скалистые горы

Rome [рóўм] Рим

Rumania [рў-мэ́й-ніä] Румы́ния

Russia [рá-шä] Россия

Sahara [сă-хä́-пă] Сахáра

Scandinavia [скæн-ді-нэ́й-віä] Скандинáвия

Scotland [скóт-лäнд] Шотлáндия

Seine [сэйн] Сéна

Siberia [сай-би́-піä] Сиби́рь

Sicily [сí-сі-лі] Сици́лия

Singapore [сі́н-гä-пōр] Сингапýр

Sofia [сóў-фіä] Софи́я

Spain [спэйн] Испáния

Stockholm [стóк-хōўм] Стóкгольм

Suez Canal [сý-із кă-нéл] Суэ́цкий канáл

Sweden [сý́-дäн] Швéция

Switzerland [суі-цä́р-лäнд] Швейцáрия

Syria [сí-піä] Си́рия

Teheran [тε-ă-рáн] Тегерáн

Thames [тэмз] Тéмза

Tiber [тáй-бäр] Тибр

Tigris [тáй-гріс] Тигр

Tokyo [тóў-кі-оў] Тóкио

Turkey [тä́р-кі] Тýрция

Ukraine [ю-крá-ін] Украи́на

Uruguay [ý-рў-гýай] Уругвáй

Union of South Africa [ю́-ніän ов саў́θ æ-фрі-кä] Южно-Африкáнский Сою́з

U.S.S.R. [ю ес ес ä́р] (*Union of Soviet Socialist Republics*) Сою́з Совéтских Социали́стических Респу́блик

U.S.A [ю эс эй] (*United States of America*) Соединённые Штáты Амéрики

Venezuela [вε-нε-зу-éлä] Венесуэ́ла

Venice [вé-ніс] Венéция

Vienna [віε-нä] Вéна

Vistula [віс-тю-лä] Ви́сла

Vosges [вож] Вогéзы

Wales [ўэ́йлз] Уэ́льс

Warsaw [ўóр-сō] Варшáва

Washington [ўó-шін-тän] Вашингтóн

White Russia [ўайт ра-шä] Белорýссия

White Sea [ўайт си] Бéлое мóре

Yalta [йäл-тä] Я́лта

Yugoslavia [ю-го-слá-віä] Югослáвия

Zurich [зю-рік] Цю́рих

Английские ненормальные глаголы
English anomalous verbs

In this list verbs which have both an irregular and a regular form are followed by an asterisk (*).

Звёздочка (*) обозначает, что глагол имеет правильную и неправильную форму.

Infinitive	Past tense	Past participle
abide жить	abode	abode
arise вставать	arose	arisen
awake* проснуться	awoke	awoke
be быть	was (s.), were (pl.)	been
bear рождать	bore	born
bear нести	bore	borne
beat бить	beat	beaten
become делаться	became	become
beget рождать	begot	begotten
begin начинать	began	begun
behold видеть	beheld	beheld
bend* сгибать	bent	bent
beseech* умолять	besought	besought
bet держать пари	bet	bet
bid велеть	bade	bidden
bind вязать	bound	bound
bite кусать	bit	bitten
bleed кровоточить	bled	bled
blow дуть	blew	blown
break ломать	broke	broken
breed порождать	bred	bred
bring принести	brought	brought
build строить	built	built
burn* жечь	burnt	burnt
burst лопнуть	burst	burst
buy купить	bought	bought
cast бросать	cast	cast
catch поймать	caught	caught
chide бранить	chid	chidden
choose выбирать	chose	chosen
cleave раскалывать	clove, cleft	cloven, cleft
cling цепляться	clung	clung
clothe* одевать	clad	clad
come прийти	came	come
cost стоить	cost	cost
creep ползти	crept	crept
cut резать	cut	cut
dare* сметь	durst	durst
deal распределять	dealt	dealt
dig копать	dug	dug

Infinitive	Past tense	Past participle
do делать	did	done
draw тащить; рисовать	drew	drawn
dream* сниться	dreamt	dreamt
drink пить	drank	drunk
drive гнать	drove	driven
dwell жить	dwelt	dwelt
eat есть	ate	eaten
fall падать	fell	fallen
feed кормить	fed	fed
feel чувствовать	felt	felt
fight сражаться	fought	fought
find найти	found	found
flee убегать	fled	fled
fling кидать	flung	flung
fly лететь	flew	flown
forbear воздерживаться	forbore	forborne
forget забывать	forgot	forgotten
forsake покидать	forsook	forsaken
freeze мерзнуть	froze	frozen
get доставать	got	got
gird* опоясывать	girt	girt
give давать	gave	given
go итти	went	gone
grind молоть	ground	ground
grow расти	grew	grown
hang* повесить	hung	hung
have иметь	had	had
hear слышать	heard	heard
heave* поднимать	hove	hove
hew* рубить	hewed	hewn
hide прятать	hid	hidden
hit ударить	hit	hit
hold держать	held	held
hurt ушибить	hurt	hurt
keep держать	kept	kept
kneel стоять на коленях	knelt	knelt
knit* вязать	knit	knit
know знать	knew	known
lade грузить	laded	laden
lay класть, нестись	laid	laid
lead вести	led	led
lean* опираться	leant	leant
leap* скакать	leapt	leapt
learn* учиться	learnt	learnt
leave уходить	left	left
lend одолжать	lent	lent

Infinitive	Past tense	Past participle
let позволять	let	let
lie лежать	lay	lain
light* освещать	lit	lit
lose терять	lost	lost
mean значить	meant	meant
meet встретить	met	met
melt* плавить	melted	molten
mow косить	mowed	mown
pay платить	paid	paid
put положить	put	put
quit* оставить	quit	quit
read читать	read	read
rend рвать	rent	rent
rid освобождать	rid	rid
ride ездить	rode	ridden
ring звонить	rang	rung
rise вставать	rose	risen
rive разрубать	rove	riven
rot* гнить	rotted	rotten
run бежать	ran	run
saw пилить	sawed	sawn
say говорить	said	said
see видеть	saw	seen
seek искать	sought	sought
seethe* кипеть	seethed	sódden
sell продать	sold	sold
send посылать	sent	sent
set ставить	set	set
shake трясти	shook	shaken
shave* брить	shaved	shaven
shed терять	shed	shed
shine светить	shone	shone
shoe обувать	shod	shod
shoot стрелять	shot	shot
show показать	showed	shown
shred* кромсать	shred	shred
shrink съёживаться	shrank	shrunk
shut закрыть	shut	shut
sing петь	sang	sung
sink опускать	sank	sunk
sit сидеть	sat	sat
slay убивать	slew	slain
sleep спать	slept	slept
slide скользить	slid	slid
sling метать из пращи	slung	slung
slink красться	slunk	slunk

Infinitive	Past tense	Past participle
slit разрезать	slit	slit
smell* пахнуть	smelt	smelt
smite ударить	smote	smitten
speed* спешить	sped	sped
speak говорить	spoke	spoken
spell* писать правильно	spelt	spelt
spend тратить	spent	spent
spill* проливать	spilt	spilt
spin прясть	spun	spun
spit плевать	spat	spat
split расколоть	split	split
spoil* портить	spoilt	spoilt
spread распространять	spread	spread
spring прыгнуть	sprang	sprung
stand стоять	stood	stood
stave* проломить	stove	stove
steal красть	stole	stolen
stick липнуть	stuck	stuck
sting жалить	stung	stung
stink вонять	stank	stunk
strew* сыпать	strewed	strewn
stride шагать	strode	stridden
strike ударить	struck	struck
string нанизывать	strung	strung
strive стараться	strove	striven
swear клясться	swore	sworn
sweep мести	swept	swept
swell* пухнуть	swelled	swollen
swim плавать	swam	swum
swing качать	swung	swung
take брать	took	taken
teach учить	taught	taught
tear рвать	tore	torn
tell сказать	told	told
think думать	thought	thought
thrive* процветать	throve	thriven
throw бросать	threw	thrown
thrust толкать	thrust	thrust
tread ступать	trod	trodden
wear носить	wore	worn
weave ткать	wove	woven
weep плакать	wept	wept
win выиграть	won	won
wind мотать	wound	wound
wring жать	wrung	wrung
write писать	wrote	written